The Dictionary
of South African Painters and Sculptors

Including Namibia

The Dictionary of South African Painters and Sculptors

Including Namibia

GRANIA OGILVIE
ASSISTED BY CAROL GRAFF

PUBLISHED BY
EVERARD READ

Published by Everard Read
Everard Read Gallery
6 Jellicoe Avenue
Rosebank
Johannesburg
South Africa

Private Bag 5
Parklands
2121
South Africa

First edition 1988

ISBN 0 620 12663 9

Edited by Matthew Seal
Cover and title-page design by Jill Paynter
Design by Everard Read, Grania Ogilvie and Carol Graff

Typesetting, reproduction, printing and binding by CTP Book Printers, Cape

BD8591

The endpaper design is part of J H Pierneef's "Lowveld"

CONTENTS

The Dictionary

LIST OF ILLUSTRATIONS

vii

ix

PREFACE

The Dictionary of South African Painters and Sculptors has been compiled to provide the most up-to-date and comprehensive survey of its kind. It contains detailed alphabetical information on over 1 800 painters, sculptors and graphic artists who were born, lived in or are presently living in South Africa or Namibia. The area, known formerly as South West Africa and more commonly today as Namibia, is included in this dictionary as the artists of this region and their work are closely affiliated with those of South Africa. For convenience the term SWA/Namibia has been used in the text.

The criteria for inclusion for both past and contemporary artists were essentially the following: those painters or sculptors who have held a solo exhibition; have participated in a major group exhibition; are represented in a public collection or whose work is on public display; have gained prizes or awards; or are an integral part of the South African or Namibian artistic heritage. No attempt has been made to supply a complete list of an artist's work – this would have made the book unwieldy – but the sections **Represented** and **References** are included to guide the reader to other sources of information. A full bibliography of works cited is supplied at the end of the book, together with a listing of useful addresses for further reference and an explanation of the abbreviations used.

Extensive research for the *Dictionary* was conducted over a period of nearly six years. Among others, the following sources were thoroughly examined: the archives of the Michaelis Art Library, Johannesburg; the Human Sciences Research Council, Pretoria; libraries of selected universities and technikons throughout South Africa; public and private galleries and their catalogues; museums; Registration Departments of Births and Deaths; and a large selection of books and periodicals published locally and overseas. Much too was gained from correspondence with artists and others. A more specific list of acknowledgements is provided on a separate page.

Carol Graff and I have benefited from the labours of previous biographers and art historians, and the research done by various institutions and in student dissertations or theses. We also take this opportunity of thanking the many contemporary artists who took the trouble to complete and return our rather daunting questionnaires; without their help and support the project would have been impossible to complete. As far as can be ascertained the information received is remarkably factual, but to double-check every single item was an impossible task. Some artists asked for certain details not to be published and we have naturally respected their wishes.

Despite all this endeavour and assistance, the compilers realise that in a book of this nature errors and misinformation can creep in. We have tried our utmost to minimise this, and apologise to any artist to whom incorrect data is attributed. Certain artists may well have been omitted who would otherwise have met our criteria for inclusion. We regret any such omissions and can only assure these artists, and the reader, that any such shortcoming is not by intent.

Perhaps only those who have attempted research in this field will be aware of the considerable difficulties encountered in locating certain artists or even finding information concerning quite major figures. Some artists felt that they were purely educationalists and should not be included in a dictionary of painters and sculptors; we would have liked to include them, but have complied with their request. We would be most grateful if readers could supply authenticated corrections or additions for any revised editions of this book.

It should be pointed out that the amount of coverage afforded to an artist does not relate to his or her "importance"; rather, it reflects the amount of reliable information available. A number of artists who by popular estimation are of particular significance are treated relatively briefly, but only for this reason. No appraisals of an artist's work have been included. Similarly, the selection of illustrations for the plates is not intended as a comment on the place of an artist or a particular work of art in the artistic life of the region; instead, we have tried to indicate the diversity of the art of South Africa and Namibia across space and time. There has been no intention to promote or otherwise endorse an individual whose work is represented here.

The information included in the entries is organised as follows:

Name: Surname followed by forenames, with married or maiden names denoted by Mrs or née in parenthesis; nicknames or commonly used names are also given in parenthesis. Major entitlements, such as RA or ARIBA, are also given.

Date and place of birth, where known.

Date and place of death, where known and where applicable.

Dates resided in South Africa; arrival in South Africa or Namibia if not born in the region and/or departure if pertinent.

Type of Artist: Whether the artist is a painter, sculptor, graphic artist, or a combination thereof; the range of subject matter and the various media used; any series or specific subject matter. This paragraph is intended as a summary and is by no means exhaustive; indeed, few artists can be pigeonholed to such a degree.

Studies: When the artist studied, where, under whom; any educational scholarships and bursaries awarded as well as qualifications gained; arranged in chronological order.

The names of present-day Technikons have been greatly simplified. These educational establishments have changed their names, at different times, from Technical Colleges, Colleges for Advanced Technical Education and finally Autonomous Technikons. At times some have been named after the towns they are situated in and others the Province. In this publication standard names have been given and they are called Technical Colleges up to 1980 and Technikons thereafter. The Diplomas awarded by these tertiary colleges change from year to year, but in general a National Diploma is followed by a Higher Diploma which in turn is followed by a Technical Diploma.

In 1955 the University of Pretoria initiated the Fine Arts Degree, however, practical classes were held at the Pretoria Technical College until 1972 when a Fine Arts Department was established.

References to the University of Natal are to the Pietermartizburg campus unless Durban is specified.

Profile: This section provides an outline of the artist's achievements and contains such information as:

1. *Membership of art societies and groups* – includes past and present membership of societies and groups throughout the world;
2. *Teaching posts held* – comprising date, position and educational establishment, or whether taught privately and where;
3. *Official positions held in the art field* – including such positions as curator of or employment in a municipal gallery, owner of or employment in a commercial gallery, art critic, moderator for an examination, etc.;
4. *Illustration and design* – itemising the illustration of books, pamphlets or periodicals, the designing of tapestries, stage and costume designs for both theatre and film, as well as architectural designs;
5. *Involvement with other arts* – in addition to visual artistic skills, whether the person concerned is or was a writer of prose or poetry, a musician, a member of the acting profession (whether actor, producer, director etc.), a photographer or a craftsman working in pottery, stained glass or enamel;
6. *Places lived in or visited* – where the artist has lived, followed by places visited, accompanied by dates whenever possible;
7. *Relationship to other artists* – artistic couples and families are a common occurrence, and connections are made between the relevant artists.

This section has not been entered in chronological order as it has not always been possible to ascertain exact dates; under these circumstances it was felt that an attempt at chronology would be misleading.

Exhibitions: The number of group and solo exhibitions listed chronologically. The date and place of the first solo exhibition are given, along with the total number of solo exhibitions and the names of the various countries in which they were held. Most artists participate in group exhibitions frequently, and in view of the difficulty of supplying an exact number, the three words several, many and numerous have been used. **Several** signifies under ten, **Many** between ten and twenty, and **Numerous** twenty and above. Where a large, more accurate figure can be ascertained, the wording **over 50**, **over 70** etc. has been employed. A number of selected major group exhibitions have also been incorporated into the listing.

Awards: Awards bestowed upon the artist are arranged according to date. These may include scholastic and travel bursaries not mentioned in ***Studies*** above.

Represented: Public galleries, museums and municipal collections, as well as university and technikon collections are listed alphabetically. Not every establishment mentioned has available a full list of its acquisitions, and there may be omissions. This list is intended to enable the reader to find a public example of the artist's work.

Public Commissions: The date (wherever possible), the artistic work and the place in which it can be found.

Publications by the artist: Books written by the artist are listed in title, date and publisher order.

References: Books are listed first under author, title of book, date, publisher, place where published, followed by periodical title and date, and finally any major catalogue, its author if known, date and publisher. Books on South African and Namibian art which recur frequently have been abbreviated, and their full titles can be found in the abbreviations list.

Johannesburg
October 1988

GRANIA OGILVIE

ACKNOWLEDGEMENTS

I would first like to thank Mr Everard Read, whose instigation, constant enthusiasm and most generous funding of the *Dictionary* have been a great encouragement; also my sincere thanks to Carol Graff whose assistance has been invaluable over the past four years. My thanks also go to Anne Howe, who helped me in the initial stages of the book, and to the staff of The Everard Read Gallery, who from time to time were called in to help, with special thanks to Anne Cowles and Julie Adler who accumulated the illustration transparencies. The most professional editing of Matthew Seal greatly improved the text, as have the invaluable words of advice and criticism of Brendan Bell; thank you both. We are also indebted to Eleanor Mary Cadell for her publishing skills and Bruce Attwood for his printing expertise.

During the years spent gathering material for this book many people throughout South Africa have been a tremendous help to us, and our thanks go to all of them. We are grateful to the artists themselves who supplied personal biographies; the South African Association of Arts and its branches; the Arts Association of SWA/Namibia, particularly Peter Strack; Universities, Technikons, public galleries and museums throughout the country which have sent information; commercial galleries for sending our questionnaire to their stable of artists, and a number of individuals who gave Carol and me substantial support and assistance.

In Johannesburg
Jonathan Frost of the Michaelis Art Library, who we thank sincerely for his unfailing helpfulness; Julia Meintjes and Sonia Begg of the Johannesburg Art Gallery; Dricus van der Walt of the Art Library of the Rand Afrikaans University; the library staff of the Africana Museum and the South African National Museum of Military History; Durant Sihlali and David Koloane of FUBA; Bill Ainslie and the staff at the Johannesburg Art Foundation; Stephen Risi of the Katlehong Art Centre, near Germiston; Karen McKerron; Caroline and Fernand Haenggi of Gallery 21; Gerard Kannberg; Chris Crake; Cyril Manganyi; Bongiwe Dhlomo; Jackie Potgieter of Shell Gallery; Matsemela Manaka; Anne Marie Grinrod, formerly of the Market Gallery.

In Pretoria
A special word of thanks to Eunice Basson, formerly of the University of Pretoria, presently of the University of South Africa, who helped us enormously; Professor Nico Roos, Professor Murray Schoonraad, Professor A E Duffey and Yvonne Rabie of the University of Pretoria, together wih Jeanne Joubert, who is now working at the Pretoria Art Museum; Katinka Kempff and the library staff at the Pretoria Art Museum; Dr Gerhard van der Waal and his staff at the Human Sciences Research Council; Roena Griesel and her staff at the headquarters of the South African Association of Arts; Lucy Alexander, formerly of the University of South Africa and presently of the South African National Gallery in Cape Town; Elbie Kaggelhoffer of the Hoffer Gallery; Aleta Michelatos; Ernst de Jongh; R W Friemelt of E Schweickerdt (Pty) Ltd.

In Pietermaritzburg
Lorna Ferguson and Melanie Hillebrand of the Tatham Art Gallery. Dr Hillebrand has since been appointed Director of the King George VI Art Gallery in Port Elizabeth, in both places she has helped us considerably. John Cannon of Cannon and Findlay; Professor Terence King and Hans Fransen of the University of Natal.

In Durban
Jill Addleson and her staff at the Durban Art Gallery; Miss J Duggan at the Killie Campbell Africana Library; Joe Thorpe of the African Arts Centre; Aidan Walsh, formerly of the Natal Society of Arts; Gordon Lowings and Elizabeth Meth of the Elizabeth Gordon Gallery; Mrs Brink of Grassroots in Westville; the Coppin Johnson Gallery.

In Cape Town
Christopher Peters of the University of Cape Town; Dr Raymund van Niekerk and his staff at the South African National Gallery; the William Fehr Collection; Louis Schachat of Die Kunskamer; Joe Wolpe; Mr Bosman of the Cape Gallery; Lieschen Heinze of the Chelsea Gallery; Desré Resnik of The Art Scene; Esther Rousso of Gallery International; Erik Laubscher and Edwine Simons of The Ruth Prowse School of Art; Professor Larry Scully and Professor C du Ry in Stellenbosch.

In the Eastern Cape
Professor Robert Brooks of Rhodes University; Joan Fourie of the Port Elizabeth Technikon; Anthony Adler.

Our thanks finally to the artists who generously gave us copyright to reproduce their works. We apologise to those whom we have been unable to contact, and hope that they approve of their inclusion.

FOREWORD
by Everard Read

Our beautiful South Africa, with its diverse peoples and constantly changing political scene, has been an inspiration and stimulation to so many wonderful artists.

I have been singularly fortunate in having a career intimately bound up with the South African art scene, and my eclectic taste has happily not restricted my appreciation of works of art to any narrow field.

The rise of the modernists in the first quarter of this century gave new incentive to those people, be they art critics, historians, artists or just interested observers, to find an accurate and yet concise definition of the meaning of the word 'art'. Lively debates have often followed learned peoples' attempts to define the parameters of what they perceive as 'art'.

As we approach the final decade of this century, we have an increasingly active visual art community producing works which often fuel this debate. What is perceived as being fine visual art in one community would not necessarily be viewed as art by another community in the same geographic area.

What is certain is that art arises out of reaction to environment and time. South Africa has always been highly stimulating to those artists who have sought to paint its landscapes which range from flat to mountainous and from deserts to rain forests. Its wildlife and plants have been painted from the earliest times. It is a great pity that names cannot be given to those marvellous artists who have left exquisite images for us to view on rock walls in various parts of our country. What an important addition their names would have been to a book such as this.

South Africa also has an almost unrivalled cultural diversity, bringing constant upheaval and an ever-changing situation. This has provided our artists with a never-ending source of material, and their art has been a clear comment on the times within which we live.

I believe that over the years a South Africanism has come to pervade the work of our painters and sculptors. It lies over and above the enormous influence the art of Europe and North America exerts on artists working here. It comes from an amalgam of many factors including our ancestry, our country, its peoples and difficulties; the haunting beauty of the bushveld and its animals; the Cape with its magnificent mountains, vineyards and architecture; the Karoo and Namib desert with their space and loneliness; our light, and the spell of our artists of the past.

If the *Dictionary of South African Painters and Sculptors* facilitates understanding of our rich heritage, then it fulfils its intentions.

THE DICTIONARY

A

AAB-TAMSEN Ines Chlotilde

Born 1926 Brits, Transvaal.

A painter and graphic artist of landscapes and still life. Works in oil, acrylic, watercolour and in various graphic media.

Studies 1943–45 University of the Witwatersrand, under Professor Heather Martienssen (1915–79) and Willem de Sanderes Hendrikz (qv); 1947–52 Pretoria Technical College, under Robert Hodgins (qv).

Profile A founder member of the SAAA and a long-time committee member. 1948–77 taught art at the Afrikaans Hoër Meisiesskool, the Girls High School, the German School and at the Technical College in Pretoria. Teaches art privately. 1952–55 Chief Art Examiner for the Transvaal Education Department.

Exhibitions She has participated in many group exhibitions in SA from 1961; 1963 SAAA Gallery, Pretoria, first of 10 solo exhibitions held in SA; 1981 Republic Festival Exhibition.

Represented Pietersburg Art Gallery; Potchefstroom Museum; Willem Annandale Art Gallery, Lichtenburg.

References SAA (under Tamsen); BSAK; AASA.

ABBOTT Clare Pauline

Born 1921 Castle Eden, County Durham, England.

Resided in SA from 1961.

A self-taught artist of wildlife, figures and abstract pictures. Works in acrylic, watercolour, gouache, ink and pencil.

Profile Two sets of game animal prints produced, each set containing 12 signed and numbered prints, published by Rowland Ward Limited. A book illustrator, illustrating *The Mammals of the Southern African Subregion*, by Reay Smithers, 1983, University of Pretoria; *South African Butterflies*, by Stephen Henning, 1984, Macmillan (SA), Johannesburg; *Rowland Ward's African Records of Big Game*, 19th edition, 1984, Game Conservation International, San Antonio, Texas, and the 20th edition entitled *Rowland Ward's Records of Big Game, Africa and Asia* in 1986; *The Atlas of Africa's Principal Mammals*, by Steven Smith, 1985, Natural History Books, Johannesburg; *Land Mammals of Southern Africa, a field guide*, 1986, Macmillan (SA), Johannesburg. She has also illustrated two small booklets, *Wetlands* for the Cape Department of Nature and Environmental Conservation and *Small Mammals of the Durban Area* for the Parks, Recreation and Beaches Department. She has recently completed 100 illustrations for *The Big Game of the World*, by Werner Trense, to be published in 1988 by Paul Parey Verlag, Hamburg, West Germany. She has produced a number of designs for tapestries, glassware, chinaware and calendars.

Exhibitions She has participated in numerous group exhibitions; 1976 Schweickerdt Gallery, Pretoria, solo exhibition.

References *SA Panorama* November 1976, December 1976, December 1981 & August 1984.

ABELMAN Justin

Born 1949 Johannesburg.

A painter of landscapes, seascapes, portraits, figures and still life. Works in acrylic and ink.

Studies 1967–70 Johannesburg School of Art, under George Boys (qv), gaining a National Diploma in Graphic Design.

Profile 1970–75 a graphic designer in advertising agencies in London and in Johannesburg. A professional dancer from 1958, studying Spanish dancing in Madrid in 1975–76. Performs under the stage name "Juan Amaya". 1976–77 travelled in Spain, France, Greece, Israel, Sweden and the USA.

Exhibitions He has participated in several group exhibitions from 1983 in the Transvaal; 1983 Trevor Coleman Gallery, Johannesburg, first of four solo exhibitions, of which one was held in Greenwich Village, New York, USA, in 1984.

ABLETT Enid Vera (Mrs Wroughton)

Born 1896.

Died 1980.

A painter of landscapes, farm and coastal scenes and flowers. Worked in watercolour, gouache and oil.

Profile Produced a number of monotypes, decoratively stained wood panels, and a series of drawings illustrating the preparations of tobacco. Lived in Cape Town. Travelled in the UK, Yugoslavia, Italy and to Zanzibar. She was actively involved in broadcasting with the SABC. A member of the National Council of Women, of which she was President of the Cape Town Branch. During WWII she was Adjutant to the Commandant of the Cape Peninsula Branch of the SA Women's Auxiliary Services and President of the Cape Town Navy League.

Exhibitions Participated in group exhibitions from 1925; held solo exhibitions in Hermanus in 1965 and in Cape Town in 1971.

Reference BSAK 2.

ABRAMS Lionel

Born 1931 Johannesburg.

A painter and graphic artist of landscapes, still life, genre, figures, interiors and abstract pictures. Works in oil, acrylic and in various graphic media, especially collotypes.

Studies 1951–53 Witwatersrand Technical College; 1954–55 mural painting and textile design at the Central School of Art, London, under Miss Batty, Gordon Crook and Alan Reynolds; 1959 Witwatersrand Technical College, gaining a National Art Teachers Certificate.

Profile 1974–75 a series of photo-pastels. 1970 a limited edition of 10 serigraphs published by the Goodman Gallery, Johannesburg. His graphics, published by Edition 21, were distributed by leading galleries in Johannesburg, Cape Town, Durban, Pretoria, London, Stockholm and throughout the USA. 1960–64 taught at Florida Park High School; until 1977 conducted his own teaching studio; 1982 took up teaching again. 1955–56 lived in Spain.

Exhibitions He has participated in numerous group exhibitions from 1959 held in SA, South America, Europe, Israel, Australia and Zimbabwe; 1957 Lawrence Adler Gallery, Johannesburg, first of many solo exhibitions held throughout SA.
Award 1965 Bronze Medal, Transvaal Academy.
Represented Durban Art Gallery; Hester Rupert Art Museum, Graaff-Reinet; Johannesburg Art Gallery; Potchefstroom Museum; Potchefstroom University for CHE; Pretoria Art Museum; Rand Afrikaans University; Sandton Municipal Collection; SA National Gallery, Cape Town; University of Natal; University of South Africa; University of the Witwatersrand; William Humphreys Art Gallery, Kimberley.
References SAA; 20C SA Art; SAP&S; SAP&D; IWAA (in addendum); SSAP; BSAK 1 & 2; SA Art; Oxford Companion to 20C Art (under SA); 3Cs; AASA; *SA Art News* 6 April 1961 & 10 August 1961; *Artlook* September 1967 & June 1969.

ADAMS John

Resided in SA 1914–21.
Studies Hanley School of Art; 1908–11 Royal College of Art, London, on a scholarship.
Profile A potter. A member of the NSA, a committee member in 1917 and President 1920–21. 1912–14 taught at the Royal College of Art, London; 1914 first Director of the Natal Technical College, where he established the pottery studio. 1919–21 on the Durban Art Gallery Advisory Committee.
Exhibitions Participated in group exhibitions with the NSA and the SA Academy.
Represented Durban Art Gallery; University of Natal.
References BSAK; AASA.

ADAMS Richard Jurgens

Born 1943 Pretoria.
A sculptor of abstract expressionistic works. Uses welded steel and ceramics.
Studies University of Pretoria, under Gunther van der Reis (qv), Larry Scully (qv), Walter Battiss (qv), Eugene Bouffa (qv) and Leo Theron (qv), gaining a BA(FA) in 1967.
Profile A member of the SAAA. From 1970 a lecturer at the Pretoria Technikon. Involved in ceramics and ceramic technology from 1967.
Exhibitions He has participated in several group exhibitions from 1976; 1976 SAAA Gallery, Pretoria, solo exhibition; 1981 Republic Festival Exhibition.
Awards 1979 Metalart Prize (Open Category); 1983 First Prize, Friends of the Durban Art Gallery Sculpture Competition.
Public Commissions 1969 cast concrete relief wall, Allied Building Society, Ermelo; 1970 welded steel panels, Jan Smuts Airport, Johannesburg; 1984 stainless steel sculpture, Durban Beach Front.
References *De Arte* September 1969; *Artlook* November 1973.

AGUIAR Marina Naomi (née Du Bruyn)
Born 1942 Winburg, Orange Free State.
An artist working in gouache, ink, wash, pencil, charcoal, various graphic media, bronze, ciment fondu, wood, resin, perspex and mixed media. Makes her own paper. Series: 1973–79 "Revelation", fibreglass panels and prints; 1974–77 "Lovers", resin sculptures; 1979–83 "Africa"; 1981–82 "Stickman", accompanied by poetry by Dorian Haarhoff; 1982–83 "Desert"; from 1983 "Bone".
Studies 1962 Orange Free State Technical College, under Michael Edwards (qv); 1963 Natal Technical College, under Mary Stainbank (qv); 1964–66 Witwatersrand Technical College, under Attie Tromp, George Boys (qv), Joyce Leonard (qv) and Phil Botha (qv), gaining a National Art Teachers Diploma; 1968 University of South Africa, under Anna Vorster (qv); 1981–83 University of South Africa, under Steven Sack (qv), Professor Karin Skawran, Joey de Jager (qv) and Johann Moolman (qv).
Profile From 1977 a member of the SAAA; 1980–83 a committee member of the Arts Association SWA/Namibia; 1984 a committee member of the East London Fine Art Society; 1985 a member of the EPSFA. 1972–73 taught art at St Andrew's School, Johannesburg; 1978 a lecturer at the Khomasdal Teachers Training College, SWA/Namibia; 1981–83 lectured at the Windhoek Academy, SWA/Namibia. Involved in acting and pottery. 1981–83 the art critic for *Die Republikein* in Windhoek. 1959–62 lived in Bloemfontein; 1963 in Durban; 1964–77 and 1979 in Johannesburg; 1978 and 1980–83 in SWA/Namibia; from 1984 in East London. 1968, 1983 and 1984 visited Europe.
Exhibitions She has participated in many group exhibitions from 1966 in SA, SWA/Namibia, France, Italy, Monaco and West Germany; 1975 Cecil Mark Gallery, Illovo, Johannesburg, first of nine solo exhibitions held in SA and SWA/Namibia.
Represented Ann Bryant Gallery, East London; Arts Association SWA/Namibia Collection.
Reference SA Arts Calendar Summer 1985–86.

AINSLIE Alan Frederick
Born 1952 Port Elizabeth.
A painter of wildlife. Works in oil and watercolour.
Studies 1972–74 East London Art School, under Jack Lugg (qv), gaining a National Diploma in Graphic Design.
Profile A graphic designer, who was Head Artist in 1975–77 at the Interstate Motor Vehicle Company and from 1978 at *SA Panorama* magazine. In 1984 his paintings were reproduced in a calendar for Impact Publishers. In 1985 he issued a portfolio of 150 limited edition prints and in 1987 a set of two prints entitled "Desert Dwellers" in a limited edition of 250, the proceeds of both being donated to The Endangered Wildlife Trust.
Exhibitions 1985 participated in a wildlife exhibition held at the Everard Read Gallery, Johannesburg; 1987 Sanderling Gallery, Johannesburg, solo exhibition.

AINSLIE Bill

Born 1934 Bedford, Cape Province.

A painter of landscapes, figures and portraits and from 1968 of abstract pictures. Works in oil.

Studies 1956–58 University of Natal, under Jack Heath (qv), gaining a BA(FA) (Hons).

Profile 1958–65 taught at Michaelhouse School, Natal, Cyrene Mission School, Rhodesia (Zimbabwe) and King Edward's School, Johannesburg. 1965–68 taught art privately. 1972 founded a teaching studio in Johannesburg which led to the registering in 1982 of the present Johannesburg Art Foundation, of which he is a Director. He initiated a joint effort which led to the establishment of the FUBA Art Centre in 1978, the Alexandra Art Centre in 1985, and in conjunction with USSALEP, the Thupelo Art Project in 1986. 1979 wrote "An Artist's Workshop", published in *The State of Art in SA*, University of Cape Town. 1968 spent a year travelling and painting in Europe, a large part of this year being spent in Spain; 1969 lived in St Ives, Cornwall. He is the great-great-grandson of James Stewart (qv).

Exhibitions 1964 Adler Fielding Gallery, Johannesburg, first of eight solo exhibitions held in SA; 1970 De Sfinx Gallery, Amsterdam, solo exhibition; he has participated in several group exhibitions from 1965 in SA, England and the USA; 1982 National Gallery, Gaborone, Botswana, Exhibition of SA Art; 1987 Johannesburg Art Gallery, Vita Art Now; 1987 Johannesburg Art Foundation, joint exhibition with David Koloane (qv), Dumisani Mabaso (qv), Tony Nkotsi (qv) and Anthusa Sotiriades (qv).

Awards 1968 Hajee Suliman Ebrahim Award, Art SA Today; 1975 Julius Robinson Award, Art SA Today.

Represented Durban Art Gallery; Johannesburg Art Gallery; Pretoria Art Museum; SA Akademie vir Wetenskap en Kuns; SA National Gallery, Cape Town; University of the Witwatersrand; William Humphreys Art Gallery, Kimberley.

References SAP&S; BSAK 1 & 2; 3Cs; AASA; *Artlook* July 1968.

AITCHISON Lynette

Born 1961 Pretoria.

An artist producing abstract pictures. Works in oil, acrylic, gouache, pencil, charcoal, crayon, resin, wax, pastel, sand, and with other organic matter. A lithographer and etcher. 1984–85 a series on "Flight Thoughts".

Studies 1979–81 Pretoria Technikon, under Ian Redelinghuys (qv), Koos den Houting (qv), Gunther van der Reis (qv), Carl Jeppe (qv), Leslie Reinhardt (qv), Daniel de Wet (qv), P de Wet and Elsabe Schady (qv), gaining a National Diploma in Graphic Art; 1984 lithography at the Intern Summer Academy of Fine Arts, Salzburg, Austria, under Professor Werner Otto and Konrad Winter; 1986 etching at the Johannesburg Art Foundation, under Russel Scott.

Profile From 1986 a member of the SAAA. A full-time Art Director. A pianist and modern ballerina, designing posters for the Sylvia Glasser dance studio in 1983. 1984 lived in Salzburg, Austria, exhibiting at the Venice Biennial in Italy.

Exhibitions She has participated in several group exhibitions from 1981 in SA and Austria.

ALEKSANDER-RISTIČ Nina Ivana

Born 1931 Zagreb, Yugoslavia.
Resided in SA from 1948.
A painter and graphic artist mainly of landscapes, but also of still life, seascapes and abstract pictures. Works in oil, watercolour, gouache, ink, wash, pencil, charcoal and in various graphic media.
Studies 1944–46 at the Istituto di Belle Arti in Perugia, Italy, under D Caputi, gaining a Higher Course Diploma; 1947 at the Accademia di Belle Arti in Florence, Italy, under Professor Vignetti.
Profile 1984–85 tapestry designs. A number of illustrations for books including *This Africa of Ours*, by M McNeile, 1957, McAlan Publishers and *Windows of The Transvaal*, by Juliet Marais Louw, 1961, Collins, Johannesburg. Numerous designs for greetings cards. 1976 visited Greece, 1982 Brazil and Peru.
Exhibitions 1954 Johannesburg, first solo exhibition; she has participated in group exhibitions from 1955 in SA; 1956, 1960 and 1964 Quadrennial Exhibitions.
Represented University of the Witwatersrand; William Humphreys Art Gallery, Kimberley.
References Art SA; SAA; BSAK; AASA.

ALERS Gerard Engelbrecht

Born 1887 Rotterdam, The Netherlands.
Died During the 1970s in Cape Town.
Resided in SA 1921–31 and from 1946.
A self-taught painter and graphic artist of landscapes. Worked in oil and in various graphic media.
Profile 1931–46 lived in Curaçao, Netherlands Antilles. A missionary and from 1946 a minister of the Dutch Reformed Church.
Exhibitions Participated in numerous groups exhibitions held throughout SA and in The Netherlands and Central America; 1931 Rotterdam, first solo exhibition; 1949 Cape Town, first of many solo exhibitions held in SA; 1964 Quadrennial Exhibition.
References Art SA; SAA; BSAK; AASA.

ALEXANDER Fritz Ludwig

Born 1902 West Berlin, Germany.
Died 1971 Cape Town.
Resided in SA from 1936.
Worked in pen and ink depicting figures and humorous scenes.
Studies 1922 passed the Trade Test of the Handswerkskammer, Berlin, having studied under the metal sculptor Karl Fohrholz; 1922–23 University of Berlin, studying History of Art; 1924–28 Kunstgewerbeschule, Charlottenburg, West Germany, studying sculpture under Professor Fritz Klimsch (1870–1960).

Profile A member and former Chairman of the SAAA. Taught art for a short period *c.*1956–57 in Cape Town. An art advisor to the Rembrandt Art Foundation and Sanlam. He was a council member of the SA National Gallery, Cape Town. In 1956 he was appointed Curator of the Jewish Museum, Cape Town. 1969–71 employed as the art correspondent for *Die Burger*. Illustrated Babel's book *Odessa* with 17 pen and ink sketches.

Exhibition 1971 SAAA Gallery, Cape Town and SA National Gallery, Cape Town, "Homage to F L Alexander", his only exhibition.

Award In 1971 the SA Akademie vir Wetenskap en Kuns honoured him for his contribution to art criticism.

Represented SA National Gallery, Cape Town.

Publications by Alexander Co-author with R F M Immelman and Percival J G Bishop of *South African Bookplates from the Percival J G Bishop Collection*, 1955, A A Balkema, Cape Town; *Art in South Africa, Painting, Sculpture and Graphic Work since 1900*, 1962, A A Balkema, Cape Town; *South African Graphic Art and its Techniques*, completed and edited by R Waher (qv), 1974, Human & Rousseau, Cape Town.

References BSAK; SASSK; LSAA; Catalogue *Homage to F L Alexander*, by Neville Dubow and Victor Holloway, 1971, SA National Gallery, Cape Town.

ALEXANDER James Edward General Sir

Born 1803.

Died 1885.

In SA 1835–37.

A British soldier who painted animals, landscapes and scenes of tribal life. Worked in watercolour.

Profile Produced woodcuts on farmhouse defence, for the supplement to the *Graham's Town Journal*, 20 August 1835. 1836–37 led an expedition from the Cape to SWA/Namibia.

Publications by Alexander *Narrative of a Voyage and of a Campaign in Kaffirland*, 2 volumes, 1837, Henry Colbourn, London—most of the plates for this book were, however, drawn by his father-in-law, Lieutenant-Colonel Michell (qv); *An Expedition of Discovery through the Countries of the Great Namaquas*, 2 volumes, 1838, Henry Colbourn, London.

References Pict Art; Pict Afr; SA Art.

ALEXANDER Jane

Born 1959 Johannesburg.

A sculptor of human and animal figurations. Works in mixed media, rhinolite plaster, bone and photo-montage.

Studies 1978–82 University of the Witwatersrand, gaining a BA(FA); 1986–87 University of the Witwatersrand, under Peter Schütz (qv), studying for an MA(FA).

Exhibitions She has participated in several group exhibitions from 1981 in SA; 1985 Cape Town Triennial; 1986 Market Gallery, Johannesburg, solo exhibition; 1988 Johannesburg Art Gallery, Vita Art Now.

Awards 1982 Standard Bank National Student Award and the Martienssen Prize, University of the Witwatersrand.
Represented University of the Witwatersrand.

ALEXANDER Keith Savel

Born 1946 Sinoia, Rhodesia (Zimbabwe).
Resided in SA from 1965.
From 1974 a painter of landscapes and wildlife. Works in oil and acrylic. A number of large series: "Namib" 1982; "Sperrgebiet" 1983 and "Eduard Bohlen" 1984–85. Prior to 1974 a sculptor of abstract works, using bronze, wood, steel and fibreglass.
Studies 1965–69 University of Natal, under Jack Heath (qv), where he gained a BA(FA)(Hons), majoring in Sculpture and History of Art.
Profile 1969 a junior lecturer in sculpture at the University of Natal. 1970 moved to Johannesburg; 1979 established a studio in White River, Eastern Transvaal. Visited SWA/Namibia in 1981, 1982, 1984 and 1985.
Exhibitions He has participated in many group exhibitions from 1970 in SA and one in Reno, Nevada, USA in 1986; 1970 Rembrandt Gallery, Cape Town, first of two solo sculpture exhibitions; 1976 Madame Haenggi Gallery, Johannesburg, first of nine solo painting exhibitions; 1978 University of Natal, Pietermaritzburg and Durban, solo exhibition; 1983 and 1985 University of the Witwatersrand, solo exhibitions.
Represented Boksburg Municipal Gallery; Nelspruit Art Gallery; Pretoria Art Museum; Sandton Municipal Collection; University of Natal; University of the Orange Free State; University of the Witwatersrand; William Humphreys Art Gallery, Kimberley.
Public Commissions 1969 sculptural mural, Psychology Department, University of Natal; 1974 steel sculptures, Administration Avenue, Pietermaritzburg.
References BSAK; *Artlook* December 1972; *Gallery* Summer 1981; *Habitat* no 32, 1978 & no 48, 1982; *SA Panorama* November 1985; *Flying Springbok* April 1987; Catalogue *Keith Alexander: the artist and his work*, 1985, Elizabeth White & Associates, Johannesburg.

ALICE Bonita Kim

Born 1962 Johannesburg.
A sculptor of figures which she uses as vehicles for social comment. Works in plaster, ciment fondu, bronze and wood.
Studies 1981–84 University of the Witwatersrand, under Neels Coetzee (qv) and Peter Schütz (qv), where gained a BA(FA).
Profile 1985 a part-time sculpture and drawing teacher at the Johannesburg Art Foundation; 1986 a part-time sculpture teacher at the Funda Centre; 1986 sculpture teacher at the Johannesburg Art, Ballet and Music School; 1987 sculpture lecturer at the University of Natal.
Exhibitions She has participated in several group exhibitions from 1984 in SA and in SWA/Namibia; 1985 Cape Town Triennial.
Award 1984 Prize Winner, New Signatures, SAAA.

ALLARD Michael John

Born 1950 Shoreham by Sea, Sussex, England.
A painter of landscapes and figures. Works in acrylic.
Studies 1969–73 Michaelis School of Fine Art, under Kevin Atkinson (qv),
Stanley Pinker (qv) and Stephen Andrews (qv), gaining a Diploma in Fine Art
in 1972 and a Post-Graduate Advanced Diploma in Fine Art in 1973, when he
was also awarded the Michaelis Prize.
Profile 1973–79 lived in London; 1979–84 in Dublin, Republic of Ireland and
from 1984 in Zimbabwe. Visits the USA three times a year and in 1982 visited
Egypt.
Exhibitions 1980 Ashley Gallery, Palm Beach, Florida, USA, first solo exhibition; 1982 Solomon Gallery, Dublin, Republic of Ireland, solo exhibition; 1984
and 1985 Karen McKerron Gallery, Johannesburg, solo exhibitions.
Award 1976 Arts Council of Great Britain Award.

ALMEIDA Orlando Conceicao de

Born 1936 Mozambique.
Resided in SA from 1961.
A self-taught sculptor of figures and abstract works. Uses mild steel, stainless
steel, brass and aluminium.
Profile A member of the SAAA and TAM, a Mozambican art group in SA.
Designs and manufactures steel furniture.
Exhibitions He has participated in several group exhibitions in Johannesburg
and Cape Town from 1984; 1983 Johannesburg, first of eight solo exhibitions
held in Johannesburg and Cape Town.
Award 1983 elected Man of the Year in the Field of Art by the Portuguese Clubs
in Transvaal.
Public Commissions 1984 Horse's Head, New Doornfontein, Johannesburg;
1985 SA Furniture Floating Trophy.
Reference *Wood Southern Africa* May 1985.

AMALER-RAVIV Arlene

Born 1953 Johannesburg.
A painter of figures, interiors and still life. Works in oil and creates collages.
Studies 1970–73 University of the Witwatersrand, under Cecily Sash (qv), Erica
Berry (qv) and Judith Mason (qv), gaining a BA(FA); 1973–74 Johannesburg
College of Education, where awarded a Higher Diploma in Education; 1981–82
Midrasha-Ramat Hasharon College, Israel, under Raffi Lavi.
Profile 1974–75 taught at the Johannesburg Art, Ballet and Music School; 1979
at the King David High School, Linksfield, Johannesburg; 1980 lectured at the
Johannesburg College of Education; 1981 taught at an art centre in Israel. From
1981 she has been involved in both theatre and film work. 1987 teaching at
Chinta Park Gallery, Johannesburg, as well as privately.

Exhibitions 1979 Market Gallery, Johannesburg, first of three solo exhibitions held in Johannesburg; she has participated in several group exhibitions from 1981 in SA and Israel; 1986 Everard Read Gallery, Johannesburg, joint exhibition with Karin Dando (qv) and Anita van der Merwe (qv); 1988 Johannesburg Art Gallery, Vita Art Now.

AMM Wendy Marion

Born 1927 Fort Victoria, Rhodesia (Mazvingo, Zimbabwe).
Resided in SA from 1970.
A painter of landscapes, portraits, still life, seascapes, figures and abstract pictures. Works in oil, watercolour, gouache and wash, draws in ink, pencil and charcoal. Additionally sculpts in clay.
Studies Part-time courses: 1968 one year at the Peter Birch Art School, Rhodesia (Zimbabwe), 1971 drawing and painting classes, Natal Technical College, 1972 at the Irish School of Painting, Suffolk, UK, under Kenneth Webb; at the City and Guilds of London Art School, and in 1972 and 1974 Heatherley School of Art, London and in 1981 through the University of South Africa.
Profile From 1970 a member of the SAAA; 1972 a founder member of the WSSA, becoming an Associate in 1978 and a Fellow in 1984; from 1973 a member of the North Coast Art Group, Natal; a member of the Highway Art Group and the Queenstown and King William's Town Groups. 1975–78 taught art privately in her studio. Whilst in Zimbabwe she was involved in costume and stage design for the theatre and in organising art competitions.
Exhibitions She has participated in group exhibitions from 1970 in SA, Zimbabwe, SWA/Namibia, Portugal, Australia and London; 1976 Rhodesia (Zimbabwe), first of five solo exhibitions; 1987 Strack van Schyndel Gallery, Johannesburg, joint exhibition with Elizabeth Illingworth Spann (qv) and Iris Vermont (qv).
Awards 1975 P W Storey Trophy; 1981 Mary Clark Floating Trophy; 1981 Meta Orton Art Group Award; 1982 P W Storey Trophy.
Represented Queenstown Municipal Collection; Randburg Municipal Collection; Willem Annandale Art Gallery, Lichtenburg.
Reference BSAK.

AMOILS Blumé

Born 1907 Cape Town.
A painter of landscapes, seascapes, portraits, figures, still life and abstract pictures. Works in oil, watercolour, gouache and wash. Additionally creates monotypes and collages.
Studies Initially under Emily Fern (qv); 1958 Witwatersrand Technical College, under James Gardner (qv) and Gert Brusseau (qv); 1959 Heatherley School of Art, London; 1960 Académie de la Grande Chaumière, Paris.
Profile A member of the Johannesburg Art Society and the Transvaal Academy. Lives in Johannesburg. 1965 lived in Milan, Italy; 1967 travelled in Southern Europe; 1970–85 lived in Lugano, Switzerland.

Exhibitions She has participated in numerous group exhibitions from 1954 in SA, Italy and Switzerland; 1961 Lidchi Gallery, Johannesburg, first of several solo exhibitions held in SA, Italy and Switzerland.
Represented Africana Museum, Johannesburg; SA Consulate, Milan, Italy; SA Embassy, Paris, France.
References SAA; AMC6; *Artlook* July 1970.

AMPENBERGER Iris (née Vining)
Born 1916 Cape Town.
Died 1981 Thaba 'Nchu, Orange Free State.
A painter of simplified figures, using large brushstrokes. Worked in oil, charcoal and watercolour and produced linocuts. A number of sculptures modelled in clay and cast in cement.
Studies Part-time at Port Elizabeth Technical College and full-time for two years *c.*1943 at the Witwatersrand Technical College, studying under Eric Byrd (qv), Maurice van Essche (qv), Phyllis Gardner (qv) and Mary Davies (qv).
Profile A member of the Bloemfontein Group, with whom she exhibited. For 17 years travelled extensively, by caravan, in SA and Rhodesia (Zimbabwe) with her husband Stefan Ampenberger (qv). The Municipal Art Museum in Tweespruit, opened in 1982, was named after Frans Claerhout (qv), and Iris and Stefan Ampenberger.
Exhibitions Participated in numerous group exhibitions with the Orange Free State Art Society and throughout SA; held joint exhibitions with her husband; 1961 Cape Town, first of several solo exhibitions; 1964 Quadrennial Exhibition; 1965 Kimberley, Kroonstad and Thaba 'Nchu, joint exhibition with Stefan Ampenberger (qv) and Frans Claerhout (qv); 1967 National Museum, Bloemfontein, solo exhibition; 1970 and 1973 William Humphreys Art Gallery, Kimberley, joint exhibitions with her husband; 1976 University of the Orange Free State, Retrospective Exhibition; 1982 National Museum, Bloemfontein, Retrospective Exhibition.
Represented National Museum, Bloemfontein; Pretoria Art Museum; University of the Orange Free State; William Humphreys Art Gallery, Kimberley.
Public Commission 1972 designed seven relief panels, cast by her husband, for the Moroko Hospital, Thaba 'Nchu.
References BSAK; AASA; LSAA; F P Scott, L Roppe & K Jonckheere, *Frans Claerhout*, 1975, Vriende Frans Claerhout, Hasselt, Belgie.

AMPENBERGER Stefan
Born 1908 Munich, Germany.
Died 1983 Thaba 'Nchu, Orange Free State.
Resided in SA from 1926.
A painter of landscapes, using large brushstrokes. Worked in oil and watercolour. A number of sculptures in cement, wonderstone and wood.

Studies During the 1930s took a number of lessons from J H Amshewitz (qv).
Profile A member of the Bloemfontein Group, with whom he exhibited. For 17 years travelled extensively, by caravan, in SA and Rhodesia (Zimbabwe) with his wife Iris Ampenberger (qv). The Municipal Art Museum in Tweespruit, opened in 1982, was named after Frans Claerhout (qv), and Stefan and Iris Ampenberger.
Exhibitions Participated in numerous group exhibitions with the Orange Free State Art Society and throughout SA; held joint exhibitions with his wife; 1926 first of several solo exhibitions; 1964 Quadrennial Exhibition; 1965 Kimberley, Kroonstad and Thaba 'Nchu, joint exhibition with Iris Ampenberger (qv) and Frans Claerhout (qv); 1968 Bloemfontein Technical College, Retrospective Exhibition; 1970 and 1973 William Humphreys Art Gallery, Kimberley, joint exhibitions with his wife; 1978 National Museum, Bloemfontein, Retrospective Exhibition.
Represented King George VI Art Gallery, Port Elizabeth; National Museum, Bloemfontein; Potchefstroom University for CHE; Pretoria Art Museum; SA National Gallery, Cape Town; University of the Orange Free State; William Humphreys Art Gallery, Kimberley.
Public Commission 1972 cast seven relief panels, designed by his wife, for the Moroko Hospital, Thaba 'Nchu.
References SAP&S; BSAK; AASA; LSAA; *Artlook* January 1968; *SA Panorama* November 1983.

AMSHEWITZ John Henry RBA
Born 1882 Ramsgate, Kent, England.
Died 1942 Muizenberg, Cape Province.
Resided in SA 1916–22 and from 1936.
A painter of portraits, landscapes and from 1921 onwards of over 200 still life paintings, also depicted historical scenes. Worked in oil, pastel, watercolour, gouache and ink. An etcher.
Studies 1898–1900 Birkbeck Institute, London; Art Academy, Edinburgh; 1902–07 received a bursary to study at the Royal Academy Schools, London, under John Singer Sargent (1856–1925), Sir Luke Fildes (1843–1927), Sir George Clausen (1852–1944), J Solomon Solomon (1860–1927) and Arthur Hacker (1858–1919). Winner of the Royal Academy Schools mural prize.
Profile 1914 elected a member of the Royal Society of British Artists. A founder member of the Johannesburg Sketch Club and a member of the SA Society of Artists. 1917–21 a cartoonist for *The Rand Daily Mail* and *The Sunday Times*, also illustrated journals. 1922–36 lived in England. Among the many books he illustrated are *Ghetto Comedies and Ghetto Tragedies* by Israel Zangwill, *The Hagadah* edited by Maurice Myers, *Myths and Legends of Ancient Israel* by Angelo Rappaport, 3 volumes, 1928, London and *A Fool on the Farm* by Leonard Flemming.
Exhibitions Participated in numerous group exhibitions from 1905 in SA, Australia, Canada, the UK, France, Hong Kong, India, Israel, Italy, Mozambique, Singapore, the USA and Zimbabwe; 1916 Johannesburg, first of numerous solo exhibitions in SA and the UK; 1943 Duncan Hall, Johannesburg, Memorial Exhibition.

Represented Africana Museum, Johannesburg; Albany Museum, Grahams-town; Ann Bryant Gallery, East London; Brakpan Municipal Collection; Durban Art Gallery; Johannesburg Art Gallery; Julius Gordon Africana Centre, Riversdale; King George VI Art Gallery, Port Elizabeth; Metropolitan Museum, New York, USA; Pretoria Art Museum; Rhodes University; SA National Gallery, Cape Town; University of Cape Town; Victoria and Albert Museum, London, UK; William Humphreys Art Gallery, Kimberley; and in public collections in India, Israel and Singapore.

Public Commissions Murals: 1907 Town Hall, Liverpool, UK; 1910 Royal Exchange, London, UK; 1921 St Michaels and All Angels Church, Boksburg, Transvaal; 1934 South Africa House, London, UK; 1935 William Cullen Library, University of the Witwatersrand; *c.*1936 Eu Tong Sen Collection, Singapore; 1937 Great Trek Panel in the Vestibule, City Hall, Pretoria; 1938 City Hall, Pretoria; 1941 two panels, Main Hall, New General Post Office, Cape Town; 1941 All Saints Church, Muizenberg, Cape Province. Numerous portrait commissions including Professor Albert Einstein, Mahatma Gandhi and other public figures.

References Sarah Briana Amshewitz, *The Paintings of J H Amshewitz RBA*, 1951, B T Batsford Ltd, London; Collectors' Guide; Art SA; SAA; SADNB; AMC1&6; DSAB; SAP&S; SAP&D; SESA; SSAP; DBA; BSAK 1 & 2; SA Art; AASA; SASSK; LSAA; *SA Art Collector* August 1947; *Artlook* January 1968; *SA Panorama* September 1983; *De Arte* September 1985.

ANCKETILL Oona (née Reason)

Born 1879 Durban.
Died 1955 Cape Town.
A painter of landscapes, portraits, still life and miniatures. Worked in oil, watercolour, charcoal and pencil. Painted portraits on ivory and retouched photographs.

Studies 1891–97 Durban Art School, under W H Tottendell Venner (qv).

Profile 1902 founded the Women's Suffrage League of SA, of which she was President in 1902 and 1907–08. Lived in Natal and the Cape.

Exhibitions Participated in group exhibitions from 1904.

Represented Tatham Art Gallery, Pietermaritzburg.

Public Commissions 1898–1900 three landscape murals for the Legislative Assembly of Natal; 1904–05 portrait of John Robinson, Provincial Council Building, Pietermaritzburg.

References Register SA & SWA; AASA.

ANDERSEN Nils Severin

Born 1897 Drammen, Norway.
Died 1972 Durban.
Resided in SA from 1911.
A painter of maritime subjects, figures, fishing villages, historical events and of landscapes often incorporating buildings. Worked in oil, watercolour, pastel and gouache. His graphic work included woodcuts, etchings and engravings.

Studies 1924–28 part-time at the Natal Technical College, under Professor O J P Oxley (qv) and Alfred Martin (qv); 1938 ceramics at the Natal Technical College.

Profile Several of his works were reproduced by E Schweickerdt, Pretoria. From 1924 a member of the NSA and its President in 1937, 1946, 1949 and 1955. 1940 appointed an Official War Artist to the Natal Command and the Royal Navy. 1942–48 taught at the Natal Technical College. Until 1911 spent his life at sea on his father's ship; 1911–13 lived at Saldanha Bay, thereafter in Durban. In 1917 travelled to Madagascar; 1919 to Mauritius and Réunion; 1923 went on a whaling expedition; 1935 visited Saldanha Bay; 1950 and 1951 SWA/Namibia; 1954 the Kalahari. Travelled extensively throughout SA.

Exhibitions Participated in numerous group exhibitions throughout SA from 1924; 1928 Durban Art Gallery, joint exhibition with Joy Krause (qv); 1931 Durban Art Gallery, first of numerous solo exhibitions held throughout SA; 1943–62 exhibited annually with E Schweickerdt, Pretoria.

Represented Africana Museum, Johannesburg; Ann Bryant Gallery, East London; Durban Art Gallery; King George VI Art Gallery, Port Elizabeth; National Museum, Bloemfontein; SA National Gallery, Cape Town; SA National Museum of Military History, Johannesburg; Tatham Art Gallery, Pietermaritzburg; University of Natal; Willem Annandale Art Gallery, Lichtenburg; William Humphreys Art Gallery, Kimberley.

Public Commissions Murals: 1930 frieze, Durban Children's Hospital; Dioramas, Durban Art Gallery; Norwegian Hall, Durban; Natal Chamber of Commerce, Durban; Natal Mercury, Durban; Sugar Association, Durban.

References Collectors' Guide; SAA; Benezit; BSAK 1 & 2; Art SWA; AASA; *The Studio* vol 119 no 563, February 1940; *Historia* vol xi no vi; *Artlook* February 1971.

ANDERSON Andrew Arthur

Born Scotland.
Died 1897.
Resided in SA from *c*.1850.

A painter of landscapes, army camp sites, flowers, trees, butterflies and places of archaeological note, often accompanied by inscriptions. Worked in watercolour.

Profile An early Scottish settler who farmed near Pietermaritzburg. From 1860 travelled extensively throughout SA, SWA/Namibia and Rhodesia (Zimbabwe), making maps and trading. 1878 served with the Frontier Light Horse in the Zulu War, 1879 transferred to the Royal Artillery. 1880–81 volunteered his service in the Transvaal War. Lived in England 1884–88, returning to SA in 1889.

Represented Africana Museum, Johannesburg.

Publications by Anderson *Twenty-five Years in a Wagon*, 2 volumes, illustrated, 1887, Chapman & Hall, republished by C Struik, Cape Town. A number of these illustrations were also used by J M Stuart in *The Ancient Gold Fields of Africa*, 1891, Express Printing Company, London.

References E C Tabler, *Pioneers of Rhodesia*, 1966, C Struik, Cape Town; Pict Art; AMC1 & 6; DSAB; Pict Afr; BSAK; Art SWA; *ANN* vol 15 no 8, December 1963.

ANDERSON Audrey Philippa (Toots)

Born 1928 Johannesburg.

A self-taught naive painter of landscapes with figures and of house portraits. Works in acrylic.

Exhibitions 1975 and 1977 Everard Read Gallery, Johannesburg, solo exhibitions.

Reference AASA.

ANDERSON Deane ARIBA MIA FRSA

Born 1906 Rondebosch, Cape Town.

Died 1982 Cape Town.

A painter of still life and of trees. Worked in oil, watercolour and ink.

Studies Bartlett School of Architecture, University College, London, under Professor Albert Richardson, gaining a BA (London) with Honours in Architecture; Slade School of Art, London, under Henry Tonks (1862–1937).

Profile A member of the International Association of Art Critics. A council member of the SAAA. 1947–54 an art critic on *The Argus* newspaper. 1955–77 taught at the Michaelis School of Fine Art. A trustee of the SA National Gallery, Cape Town. Decorated and embellished many Anglican churches in Cape Town.

Exhibitions Participated in numerous group exhibitions held in SA; 1944–45 solo exhibitions in Cairo and Alexandria, Egypt, sponsored by the Royal Air Force; 1948 first of several solo exhibitions held in Cape Town and Pretoria; 1956 and 1960 Quadrennial Exhibitions.

Represented National Gallery, Cairo, Egypt.

References Art SA; SAA; AASA.

ANDERSON Ilona

Born 1948 Johannesburg.

A painter of large figurative paintings, with a strong use of colour. Works in acrylic, watercolour, ink, charcoal, crayon, oil pastel and pastel.

Studies 1970–72 Johannesburg College of Education, under Larry Scully (qv) and Margaret McKean (qv), where gained a Teachers Training Higher Diploma; University of South Africa, where gained a Nursery School Diploma in 1975.

Profile Formerly taught at the Johannesburg Art Foundation. A designer of tapestries.

Exhibitions She has participated in many group exhibitions in SA and once in the USA, in 1982; 1979 Goodman Gallery, Johannesburg, first of four solo exhibitions; 1984–85 Four Johannesburg Painters, a touring exhibition with Ricky Burnett (qv), Robert Hodgins (qv) and Jo Smail (qv); 1985 Cape Town Triennial; 1985 Tributaries, touring SA and West Germany; 1987 and 1988 Johannesburg Art Gallery, Vita Art Now.

Award 1988 Fulbright Scholarship to the USA.
Represented Johannesburg Art Gallery; King George VI Art Gallery, Port Elizabeth; SA National Gallery, Cape Town; University of South Africa; University of the Witwatersrand.

ANDERSON John David Graham
Born 1935 Gwelo, Rhodesia (Gweru, Zimbabwe).
Resided in SA from 1959.
A painter of landscapes, seascapes, still life, figures and abstract pictures. Works in oil, watercolour, gouache, ink, wash, pencil and charcoal. A potter.
Studies 1959–64 part-time at the Michaelis School of Fine Art, under Maurice van Essche (qv), as well as privately under him.
Profile From 1984 a member of the WSSA. A medical practitioner. From 1966 a member of the Classical Guitar Society. Lived in Gwelo (Gweru), Umtali (Mutare) and Bulawayo in Rhodesia (Zimbabwe) and in Cape Town and Somerset West in SA. Has travelled throughout SA and to SWA/Namibia.
Exhibitions He has participated in many group exhibitions from 1949 in Zimbabwe, SA, the USA, and Australia; 1974 Edrich Gallery, Stellenbosch, first of six solo exhibitions.
Represented Bulawayo Museum, Zimbabwe.

ANDERSON Kathleen Winifred
Born 1878 Kokstad, East Griqualand.
Died 1968 Durban.
A painter of landscapes, townscapes, seascapes, ships, flowers, portraits, figures and genre. Worked in oil and watercolour. A series of historic buildings in Durban and the surrounding area. A number of plastercasts and etchings.
Studies 1894 Durban Art School, under W H Tottendell Venner (qv); 1899 South Kensington School, London; 1905 Crystal Palace Art School, London; 1906 animal painting at Frank Couldron's Art School, Baker Street, London, for four months; 1906 Slade School of Art, London, for six months.
Profile After her studies at Durban Art School she became an assistant teacher under W H Tottendell Venner (qv). 1905 a founder member of the NSA. A nurse at the Addington Hospital, Durban, and in the Red Cross. Served in the UK 1916–19 and was awarded the South African Medal for War Services in 1947.
Exhibitions Participated in many group exhibitions throughout SA, several in London and frequently with the NSA; 1946 and 1953 Durban Art Gallery, "Paintings of Durban" exhibitions; 1951 Durban, joint exhibition with Isa Cameron (qv); 1948–57 five solo exhibitions held in Durban.
Awards Gold, Silver and Bronze medals in Grahamstown, Pietermaritzburg and Durban for landscape and still life oil paintings.
Represented Ann Bryant Gallery, East London; Durban Art Gallery.
References Natal Art; BSAK; AASA.

ANDERSON Mala Matilda

Born 1956 Swakopmund, SWA/Namibia.

A painter working in mixed media.

Studies 1978 gained a BA(FA) from the University of Pretoria.

Profile From 1978 has taught art in Wellington and at Gordon's Bay, Cape Province.

Exhibitions She has participated in numerous group exhibitions from 1979 in SA; 1981 Republic Festival Exhibition; 1985 SAAA Gallery, Pretoria, solo exhibition.

Awards 1978 Merit Award, New Signatures, SAAA; 1979 First Prize Painting, Royal League, London.

ANDERSON Olive Margaret

Born 1938 Gatooma, Rhodesia (Kadoma, Zimbabwe).

Resided in SA from 1980.

A painter of botanical studies, landscapes, still life, seascapes and wildlife. Works in oil, acrylic, watercolour, gouache, ink, wash and pencil.

Studies 1957–59 University of Natal, under Professor Jack Heath (qv).

Profile A number of series of paintings including in 1965 25 paintings of birds; in 1970 15 of wildlife; 1972–80 over one thousand of trees and flora, insects and African artifacts; 1983–85 over two thousand biology illustrations; in 1985 30 of orchids. From 1979 she has contributed illustrations to various specialised periodicals and books including those of the Acacia fruits in *Trees of Southern Africa*, by Keith Coates Palgrave, 1977, C Struik, Cape Town; numerous illustrations for *Science Focus* volumes 5, 6 and 7 in 1983, and *Exploring Biology*, by Thienel, Pellew, Green-Thompson & Ayerst, 1985, both published by Shuter & Shooter, Pietermaritzburg; and all for *The Traditional Medical Practitioner in Zimbabwe*, by M Gelfand, 1985, Mambo Press, Gweru, Zimbabwe. 1972–80 botanical artist to the National Herbarium, Salisbury, Rhodesia (Harare, Zimbabwe); from 1983 a biology illustrator to Shuter & Shooter, Pietermaritzburg; from 1984 artist to the Institute of Natural Resources, Pietermaritzburg; from 1985 artist to the Department of Botany, University of Natal.

Exhibitions She has participated in several group exhibitions from 1971 in SA and Zimbabwe; 1977 Salisbury, Rhodesia (Harare, Zimbabwe), solo exhibition.

ANDOR Stephen

Born 1910 Budapest, Hungary.

Resided in SA from 1949.

A sculptor of figures. Works in bronze and ciment fondu.

Studies 1926–27 School of Fine Art, Budapest, under Arthur Podolini (qv).

Profile Began sculpting in 1960, prior to which he painted. Farmed in England during WWII. Lives in Johannesburg.

Exhibitions He has participated in many group exhibitions from 1962; 1967 Mona Lisa Gallery, Johannesburg, first of 11 solo exhibitions.
Represented Pietersburg Collection.
Reference BSAK.

ANDREW Richard Charles
Born 1947 Johannesburg.
A painter of landscapes and figures. Works in acrylic.
Studies 1966 Natal Technical College, under Barry Maritz (qv); 1967–69 University of Natal, under Professor Jack Heath (qv), gaining a BA and a University Education Diploma.
Profile From 1979 a member of the NSA. 1971–72 taught at Harwood Boys High School, Pietermaritzburg; 1973–74 at the Technical School, Pietermaritzburg; 1975 at Maritzburg College, Pietermaritzburg; 1977–80 at Hillcrest High School; from 1981 a lecturer in the Department of Creative Design, Natal Technikon. From 1976 a professional musician.
Exhibitions He has participated in several group exhibitions from 1979 in SA; 1980 NSA Gallery, Durban, first of two solo exhibitions in Durban; 1981 Republic Festival Exhibition.
Awards 1979 New Signatures Award, NSA; 1981 Painting Prize, Republic Festival Exhibition.
Represented Durban Art Gallery; Natal Technikon; SA Akademie vir Wetenskap en Kuns.
Reference AASA.

ANDREWS Raymond Hillary
Born 1948 East London.
A painter of figures and animals. Works on engraved wood panels in oil, silver and goldleaf. Additionally a graphic artist and a potter.
Studies 1966 Johannesburg Art School; 1967–68 under Cecil Skotnes (qv) and Ernest Ullmann (qv).
Profile 1978–79 an external tutor for the University of South Africa; 1973–74 a graphics lecturer at the University of Pretoria. 1973 illustrated *Xironga Folk Tales* published by the University of South Africa. 1969 shared a studio with Mike Costello (qv). 1969 spent six months in Malawi, 1969–71 lived in the Okavango Swamps. In 1973 he visited the Indian Ocean islands; in 1974 Japan and Taiwan; in 1977 Brazil and Australia; from 1974 he has made frequent visits to India, Nepal and Sri Lanka. The son of Victor Andrews (qv).
Exhibitions He has participated in numerous group exhibitions from 1967 in SA, Canada, Brazil, Italy, Japan, Austria, Spain, Israel, the USA, Belgium, Australia, France, Zimbabwe, West Germany and Switzerland; 1967 SAAA Gallery, Pretoria, first of 14 solo exhibitions held in SA; 1970 and 1972 National Museum, Botswana, solo exhibitions.

Award 1972 Bronze Medal, Carpi, Italy.
Represented Durban Art Gallery; National Gallery, Gaborone, Botswana; Pietersburg Collection; Potchefstroom Museum; Potchefstroom University for CHE; Pretoria Art Museum; Pretoria Technikon; Rand Afrikaans University; SA Akademie vir Wetenskap en Kuns; SA National Gallery, Cape Town; University of Durban-Westville; University of Natal; University of the Orange Free State; University of Pretoria; University of South Africa; University of the Witwatersrand; Walter Battiss Art Gallery, Somerset West; Willem Annandale Art Gallery, Lichtenburg; William Humphreys Art Gallery, Kimberley.
Public Commission 1981 mural, the State Theatre, Pretoria.
References BSAK 1 & 2; 3Cs; AASA; LSAA; *Artlook* August 1969; *SA Panorama* July 1969, June 1983 & December 1985.

ANDREWS Stephen RCA

Born 1922 Saskatoon, Saskatchewan, Canada.
A painter and graphic artist of abstract works often incorporating lettering. Works in acrylic, watercolour and in various graphic media. A creator of collages.
Studies Winnipeg School of Art, Canada; Chelsea Polytechnic and Camberwell School of Art, London; Académie Julian, Paris; Scuola del Mosaico, Ravenna, Italy and under Martin Bloch (1883–1954) in London.
Profile On leaving school he worked briefly as a cartographer. 1967 for eight months, a senior lecturer at the University of Alberta, Canada; 1969–71 a lecturer in design at the Michaelis School of Fine Art. Lived in Norway for three years and in India, the USA and Italy. On leaving SA he settled in Spain. Has travelled extensively throughout the world and revisited SA in 1979.
Exhibitions 1967 SAAA Gallery, Pretoria, first of several solo exhibitions held in SA; 1979 held solo exhibitions in Cape Town and Pretoria; he has also exhibited in Europe, the USA and Canada.
Represented Durban Art Gallery; Montreal Museum of Fine Art, Canada; National Gallery, Canada; Pretoria Art Museum; SA National Gallery, Cape Town.
References AASA; *Artlook* June 1967.

ANDREWS Victor

Born 1922 East London.
A self-taught painter of wildlife. Works in oil and pastel.
Profile For 26 years a copywriter and commercial artist for *The Daily Despatch*. Father of Raymond Andrews (qv).
Exhibitions He has participated in many group exhibitions from 1973 in SA, The Netherlands, Canada, Australia, Zimbabwe and the USA; 1969 SAAA Gallery, Pretoria, first of seven solo exhibitions held in SA and New Zealand.
References AASA; SASSK.

ANGAS George French
Born 1822 Durham, England.
Died 1886 London, England.
Resided in SA 1846–47.
Studies Thought to have studied drawing and lithography in London.
Profile Not strictly speaking a South African artist. Primarily a zoologist and an explorer who painted a number of watercolours of early South Africa, all of which have been made into lithographs. Known SA paintings by him are 19 of figures, nine of scenery and two of natural history. He travelled throughout the world and published many accounts of his travels generally illustrated with his drawings. In 1851 he settled in Australia and became a museum director in Sydney; by 1874 he had returned to England where he exhibited his work. The son of George Fife Angas, one of the founders of the colony of South Australia.
Exhibition 1948 Tate Gallery, London, SA Art Exhibition.
Represented Africana Museum, Johannesburg; British Museum, London, UK; SA Cultural History Museum, Cape Town; SA National Gallery, Cape Town; University of Natal; William Fehr Collection; Cape Town.
Publication by Angas *The Kafirs Illustrated*, 1849, J Hogarth Press, London; a facsimile reprint of the original edition with a new introduction by Frank R Bradlow, 1974, A A Balkema, Cape Town.
References Pict Art; Collectors' Guide; Afr Repos; SADNB; AMC1; DSAB; SAP&D; Pict Afr; Benezit; BSAK 1 & 2; Enc S'n A; SA Art; 3Cs; AASA; LSAA; *Apollo* October 1975, London.

ANGUS Prudence Mary (Mrs Van der Spuy)
Born 1942 Prestwick, Scotland.
Resided in SA from 1979.
A painter and graphic artist of seascapes and abstract works. Primarily an etcher, occasionally works in oil.
Studies 1968–69 Putney School of Art, London; 1969–74 Byam Shaw School of Art, London, under Geri Morgan, where gained a Byam Shaw Diploma in Fine Art and a London Diploma in Art and Design; 1975–78 Morley College, London.
Profile A member of the Chelsea Arts Club and the Print Collectors Club, Bankside Gallery, London.
Exhibitions She has participated in several group exhibitions from 1976 in the UK and Japan; 1985 Yellow Door Gallery, Cape Town, first of two solo exhibitions, the second being held in Stellenbosch.
Represented Kanagawa Prefectual Gallery, Japan; Provincial Library, Cape Town.

ANREITH Anton
Born 1754 Riegel, near Freiburg im Breisgau, South Germany.
Died 1822 Cape Town.
Resided in SA from 1777.
A sculptor in lime, brick, stucco, plaster and wood. Produced relief carvings and sculptures in the round, as well as decorations for public buildings in Cape Town in the rococo manner.

Studies 1762–76 possibly apprenticed to the sculptor, painter and architect Christian Wenzinger (1710–97) in Freiburg im Breisgau.

Profile In 1777 he joined the Dutch East India Company in Amsterdam, 1777–86 was employed as a workman and then as a carpenter in Cape Town. In 1786 was appointed Master Sculptor, leaving the Dutch East India Company in 1791. He worked with the French architect Louis-Michel Thibault (1750–1815) and the German master builder Hermann Schütte (qv). 1805–14 gave private drawing lessons in Cape Town. 1815–22 Principal of the Freemasons Technical Institute. In 1816 held an exhibition of his pupils' work, thought to have been the first art exhibition held in SA.

Represented SA Cultural History Museum, Cape Town; SA National Gallery, Cape Town.

Public Commissions 1783–85 organ loft and interior of the Lutheran Church, Strand Street, Cape Town; *c.*1787 statues for the organ, Paarl Church; 1788–89 pulpit, Groote Kerk, Cape Town; 1791–92 facade and two statues, Lutheran Church, Cape Town; 1801–04 seven symbolic statues (three survive), Lodge de Goede Hoop, Cape Town; 1803–05 Lioness and Lion Gateways, Government Gardens, Cape Town; 1805–06 New Fountain, Lion's Masks, Government Gardens, Cape Town. It is generally accepted that he also did the following work: 1785 Martin Melck Memorial, Lutheran Church, Cape Town; 1785–91 relief on parapet of Kat Balcony, entrance door and relief opposite, The Castle, Cape Town; 1791 relief for the wine cellar and Statue of Plenty, Groot Constantia, Cape Town, as well as many fanlights, pediments and carvings for houses in Cape Town.

References J Meintjes, *Anton Anrieth, Sculptor*, 1951, Cape Town; C de Bosdari, *Anton Anrieth, Africa's First Sculptor*, 1954, A A Balkema, Cape Town; Pict Art; Our Art 1; Art SA; SADNB; DSAB; SESA; SAP&D; Pict Afr; BSAK 1 & 2; Enc S'n A; SA Art; 3Cs; AASA; LSAA.

ANZISKA Doreen

Born 1920 Cape Town.

A sculptor of portraits. Works in clay, bronze, ciment fondu and wood.

Studies Michaelis School of Fine Art, under Ivan Mitford-Barberton (qv), where gained the Michaelis Prize in 1941.

Profile A member of the SAAA, of the Portrait Sculptors, London and the Federation of British Artists. Has travelled throughout Europe and to the USA, Turkey and Israel. Mother of Wendy Anziska (qv).

Exhibitions 1954 Maskew Miller Gallery, Cape Town, first solo exhibition; she has participated in numerous group exhibitions from 1962 in the UK, Paris and SA.

Award 1963 Bronze Medal, Société des Artistes Français, Paris Salon.

Represented University of Cape Town.

Public Commissions Numerous portrait bust commissions including those of General Louis Botha, Parliament, Cape Town; Professor Frank Forman, Medical Library, Cape Town; Professor J H Louw, Department of Surgery, University of Cape Town; Professor V Schrire, Groote Schuur Hospital, Cape Town; Professor Albert Einstein, Imperial College of Science and Technology, London and in the Albert Einstein College of Medicine, New York.

Reference AASA.

ANZISKA Wendy (Mrs Isaacs)

Born 1945 Cape Town.
A painter of nature and the human element. Works in oil.
Studies 1962–68 Michaelis School of Fine Art, under Professor Maurice van Essche (qv), Carl Buchner (qv), May Hillhouse (qv) and Katrine Harries (qv), where gained a Certificate in Fine and Graphic Art.
Profile Has visited the Far East, France, the UK and South America. Daughter of Doreen Anziska (qv).
Exhibitions She has participated in many group exhibitions from 1970 in SA, Australia and Israel; 1970 Wolpe Gallery, Cape Town, first of six solo exhibitions held in Cape Town; 1981 Republic Festival Exhibition.
Represented Pietersburg Art Gallery; Pretoria Art Museum; Rand Afrikaans University; SA National Gallery, Cape Town; University of Stellenbosch.
References AASA; *Artlook* June 1973; *Contrast* Summer Edition 1976; *Gallery* no 33, 1981 and Autumn 1983; *Lantern* April 1985; *Living* October 1985; *Cosmopolitan* October 1985.

APPOLLIS Tyrone Errol

Born 1957 Cape Town.
A painter and graphic artist of landscapes, portraits and figures. Works in oil, watercolour, gouache, ink, pencil, charcoal and in various graphic media. From 1981 a sculptor. From *c.*1982 a series of third-class passengers and train scenes.
Studies 1987 studying for a Diploma at the SA Foundation School, under Barbara Pitt.
Profile Several illustrations for magazines from 1985. A poet.
Exhibitions He has participated in group exhibitions in Cape Town; 1982 Rocklands Library, Mitchell's Plain, solo exhibition.
Reference *Contrast* December 1985.

ARBER Kenelm Everard

Born 1933 Manikpur, India.
A painter and sculptor of portraits and still life. Works in oil, acrylic, stone and wood.
Profile 1966–68 a Director of the Adler Fielding Gallery, Johannesburg; 1966–71 an art critic for the *Financial Gazette*. 1962–64 owner/manager of Serendipity Gallery. 1971–78 a full-time painter living in Ibiza, Majorca, and Spain.
Exhibitions He has participated in several group exhibitions from 1973 in Majorca and SA; Gallery Figuerettas, Spain, first of five solo exhibitions, three held in Spain and two in SA.
Public Commission 1972 portrait of Indra, Princess of Kapurthala, Indian Embassy, Madrid, Spain.

ARBUTHNOT Jane

Born 1819 Peterhead, Aberdeenshire, Scotland.
Died 1907 Equeefa, Natal.
Resided in SA from 1850.
Profile A large number of pencil sketches of Natal landscapes in unpublished albums. Wrote *Autographical Sketch*, 1897, unpublished, a copy of which remains in the Killie Campbell Africana Library, Durban.
References Natal Art; Shelagh O'Byrne Spencer, *British Settlers in Natal 1824–57, a biographical register*, volume 1, 1981, University of Natal Press, Pietermaritzburg.

ARGENT Charles

Born 1913 England.
Died 1982 London, England.
Resided in SA 1948–61.
A painter of landscapes, figures and still life. Worked in oil, ink and wash. In 1950 he began producing collages using materials such as bus tickets, empty tubes of paint, gold and other coloured papers, and ribbons.
Studies Birmingham College of Art, where his studies were interrupted by WWII; 1945–49 Reading University, UK, gaining a BA(FA).
Profile 1949–61 a lecturer in the History of Art and on Painting at the University of the Witwatersrand. 1961–75 held the Chair of Fine Art at Ahmadu Bello University, Zaria, Northern Nigeria. Wrote occasional articles on art whilst in SA. 1975–82 lived in London.
Exhibitions Participated in several group exhibitions from 1949 in SA; 1951 Whippman's Gallery, Johannesburg, first of nine solo exhibitions.
References SAA; BSAK 1 & 2; AASA; *SA Architectural Record* vol 37 no 8, August 1952; *SA Art News* 22 June 1961.

ARMSTRONG Frederick William ARCA

Born 1875 Durham, England.
Died 1968 Vereeniging, Transvaal.
Resided in SA from 1904.
A sculptor of portrait busts and panels. A painter in watercolour, a potter, scribe, engraver and a stained glass artist.
Studies Royal College of Art, London, gaining an Associateship with distinction.
Profile 1918 founded the Eastern Province Society of Arts and Crafts. A member of the SA Society of Artists. 1904–25 Art Master at Grahamstown School of Art and first Professor when, in 1926, it became the Fine Art Department of Rhodes University; 1929–32 taught at the Witwatersrand Technical College. 1922 and 1923 visited Victoria Falls, Rhodesia (Zimbabwe). Grandfather of Geoffrey Armstrong (qv).

Exhibitions Participated in several exhibitions in Grahamstown, Springs and Bulawayo; 1924 Grahamstown, solo exhibition; 1971 Hill High School, Johannesburg, posthumous exhibition of his paintings, sculpture and pottery.
Award 1924 Gold Medal for Pottery, Empire Exhibition, Wembley, England.
Represented Albany Museum, Grahamstown.
Public Commissions Bust of Sir William Hoy, Johannesburg Station; high relief panel of Cecil Rhodes, Town Hall, Bulawayo, Zimbabwe. Panels in Voortrekker Museum, Pietermaritzburg, in Uitenhage Town Hall and in Rhodes Great Hall, Grahamstown. Memorial stained glass in Christ Church, Grahamstown.
References SESA; BSAK 1 & 2; AASA.

ARMSTRONG Geoffrey Lawrence Vinal

Born 1945 Vereeniging, Transvaal.
A painter and sculptor of landscapes, figures and abstracts. Works in oil, acrylic, watercolour, ink, wash, pencil, charcoal, stone, wood and synthetic enamel. A graphic artist producing monotypes.
Studies Johannesburg Art School, under Joyce Leonard (qv) and George Boys (qv).
Profile 1969–75 lived and worked in England; 1976–77 lived in SA, with several visits to England; thereafter based in England, with visits to SA. Grandson of Frederick Armstrong (qv).
Exhibitions He has participated in numerous group exhibitions in SA and England; 1964 Lidchi Art Gallery, Johannesburg, first of *c*.10 solo exhibitions held in SA and England; 1971 Lidchi Gallery, Johannesburg, joint exhibition with Louis Maqhubela (qv) and Sydney Kumalo (qv); 1976 University of the Witwatersrand, Prestige Exhibition; 1977 the sole representative of SA artists at the São Paulo Bienale, Brazil; 1987 Karen McKerron Gallery, Johannesburg, joint exhibition with Claire Gavronsky (qv) and Gregory Kerr (qv).
Represented Johannesburg Art Gallery; Rand Afrikaans University; Sandton Municipal Collection; University of the Witwatersrand.
References BSAK 1 & 2; AASA; *Artlook* January 1967, December 1967 & February 1969; *SA Panorama* January 1978; *Habitat* no 56, 1983.

ARMSTRONG Juliet Yvonne

Born 1950 Durban.
A sculptor of landscapes. Works in ceramics.
Studies 1968–72 University of Natal, under Professor A Duckworth and Professor H Ditchburn (qv), where gained a BA(FA); 1973–74 Leicester Polytechnic, England, under John Cook, gaining a Postgraduate Diploma; 1979 ceramic sculpture at the University of Natal, under Professor H Ditchburn (qv), gaining an MA(FA) in 1981.
Profile From 1977 a lecturer at the University of Natal.
Exhibitions She has participated in several group exhibitions in SA; 1977 Jack Heath Gallery, Pietermaritzburg, solo exhibition; 1982 Cape Town Triennial; 1985 Cape Town Triennial.

Award 1984 joint winner of APSA National Exhibition.
Represented Durban Art Gallery; Pretoria Art Museum; Tatham Art Gallery, Pietermaritzburg; Touch Gallery, SA National Gallery, Cape Town; University of Natal, Corobrick Collection.
References 3Cs; AASA: *Sgraffiti* nos 33 & 39.

ARNOLD Ben

Born 1942 Albertsville, Johannesburg.
A sculptor of figures. Works in terracotta, plaster and bronze. Additionally sculpts friezes.
Studies Polly Street Art Centre, under Cecil Skotnes (qv) and Sydney Kumalo (qv).
Profile During the 1960s taught at the Jubilee Art Centre, Johannesburg. 1965 taught at the Zenzele Arts Project for Children in Soweto. He also taught at FUBA.
Exhibitions He has participated in many group exhibitions held in SA; 1964 Egon Guenther Gallery, Johannesburg, first of many solo exhibitions; 1981 Standard Bank, Soweto, Black Art Today; 1982 National Gallery, Gaborone, Botswana, Exhibition of SA Art; 1985 Tributaries, touring SA and West Germany.
References BSAK 1; AASA; Echoes of African Art; *Artlook* January 1961, December 1967, December 1968 & February 1969; *SA Panorama* July 1982.

ARNOLD Marion

Born 1947 London, England.
A painter of landscapes and still life. Works in oil, watercolour, pencil, mixed media and pastel. From 1984 she has made her own sculpted frames.
Studies 1966–69 University of Natal, where gained a BA in 1968 and a BA(FA) in 1969; 1970 gained a Graduate Certificate in Education, London; 1978 University of South Africa, gaining a BA with Honours in History of Art.
Profile A member of the SAAA and the SAAAH. She spent her childhood in Rhodesia (Zimbabwe). Whilst in Salisbury (Harare) she ran her own art studio and taught at a secondary school. From 1979 a lecturer in the Department of History of Art and Fine Art, University of South Africa. From 1975 an art critic, writing articles for *Herald* (1975–79), *Pretoria News*, *De Arte*, *Lantern*, *Arts Zimbabwe* and *De Kat*. Visits Zimbabwe regularly.
Exhibitions She has participated in numerous group exhibitions from 1968 held in Zimbabwe, SA, the USA and West Germany; 1970 first of three solo exhibitions held in Salisbury (Harare); 1981 SAAA Gallery, Pretoria, first of three joint exhibitions held with Wendy Ross (qv); 1982 Cape Town Triennial; 1985 Cape Town Triennial; 1985 1820 Settlers National Monument, Grahamstown, solo exhibition travelling to Johannesburg Art Gallery, Pretoria Art Museum, University of Natal and the University of the Orange Free State; 1985 Tributaries, touring SA and West Germany; 1988 Goodman Gallery, Johannesburg, joint exhibition with Mashego Johannes Segogela (qv).

Award 1985 Standard Bank Young Artists Award for Fine Art.
Represented Johannesburg Art Gallery; National Gallery, Harare, Zimbabwe; Pretoria Art Museum; SA National Gallery, Cape Town; University of the Orange Free State; University of South Africa; University of the Witwatersrand.
Publications by Arnold *Zimbabwe Stone Sculpture*, 1981, Books of Zimbabwe, Bulawayo. Wrote an essay "Confronting Paintings" in *Walter Battiss*, edited by K M Skawran and M Macnamara, 1985, Ad Donker, Johannesburg.
References *De Kat* July 1985; Standard Bank Young Artist Catalogue, 1985.

ARNOLD Vivienne

Born 1960.
A painter of abstract pictures. Works in oil and acrylic.
Exhibitions She has participated in several group exhibitions from 1983 held in Johannesburg; 1983 Things Gallery, Melville, Johannesburg, solo exhibition.

ARNOTT Bruce Murray

Born 1938 Highflats, Natal.
A sculptor, working in bronze, stone, ciment fondu, lead, wood, resin, fibreglass and acrylic.
Studies 1957–61 Michaelis School of Fine Art, under Lippy Lipshitz (qv), gaining a BA(FA) in 1960, an MA(FA) and the Michaelis Prize in 1961; 1964–65 Courtauld Institute, University of London, on a British Council Scholarship.
Profile 1980 a founder member of the Artists Guild, Cape Town. 1974 a temporary lecturer, 1978–79 a lecturer, 1980–82 a senior lecturer, from 1983 Associate Professor and Head of the Sculpture Department at the Michaelis School of Fine Art. 1970–72 Assistant Director of SA National Gallery, Cape Town. 1972–78 lived in the Drakensberg, thereafter in Cape Town.
Exhibitions He has participated in numerous group exhibitions from 1959 in SA, at São Paulo, Brazil and in West Germany; 1967 Wolpe Gallery, Cape Town, first of three major solo exhibitions; 1979 Cape Town Biennial, Invited Artist; 1985 Tributaries, touring SA and West Germany.
Represented Johannesburg Art Gallery; Pretoria Art Museum; SA National Gallery, Cape Town; Tatham Art Gallery, Pietermaritzburg; University of Cape Town.
Public Commissions 1977 "Sphinx", Baxter Theatre, University of Cape Town; 1979 "Numinous Beast", SA National Gallery, Cape Town; 1984–85 "Opera", "Drama", "Dance" and "Music", Sand du Plessis Theatre, Bloemfontein; 1985 "Regency Punch", Natal Playhouse, Durban; 1985–86 "Blacksmith", 1820 Foundation, Grahamstown; 1985–86 "Citizen", Johannesburg Centenary, Johannesburg Art Gallery.
Publications by Arnott *Lippy Lipshitz* (qv), 1969, A A Balkema, Cape Town; *Claude Bouscharain* (qv), 1977, C Struik, Cape Town; *John Muafangejo* (qv), 1977, C Struik, Cape Town.
References SAP&S; SESA; BSAK; 3Cs; AASA; LSAA; *Artlook* January 1967; *Gallery* Autumn 1982.

ARNOTT (George) Graeme

Born 1941 Salisbury, Rhodesia (Harare, Zimbabwe).
Resided in SA from 1977.
A self-taught painter of wildlife, particularly birds. Works in oil, watercolour, gouache and pencil.
Profile A trained teacher, now working full-time as an artist. Illustrated the following books: Peter Steyn, *Birds of Prey of Southern Africa*, 1982, David Philip, Cape Town and M K Rowan, *Doves, Parrots, Louries and Cuckoos of Southern Africa*, 1983, David Philip, Cape Town. During 1986 and 1987 was working on the illustrations for A Harris, *Shrikes of Southern Africa*, due to be published in 1988, by Winchester Press, Johannesburg.
Exhibitions He has participated in several group exhibitions from 1972 in Zimbabwe and SA; 1979 Cape Town, first of three solo exhibitions.

ARNOTT Lauryn

Born 1960 Kitwe, Zambia.
An artist producing drawings, paintings, and graphic works. Her pictures depict portraits and figures.
Studies Natal Technikon, gaining a Diploma in Fine Art; *c.*1985 postgraduate work at the Michaelis School of Fine Art.
Profile Lives in Cape Town.
Exhibitions She has participated in several group exhibitions from 1980 held in SA; 1981 Elizabeth Sneddon Theatre, Durban, first of three solo exhibitions, the second and third being held in Cape Town and Johannesburg respectively; 1985 Tributaries, touring SA and West Germany.
Award 1981 New Signatures Award, NSA.
Represented SA National Gallery, Cape Town.

ARRIDGE Margaret Irene Chadwick (Peggy) (Mrs IMC Farquharson)

Born 1921 Salisbury, England.
Resided in SA from 1937.
A painter of flowers, gardens, quarries, landscapes, portraits and still life. Works in oil, watercolour, gouache, pastel and pencil.
Studies Chelsea School of Art, London, and privately under Bernard Adams (*fl.*1916–39); miniature painting privately under Violet Butler (qv).
Profile From 1949 an Associate Member of the Royal Society of Miniature Painters and from 1985 of the National Society, London. She has taught art privately in Johannesburg. 1921–37 and 1950–54 lived in England. Visits England annually and has travelled in France and Italy.
Exhibitions She has participated in numerous group exhibitions in SA, in London annually and in Paris; 1959 Johannesburg, first solo exhibition.
Award 1981 Third Prize, International Artists in Watercolour Painting, Mall Galleries, London.
References BSAK; *Artlook* January 1971.

ASCHENBORN Dieter

Born 1915 Okahandja, SWA/Namibia.

A painter and a carver of landscapes and wildlife. Works in acrylic, watercolour, ink, and with a knife on Kudu skin and other leathers. Also carves wooden panels.

Studies Studied under H A Aschenborn (qv).

Profile A magazine and book illustrator and a designer of stamps. 1920 lived in Germany. During the early 1930s he farmed in the Transvaal. A former game warden at Etosha Pan, SWA/Namibia. 1963 lived in Windhoek. Son of H A Aschenborn (qv).

Exhibitions He has participated in group exhibitions in SA, SWA/Namibia and West Germany; 1965 Assembley Hall, Windhoek, exhibition of the three generations of Aschenborns; 1976 Orde Levinson Fine Art, Johannesburg, solo exhibition; 1984 E Schweickerdt Gallery, Pretoria, solo exhibition.

Public Commissions Panels for schools and hotels in Windhoek.

Represented Arts Association SWA/Namibia Collection; War Museum of the Boer Republics, Bloemfontein.

References AASA; *Animal Art of Etosha*, 1986, Department of Agriculture and Nature Conservation, Windhoek; *SA Panorama* April 1970.

ASCHENBORN Hans Anton Heinrich

Born 1888 Kiel, Germany.

Died 1931 Kiel, Germany.

Resided in SWA/Namibia and SA 1909–21.

Renowned for his graphic work. Aschenborn also painted, mainly in watercolour until 1914 and thereafter in watercolour, oil, chalk, gouache and mixed media. His subject matter was generally of wildlife and figures set in a landscape.

Studies Mainly self-taught, but received some tuition from Professor Burmester in Kassel, West Germany.

Profile A large number of his lithographs have been printed including "Afrikanische Tierkopfe", "Aschenborn's Afrikamappe", both published in 1917 in Swakopmund; three portfolios of reproductions: 10 linocuts in 1971, etchings in 1972 and lithographs in 1973, all printed by Phoenix, East Lynne, Pretoria. A large number of illustrations for books including *Ehombo* by Steinhardt, 1923, J Neumann, Neudamm; *Uit Oerwoud en Vlakte* by Sangiro; *Op Leeutemmer en Ander Vertellings* by Doctor Grosskopf and a number of his own books. His illustrations and linocuts were also used in SWA/Namibian newspapers. A writer of art reviews, poems and short stories. 1909–13 lived in SWA/Namibia; 1914–17 interned at Pietermaritzburg; 1917–20 farmed at Okahandja, SWA/Namibia; 1920–21 lived in Stellenbosch; 1921–25 in Germany; 1925–28 in East Africa; 1928–31 in Germany. Father of Dieter Aschenborn (qv) and grandfather of Hans U Aschenborn.

Exhibitions Participated in several group exhibitions in SWA/Namibia; 1965 Assembly Hall, Windhoek, exhibition of the three generations of Aschenborns; 1970 Pretoria Art Museum, Commemorative Exhibition; 1981 Arts Association SWA/Namibia Gallery, Windhoek, Commemorative Exhibition.

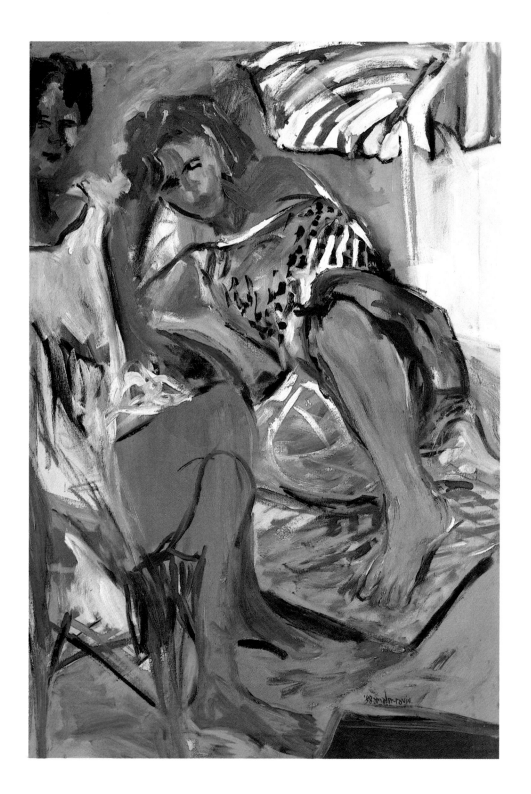

ARLENE AMALER-RAVIV
Sunday Afternoon in Armadale Road 1988
Oil on Canvas 99 × 145 cm
Mr & Mrs E A Limberis

RAYMOND ANDREWS
Flower Seller 1985
Gold, Silver & Oil on Panel 130 × 80 cm
Private

BRUCE ARNOTT
Citizen 1985
Bronze 2,25 m High excluding granite base
Johannesburg Art Gallery

KEVIN ATKINSON
Early One Morning 1985
2,4 m × 3,6 m
Durban Art Gallery

Represented Pretoria Art Museum; University of South Africa; William Humphreys Art Gallery, Kimberley.

Publications by Aschenborn Wrote and illustrated *Uit Die Lewe van 'n Gemsbok*, 1923, Juta & Company, Cape Town and *Die Adelaar and ander Afrikaanse Verhale*, 1923, Nasionale Pers, Cape Town. Wrote *Afrikanische Buschreiter*, 1926, August Scheil GmbH, Berlin, a book about his early experiences in SWA/Namibia, *Die Farm, Steppenlande* and *Die Zweite Heimat*, a book of poems with illustrations, 1981, Phoenix, East Lynne, Pretoria.

References Collectors' Guide; SAA; SADNB; DSAB; BSAK 1 & 2; SESA; Enc S'n A; Art SWA; SA Art; AASA; LSAA; *Fontein* no 3 Summer 1960; *Historia* vol 1 no 1, March 1965; *Lantern* December 1965; *SA Panorama* April 1970.

ASHBORN Colombè Marié Amabel

Born 1938 Kroonstad, Orange Free State.

A painter of landscapes, portraits, still life and of historical buildings. Works in watercolour and ink. Additionally produces serigraphs. A series of 12 watercolour and pen drawings of Church Square, Pretoria. 1985–86 a series of 10 serigraphs of Graaff-Reinet.

Studies 1959–61 Pretoria Technical College, under Ernst de Jong (qv), Peter Eliastam (qv), Albert Werth (qv), Johan van Heerden (qv), Leo Theron (qv), Carol Hamilton and Maxie Steytler, gaining a Diploma with Honours in Commercial Art.

Profile From 1965 a member of the SAAA. 1963–66 a senior lecturer in Graphic Design, Pretoria Technical College; 1973 a lecturer in Graphic Design at the University of Pretoria. 1961 designed the South West Coat of Arms. 1967–68 drew a number of illustrations for books on chemistry. 1985 moved from Pretoria to the Orange Free State. 1982 visited Pilgrim's Rest, Eastern Transvaal, 1983 Stellenbosch; 1984 spent three months on the Greek islands; 1985 in Graaff-Reinet. Married to Keith Ashborn (qv).

Exhibitions She has participated in many group exhibitions from 1977 in SA and West Germany; 1978 Hoffer Gallery, Pretoria, first of five solo exhibitions held in SA; she has also held *c.*10 solo exhibitions in private homes.

Represented Potchefstroom Museum; Potchefstroom University for CHE; University of Bophuthatswana; University of Pretoria; Willem Annandale Art Gallery, Lichtenburg.

Reference AASA.

ASHBORN Keith Denzil

Born 1940 Bloemfontein.

Until 1980 a painter of landscapes. Worked in acrylic and watercolour. From 1980 a sculptor of figures, working in welded steel.

Studies 1964–65 University of South Africa, under Professor Walter Battiss (qv); 1965–68 Pretoria Technical College, under Colombè Ashborn (qv) and Gunther van der Reis (qv).

Profile A graphic designer until 1980 and a designer of jewellery. In 1984 visited Greece and Europe. Married to Colombè Ashborn (qv).
Exhibitions He has participated in many group exhibitions from 1972 in SA; 1977 Hoffer Gallery, Pretoria, first of six solo exhibitions.
Represented Potchefstroom University for CHE; Willem Annandale Art Gallery, Lichtenburg.
Reference *Gallery* Summer 1982.

ASHTON William Percy (Bill)

Born 1925 Mooi River, Natal.
A painter of landscapes and still life. Works in acrylic, pen and ink, oil and watercolour.
Studies 1946 under Professor Gaido in Rome; 1947–48 Johannesburg School of Art; 1955–63 life classes in Johannesburg.
Profile 1959–64 a cartoonist with the *Sunday Express*. He later worked part-time for the *Sunday Express*. His cartoons have also appeared in *Die Brandwag*, *Dagbreek, Sondagnuus, Golden City Post* and *The Star*. A designer and illustrator. 1964–74 farmed in the Sabie area of the Eastern Transvaal. From 1974 he has lived in Johannesburg.
Exhibitions 1965 and 1975 solo exhibitions held in Cape Town, Johannesburg, Kimberley and Durban.
Award 1963 Special Award, Art Directors Club, New York.
Represented Africana Museum, Johannesburg.
Reference SASSK.

ATHERSTONE William Guybon Doctor

Born 1814 Nottingham, England.
Died 1898 Grahamstown.
Resided in SA from 1820.
A painter of genre, especially of tribal life. Worked in watercolour.
Profile A medical practitioner in Grahamstown, he is reputed to have performed the first operation in SA on an anaesthetised patient. He founded the Grahamstown Library and Botanical Gardens, and in 1855 the Albany Museum in Grahamstown.
Represented SA National Gallery, Cape Town.
References Pict Art; H E Hockley, *The Story of the British Settlers of 1820 in SA*, 2nd edition, 1957, Juta, Cape Town; SADNB; DSAB; SESA; SAP&D; Pict Afr; BSAK; Enc S'n A; *SA Panorama* 15 October 1967; *Lantern* 7 September 1970.

ATKINS Harry

Born 1909 Wallasey, Cheshire, England.
Died 1983 Port Elizabeth.
Resided in SA from 1947.
A sculptor of portrait busts and reliefs. Worked in stone and wood.

Studies 1923–26 Birmingham Art School, England; apprenticed in the studio of William J Boyle; 1931 Birmingham College of Art, England; also under Eric Gill (1882–1940) in London.

Profile 1931–39 taught at Small Heath Art School, Birmingham College of Art and established his own studio. 1947 taught sculpture at Port Elizabeth School of Art. 1965–72 Head of the Sculpture Department, University of Natal. 1948–65 travelled throughout SA.

Exhibitions Participated in several group exhibitions; 1981 Republic Festival Exhibition; 1983 King George VI Art Gallery, Port Elizabeth, Retrospective Exhibition.

Public Commissions Numerous commissions including that of a bust of Sir Ernest Oppenheimer; a carved relief in the Church of the Vow, Pietermaritzburg; a series of carved panels, Provincial Administration Headquarters, Pietermaritzburg; also panels in banks in Port Elizabeth and in St Andrews College and the Albany Museum in Grahamstown; 1982 crest, Port Elizabeth City Hall. Reliefs in the UK at the Universities of Birmingham, Leeds and Oxford and at the Civic Centres in Bolton and Ruislip; reliefs in Zimbabwe at the Pearl Insurance Building, Harare and Barclays Bank, Bulawayo.

Represented King George VI Art Gallery, Port Elizabeth.

References AASA; King George VI Art Gallery Retrospective Exhibition Catalogue 1983.

ATKINSON Kevin

Born 1939 Cape Town.

A painter and graphic artist of abstract pictures and abstracted landscapes, occasional use of lettering. Works in acrylic, pastel and makes serigraphs. Creates murals and large multiple canvas paintings linked by hinges. Occasionally works on aluminium sheeting.

Studies 1959–62 on Sir Abe Bailey and Government Scholarships, at the Michaelis School of Fine Art, gaining a BA(FA); 1965 Atelier 17, Paris, under Stanley Hayter (*b*.1901); University of Sussex, Brighton, England, under Jennifer Dickson; lithography under Emile Mathieu in Zurich. 1978 attained an MA(FA).

Profile 1965 a founder member of the Artists Gallery, Cape Town, of which he was Chairman in 1966; 1972 a founder member of the Space Gallery, Cape Town; 1980 a founder member and Vice-Chairman of the Artists Guild, Cape Town. 1963 co-founder and Director of the Cape Town Art Centre; 1968 Director and Founder of The Visual Arts Research Centre, Cape Town; 1970 Founder of the Cape Town Graphic Workshop. 1964 a lecturer in drawing and painting at the Cape Town Technical College; 1973 a lecturer, 1975 a senior lecuturer, later becoming an Associate Professor in Fine Art at the Michaelis School of Fine Art. During the early 1970s he became interested in photography and film-making. An art consultant with Neville Dubow and Richard Wake (qv) for the Beachfront Redevelopement Scheme, Muizenberg, Cape Province. 1964–75 made numerous study tours of Europe. Married to Patricia Pierce-Atkinson (qv).

Exhibitions He has participated in numerous group exhibitions from 1963 held throughout SA and in São Paulo, Edinburgh, Athens, Monte Carlo, Tel Aviv and in West Germany and the USA; 1967 Johannesburg, first of many solo exhibitions held in SA; 1970 Goodman Gallery, Johannesburg, joint exhibition with Richard Wake (qv); 1972 Durban Art Gallery, solo exhibition of "Conceptual Art"; 1978 University of the Witwatersrand and the University of Natal, solo exhibitions; 1979 Cape Town Biennial, Invited Artist; 1982 Cape Town Triennial; 1983 University of Stellenbosch, joint exhibition with Patricia Pierce-Atkinson (qv); 1985 Tributaries, touring SA and West Germany; 1985 University of the Witwatersrand, solo exhibition.

Award 1966 Gold Medal, SA Breweries Art Prize.

Represented Durban Art Gallery; Johannesburg Art Gallery; Johannesburg College of Education; Pretoria Art Museum; SA National Gallery, Cape Town; University of Natal; University of the Orange Free State; University of South Africa; University of Stellenbosch; University of the Witwatersrand.

Public Commissions 1970 a relief mural, joint winner with Richard Wake (qv) of the 1820 Settlers Memorial Monument Competition; numerous murals in the Cape and the Transvaal including in 1964 a mosaic mural, Dutch Reformed Church, Robertson, Cape; 1970 mural, Jan Smuts Airport, Johannesburg; 1974 mural, Forest Trust Building, Cape Town; 1975 mural, Colosseum Building, Cape Town.

References SAP&S; SAP&D; SSAP; Oxford Companion to 20C Art (under SA); 3Cs; AASA; LSAA; *Artlook* February 1971; *Habitat* no 25, 1977.

AUGUSTINUS Paul Brian Dons

Born 1952 Haderslev, Denmark.

A self-taught painter of wildlife and landscapes. Works in oil, acrylic, watercolour, gouache and pastel.

Profile He has travelled throughout Africa and lived in Mozambique, Tanzania and Kenya. Since 1977 he has lived and painted in the bush in Botswana.

Exhibitions He has participated in group exhibitions since 1980 in the USA, Botswana and Johannesburg; 1987 Everard Read Gallery, Johannesburg, solo exhibition of the illustrations for his book.

Publication by Augustinus Botswana—A Brush with The Wild, 1987, Acorn Books, Johannesburg.

AYTON Carol (Mrs Symonds)

Born 1950 Mufilira, Zambia.

Produces mixed media drawings. 1984 "Inferno Series".

Studies 1971 gained a BA(FA) from the Michaelis School of Fine Art; 1972 gained a Higher Diploma in Education from the University of Cape Town.

Profile From 1973 an Art and English teacher at various high schools in Cape Town. Regularly visits Europe, the UK and the USA.

Exhibitions She has participated in group exhibitions in The Netherlands and SA.

B

BADENHORST Francois

Born 1934 Pietersburg, Northern Transvaal.

A painter of landscapes, seascapes, still life and portraits. Works in oil, acrylic and watercolour.

Studies 1954 Giotto Academy of Arts, Johannesburg, under Sidney Goldblatt (qv).

Exhibitions He has participated in several group exhibitions from 1973 in SA and one in Gaborone, Botswana; 1974 Carlton Centre, Johannesburg, first of 25 solo exhibitions.

Represented National Gallery, Gaborone, Botswana; Pietersburg Collection.

Public Commissions A number of portraits of SA notability.

BADENHORST Philip

Born 1957 Ottosdal, Western Transvaal.

A painter of genre and abstract pictures. Works in oil, watercolour and mixed media.

Studies 1981–84 Potchefstroom University for CHE, under Nola Strauss and Basie Koen, where gained a BA(FA). Awarded the Gregoire Boonzaier Bursaries for Painting in 1983 and 1986. 1987 studying for an MA(FA) at Potchefstroom University for CHE.

Profile From 1987 a member of the SAAA. From 1985 a junior lecturer in painting at Potchefstroom University for CHE.

Exhibitions 1983 Nedbank, Potchefstroom, first of nine solo exhibitions held in Potchefstroom, Pretoria and Hout Bay, Cape Province; he has participated in several group exhibitions from 1984 in SA.

Awards 1983 Winner of the Perm Kuesta Art Festival, Potchefstroom University for CHE; 1985 Merit Award, Rolfes Impressions, Johannesburg Art Gallery.

Represented Potchefstroom Municipality; Potchefstroom University for CHE; Pretoria Art Museum; Willem Annandale Art Gallery, Lichtenburg.

BADENHORST Rina (Mrs H C de Wet)

Born 1942 Schweizer-Reneke, Western Transvaal.

A painter of landscapes, figures, portraits, still life, genre, seascapes, seagulls and abstract pictures. Works mostly in oil but also in watercolour, gouache, pencil and charcoal. 1981–82 rockscape series; 1982 glass bird series; 1982 and 1985 shell series.

Studies 1961–63 University of Pretoria, under Professor N F Nilant and H van der Westhuizen, with art classes under Gunther van der Reis (qv) and André de Beer (qv), gained a BA; 1963–64 Pretoria Teachers Training College, gaining a Higher Diploma in Education.

Profile From 1971 a member of the SAAA. 1965–66 an art teacher at the Transvalia High School, Pretoria; 1975–80 taught art privately in Port Elizabeth. From 1977 a music, literature and art critic for *Oosterlig*. 1942–60 lived in the Western Transvaal; 1961–69 in Pretoria; from 1970 in Port Elizabeth; 1976 and 1980 visited Europe.

Exhibitions She has participated in many group exhibitions in SA from 1965; 1975 University of Port Elizabeth, first of seven solo exhibitions.

Represented Potchefstroom University for CHE; Willem Annandale Art Gallery, Lichtenburg.

Public Commissions 1976–80 two portrait commissions from the Eastern Cape Development Board, Port Elizabeth.

BAILEY Beezy

Born 1962 Johannesburg.

A painter of landscapes, seascapes, portraits and figures. Works in oil, acrylic, gouache, pastel, ink, wash, pencil, charcoal, wood, driftwood and clay. A graphic artist and sculptor.

Studies 1983–86 Byam Shaw School of Art, London, where gained a Diploma in Fine Art.

Profile From 1983 annual visits to France; 1985 visited SWA/Namibia; 1987 the Cape. Brother of Jessica Bailey (qv).

Exhibitions He has participated in several group exhibitions from 1986 held in SA and the UK; 1986 Art Show Gallery, London, first of three solo exhibitions, the others being held in Cape Town and Johannesburg; 1987 Karen McKerron Gallery, Johannesburg, joint exhibition with Lulu Baily (qv) and Pippa Lea (qv).

References *Style* February 1987; *Fair Lady* March 1987; *Flying Springbok* June 1987.

BAILEY Harold G

Born Yorkshire, England.

Died Thought to have died in Pietermaritzburg.

An artist producing pen and ink drawings of buildings, characterised by accuracy. Occasionally painted landscapes.

Profile His work has been reproduced in the press both abroad and in SA, notably in the weekly *Natal Witness*. Worked for the Durban Museum. Came to SA via Kenya and Dar es Salaam.

BAILEY Jessica Mary (Mrs J Clarke)

Born 1960 Johannesburg.

A self-taught painter of figures and children's book illustrations. Works in watercolour and ink.

Profile A trained practising cellist. Married to John Clarke (qv).

Exhibitions 1979 Goodman Gallery, Johannesburg, first of two solo exhibitions held in Johannesburg.

BAILEY Stella Mary (née Chiappini)

Active during the 1940s and 1950s.

A painter, in watercolour, of figures, landscapes and objects.

Profile Illustrated *Badoli The Ox*, by Myles Bourke, 1949, Howard Timmins, Cape Town, with 12 drawings of tribal scenes (four colour reproductions) and a further two colour illustrations. 1945 married Sir John Milner Bailey, son of Sir Abe Bailey, widowed in 1946.

Represented Africana Museum, Johannesburg.

Reference AMC6.

BAILEY Wellesley

Born 1874 London, England.

Died 1954.

Resided in SA from 1913.

A painter of Cape homesteads and landscapes, in later years depicted mostly highveld landscapes. Painted mainly in watercolour and occasionally in oil.

Studies Architecture at Edinburgh School of Applied Art, and in Italy.

Profile Prior to 1913 lived in Edinburgh and London. A professional architect and a founder member of the Transvaal Art Society in 1937.

Exhibitions Participated in group exhibitions in the UK 1901–36; participated in SA exhibitions from 1925; Herbert Evans Gallery, Johannesburg, solo exhibition; 1954 Transvaal Academy, Memorial Exhibition.

References DBA; BSAK; AASA.

BAILY Sara Louise (Lulu)

Born 1961 Gorseinon, Wales.

Resided in SA from 1966.

A painter of portraits, still life, imaginary scenarios and her immediate environment. Works in oil and watercolour. A printmaker, making multiple plate colour etchings. 1983 a series of 15 colour etchings of "The Hindu Temples of Durban and Natal".

Studies 1980–83 Natal Technikon, under Jan Jordaan (qv) and Clive van den Berg (qv), gaining a Diploma in Fine Art–Printmaking, a Higher Diploma in Fine Art–Printmaking and the Emma Smith Merit Prizes and Bursaries in 1981 and 1982.

Profile 1982 illustrated a career guidance manual for the Career Information Centre, Durban. 1966, 1968–70 and 1978–85 lived in Durban; 1967 in Zululand; 1985–86 in London; 1986–88 in Johannesburg; 1988 in Cape Town. 1974 revisited Mauritius, having lived there 1961–63.

Exhibitions She has participated in several group exhibitions from 1980 in SA and one held in the Republic of China; 1987 Karen McKerron Gallery, Johannesburg, joint exhibition with Beezy Bailey (qv) and Pippa Lea (qv).

BAIN Robert Professor

Born 1912 Edinburgh, Scotland.
Died 1973.
Resided in SA from 1936.
A sculptor of portrait busts, life-size figures, smaller figures and relief heads.
Worked in bronze, terracotta, stone and wood.
Studies Trained in decorative plasterwork, architecture and design at the
Heriot-Watt College, Edinburgh; part-time classes at Edinburgh School of Art;
1947–48 Academy of Fine Arts and Artistic Lyceum, Florence, Italy, where
awarded a Diploma of the Licentiate in a Course of Sculpture and a Gold Medal
by the Commissione Ordinatrice della 1 Rassegna Sindacale Toscana delli Arti
Figurative. Became Professor in 1948.
Profile 1936 a part-time lecturer at the Natal Technical College; 1940–46 and
1948–52 a senior lecturer at the Port Elizabeth School of Art; 1953–54 Head of
the Port Elizabeth School of Art; 1955 appointed Director of the Art School at
the Witwatersrand Technical College. 1942 served as a Sapper in WWII.
Exhibitions Participated in group exhibitions in SA.
Award 1948 Gold Medal from the Palazzo Strozzi International Exhibition in
Florence.
Represented King George VI Art Gallery, Port Elizabeth; Port Elizabeth
Technikon; University of Pretoria.
Public Commission The Bronze Doors, Reserve Bank, Port Elizabeth.
References AASA; Port Elizabeth School of Art.

BAINES (John) Thomas FRGS

Born 1820 King's Lynn, Norfolk, England.
Died 1875 Durban.
Resided in SA 1842–53, 1858–65 and 1869–75.
A self-taught painter working mainly in oil, but also producing a number of
watercolours, etchings and sketches. Over 400 scenes of Africa with descriptions
written on the back. Dramatic scenes with strong use of vivid colour. Subjects
include landscapes, shipping scenes, interiors, figures, birds, animals, plants and
war skirmishes. Painted a number of portraits of Cape Town notability.
Profile An apprenticed coach painter until the age of twenty. An explorer who
made a number of botanical and entomological discoveries. A cartographer and
prospector. Sketched throughout his travels. 1842–48 lived in Cape Town and
worked as a coach painter, portrait painter and seascape artist; 1848 travelled by
ship to Algoa Bay (Port Elizabeth), to Grahamstown, where he met the explorer
W F Liddle, to Fort Beaufort, Colesberg and across the Orange River; 1849
travelled alone from Grahamstown to King William's Town; 1850 travelled with
Joseph McCabe from Grahamstown to Bloemfontein and across the Vaal River
to Potchefstroom; 1851–52 a war artist, with Major-General Somerset, in the
Eighth Frontier War; 1852–53 in Grahamstown and Port Elizabeth; 1853–55 in
England, where he learnt the art of map drawing; 1855–57 in Northern Australia
with A C Gregory; 1857 returned to England; 1858–59 travelled with Doctor

David Livingstone up the Zambesi, Rhodesia (Zimbabwe); 1860 in Cape Town; 1861–63 in SWA/Namibia travelling to Victoria Falls, Rhodesia (Zimbabwe), with J Chapman; 1864 in SWA/Namibia and Cape Town; 1865–67 in England; 1867–71 Northern Goldfields Expedition in SA and Rhodesia (Zimbabwe); 1871–73 in Natal and up to Nylstroom; 1873 attended the Zulu King Cetch-wayo's coronation as a newspaper correspondent and artist; 1873–75 in Cape Town, Port Elizabeth and Durban. Numerous prints, printed in London and Durban including: "Scenery & Events in South Africa", six plates, Ackermann & Company, London, 1852, a facsimile reprint of the 1852 edition of hand-coloured lithographs with an introduction and notes by Frank Bradlow, 1977, A A Balkema, Cape Town; "The Victoria Falls, Zambesi River", 11 plates, Day & Son, London, 1865 and "The Birds of South Africa", a portfolio of nine proof prints, with an introduction by R F Kennedy, 1973, Winchester Press, Johannesburg; facsimile lithographic reproductions of six watercolours with critical introduction and notes of plates by R F Kennedy, 1967, A Robinson Sons & Company, Johannesburg; "The Frontier Wars, 1851–1853", a portfolio, 1976, The Heritage Collection, Cape Town. A large number of illustrations and articles for books and periodicals. In 1975 a set of four stamps was produced as a commemorative issue.

Exhibitions Included in numerous group exhibitions of SA paintings; 1864 Cape Town, first solo exhibition; 1948 Tate Gallery, London, SA Art Exhibition; 1960 National Gallery, Salisbury, Rhodesia (Harare, Zimbabwe), exhibition; 1960 King George VI Art Gallery, Port Elizabeth, Centenary Festival Exhibition; 1971 Pretoria Art Museum, exhibition; 1975 Fine Arts Society, London and the University of the Witwatersrand, Commemorative Exhibitions.

Represented Africana Museum, Johannesburg; Albany Museum, Grahamstown; Central Africa Archives, Harare, Zimbabwe; Fort Beaufort Historical Museum; Julius Gordon Africana Centre, Riversdale; King George VI Art Gallery, Port Elizabeth; National Museum, Bloemfontein; Natural History Museum, London, UK; Old House Museum, Durban; Pretoria Art Museum; public libraries in Cape Town, Johannesburg and Port Elizabeth; Royal Botanical Gardens, London, UK; Royal Geographical Society, London, UK; SA Cultural History Museum, Cape Town; SA National Gallery, Cape Town; University of Cape Town; University of Natal; University of Stellenbosch; William Fehr Collection, Cape Town.

Publications by Baines *Journals of Residence in South Africa*, 2 volumes, 1842–53, edited by R F Kennedy, The Van Riebeeck Society, Cape Town; *Explorations in South-West Africa*, illustrated, 1864, Longman Green, London, reprint with introduction by F Bradlow, Heritage series, Pioneer Head, Salisbury, Rhodesia (Harare, Zimbabwe); *Shifts and Expedients of Camp Life, Travel and Exploration*, with W B Lord, illustrated, 1871, London; *The Northern Goldfields Diaries of T Baines 1869–1872*, 3 volumes, edited by J P R Wallis, 1964, Chatto & Windus, London; *The Gold Regions of South Eastern Africa*, by the late T Baines Esq FRGS, accompanied bv a biographical sketch of the author, edited by Henry Hall, 1877, Edward Stanford, London and J W C Mackay, Port Elizabeth.

References J P R Wallis, *Thomas Baines of King's Lynn*, 1941, Jonathan Cape, London, text reproduced with new illustrations, 1976, A A Balkema, Cape Town; J P R Wallis, *Thomas Baines, his art in Rhodesia*, 1956, Central African Archives, Salisbury, Rhodesia (Harare, Zimbabwe); Fay Jaffe, *They Came to South*

Africa, 1963, Howard Timmins, Cape Town; Marius and Joy Diemont, *The Brenthurst Baines*, 1975, Brenthurst Press, Johannesburg; R F Kennedy, *The Birds of South Africa painted by Thomas Baines*, 1975, Winchester Press, Johannesburg; Edward C Tabler, editor, *Baines on the Zambesi*, 1982, Brenthurst Press, Johannesburg; Collectors' Guide; Pict Art; Our Art 1; Art SA; Afr Repos; SADNB; E C Tabler, *Pioneers of Rhodesia*, 1966, C Struik, Cape Town; AMC 1 & 6; DSAB; SAP&S; SESA; Oxford Companion to Art (under SA); Pict Afr; DBA; BSAK 1 & 2; Enc S'n A; Art SWA; SA Art; 3Cs; AASA; SASSK; LSAA; *SA Panorama* April 1973 & December 1982; *De Arte* April 1979.

BAKER Clarewen

A painter working in watercolour, ink and wash.
Studies University of South Africa, under Walter Battiss (qv); Rhodes University, where attained an MFA.
Profile Teaches at East London Technical College.
Exhibitions She has participated in group exhibitions in SA; 1981 Republic Festival Exhibition.
Reference AASA.

BAKKER Kenneth

Born 1926 Cape Town.
Died 1988 Cape Town.
A painter of abstracted landscapes and seascapes. Worked in oil, acrylic, pencil and charcoal, made relief constructions with gesso, steel, perspex and plastic. 1968–71 a series of Geoniche/Geo structures; 1972–80 a series of constructions; 1981–84 a series of relief paintings with constructions; 1985–86 a series of reliefs with semi-precious stones.
Studies Continental School of Art, Cape Town, under George de Leon; 1953–55 at the Contemporary School of Art, Cape Town, under Erik Laubscher (qv).
Profile 1954–64 a member of the SAAA. Until 1955 lived in Cape Town, then moved to Simonstown. Married to Bernadine Biden (qv).
Exhibitions Participated in numerous group exhibitions from 1954 in SA and at the Venice and São Paulo Biennials; from 1955 held six joint exhibitions with Bernadine Biden (qv); 1960 and 1964 Quadrennial Exhibitions; 1968 Silberburg Gallery, Cape Town, first solo exhibition.
Award 1963 Medal—Mention of Honour, São Paulo Bienale.
Represented Ann Bryant Gallery, East London; Hester Rupert Art Museum, Graaff-Reinet; Pretoria Art Museum; SA National Gallery, Cape Town; University of the Witwatersrand; William Humphreys Art Gallery, Kimberley.
References Art SA; SAA; 20C SA Art; SSAP; BSAK 2; SA Art; Oxford Companion to 20C Art (under SA); 3Cs; AASA; LSAA; *SA Panorama* January 1969; *Lantern* June 1970; *Artlook* November 1970 & August/September 1975.

BALDINELLI Armando

Born 1908 Ancona, Italy.
Resided in SA from 1953.
A painter and graphic artist of figures, portraits, still life and elements of landscapes. Works in oil, acrylic, gouache, ink, wash, pencil, charcoal and in various graphic media, particularly woodcuts. 1963–71 abstract works. 1964–66 a number of assemblages in metal and wood. A painter of frescos and a mosaic artist.

Studies 1925–28 Academy of Fine Art, Rome; 1935–39 Istituto Superiore di Belle Arti, Modena, Italy.

Profile 1962–63 a member of Gutai Pinacoteca, Osaka, Japan. 1941–51 Professor at the Art Institute Aldini and Valeriani, Bologna. A number of book illustrations in Italy. A designer of stained glass windows; 1950–52 designed the windows of Noto Cathedral, Siracuse, Sicily, where he also painted alfrescos in the apse; 1962 designed the windows of St George's Presbyterian Church, Wolmarans Street, Johannesburg. He is also interested in cinematography and has made a number of films. 1962-63 lived in Japan; 1964 in New York. He has travelled extensively throughout the world.

Exhibitions He has participated in numerous group exhibitions from 1931 in Italy, Zimbabwe, SA, throughout Europe and in the USA; 1936 Istituto di Cultura, Bergamo, Italy, first of over 10 major solo exhibitions held in Italy; from 1953 he has held over 20 solo exhibitions in SA, the USA and Portugal; 1967 Pretoria Art Museum, Prestige Joint Exhibition with Gunther van der Reis (qv); 1975 University of the Witwatersrand, Prestige Exhibition; 1981 Republic Festival Exhibition; 1981 Rand Afrikaans University, Retrospective Exhibition; 1984 University of the Witwatersrand, Retrospective Exhibition.

Awards 1936 Diploma d'Onore, Italian Contemporary Art Exhibition, Budapest, Hungary; 1946 Diplome d'Honneur, Musée des Beaux Arts, Nancy, France; 1950 awarded the Canadian Government Prize, Venice Biennial; 1965 Artist of Fame and Promise Award.

Represented British Museum, London, UK; Civic Gallery, Bologna, Italy; Galleria d'Arte dei Contemporanei, Milan, Italy; Hester Rupert Art Musuem, Graaff-Reinet; Johannesburg Art Gallery; Modern Art Gallery, Ancona, Italy; Modern Art Gallery, Florence, Italy; National Gallery of Modern Art, Rome, Italy; Pietersburg Collection; Pretoria Art Museum; Rand Afrikaans University; SA National Gallery, Cape Town; Sogetsu Kaikan Gallery, Tokyo, Japan; University of the Witwatersrand.

Public Commissions Numerous commissions in Italy. From 1953 a large number of mosaics and murals in public buildings in SA, including at Jan Smuts Airport, Johannesburg; Hyde Park Shopping Centre, Johannesburg; Transvaal Provincial Administration Building, Pretoria; Natal Provincial Administration Building, Pietermaritzburg and in theatres, churches and educational institutions.

References Umbro Apollonio, *Baldinelli*, 1964, Edizione d'Arte Moderna, Roma; *Armando Baldinelli*, with an introduction by Albert Werth, 1974, Gallery 21, Johannesburg; SAA; 20C SA Art; SAP&S; SESA; SSAP; BSAK 1 & 2; Our Art 3; SA Art; 3Cs; AASA; LSAA; *Fontein* vol 1 no 3; *SA Panorama* November 1962, November 1982 & January 1984; *Lantern* December 1963; *Artlook* January 1967, March 1967, November 1967, September 1968, December 1969, June 1971 &

April 1973; *Habitat* no 10, 1974, no 16, 1975 & no 24, 1977; *Flying Springbok* September 1981 & January 1984; *SA Art Calendar* October/November 1981; *Gallery* Winter 1982 & Summer 1984; *Armando Baldinelli, Yesterday and Today*, 1984, University of the Witwatersrand.

BALFOUR-CUNNINGHAM Gordon see CUNNINGHAM Gordon Balfour-

BALL Cynthia Lindsay
Born 1914 Johannesburg.
A painter of landscapes, seascapes, still life and abstract pictures. Works in watercolour, gouache, ink, wash, pencil, charcoal and pastel.
Studies 1933–35 Witwatersrand Technical College, under James Gardner (qv) and Phyllis Gardner (qv); 1960–66 under Sidney Goldblatt (qv).
Profile 1972 Co-founder of the WSSA, becoming a Fellow in 1980. 1958–60 an art teacher at St Johns College, Johannesburg; 1960–66 at St Peters Preparatory School, Johannesburg; from 1975 she has taught art privately. A set and costume designer for children's theatre. 1934 went on an arts tour with James and Phyllis Gardner (qv) in Europe; 1973 on a painting holiday in Italy with Marjorie Bowen (qv); 1985 on a painting holiday in Greece with Ulrich Schwanecke (qv).
Exhibitions She has participated in group exhibitions from 1962 and frequently with the WSSA, exhibiting in SA, London and West Germany; 1969 SAAA Gallery, Pretoria, first of seven solo exhibitions held in SA; 1979 Gallery 21, Johannesburg, joint exhibition with Nicholas Garwood (qv), Diedie Marais (qv) and Ulrich Schwanecke (qv).
References BSAK; AASA.

BALLEN Lynda (née Moross)
Born 1951 Johannesburg.
An artist working with handmade paper, pigment and dye, creating two-dimensional abstract pictures.
Studies 1968–72 University of the Witwatersrand, under Cecily Sash (qv), Joyce Leonard (qv), Judith Mason (qv), Giuseppe Cattaneo (qv) and Professor Heather Martienssen (1915–79), where gained a BA(FA); 1977–78 University of New York, under John Kacere (*b*.1920), Don Eddy (*b*.1944) and Leonie Webber, where gained an MA in Art Education.
Profile From 1987 a member of the International Paper Artists and Papermakers. 1974–75 Curator of the Schlesinger Art Collection, Johannesburg. 1975–76 a teacher of Art and the History of Art at Waverley Girls High School, Johannesburg; 1975–77 taught children at the Bill Ainslie (qv) Studios, Johannesburg; 1979–80 a teacher of Art and the History of Art, Damelin College, Johannesburg; from 1981 a senior teacher of Art and the History of Art, Johannesburg Art Foundation; 1987 a teacher of Painting and Drawing, Witwatersrand Technikon. 1977–78 lived in New York; 1980–81 lived in Colorado, USA; lives in Johannesburg. 1981 travelled in South and Central America; 1981–86 has travelled extensively in Africa. Married to Roger Ballen (*b*.1950, New York), the photographer and author of *Boyhood*, 1979, Chelsea House, New York and *Dorps*, 1986, Clifton Publishers, Cape Town.

Exhibitions She has participated in many group exhibitions from 1975 held in SA and the USA; 1985 Goodman Gallery, Johannesburg, solo exhibition; 1987 Johannesburg Art Gallery, Vita Art Now; 1987 SA National Gallery, Cape Town and the Goodman Gallery, Johannesburg, joint exhibition with Philippa Hobbs (qv), Susan Rosenberg (qv) and Elizabeth Vels (qv).
Represented Pretoria Art Museum; SA National Gallery, Cape Town.

BALLENDEN Toni-Ann

Born 1953 Cape Town.
A painter of landscapes, portraits, seascapes, figures and abstract pictures. Works in oil, acrylic, pencil and craypas pastel. Additionally a potter.
Exhibitions She has participated in group exhibitions in 1987 in Johannesburg.

BALLOT Elizabeth Laetitia (Titia)

Born 1941 Clocolan, Orange Free State.
A painter of landscapes, symbolic objects and abstract pictures. Works in oil, acrylic, watercolour, ink, pencil and charcoal, also a printmaker. 1979–81 "Time & Space" series.
Studies 1960–63 through the university of Pretoria, under Zakkie Eloff (qv), Anna Vorster (qv), Leo Theron (qv) and Gunther van der Reis (qv), gaining a BA(FA).
Profile A member of the SAAA and the SAAAH. 1971–75 a part-time lecturer, 1976–80 a junior lecturer, 1981 a lecturer and from 1986 a part-time lecturer in graphic art at Potchefstroom University for CHE. 1982–85 lived in Bonn, West Germany. A number of her works have been reproduced in print form. Married to Professor Doctor G M Ballot, Head of the Art History Department, Potchefstroom University for CHE and President of the SAAA, 1979–81.
Exhibitions 1970 SAAA Gallery, Potchefstroom, first of nine solo exhibitions held in SA; she has participated in many group exhibitions from 1972 in SA; 1981 Republic Festival Exhibition; 1981 NSA Gallery, Durban, joint exhibition with Louis van Heerden (qv); 1985 Im Vogelsang 8, Bonn, West Germany, solo exhibition.
Represented Gorgen-Behrens Collection, SA Embassy, Bonn, West Germany; Potchefstroom Museum; Potchefstroom University for CHE; Pretoria Art Museum; Willem Annandale Art Gallery, Lichtenburg.
Reference AASA.

BALOYI Vincent

Born 1954 Newclare, Johannesburg.
A sculptor and painter of figures, portraits, birds, landscapes and abstracts. Works in wood, metal, oil, watercolour, gouache, ink, pencil and charcoal. A graphic artist.

Studies 1974–75 at Rorke's Drift Art Centre, under Otto Lundbohm and Carl Ellertson; 1977–81 Jasna Bufacchi Art Society, Johannesburg.
Profile 1976–80 a member of the National Art Society. Has taught art at FUBA. 1988 Guest Artist at the Funda Centre, Soweto.
Exhibitions His work has been included in group exhibitions in SA, the USA, West Germany, Italy, Greece and Israel; 1987 Shell Gallery, Johannesburg, solo exhibition; 1987 Johannesburg Art Gallery, Vita Art Now; 1988 FUBA Gallery, Johannesburg, solo exhibition.
Represented Durban Art Gallery.
Reference AASA.

BAM Diana Margaret

Born 1923 Pretoria.
A painter of landscapes, portraits, still life and abstract pictures. Works in oil.
Studies 1962 Pretoria Technical College, under Robert Hodgins (qv), Peter Eliastam (qv) and Zakkie Eloff (qv).
Profile 1960 a member of the SAAA.
Exhibitions She has participated in group exhibitions from 1964 in SA and London; Hoffer Gallery, Pretoria, solo exhibition.
Represented Willem Annandale Art Gallery, Lichtenburg.

BANDS Ann Marie

A painter of landscapes. Works in watercolour on rice-paper.
Studies c.1969–72 studied Chinese watercolour techniques privately under Madame Tang-li Chao, wife of the Chinese Ambassador to Malawi.
Exhibition 1979 Van Wouw House, Pretoria, solo exhibition.

BANKS Stella (née Bewick)

Born 1928 Germiston, Transvaal.
A painter and graphic artist of landscapes and still life. Works in oil, watercolour, charcoal, pencil and in various graphic media.
Studies 1946–48 Michaelis School of Fine Art, under Edward Roworth (qv) and Rupert Shephard (qv); 1959 Stellenbosch Technical College, under Joyce Ordbrown (qv); 1985 etching, privately under Mimi van der Merwe (qv).
Profile c.1974 a member of the SAAA; 1979 a member of the Club 997, Pretoria; 1981 a member of the WSSA.
Exhibitions She has participated in group exhibitions from 1981 in Pretoria.

BARBER Mary Elizabeth (née Bowker)

Born 1818 Gateshead, Durham, England.
Died 1899 Pietermaritzburg.
Resided in SA from 1820.
A self-taught painter of landscapes and natural history subjects. Worked in watercolour and ink.

Profile Her pen and ink illustrated journal "Wanderings in SA by Sea and Land" is in the Cory Library, Rhodes University and has been published in the *SA Library Quarterly Bulletin* (December 1962–December 1963). A botanist and entomologist. She was a member of the Berlin Ornithological Society and the Linnaean Society. Several species of plants and insects have been named after her. She wrote many papers on natural history and published a book of poems. She lived in the Eastern Cape until 1872. 1872–89 trekked to the diamond fields around Kimberley and to the goldfields of the Transvaal. 1889–92 lived in Europe. After 1892 lived alternately in Johannesburg and Pietermaritzburg. The grandmother of Ivan Mitford-Barberton (qv).
Represented Africana Museum, Johannesburg; Albany Museum, Grahamstown.
References I Mitford-Barberton, *Barbers of the Peak*, 1934, Oxford; Pict Art; H E Hockley, *The Story of the British Settlers of 1820 in SA*, second edition, 1957, Juta, Cape Town; SADNB; DSAB; Pict Art; SA Art.

BARBOURE Margaret (Peggy) (Mrs Martin)

Born in Pretoria.
A painter of portraits, particularly children's, of flowers and of figures. Works mostly in oil and pastel and occasionally in watercolour.
Studies From 1939 Natal Technical College, under Eric Byrd (qv) and Merlyn Evans (qv), where she was awarded two scholarships; 1942 introduced to oil painting by Robert Broadley (qv).
Profile From 1941, for many years, a member of the NSA. 1944 designed decorations and the dust jacket for a book of poems entitled *The House of Bread*, by Edgar H Brookes, The Knox Printing & Publishing Company, Durban. In 1947 lived in Eritrea, Ethiopia. 1949 visited England and Italy.
Exhibitions She has participated in numerous group exhibitions from *c.*1942 in SA and England; 1952 Pieter Wenning Gallery, Johannesburg, first of four solo exhibitions.
Represented Ann Bryant Gallery, East London; Durban Art Gallery; SA National Gallery, Cape Town; William Humphreys Art Gallery, Kimberley.
References Collectors' Guide; SAA; SAP&D; BSAK 1 & 2; AASA.

BARCLAY Dorothy

Born 1892 Cape Town.
Died 1940.
A painter of flowers, landscapes and seascapes. Worked in watercolour.
Studies Under George C Robinson (qv). Won a scholarship to the Regent Street Polytechnic Art School, London, for three years.
Profile Wrote and illustrated *South African Wild Flowers*, 1925, Speciality Press, Cape Town and *A Second Book of South African Wild Flowers*, 1936. Also illustrated *Die Kleinspan*, the children's supplement to *Die Huisgenoot* and *Kammastories* by Ella Mackenzie, 1930, Nasionale Pers. Contributed a number of plates to *The Flowering Plants of Africa*, a quarterly publication issued by the Botanical Research Institute, Pretoria. Niece of Ethel Dixie (qv).

Exhibitions Participated in SA exhibitions from 1933.
Represented Cape Town Library; SA Cultural History Museum, Cape Town; University of Cape Town.
References SAA; BSAK 1 & 2; AASA.

BARDAVID Reggi

Born 1945 Alexandria, Egypt.
Resided in SA from 1974.
A painter working in oil, acrylic, ink, wash, pencil and charcoal.
Studies 1980–84 Johannesburg Art Foundation, under Bill Ainslie (qv); 1985–87 studying for a BA(FA), through the University of South Africa, gaining bursaries in 1986 and 1987.
Profile 1945–56 lived in Egypt; 1956–58 in Italy; 1958–64 in Rhodesia (Zimbabwe); 1964–74 in Zaire, thereafter in SA. Has travelled in Europe, Israel and the Americas.
Exhibitions He has participated in several group exhibitions in Pretoria from 1985; 1987 Johannesburg Art Foundation, joint exhibition with Bongiwe Dhlomo (qv), Madi Phala (qv), Sam Nhlengetwa (qv) and Pat Mautloa (qv).

BARKER Paulette Dubayle

Born 1928 Mulhouse, France.
Resided in SA from 1953.
A painter and graphic artist of landscapes, interiors and exteriors, still life, figures and abstract pictures. Works in oil, acrylic, watercolour, pencil, charcoal and in various graphic media. A number of large series: 1982 "Paint Tube Series" (abstract); 1984 "Childhood Memories" (dream); 1985 "Interiors".
Studies Technical College, Mulhouse, France; extra-mural studies at the University of Natal, Durban, the University of South Africa and the Natal Technical College.
Profile A member of the NSA and a council member from 1978; 1978 a member of the WSSA; 1985 a member of D'ARTS. Taught art privately from 1976. 1928–52 lived in France; 1952–53 in England; thereafter in SA. 1985 spent four months at the Cité Internationale des Arts, Paris. Frequently visits France and England; 1984 visited West Germany and The Netherlands.
Exhibitions She has participated in many group exhibitions from 1975 in Natal and in Paris; 1982 NSA Gallery, Durban, first of 10 solo exhibitions held in SA and in Paris.
Award 1977 MOAG Award, North Coast Group, Natal.
Represented Musée des Beaux Arts, Mulhouse, France.
Reference SA Arts Calendar Summer 1985–86.

BARKER Wayne Cahill

Born 1963 Voortrekkerhoogte, Pretoria.
A painter of landscapes, still life, genre and abstract pictures. Works in mixed media and in oil on canvas.

THOMAS BAINES
The Lion Family Among the Granite Hills between Shasha and Macloutsie Rivers 1872
Oil on Canvas 51 × 66 cm
Sanlam Limited

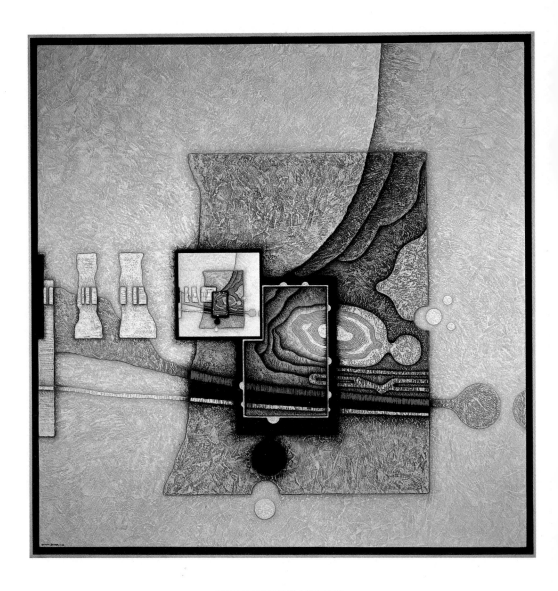

KENNETH BAKKER
Composition 1983
Gesso Low Relief 122 × 122 cm
Die Kunskamer

Studies 1981 Pretoria Technikon; 1982–83 Michaelis School of Fine Art, under Stanley Pinker (qv) and Kevin Atkinson (qv).
Exhibitions He has participated in several group exhibitions from 1984 in Johannesburg.

BARRY Jillian Elizabeth (Mrs Carman)

Born 1951 Durban.
A painter and graphic artist of still life, details from nature, figures and abstract pictures. Works in oil, acrylic, watercolour, gouache, pencil and in various graphic media. 1972–74 a series of drawings of details of the female figure; 1974–75 etchings and aquatints of details of feathers.
Studies 1969–74 University of the Witwatersrand, under Professor Heather Martienssen (1915–79), Erica Berry (qv), Robert Hodgins (qv), Cecily Sash (qv), Elizabeth Rankin and Rory Doepel, where gained a BA(FA) in 1971 and, on a Raikes Scholarship, BA(Hons) in 1974. 1974–75 Ecole Nationale Supériéure des Arts Décoratifs, Paris, under Yves Heude and Marcel Florini, on a French Government Scholarship; 1980 University of South Africa, art history under Frieda Harmsen, where gained an MA.
Profile 1975–76 a part-time assistant at the SAAA, Southern Transvaal Branch. From 1977 a senior professional officer at the Johannesburg Art Gallery.
Exhibitions 1975–76 participated in four group exhibitions held in France and Johannesburg; 1976 SAAA Gallery, Johannesburg, solo exhibition; mainly exhibited drawings and etchings. Is no longer an exhibiting artist.

BARTLETT George Richard

Born 1942 Springs, Transvaal.
A self-taught painter and sculptor of landscapes, portraits, still life, seascapes and wildlife. Works in oil, watercolour and wood.
Exhibitions 1972 Salisbury, Rhodesia (Harare, Zimbabwe), first of 10 solo exhibitions held in Rhodesia (Zimbabwe). He has held one solo exhibition in SA.
Represented National Gallery, Harare, Zimbabwe.

BARTON (Charles) Edmund

Born 1933, Newry, County Armagh, Northern Ireland.
Resided in SA from 1970.
A painter of landscapes, still life, seascapes, genre, wildlife, horse portraits and abstract pictures. Works in oil, acrylic, watercolour, gouache and wash.
Studies Mainly self-taught but *c*.1971 studied part-time at the Natal Technical College.
Profile A large amount of commercial artwork for hotels, offices and apartments, as well as industrial illustrations and graphic work. 1971 a member of the NSA. Has travelled and painted throughout Southern Africa.
Exhibitions 1973 Springs, Transvaal, first of four solo exhibitions.
Represented Africana Museum, Johannesburg; Boksburg Municipality; Sasolburg Municipality.

BASSON Albertus Johannes (Bokkie)

Born 1923 Malmesbury, Cape Province.

A painter and graphic artist of abstracted landscapes and seascapes. Works in mixed media, woodcut and linocut.

Studies 1947–48 Continental School of Fine Art, Cape Town, under Maurice van Essche (qv); 1949–51 Teachers Training College, Cape Town, under Barbara Ayres, where awarded a Teachers Training Higher Diploma; 1956–57 Central School of Art, London, under Cecil Collins *(b.*1900), Merlyn Evans (qv) and Blair Hughes-Stanton *(b.*1902).

Profile A member of the SAAA. 1952 an art teacher, 1953–68 Principal of the Hugo Naudé Art Centre, Worcester, Cape Province; 1969–70 lectured in art at the Teachers Training College, Cape Town; 1971–84 lectured in art at the University of Stellenbosch. From 1951 a weaver. 1965 a co-founder of the Artists Gallery, Cape Town. Promoted creative art teaching to children and in 1969 taught in workshops for the blind.

Exhibitions He has participated in many group exhibitions from 1959 in SA; 1959 Worcester, first of nine solo exhibitions held in the Cape Province; 1961 Cape Town, joint exhibition with Johannes Koorzen (qv); 1964 Quadrennial Exhibition; 1981 Republic Festival Exhibition.

Represented University of Stellenbosch.

References SAA; AASA.

BATHA Gerhard

Born 1937 Vienna, Austria.

Resided in SA from 1967.

A painter of landscapes, seascapes, portraits, figures, still life and abstract pictures. Works in acrylic, gouache, watercolour and oil.

Studies 1953–57 Graphic High School, Vienna, under Professor Wolfsberger; 1961–62 Summerschool, Salzburg, Austria, under Oskar Kokoschka (1886–1980).

Profile Travels, studies and paints in the USA, Italy, the UK and France.

Exhibitions He has participated in many group exhibitions from 1981 in SA; 1984 Everard Read Gallery, Johannesburg, first of two solo exhibitions.

Represented Pretoria Art Museum; William Humphreys Art Gallery, Kimberley.

References *Habitat* no 34, 1979 & no 65, 1984; *Sun* December 1985.

BATTEN Auriol Ursula

Born 1918 Pietermaritzburg.

A painter of flowers, landscapes and wildlife. Works in watercolour, ink, pencil and oil.

Studies 1935–38 University of Natal, under Eric Byrd (qv) and Professor O J P Oxley (qv), whilst majoring in botany and geography; 1941–44 Natal Technical College, under Eric Byrd (qv), Merlyn Evans (qv) and E C Fincher, as well as privately under Nils Andersen (qv).

Profile Particularly interested in drawing botanical illustrations of indigenous SA plants, which have been used in various flower books and in Douglas Hey's *Water, Source of Life*. 1939–41 taught at Estcourt High School, Natal; 1941 and 1943 at Durban Girls High School. Designed a set of stamps, "Endangered Plants of the Ciskei", to be issued in 1988. A potter, teaching this craft for several years at the East London Technical College. Lives in East London.

Exhibitions She has participated in numerous group exhibitions from *c*.1940 in SA and once in England; 1986 Pretoria Art Museum, solo exhibition; 1986 East London Museum, solo exhibition.

Award 1986 Gold Medal of The Royal Horticultural Society, London, for painting SA flowers.

Represented Durban Art Gallery.

Publications by Batten Flowers of Southern Africa, 1986, Frandsen Publishers, Johannesburg; illustrator and co-author with Hertha Bokelman of *Wild Flowers of the Eastern Cape*, among others.

References SESA; AASA; *SA Panorama* May 1986.

BATTISS Grace ARCA

Born Klerksdorp, Transvaal.
Died 1975.
A painter in oil, also a potter and weaver.

Studies Royal College of Art, London, on a Milner Scholarship.

Profile A member of the Transvaal Art Society. A former art mistress at Roedean School, Johannesburg, and at Pretoria Girls High School. Prior to her marriage to Walter Battiss (qv) in 1940 she lectured on art at the Pretoria and Johannesburg Normal Colleges.

Exhibitions Participated in group exhibitions from 1927; 1942 and 1945, joint exhibitions with Walter Battiss (qv); 1952 Van Riebeeck Festival Exhibition.

Represented Pretoria Art Museum.

References SAA; Register SA & SWA; BSAK; AASA.

BATTISS Walter Whall FRSA FIAL

Born 1906 Somerset East, Cape Province.
Died 1982 Port Shepstone, Natal.
An extremely versatile artist painting in many media in numerous different styles. Influenced by his intense interest in and study of African rock art. During the late 1940s and the 1950s painted pure abstraction. Use of strong, bright colours and symbols. From the mid 1950s calligraphic improvisations. Creator of Fook Island concept.

Studies 1927 briefly at Johannesburg Art School, under Professor A Winter Moore (qv); 1929 part-time at the Witwatersrand Technical College under Professor F W Armstrong (qv); 1930–32 full-time at the Johannesburg Teachers Training College and at the University of the Witwatersrand, awarded a Teachers Education Diploma; 1940 gained a BA(FA) through the University of South Africa.

Profile 1937 a founder member of the Transvaal Art Society; 1938–49 a member of the New Group; 1949 co-founder of the International Art Club SA; 1949 first Chairman of the SAAA, Northern Transvaal Branch; 1953 Founder and first President of the SA Council of Artists; 1954–58 an Executive committee member of the International Association of Plastic Arts, UNESCO; 1954 elected a Fellow of the Royal Society of Arts, London; 1960 a Fellow of the International Institute of Arts and Letters; 1965 an Honorary Member of the Academy of Florence; 1970 co-founder, with Cecil Skotnes (qv), of the Africa Council for Art. Taught art at numerous establishments including from 1936 his long and influential appointment at Pretoria Boys High School. Lectured on SA art in Tzaneen in 1950 and a guest lecturer on SA art at the University of London 1952–53; 1953 Principal of Arts at the Pretoria Art Centre; 1959 briefly held the Chair of Fine Arts at Rhodes University; 1964–71 Professor of Fine Arts, University of South Africa. Wrote numerous articles for magazines and newspapers throughout his life, founder of the magazines *Aurora* in 1948 and *De Arte* in 1965. 1951 published a folio of prints entitled "Fragments of Africa". In 1981 the Walter Battiss Art Museum opened in Somerset East, to which he contributed 81 of his works and a collection of personal documents and manuscripts. Lived mainly in Pretoria, but travelled and painted widely throughout his life including in 1938, 1954, 1956, 1963, 1969 and 1972 in Europe; 1948 in the Namib Desert; 1949 in Turin, Italy and in Paris; 1951 in Rhodesia (Zimbabwe); 1954 in Lourenço Marques (Maputo), Mozambique; 1961 in Tanzania and the Middle East; 1964 in the Bajun Islands, East Africa; 1965 in Saudi Arabia and Jordan; 1966 in Greece; 1967 and 1968 in the Greek islands; 1969 in Germany; 1971 in Spain and London; 1972 in the Seychelles; 1973 in London; 1974 in America; 1975 in England and Turkey; 1976 in America, Fiji, Samoa, the Hawaiian islands and Australia; 1978 in Tahiti; 1979 in America; 1980 in Greece and in 1982 in West Germany. Married to Grace Battiss (qv).

Exhibitions 1927 Masonic Hall, Rustenburg, Transvaal, first of over 80 solo exhibitions held throughout SA and in Mozambique, Botswana, the UK and SWA/Namibia; participated in numerous group exhibitions from 1929 in SA, Austria, Italy, South America, The Netherlands, West Germany, Greece and Zimbabwe; exhibited frequently with the New Group 1938–48; 1942 and 1945 joint exhibitions with Grace Battiss (qv); 1948 Tate Gallery, London, SA Art Exhibition; 1956, 1960 and 1964 Quadrennial Exhibitions; 1982 National Gallery, Gaborone, Botswana, Exhibition of SA Art; 1976 Van Wouw House, Pretoria, solo exhibition; 1979–80 Prestige Exhibition, touring art galleries and museums in Pretoria, Johannesburg, Cape Town, Pietermaritzburg, Durban, Port Elizabeth and Kimberley.

Awards 1948 Bronze Medal and Diploma, Olympiad Art Competition, Victoria and Albert Museum, London; 1964 Medal of Honour for Painting, SA Akademie vir Wetenskap en Kuns.

Represented Africana Museum, Johannesburg; Albertina Graphische Sammlung, Vienna, Austria; Ann Bryant Gallery, East London; Art Museum, Cincinnati, USA; Durban Art Gallery; Hester Rupert Art Museum, Graaff-Reinet; Johannesburg Art Gallery; King George VI Art Gallery, Port Elizabeth; Musées Royaux des Beaux Arts de Belgique, Brussels, Belgium; National Museum, Bloemfontein; National Gallery, Gaborone, Botswana; Permanent

International Woodcut Exhibition, Yugoslavia; Potchefstroom University for CHE; Pretoria Art Museum; Rand Afrikaans University; Sandton Municipal Collection; SA Akademie vir Wetenskap en Kuns; SA National Gallery, Cape Town; Tatham Art Gallery, Pietermaritzburg; Teachers Training College, Bloemfontein; University of Cape Town; University of Natal; University of the Orange Free State; University of Pretoria; University of South Africa; University of the Witwatersrand; Victoria and Albert Museum, London, England; Walter Battiss Museum, Somerset East; Willem Annandale Art Gallery, Lichtenburg; William Humphreys Art Gallery, Kimberley.

Public Commissions Murals: 1953 Culemborg Hotel, Pretoria; 1955 City Hall, Pretoria; 1961 Luxavia Airways, Johannesburg; 1959–62 Transvaal Provincial Administration Building, Pretoria; 1968 President Hotel, Johannesburg; 1968 H F Verwoerd Building, Bloemfontein; 1970 Standard Bank Building, Johannesburg.

Publications by Battiss South African Artists, 1937, Caxton Press, Pretoria; *The Amazing Bushman*, 1939, Red Fawn Press, Pretoria; *South African Paint Pot*, 1940, Red Fawn Press, Pretoria; *Homecoming*, 1945, Wallachs, Pretoria; *The Artists of the Rocks*, 1948, Red Fawn Press, Pretoria; *Bushman Art*, 1950, Red Fawn Press, Pretoria; *Fragments of Africa*, 1951, Red Fawn Press, Pretoria; *The Art of Africa*, with G H Franz, J W Grossert and H P Junod, 1958, Shuter & Shooter, Pietermaritzburg; *Limpopo*, 1965, J L van Schaik, Pretoria; *Art in a Mixed Up World*, 1965, A38, University of South Africa, Pretoria; *Nesos*, 1968, Battiss, Pretoria; *Battiss*, 1973, Art Folio, Johannesburg; *Fook Book 1*, 1973, Battiss, Pretoria; *Fook Book 2*, 1978, Battiss, Pretoria.

References Murray Schoonraad, *Walter Battiss*, 1976, C Struik, Cape Town; Murray Schoonraad and Peter Duminy, *Battiss 75*, 1981, D & S Publishers, Pietermaritzburg; *Walter Battiss*, edited by Karin Skawran and Michael Macnamara, 1985, Ad Donker, Johannesburg; Collectors' Guide; Our Art 2; Art SA; SAA; 20C SA Art; SAP&S; Oxford Companion to Art (under SA); SAP&D; SSAP; BSAK 1 & 2; Enc S'n A; SA Art; Oxford Companion to 20C Art; 3Cs; AASA; SASSK; LSAA; *Fontein* vol 1 no 3, 1960; *SA Art News* 6 April 1961 & 1 June 1961; *Artlook* February 1970, November 1970 & April 1973; *De Arte* October 1971, September 1973 & April 1982; *SA Panorama* January 1972, January 1981, April 1983 & June 1983; *Habitat* no 3, 1973; *Gallery* Summer 1982; *SA Arts Calendar* March 1983.

BAUDERT Friedrich Rudolf

Born 1911 Mvenyane (Mvunyana), Transkei.
A painter and graphic artist of landscapes. Works in watercolour, ink, pencil and in various graphic media, particularly etchings.

Profile 1980–83 a member of the Brush and Chisel Club, Johannesburg; from 1983 a member of the SAAA, 1986 a member of the Mimi van der Merwe (qv) etching studio.

Exhibitions He has participated in several group exhibitions in SA; 1986 SAAA Gallery, Pretoria, joint exhibition with Elsa Botha (qv).

BAUER Fred F

Born 1899 Vienna, Austria.
Died Johannesburg.
Resided in SA from 1935.
A city and landscape artist working in watercolour, pencil, wash, charcoal and crayon.
Studies Academy of Arts, Austria, under Anton Storch and Wilhelm von Munchausen.
Profile In 1918 served in the Austrian army, then saw service in the Argentine war. Until 1935 based in Vienna, studying and travelling frequently to the USA and Mexico. 1939–45 an Official Air Force War Artist. 1966–71 illustrations for *The SA Builder*. Lived for many years in the Drakensberg, Natal. Travelled throughout SA and revisited Vienna many times. Finally settled in Johannesburg.
Exhibitions From 1945 participated in several group exhibitions in SA, New York, Buenos Aires and in Mexico; 1945 Herbert Evans Gallery, Johannesburg, first of several solo exhibitions; 1956 Quadrennial Exhibition; 1976 Elizabeth Art Gallery, Johannesburg, joint exhibition with Adolph Jentsch (qv).
Represented A series of 750 pictures in various media entitled "The Changing Scene", Africana Museum, Johannesburg; Johannesburg Art Gallery.
References SAA; AMC1 & 6; BSAK 1 & 2; AASA.

BAWCOMBE Philip William FRSA

Born 1906 London, England.
Resided in SA from 1939/40.
A painter of landscapes and buildings. Works mainly in watercolour, but also in oil, acrylic, gouache and ink.
Profile An industrial artist. 1938 elected a Fellow of the Royal Society of Arts, London; a member of the London Sketch Club and the Chelsea Arts Club; a member of the NSA and its President in 1948. 1922 apprenticed to firm of shopfitters, later worked as a designer at Maple and Company, London, for three years; he then joined a ship-decorating company as a senior designer. 1930–38 worked in the British film industry. 1938–39 lived in Bulawayo, Rhodesia (Zimbabwe). 1939–43 served in the Camouflage Unit in the Middle East; 1943–45 an Official War Artist to the SA Forces in the Field, working in North Africa and Italy. 1953 the official designer of the Rhodes Centenary Exhibition, Bulawayo. 1962–64 designed villas on Skiathos, Greek islands. Over a period of fifteen years worked as an art director and designer of films in England; 1970–71 worked on three films in SA. Married to Pat Skilliter (qv).
Exhibitions 1944–70 participated in numerous group exhibitions in SA, Mozambique and Swaziland; 1980 Lister Gallery, Johannesburg, joint exhibition with Francois Koch (qv).
Represented Africana Museum, Johannesburg; Ann Bryant Gallery, East London; Mine Museum, Kimberley; SA National Museum of Military History, Johannesburg.

Publications by Bawcombe *Philip Bawcombe's Johannesburg*, text by Ted Scannell 1972, Rufus and Joubert, Johannesburg; *Philip Bawcombe's Kimberley*, text by Ted Scannell 1976, Rufus and Joubert, Johannesburg.
References Collectors' Guide; AMC1; BSAK 1 & 2; SA Art; AASA; *SA Panorama* September 1974 & April 1981; *Lantern* July 1978; *The World War II works of Philip Bawcombe*, by N Huntingford and R Hardy, 1981, SA National Museum of Military History, Johannesburg.

BEAUMONT Baron William Richard

Born 1877 Pietermaritzburg.
Died 1927 Isipingo, Durban.
A self-taught watercolourist. Painted landscapes generally of the Drakensberg and the Natal South Coast. A distinctive signature of BWRB.
Profile *c.*1904 practised as an architect. 1926 on the Council of the NSA. Taught at Durban Art School until his death. Son of Judge W H Beaumont, an amateur artist.
Exhibitions Participated in several group exhibitions from 1924.
Reference AASA.

BECK Sidney

Born 1936 Johannesburg.
A self-taught sculptor of figures and semi-abstract works. Uses plaster of Paris and bronze. Draws in charcoal and paints in oil.
Profile A winner of *The Star* Seaside Fund Competition, through which he travelled to London.
Exhibitions He has participated in several group exhibitions in Johannesburg from 1967; 1967 Adler Fielding Gallery, Johannesburg, first solo exhibition.
References BSAK; AASA; *SA Panorama* November 1974; *Artlook* June/July 1975.

BEERMAN Audrey

Born 1933 Cape Town.
A painter of landscapes, portraits, and figures. Works in oil, ink, pencil, craypas and charcoal. 1969–80 a series of large Cosmos flowers in landscapes; 1970–80 landscapes; 1970–85 a series of dolls painted in mixed media; 1976–82 Roses.
Studies 1967–69 under George Boys (qv); 1955 Michaelis School of Fine Art, drawing under Lippy Lipshitz (qv).
Profile 1985 an art teacher on Artists Week, Casa do Sol, Eastern Transvaal and privately. 1983 and 1985 on the panel of judges for the Brush and Chisel Club. 1959 lived in Spain.
Exhibitions She has participated in many group exhibitions from 1972 in SA; 1975 Madden Gallery, Duke Street, London, first of two solo exhibitions, the second being held in Johannesburg.

Public Commissions Portraits: 1972 Anne Scheepers, Woman of the Year, *The Star* newspaper; 1979 Desiree Wilson, Sports Woman of the Year, *Fair Lady* magazine; 1981 Donna Wurzel, Woman of the Year, *The Star* newspaper; 1984 Reeva Forman, Woman of the Year, Barclays (First National) Bank.
References AASA; *Gallery* Autumn 1987.

BEETON Jean Elizabeth Gordon

Born 1929 Pretoria.
A painter and graphic artist of genre and figures. Works in oil, charcoal and in various graphic media.
Studies 1947–48 Natal Technical College, under Cecil Todd (qv); 1952–53 six months at the Sir John Cass School of Art, London; 1962–68 University of South Africa, under Professor Walter Battiss (qv), gaining a BA(FA); 1967–68 part-time at The Visual Arts Research Centre, Johannesburg, under George Boys (qv); 1971 Pretoria Technical College, gaining a National Art Teachers Diploma.
Profile From 1968 a member of the SAAA. 1964 a part-time lecturer, 1972 a full-time lecturer, 1981 a senior lecturer, 1982 Acting Head and from 1983 Head of the Textile and Clothing Design Department, School of Art, Pretoria Technikon. 1972 visited Italy, France, Greece and the UK; 1980 Israel, Italy, Sweden and the UK. Mother of Julia Kuhlmann (qv).
Exhibitions She has participated in over 50 group exhibitions in SA from 1949; 1971 SAAA Gallery, Pretoria, joint exhibition with the author and amateur artist, B Breytenbach; 1976 SAAA Gallery, Pretoria, joint exhibition with Elsabe Schady (qv); 1981 Republic Festival Exhibition.
Represented Potchefstroom University for CHE; Willem Annandale Art Gallery, Lichtenburg.
References BSAK; AASA; *Artlook* November 1971.

BEETON Julia see KUHLMANN Julia

BEHRMANN Gail

Born 1948 Brakpan, Transvaal.
A painter of abstract pictures. Works in oil, acrylic, ink, pencil, charcoal and creates collages.
Studies 1974–76 under Bill Ainslie (qv).
Profile 1977 assisted David Koloane (qv) to establish the first Black art gallery in Johannesburg. From 1980 an art director for television drama productions, and a researcher for documentaries. 1985 a founder member of the Johannesburg Art Foundation Gallery, where she also taught in children's workshops.
Exhibitions She has participated in several group exhibitions from 1978 in Johannesburg; 1984 Karen McKerron Gallery, Johannesburg, first of two solo exhibitions; 1987 Johannesburg Art Foundation, joint exhibition with Dee Jacobs (qv), Charles Levin, Lionel Murcott (qv) and Russel Scott.

BEKKER-WILLIAMS Myfanwy Gail (Muffin)

Born 1947 Pretoria.

Resided in SA until 1976.

A painter, graphic artist and sculptor, working in many media including oil, acrylic, watercolour, gouache, pencil, charcoal, various graphic media, clay, neon, plastic, stone and ciment fondu.

Studies 1969 graduated from Pretoria Technical College with a Diploma in Fine Arts; 1970–73 ceramic technology at Pretoria Technical College, under Richard Adams (qv), Walter Battiss (qv) and Gunther van der Reis (qv); 1976 ceramics at New Mexico State University, under Bill Miles; 1978 New Mexico Junior College, under Terry Bumpass; 1979–83 various workshops in Texas.

Profile 1971–76 taught drawing and ceramics at various schools and at the Pretoria Technical College, the University of Pretoria and at the Teachers Training College in the Seychelles; 1976–81 taught ceramics and painting at various art establishments in New Mexico and Texas. From 1981 has given workshops in Texas. A number of architectural designs. Has lived in the Seychelles and from 1976 in South West USA.

Exhibitions She has participated in numerous group exhibitions from 1969 in SA and the USA; 1969 Ivan Soloman Gallery, Pretoria, first of several solo exhibitions held in SA, the Seychelles and the USA.

Public Commissions Several works in public buildings in Texas including in D F W Airport, Dallas.

BELL Caroline Frances

Born 1940 Johannesburg.

A painter of landscapes, portraits, figures and abstract pictures. Works in oil, watercolour, gouache, ink, wash and pencil.

Studies 1958–59 Harrogate School of Art, UK, gaining an Intermediate Certificate; 1959–61 Leeds College of Art, UK; 1962 part-time at Bradford College of Art, UK.

Profile 1982 a member of the WSSA and its Vice-Chairman in 1987. Has worked as a commercial artist and a designer of wall decorations. 1945–82 lived in the UK.

Exhibitions She has exhibited with the WSSA in SA and SWA/Namibia.

BELL Charles Davidson

Born 1813 Fife, Scotland.

Died 1882 Edinburgh, Scotland.

Resided in SA 1830–72.

A versatile artist travelling throughout SA. Worked in oil, watercolour, gouache and lithography, modelled in clay and executed a number of drawings using ink, pencil and/or sepia wash. His subject matter included portraits, landscapes, war scenes, figure studies, scenes of early African life (historical scenes) and caricatures. In addition to this he also painted on plates.

Profile In 1834 he accompanied Sir Andrew Smith on an expedition into the interior, from which his sketches were used as book illustrations. 1848–72 appointed Surveyor-General at the Cape. 1851 designed The Cape of Good Hope Triangle Stamp, among others; 1865–72 Chairman of the South African Mutual Life Association Society and designer of their seal; 1870 designed the Four Pound Note for the Bank of Queenstown. Designed the Harry Smith Medal. 1871 a foundation committee member of the Fine Arts Association. 1879 a committee member of the fifth SA Fine Arts Exhibition. Produced eight illustrations for Chapman's *Travels in the Interior of South Africa 1861–64*, 1868, Bell and Daldy, London; reprinted 1971, A A Balkema, Cape Town. His illustrations were also used in Andrew Smith's diary, published in 1939. He engraved illustrations for *The Blue Book*, an official publication about the Namaqua Copper Fields. He began a series of drawings of the Coats of Arms of SA families, later completed by Daniel Krynauw (qv), to whom he was related by marriage. 1813–29 lived in Scotland; 1830–72 in the Cape; 1872–82 in Scotland, revisiting SA in 1879. The town of Bellville was named after him. A musician and archaeologist.

Exhibitions Participated in group exhibitions in Cape Town and posthumously in Rhodesia (Zimbabwe); 1967 Johannesburg Library, Commemorative Exhibition; 1983 Grahamstown Festival, Commemorative Exhibition.

Award 1851 Gold Medal for the best original historical painting in oil, First Annual Exhibition of Fine Art, Cape Town.

Represented Africana Museum, Johannesburg; SA Cultural History Museum, Cape Town; SA Library, Cape Town; University of Cape Town; University of the Witwatersrand; William Fehr Collection, Cape Town.

References Pict Art; Afr Repos; A Gordon Brown, *Christopher Webb Smith*, 1965, Howard Timmins, Cape Town; SADNB; AMC1&6; DSAB; Register SA & SWA; SESA; Pict Afr; BSAK 1 & 2; SA Art; Marjorie Bull, *Abraham de Smidt, 1829–1908*, 1981, Printpak, Cape Town; 3Cs; AASA; SASSK; *ANN* June 1954; *SA Panorama* July 1969 & April 1982; *Apollo* October 1975, London.

BELL Deborah Margaret

Born 1957 Johannesburg.

A painter of figures. Works in oil and charcoal.

Studies 1975–78 University of the Witwatersrand, gaining a BA(FA) in 1977 and a BA(Hons) in 1978; 1981–85 University of the Witwatersrand, under Robert Hodgins (qv), Giuseppe Cattaneo (qv), Paul Stopforth (qv), Professor Alan Crump and Terry King (qv), being awarded an MA(FA).

Profile A founder member of Possession Arts. 1983–85 a part-time lecturer in the Department of Architecture, University of the Witwatersrand; 1985 a part-time lecturer in the Fine Arts Department, University of South Africa; 1986–87 a full-time lecturer at the University of South Africa. 1986 spent two months in Cité Internationale des Arts, Paris.

Exhibitions 1982 Market Gallery, Johannesburg, first of two solo exhibitions; she has participated in many group exhibitions from 1983 in SA; 1985 Cape Town Triennial; 1986 University of the Orange Free State, joint exhibition with Sybille Nagel (qv), Johann Moolman (qv) and Keith Dietrich (qv); 1987 exhibition of drypoints entitled "The Hogarth Series", with Robert Hodgins (qv) and William Kentridge (qv), touring SA.

Represented Durban Art Gallery; Johannesburg Art Gallery; SA National Gallery, Cape Town; Tatham Art Gallery, Pietermaritzburg; University of Natal; University of South Africa; University of the Witwatersrand.
References *De Kat* December/January 1986 & May 1986; *Fair Lady* September 1986.

BELL (Frank) Graham

Born 1910 Natal.
Died 1943 on active service with the Royal Air Force.
Resided in the UK after 1931.
A painter of portraits, landscapes and still life. Worked in oil.
Studies Durban Art School prior to 1931.
Profile 1931–34 a number of non-representational works, one of the few artists experimenting in this form of expression along with Duncan Grant (*b.*1885), William Coldstream (*b.*1908) and Geoffrey Tibble (*b.*1909). 1934–37 gave up painting and became a journalist and a critic working for such publications as *The New Statesman*. 1937 returned to naturalistic, realistic painting and was a founder member of the Euston Road School, London; *c.*1937 a member of the Artists International Association. 1939 volunteered for war service.
Exhibitions 1929 exhibited with the NSA; 1931 Durban City Hall, first solo exhibition; 1934 participated in the Objective Abstraction Exhibition, London; 1948 Tate Gallery, London, SA Art Exhibition.
Represented Durban Art Gallery; Johannesburg Art Gallery; Manchester Art Gallery, UK; SA National Gallery, Cape Town; Tate Gallery, London, UK.
Publication by Bell *The Artist and His Public*, 1939, Hogarth Press, London.
References Sir Kenneth Clark, *The Paintings of Graham Bell*, 1947, London; *Tate Gallery Catalogue—Modern British Paintings, Drawings and Sculpture*, volume 1, 1964, Oldbourne Press, London; Collectors' Guide; Register SA & SWA; SAP&D; BSAK; Oxford Companion to 20C Art; DBA; Charles Harrison, *English Art and Modernism 1900–1939*, 1981, Allen Lane, London; AASA.

BELL Peter Alan

Born 1918 Grantham, Lincolnshire, England.
Resided in SA 1947–63.
Studies 1947 Architecture at the University of Cape Town; 1948 Rhodes University, where attained a BA(FA).
Profile 1959–63 Head of the Ndaleni Art School, Natal. 1963–67 tutor in art, Memoral University, Newfoundland, Canada. 1969 curator of the Memorial University Art Gallery, Canada. Produced serigraphs.
Exhibitions He has participated in group exhibitions from 1942 in the UK, SA and Canada; 1947 Cape Town, first of many solo exhibitions held throughout SA and in Canada.
Represented SA National Gallery, Cape Town.
Reference AASA.

BELLING Ronald Robert

Born 1933 East London.

A painter of mainly aviation art, but occasionally landscapes, seascapes and abstract pictures. Works in oil, acrylic, watercolour, ink, wash, pencil and charcoal.

Studies 1948–49 part-time at the Port Elizabeth Technical College, under Professor Robert Bain (qv).

Profile From 1977 an Official War/Military Artist; 1977–78 a series of SA Air Force activities on the Angolan Border; 1979–80 a series of SA Air Force Maritime Command Activities. 1974–81 a member of the EPSFA; from 1980 of the SA Guild of Aviation Artists. An Architectural Development Officer for the Port Elizabeth City Engineering Department. Numerous illustrations for aviation books and journals.

Exhibitions 1964 Port Elizabeth, first of nine solo exhibitions held in the Eastern Cape; 1966 Cleveland, Ohio, USA, solo exhibition; he has participated in several group exhibitions from 1981.

Represented SA National Museum of Military History, Johannesburg.

References AASA; *SA Panorama* November 1978.

BENDER Desmond

Born 1958 Dundee, Natal.

A painter of natural and industrial landscapes. Works in oil, pastel and acrylic. 1985 a series of Northern Natal veld scenes; 1986 of Northern Natal coal/industrial fields.

Studies 1978–81 Natal Technikon, under Penny Siopis (qv) and Basil Friedlander (qv), gaining a Higher Diploma in Fine Arts; 1984–86 University of Natal, under Professor Terry King (qv) and Dick Leigh (qv), attaining a BA(FA).

Profile From 1981 a member of the NSA. 1984 a member of the Natal Foundation of Arts. 1982 a high school teacher at Carmel College, Durban; 1983–86 subject head, Maritzburg College, Pietermaritzburg; from 1987 Head of the Art Department, Hilton College, Natal. 1985 on the Subject Advisory Committee and a Sub-Examiner in Art History for the Natal Education Department.

Exhibitions He has participated in several group exhibitions from 1982 in Natal; 1985 Café Geneve Gallery, Durban, solo exhibition.

BENEDICK Frans L

Born 1915 Berlin, Germany.

Resided in SA from 1935.

A painter of landscapes and still life. Works in oil.

Studies Under Bill Ainslie (qv); Centre for Continuing Education, University of the Witwatersrand, under Bernice Michelow (qv) and Anton Uys.

Exhibitions He has participated in group exhibitions from 1979 in Johannesburg.

BENSON Elizabeth see MACADAM Elizabeth

BENZON Leonard Anton
Born 1944 Johannesburg.
A self-taught painter of landscapes, seascapes and figures. Works in oil. Has
painted throughout SA and in Zimbabwe.
Profile Son of Johannes Oldert (qv), who influenced his work, and Elise Laidler
(qv).
Exhibitions He has participated in numerous group exhibitions in SA; 1984
Darnall, Natal, first of many solo exhibitions.

BERESFORD Rochelle
Born Paarl.
A sculptor in ceramics of figures, also creates collages and draws in pastel.
Studies 1973 and 1977 Cape Technical College; 1980–81 Ruth Prowse School of
Art, Cape Town, where awarded the Erik Laubscher (qv) Prize for Painting;
1983 raku technique, part-time under David May.
Exhibitions She has participated in several group exhibitions from 1977 in the
Cape Province; 1984 SAAA Gallery, Pretoria, solo exhibition; 1986 Gallery
International, Cape Town, joint exhibition with Daan Verwey (qv).

BERGER Brenda Joyce
Born 1943 Port Elizabeth.
A painter and graphic artist of figurative imagery in a surreal setting. Works in
oil, mixed media and in various graphic media.
Studies 1977–78 Ruth Prowse School of Art, Cape Town, under Erik Laubscher
(qv) and Edwine Simon (qv); 1982–84 Michael Pettit School of Art, Cape Town,
under Michael Pettit (qv).
Profile From 1986 a member of the SAAA. A trained musician and music
lecturer in Cape Town. Composed the song book *Songs for Granny's Prints*, 1979,
for the International Year of the Child.
Exhibitions She has participated in several group exhibitions from 1977 in the
Cape Province; 1985 Atlantic Art Gallery, Cape Town, first of two solo
exhibitions, the second being held in Johannesburg.
Reference *International Register of Profiles*, 6th edition, 1982.

BERGER Jochen
Born 1942 Ansbach, West Germany.
Resided in SA from 1967.
A painter of landscapes, still life and figures. Works in oil and watercolour,
draws in pencil, coloured pencil, ink and mixed media. 1972–74 a series of
human situations, 1974–79 a series of artificial landscapes, 1982–84 a series of
triangles.

Studies 1961–66 Essen University, West Germany, under Professor Schardt, Professor Zander and Professor Guttschow.
Profile From 1984 a committee member of the Cape SAAA and in 1985 Chairman of its selection committee. 1969–84 a senior lecturer in the Creative Art Department, University of Stellenbosch; from 1984 Head of the Graphic Design Department, Cape Technikon. From 1979 a judge for several national art competitions.
Exhibitions He has participated in numerous group exhibitions from 1969 in SA, the USA, France, Israel and West Germany; 1970 Cape Town, first of eight solo exhibitions held in SA, West Germany and France; 1979 Cape Town Biennial, Invited Artist; 1981 Republic Festival Exhibition.
Award 1970 SA Institute of Race Relations Award, SA Breweries Biennale.
Represented Durban Art Gallery; SA National Gallery, Cape Town; University of Stellenbosch.
References AASA; *Artlook* September 1972.

BERGMANN-MAAG Ursula H A C H
Born 1920 Windhoek SWA/Namibia.
Both a painter and sculptor of landscapes, portraits, figures and still life. Works in oil, watercolour, pencil, charcoal, bronze and ciment fondu.
Studies 1940 privately under Adolph Jentsch (qv); 1946–49 Michaelis School of Fine Art, under Professor Edward Roworth (qv) and Ivan Mitford-Barberton (qv).
Profile From 1967 a member of the Arts Association SWA/Namibia. 1946–74 lived in Cape Town, thereafter in SWA/Namibia.
Exhibitions She has participated in group exhibitions from 1946 in Cape Town and SWA/Namibia; 1967 Windhoek, SWA/Namibia, first solo exhibition.
Represented Willem Annandale Art Gallery, Lichtenburg.

BERMAN Audrey Barbara
Born 1921 Bulawayo, Rhodesia (Zimbabwe).
Resided in SA from 1966.
A painter of her own experiences and surroundings. Works in oil.
Profile Began painting in 1977. From 1970 a member of the NSA and from 1984 of D'ARTS. 1985 produced leatherwork. 1982 visited the USA. Lived in Durban, moving to Cape Town in 1987.
Exhibition She has participated in several group exhibitions from 1977 in Natal and Cape Town; 1985 NSA Gallery, Durban, solo exhibition.

BERNER Dörte
Born 1942 Germany.
Resided in SWA/Namibia from 1966.
A sculptor of figures. Works in stone.

Studies Academy of Art, Nuremberg, West Germany.
Profile Married to Volker Berner, the designer and weaver.
Exhibition 1979 Cape Town Biennial.
Represented Arts Association SWA/Namibia Collection; Pretoria Art Museum;
SA National Gallery, Cape Town.
References Art SWA; AASA; LSAA.

BERNSTEIN Hilda

Born 1915 London, England.
Resided in SA 1933–64.
A self-taught painter and graphic artist working in oil, watercolour, gouache,
ink, wash, pencil, charcoal and in various graphic media. Primarily an etcher.
Profile 1971 a member of the Hampstead Artists Council in England. 1983 and
1984 a tutor at a Summer School under the auspices of the Hampstead Artists
Council. During the 1970s she designed a number of book jackets and also
illustrated books; her work has also been used on posters and cards. A writer.
1964–85 lived in London, thereafter in Herefordshire, England. She has
travelled throughout Africa.
Exhibitions She has participated in numerous group exhibitions from 1971 in
SA, the USA, West Germany, The Netherlands and the UK; 1971 Pace Gallery,
London, first of 11 solo exhibitions held in the UK, the USA, West Germany and
Zambia.
Publications by Bernstein *The World That Was Ours*, 1967, Heinemann, London;
The Terrorism of Torture, 1972, International Defence and Aid Fund, London; *For
Their Triumphs and Their Tears*, 1975, International Defence and Aid Fund,
London, republished 1980, updated edition 1985; *No. 46—Steve Biko*, 1978,
International Defence and Aid Fund, London; *Death is Part of the Process*, 1983,
Sinclair-Browne, London.

BERNSTEIN Michele

Born 1947 Johannesburg.
A painter of fantastical pictures. Works in oil. 1986 a series of dolls, puppets,
circus figures, dwarfs and toys.
Studies During the 1960s at the University of the Witwatersrand, under Cecily
Sash (qv) and Giuseppe Cattaneo (qv), where gained a BA; University of the
Witwatersrand, under Judith Mason (qv), attaining a Higher Diploma in
Education; also studied privately under Michael Pettit (qv).
Profile A member of the SAAA. During the 1970s an English teacher, from 1981
art mistress at Herzlia Highlands Primary School, Cape Town.
Exhibitions She has participated in several group exhibitions from 1984; 1986
SAAA Gallery, Cape Town, first of three solo exhibitions, the second being held
in Johannesburg.

BERRY Erica Frances Fleetwood (Mrs Mitchell) ARCA
Born 1916 Johannesburg.
A painter of still life and landscapes. Works in watercolour, oil, gouache, ink, wash, pencil and mixed media. Creates collages from her watercolours.
Studies 1931–34 Witwatersrand Technical College, gaining a National Art Teachers Diploma; 1935–39 Royal College of Art, London, under John Nash (*b.*1895) and Gilbert Spencer ARCA (*b.*1892), becoming an Associate.
Profile 1940–41 taught at Roedean School, Johannesburg; 1941–42 at Bishops Diocesan College, Cape Town; 1943–44 ran the Frank Joubert Children's Art Centre, Cape Town; 1945–46 taught at the Johannesburg School of Art; 1946–78 a lecturer at the University of the Witwatersrand. 1981 appointed art advisor to Pietermaritzburg Cathedral. Visited Israel in 1984.
Exhibitions She has participated in numerous group exhibitions from 1940 in SA; 1944 first of numerous solo exhibitions held in Johannesburg and Cape Town; 1956 Quadrennial Exhibition; 1981 Republic Festival Exhibition; 1987 Everard Read Gallery, Johannesburg, solo exhibition.
Represented Hester Rupert Art Museum, Graaff-Reinet; University of Cape Town; University of South Africa; University of the Witwatersrand.
References Collectors' Guide; SAA; 20C SA Art; BSAK 1 & 2; AASA; *Artlook* September 1970 & August/September 1974.

BERRY Ronald
Born 1951 Pretoria.
A painter of portraits. Works in oil, acrylic, watercolour and gouache, draws in pastel, ink, wash, pencil and charcoal.
Studies 1973 and 1976–77 Pretoria Technical College, under Justinus van der Merwe (qv), Gunther van der Reis (qv), Ian Redelinghuys (qv) and Jean Beeton (qv), gaining a Diploma in Fine Art.
Profile 1978–80 artist to the Post Office Museum, Pretoria, where he painted a mural; from 1983 a graphic artist with the SABC.
Exhibition *c.*1980 SAAA Gallery, Pretoria, solo exhibition.

BESTALL Cliff
Born 1947.
A graphic artist.
Profile Taught at the Natal Technical College during the 1970s.
Exhibitions 1971 Republic Festival Exhibition; 1971 Art SA Today; 1974 Durban Art Gallery, solo exhibition entitled "Prospects of Survival".
Award 1969 Phillip Frame Award, Art SA Today.
Represented Durban Art Gallery.
References BSAK 1; AASA; *Artlook* September 1969 & November 1971.

BESTER Valerie
Born 1936 Schweizer-Reneke, Western Transvaal.
A sculptor working in perspex, bronze and wood.

GERHARD BATHA
Uniondale 1987
Acrylic on Canvas 90 × 120 cm
Private

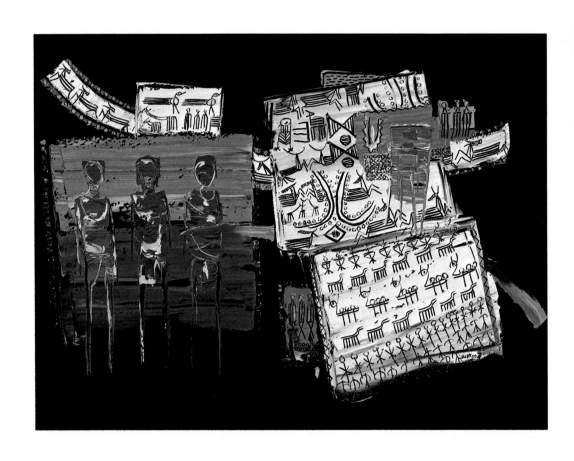

WALTER BATTISS
Palimpsest II
Oil on Canvas 90,5 × 120 cm
Pretoria Art Museum

GREGOIRE BOONZAIER
Busy Street with Table Mountain, District Six 1977
Oil on Canvas 71 × 91 cm
Artist

THOMAS BOWLER
Green Point/Old Lighthouse
Watercolour 19,8 × 29,5 cm
Private

Table Bay/Blueberg
Watercolour 23,8 × 66 cm
Private

Studies University of South Africa, attaining a BA(FA) in 1978 and an MA(FA) in 1986.

Profile From 1979 a lecturer in the Department of History of Art and Fine Art, University of South Africa. 1984 a sabbatical research programme conducted in New York and Washington DC on environment art.

Exhibitions She has participated in group exhibitions from 1980 held in Pretoria, Bloemfontein, Johannesburg and in West Germany.

Reference *De Kat* December/January 1987.

BEUKES G J

Born 1885 Prince Albert, Cape Province.

Died 1945 in the Cape.

A painter of Cape landscapes and in particular those of Afrikaner historical import. Worked in oil.

Studies Under Mrs J M Theunissen.

Profile A number of reproductions of his work have been printed by E Schweickerdt, Pretoria.

Exhibitions 1934 first Transvaal solo exhibition.

References BSAK; AASA.

BEVINGTON William George ARCA

Born 1881 East London.

Died Thought to have died in 1953 in Cape Town.

A painter of portraits, landscapes, still life, genre, Cape villages and cattle scenes. Worked in oil and watercolour. A sculptor, both a wood carver and modeller. Designed mouldings and pediments for buildings, a number of church decorations and designs for medals.

Studies 1903–06 Grahamstown School of Art, 1906 awarded a Rhodes Bursary to study at the Kensington Royal College of Art, London.

Profile A member of the SA Society of Artists. A deaf-mute who taught drawing and sculpture in King William's Town and in the 1920s at the Cape Town Art School, he also worked for *The Cape Times* as a cartoonist.

Exhibitions 1918 Cape Town, joint exhibition with Dennis Edwards (qv); participated in group exhibitions from 1924 in SA and the UK.

Represented Africana Museum, Johannesburg; Albany Museum, Grahamstown; Pretoria Art Museum; SA National Gallery, Cape Town; William Humphreys Art Gallery, Kimberley.

Public Commissions Bronze bas-relief, Court House, King William's Town; wood carvings of the "Arms of the Union" in English oak, both Houses of Parliament.

References Collectors' Guide; SAA; SADNB; SAP&S; AMC6; SAP&D; BSAK; AASA; *SA Art Collector* April 1947; *SA Panorama* December 1981.

BEYNON   Claire Lynda (Mrs Van Ammers)
Born   1960 Johannesburg.
An artist working in various graphic media, acrylic, ink, pencil, charcoal, pastel and mixed media. Combines drawings and monoprints and makes rubbings. Her paintings are a combination of abstract and representational with use of symbols. 1984 an etching and screenprint series entitled "Rebus I–VII"; 1984–85 a pastel series entitled "Even if the unfallen Adam was all of the fallen man I–IV"; 1984 a mixed media series entitled "Ashes to Ashes, Dust to Dust I–III".
Studies 1979–82 University of Natal, under Stephen Inggs (qv), gaining a BA (FA); 1983–84 Chelsea School of Art, London, under Tim Mara.
Profile 1979–82 lived in Pietermaritzburg; 1983–84 in London; 1984–85 at Nooitgedacht, Transvaal; 1986 Johannesburg; 1987 Cape Town.
Exhibitions She has participated in several group exhibitions from 1981 in SA, in Taiwan in 1983 and in London in 1984; 1985 Karen McKerron Gallery, Johannesburg, first of two solo exhibitions.

BEZUIDENHOUT   Daniël
Born   1934 Bloemfontein.
A painter of landscapes. Works in watercolour.
Studies 1958–61 Orange Free State Technical College, under Justinus van der Merwe (qv), Mike Edwards (qv) and Rose-Marie Budler (qv).
Profile From 1978 an Associate of the WSSA. From 1976 a member of the SAAA and of the Orange Free State Art Society, of which he was also a committee member. 1983 produced a calendar for the Bank of Lesotho.
Exhibitions He has participated in numerous group exhibitions from 1960 throughout SA and in London; 1979 Bloemfontein, solo exhibition.
Represented Queenstown Art Gallery; Willem Annandale Art Gallery, Lichtenburg.
Reference *Aquarelle* March 1985.

BHENGU   Gerard
Born   1910 Mundi, Natal.
A self-taught painter of portraits, genre, figures and township scenes. Works in watercolour and sepia.
Profile 1940–59 worked as an artist for Payne Brothers Department Store, Durban. From 1935 illustrated story books and readers in Zulu, also illustrated Phyllis Savory's *Bantu Fireside Tales*. Has lived in Zululand, at Mariannhill and in Durban.
Exhibitions He has participated in group exhibitions from 1936; 1948 Gallery Beaux-Arts, Johannesburg, solo exhibition; 1979 Contemporary African Art in SA, touring; 1986 Alliance Française, Pretoria, Historical Perspective of Black Art in SA Exhibition.
Represented Africana Museum, Johannesburg; Albany Museum, Grahamstown; University of Fort Hare.

References P Savory, *Gerard Bhengu – Zulu Artist,* 1965, Timmins, Cape Town; BSAK; SESA; E J de Jager, *Contemporary African Art,* 1973, Cape Town; Echoes of African Art; *Artlook* May 1972; *Lantern* June 1972; *Bantu* September 1974; *SA Panorama* May 1975.

BHENGU Titus

Born 1930 Ndwedwe, Natal.
A sculptor of figures. Works in wood.
Exhibitions He has participated in several group exhibitions in SA.

BIDEN Bernadine

Born 1913 Pretoria.
Died 1988 Cape Town.
A painter of abstract pictures with calligraphic themes. Created three-dimensional constructions. Worked in oil, acrylic, laminated wood and perspex.
Studies Worked briefly in the studio of the Canadian artist Helen Turner.
Profile Wife of Kenneth Bakker (qv).
Exhibitions Participated in group exhibitions held throughout SA; 1955 first of several joint exhibitions held with Kenneth Bakker (qv); 1960 and 1964 Quadrennial Exhibitions; 1969 Martin Melck House, Cape Town, solo exhibition.
Represented SA National Gallery, Cape Town; University of Stellenbosch.
References Art SA; BSAK; 3Cs; *Artlook* August–September 1975.

BIGGS Catharina Carolina Elizabeth (Rina) (née Pretorius)

Born 1941 Vrede, Orange Free State.
A painter of landscapes, still life, portraits, seascapes, figures, abstract pictures and wildlife. Works in oil.
Studies 1979–81 in Durban under Peter van Blommestein (qv).
Exhibitions 1972 Barberton, Transvaal, first of over 50 exhibitions held in SA and SWA/Namibia; she has participated in several group exhibitions from 1982.

BILAS Peter Gerd

Born 1952 St Pölten, Austria.
Resided in SA from 1974.
A self-taught painter of marine subjects. Works in oil.
Profile His work has been used to illustrate various maritime publications.
Exhibitions He has participated in several group exhibitions from 1982 in SA, the UK and the USA; 1982 Forum, Claremont, Cape Town, first of four solo exhibitions.

Represented Maritime Museum, The Castle, Cape Town.
Public Commission Nine paintings of Antarctic exploration for the SA Antarctic research ship, *SA Agulhas*.

BILGERI Hans

Born 1942 Austria.
Resided in SA from 1963.
A self-taught painter, sculptor and graphic artist of landscapes, figures and abstracts. Works in oil, acrylic, charcoal, ciment fondu, wood and in various graphic media, particularly woodcuts.
Profile From 1967 a member of the SAAA.
Exhibitions He has participated in several group exhibitions from 1967 in Pretoria and Johannesburg and in Austria, Israel and Australia; 1969 SAAA Gallery, Pretoria, first of four solo exhibitions held in Pretoria and Johannesburg; 1970 Herbert Evans Gallery, Johannesburg, joint exhibition with Justinus van der Merwe (qv).
References BSAK; AASA; *Artlook* April 1969 & June 1970.

BINGE-COETZEE Ferrie Francina

Born 1926 Keetmanshoop, SWA/Namibia.
A painter and graphic artist of mostly abstract works but also a number of pastel flower pieces. Works in oil, charcoal, pastel and in various graphic media.
Studies 1943 privately under Siegfried Hahn (qv) in Stellenbosch; 1953 Haagsch Akademie voor Beeldende Kunsten, The Netherlands, under Randi Doorman; 1963–66 Pretoria Technical College, under Gunther van der Reis (qv); later studied graphic techniques under Titia Ballot (qv).
Profile From 1962 a member of the SAAA and 1963–67 a committee member and Editor of their magazine, *SA Arts Calendar*; 1981 a founder member of the Artists Guild, Cape Town. 1949–53 an art correspondent in The Netherlands for *Die Burger* newspaper; 1966–67 an art critic for *Die Vaderland* newspaper. 1967–86 lived in Spain and at Tulbagh in the Cape Province. 1986 moved to Strand, Cape Province. Married Christo Coetzee (qv) in 1968.
Exhibitions She has participated in many group exhibitions from 1966 in SA; 1967 SAAA Gallery, Pretoria, first of 13 solo exhibitions held in SA and SWA/Namibia.
Represented Willem Annandale Art Gallery, Lichtenburg.
References BSAK; *Artlook* October 1967 & January 1971; *De Kat* August 1985.

BISSEKER Noel

Born 1939 Port St Johns, Transkei.
A painter, sculptor and graphic artist of landscapes, figures, abstracted landscapes and abstract works. Uses mixed media, wood, metal and "found fragments". Creates collages, constructions and serigraphs.
Studies 1956–59 Natal Technical College, gaining a National Art Teachers Diploma.

Profile 1960–63 lectured at Natal Technical College; 1965–79 a lecturer at the Witwatersrand Technical College, becoming a senior lecturer in Fine Art and Design in 1972; 1982 lectured at the Witwatersrand Technical College. From 1968 a slide photographer. 1964 spent nine months in Europe, mainly in Greece, since when he has made frequent visits to Greece and the Greek islands.

Exhibitions From 1964 he has participated in group exhibitions held in SA, West Germany, The Netherlands, Belgium, the USA, Italy and SA; 1967 Durban, first of many solo exhibitions held in SA.

Award 1985 Winner of the Trustbank Poster Competition.

Represented Cape Technikon; Johannesburg Art Gallery; Pretoria Art Museum; Rand Afrikaans University; Sandton Municipal Collection; SA National Gallery, Cape Town; University of South Africa; University of the Witwatersrand; William Humphreys Art Gallery, Kimberley.

References AASA; *Photography and Travel* July 1976.

BLACK Peter

Born 1946 Zambia.

Works in the pointillist manner using ink and pencil. His subject matter is varied and includes landscapes, still life, figures and portraits.

Studies Part-time at the Natal Technical College.

Profile 1965 an actor/dancer with PACT; 1970–72 a gallery manager in Athens, Greece; 1972 lived in Stockholm, Sweden, where he illustrated a number of magazines. Has travelled throughout Europe, SA and to Los Angeles, USA.

Exhibitions 1981 Crake Gallery, Johannesburg, solo exhibition; he has participated in several group exhibitions from 1982.

BLACK Raymond Alexander Ritchie

Born 1939 Aberdeen, Scotland.

Resided in SA from 1945.

A painter of wildlife and landscapes. Works in acrylic and gouache.

Studies 1957–59 Witwatersrand Technical College, under Phil Botha (qv), where gained a Diploma in Commercial Art and Design.

Profile 1962 a part-time lecturer in graphic design at the Port Elizabeth School of Art. A museum artist in Grahamstown. 1975 illustrated *Rats and Mice of Rhodesia* by Reay Smithers; 1977 illustrated a folio entitled *Game Birds of Southern Africa* published by Howard Swan, Johannesburg; 1980 illustrated *Rodents of Southern Africa* by G de Graaff; in 1986 working on a series of pictures for a book on kingfishers of Southern Africa. 1969–76 lived in Rhodesia (Zimbabwe).

Exhibitions He has participated in several group exhibitions from 1972 in Zimbabwe and SA; 1977 Sladmore Gallery, Johannesburg, joint exhibition with R D Digby.

Reference AASA.

BLATT Arnfried

Born 1935 Swakopmund, SWA/Namibia.
Died 1976 Swakopmund, SWA/Namibia (killed in a plane crash).
A painter of landscapes, particularly of the Namib Desert. Worked in oil, tempera and pastel.
Studies Whilst studying architecture at the University of Cape Town he took art lessons at the Michaelis School of Fine Art from Maurice van Essche (qv).
Profile An architect practising in Windhoek. Son of Johannes Blatt (qv).
Exhibitions 1968 Arts Association SWA/Namibia Gallery, Windhoek, first of several solo exhibitions in SWA/Namibia and SA; 1972 solo exhibition touring West Germany; participated in group exhibitions from 1973 in SA and SWA/Namibia; 1976 Arts Association SWA/Namibia Gallery, Windhoek, Memorial Exhibition; 1977 Ann Zinn Gallery, Cape Town, Retrospective Exhibition; 1980 Arts Association SWA/Namibia Gallery, Windhoek, SAAA Gallery, Pretoria and Swakopmund Museum, Memorial Exhibitions; 1982 Arts Association SWA/Namibia Gallery, Windhoek, Commemorative Exhibition.
Represented Arts Association SWA/Namibia Collection; Pretoria Art Museum.
References Art SWA; AASA; *Artlook* April 1975; *Gallery* Spring 1982.

BLATT Johannes

Born 1905 Trier, West Germany.
Died 1972 Windhoek, SWA/Namibia.
Resided in SWA/Namibia from 1913.
A painter of landscapes, seascapes, wildlife, figures, portraits and still life. Worked in oil, pastel, watercolour, ink, wash, pencil, charcoal and tempera; also a number of etchings.
Studies 1916 briefly under Axel Eriksson (qv) in Swakopmund; 1922–25 Schule am Lerchenfelds in Hamburg, Germany, under Professor Julius Wohlers, A Schroeder, H Rompendahl, O Beuhne and C Beckerath.
Profile A member of the Arts Association SWA/Namibia. A former art teacher at the High School, Swakopmund; in 1968 he began an art school in Windhoek; 1970 an art teacher at the German High School in Windhoek. 1913–54 lived in Swakopmund; from 1954 lived in Cape Town for a number of years, then in Windhoek. In 1971 he travelled and exhibited in Rhodesia (Zimbabwe) and in 1972 in Switzerland. Father of Arnfried Blatt (qv).
Exhibitions 1925 Ebenfalls, West Germany, first of three solo exhibitions held in Europe; 1927 Swakopmund, first of several solo exhibitions held in SWA/Namibia and SA; participated in group exhibitions from 1947 in SWA/Namibia, SA and West Germany; 1973 Arts Association SWA/Namibia Gallery, Windhoek, Memorial Exhibition; 1977 Windhoek, Retrospective Exhibition; 1980 Swakopmund Museum, Exhibition; 1985 Arts Association SWA/Namibia Gallery, Windhoek, Commemorative Exhibition.
Represented Ann Bryant Gallery, East London; Arts Association SWA/Namibia Collection, Windhoek; Pretoria Art Museum; University of South Africa; William Humphreys Art Gallery, Kimberley.
References SAA; BSAK; Art SWA; AASA.

BLEACH C Meredith

Active from 1901.

A painter of marine scenes, landscapes, figures and portraits. Worked in watercolour, oil and in various graphic media. Produced sketches of the Anglo-Boer War and WWI, depicting, both seriously and in cartoon form, military subjects and situations.

Studies Under J H Amshewitz (qv).

Profile 1920 a member of the Johannesburg Sketch Club. 1940–41 an Official War Artist, working in East and South Africa. Contributed to Charles Cutler's book *Humorous Sketches of the Campaign in German East Africa*, published in Johannesburg.

Exhibitions Participated in group exhibitions in SA from 1920.

Represented Africana Museum, Johannesburg; SA National Museum of Military History, Johannesburg.

Public Commissions Portraits of many SA political and military personalities, including the Earl of Clarendon and Admiral Sir Edward Evans.

References AMC1; SA Art; AASA; SASSK.

BLEACH R L (Jack)

A painter of landscapes and street scenes of the Cape and of East Africa. Worked in watercolour and oil.

Profile As a Lieutenant in the Union Defence Force during WWII he produced paintings of the Desert War.

Exhibitions 1944 Transvaal Art Society, Johannesburg, first solo exhibition.

BLENNERHASSET William Thomas

Born 1895 Belfast, Northern Ireland.

Died 1954 Durban.

Resided in SA from 1924.

A painter of landscapes of Natal, the Cape and Rhodesia (Zimbabwe). Worked in oil.

Studies In Dublin and in his grandfather's studio.

Profile During WWI served in the British Army and continued to do so for a period after the war. 1924–52 a member of the Durban Police Force, also worked on the advertising of the Transport Service there. Became a full-time painter on his retirement. 1952–54 President of the NSA. An advisor to the Durban Art Gallery. A well-travelled person, visiting such places as India, Iran and Russia.

Exhibitions Participated in group exhibitions from 1944 throughout SA; *c.*1947 Durban Art Gallery, solo exhibition.

Represented Durban Art Gallery.

Reference AASA.

BLOM Johannes Jacobus

Born 1948 Cape Town.

A painter of landscapes, portraits, still life, figures and abstract pictures. Works in oil, acrylic, watercolour, ink, pencil, pastel, conté and crayons. Creates collages.

Studies 1972–73 Michaelis School of Fine Art, under Kevin Atkinson (qv), Richard Wake (qv), Peggy Delport (qv) and Stanley Pinker (qv); 1980 Johannesburg College of Adult Education, under Hermine Spies (qv); 1982–84 privately under Lionel Abrams (qv); 1984 privately under Elizabeth Harington (qv).

Exhibitions He has participated in several group exhibitions from 1983 in Johannesburg and Pretoria; 1983 Gallery 21, Johannesburg, first of two solo exhibitions.

BLOM Willem Adriaan (Wim)

Born 1927 Germiston, Transvaal.

A painter of landscapes, seascapes, still life, genre, figures and interiors. Works in oil, watercolour, gouache, wash, pencil, charcoal, egg tempera and collage.

Studies 1944–47 University of the Witwatersrand, under Professor Heather Martienssen (1915–79), Willem Hendrikz (qv) and Joyce Leonard (qv), gaining a BA(FA)(Hons) and an MA(FA); 1948–50 Edinburgh University, Scotland, under Professor Talbot Rice; 1949 University of Perugia, Italy, under Professor A Cristofani; 1959 graphic techniques at the Southern Alberta Institute of Technology, Calgary, Canada; 1965 lithography at the Instituto de San Miguel de Allende, Mexico.

Profile 1951 lectured in the History of Art at the University of the Witwatersrand; 1958–59 a lecturer in Drawing and Design at the Witwatersrand Technical College; 1960–61 Curatorial Assistant at the Art Gallery of Ontario, Toronto; 1961–66 Research Curator, 1968–70 Curatorial Administrator, National Gallery of Canada, Ottawa. In 1972 he was made an Honorary Member of the Masters of Fine Arts International, New York. 1955–57 lived in Florence, Italy; 1959–70 in Canada; from 1970 in Minorca, Spain, where he is a full-time artist.

Exhibitions He has participated in numerous group exhibitions from 1948 in SA, Italy, Canada, Switzerland, Australia, West Germany and Minorca, Spain; 1954 Herbert Evans Gallery, Johannesburg, first of 26 solo exhibitions held in SA, Canada, and Minorca, Spain; 1969 Durban Art Gallery, Prestige Exhibition; 1981 Republic Festival Exhibition.

Awards 1957 Dante Alighieri Gold Medal, Florence, Italy; 1979 Medalla de honor, XVIII Salon de Primavera, Minorca; 1982 Primo Premio, International Exhibition of Painting, Mahon, Spain.

Represented Ann Bryant Gallery, East London; Ayuntamiento de Mahon, Minorca, Spain; Consejo Insular, Mahon, Minorca, Spain; Durban Art Gallery; Johannesburg Art Gallery; Kelowna Art Gallery, British Columbia, Canada; National Gallery of Canada, Ottawa; Pietersburg Collection; Pretoria Art Museum; Queen's University, Kingston, Ontario, Canada; Rand Afrikaans University; Roodepoort Art Museum; Sandton Municipal Collection; SA National Gallery, Cape Town; Tatham Art Gallery, Pietermaritzburg; Teachers Training College, Johannesburg; University of the Orange Free State; University of South Africa; University of the Witwatersrand; William Humphreys Art Gallery, Kimberley.

Publications by Blom From 1962 numerous catalogues for Canadian art galleries and travelling exhibitions including *The National Gallery of Canada, Illustrated Guide to the Collections*, 1964, Ottawa; *Italian Paintings in the National Gallery of Canada*, 1966, Ottawa; *Flemish, Dutch and German Paintings in the National Gallery of Canada*, 1966, Ottawa.

References SAA; SSAP; BSAK 1 & 2; SA Art; AASA; *Dictionary of International Biography*, volume 11, 1975, Cambridge; *SA Panorama* May 1958; *South Africana* December 1960; *SA Art News* 6 April 1961; *Artlook* March 1968, December 1969 & November 1973; *Lantern* December 1970; *Canadian Paintings, Catalogue of the Collection of the National Gallery of Canada*, 1981, Ottawa; *De Kat* December/January 1987.

BLOMKAMP Paul Christian

Born 1949 Johannesburg.

A self-taught painter and sculptor of semi-abstract works of future man and place. Works in oil, acrylic, airbrush, wood and a unique sculpture medium based on micro-ballon filler and epoxy mix. 1986 a series entitled "The Heads of State or the State of Heads". A maker and designer of stained glass windows.

Exhibitions He has participated in numerous group exhibitions from 1970; 1973 Gallery 73, Johannesburg, first of three solo exhibitions.

Public Commissions Stained glass windows or panels for: 1969 Hillbrow Microwave Tower, Johannesburg; 1972 Civic Centre Church, Johannesburg; 1977 Rosebank Union Church, Johannesburg; 1980 the State Theatre, Pretoria; 1980 Greek Orthodox Church, Melrose, Johannesburg; 1980–87 St Stithians College, Randburg, Johannesburg; began in 1986 a panel consisting of coloured wood blocks and mirror for the Germiston Civic Centre, Transvaal.

References AASA; *Gallery* Summer 1982.

BLOOM Doris Desirée

Born 1954.

A painter of landscapes and figures. Works in mixed media and oil. A graphic artist producing copper etchings, drypoints and aquatints. Also works in ceramics. Large mural designs.

Studies Witwatersrand Technical College, gaining a Diploma in Ceramics in 1974; 1976 Royal Danish Academy of Fine Art, under Professor Robert Jacobson and Professor Dan Sterup Hansen.

Profile A member of the Danske Grafikere and the Danske Billedkunstneres Forbund. *c.*1976 taught at Doornfontein Recreation Centre.

Exhibitions She has participated in group exhibitions in SA and Denmark; held solo exhibitions during the 1970s and 1980s in Johannesburg, Pretoria, Durban and in Denmark.

Represented Royal Danish National Gallery, Denmark.

Public Commissions Several murals in Denmark.

Reference *Gallery* Summer 1982.

BLORE John Richard Hockly

Born 1928 Grahamstown.
A painter of landscapes, still life, figures and abstract pictures. Works in oil, acrylic, watercolour, gouache, ink, wash, pencil and charcoal.
Studies Adult Education courses under George Boys (qv).
Profile A member of the NSA and the WSSA. Lives in Southern Natal.
Exhibitions He has participated in numerous group exhibitions in Natal; 1987 Kokstad, Natal, solo exhibition.

BODENSTEIN-FERREIRA Erna Marita

Born 1958 Pretoria.
A painter and graphic artist of social and political figures. Works in oil, pencil, charcoal and in various graphic media.
Studies 1977–80 University of Pretoria, under John Clarke (qv), Keith Dietrich (qv) and Professor Nico Roos (qv), gaining a BA(FA).
Profile A member of the SAAA. From 1981 a part-time lecturer in graphics at the University of Pretoria.
Exhibitions She has participated in many group exhibitions from 1980 in SA and SWA/Namibia; 1982 University of Pretoria, solo exhibition; 1983 SAAA Gallery, Pretoria, joint exhibition with William Steyn (qv); 1986 Gallery 21, Johannesburg, joint exhibition with Guy du Toit (qv) and Amanda Marais (qv); 1987 Gallery 21, Johannesburg, joint exhibition with John Clarke (qv), Johann Moolman (qv), Jacobus Kloppers (qv) and William Steyn (qv); 1988 SAAA Gallery, Pretoria, joint exhibition with John Clarke (qv), Jacobus Kloppers (qv) and William Steyn (qv).

BODLEY Elise

Born Paarl, Cape Province.
A botanical illustrator.
Studies At a private art school in Stockholm, Sweden.
Profile In 1948 succeeded Jean Welz (qv) as head of the Hugo Naudé Art Centre in Worcester. A former Head of the Stellenbosch Art Centre and a lecturer at the Cape Town Training College. *c.*1980 an illustrator with the Botanical Research Institute.
Exhibitions She has held a few exhibitions in SA; 1985 Botanical Department, Rand Afrikaans University, solo exhibition.
Represented Hunt Institute, Pittsburgh, USA.

BOLLAND Marguerite Una

Born 1924 Johannesburg.
A painter of her personal response to SA society and events. Works in oil, acrylic and ink. An etcher.
Studies 1941–46 Architecture at the University of Cape Town, attaining a BA in Architecture; 1947 St Martin's Art School and the Central School of Art, London; 1973 etching at the Ruth Prowse Art Centre, Cape Town.

Profile From 1963 a member of the SAAA. From 1979 a member of the Artists Guild, Cape Town. Until 1976 worked as an architect. In 1961 she illustrated *Rhymes & Verses*, Maskew Miller, Cape Town; her illustrations have also been used in magazines. A poet, who in 1985 had two poems and drawings in *The Book of Protest*. 1947–48 lived in England; 1949–59 in New Zealand and Australia, thereafter in the Cape.

Exhibitions She has participated in many group exhibitions from 1956 in Australia, SA, Japan and Botswana; 1963 SAAA Gallery, Cape Town, first of six solo exhibitions held in Cape Town and Johannesburg; 1982 National Gallery, Gaborone, Botswana, Exhibition of SA Art.

Represented Pietersburg Collection.

BOMBERG-LIPSCHITZ Rachelle

Born 1950 London, England.

Resided in SA from 1973.

A painter, working in oil, watercolour and collage, also a sculptor in clay. 1976–79 a series on "Mother & Child"; 1979–84 a series on "Space/Time"; from 1985 a series on "The Essence of Life and Self".

Studies 1974–76 Witwatersrand Technical College, gaining a Diploma in Fine Art.

Profile A member of the SAAA and the Artists Guild, Cape Town. 1972–74 travelled throughout the world working as an air stewardess. From 1976 involved with dance, particularly Jazzart.

Exhibitions She has participated in many group exhibitions from 1979 in SA; 1980 SAAA Gallery, Cape Town, first of eight solo exhibitions held in Cape Town and Johannesburg.

BONNEY Peter John

Born 1953 Strand, Cape Province.

A self-taught painter of landscapes. Works in acrylic.

Exhibitions He has participated in several group exhibitions held in Johannesburg from 1985; 1986 Crake Gallery, Johannesburg, first of two solo exhibitions.

Represented Germiston City Council Collection.

BOONZAIER Daniël Cornelis

Born 1865 Patatsrivier, Carnarvon District, Cape Province.

Died 1950 Cape Town.

Profile A cartoonist, submitting work to *Knobkerrie* in 1884, *The Cape Punch* 1888, *The Owl* 1896 and *The Cape Times* 1901, among other publications. 1899–1902 worked for *The Owl*; 1903–07 *The South African News*; 1907–10 *The Cape*; 1914 *The Sunday Post*, Johannesburg; 1915–40 *Die Burger*; 1929–31 *The Sjambok*, Johannesburg, here under the pseudonym "Nemo". A member of the SA Society of Artists. The mentor of many young artists including Moses Kottler (qv) and Pieter Wenning (qv) and father of Gregoire Boonzaier (qv). An actor and stage producer.

Exhibitions 1953 Rhodes Centenary Exhibition, Bulawayo, Rhodesia (Zimbabwe); 1973 Pretoria Art Museum, SA Cartoonists and Comic Strip Artists Exhibition.

Represented Africana Museum, Johannesburg; Johannesburg Public Library; SA National Gallery, Cape Town; University of Cape Town; University of Pretoria; University of Stellenbosch.

Publications by Boonzaier Caricatures: *Owlograms*, 1901, Cape Town; *South African News Cartoons*, 1904, Cape Town; *My Caricatures*, 1912, Cape Town; *Rand Faces*, 1915, Cape Town; *Politieke Prente uit "Die Burger"*, 3 volumes, 1916, 1917 & 1919, Cape Town; *The Springboks in New Zealand*, 1921, Nasionale Pers, Cape Town.

References J du P Scholtz, *D C Boonzaier en Pieter Wenning*, 1973, Tafelberg, Cape Town; PSA; Our Art 1; Art SA; SAA; SADNB; AMC1; DSAB; SESA; SSAP; SAP&D; Enc S'n A; BSAK 1 & 2; SA Art; 3Cs; AASA; SASSK; *Huisgenoot* 28 December 1947.

BOONZAIER Gregoire Johannes

Born 1909 Newlands, Cape Town.

A painter of landscapes, portraits, still life, seascapes and figures. Works in oil, watercolour, ink, wash, pencil and charcoal. A graphic artist, producing linocuts.

Studies Heatherley School of Art, London, under Bernard Adams (*fl.*1916–39); Central School of Art, London.

Profile A foundation member of the New Group and for a decade Chairman. For six years he was the Cape Town SAAA Representative on the Board of the SA National Gallery, Cape Town. Issued a limited edition portfolio of six watercolour and ink drawings of District Six, Cape Town. Visited Venice. Son of D C Boonzaier (qv).

Exhibitions 1931 William Derry Gallery, Cape Town, first of numerous solo exhibitions held throughout SA; 1948 Tate Gallery, London, SA Art Exhibition.

Award 1958 awarded the Medal of Honour of the SA Akademie vir Wetenskap en Kuns.

Represented Africana Museum, Johannesburg; Ann Bryant Gallery, East London; Durban Art Gallery; Hester Rupert Art Museum, Graaff-Reinet; Johannesburg Art Gallery; Julius Gordon Africana Centre, Riversdale; King George VI Art Gallery, Port Elizabeth; National Museum, Bloemfontein; Potchefstroom Museum; Pretoria Art Museum; SA Cultural History Museum, Cape Town; SA National Gallery, Cape Town; University of Cape Town; University of the Orange Free State; University of Pretoria; University of South Africa; University of Stellenbosch; Willem Annandale Art Gallery, Lichtenburg; William Humphreys Art Gallery, Kimberley.

Publication by Boonzaier Co-author with Lippy Lipshitz (qv) of *Wenning*, (qv), 1949, Unie Volkspers Bpk, Cape Town.

References F P Scott, *Gregoire Boonzaier*, 1964, Tafelberg, Cape Town; Collectors' Guide; SESA; BSAK 1 & 2; *SA Panorama* January 1963, November 1981 & June 1983.

BORBEREKI Barbara (Mrs Goldin)
Born 1941 Szolnok, Hungary.
Resided in SA from 1950.
A painter of landscapes, seascapes, portraits, still life, figures and abstract
pictures. Works in oil, acrylic, ink, pencil and charcoal. In addition to this she
works in mosaic, ceramics and creates sculptures in fibreglass, wood and bronze.
Studies Fine Art at l'Ecole des Beaux Arts, Sorbonne, Paris; drawing at
Académie de la Grande Chaumière, Paris; commercial art at l'Ecole Supérieure
des Arts Moderns, Paris; the O'Halloran Hill College of Further Education,
Adelaide, Australia, gaining an Advanced Art and Craft Certificate (jewellery).
Profile 1967 and 1973–76 a member of the SAAA; 1969 a member of the NSA.
Daughter of Zoltan Borbereki (qv) and Elizabeth Sebok (qv), sister of Daniel
Kovacs (qv).
Exhibitions She has participated in many group exhibitions from 1962 in SA and
Australia; 1970 Gallery 101, Johannesburg, solo exhibition.
Represented Touch Gallery, SA National Gallery, Cape Town.
References BSAK 1 & 2; *Artlook* April 1970 & October 1971.

BORBEREKI Zoltan
Born 1907 Ronaszek, Hungary.
Resided in SA from 1950.
A sculptor in bronze, stone, ciment fondu, wood, perspex, fibreglass, ivory and
terracotta. He is also a mosaic artist and a painter.
Studies 1928–35 Academy of Fine Arts, Budapest, Hungary. 1933–35 Italian
State Bursary for Painting (Prix de Rome Scholarship), Rome Academy.
Profile Began sculpting figures in a realistic manner. His work gradually became
semi-abstract and later abstract. 1931–33 Assistant Professor at the Academy of
Fine Arts, Budapest. From 1940 a member of the Settlement of Artists, Szolnok,
Hungary, 1941 Deputy President, UME Society of Artists, Hungary; 1947
Deputy President, Rippl-Ronai Society of Artists, Hungary. From 1956 a
member of the SAAA, of which he is presently a committee member. He has
travelled throughout Europe and the USA. Father of Barbara Borbereki (qv),
Daniel Kovacs (qv) and husband of Elizabeth Sebok (qv).
Exhibitions From 1932 has participated in over 130 group exhibitions in SA and
throughout the world; 1937 Budapest, first of over 40 solo exhibitions held
throughout the world; 1981 Republic Festival Exhibition.
Awards 1932 "Budapest" prize for painting; 1935 Franz-Josef Jubilee Prize,
Budapest; 1937 "Grand Prix", Paris World Exhibition (sculpture); 1937
"Vindobona" Medal, Vienna, Austria (sculpture); 1959 Second Prize, Royal
Society of British Sculptors; 1962 First Prize, "Arts & Religion" Competition,
Johannesburg; 1974 First Prize, National Stainless Steel Sculpture Competition,
Johannesburg.
Represented Durban Art Gallery; Hester Rupert Art Museum, Graaff-Reinet;
Johannesburg Art Gallery; Luther Museum, Wittenberg, East Germany; Museo
de Arte Moderno, Bogota, Colombia; National Gallery and National Museum of
Fine Arts, Budapest, Hungary; National Museum, Helsinki, Finland; Pretoria
Art Museum; Sandton Municipal Collection; SA National Gallery, Cape Town;
Szolnok Museum, Hungary; University of Natal; University of Pretoria; Uni-
versity of the Witwatersrand; William Humphreys Art Gallery, Kimberley.

Public Commissions 1933–45 17 monuments in Hungary; 1950–80 12 monuments in SA; also numerous commissions in SA for educational establishments, churches, public administration buildings and other organisations.

References *Zoltan Borbereki—Sculptures in Semi-Precious Stones*, 1981, published by Gallery 21, Johannesburg; Art SA; SAA; 20C SA Art; SAP&S; SESA; BSAK 1 & 2; SA Art; 3Cs; AASA; LSAA; *South Africana* January 1956; *SA Panorama* November 1958 & February 1967; *Artlook* May 1968, July 1970 & September 1971; *Habitat* no 13, 1975 & no 22, 1976.

BORMAN Johannes G

Born 1912.
Died 1981.
A painter of landscapes, still life and figures. Worked in oil and watercolour. Additionally produced a number of drawings.

Exhibitions Participated in group exhibitions including those with the National Art Society of SA; 1943 Pretoria, first of several solo exhibitions.

Represented Willem Annandale Art Gallery, Lichtenburg.

References BSAK; AASA.

BORNMAN Priscilla (née Postma)

Born 1931 Klerksdorp, Transvaal.
A painter of flowers, landscapes and still life. Works in watercolour.

Studies From 1979 several painting holidays with Marjorie Bowen (qv).

Profile From 1976 a member of the WSSA. Spends three months of each year at Arniston, Cape Province. Lives in Pietersburg, Transvaal. 1980 visited Wales and the Greek islands.

Exhibitions She has participated in many group exhibitions from 1972 in SA; 1980 Atlantic Gallery, Cape Town, first of 15 solo exhibitions.

Represented Pietersburg Collection.

BOSCH (Margaretha) Beatrix

Born 1935 Hertzogville, Orange Free State.
An artist of abstract pieces. Works in leather, clay and airbrush.

Studies 1965–66 weaving and pottery at the Johannesburg School of Art, under J Edwards and Mrs E Reck.

Profile Occasionally commissioned to do landscapes and figurative works. A member of the SAAA. 1962–67 lived in Johannesburg; 1967–69 in Nelspruit, Eastern Transvaal; from 1969 at Wilderness, Cape Province.

Exhibitions She has participated in numerous group exhibitions from 1969 in SA, Italy and Sicily; 1969 Stellenbosch, first of 28 solo exhibitions held in SA and the USA.

Award 1975 Hajee Suliman Ebrahim Award, Art SA Today.
Represented University of the Orange Free State.
Public Commissions "Prelude", the State Theatre, Pretoria; "People Move-
ment" & "Knowledge in Motion", University of Stellenbosch; "Suspension",
"Construction", "Maalstroom", "Konsensus" and "Green Zone", University of
the Orange Free State; "The Cycle", Public Library, George, Cape Province;
"Growth", Medical Center, Houston, Texas, USA; "Lava Flow", Secunda
Theatre, Transvaal; "Carnival", Nelspruit Municipality, among other commis-
sions.
References BSAK; AASA; LSAA; *Artlook* September 1969 & August/September
1975; *SA Panorama* June 1983.

BOSCH Esias

Born 1923 Winburg, Orange Free State.
A ceramicist and painter of large ceramic panels and murals. Grinds his own raw
materials.
Studies Briefly at the University of the Witwatersrand; Johannesburg School of
Art, gaining a Teachers Diploma with a distinction in portraiture; on a
three-year overseas ceramic scholarship 1950 at the Central School of Art,
London, under Dora Billington; 1951 under Ray Finch in Winchcombe and in
1952 under Michael Cardew in Cornwall.
Profile Began working in earthenware in 1954 and stoneware in 1962. In
addition to this he produces domestic ware. 1952–54 taught in Durban. 1954
moved to Pretoria; presently lives in White River, Eastern Transvaal. He has
travelled to the UK, throughout Europe and to India, Nigeria, Japan and the
USA.
Exhibitions He has participated in numerous group exhibitions in SA, the UK,
the USA and in Europe; 1954 Pretoria, first of 20 solo exhibitions.
Represented Durban Art Gallery; SA Akademie vir Wetenskap en Kuns;
University of Natal.
Public Commissions 1973 VIP Lounge, Jan Smuts Airport, Johannesburg,
among other commissions.
References Andree Bosch and Johann de Waal, *Esias Bosch*, 1988, Struik-
Winchester, Cape Town; SAA; BSAK; Our Art 3; SA Art; 3Cs; AASA; LSAA;
SA Panorama August 1962; *Artlook* August 1967 & May 1968; *De Arte* April 1979;
Gallery Autumn 1982.

BOSHOFF Adriaan Hendrik

Born 1935 Pretoria.
A self-taught painter of landscapes, seascapes, still life and figures. Works in oil.
Profile Travels extensively throughout Southern Africa.
Exhibitions 1973 Denis Hotz Gallery, Johannesburg, first of seven solo exhibi-
tions held in SA.
References AASA; *Gallery* Summer 1983.

BOSHOFF Willem Hendrik Adriaan

Born 1951 Vanderbijlpark, Transvaal.

A sculptor, painter and graphic artist of abstract works. Uses wood, mixed media, acrylic, ink and various graphic media. 1979–80 Microscopic project; 1982–83, 370-day project; 1980–86 cryptic writing project.

Studies 1970–74 Witwatersrand Technical College (Technikon), under Eben Leibrandt (qv), where gained a National Art Teachers Diploma; 1980 Witwatersrand Technical College (Technikon), under I Kruger, gaining a Higher Diploma; 1984 Witwatersrand Technikon, under I Kruger and Margaret McKean (qv), attaining a National Diploma in Technology.

Profile 1975–77 taught at Parktown Boys High School, Johannesburg; 1977–80 a lecturer, 1980–82 a senior lecturer, from 1983 Associate Director of the Department of Fine Art, Witwatersrand Technikon. From 1976 a writer of Visual Poetry. 1982 made a study visit to Austria.

Exhibitions He has participated in several group exhibitions from 1977 in SA and West Germany; 1982 Natalie Knight Gallery, Johannesburg, first of two solo exhibitions; 1985 Tributaries, touring SA and West Germany.

Publication by Boshoff Kykafrikaans, an anthology of Visual Poetry, 1980, SA.

References Habitat no 49, 1982; Gallery Autumn 1982.

BOSMAN Paul

Born 1929 South Africa.

A painter of wildlife. Best known for his pastel drawings and pencil sketches.

Studies Studied at the Witwatersrand Technical College and at the Central School of Art, London.

Profile Worked in advertising prior to becoming a full-time artist. A designer of stamps, for which he has won awards. Many limited edition prints have been made of his work. He has raised funds for wildlife conservation projects in India, Zambia, Zimbabwe, SWA/Namibia and SA. Spent his childhood in Botswana. During the late 1970s moved to Malapati, Rhodesia (Zimbabwe). From 1982 he has lived in Phoenix, Arizona, USA.

Exhibitions From 1973 he has exhibited in SA, Europe and America.

Publication by Bosman Elephants of Africa, with text by Anthony Hall-Martin, 1986, C Struik, Cape Town.

BOTHA Alice (née Brink)

Born 1914 Johannesburg.

A painter of landscapes, seascapes, still life and abstract pictures. A large number of Namaqualand and highveld landscapes. Works in watercolour, oil, acrylic, gouache, ink and pastel.

Studies Privately under Otto Klar (qv), Alfred Krenz (qv), Erik Laubscher (qv) and Michael du Toit (qv).

Profile From 1973 a member of the SAAA and from 1985 of the WSSA. Has taught art to children in Ermelo, Transvaal from 1973 and has travelled extensively in Europe since 1972.

Exhibitions 1964 Ermelo, first of nine solo exhibitions held in SA; she has participated in several group exhibitions from 1980.

Award 1986 WSSA Cream of the Crop Award, Johannesburg.

ROBERT BROOKS
Glenthorpe Farm, Grahamstown 1984
Acrylic & Oil on Board 120 × 120 cm
Douglas Reid Skinner, Cape Town

DAVID BROWN
Tightroping 1985–1986
Bronze
Height 387 cm Width 234 cm Length 630 cm
Johannesburg Art Gallery

BOTHA Andres Johannes
Born 1952 Durban.
A sculptor of figurative landscapes. Works in multi media.
Studies University of Natal, gaining a BA(FA).
Profile From 1980 on the Durban Art Gallery Advisory Committee; 1983 Chairman of the Community Arts Workshop; 1985 on the Durban Arts Visual Arts Committee. From 1979 a lecturer at the Natal Technikon.
Exhibitions He has participated in numerous group exhibitions from 1976; 1980 Market Gallery, Johannesburg, first of two solo exhibitions held in Johannesburg and Durban; 1985 Cape Town Triennial; 1985 Tributaries, touring SA and West Germany.
Represented Durban Art Gallery; Natal Technikon.

BOTHA Christina Aletta (Christa)
Born 1938 Wolmaranstad, Transvaal.
A painter of abstract works, wildlife, portraits and landscapes. Works in oil, watercolour, pencil and charcoal.
Studies 1956–59 Witwatersrand Technical College, under Professor Robert Bain (qv) and Joyce Leonard (qv), where attained a National Art Teachers Certificate.
Profile 1979–82 secretary of the Empangeni branch of the SAAA, from 1982 a member. 1960–63 an art lecturer at the Orange Free State Technikon; teaches both adults and children privately at home. Additionally a potter. Has visited art centres in Europe and the Far East.
Exhibitions 1961 Reivilo, Cape Province, first of 22 solo exhibitions held throughout SA; she has participated in several group exhibitions from 1972 in SA and in California and Brussels; 1972 University of Stellenbosch, solo exhibition; 1981 Republic Festival Exhibition; 1985 SAAA Gallery, Pretoria, joint exhibition with Deline de Klerk (qv) and Wendy Malan (qv); 1986 SAAA Gallery, Pretoria, joint exhibition with the potters David Schlapobersky and Felicity Potter.
Represented Potchefstroom Municipal Collection; Potchefstroom University for CHE; Sasolburg Municipal Collection; University of Stellenbosch; Willem Annandale Art Gallery, Lichtenburg.
Public Commission 12 paintings for the "Balieraad", Pretoria.
Reference AASA.

BOTHA David Johannes
Born 1921 Graaff-Reinet, Cape Province.
A painter and a graphic artist of landscapes, seascapes and still life. Works in oil, watercolour, ink, pencil, charcoal and in various graphic media. He is best known for his wet street scenes of the Cape.
Studies 1941 Cape Town Teachers Training College, where gained a Higher Primary Teachers Certificate; 1950–52 Camberwell School of Art, London.

Profile A member of the SAAA and a founder member of the Artists Guild in 1979. 1946–78 a senior itinerant art teacher at four high schools in Paarl, Cape Province. 1950–52 travelled throughout Europe studying art.

Exhibitions 1944 Cape Town, first of 50 solo exhibitions in SA; he has participated in over 100 group exhibitions from 1946 held in SA, Mozambique and in The Netherlands; 1956 and 1960 Quadrennial Exhibitions; 1981 Republic Festival Exhibition.

Represented Hester Rupert Art Museum, Graaff-Reinet; National Museum, Bloemfontein; Pretoria Art Museum; Rand Afrikaans University; SA Cultural History Museum, Cape Town; SA National Gallery, Cape Town; University of Stellenbosch; Willem Annandale Art Gallery, Lichtenburg.

References Art SA; SAA; 20C SA Art; IWAA; BSAK 1 & 2; 3Cs; AASA; *SA Panorama* February 1959, December 1963 & August 1979; *Artlook* September 1969.

BOTHA Elizabeth Josephine (Elza) (Mrs Miles)

Born 1938 Potgietersrus, Transvaal.

A painter and graphic artist of figures. Works in oil pastels, gouache and in various graphic media. Series on "Corsetry", "Butterflies" and "Social Commentary".

Studies 1957–61 through the University of Pretoria, under Professor Walter Battiss (qv), George Boys (qv), and Gunther van der Reis (qv) gaining a BA(FA); 1962–64 University of Pretoria, History of Art under H M van der Westhuysen, gaining an MA(FA); 1978–83 Rand Afrikaans University, under E P Engel, where gained a D Phil et Litt.

Profile 1963–64 a part-time History of Art lecturer at the Pretoria Technical College and in 1969–75 at the Rand Afrikaans University; 1977–79 an art teacher at the Hoerskool die Kruin, Johannesburg. 1972–75 a freelance art critic for *Rapport* newspaper and from 1983 for *Beeld* newspaper. Produced the jackets for a number of books, including P J Nienaber's *Digter & Digkuns*, 1971, Perskor, Johannesburg; John Miles' *Okker Bestel Twee Toebroodjies*, 1973, Buren; Abraham de Vries' *Briekwa*, 1973, Perskor, Johannesburg, and *Bliksoldate Bloei Nie*, 1975, Human & Rousseau, Cape Town and Wessel Pretorius' *Ruimte—Ark —Kolonie*, 1980, Perskor, Johannesburg. Married to the writer John Miles.

Exhibitions She has participated in several group exhibitions from 1962 in SA; 1964 Quadrennial Exhibition; 1967 Neil Sack Gallery, Pietermaritzburg, first of five solo exhibitions held in SA; 1986 SAAA Gallery, Pretoria, joint exhibition with Friedrich Baudert (qv).

Represented Potchefstroom University for CHE; Rand Afrikaans University; Willem Annandale Art Gallery, Lichtenburg.

BOTHA Etienne

Born 1956 Bloemfontein.

A painter and graphic artist of landscapes and abstract pictures. Works in oil and silkscreen.

Studies 1977–79 Orange Free State Technical College, gaining a National Diploma in Graphic Design.

Profile A member of the SAAA. 1986 Head of the Art Department, National Museum, Bloemfontein. In addition to this he is actively involved in music, pottery, stained glass, architecture, art-wood furniture and papermaking. 1981 visited France and Germany.

Exhibitions He has participated in many group exhibitions from 1977 in SA; 1978 Welkom, first of three solo exhibitions.

Represented University of the Orange Free State.

BOTHA Hardy

Born 1947 Kroonstad, Orange Free State.

A painter and graphic artist of figures, animals and carnival scenes. Works in oil, lithography and etching.

Studies 1967 gained a Diploma in Fine Art from the Orange Free State Technical College.

Profile A scenery designer for a circus where he also worked as a clown in 1972.

Exhibitions He has participated in many group exhibitions in SA, at the São Paulo Bienale in Brazil and on exhibitions in the USA and in West Germany; 1973 SAAA Gallery, Pretoria, first of several solo exhibitions held in SA; 1979 Cape Town Biennial.

Represented National Museum, Bloemfontein; Pretoria Art Museum; SA National Gallery, Cape Town; University of the Orange Free State; University of Stellenbosch.

Reference SA Panorama February 1976.

BOTHA Phil C

Born Messina, Northern Transvaal.

Studies Witwatersrand Technical College, under James Gardner (qv), T O D Davies, William Cook and J W Bramham, gaining a National Art Teachers Certificate in 1954; 1957 industrial design at the Central School of Art, London; gained a BA(FA) in 1963 from the University of South Africa.

Profile Taught at the Witwatersrand Technical College and introduced an industrial design course in c.1958. 1977 appointed Inspector of Art, Music, Drama and Ballet Education, Department of National Education.

Reference Port Elizabeth School of Art.

BOTMA Benjamin

Born 1953 Kroonstad, Orange Free State.

A painter and graphic artist of a combination of animals, people and objects. Works in oil, ink, wash, pencil, charcoal, mixed media and in various graphic media. 1986–87 "Talking Head Ostrich" series.

Studies 1975–78 University of the Orange Free State, under Leon de Bliquy (qv), gaining a BA(FA); 1980 registered for an MA(FA) at the University of the Orange Free State, under Professor Van der Berg.

Profile From 1986 a member of the SAAA, in 1987 on the executive committee of his local branch. 1980–85 lectured in printmaking, University of the Orange Free State; 1986–87 acting Head of the Fine Art Department, University of the Orange Free State.

Exhibitions He has participated in many group exhibitions from 1978 in Johannesburg; 1981 Republic Festival Exhibition; 1986 University of the Orange Free State, solo exhibition.

Represented University of the Orange Free State.

BOUFFA Eugene-Leon

Born 1912 Liège, Belgium.
Resided in SA from 1960.
A sculptor of portraits and figures. Works in stone and wood.

Studies 1923–29 studied sculpture under Georges Petit and Jacques Ochs; Académie des Beaux Arts, Brussels, Belgium.

Profile 1958–60 taught drawing at the Athenée Royale de Stanleyville, Congo (Zaire); during the 1960s and 1970s taught sculpture at Pretoria Technical College.

Exhibitions He has participated in group exhibitions in Belgium and SA; 1964 Quadrennial Exhibition.

Represented Musée de la vie Wallove, Ecole Professionnelle des Jeunes Filles, Belgium; Pretoria Art Museum; University of Pretoria.

Public Commissions Many commissions in Belgium. A statue of Christ, Seminary of St John Vianney, Pretoria; one of Field-Marshal J C Smuts, Transvaal Provincial Administration Building, Pretoria and works for the Marist Brothers Colleges in Johannesburg and Durban.

References SAA; BSAK 1 & 2; *Personality* 15 April 1965; *Artlook* October 1967.

BOUSCHARAIN Claude Marie Madeleine

Born 1922 Foëcy (Cher), France.
Resided in SA from 1951.
A painter of wide-ranging subject matter. Ships, mountains and hieratic figures recur in her work. Worked in oil until 1966, thereafter in acrylic.

Studies 1946 l'Ecole des Beaux Arts, Paris; 1947 Art Students League, New York, under Morris Kantor (*b*.1896) and Robert Beverley Hale (*b*.1901); 1950 Académie Montmartre, Paris, under Fernand Léger (1881–1955).

Profile A life member of the SAAA and a founder member of the Artists Guild, Cape Town. 1922–42 lived in Geneva, Switzerland, 1940–42 studied child psychology, 1943 returned to Paris where she worked in this field; 1946–50 lived in New York; 1966 travelled in the USA. Married to Erik Laubscher (qv).

Exhibitions She has participated in over 40 group exhibitions from 1950 in the USA, SA, Belgium, Zimbabwe and Australia; 1959 Argus Gallery, Cape Town, first of five solo exhibitions; 1963 Lidchi Gallery, Johannesburg, joint exhibition with Erik Laubscher (qv); 1979 Cape Town Biennial, Invited Artist; 1981 Republic Festival Exhibition; 1982 University of Stellenbosch, solo exhibition; 1985 Drostdy Centre, Stellenbosch, joint exhibition with Erik Laubscher (qv) and Stanley Pinker (qv).

Represented Hester Rupert Art Museum, Graaff-Reinet; National Museum, Bloemfontein; Pretoria Art Museum; Sandton Municipal Collection; SA National Gallery, Cape Town; University of the Orange Free State.

References Bruce Arnott (qv), *Claude Bouscharain*, 1977, C Struik, Cape Town; SAA; 20C SA Art; Register SA & SWA; SAP&S; BSAK 1 & 2; AASA; LSAA; *Artlook* August 1972; *To the Point* 9 September 1972.

BOWEN Marjorie Louise

Born 1920 Lüderitz, SWA/Namibia.
Resided in SA from 1920.
A painter of landscapes, seascapes and still life. Mainly works in watercolour, but also uses oil, acrylic, gouache and other media.

Studies 1936–38 East London Technical College, under Elaine Savage (qv); 1944–46 Port Elizabeth Technical College, under John Muff-Ford (qv) and Joan Wright (qv); 1939–43 under Percy V Bradshaw in London; 1965 Heatherley School of Art, London, under Professor Roy Glanville.

Profile 1972 co-founder of the WSSA, first Chairwoman and a Fellow from 1978. From 1977 a Honorary Member of Art by the Sea and from 1938 a member of the East London Society of Fine Arts. An art teacher in 1938 at the East London Technical College and since then throughout SA; 1953–77 an Adult Education lecturer in Johannesburg; from 1966 an art teacher on painting holidays in SA, Italy, the Greek islands, Spain, the Seychelles, the UK, and privately in France and Portugal. Designed stage sets for the Eva Harvey operas *Yugao* in 1967 and *Ruth and Naomi* in 1969.

Exhibitions She has participated in numerous group exhibitions from 1938 in SA, the UK, France, West Germany, Spain, Portugal and Canada; 1939 East London, first of numerous solo exhibitions; 1970 joint exhibition with Phyllis Luyt and Patricia Purvis (qv).

Represented Municipal collections in Margate and Randburg; Willem Annandale Art Gallery, Lichtenburg.

References BSAK 1 & 2; AASA; *Artlook* November 1969.

BOWLER Thomas William

Born 1812 Tring, Hertfordshire, England.
Died 1869 London.
Resided in SA 1834–68.
A painter in watercolour of scenes of both countryside and town, characterised by small figures, as well as of seascapes. A number of oils (10 known) and sketches on coloured chalk paper. From 1843 63 lithographic and two steel-engraved prints were produced in London, France and SA.

Studies Mainly a self-taught artist who studied briefly under James Duffield Harding (1798–1863) during a visit to England in 1854.

Profile Drew a number of sketches for *The Illustrated London News* and various book illustrations. Taught art privately in Cape Town, was art master at the SA College 1842–66 and taught at the Diocesan College in Cape Town. 1850–59 a Committee Member of the Cape Town Exhibitions of Fine Arts. In 1851 he introduced The Art Union of London to the Cape and became its first secretary in 1853. 1836–38 lived on Robben Island as a tutor to the children of Captain Richard Wolfe; travelled throughout the Cape and in 1844 to Natal; 1861 to the Eastern Province; 1865 to Durban; 1866 and 1868 to Mauritius; 1868 to England via Egypt.

Exhibitions 1851 Cape Town, exhibited on the First Annual Exhibition of Fine Art; 1857 Society of British Artists, London; 1859 Cape Town, solo exhibition; 1860 Royal Academy, London; 1948 Tate Gallery, London, SA Art Exhibition; 1975 Metropolitan Homes Trust Life Gallery, Cape Town, Memorial Exhibition; 1980 Pretoria Art Museum, 1981 Durban Art Gallery, 1985 SAAA Gallery, Cape Town, Exhibitions of the Metropolitan Homes Trust Life Collection.

Awards 1851 Gold Medal for the best original landscape in watercolour, First Annual Exhibition of Fine Art, Cape Town; 1858 Best Watercolour Landscape, Third Annual Exhibition of Fine Art, Cape Town.

Represented Africana Museum, Johannesburg; Albany Museum, Grahamstown; Ann Bryant Gallery, East London; Durban Local History Museum; Julius Gordon Africana Centre, Riversdale; King George VI Art Gallery, Port Elizabeth; Pretoria Art Museum; SA Cultural History Museum, Cape Town; SA National Gallery, Cape Town; Swellendam Drostdy Museum; University of Cape Town; University of Natal; University of South Africa; William Fehr Collection, Cape Town; William Humphreys Art Gallery, Kimberley; Worcester Museum, Cape Province.

Publication by Bowler *The Student's Handbook—intended for those studying art on the system of J D Harding*, 1857, Cape Town.

Prints by Bowler *Four Views of Cape Town, Cape of Good Hope*, 1844, Day & Haghe, London—reproductions of these prints were published in 1966 by A A Balkema, Cape Town with a new introduction by F R Bradlow; *The Great Meeting held in front of the Commercial Hall, Cape Town on the 4th July 1849 . . .*, dedicated to the members of the Anti-convict Association . . ., 1859, Day & Son, London; *South African Sketches*, a series of ten of the most interesting views of The Cape of Good Hope, in double tinted lithography, 1854, Day & Son, London; *The African Sketch Book*, 8 plates, 1855, Day & Son, London; *The Kafir Wars and British Settlers in South Africa*, a series of picturesque views from original sketches by T W Bowler with descriptive letterpress by W R Thompson, 1865, Day & Son, London, J C Juta, Cape Town and others; *Pictorial Album of Cape Town, with views of Simon's Town, Port Elizabeth and Graham's Town*, with historical and descriptive sketches by W R Thompson, 1866, J C Juta, Cape Town, reproduced in facsimile, 1966, C Struik, Cape Town. Several individual lithographs and two steel engravings.

References Edna and Frank Bradlow, *Thomas Bowler of The Cape of Good Hope, his life and works with a catalogue of extant paintings*, 1955, A A Balkema, Cape Town; F R Bradlow, *Thomas Bowler, His Life and Works*, 1967, A A Balkema, Cape Town; Frank Bradlow, *Thomas Bowler in Mauritius, a detail in the history of contacts between The Cape of Good Hope and Mauritius, 1866–68*, 1970, A A Balkema, Cape Town;

Collectors' Guide; Pict Art; Our Art 1; Art SA; Afr Repos; AMC1&6; DSAB; SAP&S; SESA; SAP&D; SSAP; Pict Afr; Benezit; BSAK 1 & 2; Enc S'n A; SA Art; Marjorie Bull, *Abraham de Smidt, 1829–1908*, Printpak, Cape Town; 3Cs; AASA; SASSK; LSAA; *SA Panorama* August 1959, February 1981 & December 1982; *Fontein* vol 1 no 3, 1960; *De Kat* June 1986.

BOYES Harold

A painter of SA and Mozambican coastal scenes and landscapes. Worked in watercolour and oil.
Profile A member of the SA Society of Artists. Lived in Rondebosch, Cape Town, in the early 1900s, travelling frequently along the coast from Cape Town to Lourenço Marques (Maputo), Mozambique. His picture "Gordon's Bay" was reproduced in the United SA Annual of 1934.
Exhibitions Participated in group exhibitions with the SA Society of Artists and at Lezards, Johannesburg from *c.*1915; 1933 Lezards, first Johannesburg solo exhibition.
Represented Africana Museum, Johannesburg.
References AMC6; AASA.

BOYLEY Errol Stephen

Born 1918 Pietermaritzburg.
A painter of landscapes, still life, seascapes, figures and wildlife. Works in oil.
Studies Mainly self-taught but during the early 1940s studied at the Natal Technical College.
Profile 1940–47 a professional guitar player in night-clubs. During WWII joined the Natal Field Artillery. 1948 lived in Knysna; 1954 moved to Johannesburg. Established and owned an art gallery in Ramsgate, Natal. 1985–86 lived in Underberg, Natal; 1987 in Pietermaritzburg. Has lived and worked throughout SA and visited Madagascar in 1973.
Exhibitions 1956 Herbert Evans Gallery, Johannesburg, first of many solo exhibitions held in SA.
Represented Pretoria Art Museum; University of Stellenbosch.
Public Commission 1971 commissioned by the Johannesburg Turf Club to paint a painting of Turffontein Race Course for the Victoria Turf Club, Melbourne, Australia.
References SAA; BSAK; SA Art.

BOYS George

Born 1930 Johannesburg.
A painter of abstract pictures, seascapes, landscapes and plant forms. Works in oil. Creates assemblages. 1968–75 an experimental phase, involving the graphic and photographic processes, music and astral imagery. 1972–75 Cosmos series of semi-abstract flower paintings; 1985 Mask series.

Studies 1949–53 Witwatersrand Technical College, where attained a National Art Teachers Certificate.

Profile 1954–57 lectured at Pretoria Art Centre; 1958–63 a lecturer at the Witwatersrand Technical College; 1963 Vice-Principal of the Johannesburg Art School; 1966–70 founded and taught at The Visual Arts Research Centre, Johannesburg. Teaches art privately. 1977 created a 12-part audio-visual correspondence course on painting. Has studios in Zurich, Majorca, Spain, Johannesburg and at Salt Rock in Natal.

Exhibitions He has participated in numerous group exhibitions held throughout SA and in Zurich, Seoul, Lisbon and São Paulo; 1962 Egon Guenther Gallery, Johannesburg, first of many solo exhibitions, a few of which have been held in SA, but most of them from 1975 in Zurich and latterly in the USA; 1967 Durban Art Gallery, solo exhibition; 1969 organised the first art happening in Johannesburg.

Represented Durban Art Gallery; Hester Rupert Art Museum, Graaff-Reinet; Johannesburg Art Gallery; National Gallery, Victoria, Australia; PotchefstroomMuseum; Potchefstroom University for CHE; Pretoria Art Museum; Rand Afrikaans University; Sandton Municipal Collection; SA National Gallery, Cape Town; University of the Witwatersrand.

Public Commissions 1972 stainless steel environment, vestibule, Esselen Towers, Johannesburg; 24 panels for a building facade in Pretoria; mural, SA Railways Recreation Club; 1981 mural assemblage, the State Theatre, Pretoria.

References SAA; 20C SA Art; SAP&S; SSAP; BSAK 1 & 2; Our Art 3; Oxford Companion to 20C Art (under SA); 3Cs; AASA; LSAA; *Artlook* July 1968, September 1968 & September 1970; *Habitat* no 24, 1977; *SA Panorama* January 1984.

BOZAS Diamond

Born 1923 Isipingo, Natal.

A painter of landscapes, portraits, still life and abstract pictures. Works in many media including oil, watercolour, gouache, charcoal and in various mixed media such as hessian, sand and Polyfilla.

Studies 1955–60 Chelsea School of Art, London, under Harold S Williamson (*b*.1898) and Professor Lawrence Gowing (*b*.1918). Gained a National Diploma in Design (Painting) 1959.

Profile Since 1950 a member of the NSA and a committee member 1975–79; 1978–80 Founder and Chairman of the Zululand Society of Arts, and re-elected to the Chair in 1984. From 1984 a trustee of the Natal Arts Trust, Pietermaritzburg.

Exhibitions He has participated in numerous group exhibitions from 1950 in SA and London; 1972 Anglo-Persian Galleries, Durban, first of four solo exhibitions; 1981 Republic Festival Exhibition.

Represented Natal Technikon.

Reference AASA.

BRAAK Olchert (Otto)

Born 1894 The Netherlands.
Died 1971 Pretoria.
Resided in SA from 1896.
A self-taught painter of landscapes. Worked in oil.
Profile A member of the Transvaal Art Society. 1930 Vice-President of the
Orange Free State Society of Arts and Crafts; 1937 President of the East Rand
Society of Artists. Worked for The Netherlands Bank (Nedbank) from 1913.
Travelled on painting excursions with Erich Mayer (qv). 1896–1918 lived in
Pretoria; 1918–28 in Bronkhorstspruit, Transvaal; 1928–34 in Bloemfontein;
1934–39 in Springs, Transvaal; 1939–46 in Swaziland, thereafter in Johannes-
burg, East London and Pretoria.
Exhibitions Participated in several group exhibitions with the SA Academy and
the Transvaal Art Society; 1929 Bloemfontein, solo exhibition.
Represented Africana Museum, Johannesburg.
References Collectors' Guide; AMC6; BSAK; AASA.

BRACCIALARGHE Severino

Paints under the name Severino.
Born 1943 Macerata, Italy.
Resided in SA from 1970.
A sculptor of figurative and abstract pieces. Works in stone, particularly marble
and in bronze. An etcher.
Studies National Diploma Art School, Italy.
Profile 1965–82 an architectural designer. 1985 a sculpture tutor at the Funda
Centre, Soweto. Has travelled widely throughout Africa, Europe, the USA and
South America. 1983–84 spent 15 months in Pietrasanta, Carrara, Italy,
perfecting marble and bronze techniques. Comes from a traditionally artistic
family.
Exhibitions 1983 Macerata, Italy, first of two solo exhibitions in Italy; he has
participated in several group exhibitions from 1984 in Italy and SA; 1986 Karen
McKerron Gallery, Johannesburg, first solo exhibition in SA.
Public Commissions From 1983 a number of commissions for hotels and
churches.
Reference *Gallery* Summer 1985.

BRADSHAW Brian ARCA ARE

Born 1923 Bolton, Lancashire, England.
Resided in SA 1960–78.
A painter of landscapes, seascapes, figures, portraits, genre, still life, animals and
abstract pictures. Works in oil, watercolour, gouache, ink, wash, pencil and
charcoal.
Studies 1939 Bolton College of Art, under John Gauld ARCA (*d.*1962);
Manchester College of Art; 1948–51 Royal College of Art, London, under
Robert Austin RA (1875–1973), becoming an Associate; 1951–53 Accademia
Britannica, Rome. In 1948 he gained an Art Teachers Diploma.

Profile A member of the Manchester Academy of Fine Art, the Liverpool Academy of Fine Art and the Chelsea Arts Club. 1951 elected an Associate of the Royal Society of Painters-Etchers and Engravers. 1964 founded the Grahamstown Group. 1958–60 Vice-Chairman and Founder of the British Parliamentary Committee on Art Education. 1960–78 Professor of Fine Art, Rhodes University; 1974–78 Director of the National Gallery of Rhodesia (Zimbabwe); 1979–82 a senior lecturer at Liverpool Polytechnic, UK; 1982 a senior lecturer at Bulawayo Polytechnic, Zimbabwe. Numerous illustrations for magazines, including *Harpers Bazaar*; set and programme designs for theatres in Rome, London, and in Germany. A writer and in 1954–60 an art critic for *The Bolton News* and *The Guardian* in the UK; 1982 an art critic for the *Bulawayo Chronicle*. During the 1960s a member of the Board of Governors and a sound broadcaster for the SABC; 1974–78 a TV broadcaster for the Rhodesian Broadcasting Corporation. 1923–40 lived in Lancashire, UK; 1942–47 with the British Army in North Africa, Sicily, The Netherlands and Germany; 1951–53 lived in Italy, Austria, Germany and Spain; 1955–60 in Wales; 1982–83 in Zimbabwe; from 1983 he has lived in Wales.

Exhibitions He has participated in numerous group exhibitions from 1949 in the UK, SA, Zimbabwe, Italy, Belgium and Australia; 1952 Salford, UK, first of over 40 solo exhibitions held in the UK, the USA, SA, Zimbabwe and Australia; 1964 Quadrennial Exhibition.

Awards 1949 Architecture Prize, Royal College of Art; 1950 Engraving Prize, Royal College of Art; 1951 Silver Medal, Royal College of Art; 1951 Prix de Rome (etching); 1956 British Arts Council Engraving Prize.

Represented Art galleries in Manchester, Liverpool, Bolton, Salford, Rutherston, Whitworth, Oxford, Blackburn, Tillotson and Bangor in the UK; Johannesburg Art Gallery; King George VI Art Gallery, Port Elizabeth; National Gallery, Harare, Zimbabwe; Pietersburg Collection; SABC Collection, Johannesburg; University of the Witwatersrand.

Publications by Bradshaw *The Culture Plan*, 1960; *Art and Totality*, 1969; *Bolton Bred*, 1984.

References Who's Who in Art; Who's Who in the World; Who's Who in SA; Dictionary of English Artists; Exhibitors at the Royal Academy; SAA; IWAA; BSAK; 3Cs; AASA; LSAA; *SA Panorama* November 1970.

BRANDENBERG Machiel

Born 1907 Rotterdam, The Netherlands.
Resided in SA from 1953.
A painter of portraits, still life and plants. Works in oil.

Studies 1922–31 Koninklijke Academie, Rotterdam, gaining an MA(FA); 1931–32 l'Ecole des Beaux Arts, Brussels; 1932–34 l'Ecole des Beaux Arts, Paris.

Exhibitions He has participated in group exhibitions held in SA, The Netherlands, France, Belgium, Indonesia, Finland, Canada and the USA; 1964 Quadrennial Exhibition.

Public Commissions Several public commissions by the government and royalty of The Netherlands.

References Register SA & SWA; BSAK 1 & 2 (under Bradenburg); AASA.

BRANDT Helena

Born 1941 Pretoria.
Resided in SWA/Namibia from 1946.
A sculptor of figures, wildlife, genre, landscapes and abstract forms. Works in bronze, ciment fondu, stone, wood, ceramic and resin. A graphic artist and a designer of karakul wool wall-hangings.
Studies 1962 Michaelis School of Fine Art, under Lippy Lipshitz (qv) and Katrine Harries (qv), gaining a Diploma in Fine Art; 1963–64 gained a Higher Primary Teachers Diploma.
Profile From 1965 a member of the Arts Association SWA/Namibia and 1977–79 its Vice-President. 1971–86 Principal, teacher and founder of the H B Art School, Windhoek. Has also taught part-time at the Onguediva Training College, Ovambo, in Tsumkwe, Omega and Bagani. 1985–87 a lecturer in the Department of Fine Arts, Windhoek Academy. 1982–86 Director of Gallery Goethe Street, Windhoek.
Exhibitions She has participated in group exhibitions from 1971; 1976 Arts Association SWA/Namibia Gallery, Windhoek, first of two solo exhibitions, the second being of graphic work in 1984 in Stellenbosch.
Public Commissions Fountain Group for Baines Shopping Centre; wall hangings for churches, banks and government departments; 1986 several murals for St George's Diocesan School, Windhoek.

BRAUNGER Mascha

Born 1906 Vienna, Austria.
Resided in SA from 1938.
A painter and graphic artist of semi-abstracted pictures, based on form and texture. Worked in oil, watercolour, gouache, pencil and in various graphic media.
Studies Three years at Fachklasse für Architektur und Mode under Oberbaurat Josef Hoffmann; three years at Frauenakademie under Professor Otto Friedrich.
Profile 1935–37 book illustrations and poster designs in Austria and France. 1937 a costume designer for Max Weldy Costumier, London and Paris. Has travelled in Europe and to Mexico, India and China.
Exhibitions She has participated in many group exhibitions in SA; 1964 Quadrennial Exhibition; she has held eight solo exhibitions in SA.
Represented Pretoria Art Museum.
Public Commissions Stations of the Cross, Witbank Cathedral, Transvaal; murals, St Joseph's Church, Pretoria.
References Art SA; SAA; BSAK; AASA; *Artlook* November 1968.

BREEBAART Andrew Peter

Born 1961 Somerset West, Cape Province.
A painter of abstract pictures. Works in acrylic, oil pastel, pencil and charcoal.
Studies 1983–86 Pretoria Technikon, under Gert le Grange, where gained a National Diploma in Graphic Design.

Profile From 1986 a member of the SAAA. A graphic designer. 1987 living in Amsterdam.

Exhibitions He has participated in several group exhibitions from 1984 in SA and the UK.

Awards 1986 two Drawing Awards, New Signatures, SAAA; 1986 Merit Award, Volkskas Atelier, SAAA.

Reference De Kat May 1986.

BRENTON Jahleel Vice-Admiral Sir KCB

Born 1770 Rhode Island, USA.

Died 1844 Leamington, England.

Resided in SA 1815–21.

A painter in watercolour and gouache of landscapes. A number of pencil sketches.

Profile 1787 joined the Royal Navy; 1815–21 the Naval Commissioner of the Dockyard at Cape Town. Published four works dealing with the sea and the navy. Travelled widely in the Cape.

Represented Africana Museum, Johannesburg; William Fehr Collection, Cape Town.

References Henry Raikes, editor, *Memoirs of the Life and Services of Vice-Admiral Sir Jahleel Brenton*, 1846, Hatchards, London; Pict Art; Afr Repos; AMC1 & 6; DSAB; SESA; Pict Afr; BSAK; SA Art; 3Cs; *Apollo* October 1975, London.

BREWIS Beaujolais Ruth

Born 1957 King William's Town, Cape Province.

A painter and graphic artist of mainly figures and nudes, but also of portraits and landscapes. Works in pastel, chalk, oil, acrylic, pencil, charcoal and in various graphic media. 1980–81 a series of reclining nudes; 1980–86 of portraits; 1985 of landscapes.

Studies 1980 Cape Town Institute of Art, studied briefly under Lukas van Vuuren (qv); 1984 studied briefly under George Boys (qv); from 1985 studying through the University of South Africa for a BA(FA).

Profile 1980 painted a mural for the dance club "1886" in Cape Town. Studied anatomy and trained in midwifery and operating theatre technique. From 1981 a member of Medical Arts; from 1986 a member of the Christian Art Group and the SAAA. 1979–82 visited Western Europe and the UK; 1983 Mauritius and Australia; 1983 and 1985 visited Malawi.

Exhibitions She has participated in several group exhibitions from 1980 in SA; 1980 Est. Gallery, Cape Town, first of two solo exhibitions, the second being held in Johannesburg; 1981 The Space Theatre, Cape Town, joint exhibition with Ben Dekker.

BREWIS Julia
Born 1953 Pretoria.
A painter and graphic artist of figures and portraits. Works in oil, pastel, pencil and in various graphic media. 1982–83 a series of Romantic works.
Studies 1971–73 Pretoria Technical College, under Gunther van der Reis (qv), gaining a Diploma in Fine Art; 1982–83 Cape Technikon, gaining a Higher Diploma in Fine Art.
Profile From 1982 a lecturer in Textile Design at the Cape Technikon. 1985–86 commercial artwork for Dominique Martine, New York.
Exhibitions She has participated in several group exhibitions from 1972 in SA and the USA; 1976 SAAA Gallery, Pretoria, first of three solo exhibitions.

BREWS Lee
Born 1944 Fauresmith, Orange Free State.
A painter of abstract pictures. Works in oil, gouache, ink and pencil.
Studies Johannesburg School of Art, under George Boys (qv); in Amsterdam under Clifford Flymen; Camden Art Centre, London, under Anita Ford.
Profile From the early 1970s he has lived in Paris, London and Amsterdam, frequently visiting SA and once staying for four years, during which time he opened a gallery in Cape Town. Established the Zebra I Gallery in Hampstead, London, where he now lives and is involved in publishing.
Exhibitions He has participated in numerous group exhibitions from 1972 in SA, Paris, London and Amsterdam; Gilbert Parr Gallery, London, first of eight solo exhibitions, most of which have been held in London; 1977 Johannesburg, first of three solo exhibitions held in SA; 1978 Potchefstroom University for CHE, solo exhibition.
Represented Johannesburg Art Gallery; Potchefstroom Museum.
References AASA; *Habitat* no 29, 1978.

BREYTENBACH Lois Lilla
Born 1930 Potchefstroom, Transvaal.
A painter and graphic artist of portraits, figures and abstract pictures, using linear forms. Works in oil, acrylic, watercolour, gouache, ink, wash, pencil, charcoal, conté and in various graphic media.
Studies 1948–51 Witwatersrand Technical College, under James Gardner (qv) and Phyllis Gardner (qv); 1969–71 The Visual Arts Research Centre, Johannesburg, under George Boys (qv).
Profile From *c.*1969 a member of the SAAA. 1952–54 lectured in layout and typography at the Pretoria School of Art; from 1962 has given private art tuition. From 1952 a number of her pen & ink drawings and calligraphic works have been used in advertising. Has designed sets and costumes for the theatre.
Exhibitions 1971 SAAA Gallery, Pretoria, first of two solo exhibitions; she has participated in group exhibitions from 1972 in Pretoria.
Represented University of Botswana; University of South Africa.
References BSAK; *Artlook* November 1971.

BRIDGMAN Arthur Humphrey

Born 1916 Oudtshoorn, Cape Province.

A painter of landscapes, seascapes, flowers and buildings. Works in watercolour, gouache, ink, wash and pencil.

Studies 1935–39 part-time at the SA School of Commercial and Fine Art, Cape Town, under Arthur Podolini (qv); Cape Technical College; figure drawing under Maurice van Essche (qv); 1968–71 a part-time pottery student at the Natal Technical College.

Profile During the 1950s a member of the Brush and Chisel Club and its Chairman 1957–60; from 1973 a member of the Somerset West Art Group and its Chairman 1975–79. A member of the SAAA. 1981 a portfolio entitled *Cape Countryside* published by Howard Swan, Johannesburg; 1983 published a port-folio entitled *Streets of Stellenbosch*.

Exhibitions He has participated in numerous group exhibitions from 1957 in SA; 1977 Somerset West, first of five solo exhibitions.

Reference *SA Panorama* August 1983.

BRIERS Douw Eddie

Born 1953 Hartbeesfontein, Transvaal.

A painter and graphic artist of figures and portraits. Works in acrylic, watercolour, ink, wash and in various graphic media.

Studies 1973–75 Pretoria Technical College, under Tertia Knaap (qv), gaining a Diploma in Graphic Design.

Profile A graphic designer and photographer with the Stellenbosch Museum. A ceramicist.

Exhibitions 1982 private home, Pretoria, solo exhibition; he has participated in several group exhibitions from 1984.

BRIGG Melvin Arthur (Mel)

Born 1950 Bloemfontein.

A self-taught painter of landscapes, portraits, still life, seascapes, figures and abstract pictures. Works in oil, acrylic, pencil and charcoal.

Profile 1977 Founder of the Swellendam Arts and Crafts Society. 1970–73 lived in the Orange Free State; from 1975 in Swellendam, Cape Province.

Exhibitions He has participated in many group exhibitions from 1973 held in SA; 1973 Springs, first of over 20 solo exhibitions held throughout SA.

Represented Nelspruit Municipal Gallery; University of the Orange Free State; University of Stellenbosch.

Public Commissions 1974 an oil painting for the University of the Orange Free State; 1985 an oil painting for The Royal Exchange, London; various council commissions.

Reference AASA.

BRIGHT Sheila Anne
Born 1934 Pietermaritzburg.
A painter of landscapes, seascapes and portraits. Works in oil and watercolour.
Studies 1953 Millais Art, Designing and Interior Decorating School, under P C
Patrick in Pietermaritzburg; 1954–55 life drawing and portrait painting, Natal
Technical College, under Hugh Dent (qv); 1981–85 oil painting and drawing,
under Jane Heath (qv) in Pietermaritzburg.
Profile From 1986 a member of the Midlands Arts and Crafts Society. 1952
designed a Road Safety Poster. 1954 a layout artist for Greenacres Departmental
Store, Durban.
Exhibitions She has participated in group exhibitions in Pietermaritzburg.

BRIGHTMAN Michael Peter
Born 1938 Durban.
A painter of figures. Works in oil, pencil and charcoal.
Studies 1976–84 University of South Africa, gaining a BA(FA).
Profile From 1977 a member of the SAAA. A trained veterinary surgeon.
Exhibitions He has participated in several group exhibitions from 1984 in
Pretoria and Natal.

BRINK David George Rex
Born 1923.
Died 1963 most probably in Port Elizabeth.
A woodcarver, painter and maker of puppetry.
Studies 1946 Michaelis School of Fine Art; 1952–54 assisted by Walter Battiss
(qv) in sculpture and painting; gained a BA(FA) through the University of
South Africa in 1955.
Profile 1952–54 taught woodcarving and puppetry privately, organised an
Educational Puppetry Club for Children's Theatre Incorporated, Johannesburg,
and lectured part-time at Pretoria Technical College. 1955–57 lectured at East
London School of Art; 1958 appointed Senior Lecturer and Acting Head of the
School, 1959 appointed Head of the Port Elizabeth School of Art, a position he
filled until his death.
Exhibitions Participated in numerous group exhibitions in SA; 1956 Quadren-
nial Exhibition.
References SESA; BSAK; Port Elizabeth School of Art; AASA.

BRINK Piet
Born 1950 Pretoria.
A painter and graphic artist of esoteric, city orientated, contemporary subject
matter. Works in oil, gouache, ink, pencil and in various graphic media.
Profile From c.1974 a member of the SAAA. 1974–79 and from 1982 a senior
graphic and display artist at the National Museum, Pretoria. Several of his
poems have been published in literary magazines. 1976 visited England and
Europe.

Exhibitions He has participated in several group exhibitions from 1975 held throughout SA; 1977 SAAA Gallery, Pretoria, first of four solo exhibitions; 1981 Republic Festival Exhibition; 1983 University of Natal, Pietermaritzburg, first of two joint exhibitions with Annemarie Wessels (qv).

BRISTOW Susan

Born 1952 Louis Trichardt, Northern Transvaal.
A painter, sculptor and graphic artist of landscapes, figures, abstracts, assemblages and repeat designs. Works in oil, acrylic, gouache, bronze, ciment fondu, wood, papier mache, fabrics, various graphic media and mixed media, including wax and plastic.
Studies Michaelis School of Fine Art, under Kevin Atkinson (qv), gaining an Advanced Diploma in Fine Art.
Profile Involved with "Possession", a theatre and art group.
Exhibitions She has participated in several group exhibitions in SA.

BRITTAN Mathew

Born 1948 Johannesburg.
A self-taught painter of the unfamiliar in an ordinary context, figures and landscapes. Works in oil.
Exhibition 1969 Goodman Gallery, Johannesburg, solo exhibition.
Reference BSAK.

BRITZ Cornelius Jacobus (Nelius)

Born 1943 Worcester, Cape Province.
A sculptor of abstract pieces and murals. Works in glazed ceramics. 1982 jointly with Sandra Uttridge (qv), a series entitled "Sea Shapes" and in 1985 "Living Lustres".
Studies 1971–74 Harrow School of Art, London, under Mike Casson, David Leach and Victor Magrie, gaining a Diploma in Ceramics.
Profile 1972–82 taught privately in Cape Town. A trained botanist. Has worked with Sandra Uttridge (qv) from 1981 producing large, privately commissioned murals.
Exhibitions He has participated in several group exhibitions from 1976 in SA; 1979 Gallery International, Cape Town, solo exhibition; 1982–83 Shell House, Cape Town, first of eight joint exhibitions with Sandra Uttridge (qv).
Reference SA Panorama March 1987.

BROADLEY Robert

Born 1908 Waterfoot, Lancashire, England.
Resided in SA from 1926.
A painter of landscapes, seascapes, portraits, figures and still life. Works in oil, watercolour, gouache, ink, wash, pencil and charcoal.

Studies 1922–26 on a scholarship at the Victoria School of Art, Southport, Lancashire, under Henry Percy Huggill (1886–1957).

Profile A member of the New Group. 1908–26, 1930, 1937 and 1954 lived in England; 1952 in Sweden; 1956–64 in Spain. He has lived in Durban, Johannesburg and Pretoria and is presently living in Cape Town. Has travelled extensively in Western Europe and to the Canary Islands in 1973.

Exhibitions 1932 Cape Town, first of 20 solo exhibitions, one of which was held in London and one in Spain; he has participated in numerous group exhibitions from 1948 in England, SA, Zimbabwe and the USA; 1948 Tate Gallery, London, SA Art Exhibition; 1981 Republic Festival Exhibition.

Represented Albany Museum, Grahamstown; Durban Art Gallery; galleries in Southport and Truro, England; Johannesburg Art Gallery; King George VI Art Gallery, Port Elizabeth; Pretoria Art Museum; SA Cultural History Museum, Cape Town; SA National Gallery, Cape Town; SA National Museum of Military History, Johannesburg; University of Cape Town; William Humphreys Art Gallery, Kimberley.

Public Commissions 1947 Royal Opening of the SA Parliament by King George VI, Cape Town; 1947 portrait of The Right Honourable G Brand van Zyl; 1980 portrait of The Honourable J J Loots, Speaker of the House of Assembly.

References Collectors' Guide; Art SA; SAA; SAP&S; SAP&D; SSAP; BSAK 1 & 2; SA Art; 3Cs; AASA.

BRODIE Benjamin F A

Born 1895 Parys, Orange Free State.
Died 1969 Sea Point, Cape Town.
A painter of landscapes, cityscapes and flowers. Worked in oil and watercolour.

Studies 1914 Normal College, Bloemfontein.

Profile An art lecturer with the Transvaal Education Department, at teachers training colleges in Johannesburg and Potchefstroom, also taught art at Pretoria and Potchefstroom Boys High Schools; 1937 joined the Teachers Training College, Potchefstroom, as Head of the Art Department. 1926–35 lived in Pretoria; 1935–45 in Potchefstroom; 1945–69 in Cape Town. *c.*1952 visited Europe.

Exhibitions Participated in several group exhibitions from 1930; 1944 Gainsborough Gallery, Johannesburg, first of several solo exhibitions; 1953 Rhodes Centenary Exhibition, Bulawayo, Rhodesia (Zimbabwe).

Represented National Museum, Bloemfontein.

References BSAK; AASA.

BROOKS Robert Beverley Professor

Born 1941 Springs, Transvaal.
A painter of a melange of landscapes and portraits as well as historical experiences. Usually works in oil or acrylic on 1,80 m × 1,80 m Masonite squares. He also works in various graphic media.

Studies 1961–65 Rhodes University, under Professor Brian Bradshaw (qv), gaining a BA(FA) in 1964 and an MA(FA) (cum laude) in 1965.

Profile 1961–69 a member of the Grahamstown Group; 1961–86 a member of the EPSFA. 1966 taught at Port Elizabeth Technical College and at the Art High School; 1967–72 a lecturer, then senior lecturer, School of Fine Art, Rhodes University; 1972–81 senior lecturer and Head of Department, Port Elizabeth Technical College; from 1981 Professor and Head of Department, School of Fine Art, Rhodes University. From 1985 on the Board of Trustees of the King George VI Art Gallery, Port Elizabeth. From 1982 a designer and cover illustrator of *English in Africa*, a magazine published by Nelm. 1985 drew the cover illustration for *House in Pella District*, a book of poems by Douglas Reid Skinner, published by David Philip, Cape Town. Has visited the Hebrides, Scotland. Married to Jennifer Crooks (qv).

Exhibitions He has participated in numerous group exhibitions in SA from 1961; 1973 NSA Gallery, Durban, first of four solo exhibitions.

Awards 1973 Julius Robinson Charity and Educational Trust Award on Art SA Today; 1973 Crown Cebestos Fine Art Prize.

Represented King George VI Art Gallery, Port Elizabeth.

References AASA; *Photography and Travel* November 1969; *Close Up* 6 November 1970.

BROWN David James

Born 1951 Johannesburg.

A sculptor of man and beast, man and machine. Works in bronze, wood and steel. 1983–85 a series of "Procession, Man, Animal and Machine".

Studies 1970–73 Michaelis School of Fine Art, gaining a Diploma in Graphic Design; 1974 Michaelis School of Fine Art, attaining a Postgraduate Diploma in Fine Art.

Profile Introduced to sculpture in 1975 by Cecil Skotnes (qv). From 1979 a member of the Artists Guild, Cape Town. A part-time lecturer at the Ruth Prowse School of Art, Cape Town. Married to Pippa Skotnes (qv).

Exhibitions He has participated in many group exhibitions from 1975 held in SA, Switzerland and West Germany; 1975 Cape Town, first of six solo exhibitions held in Cape Town and Johannesburg;
1985 Tributaries, touring SA and West Germany; 1987 Johannesburg Art Gallery, Vita Art Now.

Award 1986 Vita Art Now Quarterly Award Winner.

Represented Durban Art Gallery; Johannesburg Art Gallery; Pretoria Art Museum; Rand Afrikaans University; SA National Gallery, Cape Town; Tatham Art Gallery, Pietermaritzburg; University of Cape Town; University of the Witwatersrand.

Public Commissions 1985 Revenue Building, Cape Town; 1985–86 Johannesburg Centenary Sculpture Competition Winner, Johannesburg Art Gallery.

References AASA; LSAA.

BROWN John Roland

Born 1850 Port Elizabeth.

Died 1923 Grahamstown.

A watercolourist of landscapes, seascapes, genre and portraits in the English tradition.

Studies 1866–67 at the Roeland Street School of Art, Cape Town, under Thomas Mitchener Lindsay (qv) and 1867–70 at the Liverpool School of Art. In 1870 he won a Queen's Scholarship, several silver medals and was made an assistant teacher at the Liverpool School of Art, where he remained teaching for 30 years.
Profile A deaf-mute who lived in Liverpool 1867–1902, he then retired to SA, living in Port Alfred, Grahamstown, East London and Durban.
Exhibitions 1886–99 exhibited in Liverpool and London; 1916 Grahamstown, solo exhibition.
Represented Africana Museum, Johannesburg; Albany Museum, Grahamstown; William Fehr Collection, Cape Town.
References AMC1&6; DSAB; Pict Afr; DBA; Marjorie Bull, *Abraham de Smidt 1829–1908*, 1981, Printpak, Cape Town; AASA.

BRUNTON Winifred Mabel (née Newberry)
Born 1880 Cairo, Egypt.
Died 1959.
Came to SA at a very early age.
A painter of miniatures, portraits, landscapes, flowers and Egyptian subjects. Worked in watercolour, often on ivory.
Studies Known to have studied art in various places including in SA and at the Slade School of Art, London.
Profile 1912 a member of the Royal Society of British Artists and an Associate of the Royal Miniature Society; 1916 elected a Member of the Royal Miniature Society. Lived in London, in Cairo during the early 1930s and in SA at White River, Eastern Transvaal. Signed her work W.M.N.B.
Exhibitions Participated in group exhibitions in London and in SA; held eight solo exhibitions at Arlington Gallery, London.
Represented Africana Museum, Johannesburg; Egyptian Art Gallery, Cairo, Egypt; Guildhall, London, England; Johannesburg Art Gallery.
Publications by Brunton *Kings and Queens of Ancient Egypt* and *Great Ones of Ancient Egypt*, Hodder & Stoughton, London.
Reference AMC1.

BRUSSEAU Gert Johannes
Born 1901 Berlin, Germany.
Died 1961.
Resided in SA from 1936.
A painter, working in oil, of landscapes and city views. Drew portraits in pastel and produced a number of etchings.
Studies 1922–24 State Academy, Berlin, under Professor Emil Orlik (1870–1932) and Karl Hofer (1878–1955); 1925 State Academy, Munich, under Professor Karl Doener; 1926 Musée de Sculpture Comparée, Paris, under Pierre Marchand and Louis Icart.

Profile A member of the Transvaal Art Society and a foundation member of the Brush and Chisel Club. Lectured for 10 years at the Witwatersrand Technical College of Art.
Exhibitions Participated in group exhibitions from 1938 in Johannesburg; held a solo exhibition in Johannesburg.
Represented Africana Museum, Johannesburg.
References BSAK; AASA.

BUCHAN John de Villebois
Born 1938 Johannesburg.
A painter of landscapes and wildlife. Works in oil.
Studies Witwatersrand Technical College, under Professor Robert Bain (qv), awarded a Diploma in Commercial Art in 1960.
Exhibitions He has participated in group exhibitions in Johannesburg.

BUCHNER Carl Adolph
Born 1921 Somerset East, Cape Province.
A painter of portraits, figures, landscapes, still life, interiors and street scenes. Works in oil and acrylic.
Studies 1940–44 Witwatersrand Technical College, under Eric Byrd (qv), Phyllis Gardner (qv), Elizabeth Macadam (qv) and Maurice van Essche (qv), gaining a National Art Teachers Certificate.
Profile An Executive member of the SAAA. 1964 Chairman of the National Committee of the SAAA. 1944–54 taught at several Transvaal schools and at the Pretoria Art Centre; 1954 Art Inspector for the Cape Education Department; 1956 Head of the P J Olivier Art Centre, Stellenbosch; 1959–70 lectured at the Michaelis School of Fine Art. For many years a Trustee of the SA National Gallery, Cape Town. 1962 an art critic for *Die Burger*; also an art critic for *The Cape Times* and a writer of articles on art and artists for various magazines. 1967 wrote the introduction to *Van Essche*, Tafelberg, Cape Town. A painting entitled "Karroo Village" was reproduced by A A Balkema, Cape Town. 1957–58 and 1964 study tours of Europe.
Exhibitions He has participated in numerous group exhibitions in SA, Zimbabwe and Argentina; 1954 first of several solo exhibitions held in SA; 1956 and 1960 Quadrennial Exhibitions; 1982 Cape Town Triennial.
Award 1963 Artists of Fame and Promise Award.
Represented Hester Rupert Art Museum, Graaff-Reinet; Pietersburg Collection; Pretoria Art Museum; Rand Afrikaans University; SA National Gallery, Cape Town; University of the Orange Free State; University of South Africa; Willem Annandale Art Gallery, Lichtenburg; William Humphreys Art Gallery, Kimberley.
References Art SA; SAA; 20C SA Art; SAP&S; SESA; SSAP; BSAK 1 & 2; 3Cs; AASA; *Lantern* March 1953.

BUDER-MALLOWS Elvira
Born 1918 Ismailia, Egypt.
Resided in SA from 1947.
A painter of landscapes, seascapes, still life, figures and abstract pictures. Works in acrylic, watercolour, gouache, ink, wash, pencil and charcoal. Creates collages behind perspex sheets. A series entitled "Inscapes", combining geometrical forms, natural forms and textures.
Studies 1938–39 and 1940–41 Art et Publicité, Paris; 1939–40 l'Ecole des Beaux Arts, Rennes, France; 1967–71 University of South Africa, under Walter Battiss (qv), gaining a BA(FA); 1969 engraving with Bennic and Dorny in Paris.
Profile Until 1986 a member of the SAAA. Worked as a French teacher until 1970. Lives in Johannesburg.
Exhibitions 1970 Lidchi Gallery, Johannesburg, solo exhibition; she has participated in numerous group exhibitions in SA from 1971; 1981 Republic Festival Exhibition.
Represented Accademia d'Arte di Montecatini, Italy; University of the Witwatersrand.
Reference AASA.

BUDLER Rose-Marie (Mrs Jensen)
Born 1925 Kestell, Orange Free State.
A painter of landscapes, still life and figures. Works in oil, watercolour and gouache.
Studies 1943–47 Rhodes University, under Professor A Winter Moore (qv), attaining a BA(FA); 1959 University of South Africa, where gained a BA(FA)(Hons); 1960 Witwatersrand Technical College, where awarded a National Art Teachers Diploma, with a distinction in design.
Profile 1958 a founder member of the Bloemfontein Group. 1948 and 1958–60 lectured at the Orange Free State Technical College; 1949–57 lectured at the Port Elizabeth Technical College. 1961–62 an Inspectress of Art for the Cape Education Department in Port Elizabeth; 1969–85 Senior Superintendent of Education, Port Elizabeth. 1972 made a study tour of Europe.
Exhibitions 1956 Uitenhage, first of 10 solo exhibitions; she has participated in numerous group exhibitions from 1959 in SA; 1960 and 1964 Quadrennial Exhibitions.
Represented Ann Bryant Gallery, East London.
References SAA; BSAK; Port Elizabeth School of Art; AASA.

BUITENDAG Elise
Born 1941 Johannesburg.
A self-taught painter of botanical studies. Works in oil, watercolour, ink and pencil.
Profile A trained botanist. Numerous designs for cards, emblems and murals. Has illustrated books and magazines. She has also written and illustrated various botanical brochures and books. Lives in Nelspruit, Eastern Transvaal.
Exhibitions She has participated in many group exhibitions from 1973 in SA; 1982 Nelspruit, first of two solo exhibitions.

BULLEN Edith Florence

Born 1939 Evaswalde, Germany.
Resided in SA from 1953.
A painter of imaginary landscapes, still life and figures. Works in acrylic, gouache, ink and charcoal. In addition to this she also makes collages and monoprints. A number of large series: 1978–79 nudes, 1980–81 birds, from 1983 windows.
Studies 1968–69 The Visual Arts Research Centre, under George Boys (qv); 1976–79 in George Boys' Studio.
Profile A member of the SAAA from the late 1960s. A writer of short stories. Has lived in India and England, and presently lives in Johannesburg.
Exhibitions She has participated in several group exhibitions from 1958 in India and SA; 1979 Johannesburg, first of five solo exhibitions held in Johannesburg and Pretoria.

BUMSTEAD Judy Carol

Born 1952 Boksburg, Transvaal.
A painter and graphic artist with a wide range of subject matter including figures and landscapes. Works in oil, acrylic, watercolour, gouache, ink, wash, pencil, charcoal and in various graphic media. A sculptor in clay and wood and a potter from 1968.
Studies 1968–70 Pretoria School of Art, Ballet and Music; 1970–71 Pretoria Technical College; 1971–74 Johannesburg School of Art, gaining a Diploma in Fine Art and Design.
Profile 1983–84 several illustrations for *New Vision* magazine, East London. Lived in London 1975–81 and travelled extensively in Europe. Presently lives in Johannesburg.
Exhibitions She has participated in many group exhibitions from 1971 in SA and London.

BURCHELL William John

Born 1781 Fulham, London.
Died 1863 Fulham, London.
Resided in SA 1810–15.
A painter in watercolour and oil. Some pencil, ink and wash drawings of landscapes.
Studies 1796 privately under J Merigot, an aquatinter, and John Claude Notts, a topographical draughtsman, in London.
Profile 1803 elected a Fellow of the Linnaean Society. Prior to 1805 worked at the Botanical Gardens, Kew, Surrey; 1805–10 a schoolmaster and acting botanist on St Helena Island, Altantic Ocean; 1810 in Cape Town; 1811–15 collected specimens of flora and fauna during his travels throughout the Cape, discovered the Quagga, the White Rhinoceros and the Blue Wildebeest; several species of birds and plants named after him. He made *c.*500 drawings of his travels. 1815–24 lived in England; 1825–30 in Brazil.

Award 1834 awarded an Honorary Degree of Doctor of Civil Law, Oxford University, England.

Represented Africana Museum, Johannesburg; Albany Museum, Grahamstown; Hope Museum, Oxford, England; King George VI Art Gallery, Port Elizabeth; SA Cultural History Museum, Cape Town; University of the Witwatersrand.

Publication by Burchell Travels in the Interior of Southern Africa, 2 volumes, 1822 and 1824, Longmans, London (with author's illustrations), reprinted, with an introduction by A Gordon Brown, 1967, C Struik, Cape Town.

References The South African Drawings of William J Burchell, 2 volumes, edited by Helen M McKay, 1938 and 1952, University of the Witwatersrand; F Jaffe, *They Came to South Africa*, 1963, Howard Timmins, Cape Town; Pict Afr; Afr Repos; AMC1 & 6; DSAB; SESA; Pict Art; BSAK; Enc S'n A; SA Art; 3Cs; *Apollo* October 1975, London.

BURDETT-COUTTS Olivia see WATSON Olivia

BURGER Melvyn

A painter, sculptor and graphic artist of portraits, figures and abstract works. Uses mixed media, silkscreen and etching processes.

Studies 1969–72 Pretoria and Johannesburg Technical Colleges, where attained a Diploma in Fine Art.

Profile 1973 began screenprinting work for other artists. 1985 a printmaking lecturer at the Orange Free State Technical College. 1975–78 involved in textile printing; 1979–83 worked in the textile industry. 1973–79 lived in the Eastern Transvaal; 1979–83 lived in the Cape Province.

Exhibitions He has participated in numerous group exhibitions from 1973 held in Johannesburg, Pretoria, Cape Town and Bloemfontein.

BURGES Edith Kathleen (Mrs Metherell)

Born 1919 Pietermaritzburg.

A painter of landscapes, portraits, still life, figures and botanical subjects. Works in oil, watercolour and pencil.

Studies 1938–40 School of Arts and Crafts, Natal Technical College, under Merlyn Evans (qv), where awarded the Arthur May Bursary.

Profile A member of the Scottburgh Arts Club and the Upper South Coast Art Association. 1942–44 an artist with the Botanical Research Institute, where her illustrations appeared in *The Flowering Plants of South Africa* and later in *The Flowering Plants of Africa* from 1943. 1938–41 worked in pottery; 1968–69 designed a tapestry panel, now in Natalia, Pietermaritzburg. Since 1970 she has made several wall hangings using the batik method. 1940 and 1941 designed SA Christmas Stamps.

Exhibitions She has participated in many group exhibitions from 1961 in Natal.

Reference SAA.

BURNARD Margaret Lucy
Born 1933 Rhodesia (Zimbabwe).
Resided in SA from 1936.
A painter of landscapes, still life, seascapes, wildlife and abstract pictures. Works in oil, watercolour, gouache, ink, wash, pencil and charcoal.
Studies 1975 under Alfred Ewan (qv); 1980 under Anthony Strickland (qv); 1982 under Jane Heath (qv); 1985 San Raphael Art School, Spain, under Michael Still.
Profile A member of the NSA, the WSSA and the Highway Art Group. From 1979 she has held private art classes in her studio in Westville, Natal.
Exhibitions She has participated in group exhibitions from 1975 in SA and London; 1977 Durban, first of three solo exhibitions.
Represented Killie Campbell Africana Library, University of Natal, Durban.

BURNETT Martin Patrick
Born 1946 Johannesburg.
A painter of landscapes, still life and figures. Works in oil, watercolour and pencil. Additionally creates three-dimensional constructions in ceramics. 1975 a large series entitled "Dreams" and "Visions of Loneliness".
Studies 1971–74 Natal Technical College (Technikon), under Andrew Verster (qv), Patrick O'Connor (qv) and Paul Stopforth (qv); 1985 Natal Technikon, under Penny Siopis (qv), Clive van der Berg (qv) and Basil Friedlander (qv). 1971 awarded the Emma Smith Scholarship, 1982 completed a Higher Diploma in Education, majoring in painting.
Profile 1965–67 a committee member of the Artists Market, Johannesburg; from 1983 a committee member of the Natal Art Teachers Association; 1984–85 a council member of the NSA. 1972–76 a part-time drawing lecturer, Natal Technical College; 1974 assistant Visual Communications lecturer at the University of Natal; from 1983 an art teacher at Westville Boys High, Durban. 1971–76 involved in a design and silkscreen studio.
Exhibitions 1972 Bojo Gallery, Durban, first of five solo exhibitions in Durban and Johannesburg; he has participated in many group exhibitions from 1974 in Durban and Cape Town; 1982 Cape Town Triennial.
Represented Natal Technikon.
References BSAK; AASA.

BURNETT Richard Leslie George (Ricky)
Born 1949 Birmingham, England.
Resided in SA 1956–85.
A painter and sculptor of landscapes, figures and abstracted works. Uses oil, pencil, charcoal, bronze and steel.
Studies Privately under Bill Ainslie (qv).
Profile 1975 and 1983 a teacher at the Johannesburg Art Foundation. An art critic for the, now defunct, *Rand Daily Mail*. 1983–85 art advisor to BMW (SA) and the compiler of "Tributaries", an exhibition of SA work travelling in SA and West Germany. He has lived in London from 1985.

Exhibitions He has participated in several group exhibitions from 1978 in SA and West Germany; 1980 Market Gallery, Johannesburg, first of three solo exhibitions, one of which was held in London; 1982 National Gallery, Gaborone, Botswana, Exhibition of SA Art; 1984–85 Four Johannesburg Painters, a touring exhibition with Ilona Anderson (qv), Robert Hodgins (qv) and Jo Smail (qv); 1985, Tributaries, touring SA and West Germany.

BURRAGE Leslie Thomas (Ben)

Born 1909 Hove, Sussex, England.
Died 1983 Johannesburg.
Resided in SA from 1936.
A painter of a wide range of subjects. Worked in watercolour, oil, pen, charcoal, chalk and pastel. Best known for his depiction of SA military machinery and engineering, especially that used in WWII.
Studies Brighton School of Art, England.
Profile 1943–45 an Official War Artist, illustrating instruction pamphlets and producing posters on camouflage. A member of the SA National Museum of Military History Art Committee. 1936–42 contributed illustrations to *The Outspan* magazine. Designed the Hall of Remembrance, Sappersrust, Transvaal. 1929–36 lived in London; 1936–42 in Cape Town; 1942–43 in Pretoria; 1943–44 in the Middle East; 1944 in SA; 1945 in Italy; 1946 in Johannesburg, where he worked for the Strathmore Mining Group as an artist and art advisor. Designed pamphlets, posters and illustrations for SATOUR. 1946–48 cartoons by Burrage appeared regularly in *Dagbreek*. 1958–68 worked in advertising. On his retirement he became a full-time artist.
Exhibition 1981 SA National Museum of Military History, Johannesburg, solo exhibition.
Represented SA National Museum of Military History, Johannesburg.
Public Commission 1980 mural for the Wanderers Club, Johannesburg.
References BSAK; SA Art; SASSK; AASA; *The World War II Works of Burrage*, 1981, SA National Museum of Military History, Johannesburg.

BURRY Barbara Grace

Born 1909 London, England.
Resided in SA from 1952.
A painter of landscapes, still life and figures. Works in oil and watercolour.
Studies 1927–30 Brighton School of Art, England; 1957–59 under Professor Alfred Krenz (qv).
Profile A member of the SAAA and the Somerset West Art Group.
Exhibitions She has participated in numerous group exhibitions from 1960 in SA; 1962 SAAA Gallery, Cape Town, first of several solo exhibitions in SA.
Represented Pietersburg Collection.
References BSAK; AASA.

BURWITZ Nils

Born 1940 Swinemünde, Pomerania, Germany.
Resided in SA 1958–76.
A painter, sculptor and graphic artist working in oil, watercolour, gouache, ink, wash, pencil, charcoal, wood and in various graphic media. His subject matter is environments.
Studies 1960–63 University of the Witwatersrand, gaining a BA(FA); 1965 visited Europe on a two-year travel bursary from the University of the Witwatersrand; 1966 a lithography course at the School of Vision, Salzburg, Austria.
Profile Artist collaborator in the invention of the resin engraving technique. 1974 taught at Dorkay House, Johannesburg and at the Summer School of the University of the Witwatersrand; 1975 invited to lecture at the University of the Witwatersrand. 1967 a limited edition (125) of a series of nine drawings entitled "Locust Variations"; 1969, 1971 and 1972 theatre designs for Robert Kirby plays; 1973 nine serigraphs entitled "It's About Time", 1974 nine serigraphs entitled "Tidal Zone" and in 1981 "Cara O Creu?", all published by Advanced Graphics, London. 1940–45 lived in East Germany; 1946–58 in West Germany; 1958–76 in SA and from 1976 in Spain. 1966 visited Russia.
Exhibitions He has participated in over 100 group exhibitions from 1963 in Germany, SA, Australia, Chile, the UK, Greece, Italy, Norway, the USA, Yugoslavia and Spain; 1964 Lidchi Gallery, Johannesburg, first of over 40 solo exhibitions held in SA, the UK, Botswana, Yugoslavia and Spain; 1970 Durban Art Gallery, Prestige Exhibition; 1979 William Humphreys Art Gallery, Kimberley, Prestige Exhibition; 1982 Cape Town Triennial.
Awards Numerous awards for both paintings and graphics from 1962 in SA, Yugoslavia, Ireland, England, Monaco, Spain, Japan and The Americas.
Represented Durban Art Gallery; Johannesburg Art Gallery; Pietersburg Collection; Pretoria Art Museum; Rand Afrikaans University; Sandton Municipal Collection; SA National Gallery, Cape Town; University of Natal; University of the Orange Free State; University of South Africa; University of Stellenbosch; University of the Witwatersrand; Victoria and Albert Museum, London, UK; William Humphreys Art Gallery, Kimberley.
References 20C SA Art; SSAP; BSAK 1 & 2; Our Art 3; SA Art; 3Cs; AASA; LSAA; *Artlook* March 1967, November 1967, June 1969, June 1973, March 1974 & February 1975; *Habitat* no 14, 1975 & no 40, 1980; *Gallery* Winter 1982 & Spring 1983.

BUSH Rowena Elizabeth

Born 1917 Ceylon (Sri Lanka).
Resided in SA from 1962.
A painter of landscapes, portraits, still life and seascapes. Works in oil, watercolour, gouache, ink, wash, pencil and pastel. Has also produced several sculptures. 1938–60 a series of 500–600 studies of East African Indigenous Plants in watercolour.

Studies 1933–36 West of England Academy of Art, Bristol, under R E Bush and D Milner; 1936–37 London School of Interior Design, under Mr Ellerton. Gained Part I (3 years) Board of Education (UK) Teachers Certificate; Art Masters Certificate and a Diploma from the London School of Interior Design; 1969–70 sculpture at Natal Technical College, under Mary Stainbank (qv); 1979–85 various classes under Jane Heath (qv) in Pietermaritzburg.

Profile 1940–62 a member of the Kenya Art Society; 1963 of the Queenstown Art Society; 1964 of the Orange Free State Art Society; 1965 of the Highway Art Group; from 1972 a member, from 1977 an Associate and from 1984 a Fellow of the WSSA. In 1985 she was Vice-Chairman of the Natal Branch of the WSSA. 1939–40 taught art at Dar es Salaam Girls School, Tanganyika (Tanzania); 1940–43 at St Andrews School and St Georges School, Turi, Kenya; 1963–71 taught art privately in Durban. 1940–46 numerous illustrations for vernacular books. 1966 worked in pottery with Sylvia Baxter. 1917–24 lived in Ceylon (Sri Lanka); 1924–38 in England; 1938–40 in Tanganyika (Tanzania); 1940–43 in Kenya; 1944–51 in Tanzania; 1951–62 in Kenya. 1950 visited Norway; 1972 Greece; 1974 Italy; 1974 and 1978 Spain.

Exhibitions She has participated in numerous group exhibitions from 1939 in Kenya, West Germany, Portugal, London and throughout SA; 1947 Bristol Art Gallery, first of two solo exhibitions held in Tanzania; 1963 Embankment Gallery, Durban, first of 23 solo exhibitions held in SA.

Awards Has been awarded the Mary Clark and P W Storey Trophy, awarded to members of the Highway Art Group, several times.

References BSAK; AASA.

BUTLER Frank Harold (Sam)

Born 1889 Nottingham, England.

Resided in SA from 1938.

A painter of landscapes and seascapes. Worked in oil, watercolour, pen and wash.

Studies 1915–18 by correspondence through the Press Art School, London; 1920–36 also by correspondence through various art schools in London, including Heatherley School of Art; 1937 evening classes at St Margaret's School of Art, Birmingham.

Profile A member of the SA Society of Artists; 1938–69 an art master at the Diocesan College, Rondebosch, Cape Town. 1907 joined the British Army, seeing service in Egypt and Europe. 1920–36 lived in Egypt; 1937 in Birmingham, UK, thereafter in SA, travelling abroad in 1956 and 1970. Lived in Kalk Bay, Cape Province.

Exhibitions Participated in group exhibitions from 1922 in the UK and SA.

Represented SA National Gallery, Cape Town.

References SAP&D; DBA.

BUTLER Henry Captain

Resided in SA 1835–39.

A professional soldier who painted landscapes, hunting scenes and tribal genre. Worked in watercolour and produced many pen and pencil sketches.

Profile Travelled from Cape Town to Knysna in 1835, to King William's Town, the Winterberg and the Kei River in 1836, and in the hunting areas of the Eastern Cape in 1837–38. Hunted with Lieutenant William Guise (qv).
Represented Africana Museum, Johannesburg; William Fehr Collection, Cape Town.
Publication by Butler *South African Sketches, illustrative of the wild life of a hunter on the frontier of the Cape Colony, 1841*, Ackerman, London, an account of his 1837–38 journey containing 31 illustrations on 15 plates.
References Pict Art; AMC; Pict Afr; SASSK.

BUTLER Violet Victoria (née Kaul) ARMS

Born 1889 Kensington, London, England.
Died 1980.
Resided in SA from 1938.
A painter of wildlife, landscapes, flowers and portraits. Also a miniaturist. Worked in oil.
Profile 1916 elected an Associate of the Royal Miniature Society. From 1938 lived in Johannesburg. Travelled extensively in Europe and in her later years accompanied her son Peter Black, a wildlife photographer, on an annual two-month safari.
Exhibitions Participated in group exhibitions in SA and London.
Public Commissions Among the many portraits are those of King Leopold of Belgium, King George VI of England, Field-Marshal J C Smuts and of the King of Yugoslavia, which was commissioned posthumously by his Queen.
References Benezit; DBA; BSAK 1 & 2; AASA.

BUYS Jan

Born 1909 Rotterdam, The Netherlands.
Died 1985 Cape Town.
Resided in SA from 1954.
A painter of landscapes, wildlife and figures, especially of SWA/Namibia and its people. Worked in oil. His early pictures are characterised by rich colours, but increasingly he used more of the desert tones of SWA/Namibia.
Studies Academie van Beeldende Kunsten, Rotterdam, also in Antwerp and under Mees-Bouts in Heidelberg, Germany.
Profile A member of the Contemporary Art Society. *c.*1960 a part-time teacher at the Witwatersrand Technical College. During WWII worked for the Rotterdam Archives, depicting scenes of the bombed city. Lived in Johannesburg and from 1964 in Cape Town. First visited SA in 1949. Travelled extensively throughout SA and in 1961 in Lesotho; 1961–64 worked in SWA/Namibia.
Exhibitions Participated in group exhibitions in Europe, SA and SWA/Namibia; 1933 Rotterdam, first solo exhibition; 1949 Johannesburg, first of several solo exhibitions in SA.

Represented Durban Art Gallery; Gemeente, Rotterdam, The Netherlands; Hester Rupert Art Museum, Graaff-Reinet; Kroonstad Technikon; Pretoria Art Museum; SA National Gallery, Cape Town; University of Pretoria; William Humphreys Art Gallery, Kimberley.
References 20C SA Art; SAA, SAP&S; BSAK 1 & 2; Art SWA; AASA; *Artlook* March 1970.

BUYSKES Arnold Gregg

Born 1948 Cape Town.
A self-taught sculptor working in wood and stone.
Exhibitions 1981 first of four solo exhibitions held at the State Theatre, Pretoria; 1983–85 four solo exhibitions held in Durban and Cape Town.
Public Commissions 1983 "Man and Flute", Egerton College, Ladysmith, Natal; 1983 "Owl and Mouse", Klip River Primary School, Ladysmith, Natal.

BUZZARD Thelma

Born Durban.
A painter of flowers and landscapes. Works in watercolour, ink and oil, also creates collages.
Studies 1974–77 Natal Technical College, under Louis Jansen van Vuuren (qv) and Martin van der Spuy; 1977 life drawing in London under Margaret and Leonard Boden; 1978–82 University of Natal, under Andrew Verster (qv) and Diana Kenton (qv).
Profile From 1981 an Associate of the WSSA; a member of the NSA, the Highway Art Group and the North Coast Art Group. 1961–84 a member of the Natal Panel of Floral Art Judges. 1984 two Bougainvillea Portfolia and in 1985 two Azalea Portfolia published by Howard Swan Publishers, Johannesburg.
Exhibitions She has participated in numerous group exhibitions from 1978 in SA and once in London; 1979 Musgrave Centre, Durban, first solo exhibiton.
Award 1981 jointly with Wendy Amm (qv), the MOAG Award from the North Coast Art Group, Natal.

BYRD Eric

Born 1905 Durban.
Resided in SA 1936–50.
A painter of landscapes, seascapes, boating scenes, still life, portraits, figures, animals and birds. Works in watercolour and oil. Draws in pen and ink.
Studies 1925–26 Cardiff School of Art, Wales; 1927–32 Hornsey School of Art, London, under John Moody (1884–1962) and Robert Lyon; 1934 Slade School of Art, London, under Randolph Schwabe (1885–1948).

Profile 1938 a member of the New Group. A council member of the NSA. Lectured at Hornsey School of Art, Natal Technical College, the University of Natal and from 1938 at the Witwatersrand Technical College, becoming Acting Head in 1940. From 1943 again lectured at Natal Technical College. From 1950 taught at Sir George Williams College, Montreal, where he had his own studio. Provided illustrations for Hugh Tracey's book *Lalela Zulu*. Travelled in France, Italy, West Germany, the USA and Canada, where he lived after 1950.

Exhibitions He has participated in group exhibitions throughout SA and in Canada; 1943 Gainsborough Gallery, Johannesburg, first solo exhibition in SA; has held a solo exhibition in Montreal.

Represented Durban Art Gallery; SA National Gallery, Cape Town; SA National Museum of Military History, Johannesburg.

References Who's Who in Art, 6th edition, 1952; SAP&D; BSAK; AASA.

BYRNE Susan Janice

Born 1952 Johannesburg.

A painter of portraits, genre and figures. Works in oil, acrylic, watercolour, ink, pencil and mixed media. Additionally she creates collages. A number of large series entitled: 1977–84 "Court Case"; 1981–84 "Mother & Child"; from 1984 plate glass double-sided paintings; from 1984 a series of people at exhibition openings.

Studies 1971–74 University of the Witwatersrand, under Robert Hodgins (qv), Cecily Sash (qv), Erica Berry (qv) and Neels Coetzee (qv), gaining a BA(FA); 1976 obtained a Higher Diploma in Education.

Profile Taught art in 1977 at Parktown Boys High School, Johannesburg; 1978–79 art and Zulu teacher at Mondeor High School, Johannesburg; 1980, 1981 and 1984 a Zulu lecturer at the Johannesburg College of Education.

Exhibitions She has participated in several group exhibitions from 1984; 1986 Market Gallery, Johannesburg, solo exhibition.

Award 1974 Herbert Evans Prize for best student.

C

CALBURN Simon Robert Henry

Born 1938 London, England.

Resided in SA from 1952.

A painter of wildlife particularly birds. Works in watercolour, gouache and pencil. In addition to this he has painted a number of landscapes, in watercolour, crayon and ink.

Studies 1957–59 University of the Witwatersrand, where gained a BA. 1961–63 Oxford University, England, on a Bell Memorial Scholarship, where gained an MA.

Profile From 1983 a member of the Africana Museum Advisory Board. Sets of signed prints of his work were issued in 1972, 1975, 1977, 1980, 1983 and 1984. Illustrated *The Owls of Southern Africa*, with text by Alan Kemp, 1987, Struik/Winchester, Cape Town. A music critic for *The Sunday Times* and *The Weekly Mail*.

Exhibitions 1969 Lidchi Gallery, Johannesburg, first of two solo exhibitions; he has participated in numerous group exhibitions from 1971 in SA, Canada and the UK; 1981 Africana Museum, Johannesburg, Retrospective Exhibition.

Represented Africana Museum, Johannesburg.

Publication by Calburn *Calburn's Birds of Southern Africa*, 1969, Purnell, Johannesburg.

References SESA; BSAK; SA Art; AASA; *Artlook* August 1969; *SA Panorama* May 1975.

CALDECOTT Harry Stratford (Strat)

Born 1886 Kimberley, Orange Free State.

Died 1929 Cape Town.

A painter of landscapes and city scenes. Worked mainly in oil but made a number of charcoal, chalk, ink and/or pencil drawings as well as a few watercolour and gouache paintings. Painted 31 oil paintings, including scenes of the Malay Quarter in 1925 and 1927, scenes of Cape Town and of Cape Town Station.

Studies 1912 Académie Julian, Paris; 1913 l'Ecole des Beaux Arts, Paris, under Gabriel Ferrier (1847–1914); it is thought that Caldecott also studied in the Colarossi Studio and under Maurice Denis (1870–1943).

Profile A member of the K Club. In 1925 he designed the "Giraffe" poster and a number of postcards for the Kruger National Park where he had stayed for a few months sketching the bush. He was greatly interested in wildlife conservation and helped create the Kruger National Park. A founder of the Cape Branch of the SA Wildlife Protection Society and in 1926 its representative. Involved in the preservation and restoration of historic buildings. He designed a number of posters for SA Railways and drew illustrations for the publishers Nasionale Pers. An art critic and writer of articles on wildlife and historic buildings for *The South African Nation* from 1923 and for *New Frontier*, *Die Burger* and *Die Huisgenoot*, often using the pseudonyms "L'imagier" and "Y Y". Lived in Paris 1912–23, visiting Munich in 1914; 1915–18 in the Allied Forces; 1923–24 in Johannesburg; 1924–29 in Cape Town. 1926 visited Worcester; 1927 visited Clifton, Stellenbosch, Montagu and Grabouw. Married Florence Zerffi (qv) in 1924.

Exhibitions Participated in group exhibitions in Johannesburg and Cape Town from 1925; 1925 Ashbey's Gallery, Cape Town, joint exhibition with Florence Zerffi (qv); held solo exhibitions in Paris and Johannesburg; 1944 Argus Gallery, Cape Town, Memorial Exhibition; 1948 Tate Gallery, London, SA Art Exhibition; 1953 Rhodes Centenary Exhibition, Bulawayo, Rhodesia (Zimbabwe); 1956 SA National Gallery, Cape Town, Memorial Exhibition; 1983 SA National Gallery, Cape Town, Commemorative Exhibition; 1986 SA National Gallery, Cape Town, Retrospective Exhibition; 1987 William Humphreys Art Gallery, Kimberley, Exhibition.

Represented Johannesburg Art Gallery; Pretoria Art Museum; SA National Gallery, Cape Town; William Humphreys Art Gallery, Kimberley.

Public Commission 1926 stencils on the ceiling of the Diocesan College, Rondebosch, Cape Town.

References J du P Scholtz, *Strat Caldecott*, 1970, A A Balkema, Cape Town; PSA; Collectors' Guide; Our Art 1; Art SA; SAA; SADNB; 20C SA Art; DSAB; SESA; SAP&S; SSAP; BSAK 1 & 2; SA Art; 3Cs; AASA; SASSK; LSAA; *Die Huisgenoot* March 1944; SA National Gallery Catalogue, 1956, Cape Town.

CALDER Ian

Born 1955 Scottburgh, Natal.
A sculptor working in mixed media.
Studies 1976 gained a BA(FA) from the University of Natal.
Profile Teaches at the University of Natal.
Exhibitions 1985 Cape Town Triennial Exhibition.
Represented Pretoria Art Museum; Tatham Art Gallery, Pietermaritzburg; University of Natal.
References *Sgraffiti* no 33.

CALDWELL Edmund

Born 1852 Canterbury, Kent, England.
Died 1930 London, England.
A painter of landscapes, figures and animals. Several bronze animals.
Studies Under Thomas Sidney Cooper RA (1803–1902) in London; Académie Julian, Paris, under Boulanger and Lefebre.
Profile Not a South African artist, but well known in SA for his illustrations in *Jock of the Bushveld* by Sir Percy FitzPatrick, 1907, Longmans Green & Company, London; also illustrated *Elephant Hunting in East Equatorial Africa* by Neumans, 1898, *Gun and Camera in Southern Africa*, 1895 and *Animals in Africa*, 1900, both by Henry Anderson Bryden; *Big Game Shooting and Travel in South Eastern Africa* by F R N Findlay, 1903, T Fisher Unwin, London; *My Sporting Holidays* by Sir Henry Seton-Karr, 1904, Edward Arnold, London; *Lives of the Fur Folk* by M D Haviland, 1910, Longmans Green & Company, London; *African Nature Notes and Reminiscences* by F C Selous, 1908, Macmillan & Company, London. A number of his paintings were used as illustrations in *The Conservationists and The Killers* by

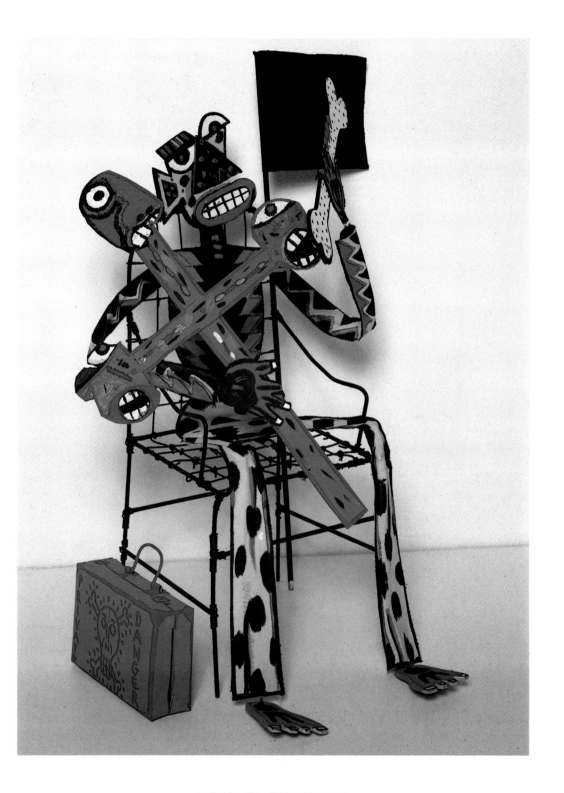

NORMAN CATHERINE
The Saint 1987
Acrylic on Canvas, Wood & Metal 89 × 71 cm
Paul Drexler
Los Angeles

GIUSEPPE CATTANEO
After the Rain, Malcome's Place
Oil on Canvas 91 × 121 cm
Julius Feinstein

John Pringle. Whilst in this country he painted a number of wildlife paintings and sculpted some animals in bronze. Most of his work was done in London from 1895 until 1919, when his eyesight failed. Travelled in Canada; 1905 Rhodesia (Zimbabwe), 1906 SA.

Exhibitions 1880–1903 exhibited in London; 1983 King George VI Art Gallery, Port Elizabeth, Edmund Caldwell's Drawings for *Jock of the Bushveld* Exhibition.

Represented William Fehr Collection, Cape Town.

References *Jock — The Art of Edmund Caldwell*, 1978, text by Jan Meiring & *The Art of Edmund Caldwell*, volume II, text by Dr F R Bradlow, 1982, Frank Read Press, Mazoe, Zimbabwe; SAA; AMC2; SESA; Benezit; DBA; BSAK; SA Art; AASA; *De Kat* December/January 1986.

CALINIKOS Constantine (Costa)

Born 1928.

Both a painter and a sculptor of landscapes, portraits, still life, figures, boats and buildings. Works in oil, watercolour, pastel, crayon and wood.

Studies Pretoria Technical College; 1957 South Kensington School of Art and the Charing Cross School of Art, London.

Exhibitions Has participated in group exhibitions from the late 1950s in the UK and in SA; 1953 Stuttaford Galleries, Johannesburg, first of several solo exhibitions; 1982 Athens, Greece, solo exhibition.

References BSAK 1; *Artlook* December 1970; *Gallery* Autumn 1982.

CALITZ Rehann

Born 1961 Upington, Cape Province.

A pastel artist of modern/contemporary landscapes. Additionally works in mixed media.

Profile An army artist and police layout artist.

Exhibition 1987 Pretoria, group exhibition.

CALLINICOS Athanasios Peter (Naso)

Born 1945 Johannesburg.

A sculptor in stone, wood and mixed media of figures.

Studies Prior to 1966 had a number of lessons under Cecil Skotnes (qv); 1966–67 The Visual Arts Research Centre, Johannesburg, under George Boys (qv); 1967–69 Farnham School of Art, England, under Ben Franklin; 1969–70 Atelier 63, The Netherlands, under Jan Dibbits; 1971 studied architecture at the University of the Witwatersrand.

Profile 1966–67 lived in Greece.

Exhibitions 1976 Market Theatre, Johannesburg, solo exhibition; he has participated in several group exhibitions from 1982 in Zimbabwe and SA.

References BSAK 1 & 2.

CAMERON Isa

Born Pietermaritzburg.
A painter of landscapes, portraits and figure groups. Worked in oil and watercolour. A graphic artist producing woodcuts.
Studies Royal College and Chelsea School of Art, London, and in Paris.
Profile A member of the NSA and the Transvaal Art Society. Lived in Natal and Johannesburg.
Exhibitions Exhibited with the Royal Portrait Society in London; participated in group exhibitions from 1930, frequently exhibiting with the SA Academy, the Orange Free State Society of Arts and Crafts, and in 1931 with the Everard Group at the Herbert Evans Gallery, Johannesburg; 1945 Gainsborough Gallery, Johannesburg, solo exhibition; 1951 Durban, joint exhibition with Kathleen Anderson (qv).
References DBA; BSAK; AASA.

CAMPBELL Laraine

Born 1941 Pretoria.
An artist producing drawings in pencil, charcoal, pastel and gouache of figures, portraits and of still life. A graphic artist making etchings and monoprints.
Studies 1968–71 Natal Technical College, under Andrew Verster (qv).
Profile 1981 a co-founder of the Parktown Life Drawing Group. 1968–74 drew illustrations for *The Sunday Tribune*, Durban; 1970–72 for *Living* magazine, Durban and in 1985 for *Calligraphy Idea Exchange*, USA. A trained flautist.
Exhibitions She has participated in many group exhibitions from 1972 in SA; 1975 Lidchi Gallery, Johannesburg, solo exhibition; 1984 Crake Gallery, Johannesburg, joint exhibition with Cecily Grant (qv) and Donna White (qv); 1984 SAAA Gallery, Pretoria, joint exhibition of etchings with Elizabeth Harington (qv), Cecily Grant (qv) and Pamela Kleinot.

CAMPBELL Thelma Martha

Born 1900 Cape Town.
A painter of birds, butterflies and fish.
Profile A staff member of the Transvaal Museum, Pretoria. Drew the frontispiece for *Fishes of Southern Africa* by J L B Smith in 1949. One of the illustrators of *Die Groot Woordeboek*, published in 1950. Drew the bird plates of the 1953 SA Airways Calendar. 1958–60 illustrator of volumes 1 and 3, and co-illustrator, with Dick Findlay (qv) of volume 2, of *Birds of the Kruger National Park*. Illustrated *The Lepidoptera of South Africa* by L Vari, 1962.
References SAA; SESA; BSAK; AASA.

CAMPBELL-QUINE Nina (née Arbuckle)

Born 1911 near Pretoria.
An extremely versatile artist, painting, sculpting and producing graphics.
Studies 1928 won the Jane Plotz Scholarship to the Witwatersrand Technical College, studied under Professor A Winter Moore (qv) and Professor F W Armstrong (qv).

Profile Works in enamel and has designed jewellery, furniture and fabric. A member of the Society of Artist Enamellers of Great Britian. A number of illustrations for books and periodicals. 1945–72 involved in theatre productions, designing sets and costumes and in lighting and choreography. 1958 taught art at St Peter's School, Johannesburg; teaches art privately. 1911–22 lived in the UK. From 1961 she has travelled to Greece, Italy and Turkey, and in 1974 to the Far East.

Exhibitions She has participated in numerous group exhibitions from 1929 in SA, Italy, the USA, Japan and the UK; 1954 New York, USA, first of 12 solo exhibitions held in SA, New York and in London, England; 1956 Quadrennial Exhibition.

Represented Hester Rupert Art Museum, Graaff-Reinet; Pietersburg Collection; SA National Gallery, Cape Town.

References Who's Who in Art; Shirley Faith Hooper, *Nina Observed*, 1978, Aspiral Press, SA; Art SA; SAA; 20C SA Art; AMC6; BSAK; AASA.

CANITZ George Paul

Born 1874 Leipzig, Germany.

Died 1959 Stellenbosch, Cape Province.

Resided in SA from 1909, settled in the Stellenbosch area in 1910.

A painter of landscapes, animals and portraits of women and SA politicians. Worked in oil and pastel.

Studies Saxon Academy, Dresden, and in Paris, Italy and The Netherlands.

Profile A member of the SA Society of Artists. From 1925 a wine farmer at Muratie, Koelenhof, near Stellenbosch. Canitz painted in his free time and lectured in art at the University of Stellenbosch. 1909–12 travelled in SWA/Namibia, Angola and in the Kalahari Desert. Travelled extensively in Natal and the Orange Free State.

Exhibitions 1924 participated in the British Empire Exhibition, Wembley, London, England; participated in several group exhibitions in SA from 1925; 1935 Darter Art Gallery, Cape Town, thought to have been the first of several solo exhibitions held in Cape Town; 1950 exhibited 24 landscapes in London, Paris and in Hamburg.

Represented National Museum, Bloemfontein; Pretoria Art Museum; SA Cultural History Museum, Cape Town; University of Stellenbosch; Willem Annandale Art Gallery, Lichtenburg.

References SAA; DSAB; SESA; BSAK 1 & 2; AASA.

CANTRELL Arthur Edward

Born 1917 Kalaw, Upper Burma.

Resided in SA from 1935.

A self-taught painter of abstracts. Works in oil. His early works, in both watercolour and oil, were of Johannesburg street scenes. A sculptor in metal.

Profile In 1959 published a portfolio, entitled *Johannesburg Sketch Book*. Travelled extensively in Europe and to Madeira, the Caribbean islands, the Middle East and throughout Africa, painting and exhibiting in each place. Married to Fayette Varney (qv).

Exhibitions 1953 SAAA Gallery, Bloemfontein, first of over 20 solo exhibitions held in SA, London, Madeira, Jamaica, Spain and Portugal; he has participated in numerous group exhibitions from 1954; 1964 Quadrennial Exhibition.
Represented Africana Museum, Johannesburg; National Museum, Bloemfontein; William Humphreys Art Gallery, Kimberley.
Public Commission With Neville Varney (qv), a Crucifixion Triptych in wood and metal for the Chapel Amador, Funchal, Madeira.
References SAA; AMC2; BSAK 1 & 2; AASA.

CANTY David

Born   1870 Mitchell's Town, Cork, Republic of Ireland.
Died   1936 Pretoria.
Resided in SA from 1889.
A painter of landscapes and occasionally of figures. Worked in watercolour.
Studies Cork Art School, Republic of Ireland.
Profile Most of his pictures were painted in the Pietersburg and Piet Retief areas where he lived from 1903 to 1921. In 1922 he moved to Pretoria. A Government stock-inspector.
Exhibitions Held solo exhibitions in Pretoria.
Represented Africana Museum, Johannesburg; University of Pretoria.
References Pict Art; AMC2; DSAB; Pict Afr; BSAK; AASA.

CAREY

Psuedonym of Marjorie Eileen Wycliffe Thompson, later Mrs J B Madden, used in order to conceal the fact that she was female.
Born   1906 Middelburg, Transvaal.
Painted portraits.
Studies Winchester School of Art, England, under Walter Bayes (1869–1956).
Profile Spent her childhood in England, returning to SA in 1928. Worked for various newspapers, mainly as a cartoonist, but also as an illustrator and advertising designer. A former Secretary of the Friday Club. Worked in both Durban and Johannesburg until her marriage in 1933.
Exhibitions Participated in group exhibitions in Durban and Johannesburg.
Represented Africana Museum, Johannesburg.
References AMC6; SASSK.

CAREY Margaret Jean Brown (Mrs B Stead)

Born   1901 Scotland.
Resided in SA from 1925.
A painter of landscapes and figures. Worked in watercolour and oil.
Studies 1924–25 Glasgow School of Art, Scotland.
Profile A member of the NSA. Lived mainly in Natal.
Exhibitions Participated in group exhibitions from 1925 in SA.
Public Commission 1936 commissioned by the National Monuments Council to portray Dingaanskraal, Natal.
References BSAK 1 & 2; AASA.

CARGILL Jillian

Born 1953 Durban.

A painter and graphic artist of portraits, genre and figures. Works in oil, acrylic, ink and in various graphic media, particularly woodcuts.

Studies 1971–73 Natal Technical College, under Andrew Verster (qv), Paul Stopforth (qv), Gavin Younge (qv) and Patrick O'Connor (qv).

Profile 1973–74 a part-time lecturer at the Natal Technical College; 1984–85 an associate member of the Johannesburg Art Foundation, where she lectures. 1985 a part-time teacher at King David High School, Johannesburg. A keen photographer, who in 1979–82 was chief photographer on the *Financial Mail*; her photographs have also been used in other periodicals including *Leadership*. 1975–76 lived in England; 1976–77 in Amsterdam; 1977 in Israel; 1978–79 in Amsterdam and Brazil.

Exhibitions She has participated in many art and photographic exhibitions from 1973 in SA; 1974 Walsh Marais Gallery, Durban, solo exhibition.

CARR John Denzil

Born 1916 Germiston, Transvaal.

A sculptor of portraits and a painter of landscapes, still life and flowers. Works in clay, metal, oil, watercolour and pencil.

Profile 1946–47 a member of the Sale Art Society, England; 1946–47 a member of the Manchester Graphic Club, England. From 1963 Chairman of the Tree Society of Southern Africa.

Exhibitions He has participated in several group exhibitions from 1946 in the UK and SA.

Publications by Carr The South African Acacias, 1976, Conservation Press, Johannesburg; *Combretaceae in Southern Africa*, 1987, Tree Society of Southern Africa, Johannesburg.

CARRUTHERS Walter Edward Royden (Roy)

Born 1938 Port Elizabeth.

A painter and graphic artist of still life and figures. Works in oil, acrylic, watercolour, gouache, ink, wash, pencil, charcoal and in various graphic media. A sculptor working in bronze and wood. 1978 "Smoker Series".

Studies 1955–56 Port Elizabeth Technical College, under Stanley Field (qv) and Joan Wright (qv), where he won a bronze medal in 1956.

Profile Until 1974 worked in advertising. 1975 lectured at the School of Visual Arts in New York, USA. Lives in the USA.

Exhibitions He has participated in group exhibitions from 1969 in France, the USA, Switzerland and the UK; 1975 Galeria de Las Americas, Puerto Rico, first of six solo exhibitions held in The Americas; 1982–83 King George VI Art Gallery, Port Elizabeth, Johannesburg Art Gallery, Pretoria Art Museum and Durban Art Gallery, Retrospective Exhibition.

Represented The Fine Art Museum of San Fransisco, California, USA; King George VI Art Gallery, Port Elizabeth; Magnus Museum, Berkeley, California; University of North Carolina, Greensboro, USA; University of Wyoming, Laramie, USA; Wichita State University, Kansas, USA.
References Hunter Nesbit (qv), *Roy Carruthers*, 1982, Retrospective Exhibition Catalogue; *Gallery* Summer 1984. Numerous overseas publications.

CARTER Beatrice Orchard

Born 1889 King William's Town, Cape Province.
Died 1939 Cape Town.
A painter of flowers.
Studies Cape Town School of Art.
Profile 1926–39 appointed artist at the Bolus Herbarium. Co-illustrator, with Mary Page (qv), of *The Genera of The Mesembryanthemaceae* written by H Herre, published in 1971 in Cape Town.
Exhibition 1966 Kirstenbosch, Cape Town, Botanical Exhibition.
Reference AASA.

CARTER Sydney

Born 1874 Enfield, Middlesex, England.
Died 1945 Harrismith, Orange Free State.
Resided in SA from 1923.
A painter of landscapes, generally incorporating trees, and of portraits. Worked in oil and gouache. A cartoonist.
Studies 1889 Buckhurst Hill Art School, England; 1890–95 Walthamstow School of Art, London, gaining an Art Teachers Certificate; 1896 National Art Training School, London; 1897–99 Royal College of Art, London, where he was awarded a British Institute Scholarship.
Profile A member of the London Sketch Club and the Johannesburg Sketch Club. 1924 elected a Fellow of the Cape Town Society of Artists; 1925 Vice-President of the Orange Free State Society of Arts and Crafts. 1927 began teaching at the Witwatersrand Technical College. Illustrated, in a similar style to that of Arthur Rackham, editions of works by authors such as Charles Dickens, Jane Austen and Charlotte Brontë. In SA illustrated books by Dorothea Fairbridge, including the well-known *Skiddle*. Travelled extensively in SA. Son of the artist Richard Carter.
Exhibitions Participated in several group exhibitions from 1894 in London, Paris and SA; held numerous solo exhibitions throughout SA; 1949 Gainsborough Gallery, Johannesburg, Commemorative Exhibition; 1974 Pretoria Art Museum, Commemorative Exhibition.
Awards 1890 Bronze Medal for Drawing from the Antique; 1898 the Gilbert Garrett Prize for Landscape.

Represented Africana Museum, Johannesburg; Albany Museum, Grahamstown; Ann Bryant Gallery, East London; Durban Art Gallery; Johannesburg Art Gallery; National Museum, Bloemfontein; Pretoria Art Museum; SA National Gallery, Cape Town; University of Pretoria; William Humphreys Art Gallery, Kimberley.

Public Commissions 1936 five landscape murals in Jeppe Street Post Office, Johannesburg. 1938 two murals in Cape Town Post Office.

Publications by Carter Wrote and illustrated *The Wonderful Adventures of Mr Fox*, *Pinkie and Pearl*, *Mr and Mrs Elephant's Golden Wedding* and *The Walrus and The Jabaru*.

References Elizabeth Carter (his widow), *Sydney Carter*, 1948, The Swan Press, Johannesburg; Collectors' Guide; SAA; SADNB; 20C SA Art; AMC2; DSAB; SESA; SSAP; Benezit; DBA; BSAK 1 & 2; Enc S'n A; SA Art; 3Cs; AASA; LSAA.

CATHERINE Norman Clive

Born 1949 East London.

An artist of genre, landscapes, figures and animals. Works in oil, acrylic, watercolour, gouache, ink, wood, fibreglass, airbrush, wire, metal, "found objects" and in various graphic media.

Studies 1967–69 East London Technical College, under Jack Lugg (qv).

Profile 1973 began collaboration on Fook Island concept with Professor Walter Battiss (qv). 1949–70 lived in East London, thereafter in the Transvaal. 1977 visited the USA and Europe, 1979 and 1980 visited the USA. Between 1982 and 1986 spent a total of two years working in New York and Los Angeles, USA.

Exhibitions He has participated in numerous group exhibitions from 1969 held throughout SA and in Italy, France, Switzerland, the UK, West Germany and the USA; 1969 Herbert Evans Gallery, Johannesburg, first of 19 solo exhibitions held in SA, SWA/Namibia, The Netherlands and the USA; 1979 Rand Afrikaans University, Retrospective Exhibition 1969–79; 1981 Republic Festival Exhibition; 1985 Cape Town Triennial; 1985 Tributaries, touring SA and West Germany; 1987 and 1988 Johannesburg Art Gallery, Vita Art Now.

Awards 1973 Cambridge Shirt Award, Art SA Today, Durban; 1981 Graphic Award, Republic Festival Exhibition.

Represented Ann Bryant Gallery, East London; Boksburg Town Council Collection; Durban Art Gallery; Johannesburg Art Gallery; Pretoria Art Museum; Rand Afrikaans University; Sandton Municipal Collection; SA National Gallery, Cape Town; Tatham Art Gallery, Pietermaritzburg; University of Natal; University of South Africa; University of Stellenbosch; University of the Witwatersrand; Walter Battiss (qv) Museum, Somerset East, Cape Province.

Reproductions by Catherine Numerous reproductions including in 1975 a self-portrait lithograph; 1977 eight coloured postcards published with Gallery 21, Johannesburg; 1978 produced "Black Face" serigraph; 1980 11 original lithographs were published by Broederstroom Press, Transvaal; 1981 "Cactus Garden", a lithograph published by Mirage Editions, Los Angeles, USA; 1983 "Identikit" lithograph published; 1984 four original lithographs published by Broederstroom Press, Transvaal.

Publications by Catherine Last Letters from the Wilderness, with poetry by Ramsay MacKay, 1978, Johannesburg Records; *Memo Book*, with Alan Cameron, to be published 1988–89.
References BSAK 1 & 2; SA Art; *The Airbrush Book*, 1980, Orbis Publishers, London; 3Cs; AASA; *The Advanced Airbrush Book*, 1984, Orbis Publishers, London; LSAA; *Artlook* November 1969 & June 1972; *Habitat* no 1, 1973, no 12, 1975 & no 21, 1976; *Deluxe* vol 1 no 1, 1977, London; Rand Afrikaans University Retrospective Exhibition Catalogue 1979; *Style* December 1980; *IDEA 164* volume 29, January 1981, Tokyo; *Sun Magazine* February 1984; *De Kat* July 1987.

CATLIN Gail Deborah

Born 1948 Johannesburg.
A painter of landscapes, portraits and figures. Works in mixed media. A creator of assemblages.
Studies Cape Town Institute of Fine Art.
Profile A member of the Artists Guild, Cape Town, and the SAAA.
Exhibitions She has participated in several group exhibitions from 1979, one of which was held in London; 1979 SAAA Gallery, Cape Town, first of five solo exhibitions; 1981 Republic Festival Exhibition; 1982 Cape Town Triennial.
Represented Durban Art Gallery; Johannesburg Art Gallery; Pietersburg Collection; SA National Gallery, Cape Town; University of Stellenbosch.
References AASA; *Gallery* Spring 1983.

CATTANEO Giuseppe

Born 1929 Milan, Italy.
Resided in SA from 1954.
A painter, sculptor and graphic artist of wide-ranging subjects. Works in oil, acrylic, watercolour, gouache, ink, wash, pencil, charcoal, various graphic media, stone, ciment fondu, plastic, metal and steel. 1970–71 produced a portfolio of six lithographs with social comments; 1981–82 a series on London Wharves.
Studies 1947–52 Scuola Superiore d'Arte del Castello, Milan, under A Piantini, S Labo and F Fedeli, where gained a Diploma. 1948–53 Scuola Serale del Nudo, Brera Academy, Milan, under Aldo Salvadori (*b*.1905); 1952–53 Accademia di Belle Arti di Brera, Milan, under Aldo Carpi (1886–1973) and Marino Marini (*b*.1901).
Profile 1960 a member of the SA Council of Artists in Johannesburg. 1963 a founder member of the Amadlozi Group. 1961–63 a part-time instructor; 1963–66 a full-time instructor; 1966–72 a part-time tutor, 1974–80 a full-time lecturer and from 1980 a senior lecturer in the Fine Arts Department, University of the Witwatersrand. From 1960 a judge on a number of South African art competitions and exhibitions. 1959–60 co-designer of the Government Pavilion, Milner Park, Johannesburg; 1962 commissioned to do a stage set for "The Red

Silk Umbrella" by J A Brown, in Johannesburg; 1962 designed St Peter's College Church, Alice, Cape Province (Ciskei); 1963 designed the stage set for "Romeo & Jeannette" by J Anouilh, in Johannesburg. A potter and stained glass artist. 1961 study travels to Italy, Switzerland, Austria, Germany, The Netherlands, England and France; 1980 sabbatical leave in Italy, France, England and the USA.

Exhibitions From 1949 he has participated in over 70 group exhibitions in Italy, Zimbabwe, America, France, Brazil, England, Monaco, West Germany, Taiwan, China, Denmark, Austria, Portugal, Israel and SA; 1956 Whippman's Gallery, Johannesburg, first of eight solo exhibitions held in Johannesburg and Durban; 1960 and 1964 Quadrennial Exhibitions; 1977 University of the Witwatersrand, Retrospective Exhibition; 1985 Tributaries, touring SA and West Germany; 1986 Amadlozi Art Centre, Johannesburg, joint exhibition with Edoardo Villa (qv).

Awards 1960 Artist of the Year, Artists of Fame and Promise; 1961 awarded honourable mention, Paris Biennial; 1966 Merit Award, SA Breweries Competition.

Represented Durban Art Gallery; Johannesburg Art Gallery; Pretoria Art Museum; Rand Afrikaans University; Sandton Municipal Collection; SA National Gallery, Cape Town; University of Natal; University of Pretoria; University of South Africa; University of the Witwatersrand.

Public Commissions 1967 six panels, Transvaal Room, President Hotel, Johannesburg; 1968 ceramic mural, Hyde Park Shopping Centre, Johannesburg.

References Art SA; SAA; 20C SA Art; SESA; SSAP; BSAK 1 & 2; Our Art 3; SA Art; Oxford Companion to 20C Art (under SA); 3Cs; AASA; LSAA; *Fontein* vol 1 no 1, 1960 & vol 1 no 3, 1960; *SA Panorama* September 1972; *Artlook* June 1973 & August/September 1974; *Habitat* no 15, 1975 & no 26, 1977.

CHAIT Laurence Anthony

Born 1943 Johannesburg.
A self-taught sculptor of portraits and abstracts. Works in stone, ciment fondu and bronze.

Profile 1975 a founder member of the Medical Art Society. A plastic and reconstructive surgeon.

Exhibitions He has participated in several group exhibitions from 1975 with the Medical Art Society; 1975 Lidchi Gallery, Johannesburg, first of three solo exhibitions.

Public Commissions 1977 portrait bust of Professor D J du Plessis, University of the Witwatersrand; 1984 and 1985 busts of Ester Adler, Professors Craib and A J Orensten, History of Medicine Museum, Johannesburg.

CHAIT Thelma

Born 1918 Bloemfontein.
A graphic artist of geo- figures and forms. During the 1950s and early 1960s painted, also draws in pen and ink. Her early graphic work was in black and white, and she began to use colour in 1965. *c.*1971 a series on "Man's Search for Meaning". Has produced numerous portfolios.

Studies 1935–40 architecture at the University of Cape Town, gaining a BA Architecture; 1954–57 part-time at the Michaelis School of Fine Art.
Profile Illustrated the book *Hello Up There*, with text by Esther Adar and Hindy Rutenberg, 1968, Howard Timmins, Cape Town. Lives in Cape Town.
Exhibitions 1957 SAAA, Cape Town, first of several solo exhibitions held in SA and in the USA in 1981; she has participated in group exhibitions from 1960 in SA, West Germany and the USA; 1964 Quadrennial Exhibition; 1979 National Museum, Bloemfontein, joint exhibition with Cecil Skotnes (qv), Olivia Scholnick (qv) and Lorraine Edelstein (qv); 1979 SAAA Gallery, Pretoria, joint exhibition with Olivia Scholnick (qv); 1981 Rand Afrikaans University, Solo Prestige Exhibition of Drawings.
Represented Hester Rupert Art Museum, Graaff-Reinet; Pietersburg Collection; Pretoria Art Museum; Rand Afrikaans University; SA National Gallery, Cape Town; University of Cape Town.
References Register SA & SWA; SAP&D; BSAK 1 & 2; SA Art; AASA; *Artlook* December 1966; *Lantern* July 1978.

CHAMBERS Richard

Born 1958 Boksburg, Transvaal.
A painter/sculptor working in oil and acrylic with ready-made objects. Often uses a spraygun or airbrush. His work is figurative with use of letterism. Two large series to date: 1980–81 "Colour classification of people in SA re Population Registration Act"; 1985–86 "SA, a gun/kill/maim/hate/bizarre/comical society".
Studies 1976–78 University of the Witwatersrand, under Giuseppe Cattaneo (qv), Robert Hodgins (qv), Paul Stopforth (qv) and Malcolm Payne (qv), gaining a BA(FA); 1979 University of the Witwatersrand, under Ulrich Louw (qv), where awarded a Higher Diploma in Education (Primary Grade); 1980 University of the Witwatersrand, under Professor Alan Crump, Paul Stopforth (qv) and Giuseppe Cattaneo (qv), attaining a BA(FA)(Hons).
Profile 1981 and 1984–85 taught art at Waverley Girls High School, Johannesburg. During his National Service in 1982 he illustrated a number of SA Defence Force publications.
Exhibitions He has participated in several group exhibitions from 1978 in Johannesburg; 1981 Olivetti Gallery, Johannesburg, first solo exhibition; 1987 Johannesburg Art Gallery, Vita Art Now.

CHAMPION David

Born 1946 East London.
A painter of landscapes and of organic abstractions. Works in oil and enamel.
Studies 1966–69 Rhodes University, gaining a Diploma in Fine Art.
Profile 1966–79 a member of the Grahamstown Group.
Exhibitions He has participated in group exhibitions in SA from the 1960s.
Reference AASA.

CHANDLER Jeff

Born 1947 Queenstown, Cape Province.
A painter and sculptor of figures. Works in oil, pencil, charcoal and ciment fondu.
Studies 1967–70 Rhodes University, under Professor Brian Bradshaw (qv); 1975–76 Rhodes University, under Professor Brian Bradshaw (qv), gaining an MFA.
Profile 1987 a member of D'ARTS; from 1977 a lecturer at the Natal Technikon.
Exhibitions He has participated in many group exhibitions from 1968 in the Eastern Cape and Natal; 1984 Café Geneve Gallery, Durban, solo exhibition.

CHAPMAN Grant Wayne

Born 1965 Johannesburg.
A painter of landscapes, still life and figures. Works in oil, watercolour, ink, pencil and charcoal.
Studies 1981 Johannesburg Art Foundation, under Bill Ainslie (qv).
Exhibitions He has participated in several group exhibitions in the Transvaal.

CHAPMAN Nigel

Born 1908 Weenen, Natal.
A self-taught painter of landscapes, still life, seascapes and wildlife. Works in watercolour and occasionally in oil.
Exhibitions He has participated in numerous group exhibitions in SA, the UK, West Germany and Italy; 1964 Quadrennial Exhibition.
References Register SA & SWA; AASA.

CHAPPELL Alan Colwill

Born 1935 Croydon, Surrey, England.
A painter of wildlife and landscapes. Works in oil, pencil, charcoal and conté.
Studies 1965 Croydon Art College, Surrey, England.
Profile 1965 a member of the Dar es Salaam Art Society. A number of illustrations for *The Standard Newspaper*, Dar es Salaam, Tanzania. 1981 issued a limited edition print in Kenya. His paintings have been used on numerous calendars and cards. 1960–70 lived in Tanzania; 1970–81 in Kenya; from 1982 in SA.
Exhibitions He has participated in numerous group exhibitions from 1964 in Tanzania, Kenya and SA; 1975 Nairobi, Kenya, solo exhibition.

CHARLESWORTH Geoffrey Terence

Born 1930 Durban.
A painter of landscapes, portraits, still life, seascapes, genre and figures. Works in oil, watercolour, ink, wash and pencil. A muralist.

Studies 1948–50 Natal Technical College, under Cecil Todd (qv), where he was awarded the 1947 Arthur May Scholarship, the 1948 Leyell Taylor Scholarship and the 1950 Emma Smith Overseas Scholarship; 1951–53 Camberwell Art School, London, under Gilbert Spencer (*b*.1891).

Profile 1954–66 a member of the NSA. 1955–65 a member of the Advisory Committee of Durban Art Gallery. Travelled throughout SA and to Europe in 1970 and 1972.

Exhibitions He has participated in numerous group exhibitions from 1949 held in SA and the UK; 1954 Van Riebeeck Galleries, Durban, first of over 30 solo exhibitions held throughout SA; 1960 Quadrennial Exhibition; 1966 Durban Art Gallery, solo exhibition; 1981 Republic Festival Exhibition.

Award 1953 P W Storey Award.

Represented Ann Bryant Gallery, East London; Durban Art Gallery; SA National Gallery, Cape Town.

Public Commission 1955 portrait of Mr Lewis, retiring Registrar of the Institute of Artists, Johannesburg.

References Art SA; SAA; BSAK; AASA.

CHASE Gillian Lesley

Born 1944 Durban.

A painter of landscapes, seascapes, still life, portraits, figures, wildlife and abstracts. Works in oil, acrylic, watercolour, gouache and ink.

Studies *c*.1961–63 Johannesburg School of Art, under Andrew Verster (qv), George Boys (qv) and Joyce Leonard (qv).

Profile 1971 taught fabric printing and painting with the Peace Corps at Mochudi, Botswana; 1972 taught at the Natal Technical College. From 1985 she has been making pots and clay sculptures. 1968 lived in Rome and painted portraits, also spent six months in Malta.

Exhibitions She has participated in many group exhibitions held in SA from 1963.

CHEALES Richard

Born 1922 New Agatha, near Tzaneen, Northern Transvaal.

A painter of landscapes, seascapes, portraits, still life and figures. Drawings of buildings in Johannesburg, sketches of artists. A series of Lesotho scenes. Works in watercolour and ink.

Studies Whilst still at high school took lessons from Joy Krause (qv).

Profile In 1961 "Basuto Market" was reproduced in the SATOUR Calendar. In 1986 he produced a series of paintings of Johannesburg to mark its centenary year. A journalist and art critic for various periodicals and Johannesburg newspapers, 1963–68 for *Die Vaderland*, 1968–76 for *The Star*, and 1976–87 for *The Citizen*. Has lived in Johannesburg since 1938.

Exhibitions He has participated in numerous group exhibitions in SA; 1944 Gainsborough Galleries, Johannesburg, first of numerous solo exhibitions.

Represented Africana Museum, Johannesburg; Pietersburg Collection.
References SAA; 20C SA Art; AASA; *South Africana* 22 June 1961; *Artlook* November 1969.

CHEMINAIS Gaby

Born 1960 Cape Town.
A sculptor working in ceramics and mixed media.
Studies 1981 attained a Diploma in Fine Art from the Michaelis School of Fine Art.
Exhibitions 1982 Cape Town Triennial; 1985 Market Gallery, Johannesburg, joint exhibition with Angela Ferreira (qv) and Louise Sherman (qv); 1985 Cape Town Triennial.
Public Commissions Mural for Strandfontein Pavilion, Cape Province; tiles for a pedestrian underpass in Durban.

CHIDELL-BRABY Rosalind

Born 1919 Durban.
Both a painter and sculptor of landscapes, seascapes, portraits, still life, wildlife and abstracts. Works in oil, watercolour, pencil, charcoal and ciment fondu. She has painted numerous portraits in watercolour.
Studies 1938–39 on a scholarship to the Natal Technical College, studying under Merlyn Evans (qv); 1970–73 sculpture under Mary Stainbank (qv).
Profile From 1981 an Associate of the WSSA and the Chairman of the Natal Branch in 1986. A member of the NSA and the Highway Art Group. From 1968 she has taught art privately. Visited SWA/Namibia in 1984/85 and 1986/87.
Exhibitions She has participated in over 80 group exhibitions from 1942 held throughout SA and in the UK and West Germany; Grassroots Gallery, Westville, Durban, solo exhibition.

CHONCO Linda Mfanafuthi

Born 1960 Ixopo, Natal.
A painter and graphic artist of landscapes, portraits, figures, still life, genre, wildlife and abstract pictures. Works in oil, acrylic, watercolour, ink, pencil and in various graphic media.
Studies Rorke's Drift Art Centre, under Jay Johnson, where gained a Diploma.
Exhibitions He has participated in several group exhibitions from 1983 in SA and Swaziland.

CHRISTIAN Malcolm

Born 1950 Durban.
A printmaker, creating silkscreens and etchings.
Studies Natal Technical College; Croydon College of Design, Surrey, England; University of Natal.
Profile A photographer. Lectured in printmaking at the University of Natal.

Exhibitions He has participated in group exhibitions in SA, the UK, West Germany and the USA; 1982 Cape Town Triennial; 1983 NSA Gallery, Durban, joint exhibition with Terence King (qv); 1985 Tributaries, touring SA and West Germany.
Represented Durban Art Gallery; Johannesburg Art Gallery; Tatham Art Gallery, Pietermaritzburg.
Reference AASA.

CHRISTIE Isabella (Ella)
Born *c.*1865 Aberdeen, Scotland.
Died 1934.
A painter of portraits and landscapes. Worked in oil.
Studies In Edinburgh.
Profile Lived at Impolweni Mission. Married to Tom Everard, the brother-in-law of Bertha Everard (qv).
Exhibition 1888 group exhibition in Edinburgh.
References Natal Art; DBA; BSAK.

CHRISTIE Valerie Iris (née Olmesdahl)
Born 1928 Piet Retief, Transvaal.
A painter of landscapes, seascapes and still life. Works in watercolour.
Studies 1949–51 Witwatersrand Technical College, under James Gardner (qv); 1977 under Marjorie Bowen (qv) and Cynthia Ball (qv).
Profile From 1977 a member of the WSSA, becoming an Associate in 1981. From 1983 a member of the Brush and Chisel Club.
Exhibitions She has participated in many group exhibitions from 1978 held in SA, the UK, West Germany and Spain.

CHRISTOL Frédéric
Born 1850 Paris, France.
A painter of landscapes and portraits. Worked in oil and in ink.
Studies Under Jean-Léon Gérome (1824–1904) and Paul-Jean Flandrin (1811–1902) in Paris.
Profile 1882–1908 worked as a missionary in Basutoland (Lesotho). Additionally worked in Italy, Switzerland and Palestine.
Exhibitions Participated in group exhibitions 1874–80 at the Paris Salon.
Publications by Christol Au Sud de l'Afrique, 2nd edition 1900, Berger-Levrault, Paris and Nancy, France; *L'Art dans l'Afrique Australe*, 1911, Berger-Levrault, Paris and Nancy, France; *Vingt-six ans au Sud de l'Afrique*, 1930, Société des Missions Evangeliques, Paris.
References AMC2; Natal Art; Pict Afr; Benezit.

CHRISTOPHER Tinka
Born 1939 Grahamstown.
A self-taught sculptor of wild and domestic animals and of figures. Works in bronze. 1987 a series of Zodiac Signs. Several private commissions in SA.
Public Commission 1986 Toyota Equestrian Statue, Sandton, Johannesburg.

CHURCH Frieda (Mrs Lane)
Born 1901 Lady Grey, Cape Province.
A sculptor of wildlife. Works in ceramics.
Studies 1930–35 Michaelis School of Fine Art.
Profile 1936–43 a lecturer in pottery at the Michaelis School of Fine Art, Cape Town.
Represented SA National Gallery, Cape Town.
References SAP&S; SA Art.

CILLIERS Mathys Wilhelm Christiaan (Thys)
Born 1956 Kimberley, Cape Province.
A painter of landscapes, still life, seascapes, figures and abstract pictures. Works in oil, acrylic, watercolour, ink, wash, pencil and charcoal.
Studies 1975–78 University of Stellenbosch, under Professor Larry Scully (qv) and Louis Jansen van Vuuren (qv), gaining a BA in Creative Arts Education; 1984–87 part-time at the Port Elizabeth Technikon, under Leon de Bliquy (qv) and Hunter Nesbit (qv).
Profile A member of the EPSFA and the GAP Group. 1981–82 an art teacher at the Lawson Brown High School, Port Elizabeth; from 1983 a lecturer at the Port Elizabeth Technikon. 1982 designed a poster for the Pieter Fourie play "Mooi Maria" which was performed at the Port Elizabeth Opera House. Lived in Kimberley until 1973; 1973–78 in Cape Town; thereafter in Port Elizabeth. Visited SWA/Namibia.
Exhibitions 1982 EPSFA Gallery, Port Elizabeth, joint exhibition with Albert Heydenrych (qv); he has participated in many group exhibitions from 1983; 1986 Port Elizabeth Technikon, solo exhibition.

CILLIERS-BARNARD Bettie
Born 1914 Rustenburg, Transvaal.
A painter and graphic artist of portraits, still life, genre, figures and abstracts. Works in oil, watercolour, acrylic, mixed media, collaged canvas and in various graphic media.
Studies 1935–37 Pretoria Teachers Training College, where obtained a Transvaal Teachers Diploma; 1938–39 evening classes under Phyllis Gardner (qv), art evaluation under Dr Maria Stein-Lessing (1915–79); 1941–44 under the guidance of Madame Stradiot-Bougnet; 1948 Koninklijke Academie voor Schone Kunsten en de Hogere Instituten, Antwerp, Belgium (Opsomer School), and in Paris under André Lhote (1885–1962); 1956 in Paris under Stanley William Hayter (*b.*1901) and graphic art under Jean Pons (*b.*1913).

Profile From 1949 a member, and from 1968 an Honorary Life Member of the SAAA; from 1974 National Vice-President of the SAAA; from 1978 Chairman of the Art Section of the SA Women's Bureaux. 1939–43 an art lecturer at the Pretoria Teachers Training College; 1940–43 a part-time art teacher at the Children's Art Centre, Pretoria; 1975–85 an external examiner for Fine Arts at the University of Pretoria. 1969 "Symbols", a portfolio of 10 lithographs published by the Goodman Gallery, Johannesburg. A designer of tapestries. 1948 lived in Belgium and Paris, returned to Paris in 1956, 1960 when studied the art of tapestry, 1964, 1971, 1981 and 1985. 1964 made a study tour of Portugal and Spain. Visited the USA in 1981 and 1985.

Exhibitions 1946 MacFadyen Hall, Pretoria, first of over 50 solo exhibitions held in SA and in London and Paris; she has participated in group exhibitions from 1949 in SA, Zimbabwe, Italy, Switzerland, Brazil, The Netherlands, West Germany, Yugoslavia, Belgium, the USA, Portugal, Austria, Israel, Australia, Peru, Bolivia and Monaco; 1960 and 1964 Quadrennial Exhibitions; 1966 Pretoria Art Museum, joint exhibition with Joan Clare (qv); 1972 Goodman Gallery, Johannesburg, joint exhibition of tapestries with Cecil Skotnes (qv); 1974 SAAA Gallery, Pretoria, Prestige Exhibition; 1978 Van Wouw House, Pretoria, Retrospective Exhibition; 1981 Republic Festival Exhibition; 1984 University of Pretoria, Retrospective Exhibition; 1987 Taipei Fine Arts Museum, Taiwan, Prestige Exhibition.

Awards 1966 Gold Medal, Transvaal Academy; 1977 Merit Award, 21st Grand Prix International d'Art Contemporain, Monte Carlo; 1978 Medal of Honour for Painting, jointly with Leo Theron (qv), SA Akademie vir Wetenskap en Kuns; 1983 Decoration for Meritorious Services by the State President; 1985 Chancellor's Medal, University of Pretoria.

Represented Ann Bryant Art Gallery, East London; Hester Rupert Art Museum, Graaff-Reinet; King George VI Art Gallery, Port Elizabeth; National Museum, Bloemfontein; Potchefstroom Museum; Potchefstroom University for CHE; Pretoria Art Museum; Randfontein Municipal Collection; Sandton Municipal Collection; SA Akademie vir Wetenskap en Kuns; SA National Gallery, Cape Town; University of Natal; University of the Orange Free State; University of Pretoria; University of South Africa; University of Stellenbosch; University of the Witwatersrand; Willem Annandale Art Gallery, Lichtenburg; William Humphreys Art Gallery, Kimberley.

Public Commissions 1963 tapestry, Transvaal Provincial Administration Building, Pretoria; 1969 mural, Orange Free State Provincial Administration Building, Bloemfontein; 1972 mural, Jan Smuts Airport, Johannesburg; 1973 tapestry, Women's Residence, University of Pretoria; 1983 tapestry, the State Theatre, Pretoria.

References Our Art 2; Art SA; SAA; 20C SA Art; SAP&S; SAP&D; SESA; SSAP; BSAK 1 & 2; SA Art; Oxford Companion to 20C Art (under SA); 3Cs; AASA; LSAA; *Fontein* vol 1 no 3, 1960; *South Africana* 4 May 1961; *SA Panorama* April 1964, November 1971, June 1983, January 1984 & March 1984; *Artlook* March 1967, April 1967, October 1967, October 1970 & October/November 1974; *SA Art Calendar* October/November 1981 & March 1983; *De Kat* May 1987.

CLAERHOUT Frans Martin

Born 1919 Pittem, Belgium.
Resided in SA from 1946.
A self-taught painter in oil of landscapes and figures, also works in pastel, ink, pencil, charcoal. A graphic artist producing monotypes and linocuts. Several murals and sculptures. Began painting in 1957, mainly scenes around the mission stations in the Orange Free State, where he was a Catholic priest. An expressionistic painter with works characterised by warm colours, impasto and elongated human forms. Painted a large number of religious scenes and a number of series of pictures, including in 1983 the "Suncatcher" series and in 1984 "Christ and Other Persons".

Profile 1958–68 a founder member of the Bloemfontein Group. 1969 built the church of Thabo ya Kreste, Thaba 'Nchu, with the help of the sculptors Gerard de Leeuw (qv), Jef Claerhout (nephew) and the artists Michael Edwards (qv) and Jacob Tladi. 1948–60 lived in the Bloemfontein area; 1960–77 at Thaba 'Nchu and from 1977 in Tweespruit, Orange Free State. The Municipal Art Museum in Tweespruit, opened in 1982, was named after Frans Claerhout, Iris Ampenberger (qv) and Stefan Ampenberger (qv).

Exhibitions He has participated in group exhibitions from 1957 in SA and annually with the Orange Free State Arts Society; 1960 and 1964 Quadrennial Exhibitions; 1961 Johannesburg, first of numerous solo exhibitions held throughout SA and in Belgium, Canada, the USA and Germany; 1965 Kimberley, Kroonstad and Thaba 'Nchu with Iris Ampenberger (qv) and Stefan Ampenberger (qv); from 1968 regular exhibitions in Belgium; 1980 Emelgem, Belgium, "De Familie Claerhout", an exhibition of six members of the Claerhout family; 1981 Republic Festival Exhibition.

Award 1979 Flemish Order of t'Manneke Uit de Mane.

Represented The Belgian Government; Hester Rupert Art Museum, Graaff-Reinet; Johannesburg Art Gallery; National Museum, Bloemfontein; Potchefstroom University for CHE; Pretoria Art Museum; Rand Afrikaans University; SA National Gallery, Cape Town; University of Natal; University of the Orange Free State; University of the Witwatersrand; Willem Annandale Art Gallery, Lichtenburg; William Humphreys Art Gallery, Kimberley.

Public Commissions Murals in mission churches throughout SA, including in Bloemfontein, Edenburg, Potchefstroom, Schweizer-Reneke, Thaba 'Nchu and Witsieshoek.

Publications by Claerhout Kromdraai, 1982, Errol Marks, Pretoria; *Sketse en gedagtes vir die Simfonie van die Sonnevanger*, a booklet available from the Roman Catholic Mission Station, Tweespruit.

References F P Scott, L Roppe, P Rock, K Jonckheere, *Frans Claerhout*, 1975, Vriende Frans Claerhout Hasselt Belgie, Drukkerij-Uitgeverij Lannoo, Belgium; Leon Strydom, *Frans Claerhout—Catcher of the Sun*, 1983, Tafelberg, Cape Town; Art SA; SAA; 20C SA Art; SAP&S; SAP&D; BSAK 1 & 2; SA Art; 3Cs; AASA; LSAA; *Artlook* August 1968, August 1969 & June 1975; *SA Panorama* June 1981 & June 1983; *Frans Claerhout*, 1978, Pretoria Art Museum Catalogue.

CLANCEY Phillip Alexander

Born 1917 Langside, Glasgow, Scotland.
Resided in SA from 1950.
A painter of landscapes and wildlife, particularly birds. Works in gouache, ink, wash and oil.

Studies 1936–37 Glasgow School of Art, Scotland.

Profile An Honorary Life Member of the Southern African Ornithological Society. 1950–52 Head of the Natal Museum in Pietermaritzburg. 1952–82 Director of Durban Museum and Art Gallery. Illustrated *The Handbook of British Birds*, 1938, H F & G Witherby, London. A taxonomist. 1939–45 served with the British Army. 1979 travelled in Europe and the USA.

Exhibitions He has participated in several group exhibitions in SA and at the Read Stremmel Gallery in Texas, USA.

Awards In 1981 the University of Natal conferred the degree of Doctor of Science on Clancey in recognition of his contribution to and knowledge of African birds; a Gill Memorial Medallist; awarded an Honorary Fellowship of the American Ornithological Union.

Represented Durban Art Gallery.

Publications by Clancey Wrote and illustrated: *Birds of Natal and Zululand*, 1964, Oliver & Boyd, Edinburgh; *Gamebirds of Southern Africa*, 1967, Purnell & Son, Cape Town; *Handlist of the Birds of Southern Mozambique*, 1970–72 Inct. Cient. Moc., Lourenço Marques (Maputo), Mozambique; *Rare Birds of Southern Africa*, 1985, Winchester Press, Johannesburg.

References SAA; SESA; BSAK; SA Art; AASA.

CLARE Joan

Born 1925 Johannesburg.
A painter of abstract pictures. Worked in casein paint until 1959, thereafter in oil.

Studies 1942–45 Witwatersrand Technical College, under Maurice van Essche (qv); 1947–49 Regent Street Polytechnic, London and Camberwell Art School, London, under Victor Pasmore (*b*.1908) and John Buckland Wright (*b*.1897); part-time at the Anglo-French Art School, London; 1975–78 University of Pretoria.

Profile c.1954–57 a member of the Contemporary Art Society. Spent eight years teaching at the Transvaal Teachers Training College for Nursery School Teachers and two years at Damelin College, Johannesburg. 1950–52 lived in New Zealand. Presently living in England.

Exhibitions She has participated in many group exhibitions held in SA, the UK, Italy, Brazil and New Zealand; 1952 Johannesburg, first of six solo exhibitions held up to 1968; 1956 Quadrennial Exhibition; 1966 Pretoria Art Museum, joint Prestige Exhibition with Bettie Cilliers-Barnard (qv).

Represented Pretoria Art Museum; University of the Witwatersrand.

References SAA; 20C SA Art; SSAP; Our Art 3; 3Cs; AASA; *Artlook* July 1968.

CLARKE Brenda

Born 1917 Johannesburg.
A self-taught painter of botanical illustrations. Works in watercolour and ink.
Profile 1985 illustrated *The South African Herbal* by Eve Palmer, Tafelberg, Cape Town and *Making Pot Pourri in South Africa* by Mavis Skene, Acorn Books, Johannesburg. Mother of John Clarke (qv).

CLARKE John Frederick Casper

Born 1946 Salisbury, Rhodesia (Harare, Zimbabwe).
Resided in SA from 1947.
A pastel and etching artist of landscapes in a fantastical manner. Also works in oil, ink, pencil and charcoal. A large amount of work in black and white. From 1978 mainly a printmaker using the intaglio process. Several series: 1978–85 "Drive-In"; 1980 "Soutpan"; 1980–84 "Leopard Stone"; 1982 "Regalia"; 1984 "Barberton"; 1985 "Beacon"; 1986 "Gwandaland".
Studies University of the Witwatersrand, under Cecily Sash (qv), Giuseppe Cattaneo (qv), Robert Hodgins (qv) and Erica Berry (qv), gaining a BA(FA) in 1968; 1969 Johannesburg College of Education, where gained a Teachers Training Higher Diploma; 1981 University of Pretoria, under Professor Nico Roos (qv), where awarded an MA(FA).
Profile A member of the SAAA, the SA Society for Cultural History and the SAAAH. 1970–78 an art teacher at various high schools; from 1978–87 a senior lecturer in the Fine Arts Department of the University of Pretoria. 1987 began lecturing at the University of South Africa. 1950–58 lived at Barberton in the Eastern Transvaal; 1959–64 in Pretoria; 1965–76 in Johannesburg; from 1976 in Pretoria. Has travelled widely in Southern Africa. The husband of Jessica Bailey (qv) and son of Brenda Clarke (qv).
Exhibitions He has participated in numerous group exhibitions in SA and West Germany; 1975 SAAA Gallery, Pretoria, first of five solo exhibitions held in SA; 1982 Cape Town Triennial; 1983 Gowlett Gallery, Cape Town, joint exhibition with Annette Pretorius (qv); 1985 Cape Town Triennial; 1985 Tributaries, touring SA and West Germany; 1987 Gallery 21, Johannesburg, joint exhibition with Erna Bodenstein-Ferreira (qv), Johann Moolman (qv), Jacobus Kloppers (qv) and William Steyn (qv); 1988 SAAA Gallery, Pretoria, joint exhibition with Erna Bodenstein-Ferreira (qv), Jacobus Kloppers (qv) and William Steyn (qv).
Awards 1982 Rembrandt Bronze Medal, Cape Town Triennial; 1984 Prize winner–Print Making, Festival of African Art, University of Zululand.
Represented Durban Art Gallery; Pretoria Art Gallery; Rand Afrikaans University; SA National Gallery, Cape Town; Tatham Art Gallery, Pietermaritzburg; University of the Orange Free State; University of South Africa; University of Stellenbosch.
References AASA; LSAA; *Bulletin* Pretoria Art Museum, April 1983; *Habitat* no 56, 1983.

CLARKE Peter

Born 1929 Simonstown, Cape Province.

A painter and graphic artist of figures in landscapes and of interiors, social events, portraits, still life and seascapes. Works in acrylic, gouache, ink, wash, pencil and in various graphic media.

Studies 1961 Michaelis School of Fine Art, under Katrine Harries (qv) and Maurice van Essche (qv); 1962–63 Rijks Academie van Beeldende Kunsten, Amsterdam, The Netherlands, under Kuno Brinks; 1978–79 Atelier Nord, Oslo, Norway, graphics under Anne Breivik.

Profile A member of the SAAA; 1984 a founder member of the Vakalisa Art Associates. 1965 awarded Accademico Onorario of the Accademia Fiorentina delle Arti des Disegno, Florence, Italy; 1975 elected an Honorary Fellow in Writing, University of Iowa, USA; 1982 awarded a Diploma of Merit in Literature, Universita delle Arti, Italy; 1983 awarded a Diploma of Merit in Art, Accademia Italia; 1983 elected an Honorary Member of the Museum of African American Art, Los Angeles, USA; 1984 elected an Honorary Doctor of Literature, World Academy of Arts and Culture, Taipei, Taiwan. 1979 an art teacher at Kleinberg Primary School, Ocean View, Cape Province. From 1979 voluntarily teaches children in Ocean View. Has illustrated books published in SA, Sweden, Germany, Switzerland, Nigeria and the UK. From the 1950s has written short stories, essays and is an internationally recognised poet. 1962–63 and 1978–79 visited Europe. He has also visited the USA, Botswana and Israel.

Exhibitions He has participated in numerous group exhibitions from 1951 in SA, Yugoslavia, West Germany, Brazil, Austria, Italy, The Netherlands, Belgium, the USA, Argentina, Norway, Botswana, Japan, Switzerland and the UK; 1957 Golden City Post, Cape Town, first of numerous solo exhibitions held in SA, Nigeria, Kenya, Australia, the USA, Norway and Israel; 1982 National Gallery, Gaborone, Botswana, Exhibition of SA Art.

Represented Fisk University, Nashville, Tennessee, USA; King George VI Art Gallery, Port Elizabeth; Kunsthalle der Stadt, Bielefeld, West Germany; Library of Congress, Washington DC, USA; Museum of African American Art, Los Angeles, USA; Museum of Contemporary Art, Skopje, Yugoslavia; National Gallery, Gaborone, Botswana; Pretoria Art Museum; SA National Gallery, Cape Town; Stichting Afrika Museum, Bergen Dal, The Netherlands; University of South Africa; Willem Annandale Art Gallery, Lichtenburg; William Humphreys Art Gallery, Kimberley.

References Art SA: SAA; SAP&D; SESA; BSAK 1 & 2; 3Cs; AASA; LSAA; Echoes of African Art; *South Africana* April 1958; *SA Panorama* November 1961; *Personality* 21 May 1970; *Soul Motion III: Peter Clarke—South African Artist-Poet*, introduction by Professor David Driskey, 1973, Fisk University, Tennessee, USA, Exhibition Catalog.

CLARKSON Anthony Charles Vernon

Born 1943 Durban.

A painter of wildlife, particularly birds. Works in oil and gouache.

Studies 1961–66 University of Natal, where he gained a BA in Architecture.

Profile A practising architect in Ladysmith. Has illustrated a number of books, including *Where To See Birds*, published in 1979, *Natal Bird Atlas*, 1980, University of Natal Press, Durban and *Birds of The Drakensberg*, 1986, published by The Wildlife Society. Has travelled throughout SA and to Kenya, Tanzania and Mozambique on bird-watching holidays.
Exhibitions He has participated in several group exhibitions from 1983 in Natal and Johannesburg; 1985 Richards Bay, Natal, only solo exhibition.

CLAUDIUS Hendrik

Born *c.*1655 Breslau, Saxony, Germany.
Died After 1697.
Resided in SA 1682–*c.*1688 when he was banished to Mauritius and Batavia. It is thought he returned to the Cape, and was living there in 1693.
A painter of birds, animals and plants. Worked in watercolour.
Profile An apothecary sent in 1682 by the Dutch East India Company to the Cape to gather medicinal plants. He also collected for Baron von Rhude's herbarium. 1685 joined the Namaqualand expedition of Olof Bergh and kept a journal of the venture which he illustrated with the animals and plants he had seen. Illustrated *Voyage de Siam*, 1686, Paris and *Second Voyage*, 1689, Paris, both by Father Tachard, and *Rariorum Africanarum Plantarum* by Johannes Burman, 1838, Amsterdam, containing 100 botanical illustrations made at the Cape by Claudius. His work is reproduced in Simon van der Stel's *Journal of his Expedition to Namaqualand*, edited by G Waterhouse, 1932, Longmans, London; and in *The Journal of South African Botany*, volume 13, 1947.
Represented Africana Museum, Johannesburg; British Museum, London, England; Library of Trinity College, Dublin, Republic of Ireland; SA Library, Cape Town; University Library, Marburg, West Germany.
References Anna H Smith, *Claudius' Watercolours in the Africana Museum*, 1952, Africana Museum, Johannesburg; Pict Art; Afr Repos; SADNB; AMC2; DSAB; SESA; Pict Afr; BSAK 1 & 2; 3Cs; *ANN* xv 116, xiv 74 and xii 242.

CLAYTON Harry

Born 1864 Nottingham, England.
Died 1938 Paris.
Resided in SA 1885–1932.
A painter of landscapes and city scenes, specifically of Johannesburg. Worked in watercolour and oil. Drew many pencil sketches and portraits in pencil of his wife, Ida May Clayton (qv).
Profile An architect and surveyor responsible for a number of buildings in Johannesburg and Natal. 1907 Honorary Treasurer of the Society of Architects, SA Branch. 1910 elected to the council of the Association of Transvaal Architects. A Captain in WWI in the Royal Field Artillery. 1885 lived in Pietermaritzburg; 1888 in Barberton, Eastern Transvaal; 1889 in Johannesburg; 1899–1902 in Durban, then in Johannesburg until 1932, when he returned to the UK to Market Deeping, Lincolnshire. 1904 went overseas for six months, thereafter he went abroad every two years. Died in the British Hospital in Paris whilst returning to the UK from Italy.

Exhibitions Participated in group exhibitions from 1925 in SA; 1929 Herbert Evans Gallery, Johannesburg, solo exhibition.
Represented Africana Museum, Johannesburg.
References Anna H Smith, editor, *Sketches by Ida May Stone and Harry Clayton*, 1976, Ad Donker, Johannesburg; Afr Repos; AMC2.

CLAYTON Ida May (née Stone)

Born 1867 Gold Run, California, USA.
Died 1932 Nylstroom, Transvaal.
Resided in SA from *c*.1885.
A number of drawings of early Johannesburg and of mining camps at Spitzkop in 1886–87 and Barberton in 1887. Worked in watercolour, pastel and crayon.
Studies Possibly studied at an art school in California.
Profile 1902 a founder of the Martha Washington Club, Johannesburg. Worked with her husband Captain Harry Clayton (qv). 14 of her drawings were used in *Pictorial History of Johannesburg*, 1956, Juta & Company, Cape Town; nine of her illustrations were used in *A History of Johannesburg: The Early Years*, 1964, by G A Leyds .
Exhibition 1956 nine drawings exhibited at the Public Library, Johannesburg.
Represented Africana Museum, Johannesburg.
References Anna H Smith, editor, *Sketches by Ida May Stone and Harry Clayton*, 1976, Ad Donker, Johannesburg; AMC2; DSAB; Pict Afr; AASA.

CLOETE Phillip

Born 1936 Wynberg, Cape Town.
A self-taught painter of landscapes and seascapes. Works in watercolour and pastel.
Profile Limited edition prints and a number of calendars incorporating his work have been published.
Exhibitions He has participated in group exhibitions from 1980 and has held solo exhibitions from 1981.

CLOGG Nicky

Born 1924 Cheshire, England.
Resided in SA 1933–57 and from 1977.
An artist working in coloured pencils, oil, watercolour, wash and charcoal. A sculptor in ciment fondu.
Profile From 1979 a member of the Fish Hoek Art Society and from 1980 of the SAAA. 1957–77 lived in Rhodesia (Zimbabwe).
Exhibitions Has participated in numerous group exhibitions from 1980 in the Cape; 1984 Kirstenbosch Exhibition Hall, Cape Town, solo exhibition.

CLOUTS Anita
Born 1912 Cape Town.
A painter of abstract pictures. Works in oil.
Studies 1962 under Cecil Skotnes (qv); 1963–66 under Pearl Cohen (qv).
Profile A former professional dancer with African Theatres.
Exhibitions She has participated in several group exhibitions from 1966 in Johannesburg and Durban; 1969 Netherlands Bank (Nedbank), Johannesburg, first of five solo exhibitions held in Johannesburg and Durban.
References BSAK; *Artlook* December 1969 & April 1971.

CLUR Denise (née Barker)
Born 1933 Uitenhage, Cape Province.
A painter and graphic artist with wide-ranging subject matter. Works in many different media. A number of sculptures in clay.
Studies 1967 University of the Witwatersrand, under Erica Berry (qv) and Cecily Sash (qv); part-time courses in England, Durban and Johannesburg under a variety of artists.
Profile 1970 a member of the SAAA. A science teacher at various educational establishments. A number of illustrations for magazines, a writer of short stories and a potter.
Exhibitions She has participated in many group exhibitions from 1965 in SA.
Represented Potchefstroom University for CHE; Willem Annandale Art Gallery, Lichtenburg.
Reference AASA.

COETSEE Johan
Born 1939 Pietersburg, Northern Transvaal.
A painter of figures. Works in oil and acrylic.
Studies 1958–62 Pretoria Technikon, under Robert Hodgins (qv) and Zakkie Eloff (qv), gaining a National Art Teachers Diploma; 1963 Batik Studio Edith Müller-Ortloff, Meersburg, West Germany.
Profile 1966–67 a lecturer at Pretoria Technical College. From 1967 Head Artist for the Bureau of Heraldry, Pretoria. Produces batik tapestries, wall panels and designs for woven tapestries. 1961 visited Israel and Greece; 1963 the UK and West Germany; 1966 Europe and the USA; 1969 Europe.
Exhibitions He has participated in many group exhibitions from 1960 in SA, Italy and Belgium; 1962 Gallery 101, Johannesburg, first of four solo exhibitions.
Public Commissions 1970 oil panel, "Music in the Woods", University of Pretoria; 1973 10 religious batik panels, Dutch Reformed Church Hall, Waterkloof, Pretoria; 1980 tapestry design, Nylstroom City Hall, Transvaal.
References *SA Panorama* October 1962; *Lantern* June 1970; *Die Brandwag* December 1974; *SA Panorama* October 1975; *Rooi Rose* March 1976; *Lantern* December–February 1977.

COETZEE Anton

Born 1958 Pretoria.
Mainly a graphic artist who also works in charcoal and mixed media. His works are social/political.
Studies 1977–81 University of Pretoria, gaining a BA Architecture (cum laude); 1987 University of South Africa, studying for a BA(FA).
Profile From 1980 a member of the SAAA. 1981–87 practised as an architect. 1987 a lecturer at the Witwatersrand Technikon. 1985 presentation drawings and the cover for *UIA International Architect* magazine.
Exhibitions He has participated in many group exhibitions from 1981 in the Witwatersrand.
Award 1984 Award of Merit, New Signatures, SAAA, Pretoria.

COETZEE Christo

Born 1929 Turffontein, Johannesburg.
A painter of still life, genre, figures and abstract pictures. Works in oil and mixed media. Creates assemblages, using perspex in his palimpsestic superimpositions. 1947–53 figurative pictures; 1953–56 abstract pictures; 1956–64 assemblages; 1964–73 Neo Baroque; from 1974 Protest and Hypermannerist.
Studies 1947–50 University of the Witwatersrand, under Professor Heather Martienssen (1915–79) and Marjorie Long (qv), gaining a BA(FA); 1951–52 on a postgraduate study bursary at the Slade School of Art, London, under Professor William Coldstream (*b.*1908); 1956 studied on an Italian Government Travelling Scholarship (shared with the Australian artist Sidney Nolan) in Italy; 1959–60 on a Japanese Government Travelling Scholarship at the University of Kyoto, Japan, under Professor Ijima; Gutai Group, Osaka, Japan, under Jiro Yoshihara.
Profile 1947–51 a member of the Witwatersrand Group and 1958–63 of the Gutai Group, Osaka, Japan. 1968 illustrated the cover of *The Penguin Book of South African Verse*; 1974 the cover of *Woorde vir 'n Wind Harp* by Wessel Pretorius; 1978 *Donderdag of Woensdag*, by John Miles and in 1978 *Ontwikkeling van de Afrikaanse Fondeer* by L W B Binge. 1929–51 lived in Johannesburg; 1951–56 in London; 1956–64 in Paris, spending 1959 & 1960 in Osaka, Japan; from 1964 he has lived in Spain, spending half of each year at Tulbagh in the Cape from 1972. Has travelled extensively. First married Marjorie Long (qv) and in 1968 Ferrie Binge Coetzee (qv).
Exhibitions He has participated in numerous group exhibitions from 1949 in SA and in the UK, France, Japan, the USA, Italy, Belgium, Canada, Australia, SWA/Namibia, Spain, The Netherlands, West Germany and Greece; 1951 IDB Gallery, Cape Town, first of *c.*40 solo exhibitions held in SA, the UK, the USA, France, Japan, Italy, Belgium, Spain and China; 1965 Pretoria Art Museum, Retrospective Exhibition; 1973 Potchefstroom University for CHE, Prestige Exhibition; 1975 Rand Afrikaans University, Prestige Exhibition; 1978 University of Stellenbosch, Prestige Exhibition; 1981 Republic Festival Exhibition; 1983 Pretoria Art Museum, Retrospective Exhibition; 1987 Rand Afrikaans University, Prestige Exhibition; 1988 Johannesburg Art Gallery, Vita Art Now.

Awards 1961 Award Winner, Art of Assemblage Exhibition, Museum of Modern Art, New York, USA; 1983 Medal of Honour for Painting, SA Akademie vir Wetenskap en Kuns.

Represented Beaverbrook Art Gallery, Canada; Durban Art Gallery; Hester Rupert Art Museum, Graaff-Reinet; Idemitsu Collection, Japan; Johannesburg Art Gallery; Pietersburg Collection; Potchefstroom Museum; Potchefstroom University for CHE; Pretoria Art Museum; Rand Afrikaans University; Roodepoort Museum; Sandton Municipal Collection; SA Akademie vir Wetenskap en Kuns; SA National Gallery, Cape Town; University of Cape Town; University of Natal; University of the Orange Free State; University of Pretoria; University of South Africa; University of Stellenbosch; University of the Witwatersrand; Willem Annandale Art Gallery, Lichtenburg; William Humphreys Art Gallery, Kimberley.

Public Commissions 1971 tapestry for Jan Smuts Airport, Johannesburg; 1980 fire curtain, Drama Theatre, the State Opera House, Pretoria.

References Art SA; SAA; 20C SA Art; SAP&S; SSAP; BSAK 1 & 2; SA Art; Oxford Companion to 20C Art (under SA); 3Cs; AASA; LSAA; *South Africana* 4 May 1961; *Artlook* January 1967, February 1969, April 1971 & January 1973; *Lantern* June 1971 & April 1984; *De Kat* August 1985; *Christo Coetzee*, Exhibition Catalogue, 1983, Pretoria Art Museum.

COETZEE Cyril

Born 1959 Grahamstown.

A painter of genre and figures. Works in oil.

Studies 1983 gained an MFA from Rhodes University.

Exhibition 1985 Cape Town Triennial.

Awards 1980 Purvis Prize for Fine Art, Rhodes University; 1982 National Building Society National Inter-Art Schools Competition.

Represented Rhodes University.

COETZEE Herbert Herold

Born 1921 Cape Town.

A painter of landscapes, seascapes, portraits, figures and still life. Works in oil, acrylic, gouache, ink and charcoal.

Studies c.1949 six months part-time at the Continental School of Art, Cape Town, under Maurice van Essche (qv); 1958–60 Koninklijke Academie voor Schone Kunsten en de Hogere Instituten, Antwerp, Belgium, under Professor Julien Creytens (b.1897), Professor Jan Vaerten (1909–80) and Professor F van der Spiet, on a study bursary.

Profile 1951–54 a member of the Executive Committee of the SA Society of Artists. 1968–81 lectured at the Cape Technical College. 1975–76 a judge for school and art society exhibitions. A trained singer. Has travelled extensively in Europe in 1959, 1973 and 1985.

Exhibitions He has participated in numerous group exhibitions from 1952 in SA and once in Antwerp; 1956 SAAA Gallery, Cape Town, first of 12 solo exhibitions held in SA; 1956 Quadrennial Exhibition; 1981 Republic Festival Exhibition.

Represented Ann Bryant Gallery, East London; Hester Rupert Art Museum, Graaff-Reinet; Pretoria Art Museum; Rand Afrikaans University; University of Cape Town; University of the Orange Free State; University of the Witwatersrand.

Public Commissions From 1956 several landscape commissions for military and commercial offices; many portrait commissions, including 1981–85 seven portraits of Officials of the University of the Orange Free State.

References Art SA; SAA; BSAK; 3Cs; AASA.

COETZEE Johannes Cornelius (Neels)

Born 1940 Bethal, Transvaal.

A sculptor of abstract pieces. Works in bronze.

Studies 1963 gained a BA from the University of Natal; 1963–65 Hornsey College of Art, London, where he was awarded a Post-Graduate Diploma; 1965–66 a guest student on a Belgian–South African Cultural Agreement Scholarship, at the Koninklijke Academie voor Schone Kunsten en de Hogere Instituten, Antwerp, Belgium; 1966–67 Royal College of Art, London, attaining a Senior Certificate; 1970 gained a National Art Teachers Diploma; 1986 University of the Witwatersrand, gained an MA(FA) (cum laude).

Profile 1968–69 a part-time lecturer at the Witwatersrand Technical College; 1970–73 a lecturer at the Pretoria Technical College; 1973–85 a lecturer and from 1986 a senior lecturer at the University of the Witwatersrand. 1974 introduced bronze foundry work at the University of Witwatersrand. 1976 Acting Head of the Fine Arts Department, University of the Witwatersrand. 1982 a visiting lecturer at the University of Cape Town; 1974–76 a member of the Board of the Faculty of Education, University of the Witwatersrand; 1975–76 and 1984–85 a member of the Board of the Faculty of Arts, University of the Witwatersrand; until 1985 a member of the University of the Witwatersrand Galleries Management Committee; a member of the Acquisitions and Exhibitions Committee for the University of the Witwatersrand Art Galleries. 1978 visited Italy and the UK; 1980 visited the USA.

Exhibitions He has participated in group exhibitions from 1967 held throughout SA and in the UK, Australia, Chile, the USA and West Germany; 1978 Metalart Competition, Guest Artist; 1978 Johannesburg, solo exhibition; 1980 Metalart Guest Artists Exhibition, with Edoardo Villa (qv), Johann van Heerden (qv), Gavin Younge (qv) and Ian Redelinghuys (qv); 1985 Cape Town Triennial; 1985 Tributaries, touring SA and West Germany.

Awards 1970 first prize, AMCOR competition for a civic sculpture in Newcastle, Natal; 1977 Metalart Prize (closed category); 1981 award winner, Almaks National Sculpture Competition.

Represented Durban Art Gallery; Johannesburg Art Gallery; University of Cape Town; University of Natal; University of South Africa; University of the Witwatersrand.

Public Commissions Numerous trophies and awards from 1974; 1980 untitled hanging sculpture, the State Theatre, Pretoria.
References BSAK; 3Cs; AASA; LSAA; *Habitat* no 10, 1974, no 27, 1977 & no 32, 1978; *De Arte* April 1977.

COETZEE Johannes Hendrik

Born 1947 Uganda.
Resided in SA from 1958.
A painter of landscapes and figures. Works in oil, watercolour and charcoal.
Studies 1966–70 Peninsula Technical College, where he gained a Diploma in Commercial Art in 1969 and a Certificate in Commercial Art in 1970.
Profile From 1977 a member of the SAAA; from 1980 Vice-Chairman of the Bellville region of the SAAA. 1985 illustrated Carolyn Stuyvesant's *Storytime in Africa Books 1–5*.
Exhibitions He has participated in several group exhibitions from 1976; 1977 Johannesburg, first of four solo exhibitions.

COETZEE Neels see COETZEE Johannes Cornelius

COETZEE Pieter Jacobus

Born 1948 Johannesburg.
A graphic artist and sculptor. His graphic works are figurative screenprinted images incorporating mixed media collages. His sculptures are abstract statements about Africa; works in wood, metal, neon and in other mixed media.
Studies 1969–73 Witwatersrand Technical College (Technikon), where gained a National Art Teachers Diploma; 1979 gained a Higher Diploma in Graphic Design; 1986–87 Witwatersrand Technikon, on a National Diploma in Fine Arts Course.
Profile From 1975 a member of the SAAA. 1974–80 a senior lecturer at the Witwatersrand Technical College; 1980–85 Head of the Fine Art Department and from 1985 Associate Director of the Witwatersrand Technikon. He has completed numerous commercial design projects.
Exhibitions He has participated in several group exhibitions from 1975 in Pretoria and Johannesburg; 1980 Collector's Gallery, Johannesburg, first of two solo exhibitions.
Represented Pietersburg Collection.

COETZEE Ronald

Born 1924 Coventry, Warwickshire, England.
Resided in SA from 1947.
A painter and graphic artist of animals, figures, landscapes and seascapes. Works in watercolour, ink and wash, occasionally in oil and more frequently in the various graphic media.

Studies 1937–39 gained a scholarship to Coventry School of Art, England, under Walter Ashworth and Archibald Macdonald.
Profile Works in the commercial art field.
Exhibitions He has participated in several group exhibitions from 1952 in Durban.

COETZER Wenselois Johann

Born 1947 Johannesburg.
A painter of landscapes, seascapes, portraits, still life, figures and wildlife. Works in oil, ink, pencil, charcoal and pastel.
Studies Under his father W H Coetzer (qv).
Profile A member of the Brush and Chisel Club and its Chairman in 1984; a member of the Benoni Art Society. 1968–71 lived in London. A trained aeronautical engineer.
Exhibitions He has participated in numerous group exhibitions from 1977.

COETZER Willem Hermanus FRSA FIAL FIBA

Born 1900 Tarkastad, Cape Province.
Died 1983 Johannesburg.
A painter of landscapes, still life, portraits and historical paintings. Worked in oil and pastel. A number of etchings, woodcuts and modelled sculpture.
Studies 1928–30 and 1934–35 Regent Street Polytechnic College, London, under Harry Watson RBS (1871–1936) and Giffard H Lenfestey RBA ARCA (*b.*1872); 1934 Central School of Art, London, etching under William Palmer Robins (*b.*1882).
Profile 1948 Co-founder and President of the Brush and Chisel Club and a member of the Africana Advisory Committee. 1917–25 a wheelwright coach-builder, thereafter a full-time artist. 1939 taught art appreciation at Potchefstroom Teachers Training College. 1938 designed 10 postage stamps and souvenirs for the Great Trek Centenary; 1948 designed the marble frieze and from 1953 15 tapestries for the National Voortrekker Monument, Pretoria. In 1969 800 etchings by him were given to the City of Johannesburg; these were reproduced by E Schweickerdt, Pretoria. Designed logos and a further two sets of stamps. In 1952 the W H Coetzer Primary School, Klipriviersberg, Johannesburg, was named after him. 1900–28 lived in SA, visiting the UK in 1925; 1928–30 lived in the UK with visits in 1928 to Germany, 1929 to France, Italy and Switzerland, 1930 to Germany, Austria, Italy, France and Spain; 1931–34 lived in SA; 1934–35 in the UK; from 1935 in SA with visits to London in 1948 and 1971. Father of W J Coetzer (qv).
Exhibitions Participated in group exhibitions from 1948 in SA and in the UK; 1928 Lezards, Johannesburg, first of numerous solo exhibitions held throughout SA; 1948 Tate Gallery, London, SA Art Exhibition; 1970 Rand Afrikaans University, Retrospective Exhibition of Historical Work; 1974 Herbert Evans Gallery, Johannesburg, Retrospective Exhibition of Still Life Work; 1980 80th Birthday Exhibition, Johannesburg Art Gallery.

Awards 1930 Regent Street Polytechnic Prize for still life; 1965 Special Medal, SA Akademie vir Wetenskap en Kuns for historical work.

Represented Africana Museum, Johannesburg; Ann Bryant Gallery, East London; Collection of Queen Elizabeth II, England; Durban Art Gallery; Hester Rupert Art Museum, Graaff-Reinet; Johannesburg Art Gallery; Julius Gordon Africana Centre, Riversdale; National Museum, Bloemfontein; Potchefstroom Museum; Potchefstroom University for CHE; Pretoria Art Museum; Rand Afrikaans University; SA Akademie vir Wetenskap en Kuns; SA National Gallery, Cape Town; University of Natal; University of Pretoria; University of Stellenbosch; War Museum of the Boer Republics, Bloemfontein; William Humphreys Art Gallery, Kimberley.

Portraits painted by Coetzer Painted portraits of SA notability, including The Honourable D J Strijdom, Dr D F Malan, General J B M Hertzog, the Reverend J D Kestell and Jan Cilliers.

Public Commission 1963 historical mural, Transvaal Provincial Administration Building, Pretoria.

Publications by Coetzer *My Kwas Vertel*, 1947, Boek-en-Kunssentrum, Johannesburg; *W H Coetzer, 80*, autobiography, 1980, Cum Books, Roodepoort; *Pen Sketse/Sketches*, 1981, Cum Books, Roodepoort; *W H Coetzer, Stillewes/Still Lifes*, 1982, Cum Books, Roodepoort.

References Collectors' Guide; Our Art 1; Art SA; SAA; 20C SA Art; AMC2 & 6; SAP&S; IWAA; SSAP; BSAK 1 & 2; SA Art; 3Cs; AASA; LSAA; *Die Huisgenoot* 14 February 1947; *Die Brandwag* 31 December 1954 & 8 January 1965; *SA Panorama* November 1963 & May 1981; *Artlook* April 1969; *ANN* September 1969.

COHEN Pearl

Born 1908 London, England.

A painter of cityscapes, harbour scenes and of portraits. Worked in oil.

Studies Michaelis School of Fine Art, Witwatersrand Technical College, the Byam Shaw School of Art, London and privately under Sidney Goldblatt (qv) and Lionel Abrams (qv).

Profile A member of the Transvaal Art Society and the Brush and Chisel Club. Taught art privately.

Exhibitions Participated in group exhibitions from 1954 in SA; 1962 Gallery 101, Johannesburg, joint exhibition with Sylvia Freedman (qv); 1965 first of four solo exhibitions held in Johannesburg.

Represented Durban Art Gallery.

References SAA; BSAK; AASA; *Artlook* March 1970.

COHEN Robyn Yael

Born 1963 Johannesburg.

A painter of landscapes, still life, figures, and interiors. Works in oil and mixed media. A sculptor, photographer and a collage maker.

Studies 1982–85 University of the Witwatersrand, gaining a BA(FA), a Merit Award for Painting and the 1985–86 Giovanna Milner Travel Scholarship; 1986 University of the Witwatersrand, registered for an MA(FA).

Exhibitions She has participated in several group exhibitions from 1984 in Johannesburg and Pretoria; 1986 Market Gallery, Johannesburg, joint exhibition with Lulu Davis (qv) and Lea Henorain (qv).

Awards 1984 Merit Award, Rolfes Impressions '84, Johannesburg Art Gallery; 1984 First Prize Drawing and First Prize Mixed Media Work, New Signatures, SAAA, Pretoria.

COLE Phillip Tennyson

Born 1862 London, England.
Died Thought to have died in 1939.
Resided in SA from *c*.1890.
A painter of genre, interiors and portraits. Worked in watercolour and oil.

Profile His sitters included Cecil John Rhodes, Lord Milner and the Duke of Norfolk. 1897 a founder member of the SA Society of Artists. 1900 accompanied Dr Carel Peters on an expedition up the Zambezi. Lived in London and Cape Town, thought to have returned to England prior to 1927. Travelled widely in Australia and New Zealand.

Exhibitions Participated in group exhibitions in the UK; 1882 held a solo exhibition in London.

Represented Albany Museum, Grahamstown; Johannesburg Art Gallery; Melbourne Museum, Victoria, Australia.

References SADNB; Bénézit; DBA; AASA.

COLEMAN Trevor

Born 1936 Johannesburg.
A painter and graphic artist of landscapes, still life and abstract pictures. Works in oil, acrylic, watercolour, gouache, ink, wash, pencil, charcoal and in various graphic media, particularly monotypes. 1960–66 organic textured paintings; 1966–72 hard edge paintings; 1972–83 landscape and collage paintings. Several large series: 1978 "SWA"; 1981–82 "India–Inspiration"; 1985 "Seychelles".

Studies 1958–60 Witwatersrand Technical College, under Professor Robert Bain (qv); 1961 part-time at the Central School of Art, London.

Profile 1961–65 a member of the Hampstead Art Society; a member of the SAAA of which he was a Transvaal Committee Member 1967–73. An art teacher in 1966 at The Visual Arts Research Centre, Johannesburg; has also taught privately. 1977–85 established and ran the Trevor Coleman Gallery, Johannesburg. 1981–83 editor of *Gallery* magazine, Johannesburg. A potter and a photographer. 1961–65 lived in London. Visited India in 1978, 1979 and 1980; Burma, Thailand and Sri Lanka in 1980; Morocco in 1981 and Australia in 1982.

Exhibitions He has participated in many group exhibitions from 1959 in SA and the UK; 1961 London, first of eight solo exhibitions held in London and 11 held in SA.

Represented Johannesburg Art Gallery; Museum of Modern Art, New Delhi, India; Pietersburg Collection; Rand Afrikaans University; University of the Witwatersrand; Victoria and Albert Museum, London, England.
References BSAK; AASA; *Artlook* February 1967, August 1969, April 1970 & August 1973.

COLLET Rhona (née Brown)

Born 1922 Pretoria.
A painter of mixed panels of indigenous flowers, fruits and grasses. Works in watercolour and ink.
Studies 1940–44 University of Natal, under Professor O J P Oxley (qv) and Rosa Hope (qv), where she attained a BA(FA); University of South Africa, where she attained a BA(FA)(Hons) and a National Art Teachers Certificate.
Profile Taught for five years at St Michael's School, Bloemfontein, and later at several schools in the Transvaal. 1943–46 and 1967–70 an artist with the Botanical Research Institute where she contributed illustrations to *The Flowering Plants of Africa*. Black and white illustrations for *Flora of Southern Africa*, *Bothalia*, and *A Field Guide to the Trees of Southern Africa*, by Eve Palmer, 1972.
Exhibitions She has participated in group exhibitions of botanical work at Pretoria Art Museum and the University of the Witwatersrand; she has held several solo exhibitions.
Public Commission Roll of Honour for the SA Air Force Memorial in Pretoria.
References SAA; AASA.

COLLIER Joy (Mrs Anthony Millar)

Born 1914 London, England.
Resided in SA from 1947.
An artist depicting landscapes, cityscapes, portraits, figures, genre and buildings. Works in ink and wash.
Studies In London and Geneva.
Profile Numerous illustrations for books. Lives in Cape Town.
Represented Africana Museum, Johannesburg; East London Municipal Library.
Publications by Collier *Stellenbosch Revisited*, 1959; *Portrait of Cape Town*, 1960, Nasionale Boekhandel, Cape Town; *Frontier Post—the Story of Grahamstown*, 1961; *The Purple and the Gold—the Story of Pretoria and Johannesburg*, 1965, Longmans SA.
References AMC6; BSAK; AASA.

COLLINS Ray (Mrs)

Born 1920 Durban.
A painter of portraits and still life. Works in oil and watercolour.
Studies 1936–38 Natal Technical College.
Exhibitions She has participated in several group exhibitions from 1938.

COMERFORD Jonathan Ambrose

Born 1961 Cape Town.

A graphic artist of social, political and abstract pictures. Produces silkscreens, etchings, linocuts and woodcuts, also works in pencil, charcoal and creates collages.

Studies 1980 Cape Technikon; 1981 for six months, 1983–85 and in 1986 for six months, courses at the Ruth Prowse School of Art, Cape Town, under Edwine Simon (qv) and Erik Laubscher (qv), where he was awarded a Diploma in Fine Art.

Profile 1986 spent six months as an assistant lecturer at the Ruth Prowse School of Art, Cape Town.

Exhibitions He has participated in several group exhibitions from 1983 in SA; 1986 Cape Gallery, Cape Town, solo exhibition.

Award 1983 Merit Award, Rolfes Impressions '83, Johannesburg Art Gallery.

COMFIELD John F

Born 1799 England.

Resided in SA from 1820.

A painter of landscapes. Worked in watercolour.

Profile Taught at the English Grammar School in Cape Town, and in 1829 opened his own drawing and writing school. Two of his works were included among the earliest lithographs made by R Middleton in the Cape. Lived in Port Elizabeth until 1824, when he moved to Cape Town.

Rrepresented SA Public Library, Cape Town; William Fehr Collection, Cape Town.

References Pict Art; H E Hockley, *The Story of the British Settlers of 1820 in SA*, 2nd edition, 1957, Juta, Cape Town; Pict Afr.

CONNEL Mary E (Mrs Stutterheim)

Born 1917 York, England.

Resided in SA from 1933.

A painter of SA flora. Works in watercolour, ink and pencil.

Studies 1936 Witwatersrand Technical College, under James Gardner (qv).

Profile 1936–42 an artist with the Botanical Research Institute for which she produced 121 colour illustrations for *The Flowering Plants of Africa;* also drew illustrations for *Farming in SA* for the Department of Agriculture; *Noxious Weeds of SA*, 1939; *Succulent Euphorbiae*, 1941; *Trees and Shrubs of the Kruger National Park*, 1951; *Grasses and Pastures of SA*, 1954; *Common Weeds of SA*, 1966 and the periodical *Flora of Southern Africa*.

Exhibition Participated in a group exhibition of botanical work at the Pretoria Art Museum.

Reference SAA.

BETTIE CILLIERS-BARNARD
Cosmic Experience 1986–87
Oil & Collage on Canvas 120 × 120 cm
Artist

CHRISTO COETZEE
Still Life with Face
Mixed Media on Canvas 120 × 123 cm
The Everard Read Gallery

CONRADIE Helene

Born 1931 Stellenbosch, Cape Province.

A sculptor in ceramics of birds. A painter of landscapes, still life, figures, wildlife and abstract pictures. Works in oil and watercolour.

Studies Privately under Sidney Goldblatt (qv); evening classes at the University of the Witwatersrand, Witwatersrand Technical College, Pretoria Technical College and at the Hammersmith School of Arts and Crafts in London in *c.*1956; 1972–73 studied ceramic technology under Hans Bohn at the Pretoria Technical College.

Profile From 1978 a member of the Knysna Arts and Crafts Society and from 1974 of the APSA.

Exhibitions She has participated in many group exhibitions in SA from 1956.

Reference AASA.

COOK Agatha Minnie

Born 1908 Durban.

A painter of landscapes, portraits, still life, seascapes, genre and figures. Works in oil, watercolour and gouache.

Studies Under her mother, Agnes Waller (qv); 1963–73 under Rosa Hope (qv); 1966 figure drawing at the Natal Technical College.

Profile 1977 a founder member of the North Coast Art Group; a member of the SAAA, the WSSA and a Life Member of the NSA. 1971 visited Portugal and in 1985 Spain.

Exhibitions She has participated in numerous group exhibitions in SA; 1964 Pabros Theatre, Durban, solo exhibition; 1966 Klynsmith Gallery, Johannesburg, joint exhibition with Rosa Hope (qv); 1978 NSA Gallery, Durban, joint exhibition with Anne Frost (qv); 1987 NSA Gallery, Durban, joint exhibition with Carol Thompson (qv) and Professor Jan Zaal (qv).

Represented Killie Campbell Africana Library, University of Natal, Durban.

COOK Daniel Edmund

Born 1947 Johannesburg.

A painter of landscapes and abstract pictures. Works in oil, acrylic, watercolour, gouache and pencil.

Studies 1966–67 Natal Technical College; 1968–72 University of the Witwatersrand, under Cecily Sash (qv), Robert Hodgins (qv) and Giuseppe Cattaneo (qv), gaining a BA(FA).

Profile 1974–77 a lecturer at the Natal Technical College; 1977–78 lectured at the Johannesburg College of Education; 1978–79 a lecturer at the University of South Africa; 1979–82 a senior lecturer at the Witwatersrand Technical College (Technikon); from 1982 a senior lecturer at the Natal Technikon.

Exhibitions He has participated in several group exhibitions from 1975 in SA; 1975 NSA Gallery, Durban, first of two solo exhibitions, the second being held in Johannesburg.

Represented Pietersburg Collection; University of Stellenbosch.

COOK Ronald James

Born 1940 Auckland, New Zealand.
Resided in SA from 1966.
A painter of landscapes, portraits and wildlife, specifically of birds. Works in oil, acrylic, watercolour and gouache.
Studies 1959–60 part-time at the Elam School of Fine Art, New Zealand; 1960–65 portraiture privately under A Robinson in New Zealand.
Profile 1960–65 a member of the New Zealand Fellowship of Artists; 1981–82 a member and from 1982 a Fellow of the SA Aviation Art Guild. Until 1985 a freelance commercial artist working in the advertising field, since when he has painted full-time. 1961–65 designed backdrops for theatres in New Zealand; 1967–71 designed numerous stands and pavilions for showgrounds in Johannesburg.
Exhibitions He has participated in several group exhibitions from 1960 in New Zealand and SA.
Reference BSAK.

COOKE-TONNESEN Wendy Jennifer

Born 1945 Johannesburg.
A painter of portraits, figures and abstract pictures. Works in oil, acrylic, watercolour, ink, wash, pencil, charcoal and pastel, also creates collages.
Studies 1960–62 Natal Technical College, gaining a Diploma in Commercial Art; private tuition under George Boys (qv).
Profile From 1983 a member of the WSSA. 1973 an art teacher at Newcastle Technical College, Natal. From 1974 has taught art privately. Lived in Durban until 1972, in Newcastle until 1978, thereafter in Benoni.
Exhibitions She has participated in many group exhibitions in SA, West Germany and the USA; 1977 Newcastle, Natal, first of five solo exhibitions.

COOPER Charlotte Mary

Born 1954 Vancouver, British Columbia, Canada.
Resided in SA from 1979.
A painter and graphic artist working in oil, acrylic, ink, wash, pencil, charcoal, airbrush, various graphic media and in perspex with inlays. Produces computer graphics. She depicts racial archetypes and individual archetypal combinations which are derived through astrological and psychic means.
Studies 1973–74 University of British Columbia; 1974–75 at a private art school in Paris, 1975–76 Sorbonne, Paris; 1976–77 University of Paris; 1977–79 University of Concordia, Montreal, Canada. Gained a BA(FA).
Profile 1985 and 1986 a guest lecturer at the Witwatersrand Technikon. Since 1982 she has also worked as a commercial artist. Travelled extensively in Europe, the USA, Egypt and Israel.
Exhibitions She has participated in several group exhibitions from 1979 in Toronto and SA; 1980 Crake Gallery, Johannesburg, first of four solo exhibitions; 1981 Republic Festival Exhibition.

Public Commission 1979 large mural, Toronto, Canada.
References *La Estacian Azul*, a book of poems about Cooper, by Jaime Rosa, 1980; AASA.

COOPER Claudia

Born 1953 Graaff-Reinet, Cape Province.
A painter and a sculptor of abstracts, figures, still life and landscapes. Works in oil, gouache, ink, pencil, charcoal, stone, clay and slate. A graphic artist working in various graphic media.
Studies 1974 White House School of Design, Cape Town; 1977 film-making at the Rice Media Center, Houston, Texas, USA; 1977–80 ceramics, printmaking and jewellery, Museum School, Houston, Texas, USA.
Profile 1977–79 a technical assistant in the ceramics department, Museum School, Houston, Texas, USA. 1984 taught art privately in Graaff-Reinet; 1985 an art teacher at the Torah Academy, Johannesburg.
Exhibitions She has participated in several group exhibitions in SA and the USA from 1978; 1982 Things Gallery, Johannesburg, first of two solo exhibitions held in Johannesburg.
Awards 1978 Student Association Award, Museum School, Houston, Texas, USA; 1979 Womans Award, Museum School, Houston, Texas, USA.
Represented Johannesburg Art Gallery.

COOPER Esmé Margaret

Born 1918 Pretoria.
A self-taught painter and graphic artist of landscapes, still life, seascapes, figures, wildlife and botanical studies. Works in oil, acrylic, watercolour, ink, wash, pencil and in various graphic media, particularly linocuts.
Profile 1983 a member of the SAAA; 1984 a member of Club 997, Pretoria, and of the Boksburg Art Society. Teaches the art of watercolour privately.
Exhibitions She has participated in numerous group exhibitions from 1981 in Pretoria.

COOPMANS Maria Paula Magdalena Monique

Born 1940 Roermond, The Netherlands.
Resided in SA from 1972.
A sculptor of figures, genre and portraits in an abstracted manner. Works in bronze, stone, ciment fondu, wood and plaster of Paris.
Studies 1958–62 Stads Academie voor Toegepaste Kunsten, Maastricht, The Netherlands; 1962–66 Jan van Eyck Academie, Maastricht, under Fred Carasso, gaining an MFA (cum laude); 1966–68 on a scholarship from the Austrian Government at the Akademie für Bildenden Kunste, Vienna, under Professor Fritz Wotruba (1907–75).

Profile 1967–68 worked for Austrian TV, designing sets and making puppets. 1968–72 an art teacher at the High School, Roermond, The Netherlands; 1974 a lecturer at the University of Stellenbosch; 1975–76 a sculpture lecturer at the University of the Witwatersrand. 1971 designed a mini zoo and sculptural reliefs in Roermond; 1980 visited South America. Peruvian Inca art inspired her painting of a relief mural at the Craighall Community Centre, Johannesburg.
Exhibitions She has participated in several group exhibitions from 1966 in The Netherlands, Austria and SA; 1976 Fabian Fine Art, Cape Town, first of three solo exhibitions held in Cape Town and Johannesburg.
Awards 1966 Prize of the City of Maastricht, The Netherlands; 1975 Metalart Prize (amateur category).
Represented Pietersburg Collection.
Public Commissions A number of relief works and sculptures in The Netherlands and SA.
References AASA; *Habitat* no 30, 1978.

COPE Lesley (née Luitingh)

Born 1921 Lydenburg, Transvaal.
Died 1988 Nelspruit, Eastern Transvaal.
A painter of landscapes, figures, still life and town scenes. Worked in oil.
Studies Camberwell School of Art, London, under Sir William Coldstream (*b*.1908) and Victor Pasmore (*b*.1908).
Profile A book illustrator, often working with Sue Hart on her children's and conservation books, most recently on *Secret of the Sycamore Tree*, 1983, Johannesburg. Married the writer, Jack Cope. Lived in the Eastern Transvaal and in the Cape.
Exhibitions 1951 Cape Town, first of several solo exhibitions.
References Register SA & SWA; *South Africana* 6 April 1961.

COPNALL Edward Bainbridge

Born 1903 Cape Town.
Died 1973 Littlebourne, Kent, England.
A sculptor and painter of portraits, portrait busts and large architectural works.
Studies Goldsmiths College, London, and the Royal Academy Schools, London.
Profile His portrait busts include those of Sir Winston Churchill and Edward Heath. A corresponding member of the National Society of American Sculptors. A former President of the Royal Society of Sculptors. 1951 Master and later Headmaster of the Sir John Cass School of Art, London. Lived in England. Nephew of the portrait painter Frank Copnall (*b*.1870).
Exhibitions Participated in group exhibitions regularly in the UK.
Public Commission Le Cerf, Stag Place, Victoria, London.
References Who's Who in Art, 16th edition, 1972; Bénézit; DBA.

COSTELLO Michael Alan

Born 1948 Cala, Transkei.

A sculptor, painter and graphic artist producing both representational and abstract works. Uses many media, but most particularly natural woods and oil.

Studies East London Technical College, under Jack Lugg (qv) and Brian Walsh.

Profile Involved in the writing of prose and poetry, theatre direction and design, as well as photography. 1969 shared a studio with Raymond Andrews (qv). 1974 visited the USA, the UK, The Netherlands, France, Spain, Italy, Switzerland and Germany; 1978 visited the Seychelles.

Exhibitions He has participated in numerous group exhibitions in SA, Italy, the Seychelles, The Netherlands and the USA; 1968 Cala, Transkei, first of 15 solo exhibitions; 1981 Republic Festival Exhibition.

Public Commission 1972 large mural, Roodepoort, Transvaal.

Represented University of Stellenbosch.

References BSAK 1 & 2; AASA; *Habitat* no 25, 1977; *Gallery* Summer 1981.

COTTRELL Kent (Mrs)

Born 1887 England.

A painter of portraits and genre of African people. Worked in oil and pastel.

Studies In Paris.

Profile Spent some years prior to the end of WWI in SA, then joined an artists' colony in Cornwall. Lived in London until the beginning of WWII when she returned to SA. Travelled widely in Africa.

Exhibitions Participated in group exhibitions in SA from 1941; 1941 Johannesburg, first of several solo exhibitions held in SA.

Publications by Cottrell *Sunburnt Sketches of Africa*, 1953, CNA, Johannesburg; *More than Sunburnt*, 1958, CNA, Johannesburg.

References BSAK; AASA.

COULSON Elizabeth Jane Dalrymple

Born 1897 Ficksburg, Orange Free State.

A painter of landscapes, portraits and still life. Worked in oil, watercolour and pencil.

Studies 1916–17 Durban School of Art, under John Adams (qv).

Profile 1918–19 an assistant teacher at the Grahamstown School of Art. A potter.

COUZYN Elizabeth

Born 1925 Pretoria.

Died 1979 France.

A painter in mixed media of figures, still life and flowers. Religious and Mother & Child themes run through her work.

Studies 1940–44 Pretoria Art Centre, under Le Roux Smith Le Roux (qv); 1948–50 under Herman Wald (qv) in Johannesburg; 1955 in Vienna, under Professor Paux; 1963–64 Schule Des Sehens, Salzburg, Austria, under Oskar Kokoschka (1886–1980).
Profile 1940–44 Secretary of the Pretoria Art Centre. 1955 lived in Vienna; 1959 in Salzburg and from 1965 in SA. 1976–77 visited Israel and Greece. Married to the opera singer Dawie Couzyn.
Exhibitions 1963–67 held solo exhibitions in Austria, Germany and throughout SA.
Represented University of Pretoria.
Reference BSAK.

COWAN John

Born 1951 Durban.
A painter working in acrylic.
Studies 1973 gained a Diploma from the Natal Teachers Training College; 1976 a postgraduate course at Oxford Polytechnic, England.
Profile 1982 a lecturer at the Natal Technikon.
Exhibition 1982 Cape Town Triennial.
Represented Durban Art Gallery; Oxford College Art Gallery, England; William Humphreys Art Gallery, Kimberley.

CRAIG Frank Barrington (Barry)

Born 1902.
Died 1951.
Active in SA during the 1920s and 1930s.
A painter of portraits and landscapes. Worked in watercolour and oil.
Studies Slade School of Art, London.
Profile 1926–33 Professor of Fine Art, Michaelis School of Art. Returned to London sometime after 1934. A member of the New English Art Club from 1946.
Exhibitions Participated in group exhibitions in England from 1925 and in SA from 1927.
Represented Africana Museum, Johannesburg; University of Cape Town.
References AMC2; DBA; BSAK.

CROESÉR Michael Peter Laubser

Born 1919 Amersfoort, Transvaal.
A painter of landscapes, seascapes, still life and wildlife. Works in oil, watercolour, gouache, ink, wash, pencil, charcoal and pastel.
Studies 1964–66 under the guidance of Cecil Thornley Stewart (qv).
Profile 1974–80 a member of the Pietersburg Art Society. Three portfolios printed by Howard Swan, Johannesburg: "The Bushveld" in 1978, "SA Wildlife" in 1979 and "The Garden Route" in 1983. Until 1963 lived in Rhodesia (Zimbabwe), 1963–80 in the Eastern Transvaal Lowveld and from 1980 in Knysna. 1976 and 1983 visited SWA/Namibia; he has made several painting trips to Zimbabwe and Botswana.

Exhibitions He has participated in several group exhibitions held in SA, West Germany and Portugal; 1952 Salisbury, Rhodesia (Harare, Zimbabwe), first of 12 solo exhibitions held in Zimbabwe and SA.
Represented Pietersburg Collection.
References BSAK; AASA; *Artlook* December 1972.

CRONJÉ Dawid Andreas (André)

Born 1956 Hopetown, Cape Province.
A painter and graphic artist of modern life. Works in oil, acrylic, watercolour, gouache, ink, wash, pencil, charcoal and silkscreen. 1980–81 a series entitled "Triangle"; 1985–87 a series entitled "Cloth/Clothes".
Studies 1977–81 Pretoria Technikon, under Gunther van der Reis (qv), Leslie Reinhardt (qv) and Ian Redelinghuys (qv), gaining a National Diploma in Fine Art and a Higher Diploma in Fine Art (Painting).
Profile From 1981 a lecturer at the Pretoria Technikon. 1984 and 1986 stage designs for plays produced at the Grahamstown Arts Festival. 1985–87 experimenting with fabrics, creating wall hangings, curtains and clothes. 1985 visited Spain, France, London and New York.
Exhibitions He has participated in several group exhibitions from 1979 in Pretoria and Durban; 1981 Republic Festival Exhibition; 1981 SAAA Gallery, Pretoria, first of two solo exhibitions.
Award 1987 Best Designer of the Year.

CROOKS Jennifer Lynne

Born 1943 Uitenhage, Cape Province.
A painter of landscapes. Works in oil.
Studies 1962–65 Rhodes University, under Professor Brian Bradshaw (qv), gaining a BA(FA); 1981 Rhodes University, under Josua Nell (qv), gaining an MFA.
Profile A member of the Grahamstown Group. An art teacher at the Diocesan School for Girls, Grahamstown and a lecturer in clothing design at Port Elizabeth Technikon. 1983 and 1985 visited Greece. Married to Professor Robert Brooks (qv).
Exhibitions She has participated in numerous group exhibitions from 1965 in SA and West Germany; 1976 Leader Gallery, Grahamstown, first of three solo exhibitions held in the Eastern Province; 1985 Cape Town Triennial.
References AASA; *Fair Lady* 5 July 1978.

CROSBY Beatrice

Born 1893 London, England.
Resided in SA from 1921.
A painter of landscapes, city scenes, portraits, still life, figures and flowers. Worked in oil, watercolour, wash, pencil and charcoal. Produced copper etchings.

Studies Regent Street Polytechnic, London, under George P Gaskell (1868–1934), gaining a one-year scholarship; Académie de la Grande Chaumière, Atelier Colarossi and Académie Julian, Paris; refresher courses at the Witwatersrand Technical College, under James Gardner (qv).

Profile c.1930 a member of the Transvaal Art Society; c.1935 a member of the Brush and Chisel Club, being made an Honorary Life Member in 1970; a Fellow and founder member of the WSSA and a past committee member of the SAAA. Contributed articles to various art magazines. A violinist. Lived in Rhodesia (Zimbabwe), SWA/Namibia and SA.

Exhibitions She has participated in group exhibitions in the UK and from 1945 in SA; 1969 Marjorie Bowen Gallery, Johannesburg, first solo exhibition.

Represented Africana Museum, Johannesburg.

Public Commission Portrait of Sir John Clayden, ex-Chancellor of the Central African Federation.

References AMC6; BSAK; *Artlook* October 1969.

CROSLAND ROBINSON George see ROBINSON George Crosland

CROSS Marion Edith Martha

Born 1955 Düsseldorf, West Germany.
Resided in SA from 1956.
A painter of landscapes, portraits, still life, figures and abstract pictures. Works in oil, acrylic, watercolour, gouache, ink, pencil and charcoal.

Studies Oil painting under Eileen Smithers; Johannesburg Art Foundation under Bill Ainslie (qv).

Profile A potter and a weaver. 1982 visited Germany, 1984 Spain.

Exhibitions She has participated in several group exhibitions in Johannesburg from 1985.

CROUSE Reshada

Born Plettenberg Bay, Cape Province.
A painter of portraits. Works in oil.

Studies 1969–73 University of Natal, under Dr Raymond van Niekerk, gaining a BA(FA); 1976–79 Michaelis School of Fine Art, under Professor Neville Dubow, where she was awarded an MA(FA) and in 1978 a Higher Diploma in Education (Primary Grade); 1979–81 St Martins School of Art, London, where awarded an Advanced Diploma in Painting.

Profile 1981–84 worked as a commercial artist.

Exhibitions She has participated in several group exhibitions from 1981 in the UK and SA; 1982 Market Gallery, Johannesburg, first of two solo exhibitions held in Johannesburg and Durban; 1985 Cape Town Triennial.

Public Commission 1987 Portrait of the Mayor of Cape Town.

References *Fair Lady* September 1986; *Style* November 1987.

CROWE Richard Joseph John

Born 1955 Colleen Bawn, Rhodesia (Zimbabwe).

A painter and graphic artist of symbolic and abstract pictures. Works in oil, acrylic, gouache, ink, wash, various graphic media and in ceramics.

Studies 1973–81 Rhodes University, under Professor Brian Bradshaw (qv), gaining a BA(FA)(Hons), an MFA (cum laude) and a Higher Diploma in Education; 1982–85 courses at the Institut für Kunstgeschichte, Munich, West Germany, under Professor F Mütherich; 1985 on a Human Sciences Research Council Scholarship to Trinity College, Dublin, Republic of Ireland, under Roger Halley.

Profile 1973–79 a member of the Grahamstown Group; from 1984 a member of the GAP Group and its organiser in 1985. 1981 an art teacher at Fairmont High School, Cape; 1982–85 a lecturer in the School of Art and Design at Port Elizabeth Technikon. He has done extensive research into illustrated medieval manuscripts, for which he has travelled throughout Europe.

Exhibitions He has participated in many group exhibitions from 1975 in SA; 1980 Rhodes University, solo exhibition; 1985 Tributaries, touring SA and West Germany.

Represented University of the Witwatersrand.

CRUISE Wilma

Born 1945 Johannesburg.

A sculptor of figures. Works in wood and ceramics.

Studies 1969–70 University of South Africa, under Professor Walter Battiss (qv); 1984–85 Witwatersrand Technical College, under Karin Boyum, gaining a National Diploma in Ceramic Science; 1987 returned to the University of South Africa to continue the BA(FA) course.

Profile A member of the APSA and in 1985–86 Chairman of the Southern Transvaal Branch. 1972–85 taught ceramics privately in Springs, Richards Bay and Sandton. She has written a number of articles for *Sgraffiti*, a ceramics magazine.

Exhibitions She has participated in many group exhibitions from 1970 in Johannesburg; 1983 Beuster Skolimowski Gallery, Pretoria, first of three solo exhibitions.

Represented Pietersburg Collection; University of Natal (Corobrik Collection).

Public Commission Barclays (First National) Bank, George.

CUAIRAN Florencio

Born 1895 Barcelona, Spain.

Resided in SA from 1938.

A sculptor in bronze, stone, marble, copper, wood and clay. Generally depicted animals, but during the 1940s he began sculpting human heads in brass, and Mother & Child groups.

Studies Barcelona Art School and in Madrid.

Profile Taught sculpture privately. Lived in Cape Town.

Exhibitions Participated in group exhibitions in Madrid, London, Johannesburg and Cape Town; 1930 exhibition in Barcelona, Spain; 1938 joint exhibition with Gregoire Boonzaier (qv); 1944 Johannesburg, solo exhibition; 1948 Maskew Miller Gallery, Cape Town, exhibition of religious sculptures.
Award 1930 Gold Medal, Madrid Exhibition of Fine Art.
Represented Barcelona Museum, Spain; SA National Gallery, Cape Town; University of Cape Town.
Public Commissions Black Panther, granite, Government House, Pretoria; Transvaal Crest, stinkwood, Transvaal Provincial Administration Building, Pretoria; 1957 pediment on KWV Headquarters, Paarl, Cape Province.
References Art SA; SAA; SAP&S; BSAK 1 & 2; SA Art; AASA.

CULL Cleone

Born 1946 Upington, Cape Province.
A painter of landscapes and portraits. Works in oil.
Studies Rhodes University, gaining a BA(FA), an Art Teachers Diploma in 1969 and an MFA in 1975.
Profile A member of the Grahamstown Group. Taught at Belgravia Art High School and West Bank High School, East London, before joining the staff of the Port Elizabeth Technikon. She became Head of the Department of Foundation Studies there in 1981.
Exhibitions She has participated in many group exhibitions from 1976 in SA; 1981 Republic Festival Exhibition.
Represented Ann Bryant Gallery, East London.
References Port Elizabeth School of Art; AASA.

CUNNINGHAM Gordon Balfour-

Born 1925 Johannesburg.
A sculptor of wildlife. Works in bronze, stone and wood. A painter of landscapes, still life and wildlife. Works in watercolour, oil, acrylic, gouache, ink, wash, pencil and charcoal.
Profile A member of the WSSA. A qualified architect, practising in Pietermaritzburg and working on many projects in SA and in the USA. Designed two stamps for the Philatelic Services, the Official Crest and Flag for KwaZulu and the Emblem for the Natal Provincial Administration. A number of illustrations for various magazines and other publications. Drew the comic strip series "Trail Tales" for children's wildlife conservation education. As a child lived in Zululand and the Northern Cape. He has travelled in the UK, the USA and the Far East.
Exhibitions He has participated in many group exhibitions from 1952 in SA and the USA; 1952 Durban, joint exhibition with Jack Lugg (qv); 1981 Republic Festival Exhibition; 1986 Schweickerdt Gallery, Pretoria, solo exhibition.
References BSAK 1 & 2; AASA; *Artlook* August 1967.

CUNNINGHAM Jeremy Mark

Born 1958 Bulawayo, Rhodesia (Zimbabwe).

A sculptor in bronze, stainless steel, stone, ciment fondu, wood, ceramics and other media. Draws in pencil and charcoal and works in various graphic media. His subject matter includes figures, figure groupings and landscapes. Prior to 1983 he depicted landscapes and mechanical structures, since 1983 figures in motion, in urban settings, interacting in balance and in circus situations.

Studies 1980–83 University of Natal, under Professor Murray Schoonraad and R H D Davies, gaining a BA(FA) majoring in sculpture, with a First Class for his final year and a Certificate of Merit.

Profile From 1982 a member of the SAAA. From 1984 a number of show pavilions for the Department of Agriculture. 1985 a part-time lecturer at the University of Natal. From 1986 he has been living in England.

Exhibitions Has participated in many group exhibitions from 1976 in SA and Zimbabwe; 1985 Crake Gallery, Johannesburg, first of three solo exhibitions held in Johannesburg and Durban.

Award 1983 Merit Award, Rolfes Impressions '83, Johannesburg Art Gallery.

CURNICK Cheryl

Born 1946 Transvaal.

A painter of landscapes and abstracted pictures. Works in watercolour, acrylic, gouache, ink, wash and in pencil.

Studies 1965–67 Natal Technical College, under Barry Maritz (qv), gaining a Diploma in Commercial and Applied Art.

Profile From 1978 a member of the WSSA, becoming an Associate in 1983 and a Fellow in 1987. A committee member of the Executive Board of the WSSA. Teaches art through workshops. Sister of Janeen du Toit (qv).

Exhibitions She has participated in many group exhibitions from 1980 in SA and with the WSSA in London; 1980 Benoni, first of several solo exhibitions.

CURRIE-WOOD Edin Godfrey

Born 1919 at sea on *The Edinburgh Castle*.

Resided in SA from 1919.

A painter of landscapes and figures. Works in oil, acrylic and ink.

Studies 1945–46 part-time at Natal Technical College, under Cecil Todd (qv).

Profile From 1959 a member of the NSA, 1962–64 Vice-President and in 1965–67 its President. Became a full-time painter in 1985. 1919–71 lived in Durban; from 1971 in Johannesburg. Visited Mexico in 1982.

Exhibitions He has participated in many group exhibitions from 1951 in the UK and SA; 1960 Lidchi Gallery, Johannesburg, first of 13 solo exhibitions held in Johannesburg, Durban and Cape Town; 1964 Quadrennial Exhibition; 1981 Republic Festival Exhibition.

Represented Durban Art Gallery; Hester Rupert Art Museum, Graaff-Reinet; Pietersburg Collection.

References SAA; 20C SA Art; BSAK; AASA; SASSK.

CUSSONS Sheila

Born 1922 Piketberg, Cape Province.

A painter of figures, landscapes, portraits, still life and abstract pictures. Works in oil, acrylic, watercolour, gouache, pastel, charcoal and ink. A series of Natal Indian dancers and festivals.

Studies 1939–43 University of Natal, under Professor O J P Oxley (qv) and Rosa Hope (qv), gaining a Teaching Diploma in Fine Art; 1947 six months at Camberwell Polytechnic, London, under Victor Pasmore (b.1908); 1948–50 etching under Theo Berrendonck in Amsterdam, The Netherlands.

Profile 1943–44 a lecturer in life drawing at the University of Natal; 1944–45 a lecturer at the Pietermaritzburg Technical College; 1946 taught at the Hugo Naudé Art Centre, Worcester. An author of prose and poetry and winner of many literary awards. 1947–48 lived in London; 1948–56 in Amsterdam; 1956–82 in Barcelona, Spain; 1982–85 in Cape Town; from 1986 in Barcelona and Cape Town.

Exhibitions She has participated in group exhibitions from 1942 in SA; 1943 University of Natal, first of seven solo exhibitions held throughout SA and in Amsterdam and Barcelona; 1984 SAAA Galleries in Cape Town and Bellville, Retrospective Exhibition.

Represented University of Natal.

Reference BSAK.

CUTLER Richard

Born 1927 Pretoria.

A painter and graphic artist of landscapes, portraits, still life, genre and abstract pictures. Works in oil, acrylic, ink and in various graphic media.

Studies During the 1960s studied the history of art at the Sorbonne, Paris, under René Huyghe; 1979–85 studied privately under Ruth Levy (qv).

Profile A photographer and food critic. 1953 a partner of the Constance Stuart Studio with Herman Hahndiek (qv). 1961–71 lived in Paris. Has travelled extensively in Europe, The Americas and to the Far East.

Exhibitions 1981 Carriage House Gallery, Johannesburg, first of two solo exhibitions held in Johannesburg and Pretoria.

D

DALLE RIVE Olga Luigia (Mrs De Giovanni)
Born 1946 Italy.
Resided in SA from 1957.
A painter of landscapes, seascapes, still life and figures. Works in oil and watercolour.
Studies 1976–84 under Patricia Purvis (qv).
Profile From 1980 a member of the Brush and Chisel Club; 1980–86 a member of the WSSA; 1985 a member of the Artists Market Association.
Exhibitions She has participated in several group exhibitions from 1980 in Johannesburg and Pretoria.

DALY Nicholas (Niki)
Born 1946 Cape Town.
A children's book illustrator in mixed media.
Studies 1967–70 Cape Technical College, under W Bruce Franck (qv), gaining a Diploma in Graphic Design.
Profile 1974–79 a part-time lecturer at East Ham Polytechnic, London; from 1983 Head of Graphic Design, University of Stellenbosch. He has illustrated *The Little Girl who Lived Down the Road, Vim the Rag Mouse, Maybe It's a Tiger, Joseph's Other Red Sock, Leo's Christmas Surprise, I Want to See the Moon, Not So Fast Songololo* and six titles for the Walker Book Storytime series. A record by him, entitled *Living in The Suburbs*, was released by Warner Brothers in 1984. He has also written and arranged music for animated films and puppet theatres. Lived in London 1971–80.
Exhibitions 1982 SAAA Gallery, Bellville, solo exhibition; he has participated in group exhibitions from 1983.
Awards 1978 British Arts Council and Provincial Booksellers Awards for Illustration.
References **Fair Lady** 29 May 1985; *Style* June 1982 & June 1984.

DANDO Karin Margaret
Born 1961 Johannesburg.
A painter and graphic artist of figures and abstract pictures. Works in oil and various graphic media, particularly etchings.
Studies 1979–82 University of the Witwatersrand, under Professor Alan Crump, gaining a BA(FA)(Hons); 1983 Atelier 17, Paris, under Stanley William Hayter (*b.*1901); 1983 International Sommerakademie, Salzburg, Austria, under Professor Werner Otto; 1983–85 Akademie der Bildenden Kunste, Vienna, Austria, under Professor Wolfgang Hollegha.
Profile 1982 taught etching at the Johannesburg Art Foundation. 1983 lived in Paris. 1984–85 spent four months on Majorca working with Nils Burwitz (qv). From 1984 she has lived in Austria, but has visited SA several times.

153

Exhibitions She has participated in many group exhibitions from 1981 in SA, Vienna, Salzburg and in England and Taiwan; 1986 Everard Read Gallery, Johannesburg, joint exhibition with Arlene Amaler-Raviv (qv) and Anita van der Merwe (qv).
Awards 1981 Second Prize, 1982 First Prize (graphics), New Signatures, SAAA.

DANIELL Samuel

Born 1775 Chertsey, Surrey, England.
Died 1811 Ceylon (Sri Lanka).
Resided in SA 1799–1803.
A painter and graphic artist of landscapes, figures, animals and hunting scenes. Worked in watercolour, ink and wash. Made aquatints and engravings.
Studies East India College, Haileybury, Hertfordshire, England, under Thomas Medland (*d.*1833).
Profile A member of the staff of the Governor of the Cape of Good Hope, Sir George Yonge. 1800 undersecretary to John Barrow; 1800 secretary to Doctor William Somerville, with whom he went to Graaff-Reinet; 1801–02 secretary and draughtsman to the Truter and Somerville expedition to Bechuanaland (Botswana); 1804 lived in London; 1805–11 lived in Ceylon (Sri Lanka). Illustrated J Barrow's *A Voyage to Cochinchina*, 1806, London and *Travels into the Interior of Southern Africa*, second edition, volume 1, 1806, London. Nephew of Thomas Daniell (1749–1840) and brother of William Daniell (1769–1837), both of whom were artists.
Exhibitions 1792 and 1793 exhibited at the Royal Academy, London; 1948 Tate Gallery, London, SA Art Exhibition.
Represented Africana Museum, Johannesburg; King George VI Art Gallery, Port Elizabeth; SA National Gallery, Cape Town; University of Cape Town; William Fehr Collection, Cape Town.
Reproductions of Daniell's work 1804–05 a large folio containing 30 coloured aquatints was published in two parts entitled *African Scenery and Animals* (see below). Two other sets of sketches are attributed to him although published posthumously, *Sketches of South Africa* in 1821 and *Twenty varied subjects of the Tribe of Antelope* in 1832. *Sketches Representing the Native Tribes, Animals and Scenery of Southern Africa*, 1820, 48 etchings by William Daniell after Samuel Daniell's original sketches, W Daniell and Wood, London.
References Thomas Sutton, *The Daniells, Artists and Travellers*, 1954, Bodley Head, London; *African Scenery and Animals*, a facsimile edition with introduction by F R Bradlow, 1976, A A Balkema, Cape Town; Pict Art; Afr Repos; SADNB; AMC 2 & 6; DSAB; Oxford Companion to Art (under SA); SAP&D; SESA; Pict Afr; Benezit; BSAK 1 & 2; SA Art; 3Cs; *Apollo* October 1975, London.

DANNHAUSER Valerie Decima

Born 1926 Paarl, Cape Province.
A painter and sculptor of landscapes, seascapes, portraits and figures. Works in watercolour, ink, wash and ciment fondu.

Studies 1945–49 Michaelis School of Fine Art, under Professor Edward Roworth (qv), Ivan Mitford-Barberton (qv) and Professor Rupert Shephard (qv), where gained a BA(FA); 1969 Cape Technical College, gaining a Secondary Teaching Diploma; 1974 Ruth Prowse Art Centre, Cape Town, under Erik Laubscher (qv).

Profile 1980–85 taught art privately. 1926–45 lived in Paarl; 1945–52 in Cape Town; 1952–53 in King William's Town; 1953–69 in Beaufort West, thereafter in Cape Town. 1963 visited the Far East; 1970 Mauritius; 1972 Europe; 1975 Scandinavia, Switzerland and France; 1979 Europe and Israel; 1981 the USA; 1983 the Greek islands, Turkey and Israel; 1984 Portugal; 1985 the Far East. Visits SWA/Namibia annually.

Exhibitions She has participated in several group exhibitions from 1977; 1979 The Venue, Sea Point, Cape Town, first of four solo exhibitions.

D'ARCY THOMPSON Molly

Born 1908 Broughty Ferry, Angus, Scotland.
Resided in SA from 1951.
A painter and graphic artist of African life, figures in movement and flower paints. Works in oil, gouache, ink, wash and in various graphic media, particularly lithography.

Studies Studied briefly under André Lhote (1885–1962) in Paris; Edinburgh College of Art, under Sir William Gillies (1898–1973); Westminster School of Art, under Bernard Meninsky (1891–1950); Central School of Art, London, where gained a Diploma.

Profile 1952–63 taught art at the Silver Star Club, Salt River, Cape Town; has also taught art privately.

Exhibitions Participated in many group exhibitions from 1930 in the UK, SA, West Germany and Italy; 1953 HAUM Gallery, Cape Town, first of seven solo exhibitions, five held in the Cape, one in London and one in Edinburgh; 1956 and 1964 Quadrennial Exhibitions.

Represented Ann Bryant Gallery, East London; SA National Gallery, Cape Town.

Publications by D'Arcy Thompson *Call the Wind*, 1971, David Philip, Cape Town; *Forgotten Corners of the Cape*, 1981, John Malherbe, Cape Town; *Mopsy's Story*, 1984, John Malherbe, Cape Town.

References Art SA; BSAK 2; SAA; AASA.

DARDAGAN Roxandra

Born 1962 Salisbury, Rhodesia (Harare, Zimbabwe).
Resided in SA from 1981.
A graphic artist depicting landscapes and portraits.

Studies 1981–84 Rhodes University, under Professor Robert Brooks (qv), gaining a BA(FA); 1985 began an MFA course at Rhodes University.

Profile 1984 produced, together with Shaun Naidoo, a slide show entitled "Monumentality". 1986–87 book jacket, poster and programme designs.

Exhibitions She has participated in several group exhibitions from 1982 in SA and Zimbabwe.
Represented Rhodes University.

DARROLL Gail Denise

Born 1952 Cape Town.
A self-taught painter of birds. Works in watercolour.
Profile 1976–78 a member of the administrative staff of the University of Cape Town in the Departments of Microbiology and Botany. Here she studied birdlife and was involved in the preparation of scientific drawings to illustrate articles by the academic staff, for inclusion in international journals. 1980–85 illustrated *Ducks of Sub-Saharan Africa*, by Professor G L Maclean, 1986, Acorn Books, Johannesburg. From 1982 has lived at Wilderness, Cape Province.
Exhibitions 1980 Cape Town, solo exhibition; she has participated in several group exhibitions in Johannesburg from 1984; 1984–87 took part in three international group exhibitions at the Everard Read Gallery and in 1987 at the Read Stremmel Gallery in the USA; 1986 Everard Read Gallery, Johannesburg, exhibition of the original paintings of *Ducks of Sub-Saharan Africa*.
References AASA; *SA Panorama* November 1986.

DAVIES Eirys

Born 1920 Wales.
Resided in SA *c.*1946–59.
A painter of portraits in oil.
Studies Slade School of Art, London, under Sir William Rothenstein (1872–1945), where attained a Fine Arts Diploma; St Martin's School of Art, London and in St Ives, Cornwall.
Profile 1947–59 an art lecturer at Natal Technical College, University of Natal, Witwatersrand Technical College and the University of the Witwatersrand.
Exhibitions She has participated in group exhibitions in England, Wales, Canada and SA and held solo exhibitions in Durban, Johannesburg and Cape Town.
Represented Ashmolean Museum, Oxford, UK; National Museum of Wales, UK.
References SAA; AASA.

DAVIES (Owen) Llewellyn

Born 1950 Bulawayo, Rhodesia (Zimbabwe).
Resided in SA from 1973.
A self-taught sculptor of wildlife, figures and portrait busts. Works in bronze. Casts his own work.
Exhibitions He has participated in group exhibitions from 1985 in SA.
Public Commissions 1978 "The Cane Cutter", 1980 "Deja Vu" and "The Penny Whistler", Tongaat, Natal.

W H COETZER
Nagmaal 1934
Oil on Canvas 66,3 × 87 cm
Durban Art Gallery

GAIL DARROLL
Knysna Loeries 1988
Watercolour 56 × 46 cm
Peter Gain

LEON DE BLIQUY
The Rain Bull 1987
Egg Tempera on Canvas 140 × 140 cm
P J de Bruyn

ERNST DE JONG
Planet of Mangoes 1979
Oil on Canvas 100 × 150 cm
Artist

DAVIES Mary Alison
Born 1916 Port Elizabeth.
An artist depicting landscapes, seascapes and town scenes. Works in ink and wash.
Studies Port Elizabeth Technical College; Chelsea School of Art, London, under Robert Medley (*b*.1905); Royal College of Art, London, under Barnett Freedman (1901–58), Gilbert Spencer (*b*.1892), Roland Vivian Pitchforth (qv) and engraving under Robert Austin (1895–1973).
Profile 1940–52 lectured at the Witwatersrand Technical College; 1954–59 lectured at the American Community School, Athens, Greece. 1959–62 lived in England, thereafter in SA. Works at the Transvaal Museum, Pretoria.
Exhibitions 1942 Johannesburg, solo exhibition; 1952 Van Riebeeck Festival Exhibition.
References SAA; AASA.

DAVIS Arthur Savile
Born 1891 Johannesburg.
Died 1975.
A painter of mining scenes, views of early Johannesburg and the docks in Durban. Worked in watercolour and oil.
Studies Slade School of Art, London, under Henry Tonks (1862–1937) and Hutchison; under A E Gyngell (qv) in Johannesburg.
Profile A mining engineer and part-time painter. A member of the Johannesburg Sketch Club and the Transvaal Art Society.
Exhibitions Participated in group exhibitions from 1926 in SA and in London.
Represented Africana Museum, Johannesburg.
References Collectors' Guide; SAA; AMC2; DBA; AASA.

DAVIS Peter
Born 1932.
A self-taught sculptor of figures and abstracts. Works in wood and occasionally in bronze.
Exhibitions He has participated in group exhibitions from 1966; 1968 Lidchi Gallery, Johannesburg, first of several solo exhibitions.
References BSAK 1; *Artlook* May 1968 & March 1970.

DAVIS William John (Bill)
Born 1933 Assam, India.
Resided in SA from 1938.
A sculptor of both figurative and abstract works. Uses bronze, stone, ciment fondu, wood and ivory. Paints, draws and produces graphics.
Studies 1951–54 Michaelis School of Fine Art, under Professor Lippy Lipshitz (qv), where he gained a Diploma in Fine Art; 1955–57 drawing at the Ryksnormaal School, Amsterdam; 1957–62 Rijksakademie van Beeldende Kunsten, Amsterdam, under Professor V P S Esser, on a Dutch/SA Student Exchange Bursary.

Profile A member of the SAAA and Chairman of the Worcester Association of Arts. 1963–65 an art master at the South African College Schools, Cape Town; 1966 a lecturer in sculpture at the Michaelis School of Fine Art; 1966–71 lectured in life drawing at the School of Architecture, University of Cape Town. 1957 visited Israel, 1957, 1959 and 1974 Greece and in 1962 France.

Exhibitions He has participated in group exhibitions from 1960 in Amsterdam, SA and at the Venice Biennial in 1964 and the São Paulo Bienale in 1965; 1962 Amsterdam, first of 15 solo exhibitions held in Amsterdam and throughout SA; 1979 Invited Artist, Cape Town Biennial; 1987 Die Kunskamer, Cape Town, Special Exhibition on the occasion of the publication of his book on Genesis Woodcuts.

Awards 1961 Prix de Rome; 1963 Graphic Art Prize, Cape Salon; 1966 Sculpture Prize, SA Breweries Competition; 1967 Sculpture Prize, Cape Art.

Represented Ann Bryant Gallery, East London; Hugo Naude Art Centre, Worcester; Municipal Collection, Amstelveen, The Netherlands; Pretoria Art Museum; Touch Gallery, SA National Gallery, Cape Town; University of Cape Town; University of the Orange Free State; Willem Annandale Art Gallery, Lichtenburg; William Humphreys Art Gallery, Kimberley.

Public Commissions Various medals and portrait busts; Meulsloot Monument, Stellenbosch; wall relief, Nico Malan Opera House, Cape Town; Chapel doors, University of Cape Town; sculptures for St Bernard's Church, Newlands, the Roman Catholic Church, Durbanville and St Thomas' Church, Rondebosch.

References SAA; SESA; 3Cs; AASA; *Artlook* May 1971.

DAY Mark Cedric

Born 1958 Rhodesia (Zimbabwe).
Resided in SA from 1965.
A painter and graphic artist of landscapes, portraits, still life, figures and abstract pictures. Works in acrylic, watercolour, gouache, ink, wash, pencil, charcoal, graphite, airbrush, woodcut, linocut, silkscreen and resin.

Studies 1975–79 Witwatersrand Technical College, under Johan van Heerden (qv), Noel Bisseker (qv), Claude van Lingen (qv), Johann Moolman (qv), Jo Smail (qv) and Nico van Rensburg (qv).

Profile Has produced a number of book illustrations.

Exhibitions He has participated in several group exhibitions from 1977 in SA; 1985 Crake Gallery, Johannesburg, solo exhibition.

Reference Habitat no 67, 1985.

DE BEER André

Born 1933 Potchefstroom, Transvaal.
A painter of landscapes, portraits, still life, seascapes, genre and figures. Works in oil, watercolour, ink, pencil, charcoal and pastel.

Studies 1951–53 University of Pretoria, gaining a BA; 1954 Teachers Training College, Pretoria, specialising in art and obtaining a Higher Diploma in Education; 1957–60 University of South Africa, where gained a BA(FA); 1969–70 University of Pretoria, under Professor F G E Nilant, where he was awarded an MA(FA).

Profile A member of the National Art Society of SA and its Chairman 1964–70. 1964–70 also a member of the Curatorium of the Pretoria Art Museum. 1955–58 an art teacher at Oost-Eind School, Pretoria; 1958–70 an art lecturer, then a senior lecturer in the Art Department, 1970–78 Head of the Art Department and 1979–83 Vice-Rector, Pretoria College of Education. Became a full-time painter in 1983. 1975–77 a part-time political cartoonist for *Hoofstad* newspaper, Pretoria, also a number of illustrations for various periodicals.

Exhibitions He has participated in numerous group exhibitions from 1960 in SA; 1968 Schweickerdt Gallery, Pretoria, first of eight solo exhibitions held in SA; 1981 Republic Festival Exhibition.

Represented Willem Annandale Art Gallery, Lichtenburg.

References BSAK, AASA; SASSK; *Artlook* November 1968 & January 1971.

DE BLIQUY Leon Paul

Born 1943 Johannesburg.

A painter and graphic artist of mythological and literary themes, incorporated into landscapes, portraits, still life, figures, animals and abstract pictures. Works in watercolour, tempera, egg tempera, casein tempera, fresco, mural painting techniques, oil, acrylic, gouache, ink, pencil, charcoal and in various graphic media. 1967 a series of "Walls and Houses"; 1968 of "Interiors"; 1970 of "Boats and Reflections"; 1970 of "Figures and Fruit"; 1971–72 of "Greek Poems"; 1971–72 of "Flight over Africa"; 1974 of "The Flemish Bride"; 1976 of "African Mythology"; 1977 of "Death and Regeneration of the Mantis Child"; 1978–79 of "Myths of Rain"; 1980 of "Lament for Ignacio Sanchy Mejias"; 1981 of "Marine Genesis–Shell"; 1983 of "Genesis".

Studies 1962–63 Michaelis School of Fine Art, under Neville Dubow, Carl Buchner (qv) and Katrine Harries (qv); 1964–67 part-time at the Cape Technical College, gaining a National Printers Diploma in 1965 and a Certificate in Commercial Art in 1967; 1971–72 and 1975–76 Koninklijke Academie voor Schone Kunsten en die Hogere Instituten, Antwerp, Belgium; 1979 University of the Orange Free State, gaining a BA(FA); 1983 Port Elizabeth Technikon, where awarded a National Diploma in Technology (Graphic Art); 1985 Rhodes University, under Professor Robert Brooks (qv), where attained an MFA.

Profile 1971 a portfolio of coloured lithographs, produced at the Koninklijke Academie in Antwerp. 1974 a committee member of the SAAA, Cape Town Branch and in 1977–80 of the SAAA, Orange Free State Branch. 1982–83 a member of the EPSFA. 1982 a selector for the Cape Town Triennial; 1983 on the King George VI Art Gallery, Port Elizabeth, Acquisition Committee and Board of Trustees. 1963–69 worked as a commercial artist; 1969–71 the owner and manager of the Dorp Street Studio and a part-time lecturer at the Cape Technical College and at the Cape Town Art Centre; 1973–75 a lecturer at the Cape Technical College; 1976–79 a lecturer at the University of the Orange Free State; 1980–86 Head of the Drawing Department, Port Elizabeth Technikon. 1971 first of several visits to Europe.

Exhibitions He has participated in numerous group exhibitions from 1967 held in SA, Belgium, Monaco, the USA, West Germany and China; 1967 Adler Fielding Gallery, Johannesburg, first of 23 solo exhibitions held in SA and Belgium; 1970 and 1972 Stellenbosch Museum, solo exhibitions; 1973 and 1975 Bloemfontein Museum, solo exhibitions; 1977 University of the Orange Free State, solo exhibition; 1981 Republic Festival Exhibition; 1983 King George VI Art Gallery, Port Elizabeth, solo exhibition.
Awards 1967 Painting Prize, Cape Art; 1975 Cape Tercentenary Foundation Award.
Represented King George VI Art Gallery, Port Elizabeth; National Museum, Bloemfontein; Pretoria Art Museum; SA National Gallery, Cape Town; Sterckshof Museum, Antwerp, Belgium; University of the Orange Free State; William Humphreys Art Gallery, Kimberley.
Public Commissions 1978 stainless steel relief sculpture, Student Centre, University of the Orange Free State; 1979 mural painting, Hotel President, Bloemfontein; 1986 mural, Johannesburg Consolidated Investment Building, Johannesburg.
References BSAK 2; AASA.

DE BOOM Marcella

Born 1945 Pretoria.
A painter and a sculptor of landscapes, portraits and figures. Works in acrylic, watercolour, ciment fondu and ceramics.
Studies 1962–63 Cornell University, USA, under Professor N Daly; 1963–66 through the University of Pretoria, under Gunther van der Reis (qv), where gained a BA(FA).
Profile A member of the SAAA.
Exhibitions She has participated in group exhibitions from 1967 in SA; 1970 Pretoria, solo exhibition; 1981 Republic Festival Exhibition.
Represented University of Pretoria.
Reference AASA.

DE BRUYN Linky (née Stoker)

Born 1941 Pretoria.
An artist who regards any medium as a challenge and finds that the medium and often the style dictate the subject matter.
Studies 1960–62 Pretoria Technical College (Technikon), under Ernst de Jong (qv), Peter Eliastam (qv), Robert Hodgins (qv) and Zakkie Eloff (qv), where she attained a National Diploma in Graphic Design; 1981 Pretoria Technikon, under Gert le Grange, gaining a Higher Diploma in Graphic Design (cum laude).
Profile From 1960 a member of the SAAA and from 1985 of the APSA. 1963–65 a lecturer in basic and graphic design, Pretoria Technical College, continuing to lecture there on a part-time basis in 1975, 1981 and 1985. From 1963 a commercial artist, involved in poetry, calligraphy and graphic design. 1963, 1965, 1973, 1983 and 1985 visited Europe and the USA.
Exhibitions She has participated in several group exhibitions from 1966 in SA; 1975 SAAA Gallery, Pretoria, solo exhibition.

DEICHMANN Johan Reinder

Born 1953 Pretoria.

A painter of fantasy landscapes, still life and abstract pictures. Works in oil, acrylic, watercolour, gouache, ink, wash, pencil and charcoal. Creates collages.

Studies 1976 University of Pretoria, under Professor Nico Roos (qv), gaining a BA Education—Art; 1980 University of Pretoria, under Professor F G E Nilant, where he attained a BA Honours—History of Art.

Profile From 1984 a member of the SAAA and a board member in 1986. 1977–82 an art teacher at the Afrikaanse Hoër Seunsskool, Pretoria; 1983 at Waterkloof Hoër Skool, Pretoria; 1984–86 at Carmel High School, Pretoria. From 1987 a full-time artist. November 1985–March 1986 lived in Paris, at the Cité Internationale des Arts. 1982–83 spent four months in Greece.

Exhibitions 1982 Mini Gallery, Pretoria, first of eight solo exhibitions of which one was held in the SA Embassy in Paris; he has participated in several group exhibitions from 1984 in SA and once in Paris.

DE JAGER Albert

Born 1925 Bloemfontein.

A painter of landscapes, cottages and historical buildings. Works in watercolour.

Studies 1944–48 Orange Free State Technical College.

Profile The Art Director of an Afrikaans magazine in Cape Town. A past music critic and cartoonist for various newspapers and magazines.

Exhibition 1986 Atlantic Art Gallery, Cape Town, solo exhibition.

Reference SASSK.

DE JAGER Daniël Jacobus

Born 1936 Germiston, Transvaal.

A sculptor of both figurative and abstract works.

Studies Witwatersrand Technical College, under James Gardner (qv).

Profile A member of the Pretoria Art Society. 1965 and 1968 spent three months in Europe, since 1979 has visited Europe annually.

Represented University of Cape Town; War Museum of the Boer Republics, Bloemfontein.

Public Commissions Hertzog Monument, Bloemfontein; Strijdom Monuments in Pretoria and Nelspruit; Smuts Monument, Pretoria; "Banneling" ("The Exile"), Bloemfontein; abstract works in Warmbaths and at the State Theatre, Pretoria; Giraffes, Nature Conservation Building, Pretoria; Delville Wood Monument, France; among numerous others in libraries, airports and various other public buildings.

References BSAK 1 & 2; SA Art; 3Cs; AASA; *Artlook* October 1968.

DE JAGER Joey

Born 1949 Tzaneen, Northern Transvaal.

A painter of landscapes, portraits and figures. Works in oil.

Studies 1968–71 and 1976 University of Pretoria, under Professor Nico Roos (qv) and Gunther van der Reis (qv), gaining a BA(FA) in 1971 and a BA(Hons) in 1976.

Profile A member of the SAAAH. From 1973 a lecturer in the Department of History of Art and Fine Art, University of South Africa. From 1975 Chief Examiner in Art for the Joint Matriculation Board.
Exhibitions He has participated in several group exhibitions from 1979; 1980 SAAA Gallery, Pretoria, joint exhibition with J P van der Walt (qv).
Represented University of the Orange Free State.

DE JONG Ernst

Born 1934 Pretoria.
A painter of landscapes, still life, seascapes, figures and of abstract pictures. Works in oil, watercolour, ink, pencil, charcoal and gold leaf. A graphic artist, producing serigraphs. A large series of constructivist relief paintings in gold leaf and oil; "Flower" series; "Fruit" series; "Underwater and Sea Images" series; "Rocks and Boulders" series.
Studies 1952–56 on a full scholarship at the University of Oklahoma, USA, stone lithography under Professor Amelio Amero, design under Professor Eugene Bavinger and painting under Professor John O'Neil, gaining a BA(FA).
Profile 1958–60 lectured in design at the Pretoria Technical College; 1972–74 lectured in design at the University of Pretoria; 1977–79 lectured in design and painting at the University of Pretoria. From 1958 Managing and Creative Director of the Ernst de Jong Studios (Pty) Ltd, Pretoria, working in commercial and graphic design as well as in film. In 1979 he opened the Ernst de Jong Studio Gallery. A member of the Board of the Bureau of Heraldry. He has worked in the advertising industry from 1963. From 1968 he has produced a large number of designs for postage stamps; 1974 designed a tapestry for the Springs Civic Centre; designs for commemorative gold medallions in 1976 for the Transkei and in 1978 for Bophuthatswana; 1984 designed the "Cape St Francis" pendant. Has also designed several private residences in Pretoria, including his own. 1952–57 lived in the USA, has travelled extensively and frequently in the USA and in Europe.
Exhibitions 1956 University of Oklahoma, first of 26 solo exhibitions in the USA, SA and Italy; he has participated in numerous group exhibitions from 1960 in SA, the USA, Canada, Switzerland, Italy and Belgium; 1961 Gallery 101, Johannesburg, joint exhibition with Robert Hodgins (qv); 1988 Pretoria Art Museum, exhibition.
Awards 1956 Letzeiser Award for Best Student, University of Oklahoma; 1987 Dashing/SDSA Crystal Award for Outstanding Design Achievement.
Represented Ann Bryant Gallery, East London; Hester Rupert Art Museum, Graaff-Reinet; Pretoria Art Museum; Rand Afrikaans University; University of Natal; University of the Witwatersrand.
Public Commissions Over 30 public murals, including: 1961 mosaic murals, Transvaal Provincial Administration Building; Pretoria; 1968 mural, Jan Smuts Airport, Johannesburg; 1972 gold leaf relief mural, Banking Hall, United Building Society, Pretoria; 1972 mural, Natal Provincial Administration Building, Pietermaritzburg; 1976 two murals, Rustenburg Civic Centre. 1980–81 "Fantasia", a fire curtain, the State Theatre, Pretoria; 1984 sculpture "Earth and Space", Library, Germiston Civic Centre, Transvaal.

Reproductions by De Jong Numerous portfolios of his work have been printed: 1969 *Oklahoma*, 12 serigraphs; 1974 *Springs*, four serigraphs; 1974 *Shells*, four serigraphs; 1974 *Dance*, four serigraphs; 1975 *Shield*, six lithographs; 1976 *Night Passage*, eight lithographs; 1977 *White Bird*, one serigraph, included in a portfolio by 10 SA printmakers; 1977 *Western Images*, four serigraphs; 1983 *Flowers*, four serigraphs.
References Collectors' Guide; Art SA; SAA; 20C SA Art; BSAK 1 & 2; SA Art; AASA; LSAA; *SA Panorama* November 1958, April 1976 & January 1984; *Artlook* April 1967 & September 1967.

DE JONGH Gabriel Cornelis

Born 1913 Amsterdam, The Netherlands.
Resided in SA from 1921.
A painter of landscapes, still life, seascapes, wildlife, religious subjects and paintings inspired by classical music. Works in oil, watercolour, ink and pencil. A graphic artist producing etchings.
Studies Michaelis School of Fine Art; Slade School of Art, London; woodcarving under H V Meyerowitz (qv) in Cape Town; photo-lithography at *The Cape Times*; also studied under his father Tinus de Jongh (qv).
Profile A war artist depicting scenes in France, England, Belgium and The Netherlands. Has travelled in South America and Europe. He built an art gallery at the Lanzerac Hotel in Stellenbosch to display the life in pictures of Tinus de Jongh (qv).
Exhibitions He has participated in numerous group exhibitions in SA; 1946 Maskew Miller Gallery, Cape Town, first solo exhibition.
Represented Ann Bryant Gallery, East London; National Museum, Bloemfontein; University of Cape Town; University of Stellenbosch.
References Collectors' Guide; AASA.

DE JONGH Marthinus Johannes (Tinus)

Born 1885 Amsterdam, The Netherlands.
Died 1942 Bloemfontein.
Resided in SA from 1921.
A prolific painter of landscapes, street scenes and interiors. His landscapes are generally mountainous and frequently incorporate a gabled farmhouse. Worked in oil. A graphic artist producing etchings.
Studies 1900–02 Ambachtsscholen, Amsterdam, where he studied decorating and was awarded the First Prize presented by Paul Kruger. Until 1906 studied at various art schools in The Netherlands.
Profile A member of the SA Society of Artists. Well-known in The Netherlands, where he was commissioned to paint a series of views of The Old Dam in Amsterdam for Queen Wilhelmina. Travelled extensively throughout SA.
Exhibitions 1922 Johannesburg, first of numerous solo exhibitions in SA, London and Rhodesia (Zimbabwe); participated in group exhibitions from 1925; 1981 Total Gallery, Johannesburg, Memorial Exhibition.

Represented Albany Museum, Grahamstown; Ann Bryant Gallery, East London; Durban Art Gallery; Julius Gordon Africana Centre, Riversdale; National Museum, Bloemfontein; Potchefstroom Museum; Pretoria Art Museum; Rand Afrikaans University; Rijksmuseum, Amsterdam, The Netherlands; SA Cultural History Museum, Cape Town; SA National Gallery, Cape Town; Stedelik Museum, Amsterdam, The Netherlands; Tinus de Jongh Memorial Gallery, Stellenbosch; University of South Africa; University of Stellenbosch; Willem Annandale Art Gallery, Lichtenburg.

Public Commission 1923 Groote Schuur Hospital, medical illustrations for training purposes.

References Art SA; SAA; 20C SA Art; SADNB; DSAB; SESA; DBA; BSAK 1 & 2; SA Art; 3Cs; AASA; Tinus de Jongh Gallery Catalogue, Stellenbosch.

DE KLERK Deline

Born 1956 Delareyville, Transvaal.

A painter of figurative and symbolic images in unconventional landscapes and interiors. Works in oil, acrylic, watercolour and mixed media. A photographer and a graphic artist.

Studies 1975–78 University of Pretoria, under Professor Nico Roos (qv), gaining a BA(FA); 1979 University of Pretoria, where attained a Higher Diploma in Education.

Profile From 1975 a member of the SAAA. In 1980 founded, with her husband Willi Lottering (qv), The Art Studio, Pretoria, where she lectures and designs. 1980 a lecturer at the Pretoria Central Technical Institute; 1985 at the Pretoria Technikon; 1987 a part-time lecturer at the University of Pretoria. Has lived in Pretoria from 1975. Visited Europe in 1979.

Exhibitions She has participated in many group exhibitions from 1978 in SA; 1980 Ernst de Jong Gallery, Pretoria, first of three solo exhibitions; 1984 Gallery 21, Johannesburg, first of several joint exhibitions held with Willi Lottering (qv); 1985 SAAA Gallery, Pretoria, joint exhibition with Wendy Malan (qv) and Christa Botha (qv).

Happenings staged by Willi Lottering (qv) and Deline de Klerk "Colour Fields", April 1982; "Archaeological Finds", July 1983; "Sound and Expression", February 1984; "Human Ecology", November 1985.

Awards 1978 First Prize Painting and Merit Award Graphics, New Signatures, SAAA.

DE LEEUW Gerard

Born 1912 Amsterdam, The Netherlands.

Died 1985 Johannesburg.

Resided in SA from 1932.

A sculptor of portrait busts, figures, animals, birds and anthropological subjects. Worked in bronze. A series on witchdoctors. From 1937 he did most of his own casting, using the cire perdue casting method. An etcher.

Studies 1929–32 various art schools including the Antwerp Academy; 1948–50 studied casting at foundries in England, France and at Leyden in The Netherlands.

Profile 1932–36 shared Palm Studio, Cape Town, with Lippy Lipshitz (qv) and Wolf Kibel (qv), thereafter lived in Johannesburg. *c.*1937 travelled the Platteland selling paintings for a few years.

Exhibitions Participated in numerous group exhibitions from 1941 in SA, Italy, Brazil and Zimbabwe; 1964 Quadrennial Exhibition; 1980 Pretoria Art Museum, Retrospective Exhibition.

Award 1949 SA Academy Silver Medal for Sculpture.

Represented Hester Rupert Art Museum, Graaff-Reinet; Pretoria Art Museum; SA National Gallery, Cape Town; University of the Orange Free State; Willem Annandale Art Gallery, Lichtenburg; William Humphreys Art Gallery, Kimberley.

Public Commissions 1952 portrait of Minister Tom Naudé; 1954 Pelicans, Receiver of Revenue, Johannesburg; 1954 portrait of Minister Ben Schoeman, SA Railways; 1958 wall panels, Medfontein Building, Bloemfontein; 1964 Figure of Christ, Roman Catholic Church, Bloemfontein; 1968 statue of H F Verwoerd, Provincial Administration Building, Bloemfontein; 1971 Founder, SEIFSA, Johannesburg and Durban; 1972 Lucifer, Thaba ya Kreste Catholic Church, Thaba 'Nchu.

References Matthys J Strydom, *Gerard de Leeuw*, 1979, Suid Kaap Uitgewery; Collectors' Guide; Art SA; SAA; 20C SA Art; BSAK 1 & 2; SA Art; 3Cs; AASA; LSAA; *Artlook* October 1969.

DELPORT Peggy (Mrs Archer)

Born 1937 Paarl, Cape Province.

A painter of landscapes and figures. Works in oil and wash. A graphic artist producing serigraphs. "Valley" series, studies of poverty and deprivation.

Studies 1955–59 Michaelis School of Fine Art; 1979 Ruskin School of Drawing, Oxford University, England.

Profile 1965 Foundation member of the Artists Gallery, Cape Town. 1963 a lecturer in graphic design at the Michaelis School of Fine Art; 1972–73 visiting artist in the Printmaking Department, Brighton Art School, UK; from 1980 a lecturer at the Michaelis School of Fine Art. Until 1978 an organiser of workshops and a trustee and co-ordinator of art programmes for the Community Arts Project. 1972–73 and 1979–80 lived in England.

Exhibitions She has participated in group exhibitions from 1963; 1968 Cape Town, first solo exhibition; 1982 National Gallery, Gaborone, Botswana, Exhibition of SA Art; 1985 Tributaries, touring SA and West Germany.

Awards 1965 Painting Prize, Thames & Hudson Award from Cape Salon; 1966 Best Student, Artists of Fame and Promise, Adler Fielding Gallery, Johannesburg; 1966 First Prize for Graphics, Cape Art '66, Cape Town; 1968 Bronze Medal, Art Prize 1968, SA Breweries, Cape Town.

Represented Ann Bryant Gallery, East London; Pretoria Art Museum; SA National Gallery, Cape Town.

References Register SA & SWA; SAP&D; BSAK 1 & 2; 3Cs; AASA.

DELPORTE Wilfred Alec

Born 1937 Kimberley, Cape Province.
A sculptor, painter and graphic artist of figures and abstract works. Uses metal, stone, wood, oil, various graphic media and enamel.
Studies 1960 Polly Street Art Centre, Johannesburg, under Cecil Skotnes (qv); 1976 British Arts Council Scholarship to study graphics and sculpture at Cardiff College of Fine Art and Design, Wales.
Profile 1983 a member of the SAAA, Pretoria and until 1984 of the Kimberley Society of Arts. In 1985 became a member of the International Sculptors Center, Washington DC, USA. Taught art in 1962 at a primary school in Kimberley and 1963–65 at a high school in Kimberley. Has travelled in England, Wales, France and The Netherlands. Lives in Kimberley.
Exhibitions He has participated in numerous group exhibitions from 1963 in SA, Wales, Paris, West Germany and Spain; 1970 William Humphreys Art Gallery, Kimberley, first of 12 solo exhibitions held in SA.
References AASA; *SA Panorama* November 1974; *Lantern* May 1977.

DE MEILLON Henry Clifford

Died *c.*1856 Port Elizabeth.
Resided in SA from 1823.
A self-taught artist of scenes of Cape Town, botanical studies and historical events. Worked in watercolour.
Profile A number of the illustrations used in *Travels in South Africa*, by George Thompson, 1927 and *Letters from The Cape by Lady Gordon Duff*, by Dorothea Fairbridge, 1927, were by De Meillon. Sixteen hand-coloured lithographs of Cape Town were produced by George Greig, Cape Town, in 1832 and later inserted in Greig's *Cape Almanacs* 1832–35. Lithographs of De Meillon's work were also produced by Day & Hage, London. Until 1838 he lived in Cape Town, thereafter in the Eastern Cape.
Represented Africana Museum, Johannesburg; SA Cultural History Museum, Cape Town; University of Natal; William Fehr Collection, Cape Town.
References Anna H Smith, *Cape Views and Costumes, watercolours by H C de Meillon*, 1978, Brenthurst Press, Johannesburg; Pict Art; Afr Repos; SADNB; AMC2; SESA; Pict Afr; BSAK; SA Art; 3Cs; *ANN* September 1946; *Apollo* October 1975, London.

DE NECKER Francois

Born 1944 Orange Free State.
A painter of landscapes and abstract pictures. Works in oil and water-colour.
Studies Witwatersrand Technical College, under Judith Mason (qv), Claude van Lingen (qv), Anna Vorster (qv) and Joyce Leonard (qv); The Visual Arts Research Centre, Johannesburg, under George Boys (qv).

Profile 1968 worked in advertising in Johannesburg. 1974 a lecturer in the Fine Art Department, University of Pretoria; 1981 Head of the Art Department, Windhoek College of Education; 1983 established an art department at the Academy for Tertiary Education, Windhoek.

Exhibitions He has participated in group exhibitions in SA and SWA/Namibia; 1978 Hoffer Gallery, Pretoria, first of several solo exhibitions held in SA and SWA/Namibia; 1981 Republic Festival Exhibition.

Represented Arts Association SWA/Namibia Collection; University of Natal.

References AASA; PS/N.

DEN HOUTING Jacobus Johannes (Koos)

Born 1939 Alicedale, Cape Province.

A sculptor of portraits, figures and abstract pieces in figurative, traditional and abstract styles. Works in bronze, stone, ciment fondu and wood. 1975–85 a large series entitled "The Relation between Human and Bird Forms".

Studies 1963 Witwatersrand Technical College, under Phil Kolbe (qv), gaining a National Diploma in Art and Design; 1978 Pretoria Technical College, under Justinus van der Merwe (qv), attaining a Higher Diploma in Sculpture.

Profile 1967–72 a committee member and from 1975 a member of the SAAA, Pretoria. 1964 taught art in Durban and from 1965 Head of the Sculpture Department, Pretoria Technikon. 1970–80 taught jewellery and enamelling. Cover illustrations in 1977 for the *SA Aloe and Succulent Society Journal*. 1960–61 lived in Bloemfontein, 1962–63 in Johannesburg, 1964 in Durban and from 1965 in Pretoria. Visited Paraguay in 1981.

Exhibitions 1966 The Gallery, Johannesburg, first of 10 solo exhibitions held in Johannesburg and Pretoria; he has participated in numerous group exhibitions in SA from 1967; 1980 Rand Afrikaans University, Retrospective Exhibition; 1981 Republic Festival Exhibition; 1982 Gallery 21, Johannesburg, joint exhibition with F J Yssel (qv).

Awards 1973 Metalart Prize (Open Category); 1985 joint winner of the Hans Merensky Sculpture in Wood Competition with Guy du Toit (qv).

Represented Municipal collections of Pietersburg, Estcourt and Secunda; William Humphreys Art Gallery, Kimberley.

Public Commissions 1970 wood panel, Jan Smuts Airport, Johannesburg; 1983 emblem, SA Police Headquarters, Pretoria.

References BSAK; AASA.

DENT Hugh Railton

Born 1927 Pietermaritzburg.

A painter of landscapes, portraits and figures. Works in oil, ink, wash, pencil and charcoal.

Studies 1947 and 1950–52 University of Natal, under Rosa Hope (qv) and Geoffrey Long (qv), where gained a BA(FA); 1953 City and Guilds School, London, under Middleton Todd and Henry Wilkinson, gaining a Certificate of Merit; 1974–75 Rhodes University, under Professor Brian Bradshaw (qv) and Josua Nell (qv), where attained an MFA in art and nature conservation.

Profile 1974–76 a member of the Grahamstown Group. 1955, 1956 and 1960–73 a Senior Ranger and Field Officer with the Natal Parks Board and the Wilderness Leadership School; 1958–59 a lecturer in Fine Art, Natal Technical College (Technikon); 1976 substitute senior lecturer in Fine Art, University of Fort Hare; 1977–79 a senior lecturer in Fine Art, 1980–83 Director of Fine Art, 1984–87 a senior lecturer in Drawing, at the Natal Technikon. 1977 Education Officer, National Gallery of Rhodesia (Zimbabwe). Visited London and the UK in 1953, 1963, 1973, 1976 and 1983; France, The Netherlands, Switzerland and Italy in 1953; the USA in 1974 and 1978; Paris in 1983.
Exhibitions He has participated in several group exhibitions from 1975 held throughout SA.
Public Commissions 1963 several posthumous portraits for St John's College, Johannesburg and in 1983 a posthumous portrait for the University of Natal, Durban.

DE ROUBAIX Tina

Born 1952 Boksburg, Transvaal.
A painter of landscapes and in 1980–81 of figures in a fantastical and impressionistic manner. Works in batik.
Studies 1966–68 Pretoria School of Art, Ballet and Music, under Elsa Lamb (qv) and Danie de Wet (qv); 1969 Pretoria Technical College, under Justinus van der Merwe (qv) and Jean Beeton (qv).
Profile 1958–69 lived in Swaziland; from 1980 in Nottingham Road, Natal, where she runs the Braemar Gallery with her husband Wim de Roubaix (qv). 1981–83 a children's art teacher at the Braemar Gallery; 1985 a founder member of the Midlands Meander Group. From 1985 an art teacher at Kings School, Natal.
Exhibitions She has participated in many group exhibitions from 1971 in SA and West Germany.
References SA *Garden & Home* September 1983 & December 1986.

DE ROUBAIX Wim

Born 1951 Pretoria.
A painter, graphic artist and sculptor of abstracted works often incorporating figures and animals. Works in oil, watercolour, gouache, ink, wash, pencil, various graphic media, wood, wax, metal, particularly lead, plaster of Paris, ceramics and enamel.
Studies 1967–69 Pretoria School of Art, Ballet and Music, under Elsa Lamb (qv) and Danie de Wet (qv); 1970 Pretoria Technical College, under Danie de Wet (qv).
Profile From 1980 has lived in Nottingham Road, Natal, where he runs the Braemar Gallery with his wife Tina de Roubaix (qv). In 1981 began teaching at the Braemar Gallery. From 1984 a founder member of the Midlands Arts and Crafts Society; 1985 a founder member of the Midlands Meander Group. 1970–73 designed and manufactured stained glass for an Anglican Church in Port Shepstone as well as for private homes.

Exhibitions He has participated in many group exhibitions from 1971 in SA and Swaziland; 1984 Pretoria, first of two solo exhibitions held in SA and Boston, USA.
References *SA Garden & Home* September 1983 & February 1986.

DE SMIDT Abraham

Born 1829 Cape Town.
Died 1908 Brighton, Sussex, England.
Resided in SA until 1890.
A painter of Cape Province landscapes. Worked in watercolour and gouache, and occasionally, in the 1880s, in oil.
Studies 1840–45 South African College, Cape Town, art under Thomas Bowler (qv) and land-surveying.
Profile 1848 a civil servant in the Surveyor-General's Department; 1852 a surveyor under Charles Bell (qv); 1863 Assistant Surveyor-General; 1872–89 Surveyor-General at the Cape. 1852 a committee member of the Second Exhibition of Fine Arts, Cape Town; 1858 Honorary Secretary of the Third Exhibition of Fine Arts, Cape Town; 1866 a committee member of the Fourth Exhibition of Fine Arts, Cape Town; 1871 instrumental in the founding of the SA Fine Arts Association, also organised its first exhibition, a committee member on the second exhibition in 1872, the third exhibition in 1875, the fourth exhibition in 1877, the fifth exhibition in 1879 and the sixth exhibition in 1880. Influential in the affairs of the SA Drawing Club. A well-known art collector who exhibited his collection of paintings in Cape Town. 1872 a Trustee for the T B Bayley Bequest of 30 paintings which became the nucleus of the SA National Gallery, Cape Town, in whose formation and foundation he was actively involved and of which he was a Trustee until 1895. For a number of years he owned Groote Schuur, which he let from 1873–76 to the Governor for use as his summer residence and lived in himself from 1876 to 1878. A friend of Daniel Krynauw (qv) for many years. 1849–50 travelled to Grahamstown; 1853–54 to Fort Beaufort and Stockenstrom; 1857 to St Helena, England, Belgium, Germany, Switzerland and Italy; 1864 to Swellendam, Knysna and Caledon; 1879 to England, France, The Netherlands, Germany, Italy and Switzerland; 1890–1905 lived in Southampton, Eastbourne and Brighton, England, travelling to Europe in 1891 to collect works of art for the SA National Gallery, Cape Town.
Exhibitions Participated in group exhibitions in Cape Town and Port Elizabeth 1852–90 with the SA Fine Arts Association; 1886 included in the Colonial and Indian Exhibition in London; 1890–93 exhibited with the Shipton Art Society, England; 1974 SA National Gallery, Cape Town, Memorial Exhibition.
Awards 1877 Gold Medal, SA Fine Arts Association Exhibition; 1881 and 1885 Silver Medals, SA Fine Arts Association Exhibition.
Represented Africana Museum, Johannesburg; Julius Gordon Africana Centre, Riversdale; Municipal Council Chambers, Fort Beaufort; SA National Gallery, Cape Town; William Fehr Collection, Cape Town.

Articles by De Smidt "An Art Gallery for South Africa", *Cape Monthly Magazine* March 1871; "Dutch East Indiamen attacking while sheltering in Saldanha Bay", *ANN* vol 18 no 8, December 1969; also had a number of articles published in *The Cape Argus*.

References Majorie Bull, *Abraham de Smidt 1829–1908, Artist and Surveyor-General of the Cape Colony*, 1981, Cape Town; Afr Repos; SADNB; AMC2; DSAB; SESA; Pict Afr; Bénézit; BSAK; 3Cs; AASA; *ANN* vol 4 no 3, June 1947; *Die Staatsamptenaar* April 1951; "Abraham de Smidt 1829–1908", SA National Gallery Catalogue, 1974, Cape Town.

DESMOND Nerine Constantia FIAL

Born 1908 Constantia, Cape.

A painter, sculptor and graphic artist of landscapes, seascapes, portraits, still life and figures. Works in watercolour, oil, pencil, charcoal, wood, bronze and in various graphic media. A series of Basuto hut designs, numerous pastoral scenes, paintings of the Herero Women of SWA/Namibia and Voortrekker scenes.

Studies 1924 Cape Town Art School, under W G Bevington (qv) and C S Groves (qv); 1938 etching and aquatints, London County Council Art School; night-classes at the Chelsea School of Art, London, and at Académie de la Grande Chaumière, Paris.

Profile A member of the New Group. 1961 elected a Fellow of the International Institute of Arts and Letters. 1960 and 1966 an art teacher at Springfield Convent, Cape Town. 1966 Curator of the Tatham Art Gallery, Pietermaritzburg. 1961 designed the one cent postage stamp. A writer of short stories, children's books, plays and poetry. Illustrated *Tales from the Malay Quarter*, by I D du Plessis, 1981 and *Bantu Tales*, by Pattie Price, among others. Painted "The Cavalcade, Basutoland" which was reproduced by E Schweickerdt, Pretoria. Spent her childhood in Pretoria, returning to the Cape in 1920. During the 1940s she crossed the Maluti Mountains in Basutoland (Lesotho), alone on a pony, painting the countryside and its people. 1949 travelled in SWA/Namibia and in 1954 along the East African coast. Has also travelled in Spain. Lives in Stellenbosch.

Exhibitions She has participated in group exhibitions from 1918 in SA, the UK, Brazil, the USA, Australia and West Germany; 1935 Cape Town, first of numerous solo exhibitions; 1948 Tate Gallery, London, SA Art Exhibition; 1956, 1960 and 1964 Quadrennial Exhibitions; 1981 Republic Festival Exhibition.

Represented Ann Bryant Gallery, East London; Durban Art Gallery; Johannesburg Art Gallery; Julius Gordon Africana Centre, Riversdale; King George VI Art Gallery, Port Elizabeth; National Museum, Bloemfontein; Pietersburg Collection; Pretoria Art Museum; SA Cultural History Museum, Cape Town; SA National Gallery, Cape Town; University of Cape Town; University of the Orange Free State; University of Pretoria; University of Stellenbosch; Wellington Art Collection; Willem Annandale Art Gallery, Lichtenburg; William Humphreys Art Gallery, Kimberley.

Public Commissions Murals in public buildings in Cape Town and Johannesburg.

References PSA; Collectors' Guide; Art SA; SAA; SAP&D; SESA; BSAK 1 & 2; Art SWA; SA Art; AASA; *Artlook* October 1970.

DE VILLIERS Adrian

Born 1951 Cape Town.

A sculptor of figures and personalised rituals. Works in bronze, wood and mixed media.

Studies 1969–72 Pretoria and Witwatersrand Technical Colleges, under Neels Coetzee (qv) and Eben Leibrandt (qv), gaining a Diploma in Fine Art; 1973–77 St Martin's School of Art, London, under Anthony Caro (*b*.1924) and Philip King (*b*.1934), where he attained a First Class BA Honours and was awarded a British Council Grant in 1979.

Profile 1976–80 a member of the London Performance Co-op; 1978 a founder of Cumbria Community Arts, UK. From 1985 a member of the SAAA. 1978–79 a tutor in sculpture and drawing, Ulverston Adult Education Centre, Cumbria, UK; 1983–84 a lecturer in sculpture and drawing, Orange Free State Technikon; from 1985 a senior lecturer in sculpture at the University of Bophuthatswana. 1973–80 lived in the UK.

Exhibitions He has participated in many group exhibitions from 1971 in SA and two in the UK; 1985 Gallery 21, Johannesburg, solo exhibition.

Award 1973 Education Trust Award, Art SA Today.

Reference AASA.

DE VILLIERS Izak Benjamin

Born 1951 Johannesburg.

A painter and graphic artist working in oil, acrylic, watercolour, ink, wash, pencil, pastel, charcoal and in various graphic media. Series of paintings entitled "Revelations" and "Two-Twenty Volts".

Studies 1976–79 University of Pretoria, under Professor Nico Roos (qv) and John Clarke (qv), where he gained a BA(FA).

Profile 1977 co-founder and a committee member of the University of Pretoria Film Society. 1980–81 graphics assistant at the University of South Africa. 1981 a set painter for PACT. 1975 lived in Amsterdam, The Netherlands; 1976–81 in Pretoria; 1982–84 in Cape Town, thereafter in Johannesburg.

Exhibitions He has participated in many group exhibitions from 1981 in Pretoria and Johannesburg; 1982 Pepper Studio, Cape Town, solo exhibition; 1984 own studio, Cape Town, two joint exhibitions with Kobus Kloppers (qv); 1985 Gallery 21, Johannesburg, joint exhibition with Julian Venter (qv); 1986 St Mary's Diocesan School for Girls Art Gallery, Pretoria, solo exhibition.

Awards 1979 First Prize Graphics, New Signatures, SAAA; 1987 a finalist in the Volkskas Atelier Exhibition, SAAA Gallery, Pretoria. Represented Pretoria Art Museum; University of South Africa.

Reference SA Arts Calendar Autumn 1986.

DE VILLIERS Pierre Francois

Born 1921 Cape Town.

A painter of landscapes, still life, seascapes and wildlife. Works in oil and acrylic. Series of paintings of the Malay Quarter, Cape Town and of flowers.

Studies 1930 privately under Maggie Laubser (qv) in Cape Town; 1937 drawing lessons at the Cape Technical College.

Profile From 1974 a member of the NSA and from 1982 of the SAAA. A musician, who between 1976–82 was Principal of the Pierre de Villiers School of Music in Durban. 1921–67 lived in Cape Town; 1967–82 in Durban and from 1982 in Pretoria.

Exhibitions He has participated in many group exhibitions in Durban; 1974 Royal Hotel, Durban, first of 10 solo exhibitions held in Durban.

Reference Register SA & SWA (in addendum).

DE VILLIERS Stephen

Born 1923 Kimberley.

A painter.

Studies Cape Town Teachers Training College; 1948–49 Continental School of Art, Cape Town, under Maurice van Essche (qv); Michaelis School of Fine Art; Accademia di Belle Arti, Florence, where studied stage design and decor on a Cape Centenary Foundation Scholarship for Study Travel in 1959.

Profile 1961 taught at the Cape Town Training College; 1969–77 taught at the Michaelis School of Fine Art.

Exhibitions He has participated in group exhibitions held throughout SA and in São Paulo, Brazil.

References SAA; Register of SA & SWA; AASA.

DEWAR John Harvey

Born 1929 East London.

A painter of landscapes, seascapes, still life, figures and abstract pictures. Works in oil, acrylic, pencil, charcoal and pastel. 1986 Halley's Comet Series; 1986 a series of 10 Cape landscapes. A sculptor.

Studies 1951–52 City and Guilds of London Art School.

Profile 1950–57 studied architecture. 1975–85 and from 1987 an art critic for *The Star* newspaper. Has written numerous articles and some poetry. Stained glass designs for a church in Botswana. Has lived in the UK, France, Spain, Greece, the Cape and Transkei, presently lives in Johannesburg.

Exhibitions He has participated in numerous group exhibitions from 1956 in SA; 1968 Gallery 101, Johannesburg, first of two solo exhibitions.

References BSAK; *Artlook* August 1968.

DE WET Barend Petrus

Born 1956 Boksburg, Transvaal.

An artist working in oil, bronze, stone, wood, steel, cardboard and rusted steel. 1985 "Cardboard" series; 1986 "Wood" series; 1987 "Rusted steel" series.

Studies 1980–83 Michaelis School of Fine Art, under Bruce Arnott (qv) and Professor Neville Dubow, gaining a Diploma in Fine Art.

Profile 1983–85 set designs and sculpture props for theatres. 1957–76 lived in Boksburg; 1976–77 in Pretoria; 1978–80 in Johannesburg, thereafter in Cape Town.

Exhibitions He has participated in several group exhibitions from 1984 in SA; 1985 Woodstock, Cape Town, first of three solo exhibitions; 1988 Karen McKerron Gallery, Johannesburg, joint exhibition with Philippa Graff (qv) and Lea Henorain (qv).

Award 1985 Zolner prize, New Visions Exhibition, Market Gallery, Johannesburg.

Represented SA National Gallery, Cape Town.

Reference *Style* November 1984.

DE WET Daniël Jacobus Steyn (Danie)

Born 1944 Bethal, Transvaal.

A painter of landscapes, still life and figures. Works in oil, acrylic, watercolour and pencil. 1983 a series on "Social Comment", 1985 "Symbolic Landscapes."

Studies 1963–66 Pretoria Technical College, under Leo Theron (qv), attaining a National Diploma in Graphic Design in 1965 and a National Art Teachers Diploma in 1966; 1972–73 a six-month course at the University of Newcastle-upon-Tyne, England, under Mr Dobson; 1973 a six-month course at the Akademie der Bildenden Kunste, Munich, West Germany, studying under Professor K F Dahmen; 1983 privately under Anna Vorster (qv); 1983 attained a Higher Diploma in Fine Arts.

Profile 1978–84 a member of the SAAA, of which he was a member of the Board in 1982. 1967–69 a full-time lecturer and 1969–72 a part-time lecturer at the Pretoria Technical College (Technikon); 1967–69 a part-time lecturer, 1969–72 a full-time lecturer at the Pretoria School of Art, Ballet and Music; from 1975 a lecturer at the Pretoria Technikon. From 1969 a stained glass artist, working with Leo Theron (qv) 1972–75; 1974 illustrated a children's book in Welkom, Orange Free State.

Exhibitions He has participated in many group exhibitions from 1968 in SA; 1981 Republic Festival Exhibition; 1983 Ivan Solomon Gallery, Pretoria Technikon, first of two solo exhibitions.

Reference *SA Arts Calendar* Spring 1985.

DE WET Eone

Born 1928 Bloemfontein.

A sculptor of symbolic wall sculptures. Works in bronze, stone, wood, copper, brass and silver.

Studies 1950 Rhodes University, under Professor Austin Winter Moore (qv) and Cecil Todd (qv), gaining a BA(FA); 1952 Michaelis School of Fine Art, under Maurice van Essche (qv) and Lippy Lipshitz (qv); 1953 Central School of Art, London, under Alan Davie (*b*.1920), Robert Adams (*b*.1917) and Eduardo Paolozzi (*b*.1924).

Profile 1952 an art teacher at the Pretoria High School for Girls and in 1957 at the Child Art Centre in Pretoria.

Exhibitions 1951 Constance Stuart Studio, Pretoria, solo exhibition; she has participated in numerous group exhibitions from 1953 in SA, the UK and Switzerland.

Award 1962 Prize Winner, Artists of Fame and Promise, Adler Fielding Gallery, Johannesburg.

Public Commissions 1968 two murals and the doors of the VIP Lounge, Jan Smuts Airport, Johannesburg; 1970 mural, main entrance hall, Civitas, Pretoria; 1974 façade of Springs City Hall, Transvaal; 1982 crest for Civic Centre, Phalaborwa, Transvaal; doors for The Parliament of Venda, among others.

References BSAK 1 & 2; AASA; *Lantern* January–March 1957 & March 1972; *Die Huisgenoot* 10 August 1962; *Sarie Marais* 2 June 1971; *Personality* 11 February 1972; *Artlook* April 1972; *SA Panorama* December 1975; *Style* September 1981.

DE WET Frederik Willem

Born Late 1790s Cape Town.

Died After 1860.

Profile Made woodcuts and engravings of Cape Town, which were often reproduced in newspapers. 1833 designed a seal for the Cape Town Literary Society. Made maps of SA and of Cape Town. Illustrated *Verhandeling* by Changuion in 1832 and *The Cape Almanac* of 1834–41. A Police Office clerk at the Cape 1815–57.

References Pict Art; Pict Afr; 3Cs.

DHLOMO Bongiwe

Born 1957 Vryheid, Natal.

A graphic artist of socio-political wood- and lino-cuts.

Studies 1978–79 Rorke's Drift Art Centre, Natal.

Profile 1976–77 worked as a secretary in Durban. Presently Project Co-ordinator the Alexandra Art Centre, Johannesburg. Married to Pat Mautloa (qv).

Exhibitions She has participated in numerous group exhibitions in SA and West Germany; 1987 Johannesburg Art Foundation, joint exhibition with Madi Phala (qv), Reggie Bardavid (qv), Sam Nhlengetwa (qv) and Pat Mautloa (qv).

Represented Durban Art Gallery.

References Echoes of African Art; *ADA* 5.

DICKS Gertruida S M

Born 1940 Graaff-Reinet, Cape Province.

A painter of genre and figures. Works in acrylic, ink, pencil and charcoal. 1984–85 a series of complex personalities and complex relationships; 1986 a series of home and close relationships.

Studies University of South Africa, under Johann Moolman (qv), gaining a BA(FA) in 1985.

Profile From 1967 a member of the Arts Association SWA/Namibia and a committee member in 1987; from 1986 a member of the SAAAH. 1986 an art teacher at Windhoek High School; 1987 an art lecturer at The Academy, Windhoek.

Exhibitions She has participated in several group exhibitions from 1970; 1986 first solo exhibition.

Award 1985 Painting Award, STANSWA Biennale, Windhoek.

DIEMONT A Rose S

Born 1889 Dublin, Republic of Ireland.
Died 1954 Cape Town.
Resided in SA from 1911.
A painter of landscapes and the wild flowers of the Western Cape. Worked in oil, pastel and watercolour.

Studies Studied art and music in Dublin.

Profile Produced a number of works in pewter. Taught art in Oudtshoorn, Cape Province.

Exhibition Participated in the 1936 Empire Exhibition, Johannesburg.

Represented University of Stellenbosch.

References BSAK; AASA.

DIETRICH Keith Hamilton

Born 1950 Johannesburg.
A painter and graphic artist of portraits and still life. Works in oil, watercolour, pastel and in various graphic media.

Studies 1971–74 University of Stellenbosch, gaining a BA(FA); 1976–77 Koninklijke Academie voor Schone Kunsten en die Hogere Instituten, Antwerp, Belgium, on a Maggie Laubser Bursary, where awarded a Post-Graduate Diploma; 1980–83 University of South Africa, through which he attained an MA(FA).

Profile 1979–81 a member of the SAAA; 1986 on the Market Gallery Advisory Board. 1978–80 a lecturer at the University of Pretoria; from 1981 a lecturer at the University of South Africa. From 1975 a number of cover illustrations for HAUM Publishers, Cape Town. 1975–77 and 1980 travelled extensively in Europe; 1981 in the USA.

Exhibitions He has participated in over 40 group exhibitions in SA, Belgium, West Germany and Botswana; 1982 Cape Town Triennial; 1982 National Gallery, Gaborone, Botswana, SA Art Exhibition; 1983 University of Stellenbosch, first of four solo exhibitions; 1985 Cape Town Triennial; 1985 Tributaries, touring SA and West Germany; 1986 University of the Orange Free State, joint exhibition with Sybille Nagel (qv), Johann Moolman (qv) and Debbie Bell (qv).

Represented Johannesburg Art Gallery; Nelspruit Art Museum; Pretoria Art Museum; SA National Gallery, Cape Town; University of Natal; University of the Orange Free State; University of South Africa; University of Stellenbosch; University of the Witwatersrand; William Humphreys Art Gallery, Kimberley.
References 3Cs; AASA; LSAA.

DIKGALE Noah

Born *c.*1959 Durban.
A carver of wood sculptures. A graphic artist producing linocuts of figures and Biblical themes.
Studies Graduated from Rorke's Drift Art Centre, Natal, in 1978.
Profile Trained as a carpenter.
Exhibitions He has participated in group exhibitions in SA and West Germany.

DILL Dieter Eugen

Born 1944 Feldrennach, West Germany.
Resided in SA from 1971.
A sculptor, painter and graphic artist of abstract works. Uses steel, acrylic, pencil and various graphic media.
Studies 1964–69 Fachhochschule für Gestaltung, Pforzheim, West Germany, under Professor R Reiling, Professor H Stark and Professor F Vahle, gaining a Degree, graduating in design.
Profile From 1971 a senior lecturer in jewellery design at the University of Stellenbosch. An enamellist and jeweller.
Exhibitions He has participated in numerous group exhibitions from 1968 in West Germany, Greece, Austria, France, the USA, Japan and SA; 1972 University of Stellenbosch, first of four solo exhibitions held in SA and West Germany; 1981 Republic Festival Exhibition.
Awards Several awards for jewellery design.
Represented SA National Gallery, Cape Town; Schmuck Museum, Pforzheim, West Germany; University of Stellenbosch.
Reference AASA.

DINGEMANS Johannes Wilhelmus (Jan)

Born 1921 Breda, The Netherlands.
Resided in SA from 1948.
A painter of figures, still life and abstract pictures. Works in oil.
Studies 1943–45 Academy of Art, Tilburg, The Netherlands, gaining a Teaching Diploma; 1946 Koninklijke Academie voor Schone Kunsten en de Hogere Instituten, Antwerp, Belgium.
Profile Worked as a display artist in Johannesburg.
Exhibitions He has participated in numerous group exhibitions in The Netherlands, SA and the USA; 1956 and 1960 Quadrennial Exhibitions.

Represented African and Primitive Art, New York, USA; Hester Rupert Art Museum, Graaff-Reinet; Willem Annandale Art Gallery, Lichtenburg.
References Collectors' Guide; SAA; BSAK; AASA; *SA Art News* 10 August 1961.

DINGEMANS Waalko

Born 1912 Gorinchem, The Netherlands.
A painter of landscapes, portraits, seascapes and figures. Works in oil, water-colour and pencil.
Studies Rijksmuseum School for Art Teachers, Amsterdam; Rijks Academie voor Beelende Kunsten, under Professor Johannes H Jurres (1875–1946) and Professor Wolter, where gained a Queen Wilhelmina Scholarship.
Profile 1955 lived in Salisbury, Rhodesia (Harare, Zimbabwe).
Exhibitions 1939 Utrecht, first of five solo exhibitions held in The Netherlands; he has held several solo exhibitions in SA and four in Rhodesia (Zimbabwe).
Public Commissions Portraits of Rhodesian, Northern Rhodesian and Nyasa-land politicians; 1961 portrait of the former SA State President, C R Swart.
References SAA; AASA; *Artlook* November 1971.

DINSDALE John

Born 1951 Eshowe, Natal.
Draws portraits in pencil.
Studies Natal Technical College.
Profile An art director for a retail outlet.
Exhibition 1982 Cape Town Triennial.

DISNER Solly

Born 1909 Nidz, Lithuania (Lithuanian SSR).
Died 1985 Cape Town.
Resided in SA from 1927.
A self-taught sculptor working in wood, bronze, verdite, marble and ivory. Initially sculpted portraits, but later his work became increasingly abstract.
Profile Began sculpting in 1940. Lived in Cape Town.
Exhibitions 1960 first solo exhibition in Cape Town; 1962 Adler Fielding Gallery, Johannesburg, Retrospective Exhibition; participated in group exhibitions from 1964.
Represented SA National Gallery, Cape Town; William Humphreys Art Gallery, Kimberley.
References Art SA; SAA; 20C SA Art; SESA; BSAK; 3Cs; AASA; *Jewish Affairs* November 1962.

DITCHBURN Hilda Professor

Born in the Orange Free State.
A ceramicist.
Studies Obtained a BA(FA) from the University of Natal; after WWII attended the Central School of Art, London.
Profile 1941–81 lectured in ceramics at the University of Natal.
Exhibitions Participated in group exhibitions throughout SA.
Represented University of Natal.
Reference Sgraffitti no 26.

D'IVRY-RUSSELL Ursula Garrett

Born 1940 Johannesburg.
A painter of landscapes, semi-abstracted seascapes, wildlife in imaginary abstract settings and of abstract pictures. Works in acrylic, watercolour, ink, wash, pencil and charcoal. "Bushveld Dream", a series of small animal-life in dream habitat; "Nature Meditation", a series of spatially isolated forms.
Studies 1964 under Robert Hunter Craig and Trevor Wood in Rhodesia (Zimbabwe); from 1976 aided by Majorie Bowen (qv), Ulrich Schwanecke (qv), George Boys (qv) and Cora Lawson (qv).
Profile From 1981 a member of the WSSA, becoming an Associate in 1983. From 1982 a member of the SAAA. Illustrated *Zimbabwe Cavalcade*, written by her father B G Paver, 1950, CNA, SA. 1960–75 lived in various national parks in Rhodesia (Zimbabwe). 1974/75 visited Kenya.
Exhibitions She has participated in numerous group exhibitions from 1965 held in Zimbabwe, SA, the USA and the UK; 1967 Meikles Hotel, Salisbury, Rhodesia (Harare, Zimbabwe), solo exhibition.
Award 1968 First Prize Painting, Festival of Arts Exhibition, Salisbury, Rhodesia (Harare, Zimbabwe).
Publication by d'Ivry-Russell Dzokuti in the Bush, illustrated with pen and ink drawings, 1960, Peter Davies, London.
Represented Margate Art Gallery; National Gallery, Harare, Zimbabwe.

DIXIE Ethel May

Born 1876 Cape Town.
Died 1973 Cape Town.
A self-taught painter of wild flowers. Worked in watercolour.
Profile Began painting in 1900. 1966 awarded an Honorary Life Membership of the Botanical Society of SA. Illustrated *Flora of South Africa* by Rudolph Marloth, 1913, published by William Wesky, London. Among numerous other illustrations for botanical books and periodicals, she contributed a number of plates to *The Flowering Plants of Africa*, a quarterly publication issued by the Botanical Research Institute. Aunt of Dorothy Barclay (qv) and great-aunt of Margaret Rundle (qv).

Exhibition 1966 Kirstenbosch, Cape Town, botanical exhibition.
Represented Africana Museum, Johannesburg; National Botanical Gardens, Kirstenbosch, Cape Town; SA National Gallery, Cape Town; William Fehr Collection, Cape Town.
Publication by Dixie *Wild Flowers of the Cape of Good Hope*, 1953, Janda Press, Cape Town.
References SAA; AMC2&6; SESA; BSAK; AASA.

DIXON Leng

Born 1916 Cape Town.
Died 1968 Cape Town.
Watercolour and line drawings of animals and Cape scenes, particularly of the Cape Malay Quarter, also known to have painted a number of oils, murals and decorative designs.
Studies 1937–38 Camberwell School of Art, London, under John Cosmo Clark RA (1897–1967), Eric Fraser (*b*.1902) and Roland Vivian Pitchforth (qv); 1938–39 further studies in Paris.
Profile 1938–54 a member and sometime Vice-Chairman of the New Group. A book illustrator, whose illustrations include those for *Not for Me The Wilds* by Barbara Carr and *Almost Forgotten, Never Told* by Lawrence Green. Married to Phay Hutton (qv).
Exhibitions 1945 and 1946 Gainsborough Galleries, Johannesburg, joint exhibitions with Phay Hutton (qv); 1948 Tate Gallery, London, SA Art Exhibition; 1952 Cape Town, first of numerous solo exhibitions held in SA and abroad; 1956 and 1960 Quadrennial Exhibitions.
Represented Ann Bryant Gallery, East London; SA National Gallery, Cape Town.
Publication by Dixon *Leng Dixon, Malay and Cape Sketches*, introduction by Ruth Prowse (qv), 1952, Maskew Miller, Cape Town.
References Collectors' Guide; Art SA; SAA; SAP&D; BSAK 1 & 2; AASA.

DIXON Mark Lawrence

Born 1957 Cape Town.
A painter and graphic artist of landscapes and abstract pictures. Works in oil, acrylic, watercolour, gouache, ink, pencil and in various graphic media, particularly woodcuts. Creates collages and assemblages. 1980–81 a series entitled "Today's News Today"; 1983–84 a series entitled "The Tulbagh Droebane Works"; 1985–86 a watercolour series entitled "Sound Cycle".
Studies 1978–81 Ruth Prowse School of Art, Cape Town, under Erik Laubscher (qv), gaining a Fine Arts Diploma in Painting and Photography; he was awarded the 1980 Prize for Painting and the Ruth Prowse Trust Fund Bursary in 1980 and 1981.
Profile A potter of Raku pots. A maker of sets and props for theatres and a stage manager of threatre productions. 1987 painted fabrics under the Suma label. 1983–84 lived in the Tulbagh Valley, thereafter in Cape Town.

Exhibitions He has participated in numerous group exhibitions from 1980 held throughout SA; 1981 SAAA Gallery, Cape Town, first of six solo exhibitions; 1982 Cape Town Triennial; 1986 SAAA Gallery, Cape Town, joint exhibition.
Award 1981 BANKOVS Prizes for Oil Painting and Drawing.
Represented Pietersburg Collection; SA National Gallery, Cape Town; University of the Western Cape.
References AASA; *Fair Lady* September 1986.

DIXON Percy RI

Born 1862.
Died 1924.
Known to have been in SA *c.*1893–*c.*1909.
A painter of landscapes and coastal scenes. Worked in watercolour.
Profile 1915 elected to the Royal Institute of Painters in Watercolour. Lived in London and Cape Town. 1893 visited Durban.
Exhibitions Participated in group exhibitions 1886 and 1909 in the UK and in 1892 and 1903 in Cape Town; held a solo exhibition at Dowdswell Gallery, London; 1976 included in the English and SA Watercolour Exhibition, SA National Gallery, Cape Town.
Represented Africana Museum, Johannesburg; SA National Gallery, Cape Town.
References AMC6; DBA; BSAK 2; AASA.

DLAMINI Nelisiwe Patience

Born 1957 Nyanyadu, Dundee, Natal.
A painter of landscapes, portraits, still life, figures, wildlife and abstract pictures. Works in oil, acrylic, watercolour, wash, pencil and charcoal. A graphic artist and a sculptor in clay with glazes.
Studies 1978 spent four months at Rorke's Drift Art Centre, under Jules van de Vijver (qv) and Ada van de Vijver (qv); 1979–80 Rorke's Drift Art Centre, under Gabrielle and Carl Ellertson, Eric Mbatha (qv) and Carl Bethke, gaining a Diploma in Fine Art.
Profile 1980–82 a member of the Abangni Youth Centre. 1982–85 taught arts and crafts in the Pietermaritzburg area. A classical musician, potter, enameller and a commercial artist. From 1985 has lived at Umlazi near Durban.
Exhibitions From 1982 he has participated in several group exhibitions in SA.
Represented University of Fort Hare.

DOLD Mary-Rose

Born 1927 King William's Town, Cape Province.
Mainly a graphic artist but also a painter. She works in various graphic media, oil, acrylic, watercolour, ink and pencil. Her subject matter includes landscapes, still life, genre and figures. Recently she has concentrated on very large hand-rubbed linocuts, with recurring series of "Farm Scenes", "Scenes from a Farm Childhood" and "Swimming Pool".

Studies 1943–47 Rhodes University, under Professor Austin Winter Moore (qv), Natalie Guiton and Jack Heath (qv), gaining a BA(FA) and being awarded the Purvis Prize in 1947.

Profile A member of the EPSFA, who has spent many terms as a committee member, was a former President and is now an Honorary Life Member. A member of the Board of Trustees of the King George VI Art Gallery, Port Elizabeth. 1948 an art teacher at the Grahamstown Training College and at the Johan Carinus Art Centre in Grahamstown; *c.*1959–66 taught at the Port Elizabeth Technical College.

Exhibitions She has participated in numerous group exhibitions from 1958 in SA and once in West Germany; 1972 Hester Rupert Art Museum, Graaff-Reinet, first of 14 solo exhibitions held in SA; 1981 Republic Festival Exhibition.

Represented Ann Bryant Gallery, East London; Hester Rupert Art Museum, Graaff-Reinet; King George VI Art Gallery, Port Elizabeth; Potchefstroom Museum; Turnhalle, Windhoek, SWA/Namibia.

DOMSAITIS Pranas

Born 1880 Cropiens, Postnicken, East Prussia.
Died 1965 Rondebosch, Cape Town.
Resided in SA from 1949.

A painter of religious scenes, village and farm scenes, still life, particularly flowers, of portraits, figures and in the late 1960s a few abstract pictures. Worked in oil, charcoal, pencil, crayon, pastel and watercolour. A graphic artist who produced monotypes, etchings and lithographs. His work is characterised by deep, strong colours, a heavy outline and the themes of refugees and the Karoo.

Studies 1907–10 Academy of Fine Art at Königsberg, East Prussia, under Professor Ludwig Dettmann (*b.*1865); 1910–12 in Berlin, under Lovis Corinth (1858–1925), further studies in Paris, Florence, London and Amsterdam.

Profile Influenced by the German Expressionists, Georges Rouault (1871–1958) and Edvard Munch (1863–1944), the latter he met on a trip to Norway in 1914. A member of the SA Society of Artists. 1938 a member of the New Group. Illustrated *Die Seele Des Ostens* by Karl Scheffler. A number of his works were reproduced by E Schweickerdt, Pretoria. He sewed wall tapestries and embroideries. A Lithuanian, born Franz Domscheit, he changed his name to the present spelling in 1920, but continued to sign pictures in his original name until 1938. Farmed in East Prussia until the age of 27; 1910–14 travelled in Germany, Italy, France, England, The Netherlands and Norway, 1912 lived in Petersburg, Russia for six months; 1914–18 in Berlin and Lithuania, serving in the army; 1919–24 travelled in Austria and Bavaria, where he began collecting medieval nativity figures from monasteries; 1925–29 travelled in Austria, East Prussia, Romania and Turkey; 1929–44 lived in Berlin and travelled throughout Europe; 1944–49 in Austria; 1949–65 in Cape Town, visiting the Karoo, Transkei, Orange Free State and the Transvaal in 1958. 1929 married the professional singer, Adelheid Armhold, who from 1949 lectured at the University of Cape Town.

Exhibitions 1918–49 participated in numerous group exhibitions in Berlin, Austria, East Prussia, Romania and Turkey; 1919–37 held solo exhibitions in Breslau, Essen, Hamburg, Berlin and Istanbul; participated in numerous group exhibitions in SA from 1949 and in New York, Toronto, São Paulo and Bulawayo; 1949 SA National Gallery, Cape Town, first of over 20 solo exhibitions in SA; 1960 and 1964 Quadrennial Exhibitions; 1966 SAAA Gallery, Pretoria, Prestige Exhibition; 1966 Adler Fielding Gallery, Johannesburg, Memorial Exhibition; 1966 SA National Gallery, Cape Town and Pretoria Art Museum, Commemorative Exhibition; 1968–69, 1970 and 1971 Gallery 101, Johannesburg, Memorial Exhibition; 1970 Bielefeld, West Germany, Memorial Exhibition; 1978 Rand Afrikaans University, Memorial Exhibition; 1978 University of Hawaii, Honolulu, Retrospective Exhibition.

Award 1964 Prizewinner, Artists of Fame and Promise Exhibition.

Represented Art galleries in Lübeck, Königsberg, Munich, Stettin, Hanover and Hamburg, West Germany; Berlin National Gallery, Germany; Durban Art Gallery; Hester Rupert Art Museum, Graaff-Reinet; Johannesburg Art Gallery; King George VI Art Gallery, Port Elizabeth; National Gallery, Harare, Zimbabwe; National Museum, Bloemfontein; Pretoria Art Museum; SA National Gallery, Cape Town; University of Cape Town; University of the Orange Free State; University of Stellenbosch; University of the Witwatersrand; Willem Annandale Art Gallery, Lichtenburg; William Humphreys Art Gallery, Kimberley.

References Elsa Verloren van Themaat, *Pranas Domsaitis*, 1976, C Struik, Cape Town; Art SA; SAA; 20C SA Art; DSAB; SAP&S; SAP&D; SESA; SSAP; Bénézit (under Domscheit, Frans); BSAK 1 & 2; Our Art 3; SA Art; 3Cs; AASA; LSAA; *SA Art News* 6 April 1961; *Artlook* December 1967 & February 1968; *Pranas Domsaitis 1880–1965*, SA National Gallery, Cape Town, Catalogue, November 1966; University of Hawaii Catalog by Murray Turnball, 1978.

DONALDSON Kim

Born 1952 Umtali, Rhodesia (Mutare, Zimbabwe).
Resided in SA from 1973.
A painter of wildlife and landscapes. Works in pastel, oil, watercolour and acrylic.

Studies 1964–69 privately under Mr Forsyth; 1976 privately under David MacGregor (qv).

Profile From 1975 a member of the WSSA, becoming an Associate in 1979. 1973–77 a commercial artist for various advertising agencies and newspapers. From 1979 a number of prints of his work have been made. He has travelled extensively in Zimbabwe, Botswana, SWA/Namibia and SA. Presently living in Florida, USA.

Exhibitions 1976 La Petite Gallery, Cape Town, first of 16 solo exhibitions held in SA and in the UK; he has participated in numerous group exhibitions from 1977 held throughout SA and in West Germany and the USA.

Reference AASA.

DONDE Michelle Ilana

Born 1959 Johannesburg.

A sculptor of the multiplication of familiar objects. Works in bronze, ceramics, steel, lead, glass and oil.

Studies Witwatersrand Technikon, gaining a National Diploma in Fine Art in 1980 and a Higher Diploma in Fine Art and Sculpture in 1987.

Profile 1980 designed and built stage sets for the Alwyn Davies Theatre, Johannesburg; 1982–83 worked as a commercial artist. 1982–84 on a part-time basis taught general, life and geometric drawing as well as volume design at the Witwatersrand Technikon; 1983 taught drawing and watercolour painting at the Inscape School of Interior Design, Johannesburg; 1984–87 a part-time tutor in the Department of Architecture, University of the Witwatersrand. 1968 visited South America; 1969, 1972, 1976, 1981 and 1986 visited Israel; 1972 Greece, Austria and the UK; 1973 the UK and the USA; 1974 and 1976 the Far East; in 1982 she spent six months in Europe; 1986 visited Italy and the USA; 1987 the UK. 1987–88 living and working in Jerusalem, Israel.

Exhibitions She has participated in several group exhibitions from 1979 in SA; 1987 Goodman Gallery, Johannesburg, solo exhibition of drawings and sculpture.

Represented SA National Gallery, Cape Town.

DOUGLASS Frank

Born 1907 England.

Died 1975.

A self-taught painter of still life, figures, landscapes and city scenes. Worked in oil.

Profile Began painting late in life. A well-known broadcaster and actor. Lived in Johannesburg.

Exhibitions Participated in group exhibitions from 1964 in SA; 1964 first of many solo exhibitions held in SA; 1972 Hester Rupert Art Museum, Graaff-Reinet, solo exhibition; 1980 SAAA Gallery, Johannesburg, Memorial Exhibition.

Represented Ann Bryant Gallery, East London; Hester Rupert Art Museum, Graaff-Reinet; King George VI Art Gallery, Port Elizabeth; National Museum, Bloemfontein.

Reference *Artlook* August 1972

DOWNING Peter Hilton

Born 1944 Nababiep, Namaqualand.

A painter of landscapes, figures and wildlife. Works in watercolour, oil, ink and wash. A sculptor of abstracts and wildlife in wood.

Studies Several private lessons under Johannes Blatt (qv).

Profile From 1969 a member of the Arts Association SWA/Namibia, from 1983 a member of the SAAA; 1969–71 a commercial artist for Nature Conservation in Windhoek; 1971–73 taught Okavangos new furniture designs and art in Rundu with the First National Development Corporation; 1973–74 an artist for the First National Development Corporation in Pretoria. 1977–82 Editor of *Rössing News*. 1984 freelance work for advertising agencies. 1956–58 lived in Kenya and Uganda; from 1979 he has lived in Swakopmund, SWA/Namibia.

Exhibitions 1971 Arts Association SWA/Namibia Gallery, Windhoek, first of 10 solo exhibitions held in SWA/Namibia; he has participated in many group exhibitions from 1981 in SWA/Namibia and SA.
Award 1981 Standard Bank Award.
Represented Arts Association SWA/Namibia Collection.
Public Commissions 1973 wood carvings, Civic Centre, Walvis Bay; 1975 wood carvings, Canyon Hotel, Keetmanshoop; 1975 wood carvings, Crematorium, Windhoek; 1979 large oil, SWAWEK, Windhoek; 1985 wooden plaque, SWALU, Windhoek.
References BSAK; PS/N.

DOYLE Jean

Born 1930 Wynberg, Cape Town.
A sculptor of figures and wildlife. Works in bronze.
Studies 1961–63 Cape Town Training College, under Stephen de Villiers (qv), gaining a Higher Primary Teachers Certificate; 1983 SA Institute of Foundrymen, under Dr A Koursaris.
Profile A member of the SAAA; 1964 taught at the Alicedale Primary School, Cape Province; from 1976 a sculpture teacher at Studio 6, Wynberg, Cape Town; 1978–81 at Cape Town Art Centre and in 1986 at Disa House, Cape Town. 1970–71 illustrated Douglas Hey's articles for *Die Burger*; 1975 designed a birds of prey identification poster for the Department of Nature and Environmental Conservation; 1983 illustrations for a medical textbook, by K E Sapire. 1971–75 a restorer with the Department of Nature and Environmental Conservation. In 1983 she opened a bronze foundry in Cape Town and was elected a member of the SA Institute of Foundrymen. 1980 visited the USA.
Exhibitions From 1980 she has participated in several group exhibitions in the USA and SA; 1980 The Venue, Sea Point, Cape Town, first of five solo exhibitions held in SA and SWA/Namibia.
Represented Pietersburg Collection; University of the North.
Public Commissions Several portrait busts from 1980; 1984 "Just Nuisance", Simonstown; 1984 Commemorative plaque of Mansergh, Cape Agulhas.
Reference SA Art Calendar vol 10 no 3.

D'OYLY Charles Sir

Born 1781 India.
Died 1845 Ardenza, near Leghorn, Italy.
Resided in SA 1832–33.
A painter of landscapes, genre, street scenes and homesteads. Worked in watercolour and oil. Numerous sketches in pencil, ink and wash.

Studies c.1819 a number of lessons from George Chinnery (1748–1847).

Profile 1833–38 a senior member of the Marine Board of the Customs, Salt and Opium Board for the East India Company in India. 1824 co-founder and President of the Behar School of Athens (a society in Patna, Bengal, India) with Christopher Webb Smith (qv) acting as Vice-President. He also established a private printing press, producing many of his own prints in India. Only one SA print, an engraving entitled "Tom Raw, the Griffin", printed by R Ackerman, 1828, London. 1785–96 lived in England; 1796–1838 in India, retired to Italy. Travelled throughout the Western Cape in 1832, and revisited the Cape briefly in 1838.

Exhibition 1948 Tate Gallery, London, SA Art Exhibition.

Represented Africana Museum, Johannesburg; Cape Archives, Cape Town; Newton Library, Cambridge, England (with Webb Smith (qv)); William Fehr Collection, Cape Town.

Publications by D'Oyly *The European in India*, 1813; *Antiquities of Dacca*, 1814, London; *Sketches of the New Road*, 1830, Calcutta. In collaboration with C Webb Smith (qv), the scenery of the illustrations in *Feathered Game of Hindostan*, 1828 and *Oriental Ornithology*, 1829.

References *The Cape Sketch Book of Sir Charles D'Oyly*, introduction by A Gordon Brown, 1968, A A Balkema, Cape Town; Pict Art; Afr Repos; A Gordon Brown, *Christopher Webb Smith*, 1965, Howard Timmins, Cape Town; SADNB; AMC2&6; DSAB; SESA; Pict Afr; BSAK 2; 3Cs; SASSK; *ANN* vol 12 no 8, December 1957; *Apollo* October 1975, London.

DRAKE Elizabeth

Born 1866 Rochester, Kent, England.
Died 1954.
Resided in SA from 1937.

A painter of architectural subjects, especially cathedrals and other London buildings, of landscapes, portraits and miniatures. Worked in watercolour.

Studies Rochester and Westminster Art Schools; three months at l'Atelier Colarossi in Paris; also trained, by her father, as an architect and surveyor.

Profile Taught art at schools in Rochester, Kent and elsewhere in the UK, as well as privately. Produced architectural drawings for the Kent and Sussex Archaeological Societies, lithographic work for the Natural History Department of the British Museum and illustrations for the Royal Medical Society and *Windsor Magazine*. c.1922 painted 12 watercolours of garden scenes illustrating Dorothea Fairbridge's *The Gardens of South Africa*. Visited SA and Rhodesia (Zimbabwe) regularly from 1922, before finally settling in SA in 1937.

Exhibitions Participated in group exhibitions in the UK and from 1928 in SA.

Represented SA National Gallery, Cape Town; University of Cape Town.

References SAP&D; BSAK 1 & 2; *Outspan* May 1946.

DRONSFIELD John Marsden

Born 1900 Oldham, Lancashire, England.
Died 1951 Cape Town.
Resided in SA from 1939.
A painter of figures, especially Cape figures, with a strong use of line. Worked in oil and ink.

Studies Mainly self-taught but studied briefly at the Manchester Art School, England.

Profile 1948 a founder member of the International Art Club SA. A stage and costume designer in 1923 with Sybil Thorndike in London, and in SA in 1940 for a ballet by Dulcie Howes at the Little Theatre, Cape Town and 1945–48 for Davies and Vanne Productions. A producer of plays. 1930 worked in London as a commercial artist and designer. A designer of pavilions for exhibitions including in 1940 for the British Board of Trade, World Fair, New York. 1941 co-organiser of the exhibition entitled "African Native Art". He illustrated a number of books including the new edition of *The Week End Book*, 1936, Nonesuch Press, England. Two portfolios of graphic work produced in 1956, by Janda Press, Cape Town, entitled "Fifteen African Improvisations", in an edition of 120 and "Fifty African Improvisations", in an edition of 80. A talented musician and poet.

Exhibitions 1939 Maskew Miller Gallery, Cape Town, first of six solo exhibitions held prior to 1948 in Cape Town, Johannesburg and Durban; participated in numerous group exhibitions in SA, Italy and Brazil; from 1940 often exhibited with Cecil Higgs (qv) and Lippy Lipshitz (qv); 1948 Tate Gallery, London, SA Art Exhibition; 1955 SA National Gallery, Cape Town, Memorial Exhibition; 1966 Wolpe Gallery, Cape Town, Memorial Exhibition; 1968 Durban Art Gallery, SA National Gallery, Cape Town and Tatham Art Gallery, Pietermaritzburg, joint exhibition with Lippy Lipshitz (qv) and Cecil Higgs (qv); 1977 Cape Town Festival Exhibition.

Represented Africana Museum, Johannesburg; Durban Art Gallery; Johannesburg Art Gallery; Pretoria Art Museum; SA National Gallery, Cape Town; University of Cape Town; University of the Orange Free State; University of the Witwatersrand; Wigan Gallery, Lancashire, England; William Humphreys Art Gallery, Kimberley.

Publications by Dronsfield *Non-Europeans Only*, a limited edition of 350 books of drawings, 1942, Dennis Bullough Publishers, Cape Town; *Satires and Verses*, edited by Dennis Hatfield Bullough, 1955, Oxford University Press, England.

References PSA; Collectors' Guide; Art SA; SAA; SADNB; 20C SA Art; SAP&S; Oxford Companion to Art; SAP&D; SESA; SSAP; BSAK 1 & 2; AASA; LSAA; *Die Huisgenoot* vol 26 no 980, 3 January 1941; *SA Architectural Record* August 1943; *Artlook* December 1966; *Memorial Exhibition of Works by John Dronsfield*, catalogue, 1955, SA National Gallery, Cape Town.

DUARTE Izidro

Born 1942 Portugal.
Resided in SA from 1953.
A painter of the African environment. Works in watercolour, gouache, ink and oil.

Studies 1959–61 Witwatersrand Technical College, under Professor Robert Bain (qv), Phil Botha (qv), George Boys (qv), Joyce Leonard (qv) and Anna Vorster (qv), gaining a Commercial Art Certificate; 1964–65 Camden Art Institute, London.

Profile 1962–63 and 1968–69 children's book illustrations for Afrikaanse Pers. Has lived in Mozambique, Northern Transvaal, Natal, in the Drakensberg and the Transkei.

Exhibitions He has participated in several group exhibitions from 1969 in SA; 1970 Johannesburg, first of three solo exhibitions.

DUFF George

Resided in SA *c.*1840–64.

A painter of buildings, figures and heads. Worked in watercolour.

Profile Contributed articles and poems to extant Cape Town magazines. Went to Port Elizabeth in 1840, and in 1846 walked from there to Cape Town.

Represented Africana Museum, Johannesburg; William Fehr Collection, Cape Town.

References Pict Art; AMC2 & 6; Pict Afr; J A Verbeek, *Natal Art Before Union*, 1974, University of Natal Library.

DUMBLETON Bertram W

Born 1896 George, Cape Province.

Died 1966 Cape Town.

A painter of landscapes, figures and portraits. Worked in tempera and watercolour.

Studies 1914–15 and 1918–20 Regent Street Polytechnic, London; 1928–30 Académie Julian, Paris, under Professor P A Laurens (1870–1934).

Profile A member of the SA Society of Artists. 1941–46 a lecturer at the Michaelis School of Fine Art and later at the Fish Hoek Art Society. 1915–18 in the British Forces. 1920–25 lived in SA; 1925–27 in the UK; 1928–30 in Paris; 1930–38 in the UK and from 1938 in SA.

Exhibitions 1926–38 exhibited at the Royal Academy and throughout the UK; participated in group exhibitions in SA from 1947.

Represented Albany Museum, Grahamstown; SA National Gallery, Cape Town; University of Cape Town.

References Art SA; SAA; SAP&S; DBA; BSAK 1 & 2; AASA.

DUMILE see MHLABA Zwelidumile Mxgazi

DUNBAR VAN WEZEL Maggie

Born 1946 Johannesburg.

A painter of figures and genre. Works in acrylic, conté and wash.

Studies 1964–68 Johannesburg School of Art, under George Boys (qv) and Joyce Leonard (qv), gaining a National Art Teachers Diploma; 1969 The Visual Arts Research Centre, Johannesburg, under George Boys (qv); 1983–84 Witwatersrand Technikon, under M Marais.

Profile 1985 a member of the Factory II, an arts workshop in Doornfontein, Johannesburg. 1980–85 Head of the Art Department, Jeppe High School for Girls, Johannesburg. 1987 teaching at Parktown Convent, Johannesburg.
Exhibitions She has participated in several group exhibitions from 1970 in SA; 1978 Market Gallery, Johannesburg, joint exhibition with Agnes Bekes; 1985 Market Gallery, Johannesburg, first of two solo exhibitions.
Represented Rand Afrikaans University.

DUNJEY Judy Grace

Born 1953 Bulawayo, Rhodesia (Zimbabwe).
A painter of wildlife and landscapes. Works in oil.
Studies 1971–73 Bulawayo Technical College, gaining a Diploma in Commercial Art.
Profile 1974–76 a commercial artist; 1976–83 lived and worked in Hwange National Park, Zimbabwe; from 1983 a display artist at the Natural History Museum, Bulawayo. Has travelled throughout Zimbabwe and to Botswana, Kenya and Malawi.
Exhibitions 1984 John Boyne Gallery, Harare, joint exhibition with S Burr; 1984 Naakes Art, Bulawayo, first of two solo exhibitions; she has participated in several group exhibitions in Zimbabwe from 1985.

DUNN Normand Robertson

Born 1917 Leven, Fife, Scotland.
Died 1988 Swellendam, Cape Province.
Resided in SA from 1946.
A painter of sophisticated primitivism with emphasis on people, both in unusual situations and under normal living conditions. Worked in acrylic on board.
Studies 1936–40 Edinburgh College of Art, under William Gillies (1898–1973), William McTaggart (*b*.1903) and John Maxwell (1905–63), gaining a D A (Edin), on an Andrew Grant Scholarship to college, awarded an Andrew Grant Post-Graduate Scholarship in 1940.
Profile 1946–75 Art Director at Hilton College, Natal, where an art gallery has been named after him. 1947–56 contributed cartoons to *The Natal Witness* under the pseudonym "Falk" and to other publications under his own name.
Exhibitions Participated in numerous group exhibitions from 1960 in SA; 1960 Quadrennial Exhibition; 1969 Neil Sack Gallery, Pietermaritzburg, first of five solo exhibitions.
Represented SA National Gallery, Cape Town.
References SAA; AASA; SASSK; *Artlook* January 1969; *Gallery* Winter 1987.

DUNSFORD-WHITE Ailsa Mary

Born 1926 King William's Town, Cape Province.
A painter of landscapes, portraits, still life, figures, wildlife and circus fantasies. Works in oil, acrylic, watercolour, gouache, ink, wash, pencil, charcoal and cloth appliqué.

Studies 1944–47 Natal Technical College, under Eric Byrd (qv) and Cecil Todd (qv), gaining a National Art Teachers Certificate and being awarded the Arthur May Scholarships of 1945, 1946 and 1947; 1949 Continental School of Art, Cape town, under Maurice van Essche (qv).
Profile From 1979 an Associate of the WSSA, 1983–85 Chairman of the Johannesburg, Pretoria and Vereeniging Regional Branch. 1948 taught art at St Anne's Diocesan College, Natal; 1949–53 at Wynberg Girls High, Cape Town; 1968–76 at Bryanston High School, Johannesburg, and in 1977 at Damelin College, Johannesburg. A number of murals in gouache for De Vaal Hotel, Oranjezicht, Cape Town. Has travelled throughout SA and to Italy in 1976.
Exhibitions She has participated in many group exhibitions from 1980 in SA and in London in 1983; 1980 Rosebank, Johannesburg, solo exhibition.
Represented Hugo Naudé Centre, Worcester, Cape Province.

DUNSTON DE PAOLA Lola
Born 1922 Rome, Italy.
Resided in SA from 1946.
A painter and graphic artist of landscapes, portraits, seascapes, figures, wildlife and abstract pictures. Works in many media. 1978 a series of 20 oil paintings on Dante's "Divina Commedia".
Studies Part-time at Accademia di Belle Arti, Rome; Heatherley School of Art, London.
Profile 1969 a member of the Academy of St Nicola of Greece; 1970 of the Club Artistico CEDAR, Rome; 1970 of the Association des Beaux Arts de Cannes; 1971 of the Society of Graphic Artists, London, among others in France, England and Italy. From 1980 a council member of the SAAA, Northern Transvaal Branch. 1980 elected a Fellow of the International Biographical Association. A writer of poetry and a musician. She has travelled and lived throughout Europe.
Exhibitions She has participated in numerous group exhibitions from 1959 in SA, Italy, France and the UK; 1970 Gallery Latin, Hamburg, West Germany, first of nine solo exhibitions held in Italy, Greece and SA; 1981 Republic Festival Exhibition.
Awards From 1970 a number of medals and prizes from art competitions in Italy, France and the UK.
Represented Musée de Picardie, France; National Cultural History and Open-Air Museum, Pretoria; Pietersburg Collection; Pretoria Art Museum; University of Pretoria; Willem Annandale Art Gallery, Lichtenburg.
Publications by Dunston Far faraway, 1973 (poetry); *Young Pretoria*, 1975 (historical); *Yonder*, 1976 (poetry); *Echoes*, 1981 (poetry), all published by Dunston, Pretoria.
References International Directory of Art, editions 1974–75, 1977–78, 1983–84; *Contemporary Personalities*, 1983; *The Worlds Who's Who of Women*, 1980; *The International Who's Who of Intellectuals*, 1978 and 1981, Cambridge, England; *International Register of Profiles*, edition 6, 1982; *American Biographical Institute for Biographical Reference Work*, 1986; AASA; *Artlook* April 1973.

DUNSTONE Albert Edward

Born 1871 Ireland.
Died 1950 Johannesburg.
Resided in SA from the early 1890s.
A painter of landscapes and scenes of early Johannesburg. Worked in water-
colour.
Represented Africana Museum, Johannesburg (sketches dated 1894–1900).
References AMC2; Pict Afr.

DU PLESSIS Alfrieda

Born 1952 Bloemfontein.
A painter of semi-abstract landscapes, portraits, still life and figures. Works in
oil, acrylic and pastel.
Studies 1970–74 Pretoria Teachers College, gaining a Teaching Diploma;
1976–79 University of South Africa, where gained a BA(FA).
Profile 1975–79 a teacher working for the Transvaal Education Department;
1981–84 lectured at the University of the Orange Free State; 1986 and 1987
resumed her position with the Transvaal Education Department; 1988 teaching
at the Conservatoire, Windhoek, SWA/Namibia. 1980 spent a year travelling in
the UK and throughout Europe.
Exhibitions She has participated in several group exhibitions from 1981 in SA;
1988 Karen McKerron Gallery, Johannesburg, first of two solo exhibitions, the
second being held in SWA/Namibia.
Represented Pretoria Art Museum.

DU PLESSIS (Hercules) Enslin

Born 1894 Standerton, Transvaal.
Died 1978 Bromley, London.
Resided in SA until 1922 when he emigrated to England, but made frequent
visits to SA thereafter.
A self-taught painter and graphic artist of interiors, landscapes, figures and still
life. Worked in oil, watercolour and lithography.
Profile 1928 began painting in earnest. 1929 a member of the London Group; a
member of the London Artists Association, 1935 a member of the New Group.
1912–14 a practising journalist; 1914–18 served in the armed forces; 1918–22 a
journalist on *The Star* newspaper, Johannesburg; 1923–56 in London with the
Argus Newspaper Group. Thereafter a full-time painter. Painted in the UK,
France, Spain and the Scilly Isles.
Exhibitions 1928 London, first solo exhibition; participated in group exhibitions
in London from 1929 and in SA from 1938; 1935 a representative of British Art
in the World Exhibition, Brussels, Belgium; 1944 Gainsborough Gallery,
Johannesburg, first of several solo exhibitions held in SA; 1948 Tate Gallery,
London, SA Art Exhibition; 1948 joint exhibition with Edward Wolfe (qv); 1970
Pretoria Art Museum, Retrospective Exhibition; 1972 Pieter Wenning Gallery,
Johannesburg, Prestige Exhibition; 1978 SA National Gallery, Cape Town,
Commemorative Exhibition.

Award 1972 Medal of Honour for Painting, SA Akademie vir Wetenskap en Kuns.

Represented Arts Council and British Council, London, UK; Bristol, Cardiff and Manchester galleries, UK; Durban Art Gallery; Johannesburg Art Gallery; Julius Gordon Africana Centre, Riversdale; King George VI Art Gallery, Port Elizabeth; Pretoria Art Museum; SA Akademie vir Wetenskap en Kuns, Pretoria; SA National Gallery, Cape Town; SA National Museum of Military History, Johannesburg; Tatham Art Gallery, Pietermaritzburg; University of Pretoria; University of South Africa; University of Stellenbosch; University of the Witwatersrand; William Humphreys Art Gallery, Kimberley.

References Collectors' Guide; Our Art 2; Art SA; SAA; 20C SA Art; SAP&S; BSAK 1 & 2; 3Cs; AASA; LSAA; *South Africana* September 1957; *Artlook* October 1968 & November 1973; *SA Arts Calendar* September 1983; 1972 Catalogue by Albert Werth, Pieter Wenning Gallery, Johannesburg.

DU PLESSIS Gavin

Born 1952 Cape Town.

A painter of abstracted and abstract pictures. Works in oil, acrylic, watercolour, ink, wash, pencil, airbrush and pastel crayon. 1977–80 a large series of pen and ink drawings; 1980s pastel and oil series "Götterdämmerung".

Studies 1971–73 Cape Technical College, under Joram Rosov; 1974–77 Croydon College of Design and Technology, UK, studying theatre design, in which he gained a Diploma.

Profile A member of the Artists Guild, Cape Town. 1986 a part-time lecturer in drawing at the Professional School of Dress Designing, Cape Town. Organiser and owner of the "Atelier Julian" School of Art, Cape Town. From 1980 collaborated with Johan Cloete on various concert and film productions. 1975 visited The Hague, The Netherlands.

Exhibitions He has participated in several group exhibitions from 1974 in SA; 1974 Neels Gallery, Cape Town, first of six solo exhibitions; 1979 NSA Gallery, Durban, joint exhibition with Bill Davis (qv).

Represented Pietersburg Collection.

Public Commissions 1980 and 1983 murals in Eikendal Library and Kraaifontein Library, both in Kraaifontein, Cape Province.

References *The South Easter* October/November 1985.

DU PLESSIS Hannes

Born 1950 Hennenman, Orange Free State.

A painter in oil and acrylic and a sculptor in bronze, stone and wood of realistic landscapes, abstracted animals, figures and portraits.

Studies 1969–72 Pretoria Technical College, gaining a Diploma.

Profile A member of the SAAA. A number of illustrations for commercial magazines.

Exhibitions 1978 Northcliff, Johannesburg, first of four solo exhibitions in SA; he has participated in several group exhibitions from 1980 in SA.
Represented Potchefstroom University for CHE; Standerton Municipal Collection.

DU PLESSIS Johann

Born 1953 Frankfort, Orange Free State.
A painter of symbolistic figures and portraits. Works in pencil, watercolour and wash; creates collages.
Studies 1973–74 University of the Orange Free State, where studied architecture; 1976 Orange Free State Technikon; 1977–80 University of the Orange Free State, under Leon de Bliquy (qv), gaining a BA(FA) and a Higher Diploma in Education.
Profile A member of the SAAA. 1980–85 an art teacher at the Eunice School for Girls, Bloemfontein; 1986 an art teacher at the Johannesburg Art, Ballet and Music School. 1981 visited Europe.
Exhibitions He has participated in many group exhibitions from 1978 held in SA, Monaco and Canada; 1979 Sterreweg Teater, Bloemfontein, first of 11 solo exhibitions held in SA; 1985 SAAA Gallery, Pretoria, joint exhibition with Evette Weyers (qv); 1987 Verwoerdburg Association of Arts Gallery, joint exhibition with Guy du Toit (qv), Maryna Huyser (qv) and Evette Weyers (qv); 1987 SAAA Gallery, Pretoria, joint exhibition with Annette Pretorius (qv).
Award 1983 Santam Best Art Teacher Award, Orange Free State.
Represented Bloemfontein Municipality; Durban Art Gallery.
Reference SA Arts Calendar Spring 1985.

DU PLESSIS Johannes

Born 1953 Hofmeyr, Cape Province.
A painter of landscapes. Works in watercolour, pencil and charcoal. A series of animal skulls, painted in oil. A sculptor, working in ceramics, of abstracted heads.
Studies 1968–70 studied privately under Maureen Quin (qv); 1975–79 Port Elizabeth Technical College (Technikon), under Phil Kolbe (qv) and Hylton Nel (qv), gaining a Higher Diploma in Fine Arts.
Profile A part-time artist at a silkscreen company. 1982 illustrated the Loerie series of books, Maskew Miller, Cape Town. A potter.
Exhibitions He has participated in several group exhibitions from 1982 in SA; 1985 Artscene, Cape Town, first of three solo exhibitions.
Represented Port Elizabeth Technikon.

DU PLESSIS Leon

Born 1949 Krugersdorp, Transvaal.
Both a painter and a sculptor.
Studies 1972 gained a BA(FA) (cum laude) from the University of the Witwatersrand; 1980 gained an MA(FA) through the University of South Africa; 1980 a course in film theory and practice at New York University, USA.

Profile 1974 a lecturer, 1979 Head of Fine Arts, 1980 Associate Professor at the University of South Africa. 1976–77 wrote art reviews for *Pretoria News*. 1981 wrote "American Reflections—South African Realities", published in *The Bloody Horse*, Johannesburg.

Exhibitions Has participated in several group exhibitions from 1973 in SA and the USA; 1978 University of the Witwatersrand, joint exhibition with Professor Alan Crump; 1980 University of the Witwatersrand, solo exhibition.

Awards 1972 Henri Lidchi Award for Drawing; 1973 Elizabeth Macadam Overseas Scholarship; 1973 Herbert Evans Award for Painting; 1974 Vick International Art Award for Design.

Represented University of South Africa.

Performances, Videos 1980 Summer Arts Fair, Central Park, New York; 1980 Experimental Workshop, University of Southern California, Los Angeles.

DURING (George) Diederick

Born 1917 Roodepoort, Transvaal.

A painter of landscapes, seascapes and figures. Works in oil, acrylic, tempera and mixed mida.

Studies *c.*1944 Witwatersrand Technical College, under Maurice van Essche (qv).

Profile Lives in Florida, Transvaal.

Exhibitions He has participated in numerous group exhibitions from 1946; 1947 Bothner's Gallery, Cape Town, first of numerous solo exhibitions held in SA; 1956, 1960 and 1964 Quadrennial Exhibitions; 1981 Republic Festival Exhibition.

Award 1949 jointly with Johannes Meintjes (qv), winner of *Die Vaderland*'s Award for the Most Original SA Work of Art.

Represented Hester Rupert Art Museum, Graaff-Reinet; Indianapolis Art Gallery, USA; National Gallery, Harare, Zimbabwe; Pretoria Art Museum; Roodepoort City Council; University of the Witwatersrand.

References 20C SA Art; AASA; *Artlook* March 1967.

DUTILLEUX Liane Ditta (Mrs Smith)

Born 1947 Luxembourg.

Resided in SA from 1953.

A painter of portraits and figures. Works in oil.

Studies 1966–69 Witwatersrand Technical College, under Joyce Leonard (qv), Claude van Lingen (qv) and Zoltan Borboreki (qv), where attained a Teaching Diploma in Fine Art.

Profile During the 1960s a member of the SAAA. 1980–81 illustrations for *The Reader*. Married to Richard Smith (qv).

Exhibitions From 1969 she has participated in several group exhibitions.

Public Commissions Several portrait commissions including in 1985 one of Lesley Barrit, for *People Magazine*, Johannesburg and in 1987 of Saira Essa, for *The Star*.

DU TOIT Guy Pierre
Born 1958 Rustenburg, Transvaal.
A sculptor of abstract works and absurd, mechanical machines often military. Defensive sculptures called "Stopalls" against offensive called "Killalls". Works in bronze, stone, ciment fondu, wood, sandstone, steel, brass and ceramics. Draws in ink, pencil and charcoal.
Studies 1979–82 University of Pretoria, under Professor Nico Roos (qv) and Mike Edwards (qv), where gained a BA(FA); 1983 awarded the Emil Schweickerdt Bursary for a study tour of Europe.
Profile From 1979 a member of the SAAA. 1983–86 a technical assistant at the University of Pretoria. From 1987 an art teacher at the Johannesburg Art, Ballet and Music School. A potter. A number of visits to SWA/Namibia from 1977, including one year spent on National Service there.
Exhibitions He has participated in many group exhibitions from 1982 in SA and SWA/Namibia; 1984 SAAA Gallery, Pretoria, first of three solo exhibitions; 1985 Cape Town Triennial; 1986 Gallery 21, Johannesburg, joint exhibition with Amanda Marais (qv) and Erna Bodenstein-Ferreira (qv); 1987 Gallery 21, Johannesburg, joint exhibition with Maryna Huyser (qv); 1987 Verwoerdburg Association of Arts Gallery, joint exhibition with Johann du Plessis (qv), Maryna Huyser (qv) and Evette Weyers (qv); 1987 and 1988 Johannesburg Art Gallery, Vita Art Now.
Awards 1982 Sculpture Prize, New Signatures, SAAA, Pretoria; 1985 joint winner of Hans Merensky Sculpture in Wood Competition with Koos den Houting (qv); 1986 Vita Quarterly Award Winner; 1987 *Style* Lighting Design Award, Johannesburg; 1987 Merit Award, Hans Merensky Foundation Sculpture in Wood Competition; 1987 Corona del Mar Young Artist Award for Sculpture.
Represented Pretoria Art Museum; Tatham Art Gallery, Pietermaritzburg; University of the Orange Free State; University of Pretoria.
Reference *Africa Insight* vol 14 no 3, 1984.

DU TOIT Janeen Lilian
Born 1943 Johannesburg.
A painter of landscapes and abstract pictures. Works in watercolour, oil, acrylic, gouache, ink, wash and pencil. A sculptor, using found objects, of environmental sculptures. A photographer.
Studies 1974–77 University of South Africa, under Professor Leon du Plessis (qv), where gained a BA(FA); 1985 University of South Africa, under Professor Leon du Plessis and Alan Crump, where awarded an MA(FA).
Profile From 1982 a member of the WSSA, becoming an Associate in 1987. A committee member of the Executive Board of the WSSA. Teaches art through workshops. Sister of Cheryl Curnick (qv).
Exhibitions She has participated in numerous group exhibitions from 1976 in SA; 1981 Olivetti Gallery, Johannesburg, solo exhibition.
Represented University of the Witwatersrand (photographs).

DU TOIT Michael Frederick Horn

Born 1925 Potgietersrus, Northern Transvaal.
A painter of landscapes, portraits, still life, seascapes and wildlife. Works in oil and watercolour.
Studies 1943–46 Witwatersrand Technical College, under James Gardner (qv), Maurice van Essche (qv) and E Renfield, where gained a Teachers Diploma in Art.
Profile From 1960 a member of the WSSA. Taught art in 1946 in Ermelo and privately from 1961 in Rooiberg, Thabazimbi and Warmbaths, Transvaal.
Exhibitions He has participated in several group exhibitions from 1946 in SA and West Germany; 1947 Ermelo, first of 32 solo exhibitions held in SA and SWA/Namibia.
Reference AASA.

DU TOIT Paul

Born 1922 Noordehoek, Cape Province.
Died 1986 Stellenbosch.
A painter of landscapes and abstract pictures. From 1961 sea themes. Worked in oil, acrylic (after 1958), watercolour and ink.
Studies 1944–46 under Jean Welz (qv) at the Hugo Naudé Art Centre in Worcester; 1955 briefly at l'Ecole des Beaux Arts, Paris and at l'Académie de la Grande Chaumière.
Profile 1955–58 toured Europe; 1959–61 lived on a farm in the Paarl area; 1961–68 in Cape Town; 1968–74 in London, thereafter in Cape Town.
Exhibitions 1945 Argus Gallery, Cape Town, joint exhibition with Jean Welz (qv); 1949 SAAA Gallery, Cape Town, first solo exhibition; participated in group exhibitions from 1950 throughout SA and in Brazil, Italy, Belgium and France; 1964 Quadrennial Exhibition; 1976 Pretoria Art Museum, Retrospective Exhibition; 1979 University of Stellenbosch, exhibition; 1981 Republic Festival Exhibition; 1984 University of the Orange Free State, exhibition.
Award 1984 Medal of Honour, SA Akademie vir Wetenskap en Kuns.
Represented Hugo Naudé Art Centre, Worcester; King George VI Art Gallery, Port Elizabeth; National Museum, Bloemfontein; Pretoria Art Museum; SA National Gallery, Cape Town; University of the Orange Free State; University of Stellenbosch; Willem Annandale Art Gallery, Lichtenburg; William Humphreys Art Gallery, Kimberley.
References Art SA; SAA; 20C SA Art; SAP&S; SSAP; BSAK 1 & 2; AASA; LSAA; *De Kat* March 1987; *Paul du Toit*, Pretoria Art Museum Catalogue, 1976.

DU TOIT Susan

Born 1955 Pretoria.
A painter and graphic artist of social symbolism in domestic scenes. Works in oil and various graphic media. 1976–80 a series of abstract landscapes; 1980–83 of poetic landscapes; from 1983 of genre.

Studies 1973–74 University of Pretoria, under Eben van der Merwe (qv), gaining a BA(FA); 1983–84 Boston Museum School, USA, under John Brennan; 1984–85 began an MA(FA) at Massachusetts College of Art, USA, under Henry Isaacs and Dan Kelleher.

Profile From 1986 a member of the SAAA. 1984–85 a lithography instructor at Massachusetts College of Art, Boston, USA. 1982 made low fire clay vessels. 1977–79 lived in London; 1983–85 in Boston, USA. 1977, 1978 and 1979 visited Paris, 1982 Japan, 1983, 1984 and 1985 New York.

Exhibitions 1977 SAAA Gallery, Pretoria first of seven solo exhibitions, one of which was held in London; she has participated in many group exhibitions from 1980 in SA, the USA, West Germany and Italy; 1981 Republic Festival Exhibition.

Reference AASA.

DUXBURY Mary E

Born Somerset East, Cape Province.
Died 1967 Somerset East, Cape Province.
Primarily an illuminist and scribe, who also painted watercolours and decorated wood panels. Her motifs included SA animals, birds, flowers and regimental badges.

Studies Rhodes University, under Professor F W Armstrong (qv); Edinburgh College of Art, Scotland, under Irene Wellington.

Profile A member of the Transvaal Art Society. Taught voluntarily at the Polly Street Art Centre, Johannesburg.

Exhibitions Participated in group exhibitions in SA; 1946 Constantia Gallery, Johannesburg, first solo exhibition.

Represented Houses of Parliament, Cape Town.

Public Commissions Numerous illuminated manuscripts including in 1947 the Addresses from Pretoria and Johannesburg to the Royal Family; the Book of Remembrance for the Sapper Association; the Roll of Honour of SA War Dead in WWII for the National War Memorial Health Foundation.

References SAA; SESA; BSAK; AASA.

DYER Irene

Born 1890 Perth, Australia.
Died 1954 Durban.
Resided in SA from 1925.
From 1929 a painter of landscapes; worked in watercolour and occasionally in oil.

Exhibitions Held numerous solo exhibitions at Lezards, Johannesburg.

Represented Pretoria Art Museum.

Reference AASA.

DYKMAN Henry John

Born 1893 Pretoria.
Died 1972 Johannesburg.
A painter of flowers, landscapes and portraits. Worked in oil.
Studies Under his father John Frederick Dykman senior, an amateur painter.
Profile A professional paint chemist living in Natal. Came from a family of flower painters, brother of John Frederick Dykman (qv), uncle of Jeanette Dykman (qv).
Exhibitions 1952, 1953 and 1954 solo exhibitions held at the Pieter Wenning Gallery, Johannesburg.
Represented Ann Bryant Gallery, East London; Willem Annandale Art Gallery, Lichtenburg.
References Collectors' Guide; BSAK 2; AASA.

DYKMAN Jeanette

Born 1938 Johannesburg.
A painter of flowers, particularly roses.
Studies Tuition from her father John Dykman (qv).
Profile From 1982 she has lived partly in Johannesburg and partly in La Jolla, California, USA. Daughter of John F Dykman (qv), niece of Henry J Dykman (qv).
Exhibitions She has participated in many group exhibitions in SA from 1970; 1971 SA House, London, first of several solo exhibitions held in the UK, Switzerland, SA and the USA.
Represented Municipal collections of Springs, Randfontein, Brakpan, Krugersdorp and Newcastle; Museum of Modern Art, New York, USA; University of the Witwatersrand.
References AASA; *Gallery* Winter 1982.

DYKMAN John Frederick

Born 1897 Cape Province.
Died 1974 Johannesburg.
A painter of landscapes, seascapes and still life.
Studies *c.*1918 Chelsea School of Art, London.
Profile A professional sign-writer, who held the contract for the first advertising on the Johannesburg trams and buses. 1930 painted pantomime sets for the Hippodrome in Johannesburg. Brother of Henry John Dykman (qv), father of Jeanette Dykman (qv).
Exhibition 1949 Johannesburg, first solo exhibition.
Reference AASA.

DZIOMBA Elsa Hermine

Born 1906 Dt'Eylau, Germany.
Died 1970 Johannesburg.
Resided in SA from 1933.

A sculptor of both realist and abstract works. Depicted universal themes; her pieces are related to the human form but are stylised. She was influenced by African tribal sculpture and sensitive to the texture of her material, using the grain in her work. Worked in wood, stone, marble, malachite, ivory, verdite and various other semi-precious stones.

Studies Five years at Kunst Akademie, Berlin, under Professor Becker; Académie de la Grande Chaumière, Paris, winning a bursary for further studies in Germany and The Netherlands.

Profile 1938 a member of the New Group. She was commissioned to make numerous portrait busts.

Exhibitions Participated in group exhibitions from 1936 throughout SA and in Arnhem (Netherlands), London and Venice; 1938 Cape Town, first solo exhibition; 1941 Pretoria, joint exhibition with Jack Lugg (qv) and Gabor Tallo; 1945 Constantia Gallery, Johannesburg, first of several joint exhibitions with Jean Welz (qv); 1948 Tate Gallery, London, SA Art Exhibition.

Awards 1953 prize winner at the International Sculpture Competition, Tate Gallery, London, Granite Maquette—Monument to an Unknown Political Prisoner; 1963 Silver Medal, Chamber of Mines, Transvaal Academy.

Represented Hester Rupert Art Museum, Graaff-Reinet; Johannesburg Art Gallery; Pretoria Art Museum; SA National Gallery, Cape Town.

Public Commissions 1937 designed the SA part of the Coronation Medal; bronze relief, Bank of Athens, Johannesburg; 1948 bust of Dr Robert Broom, Transvaal Museum, Pretoria and Sterkfontein Caves, Krugersdorp, Transvaal; 1955 portal statues, Receiver of Revenue Building, Johannesburg; 1961 statue, Afrikaans Girls High School, Pretoria.

References Collectors' Guide; Our Art 2; Art SA; SAA; 20C SA Art; SAP&S; SA Art; 3Cs; AASA; *Libertas* May 1947; *Artlook* December 1969 & June 1970.

E

EALES Yvonne
Born 1920 Dannhauser, Natal.
Died 1987 in a motor accident.
A painter of landscapes, portraits, still life and seascapes. Worked in water-colour, oil and ink.
Studies 1974–85 painting holidays under Alfred Ewan (qv), Ulrich Schwanecke (qv), George Boys (qv) and Marjorie Bowen (qv).
Profile From 1965 a member of the Grahamstown Art Society and its Chairman in 1985 and 1986. From 1973 a member of the Queenstown Art Society and from 1974 of the EPSFA. A member of the WSSA from 1975, becoming an Associate in 1979. A needlewoman. In 1956–57 she made a six-month tour of Europe.
Exhibitions Participated in numerous group exhibitions from 1966 in SA and one in SWA/Namibia; 1977 1820 Settlers Museum, Grahamstown, first of two solo exhibitions.

EDDIE James
Born 1916.
A painter of portraits and still life, particularly flowers. Works in oil.
Studies c.1936 studied commercial art in Cape Town; later studied at the Michaelis School of Fine Art.
Profile Lived in Europe, mainly in Greece, prior to 1935. It is thought that he has returned to Europe.
Exhibitions Known to have exhibited in SA from 1943.
Represented SA National Gallery, Cape Town; University of Cape Town.
References SAA; SAP&S.

EDELSTEIN Lorraine
Born 1929 Bulawayo, Rhodesia (Zimbabwe).
Resided in SA from 1960.
A sculptor of figures and abstract pieces. Works in stone, wood and bronze.
Studies 1961–62 a part-time sculpture student at the Michaelis School of Fine Art, under Professor Lippy Lipshitz (qv).
Profile From 1980 a member of the Artists Guild, Cape Town. 1968–70 taught sculpture privately. 1977 lived in Pietrasanta, Italy, revisited Italy in 1980, 1981 and 1985. 1982 visited Zimbabwe; 1983 visited Karnak, Egypt; 1984 visited The Hermitage in Leningrad and Moscow, Russia. Visits London annually and has lived and worked in Israel.
Exhibitions She has participated in numerous group exhibitions from 1961 in Zimbabwe, SA, the UK and Italy; 1976 SAAA Gallery, Cape Town, first of seven solo exhibitions; 1979 National Museum, Bloemfontein, joint exhibition with Thelma Chait (qv), Cecil Skotnes (qv) and Olivia Scholnick (qv).

Award 1975 Prize Winner, New Signatures, SAAA, Cape Town.
Represented National Gallery, Harare, Zimbabwe; SA National Gallery, Cape Town; William Humphreys Art Gallery, Kimberley.
Public Commission 1979 Persian travertine spiral sculpture, New Stock Exchange Building, Johannesburg.
Reference Habitat no 32, 1978.

EDWARDS (Henry) Dennis

Born 1861.
Died 1921.
A painter of landscapes. Worked in watercolour and oil.
Profile A member of the SA Society of Artists. Came to SA in 1879, working for *The Graphic* as a war correspondent. In 1880 he began his own printing and publishing company in Cape Town and illustrated many of the directories and guides that this company published. From 1890 he published the weekly *Cape Register*, to which he contributed cartoons, often under the pseudonym "Grip".
Exhibitions Participated in group exhibitions from 1903 in SA; 1918 Cape Town, joint exhibition with W G Bevington (qv).
Represented SA Cultural History Museum, Cape Town; William Fehr Collection, Cape Town.
References AASA; SASSK.

EDWARDS Ethel M

A painter of landscapes. Worked in oil.
Studies Under Frank Brangwyn (1867–1956).
Profile 1901 a member of the SA Drawing Club, later a member of the SA Society of Artists. *c.*1897 taught drawing in Cape Town.
Exhibitions Participated in group exhibitions from 1902 in SA.
Represented SA Cultural History Museum, Cape Town.
Reference AASA.

EDWARDS Marc Damon

Born 1958 Pretoria.
A sculptor of portraits, still life, figures and investigations into objects and environments. Works in bronze, stone, ciment fondu, wood and mixed media.
Studies 1978–82 Pretoria Technikon, under Gunther van der Reis (qv) and Ian Redelinghuys (qv), gaining a National Diploma in Fine Art in 1980 and a Higher Diploma in Fine Art in 1983; 1984 University of South Africa.
Profile From 1982 a member of the SAAA and from 1983 of the Independent Visual Arts Council. 1982–84 a lecturer at Pretoria Technikon; 1984 a part-time lecturer at the University of Pretoria; from 1985 a lecturer at the Witwatersrand Technikon. 1984 on the judging panel of the SAAA New Signatures Exhibition. Has travelled extensively in South Africa and in SWA/Namibia from 1979. 1983–84 travelled in Europe.

Exhibitions He has participated in many group exhibitions from 1979 in SA; 1981 Republic Festival exhibition; 1983 Market Gallery, Johannesburg, solo exhibition.

Awards 1979, 1980 and 1981 Prize Winner, New Signatures, SAAA; 1984 Haggie Award, Market Gallery, Johannesburg.

Reference AASA.

EDWARDS Michael Henry Keith (Mike)

Born 1938 Port Elizabeth.

A sculptor of figures, portraits, still life and landscapes in both figurative and abstracted manner. Works in bronze, stone, ciment fondu and wood. A graphic artist.

Studies 1957–60 Port Elizabeth Art School, under John Hooper (qv), Joan Wright (qv) and Betsy Fordyce (qv), gaining a National Art Teachers Certificate; 1978–82 University of Pretoria, under Professor F G E Nilant and Professor Nico Roos (qv), gaining a BA(FA).

Profile 1966–74 a member of the Bloemfontein Group; a member of the SAAA. 1961–72 a lecturer, then a senior lecturer at the Orange Free State Technical College, appointed Vice-Head of the Fine Arts Department in 1967; from 1973 a senior lecturer in the Fine Arts Department at the University of Pretoria, presently Head of Sculpture. 1960–62 theatre designs in Port Elizabeth and Bloemfontein. 1966–69 construction of the stained glass, designed by Eben van der Merwe (qv), for the Orange Free State Provincial Building, Bloemfontein. He has travelled throughout Europe and the USA visiting art schools, bronze foundries, glass works etc. In 1985 he spent two months working at the Mariani Foundry in Italy.

Exhibitions He has participated in numerous group exhibitions from 1959 held throughout SA and in Harare, Zimbabwe and Washington DC, USA; 1964 Quadrennial Exhibition; 1973 joint exhibition with Eben van der Merwe (qv); 1971 SAAA Gallery, Pretoria, first of four solo exhibitions.

Award 1959 Port Elizabeth Municipal Silver Medal.

Represented National Museum, Bloemfontein; Potchefstroom Museum; Potchefstroom University for CHE; Pretoria Art Museum; Rand Afrikaans University; University of the Orange Free State; University of Pretoria; Willem Annandale Art Gallery, Lichtenburg; William Humphreys Art Gallery, Kimberley.

Public Commissions A large number of public commissions from 1959, including in 1959 "Tragedy & Comedy", Little Theatre, Athenaeum Club, Port Elizabeth; 1963 an abstract bronze, Netherlands Bank (Nedbank), Bloemfontein; 1969 a ciment fondu Christ, Thaba ya Kresta Catholic Church, Thaba 'Nchu; 1970 relief panels, Central Government Building, Bloemfontein; 1972–74 stainless steel piece, Civitas Building, Pretoria; 1983–85 bronze panel I, Delville Wood Museum, Congueval, France; also portrait busts of Presidents, public figures and fellow artists.

References BSAK 1 & 2; AASA; Port Elizabeth School of Art; LSAA.

EGERSDORFER Heinrich (Heiner)

Born 1853 Nuremberg, Germany.
Died 1915 London, England.
Resided in SA 1879–85 and 1895–1910.
A painter of wildlife and Boer genre. Worked in watercolour. A trained lithographer.
Profile A Boer War artist. A large number of drawings and cartoons, which were often used in illustrated papers including *The SA Illustrated News*, published 1884–85 in Cape Town. His work also appeared in *The Press*, *The Johannesburg Times*, *The Sunday Times*, *The South African Review*, *The Owl* and *The Cape Argus*. His cartoons feature in *The SA Review Book of 50 Famous Cartoons: a unique souvenir of the Anglo Boer war 1899–1900*, 1900, SA Review, Cape Town. During the 1890s a large series entitled "Sketches of South African Life" was reproduced as postcards. Prior to 1879 lived in England and Ireland, 1885–95 in Australia, 1910–15 in England. Travelled extensively in SA, SWA/Namibia and Rhodesia (Zimbabwe).
Exhibition 1902 exhibited on the first SA Society of Artists Exhibition.
Award 1910 prize winner, SA National Union Exhibition.
Represented Africana Museum, Johannesburg; Pretoria Art Museum; William Fehr Collection, Cape Town; William Humphreys Art Gallery, Kimberley.
References Eric Rosenthal, *Heinrich Egersdorfer*, 1960, Nasionale Boekhandel, Cape Town; Pict Art; SADNB; AMC3&6; DSAB; SESA; Pict Afr; BSAK 1 & 2; SA Art; 3Cs; AASA; SASSK; *ANN* March 1964.

EICHBAUM Heinrich Alexander

Born 1914 Magdeburg, Germany.
Resided in SA from 1938.
A painter of landscapes and seascapes. Works in watercolour and pastel.
Profile 1956–83 a member of the Arts Association SWA/Namibia; from 1984 of the Fish Hoek Art Society and the Muizenberg Association of Arts and Crafts. 1932–35 an art critic in Dresden; 1937–38 lived in London; 1938–42 in Cape Town; 1942–56 in Johannesburg; 1956–83 an art critic in Windhoek; thereafter lived in Muizenberg, Cape Province.
Exhibitions He has participated in several group exhibitions from 1962 in SWA/Namibia, SA and West Germany; 1962 Lüderitz, SWA/Namibia, first of 12 solo exhibitions held in SWA/Namibia and SA, with one held in London and one in Düsseldorf, West Germany.
Represented Arts Association SWA/Namibia Collection.
References Art SWA; AASA.

EIDELMAN Angela Frances

Born 1936 Kent, England.
Resided in SA from 1948.
A self-taught painter and graphic artist of landscapes and seascapes. Works in watercolour, gouache and in various graphic media.
Profile A member of the WSSA, becoming an Associate in 1986. Teaches art privately.

Exhibitions She has participated in numerous group exhibitions in the Transvaal.
Public Commission 1986 Resurrection, St James Church, Boystown, Transvaal.

ELAHI Alice (Brooke)

Born Cape Town.

A painter of landscapes, seascapes and flowers. Works in oil, acrylic, gouache, watercolour, ink, pencil, charcoal and mixed media. Several large series: *c.*1971–74 "Orchards in Blossom"; *c.*1974–76 "Snow Landscapes"; *c.*1980 "Harbour Scenes, Cape Town Docks"; 1980–83 "Red Vineyards, De Doorns"; "Mountain Landscapes, Seweweekspoort, Karoo and Golden Gate Areas"; "Namaqualand and Flower Farms"; "Beach Studies with Figures, Cape"; from 1980 "Namib Desert, Dunescapes and Skeleton Coast".

Studies Continental School of Art, Cape Town, under Maurice van Essche (qv); Anglo-French Art Centre, London; Camberwell School of Art, London, under Victor Pasmore (*b.*1908); studied stained glass techniques at the Central School of Art, London; Hampstead School of Art, London, under Ruskowski.

Profile Organising Secretary of the University of Cape Town Art Society, whilst studying there for a Bachelor of Science degree. An invited member of the Women's International Art Club, London; a member of SAAA. During the early 1970s taught life drawing with Anna Vorster (qv) in Pretoria. She has travelled throughout SA and SWA/Namibia.

Exhibitions She has participated in numerous group exhibitions from 1952 held throughout SA and in Zimbabwe, West Germany and Portugal; 1981 Republic Festival Exhibition; she has held several solo exhibitions in Pretoria, Johannesburg, and in SWA/Namibia.

Award 1968 First Prize with Elizabeth Lamb (qv) and Malcolm Payne (qv), New Signatures, SAAA.

Represented Embassies in Tel Aviv, Teheran and Munich, West Germany; galleries in Pietersburg and Swakopmund; Pretoria Art Museum; SA House, London, England; Willem Annandale Art Gallery, Lichtenburg.

References AASA; *Artlook* September 1968; *Lantern* March 1977; *Femina* 27 March 1985.

ELIASTAM Peter

Born 1934.

An artist producing collages of landscapes, flowers and religious works. Concerned with war and aggression and their consequences.

Profile During the 1960s taught at the Pretoria Technical College. 1961 designed the triangular motif of the SAAA.

Exhibitions He has participated in group exhibitions in SA; 1973 Lidchi Gallery, Johannesburg, first of several solo exhibitions; 1973 Durban Art Gallery, Prestige Exhibition "Homage to the Messiah".

References *SA Arts Calendar* May 1973; *Artlook* July 1973.

ELIOVSON Sima

Born 1919 Cape Town.
A painter of flowers and landscapes. Works in oil, watercolour and Chinese ink.
Studies An art course at the Witwatersrand Technical College; privately under
Joyce Leonard (qv) and George Boys (qv), and Sumi-e (ink) painting under
Gofu Sano in Kyoto, Japan.
Profile A writer of eleven horticultural books. A photographer, occasionally
using her photographs to illustrate her book and magazine publications. Several
visits to Namaqualand from 1951 and to Israel from 1964. She has made
extensive trips throughout the world, lecturing and photographing gardens.
Exhibitions She has participated in several group exhibitions in SA from 1976.
Publications by Eliovson *Little Umfaan*, 1943, privately printed for charity; a
short story in *South African New Writing:* "The Oriental Dancer", 1966; *Flowering
Shrubs, Trees and Climbers*, 1951, Howard Timmins, Cape Town, 8th edition
enlarged and republished as *Shrubs, Trees and Climbers for Southern Africa*,
Macmillan (SA), Johannesburg; *South Africa, Land of Sunshine*, 1953; *South African
Wild Flowers for the Garden*, 1955, Howard Timmins, Cape Town, revised and
republished as *Wild Flowers of Southern Africa*, 1984, Macmillan (SA), Johannesburg; *Johannesburg, The Fabulous City*, 1957; *The Complete Gardening Book*, 1960,
Howard Timmins, Cape Town, revised 1974, Macmillan (SA), Johannesburg,
revised 1988, Howard Timmins, Cape Town; *This is South Africa*, 1962;
Discovering Wild Flowers in Southern Africa, 1962, Howard Timmins, Cape Town;
Proteas for Pleasure, 1965, Howard Timmins, Cape Town, revised 1973, Macmillan (SA), Johannesburg; *Johannesburg, City of Gold*, 1965, Frameworthy; *Bulbs
for the Gardener*, 1967, Howard Timmins, Cape Town; *Gardening the Japanese Way*,
1970, Howard Timmins, Cape Town; *Namaqualand in Flower*, 1972, Macmillan
(SA), Johannesburg; *Garden Beauty of South Africa*, 1979, Macmillan (SA),
Johannesburg; *Garden Design for Southern Africa*, 1985, Macmillan (SA), Johannesburg.
References BSAK 1 & 2; AASA.

ELLIOT Colin Francis Kilpin

Born 1906 Paarl, Cape Province.
Died 1966 Port Elizabeth.
A painter of landscapes. Worked in watercolour and oil.
Profile Primarily a Magistrate who, upon retirement, opened an art gallery in
Schoenmakerskop, Port Elizabeth.
Exhibitions 1946 Somerset East, joint exhibition with G P Canitz (qv);
participated in numerous group exhibitions with his wife Margaret Oliphant, a
potter; held many solo exhibitions throughout SA.

ELLIOT Dale Alan Leslie

Born 1946 Queenstown, Cape Province.
A self-taught painter of landscapes, seascapes, still life, figures and wildlife.
Works in oil, watercolour and ink.

PAUL DU TOIT
Cedarberg Landscape
Oil on Board 43 × 48,5 cm
Die Kunskamer

ZAKKIE ELOFF
Late Afternoon
Oil on Canvas 90 × 120 cm
U Schwitter

Profile From 1957 a member of the Queenstown Art Society and its President in 1986; from 1960 a member of the East London Society of Fine Arts, the EPSFA and the Orange Free State Society of Fine Arts; from 1983 a member of the WSSA. 1970–80 an Attorney. 1981 established the Penny Lane Art Studios in Queenstown. 1983 and 1984–85 co-leader of painting holidays in the Drakensberg. 1984–86 issued lithographs of Queen's College, Queenstown and St Andrew's College, Grahamstown.

Exhibitions He has participated in numerous group exhibitions from 1961 in SA; 1967 Edrich Gallery, Stellenbosch, first of 13 solo exhibitions held in SA; 1984 SAAA Gallery, Pretoria, joint exhibition with Wendy Malan (qv), Ulrich Schwanecke (qv) and Gordon Vorster (qv).

Represented Queenstown Art Gallery.

ELLISON Gabriel MBE

Born 1930 Lusaka, Northern Rhodesia (Zambia).

A painter of landscapes, portraits and wildlife; works in oil, acrylic, watercolour, gouache, ink, wash, pencil and charcoal. A graphic artist, an embroiderer and a maker of collages.

Studies Privately in England.

Profile A Fellow of the British Display Society, of the Royal Society of Arts and a member of the Society of Industrial Artists and Designers. 1962–73 Chief Graphic Artist for the Information Services of the Government of Zambia. Murals and paintings used in official exhibitions and Trade Fair stands in Africa and Europe. Many illustrations for textbooks, tourism pamphlets and posters. From 1964 she has designed the majority of the Zambian stamps and two sets of stamps for Swaziland. She has also designed the one and two ngwee coins and most of the Zambian medals and decorations.

Exhibitions She has participated in numerous group exhibitions in Zambia, SA, East and West Germany, Hungary, the UK, Zimbabwe, Czechoslovakia, the USA and Japan; 1955 Zambia, first of numerous solo exhibitions held in Zambia, the UK and Majorca.

Awards 1965 appointed a Member of British Empire by the UK Government; 1967 awarded Grand Officer of the Order of Distinguished Service by the Zambian Government—both awards for service in the field of art and design.

Represented Zambia National Collection.

Public Commissions Murals in Lusaka Airport; Pamodzi Hotel, Lusaka; Intercontinental Hotels in Lusaka and Livingstone and in the Mulungushi Hall, Lusaka; designs for a mosaic in Barclays Bank, Lusaka; official gifts of paintings to H M Queen Elizabeth II of England in 1980 and to the Prince and Princess of Wales on the occasion of their wedding.

ELOFF René (née Van Zyl)

Born 1939 Pretoria.

A painter and graphic artist of landscapes, wildlife, still life and figures. Works in oil, mixed media and in various graphic media.

Studies 1957 University of Pretoria, under Walter Battiss (qv); 1958 Pretoria Technical College, under Robert Hodgins (qv) Zakkie Eloff (qv) and Ernst de Jong (qv). Gained a National Art Teachers Certificate in 1960.

Profile 1961–62 a junior lecturer at the Pretoria Technical College. 1982 designed a tapestry for the town of Nelspruit in the Eastern Transvaal. 1962–68 lived in the Etosha Game Reserve, SWA/Namibia. From 1969 she has lived and worked in the Eastern Transvaal Lowveld. Married to Zakkie Eloff (qv).

Exhibitions She has participated in group exhibitions and held solo exhibitions from 1961; 1987 University of Pretoria, joint Retrospective Exhibition with Zakkie Eloff (qv).

References SAA (under Van Zyl Eloff); AASA; *SA Art News* 10 August 1961.

ELOFF Stephanus Johannes Paulus (Fanie)

Born 1885 Pretoria.

Died 1947 Pretoria.

A sculptor of small statuettes and portrait busts of his family and friends. 1914–32 portrait busts of Afrikaner leaders and 1932–41 a large series of dancers and athletes. Worked in bronze and marble.

Studies 1908–14 sculpture in Paris under the Swedish sculptor David Edstrom (*b*.1873).

Profile Influenced by Auguste Rodin (1840–1917), whom he met in 1908, and Aristide Maillol (1861–1944). 1912 elected a member of the Paris Union Internationale des Beaux Arts et Lettres. Lived in Paris 1908–14, 1920–25 and 1932–41, in SA 1914–20, 1925–32 and 1941–47.

Exhibitions 1929 Johannesburg, joint exhibition with J H Pierneef (qv); 1947 Pretoria, Retrospective Exhibition; 1948 Christi Gallery, Pretoria, Memorial Exhibition; 1948 Tate Gallery, London, SA Art Exhibition.

Award 1944 Medal of Honour for Sculpture, SA Akademie vir Wetenskap en Kuns.

Represented British Museum, London, UK; Johannesburg Art Gallery; Musée d'Art Moderne, Paris, France; Pretoria Art Museum; SA National Gallery, Cape Town; Transvaal Museum, Pretoria; University of Pretoria.

Public Commissions 1929 Discus Thrower, Loftus Versfeld Stadium, Pretoria; decorative vases on antelope heads, Union Buildings Pretoria.

References SK; Collectors' Guide; Our Art 2; Art SA; SAA; SADNB; 20C SA Art; SAP&S; SESA; BSAK 1 & 2; 3Cs; Enc S'n A; AASA; *SA Digest* 28 April 1972.

ELOFF Zacharias (Zakkie)

Born 1925 Waterberg District, SWA/Namibia.

A painter and graphic artist of wildlife. Works in oil, watercolour, ink, wash, monotype and etching.

Studies Pretoria Boys High School, under Walter Battiss (qv); Witwatersrand Technical College, under Maurice van Essche (qv), James Gardner (qv) and Phyllis Gardner (qv); 1957 graphic techniques at the Central School of Art, London; etching under Dolf Rieser (qv).

Profile 1958–62 taught at Pretoria Technical College and 1961–62 for the University of Pretoria. He has illustrated various books. 1962–68 worked as a Game Ranger in the Etosha Game Reserve, SWA/Namibia. From 1969 he has lived and worked in the Eastern Transvaal Lowveld. Married to René Eloff (qv).
Exhibitions He has participated in group exhibitions from 1942 in SWA/Namibia, SA, the UK, Spain, Israel, Argentina, Australia and at São Paulo, Brazil in 1961; 1953 Pretoria, first of several solo exhibitions; 1987 University of Pretoria, joint Retrospective Exhibition with René Eloff (qv).
Represented Ann Bryant Gallery, East London; Hester Rupert Art Museum, Graaff-Reinet; Pretoria Art Museum; University of Pretoria; University of South Africa; Willem Annandale Art Gallery, Lichtenburg; William Humphreys Art Gallery, Kimberley.
Public Commission 1973 three paintings for Jan Smuts Airport, Johannesburg.
References Art SA; SAA; 20C SA Art; BSAK 1 & 2; Our Art 3; Art SWA; SA Art; 3Cs; AASA; LSAA; *SA Art News* 10 August 1961; *Artlook* October 1969; *SA Panorama* April 1976.

EMANUEL Joan

Born 1937 Ladysmith, Natal.
A painter of abstract works. Works in oil and charcoal.
Studies 1982 privately under Jane Heath (qv) in Pietermaritzburg; 1983 extra-murally at the University of Natal, under Andrew Verster (qv); 1984 under Diana Kenton (qv).
Profile A member of the North Coast Art Group and the NSA.
Exhibitions She has participated in several group exhibitions from 1975 in Durban; 1984 NSA Gallery, Durban, solo exhibition.

EMSLEY Paul

Born 1947 Glasgow, Scotland.
Resided in SA from 1949.
A painter of landscapes, portraits and figures. Works in oil, acrylic, watercolour, ink, wash, pencil, charcoal, crayon, chalk and pastel. 1979–80 a series of Table Mountain as a psychological and political symbol; 1981–82 a series on the dilemma of white SA.
Studies 1969 Cape Technical College, gaining a National Diploma in Graphic Design.
Profile From 1975 a member of the SAAA; from 1981 of the Artists Guild, Cape Town. 1976 a lecturer at the Cape Technical College; 1978 at the Ruth Prowse School of Art and from 1983 at the University of Stellenbosch. From 1970 he has worked as an illustrator. 1976–77 lived in England.
Exhibitions He has participated in many group exhibitions from 1978 in SA and the USA; 1981 University of Stellenbosch, first of three solo exhibitions; 1982 Cape Town Triennial; 1985 Cape Town Triennial.

Represented Johannesburg Art Gallery; SA National Gallery, Cape Town; University of Stellenbosch; University of the Witwatersrand.
References AASA; *Gallery* Spring 1982.

ENGELA Johan

A painter of landscapes, portraits, still life and seascapes. Worked in oil, watercolour, gouache, pastel and egg tempera.
Profile Lived in the Cape.
Exhibitions Participated in group exhibitions in SA during the 1940s and 1950s; Gainsborough Gallery, Johannesburg, first of *c.* four solo exhibitions.
Represented University of Stellenbosch; Willem Annandale Art Gallery, Lichtenburg.

ENGLISH André

Born 1936 Johannesburg.
A self-taught painter of wildlife. Works in gouache.
Profile He has lived in the Kruger National Park since 1963. 1970 painted a number of paintings for the National Parks Board offices.
Exhibitions He has participated in several group exhibitions from 1974 in Johannesburg, Pretoria and Nelspruit.

ENGLISH John Mayne

Born 1922 Malvern, Worcestershire, England.
Resided in SA from 1937.
A painter, working in watercolour, ink and wash, and a sculptor, working in wood. He depicts landscapes, genre, wildlife, urban scenes and buildings.
Profile 1968 a member of the Grahamstown Art Society. A trained, practising architect. Nephew of Grace English, Royal Academician.
Public Commission 1980 a view of the harbour of circa 1860, Port Alfred Municipality.
Publications by English *The Story of Buck Horns*, 1970, and *Warthog Story*, 1975, Grocott and Sherry Printers, Grahamstown.

ENSLIN George

Born 1919 Richmond, England.
Died 1972 Aegina, Greece.
Resided in SA from 1920.
A painter of landscapes, genre and scenes of the Cape Malay Quarter and Fishing Villages. Worked in oil. Known to have painted in SWA/Namibia.

Studies 1938–39 under Arthur Podolini (qv) in Cape Town; 1946 Continental School of Art, Cape Town, under Maurice van Essche (qv); 1949 Heatherley School of Art, London; 1950 Académie de la Grande Chaumière, Paris; 1950 sculpture at Carrara Academy, Italy.

Profile Travelled extensively throughout the world. Visited Japan six times, where he learnt the Japanese arts of pottery, woodblock printing and enamel work. From 1967 he lived in Greece.

Exhibitions 1948 Cape Town, first of numerous solo exhibitions held in SA and SWA/Namibia; participated in group exhibitions from 1952 in SA and Zimbabwe; 1956 and 1960 Quadrennial Exhibitions; 1981 posthumously exhibited in Japan with his wife, Noriko, a painter in the Japanese Sumi-e tradition and a designer of jewellery.

Represented Durban Art Gallery; National Museum, Bloemfontein; Pretoria Art Museum; Rand Afrikaans University; University of the Orange Free State; University of Pretoria; University of Stellenbosch; University of the Witwatersrand; William Humphreys Art Gallery, Kimberley.

References Art SA; SAA; 20C SA Art; BSAK 1; Art SWA; AASA; *Artlook* June 1970.

ERASMUS David

Born 1930 Kenya.
Resided in SA from 1936.
A painter of landscapes and seascapes. Works in acrylic.
Profile A retired Engineer.
Exhibitions He has participated in several group exhibitions from 1966 in SA; 1966 Welkom, solo exhibition.

ERASMUS Derrick

Born 1934 Balfour, Transvaal.
A painter and graphic artist of masks at varying degrees of abstraction. Works in oil, acrylic, watercolour, gouache, wash, pencil, bronze, wood, various graphic media and in mixed media such as collage, frottage, papier mache and plaster.

Studies 1956 gained a National Art Teachers Certificate from the Witwatersrand Technical College, having studied under James Gardner (qv); 1957 part-time at the Central School of Art, London, under Mervyn Peake (1911–68); 1982 gained a Higher Diploma in Painting and in 1985 a Masters Diploma in the Technology of Painting from the Port Elizabeth Technikon, having studied under Alexander Podlashuc (qv).

Profile From 1970 a member of the EPSFA and at one time a committee member. 1957 an art teacher at Parktown Boys High School, Johannesburg and the Eltham Green Secondary Modern School in London; 1967–69 a visiting lecturer at Flatford Mill Field Centre, Suffolk; 1970–72 a lecturer, 1972–87 a senior lecturer and in 1987 Acting Head of the Foundation Studies Department at the Port Elizabeth Technikon. Numerous illustrations for botanical and natural history books for both the Royal Botanical Gardens, Kew, Surrey and the Natural History Museum, London. 1957–70 lived in London and travelled extensively in Europe. Nephew of the composer M J Erasmus.

Exhibitions He has participated in numerous group exhibitions from 1960 in the UK, SA and the USA.

Represented Carnegie Mellon University, Pittsburgh, Pennsylvania, USA; the Herbarium, Royal Botanical Gardens, Kew, Surrey, UK; King George VI Art Gallery, Port Elizabeth; Natural History Museum, London.

ERASMUS Linette

Born 1960 Brakpan, Transvaal.

A painter and graphic artist of still life, figures, animals and abstract pictures. Works in oil, pencil, charcoal and in various graphic media. 1985–87 a series entitled "Knights in Shining Armour".

Studies 1975–78 Johannesburg Art, Ballet and Music School; 1979–85 University of Pretoria, under Professor Nico Roos (qv), gaining a BA(FA) in 1982 and a Teachers Training Higher Diploma in 1983; she began an MA(FA) course in 1985.

Profile A member of the Northern Transvaal Art Society. 1984–85 a teaching assistant at the University of Pretoria. Creates sculptural and functional pottery. 1986–87 spent six months in Venda.

Exhibitions She has participated in several group exhibitions in SA from 1981; 1985 University of Pretoria, solo exhibition.

ERASMUS Petronella Margaretha (Nel)

Born 1928 Bethal, Transvaal.

A painter of the metamorphoses of various combinations of landscapes, portraits, still life, seascapes, genre, figures, and animals and their use as source material for further formal exploration. Although her work is frequently abstract in appearance it is firmly rooted in the forms and patterns of nature. Works in oil, acrylic, gouache, ink, wash, pencil and charcoal. Numerous series of paintings including "Nocturne", "Human Body", "Dog", "Bird", "Lamp and Light", "Horse", "Ophelia", "Portrait", "Crucifixion", "Human Temple" and "Music".

Studies 1946–50 University of the Witwatersrand, under Joyce Leonard (qv) and Heather Martienssen (1915–79), gaining a BA(FA); 1951–52 Witwatersrand Technical College, under Phyllis Gardner (qv), where awarded a National Art Teachers Certificate; 1952 privately under the Czech–German painter, Gina Berndtson; 1952–55 the Sorbonne, Paris, under Soureau; Académie Ranson, Paris, under Selim, Gustave Singier (b.1909) and Fiorini and at l'Ecole des Beaux Arts, Paris, under Edouard Goerg (1839–1969), awarded Etudiant Libre.

Profile A member of the SAAA. 1952 an art teacher at the Johannesburg High School for Girls. 1957–64 a Professional Assistant, 1964–77 Curator, then Director of the Johannesburg Art Gallery. Illustrated *Put-sonder-water* and *Christine* by Bartho Smit and *Boot in die Woestyn* by Marlise Joubert. Designed the record cover of "Interludes" for Continental Records. She has written articles in museological and related publications. 1952–55 visited Italy, Greece, Austria, Germany, The Netherlands, Spain and Switzerland. 1982 visited Taiwan and Japan. She has also visited the Namib Desert and India.

Exhibitions She has participated in numerous group exhibitions from 1950 in SA, France, Belgium and Brazil; 1957 Lidchi Gallery, Johannesburg, first of 16 solo exhibitions; 1960 and 1964 Quadrennial Exhibitions; 1972 University of the Witwatersrand and Rand Afrikaans University, Prestige Exhibition; 1981 Rand Afrikaans University, Prestige Exhibition; 1985–86 University of the Orange Free State, SA National Gallery, Cape Town, Pretoria Art Museum and Potchefstroom Museum, Retrospective Exhibition.

Represented Hester Rupert Art Museum, Graaff-Reinet; Johannesburg Art Gallery; Pietersburg Collection; Pretoria Art Museum; Rand Afrikaans University; SA National Gallery, Cape Town; University of the Orange Free State; University of Stellenbosch; University of the Witwatersrand; Willem Annandale Art Gallery, Lichtenburg.

References M Seuphor, *Dictionary of Abstract Painting*, 1957, Hazan, Paris; M Seuphor, *Abstract Painting: Fifty years of accomplishment from Kandinsky to the present*, 1961, Harry N Abrams, New York; SA; SAA; 20C SA Art; *Gees van die wingerd, Republiek van Suid-Afrika*, edited by D J Opperman, 1968, Human & Rousseau, Cape Town; SAP&S; SSAP; SAGAT; Bénézit; BSAK 1 & 2; *The World's Who's Who of Women*, edited by E Kay, 1978, International Biographical Centre, Cambridge, UK; 3Cs; AASA; LSAA; *South Africana* September 1958; *Fontein* vol 1 no 1, Winter 1960; *SA Art News* 6 April 1961; *Vogue South Africa* no 2, Spring/Summer 1962; *Lantern* vol XII no 1, July–September 1962; *South African Digest* 1 August 1969; *Artlook* January 1973; *Fair Lady* 24 July 1974 and in its supplement 24 November 1976; *SA Arts Calendar* November 1977, August 1981, March 1983, March 1984 & Autumn 1986.

ERIKSSON Axel Francis Zeraava

Born 1878 Omaruru, SWA/Namibia.
Died 1924 Warmbad, SWA/Namibia.
A painter of landscapes, particularly of the diamond fields and of tribal figures, especially of Nama women. Worked in gouache and oil.

Studies 1903–05 awarded a bursary to study at the Berlin Academy.

Profile 1905 illustrated *Wild und Hund* magazine, Berlin. 1916 taught art in Swakopmund. 1903–09 lived in Berlin, Germany; 1909–19 in Swakopmund; 1919–24 in Lüderitz.

Exhibitions 1913 Swakopmund, first of several solo exhibitions held in SWA/Namibia; 1978 Arts Association SWA/Namibia Gallery, Windhoek, Commemorative exhibition.

Represented Arts Association SWA/Namibia Collection; Hall of Assembly, Windhoek.
References SAA; BSAK 1; Art SWA; 3Cs; AASA.

ERNST Johanna Petronella

Born 1932 Waterberg, Northern Transvaal.
A painter and graphic artist of landscapes, seascapes and still life. Works in oil, watercolour, gouache, mixed media and in various graphic media. More recently she has been painting abstract pictures.
Studies Potchefstroom Normal College, where she gained a Transvaal Teachers Diploma; University of South Africa, under Professor Walter Battiss (qv), gaining a BA(FA); University of Pretoria, under Professor F G E Nilant, attaining an MA (History of Art).
Profile A lecturer at the Pretoria College of Education; 1954–84 an art teacher at both primary and high schools levels in the Transvaal. Illustrated children's stories for Daan Retief Publishers, Pretoria.

ESMONDE-WHITE Eleanor Frances (Mrs Laurano)

Born 1914 Dundee, Natal.
A painter and graphic artist from 1952 of genre and the life and occupations of women. Works in oil with a large amount of graphic work including African-inspired woodcuts. Murals in egg tempera and tapestry designs.
Studies 1932–34 University of Natal, under Professor O J P Oxley (qv); 1935–36 Royal College of Art, London, under Sir William Rothenstein (1872–1945), Gilbert Spencer (*b*.1892) and Eric Ravilious (1908–42); 1937 British School, Rome; 1935–37 awarded the Herbert Baker Scholarship to study mural painting in London and Italy.
Profile 1938–54 a member of the New Group. 1949–50 lectured in design at the Michaelis School of Fine Art, 1951–60 established and taught in the Department of Design there. 1952 illustrated *As Jy Kan Fluit op Hierdie Maat*, by Frieda Linde, also illustrated children's books for John Malherbe and Human & Rousseau, Cape Town. 1959 designed stage sets and costumes for ballet and opera, performed at the University of Cape Town; 1963 stage and costume designs for CAPAB dramas. 1935–49 lived mainly in England with occasional trips to SA; 1949–60 in SA; 1960–61 in Cyprus; from 1980 she has lived in Greece. 1951 and 1952 visited St Helena, 1958 Cyprus.
Exhibitions 1952 Cape Town, first of many solo exhibitions held in Cape Town, Johannesburg and Bloemfontein; she has participated in group exhibitions from 1962 in SA, Italy, Brazil, Zimbabwe, the UK, Yugoslavia, the USA, Belgium and West Germany; 1956 and 1960 Quadrennial Exhibitions.
Awards 1936 Prix de Rome; 1952 Cape Tercentenary Foundation Award for Design.

Represented Durban Art Gallery; Hester Rupert Art Museum, Graaff-Reinet; Johannesburg Art Gallery; Pietersburg Collection; Pretoria Art Museum; SA National Gallery, Cape Town; University of the Orange Free State; University of the Witwatersrand; William Humphreys Art Gallery, Kimberley.

Public Commissions Murals: 1935–37 SA House, London, with Le Roux Smith Le Roux (qv); 1938 *Queen Elizabeth* Liner with Le Roux Smith Le Roux; 1938 Science Museum, London; 1942 New Law Courts, Johannesburg; 1951 Overland Pavilion, Festival of Britain, South Bank, London; 1952 Van Riebeeck Tercentenary Festival; 1952 mosaic, Cape Province Library, Cape Town; 1966 tapestry, Welkom Civic Theatre; 1969 tapestry, Divisional Council Chamber, Cape Town; 1972 tapestry, Nico Malan Opera House, Cape Town; 1977 tapestry, Baxter Theatre, Cape Town.

References Art SA; SAA; 20C SA Art; SAP&S; SAP&D; BSAK 1 & 2; SA Art; 3Cs; AASA; LSAA; *SA Art News* 6 April 1961 & 22 June 1961; *Fair Lady* 1 May 1968; *SA Panorama* September 1983.

ESTCOURT Kathleen (Vicomtesse de Sarigny) ARMS

Born 1906 England.
Died 1968.
Resided in SA from 1948.
A painter of portraits, flower pieces and of miniatures.
Studies Under Ethel Wallace.
Profile An Associate member of the Royal Miniature Society.
Exhibitions Participated in group exhibitions in London and SA; 1956 Greenwich Gallery, Johannesburg, first solo exhibition held in SA.
Reference AASA.

EVANS Merlyn Oliver

Born 1910 Cardiff, Wales.
Died 1973 London, England.
Resided in SA 1938–42.
A painter of abstract paintings *c.*1930, thereafter of more surrealistic paintings, incorporating figures. A sculptor and an etcher.
Studies 1927–30 Glasgow School of Art, Scotland, where he won a travelling scholarship, through which he visited France, Germany, Denmark and Sweden; 1931–33 Royal College of Art, London; 1934–36 engraving under Stanley William Hayter (*b.*1901) in Paris.
Profile 1952 a member of the London Group; 1953 a member of the International Group. A member of the Durban Art Gallery Advisory Committee. 1938–42 a lecturer at the Natal Technical College; 1942–46 served with the 8th Army in North Africa, Syria and Italy; from 1946 a lecturer at the Central School of Art, London.

Exhibitions Participated in group exhibitions from 1936 in London and SA; 1939 first-ever solo exhibition held at the City Art Gallery, Durban, and the first of numerous solo exhibitions for him held in SA and the UK; 1948 Tate Gallery, London, SA Art Exhibition; 1956 Whitechapel Art Gallery, London, Retrospective Exhibition; 1973 Victoria and Albert Museum, London, Retrospective Exhibition.

Represented Durban Art Gallery; Johannesburg Art Gallery; Pretoria Art Museum; SA National Gallery, Cape Town; Tate Gallery, London, UK.

Public Commission Natal Technical College, mural with his students Beryl Newman (qv) and Alex Wagner (qv) (now demolished).

References SAA; *Tate Gallery Catalogue—The Modern British Paintings, Drawings and Sculpture*, volume 1, 1964, Oldbourne Press, London; SAP&D; Benezit; DBA; BSAK 1; AASA.

EVENDEN Charles Alfred

Born 1894 London, England.
Died 1961 Durban.
Resided in SA from 1924 in Durban.

Profile 1924–53 the cartoonist for *The Natal Mercury* working under the pseudonym "Evo". Founder of "The Memorable Order of Tin Hats" in Durban in 1927, reigniting the comradeship of First World War ex-servicemen in SA and later overseas. Prior to coming to SA he lived in Australia.

Represented Africana Museum, Johannesburg.

Publication by Evenden *Old Soldiers Never Die*, 1952, Robinson, Durban, autobiographical.

References SADNB; AMC3; SASSK.

EVERARD (Amy) Bertha (née King)

Born 1873 Durban.
Died 1965 Carolina, Eastern Transvaal.

A painter of landscapes in a stylised manner with a strong use of line and colour. Worked in oil. 1916 "Moon & Shadow" series; 1925 "Forest scenes, Paris" series; 1926 "Delville Wood" series (war-devastated landscapes). Painted a number of portraits.

Studies 1893–94 Slade School of Art, London; 1894–96 Herkomer School of Art, Bushey, Hertfordshire, England, under Professor Hubert Herkomer (1849–1942); 1896–97 Westminster School of Art, London, under W Mouat-Loudan (*b*.1860); 1897–99 St Ives School of Landscape Painting, Cornwall, England, under Julius Olsson (1864–1942); 1925–26 informally in Paris.

Profile 1918 a member of the SA Society of Artists. 1900 gained an Ablett Teachers Certificate from the Royal Drawing Society of Great Britain and Ireland; 1900–01 a visiting teacher at Walthamstow Hall, Sevenoaks, Kent; 1902–03 Art Mistress at Pretoria High School for Girls and at the Pretoria

Technical College. Five reproductions of her work have been published: in 1910 "Peace of Winter", in 1924 "Moonrise", in 1926 "Delville Wood", "Pale Hillside" and in 1932 "Banks of Komatie". Illustrated "Country Rhymes for Children" by Edith King (qv), (unpublished, these illustrations are housed in the Pretoria Art Museum). 1915 designed a banner for The Eunice School, Bloemfontein (where Edith King was Headmistress). 1891–93 studied music in Vienna, becoming an accomplished pianist. She wrote articles on art, including "Modern Art in Europe" for the Natal Technical College magazine in 1926. Designed the Carolina Anglican Church. 1874–1902 lived in England; 1902–21 in the Transvaal; 1921–22 in Cape Town; 1922–25 in Hertfordshire, England; 1925–26 in France and England; 1926–65 in the Transvaal. Sister of Edith King (qv), mother of Rosamund Everard-Steenkamp (qv) and Ruth Everard-Haden (qv), who together were known as the Everard Group. Grandmother of Leonora Haden (qv).

Exhibitions Participated in group exhibitions from 1899 in England, France and SA; 1916 Bloemfontein, first of several solo exhibitions held in London, Bloemfontein and Johannesburg; 1931 Herbert Evans Gallery, Johannesburg, first exhibition of the Everard Group; 1935 University of Pretoria, Exhibition of the Everard Group; 1967 Adler Fielding Gallery, Johannesburg, Pretoria Art Museum and the Tatham Art Gallery, Pietermaritzburg, Retrospective Exhibition of the Everard Group; 1982 Tatham Art Gallery, Pietermaritzburg, Retrospective Exhibition of the Everard Group.

Represented Durban Art Gallery; Johannesburg Art Gallery; National Museum, Bloemfontein; Pretoria Art Museum; SA House, London, UK; SA National Gallery, Cape Town; Tatham Art Gallery, Pietermaritzburg; University of Pretoria; Washington Art Gallery, Washington DC, USA; William Humphreys Art Gallery, Kimberley.

References Frieda Harmsen, *The Women of Bonnefoi*, 1980, J L van Schaik, Pretoria; Our Art 2; Art SA; SAA; DSAB; SAP&S; SESA; SSAP; DBA; BSAK 1 & 2; SA Art; 3Cs; AASA; LSAA.

EVERARD-HADEN Ruth

Born 1904 Nottingham Road, Natal.
A painter of landscapes, particularly of the Eastern Transvaal, seascapes of the Natal North Coast, portraits, figures and of religious scenes. Worked in oil, prior to 1923 worked in watercolour and produced a number of linocuts in 1925.

Studies 1921–22 part-time at the Cape Town School of Art, under G C Robinson (qv); 1922–23 studied drawing at the Slade School of Art, London, under Henry Tonks (1862–1937); 1923–27 Académie Colarossi, Paris, under Guerin, at various other academies in the Rue de la Grande Chaumière and briefly in 1927 under André Lhote (1885–1962) in Paris; 1925 a three-week course in the art of linocuts, under Eric Hesketh Hubbard (1892–1957) in Salisbury, England.

Profile Owing to her failing eyesight she has not painted since 1956. Studied both music and literature. 1922–23 lived in England; 1923 visited Venice,

Florence, Padua, Milan and Rome, Italy; 1923 spent the summer on a painting holiday in France; 1923–26 based in Paris, in 1925 visited Normandy, France and Salisbury, England, in 1926 visited Delville Wood, France, with her mother, and the Salisbury area, England; 1927 visited St Tropez and Avignon, France, with Edith King (qv); 1928 in SA; 1929/30 went on a brief visit to England and Paris. Lives near Carolina in the Eastern Transvaal. Daughter of Bertha Everard (qv), sister of Rosamund Everard-Steenkamp (qv) and niece of Edith King (qv), who together were known as the Everard Group. Sister-in-law of Isabella Christie (qv) and mother of Leonora Haden (qv).

Exhibitions Participated in group exhibitions from 1925 in Paris, England and SA; 1931 Herbert Evans Gallery, Johannesburg, first exhibition of the Everard Group; 1935 University of Pretoria, exhibition of the Everard Group; 1948 Tate Gallery, London, SA Art Exhibition; 1956 Quadrennial Exhibition; 1967 Adler Fielding Gallery, Johannesburg, Pretoria Art Museum and the Tatham Art Gallery, Pietermaritzburg, Retrospective Exhibition of the Everard Group.

Represented Johannesburg Art Gallery; Pretoria Art Museum; SA House, London, UK; SA National Gallery, Cape Town; Tatham Art Gallery, Pietermaritzburg; William Humphreys Art Gallery, Kimberley.

Public Commission 1932 "Supper at Emmaus", Church of the Resurrection, Carolina, Eastern Transvaal.

References Frieda Harmsen, *The Women of Bonnefoi*, 1980, J L van Schaik, Pretoria; Collectors' Guide; Our Art 2; SSAP; Bénézit; AASA.

EVERARD-STEENKAMP Rosamund King

Born 1907 Carolina, Eastern Transvaal.
Died 1946 England (crashed whilst flying a Spitfire).
A painter of Eastern Transvaal landscapes. Worked in oil. A number of still-life paintings.

Profile No formal art training but learnt from her mother Bertha Everard (qv). A member of the New Group. A talented musician, farmer and a qualified pilot. 1907–19 lived in the Transvaal; 1919–21 in Bloemfontein; 1922–25 in England, France and Italy; 1926–37 in SA; 1937–38 travelled to England via North Africa. Daughter of Bertha Everard (qv), sister of Ruth Everard-Haden (qv) and niece of Edith King (qv), who together were known as the Everard Group. Sister-in-law of Isabella Christie (qv) and aunt of Leonora Haden (qv). 1939–42 married to Nicholas Steenkamp.

Exhibitions Participated in group exhibitions from 1924 in England, France and SA; 1931 Herbert Evans Gallery, Johannesburg, first exhibition of the Everard Group; 1935 University of Pretoria, exhibition of the Everard Group; 1967 Adler Fielding Gallery, Johannesburg, Pretoria Art Museum and the Tatham Art Gallery, Pietermaritzburg, Retrospective Exhibition of the Everard Group.

Represented Durban Art Gallery; Pretoria Art Museum; SA National Gallery, Cape Town; Tatham Art Gallery, Pietermaritzburg; William Humphreys Art Gallery, Kimberley.

References Frieda Harmsen, *The Women of Bonnefoi*, 1980, J L van Schaik, Pretoria; Our Art 2; SAA; SSAP; BSAK 1; 3Cs; AASA; LSAA.

EVERETT Frederic Frith

Born Norwich, England.
Died 1934 Grahamstown.
Resided in SA from *c.*1890.
A painter of landscapes and figures.
Profile 1902–20 on the managing committee of the Grahamstown Fine Art Association. A partner in Well and Company, chemists.
Exhibitions Participated in group exhibitions 1882–90 in the UK and from 1903 in SA.
Represented Albany Museum, Grahamstown.

EWAN Alfred

Born 1910 Dundee, Angus, Scotland.
Died 1981.
Resided in SA from 1944.
A painter of landscapes. Worked in watercolour and crayon.
Studies Dundee College of Art.
Profile A member of the WSSA. Taught art in the UK at the Bluecoat School, Liverpool and was the Head of the Art Department at Kingston High School. 1953–65 a lecturer in Art History at Rhodes University; thereafter an art lecturer at the Ndaleni Training College, Natal. 1910–36 lived in Dundee; 1936–40 in Liverpool; 1940–44 served in WWII. Father of Fiona Rowett (qv).
Exhibitions Participated in group exhibitions from 1934 in the UK, SA, the USA and West Germany; 1943 first of numerous solo exhibitions held in SA; 1956 Quadrennial Exhibition.
Represented Ann Bryant Gallery, East London; Fort Beaufort Historical Museum; Hester Rupert Art Museum, Graaff-Reinet; King George VI Art Gallery, Port Elizabeth; Tatham Art Gallery, Pietermaritzburg.
References SAA; DBA; BSAK 1; AASA; *Artlook* July 1968; *SA Panorama* January 1977.

EWERT Juanita Jessica (Nina)

Born 1953 Robertson, Cape Province.
A painter of landscapes, still life and figures. Works in oil, watercolour, ink and pencil.
Studies 1971–74 University of Stellenbosch, under Professor Otto Schröder (qv), G Shultz, P Niehaus-Bouma and Jochen Berger (qv), gaining a BA(FA) (Education).
Profile 1975 an art teacher at Bellville High School; 1976–79 at Durbanville High School. 1985 illustrations for Maskew Miller Publishers, Cape Town.
Exhibitions 1985 participated in a group exhibition; 1986 Stellenbosch, solo exhibition.

F

FABIAN Anita Ann

Born 1934 Middelburg, Cape Province.

A painter and graphic artist of botanical paintings in a realistic manner and of landscapes in an expressionistic manner. Works in watercolour, gouache and in various graphic media.

Studies 1950–52 Michaelis School of Fine Art, under Maurice van Essche (qv), Rupert Shephard (qv), Eleanor Esmonde-White (qv) and Katrine Harries (qv).

Profile From 1984 a member of the WSSA. Illustrated *Transvaal Wild Flowers*, text by Gerrit Germishuizen, 1982, Macmillan (SA), Johannesburg.

Exhibitions She has participated in several group exhibitions from 1973 in SA; 1976 Pieter Wenning Gallery, Johannesburg, first of three solo exhibitions.

Represented Arts Association SWA/Namibia Collection.

FANNING Charles

Resided in SA from *c*.1853.

A painter of portraits. Produced many accurate sketches of landscapes.

Profile An art master at Tot Nut van't Algemeen School and the SA Institute, Cape Town. Mentioned in the *Schröder Art Momento*, by W H Schröder (qv). Lived in Cape Town.

Exhibition Participated in a group exhibition in 1851 in Cape Town.

References Pict Art; Pict Afr.

FASCIOTTI Titta

Born 1927 Bergamo, Italy.

Resided in SA from 1948.

A painter of landscapes, still life, seascapes and figures. Works in oil, acrylic, watercolour, ink, wash, pencil and charcoal. A series of Karoo and African Tribal scenes.

Studies 1944–48 Accademia di Belle Arti, Carrara, Bergamo, Italy, under Professor Achille Funi; 1952–55 privately under W G Wiles (qv).

Profile A member of the WSSA, the Brush and Chisel Club, Circolo Artistico Bergamasco, Italy and the Accademia di Belle Arti, Florence. He has travelled throughout SA and Western Europe and lived in Italy in 1969.

Exhibitions He has participated in numerous group exhibitions from 1953 in SA, Australia, Italy, the USA and the UK; 1963 Johannesburg, first of 31 solo exhibitions held in SA, and one held in Italy.

References BSAK 1; AASA.

FASSLER ROSS Stephanie

Born 1941 Johannesburg.
A painter and stained glass artist of decorative flower pieces. Works in oil, watercolour, ink and pencil. Creates mosaics, glass sculptures, stained glass windows and lampshades.
Studies 1959–62 University of the Witwatersrand, under Professor Heather Martienssen (1915–79), gaining a BA(FA); mosaic work under Cecily Sash (qv).
Profile Teaches privately. An illustrator of children's books and a designer of tapestries. Lived in England, working as an apprentice in the John Piper Studio for eighteen months.
Exhibitions She has participated in numerous group exhibitions from 1963 in the UK and SA; 1975 Pieter Wenning Gallery, Johannesburg, solo exhibition.
Public Commissions Several commissions for stained glass windows in SA and Botswana, including in 1966 for the Rand Water Board Building, Johannesburg; 1974 Senate Chamber, University of the Witwatersrand; Christ Church, Constantia, Cape Town; All Saints Church, Vanderbijlpark, Transvaal; St Anne's Diocesan College, Natal.

FAULDS Jutta

Born 1933 Bonn, West Germany.
Resided in SA from 1960.
An artist who works in oil, watercolour, gouache, ink, wash, mixed media, paper and fabric collage. Her pictures are abstract and fantastical.
Studies Attended part-time classes under Jane Heath (qv) in Pietermaritzburg.
Profile A member of the NSA and from 1983 of the Midlands Arts and Crafts Society, of which she is a founder and President. A designer and maker of garments, fabric wall hangings and church embroideries.
Exhibitions She has participated in numerous group exhibitions from 1968 in Durban and Pietermaritzburg; 1975 Pietermaritzburg, solo exhibition.
Reference *Darling* September 1979.

FERGUSON John Kenneth

Born 1885 Durban.
Died 1967 Durban.
A self-taught painter of landscapes, seascapes and harbour views. A number of paintings of early Johannesburg. Worked in watercolour and oil.
Profile A member of the Johannesburg Sketch Club and *c*.1943 of the NSA. 1895 an apprenticed sign-writer, 1899–1920 a sign-writer for Herbert Evans in Johannesburg; 1933 a poster designer and scene painter for African Theatres, Johannesburg. Educated in Australia, he lived and travelled in many parts of the world, including SA from 1910–12 and again from before WWII until his death.
Exhibitions Participated in group exhibitions from 1920; 1945 Lezards, Johannesburg, joint exhibition with Natalie Field (qv); held several solo exhibitions in Johannesburg and Durban; 1966 Durban Art Gallery, Retrospective Exhibition.
Represented Ann Bryant Gallery, East London; Durban Art Gallery; SA National Gallery, Cape Town; William Humphreys Art Gallery, Kimberley.

Public Commissions Two large paintings of Durban Bay in 1850 and 1950, Durban Club; mural, Allied Building Society, Durban (repainted in 1971 by Mrs Armie Hill)
References SAA; AASA.

FERGUSON Wendy

Born 1939 Durban.
A painter and graphic artist of landscapes, portraits, figures and abstract pictures. Works in oil, acrylic and in various graphic media. A sculptor working in clay and a weaver of large soft sculptures and wall hangings.
Studies 1974–75 under Diamond Bozas (qv); 1976 through a George Boys (qv) correspondence course.
Profile A founder member of the Zululand Society of Arts and its Chairman 1979–81 and 1984–85. Has lived in Zululand from 1962.
Exhibitions She has participated in many group exhibitions from 1975 in SA.

FERN Emily Isabel

Born 1881 Ballarat, Victoria, Australia.
Died 1953 Johannesburg.
Resided in SA from *c.*1890.
A painter of flowers, landscapes, portraits and figure studies. Worked in oil, pastel, pencil and wash. Produced linocuts and etchings.
Studies 1901 Port Elizabeth School of Art, under H C Leslie (qv); 1904 pastel drawing under G S Smithard (qv); 1913 Johannesburg School of Art; 1916 under J H Amshewitz (qv); 1920–22 Slade School of Art, London, under Henry Tonks (1862–1937), Wilson Steer (1860–1942) and etching under Frank Emmanuel, gaining a Royal Drawing Art Teachers Certificate; 1933 and 1949 at the André Lhote (1885–1962) Academy, Paris.
Profile 1916 a founder member of the Johannesburg Sketch Club and the Friday Club; 1918 a member of the SA Society of Artists. A member of the EPSFA, the Transvaal Art Society and the Brush and Chisel Club. Taught art privately in Johannesburg. 1926–30 and in 1934 taught at the Witwatersrand Technical College. 1931–34 lived in Europe; 1949 revisited Europe.
Exhibitions Participated in group exhibitions from 1914 in SA and Paris and 1931–34 in the UK; 1925 Johannesburg, first solo exhibition; 1965 Klynsmith Gallery, Johannesburg, Memorial Exhibition.
Awards 1914 two Gold Medals for Portraiture, Johannesburg Eisteddfod.
Represented Africana Museum, Johannesburg; Ann Bryant Gallery, East London; SA National Gallery, Cape Town.
References Collectors' Guide; SAA; AMC3&6; SAP&S; BSAK 1; AASA; *Historia* 8 no 3, September 1963 & no 4, December 1963.

FERREIRA Angela Maria

Born 1958 Lourenço Marques (Maputo), Mozambique.
Resided in SA from 1977.
A sculptor of surreal observations of her environment. Works in bronze, wood, fibreglass, resin, ceramics and aluminium.

Studies 1978–83 Michaelis School of Fine Art, under Bruce Arnott (qv), gaining a BA(FA) in 1981 and being awarded the Michaelis Prize and an MA(FA) in 1983.

Profile From 1982 an associate member of the Artists Guild, Cape Town. From 1984 a lecturer in sculpture at the Cape Technical College. 1982 designed a stage set for the Glass Theatre, Cape Town.

Exhibitions 1983 Michaelis School of Fine Art Gallery, solo exhibition; she has participated in many group exhibitions from 1984 in SA; 1985 Café Geneve Gallery, Durban, joint exhibition with Gaby Cheminais (qv); 1985 Market Gallery, Johannesburg, joint exhibition with Gaby Cheminais (qv) and Louise Sherman (qv); 1985 Cape Town Triennial.

Represented University of Cape Town.

Public Commission 1982 murals for the Pavilion, Strandfontein, Cape Province.

FERRI Fleur

Born 1929 Pretoria.

Primarily a portrait painter but also paints landscapes, still life, seascapes, genre, figures and abstract pictures. Works in oil, acrylic, watercolour, gouache, ink, wash, pencil, charcoal and in gold leaf on wood.

Studies 1945–46 gained an Arthur May scholarship to the Natal Technical College, studying under Eric Byrd (qv); 1947 Witwatersrand Technical College.

Profile 1950–57 designed and built exhibition stands for the Rand Show and other national exhibitions, for which she has gained a number of medals. 1954–56 lived in Italy. She has travelled throughout Europe.

Exhibitions 1947 Truter Gallery, Pretoria, first of 16 solo exhibitions; she has participated in numerous group exhibitions from 1962 in SA; 1981 Republic Festival Exhibition.

Represented Africana Museum, Johannesburg; Houses of Parliament, Cape Town; King George VI Art Gallery, Port Elizabeth; Pietersburg Collection; Potchefstroom Art Museum; Pretoria Art Museum; University of Cape Town; Willem Annandale Art Gallery, Lichtenburg.

Public Commissions 1985–86 a six-metre painting of the SA Parliament Cabinet Ministers of the last Sitting of the Westminster System of Government. Numerous portrait commissions of SA notability and University Chancellors, including those of State Presidents P W Botha, Marais Viljoen, J B Vorster and Dr Nico Diederichs.

Publication by Ferri *Born on a Breeze*, an illustrated book of prose and poetry, 1983, Triad Publishers, USA.

References SAA; BSAK 1; AASA; *Dictionary of International Biography*, volume 18, General Editor E Kay, 1984, International Biographical Centre, Cambridge, UK; *World's Who's Who of Women*, edited by E Kay, 1984, International Biographical Centre, Cambridge, UK; *International Book of Honor*, 1985, American Biographical Institute, Raleigh, North Carolina, USA; *Who's Who of Southern Africa*, 68th edition, 1985, Argus, Johannesburg; *De Arte* May 1967; *Femina* 7 August 1969; *Habitat* no 31, 1978 & no 58, 1983; *SA Panorama* April 1980; *Fair Lady Who's Who in SA*, 1983; *SA Digest* January 1983; *SA Arts Calendar* May 1983; *Gallery* Autumn 1983.

FIELD Natalie (Mrs Nash)

Born 1898 London, England.
Died 1977 Umkomaas, Natal.
Resided in SA from 1898.
A painter of flowers, figures and portraits. Worked in oil and pastel. A miniaturist.
Studies 1916–22 Slade School of Art, London, under Henry Tonks (1862–1937), Wilson Steer (1860–1942) and Ambrose McEvoy (1878–1927) and the Westminster School of Art, under Walter Sickert (1860–1942).
Profile A member of the SA Society of Artists. 1937 a founder and in 1938–39 President of the Transvaal Art Society. A Life Member of the SAAA and an Honorary Life Member of the NSA, of which she was also a founder.
Exhibitions Participated in group exhibitions in SA; 1930 Durban, first of many solo exhibitions held in SA; 1945 Lezards, Johannesburg, joint exhibition with John Ferguson (qv).
Represented Africana Museum, Johannesburg; SA National Gallery, Cape Town; SA National Museum of Military History, Johannesburg; William Humphreys Art Gallery, Kimberley.
References SAA; SAP&S; BSAK 1 & 2; AASA.

FIELD Stanley ARCA

Born 1908 London, England.
Resided in SA from after WWII until 1958.
A painter in watercolour.
Studies St Martin's School of Art, London, on a scholarship; Royal College of Art, London, under Professor Gilbert Spencer (b.1892) and Sir William Rothenstein (1872–1945), on a senior art scholarship. Became an Associate of the Royal College of Art in 1933.
Profile 1934 taught on the panel of the London County Council; 1936 taught commercial design at Reiman School of Art, London; 1937–38 taught life and portrait painting at the Bath School of Art; 1939 taught drawing and painting at the Southend School of Art. During WWII he was involved in teaching painting and drawing to servicemen, lectured on art appreciation for the Workers Education Department and was appointed an Official War Artist. After 1945 taught at Gravesend School of Art and Borough Polytechnic, London. A lecturer at the Witwatersrand Technical College; 1954–58 a senior lecturer, then Head of the Port Elizabeth Technical College. 1958 emigrated to Australia.
Exhibitions Participated in several group exhibitions in SA from 1947; 1956 Quadrennial Exhibition; held several solo exhibitions in SA.
Represented King George VI Art Gallery, Port Elizabeth.
References Art SA; Port Elizabeth School of Art.

FIELD T Dymond

Born Tunbridge Wells, Kent, England.
A painter of landscapes. Worked in oil and watercolour.
Studies Thought to have studied at the Slade School of Art, London, and at the Brighton School of Art, Sussex, England.

Profile A member of the SA Society of Artists and the K Club. Lived in Fish Hoek. 1917–18 on active service in SWA/Namibia and Europe.
Exhibitions Participated in group exhibitions with the SA Academy in 1925 and with the SA Society of Artists.
References *The Arts in SA*, edited by WHK, 1933–34, The Knox Printing & Publishing Company, Durban; AASA.

FIELD Thelma Christine

Born 1926 Durban.
A painter of landscapes, seascapes, still life and abstract pictures. Works in watercolour, oil, wash and charcoal.
Studies Natal Technical College; summer school, University of the Witwatersrand, under Erica Berry (qv); studied under Sidney Goldblatt (qv), Bill Ainslie (qv), Giorgio Pasqualucci and Marjorie Bowen (qv).
Profile From 1974 a member of the WSSA, presently an Associate. 1974–78 Honorary Secretary of the WSSA. From 1980 a member of the Brush and Chisel Club.
Exhibitions She has participated in numerous group exhibitions from 1972 in SA, SWA/Namibia, Italy, the UK and West Germany; 1982 New Mbabane Library, Swaziland, solo exhibition.
Award 1972 Gold Medal for oil paintings exhibited at Alfa Romeo Second National Exhibition for Contemporary Art, Rome.

FIELDING Aubrey

Born 1903 Potchefstroom, Transvaal.
Died 1981.
A painter of landscapes. Worked in oil.
Studies Regent Street Polytechnic, London; Heatherley School of Art, London, under Bernard Adams (*fl.*1916–39).
Profile Co-director of the Adler Fielding Gallery, Johannesburg. Elected a member of the Oxford Art Society. A scenery painter at The Old Vic, London.
Exhibitions Participated in group exhibitions in SA and in the UK; Durban Art Gallery, joint exhibition with John Littlejohns (qv); 1958 Lawrence Adler Gallery, Johannesburg, Retrospective Exhibition of Thirty Years' Work; 1975 Gallery 101, Johannesburg, solo exhibition.
References SAA; DBA; BSAK 1.

FINCH-DAVIES Claude Gibney

Born 1875 India.
Died 1920 Cape Town.
Resided in SA from 1893.
A painter of birds. Worked in watercolour.

Profile 1907–15 wrote a number of articles for the *Journal of the South African Ornithologist's Union*, 1918–20 two articles for *South African Journal of Natural History* and 1919–20 two articles appeared in *The Ibis*. His illustrations also appeared in the above-mentioned publications as well as in others. In addition he illustrated *The Game-birds and Water-fowl of South Africa*, by Major Boyd Horsburgh, 1912, Witherby & Company, London, with 69 plates; produced one plate for *A Practical Handbook of British Birds*, 1912, Witherby & Company, London, and seven plates of his were used in *The Canaries, Seedeaters and Buntings of Southern Africa*, edited by C J Skead, 1960. A Lieutenant in the Cape Mounted Riflemen. Travelled extensively in SA; 1914–18 lived in SWA/Namibia, 1919 in Pretoria and 1920 in Cape Town.

Represented British Museum, Natural History, London, UK; complete folio of over 900 paintings, Transvaal Museum, Pretoria.

References *Claude Gibney Finch-Davies 1875–1920*, with text by Alan C Kemp, 1976, Transvaal Museum, Pretoria; *The Birds of Prey of Southern Africa*, with text by Alan C Kemp, 1980, Winchester Press, Johannesburg; *Birds of Southern Africa*, with text by Alan C Kemp, 1982, Winchester Press, Johannesburg; *The Bird Paintings of C G Finch-Davies*, introduction by Alan C Kemp, 1984, Winchester Press, Johannesburg; *Gamebirds & Waterfowl of Southern Africa*, with a foreword by Patrick Horsburgh and text by Alan C Kemp, 1986, Winchester Press, Johannesburg; SAA; SESA; BSAK 1 & 2; SA Art; Art SWA.

FINDLAY Bronwen Eunice

Born 1953 Pietermaritzburg.

A painter of landscapes, urban scenes, animals, birds and still life, particularly flowers. Works in oil.

Studies 1973–76 Natal Technical College; 1978–81 University of Natal, gaining a BA and a Higher Diploma in Education.

Profile From 1984 a member of the NSA. From 1981 an art teacher at Mansfield Boys High School, Durban. In 1986 she was one of four artists commissioned to do an etching for a portfolio for the Playhouse in Durban. Visits Swaziland and Botswana. 1987 spent three months at the Cité Internationale des Arts in Paris.

Exhibitions 1977 Walsh-Marais Gallery, Durban, first of four solo exhibitions, three held in Durban and one in Cape Town; she has participated in several group exhibitions from 1985 in SA; 1985 SAAA Gallery, Pretoria, joint exhibition with Andrew Verster (qv) and Clive van der Berg (qv); 1986 NSA Gallery, Durban, joint exhibition with Jeremy Wafer and Virginia MacKenny (qv).

Represented Durban Art Gallery; Natal Technikon.

FINDLAY Richard (Dick)

Born 1928 Pretoria.

A painter known for his pictures of birds and botanical subjects in watercolour. He has also worked in most media and painted many subjects in a realistic style.

Profile His illustrations have appeared in 10 books and in over 50 different periodicals. 1968 produced a portfolio of 12 prints of SA animals in an edition of 650. A writer of plays and articles for magazines. A designer of stamps and coins. A cousin of Minette van Rooyen (qv).

Exhibitions He has participated in numerous group and solo exhibitions from 1960 in SA, Japan, Belgium, the UK, Austria and Israel.

Represented Mafikeng Museum; Nylstroom Municipal Collection; Pietersburg Collection; Pretoria Art Museum; University of Cape Town; University of Pretoria; Walter Battiss Museum, Somerset East.

Public Commission A mural at Jan Smuts Airport, Johannesburg.

References SAA; SESA; BSAK 1 & 2; SA Art; AASA; *Fontein* vol 1 no 2, 1960; *SA Panorama* September 1961, March 1972 & May 1985.

FITZROY Viola Mary (Mrs Du Toit)

Born 1907 Johannesburg.

A painter and graphic artist of landscapes, seascapes and still life. Works in watercolour, ink, wash, pencil and in various graphic media.

Profile A calligrapher. *c.*1956 briefly a member of the SA Society of Artists. Teaches the art of watercolour privately. Prior to 1932 a journalist on *The Cape Argus*, thereafter a writer of books.

Exhibitions She has participated in many group exhibitions in SA from the 1950s; 1965 Cape Town, first of *c.*10 solo exhibitions.

Publications by Fitzroy She has written and illustrated *Cabbages and Cream*, 1948, Howard Timmins, Cape Town; *Morning's at Seven*, 1949, Howard Timmins, Cape Town; *Under Your Green Thumb*, 1952, SA Book Centre, Cape Town; *Eat and be Merry*, 1952, Howard Timmins, Cape Town; *Down to Earth*, 1952, Howard Timmins, Cape Town; *Dark Bright Land*, 1955, Maskew Miller, Cape Town; *When The Slave Bell Tolled*, 1970, Howard Timmins, Cape Town.

FLANAGAN Doreen

Born 1923 Wankie, Rhodesia (Hwange, Zimbabwe).

Resided in SA from 1961.

A self-taught painter of wildlife, particularly birds, and of still life. Works in oil, acrylic, watercolour and gouache.

Profile From 1975 a member of the SAAA and from 1983 of the Verwoerdburg Art Society. 1959 designed, with her husband, the backdrop for "The Reluctant Mermaid", a film by Carr-Hartley. 1950–60 lived in Nairobi, Kenya; 1960–61 at Broken Hill in Northern Rhodesia (Zambia). Spent two years travelling in a home-built caravan to game areas in Kenya, Uganda, Congo (Zaire), Tanganyika (Tanzania), Northern Rhodesia (Zambia), Rhodesia (Zimbabwe), Mozambique, SWA/Namibia and SA. Married to James Flanagan (qv).

Exhibitions 1959 Nairobi, Kenya, first of seven solo exhibitions held in Kenya, Zimbabwe, Zambia and SA; 1984 Schweickerdt Art Gallery, Pretoria, joint exhibition with James Flanagan (qv).

FLANAGAN James Michael

Born 1922 Germiston, Transvaal.
A painter of wildlife. Works in oil, gouache, ink and pencil.
Studies 1937–38 Pretoria Boys High School, under Walter Battiss (qv).
Profile From 1975 a member of the SAAA and from 1983 of the Verwoerdburg Art Society. Designed covers for Readers Digest in 1969 and 1971. 1959 designed, with his wife, the backdrop for "The Reluctant Mermaid", a film by Carr-Hartley. 1950–60 lived in Nairobi, Kenya; 1960–61 at Broken Hill in Northern Rhodesia (Zambia). Spent two years travelling in a home-built caravan to game areas in Kenya, Uganda, Congo (Zaire), Tanganyika (Tanzania), Northern Rhodesia (Zambia), Rhodesia (Zimbabwe), Mozambique, SWA/Namibia and SA. Married to Doreen Flanagan (qv).
Exhibitions 1959 Nairobi, Kenya, first of seven solo exhibitions held in Kenya, Zimbabwe, Zambia and SA; 1984 Schweickerdt Art Gallery, Pretoria, joint exhibition with Doreen Flanagan (qv).

FLECK Otto Julius Carl

Born 1902 Berlin, Germany.
Died 1960.
Resided in SA from 1936.
A painter of landscapes and portraits. Worked in oil and pencil.
Studies Kassel Academy under Ewald Duelberg; Berlin Academy, under Karl Hofer (1878–1955).
Profile A former official restorer for the artworks in the Michaelis Collection, Cape Town, the SA National Gallery, Cape Town and the Johannesburg Art Gallery.
Exhibitions 1938 Lezards, Johannesburg, first of more than three solo exhibitions held in SA.
Represented National Museum, Bloemfontein.
Reference SAA.

FLEISCHER Michael

Born 1915 Turda, Romania.
Resided in SA from 1963.
A sculptor of animals and figures. Works in bronze.
Studies Scoala de Arte si Meserie, Romania, under Professor Zarina; Kunst Akademie, Stuttgart, West Germany; studied classical art in Rome, Paris and Madrid; 1946 Kunst Akademie, Munich, West Germany.
Profile A member of the SAAA and the Munich Art Society, West Germany. 1964–74 Chairman of Living Arts Exhibition. 1964–74 several architectural designs.
Exhibitions He has participated in numerous group exhibitions in Romania, West Germany and SA; he has held over 100 solo exhibitions in Romania, West Germany and SA; 1987 Strack van Schyndel Gallery, Johannesburg, joint exhibition with his daughter, Rebecca.

Represented University of the Orange Free State.
Public Commissions 1964 large flora and fauna wall panel, Legislative Building, Windhoek. Numerous commissions for churches and hospitals in SA and overseas.
References BSAK 1; *Artlook* November 1968, October 1969 & September 1972.

FLEISCHMAN Erich

Born 1899 Riga, Latvia (Latvian SSR).
Resided in SA from 1934.
A painter of landscapes and seascapes. Worked in oil and watercolour.
Studies 1915–18 received painting instruction in Moscow under Tichomiroff (*b*.1867); 1921 graduated from the Academy of Fine Art, Odessa; 1921–22 the Studio, Berlin, under Professor Erdmann (*b*.1845) of the Academy of Fine Art, Berlin.
Profile A member of the SAAA. Until 1950 a minister of the church, thereafter a full-time artist. Lived in the Eastern Cape.
Exhibitions Participated in over 80 group exhibitions in SA; from 1950 he held numerous solo exhibitions in SA.
Represented Ann Bryant Gallery, East London; Pretoria Art Museum; Pretoria Teachers Training College.
Public Commission Backdrop mural in the East London Museum.

FLEMING Francis Patrick

Born 1823 England.
Died 1895 Torquay, England.
Resided in SA 1849–54.
A painter of landscapes, natural history subjects and tribal genre. Worked in watercolour and pencil, also produced some engravings.
Profile 1849–53 Chaplain to the British Forces in King William's Town and 1854–58 in Mauritius.
Represented Africana Museum, Johannesburg; East London Museum.
Publications by Fleming Illustrated and wrote, *Kaffraria and its inhabitants*, 1853; *South Africa, A geography and natural history*, 1856, London; *Mauritius*, 1862, London.
References Pict Art; AMC3; Pict Afr.

FLYNN Alma Mary (née Haarhoff) (Mrs Will)

Born 1917 Germiston, Transvaal.
A portrait painter and occasionally a painter of landscapes, still life and figures. Works in oil and pastel.
Studies 1935–47 on a bursary at Port Elizabeth Technical College, under Francis Pickford Marriott (qv) and John Muff-Ford (qv), where gained a National Art Teachers Certificate.

Profile An Honorary Life Member of the SAAA. 1938 a part-time art teacher, Port Elizabeth Technical College and the Collegiate School for Girls, Port Elizabeth; 1946 at the Witwatersrand Technical College. 1985 official portrait painter to the SA Defence Force. She has travelled and painted in the UK, France, Italy, Switzerland, Spain, the Greek islands and Portugal.

Exhibitions She has participated in over 70 group exhibitions in SA and the UK; 1970 Herbert Evans Gallery, Johannesburg, first solo exhibition; 1981 Republic Festival Exhibition.

Represented Hester Rupert Art Musuem, Graaff-Reinet; King George VI Art Gallery, Port Elizabeth; Pietersburg Collection; Rand Afrikaans University; Willem Annandale Art Gallery, Lichtenburg.

Public Commissions Numerous portrait commissions of political, educational and business notability, including State President P W Botha and his wife Mrs Elize Botha; Mrs Tini Vorster, the wife of the late State President, Mr John Vorster; Mrs Helen Suzman, MP; Dr F E Karthack and M W Richards, Chairmen of the Council, University of the Witwatersrand.

References Register SA & SWA; AASA; *World Encyclopedia of Contemporary Artists*, 1984, Seledizioni, Italy; *World's Who's Who of Women*, edited by E Kay, 7th edition, 1984, International Biographical Centre, Cambridge, UK; *Dictionary of International Biography*, vol 19; *International Directory of Distinguished Leadership*, vol 1, American Biographical Institute, Raleigh, North Carolina, USA; *International Book of Honor*, 1985, American Biographical Institute, Raleigh, North Carolina, USA; *Who's Who of Southern Africa*, 1986–87, Johannesburg; *Foremost Women of the Twentieth Century*, 1987, Biographical Publications, Cambridgeshire, UK; *Five Thousand Personalities of the World*, 1987, American Biographical Institute, Raleigh, North Carolina, USA; *Artlook* August 1968 & October 1971; *Habitat* no 15, 1975; *SA Panorama* September 1977.

FOGARTY Peter Roland

Born 1938 Bulawayo, Rhodesia (Zimbabwe).

A painter of landscapes and wildlife. Works in egg tempera, oil, watercolour and gouache.

Studies 1957–59 University of Natal, gaining a BA.

Profile 1960–82 in the Diplomatic Service. 1981 illustrated *Birds of Zimbabwe*, by M P Stuart Irwin, Quest Publishing, Salisbury (Harare). In 1981 drew designs for Zimbabwe Bank Notes. 1963–67 lived in London; 1970–72 in Cape Town; 1976–78 in Paris; thereafter in Zimbabwe.

Exhibitions He has participated in several group exhibitions from 1972 in Zimbabwe and in London, UK; 1966 Rhodesia (Zimbabwe) House, London, first of four solo exhibitions; 1986 Tryon Gallery, London, joint exhibition.

Public Commission 1972 a series of 12 bird paintings for the Rhodesia Ministry of Information, Immigration & Tourism, published as prints by the Government Printer.

FONTAINE Gregory Roger

Born 1954 Cape Town.

A painter of abstract pictures. Works with oil pastel sticks which he fingerpaints and fingerpresses.

Studies 1968–69 Cape Town Art Centre.
Exhibitions He has participated in a number of group exhibitions from 1985 in Cape Town.

FORBES Ernest William Temple
Born 1915 Cape Town.
A painter of wildlife. Works in watercolour, oil, acrylic and ink. A large series of butterflies.
Profile Illustrations for Dr Sue Hart's nature articles in *The Cape Times*, *The East London Daily Despatch*, *Quagga* and *The Lowvelder*.
Exhibitions He has participated in group exhibitions in Johannesburg.
Reference SA *Panorama* January 1985.

FORBES Mark Alexander
Born 1961 Johannesburg.
A sculptor of wildlife, figures and abstract pieces. Works in bronze, stone and wood.
Studies Studied the history of art in The Netherlands, Belgium, Scotland, Italy, Austria, Hungary, France, England and Greece. Presently studying for a BA(FA) through the University of South Africa.
Exhibitions He has participated in many group exhibitions from 1983 in SA; 1983 Akis Gallery, Johannesburg, first of two solo exhibitions.
Public Commissions 1982 Monument to the Fallen, Middelburg, Transvaal; 1982 Officers Statue, Military Academy, Saldanha Bay, Cape Province; various other military commissions.

FORD George Henry
Born 1809 England.
Died 1872 England.
Resided in SA 1820–37.
A painter of portraits, landscapes, animals, butterflies and birds. Worked in watercolour. A graphic artist who made lithographs.
Profile 1834–36 accompanied Dr Andrew Smith on his expedition into the interior. He was responsible for most of the illustrations in *Zoology of South Africa* by Dr Andrew Smith, 1849, of which a facsimile edition was published in 1973 by Winchester Press, Johannesburg, in 3 volumes. Illustrated *South African Butterflies* by R Trimem, 1862–66. After leaving SA worked at the British Museum. Son of J E Ford, a painter of miniatures.
Represented University of the Witwatersrand.
References Pict Art; Pict Afr; SA Art; H E Hockley, *The Story of the British Settlers of 1820 in SA*, 2nd edition, 1957, Juta, Cape Town; A Gordon Brown, *Christopher Webb Smith* (qv), 1965, Howard Timmins, Cape Town; SESA.

FORD James

Resided in SA from 1880.

A painter of landscapes. Worked in various media.

Profile He was invited to SA to teach art at the Cape Town School of Art by the SA Fine Art Association. He also held classes for the students of the SA College. Grandson of J E Ford, a Cape Town miniaturist.

Exhibitions He participated in a number of group exhibitions in Cape Town and in London. In 1899 his painting entitled "Holiday in Cape Town in the 20C" was exhibited in the Standard Bank building in Cape Town, and in 1980 formed part of the exhibition "Images of the Cape" mounted at the SA National Gallery, Cape Town.

References Marjorie Bull, *Abraham de Smidt 1829–1908*, 1981, Printpak, Cape Town; Pict Afr; AASA.

FORD Simon Gerard

Born 1952 Cape Town.

A painter and printmaker with a wide-ranging subject matter. Works in mixed media, acrylic, gouache, ink, wash, charcoal, pencil and in various graphic media, particularly screenprinting; creates collages. 1982–83 a series of 36 fine art posters in silkscreen entitled "Street Graphics".

Studies 1978–83 Michaelis School of Fine Art, under Jules van de Vijver, gaining a BA(FA) in 1981 and an MA(FA) in 1983.

Profile 1981–83 a printmaking demonstrator at the Michaelis School of Fine Art; 1984 a part-time teacher of graphic design, Johannesburg Art Foundation; 1985 a part-time lecturer in graphic design and perceptual studies, 1986 a lecturer in graphic design, Witwatersrand Technikon. 1982 visited London, Paris, Zurich, New York, Washington DC, Munich and Venice, whilst working on "Street Graphics".

Exhibitions He has participated in several group exhibitions from 1983 in SA and in West Germany; 1984 Market Gallery, Johannesburg, first of two solo exhibitions; 1985 Tributaries, touring SA and West Germany; 1987 Johannesburg Art Gallery, Vita Art Now.

Represented SA National Gallery, Cape Town.

FORDYCE Betsy Burns (née Moffat)

Born 1907 Dunblane, Scotland.

Died 1981 Port Elizabeth.

Resided in SA from 1949.

A painter and graphic artist of flowers, landscapes and seascapes. Worked in oil, watercolour, acrylic and in various graphic media.

Studies 1925–30 Glasgow School of Art, gaining a Diploma in Art.

Profile 1930–38 designed and painted scenery for the Scottish National Theatre. 1942–47 taught in India; 1947–49 taught in Scotland; 1950–69 taught at Port Elizabeth Technical College and extra-murally at various schools. Travelled widely in Europe, the USA, India and Egypt.

Exhibitions Participated in group exhibitions in Scotland, India and in the Eastern Province, SA; 1973 SAAA Gallery, Pretoria, solo exhibition.
Represented King George VI Art Gallery, Port Elizabeth; Port Elizabeth Technikon.
References Port Elizabeth School of Art; AASA; *SA Arts Calendar* September 1973.

FORT E A Sheila

Born 1906 Aberdeen, Scotland.
Died 1978 Cape Town.
A painter of still life, particularly flowers. Worked in a wide range of media including oil and watercolour.
Studies Michaelis School of Fine Art; two years at Gray's School of Art, Aberdeen, Scotland; South Kensington School of Art, London; Slade School of Art, London, and Hornsey School of Art. Further research into stained glass processes in Munich, Bruges (Brugge) and Paris.
Profile An illuminator, a stained glass artist and an heraldic artist. A master jeweller and a decorator of china. A founder member, councillor and former Chairman of both The Seven Arts Club and the Heraldry Society of SA. A former Chairman of the Western Cape Branch of the SAAA and National Chairman of the SA Soroptimist Club. For many years an art teacher at the Zonnebloem College, Cape Town.
Exhibitions Participated in group exhibitions in SA; 1978 SAAA Gallery, Cape Town, Memorial Exhibition.
Public Commissions Numerous illuminated addresses, including in 1947 one to the Royal Family from the Union and Rhodesian Governments, Cape Town and Kimberley cities, and the SA Jewish community. In 1953 the Union Government's Coronation Address to Queen Elizabeth II. During the 1970s she made the stained glass panel in St Mary's Church, Woodstock, Cape Town.
References SESA; BSAK 2.

FOURIE Joan (née Bender)

Born 1938 Bloemfontein.
A painter and graphic artist of landscapes, portraits, still life, figures and abstract pictures. Works in oil, acrylic, wash, pencil, charcoal and in various graphic media. Occasionally creates sculptures in bronze.
Studies 1956–57 Graaff-Reinet Teachers Training College; 1958 under F L Alexander (qv) and Katrine Harries (qv) in Cape Town; 1974–78 and 1980–81 University of South Africa, under Professor Rayda Becker and Professor Leon du Plessis (qv), gaining a BA in History of Art in 1978 and BA Honours in History of Art in 1981; 1987 began an MA in History of Art course at the University of the Orange Free State, under Professor D J van den Berg.

Profile From 1965 a member of the EPSFA, 1979 President of the EPSFA and for many years a committee member. From 1985 a member of the Board of Trustees of the King George VI Art Gallery, Port Elizabeth, also a member of its Selection Committee. A member of the SAAAH and Vice-President of the Soroptomist Club International Eastern Province branch. 1958–60 an art teacher at various high schools; 1961–64 an art teacher at the Port Elizabeth Technical College; 1964–70 Head of the Joan Fourie Art School, Port Elizabeth; 1982–83 Head of the Art Department of the Lawson Brown High School, Port Elizabeth; from 1985 Director and Head of the School of Art and Design, Port Elizabeth Technikon. A set-designer for various productions in the Eastern Province. A classical pianist.

Exhibitions She has participated in numerous group exhibitions from 1962.

Public Commission 1983 large batik, Dutch Reformed Church, Grasvoelkop, Port Elizabeth.

FOWLER Catherine

Born 1935 Aberdeen, Scotland.

Resided in SA from 1943.

A painter of landscapes, portraits, still life, genre, figures and abstract pictures. Works in oil, watercolour, ink, wash, pencil and charcoal; also creates collages.

Studies 1972–85 under Jane Heath (qv) in Pietermaritzburg.

Profile A member of the WSSA, the SAAA and the Midlands Arts and Crafts Society. Wife of John Cannon, a Director of Cannon and Findlay Fine Art Gallery, Pietermaritzburg.

Exhibitions She has participated in numerous group exhibitions in Natal; 1981 Republic Festival Exhibition.

Reference AASA.

FOX Kathleen Mary

Born 1948 Durban.

A painter of the incongruity of juxtaposed objects, often in an implied world of conflict. Works in oil.

Studies 1966–69 Natal Technical College, under Bailey-Searle, where gained a Teaching Diploma in Fine Arts; 1980–82 Michael Pettit School of Art, Cape Town, under Michael Pettit (qv).

Profile From 1984 a member of the SAAA. 1970 an art teacher at Empangeni High School and Bushlands, Durban; 1975–76 established her own art school in Durban. Lives in Cape Town.

Exhibitions She has participated in several group exhibitions from 1981 in SA; 1986 SAAA Gallery, Cape Town, solo exhibition.

FRADAN Cyril

Born 1928 Johannesburg.

A painter and graphic artist of landscapes, portraits, seascapes, figures and abstract pictures. Works in oil, acrylic, ink, wash, pencil, charcoal and in various graphic media. 1981 Church series on St Helena.

Studies Prior to 1950 gained a BA from the University of the Witwatersrand; 1951–52 Scuola Graffica, Rome.

Profile 1950 taught art history at the University of the Witwatersrand; 1951–60 an art teacher at the Overseas School, Rome; 1962 taught art history at the London College of Painting, London; 1963 at the Guildford School, Surrey; 1966 at the Sir John Cass School of Art, London. Numerous theatre designs in SA and in England. A small festival of art and music is held annually at his home in London. He has lived and travelled in England, Europe, and the Far East.

Exhibitions He has exhibited in Europe and throughout SA from 1948.

Represented King George VI Art Gallery, Port Elizabeth; Pretoria Art Museum; SA National Gallery, Cape Town.

References AASA; LSAA; *Artlook* January 1968 & February/March 1976; *Habitat* no 20, 1976.

FRANCK (William) Bruce

Born 1907 Mowbray, Cape Province.
Died 1970 Mowbray, Cape Province.
A self-taught painter in watercolour, also a number of drawings.

Profile 1922–29 apprenticed to a printing firm in Cape Town where he learnt lithography and commercial art. 1940 designed two covers for *Die Huisgenoot*. 1947–48 a part-time assistant in commercial art at the Michaelis School of Fine Art; 1960–70 the first full-time lecturer in printing and industrial art at the Cape Technical College. His District Six studies were published by Longmans, Cape Town, in 1967.

Exhibitions Participated in group exhibitions throughout SA and in London, Paris and Jerusalem; 1960 Quadrennial Exhibition.

Represented SA National Gallery, Cape Town; University of South Africa.

Publication by Franck Fishermen of the Cape, a posthumous collection of drawings by Franck, with text by Frank Robb, 1975/76, Longmans, Cape Town.

References Art SA; SAA; SAP&D; BSAK 1; AASA.

FRANCOIS Leo Auguste RBC

Born 1870 Chemnitz, Luxembourg.
Died 1938 Durban.
Resided in SA from 1897, visited SA 1891–96.
A painter of landscapes. Worked in oil and pastel, also produced dry-point etchings.

Studies Leipzig University, under Giuseppe Donadini; in Rome under Hendrik Siemiradzki (1843–1902); Wettiner Gymnasium, Dresden, and with the Pre-Raphaelites in London.

Profile Took up painting seriously in 1910. 1918 first of seven terms as President of the NSA of which he was a Life Member. 1925 founded and in 1926 was first President of the South African Institute of Art. 1926 Honorary Fellow of the Rhodesian (Zimbabwean) Society of Fine Arts. 1929 on the Advisory Board of Durban Art Gallery. 1929 Diploma Member of the Royal British Colonial Society of Artists, London. An art critic for *The Natal Mercury* under the nom-de-plume "Vermilion", also a music critic and writer of essays. Prior to living in London, he travelled extensively in Europe and the Near East. 1897 lived in East Griqualand (Eastern Cape); 1910 in Kimberley; 1914 in Durban. A Commemorative Bursary has been instituted in his name at the Natal Technical College (Technikon).

Exhibitions Participated in group exhibitions from 1924; held numerous solo exhibitions throughout SA; 1940 SA Academy, Memorial Exhibition; 1941 Durban Art Gallery, Memorial Exhibition; 1943 Gainsborough Gallery, Johannesburg, Memorial Exhibition.

Represented Africana Museum, Johannesburg; Ann Bryant Gallery, East London; Bulawayo Gallery, Zimbabwe; Durban Art Gallery; King George VI Art Gallery, Port Elizabeth; SA National Gallery, Cape Town; University of Natal; William Humphreys Art Gallery, Kimberley.

References The Arts in SA, edited by WHK, 1933–34, The Knox Printing & Publishing Company, Durban; SAA; SADNB; DSAB; AMC6; SAP&D; BSAK 1 & 2; Enc S'n A; 3Cs; AASA.

FRANK Audrey

Born 1905 Durban.

A painter of genre, figures and markets. Works in oil, watercolour, pastel and charcoal.

Studies Durban School of Art; Reiman School of Art, London.

Profile A member of the New Group. Taught at art schools in Durban, Johannesburg, Port Elizabeth and Bloemfontein. During the 1950s Principal of the Frank Joubert Art Centre for Children, Cape Town. Worked in a ceramic studio at Olifantsfontein, Transvaal.

Exhibitions Known to have participated in group exhibitions between the 1920s and the 1960s; 1960 Quadrennial Exhibition.

Reference AASA.

FRASER Janet

Born 1944 Cape Town.

A sculptor creating environmental constructions and assemblages. Works in bronze, wood and metal. Draws in ink and charcoal.

Studies 1962–66 Michaelis School of Fine Art; 1966–67 St Martin's School of Art, London.

Profile 1948–57 lived in England. Presently living in London.

Exhibitions Participated in group exhibitions in SA during the 1960s and the 1970s; 1968 Wolpe Gallery, Cape Town, solo exhibition; 1971 Lidchi Gallery, Johannesburg, solo exhibition.

Award 1968 Merit Award, SA Breweries Exhibition.
Represented SA National Gallery, Cape Town; William Humphreys Art Gallery, Kimberley.
References SAP&S; BSAK 1; Oxford Companion to 20C Art; AASA.

FREEDMAN Sylvia

Born 1917 Krugersdorp, Transvaal.
Known to have painted figures and yachts. Works in oil, wax, tempera and egg tempera. A graphic artist producing monotypes.
Studies Part-time studies at the Witwatersrand Technical College; also studied under Sidney Goldblatt (qv), Anna Vorster (qv) and Lionel Abrams (qv).
Profile Presently living in Australia.
Exhibitions Participated in group exhibitions in SA during 1950s and the 1960s; 1960 & 1964 Quadrennial Exhibitions; 1962 Gallery 101, Johannesburg, joint exhibition with Pearl Cohen (qv); 1962 Johannesburg, solo exhibition.

FREEMANTLE Frances

Born 1897 Harrismith, Orange Free State.
A painter of flowers and still life. Worked in oil.
Studies 1913 Pretoria Royal Drawing Society (exam passed with Honours); under Joyce Ordbrown (qv) in Johannesburg.
Profile Began painting in 1952. Daughter of Josina Letty (qv) and sister of Cythna Letty (qv).
Reference SAA.

FREUND Merle (Mrs Osrin)

Born 1939 Bloemfontein.
A sculptor of figures. Works in stone.
Studies 1957–60 Michaelis School of Fine Art, under Lippy Lipshitz (qv); 1960–61 Staatliche Kunstakademie, Düsseldorf, under Manfred Sieler, on a West German State Bursary.
Profile Lived in Cape Town and since 1968 in England.
Exhibitions She participated in group exhibitions in SA during the 1960s and the 1970s.
Represented SA National Gallery, Cape Town; William Humphreys Art Gallery, Kimberley.
References SAA; SAP&S; SESA; 3Cs; AASA.

FRIEDLAND Miriam

Born 1939 Johannesburg.
A fibre artist and a graphic artist of abstract works.
Studies 1955–57 commercial art at the Witwatersrand Technical College; part-time at the Central School of Art, London; Banff School of Art and Music, Canada.

Profile In 1978 spent several months in the USA and Canada, where she furthered her studies.

Exhibitions She has participated in numerous group exhibitions from 1965 in SA; 1968 Avant Garde Gallery, Johannesburg, first of two solo exhibitions.

Represented Durban Art Gallery.

Public Commission 1978 12 stitched panels, The Royal Residence of the late King Sobhuza of Swaziland.

Reference SA Panorama March 1982.

FRIEDLANDER Basil Arnold

Born 1947 King William's Town, Cape Province.

An artist depicting landscapes, portraits, still life and figures. Works in oil, coloured pencil and charcoal.

Studies 1965–70 University of Natal, under Professor Jack Heath (qv) and Professor A Duckworth, gaining a BA(FA).

Profile From 1973 a member of the NSA. 1971–72 an assistant teacher, Durban Commercial High; 1973–77 a lecturer and from 1978 a senior lecturer at the Natal Technikon. 1978–83 an art critic for *The Natal Mercury*.

Exhibitions He has participated in numerous group exhibitions from 1971 held in SA; 1973 Walsh Marais Gallery, Durban, first of five solo exhibitions held in Durban, Cape Town, Johannesburg and Pietermaritzburg.

Represented Durban Art Gallery; Margate Art Gallery; Pretoria Art Museum.

FRIEDRICH Anna

Born 1929 Amsterdam, The Netherlands.

Resided in SA from 1952.

A painter of landscapes, seascapes, architectural works, old ships and wildlife. Works in acrylic, watercolour, ink, wash and pencil.

Studies 1957 part-time at the Michaelis School of Fine Art, under Maurice van Essche (qv); 1978 part-time at Migros Schule, Switzerland, under P Ebner; 1985 part-time at the Ruth Prowse School of Art, Cape Town, under Erik Laubscher (qv).

Profile From 1986 a member of the SAA. 1929–52 lived in The Netherlands; 1957–60 in SWA/Namibia; 1961–66 and 1978–80 in Switzerland.

Exhibitions She has participated in several group exhibitions in the Cape from 1985.

FRIES Laura

Born in the Vryheid District, Natal.

A painter of landscapes, generally incorporating buildings and of historical street scenes of Johannesburg; also depicts flowers. Works in watercolour and oil.

Studies 1928–30 Witwatersrand Technical College; privately under G J Brusseau (qv) and Norma Ingram (qv); 1953 part-time at the Witwatersrand Technical College.

NEL ERASMUS
Purple 1984
Acrylic on Canvas 84 × 112 cm

ROSAMUND KING EVERARD
Barberton
Oil on Canvas 101,7 × 127 cm
Durban Art Gallery

Profile A member of the SAAA and the Brush and Chisel Club. Lived in Johannesburg.
Exhibitions Participated in group exhibitions with the SAAA and the Brush and Chisel Club from 1940; 1970 first of three solo exhibitions held in Johannesburg.
Represented Africana Museum, Johannesburg.
Reference AMC3.

FROOME Bertha

Born 1880 Barnet, Hertfordshire, England.
Died 1978 Durban.
A painter of flowers. Worked mainly in watercolour, but also in pastel and oil.
Studies 1894–98 South Kensington School of Art, London; Durban Art School, under W H Tottendell Venner (qv).
Profile 1938 President of the NSA. A former art mistress at the Coast High School, Durban. Travelled extensively throughout SA and in Europe.
Exhibitions Participated in group exhibitions held throughout SA.
Represented Durban Art Gallery.
References BSAK 1; AASA.

FROST Anne

Born 1913 Prieska, Cape Province.
A painter of landscapes, portraits, still life, figures and abstract pictures. Works in oil, acrylic from 1980, watercolour, gouache, ink and wash. A graphic artist producing monotypes from 1980. 1977–85 simplified landscapes in limited colour schemes with emphasis on form.
Studies 1947 Port Elizabeth Technical College, under Joan Wright (qv), Robert Bain (qv) and John Heath (qv); 1955–59 Pretoria Technical College, under Robert Hodgins (qv); 1961–68 University of South Africa, under Professor Walter Battiss (qv) and Professor K Skawran; University of Pretoria, under Professor F G E Nilant. Gained a National Art Teachers Certificate, a Certificate in Design, a BA(FA) in 1964 and an MA(FA) in 1970.
Profile A member of the SAAA. Taught art at high schools in Pretoria and in 1960–61 at the Pretoria Teachers Training College. 1955–57 studied pottery at the Pretoria Technical College. She has travelled throughout SA and in 1973 to Europe; in 1980 to the Greek islands, England and Wales; in 1985 visited Israel.
Exhibitions She participated in several group exhibitions in Port Elizabeth and Uitenhage during the 1950s; 1971 SAAA Gallery, Pretoria, first of six solo exhibitions; 1973 NSA Gallery, Durban, joint exhibition with A Minnie Cook (qv).
Represented Willem Annandale Art Gallery, Lichtenburg.

FUMAGALLI Fausto

Born 1928 Bergamo, Italy.
Resided in SA from 1968.
A painter of landscapes, seascapes, still life, figures, animals and abstract pictures. Works in oil, acrylic, watercolour, pencil and charcoal.

Studies Academy of Art, Carrara, Bergamo, Italy; Academy of Art, Brera, Milan, Italy.

Profile A set designer, decorator and mosaic artist working both in Italy and SA. Taught at the Dante Alighieri Art School in Italy. He has travelled throughout Europe and in South America and Southern Africa.

Exhibitions 1954 Bergamo, Italy, first of eight solo exhibitions in Italy, South America and SA; he has participated in group exhibitions from 1962 in Italy and SA.

Awards Silver Medal, Bergamo; Golden Brush in Bari, Bronze Medal, S Fedele, Milan.

Public Commission 1966 mural in Bergamo.

G

GABASHANE Daniel Gordon
Born 1949 Western Township, Johannesburg.
A painter and a graphic artist of landscapes, still life, figures, urban scenes and abstract pictures. Works in oil, acrylic, watercolour, gouache, pencil, charcoal, ink, wash and in various graphic media. Sculpts in wood and clay. 1978 "The Warrior", a series of six linocuts.
Studies 1974 Rorke's Drift Art Centre, under Otto Lundbohm; 1977 Rorke's Drift Art Centre, under Jules van de Vijver (qv).
Profile c.1978 taught at the Mofolo Art Centre, Soweto; 1979 taught graphic art at the The Open School, Johannesburg. A designer of posters.
Exhibitions He has participated in several group exhibitions in Johannesburg and one travelling to West Germany; 1979 FUBA, Johannesburg, joint exhibition with R Mafafo.

GAGE Cheryl Winsome (Mrs Bolleurs)
Born 1950 Potgietersrus, Transvaal.
A painter of conceptual landscapes, portraits, still life, figures and abstract pictures. Works in oil, acrylic, watercolour, gouache, pencil and charcoal. 1979–84 a series of symbolic portraits.
Studies Gained an MA(FA) in 1984 from the University of the Witwatersrand, studying under Terence King (qv) and Robert Hodgins (qv).
Profile From 1979 a part-time lecturer in graphic design at the Witwatersrand Technikon.
Exhibitions She has participated in group exhibitions from 1980; 1985 Shell Gallery, Johannesburg, solo exhibition.

GALGUT Bess
Born 1925 Johannesburg.
A sculptor of abstract pieces, portraits and figures. Works in bronze, stone, wood, resin and cement. Paints in oil and draws in pencil.
Studies 1941–43 Witwatersrand Technical College, under James Gardner (qv); 1956 part-time under Mary Stainbank (qv) in Durban.
Profile From 1945 a member of the NSA. 1957–66 assistant to the sculpture lecturer, Mary Stainbank (qv), at the Natal Technical College; 1960–66 a lecturer in the history of art and in life drawing at the Natal Technical College; 1966–70 part-time lecturer in art at the Indian University, Salisbury Island, Durban. Teaches art privately. 1944 costume and set designs in Johannesburg and illustrations for *Five-Thirty* magazine. From 1946 she has lived in Durban, where she has continued to design costumes and sets and to act in local drama productions.

Exhibitions She has participated in several group exhibitions from 1944 in SA and Australia; 1975 Overport City, Durban, first of three solo exhibitions.
Public Commissions A number of murals and sculptures for hotels, restaurants and night clubs in Johannesburg and Durban.

GALPIN Annie (née I'Ons)

Born 1864.
Died 1919 Grahamstown.
A painter of figures, portraits and landscapes. Initially worked in oil, then in watercolour on silk.
Studies Taught oil painting by Frederick T I'Ons (qv).
Profile The great-grand-daughter of Frederick T I'Ons (qv).
References *ANN* vol 2 no 96, vol 9 no 143 & vol 22 no 314.

GARDHAM Agatha (née Altham)

Born 1894.
Died 1980.
A painter.
Profile 1934 a committee member and 1964–78 Secretary of the EPSFA. Taught art in Natal and in Rhodesia (Zimbabwe). 1931 settled in Port Elizabeth. 1931–50 married to H C Gardham, the Principal of the Port Elizabeth Technical College.
Exhibitions Participated in group exhibitions in Cape Town, East London and Port Elizabeth; 1980 EPSFA held a Retrospective Exhibition of her work.

GARDNER James Major ARCA (Sculpture, London), FRSA

Born 1894 Fulham, London, England.
Resided in SA 1921–55.
A portrait sculptor and maker of medallions.
Studies Putney School of Art, London, under John Bowyer (*b.* 1872); City and Guilds School of Art, London, under Innes Fripp (*b.*1867) and Thomas Tyrrell (1857–1928); Royal College of Art, London, under Sir William Rothenstein (1872–1945) and Professor Francis Derwent Wood RA (1871–1926), becoming an Associate. While at the Royal College of Art he won the British Institute Scholarship in Sculpture for further study at the Italian School in Cairo, Egypt; studied under Antonio Mancini (1852–1930).
Profile A Fellow of the Royal Society of Arts. A member of the Institute of South African Architects. 1921–32 Principal of Port Elizabeth School of Art (Technical College); 1932–55 Principal of the Witwatersrand Technical College; 1955 an art lecturer at the University of Massachusetts and Williston Academy, USA. Later settled in Canada. Married to Phyllis Gardner (qv).

Public Commissions Port Elizabeth: 1928 Collegiate War Memorial; 1924–29 War Memorial (Cenotaph); sculpture on Walmer War Memorial. Johannesburg: mural, Chamber of Mines Building; mural, His Majesty's Theatre; artwork, the Railway Station. Pretoria: Virgin Mary and Joseph sculpture, Roman Catholic Cathedral; granite group, SA Perm Building. Vereeniging, Transvaal: artwork, the SA Mutual Building. Kimberley: artwork, SA Perm Building.
References Collectors' Guide; SAA; Port Elizabeth School of Art; AASA.

GARDNER Phyllis (née Fisher) ARCA

Born 1901 Jersey, Channel Islands.
Resided in SA 1930–55.
A painter of portraits and landscapes. Worked in watercolour and oil.
Studies Beckenham School of Art, Kent, England; Bournemouth School of Art, England; 1922 Royal College of Art, London, under Sir William Rothenstein (1872–1945), becoming an Associate. Awarded the Royal College of Art Continuation Scholarship July 1924–25 to study wood-engraving, etching, embroidery, pottery and architecture.
Profile 1925–30 taught art at Lincoln Girls High School, England; 1930–32 at Port Elizabeth Art School (Technical College); 1933–34 lectured at the Witwatersrand Technical College. Married to James Gardner (qv).
Exhibitions Participated in group exhibitions in London, Paris and SA; 1949 Constantia Gallery, Johannesburg, solo exhibition.
Represented Africana Museum, Johannesburg.
Public Commissions 1939 designed the Coat of Arms for the SA Defence Force Exhibit at Milner Park, Johannesburg. Other commissions include murals for His Majesty's Theatre, Johannesburg and the Chamber of Mines Building, Johannesburg, with her husband, as well as those surrounding the proscenium in the Port Elizabeth City Hall.
References Collectors' Guide; SAA; AMC3; BSAK 1; Port Elizabeth School of Art; AASA.

GARIZIO Gian-Piero

Born 1931 Brusnengo, Northern Italy.
Resided in SA from 1953.
A self-taught painter of landscapes, still life, seascapes, genre and figures. Works in oil, acrylic, pencil and charcoal. 1973 a series of District Six, Cape Town.
Profile His work frequently appears in company calendars and journals.
Exhibitions He has participated in numerous group exhibitions from 1973 in SA; 1975 Lister Gallery, Johannesburg, first of seven solo exhibitions.
Represented Willem Annandale Art Gallery, Lichtenburg.

GARWOOD Nicholas John Blakeley

Born 1924 Johannesburg.
A painter of portraits and abstract pictures. Works in watercolour, gouache and acrylic.

Studies 1969–71 under Sidney Goldblatt (qv).

Profile A member of the WSSA, becoming an Associate in 1979 and Chairman in 1979, 1980 and 1986, also acting as Secretary from 1980. A dental surgeon. Has visited Europe.

Exhibitions From 1970 he has participated in many group exhibitions in SA, twice in London and once in West Germany and SWA/Namibia; 1972 President Gallery, Johannesburg, first of three solo exhibitions held in the Transvaal; 1979 Gallery 21, Johannesburg, joint exhibition with Cynthia Ball (qv), Diedie Marais (qv) and Ulrich Schwanecke (qv).

GASSNER Charles (Carel Antoon)

Born 1915 Enschede, The Netherlands.
Died 1977 Cape Town.
Resided in SA from 1948.
A painter and a graphic artist of abstracted landscapes and totally abstract pictures. Depicted still life, animals and figures. Worked in mixed media.

Studied 1936–39 Reiman Schule, Berlin; 1946–47 Art Academy, The Hague, under Professor Cox.

Profile 1950–53 lived in Australia, where he was a member of the Contemporary Australian Art Society.

Exhibitions Participated in group exhibitions in Australia and SA; 1950 first of many solo exhibitions held in SA and Australia; 1960 Galerie Grauze, Paris, solo exhibition; 1974 William Humphreys Art Gallery, Kimberley, solo exhibition; 1975 exhibited on the São Paulo Bienale, Brazil; 1977 Wolpe Gallery, Cape Town, Memorial Exhibition; 1984 SAAA Gallery, Cape Town, Memorial Exhibition; 1985 Kuns Oweral, Stellenbosch, Memorial Exhibition.

Represented SA National Gallery, Cape Town; William Humphreys Art Gallery, Kimberley.

References BSAK 1; AASA; *Artlook* March 1967; *SA Panorama* February 1976.

GAVIN Femma

Born 1935 Wynberg, Cape Province.
A painter and a graphic artist of figures and landscapes. Works in oil and in various graphic media.

Studies 1966 The Visual Arts Research Centre, Johannesburg, under George Boys (qv); 1970–71 graphic art, University of the Witwatersrand, under Giuseppe Cattaneo (qv).

Profile A member of the SAAA. From 1969 she has taught art privately in Johannesburg.

Exhibitions She has participated in several group exhibitions from 1968 in Durban, Johannesburg and Pretoria; 1970 NSA Gallery, Durban, first of two solo exhibitions held in Durban and Johannesburg.

Reference SA Art.

GAVRONSKY Claire Alison

Born 1957 Johannesburg.

A painter and a sculptor of machines and figures. Works in oil, watercolour, pencil, charcoal, bronze, ceramics and mixed media. Her subject matter deals with the current situation in SA, with specific reference to "true mythological and deeprooted" Africa versus the colonialised model.

Studies 1976–78 Witwatersrand Technical College, under Claude van Lingen (qv), Johann Moolman (qv), Jo Smail (qv) and Suzette Munnick, gaining a National Diploma in Fine Art; 1978–81 Witwatersrand Technical College (Technikon), under Robert Reedy, gaining a Higher Diploma in Fine Art; 1986–87 on a scholarship from the Italian Government at Il Bisonte Scuola Internazionale della Grafica, Florence, under Professor Giulietti; 1987 a three-month course at Cité Internationale des Arts, Paris.

Profile 1984–85 a lecturer in ceramic sculpture and drawing at the Witwatersrand Technikon; 1987 a lecturer in painting and drawing at the College Consortium International Studies, Florence, Italy. From 1985 she has lived in Florence, where she teaches at the Lorenzo de Medici Art School.

Exhibitions She has participated in numerous group exhibitions from 1978 in SA, Monaco, Italy and the UK; 1980 Things Gallery, Johannesburg, first of eight solo exhibitions, one of which was held in the USA; 1981 Republic Festival Exhibition; 1982 National Gallery, Gaborone, Botswana, Exhibition of SA Art; 1985 Cape Town Triennial; 1987 Karen McKerron Gallery, Johannesburg, joint exhibition with Gregory Kerr (qv) and Geoffrey Armstrong (qv); 1988 Johannesburg Art Gallery, Vita Art Now.

Award 1987 Second Prize, 8th Cleveland County International Drawing Biennale, UK.

Represented Cleveland County National Collection, UK; Durban Art Gallery; University of South Africa.

References De Kat December/January 1986; Sgraffiti no 42.

GEFFEN Lara

Born 1943 Johannesburg.

A painter of landscapes, portraits, still life and seascapes. Works in oil, acrylic and gouache.

Profile Began painting in 1975, also works in fabrics, creates batiks, silkscreens, prints on fashion garments and produces other craftwork. A part-time teacher of painting to handicapped people. 1976–84 lived in Switzerland and West Germany.

Exhibitions She has participated in several group exhibitions from 1977 in Switzerland and SA; 1977 Basle, Switzerland, first of two solo exhibitions, the second being held in Cape Town.

GELB Pearl

Born 1909 SA.

A graphic artist of abstract works. Creates coloured etchings, serigraphs and woodcuts.

Studies Studied in Cape Town and on overseas study tours.
Exhibitions She has participated in many group exhibitions from 1952 in SA; 1968 Cape Town, first of over four solo exhibitions held in SA.
Reference Artlook April 1973.

GELDENHUYS Daniella

Born 1918 Koffiefontein, Orange Free State.
A sculptor of figures and portrait busts. Works in bronze.
Studies 1945–46 and 1949–51 Michaelis School of Fine Art, under Edward Roworth (qv) and Ivan Mitford-Barberton (qv); 1955 studied painting under Henri Goetz (*b.*1909) and modelling under Ossip Zadkine (1890–1967) in Paris.
Profile A Committee Member of the Orange Free State Art Society for over 36 years and from 1985 an Honorary Life Member; a member of the SAAA and an art advisor to the local branch in Bloemfontein. 1954 co-designer and executor of the portals for the Free State Festival. Travelled extensively in Europe during the 1950s.
Exhibitions She has participated in group exhibitions from 1949 throughout SA; 1949 Bloemfontein, first of many solo exhibitions; 1981 Republic Festival Exhibition.
Represented Durban Art Gallery; University of the Orange Free State.
Public Commissions Portrait head of Abraham Fischer, University of the Orange Free State; bust of Andre Huguenot for the Andre Huguenot Theatre, Bloemfontein, commissioned by SUKOVS. Numerous portrait busts in public centres including in the Johannesburg Civic Centre; Transvaal Provincial Administration Building, Pretoria; Houses of Parliament, Cape Town; Orange Free State Provincial Administration Building, Bloemfontein and in universities and other educational buildings.
References Who's Who in SA, 1961, Vitae; SAA.

GEORGE John William

Born 1837 London, England.
Died 1908 Johannesburg.
Resided in SA from 1859.
A painter of landscapes. Worked in watercolour.
Profile Lived in Grahamstown, Kimberley and later in Johannesburg. Brother of the English watercolourist and architect Sir Ernest George (1839–1922).
Exhibitions Participated in group exhibitions from 1870 in SA.
Represented Africana Museum, Johannesburg; Albany Museum, Grahamstown; William Fehr Collection, Cape Town.
References Pict Art; AMC3; Pict Afr.

GERBER Hendriena Wihelmina (Rina) (née Grobler)

Born 1945 Cathcart, Cape Province.
A painter of spatial studies in colour and movement inspired by landscapes integrated with archetypal symbolism. Works in oil on wood.

Studies 1978–80 University of South Africa, under Alan Crump, gaining a BA(FA).

Profile From 1972 a member of the SAAA. 1987 held a teaching workshop at the EPSFA. 1983–85 a freelance art critic for *Oosterlig*. In 1985 she began playing the classical guitar.

Exhibitions She has participated in several group exhibitions in the Eastern Province; 1983 Port Elizabeth, first of two solo exhibitions.

Represented King George VI Art Gallery, Port Elizabeth.

GERHARDO see OLIVIER Gerhardus

GERMISHUYS Eben Wessel

Born 1937 Hoopstad, Orange Free State.

A sculptor working in bronze, stone, ciment fondu, wood and steel. 1962–70 Biblical figures and themes; 1970–82 abstract constructions; from 1982 realistic figures.

Studies 1958–61 Witwatersrand Technical College, under Phil Kolbe (qv) and Phil Botha (qv), gaining a National Art Teachers Diploma; 1979–83 University of South Africa, attaining a BA(FA); from 1984 studying for an MA(FA) at the University of Pretoria.

Profile From 1971 a member of the SAAA. From 1962 an art teacher at Florida Hoërskool and later at Langenhoven Hoërskool, Pretoria, where from 1977–84 he was appointed Vice-Head and then Head of the Art Department. 1985 Deputy Head of the Pretoria Art, Ballet and Music School; 1986 Temporary Head of the Pretoria Art, Ballet and Music School. 1984 wrote a series of articles on art for the *Transvaler*. Spent three months studying art in Europe.

Exhibitions He has participated in numerous group exhibitions in SA from 1963; 1971 SAAA Gallery, Pretoria, first of five solo exhibitions; 1981 Republic Festival Exhibition.

Represented Pietersburg Collection; Willem Annandale Art Gallery, Lichtenburg.

Public Commissions Numerous commissions including a bust of President C R Swart, Randfontein; bust of Prime Minister J Vorster, Transvaal Provincial Administration Building, Pretoria; rugby statue, Loftus Versveld Stadium, Pretoria; 1975 wooden mural, George Stegman Hospital, Saulspoort, Bophuthatswana; 1977 stained glass windows, Rustenburg Church; 1985–86 wooden and glass mural panel, George Hospital, Cape Province.

References BSAK 1; AASA.

GERRYTS Beeuwen Adriaan

Born 1936 Kuilsrivier, Cape Province.

A painter of landscapes, seascapes, still life and wildlife. Works in oil.

Studies 1970–74 privately under Otto Klar (qv).

Profile A minister of religion in the Dutch Reformed Church. 1962–74 lived in Pretoria; 1974–82 in Durban, thereafter in Roodepoort, Transvaal.
Exhibitions From 1972 he has held 18 solo exhibitions in halls, galleries and private residences.

GETSY Franco

Born 1946 Bizana, Transkei.
A painter, working in oil, acrylic, ink, pencil and in various graphic media. A sculptor, working in ciment fondu, clay and with fabrics.
Profile A member of D'ARTS. Teaches airography at monthly workshops in Durban. A musician, dancer and dress designer. 1969 visited North Africa, and has also visited the Balearic Islands in the Mediterranean.
Exhibitions He has participated in several group exhibitions from 1965 in SA; 1968 Tiles Club, Durban, first of seven solo exhibitions.

GEVERS RAY Ute

Born 1951 Natal.
A sculptor of abstract pieces dealing with the concept of the environment and objects of veneration. Works in clay.
Studies 1972–75 University of Natal, under Professor Hilda Ditchburn (qv) and Malcolm MacIntyre Read, gaining a BA(FA); 1977 University of Natal, where gained a Higher Diploma in Education.
Profile A ceramicist, creating functional ware. A committee member of the APSA and a member of the NSA. 1978–82 a teacher at Durban High School; from 1983 a ceramics lecturer at the Natal Technikon.
Exhibitions She has participated in several group exhibitions from 1973 in Natal.

GIBSON Janet Mary (née Sands)

Born 1908 Aldeburgh, Suffolk, England.
Died 1985 Kloof, Natal.
Resided in SA from *c.*1912.
A painter of genre, wildlife, botanical and ornithological subjects. Worked in watercolour. In addition she worked in stained glass, mosaic and produced decorative embroidery.
Profile Lived in Natal.
Publications by Gibson *Wildflowers of Natal, Coastal* in 1975 and *Wildflowers of Natal, Inland* in 1979.

GIBSON Perla Siedle

Born 1888 Durban.
Died 1971 Durban.
A painter of portraits and Natal flora. Worked in oil.

Studies 1909 portraiture under Professor Linde-Walther (*b*.1868) in Berlin; under Robert Gwelo Goodman (qv) in Cape Town.

Profile A member of the SA Society of Artists and the NSA. She studied music in Berlin in 1907, returning to SA in 1923. An accomplished singer and musician, known as the Lady in White, who sang to the troop ships at Durban harbour during WWII.

Exhibitions Participated in group exhibitions in SA, the UK and France; she held solo exhibitions in SA, Rhodesia (Zimbabwe) and the UK.

Award 1932 Gundlefinger Award, NSA.

Represented Durban Art Gallery.

References DBA; BSAK 2; AASA.

GILL Colin Unwin RA

Born 1892 Bexley Heath, Kent, England.

Died 1940 Johannesburg.

Resided in SA from 1938.

A painter of historical murals, genre and portraits.

Studies Slade School of Art, London, under Henry Tonks (1862–1937) and Wilson Steer (1860–1942), where in 1913 he was the first winner of the British Prix de Rome Scholarship.

Profile During WWI served in France and was later appointed an Official War Artist. 1922–25 taught composition at the Royal College of Art, London. 1924 appointed a Royal Academician. 1926 a member of the New English Art Club, London.

Exhibitions Participated in group exhibitions from 1914 with the New English Art Club and later in SA; 1941 Argus Gallery, Cape Town, Memorial Exhibition.

Public Commissions Numerous commissions in England including in 1925 "The Colonists, 1826", for the British Empire Exhibition, Wembley, later donated to the University of the Witwatersrand; 1928 the "Defeat of the Danes" for St Stephen's Hall, Westminster, London; 1938 two murals for the Johannesburg Magistrates Court (one completed, second incomplete in charcoal).

Represented Johannesburg Art Gallery; Tate Gallery, London, UK; University of the Witwatersrand.

Publication by Gill Under the pen name "Richard Saxby" and jointly with his wife Una Long, *Five Came to London*, 1938.

References SAA; *Tate Gallery Catalogue—The Modern British Paintings, Drawings and Sculpture*, volume 1, 1964, Oldbourne Press, London; DBA; BSAK 1; SA Art; AASA; *Studio* vol 122, December 1941.

GILL Marion

Born 1879 United Kingdom.

Died 1959 United Kingdom.

Resided in SA 1924–57.

A painter and graphic artist of birds, flowers and landscapes. Worked in watercolour and in various graphic media.

Studies Slade School of Art, London; Newcastle School of Art, England; woodblock colour printing at Edinburgh College of Art, Scotland.
Profile Illustrated *A First Guide of South African Birds* by Leonard Gill in 1936; wrote *Our Wagtails* in 1949, which was illustrated with photographs by Leonard Gill.
Exhibitions Participated in group exhibitions in Edinburgh, Paris and SA; 1933 Cape Town, first solo exhibition.
Represented SA National Gallery, Cape Town.
References *The Arts in SA*, edited by WHK, 1933–34, The Knox Printing & Publishing Company, Durban; SAA; SAP&D; BSAK 2; SA Art; 3Cs; AASA.

GILPIN Robert Findley

Born 1950 Cape Town.
A painter of landscapes, portraits, still life and figures. Works in oil, watercolour, pencil and pastel.
Studies At the Johannesburg Art Foundation.
Exhibitions He has participated in several group exhibitions in Johannesburg and Lichtenburg.
Awards 1981 awarded R500 for self-portrait and still life paintings, Southern Life Exhibition for the Disabled.

GLASER Marcus

Born 1936 Johannesburg.
An artist working in watercolour and ink. An etcher.
Studies 1956 Michaelis School of Fine Art, under Lippy Lipshitz (qv); 1958 Chelsea School of Art, London.
Profile 1965–68 artist to *The Cape Argus*. Has published several books comprising prose, poetry and graphics.
Exhibitions Participated in group exhibitions from 1959; 1960 Lidchi Gallery, Johannesburg, first of over 10 solo exhibitions.
References Art SA; SAA; *Artlook* March 1967 & October 1970.

GLOSSOP Allerley (Joe)

Born 1870 Twickenham, Middlesex, England.
Died 1955 Lions River, Natal.
Resided in SA from 1900.
A painter and graphic artist of landscapes including figures, animals and habitations. Occasionally painted portraits. Worked in oil, pastel, watercolour, gouache and in various graphic media, particularly etchings and linocuts.
Studies Three years at the Slade School of Art, London, modelling under the sculptor Sir George Frampton (1860–1928) and painting under Sir Charles Holroyd (1861–1917); Central and Westminster Schools of Art, London, under William Mouat-Loudan (1868–1925); two years at G F Cook's School, London; also under Arthur J Elsley (*b.* 1861) and Solomon J Solomon (1860–1927).

Profile On the council of the SA Society of Artists, a member of the NSA, and in 1949, at its inception, a member of the Brush and Chisel Club. Reputed to have been a Freemason. 1947 Lesotho presented her painting of Thaba Bosigo to Princess Elizabeth as a wedding present. 1902–17 farmed at Wellington, Cape, where she took an active part in artistic life; 1917–24 based in Johannesburg, travelling throughout SA by waggon; from 1925 lived near Lions River, Natal, where she farmed. Visited the South of England frequently and in 1932 took a studio in Camden Hill Gardens, London, intending to work in studios in both SA and the UK. During WWII lived in England. Included in Edward Roworth's (qv) essay "Landscape Art in SA", 1917, Studio Publication, *Art of the British Empire Overseas.*

Exhibitions Participated in group exhibitions from 1902 in SA and London; held several solo exhibitions throughout SA and in London; 1924 Taylor Art Gallery, Durban, joint exhibition with Charles E Peers (qv).

Represented Albany Museum, Grahamstown; Ann Bryant Gallery, East London; Bulawayo Art Gallery, Zimbabwe; Durban Art Gallery; Johannesburg Art Gallery; National Museum, Bloemfontein; Pretoria Art Museum; SA National Gallery, Cape Town; University of Cape Town; William Humphreys Art Gallery, Kimberley.

References Collectors' Guide; SAA; SADNB; DSAB; SAP&S; SSAP; BSAK 1 & 2; 3Cs; AASA.

GLUCKMAN Judith

Born 1915 Johannesburg.
Died 1961 Johannesburg.
A painter and graphic artist of figures, heads and still life. Worked in oil, pastel, crayon, pencil, charcoal and in various graphic media.

Studies 1934 Witwatersrand Technical College, under Emily Fern (qv), James Gardner (qv) and Alan Gourley; 1937 Académie de la Grande Chaumière, Paris, under Colarossi; also at the Académie Ranson, under Mandelbaum; 1948 sculpture under Ossip Zadkine (1890–1967) in Paris.

Profile A member of the New Group. Married to Adam Leslie, the well-known theatrical personality. A friend of Alexis Preller (qv). 1937–38 lived in Paris and The Netherlands; 1939 in Johannesburg; 1941 in Cape Town; 1948 visited Europe.

Exhibitions Participated in group exhibitions held throughout SA and in Paris, London, New York and Rome; 1939 Johannesburg, first of several solo exhibitions held in Johannesburg, Cape Town and Pretoria; 1973 Pretoria Art Museum, Commemorative Exhibition.

Represented Pretoria Art Museum; SA National Gallery, Cape Town.

References SAA; AASA; *Artlook* March 1973.

GOBA Vela Newell

Born 1955 Inanda, Natal.
Both a painter and a sculptor of portraits and figures. Works in watercolour, ink, wash, pencil and wood.

Studies Two months at Rorke's Drift Art Centre; 1980 Cleaver-Hume College, where gained a Certificate in Art Training by Nature's Method and in Commercial Art.
Profile From 1981 a cartoonist on *Ukusa*, also contributes to *The Sunday Tribune Herald*, *The Echo*, a supplement to *The Natal Witness*, and *Umafrica*.
Exhibitions He has participated in several group exhibitions.
Reference SASSK.

GOEDHALS Neil John

Born 1957 East London.
A painter, sculptor and graphic artist of diverse subjects. Works in oil, acrylic, watercolour, gouache, ink, wash, pencil, charcoal, mixed media, stone, wood and in various graphic media.
Studies 1980–83 University of Natal, gaining a BA(FA); 1986–87 registered for an MA(FA) at the University of the Witwatersrand, on a University Bursary.
Profile 1983 a member of Possession Arts and from 1986 of the SAAAH. 1984 set designs for the Market Theatre, Johannesburg and in 1986 poster designs. 1982 released a record with the "Prisoners Go-Go Band".
Exhibitions He has participated in many group exhibitions in Johannesburg and Pretoria; 1985 Cape Town Triennial.

GOEDVRIEND Theodoor Franciscus (Theo)

Born 1879 De Steeg, Rheden, The Netherlands.
Died 1969 Warnsveld, The Netherlands.
Resided in SA 1936–41.
A painter of landscapes, city scenes, portraits and flower studies, his depictions of mushrooms being especially notable. Worked in tempera on wood and in oil. An etcher.
Studies 1897 under A J Derkinderen (*b.*1859); 1899 Kunstnijverheid School, Amsterdam; in Hilversum, The Netherlands, under Theo van Hoytema (1863–1917); also in Italy.
Profile A member of the Arte et Amicitige. 1938 taught art history at the University of Pretoria. During the 1920s lived on Lake Garda, Italy; 1936–41 in Pretoria; 1941–44 imprisoned in Japanese prisoner of war camps; 1945 returned to The Netherlands.
Exhibitions 1937 Gainsborough Gallery, Johannesburg, first of several solo exhibitions held in SA; 1939 Retrospective Exhibition held in The Netherlands.
Represented Arnhem Museum, The Netherlands; Dordrecht Art Museum, The Netherlands; Frans Hals Museum, Haarlem, The Netherlands; Pretoria Art Museum; Rijks Museum, Amsterdam, The Netherlands; University of Pretoria; William Humphreys Art Gallery, Kimberley.
References Johan Wesselink, *De Schilder Theo Goedvriend*, 1954, N V Gebr. Forner & Keuning, Wageningen, Nederland; DSAB; Bénézit; BSAK 1 & 2; AASA.

GOLDBERG Harry

Born 1906 Johannesburg.
A painter of figures and portraits. Works in acrylic.
Studies From 1973 part-time under Bill Ainslie (qv).
Exhibitions He has participated in group exhibitions from 1983 in Johannesburg; 1985 Market Gallery, Johannesburg, first of two solo exhibitions.

GOLDBERG (Louis) Michael

Born 1952 Johannesburg.
An artist creating assemblages.
Studies Michaelis School of Fine Art, gaining a BA(FA); studying for an MA(FA) through the University of South Africa.
Profile On the Committee of the Market Gallery, Johannesburg.
Exhibitions 1978 solo exhibition; 1981 Market Gallery, Johannesburg, joint exhibition with Paul Stopforth (qv); 1985 Cape Town Triennial; 1986 Market Gallery, Johannesburg, solo exhibition.
Represented Johannesburg Art Gallery; SA National Gallery, Cape Town; University of the Witwatersrand.
Reference AASA.

GOLDBLATT Sidney

Born 1919 Johannesburg.
Died 1979 Magoebaskloof, Northern Transvaal.
A highly versatile artist. Painted cityscapes, birds, animals, landscapes, still life, genre and figures. From 1958 became more abstracted, by 1970 abstract. Worked in oil, gouache and acrylic. 1955 began working with linoleum. Non-figurative sculpture in silver, aluminium and both green and black bronze. From 1966 a series of monochrome collages, in silver or brown, made of oil paint, linoleum and hessian. From 1972 worked in acrylic and mixed media. A graphic artist.
Studies *c.*1940 evening classes at the Witwatersrand Technical College, under Eric Byrd (qv) and James Gardner (qv); 1949 Anglo-French Art Centre, London; 1950 under André Lhote (1885–1962) and Fernand Léger (1881–1955) in Paris; 1952 sculpture at the Sir John Cass School of Art, London, under Edward Copnall (qv).
Profile 1953 opened Gallery Independent, Johannesburg, with nine others; 1954 founded the Giotto Art Academy, Johannesburg, with Ina Mansch; 1955 began his own private art school. A Committee Member of the Transvaal Art Society. A judge on Artists of Fame and Promise Exhibitions. 1977 designed wine labels for Rebel Bottle Store. 1951 visited Italy; 1957–58 lived for six months in Marbella, Spain, also visited Italy, Switzerland, France and spent three months in England; 1969 visited Israel, the Greek islands, Athens, Istanbul and London; 1972 visited Toronto, the USA and headed an art tour of Europe; 1975 visited Scandinavia; 1979 visited SWA/Namibia.

Exhibitions 1948 Jewish Guild Memorial Hall, Johannesburg, first of 15 solo exhibitions held in SA, The Netherlands and Israel; participated in group exhibitions from 1953 in Yugoslavia, Belgium, Italy, Zimbabwe, West Germany, the USA, Italy, Brazil and SA; 1956, 1960 and 1964 Quadrennial Exhibitions; 1979 Rand Afrikaans University, Prestige Exhibition; 1980 Atlantic Art Gallery, Cape Town, Retrospective Exhibition of SWA/Namibian works; 1981 Pretoria Art Museum, Retrospective Exhibition.

Award 1967 Cambridge Shirt Award on the Art SA Today Exhibition, Durban.

Represented Ann Bryant Gallery, East London; Durban Art Gallery; Hester Rupert Art Museum, Graaff-Reinet; Israel Museum, Jerusalem; King George VI Art Gallery, Port Elizabeth; Pietersburg Collection; Pretoria Art Museum; Rand Afrikaans University; SA National Gallery, Cape Town; University of the Witwatersrand; William Humphreys Art Gallery, Kimberley.

References Our Art 2; Art SA; SAA; SAP&S; SSAP; BSAK 1 & 2; SA Art; 3Cs; AASA; LSAA; *Lantern* March/June 1959 & November/December 1971; *Art News and Review* 6 June 1959; *Artlook* July 1969, May 1970 & September 1971; *SA Panorama* December 1970; *Gallery* Summer 1981; Retrospective Exhibition Catalogue, 1981, Pretoria Art Museum.

GOLDIN Alice

Born 1925 Vienna, Austria.
Resided in SA from 1948.

A painter and a graphic artist of landscapes, seascapes and still life. Works in mixed media and in various graphic media, particularly woodcuts and screen-prints. Series of "Musicians", "Trees", "Rocks" and "Seasons".

Studies 1955–60 Pretoria Technical College, under Robert Hodgins (qv); 1965 in Rome, Italy, under S Giuliani; 1978 Camden Institute for Adult Education, London, England, screenprinting under Miss Greenfield.

Profile From 1960 a member of the SAAA; a member of the Artists Guild, Cape Town. 1984 illustrated *Gebed vir Wilhelm*, a book of poetry by Phil du Plessis. 1938–48 lived in England; 1948–71 lived in Pretoria, thereafter in the Cape Province. 1964–65 visited Rome; 1978 London and in 1984 Jerusalem. In 1986 she spent four months at the Cité Internationale des Arts, Paris.

Exhibitions 1959 Lidchi Gallery, Johannesburg, first of 37 solo exhibitions, two of which were held in London in 1978 and one in 1985; she has participated in numerous group exhibitions from 1960 throughout SA and in Italy, West Germany, Zimbabwe, the UK, the USA and France; 1960 and 1964 Quadrennial Exhibitions; 1981 Republic Festival Exhibition.

Represented Hester Rupert Art Museum, Graaff-Reinet; King George VI Art Gallery, Port Elizabeth; Potchefstroom Museum; Potchefstroom University for CHE; Pretoria Art Museum; Rand Afrikaans University; SA National Gallery, Cape Town; University of Cape Town; University of Stellenbosch; University of the Witwatersrand; Willem Annandale Art Gallery, Lichtenburg; William Humphreys Art Gallery, Kimberley.

References SAA; SAGAT; BSAK 1; SA Art; 3Cs; AASA; *Artlook* August 1967, September 1969 and June 1971; *SA Arts Calendar* vol 2 no 6, July 1977; *Gallery* Winter 1983.

GOLDSMID Erica

Born 1921 Lourenço Marques (Maputo), Mozambique.
Resided in SA from 1934, arriving from Rio de Janeiro.
Both a painter and sculptor of figures, still life and abstracts. Works in oil and bronze. An etcher.

Studies 1961–63 University of the Witwatersrand, under Cecily Sash (qv); 1963–65 under Lionel Abrams (qv); 1968 briefly at the Positano Art Workshop in Italy, under Eugene Charlton; 1969 sculpture at the Whitechapel School of Art, London; 1970 briefly at the International School in Spain, under Harry Thubron and Terry Frost (b.1915).

Profile A member of the SAAA. 1950–82 made several visits to France; 1969 visited England and in 1981 the USA.

Exhibitions She has participated in many group exhibitions from 1964 in SA and in the USA; 1972 Gallery 101, Johannesburg, first of two solo exhibitions.

GOODMAN Robert Gwelo

Born 1871 Taplow, England.
Died 1939 Cape Town.
Resided in SA from 1886.
Adopted the name "Gwelo" in 1900.
A painter of landscapes and street scenes. 1900 sketched the battlefields of the Anglo-Boer War. Painted Cape homesteads 1916–24, flowers from 1918, interiors of Newlands House 1919–22 and the occasional portrait at the beginning of his career. Worked in oil, pastel and watercolour.

Studies Evening classes under J S Morland (qv) in Cape Town; 1895 at the Académie Julian, Paris, under William Bouguereau (1825–1905), Constant Bachet and Gabriel Ferrier (1847–1914), gaining a special medal in 1897.

Profile A member of the SA Society of Artists and an Honorary Member of the Johannesburg Sketch Club. Illustrated *Historic Houses of South Africa*, by Dorothea Fairbridge, in 1922. Involved in the restoration of Newlands House and The Old Brewery, Newlands, Cape Town, both of which he lived in. Designed the Community Centre, houses and other buildings at Tongaat, Natal, a house for his daughter in Killarney Road, Johannesburg and a number of alterations for existing residences. 1886–94 lived in Cape Town; 1894–97 in France; 1897–1915 lived in England, visiting SA several times; 1903 and 1905 visited India; 1907 travelled in Italy, Spain, Ireland, Scotland and to the Lake District in England; 1910 visited Venice; 1915 returned to SA, settling in Cape Town; 1916 visited SWA/Namibia; 1917 spent six months in Johannesburg, painting mine dumps; 1918–19 visited the Drakensberg and Durban; 1924 visited London. Included in Edward Roworth's (qv) essay "Landscape Art in South Africa", 1917, Studio Publication, *Art of the British Empire Overseas*.

Exhibitions Participated in group exhibitions from 1898 in the UK, Paris, San Francisco, SA and posthumously in Rhodesia (Zimbabwe); 1901 Technical Institute, Queen Victoria Street, Cape Town, first of several solo exhibitions held in SA and in England; 1919 Durban Art Gallery, solo exhibition; 1948 Tate Gallery, London, SA Art Exhibition.

Awards 1915 Gold Medal for pastel drawing at San Francisco International Exhibition; 1915 Silver Medal, Panama Pacific International Exhibition.

Represented Africana Museum, Johannesburg; Albany Museum, Grahamstown; Durban Art Gallery; galleries in Birmingham, Liverpool, Manchester and Oldham, UK; Johannesburg Art Gallery; Julius Gordon Africana Centre, Riversdale; King George VI Art Gallery, Port Elizabeth; National Gallery, Canada; National Museum, Bloemfontein; Pretoria Art Museum; SA National Gallery, Cape Town; Tatham Art Gallery, Pietermaritzburg; Toronto Gallery, Canada; University of Cape Town; University of Natal; William Humphreys Art Gallery, Kimberley.

Public Commissions 1929 10 murals for SA House, London. 1936 murals for the staircase at Monterey, Cape Province.

References Joyce Newton-Thompson, *Gwelo Goodman—South African Artist*, 1951, Howard Timmins, Cape Town; Collectors' Guide; Our Art 1; Art SA; SAA; SADNB; DSAB; SAP&S; SAP&D; SESA; SSAP; Pict Afr; Bénézit; DBA; BSAK 1 & 2; Art SWA; SA Art; 3Cs; AASA; LSAA; *SA Panorama* September 1983.

GORDON Robert Jakob

Born 1743 Doesburg, The Netherlands.
Died 1795 Cape Town.
Resided in SA from 1777.
A painter of landscapes, views of Cape Town and Simonstown, figures, plants and animals. Worked in watercolour.

Profile His paintings are of historical interest owing to their early date. A Colonel in the Dutch Forces, an explorer, botanist, geographer, cartographer and draughtsman. 1777–86 explored throughout the Cape; 1779 named the Orange River. 1789 introduced Merino sheep to SA.

Exhibition 1952 included in the Van Riebeeck Tercentenary Festival Exhibition.

Represented Rijks Museum, Amsterdam, *c.*400 drawings.

References Pict Art; Afr Repos; AMC3; DSAB; SESA; Pict Afr; BSAK 1 & 2; Enc S'n A.

GORVY Rhona Adele

Born 1921 Springs, Transvaal.
A sculptor, graphic artist and painter of figures. Works in stone, bronze, etching, monotype, linocuts, ink, pencil, charcoal and oil. 1973 a series of drawings entitled "Adam & Eve"; five series of etchings: 1977 "In Search of Freedom"; 1977 "Man with a Rope"; 1979 "Time"; 1980 "Battered Baby"; 1985 "The Dream and the Abuse" (drugs).

Studies 1966–70 The Visual Arts Research Centre, Johannesburg, under George Boys (qv) and Joyce Leonard (qv).

Profile A member of the SAAA. 1970 co-founder of "The Groop". 1968 wrote *The Boyhood of Grieg*, a play for children. From 1975 a designer of both sets and costumes for children's theatre. 1979–80 artistic co-ordinator of children's theatre productions, Johannesburg. A poet.

Exhibitions She has participated in many group exhibitions from 1966 in SA and in London; 1970 Helen de Leeuw Gallery, Johannesburg, first of six solo exhibitions, two of which were held in the USA.
Award 1970 Drawing Award, New Signatures.
Represented Potchefstroom University for CHE; Willem Annandale Art Gallery, Lichtenburg.
References IWAA; *Dictionary of International Biography*, 1984, International Biographical Centre, Cambridge, UK; *International Who's Who of Women*, Melrose Press, Cambridge, UK; AASA; *Artlook* November 1970.

GOTTHARD Charles

Born 1951 Johannesburg.
A sculptor of wildlife, figures and abstract pieces. Works in ceramics and bronze.
Studies 1971–74 Witwatersrand Technical College, under Spies Venter (qv), gaining a Diploma in Architectural Ceramics.
Profile A potter, making functional ware. 1977 a lecturer in figure drawing at the Witwatersrand Technical College; 1978 ceramic sculpture lecturer at Rustenburg Technical College; from 1979 he has taught art privately. A cousin of Jan Schutte (qv).
Exhibitions He has participated in many group exhibitions from 1973 in SA; 1973 Helen de Leeuw Gallery, Pretoria, first solo exhibition.
Award 1976 Brickor Award for sculpture.
Represented Potchefstroom Museum; Pretoria Art Museum; Touch Gallery, SA National Gallery, Cape Town; Willem Annandale Art Gallery, Lichtenburg; William Humphreys Art Gallery, Kimberley.
Public Commissions 1976 abstract ceramic mural, Alberton Civic Centre; 1977 abstract ceramic fountain, Ficksburg Sentra Oes, Orange Free State; 1981 ceramic figurative sculpture, the State Theatre, Pretoria; 1984 abstract ceramic panel, Pietersburg Civic Centre, Transvaal; 1984 nine stained glass panels embedded in a ceramic abstract form, Louis Trichardt Civic Centre, Transvaal; 1985 ceramic and bronze fountain, Witbank Theatre, Transvaal.
References G Clerk & L Wagner, *Potters of Southern Africa*, 1974, C Struik, Cape Town; AASA; LSAA; *Artlook* October/November 1975.

GOTTLIEB Vivian

Born 1939 Cape Town.
A painter of landscapes, seascapes and still life. Works in watercolour. 1984 a series of Cape landscapes, 1985 of flowers and of Biblical visions.
Studies 1957–61 Michaelis School of Fine Art, under Rupert Shephard (qv), gaining a Diploma in Graphic Art and Design.
Profile From 1970 a member of the SAAA. 1971–73 taught at the Cape Town Art Centre; 1977–79 through the SA Institute of Race Relations; 1980–82 taught art therapy in Valkenberg, Cape Town; from 1982 she has taught art privately. Published a limited edition portfolio entitled "Airs, Waters and Places".

Exhibitions 1970 Cape Town, first of nine solo exhibitions, one of which was held in Switzerland; she has participated in several group exhibitions from 1971 in SA and one in Switzerland.
Represented SA National Gallery, Cape Town; William Humphreys Art Gallery, Kimberley.

GOUDEMOND Louise Marguerite

Born 1935 San Diego, California, USA.
Resided in SA from 1965.
A painter of landscapes, portraits, still life, figures, wildlife and abstract pictures. Works in oil, watercolour, gouache and ink. 1979 a series of "Clowns".
Studies 1954–56 Lynchburg, Virginia; 1956–58 University of Virginia, under Emil Schnellock and Cecere, gaining a BA(FA).
Profile 1975–81 Art Mistress and Art Director at the Saheti School, Johannesburg; 1982–85 Art Mistress at St Martin's School, Johannesburg. Lived in the USA until 1959, 1959–62 lived in France, 1962–64 in the USA.
Exhibitions 1960 Chateauroux, France, first of five solo exhibitions; she has participated in several group exhibitions from 1978 in SA; 1979 Charles Gallery, Melville, Johannesburg, Retrospective Exhibition; 1988 Karen McKerron Gallery, Johannesburg, joint exhibition with Veronica Ramsay and Maeve Dewar.

GOWER Stella Isabel

Born 1894 Cape Town.
A painter of flower studies.
Studies Grahamstown School of Art, under Professor F W Armstrong (qv).
Profile Taught art at schools in Graaff-Reinet and Pretoria. 1921–24 worked at the Division of Botany, Pretoria (now the Botanical Research Institute) with Dr Pole-Evans. 1942–45 worked for the Pretoria Publicity Association. Numerous botanical illustrations including 40 plates in *Pretoria Wild Flowers*, and illustrations for *Flowering Plants of Africa*, a Botanical Research Institute publication. Designed the protea motif for the SA 3d and 6d coins.
References SAA; AASA.

GRADWELL-SLABBERT Margaret Louise

Born 1956 Pretoria.
A painter and graphic artist of landscapes and city scenes, wildlife and abstract pictures. Works in oil, watercolour, gouache, pencil and in various graphic media on hand-made paper.
Studies 1974–77, 1978 and from 1985 at the University of Pretoria, under Professor Nico Roos (qv), gaining a BA(FA) in 1977 and a Higher Diploma in Education in 1978; currently studying for an MA(FA).
Profile A member of the SAAA. 1980 technical graphics assistant, 1981 a junior lecturer, from 1982 a lecturer in drawing at the University of Pretoria.

Exhibitions She has participated in several group exhibitions from 1978 in SA and once in Australia in 1977; 1981 University of Pretoria, first of two solo exhibitions.
Represented Pietersburg Collection; Pretoria Art Museum; University of the Orange Free State.

GRAFF Philippa

Born 1959 Johannesburg.
A painter of landscapes. Works in mixed media.
Studies 1977–82 Michaelis School of Fine Art, gaining a BA(FA).
Profile 1983 visited art museums in the USA and Europe. 1984–87 taught children at the Torah Academy, Johannesburg. From 1987 has taught at Redhill Primary School, Johannesburg.
Exhibition 1988 Karen McKerron Gallery, Johannesburg, joint exhibition with Lea Henorain (qv) and Barend de Wet (qv).

GRAHAM Diana Hope

Born 1947 Queenstown, Cape Province.
A painter of conceptual landscapes and figures. Works in oil.
Studies 1978–81 studied under Hillary Graham (qv).
Profile A member of the GAP Group. Married to Hillary Graham (qv).
Exhibitions She has participated in several group exhibitions from 1983 in SA.

GRAHAM Hillary

Born 1943 Graaff-Reinet, Cape Province.
A painter of symbolic and narrative landscapes and figures. Works in oil. A continuing series entitled "Maharg" (his surname reversed).
Studies 1963–67 Rhodes University, under Professor Brian Bradshaw (qv), gaining an MFA (cum laude).
Profile 1964–80 a founder member of the Grahamstown Group. 1968 taught art at Queensborough High School, Durban, and at Greenside High School, Johannesburg. 1969 a lecturer in the History of Art and in Fine Art at the University of South Africa; 1971 a lecturer and 1973–82 a senior lecturer at Port Elizabeth Technical College (Technikon); from 1983 a senior lecturer in the Fine Arts Department, University of Fort Hare. Married to Diana Graham (qv).
Exhibitions He has participated in numerous group exhibitions from 1964 held in SA; 1981 Port Elizabeth Technikon, first solo exhibition; 1986 Everard Read Gallery, Johannesburg, joint exhibition with Paul Stopforth (qv) and Richard Smith (qv); 1987 Johannesburg Art Gallery, Vita Art Now.
Awards 1966 and 1967 Purvis Prize for Fine Art, Rhodes University.
Represented Port Elizabeth Technikon; University of South Africa.
References Port Elizabeth School of Art; AASA.

GRANDISON Sheila

Born 1951 Loughborough, Leicestershire, England.
An artist working in crayon on paper.
Studies 1975 gained a BA(FA) from the University of the Witwatersrand; 1982 gained an MA(FA) from the University of the Witwatersrand; 1984 gained an MA in Art History and Theory from the University of Essex, England.
Exhibition 1985 Cape Town Triennial.

GRANT Cecily Charlene

Born 1946 Johannesburg.
A painter and graphic artist of landscapes, still life, genre and figures. Works in oil, watercolour, gouache, ink, wash, pencil, charcoal and etching.
Studies 1965 Johannesburg Art School, under George Boys (qv) and Joyce Leonard (qv); 1966 The Visual Arts Research Centre, Johannesburg, under George Boys (qv); 1967 University of South Africa, under Professor Walter Battiss (qv) and later under Nina Romm (qv); 1969 privately under Cecil Skotnes (qv); 1983–84 studied etching under and worked with Elizabeth Harington (qv).
Profile 1984 a member of the WSSA. 1968 visited Scotland; 1974 Greece; 1976 Florence, Italy; 1980 and 1983 London.
Exhibitions She has participated in many group exhibitions from 1984 in Johannesburg and Pretoria; 1984 Crake Gallery, Johannesburg, joint exhibition with Laraine Campbell (qv) and Donna White (qv); 1984 SAAA Gallery, Pretoria, joint exhibition with Elizabeth Harington (qv), Laraine Campbell (qv) and Pamela Kleinot.

GRANT David Llewellyn

Born 1950 Ladysmith, Natal.
A painter of landscapes and abstract pictures. Works in oil, acrylic, watercolour, gouache and ink.
Studies 1968–71 and 1974–76 Rhodes University, under Professor Brian Bradshaw (qv), Thomas Matthews (qv) and Robert Brooks (qv), gaining a BA in 1970, a University Education Diploma in 1971, a BA(FA) in 1975 and an MFA in 1976.
Profile 1974–76 a member of the Grahamstown Group; from 1977 a member of the East London Society of Fine Arts. 1976 an art teacher at the Belgravia Art Centre, East London; 1977–82 an art teacher at the West Bank High School, East London.
Exhibitions He has participated in group exhibitions from 1974 in Zimbabwe and SA; 1976 Pretoria, joint exhibition with Thomas Matthews (qv); 1980 Carlton Centre, Johannesburg, solo exhibition; 1981 Republic Festival Exhibition; 1983 Port Elizabeth, joint exhibition with Tony Swift (qv).
Reference AASA.

GRAVETT Willem Hendrik

Born 1917 Middelburg, Transvaal.

A painter and graphic artist of landscapes, portraits, still life and figures. Works in watercolour, ink, pencil and in various graphic media.

Studies 1939 under Arthur Podolini (qv) in Cape Town; 1947–48 part-time at the Chelsea School of Art, London; 1949 l'Ecole des Beaux Arts, Paris; 1949 part-time at the Académie Julian, Paris; 1951 Académie Lhote, Paris, under André Lhote (1885–1962).

Profile 1939–40 shared a studio with Harry Trevor (qv). From 1975 a life member of the SAAA; 1965 a founder member of the Artists Gallery, Cape Town. 1964–75 Director of the Michaelis Collection, Cape Town; 1972 Commissioner of the RSA Exhibition; 1973 Commissioner of the São Paulo Bienale, Brazil; 1974 a member of the selection board for the RSA Exhibition. A former art critic working for a number of newspapers. 1939–44 lived in Cape Town; 1944–46 in Johannesburg; 1946–48 in London; 1948–52 in Paris; 1952–54 in Sweden; 1954–55 in Johannesburg; 1955–75 in Cape Town, thereafter in Clanwilliam, Cape Province. He has travelled extensively in Europe and to America and Iceland.

Exhibitions He has participated in many group exhibitions from 1940 in SA, West Germany, Italy and France; 1942 Stellenbosch, first of six solo exhibitions one of which was held in Sweden in 1953; 1964 Quadrennial Exhibition; 1974 William Humphreys Art Gallery, Kimberley, solo exhibition; 1981 Republic Festival Exhibition; 1982 Rand Afrikaans University, solo exhibition.

Represented Johannesburg Art Gallery; SA National Gallery, Cape Town; William Humpreys Art Gallery, Kimberley.

References SAA; IWAA; BSAK 1 & 2; 3Cs; AASA.

GRAY Douglas Awdry (Ginger)

Born 1911 Bloemfontein.

A painter of wildlife; works in watercolour, ink and pencil.

Profile A fully trained engineer, now retired. From 1983 a member of the WSSA. He has illustrated two books by Dennis Winchester Gould: *Mukoba, Where Lions Roar*, 1985, Ridgeback Publishers, Johannesburg and *Wilderness Window*, 1986, Ridgeback Publishers, Johannesburg, and in 1986 three book covers for *The Hour of The Elephant*, *Deep Pulse* and *Mapela's Mountain*. 1937–39 lived in Kimberley, 1945–60 in Cape Town, thereafter in Johannesburg. He has travelled throughout Southern Africa. Father of the writer Stephen Gray.

Publication by Gray Wrote and illustrated *The Adventures of Mick the Monk in Kruger Park*, 1982, Chris van Rensburg Publishers, Johannesburg.

GRAY Douglas Raphael

Born 1950 Johannesburg.

A self-taught painter of wildlife. Works in acrylic.

Profile A member of the Artists Market. 1987 visited the Etosha Pan, SWA/Namibia.

Exhibition 1987 Crake Gallery, Johannesburg, solo exhibition.

GREAVES Constance Helen

Born 1882 Brighton, Sussex, England.
Died 1966 Cala, Transkei.
Resided in SA 1910–20 and from 1930.
A painter of portraits and figure studies. Worked in watercolour.
Studies Brighton Art School and Sussex Women's Art Club.
Profile A member of the NSA, the SA Society of Artists and the SA Institute. A number of her works were reproduced by E Schweickerdt, Pretoria. Lived in Natal and in the Transkei.
Exhibitions 1930 Bloemfontein, first of several solo exhibitions in SA; 1934–39 held solo exhibitions and participated in group exhibitions in London. Participated in the exhibitions held at the Paris Salons.
Award 1930 Gundelfinger Award, NSA.
Represented Africana Museum, Johannesburg; Ann Bryant Gallery, East London; Durban Art Gallery; Queenstown Gallery; SA National Gallery, Cape Town; University of Cape Town.
References AMC3; SAP&D; DBA; BSAK 1 & 2; SA Art; AASA.

GREEN Harold (Herold)

Born 1930 Durban.
Died 1979 Cape Town.
A painter of witty parodies of classical artworks. Worked in oil.
Exhibitions 1975 Fabian Fine Art, Cape Town, first of two solo exhibitions; 1980 posthumously included in the SA National Gallery group exhibition, "20thC Still Life".
Represented SA National Gallery, Cape Town.

GREEN Valerie Mary

Born 1948 Port Elizabeth.
A painter of landscapes, seascapes, portraits, figures, still life and genre. Works in oil, watercolour, gouache, ink, wash, pencil, charcoal, pastel and airbrush.
Studies 1965–66 Witwatersrand Technical College, under Phil Botha (qv); 1966–67 East London Technical College, under Jack Lugg (qv); 1968–69 Port Elizabeth Technical College, under Phil Kolbe (qv) and Hunter Nesbit (qv); 1970–71 Natal Technical College, under Bailey-Searle, gaining a Diploma in Fine Art.
Profile A member of the EPSFA. From 1975 has taught and choreographed at her own modern dance school in Port Elizabeth. She has held four large dance-art shows at the Grahamstown Festival.
Exhibitions She has participated in many group exhibitions from 1975 in SA; 1976 EPSFA Gallery, Port Elizabeth, first of five solo exhibitions; 1981 Republic Festival Exhibtion.
Public Commission 1975 a large batik for the University of Port Elizabeth.
Represented King George VI Art Gallery, Port Elizabeth, on loan to the City Hall; SA National Gallery, Cape Town.
References AASA; *Gallery* Spring 1985; *SA Arts Calendar* Summer 1985–86.

GREENBLATT Francine Scialom

Born 1951 Cairo, Egypt.
Resided in SA from 1960.
A painter and graphic artist depicting figures with a psycho-sexual-social nature. Works in oil and mixed media on paper and in various graphic media.
Studies 1969 University of the Witwatersrand; 1972 gained a BA(FA) from the Michaelis School of Fine Art.
Profile 1986 a committee member of the SAAA, Cape Town. 1973 a lecturer in painting, drawing and basic design at the Cape Town Art Centre. 1973 joined the Graphic Workshop, Cape Town, and in 1975 published the Graphic Workshop portfolio. From 1978 she has run her own study workshop in Wynberg, Cape Town. 1985 cover illustration for *Sephardi Jews—25 years, Cape Town*, ABC Press, Cape Town; 1986 cover illustration for *Father and Son*, by Rabbi N L Marcus and Rabbi B Marcus, Johannesburg. 1956 lived in Cairo, Egypt; 1958 in Nairobi, Kenya; 1960 in Dakar, Senegal. 1985–86 visited Japan.
Exhibitions She has participated in many group exhibitions from 1976 in SA, the USA and France; 1977 Fabian Fine Art Gallery, Cape Town, first of seven solo exhibitions one of which was held in Paris, one in Basle and one in New York.
Reference *Cimaise* no 178–179, 1986, Paris, France.

GREENBLATT Nanette

Born 1952 Cape Town.
An artist producing oil paintings and drawings.
Studies Studied architecture for three years; gained a BA(FA) from the Wimbledon School of Art, London.
Exhibitions She has participated in group exhibitions in the Western Cape; 1981 Republic Festival Exhibition; 1980 SAAA Gallery, Western Cape, solo exhibition.

GREIG Barbara

Born 1924 Cape Town.
A painter and sculptor, working in many media.
Studies York School of Art, England, and at the Port Elizabeth Technical College.
Profile She has lived in England, Egypt, Spain and SA. 1971–72 visited South America. Married to Desmond Greig (qv), with whom she established a bronze foundry for casting in the cire perdue method.
Exhibitions She has participated in numerous group exhibitions throughout SA and in London, Barcelona, Spain and Washington, DC; 1958 Port Elizabeth, solo exhibition; she has also held solo exhibitions in Johannesburg and Pretoria.
Represented Hester Rupert Art Museum, Graaff-Reinet; Pretoria Art Museum.

Public Commissions Architectural mural sculptures and fountains in hotels and public buildings in Johannesburg, Pretoria, Port Elizabeth and Durban. 1960 mural, Port Elizabeth Oceanarium; 1973 "Growth Forms", Jan Smuts Airport, Johannesburg; ceramic panel of Pentacosta, Roman Catholic Church, Moll Street, Kroonstad, Orange Free State.
References SAA; 20C SA Art; Register SA & SWA; BSAK 1; SA Art, AASA; LSAA; *Artlook* October 1967, June 1968 & November 1968.

GREIG Desmond Allistair
Born 1926 Cape Town.
A sculptor of figures and abstracts. A series of abstracted variations on the male torso. Works in bronze and wood.
Studies 1948–50 University of Stellenbosch.
Profile A novelist and poet, writing *The Country House* in 1969; *The Angel Upstairs* in 1970, a volume of short stories, and three children's novels in 1985. His poems are included in the *Penguin Book of SA Verse*, 1972. He has published numerous literary magazines and was the founder, publisher and editor of *Artlook* in 1966. In 1985 he won the Sanlam Prize for Youth Literature. 1971–72 visited South America; 1973–85 frequent visits to Spain. Married to Barbara Greig (qv), with whom he established a bronze foundry for casting in the cire perdue method.
Exhibitions He has participated in numerous group exhibitions from 1961 in Johannesburg and in Spain; 1962 Johannesburg, first of 12 solo exhibitions of which three have been in Barcelona, Spain.
Represented Pretoria Art Museum.
References BSAK 1; AASA.

GRELLIER Henry Harley
Born 1879 St Catherine's, Ontario, Canada.
Died 1943 Stellenbosch, Cape Province.
Resided in SA from 1895.
A sculptor of figures. Worked in wood, bronze and stone.
Studies 1902 Slade School of Art, London; 1903 in Rome.
Profile 1881–95 lived in England; 1895–1902 lived in Pietersburg, where he worked as a clerk for the Natal Bank; 1903 in Pretoria. 1904 a commercial artist in Durban; from 1906 a civil servant in Durban and Mapumulu, Natal and a magistrate in Grahamstown and Queenstown. Retired to Cape Town, later moving to Stellenbosch. A set of six comic postcards by him were printed by John Singleton and Son, Durban. Married to Joyce Ordbrown (qv).
Public Commissions c.1905 Dick King Memorial, Durban (unveiled 1915); carvings for Queenstown Cathedral; numerous fanlights, including those for the Land Bank, Cape Town, the United Building Society, Cape Town and the City Hall, Stellenbosch.
References SAA; BSAK 1; SA Art; AASA.

GRIFFITH Richard Edward

Born 1916 Barry, South Glamorgan, Wales.
Resided in SA from 1946.
A self-taught painter of landscapes, figures and genre. Works in gouache. A sculptor.
Profile Until 1984 an illustrator, cartoonist and freelance commercial artist. The Art Director of an advertising company for eight years.
Exhibitions He has participated in several group exhibitions from 1980 in Johannesburg ; 1960 Stuttafords, Johannesburg, solo exhibition.
Reference SASSK.

GROBBELAAR Barend Johannes Christoffel

Born 1938 Johannesburg.
A sculptor of figures, portraits and abstract pieces. Works in bronze, stone, ciment fondu, wood, terracotta and steel.
Studies 1957–59 Heidelberg Teachers Training College, gaining an Art Teachers Diploma; 1963–67 University of South Africa, under Professor Walter Battiss (qv), gaining a BA(FA); 1977–80 University of Pretoria, under Mike Edwards (qv) and Professor Nico Roos (qv), attaining an MA(FA).
Profile A member of the SAAA. 1960–69 a senior assistant art teacher at Josua Naudé Primary School, Roodepoort; 1969 a senior assistant art teacher at Florida High School, Transvaal; 1970 an art lecturer at the Goudstad Teachers Training College, Johannesburg; 1971 a lecturer at the Johannesburg Art, Ballet and Music School; 1972–81 lectured at Potchefstroom University for CHE. Teaches art privately. 1960–66 a set designer and actor for the Roodepoort Amateur Theatrical Organisation. He has travelled throughout Europe.
Exhibitions He has participated in several group exhibitions from 1970 in SA; 1976 Potchefstroom, first of three solo exhibitions; 1980 University of Pretoria, solo exhibition; 1981 Republic Festival Exhibition; 1983 Potchefstroom Museum, solo exhibition.
Award 1979 Metalart Prize, Student Section.
Represented Potchefstroom Museum.
Public Commissions 1979–80 architectonic sculpture, Potchefstroom University for CHE; 1983 two trophies for Landbouskrywers Vereeniging (Agriculture Writers Association), Transvaal; 1985 fountain, Potchefstroom Technical High School.
Reference AASA.

GROBBELAAR Hester Martha (Hettie)

Born 1948 Pretoria.
A painter primarily of flowers, but also of landscapes. Works in watercolour, oil, ink, wash, pastel and mixed media.
Studies 1968–71 Pretoria College of Education, under André de Beer (qv), Frank Gerber and Piet van der Merwe, gaining a Higher Diploma in Education.

Profile From 1983 a member of the WSSA. A teacher of disabled children. 1984–85 wrote the lyrics of an operetta entitled "Koning Lysterbaard", which was performed in Sasolburg, Orange Free State. 1981 visited the Greek islands with a group of SA artists.
Exhibitions She has participated in several group exhibitions in SA; 1974 Schweickerdt Gallery, Pretoria, first of three solo exhibitions.

GROBBELAAR Suzette

Born 1955 Rustenburg, Transvaal.
A painter and graphic artist of landscapes. Works in oil, acrylic and in various graphic media, particularly silkscreens and the intaglio processes.
Studies 1979–82 University of Pretoria, under Professor Nico Roos (qv), gaining a BA(FA).
Profile From 1983 a part-time lecturer at the University of Pretoria.
Exhibitions She has participated in many group exhibitions in SA from 1981; 1981 Republic Festival Exhibition; 1985 Aleta Michaletos Gallery, Pretoria, solo exhibition.
Awards 1983 First Prize for Graphic Art, New Signatures, SAAA; 1983 Emil Schweickerdt Study Bursary; 1984 Second Prize, National Art Festival, University of Zululand.

GROGAN Tony

Born 1940 Port Elizabeth.
A painter and graphic artist of landscapes, genre and portraits. Works in oil, watercolour, ink, wash, pencil and in various graphic media.
Studies 1958–60 Rhodes University, under Professor Cecil Todd (qv); 1963 East London Technical College, under Jack Lugg (qv); 1968–70 Port Elizabeth Technical College, under Alexander Podlashuc (qv); 1970–73 University of South Africa.
Profile 1970–73 a member of the EPSFA; 1963–65 an art teacher at Selbourne High School, East London; 1968–72 an art teacher at the Commercial High School, Port Elizabeth; 1973 at the Belgravia Art Centre, East London. He has illustrated numerous books and articles of a humorous nature. From 1974 he has been the staff cartoonist for *The Cape Times*. 1964–65 lived in East London; 1967–73 in Port Elizabeth, thereafter in Cape Town. Travelled widely in SA and SWA/Namibia.
Exhibitions He has participated in group exhibitions from 1968 in SA; 1970 Port Elizabeth, first of seven solo exhibitions held in SA.
Publications by Grogan The author of eleven books, including *A South African Sketchbook*, 1984, Don Nelson, Cape Town; *Vanishing Cape Town*, 1985, Don Nelson, Cape Town.
Reference SASSK.

GROSSERT John Watt

Born 1913 Tweedie, Natal.

A painter and graphic artist of landscapes, portraits and still life. Works in oil, watercolour, ink, wash, pencil, charcoal and in various graphic media. Carves in wood.

Studies 1930–34 on an Art Teachers Scholarship to the University of Natal, studying under Professor O J P Oxley (qv) and gaining a BA(FA) and a National Art Teachers Certificate; 1938–42 extra-murally at the University of Natal, under Professor O J P Oxley (qv), attaining an MA(FA); 1964–68 extra-murally at the University of Stellenbosch, under Professor Otto Schröder (qv), where awarded a PhD.

Profile From 1935 a member of the NSA and the SAAA; 1952 a member of the Society for Education through Art (British); 1954 a founder member of the International Society for Education through Art. 1935–48 an art teacher with the Durban-Natal Education Department; 1936–47 a part-time lecturer in art at the Natal Technical College (Technikon); 1948 founded the Ndaleni Art Centre, Natal; 1948–53 Organiser of Arts and Crafts in Natal for the African Schools of the Natal Education Department; 1954–62 Pretoria Inspector of Arts and Crafts for African Schools and Colleges; 1963–74 Professor of Fine Art at the University of the Durban-Westville. 1935–84 numerous illuminated manuscripts. 1920–48 lived in Durban; 1949–59 in Pietermaritzburg; 1960–62 in Pretoria; 1963–76 in Westville, Natal; 1976–84 in Cork, Ireland, where he painted a series of 17 paintings of the University College, Cork; from 1984 he has lived in Natal. 1936 made a study tour of Europe; 1958 on a Carnegie Travel Grant, visited Canada, the USA and Europe; 1968 travelled in Europe.

Exhibitions He has participated in numerous group exhibitions from 1936 in SA and the Republic of Ireland; 1978 Walsh-Marais Gallery, Durban, solo exhibition, also held a solo exhibition in Cork.

Represented Durban Art Gallery; Natal Technikon.

Reference AASA.

GROSSET William Leonard

Born 1904 Devon, England.

Resided in SA from 1916.

A painter of landscapes and town scenes. Works in oil.

Studies An apprenticed lithographic artist for five years with Hortors, Johannesburg; evening classes at Woolwich Polytechnic, London; Witwatersrand Technical College, under Sidney Carter (qv), Emily Fern (qv) and Elizabeth Macadam (qv).

Profile A former resident designer at the Alexander Theatre, Johannesburg.

Exhibitions 1964 Pieter Wenning Gallery, Johannesburg, first of over three solo exhibitions.

Represented Africana Museum, Johannesburg; Willem Annandale Art Gallery, Lichtenburg.

References SAA; AMC6; BSAK 1..

GROVES Charles Sidney ARCA

Born 1878 Leicester, England.
Died 1964 Cape Town.
Resided in SA from 1905.
A painter of landscapes and figures. Worked in watercolour, and in stained glass, also produced illuminated manuscripts.
Studies Leicester College of Art; 1900 Royal College of Art, London, on a scholarship.
Profile 1928–29 President of the SA Society of Artists; a member of the Eastern Province Society of Art and Crafts. 1905 assistant master at the Grahamstown School of Art; 1910–24 taught at the Cape Town School of Art; 1926–38 a lecturer at the Michaelis School of Fine Art, Cape Town. Father of Mary E Groves (qv).
Exhibitions Participated in group exhibitions throughout SA and internationally; held solo exhibitions in SA; 1975 included in "Fifty Years of the Michaelis School of Fine Art" exhibition, SA National Gallery, Cape Town.
Awards 1928 Third Prize, Gundelfinger Award, NSA; 1930 First Prize, Gundelfinger Award, NSA.
Public Commission Stained glass window, Smuts Hall, University of Cape Town, assisted by Mary Groves (qv).
Represented Albany Museum, Grahamstown; SA National Gallery, Cape Town; University of Cape Town; 1820 Settlers Memorial Museum, Grahamstown.
References *The Arts in SA*, edited by WHK, 1933–34, The Knox Printing & Publishing Company, Durban; SAA; SAP&S; SAP&D; BSAK 1 & 2; AASA.

GROVES Mary Elsie (Mrs Buchecker)

Born 1913 Cape Town.
An artist, working in stained glass and illuminating manuscripts.
Studies 1931–33 Michaelis School of Fine Art; 1934–36 Central School of Art, London, UK; Kunstgewerbe Schule, Vienna, Austria; jewellery and design at Leicester School of Art, England. Gained a BA(FA) in 1933 and a MA(FA) in 1937.
Profile An art lecturer in the History of Art, Practical Art and Design. 1938–39 an assistant lecturer at the Michaelis School of Fine Art; 1939–79 taught at the Faculty of Education, University of Cape Town. Daughter of Charles Groves (qv).
Public Commissions Assisted Charles Groves (qv) with the stained glass windows, Smuts Hall, University of Cape Town. Executed lights for churches in Knysna, Mowbray and Durbanville, all in the Cape Province.
Represented SA National Gallery, Cape Town.

GUEDES Amancio d'Alpoim (Pancho) Professor

Born 1925 Lisbon, Portugal.
A painter, sculptor and graphic artist.
Studies Studied architecture at the University of the Witwatersrand.
Profile Practised as an architect in Mozambique for 25 years. 1975 became Professor of Architecture at the University of the Witwatersrand.

Exhibitions He has exhibited in SA, São Paulo, Venice and in the USA.
Award *c.*1978 Comendador of the Ordem de Santiago da Espada (conferred by the President of Portugal).
References BSAK 1; *Habitat* no 36, 1979.

GUHRS Pamela Anne

Born 1946 Zomba, Nyasaland (Malawi).
A painter of figures and wildlife. Works in oil, watercolour, gouache, ink, wash, pencil and charcoal.
Studies University of the Witwatersrand, under Cecily Sash (qv), Judith Mason (qv), Giuseppe Cattaneo (qv) and Robert Hodgins (qv), gaining a BA(FA).
Profile Taught at Yeoville Convent, and in 1971–72 at the Johannesburg Art, Ballet and Music School; 1985 lectured at the Centre for Continuing Education, University of the Witwatersrand. 1977–84 and from 1986 she has lived in the Luangwa Valley, Zambia. Married to Vic Guhrs (qv).
Exhibitions She has participated in several group exhibitions in SA; 1986 Crake Gallery, Johannesburg, first of two solo exhibitions.

GUHRS Vic

Born 1943 Germany.
Resided in SA from 1965.
A painter and graphic artist of wildlife. Works in oil, pencil, charcoal and in various graphic media.
Studies 1968–70 The Visual Arts Research Centre, Johannesburg, under George Boys (qv).
Profile A member of the Society of Animal Artists, New York. A number of cover illustrations for magazines and pamphlets. 1977–84 and from 1986 he has lived in the Luangwa Valley, Zambia. Married to Pam Guhrs (qv).
Exhibitions He has participated in numerous group exhibitions from 1974 in SA and the USA; 1974 Gallery 101, Johannesburg, first of two solo exhibitions held in Johannesburg.
Award 1983 Gold Medal for Artist of the Year, Game Conservation International Exhibition, San Antonio, Texas, USA.
Represented New York Zoological Society, USA; Pietersburg Collection.
Public Commission 1980 a painting of a Black Rhinoceros was commissioned by the Zambian Government and given to HRH The Duke of Edinburgh.
Reference AASA.

GUISE William Vernon Lieutenant

Resided in SA 1835–39.
A painter of landscapes and animals of the Eastern Cape. Worked in watercolour, pencil and wash.

Profile A soldier on the Eastern Frontier. Hunted with Captain H Butler (qv).
Represented William Fehr Collection, Cape Town.
References Pict Art; Pict Afr.

GULSTON Geraldine

Born 1921 Benoni, Transvaal.
A painter of landscapes, seascapes, portraits, still life and abstract pictures.
Works in oil, acrylic, watercolour, gouache, ink and wash. 1980–84 a series of
large watercolour paintings of flowers; 1986–87 large paintings of scenery.
Studies 1941 teachers training and painting courses at the Natal Technical
College; 1948–51 part-time on an arts and crafts course at the Natal Technical
College.
Profile From 1969 a member, and from 1980 Secretary, of the Kloof Art Circle,
Natal. 1970 a member of the Highway Art Group; *c.*1980 a member of the
WSSA. 1984 taught art privately. A potter and a weaver. She has lived
throughout SA and in SWA/Namibia. 1951 visited England; 1974 Israel; 1981
Canada.
Exhibitions She has participated in numerous group exhibitions with the
Highway Art Group.

GUMEDE Samuel Zamokwakhe

Born 1955 Bergville, Natal.
A sculptor of figures. Works in wood and ciment fondu. A large series of small
wood carvings.
Studies Carpentry at Mariannhill Monastery, under Father Florian Langman;
at the Community Arts Workshop, Durban, under Gerrit Swart (qv).
Exhibitions He has participated in group exhibitions from 1985 at the Community Arts Workshop, Durban and at the African Arts Centre in Durban.

GUNDERSEN Alfred

Born 1926 Johannesburg.
A painter of landscapes and seascapes. Works in watercolour.
Studies 1942–45 Natal Technical College, under George Howe.
Profile Illustrated *Some South African Monuments*, edited by D Hatfield, 1967,
Purnell & Sons, Cape Town. Until 1982 worked in advertising, thereafter a
full-time artist.
Exhibitions He has participated in numerous group exhibitions in Johannesburg; 1962 Gainsborough Gallery, Johannesburg, first of two solo exhibitions.

ROBERT GWELO GOODMAN
Farm Homestead, Franschhoek Valley
Oil on Canvas 150 × 184 cm
The Tongaat–Hulett Group

HILLARY GRAHAM
Bridal Dance 1985
Oil on Canvas 150 × 156 cm
The Everard Read Gallery

GUNTER Elizabeth

Born 1957 Heidelberg, Cape Province.

A painter of figures and portraits. Works in oil, pencil and charcoal.

Studies 1975–78, 1980–81 and 1982–85 University of Stellenbosch, under Victor Honey, Louis Jansen van Vuuren (qv) and Paul Emsley (qv), where attained a BA(FA) in 1978, BA(FA)(Hons) in 1980 and an MA(FA) in 1985. 1981–82 awarded a Maggie Laubser Bursary.

Profile A member of the SAAA. 1979 taught at the Tygerberg Art Centre, Cape Town; lectured at the Hewatt Training College in Athlone, Cape Town.

Exhibitions She has participated in several group exhibitions from 1982 in the Cape; 1985 Dorp Street Museum, Stellenbosch, first of two solo exhibitions.

GYNGELL Albert Edmund

Born 1866 Wordsley, Worcestershire, England.

Died 1949 Johannesburg.

Resided in SA from 1893.

A painter of landscapes in oil. Drew portraits in charcoal.

Studies c.1890 Royal Academy Schools, London; under Sir Hubert Herkomer (1849–1914) at the Bushey School of Art, Hertfordshire, England.

Profile 1899–1902 a mine storekeeper and stationmaster at Okiep, Namaqualand. 1910 lectured at the Teachers Training College, Johannesburg; 1911–28 first Curator of the Johannesburg Art Gallery and a teacher at the Normal College, Johannesburg; a part-time art teacher at Roedean School, Johannesburg. 1924–49 a member of the Consultative Committee on Fine Arts, Johannesburg Public Library. Wrote reviews for the *SA Architectural Record*.

Exhibitions Participated in group exhibitions from 1890 in London and throughout SA; 1928 Lezards Johannesburg, first solo exhibition.

Represented Africana Museum, Johannesburg; Johannesburg Art Gallery; William Humphreys Art Gallery, Kimberley.

Public Commissions Portraits of Mayors of Johannesburg in the City Hall; portraits of General Louis Botha and Mrs Annie Botha.

References SAA; AMC3 & 6; DSAB; Pict Afr; DBA; BSAK 1 & 2; AASA.

H

HABER Robert

Born 1929 Los Angeles, California, USA.
Resided in SA from 1940.
A painter of landscapes, still life and seascapes. Works in watercolour.
Studies 1948–52 University of the Witwatersrand, under Professor Heather Martienssen (1915–79), Erica Berry (qv) and Majorie Long (qv), gaining a BA(FA).
Profile 1955–57 lived in Europe. He has lived periodically in the USA and has travelled throughout the world.
Exhibitions He has participated in several group exhibitions from 1961 in SA; 1961 Johannesburg, solo exhibition.

HADEN Leonora Everard

Born 1937 Benoni, Transvaal.
A painter of landscapes, still life and seascapes. Works in oil, watercolour and pastel. 1983–85 a large series of interiors and landscapes.
Studies 1955–60 University of Natal, under Professor John Heath (qv), gaining BA(FA)(Hons).
Profile 1963 taught art at St Andrew's School, Johannesburg. She has lived in the Eastern Transvaal and Natal. Daughter of Ruth Everard Haden (qv), niece of Rosamund Everard-Steenkamp (qv) and grand-daughter of Bertha Everard (qv).
Exhibitions She has participated in many group exhibitions from 1960 in SA; 1960 Quadrennial Exhibition; 1976 SAAA Gallery, Pretoria, first of four solo exhibitions.
Represented Pretoria Art Museum; Tatham Art Gallery, Pietermaritzburg; University of Natal.
References Art SA; SAA; BSAK 1.

HAGER Carl Otto

Born 1813 Dresden, Germany.
Died 1898 Stellenbosch, Cape Province.
Resided in SA from 1838.
A painter of portraits. Worked in oil.
Studies 1828–30 Royal Academy of Arts, Dresden.
Profile An architect who in 1840 designed St Mary's Cathedral, Cape Town. From 1841 lived in Stellenbosch, painting portraits and murals for its neighbouring communities. During the 1860s helped design the neo-Gothic church in Clanwilliam, and was wholly responsible for the church in Fraserburg and the

Theological Training School in Stellenbosch. In 1863 he was commissioned to extend and rebuild the Stellenbosch Lutheran Church in Dorp Street. During the 1870s he designed churches in Heidelberg, Caledon and Oudtshoorn, Ceres, Tulbagh, Calitzdorp and Ladismith, Cape Province. In the 1880s he designed the old Main Building of the University of Stellenbosch; 1845–46 visited Germany. 1858 owned and ran a photographic studio in Cape Town, which in 1864 he moved to Stellenbosch.

References *Autobiography of Carl Otto Hager, Architect and Artist*, translated by Elizabeth J Hager, 1960, Johannesburg; DSAB; Pict Afr; 3Cs.

HAGG Gerard

Born 1950 Ryswyk, The Netherlands.
Resided in SA from 1967.
A sculptor of process art, derived from SA traditional technical constructions. Works in stone, wood, forged iron, rope and rubber belts. Several series: 1980–84 "Procrustes' Bed"; 1981–83 "Archaeological Shelters"; 1982 "Levers"; 1982–83 "Archaeological Weapons"; 1984–85 "Ox Wagon"; 1984–85 "Weaving Loom".

Studies 1969–72 through the University of Pretoria, under Eugene Bouffa (qv), where gained a BA(FA); 1979 University of South Africa, under Professor Karin Skawran, gaining a BA(FA) with Honours in History of Art; 1981–84 University of South Africa, under Leon du Plessis (qv) and Alan Crump, where awarded an MA(FA).

Profile From 1982 a member of the SAAA, 1983 Secretary of the Orange Free State Art Association. 1973–79 a sculpture lecturer at the University of South Africa; 1980–86 a senior lecturer and Head of the Department of Fine Art, University of the Orange Free State. 1987 moved to Pretoria.

Exhibitions He has participated in several group exhibitions from 1975 in SA; 1985 Studio Gallery, University of the Witwatersrand, joint exhibition; 1985 Cape Town Triennial.

Award 1975 Logan's University Bookshop Award, Art SA Today.

Represented University of the Witwatersrand.

References AASA; LSAA.

HAHN Siegfried

Born Randfontein, Transvaal.
A painter of landscapes. Works in oil.
Studies Began architectural studies at the University of the Witwatersrand; 1934–35 Michaelis School of Fine Art; from 1935 Royal Academy Schools, London, on a bursary, 1937 awarded the Turner Gold Medal and a scholarship.

Profile A member of the New Group. 1942–43 an art lecturer at Stellenbosch Technical College. Has lived in Europe and the USA. In 1973 he became a US citizen.

Exhibitions He participated in group exhibitions in SA during the 1930s and the 1940s; 1942 first solo exhibition in SA; 1945 Schweickerdt Gallery, Pretoria, solo exhibition.

Represented Johannesburg Art Gallery; SA National Museum of Military History, Johannesburg.
Reference AASA.

HAHNDIEK Herman Johannes

Born 1907 Utrecht, The Netherlands.
Resided in SA from 1948.
A painter of iconographics. Works in oil.
Studies Private tuition in arts, applied arts and photography.
Profile A member of the SAAA. Lectured part-time at the Pretoria Technical College and at the Ruth Prowse Art Centre, Cape Town. 1950 ran the Vincent Gallery, Pretoria; 1953 a partner of the Constance Stuart Studio with Richard Cutler (qv) and Dotman Pretorius; 1956 set up his own photograph studio in Pretoria; 1962 ran the Henri Lidchi Gallery in Cape Town; 1965 started the Strand Galleries, with Eljra Solomon; 1966 manager of a Persian carpet firm; 1979 became a full-time painter. Contributed a number of articles to overseas magazines. 1960 wrote *Beeldhouwers in Beeld*, a pocket book on post-war Dutch sculptors. 1958–61 lived in The Netherlands.
Exhibitions He has participated in several group exhibitions in SA and SWA/Namibia; 1964 Military Academy, Saldanha, Cape Province, first of 14 solo exhibitions held in SA.
Reference BSAK 1.

HALDEMAN Winnifred Josephine

Born 1914 Moose Jaw, Saskatchewan, Canada.
Resided in SA from 1950.
A painter of landscapes, still life, seascapes and abstract pictures. Works in oil, watercolour, gouache, ink wash, pencil, charcoal and wood. An etcher.
Studies Privately with Elizabeth Kruger (qv) at Club 997, Pretoria; etching under Mimi van der Merwe (qv); woodcarving under L Watson.
Profile A member of Club 997 and the WSSA. Involved in acting and dancing; a founder of the Regina Ballet Company. Lived in Regina, Saskatchewan, Canada until 1950.
Exhibitions She has participated in many group exhibitions in SA from 1981.

HALL Gina

Born 1956 Cape Town.
A painter of SWA/Namibian and Namaqualand landscapes and of flowers. Works in oil, acrylic, watercolour, gouache, ink and wash.
Studies 1976 private studies in Ventimiglia, Italy, under Constanza de Roacio; 1977 studied under the restorer Philip Pound in London; 1978 under Tom Keating (1917–84) in London; 1979–84 in the studio of Gordon Vorster (qv).

Profile A member of the SAAA. Has travelled extensively in Southern Africa. Married to Gordon Vorster (qv).
Exhibitions She has participated in numerous group exhibitions in SWA/ Namibia, SA, Austria, West Germany and the USA; 1985 Hoffer Gallery, Pretoria, first of two solo exhibitions, the second being held in the USA.

HALL James Oliver

Born 1916 New Zealand.
A sculptor and a potter.
Studies 1938–39 Dunedin School of Art, New Zealand; 1946–49 Slade School of Art, London, under F E McWilliam (*b*.1909), gaining a Diploma in Fine Art in 1949; Camberwell School of Art, London, under Jacob Drew and R Kendall.
Profile Taught sculpture at the Natal Technical College.
Exhibitions He has participated in group exhibitions in Durban and in London.
Award 1960 a finalist in the African Life Sculpture Competition.
Represented Hanley Art Gallery, Stoke-on-Trent, England.
Public Commissions 1959 ceramics, Holy Trinity Church, Durban; 1959 ceramics, University of Natal; 1961 ceramics, Ocean Terminal, Durban; 1962 fibreglass sculpture, Ocean Terminal, Durban.
References SAA; SESA; AASA.

HALL John Colin

Born 1920 Harrow-on-the-Hill, Middlesex, England.
Resided in SA from 1948.
A painter of landscapes, genre and of architectural subject matter, especially of antiquity. Works in watercolour, ink and wash. From 1984 he has painted miniature watercolours.
Studies 1937–38 Regent Street Polytechnic, London, under Harold Brownsword (*b*.1885).
Profile 1975–76 "The Cries of Cape Town", sets I, II and III, published by Howard Swan, Johannesburg; "Fruit of the Vine", a portfolio of four water-colours; "Homes of Heritage", a series of pen and ink sketches published by Hall. From 1969 has had several articles published in *The Cape Times*. 1920–41 lived in Harrow, UK; 1941–46 served in India, with the Third Gurkha Regiment; 1946–48 in the UK; thereafter in the Cape.
Exhibitions 1975 Cottage Gallery, Claremont, Cape Town, joint exhibition with John Anderson (qv); 1972 Edrich Gallery, Stellenbosch, first of four solo exhibitions.
Represented Africana Museum, Johannesburg.

HALL Laurence Scott

Born 1938 Limerick, Republic of Ireland.
Resided in SA from 1963.
A painter of landscapes, seascapes, portraits, figures and still life. Works in oil and watercolour.

Studies 1955–57 Croydon College of Art, England, under David Owen, Fred Austin and Dennis Bailey.
Profile A graphic designer. 1963–66 lived in Cape Town, thereafter in Johannesburg.
Exhibition 1986 Crake Gallery, Johannesburg, solo exhibition.

HALLIER Michael Glen Thomas Professor

Born 1942 Pretoria.
A painter of landscapes. Works in oil. A graphic artist.
Studies 1962–65 University of the Witwatersrand, under Professor Heather Martienssen (1915–79), Giuseppe Cattaneo (qv) and Cecily Sash (qv), gaining a BA(FA); 1971 Rhodes University, under Professor Brian Bradshaw (qv), attaining an MFA.
Profile 1971–73 a member of the Grahamstown Group; 1972–77 a lecturer, 1978–79 a senior lecturer and from 1980 Professor at the University of Fort Hare. Visited Greece in 1978, 1982 and 1985.
Exhibitions 1965 Johannesburg College of Education, joint exhibition; he has participated in numerous group exhibitions from 1966 in SA, West Germany, the USA, Switzerland and the UK; 1971–72 Albany Museum, Grahamstown, solo exhibition; 1974 University of Fort Hare, solo exhibition.
References BSAK 2; AASA.

HALSTED Fee Elizabeth

Born 1958 Bulawayo, Rhodesia (Zimbabwe).
A painter of landscapes, figures, wildlife and abstract pictures. Works in oil, acrylic and watercolour. A ceramicist.
Studies 1977 and 1979–83 University of Natal, under Michael Taylor, Juliet Armstrong (qv) and David Middlebrook, gaining a BA(FA) and an Advanced Diploma in Ceramics.
Profile From 1982 a member of the APSA and from 1984 of the NSA. 1984–85 a ceramics teacher at the Natal Technikon. Lived in Rhodesia (Zimbabwe) until 1976; 1976–77 in Ireland, thereafter lived in SA. Has visited Greece and Turkey.
Exhibitions She has participated in numerous group exhibitions from 1980 in SA; 1984 Café Geneve Gallery, Durban, first of two solo exhibitions; 1985 Cape Town Triennial.
Award 1987 winner of the Corona Del Mar Young Artists Award.
Represented Durban Art Gallery; SA National Gallery, Cape Town; Tatham Art Gallery, Pietermaritzburg; University of Natal; University of South Africa.
Reference Sgraffiti no 40.

HAMMAR August

Born 1856 Lund, Sweden.
Died 1931 Pietermaritzburg.
Resided in SA from 1879.
A painter of landscapes. Worked in watercolour and oil.

Profile Trained as a civil engineer in Sweden in 1877. 1879 lived at the Swedish Mission at Rorke's Drift in Natal, where he sketched incidents of the Zulu War (engravings based on two of these sketches appeared in *The Graphic*, London) and joined Baker's Horse as a trooper. 1881 a land surveyor; 1884–85 travelled with Dr Aurel Schulz to Victoria Falls, Rhodesia (Zimbabwe), via Pretoria and Rustenburg; 1889 in Pietermaritzburg; 1890–1915 Government Surveyor to the Colony of Natal, travelling to the Zululand/Transvaal border in 1893 and the Natal and Zululand coasts in 1910. The area of Hammarsdale was named after him.

Exhibitions Thought to have exhibited in Pietermaritzburg under the name "Mr Dauber"; 1985 Tatham Art Gallery, Pietermaritzburg and Durban Art Gallery, Retrospective Exhibition.

Publication by Hammar Jointly with Aurel Schulz, *The New Africa*, 1897.

References Register SA & SWA; *SA Survey* 11 (5), 1968; *August Hammar*, catalogue, 1985, Tatham Art Gallery, Pietermaritzburg.

HARBER Karen

Born 1956.

An artist known to work in clay, paper, ink and watercolour.

Studies 1975–78 University of the Witwatersrand, gaining a BA(FA); 1986 registered for an MA(FA) at the University of South Africa.

Profile 1984–85 taught art at Grantley Private School, Johannesburg; 1987–88 part-time involvement with the Ekimeling School in Soweto.

Exhibitions She has participated in several group exhibitions from 1978 in Johannesburg.

HARINGTON Elizabeth (née Willot-West)

Born 1935 Pretoria.

A painter and graphic artist of nudes and anatomical works, often uses the theme of crucifixion.

Studies 1963 gained a BA(FA) from the University of the Witwatersrand; 1977–79 studied etching at the Art Students League, New York, under Roberto Delamonica; *c.*1977 at the University of North Carolina, USA.

Profile 1964–66 studied music. Has lived in New York from 1985, but has continued to exhibit in SA.

Exhibitions She has participated in group exhibitions in SA, New York and West Germany; 1981 Gowlett Gallery, Cape Town, first of 10 solo exhibitions held in SA; 1984 SAAA Gallery, Pretoria, joint exhibition with Laraine Campbell (qv), Cecily Grant (qv) and Pamela Kleinot; 1987 Johannesburg Art Gallery, Vita Art Now.

Awards 1956 Henri Lidchi Drawing Prize; 1964 Herbert Evans Painting Prize for the best student of the year, University of the Witwatersrand; 1979 Graphic Award for best student, Art Students League, New York; 1980 Bellville Grafik '80; 1986 Nessa Cohen Memorial Fund Award.

Represented Art Students League, New York, USA; Pretoria Art Museum.

Reference *Gallery* Spring 1982.

HARLING Frank

Born 1910 Lancaster, Lancashire, England.
Resided in SA from 1939.
A self-taught painter of trans-realist paintings. Works in oil, watercolour, gouache, pastel, ink, pencil and charcoal.

Exhibitions 1948 Tate Gallery, London, SA Art Exhibition; participated in a group exhibition in Johannesburg in 1961; 1985 Gallery 21, Johannesburg, solo exhibition.

Represented Beaufort West Museum; Willem Annandale Art Gallery, Lichtenburg.

References BSAK 1; AASA.

HARRIES Katrine

Born 1914 Berlin, Germany.
Died 1978 Cape Town.
Resided in SA from 1939.
An artist best known for her graphic work. Until 1944 a painter of portraits. Worked in oil.

Studies 1931–33 Studien Ateliers für Malerei und Plastik, Berlin-Charlottenburg, under Robert Erdmann (*b*.1872); 1933–38 Vereinigte Staatsschulen für Freie und Angewandte Kunst, Berlin, under Ferdinand Spiegel (1879–1950).

Profile In 1950 became a part-time lecturer, 1960 a full-time lecturer and in 1970 a senior lecturer at the Michaelis School of Fine Art, Cape Town. She began the Graphic Department there. Her first illustrations in SA were in *Trek*, 7 December 1938 and 18 January 1940. In 1948 she began her illustrations for *Die Huisgenoot*, and in 1949–59 produced numerous illustrations for *Sarie Marais*. She has also illustrated a large number of books in SA, including *Die Avontuur van Pinokkio*, by Carlo Collodi, authorised translation by Marie Malherbe, 1940, Nasionale Pers, Cape Town, reprinted 1962; *Raka*, by N P van Wyk Louw, 1966, limited edition, Nasionale Pers, Cape Town; *Die Mooiste Afrikaanse Sprokies*, by P W Grobbelaar, 1968, Human & Rousseau, Cape Town. In 1949 she visited France; 1954–55 and 1960–61 visited West Germany. In 1977 the SA Library Association Illustrations Award was named after her.

Exhibitions Participated in group exhibitions from 1940 in SA and in Yugoslavia, Rhodesia (Zimbabwe), Italy, Brazil, The Netherlands and the USA; 1948 first of three solo exhibitions; 1956 and 1960 Quadrennial Exhibitions; 1978–79 SA National Gallery, Cape Town, Pretoria Art Museum, Johannesburg Art Gallery, Durban Art Gallery, Retrospective Exhibition.

Awards 1952 lithography prize at the Van Riebeeck Tercentenary Exhibition; 1956 won a prize for her design of the catalogue cover for the First Quadrennial Exhibition; 1964, 1969, 1974 and 1977 SA Library Association "Hoogenhout Award" for best illustrated children's book; 1973 Medal of Honour for Graphic Art, SA Akademie vir Wetenskap en Kuns.

Public Commission 1951 a United Nations Organisation stamp commemorating Human Rights Day.

Represented Ann Bryant Gallery, East London; Durban Art Gallery; Hester Rupert Art Museum, Graaff-Reinet; Johannesburg Art Gallery; Pretoria Art Museum; Sandton Municipal Collection; SA National Gallery, Cape Town; University of South Africa; William Humphreys Art Gallery, Kimberley.
References J du P Scholtz, *Katrine Harries*, 1978, Tafelberg, Cape Town; Art SA; SAA; 20C SA Art; SAP&D; BSAK 1 & 2; Our Art 3; 3Cs; AASA; LSAA; *SA Libraries*, vol 46, July 1978; *De Arte* April 1979; *K Harries*, catalogue, 1979, Johannesburg Art Gallery.

HARRIS William Cornwallis Sir

Born 1807 Wittersham, Kent, England.
Died 1848 Surwur, near Poona, India.
Resided in SA 1836–37.
A painter of animals, figures and portraits, especially tribal chiefs. Worked in watercolour.
Profile 1823 entered the East India Company's Bombay Engineers, becoming a Captain in 1834 and a Major in 1843. Sent to SA on sick leave, he hunted and explored the country, travelling from Port Elizabeth through Kuruman to the far northern Transvaal and returning to Cape Town. Discovered the Sable, previously known as Harrisbuck. Harris was knighted in 1844 after a mission to Abyssinia, Ethiopia in 1841–43. A number of lithographic prints of his work were produced: "Portraits of the Game and Wild Animals of Southern Africa", 1840–41, a columbia folio containing 30 lithographic prints in five parts published by W Pickering, London, later reissued in book form (see below); "Illustrations of the Highlands of Aethiopia" 1844, a large quarto of lithographs, published by Dickinson & Son, London.
Represented Africana Museum, Johannesburg; William Fehr Collection, Cape Town.
Publications by Harris *Narrative of an Expedition into Southern Africa*, 1838, American Mission Press, Bombay, containing four lithographic plates and a map, a second edition published by John Murray, London, 1839, under the title *The Wild Sports of Southern Africa*, and numerous later facsimiles, the most recent being in 1987 by C Struik, reproduced from the 1967 edition; *Portraits of the Game and Wild Animals of Southern Africa*, 1844, Pelham Richardson, London, and numerous later facsimiles, the most recent being in 1986 by Galago Publishing, Alberton; *The Highlands of Aethiopia*, 1844, Longmans, London, 3 volumes.
References Pict Art; Afr Repos; A Gordon Brown, *Christopher Webb Smith*, 1965, Howard Timmins, Cape Town; AMC3; SESA; Pict Afr; BSAK 1 & 2; Enc S'n A; SA Art; *Lantern* September 1962.

HARRISON Mildred Rhodes

Born 1888 London, England.
A sculptor of figures. Worked in ceramics.
Studies Painting and sculpture at the London County Council School.
Exhibitions Participated in group exhibitions in SA; she held several solo exhibitions in various centres in SA.

HARRS Hannes

Born 1927 Eckernförde, Germany.
Resided in SA from 1950.
An artist working mainly in woodcuts and occasionally in oil of figurative and abstract expressionistic pictures. Sculpts in wood.
Studies 1943–44 under Carl Lambertz; 1957–60 awarded a study bursary to the Witwatersrand Technical College, where gained a Diploma in Commercial Art with Honours.
Profile A member of the SAAA. 1970 produced an edition of 12 woodcuts, published by Egon Guenther; 1976 produced an edition of 12 woodcuts, published by Gerd Mathies.
Exhibitions He has participated in numerous group exhibitions from 1961 in SA, South America, West Germany, Austria, Spain, Australia, Israel, Yugoslavia and Monaco; 1961 Egon Guenther Gallery, Johannesburg, first of many solo exhibitions held in SA, SWA/Namibia and West Germany; 1981 Republic Festival Exhibition.
Represented Johannesburg Art Gallery; National Museum, Bloemfontein; Pretoria Art Museum; Rand Afrikaans University; University of the Witwatersrand; William Humphreys Art Gallery, Kimberley.
Public Commissions 1971 sculpture, Jan Smuts Airport, Johannesburg; numerous works commissioned from 1970 for hotels in Johannesburg, Durban, Plettenberg Bay, Maseru and Thaba 'Nchu.
References BSAK 1 & 2; 3Cs; AASA; LSAA; *Artlook* February 1967 & June 1971.

HART Deirdre

Born 1946 Johannesburg.
A painter and graphic artist of surrealistic still life set in fantasy African landscapes. Works in watercolour, pencil and in various graphic media.
Studies 1964–65 Johannesburg School of Art; 1965–66 Natal Technical College, gaining a Diploma in Commercial/Graphic Art; 1981 and 1983 privately under Andrew Verster (qv) and Diana Kenton (qv).
Profile A member of the NSA. From 1983 has taught art privately to children. 1972 and 1980–82 drew illustrations for sets of school readers published by Juta & Company, Cape Town.
Exhibitions She has participated in several group exhibitions from 1975 in SA; 1984 Grassroots Gallery, Westville, Natal, solo exhibition.

HART William (Bill)

Born 1928 Heidelburg, Transvaal.
Both a painter and a sculptor working in many different media with a wide-ranging subject matter. His style is one of abstract expressionism with use of mystic symbolism. 1979–80 a series of "Mythical Villages".
Studies Witwatersrand Technical College, under James Gardner (qv) and Douglas Portway (qv); 1949 l'Ecole des Beaux Arts, Paris; 1950–51 St Martin's School of Art, London, under Anthony Caro (*b*.1924).

Profile A member of the Pentwith Society, St Ives, England. 1955–65 an art director in the Killarney Film Studio. During the 1960s taught at the Jubilee Centre, Johannesburg, 1969 founded the Mofolo Park Art Centre in Soweto. 1968–70 a cultural officer in the Johannesburg Non-European Affairs Department. From 1949 has lived in London, St Ives (Cornwall), Paris, Toronto and SA. He has travelled throughout Europe, Canada and the USA.

Exhibitions 1966 Goodman Gallery, Johannesburg, first of 21 solo exhibitions held in SA, the UK and Canada; he has participated in numerous group exhibitions from 1968 in SA, Australia, the UK, The Netherlands, West Germany, Canada, the USA and Israel.

Represented William Humphreys Art Gallery, Kimberley.

Public Commissions Three large panels, Jan Smuts Airport, Johannesburg; relief mural in the Natal Provincial Administration building "Natalia", Pietermaritzburg; three hundred panels, Sun City, Bophuthatswana, as well as numerous large murals for corporate buildings in SA and Canada.

References BSAK 1; AASA; *Artlook* March 1967, May 1968, August 1969, August 1972 & February 1974.

HARVEY Russell

Born 1904 Klerksdorp, Transvaal.

Died 1963 Cape Town.

A painter of portraits and figures. Worked mainly in oil, also created large murals for company exhibition stands. A graphic artist.

Studies A correspondence course in commercial art with John Hassall (*b.*1868), a London poster artist; 1925 evening classes, Cape Town School of Art; 1925–26 Michaelis School of Fine Art, sculpture under Herbert Meyerowitz (qv); 1925–26 a six-month study tour of Europe.

Profile Until 1930 a freelance commercial artist; 1930–32 on the art staff of *The Cape Times*; 1932–44 a designer and later a director of J Walter Thompson Advertising; 1944–51 a freelance designer, painter and sculptor; 1951–63 a lecturer in graphic design at the Michaelis School of Fine Art. 1914–18 lived in SWA/Namibia.

Exhibitions Participated in group exhibitions from 1938; 1938 Cape Town, joint exhibition with Lippy Lipshitz (qv); 1944 Cape Town, solo exhibition; 1964 SA National Gallery, Cape Town, Memorial Exhibition.

Represented SA National Gallery, Cape Town.

References Art SA; SAA; 20C SA Art; DSAB; SAP&S; SAP&D; BSAK 1 & 2; AASA.

HASKIN Ronald John

Born 1932 Cape Town.

A painter of landscapes, seascapes, portraits and wildlife. Works in oil, acrylic, watercolour, pencil and charcoal. 1962–63 a series entitled "Paintings in France"; 1984 a series entitled "Paintings in Israel".

Studies 1956 The Contemporary School of Art, Cape Town, under Erik Laubscher (qv).

Profile 1956–58 & 1969–72 a member of the SAAA, 1957–58 a committee member of the Western Province Branch; 1959–63 a member of the Eastern Province Arts and Crafts Society; 1975–76 a member of the Artists Gallery, Cape Town. 1961–62 visited France; 1965, 1968, 1970–71, 1976 and 1982 visited Israel.

Exhibitions He has participated in many group exhibitions from 1959 in SA; 1960 Arts Hall, Port Elizabeth, first of four solo exhibitions.

Reference BSAK 1.

HASSAN Kay

Born 1956 Alexandra, Johannesburg.

A sculptor, painter and graphic artist of figures, portraits, and abstract pieces. Works in wood, oil, acrylic, ink, pencil, charcoal and in various graphic media.

Studies 1978–80 Rorke's Drift Art Centre, Natal, gaining a Diploma in Fine Art.

Profile 1977 a member of the Creative Youth Association, Diepkloof, Soweto; 1981 a founder member of Artimo. 1984–86 a part-time teacher at the Alliance Française, Diepkloof, Soweto. He has visited London and Scotland.

Exhibitions He has participated in several group exhibitions from 1980 in SA, the UK, West Germany and Denmark; 1984 Market Gallery, Johannesburg, solo exhibition.

HATHORN Molly Maitland (Mrs Bloom)

Born 1918 Johannesburg.

A painter of genre and figures. Works in oil, gouache, pencil and charcoal.

Studies Three years at the Academy of Fine Arts, Munich, under Max Dörner (1870–1939); two years at the Berlin Academy of Fine Art, under Professor Arple; the Bauhaus, Dessau, under Professor Paul Scheurich (1883–1945).

Exhibitions She has participated in group exhibitions in SA, and in Berlin, Amsterdam and London. She has held solo exhibitions in Durban and Johannesburg.

Reference SAA.

HAUSER Nicholas Peter

Born 1958 Blackpool, Lancashire, England.

Resided in SA from 1970.

A painter of figures, landscapes and Biblically based themes. Works in oil, acrylic, ink, pencil and charcoal. 1979–82 a series on "Nebuchadnezzar II"; 1981 a ceramic series of "Clay Tablets"; 1981–85 a series of drawings and paintings of "Black on Black", using black paper. Creates ceramic sculptures and designs for earthenware.

Studies 1977–78 Port Elizabeth Technical College, under Hylton Nel (qv), Hillary Graham (qv) and Neil Rodger (qv); 1981–82 Orange Free State Technikon, gaining a Higher Diploma in Fine Art, majoring in painting.

Profile 1985 a member of The Slaughterhouse, a group consisting of a photographer, a ceramic artist and Hauser. 1981 lectured in drawing at the Orange Free State Technikon; 1983 lectured at the Johannesburg Art Foundation; 1983–84 a lecturer in drawing for ceramic students at the University of the Witwatersrand. From 1984 he has worked in the music industry, as a singer with the group "Mango Groove" and later with "Khaki Monitor". From 1981 a writer of poetry and prose for various magazines in SA including *Art Director Magazine.*
Exhibitions He has participated in several group exhibitions from 1978 in SA; 1978 EPSFA Gallery, Port Elizabeth, first of three solo exhibitions.

HAW Christopher Bruce

Born 1941 Howick, Natal.
A painter of landscapes, portraits, seascapes and figures. Works in oil, watercolour, gouache and charcoal.
Studies 1956–59 Natal Technical College, under George Howe.
Profile From 1975 a member of the NSA, the WSSA, the Highway Art Group and the North Coast Art Group. An Associate of the WSSA. From 1975 an art tutor in Westville, Natal. A number of illustrations for the magazine *Scope.*
Exhibitions He has participated in numerous group exhibitions from 1968 in SA; 1970 Durban, first of over 70 solo exhibitions.
Award 1975 Ernest Oppenheimer Memorial Trust Award, SA Art Today.
Represented Durban Art Gallery; Queenstown Gallery; Willem Annandale Art Gallery, Lichtenburg.

HAY Jean

Born 1929 Northern Transvaal.
A painter of landscapes, seascapes, wildlife and floral subjects. Works in oil.
Studies 1949–52 International Correspondence School, London, under G T Gillespy FRSA and Dr Brooks, gaining a Diploma in Commercial Illustrating.
Profile 1956 a member of the Bulawayo Art Club, Rhodesia (Zimbabwe). From 1974 numerous designs for calendars and Christmas cards in SA and Rhodesia (Zimbabwe). 1931–79 lived in Rhodesia (Zimbabwe). 1983 travelled to Europe.
Exhibitions She has participated in several group exhibitions from 1970 in Rhodesia (Zimbabwe) and SA; 1974 Hadden & Sly Gallery, Bulawayo, Rhodesia (Zimbabwe), first of eight solo exhibitions held in Rhodesia (Zimbabwe) and SA.

HAYSOM Shayne Rosalind

Born 1950 Cape Town.
A sculptor of animals. Works in bronze and wood.
Studies 1968–70 University of Natal, under Professor Jack Heath (qv) and Jane Heath (qv); 1979–80 C W Post College, Long Island, New York.

Profile From 1981 a member of the Society of Animal Artists, USA. Lives in the USA. Daughter of Patricia Vaughan (qv) and Paul Wiles (qv), grand-daughter of W G Wiles (qv), niece of Brian Wiles (qv) and Lucy Wiles (qv).
Exhibitions She has participated in several group exhibitions from 1977 in SA and the USA; 1982 New York, solo exhibition.
Represented Genesee Wildlife Art Museum, Rochester, New York, USA.
Reference *Sports Afield* November/December 1985.

HAYWARD FELL Carol Patricia

Born 1952 Durban.
A sculptor of figures and abstract pieces. Works in ceramics. 1979–80 tetrahedron forms; 1980–85 developed crystalline glazes; 1982–83 sculptural panels consisting of several face masks in porcelain and stoneware mounted on to wood. Creates non-functional multi-coloured, slip-painted porcelain vessels.
Studies 1971–74 University of Natal, under Professor Hilda Ditchburn (qv) and Malcolm McIntyre Reid, gaining a BA(FA); 1976 University of Natal, attaining a Higher Diploma in Education.
Profile From 1978 a member of the NSA and from 1979 a committee member of the Natal branch of the APSA and its Vice-Chairman 1982–84. 1977–78 an art teacher at Danville Park Girls High School, Durban; 1978–84 a ceramics lecturer at the Natal Technikon. From 1980 a Technikon Moderator in ceramic history. 1982–85 wrote several articles for *Sgraffiti*, an APSA publication.
Exhibitions She has participated in numerous group exhibitions held throughout SA from 1975.
Represented Durban Art Gallery; Durbanville Clay Collection; King George VI Art Gallery, Port Elizabeth; Natal Technikon; Pretoria Art Museum; Tatham Art Gallery, Pietermaritzburg; University of Natal.
Reference *Living* November 1985.

HAZELL Beatrice

Born 1864 Maidstone, Kent, England.
Died 1946 Ceres, Cape Province.
Resided in SA from 1885.
A painter of still life and landscapes. Her early work is mainly of Cape flowers and fruit. Worked in oil and watercolour.
Studies Cape Town School of Art, under G C Robinson (qv); in England under George Vicat Cole (1833–93), Frederick Stratton and Frederick Williamson.
Profile A member of the SA Society of Artists and the SA Drawing Club. *c*.1911 taught still-life drawing in her Cape Town studio. Travelled extensively in SA and Europe and produced many watercolour sketches of the places she visited.
Exhibitions Participated in group exhibitions from 1903 in SA and the UK; held her first solo exhibition in Cape Town.
Represented Africana Museum, Johannesburg.
References AMC7; BSAK 1; AASA.

HEATH Bronwen Jane (Jinny)

Born 1944 England.

A painter working in acrylic and mixed media.

Studies 1966 attained a BA(FA) from the University of Natal.

Profile A lecturer at the University of Natal. Daughter of Jack Heath (qv) and Jane Heath (qv).

Exhibitions She has participated in group exhibitions in Natal; 1982 Cape Town Triennial; 1986 Tatham Art Gallery, Pietermaritzburg, exhibition of works by the Heath family.

Represented Durban Art Gallery; Natal Technikon; SA National Gallery, Cape Town; Tatham Art Gallery, Pietermaritzburg.

HEATH Jane Tully ARCA

Born 1913 Cumberland, England.

Resided in SA from 1946.

A painter of landscapes, portraits, genre, figures, still life and abstract pictures. Works in oil, watercolour, gouache, ink, wash, pencil and charcoal.

Studies 1932–37 Birmingham College of Arts and Crafts, under Harold H Holden (b.1885); 1937–41 Royal College of Art, London, under Professor Gilbert Spencer (b.1892), gaining an Associateship and a Gold Medal.

Profile 1947–52 a member of the EPSFA. 1949–53 a part-time lecturer in painting and drawing, Port Elizabeth Technical College; 1953–68 an art lecturer at the University of Natal; from 1968 she has taught art privately. 1950–62 illustrations for educational books by Victor Pohl, published by the Oxford University Press, England, as well as for various daily and weekly publications. 1958–68 visited Kenya, Uganda and Greece. Married to John Heath (qv), mother of Bronwen Heath (qv).

Exhibitions She has participated in group exhibitions held in Port Elizabeth and in Natal; 1956 Quadrennial Exhibition; held a solo exhibition in Kenya; 1972 SAAA Gallery, Cape Town, joint exhibition with Carola Brotherton, with whom she has had additional joint exhibitions in Pretoria and Benoni; 1986 Tatham Art Gallery, Pietermaritzburg, exhibition of works by the Heath family.

Represented Durban Art Gallery; SA National Gallery, Cape Town; Tatham Art Gallery, Pietermaritzburg; University of Natal.

Public Commissions 1948–51 murals at the Children's Orthopaedic Hospital and the King Edward Hotel, Port Elizabeth, both with her husband.

References SAP&S; BSAK 1; AASA.

HEATH John Charles Wood (Jack) Professor ARCA

Born 1915 Cannock, Staffordshire, England.

Died 1969 Pietermaritzburg.

Resided in SA from 1946.

Worked in all drawing media and from 1946 in oil. His pictures were abstract or of religious subjects or arid landscapes.

Studies 1932–36 Birmingham School of Art; 1936–39 Royal College of Art, London, under Malcolm Osborne (*b*.1880) and Robert Austin (1895–1973), where specialised in etching and was awarded an Associateship in engraving.
Profile 1946 a lecturer at Rhodes University; 1947–53 Head of the Art Department at the Port Elizabeth Technical College; 1953–69 Professor of Fine Art at the University of Natal, where an art gallery has been named after him. Married to Jane Heath (qv), father of Bronwen Heath (qv).
Exhibitions Participated in group exhibitions from 1956; 1956 Quadrennial Exhibition; 1976 Jack Heath Gallery, Pietermaritzburg, Commemorative Exhibition; 1986 Tatham Art Gallery, Pietermaritzburg, exhibition of works by the Heath family.
Represented Imperial War Museum, London, UK; University of Natal.
Public Commissions 1948–51 murals at the Children's Orthopaedic Hospital and the King Edward Hotel, Port Elizabeth, both with his wife.
References Art SA; SAA; DBA; BSAK 1; AASA.

HEMP Doreen Gail
Born 1939 Johannesburg.
A painter of figures. Works in mixed media. A photographer.
Studies Drawing at the Witwatersrand Technical College, under Wim Blom (qv); basic design at the Centre for Continuing Education, University of the Witwatersrand, under Rory Doepel; 1979 design under Peggy Wolstenholme; 1980–85 University of South Africa, gaining a BA(FA).
Profile 1984–85 organised the "Women's Festival of Art"; from 1985 a committee member of the APSA; from 1986 a member of the SAAAH. She has drawn a number of illustrations for Kirstenbosch Botanical Gardens and in 1985 designed the Atteridgeville (Transvaal) Coat of Arms. Actively involved in pottery, enamelling and glassmaking.
Exhibitions She has participated in several group exhibitions from 1985.

HENCKERT (Hermann) Hans-Joachim
Born 1906 Rehoboth, SWA/Namibia.
A painter of landscapes, portraits, seascapes and wildlife. Works in oil.
Studies 1924–26 private tuition from Professor Wilhelm Kuhnert (1865–1926).
Profile 1976 a painting of a stalking leopard used as the title picture for *The SWA Annual*. 1983 designed a set of stamps for SWA/Namibia.
Exhibitions He has participated in several group exhibitions from 1947 in SWA/Namibia and West Germany; 1968 Windhoek, first of four solo exhibitions held in SWA/Namibia and West Germany.
Awards STANSWA Awards 1981 and 1983.
Represented SWA/Namibia Administration Building, Windhoek.
References Art SWA; AASA; PS/N.

HENDERSON Hilda

Born Cape Town.
Both a painter and a sculptor. Works in many media.
Studies In Port Elizabeth under J W D Muff-Ford (qv), Joan Wright (qv), Professor Robert Bain (qv) and Professor Harry Atkins (qv).
Profile A member of the SAAA, the EPSFA, the SA Society of Artists and of the Disa Art Club, Cape Town. An amateur actress and producer. A member of the Cape Town Writers Club.
Exhibitions She has participated in numerous group exhibitions in SA.

HENDRIKS (Petrus) Anton Dr

Born 1899 Rotterdam, The Netherlands.
Died 1975 Paris.
Resided in SA 1926–75.
A painter of portraits, landscapes and still life. Worked in oil. 1933–37 painted several murals.
Studies Rotterdam Academy, The Netherlands and in Paris.
Profile On the War Artists Advisory Committee during WWII; 1961 and 1962 a committee member of the SA Council of Arts. 1928–33 Principal of the Art School, Pretoria Technical College; 1937–64 Curator/Director of the Johannesburg Art Gallery, 1964–67 consultant and restorer to the Johannesburg Art Gallery. In 1958 he wrote, with Otto Schröder (qv), a monograph on Adolph Jentsch (qv), which was published in Swakopmund, SWA/Namibia. Retired to Cape Town, died on a visit to Paris.
Exhibitions Participated in group exhibitions from 1931 in The Netherlands, France, Rhodesia (Zimbabwe) and SA; 1933 MacFadyen Hall, Pretoria, solo exhibition; 1948 Tate Gallery, London, SA Art Exhibition; 1975 Johannesburg Art Gallery, exhibition entitled "A Tribute to Doctor P A Hendriks".
Award 1965 awarded an Honorary Doctorate of Philosophy from the University of the Witwatersrand for services to art and to the Johannesburg Art Gallery.
Represented Africana Museum, Johannesburg; Durban Art Gallery; Johannesburg Art Gallery; King George VI Art Gallery, Port Elizabeth; Pretoria Art Museum; SA Akademie vir Wetenskap en Kuns; SA National Gallery, Cape Town; University of Pretoria; University of the Witwatersrand.
Public Commissions 1967 portrait of the retiring Principal of the University of the Witwatersrand, Professor I D MacCrone. Murals: Pretoria City Hall; Johannesburg Post Office; General Mining Building, Johannesburg; Voortrekker Gedenksaal, Pretoria.
References Collectors' Guide; Art SA; SAA; SAP&D; BSAK 1 & 2; SA Art; 3Cs; AASA; *SA Panorama* January 1960; *SA Digest* 26 November 1965.

HENDRIKZ Willem de Sanderes

Born 1910 Brandfort, Orange Free State.
Died 1959 Plettenberg Bay, Cape Province.
A sculptor of figures, animals and universal themes. Worked in bronze, concrete, stone, wood and verdite. Architectural sculpture for the decoration of buildings. Many portrait busts, of which the most well known is that of Mahatma Gandhi which was bought by the Indian Government in 1947.

Studies 1928–33 studied architecture at the University of the Witwatersrand, gaining an MA; 1934 London School of Art, under John Skeaping (*b*.1901) and stone carving under a stone-mason; 1936 sculpture at the Royal Academy, Amsterdam and at the Royal College of Art, Copenhagen; 1944 studied art education at the Columbia University, New York, USA, gaining an MA; 1950–51 studied casting methods in Amsterdam and Copenhagen.

Profile A member of the New Group and an Adjudication Committee member of the SA Academy. An art critic under the nom de plume "Gideon Malherbe". 1937–45 a lecturer in fine art at the University of the Witwatersrand, thereafter a full-time sculptor. Created stage décor for the theatre, including for "Die Rooi Pruik", a Siegfried Mynhardt production which toured SA. 1940–43 worked in the Camouflage Department of the SA Defence Force. 1934 lived in London, spending three months in The Netherlands; 1936 in Europe; 1950–51 lived on a barge on the Dutch, German and French canals and visited Denmark and Belgium.

Exhibitions Participated in group exhibitions in SA, Rhodesia (Zimbabwe), the UK and Belgium; 1934 Cooling Gallery, London, first of several solo exhibitions held in London, Johannesburg and Pretoria; 1948 Tate Gallery, London, SA Art Exhibition; in 1950 his figure of "Rain" was exhibited for six months in Middelheim Park, Antwerp, Belgium.

Award 1948 Silver Medal for Sculpture, SA Academy.

Represented Johannesburg Art Gallery; Pretoria Art Museum; SA National Gallery, Cape Town.

Public Commissions 1935 two panels for the Red Cross House, Johannesburg; 1937 six wall panels, Escom House (Van Eck House, now demolished), Johannesburg; 1939 two lions, Reserve Bank Building, Johannesburg; 1945 six-panelled door, Volkskas Building, Johannesburg; 1948–49 panel of relief work, East London Museum; 1949 "Young Gods in Pain", Memorial for SA Medical Corps, Ingram's Building, Johannesburg; 1950 relief work, Customs Building, Johannesburg; 1953 "Mother and Child" Memorial, Sanlam Building, Johannesburg; 1953 bronze figure, SABC Building, Cape Town; 1953–54 doors for Volkskas Building, Bloemfontein, Tanganyika House, Salisbury, Rhodesia (Harare, Zimbabwe), Volkskas Building, Pretoria, Reserve Bank Building, East London and for Sanlam Building, Johannesburg; 1956 two Kudu bulls, Volkskas Building, Pretoria; 1958 bronze door, General Mining Building, Johannesburg.

Articles by Hendrikz "Art in Architecture", *SA Architectural Record* April 1948; "Sculpture in Relation to Architecture", *SA Architectural Record* November 1955.

References Collectors' Guide; Our Art 2; Art SA; SAA; SADNB; 20C SA Art; Oxford Companion to Art (under SA); SAP&D; SESA; SA Art; 3Cs; AASA; LSAA; *Die Brandwag* February 1946; *SA Architectural Record* June 1950 & August 1959; *SA Panorama* August 1958 & January 1960; *Die Huisgenoot* 8 Mei 1959.

HENDRY Mary Buik

Born 1934 Kalk Bay, Cape Province.

A painter of landscapes and genre in a naive style. Works in oil and acrylic, models animals in pottery.

Profile From 1969 a member of the Fish Hoek Art Society. 1984 illustrated a children's poem by Leon Rousseau, published by Rubicon Press, Cape Town. 1961–69 lived in London, where she attended Greater London Council art classes.

Exhibitions She has participated in several group exhibitions from 1975 in SA and one in Switzerland; 1981 Republic Festival Exhibition; 1981 Gallery International, Cape Town, first of four solo exhibitions, one of which was held in Johannesburg.

Represented Pietersburg Collection.

Reference AASA.

HENKEL Caesar Carl Hans

Born 1841.

Died in the Eastern Province.

Resided in SA from 1857.

A painter of landscapes, which today are of historical importance. Worked in oil.

Profile Initially he was a clerk to Baron Stutterheim and later a civil servant, whose posts included, 1889–98, that of Conservator of Forests in the Transkeian Territories. Drew a map of the Transkei and Pondoland. Wrote two books on forestry and illustrated his own book on the Transkei in 1903.

Represented Africana Museum, Johannesburg; East London Museum.

References AMC3; Pict Afr.

HENKEL Irmin

Born 1921 Renburg, Hanover, Germany.

Died 1977 Pretoria.

Resided in SA from 1951.

A self-taught artist of portraits, still life (mainly from 1970), landscapes (a few in Europe in 1951 and in SA after 1969) and nudes (after 1969). Worked in oil, tempera, watercolour, charcoal and sepia. From 1965 a number of sculptures, mainly of portrait busts.

Profile A fully trained orthopaedic surgeon. Had an interest in photography and played a number of instruments including the piano and the ukelele. Designed and built his own studio in Pretoria. During WWII he served in the German Armed Forces as a doctor; 1946 escaped to Switzerland; 1947 lived in the Locarno/Ascona district of Switzerland; 1949 visited Italy; 1950–51 in Switzerland; thereafter in SA, visiting Europe in 1961 and 1965.

Exhibitions Participated in group exhibitions from 1943 in Germany and SA; 1946 Bonn, solo exhibition in Germany; 1951 University of Pretoria, first of three solo exhibitions held in SA; 1960 Quadrennial Exhibition; 1966 Pretoria Art Museum, Prestige Exhibition of 70 portraits; 1969–70 an exhibition of the preparatory sketches and paintings for the "Group Portrait of the First South African Republican Cabinet" toured SA; 1977 University of the Orange Free State, solo exhibition; 1978 Pretoria Art Museum, Memorial Tribute; 1979 Van Wouw House, Pretoria, Memorial Exhibition.

Represented Africana Museum, Johannesburg; Bonn Municipal Collection, West Germany; Engelenberg House, Pretoria; municipal collections in Klerksdorp, Krugersdorp, Potchefstroom, Sasolburg and Pietersburg; Pretoria Art Museum; Pretoria Medical School; SA Akademie vir Wetenskap en Kuns; University of the Orange Free State; University of Port Elizabeth; University of Pretoria; University of South Africa; University of Stellenbosch; Willem Annandale Art Gallery, Lichtenburg.

Public Commissions 1964–69 "First Republican Cabinet", including four Deputy Ministers, 18' x 10', Houses of Parliament, Cape Town; numerous portraits of SA statesmen and other notability, including Presidents C R Swart in 1962, 1964, 1967 and 1969 and J J Fouche in 1969, 1970 and 1977; Prime Ministers D F Malan in 1951, H F Verwoerd in 1964 and 1968 and B J Vorster in 1967 and 1971. Portraits of university Chancellors and Rectors. A number of his portraits have been used as postage stamps including in 1966 Dr H F Verwoerd, 1968 J J Fouche and General J B M Hertzog and in 1969 Professor Chris Barnard.

References Margot Henkel and Professor Karin Skawran, *Irmin Henkel*, 1983, Butterworth Publishers, Pretoria; AMC7; BSAK 1 & 2; 3Cs; AASA; *SA Panorama* November 1967 & April 1969.

HENLEY Priscilla

Born 1931 Sherbourne, Dorset, England.
Resided in SA from 1962.
A painter of wildlife, particularly birds. Works in acrylic and pencil.
Studies Six months in Pietermaritzburg, under Jane Heath (qv).
Profile A member of the Natal Midlands Arts & Crafts Society. 1977–85 eight limited edition portfolios of birds published privately. 1931–48 lived in England; 1948–52 in Kenya; 1952–56 in Uganda; 1956–62 in Kenya, to which she returns frequently. Visits Botswana annually.
Exhibitions She has participated in many group exhibitions from 1977 in SA.

HENNESSY Esmé Frances (née Franklin) Professor
MSc, PhD (Natal), Sci Nat, FLS
Born 1933 Umzinto Natal.
A botanical illustrator working in watercolour, ink, wash and pencil.
Profile A trained botanist, gaining a Doctorate in Botany in 1983. In the botanical field she has written numerous articles and books and has done substantial research. She is a member of many botanical societies and began teaching botany in 1956. She is currently an Associate Professor at the University of Durban-Westville. 1986 elected a founder member of the Association of Botanical Artists, London. Her illustrations have been included in *Veld and Flora* 1971–75, in *Flowering Plants of Africa* from 1976 and in the *American Orchid Society Bulletin* from 1981. In 1977 her portfolio entitled "Wild Fruits of South Africa" was published by Howard Swan, Johannesburg. In 1981 she illustrated *Orchids of Africa*, with text by J Stewart, Macmillan (SA), Johannesburg.

Exhibitions She has participated in many group exhibitions from 1967 in SA, the USA and the UK; 1981 Everard Read Gallery, Johannesburg, solo exhibition.
Award 1984 Group Gold Medal, Royal Horticultural Society, England.
References AASA; *SA Garden & Home* November 1973; *Fair Lady* April 1978.

HENNING Mieke

Born 1955 Bloemfontein.
A sculptor and graphic artist of abstract pieces. Works in stone and in various graphic media.
Studies 1978–82 Koninklijke Academie voor Kunst en Vormgeving, 'sHertogenbosch, The Netherlands, gaining a Certificate in 1982.
Profile From 1986 a member of the SAAA. From 1985 has lived in Somerset West in the Cape.
Exhibitions She has participated in group exhibitions from 1982 in The Netherlands and SA; 1983 first of three solo exhibitions held in The Netherlands and two in SA.
Public Commission 1985 two sculptures for 'sHertogenbosch, The Netherlands.

HENORAIN Lea

Born 1959 Sante Fé, Argentina.
Resided in SA from 1983.
A painter of the human figure. Works in oil, acrylic, gouache, wood and industrial materials such as plastic, metal, fabric, glass and wax.
Studies 1980–83 Tel Aviv School of Art, Israel; 1983–86 Witwatersrand Technikon, gaining a National Diploma in 1984 and a Higher Diploma in 1986.
Profile Taught art in 1980 for the Education Department, Haifa, Israel and in 1982 at a recreation centre in Israel. In 1982 her illustrations appeared in *Yediot Ahronot*, an Israeli daily newspaper.
Exhibitions She has participated in several group exhibitions in Johannesburg and Pretoria from 1983; 1986 Market Gallery, Johannesburg, joint exhibition with Robyn Cohen (qv) and Lulu Davis (qv).
Award 1984 Merit Award, Rolfes Impressions '84 Exhibition, Johannesburg Art Gallery.
Public Commission 1982 mural, Shabtai Levy Orphanage, Haifa, Israel.
References *Fair Lady* 30 May 1984; *Beeldende* 5 October 1984.

HENRY Hilda Madeline (née Montgomerie)

Born 1875.
Died 1963.
A painter of landscapes. Worked in watercolour.
Exhibition 1938–39 participated in the 8th Annual Exhibition of Contemporary Art, SA National Gallery, Cape Town.
Represented Africana Museum, Johannesburg.
Reference AMC7.

HERMANN (Heinrich) Wilhelm

Born 1841 Frankfurt-am-Main, Germany.
Died 1916 Cape Town.
Resided in SA from 1875.
A painter of landscapes, mainly of Cape views and Knysna Forest scenes. Worked in oil, watercolour and pencil.
Studies Art and photography in Germany, where he won a travelling scholarship to SA 1869–71.
Profile Art Master at the Diocesan and SA Colleges in Cape Town. During the 1870s he established a photographic studio and from 1875 he worked as a professional photographer.
Exhibitions 1871 included in the SA Fine Arts Association Exhibition; 1871 Cape Town, joint exhibition with F R Lee (qv); 1886 included in the Colonial and Indian Exhibition, London; 1976 SA National Gallery, Cape Town, included in "English and SA Watercolours in the SA National Gallery" Exhibition.
Represented Africana Museum, Johannesburg; SA National Gallery, Cape Town; University of Stellenbosch.
References AMC3; SAP&S; SAP&D; Pict Afr; BSAK 1; 3Cs; AASA.

HERMER Manfred

Born 1915 Volksrust, Transvaal.
A painter of landscapes and buildings. Works in oil on paper.
Profile A qualified, practising architect.
Exhibitions 1974 Gallery 101, Johannesburg, first of three solo exhibitions held in SA, also held one solo exhibition in London.
Publication by Hermer *The Passing of Pageview*, 1978, Ravan Press, Johannesburg.

HERTSLET Rosalind

Born 1923 East London.
A painter in oil. A muralist and a maker of fabric assemblages.
Studies 1944–47 Witwatersrand Technical College.
Profile 1954 a committee member of the Contemporary Art Society. Taught oil painting and drawing. 1956–59 lived in London, Spain and Ibiza. Prior to 1959 married to Douglas Portway (qv).
Exhibitions She has participated in group exhibitions from 1946 in SA; 1948 Tate Gallery, London, SA Art Exhibition; 1974 Goodman Gallery, Johannesburg, solo exhibition; 1981 Republic Festival Exhibition; 1983 Studio Gallery, University of the Witwatersrand, two solo exhibitions.

HERZOG Heidi

Born 1905 Switzerland.
Died 1967.
Resided in SA from 1951.
From 1931 a painter of flower studies, portraits and landscapes. Worked in oil and pastel.

Studies In France under André Dunoyer de Segonzac (1884–1974) and Marc Chagall (1887–1985); under Professor Brenne of the Munich Academy and in Italy.

Profile A member of the SAAA. 1931 spent eight months in Italy, before living in Aix-en-Provence, France.

Exhibitions Participated in group and solo exhibitions in the South of France; participated in group exhibitions in SA; 1961 Constantia Gallery, Johannesburg, first of six solo exhibitions held in SA; 1967 Wolpe Gallery, Cape Town, first of five posthumous exhibitions held in Cape Town, Johannesburg and Pretoria; 1972 Lidchi Art Gallery, Johannesburg, Retrospective Exhibition; 1974 William Humphreys Art Gallery, Kimberley, Retrospective Exhibition; 1977 SAAA Gallery, Johannesburg, Retrospective Exhibition; 1983 Hoffer Art Gallery, Pretoria and Rand Afrikaans University, Retrospective Exhibition.

Represented Chester Beatty Collection, London, England; Kunstmuseum, Basle, Switzerland; Rand Afrikaans University; William Humphreys Art Gallery, Kimberley.

References BSAK; AASA; *SA Art News* 1 June 1961; *Artlook* April 1968; Retrospective Exhibition Catalogue, 1983, Rand Afrikaans University.

HESSELBARTH Bernhard Franz (Berne)

Born 1903 Johannesburg.

A painter of landscapes, seascapes and still life. Works in oil and pastel.

Studies c.1927 Witwatersrand Technical College under Sidney Carter (qv) and Emily Fern (qv); privately under Cecil Thornley Stewart (qv), Leonard Richmond ROI and under Don Madge (qv) in Pretoria.

Profile A member of the SAAA and the Brush and Chisel Club. Has taught art privately. A dance band leader and an amateur actor. 1903–32 lived in Johannesburg; 1932–48 in Pietersburg; 1948–62 in the Northern Transvaal and from 1962 in Pretoria. Has travelled extensively in SA and made many painting trips with Erich Mayer (qv) and Cecil Thornley Stewart (qv).

Exhibitions He has participated in numerous group exhibitions from c.1936 in SA and once in London; 1934 Pietersburg, first of numerous solo exhibitions held throughout SA.

Represented Durban Art Gallery; Pietersburg Collection; Pretoria Art Museum; Willem Annandale Art Gallery, Lichtenburg.

References BSAK 1; AASA; *Artlook* February 1971.

HEYDENRYCH Albertus B

Born 1953 Fort Beaufort, Cape Province.

A painter of landscapes, figures, social comment and town scenes. Works in pastel, acrylic, mixed media and with found objects.

Studies 1972–77 Rhodes University, gaining a BA(FA) in 1975, an MFA in 1976 and a Higher Diploma in Education in 1977.

Profile 1972–77 a member of the Grahamstown Group; 1980–82 taught at the Lawson Brown High School, Port Elizabeth; 1983–86 a senior lecturer at the School of Art and Design, Orange Free State Technikon.

Exhibitions He has participated in numerous group exhibitions throughout SA and has held three solo exhibitions.

Represented Orange Free State Technikon; Rhodes University; University of the Orange Free State.

HEYNS Michael Ferreira

Born 1946 Potchefstroom, Transvaal.

An artist of elements taken from life. Creates oil paintings and mixed media drawings. Several series: 1969–76 "Seeds, Flowers and Fruit"; 1979–80 "Butterflies"; 1979–81 "Figures and Pierrots"; 1981–83 "Denims"; 1983–85 "Portraits of Torsos".

Studies 1964–67 through the University of Pretoria, under Gunther van der Reis (qv) and Jean Beeton (qv), gaining a BA(FA).

Profile A member of the SAAA. A designer of warp-painted tapestries, woven by his wife, Susan.

Exhibitions He has participated in over 60 group exhibitions from 1967 in SA; 1969 SAAA Gallery, Pretoria, first of over 20 solo exhibitions held in SA; 1981 Republic Festival Exhibition; 1987 Johannesburg Art Gallery, Vita Art Now.

Awards 1967 Painting Prize, New Signatures, SAAA, Pretoria; 1980 SA Wool Board Design Prize.

Represented Klerksdorp Municipal Collection; Potchefstroom Art Museum; Pretoria Art Museum; Sasolburg Municipal Collection; University of Bophuthatswana; University of Pretoria; Willem Annandale Art Gallery, Lichtenburg; William Humphreys Art Gallery, Kimberley.

References BSAK 1; AASA; *Lantern* May 1981.

HIGGS Cecil

Born 1900 Thaba 'Nchu District, Orange Free State.

Died 1986 Cape Town.

A painter of marine life, seascapes, landscape, still life and from 1935 figures, particularly nudes. From 1946 the theme of the sea ran through her paintings. Painted many pictures of cats. Worked in oil, watercolour, and from 1948 in mixed media. Numerous drawings in ink, crayon, pencil, charcoal and chalk. A number of monotypes from 1958.

Studies c.1919 Grahamstown School of Art; 1920–33 Byam Shaw Art School and Goldsmith's College of Art, London, the Royal Academy Schools under Walter Sickert (1860–1942), the Walter Sickert School, Camden Town, various Paris studios including l'Académie de la Grande Chaumière and under André Lhote (1885–1962).

Profile 1971–74 unable to paint in oil due to a shoulder injury, she worked in mixed media. 1939 a member of the New Group; 1948 a member of the International Arts Club in SA. Illustrated *Stellenbosch Days* by Nora Henshilwood, 1951, A A Balkema, Cape Town and *Kelp Coast*, 1976, David Philip, Cape Town, *Leonardo The Florentine* by Leon Rousseau, 1962, Oxford University Press, Cape Town, *Magdalene Retief* by Uys Krige, 1940, Unie Volkspelers, Cape Town, 2nd revised edition, and *Nerina van Drakenstein* by A C Bouman, 1937, HAUM, Cape Town. 1900–20 lived in the Orange Free State; 1920–33 in London and Paris; 1933–35 in the Orange Free State; 1935–46 in Stellenbosch; 1946 in Green Point, Cape Town; 1947–62 in Sea Point, Cape Town; 1962–63 in Mouille Point, Cape Town; from 1964 at Onrust, Cape Province. 1939 visited Paris and London; in 1952 the Wild Coast and in 1965 England, France, The Netherlands and Italy.

Exhibitions Participated in group exhibitions from 1920 in England with the London Group and the New English Art Club and in SA from 1929; she has also exhibited in Yugoslavia, Italy, Zimbabwe and Brazil; 1936 University of Stellenbosch, first of numerous solo exhibitions held in SA; 1938 Stellenbosch, joint exhibition with René Graetz, Maggie Laubser (qv) and Lippy Lipshitz (qv); 1940 first of several joint exhibitions with Lippy Lipshitz (qv) and John Dronsfield (qv); 1948 Tate Gallery, London, SA Art Exhibition; 1953 National Museum, Bloemfontein, exhibition; 1956 and 1960 Quadrennial Exhibitions; 1968 Tatham Art Gallery, Pietermaritzburg, Durban Art Gallery and SA National Gallery, Cape Town, joint exhibition with John Dronsfield (qv) and Lippy Lipshitz (qv); 1975 SA National Gallery, Cape Town, William Humphreys Art Gallery, Kimberley, Pretoria Art Museum, Durban Art Gallery, Prestige Retrospective Exhibition; 1978 SAAA Gallery, Cape Town, Retrospective Exhibition; 1980 Wolpe Gallery, Cape Town, 80th Anniversary Exhibition.

Award 1963 Medal of Honour for Painting, SA Akademie vir Wetenskap en Kuns.

Represented Durban Art Gallery; Hester Rupert Art Museum, Graaff-Reinet; Johannesburg Art Gallery; King George VI Art Gallery, Port Elizabeth; National Museum, Bloemfontein; Pretoria Art Museum; Rand Afrikaans University; Sandton Municipal Collection; SA Akademie vir Wetenskap en Kuns; SA National Gallery, Cape Town; Tatham Art Gallery, Pietermaritzburg; University of the Orange Free State; University of Pretoria; University of South Africa; University of Stellenbosch; University of the Witwatersrand; William Humphreys Art Gallery, Kimberley.

References Victor Holloway, *Cecil Higgs*, 1974, C Struik, Cape Town; Collectors' Guide; PSA; Our Art 2; Art SA; SAA; 20C SA Art; SAP&S; Oxford Companion to Art (under SA); SAP&D; SESA; SSAP; BSAK 1 & 2; SA Art; Oxford Companion to C20 Art (under SA); 3Cs; AASA; LSAA; *Die Huisgenoot* 3 January 1941; *SA Art News* 18 May 1961; *Lantern* June 1966; *SA Panorama* June 1971; *Artlook* July 1972; *SA Oorsig* 3 September 1976; *De Arte* April 1983 & September 1983; *Gallery* Winter 1984; *De Kat* September 1986; Prestige Retrospective Exhibition Catalogue, 1975.

HILHORST Gerrit

Born 1945.

A painter and graphic artist, producing watercolours and serigraphs.

Studies 1962 studied for a National Art Teachers Diploma in Fine Art at the Pretoria Technical College.
Exhibitions He has participated in group exhibitions in SA from 1962.
Award 1973 Cambridge Shirt Award, Art SA Today.
Represented SA National Gallery, Cape Town; University of South Africa; University of Stellenbosch.
References BSAK 1; 3Cs; AASA.

HILL Leta (née Redford)
Died 1973 Cape Town.
A painter on tiles, of flowers, birds, old cottages and houses.
Profile A potter, who prior to WWII began the Pottery Department at the Michaelis School of Fine Art.
Exhibitions Participated in group exhibitions from 1945 in SA.
Public Commissions Numerous commissions for painted tiles for buildings in Cape Town.

HILLHOUSE Mary Ellen (May)
Born 1908 Stellenbosch District, Cape Province.
A painter, who works in oil, watercolour, gouache, ink, wash, pencil and charcoal. A graphic artist producing monoprints.
Studies 1921–26 Natal Technical College, under Professor O J P Oxley (qv); 1938–39 privately under Martin Bloch (1883–1954) in London.
Profile During the 1940s a member of the New Group; a member of the SAAA; 1965 a founder member of the Artists Gallery, Cape Town. 1926–38 worked as a commercial artist. 1942–43 an art critic for *The Cape Times*. 1959–68 a lecturer in design, Michaelis School of Fine Art. Illustrated *The Afrikaans Children's Encyclopaedia* and *Savage Hinterland*, by Victor Pohl, among other books. Lives in the Cape. 1952 revisited Europe.
Exhibitions She has participated in numerous group exhibitions from the 1940s; 1944 Cape Town, first of numerous solo exhibitions in SA, Italy, Zimbabwe, Brazil and Greece; 1956 and 1960 Quadrennial Exhibitions; 1979 SA National Gallery, Cape Town, Retrospective Exhibition, touring SA.
Awards 1979 Cape Art Medal for Services to Art, SAAA Western Cape; 1980 awarded the Medal of Honour for Painting, SA Akademie vir Wetenskap en Kuns.
Represented Durban Art Gallery; Hester Rupert Art Museum, Graaff-Reinet; Johannesburg Art Gallery; King George VI Art Gallery, Port Elizabeth; Pretoria Art Museum; SA National Gallery, Cape Town; University of Cape Town; University of the Witwatersrand; Willem Annandale Art Gallery, Lichtenburg; William Humphreys Art Gallery, Kimberley.
References Collectors' Guide; PSA; Our Art 2; Art SA; SAA; 20C SA Art; SAP&S; SAP&D; SESA; SSAP; BSAK 1 & 2; 3Cs; AASA; LSAA.

HILSON Barbara Hazel

Born 1937 Livingstone, Northern Rhodesia (Maramba, Zambia).
A painter of landscapes, seascapes, portraits, still life and figures. Works in oil and watercolour.
Studies 1954–55 part-time at East London Technical College, under Jack Lugg (qv); a correspondence course with George Boys (qv).
Profile A member and committee member of the East London Society of Fine Art.
Exhibitions She has participated in several group exhibitions from 1976 in the Eastern Cape; 1986 Ann Bryant Gallery, East London, solo exhibition.

HINWOOD Lionel John Hewitt

Born 1936 Johannesburg.
A self-taught painter and graphic artist of landscapes, abstract and Op art works. Uses oil, acrylic, gouache and various graphic media.
Profile From 1978 a member of the Artists Market Association. 1970 designed the set and directed the plays "Salome" by Oscar Wilde and "The Eagle Has Two Heads" by Jean Cocteau, in Johannesburg. An actor in Rhodesia (Zimbabwe) 1958–65, and in Johannesburg and Durban, 1968–78.
Exhibitions He has participated in several group exhibitions from 1960 in Zimbabwe and SA; 1978 Trevor Coleman Gallery, Johannesburg, first of three solo exhibitions in Johannesburg and Pretoria; 1981 Republic Festival Exhibition.
Public Commission 1972 eight panels depicting aloes, Satara Camp, Kruger National Park.
Reference AASA.

HIRSCHSOHN Helen Pamela (Pam)

Born 1936 Cape Town.
A painter of landscapes, seascapes and still life. Works in oil and pastel.
Studies 1954–56 and 1960 Michaelis School of Fine Art, under Rupert Shephard (qv) and Eleanor Esmonde-White (qv).
Profile 1982 visited Greece; 1983–84 visited France and Namaqualand; 1985 Italy and Madeira; 1985–86 Spain and the Karoo.
Exhibitions 1983 Gowlett Gallery, Cape Town, first of five solo exhibitions in Cape Town and Pretoria; 1985 Cape Town Triennial.

HLEZA Austin

Born 1949 Mpuluzi, Swaziland.
A sculptor in ceramics of vehicles and a graphic artist.
Studies 1971–73 Small Enterprises Development Centre in Mbabane, Swaziland.

Profile A member of the APSA and the Swaziland Art Society. 1982 a lecturer in ceramics at Ezulweni Handicraft Training Centre, Swaziland.
Exhibitions He has participated in several group exhibitions in SA from 1984; 1985 Cape Town Triennial.
Represented University of Natal; University of the Witwatersrand.
Reference *Sgraffiti* no 34.

HLUNGWANI Jackson

Born 1923.
A self-taught sculptor of religious works and of symbolic animals. Works in wood.
Profile 1946 ordained into the African Zionist Church. A member of Bozz Art. Lives in Mbokote, Gazankulu.
Exhibitions He has participated in group exhibitions from 1985 in SA; 1985 Bozz Art Foundation Exhibition, touring to Johannesburg, Cape Town and Durban, with Nelson Mukhuba (qv), Hendrick Nekhofhe (qv) and Dr Phatuma Seoka (qv); 1985 Tributaries, touring SA and West Germany; 1987 and 1988 Johannesburg Art Gallery, Vita Art Now.
Public Commission 1988 three works for the foyer of the African Studies Building, University of Cape Town.
Represented Irma Stern Museum, University of Cape Town; SA National Gallery, Cape Town; University of the Witwatersrand.

HOBBS Philippa Anne

Born 1955 Johannesburg.
A printmaker, working in woodcuts, silkscreens and etchings. Creates collages of etchings, makes paper and works in pastel. Her subject matter is predominantly of interiors in a contemporary vein as well as abstract with the use of lettering. 1984–86 "Babel" series; from 1986 "Purging" series.
Studies 1973–75 Witwatersrand Technical College (Technikon), under Claude van Lingen (qv), gaining a National Diploma in Fine Art; 1977–78 Philadelphia College of Art, USA, under Michael Lasuchin (*b*.1923); 1986 Witwatersrand Technikon, under Willem Boshoff (qv), gaining a Higher Diploma in Printmaking.
Profile 1979–84 a lecturer and from 1984 Head of the Printmaking Department, Witwatersrand Technikon. 1973 and 1987 visited Italy.
Exhibitions She has participated in several group exhibitions from 1975 in SA; 1976 Space and Design Gallery, Johannesburg, joint exhibition with Roland Metcalfe (qv); 1981 Market Gallery, Johannesburg, first of three solo exhibitions; 1982 Cape Town Triennial; 1983 Ernst de Jong Gallery, Pretoria and Goodman Gallery, Johannesburg, joint exhibition with Susan Rosenberg (qv); 1985 Cape Town Triennial; 1987 SA National Gallery and Goodman Gallery, Johannesburg, joint exhibition with Linda Moross Ballen (qv), Susan Rosenberg (qv) and Elizabeth Vels (qv); 1988 Johannesburg Art Gallery, Vita Art Now.

Awards 1975 First Prize for Printmaking, New Signatures, SAAA; 1975 Witwatersrand Technical College (Technikon), Fine Art Award; 1987 Merit Award, Volkskas Atelier Competition; 1987 Witwatersrand Technikon Medal; 1987 Chamber of Mines Award, Witwatersrand Technikon.

Represented Africana Museum, Johannesburg; Johannesburg Art Gallery; Pretoria Art Museum; Rand Afrikaans University; SA National Gallery, Cape Town; University of the Orange Free State; University of South Africa.

HODGE Simon Prince RI

Born 1903 Glasgow, Scotland.
Died 1973 Edinburgh, Scotland.
Resided in SA 1928–32 and 1950–63.
A painter of wildlife, landscapes, figures and genre. Worked mainly in water-colour.

Studies Glasgow School of Art, under Maurice Griffenhagen and in London under Iain Macnab (1890–*c*.1970).

Profile A member of the Royal Institute of Painters in Watercolour, London; 1931–32 President of the Johannesburg Friday Club. 1953 designed the Schlesinger Pavilion, Rhodes Centenary Exhibition, Salisbury (Harare, Zimbabwe). 1958–59 travelled in East Africa, North Africa and Spain. 1963–67 lived in Ibiza; 1967–72 lived in Majorca. Married to the actress Eileen Goudvis (1908–71).

Exhibitions 1933–40 exhibited in London; exhibited with the Pieter Wenning Gallery, Johannesburg, from 1954; 1965 exhibited in Glasgow.

Public Commission Five oil paintings for the Stevenson Hamilton Gallery/Library, Skukusa, Kruger National Park.

References SAA; DBA; BSAK 1 & 2; AASA.

HODGINS Robert Griffiths

Born 1920 Dulwich, London, England.
Resided in SA from 1953, visited SA in 1938.
A painter and graphic artist of figures and urban life. Works in oil, acrylic, tempera and in various graphic media. Since 1959 a series entitled "UBU, variations on Alfred Jarry's character".

Studies 1947–50 part-time, 1950–53 full-time at the Goldsmith's College of Art, University of London, gaining a National Diploma in Design (Painting).

Profile 1940–45 served in the armed forces in Egypt. 1954–62 taught painting and drawing at the Pretoria Technical College; 1962–66 a journalist, art critic and then Assistant Editor of *Newscheck*. 1966–83 a lecturer, then a senior lecturer in the Department of Fine Art, University of the Witwatersrand.

Exhibitions He has participated in numerous group exhibitions from the early 1950s in SA; 1955 Lidchi Gallery, Johannesburg, first of over 20 solo exhibitions; 1960 Quadrennial Exhibition; 1961 Gallery 101, Johannesburg, joint exhibition with Ernst de Jong (qv); from 1970 several joint exhibitions with Jan Neethling (qv); 1979 Cape Town Biennial; 1984–85 Four Johannesburg Painters, a touring exhibition with Ilona Anderson (qv), Ricky Burnett (qv) and Jo Smail (qv); 1985 Tributaries, touring SA and West Germany; 1985 Cape Town Triennial; 1986 Grahamstown Festival, "Images 1953–86", Retrospective Exhibition, touring SA; 1987 "The Hogarth Series", joint exhibition with Deborah Bell (qv) and William Kentridge (qv), touring SA; 1987 and 1988 Johannesburg Art Gallery, Vita Art Now.
Awards 1955 Transvaal Art of Today Best Young Artist Award, Pretoria Centenary Exhibition; 1986 Vita Quarterly Award Winner; 1987 Vita Annual Award Winner.
Represented Johannesburg Art Gallery; Pretoria Art Museum; SA National Gallery, Cape Town; University of South Africa; University of the Witwatersrand; William Humphreys Art Gallery, Kimberley.
References SAA; SAP&S; BSAK 1; AASA; *Artlook* January 1973; *Habitat* no 5, 1973; *De Arte* September 1984; *De Kat* June 1986.

HODNETT Noel

Born 1949 Gatooma, Rhodesia (Gadoma, Zimbabwe).
A painter of landscapes. Works in oil.
Studies Gained a BA(FA) from Rhodes University in 1971.
Profile 1969–78 a member of the Grahamstown Group. 1971–74 a pottery instructor at Rhodes University; 1972–74 a technician and from 1975 a lecturer in the Department of Fine Art, Rhodes University.
Exhibitions He has participated in numerous group exhibitions from 1971 in SA and in Zimbabwe; 1985 Cape Town Triennial.
Award 1971 Purvis Prize for Fine Art, Rhodes University.
Represented Pietersburg Collection; University of the Witwatersrand.

HOEFSLOOT Tjeerd Adrianus Johannes (Ted)

Born 1930 Amsterdam, The Netherlands.
Resided in SA from 1955.
A painter of landscapes and figures. Works in oil, acrylic and ink.
Studies 1946–51 Amsterdam School of Graphic Arts, where studied lithography and advanced drawing.
Profile 1981 Vice-Chairman of the Artists Market. 1978 illustrated *Cape Wine Estates* by C Pama, 1980 Ad Donker, Johannesburg. 1955–69 lived in Cape Town and from 1969 in Johannesburg. 1979, 1982 and 1985 spent several months in the UK.
Exhibitions He has participated in several group exhibitions from 1962 in SA; 1963 Stellenbosch, first of nine solo exhibitions held in SA.
Reference *Habitat* no 42, 1980.

HOFFE Jacqueline

Born 1932 Durban.

A painter of landscapes, seascapes, portraits and figures in an atmospheric, evocative, semi-representational manner. Works in oil, watercolour, gouache, ink, wash, pencil and charcoal.

Studies 1964–68 under Bill Ainslie (qv).

Profile 1980–85 lived in SWA/Namibia, thereafter in Johannesburg.

Exhibitions She has participated in many group exhibitions in SA; 1981 Everard Read Gallery, Johannesburg, solo exhibition.

Represented SA Embassy, Tokyo, Japan; Windhoek Municipal Gallery.

HOFMANN Eugen Herbert

Born 1941 Nürnberg, Germany.

Resided in SA from 1969.

A self-taught sculptor of animals, figures and abstract pieces. Works in brass, copper and steel sheeting.

Exhibitions He has participated in numerous group exhibitions from 1985 in SA and once in Germany; 1986 Crake Gallery, Johannesburg, solo exhibition; 1987 Laura's Collection, Johannesburg, joint exhibition with Jean Solombre.

HOJEM Linda

Born 1961 Upington, Cape Province.

A painter of figures and portraits. Works in mixed media; also a graphic artist.

Studies 1978–81 University of the Witwatersrand, under Professor Alan Crump, Robert Hodgins (qv) and Paul Stopforth (qv), gaining a BA(FA)(Hons); 1980 awarded the Anya Millman Scholarship for study and travel; 1984 University of the Witwatersrand, gaining honours in History of Art.

Profile A member of the SAAA. 1984 an assistant at the Gertrude Posel Gallery, University of the Witwatersrand; 1985 an assistant at the Market Gallery, Johannesburg.

Exhibitions Participated in many group exhibitions from 1978 in Johannesburg, Pretoria and Cape Town; 1985 Cape Town Triennial.

Awards 1981 Merit Award, and 1983 First Prize Painting and First Prize Drawing, New Signatures, SAAA, Pretoria.

Represented University of South Africa.

HOLLANDER Oscar

Born 1864 Cologne, Germany.

Resided in SA from 1889.

A painter of Karoo landscapes. Worked in oil and watercolour.

Studies In Amsterdam and under George C Robinson (qv) in Cape Town.

Profile Lived for the larger part of his life at Carnarvon in the Cape. 1924–26 in Europe.

Exhibition 1921 Lezards, Johannesburg, solo exhibition.

References BSAK 1 & 2; AASA.

HOLLOW Patrick

Born 1941 SA.
A graphic artist producing linocuts of urban life and of figures.
Studies Assisted by Cecil Skotnes (qv), otherwise self-taught.
Profile A founder member of the Nyanga Art Group. Teaches at the Nyanga Art
Centre, Cape Province.
Exhibitions He has participated in group exhibitions in Cape Town.
Reference ADA no 3, 1987.

HOLM Cornelia

Born 1943 Berlin, Germany.
Resided in SA from 1947.
Both a painter and a sculptor of landscapes, still life and figures. Works in oil,
watercolour, bronze, ceramics and wood. A graphic artist.
Studies 1962–64 Pretoria Technical College, under Anna Vorster (qv), Zakkie
Eloff (qv), Robert Hodgins (qv), Gunther van der Reis (qv) and Leo Theron
(qv).
Profile A member of the SAAA. From 1982 has taught at Berg-en-Water Art
School, Hartebeespoort, Transvaal. 1972 illustrations for Eric Holm's *Beetles*;
1979 stage designs for "Façade" by Sir William Walton. A musician who plays
the violin and sings, and a writer of plays and poems. 1947–64 lived in the
Transvaal; 1964–66 in Berlin; 1970–74 in Cape Town; 1974–76 in the Transvaal; 1976–81 in Cremona, Italy; from 1981 in the Transvaal. Daughter of Elly
Holm (qv).
Exhibitions She has participated in several group exhibitions from 1963 in SA;
1964 Schweickerdt Gallery, Pretoria, first of five solo exhibitions one of which
was held in Italy.
Public Commissions 1976 mural, Barberton Library, Transvaal; 1978 ceramic
tile mural, Stellenbosch; 1979 ceramic tile mural, Jan Smuts Airport, Johannesburg.
Reference BSAK 1.

HOLM Elly

Born 1911 Koblenz, Germany.
Resided in SA from 1935.
A painter and graphic artist working in oil, watercolour, gouache, ink, pencil,
charcoal, pastel, etching and fresco. A sculptor working in bronze, slate, sgraffito
and terracotta. Her subject matter covers landscapes, still life, figures, portraits
and wildlife.
Studies 1929–33 Academy of Art, Leipzig, Germany, under Professor Horst-
Schulze; 1934 privately at Dresden Art Gallery and the Kaiser Friedrich
Museum, Berlin.

WILLEM DE SANDERES HENDRIKZ
Mariga
Bronze 117,7 cm High
Johannesburg Art Gallery

ROBERT HODGINS
Sphinx and so forth 1987
Oil & Acrylic on Canvas 231 × 201 cm
University of the Witwatersrand

Profile 1955–59 taught art privately in Pretoria. Illustrated in 1951 *Shangani* by Oswald Pirow; in 1972 *Die Houtvrou* by C Lohann; in 1973 *Afrikanische Erzälungen* by H Trümpelmann; in 1973 *Jan Frederik in die Toring* by C Lohann; in 1974 *Vom Deutschen Leben* by H Trümpelmann; in 1974 *Die Slapers* by C Lohann; in 1976 *Roeland* by Louise Behrens. A number of stained glass windows for churches in Randburg, Tierpoort and for the Goudstad College of Education, Johannesburg. 1919–33 lived in Leipzig; 1933–35 in Berlin; 1935–39 in Durban; 1939–45 in Berlin and from 1945 near Pretoria. She has travelled throughout Europe and to Zimbabwe and SWA/Namibia. Mother of Cornelia Holm (qv).
Exhibitions She has participated in several group exhibitions in SA; 1938 City Hall, Durban, first of over 60 solo exhibitions held throughout SA and West Germany; 1986 University of Pretoria, Prestige Retrospective Exhibition.
Represented University of the Orange Free State.
Public Commissions Numerous commissions for banks, churches, government departments, libraries and educational establishments.
Publication by Holm *Affchen Jups*, 1945.
References BSAK 1 & 2.

HOLO Sydney

Born 1952 Bellville, Cape Province.
A graphic artist producing linocuts of urban life.
Studies Received a scholarship to attend night classes at the Michaelis School of Fine Art; also studied under Cecil Skotnes (qv); ceramics under Bruce Holford.
Profile A founder member of the Nyanga Art Group. Teaches ceramics, painting and graphics at the Nyanga Art Centre, Cape Province.
Exhibitions He has participated in group exhibitions in Cape Town.
Reference *ADA* no 3, 1987.

HÖN Eugene Peter

Born 1958 Bellville, Cape Province.
A sculptor of figurative pieces. Works in ceramics.
Studies 1979–85 Michaelis School of Fine Art, under John Nowers (qv) and Bruce Arnott (qv), gaining a BA(FA) in 1982 and an MA(FA) in 1985.
Profile From 1986 a lecturer in the Ceramics Department at the Witwatersrand Technikon.
Exhibitions He has participated in several group exhibitions from 1983; 1985 Michaelis School of Fine Art Gallery, Cape Town, solo exhibition; 1988 Market Gallery, Johannesburg, solo exhibition.
Represented Johannesburg Art Gallery; SA National Gallery, Cape Town.
References *De Kat* May 1986; *Ceramix* July 1987.

HOOPER John ARCA

Born 1926 Southampton, Hampshire, England.
Resided in SA 1954–61.
A sculptor of figures, architectural sculptures and portraits. Works in stone, wood, clay, metal and concrete.

Studies Bournemouth College of Art, Dorset, UK, gaining a National Diploma in Art (Sculpture); Royal College of Art, London, under Frank Dobson (1888–1963) and John Skeaping (*b*.1901), where gained a continuation scholarship for a further year of study under Sir Jacob Epstein (1880–1959) and became an Associate.
Profile 1956–58 a lecturer at the Port Elizabeth Technical College; 1958–61 a lecturer at the University of Natal.
Exhibitions He has participated in group exhibitions in the UK and in 1960 and 1961 in SA; 1960 Quadrennial Exhibition.
Represented University of Natal.
Public Commission Relief work, Ships Terminal Building, Durban Harbour.
Reference Port Elizabeth School of Art.

HOPCROFT Clive John

Born 1936 Nottingham, England.
Resided in SA from 1969.
A painter of wildlife and landscapes. Works in watercolour and gouache.
Profile A member of the WSSA. A keen bird-watcher.
Exhibitions He has participated in several group exhibitions in Johannesburg from 1980.

HOPE Rosa Somerville ARE

Born 1902 Manchester, England.
Died 1972 Kokstad, Natal.
Resided in SA from 1935.
Primarily an etcher but also a painter of landscapes, portraits, figures and religious paintings. Worked in gouache and oil. Frequently painted the Drakensberg Mountains and the Transkei.
Studies 1919 Slade School of Art, London, under Henry Tonks (1862–1937), Wilson Steer (1860–1942) and John Wheatley (qv), later at the Central School of Art, London, both on scholarships.
Profile A member of the SA Society of Artists and the NSA. 1923 an Associate of the Royal Society of Painter-Etchers and Engravers, London. 1935–38 taught etching and drawing at the Michaelis School of Fine Art; 1938–57 a senior lecturer at the University of Natal. Her mother was an art teacher and her sister, Muriel Hollinger, a recognised portraitist in England.
Exhibitions Participated in group exhibitions from 1936 in SA, the UK, Sweden, Austria and the USA; held her first solo exhibition at the Rembrandt Gallery, London; 1966 Klynsmith Gallery, Johannesburg, joint exhibition with Minnie Cook (qv); 1977 University of Natal, Retrospective Exhibition.
Award 1926 Prix de Rome for her painting entitled "Adoration of the Shepherds".

Represented Africana Museum, Johannesburg; Ann Bryant Gallery, East London; British Museum, London, UK; Durban Art Gallery; Manchester City Art Gallery, UK; National Gallery, Wales; Pretoria Art Museum; SA National Gallery, Cape Town; State Museum of Eastern Slovakia, Yugoslavia; Tatham Art Gallery, Pietermaritzburg; University of Natal; Victoria and Albert Museum, London, UK.
Public Commissions Portraits for the University of Natal, including that of the Rector and Chancellor, Professor E G Malherbe.
References SAP&D; DBA; BSAK 1; 3Cs; AASA.

HOWARTH Florence Nightingale (née Blakey)

Born 1878 Wakefield, Yorkshire, England.
Died Some time after 1965.
Resided in SA from the early 1900s.
A painter of landscapes of the Witwatersrand. Worked in oil.
Studies 1911 Mrs Arnott's sketching classes.
Profile Married to E G Hilner of Rand Mines, widowed 1913, remarried 1922.
Represented Africana Museum, Johannesburg.
Reference AMC7.

HULLEY Wallace Hugh

Born 1931 Pietermaritzburg.
A self-taught painter of landscapes, seascapes, portraits, figures, still life and wild-life. Works in watercolour, ink, pencil and oil. Creates large ceramic wall panels.
Profile An Associate member of the WSSA, a member of the Brush and Chisel Club and the British Fine Art Trade Guild. Has illustrated a number of children's books and drew the maps and wildlife drawings for *This is Botswana*. A potter. Has travelled extensively throughout the world and in 1986 visited the Greek islands.
Exhibitions He has participated in numerous group exhibitions held in SA, the UK, West Germany, Italy, Spain, Portugal and the USA; *c.*1969 Marjorie Bowen Gallery, Johannesburg, first of 20 solo exhibitions.
Represented Potchefstroom Museum; University of the Orange Free State; Willem Annandale Art Gallery, Lichtenburg.
Public Commission In 1987 he was commissioned to create a metal sculpture entitled "Birds in Flight" for a Krugersdorp building complex.
References BSAK 2; AASA.

HULME Mairn

Born 1900 East London.
A self-taught botanical artist who worked in ink.
Profile Lived in Natal, then in England and Australia until the outbreak of WWII when she returned to SA.
Publication by Hulme 1954 author and illustrator of *Wild Flowers of Natal*.
Reference SAA.

HUMPHRIS Dorothy Ella Summerton (née Levyns)

Born 1906 Johannesburg.
Died 1965 Kenilworth, Cape Town.
A painter of portraits, figures, wildlife, genre and street scenes. Worked in pastel, watercolour and oil.
Studies A mainly self-taught artist who majored in anthropology at the University of Cape Town and studied art briefly at the Heatherley School of Art, London and at the American School of Art, Fontainebleau, France.
Profile 1933–50 an illustrator on *The Cape Argus* under the pseudonym "Dorelle". Drew dust covers and illustrations for books by Lawrence Green and worked in commercial art printing with McManus Bros. Two series entitled "Cries of Cape Town" and "South of the Equator" were reproduced as table mats.
Exhibitions Participated in group exhibitions until 1958 in Johannesburg, Pretoria and Cape Town; held her first solo exhibition in Johannesburg.
Represented Africana Museum, Johannesburg; University of Cape Town.
References SAA; DSAB; AASA; AMC6 (under Dorelle).

HUNTLY Jeff

Born 1931 Bindura, Rhodesia (Zimbabwe).
Resided in SA from 1983.
A painter of African and British birds, wildlife and landscapes. Works in acrylic, watercolour, gouache and ink.
Studies Johannesburg School of Art, under George Boys (qv); privately under David Reid-Henry.
Profile 1972–82 wrote for the *Rhodesia Herald*, 1983–84 for *Pretoria News* and from 1983 for *The Star*, Johannesburg and *The Natal Witness*, Pietermaritzburg. Has written and illustrated articles for periodicals including *African Wildlife*, *Custos* and *Toktokkie*. In 1973 designed 15 Rhodesian postage stamps. Has designed coins for the Zimbabwean Government. 1967 spent a year in the Wankie (Hwange) Game Reserve. Lives in Pietermaritzburg.
Exhibitions He has participated in numerous group exhibitions from 1958 in Zimbabwe, SA and the UK; 1964 Adler Fielding Gallery, Johannesburg, first of six solo exhibitions, five of which have been held in Zimbabwe.
Publications by Huntly Wrote and illustrated *Veld Sketchbook*, 1974, Books of Rhodesia, Bulawayo; *Veld Sketchbook Two*, 1976, Pioneer Head, Harare, Zimbabwe.
References BSAK 1; *Artlook* November 1969.

HUTT Grethe (Schonken)

Born Brandfort, Orange Free State.
A painter of landscapes and street scenes. Works in oil. A graphic artist.
Studies Part-time at the Michaelis School of Fine Art; privately under Jean Welz (qv); at the Anglo-French Art Centre, England; at the Heatherley School of Art, London; colour lithography at the Central School of Art, London, and in Paris.

Profile Began painting *c.*1948. Has illustrated Afrikaans children's books. Has visited SWA/Namibia.

Exhibitions She has participated in group exhibitions in SA, Yugoslavia and São Paulo, Brazil; 1960 Quadrennial Exhibition; she has held several solo exhibitions in Cape Town, Johannesburg and Harare, Zimbabwe.

Represented Arts Association SWA/Namibia Collection.

References Art SA; AASA.

HUTTON Phay

Born 1920 Faversham, Kent, England.

Resided in SA from 1939.

A painter of landscapes, portraits, seascapes and figures. Works in oil, gouache and wash. A muralist.

Studies Five years at the Camberwell School of Art, London, under Cosmo Clark (*b.*1897), Eric Fraser (*b.*1902) and Roland Vivian Pitchforth (qv).

Profile A member of the New Group. 1950 taught at the Michaelis School of Fine Art. Married to Leng Dixon (qv).

Exhibitions She has participated in several group exhibitions in SA; 1945 and 1946 Gainsborough Galleries, Johannesburg, joint exhibitions with Leng Dixon (qv); 1956 and 1960 Quadrennial Exhibitions; 1964 SAAA Gallery, Cape Town, solo exhibition.

References Collectors' Guide; Art SA; SAA; BSAK 1 & 2; AASA.

HUYSER Maryna

Born 1959 Potchefstroom, Transvaal.

A painter, graphic artist and sculptor of landscapes, portraits, figures, animals and abstract pieces. Works in oil, acrylic, watercolour, gouache, ink, wash, pencil, charcoal, various graphic media, bronze, stone and wood. A series entitled "Dance" in 1984, "Movement in Time" in 1985 and "Sex" in 1987.

Studies 1976–77 Johannesburg Art, Ballet and Music School; 1978–81 University of Pretoria, under Professor Nico Roos (qv) and John Clarke (qv).

Profile 1987 a member of the SAAA. 1984 a graphics teacher, Johannesburg Art Foundation. 1984 a number of illustrations for books published by HAUM, Cape Town. 1982 wrote and illustrated 120 poems. 1986 lived in SWA/Namibia.

Exhibitions She has participated in several group exhibitions from 1984; 1984 Market Gallery, Johannesburg, first of four solo exhibitions; 1985 Cape Town Triennial; 1987 Verwoerdburg Association of Arts, joint exhibition with Johan du Plessis (qv), Guy du Toit (qv) and Evette Weyers (qv); 1987 Gallery 21, Johannesburg, joint exhibition with Guy du Toit (qv).

Award 1981 Drawing Prize, New Signatures, SAAA, Pretoria.

HUŸZERS Josef Pohl

Born 1946 Boksburg, Transvaal.

A sculptor of works of socio-political concern. Works in sandcast aluminium and mixed media. 1984–86 "Opus I" series; 1986–87 "Alternative Trophies and Monuments" series.

Studies 1966–67 industrial design at the Johannesburg School of Art; 1980–84 Pretoria Technikon. Gained a National Diploma in Art and Design and a Higher Diploma in Sculpture.

Profile From 1980 a member of the SAAA. 1959–64 lived in Pretoria; 1966–67 in Johannesburg; 1968–69 in Port Elizabeth; 1970–71 in District Six, Cape Town; 1972–77 in Magoebaskloof, Transvaal; from 1978 in Pretoria. Has travelled extensively in SA and throughout Europe.

Exhibitions He has participated in several group exhibitions from 1981 in SA; 1986 Pretoria Art Museum, solo exhibition; 1987 Market Gallery, Johannesburg, two solo exhibitions.

Award 1983 Ingram Anderson Prize.

Reference *SA Arts Calendar* Autumn 1987.

I

ILLINGWORTH SPANN Elizabeth see SPANN Elizabeth Illingworth

INGGS Stephen Charles

Born 1955 Cape Town.

A multifarious graphic artist. 1982–83 a series of landscape images altered by the intrusion of signs/objects with metaphoric overtones.

Studies 1976–78 Natal Technical College, gaining a National Diploma in Fine Art; 1979–80 on an Emma Smith Scholarship at Brighton Polytechnic, England, under Harvey Daniels, Tim Mara and Laurence Preece, where awarded a Postgraduate Diploma in Printmaking.

Profile A member of the Artists Guild, Cape Town. 1981–84 a lecturer in printmaking, University of Natal; from 1985 a lecturer in printmaking at the Michaelis School of Fine Art.

Exhibitions He has participated in many group exhibitions from 1979 in SA, Taiwan, the UK and Germany; 1982 Cape Town Triennial; 1983 NSA Gallery, Durban, solo exhibition; 1985 Tributaries, touring SA and West Germany.

Represented Durban Art Gallery; Tatham Art Gallery, Pietermaritzburg.

Reference AASA.

INGRAM Norma

Born 1907 Edinburgh, Scotland.

Resided in SA 1938–62.

A painter of landscapes, cityscapes, portraits, animals, still life, particularly flowers and of interiors and industrial buildings. Works in oil and watercolour. 1954–65 a series of six Johannesburg panoramas.

Studies 1921 Edinburgh College of Art; 1923 Royal Scottish Academy, under John Bowie (1860s–1914); postgraduate studies, Académie Julian, Paris; Slade School of Art, London, under Professor Randolph Schwabe (1885–1948); animal painting under William Walls (1860–1942).

Profile A member of the Society of Scottish Women Artists, the British Empire Arts Society, the Brush and Chisel Club and a foundation member and first President of the Johannesburg Society of Arts. Lived in Johannesburg. From 1962 has lived in England. While resident in SA, visited Europe.

Exhibitions Participated in group exhibitions from 1923 in Europe and SA; 1951 Herbert Evans Gallery, Johannesburg, first of several solo exhibitions held in SA and the UK.

Represented Africana Museum, Johannesburg.

Public Commission 1956 portrait of Dr W A Hoernlé for the Johannesburg Co-ordinating Council of Social Welfare Organisations.

References SAA; AMC3 & 7; BSAK 1; AASA; *SA Art News* 22 June 1961.

INGRAMS Joseph Forsyth FRGS

Born 1862 Belfast, Northern Ireland.
Died 1923 Red Hill, Durban.
A painter of landscapes, ships and seascapes. Worked in oil and watercolour. A number of Boer War sketches and paintings of scenes of historical importance in Natal.
Profile A prolific artist, particularly after 1910. From 1895 held various Government posts; 1903 a magistrate in Dundee; 1917 in Howick; later lived in Pietermaritzburg. Served in the Zulu wars and the Anglo-Boer War. Wrote several books on Natal and practised as a journalist, having several papers published in geographical journals. He was a correspondent for *South Africa*, a London weekly. 1879 travelled in Pondoland and Swaziland.
Publications by Ingrams Poems of a Pioneer, 1893, reprinted 1921, Times Printing Co., with biography by Charles W Cowen; *The Story of an African Seaport*, also illustrated by Ingrams, 1899, G Coester, Durban.
References SESA; Natal Art; Pict Afr.

I'ONS Frederick Timpson

Born 1802 Islington, Middlesex, England.
Died 1887 Grahamstown.
Resided in SA from 1834.
Although he had lessons from the sculptor John Francis, in his early youth, mainly a self-taught painter of figures, Boer life, portraits of tribal chiefs and other notability, as well as of landscapes. Worked in oil, watercolour, pen and wash.
Profile Prior to 1834 owned an art school in Marylebone, London, where taught drawing, painting, handwriting and commercial subjects. 1834–35 a volunteer in the Sixth Frontier War. After 1850 taught art privately in Grahamstown. Travelled throughout the eastern Cape Province. A cartoonist, drawing "The Aquila Caricatures", consisting of 14 caricatures of Sir Andrew Stockenström, the Lieutenant-Governor, engraved and published in England c.1838. A number of his lithographs have been reprinted. Involved in the stage decoration of theatre productions in Grahamstown. In 1979 his picture of the "Briefstok" runner was used on one of the Commemorative International Philatelic Exhibition Medals. The great-grandfather of Annie Galpin (qv).
Exhibitions 1948 Tate Gallery, London, SA Art Exhibition; 1976 SA National Gallery, Cape Town, included in "English and SA Watercolours in the SA National Gallery Exhibition".
Represented Africana Museum, Johannesburg; Albany Museum, Grahamstown; Fort Beaufort Historical Museum; King George VI Art Gallery, Port Elizabeth; SA National Gallery, Cape Town; University of Stellenbosch; William Fehr Collection, Cape Town; William Humphreys Art Gallery, Kimberley; 1820 Settlers Memorial Museum, Grahamstown.
References J Redgrave and E Bradlow, *Frederick I'Ons, Artist*, 1958, Maskew Miller, Cape Town; Pict Art; Collectors' Guide; Afr Repos; SADNB; AMC3&7; DSAB; SAP&S; SAP&D; SESA; Pict Afr; BSAK 1 & 2; SA Art; 3Cs; AASA; LSAA.

IRVING NICHOLSON Edgar

Born 1920 Johannesburg.

A painter of landscapes, portraits, still life, interiors, night street scenes, genre and figures. Works in oil, watercolour, gouache, enamel and silver. A calligrapher.

Studies 1946 Witwatersrand Technical College, under James Gardner (qv) and Phyllis Gardner (qv); 1947–50 Beckenham School of Art, Kent, UK, under Thomas Freeth; 1950–52 Royal College of Art, London, under Ruskin Spear (*b*.1911). Gained an Art Teachers Diploma (UK), a National Diploma in Design and Painting (UK), a National Certificate in Crafts (UK) and a Diploma in Gemmology.

Profile 1960–68 taught graphic design at the Witwatersrand Technical College and from 1968 at the Port Elizabeth Technical College (Technikon). 1970–80 an art critic on the *Evening Post*, Port Elizabeth. He has lived in the UK, Germany, France and in SA.

Exhibitions He has participated in group exhibitions from 1945 in the UK and SA; 1949 Hamburg, West Germany, first of 23 solo exhibitions held in the UK, Germany and throughout SA.

Represented Africana Museum, Johannesburg; galleries in Brighton, UK and Zurich, Switzerland; Tatham Art Gallery, Pietermaritzburg; University of Port Elizabeth; University of the Witwatersrand.

References Collectors' Guide; BSAK 1; AASA.

ISAACSON Edward

Born 1963 Orkney, Transvaal.

A sculptor of figures, portraits, wildlife, still life and of abstract pieces. Works in bronze, stone, ciment fondu, wood and stainless steel.

Studies 1979–80 under Effie Joffee; 1981 six months at the Witwatersrand Technikon.

Profile 1985 visited New York, USA.

Exhibitions He has participated in several group exhibitions from 1983 in Johannesburg and the USA.

Represented Pietrasanta Fine Arts, New York, USA.

IVANOFF Victor Archipovich

Born 1909 Vilna, Russia.

Resided in SA from 1937.

A painter of landscapes, seascapes, portraits, figures and animals, particularly horses. Works in oil and sepia.

Studies 1920 South Slavia Cossack Cadet School, under N Karpoff; 1926–29 architecture in Yugoslavia; 1951 in Rome under Alessio Issupoff; 1957–59 in Paris, Munich and Vienna.

Profile A cartoonist and illustrator. 1937–72 a cartoonist for *Die Vaderland* and other newspapers; 1957–59 drawings for various newspapers and periodicals in Vienna, Paris, Brussels and Munich. After 1972 his work appeared in *The Citizen* and *Die Republikein*. During his three-year study tour of Europe he also studied singing in Vienna. He sang for the German and American radio services in Germany and for the Johannesburg Municipal Opera (1944–56). 1926 lived in Tunisia.

Exhibitions He has participated in group exhibitions of both paintings and cartoons in SA and in Munich, West Germany; held over 10 solo exhibitions in the Transvaal; 1973 Rand Afrikaans University, Retrospective Exhibition of his Cartoons.

Represented Cartoons: Africana Museum, Johannesburg; National Cultural and Open-Air Museum, Pretoria; Potchefstroom Museum; Rand Afrikaans University; University of Cape Town; University of the Orange Free State.

Publication by Ivanoff *Die Tweede Wereldoorlog in Spotprente*, 1946, Afrikaanse Pers, Johannesburg.

References SAA; SASSK; *SA Panorama* July 1958.

J

JACKSON Barbara

Born 1949 Cape Town.

A sculptor of figures. Works in clay.

Profile Has written two books on ceramics. Teaches at the Community Arts Project, Cape Town and at her Green Point studio.

Exhibitions She has participated in numerous group exhibitions from 1977.

JACOBS Dee

Born 1938 Johannesburg.

A painter of still life, figures and abstract pictures. Works in oil, acrylic, watercolour, gouache, ink, wash, pencil and charcoal. A graphic artist, a maker of collages and a sculptor in stone, ciment fondu, steel and clay.

Studies 1962–65 Da Vinci School of Fine Art, Johannesburg, under Carlo Sdoya (qv); from 1984 at the Johannesburg Art Foundation, under Bill Ainslie (qv); 1986 Vermont Studio School, USA, under Professor Maurice Lowe.

Profile A trained dancer.

Exhibitions She has participated in several group exhibitions held in Johannesburg; 1987 Helen de Leeuw, Johannesburg, first solo exhibition; 1987 Johannesburg Art Foundation, joint exhibition with Gail Behrmann (qv), Charles Levin (qv), Lionel Murcott (qv) and Russel Scott.

JACOBSON Naomi Deborah

Born 1926 Windhoek, SWA/Namibia.

A sculptor of wildlife, figures, portraits of the ethnic people of SWA/Namibia and heads of Southern African leaders as well as other notable personalities. Works in bronze, steel, brass and ciment fondu.

Studies Michaelis School of Fine Art, under Professor Edward Roworth (qv), where gained a Diploma; also part-time study 1968–74 under Bernard Meadows (*b*.1915) and F E McWilliam (*b*.1909) in London and in 1981, 1982 and 1983 at Forte de Marmi, Rome, Italy.

Profile Designs needlework patterns and paints on fabric. 1950–70 a member of the Arts Association SWA/Namibia. Involved in acting and singing ventures in Windhoek.

Exhibitions 1958 Windhoek, first of five solo exhibitions held in SWA/Namibia, SA and the USA.

Represented Rand Afrikaans University; University of Cape Town; University of Pretoria; University of the Witwatersrand.

Public Commissions 1966 Springbok Fountain, Beaufort West, Cape Province; 1967 Springbok Fountain, Windhoek; 1973 steel structure, Permanent Building Society, Johannesburg; Flamingo Fountain, Permanent Building Society, Windhoek; steel structure, Germiston, Transvaal; SA Dramatist, the State Theatre, Pretoria.

References BSAK 1; SA Art; AASA.

JAHOLKOWSKI George

Born 1914 Baku, Russia.
Died 1980.
Resided in SA from 1955.
A sculptor in metal, generally welded sheet copper. His works are both realistic and semi-abstract, capturing the character of animals and the human form. Religious themes.
Studied Architecture at the University of Warsaw, Poland; 1936–37 Ecole des Beaux Arts, Paris; 1947–49 Hammersmith School of Art, London; 1957–58 Michaelis School of Fine Art, under Lippy Lipshitz (qv) and Maurice van Essche (qv).
Profile Married the pianist Virginia Fortescue.
Exhibitions Participated in group exhibitions held throughout SA from 1958; 1959 SAAA Gallery, Cape Town, first of several solo exhibitions; 1960 Quadrennial Exhibition.
Represented Hester Rupert Art Museum, Graaff-Reinet; SA National Gallery, Cape Town.
References Art SA; SAA; 20C SA Art; SAP&S; SESA; BSAK 1 & 2; SA Art; 3Cs; AASA; *Fontein* no 3, 1960; *SA Arts Calendar* February 1980.

JALI Thamsanqa Rutherford (Thami)

Born 1955 Durban.
A painter, sculptor and a graphic artist working in acrylic, pencil, charcoal, wood and in various graphic media. From 1982 a series on "Birth".
Studies 1981–82 Rorke's Drift Art Centre, under Jay Johnson, where gained an Art Certificate; 1983–84 ceramics at Natal Technikon, under Huby Wiid (qv).
Profile 1983–84 founder of Art Communications; from 1985 a member of the Clermont Art Society. 1983–84 created functional and sculptural pottery. 1955–62 lived in Lamontville, Durban; 1963–75 in Clermont, Pinetown; 1976–82 in Sikhawini, Empangeni and from 1983 in Umgababa, Natal.
Exhibitions Has participated in several group exhibitions in SA and once in Swaziland in 1983.
Award 1982 First Prize in Sculpture, Festival of African Arts, University of Zululand.
References Echoes of African Art; *Staffrider* April 1982.

JAMMET Claude

(1977–87 painted under the name Jammet-Tait)
Born 1953 Salisbury, Rhodesia (Harare, Zimbabwe).
Resided in SA from 1973.
A self-taught painter of landscapes, seascapes, wildlife, figures and portraits. Works in oil, watercolour and pencil. 1983 "Rooi Dak", a series on one house in Knysna; 1984 "Knysna Story", a series of important buildings and places in Knysna; 1985 a series on the Comores; 1986 "The Actors", a series on the members of the cast of "Caliban".

Profile 1983–85 Director of the Tait Gallery, Knysna. 1986 produced and directed "Caliban", a personal interpretation of the Arthurian tales. 1955–63 lived in Kenya; 1963–67 in India; 1967–73 in Japan; 1973–78 in SA; 1978–80 in France; thereafter in Knysna, Cape Province.

Exhibitions She has participated in many group exhibitions from 1975 in SA and once in Paris in 1979; 1983 Lookout Art Gallery, Plettenberg Bay, first of four solo exhibitions held in SA.

JANDER Peter John

Born 1954 Cape Town.

A self-taught painter of landscapes, seascapes, genre and wildlife. Works in oil, watercolour and pastel.

Profile Teaches art privately. A number of his paintings have been used in calendars. 1982 visited The Netherlands, Munich in West Germany and Ghent, Belgium.

Exhibitions He has participated in several group exhibitions in SA and two in The Netherlands; 1985 Chelsea Gallery, Wynberg, Cape Town, solo exhibition.

JANSEN VAN VUUREN Louis

Born 1949 Middelburg, Transvaal.

A painter and graphic artist of human figures and animals in fantasy or local landscapes. Works in oil, watercolour, pencil, charcoal and in various graphic media. 1984 a series of paintings, drawings and photographs of Crossroads, Cape Town.

Studies 1967–70 University of Stellenbosch, under Otto Schröder (qv) and Jochen Berger (qv), gaining a BA in Creative Arts; 1976 University of Stellenbosch, under Otto Schröder (qv), gaining a BA with Honours in History of Art (cum laude).

Profile A member of the SAAA, 1980–86 a committee member and Chairman of the SAAA Western Cape Branch in 1986. 1984 Chairman of the Fundraising Art Auction for Hunger Relief in the Western Cape. 1973 a lecturer in fine arts at the Natal Technical College; 1974–82 Head of the Painting Department, University of Stellenbosch; from 1984 a lecturer in graphic design at the Michaelis School of Fine Art. 1986 elected to the Board of Trustees and the Selection Committee of the SA National Gallery, Cape Town. 1985–86 illustrations for book covers for Tafelberg, Cape Town and for *De Suid Afrikaan*. 1985–86 designed posters for CAPAB; 1986 editorial illustrations for *Leadership* magazine. Frequent visits to Europe and the USA.

Exhibitions 1966 Middelburg, Transvaal, first of 10 solo exhibitions; he has participated in over 50 group exhibitions from 1972 in SA and the USA; 1979 Cape Town Biennial; 1981 Republic Festival Exhibition.

Represented University of Stellenbosch.

JAROSZYNSKA Karin Synmove Aurora

Born 1937 Helsinki, Finland.
Resided in SA from 1957.
A painter and graphic artist of figures in a surrealistic and fantastical manner. Works in oil, acrylic, watercolour, gouache, ink and wash, pencil, charcoal, jute and in various graphic media. A number of pen and ink series including in 1965 the "Circus" series and in 1985 the "Rialto Suite".
Studies 1951–57 Ateneum, Academy of Fine Arts, Finland, under Professor E Koponen, Professor Samuel Vanni (*b*.1908) and A Tuhka, gaining a Diploma.
Profile A member of the Maison des Artistes, Paris. 1961–77 taught painting, drawing and sculpture privately. Married to Tadeusz Jaroszynski (qv).
Exhibitions She has participated in numerous group exhibitions from 1965 in SA, Finland, the UK, Yugoslavia, West Germany, Spain, the USA, Norway, Italy, Monaco and Switzerland; 1965 Gallery 101, Johannesburg, first of numerous solo exhibitions held in SA, Finland and France; 1976 University of the Witwatersrand, joint exhibition with Tadeusz Jaroszynski (qv); 1987 Johannesburg Art Gallery, Vita Art Now.
Award 1986 Vita Quarterly Award Winner.
Represented Durban Art Gallery; Johannesburg Art Gallery; Leeds City Art Gallery, UK; Pietersburg Collection; Potchefstroom University for CHE; Pretoria Art Museum; Rand Afrikaans University; Sandton Municipal Collection; SA National Gallery, Cape Town; University of the Witwatersrand.
References SAP&D; BSAK 1 & 2; 3Cs; AASA; *Artlook* April 1971 & May 1972; *Gallery* Winter 1985.

JAROSZYNSKI Tadeusz

Born 1933 Makanska, Yugoslavia.
Resided in SA from 1957.
A painter with a wide-ranging subject matter, including still life, animals, figures and abstract pictures. Works in many media, particularly oil, gouache, pencil and wash.
Studies 1953–57 Ateneum, Academy of Fine Arts, Finland, gaining a Diploma.
Profile A member of the Maison des Artistes, Paris. Became a full-time painter in 1972. Husband of Karin Jaroszynska (qv).
Exhibitions He has participated in numerous group exhibitions in SA, France, Switzerland, West Germany, Spain, Yugoslavia, Norway, Monaco and Sweden; 1970 Johannesburg, first of several solo exhibitions held in SA; 1976 University of the Witwatersrand, joint exhibition with Karin Jaroszynska (qv); 1979 Galerie Romanet, Paris, first solo exhibition held in France.
Award 1967 First Prize, Transvaal Academy.
Represented Durban Art Gallery; Pietersburg Collection; Pretoria Art Museum; Rand Afrikaans University; Sandton Municipal Collection; SA National Gallery, Cape Town; University of the Witwatersrand.
References Pierre Mazars, *Jaroszynski*, 1979, Galerie Romanet, Paris; BSAK 1 & 2; 3Cs; AASA; *Artlook* October 1970 & February 1974.

JARZIN-LEVINSON Sheila

Born 1937 Johannesburg.
A painter of abstracted landscapes and abstract pictures. Works in oil.
Studies 1973–79 under Giuseppe Cattaneo (qv).
Profile She had made several study tours of Europe and Israel.
Exhibitions 1975 Lidchi Gallery, Johannesburg, first of two solo exhibitions; she has participated in several group exhibitions from 1978 in Johannesburg; 1985 Everard Read Gallery, Johannesburg, joint exhibition with Melissa Lipkin (qv).
Reference *Gallery* Spring 1985.

JASVEN Ben

Born 1933 Cape Town.
A painter and a sculptor.
Studies Witwatersrand Technical College, under James Gardner (qv).
Exhibitions Participated in group exhibitions in Johannesburg during the 1960s; 1963 Johannesburg, solo exhibition.
References SAA; *SA Art News* 6 April 1961.

JELLINEK Anne

Born 1923 Hamburg, Germany.
Resided in SA from 1936.
A painter and graphic artist of landscapes, seascapes, genre, figures and abstract pictures. Works in oil, watercolour and in various graphic media.
Studies 1942–44 under Maurice van Essche (qv); 1964–68 privately under Sidney Goldblatt (qv); 1970–71 privately under George Boys (qv); 1976 privately under Bill Ainslie (qv).
Profile A member of the SAAA. 1972–73 extensive study tours of England, Europe and Israel.
Exhibitions She has participated in numerous group exhibitions from 1963 in SA; 1968 Nedbank Gallery, Johannesburg, first of four solo exhibitions in Johannesburg.
Represented Willem Annandale Art Gallery, Lichtenburg.
References BSAK 1; *Artlook* December 1970.

JENKINS Patricia ARCA

Born 1933 Livingstone, Northern Rhodesia (Maramba, Zambia).
A sculptor.
Studies 1950–52 Bournemouth Municipal College, UK; 1955 Michaelis School of Fine Art, under Lippy Lipshitz (qv); 1955–58 Royal College of Art, London, under John Skeaping (*b*.1901), becoming an Associate.
Exhibitions She has exhibited in SA, Zimbabwe, Kenya and Greece.
Public Commission Fibreglass fountain group of seagulls in flight, Parkade, Cape Town.
Reference SAA.

JENNINGS Sidney (John)

Born 1899 Pretoria.

Died 1981 Pretoria.

Both a painter and a sculptor of landscapes, portraits, still life, seascapes, buildings, figures and wildlife. Worked in oil, acrylic, watercolour, ink, pencil, pastel, charcoal, wood, papier-mache, mosaic, enamel, batik, appliqué and beads. Produced large fabric wall hangings and handknotted mats. 1939–45 scenes of Cairo, Tripoli, Naples and Jerusalem.

Studies Witwatersrand Technical College, under Anton Hendriks (qv); privately under Marcelle Piltan (qv) and Monica MacIvor (qv).

Profile 1922–81 taught art privately in Rustenburg and Pretoria. A fully trained piano teacher. Visited Europe several times and Greece over 12 times.

Exhibitions Participated in numerous group exhibitions from the 1930s in SA; 1935 Hartley Hall, Pretoria, first of many solo exhibitions held in SA and Greece; 1987 Menlo Park and the SAAA Gallery, Pretoria, Commemorative Exhibitions.

Represented Pretoria Art Museum; SA National Museum of Military History, Johannesburg.

JENSEN Berrell Elizabeth

Born 1938 South Africa.

Resided in SA until 1968.

A sculptor of landscapes, seascapes, figures, abstract works, prehistoric earth forms, primitive religions and microscopic life. Works in bronze, copper, silver, brass, steel and ciment fondu.

Profile 1958 an art lecturer at the Johannesburg School of Art; 1983 an art lecturer at the Architectural Association, London. 1968–72 lived in Greece; 1972–75 in England; 1975–80 in Ireland and from 1980 in London.

Exhibitions She has participated in numerous group exhibitions from 1960 in SA, Greece, Republic of Ireland, England and Northern Ireland; 1960 Pabros Theatre, Durban, first of 16 solo exhibitions held in SA, Greece, Republic of Ireland, England and Northern Ireland.

Represented Hester Rupert Art Museum, Graaff-Reinet.

Public Commissions Numerous murals, sculptures and relief panels in hotels, commercial and industrial buildings in SA, Northern Ireland and England, including in 1965 a panel for the Rosebank Library, Johannesburg; 1967 a panel for the National Institute for Personnel Research, Johannesburg; 1971 a mural in the VIP Lounge, Jan Smuts Airport, Johannesburg.

References SAA; 20C SA Art; BSAK 1; AASA; *Artlook* October 1967 & July 1968.

JENSMA Wopko

Born 1939 Ventersdorp, Transvaal.

A graphic artist producing woodcuts, linocuts and monotypes of figures, animals and African themes.

KARIN JAROSZYNSKA
The Horseman 1984
Oil on Canvas 129 × 176 cm
Private

TADEUSZ JAROSZYNSKI
Two Women 1987
Oil on Canvas 89 × 116 cm
The Everard Read Gallery

ADOLPH JENTSCH
Nach Dem Regen 1939
Oil on Canvas 68 × 98 cm
Christo Wiese

KEITH JOUBERT
Quagga 1988
Oil on Canvas 180 × 165 cm
Gert Gertzen

Studies Gained a BA(FA) in 1964 from the University of Pretoria; also studied at Pochefstroom University for CHE.

Profile Taught art at schools in Mozambique; during the late 1960s taught art at schools in Botswana. 1965–67 a translator of novels for APB Publishers. A multilingual poet.

Exhibitions He has participated in group exhibitions from 1960 in SA, the USA and the UK; has held solo exhibitions in Johannesburg.

Represented Durban Art Gallery; SA National Gallery, Cape Town; University of the Witwatersrand; William Humphreys Art Museum, Kimberley.

References BSAK 1 & 2; AASA; *Artlook* January 1969 & February 1970; *De Arte* September 1969; *Garden & Home* August 1976.

JENTSCH Adolph Stephan Friedrich

Born 1888 Deuben, Dresden, Germany.
Died 1977 Windhoek, SWA/Namibia.
Resided in SWA/Namibia from 1938.
A painter of SWA/Namibian landscapes. Worked in watercolour and oil. A lithographer.

Studies Six years at Dresden Staatsakademie für Bildende Kunste, under Otto Gussmann (*b*.1869), Karl Kühl (*b*.1864) and Oskar Zwintscher (1870–1916) and on a travel grant award in France, Italy, London and The Netherlands.

Profile Influenced by Chinese art and interested in Oriental philosophy and yoga. 1927 illustrated a children's book; 1973 five paintings reproduced as stamps; a number of his paintings have been reproduced by Orde Levinson. 1938–47 travelled extensively in SWA/Namibia, eventually settling near Dordabis.

Exhibitions Participated in group exhibitions in SWA/Namibia, SA, Italy, Zimbabwe, The Netherlands, Belgium and West Germany; 1938 Windhoek, SWA/Namibia, first of many solo exhibitions held in SWA/Namibia and SA; 1956, 1960 and 1964 Quadrennial Exhibitions; 1958 SAAA Gallery, Pretoria, Johannesburg Art Gallery and SAAA Gallery, Cape Town, exhibition of Gruppe Funf (Group 5) consisting of Adolph Jentsch, Otto Schröder (qv), Fritz Krampe (qv), Joachim Voigts (qv) and Heinz Pulon (qv); 1958 Windhoek, 70th Birthday Retrospective Exhibition; 1966 Johannesburg Art Gallery, Prestige Exhibition; 1967 Pretoria Art Museum, Prestige Exhibition; 1968 Windhoek, 80th Birthday Retrospective Exhibition; 1969 SA National Gallery, Cape Town, Prestige Exhibition; 1970 Pretoria Art Museum, Retrospective Exhibition; 1974 Arts Association SWA/Namibia Gallery, Windhoek and Gallery 101, Johannesburg, Retrospective Exhibitions; 1976 Elizabeth Art Gallery, Johannesburg, joint exhibition with Fred Bauer (qv); 1977 Windhoek, Commemorative Exhibition; 1977 Die Kunskamer, Cape Town, joint exhibition with Fritz Krampe (qv); 1978 Windhoek, Commemorative Exhibition.

Awards 1913 Koniglich-Sachsische Staatsmedaille für Kunst und Wissenschaft; 1958 Order of Merit, First Class, Federal Republic of West Germany; 1962 Medal of Honour for Painting, SA Akademie vir Wetenskap en Kuns.

Represented Arts Association SWA/Namibia Collection; Durban Art Gallery; Hester Rupert Art Museum, Graaff-Reinet; Johannesburg Art Gallery; King George VI Art Gallery, Port Elizabeth; Pietersburg Collection; Pretoria Art Museum; Rand Afrikaans University; SA Akademie vir Wetenskap en Kuns; SA National Gallery, Cape Town; State Museum, Windhoek; University of the Orange Free State; University of Pretoria; University of South Africa; University of Stellenbosch; William Humphreys Art Gallery, Kimberley.

References O Schröder and P A Hendriks, *Adolph Jentsch*, 1958, Swakopmund; Olga Levinson, *Adolph Jentsch*, 1973, Human & Rousseau, Cape Town; Our Art 1; Art SA; SAA; 20C SA Art; SAP&S; Oxford Companion to Art (under SA); SAP&D; SSAP; Bénézit; BSAK 1 & 2; SA Art; Art SWA; 3Cs; AASA; LSAA; *Fontein* no 1, 1960; *Artlook* September 1968; *SA Panorama* March 1975; *De Arte* April & September 1975; *Art International* April/May 1976; *Gallery* Winter 1984.

JEPPE Barbara Joan

Born Pilgrim's Rest, Eastern Transvaal.
A painter of botanical studies, butterflies and wildlife. Works in watercolour.
Profile A member of the SAAA. Numerous illustrations for botanical periodicals and for the books *Cycads of South Africa* by Cynthia Giddy, *Weeds of Crops and Gardens in Southern Africa* by CIBA-GEIGY, as well as her own (see below). Mother of Leigh Voigt (qv) and Carl Jeppe (qv).
Exhibitions She has participated in several group exhibitions in SA; has held two solo exhibitions at the Everard Read Gallery, Johannesburg.
Publications by Jeppe Wrote and illustrated *Trees and Shrubs of the Witwatersrand, South African Aloes, Natal Wildflowers, Guide to Acacias of Southern Africa* and *South Africa is my Garden*, 1984, Delta Books, Johannesburg.
References AMC7; SESA; AASA; *SA Panorama* June 1978.

JEPPE Carl Victor Biccard

Born 1949 Krugersdorp, Transvaal.
A draughtsman working in pencil, charcoal and watercolour, of figures and portraits.
Studies 1970 Pretoria Technical College (Technikon), under Gunther van der Reis (qv), Leslie Reinhardt (qv), Koos den Houting (qv) and Neels Coetzee (qv), gaining a National Diploma in Fine Art in 1980 and a Higher Diploma in Fine Art in 1984.
Profile 1970–84 a council member of the SAAA. From 1978 a lecturer at the Pretoria Technical College (Technikon). 1980 a selector for the Olivetti Gallery; 1980–84 a selector for the SAAA Gallery, Northern Transvaal; 1979–84 a judge on the New Signatures Competition, SAAA, Pretoria; 1984–85 a committee member of the Ivan Solomon Gallery, Pretoria Technikon. Son of Barbara Jeppe (qv) and brother of Leigh Voigt (qv).

Exhibitions He has participated in several group exhibitions from 1970 in SA and West Germany; 1976 SAAA Gallery, Pretoria, first of three solo exhibitions; 1981 Republic Festival Exhibition.
Represented Pretoria Art Museum.
References AASA; *Habitat* no 50, 1982.

JESSNITZ Erich Reinhart

Born 1951 Duiwelskloof, Northern Transvaal.
A sculptor of abstract expressionistic pieces. Works in wood and steel.
Studies 1972–74 Pretoria Technical College, being awarded a National Diploma in Art and Design.
Exhibition 1984 Pretoria, participated in a group exhibition.

JOHNSON Christopher Charles Bonsall

Born 1961 Bulawayo, Rhodesia (Zimbabwe).
Resided in SA from 1980.
A painter of landscapes, still life, figures and portraits. Works in oil, acrylic, watercolour, gouache, ink and wash.
Studies 1980–85 Rhodes University, under Josua Nell (qv), Robert Brooks (qv) and Thomas Matthews (qv), gaining a BA(FA) in 1983 and an MFA (cum laude) in 1985.
Profile 1984–85 a tutor at Rhodes University. A singer, poet and actor. Lives in Johannesburg.
Exhibitions He has participated in several group exhibitions in SA from 1984.

JOHNSON Jenny

An artist working in many media, including ceramics.
Studies Witwatersrand Technikon, gaining a Diploma in Graphic Design in 1976; 1982–86 studied under Gael Neke (qv).
Profile From 1981 a creative director of a graphic design studio in Johannesburg.
Exhibitions She has exhibited with the APSA from 1982.
Represented Durban Art Gallery; Willem Annandale Art Gallery, Lichtenburg.

JOHNSON Magdalene Maria (Madge) (Mrs Kuyk)

Born 1900 Vlakteplaas District, Oudtshoorn, Cape Province.
A painter of mainly portraits and wildflowers, but also of landscapes, seascapes and still life. Works in pastel, oil, watercolour, gouache and ink. Models in clay. From 1953 miniature portrait paintings.
Studies 1923–26 a part-time course in art through the International Correspondence School, London, gaining a Diploma; 1952 a number of lessons at l'Ecole des Beaux Arts, Paris.

Profile From 1928 a member of the SA Society of Artists. 1924 illustrated the *Daghreek* series of Afrikaans reading books for kindergartens. A number of her poems have been published in *The Cape Times, The Cape Argus* and *Garden & Home*. Has visited Europe several times.

Exhibitions She has participated in numerous group exhibitions in SA from 1928; 1948 Modern Homes Art Gallery, Cape Town, joint exhibition with J A Smith (qv), and again at the Bellville Civic Centre in 1949.

Reference BSAK 2.

JOHNSTONE Jennifer Ann

Born 1944 Johannesburg.

A painter of abstracted landscapes. Works in oil, acrylic, watercolour, ink, wash, pencil and charcoal.

Studies 1977–82 University of South Africa, under Marion Arnold (qv), gaining a BA(FA); 1982–84 Natal Technikon, under Dan Cook (qv).

JONES Basil Louis

Born 1917 Simonstown, Cape Province.

Works in wood and stone, creating figures and bird forms in a simplified manner.

Studies Mainly a self-taught sculptor, but guided by Lippy Lipshitz (qv) and Mary Stainbank (qv).

Profile 1977–86 taught carving privately in Durban, prior to 1977 an art director for a publishing company. Lived in Cape Town, in Kimberley where he was involved in acting, and subsequently in Durban. Father of Marjorie Jones (qv).

Exhibitions He has participated in several group exhibitions from 1960 in SA; *c*.1960 NSA Gallery, Durban, first of *c*.18 solo exhibitions held in SA.

Represented William Humphreys Art Gallery, Kimberley.

References BSAK 1 & 2; *Artlook* May 1974.

JONES Graham Ashdown

Born 1958 Gwelo, Rhodesia (Gweru, Zimbabwe).

Resided in SA from 1963.

Both a painter and a sculptor of landscapes, portraits, genre, figures, animals, universal themes and abstract pieces. Works in oil, acrylic, pencil, charcoal, bronze, stone, ciment fondu, wood, paper, wire and ceramics.

Studies 1980–83 Port Elizabeth Technikon, under Hylton Nel (qv), Neil Rodger (qv), Hillary Graham (qv), Phil Kolbe (qv), Leon de Bliquy (qv), Alexander Podlashuc (qv) and Marianne Podlashuc (qv), gaining a National Diploma in Fine Art (sculpture) in 1982 and a Higher Diploma in Fine Art (sculpture) in 1983.

Profile 1986 a member of the SAAA, Bloemfontein; from 1986 a member of the Knysna Arts and Crafts Society; 1987 a member of the EPSFA. 1985 a teacher in sculpture, drawing and history at the Johan Carinus Art Centre, Grahamstown; 1985–86 a lecturer in sculpture and drawing at the Orange Free State Technikon; 1987 a temporary lecturer in sculpture at the Port Elizabeth Technikon. 1958–63 lived in Rhodesia (Zimbabwe); 1963–70 lived in Knysna, Cape Province, thereafter based there. 1981 visited Zimbabwe and Malawi; has travelled extensively in SA.
Exhibitions He has participated in several group exhibitions from 1981.

JONES Marjorie Ann (Mrs Roderick)

Born 1944 Cape Town.
A painter of landscapes, figures and abstract pictures. Works in oil and acrylic. Sculpts in wood, stone, ciment fondu and ceramics. A graphic artist producing monoprints.
Studies 1965–69 Natal Technical College, under Mary Stainbank (qv) and Kate Ambrosius.
Profile 1970–72 taught ceramics at the Natal Technical College; 1975–80 taught sculpture and ceramics privately in Durban. Daughter of Basil Jones (qv).
Exhibitions She has participated in several group exhibitions from 1969 in SA; 1973 NSA Gallery, Durban, first of three solo exhibitions held in SA.

JONES Simon Rhys

Born 1951 Lagos, Nigeria.
Resided in SA from 1955.
A painter of landscapes, seascapes, portraits, still life and figures. Works in acrylic. Series of figures in stylised landscapes, of flowerpieces and of portraits.
Studies 1970–72 Cape Technical College, gaining a Diploma in Graphic Design.
Profile Designed the first two covers for *Odyssey* magazine. 1979 lived on a farm at Overhex, Worcester, Cape Province. Son of Mary Hart and brother of the illustrator Nikki Jones.
Exhibitions 1975 Goodman-Wolman Gallery, Cape Town, first of nine solo exhibitions; he has participated in group exhibitions from 1979; 1982 Cape Town Triennial; 1985 Cape Town Triennial.
Represented King George VI Art Gallery, Port Elizabeth; Pietersburg Collection; Pretoria Art Museum; SA National Gallery, Cape Town; University of the Orange Free State.
References AASA; LSAA; *Lantern* April 1982.

JORDAAN Jan Willem

Born 1949 Springs, Transvaal.
A painter, sculptor and graphic artist. Works in oil, acrylic, watercolour, gouache, ink, wash, pencil, charcoal, mixed media, stone, ciment fondu, wood and in various graphic media. During the mid 1970s a series of wildlife landscapes in watercolour, woodcut/silkscreen and of figures in wood, stone and clay; during the 1980s a series of abstract dreamscape colour etchings and abstract figurative etchings and watercolours; in 1987 abstracted portraits and symbolic landscapes in oil and etching.

Studies 1970–73 University of Pretoria, gaining a BA(FA).
Profile A member of the NSA. 1974 taught history of art at Potchefstroom University for CHE; from 1975 a lecturer in printmaking at the Natal Technikon. In 1984 worked at Cité Internationale des Arts, Paris.
Exhibitions He has participated in group exhibitions from 1973 in SA, Zimbabwe, Taiwan and France; 1973 Barcelona Fine Art Gallery, Johannesburg, first of six solo exhibitions, one of which was held in Paris in 1984; 1974 Potchefstroom University for CHE, solo exhibition; 1981 University of Natal, solo exhibition.
Represented Durban Art Gallery; Natal Technikon; National Gallery, Harare, Zimbabwe; Potchefstroom University for CHE; University of Pretoria.

JOSEPH-AYRES Freda

Born 1944 Neath, Wales.
Resided in SA from 1966.
A painter of landscapes, seascapes, portraits, figures, still life, wildlife and abstract pictures. Works in oil, acrylic, watercolour, gouache and wash. A potter. A number of large series: 1979–80 animal portraits; 1980 flowers; 1982 still life of shirts in surrealistic and fantastical surroundings; 1985 French landscapes.
Studies Was taught privately in 1979–81 by Nicholas Gallaway; 1981–84 by Ruth Levy (qv); 1984 by Thelma Buzzard (qv); 1985 by Athelene Waters, Jennifer Johnstone (qv) and John Smith.
Profile 1984 a member of the NSA; 1985 of the North Coast Art Group; 1985 of the Inner Circle Art Group. 1982 published four sets of flower prints in a limited edition of 500. 1983–84 lived in Wales, visited France in 1985.
Exhibitions She has participated in several group exhibitions in SA from 1980; 1982 Crake Gallery, Johannesburg, first of two solo exhibitions.

JOSSEL Rosalind Vivian

Born 1937 Johannesburg.
A painter of still life. Works in oil. Paints the confrontation between Western and African cultures by the use of pattern.
Studies University of South Africa, studying for a BA(FA).
Exhibitions She has participated in several group exhibitions from 1966.

JOSSELSOHN Gail

Born 1944 Johannesburg.
A painter of landscapes, seascapes and still life. Works in dye on silk and paints murals.
Studies 1960–65 studied industrial design at the Witwatersrand Technical College, under Phil Botha (qv) and gained a Diploma.
Profile A potter. Visited the Greek islands in 1982 and Mauritius.
Exhibitions She has participated in several group exhibitions in Johannesburg.

JOUBERT Annebel (Mrs Klopper)

Born 1957 Bloemfontein.

A sculptor of figures in a landscape or interior. Works in bronze and mixed media, including fibreglass, wood and plaster. 1981 a series of female and male figures; 1981 and 1985 series of groups of figures. A graphic artist.

Studies 1975–78 University of Pretoria, under Mike Edwards (qv) and John Clarke (qv), gaining a BA(FA); 1979 University of Natal, gaining a Higher Diploma in Education; 1980–82 University of Natal, under Henry Davies, gaining an MA(FA).

Profile 1982 an art teacher at St Mary's Diocesan School for Girls, Pretoria. 1983–85 set and costume designs for theatre productions in Pretoria. 1982–86 taught pottery. 1960–65 lived in Australia; 1971–74 in the Orange Free State, visited Europe in 1973, 1984 and 1985. Lives in Pretoria.

Exhibitions 1981 Jack Heath Gallery, University of Natal, Pietermaritzburg, solo exhibition; participated in a group exhibition in 1985 in Pretoria.

Awards 1978 Merit Award for Graphics and Second Prize for Sculpture, New Signatures, SAAA.

Represented University of Natal.

JOUBERT Keith Eric

Born 1948 Johannesburg.

A self-taught painter of wildlife and figure impressions. Multiple vignettes and studies of animals, birds and figures. Works in oil and watercolour.

Studies 1963–67 Witwatersrand Technical College, under Phil Botha (qv).

Profile Since 1974 he has lived and worked in the Eastern Transvaal, Botswana, Zambia, Zimbabwe and SWA/Namibia. Several sets of prints of his work have been produced including "The Biggest of the Big Five", a limited edition of 850 in 1987.

Exhibitions He has participated in several group exhibitions from 1975 in SA, West Germany, France, frequently in the USA and annually at the World Wilderness Congress, Denver, Colorado and at Game Coin in San Antonio, Texas; 1975 Lister Gallery, Johannesburg, first of six solo exhibitions held in SA, the UK and in 1987 in the USA.

References AASA; *SA Panorama* January 1978 & September 1984.

JUDD Eric George

Born 1935 Springs, Transvaal.

A self-taught painter of landscapes, seascapes, aloes, trees and other plants, ships, boats and harbours, vernacular architecture and interiors. Works in watercolour, gouache, ink, wash and pencil. 1978–85 a series of animal-drawn vehicles with historic military backgrounds; 1980 a series of historic interiors, KWV Restaurant, Stellenbosch; 1985 a series of the Groot Winterhoek Wilderness Area; 1986 a series of Namaqualand flowers; 1986 a series of the Fish River Canyon.

Profile Until 1973 a commercial artist. In addition to his book on aloes (see below), he has also drawn aloe illustrations for *Farmers Weekly* in 1969 and *False Bay Echo* in 1986. In 1978 he designed the Kirstenbosch Postal Cover. 1935–58 and 1962–69 lived in the Transvaal; 1958–61 in Durban; in 1961 he lived in Rhodesia (Zimbabwe); from 1969 he has lived in Cape Town. Visited Europe.

Exhibitions He has participated in several group exhibitions from 1973 in SA; 1973 De Brug Gallery, Claremont, Cape Town, first of 20 solo exhibitions held in Cape Town and Johannesburg.

Represented Vanderbijlpark, Municipal Library, Transvaal.

Publication by Judd *What Aloe is That?*, 1976, Purnell, Cape Town.

Reference AASA.

JUTA Jan Carel

Born 1897 Kenilworth, Cape Town.

A painter of portraits.

Studies Under Hugo Naudé (qv); Slade School of Art, London, under Henry Tonks (1862–1937) and Ambrose McEvoy (1878–1927); British School in Rome, Italy; Académie Française, Paris, France; Academia de las Bellas Artes, Madrid, Spain; under André Lhote (1885–1962) in Paris.

Profile A member of the New Group; 1917 a member of the SA Society of Artists. Illustrated *Sea & Sardinia* by D H Lawrence; *The Cape Peninsula* by Rene Juta and *Background in Sunshine*, his memoirs. Lived in Washington DC, USA. Son of Sir Henry Juta, Speaker in the Cape House of Assembly.

Exhibitions Participated in group exhibitions in France and SA from 1925.

Represented National Portrait Gallery, London, UK; University of Texas, Austin, USA; Victoria and Albert Museum, London, UK.

Public Commissions 1933 nine murals for SA House, London; 1936 historical murals for Pretoria City Hall; glass frontage for Anglo American Building, Johannesburg; murals *SS Queen Mary* and *SS Queen Elizabeth*; murals for the Royal Institute of British Architects, London.

References SAA; Afr Repos; Pict Afr; DBA; BSAK 1 & 2; AASA; *South Africana* April 1958; *SA Panorama* September 1983.

K

KADAK Tiiu (Mrs Kaul-Andries)

Born 1907 St Petersburg (Leningrad), Russia.
Resided in SA from 1948.
A botanical artist working in watercolour.
Studies 1935 gained a BA(FA) from the University of Tartu, Estonia (Estonian SSR).
Profile Prior to 1948 a Director of the Arts and Crafts Museum, an editor, schoolteacher and inspector of homecrafts at the Chamber of Domestic Sciences, all in Tallinin, Estonia. A journalist and a writer, whose books have been published in Europe. Her works have been reproduced in periodicals and on Christmas cards in SA; eight colour prints of "South African Wild Flowers" printed in Tokyo in 1968 and 1969.
Exhibitions From *c.*1968 she has participated in numerous group exhibitions held throughout SA and in Italy, Canada and the USA; 1970 Rome, first of several solo exhibitions held in Italy, SA and Sweden.
Represented Africana Museum, Johannesburg; Botanical Library, Australia; Botanical Research Institute, Pretoria; Hunt Institute, Pittsburgh, Pennsylvania, USA; Queenstown Art Gallery.
Publications by Kadak 1936–47 three books published in Europe on arts and crafts; *A Bouquet of Wild Flowers*, 1964, Johannesburg.
References AMC3; AASA; *Artlook* August 1971; *SA Panorama* August 1971.

KAHN Maurice

Born 1943 Johannesburg.
A printmaker of etchings, serigraphs and lithographs. His works depict fantasy landscapes. A series on leaves. In 1973 he printed a portfolio entitled "Graphic Art in Honour of Heather Martienssen"; 1985 "Aspects of Israel", a portfolio of six works.
Studies 1964 gained a BA(FA) from the University of the Witwatersrand, studying under Cecily Sash (qv), Erica Berry (qv) and Giuseppe Cattaneo (qv); 1965 gained a Transvaal Teachers Higher Diploma; in 1968 began studying for an MA(FA).
Profile 1966–69 taught at various Johannesburg schools; 1970 lectured in graphic art at the Witwatersrand Technical College; 1971–76 a senior lecturer at the University of Durban-Westville. While living in Durban he established a graphics workshop. 1973–74 made a study tour of Europe. 1976 emigrated to Israel and became a lecturer at the Bezalel School of Art, University of Jerusalem.
Exhibitions He has participated in group exhibitions from the early 1960s in SA, Belgium, The Netherlands, West Germany, Australia and Israel; 1968 Walsh-Marais Gallery, Durban, first of over 10 solo exhibitions held in SA.
Awards 1963 Henri Lidchi Prize for Drawing; 1964 Herbert Evans Memorial Prize for Painting; 1967 Cambridge Shirt Award, Art SA Today.

Represented Durban Art Gallery; Pietersburg Collection; Pretoria Art Museum; Sandton Municipal Collection; SA National Gallery, Cape Town; University of South Africa; University of the Witwatersrand.
References AASA; *Artlook* April 1968, November 1970 & December 1970.

KANE Dennis Raymond

Born 1922 Lower Tugela, Natal.
A self-taught painter of landscapes, still life and seascapes. Works in oil, acrylic and gouache. Creates mixed media collages.
Profile 1975 Chairman of Art by the Sea; 1978 co-founder of the Port Shepstone Art Group. 1975–79 taught art in Port Shepstone; 1979–85 a demonstrator at Treverton College, Cedara, Natal. Lived in Johannesburg and in Port Shepstone and presently in Mooi River, Natal, travelled to SWA/Namibia, Israel and Greece.
Exhibitions He has participated in many group exhibitions in SA from 1970; 1986 Johannesburg, first solo exhibition.
Award 1979–80 First Prize for an oil painting, Midlands Expo, Greytown, Natal.
Represented Willem Annandale Art Gallery, Lichtenburg.

KAPLAN Sylvia

Born Rayton, Transvaal.
A painter working in oil, watercolour, gouache, ink, pencil, charcoal and in hand-made paper.
Studies Part-time during the 1950s under Annemarie Oppenheim (qv) and under Matthew Whippman (qv) in Johannesburg; part-time during the 1960s at the Natal Technical College; 1977–80 at the State University, New York.
Profile From 1963 a council member of the NSA of which she was President in 1967–69 and 1980–82, in 1976 appointed Honorary Life Vice-President; 1981–84 National President of the SAAA, in 1984 appointed Honorary Life Vice-President; 1978 a member of the Mamaroneck Artists Guild, New York. An Associate of the WSSA. 1981–84 a Trustee of the SA National Gallery, Cape Town. From 1982 a Trustee of the African Arts Centre, Durban and on the Advisory Committee of NAPAC Art Works, Durban. 1982–85 on the Visual Arts Committee, Durban, and its Chairman since 1985. From 1985 a Director of the Board of the Durban Arts Association. She has lectured on American Art in Durban, Johannesburg and Pietermaritzburg. Appointed to the selection committees of the 1985 Women's Student Award, Left Bank Art Exhibition; the Volkskas Atelier Award and in 1983 and 1985 the WSSA National Exhibitions. 1963–75 organiser and convenor of Art South Africa Today Exhibition in Durban. In 1977 she gave up her practice as a medical doctor and became a full-time painter. She has lived in Durban from 1953.

Exhibitions From 1978 she has participated in many group exhibitions in New York, SA, West Germany, Portugal, the UK and The Netherlands; 1984 NSA Gallery, Durban, solo exhibition; 1987 Strack van Schyndel Gallery, Johannesburg, joint exhibition with Michelle Davies and Evette Weyers (qv).
Represented Durban Art Gallery; Natal Technikon.
References AASA; *SA Arts Calendar* vol 6, 1981 & April 1982; *Anima* Winter 1984.

KARK Naomi

Born 1932 Johannesburg.
A painter of landscapes, portraits, figures and genre. Works in oil, acrylic, ink, wash and pencil; also creates montages. 1983–87 a series of her personal interpretation of socio-political figures in mixed media.
Studies 1966–68 under Sidney Goldblatt (qv); 1968 still-life painting at the University of the Witwatersrand, under Erica Berry (qv); 1979–87 study groups under Joyce Leonard (qv).
Profile A freelance journalist writing articles for *Artlook*, *The SA Jewish Times* and *The Citizen*. From 1977 she has spent a considerable amount of time in the USA.
Exhibitions 1968 Mona Lisa Gallery, Johannesburg, joint exhibition with Stephanie Watson (qv); she has participated in many group exhibitions from 1968 in SA and once in Toronto, Canada; 1972 Nedbank Gallery, Johannesburg, solo exhibition.
Reference *Artlook* March 1972.

KASS Stephen

Born 1942.
A sculptor.
Profile 1975–79 a lecturer at the Michaelis School of Fine Art.
Exhibitions He has participated in group exhibitions in SA; 1971 Republic Festival Exhibition.
Award 1969 Oppenheimer Trust Award, Art SA Today.
Represented Durban Art Gallery.
References BSAK 1; AASA.

KATZ Hanns Ludwig

Born 1882 Karlsruhe, Germany.
Died 1940 Johannesburg.
Resided in SA from 1936.
A painter of landscapes, figures, portraits and still life. Worked in oil, watercolour, pastel and charcoal.
Studies Universities of Berlin and Heidelberg and at the Karlsruhe School of Art, under Professor Wilhelm Trübner (1851–1917).
Exhibitions Exhibited in Berlin, Frankfurt and Munich; 1940 and 1961 Lawrence Adler Gallery, Johannesburg, Memorial Exhibitions.
References SAA; AASA.

KAY Clive

Born 1944 Rhodesia (Zimbabwe).
Mainly a self-taught painter of landscapes and wildlife. Works in acrylic.
Studies Private tuition from the British artist Allan Carter while living in the UK for 18 months and from the Canadian Robert Bateman while in Toronto for 10 years.
Exhibitions 1984 Sandton Gallery, Johannesburg, solo exhibition; 1985 Everard Read Gallery, Johannesburg, group exhibition.

KAY Dorothy Moss ARBC (née Elvery)

Born 1886 Greystones, County Wicklow, Ireland.
Died 1964 Port Elizabeth.
Resided in SA from 1910. Settled in Port Elizabeth in 1916.
A painter and graphic artist of portraits, self-portraits and genre. Worked in oil, gouache, watercolour, ink, wash, crayon and in various graphic media. A number of ceramic pieces and frescos.
Studies 1900 Dublin Metropolitan School of Art, where associated with Sir William Orpen (1878–1931); 1900 Royal Hibernian Academy School, under John Butler Yeats (1839–1922) and Walter Osborne (1859–1903), where she was awarded the Taylor Art Scholarship several times; later studied at the Louvre, Paris.
Profile 1918 a founder member of the Eastern Province Society of Arts and Crafts; a member of the SA Society of Artists; 1924 a member of the Royal British and Colonial Society of Arts. A part-time teacher at the Port Elizabeth Technical College. From 1929 she drew several illustrations for *The Outspan* periodical. 1929 executed designs for manufacturers' labels. 1929–34 two etchings reproduced in "Fine Prints of the Year", Michael Salaman Publishers, London. Married to Dr Hobart Kay FRCS, through whom she was able to paint a number of pictures of hospital activities, which were commissioned by the Government in 1940–45 to record the war effort on the home front. Mother of Joan Wright (qv) and sister of the British artist Beatrice, Lady Glenavy.
Exhibitions Participated in group exhibitions from 1902 in SA, the UK, Yugoslavia, West Germany, Italy, Brazil and Rhodesia (Zimbabwe); 1922 St George's Hall, Grahamstown, first of several solo exhibitions; 1955 Eastern Province Society of Arts and Crafts, Retrospective Exhibition; 1956, 1960 and 1964 Quadrennial Exhibitions; 1965 Port Elizabeth, Retrospective Exhibition; 1966 Pretoria Art Museum and Durban Art Gallery, Retrospective Exhibition; 1982 SA National Gallery, Cape Town, Prestige Retrospective Exhibition.
Represented Africana Museum, Johannesburg; Albany Museum, Grahamstown; Ann Bryant Gallery, East London; Durban Art Gallery; Johannesburg Art Gallery; King George VI Art Gallery, Port Elizabeth; Pretoria Art Museum; Queenstown Art Gallery; SA National Gallery, Cape Town; SA National Museum of Military History, Johannesburg; University of Pretoria; University of the Witwatersrand; William Humphreys Art Gallery, Kimberley; 1820 Settlers Memorial Museum, Grahamstown.

Public Commissions Numerous portraits of public figures, including mayoral portraits for Port Elizabeth, Uitenhage, Graaff-Reinet and Grahamstown. Murals: 1936 Climax Rock Drilling Company, Empire Exhibition; 1943 Reserve Bank, Port Elizabeth; 1946 General Motors, Port Elizabeth (now at Port Elizabeth Technikon); 1946 SABC, Grahamstown.

References Art SA; SAA; SADNB; 20C SA Art; DSAB; SAP&S; SAP&D; AMC7; SESA; DBA; BSAK 1 & 2; 3Cs; PESA; AASA; LSAA; *SA Panorama* July 1958.

KAYE Nell

Born 1912 Johannesburg.
Died 1969 Rondebosch, Cape Town.
A sculptor in bronze of portraits. A graphic artist.

Studies 1930–34 Witwatersrand Technical College, sculpture under Professor F W Armstrong (qv) and James Gardner (qv); during the 1950s at the Michaelis School of Fine Art, under Lippy Lipshitz (qv).

Profile 1966–67 Vice-Chairman and 1967–68 Chairman of the SAAA, Cape Town. 1965 opened her own art school, The Chelsea Art Studio in Cape Town.

Exhibitions 1959 Cape Town, first of several solo exhibitions held in SA; participated in group exhibitions from 1960 in SA and in Italy; 1960 and 1964 Quadrennial Exhibitions; 1968 Stellenbosch, joint exhibition with Frank Spears (qv); 1970 SAAA Gallery, Johannesburg, Memorial Exhibition.

Award 1970 posthumously awarded an SAAA Medal.

Represented Hester Rupert Art Museum, Graaff-Reinet; Pretoria Art Museum; SA National Gallery, Cape Town; University of Cape Town; University of Stellenbosch; University of the Witwatersrand; William Humphreys Art Gallery, Kimberley.

Public Commissions Portrait bust of Professor M van den Ende of the University of Cape Town and many other portrait busts of public figures.

References Art SA; SAA; SA Art; 20C SA Art; SAP&S; SESA; BSAK 1 & 2; 3Cs; AASA; *Artlook* March 1968, February 1969 & February 1970.

KEMP-BEZUIDENHOUT Jaco

Born 1941 Elim, Northern Transvaal.
A painter and graphic artist of figures, man and his environment, abstracted heads and abstract pictures. Works in acrylic and in various graphic media, including linocuts and monotypes; also produces drawings. 1968 a series of "Romanesque Heads".

Studies 1961–63 Pretoria Technical College, under Robert Hodgins (qv), Zakkie Eloff (qv), Gunther van der Reis (qv), Anna Vorster (qv) and Leo Theron (qv), attaining a Diploma in Graphic Design; 1964 made a study tour of Europe and studied under Fedor Ganz in Athens; 1967 tutored by Kevin Atkinson (qv) in Cape Town; 1967–69 University of South Africa, attaining a BA(FA).

Profile 1965–67 a part-time lecturer at the Pretoria Technical College; 1968 a part-time lecturer at the Cape Town Art Centre; 1971 a part-time lecturer at the Ruth Prowse Art Centre, Cape Town and the Cape Town Art Centre. 1974–79 managed the Goodman-Wolman Gallery, Cape Town. Moved to Cape Town in 1967, in 1979 left for Europe, where he settled in Amsterdam, The Netherlands. 1971–72 visited Europe.

Exhibitions Participated in group exhibitions during the 1960s and 1970s in SA; 1966 Walter Schwitter Gallery, Pretoria, joint exhibition with Tertia Knaap (qv); 1972 SAAA Gallery, Cape Town, first solo exhibition.

Represented Potchefstroom University for CHE; SA National Gallery, Cape Town; University of South Africa; University of Stellenbosch.

References AASA; *Artlook* May 1972 & January 1974; *De Arte* April 1978.

KEMPFF Catharina Jacoba (Katinka)

Born 1922 Den Helder, The Netherlands.
Resided in SA from 1936.
A painter of landscapes and still life. Works in oil and watercolour.

Studies 1940–42 Pretoria Teachers Training College, under Bettie Cilliers-Barnard (qv); 1966-68 Potchefstroom University for CHE, under Professor Dekker and Muller Ballot, where gained a BA(Hons) cum laude.

Profile A member of the SAAA and of the SAAAH. 1943–47 taught at Pretoria Afrikaans High School for Girls; 1950–61 taught art privately; 1962–63 taught at the Potchefstroom Teachers Training College. 1949–55 an Examiner for Matriculation Art, Transvaal; from 1969 Education Officer, Assistant Director, then Deputy Director of the Pretoria Art Museum; from 1978 an Examiner for Matriculation Art, Joint Matriculation Board. Visited Greece in 1985.

Exhibitions She has participated in several group exhibitions from 1955 in the Transvaal.

KENDALL Franklin Kaye FRIBA

Born 1870 Melbourne, Australia.
Died 1948 Rondebosch, Cape.
A painter and a qualified architect.

Studies Architecture at University College, London.

Profile 1894 became an Associate, and in 1912 a Fellow of the Royal Institute of British Architects. In 1896 he joined the practice of Sir Herbert Baker, for which he restored Groot Constantia after a fire in 1925; he was also involved in the design of the Rhodes University campus and in 1931, with Brian Mansergh, the design of the Anglican Church House, Victoria Street, Cape Town. 1902 Founder and a council member of the Cape Institute of Architecture; a committee member and President in 1916–17 of the SA Drawing Club, thereafter the SA Society of Artists; also a member of the Fine Arts Association, the Owl Club and a Trustee of the SA National Gallery, Cape Town. Restored and designed Cape Dutch furniture. Assisted in the formation of the School of Architecture, Cape Town.

Award 1936 Bronze Medal awarded by the Cape Institute of Architects.
Publication by Kendall *The Reconstruction of Groot Constantia*, 1926.
References *The Arts in SA*, edited by WHK, The Knox Printing & Publishing Company, Durban; DSAB; BSAK 1; 3Cs; AASA.

KENNEDY Katherine

Born 1885 Colesberg, Cape Province.
Died 1958 Johannesburg.
A painter of still life and scenes of Johannesburg. Worked in oil.
Studies 1906 under Adela Seton-Tait (qv) in Johannesburg.
Exhibitions Exhibited with the SA Academy in 1921, 1925, 1932 and 1935.
Represented Africana Museum, Johannesburg.
References AMC3; BSAK 1; AASA.

KENTON Diana Cecile

Born 1945 Cape Town.
A painter of landscapes, figures and abstract pictures. Works in oil, acrylic, ink and pencil. 1979–82 "Dune-Forest" series; from 1983 "Mountain" series.
Studies 1974 University of the Witwatersrand, under Professor Heather Martienssen (1915–79), Cecily Sash (qv), Robert Hodgins (qv), Erica Berry (qv) and Joyce Leonard (qv); 1985 University of Natal.
Profile From 1977 a member of the SAAA. 1975 a lecturer/tutor in the History of Art Department, University of the Witwatersrand; 1976 a lecturer in the Fine Arts Department, University of Durban-Westville; 1977–84 a part-time lecturer in the School of Architecture, University of Natal, Durban; 1978–82 a course leader for extra-mural studies, University of Natal, Durban; 1979–81 a lecturer in Fine Art, Natal Technikon; 1983–85 a part-time studio master in the Fine Arts Department, University of Natal, Pietermaritzburg. 1978–84 a selector for SAAA Natal exhibitions. 1979–81 on the Advisory Committee of the Friends of Durban Art Gallery; 1982 on the Steering Committee of the Natal Artists Guild; 1982–84 a co-opted member of the Durban Art Gallery Advisory Committee; 1984–85 on the Advisory Committee of the Durban Arts Association. 1978–81 a freelance art critic for *The Daily News*; 1982–83 an art critic on *The Sunday Tribune*; from 1975 a number of her essays and articles have been published in various periodicals.
Exhibitions She has participated in numerous group exhibitions in SA from 1973; 1982 Cape Town Triennial; 1982 NSA Gallery, Durban, first of three solo exhibitions held in Durban, Pietermaritzburg and Johannesburg; 1985 Cape Town Triennial.
Awards 1973 Henri Lidchi Prize for Drawing; 1973–74 Anya Millman Scholarship for Overseas Travel.
Represented Durban Art Gallery; Natal Technikon; University of the Witwatersrand.
References AASA; *SA Arts Calendar* Spring 1985.

KENTRIDGE William Joseph

Born 1955 Johannesburg.

Works in charcoal, ink, wash, pastel, pencil, oil and in various graphic media. Occasionally sculpts. 1979 "Exhibition", a series of 30 monoprints; 1981 "Domestic Scenes", a series of 40 etchings; 1985–86 "Dreams of Europe", a series of drawings.

Studies 1976–78 Johannesburg Art Foundation, under Bill Ainslie (qv).

Profile In 1976 Kentridge gained a BA in Political/African Studies from the University of the Witwatersrand and in 1981–82 studied Theatre at Ecole Jacques Lecoq in Paris. Since 1976 he has been a co-founder, member, actor, director, stage and poster designer for the Junction Avenue Theatre Company and for the Market Theatre, Johannesburg. 1980–82 taught graphics at the Johannesburg Art Foundation. 1980 wrote and directed "Dikhitsheneng" for Junction Avenue; 1981 co-directed "Howl at the Moon", a 40-minute video; 1983 wrote, directed and edited "Salestalk", a 30-minute 16 mm film; he has also been involved in several other drama productions.

Exhibitions He has participated in many group exhibitions in SA from 1974, as well as one in Paris and one in New York; 1979 Market Gallery, Johannesburg, first of 11 solo exhibitions; 1985 Cape Town Triennial; 1985 Tributaries, touring SA and West Germany; 1986 Simon Neuman Gallery, New York, solo exhibition; 1987 "The Hogarth Series", with Deborah Bell (qv) and Robert Hodgins (qv), touring SA; 1987 Vanessa Devereux Gallery, London, solo exhibition; 1987 solo exhibition travelling to the 1820 Settlers National Monument, Grahamstown, Tatham Art Gallery, Pietermaritzburg, University of the Witwatersrand, University of South Africa and Durban Art Gallery; 1988 Johannesburg Art Gallery, Vita Art Now; 1988 Gallery International, Cape Town, joint exhibition with Simon Stone (qv).

Awards 1981 First Prize, National Graphic Competition, Bellville; 1982 joint winner of the Red Ribbon Award in New York for the film "Howl at the Moon"; 1984 joint winner of the Olive Schreiner Award for the play "Randlords & Rotgut"; 1985 Cape Triennial Merit Award; 1986 New Visions Award, Market Gallery; 1987 Standard Bank Young Artist Award; 1987 Vita Quarterly Award Winner.

Represented Durban Art Gallery; Johannesburg Art Gallery; King George VI Art Gallery, Port Elizabeth; Pietersburg Collection; Pretoria Art Museum; SA National Gallery, Cape Town; Tatham Art Gallery, Pietermaritzburg; University of South Africa; University of the Witwatersrand; William Humphreys Art Gallery, Kimberley.

References BSAK 2; *Gallery* Spring 1985; *De Kat* December/January 1986 & December/January 1987.

KERR Gregory John

Born 1949 Johannesburg.

A painter of landscapes, portraits, still life, genre, figures and abstract pictures. Works in oil, acrylic, watercolour, gouache, ink, wash and pencil. 1983 a series of paintings and drawings based on "The Death of Marat".

WILLIAM KENTRIDGE
New Modder 1988
Charcoal and Pastel 135 × 105 cm
Die Kunskamer

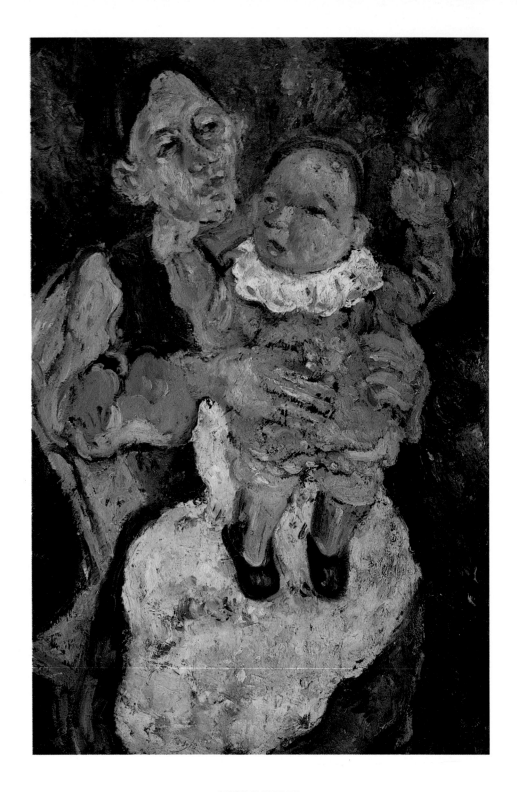

WOLF KIBEL
Mother and Child
Oil on Board 75 × 50 cm
Private

Studies 1969–71 University of the Witwatersrand, under Giuseppe Cattaneo (qv), Erica Berry (qv), Robert Hodgins (qv) and Cecily Sash (qv); 1974–76 University of South Africa, under Leon du Plessis (qv) and Alan Crump, gaining a BA(FA); 1978 Whitemore Richards Overseas Scholarship to the University of Georgia, USA, in 1979 studying under Johansen, Collier and Wachowiak; 1983 several months of research at the University of Georgia, USA, gaining a PhD in 1985.

Profile From 1976 a lecturer, then Associate Head of the Johannesburg College of Education until 1988; 1976–78 an occasional tutor in painting and drawing at the Centre for Continuing Education, University of the Witwatersrand; 1979 teaching assistant to Professor Graham Collier at the University of Georgia, USA;

Exhibitions He has participated in several group exhibitions in SA from 1967; 1982 Beuster-Skolimowski Gallery, Pretoria, first of four solo exhibitions held in Pretoria and Johannesburg; 1987 Johannesburg Art Gallery, Vita Art Now; 1987 Karen McKerron Gallery, Johannesburg, joint exhibition with Claire Gavronsky (qv) and Geoffrey Armstrong (qv).

Award 1983 Olivetti-Rugantino Prize.

Represented Johannesburg College of Education.

Reference "The Death of Marat", *Apelles* (Georgia Arts Journal) vol 1, 1984.

KETYE Ellington (Duke)

Born 1943 Orlando East, Transvaal.

A sculptor, painter and graphic artist of landscapes, portraits, wildlife, figures and abstract pieces. Works in clay, wood, ciment fondu, bronze, acrylic, watercolour, ink, wash, pencil, charcoal and in various graphic media.

Studies 1961 Lumko Art Centre, Queenstown; 1963–65 St Francis College, Mariannhill, Natal, under Josepha Selhorst (Sister Mary Pientia) (qv).

Profile From 1972 a member of the NSA; 1976 a founder member of the Mariannhill Art Centre; 1985 a member of the Vhavenda Art Foundation. 1976–78 an art teacher at St Francis College, Mariannhill, where he also ran an art gallery; 1983–85 taught at Khalaba Art and Silkscreen, Venda. 1979 illustrations for the *Zulu Good News Bible*, The Bible Society of SA. A potter, working in 1974–75 at the London Potters in Bryanston, Johannesburg; 1980–81 at Emithini Potteries, Port Edward and in 1983–84 at the Thabo Potters, Makhado, Venda.

Exhibitions 1968 Mona Lisa Gallery, Johannesburg, first of six solo exhibitions held in SA; he has participated in several group exhibitions from 1971 in SA and in 1972 in New York; 1975 Washington DC, USA, solo exhibition; 1977 NSA Gallery, Durban, joint exhibition with Charles S Nkosi (qv) and Michael Ntuli.

Represented University of Fort Hare.

Public Commissions 1974 wooden panels depicting animals, Library and Municipal Buildings, Walvis Bay; 1976 wood panels, Umtata Seminary, Transkei; 1976 a wooden portrait bust of Father Franz Pfanner, the Founder of Mariannhill; 1978 murals, Beer Hall, Glebelands, Durban and in a Catholic church in QwaQwa.

References BSAK 1; Echoes of African Art.

KEYSER Andreas Werner
Born 1938 Pretoria.
A painter of landscapes. Works in oil, watercolour and gouache.
Profile A geologist.
Represented His work is represented in many SA embassies abroad.

KGOBE Paule
Born 1955 Johannesburg.
A painter and a sculptor of portraits and figures. Works in acrylic, watercolour, gouache, ink, wash, pencil, charcoal, stone, ciment fondu and wood. A graphic artist.
Studies 1984 at FUBA, Johannesburg.
Exhibitions Has participated in group exhibitions from 1982 in Zululand, Soweto and Johannesburg; 1982 National Gallery, Gaborone, Botswana, Exhibition of SA Art.

KHALIENYANE Mamajoro Anna
Born 1942 Bloemfontein District.
A painter of landscapes, portraits and animals. Works in oil, watercolour, pencil and charcoal.

KHUMALO Dumisani Ozias
Born 1961 Glencoe, Natal.
A painter, sculptor and graphic artist of landscapes, seascapes and abstract pieces. Works in oil, acrylic, charcoal, various graphic media and in clay.
Studies 1986–87 Katlehong Art Centre, under Steven Risi; 1987 Funda Centre, Soweto, under Lindi Solomons.
Exhibitions He has participated in several group exhibitions fom 1986 in the Transvaal.

KIBEL Wolf
Born 1903 Grodzisk, Poland.
Died 1938 Cape Town.
Resided in SA from 1929.
A painter in oil and watercolour. Numerous drawings in pastel, chalk, pen, crayon and wax among other mixed media. Produced monotypes, etchings and woodcuts. His subject matter was diverse and included landscapes, portraiture, figures, nude studies, still life, Jewish genre, Biblical scenes, street scenes, interiors and scenes from his childhood.
Studies 1923–25 informal art training in Vienna, Austria.

Profile Influenced by German Expressionism, his work was frequently distorted and simplified with the use of sombre colours. In 1931 he stayed for several weeks with Hugo Naudé (qv) where he learnt the art of etching. 1933–37 shared Palm Studio with Lippy Lipshitz (qv) where they both taught art. 1903–23 lived in Poland; 1923 escaped to Czechoslovakia; 1923–25 lived in Vienna, Austria and Jerusalem, Israel. 1925–29 in Tel Aviv, Israel and from 1929 in Cape Town.

Exhibitions Participated in group exhibitions in SA; 1934 held joint exhibitions with Lippy Lipshitz (qv); 1931 Martin Melck House, Cape Town, first of several solo exhibitions; 1942 Argus Gallery, Cape Town, Memorial Exhibition; 1947 Constantia Galleries, Johannesburg, Memorial Exhibition; 1948 Tate Gallery, London, SA Art Exhibition; 1950 SA National Gallery, Cape Town, Memorial Exhibition; 1953 Rhodes Centenary Exhibition, Bulawayo, Rhodesia (Zimbabwe); 1963 Lidchi Gallery, Johannesburg, Memorial Exhibition; 1965 Wolpe Gallery, Cape Town, Memorial Exhibition; 1965 SAAA Gallery, Pretoria, Memorial Exhibition; 1966 Pretoria Art Museum, Special Commemorative Exhibition; 1976 SA National Gallery, Cape Town, Retrospective Exhibition, travelling throughout SA.

Represented Durban Art Gallery; Johannesburg Art Gallery; King George VI Art Gallery, Port Elizabeth; Pretoria Art Museum; SA National Gallery, Cape Town; Tatham Art Gallery, Pietermaritzburg; University of Cape Town; University of the Orange Free State; University of South Africa; University of Stellenbosch; University of the Witwatersrand; William Humphreys Art Gallery, Kimberley.

Public Commissions 1929 the decorations of the Alhambra Cinema, Cape Town, with others; also the Plaza Cinema, Pretoria.

References Neville Dubow and Frieda Kibel (wife), *Wolf Kibel*, 1968, Human & Rousseau, Cape Town; PSA; Collectors' Guide; Our Art 2; Art SA; SAA; 20C SA Art; DSAB; SAP&S; Oxford Companion to Art (under SA); SAP&D; SESA; SSAP; BSAK 1 & 2; 3Cs; AASA; LSAA; *Gallery* Autumn 1982.

KIDD Mary Catherine

Born 1914 East London.

A painter of flora.

Studies Slade School of Art, London, under Randolph Schwabe (1885–1948); Royal Academy Schools, London, under Sir Walter Russell (1867–1949); Central School of Art, London, under Miss Batty and in The Netherlands under Louis Hartz.

Profile Contributed illustrations to the Botanical Research Institute's publication, *The Flowering Plants of Africa*. Commissioned by the Cape Provincial Council to illustrate volumes 1 & 2 of *Protected Wild Flowers of the Cape Province*.

Publications by Kidd Author and illustrator of *Wild Flowers of the Cape Peninsula*, *Some South African Edible Fungus* and *Some South African Inedible Fungus*.

Reference SAA.

KIDDIE Alexander Cameron

Born 1927 Kimberley, Cape Province.

Known to have painted still life paintings in gouache.

Studies 1946–48 Rhodes University, gaining a BA(FA); 1949–50 Port Elizabeth Technical College, under Jack Heath (qv), where he was awarded the Drawing Prize; 1951–52 studied Painting and Drawing at the Regent Street Polytechnic, London; 1958–59 studied Basic Design and Life Drawing, Central School of Art, London.

Profile 1949–50 a part-time student and a part-time lecturer at the Port Elizabeth Technical College; 1953 a teacher with the London County Council; 1953–58 worked in the family business in Kimberley; 1959 a lecturer in Basic Design and Life Drawing at the University of Natal; 1960–68 taught full-time and 1968–78 on a part-time basis at the Port Elizabeth Technical College. From 1970 involved in the design of scenery and costumes for theatre productions, and in 1975 he spent three months, working full-time, as a painter for CAPAB. In 1978 became a professional designer.

Exhibitions 1960 Johannesburg, solo exhibition; 1960 and 1964 Quadrennial Exhibitions.

References Port Elizabeth School of Art; AASA.

KING Edith Luise Mary

Born 1869 Pietermaritzburg.

Died 1962 Carolina, Eastern Transvaal.

A painter of landscapes, still life and close-ups of plants and rocky pools. Worked in watercolour on thin, brittle, buff-coloured paper. A number of linocuts and clay pots. Rhythmical pictures, with the use of heavy line and strong colour.

Studies 1903–05 life classes at Bristol Municipal School of Art, England; *c.*1905 gained an Ablett Teachers Certificate from the Royal Drawing Society of Great Britain and Ireland; 1925–27 informal art training in Paris.

Profile The main organiser of the Everard Group. A member of the New Group. 1894–1905 taught in England; 1905–07 taught at the Eunice School for Girls, Bloemfontein, 1913–23 Headmistress. 1929 wrote articles for *The Outspan* magazine. 1870–74 lived in Natal; 1874–1904 in England, 1905–23 in Bloemfontein, spending 1908–12 at Bonnefoi, Carolina, Eastern Transvaal, with the Everards; 1923–29 in England and France, 1927 visited St Tropez and Avignon, South of France, with Ruth Everard-Haden (qv); 1929–62 in the Eastern Transvaal, travelling to Europe and extensively in SA during the 1940s and early 1950s. Sister of Bertha Everard (qv), aunt of Ruth Everard-Haden (qv) and Rosamund Everard-Steenkamp (qv), who together were known as the Everard Group; the great-aunt of Leonora Haden (qv).

Exhibitions Participated in group exhibitions from 1931, frequently with the Everard Group; 1956 and 1960 Quadrennial Exhibitions; 1967 Adler Fielding Gallery, Johannesburg, Pretoria Art Museum and Tatham Art Gallery, Pietermaritzburg, Retrospective Exhibition of the Everard Group.

Represented Johannesburg Art Gallery; King George VI Art Gallery, Port Elizabeth; National Museum, Bloemfontein; Pretoria Art Museum; SA National Gallery, Cape Town; Tatham Art Gallery, Pietermaritzburg; William Humphreys Art Gallery, Kimberley.

Publications by King A poet of mainly children's verse, writing *Country Rhymes for Children*, 1909, Blackwell, Oxford, UK; *Veld Rhymes for Children*, 1911, Longmans Green, London; *Bloemfontein—An Impression in Verse*, with Mary Littlewood, 1919, Bloemfontein; *Delville Wood Poems*, 1925; *Forms and Fancies*, 1926, Oxford, UK; *Fifty Country Rhymes*, 1926.

References F Harmsen, *The Women of Bonnefoi*, 1980, Van Schaik, Cape Town; Our Art 2; Art SA; SAA; DSAB; SSAP; BSAK 1 & 2; 3Cs; AASA; LSAA.

KING Terence Howard Professor (Terry)

Born 1947 Durban.

A painter of landscapes and abstract pictures. Works in oil, acrylic, ink and pencil.

Studies 1966–69 University of the Witwatersrand, under Professor Heather Martienssen (1915–79), gaining a BA(FA); 1970 University of Natal, gaining a University Education Diploma; 1974–78 University of the Witwatersrand, under Robert Hodgins (qv), where attained an MA(FA).

Profile From 1972 a member of the NSA and from 1984 a member of the SAAAH. 1972–76 taught art at the Natal Technical College; 1977–78 a lecturer at the University of South Africa; 1979–85 lectured at the University of the Witwatersrand and from 1985 Head and Professor, Fine Arts Department, University of Natal. 1972 a Committee Member of the Durban Art Gallery Association; 1975–76 a Council Member of the NSA; 1985 on the Advisory Committee of the Tatham Art Gallery, Pietermaritzburg.

Exhibitions Participated in many group exhibitions in SA from 1972 and one in Australia in 1973; 1973 NSA Gallery, Durban, first of six solo exhibitions held in Durban and Johannesbug; 1974 SAAA Gallery, Johannesburg, joint exhibition with Anthony Starkey (qv); 1982 Market Gallery, Johannesburg, joint exhibition with Peter Schütz (qv); 1983 NSA Gallery, Durban, joint exhibition with Malcolm Christian (qv).

Represented Durban Art Gallery; SA National Gallery, Cape Town; Tatham Art Gallery, Pietermaritzburg; University of the Witwatersrand.

References SAP&D; AASA.

KINGSBURY Phyllis M

Born 1896 Somerset, England.

Died Johannesburg.

Resided in SA from 1921.

A painter and graphic artist of landscapes, incorporating figures and domestic animals, and of flowers and urban subjects. Worked in watercolour, oil and in drypoint.

Studies 1916–20 Taunton College of Art, Somerset, England, under Fred Mason.
Profile A member of the Somerset Society of Artists, the Transvaal Art Society and the Brush and Chisel Club. Taught art briefly at Taunton College of Art. Travelled widely throughout SA. Lived in Johannesburg.
Exhibitions Participated in many group exhibitions in the UK and SA; 1953 Johannesburg, first of several solo exhibitions held in SA.
Represented Africana Museum, Johannesburg.
References SAA; AMC3; AASA.

KIRCHOFF Peter

Born 1893 Magdeburg, Germany.
Resided in SA from 1931.
A sculptor in various media, including bronze, marble and stone.
Studies Hamburg School of Art, Germany, studying sculpture and pottery.
Profile A member of the Transvaal Art Society.
Exhibitions Participated in group exhibitions in Hamburg and throughout SA; 1966 Republic Festival Exhibition.
Public Commissions Medallions of Poets and Scholars, Johannesburg Library; marble frieze, Voortrekker Monument, Pretoria; reliefs, Receiver of Revenue Building, Johannesburg; proscenium and reliefs, Germiston Town Hall; decorative stonework and bronze reliefs for the Reserve Bank, Pretoria and for Barclays (First National) Bank Head Offices, Pretoria and Johannesburg.
References SAA; BSAK 1 & 2; SA Art; AASA.

KIRKWOOD Fiona Mary

Born 1949 Irving, Scotland.
Resided in SA from 1975.
An artist creating three-dimensional fibre works, who recently has incorporated paint into her pieces. Her work is abstract, relating to the human spirit. 1980–83 a series of "Trees and Roots"; from 1985 a series of "Soul Bearers".
Studies 1967–71 Glasgow School of Art, Scotland, under Kathleen Whyte, gaining a Diploma in Art; 1980–83 University of Natal, gaining an MA(FA) in Fibre Sculpture.
Profile A member of the NSA and D'ARTS. 1975–76 and 1984–86 a part-time lecturer at the Natal Technikon; 1977–83 a junior lecturer in art education, University of Durban-Westville. From 1978 a lecturer in art at the Centre for Adult Education, University of Natal. 1985 architectural/fibre sculpture designs for "Lofties Rhythmic Rocket", a production held at the Natal Playhouse, Durban. 1980–81 visited India; 1984 and 1986 the USA; 1986 Canada, Australia, Papua New Guinea and Fiji.
Exhibitions She has participated in many group exhibitions from 1972 in Scotland and SA; 1981 NSA Gallery, Durban, solo exhibition; 1982 Rand Afrikaans University, solo exhibition.
Represented Durban Art Gallery.
Public Commission 1974 Tapestry for the Council Chambers, Kilmarnock, Scotland.
Reference SA Arts Calendar June/July 1982.

KLAR Otto Professor

Born 1908 Vienna, Austria.

Resided in SA from 1939.

A painter of landscapes, portraits, figures, religious themes and still life, particularly of flowers. From 1958 to the mid 1960s painted a number of abstract works.

Studies Vienna Academy of Arts, Austria.

Profile Taught art in Pretoria. A number of his works have been reproduced by E Schweickerdt, Pretoria.

Exhibitions Participated in numerous group exhibitions held throughout Europe and in SA; held several solo exhibitions in SA; 1952 Van Riebeeck Tercentenary Exhibition; 1960 Quadrennial Exhibition; 1964 Milan, Italy, solo exhibition; 1966 Republic Festival Exhibition.

Award 1962 awarded Honorary Professorship from the President of Austria on the recommendation of the Vienna Academy of Art.

Represented Ann Bryant Gallery, East London; Durban Art Gallery; Pretoria Art Museum; University of the Witwatersrand.

References SAA; AASA; *SA Panorama* November 1958.

KLEIN Magrietha Elizabeth (Rita)

Born 1945 Nylstroom, Northern Transvaal.

A painter of landscapes, seascapes and of details of nature. Works in oil, water-colour, ink and pencil. 1982–83 "SWA/Namibia" series; 1983–84 "Golden Gate" and "Cape Mountain" series; 1984–85 "Rock Formations" and "Crystal" series.

Studies 1968 privately under Elizabeth Couzyn (qv); 1969–72 University of South Africa, under Anna Vorster (qv); 1972–76 University of South Africa.

Profile A member of the SAAA. Illustrated *Rond en Bont*, by Marlene Serfontein, 1985, Daan Retief Publishers, Pretoria, and several magazines. Creates leather-works and mosaics.

Exhibitions 1977 private house, Pretoria, first of seven solo exhibitions; she has participated in several group exhibitions in SA from 1981.

Represented Nylstroom Municipal Collection; Pietersburg Collection; Potchef-stroom Museum.

KLOPCANOVS Alexander

Born 1912 Tashkent, Turkestan (Usbek SSR).

Resided in SA from 1949.

A painter of landscapes and figures. Works in oil, charcoal and other media.

Studies Riga Fine Art Academy, Latvia (Latvian SSR); Royal Art Academy, Stockholm, Sweden.

Profile 1949 founded the Kalahari Pottery Studio in Cape Town. Later works signed Alexander Klopcanovs Westarde.

Exhibitions 1962 Pieter Wenning Gallery, Johannesburg, first of many solo exhibitions.

References G Clark & L Wagner, *Potters of Southern Africa*, 1974, Struik Publishers, Cape Town/Johannesburg; AASA.

KLOPPERS Jacobus Joubert Krige (Kobus)
Born 1959 Nelspruit, Eastern Transvaal.
A painter and graphic artist of his own personal mythology. Works in oil, watercolour, ink and in various graphic media.
Studies 1977–80 University of Pretoria, under Professor Nico Roos (qv), Keith Dietrich (qv) and John Clarke (qv), gaining a BA(FA).
Profile In 1984 he established a private art school in Wynberg, Cape Town, with Izak de Villiers (qv). 1984 a part-time lecturer at the Wynberg Art Centre. A commercial artist. In 1982 he made a 30-minute video for the Zinc Shop Show, Pretoria. 1985 lived in McGregor, Cape Province and from 1986 in Cape Town.
Exhibitions 1980 University of Pretoria, solo exhibition; he has participated in several group exhibitions from 1981 in Pretoria and Cape Town; 1984 his studio, Wynberg, Cape Town, joint exhibition with Izak de Villiers (qv); 1987 Gallery 21, Johannesburg, joint exhibition with John Clarke (qv), Erna Bodenstein-Ferreira (qv), William Steyn (qv) and Johann Moolman (qv); 1988 SAAA Gallery, Pretoria, joint exhibition with John Clarke (qv), Erna Bodenstein-Ferreira (qv) and William Steyn (qv).
Award 1980 First Prize, New Signatures, SAAA, Pretoria.

KLUGE Jacqueline Susanna
Born 1921 Pretoria.
A painter of landscapes, wildlife and still life in oil and of flowers, both cultivated and wild, in watercolour. A graphic artist.
Studies From 1964 took a number of lessons in art and pottery at the Pretoria Technical College.
Profile 1980–85 secretary of Art in the Parks, Pretoria. 1946 a series of wild animals in pewter; 1947 a series of wild animals in leather; also makes tapestries and batiks. Lived *c.*1946 in the Umfolozi Game Reserve, Natal, now lives in Hartbeeshoek, Pretoria, and travels annually to Namaqualand to paint its flowers.
Exhibitions She has participated in numerous group and solo exhibitions in SA.

KNAAP Tertia Venda
Born 1939 Potchefstroom, Transvaal.
A sculptor and a painter, working in acrylic, pencil, wood, various metals and mixed media.
Studies 1958–60 Natal Technical College, under Mr Bailey-Searle, where gained a National Diploma in Art and Design and won the Emma Smith Scholarship in 1960; 1968–72 University of South Africa, under Professor Walter Battiss (qv); 1972 British School of Art, Athens, Greece; 1974 and 1978–82 University of South Africa, attaining an MA(FA).

Profile 1965–80 a member of the SAAA. 1963–80 a senior lecturer at the Pretoria Technical College; 1980–84 a lecturer at the Michaelis School of Fine Art; from 1984 she has taught at her own art school in Onrus River, Cape Town. Designed medals for the University of South Africa, including its 1973 Centenary Medal, and for the Pretoria Technical College in 1977 and 1980. Illustrations for several scientific papers. Visited Greece in 1963, 1968 and 1972.

Exhibitions She has participated in many group exhibitions from 1966 in SA, two in the USA and one in Belgium; 1966 Walter Schwitter Gallery, Pretoria, joint exhibition with Jaco Kemp-Bezuidenhout (qv); 1970 SAAA Gallery, Pretoria, first of three solo exhibitions; 1979 Pretoria Art Museum, exhibition of "13 Specialists in (Re)search of a Ritual Object".

Represented Pretoria Art Museum; SA National Gallery, Cape Town; University of South Africa; University of Stellenbosch.

References AASA; LSAA.

KNUDSEN Heinrich E

Born 1816 Bergen, Norway.
Died 1864 Pfarre Hattejilddalen, Norway.
Resided in SWA/Namibia and SA 1841–53.

A trained lithographer and a painter in watercolour, of genre, buildings and portraits, the latter being mostly of tribal peoples and their chiefs. A number of drawings.

Profile A missionary and physical scientist of the Rhenish Missionary Society. 1841–51 lived in Bethanie, SWA/Namibia, visiting Windhoek on numerous occasions. 1851–53 lived in Tulbagh, Cape Province; 1853 returned to Norway. His work is thought to have been represented in the Archives of the Rhenish Mission at Barmen, Germany.

Reference Art SWA.

KOBELI Eli

Born 1932 Kroonstad, Orange Free State.
A painter of urban life, figures and abstract pictures. Works in oil, gouache, watercolour and pastel.

Studies 1958 Polly Street Art Centre, Johannesburg, under Cecil Skotnes (qv); also taught by the Reverend Hall Duncan, an American missionary.

Profile A member of Artists under the Sun. 1971 lived in Kroonstad, returning to Johannesburg in 1977. Has lived in both Alexandra and in Soweto, Johannesburg.

Exhibitions He has participated in group exhibitions in SA, the UK and the USA; 1980 Gallery 21, Johannesburg, solo exhibition; 1982 National Gallery, Gaborone, Botswana, Exhibition of SA Art.

References BSAK 1; AASA (both under Kobeleli).

KOBOKA Welcome Mandla

Born 1941 Johannesburg.
A painter of figures. Works in oil, watercolour, ink and charcoal.
Studies 1961 Jubilee Centre, Johannesburg, under Cecil Skotnes (qv) and Ephraim Ngatane (qv).
Profile A member of the WSSA and the Artists Market. Teaches art at FUBA and in Diepkloof and Orlando, Soweto.
Exhibitions He has participated in numerous group exhibitions from 1964; 1970 Johannesburg, first of eight solo exhibitions; 1981 Standard Bank, Soweto, Black Art Today Exhibition.
Represented University of Fort Hare.
References BSAK 1; AASA; Echoes of African Art; *SA Panorama* July 1982.

KOCH Francois Daniel Retief

Born 1944 Johannesburg.
A painter of landscapes, seascapes, portraits, still life, wildlife and figures. Works in oil, watercolour, pencil and charcoal.
Studies 1960–62 Witwatersrand Technical College, under Professor Robert Bain (qv), where awarded a Diploma in Commercial Art.
Profile Since 1962 he has worked as an illustrator for several publishing companies. 1963–66 a layout artist for a weekly magazine; 1966–69 worked for an advertising agency, thereafter a full-time artist. Numerous paintings by him have been reproduced in calendars. From 1983 has been living in George, where he owns an art gallery. He has travelled extensively in SA and in SWA/Namibia. Brother of Johann Koch (qv) and Martin Koch (qv).
Exhibitions He has participated in numerous group exhibitions from 1962 in SA; 1971 Little Theatre, Pretoria, first of over 20 solo exhibitions; 1980 Lister Gallery, Johannesburg, joint exhibition with Philip Bawcombe (qv).
References BSAK 1; AASA; SASSK; *Artlook* March 1974.

KOCH Johann Robert Francis

Born 1948 Johannesburg.
A painter of landscapes, still life, wildlife, portraits and figures. Works in oil, watercolour, ink and pencil.
Studies 1969 Witwatersrand Technical College.
Profile A member of the SAAA. Lives and paints in the Northern Transvaal, owning an art gallery in Potgietersrus. Brother of Francois Koch (qv) and Martin Koch (qv).
Exhibitions He has participated in numerous group exhibitions from 1974 in SA and one which travelled throughout Europe and the USA; 1975 Schweickerdt Gallery, Pretoria, first of six solo exhibitions held in SA.
Represented Pietersburg Collection.
Public Commission 1983 a series of six paintings for Potgietersrus Municipality.
Reference AASA.

KOCH Marthunus Stephanus (Martin)
Born 1940 Pretoria.
A painter of landscapes, seascapes, still life, wildlife and portraits. Works in oil, watercolour, ink and pencil.
Studies 1957–58 commercial art at the Witwatersrand Technical College, under Professor Robert Bain (qv).
Profile 1978–79 taught art privately in Pretoria. 1969–78 numerous visits to the USA; he has also visited South America and Europe. Brother of Francois Koch (qv) and Johann Koch (qv).
Exhibitions Numerous group exhibitions from 1955 in SA and in the USA in 1973 and 1975; he has held *c*.50 solo exhibitions in SA and the USA.
Represented Africana Museum, Johannesburg; Potchefstroom University for CHE.
Public Commission 1967 a 10 ft × 6 ft painting of the March Past for the 1966 Republic Festival in Pretoria commissioned by the SA Defence Force.
Reference BSAK 1.

KOENIG Dezso
Born 1902 Budapest, Hungary.
Died 1972 Johannesburg.
Resided in SA from 1931.
A painter of figures, still life, city scenes and landscapes. Worked in oil and crayon.
Studies 1914–17 Hungarian Royal Academy, where he won a scholarship for further studies in Germany, France and Italy.
Profile 1948 a founder member of the Brush and Chisel Club, also a member of the Transvaal Art Society. 1939–45 served in the SA Armed Forces. During this period he was involved with art therapy for convalescing soldiers in Egypt and Johannesburg. 1957 designed the set for a production of "Madame Butterfly" in the City Hall, Johannesburg. 1955–56 lived in London, returning there in 1962.
Exhibitions Participated in group exhibitions from 1918 in Europe, Egypt, the UK, the USA and SA; 1937 Durban Art Gallery, first of many solo exhibitions in SA; 1955 Imperial Institute, London, solo exhibition; 1972 Johannesburg, solo exhibition.
Represented Africana Museum, Johannesburg; Pretoria Art Museum; SA National Museum of Military History, Johannesburg.
References SAA; AMC3; BSAK 1; *Artlook* August 1970, April 1972 & August 1978.

KOLBE Isabella Johannah
Born 1856 George, Cape Province.
Died 1919 The Cape.
A painter of portraits. Worked in oil and crayon.
Studies Cape Town School of Art, under James Ford (qv); 1884 in Düsseldorf, Germany, under A Schluter (1858–1928), also at Eiserfeld and Munich, Germany.
Profile Taught art privately and in schools. Travelled in Europe, residing there from the late 1890s until 1908. Lived in Cape Town. Bad eyesight terminated her career.
Public Commissions Portraits of the Governors of the Cape, Sir H G R Robinson and Sir H B Loch.
Reference AASA.

KOLBE Philipps (Phil)

Born 1932 London, England.

A sculptor of figures and abstract pieces. Works in bronze, stone, ciment fondu and wood. A graphic artist.

Studies 1951–54 Witwatersrand Technical College, under Elizabeth Macadam (qv), James Gardner (qv) and Edoardo Villa (qv), where won the Gold Medal in 1951, 1952, 1953 and 1954 and was awarded a National Art Teachers Diploma in 1954; 1957 Accademia di Brera, Milan, Italy, under Marino Marini (*b.*1901) and at the Carrara Academy, Italy.

Profile From 1964 a member of the EPSFA and its President 1972–73, Honorary Life Vice-President from 1974. 1955–56 a teacher at the Child Art Centre, Pretoria and a lecturer at the Pretoria Technical College; 1959–64 a lecturer at the Witwatersrand Technical College; 1964–70 Head of the Fine Art Department and from 1975 a senior lecturer at the Port Elizabeth Technical College (Technikon). 1956 worked as a potter at Bury St Edmunds, Suffolk, England and 1957–59 owned a pottery studio on the South Coast of Natal. 1985 visited Portugal for research purposes for the Prester John Monument Commission.

Exhibitions He has participated in numerous group exhibitions from 1954 in SA; 1981 Republic Festival Exhibition; 1981 King George VI Art Gallery, Port Elizabeth, solo exhibition.

Represented Hester Rupert Art Museum, Graaff-Reinet; King George VI Art Gallery, Port Elizabeth; Pretoria Art Museum; Rand Afrikaans University; Walter Battiss Museum, Somerset East.

Public Commissions 1960 eight life-size carvings, Government Pavilion, Johannesburg; 1966 foyer panel, Nasionale Bouvereniging, Port Elizabeth; 1966 rose window, 1972 bronze doors, 1981 bronze dove, Pearson Street Congregational Church, Port Elizabeth; 1968 Mother & Child, Commercial High School, Cradock, Eastern Province; 1970 façade sculpture and mosaic panel, New Municipal Building, Port Elizabeth; 1971 symbolic window panels and foyer panel, Port Elizabeth Technical College (Technikon); 1971 three mosaic panels, SA Institute of Medical Research, Port Elizabeth; 1972 sculptural façade, Port Elizabeth Museum; 1975 bronze trophies for the SA Angling Union; 1977 wood carving, Sanlam Building, Port Elizabeth; 1980 relief panel for Stannic, Norwich Union Centre, Port Elizabeth; 1983 portrait bronze of Dr Gerrit Viljoen, Rand Afrikaans University; 1984 portrait bronze of General Louis Botha, Union Buildings, Pretoria; 1985–86 bronze with enamel panel insets, Prester John Monument, Port Elizabeth.

References BSAK 1 & 2; Port Elizabeth School of Art; AASA; *Artlook* December 1968, December 1971 & August 1972.

KOLOANE David Nthubu

Born 1938 Alexandra, Johannesburg.

A painter of figures and abstract pictures. Works in acrylic, watercolour, gouache, ink, wash, pencil and charcoal.

Studies 1974–77 under Bill Ainslie (qv); 1983 Birmingham Polytechnic, England; 1983 attended the Triangle Workshop, New York, USA; 1984–85 University of London, on a British Scholarship, gaining a Diploma in Museum Studies.

Profile 1977 a co-founder of the first Black art gallery in Johannesburg. From 1981 a member of FUBA, 1981–83 Head of the FUBA Fine Arts Department, 1983–85 compiler of the FUBA Newsletter Catalogue and from 1986 to 1988 the gallery curator. 1983 a member of the Triangle International Artists Workshop, New York, USA. 1981–82 articles by him were published in *Bonanza* and *Staffrider* periodicals; 1986–88 numerous articles for various periodicals including *Art*. 1985 on the panel of judges of the African Arts Festival, University of Zululand, a co-ordinator of the Botswana Arts Festival, a co-leader of the USSALEP–FUBA workshop and on the judging panel of the SANCA Poster Competition. 1983–85 lived in London. 1983 and 1984 visited New York; 1983 Birmingham, England.

Exhibitions He has participated in numerous group exhibitions from 1975 in SA, the USA, the UK and in Paris, France; 1976 Johannesburg, first solo exhibition; 1982 National Gallery, Gaborone, Botswana, Exhibition of SA Art; 1985 Tributaries, touring SA and West Germany; 1987 Johannesburg Art Gallery, Vita Art Now; 1987 Johannesburg Art Foundation, joint exhibition with Bill Ainslie (qv), Dumisani Mabaso (qv), Tony Nkotsi (qv) and Anthusa Sotiriades (qv).

Represented National Gallery, Gaborone, Botswana; University of Zululand.

References Echoes of African Art; *True Love* December 1985.

KONQOBE Percy Ndithembile

Born 1938/39 Nigel, Transvaal.

A sculptor of figures in rural and religious settings. Began producing clay sculptures in 1971 and from 1986 his clay sculptures have been cast in bronze.

Profile From 1973 a Sangoma (indigenous healer) in Soweto. During the early 1980s he made several visits to Europe, attending international Shaman symposia. Prior to 1988 he worked under the name Kuphe.

Exhibition 1988 Goodman Gallery, Johannesburg, solo exhibition.

KONYA A Sandor

Born 1891 Budapest, Hungary.

Died 1976.

Resided in SA from 1928.

A painter of figures, portraits and landscapes. Worked in oil and watercolour, and produced a number of monotypes.

Studies In Budapest and Paris, France.

Profile A member of SAAA. 1930 co-founder, with H V Meyerowitz (qv), of the SA School of Applied Arts, Cape Town. Designed stamps and stage decorations and was employed as an art director to a film company. A trained architect. 1934–38 lived in China. While in SA lived in Cape Town and Pretoria.

Exhibitions Participated in group exhibitions in SA from 1949. Exhibited his graphics in Paris and New York.
References The Arts in SA, edited by WHK, The Knox Printing & Publishing Company, Durban; BSAK 1 & 2; *Artlook* April 1971.

KOORZEN Johannes Nicholas

Born 1931 Griquatown, Cape Province.
A painter and graphic artist of landscapes.
Studies 1954 studied under Barbara Eyre, gaining a Higher Primary Teachers Certificate in Art; Die Akademie der Bildenden Kunste, Munich, West Germany, under Professor Ernst Geitlinger.
Profile 1964 a founder member of the Artists Gallery, Cape Town.
Exhibitions He has participated in group exhibitions from the early 1960s in SA; held solo exhibitions during the 1960s at the SAAA Gallery, Cape Town; 1966 Republic Festival Exhibition.
References SAA; BSAK 1; AASA.

KOPPE Penelope Anne DA, FRSA

Born 1944 Cairo, Egypt.
Resided in SA from 1975.
A painter of landscapes, wildlife and abstract pictures. Works in watercolour, gouache, ink, wash and gold.
Studies Four years at the Glasgow School of Art, Scotland, gaining a Diploma in Design and Crafts; two years at l'Ecole Nationale Supérieure des Arts Decoratifs, Paris, where attained a Certificate in Design; awarded a Post Diploma Scholarship to the Glasgow School of Art; studied in Italy for a year on an Industrial Art Bursary.
Profile An Associate of the WSSA. Taught at Manchester College of Art and Design, England. An architectural, interior, textile and furniture designer. Lived in India until 1954, followed by several years spent living and travelling in Europe.
Exhibitions She has participated in group exhibitions from 1966 in the UK, France and SA; 1985 Sandton City, Johannesburg, first of three solo exhibitions, the third being held in Bath, England.

KORN Herman Dr

Born 1908 Segerde, Germany.
Died 1946 Windhoek, SWA/Namibia.
Resided in SWA/Namibia from 1935.
A painter of animals and landscapes. Worked in watercolour.
Profile A trained geologist. Spent two and a half years during WWII in the Namib Desert with Dr Henno Martin, who wrote about their experience in his book, *The Sheltering Desert*, 1957, William Kimber, London; third English edition, 1983, Ad Donker, Johannesburg.

Exhibitions 1948 posthumously included in an Arts Association SWA/Namibia group exhibition and in 1962 in "Art in SWA" at the SA National Gallery, Cape Town.
Represented Arts Association SWA/Namibia Collection.
References BSAK 2; Art SWA; AASA; *Garden & Home* October 1984.

KORS Stanislaw

Born 1935 Lublin, Poland.
Resided in SA from 1982.
A painter and graphic artist of current infra-realistic images. Works in oil, gouache, mixed media, charcoal and in various graphic media.
Studies 1961–67 Academy of Fine Arts, Wroclaw, Poland, under Professor Stanislaw Dawski and Professor Alfons Mazurkiewicz, gaining an MA(FA).
Profile 1967–81 a member of the Polish Artists Association. 1964–81 various designs for theatre, tapestry and architectural features, Poland. Has lived in Poland, Norway and Austria, and has visited Germany, France, Italy, the USA and Russia.
Exhibitions He has participated in many group exhibitions from 1971 in Poland, France, Norway, West Germany, the USA, Argentina and SA; 1982 Ernst de Jong Gallery, Pretoria, first of three solo exhibitions held in SA.
Reference *De Kat* December/January 1987.

KORZENNIK Mickey Myer

Born 1930 Cape Town.
A sculptor in bronze of figures and abstracted pieces. A muralist working in concrete, timber, stainless steel, vitreous enamel, aluminium and glass, among other media. A graphic artist.
Studies Mainly self-taught with a number of lessons in 1956 in Israel, under Marcel Yanco and Naftali Bezem.
Profile 1954–57 an official Kibbutz artist in Israel. 1986 the title, illustration and design of *The Dreamer Man*, by John Brett Cohen, limited private edition.
Public Commissions Numerous murals for company headquarters, banks, building societies, churches, synagogues and mosques in the Transvaal; and for the State Theatre, Pretoria; the Civic Centre, Johannesburg; New Municipal Library, Vanderbijlpark, Transvaal; Indian Welfare Headquarters, Lenasia, Transvaal.
Reference BSAK 1.

KOTTLER Moses

Born 1892 Joniskis, Kovno, Lithuania (Lithuanian SSR).
Died 1977 Johannesburg.
Resided in SA from 1915.
A sculptor of portrait busts and figure studies, a large number of public monuments and low-relief architectural panels. Worked in bronze, stone, cement, artificial stone, clay and wood. His sculpture is simplified with a strong African feeling. A painter working in oil, during 1911–24, of portraits, still life, landscapes and scenes of the Cape Malay Quarter. Produced some watercolour and pastel sketches of figures prior to 1928.

Studies A self-taught sculptor. 1910 painting at Bezalel School of Art, Jerusalem, established by Professor Boris Schatz (1867–1932), for six months; 1911–13 Die Akademie der Bildenden Kunste, Munich, Germany, under Carl Becker (*b*.1862) and Hugo von Habermann (1849–1921).

Profile A member of the SA Society of Artists. 1938 a member of the New Group. 1956–62 on the Advisory Committee of the Johannesburg Art Gallery. 1912 first visit to Oudtshoorn, Cape Province; 1913–14 visited Paris, studying sculpture in the various art galleries, influenced by Cubism and by Rodin; 1914–15 in London; 1915–16 in Oudtshoorn; 1916–22 in Cape Town; 1922 visited London and Paris; 1923–29 in Cape Town; 1929 in London; 1930–32 in London, France and Italy; 1932 visited Oudtshoorn; 1932–77 in Johannesburg. 1953–54 a three-month visit to Europe; 1965 visited Europe; 1967 Europe and Israel.

Exhibitions Participated in group exhibitions from 1916 in SA and from 1929 in London with the London Group; he also participated in group exhibitions in Rhodesia (Zimbabwe), Italy and Brazil; 1920 City Hall, Cape Town and 1932 MacFadyen Hall, Pretoria, solo exhibitions; 1924 Cape Town, joint exhibition with Daphne Taylor; 1948 Tate Gallery, London, SA Art Exhibition; 1960 Quadrennial Exhibition; 1974–75 Pretoria Art Museum, Johannesburg Art Gallery and SA National Gallery, Cape Town, Retrospective Exhibition; 1977 Johannesburg Art Gallery, exhibition entitled "A Tribute to Moses Kottler"; 1978 Johannesburg Art Gallery, Memorial Exhibition; 1978 SAAA Gallery, Bellville, Memorial Exhibition.

Awards 1949 SA Academy Gold Medal; 1962 Medal of Honour for sculpture, SA Akademie vir Wetenskap en Kuns.

Represented Africana Museum, Johannesburg; Durban Art Gallery; Hester Rupert Art Museum, Graaff-Reinet; Johannesburg Art Gallery; National Portrait Gallery, London, UK; Pretoria Art Museum; SA Akademie vir Wetenskap en Kuns; SA National Gallery, Cape Town; University of Cape Town; University of the Orange Free State; University of Pretoria; University of Stellenbosch; University of the Witwatersrand; War Museum of the Boer Republics, Bloemfontein; William Humphreys Art Gallery, Kimberley.

Public Commissions Among his numerous public commissions are: 1932 eight figures, Johannesburg Library; 1935 "Figures of Justice", Magistrates Courts, Johannesburg; 1941 "Mother Earth", "Labour" and "Science", Anglo American Corporation Building, Johannesburg; 1950 bronze statue of President T F Burgers, Burgers Park, Pretoria; 1954 SA Air Pioneers, Sir Pierre van Ryneveld & Sir Quintin Brand, Jan Smuts Airport, Johannesburg; 1957 "Man & Woman", Population and Registration Building, Pretoria (later moved to Kimberley); 1957 three figures and Sea Nymph fountain groups, General Mining Building, Johannesburg; 1958 stone relief of St Andrew, St Andrew's Church, Kensington, Johannesburg; 1961 Fountain Group, Civic Centre, Stilfontein, Transvaal; 1962 "Striving", Transvaal Provincial Administration Building, Pretoria; 1965 "Serenity and Love", Rand Water Board, Johannesburg; 1976 War Memorial, University of the Witwatersrand. Portrait busts of notabilities, including President T F Burgers, Generals De Wet, Smuts, Hertzog and Louis Botha, and Sir Max Michaelis.

MOSES KOTTLER
Meidjie 1926
Cypress Wood 155,5 cm High
Johannesburg Art Gallery

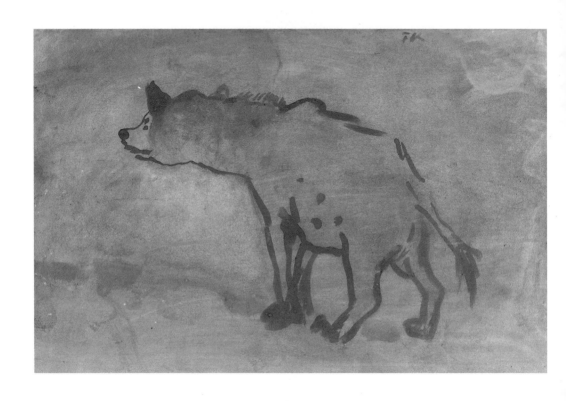

FRITZ KRAMPE
Hyena
Gouache on Cartridge Paper on Board 64 × 97,4 cm
Johannesburg Art Gallery

FRANÇOIS KRIGE
Kung Hunter 1984
Oil on Canvas 65 × 57,5 cm
Die Kunskamer

SYDNEY KUMALO
Two Bulls
Bronze 120 cm High
Pretoria Art Museum

References J du P Scholtz, *Moses Kottler, His Cape Years*, 1976, Tafelberg, Cape Town; Collectors' Guide; Our Art 1; Art SA; SAA; 20C SA Art; AMC3; SAP&S; Oxford Companion to Art (under SA); SESA; SSAP; BSAK 1 & 2; Enc S'n A; SA Art; J du P Scholtz, *Oor Skilders en Skrywers*, 1979, Tafelberg, Cape Town; 3Cs; AASA; LSAA; *SA Architectural Record* 1933; *Lantern* vol 4 no 3, 1955; *South Africana* February 1957; *Bulletin Pretoriase Kunsmuseum* 8 (4), October 1974; *Artlook* November 1974; *SA Panorama* April 1975; A J Werth, Retrospective Exhibition Catalogue, 1974–75, Pretoria Art Museum.

KOTZÉ Jeanne (Mrs Louw)

Born 1929 Lichtenburg, Western Transvaal.

A painter of landscapes, portraits, still life and figures. Works in oil, acrylic, watercolour, ink, conté and mixed media; also in mosaic, ceramic, cement and stained glass; produces textile designs. A lithographer and etcher.

Studies 1947–51 University of Natal, under Professor O J P Oxley (qv), Geoffrey Long (qv), Rosa Hope (qv) and Hilda Rose (qv), gaining a BA(FA)(Hons); 1950 won the Emma Smith Scholarship for Overseas Studies; 1952–53 Accademia di Belle Arti, Ravenna, Italy, under Professor Renato Signorini and Professor René Jaudon; 1953–54 l'Ecole Nationale Supérieure des Beaux Arts, Paris, under Professor Leoncillo; 1954–56 l'Instituto Statale d'Arte, Rome, under Signorina Castellucci; from 1985 University of Pretoria, under Professor Nico Roos (qv).

Profile From 1960 a member of the SAAA. 1958–60 a lecturer in mosaics at the Positano Art Workshop, Italy; from 1975 a lecturer in Visual Design and Painting in the Department of Fine Arts, University of Pretoria. An article on Byzantine mosaics by her was published in *Lantern* June 1968. 1952–60 lived in Europe.

Exhibitions She has participated in numerous group exhibitions in SA and in one in Italy; 1981 Republic Festival Exhibition.

Represented Pretoria Art Museum; University of Natal.

Public Commissions Numerous murals in mosaic, concrete, ceramic and egg tempera for company headquarters, banks, churches, hospitals and in 1951 for the University of Natal; 1963 University of the Orange Free State; 1968 Louis Trichardt Memorial, Lourenço Marques (Maputo), Mozambique; 1969 General Post Office, Skukuza, Kruger National Park; 1970 Inland Revenue Offices, Port Elizabeth; 1971 Jan Smuts Airport, Johannesburg; 1980 the State Theatre, Pretoria.

References SAA; BSAK 1; SA Art; AASA; LSAA.

KOVACS Daniel Stephen Borbereki-

Born 1943 Szolnok, Hungary.

Resided in SA from 1950.

A sculptor of semi-abstract female torsos, animals, universal themes and abstract pieces. Works in bronze, stone, ciment fondu and wood.

Profile 1969–70 lived in Spain, has frequently visited France. Son of Zoltan Borbereki (qv) and Elizabeth Sebok (qv), brother of Barbara Borbereki (qv).

Exhibitions He has participated in many group exhibitions from 1973 in SA, France, Belgium and Monaco; 1974 Johannesburg, first of four solo exhibitions in Johannesburg and Cape Town; 1981 Republic Festival Exhibition; 1986 SAAA Gallery, Pretoria, joint exhibition with the textile designer Z Suzsenna Haraszti.

Awards 1973 First Prize, New Signatures, SAAA, Pretoria; 1978 Gold Medal, Grand Prix d'Automne, Lyons, France; 1979 First Prize, XV Grand Prix International de la Côte d'Azur, Cannes, France.

Represented Rand Afrikaans University.

References AASA; *Habitat* no 22, 1976.

KRAFFT Marianne

Born 1906 Pommern, Germany.

Resided in SWA/Namibia from 1935.

A painter of landscapes, portraits and seascapes. Works in oil, watercolour and other media. A muralist.

Studies Studied for four years in Berlin, under Johannes Itten.

Profile A tapestry designer, founding Weberei Krafft, a weaving studio in SWA/Namibia. Daughter of August Stauch, a well-known discoverer of diamonds in SWA/Namibia.

Exhibition 1980 Arts Association SWA/Namibia, solo exhibition.

Represented Arts Association SWA/Namibia Collection.

References Art SWA; AASA.

KRAMER John Barnett

Born 1946 Worcester, Cape Province.

A painter of buildings and street scenes. Works in oil and acrylic.

Studies 1966–68 Michaelis School of Fine Art, under May Hillhouse (qv), Carl Buchner (qv) and Bill Davis (qv), gaining a Diploma in Fine Art.

Profile A member of the Artists Guild and the SAAA. An exhibition designer for the SA Museum, Cape Town. 1974 toured Europe and England.

Exhibitions He has participated in many group exhibitions from 1971 in SA; 1981 Republic Festival Exhibition; 1981 SAAA Gallery, Cape Town, solo exhibition; 1982 Cape Town Triennial.

Award 1975 Second Prize for Painting, New Signatures, SAAA.

Represented Durban Art Gallery; King George VI Art Gallery, Port Elizabeth; SA National Gallery, Cape Town; University of the Orange Free State.

References 3Cs; AASA.

KRAMPE Fritz

Born 1913 Berlin.

Died 1966 Anaikatty Jungle, Ootacamund, India (gored by the tusk of a elephant).

Resided in SWA/Namibia from 1951, having spent six months in Cape Town. A painter of wildlife, figures and portraits. Worked in oil, pastel, watercolour, gouache, mixed media, ink and wash. A large amount of graphic work, particularly lithographs. A number of mural commissions.

Studies 1931–32 Vereinigen Staatsschulen für Freie und Angewandte Kunst, Charlottenburg, Berlin, under Professor Ferdinand Spiegel; 1933 Munich Fine Arts Academy, under Professor Hess; 1935–39 Prussian Academy of Art, Berlin, becoming a master student.

Profile 1947–50 illustrated editions of such literary works as *Peer Gynt*, *Moby Dick* and *Reynard The Fox*. 1932–33 voyaged along the Siberian coast; 1934 on military training in Berlin; 1934 in Munich; 1936 in the German Armed Forces; 1941–46 a Prisoner of War in Egypt, Palestine and Australia; 1947–50 in Berlin; thereafter lived in Windhoek. Travelled extensively through Southern and East Africa; 1966 visited the Middle East, Pakistan and India. A memorial award, "The Fritz Krampe Award", is made annually by the Madras Art Club, India.

Exhibitions 1951 Cape Town, first of numerous solo exhibitions; participated in group exhibitions from 1952 in SA, Zimbabwe, Brazil, Italy, West Germany, The Netherlands and Belgium; 1956 and 1960 Quadrennial Exhibitions; 1958 SAAA Gallery, Pretoria, Johannesburg Art Gallery and SAAA Gallery, Cape Town, exhibition of the Gruppe Funf (Group 5) consisting of Fritz Krampe, Adolph Jentsch (qv), Otto Schröder (qv), Joachim Voigts (qv) and Heinz Pulon (qv); 1967–68 Johannesburg Art Gallery, SA National Gallery, Cape Town and in Kimberley, Commemorative Exhibition; 1968, 1971, 1979, 1983, Arts Association Gallery SWA/Namibia, Windhoek, Commemorative Exhibitions; 1977 Die Kunskamer, Cape Town, joint exhibition with Adolph Jentsch (qv); 1977 Madras Art Club, India, Retrospective Exhibition.

Represented Arts Association SWA/Namibia Collection; Hester Rupert Art Museum, Graaff-Reinet; Johannesburg Art Gallery; Pretoria Art Museum; SA National Gallery, Cape Town; University of Cape Town; University of the Orange Free State; University of Stellenbosch; William Humphreys Art Gallery, Kimberley.

References Our Art 2; Art SA; SAA; 20C SA Art; DSAB; SAP&D; SESA; SSAP; BSAK 1 & 2; Art SWA; SA Art; 3Cs; AASA; LSAA; *Lantern* June 1967; *Fontein* Winter 1970; *Fritz Krampe 1913–1966*, 1967, SA National Gallery Catalogue.

KRAMS Isolde Ingeborg

Born 1961 Münstermaifeld, West Germany.

Resided in South Africa from 1974.

A sculptor of figures and furniture. Works in ciment fondu, resin, fibreglass, bronze, oil and with ready-made objects.

Studies 1984 gained a BA(FA) from the University of the Witwatersrand; 1988 studying for an MA(FA) at the University of the Witwatersrand.

Profile Spent six months at Cité Internationale des Arts, Paris.

Exhibition 1985 Cape Town Triennial; 1987 Johannesburg Art, Ballet and Music School, exhibition; 1988 Johannesburg Art Gallery, Vita Art Now.

Awards 1982 National Student Fine Art Competition; 1984 Merit Award in Sculpture, New Signatures, SAAA; 1984 Martienssen Prize, Student Competition, University of the Witwatersrand; 1984 Anya Millman Scholarship for Overseas Travel.

Represented Durban Art Gallery; University of the Witwatersrand.

Reference *De Kat* December/January 1986.

KRAUSE Agnes Joy (Mrs Weeber)

Born 1906 Pietersburg, Northern Transvaal.

A painter of landscapes, seascapes, still life and figures. Works in watercolour and oil. An etcher.

Studies 1925–27 Natal Technical College, under Professor O J P Oxley (qv) and Alfred Martin (qv). Awarded the Baron Beaumont Bursary in 1927.

Profile 1928–40 a member of the NSA; 1973 a co-founder of the WSSA, of which she is an Associate; a member of the SAAA. 1938–41 an art mistress at Pietersburg High School. 1906–72 based in Pietersburg, thereafter in Cape Town. Has travelled extensively in Europe and to the USA.

Exhibitions She has participated in numerous group exhibitions from 1928 in SA; 1928 Durban, first of 10 solo exhibitions.

Represented Pietersburg Collection.

References BSAK 1 & 2; AASA; *Artlook* September 1970.

KRENZ Alfred Frederic Professor (honoris causa)

Born 1899 Vienna, Austria.

Died 1980 Cape Town.

Resided in SA from 1949 in Cape Town.

A painter of portraits, figures, nudes, landscapes, harbour scenes, street scenes and still life. Worked in oil, ink, charcoal, watercolour, crayon and tempera. A graphic artist producing linocuts and silkscreens. A series on the Cape Malay Quarter. Tended towards abstraction from 1957.

Studies 1915–16 Kunstgewerbeschule, Vienna, under Professor Franz Czizek and Professor Oskar Strnad; 1918–26 Academy of Fine Arts, Vienna, under Josef Jungwirth (1869–1950) and Karl Sterrer (*b*.1885), in 1922 graduated to the Meisterschule, under Professor Rudolph Bacher; 1929–31 Amédée Ozenfant's Academy, Paris, France.

Profile Taught briefly in Stellenbosch; 1952 opened the Krenz Art School in Rondebosch, Cape Town. 1952 a member of the New Group. 1926–29 lived in Italy; 1929–31 in Paris, France; 1932–38 in Vienna, Austria; 1938–49 in The Netherlands and in Paris. 1943 served with the Luftwaffe in Paris. 1954 toured North and South America, Haiti and Tenerife; 1962 visited Curaçao, the Netherlands Antilles; 1968–71 and 1972 Israel; 1970 and 1974 Spain; travelled widely in Southern Africa and spent three months of each year in Europe, mostly in Spain.

Exhibitions Participated in group exhibitions from 1928 in Europe, SA, Rhodesia (Zimbabwe) and Brazil; 1931 Galleria Micheli, Milan, Italy, first of many solo exhibitions held in Europe and Curaçao, the Netherlands Antilles; 1938 Argus Gallery, Cape Town (paintings sent from abroad), first of many solo exhibitions held in Cape Town, Johannesburg, Pretoria and Bellville; 1956, 1960 and 1964 Quadrennial Exhibitions; 1975 Pretoria Art Museum and SAAA Gallery, Pretoria, Prestige Retrospective Exhibition.

Awards 1926 The Vienna Prix de Rome; 1958 awarded the title Professor (honoris causa) by the Austrian Government following the Salzburg Festival Exhibition; 1967 Medal of Honour for Painting, SA Akademie vir Wetenskap en Kuns.

Represented Albertina Gallery, Vienna, Austria; Ann Bryant Gallery, East London; Hester Rupert Art Museum, Graaff-Reinet; Johannesburg Art Gallery; King George VI Art Gallery, Port Elizabeth; National Gallery, Budapest, Hungary; Palais des Beaux Arts, Brussels, Belgium; Pietersburg Collection; Pretoria Art Museum; SA Akademie vir Wetenskap en Kuns; Salzburg Art Gallery, Austria; SA National Gallery, Cape Town; University of Cape Town; University of Pretoria; University of Stellenbosch; University of the Witwatersrand; Willem Annandale Art Gallery, Lichtenburg; William Humphreys Art Gallery, Kimberley.

References Our Art 2; Art SA; SAA; 20C SA Art; SAP&S; SAP&D; SSAP; BSAK 1 & 2; 3Cs; AASA; LSAA; *Lantern* September 1960; *Artlook* September 1968 & June 1972; *SA Panorama* October 1973; Retrospective Exhibition Catalogue, 1975, Pretoria Art Museum.

KRIEDEMANN Lambert

Born 1951 Uitenhage, Cape Province.

A painter of mainly Cape landscapes and seascapes, also depicts portraits, still life, genre, figures, wildlife, architectural drawings and paintings, and paints abstract pictures. Works in oil, acrylic, watercolour, gouache, pastel, egg tempera and pencil. Occasionally works in ink, wash, charcoal and in various graphic media.

Studies 1972 Ruth Prowse Art Centre, Cape Town, under Erik Laubscher (qv) and Edwine Simon (qv).

Profile From 1978 a member of the SA Society of Artists and from 1984 of the SAAA. 1984 a founder member of Art in the Avenue, Cape Town. 1970–71 a trainee trapeze artist. 1971–75 worked as a freelance architectural designer, and as a freelance designer in film and theatre, thereafter a full-time artist. His work has been reproduced on stamps and in calendars. In 1980 four watercolours of Cape Dutch buildings were reproduced as prints. 1982 studied calligraphy and illumination under M Roberts. 1969 on military service in SWA/Namibia; 1973–74 visited Spain and the Balearic Islands; 1984 visited Portugal and West Germany. Lives in Cape Town.

Exhibitions He has participated in many group exhibitions from 1975 in SA, once in England in 1983 and once in Spain in 1973; 1978 Barclays (First National) Bank Gallery, Rondebosch, Cape, first of 12 solo exhibitions.

KRIEL Sandra

Born 1952 Cape Town.
Known to paint abstract pictures in oil.
Studies 1972–75 graphic art at the University of Stellenbosch; 1976–80 Koninklijke Academie voor Schone Kunsten en de Hogere Instituten, Antwerp, Belgium.
Profile Has taught art in Stellenbosch.
Exhibitions 1979 Cape Town Biennial; 1982 Cape Town Triennial.
Represented University of Stellenbosch.
Reference AASA.

KRIGE François

Born 1913 Uniondale, Cape Province.
A painter of landscapes, seascapes, still life, wildlife, portraits and figures. Works in oil, watercolour, ink, pencil and charcoal. A woodcarver and graphic artist.
Studies Michaelis School of Fine Art, under H V Meyerowitz (qv) and at the Koninklijke Academie voor Schone Kunsten en de Hogere Instituten, Antwerp, Belgium; 1934–37 in Spain under Vasquez Diaz, sponsored by Victor Kark.
Profile A member of the New Group and of the SAAA. 1941–45 an Official SA War Artist in Egypt and Italy. Illustrated *Jaffie*, by Eitemal (W J du P Erlank); *Sol y Sombra*, by Uys Krige, with his Spanish drawings; *Their Secret Ways*, by V Pohl and *Wit Wyne van Suid Afrika*, by W A de Klerk. He has travelled in Europe and in SWA/Namibia. Son of the writer Sannie Uys and brother of the poet Uys Krige.
Exhibitions He has participated in numerous group exhibitions in SA, one in West Germany and one in Venice, Italy; joint exhibitions with Geoffrey Long (qv); 1934 Johannesburg, first of numerous solo exhibitions held in SA; 1948 Tate Gallery, London, SA Art Exhibition; 1960 Quadrennial Exhibition.
Award 1949 Medal of Honour, SA Akademie vir Wetenskap en Kuns.
Represented Hester Rupert Art Museum, Graaff-Reinet; Johannesburg Art Gallery; Julius Gordon Africana Centre, Riversdale; King George VI Art Gallery, Port Elizabeth; National Museum, Bloemfontein; Potchefstroom Museum; Pretoria Art Museum; SA Akademie vir Wetenskap en Kuns; SA National Gallery, Cape Town; University of the Orange Free State; University of Pretoria; University of Stellenbosch; William Humphreys Art Gallery, Kimberley.
References *François Krige Drawings*, 1971, Tafelberg, Cape Town; PSA; Collectors' Guide; Our Art 2; Art SA; SAA; 20C SA Art; AMC3 & 7; SAP&S; SAP&D; SSAP; BSAK 1 & 2; Art SWA; 3Cs; AASA; LSAA.

KRUGER Braam

Born 1950 Boksburg, Transvaal.
A painter, sculptor and graphic artist, working in oil, acrylic, watercolour, gouache, ink, wash, pencil, enamel, charcoal, wood, ceramics, the encaustic processes and in various graphic media. 1982 three-dimensional paintings in plastic; 1985 "Batman" series; 1985–86 "Black" paintings; 1987 working on a series of paintings with Simon Stone (qv).

Studies 1974–79 Pretoria Technical College (Technikon), under Gunther van der Reis (qv), gaining a Teachers Diploma in Art; 1980 Frans Masereel Centrum voor Grafiek, Kasterlee, Belgium.

Profile From 1979 a member of the SAAA; 1984 founder of the SA Alternative Monuments Commission. 1984 a lecturer in painting, Cape Technikon. 1977 produced a series of etchings illustrating *Laatnagvrese*, a book of poems by Wessel Pretorius; 1986 illustrations and cover of a book of short stories by Jan Strydom. 1970 a scenic painter for PACT. Has lived in the Cape Province and presently in Johannesburg. 1978 visited New York; 1979 Paris; 1979–80 in Antwerp, Belgium.

Exhibitions He has participated in numerous group exhibitions from 1974 in SA, West Germany, Belgium and the USA; 1975 own studio, Pretoria, first of *c*.20 solo exhibitions, one of which was held in Belgium; 1978 Rand Afrikaans University, solo exhibition; 1979 exhibition of pottery and ceramics; 1985 Cape Town Triennial; 1987 Johannesburg Art Gallery, Vita Art Now.

Represented Bellville Municipal Gallery; Pietersburg Collection; Pretoria Art Museum; Pretoria Technikon; SA National Gallery, Cape Town; Sterckshof Museum, Antwerp, Belgium; Ministry for Culture, Belgium; University of Natal; University of Pretoria; Walter Battiss Museum, Somerset East; Willem Annandale Art Gallery, Lichtenburg.

Public Commissions 1974 mural for the Pretoria Technical College; 1983–84 portrait for the SA Nursing Council.

References 3Cs; AASA; *Style* March 1985; *De Kat* April 1986; *SA Arts Calendar* Winter 1986.

KRUGER Elizabeth Wilhelmina

Born 1912 Koppies, Orange Free State.

A painter and graphic artist of landscapes, seascapes, still life, portraits and figures. Works in oil, watercolour, gouache, ink, wash, pencil, charcoal and in various graphic media.

Studies 1964 portraits and life drawing at the Pretoria Technical College (Adult Education); 1983 etching under Mimi van der Merwe (qv).

Profile A member of the WSSA, the Brush and Chisel Club and Club 997, Pretoria. From 1962 has taught art privately in Pretoria. A designer of SA motifs for the making of bobbin lace. 1979 visited Spain, France and the UK.

Exhibitions She has participated in several group exhibitions in Pretoria and Johannesburg from 1981.

KRÜGER Johanna Petronella (Mrs Wessels)

Born 1954 Eldoret, Kenya.

Resided in SA from 1964.

A painter of landscapes, portraits, and figures. Works in oil, watercolour and pencil. A sculptor working in bronze and stone. 1985 a series of Welkom's flamingos; 1986 a series entitled "Nineteen Eighty Six".

Studies 1970–71 Johannesburg Art, Ballet and Music School; 1972–74 Witwatersrand Technical College, under Phil Botha (qv), Claude van Lingen (qv) and Nico van Rensburg (qv), gaining a National Senior Diploma in Fine Arts.
Profile A member of the WSSA; 1987 Chairlady of the Goldfields Art Group. 1978 taught painting part-time at Orange Free State Technical College. 1978–80 Head of the Art Department of the War Museum of the Boer Republics, Bloemfontein. Has a keen interest in photography. 1969–74 lived in Johannesburg; 1975–81 in Bloemfontein, thereafter in Welkom. 1986 visited SWA/Namibia.
Exhibitions She has participated in several group exhibitions from 1968 in SA; 1975 Bloemfontein Checkers Arcade, solo exhibition.
Award 1986 Artist of the Year, Welkom Branch of the WSSA.
Public Commission 1986 Portrait of the Mayor of Welkom for the Odendal Hall.

KRUGER-HAYE Dietrich Joachim Ernst (Dieter)

Born 1921 Sophienau, Germany (Poland).
Resided in SA from 1952.
A sculptor of figures, animals and abstract pieces. Works in wood and polyurethane. 1971–74 produced a wildlife series for the SWA/Namibian Administration.
Studies 1949–53 informal studies in woodcarving in Germany, and cabinet making, drawing, furniture and interior design in the Cape.
Profile From 1970 a member of the SAAA and from 1963 a life-member of the Cape Town Photographic Society. 1956–86 a cabinet-maker and interior designer, thereafter a full-time sculptor. 1961–85 ran his own workshop where he trained apprentices in cabinet making. 1921–42 lived in Germany, 1943–48 in Egypt; 1948–52 in Germany. He has travelled throughout SA and SWA/Namibia photographing wildlife.
Exhibitions He has participated in many group exhibitions from 1971 in SA and five in Germany during 1976–78; 1974 Stellenbosch, first of five solo exhibitions held in SA.
Public Commissions Many commissions for furniture, architectural works, coats of arms, plaques and trophies.

KRYNAUW Daniel

A painter of landscapes, portraits, figures and buildings. Worked in watercolour, pencil and wash.
Studies c.1852 under Thomas Bowler (qv).
Profile A member of the SA Fine Arts Association. In 1871 he was a committee member and the treasurer for the SA Fine Arts Exhibition. 1859–85 a Government Land Surveyor in Cape Town. Travelled overseas frequently. He completed the drawings begun by Charles Bell (qv), to whom he was related by marriage, of the Coats of Arms of SA families. A friend of Abraham de Smidt (qv) for many years.

Exhibitions Participated in group exhibitions from 1852 in Cape Town.
Represented Africana Museum, Johannesburg; SA Cultural History Museum, Cape Town; SA Library, Cape Town; William Fehr Collection, Cape Town.
References Pict Art; AMC3; Pict Afr; Marjorie Bell, *Abraham de Smidt 1829–1908*, 1981, Printpak, Cape Town; BSAK 1.

KUHLMANN Julia Ann (née Beeton)

Born 1955 Pretoria.
A painter of narrative landscapes. Works in oil, acrylic, pencil and mixed media. Makes collages using fabrics and yarns.
Studies 1973–76 Michaelis School of Fine Art, under Stanley Pinker (qv) and Jules van de Vijver (qv), gaining a BA(FA); 1977–78 University of Pretoria, under Mike Edwards (qv).
Profile From 1979 a member of the SAAA. 1977–79 a junior lecturer in fine art, University of Pretoria; 1982–85 a part-time lecturer in printmaking, Witwatersrand Technikon. Illustrated *Atletiekpret vir die Jongspan*, by Botha de Villiers, 1979, Janssoniussheyns, Ficksburg; *Lip from Southern African Women*, 1983, Ravan Press, Johannesburg. Daughter of Jean Beeton (qv).
Exhibitions She has participated in several group exhibitions in SA from 1977; 1982 and 1985 Cape Town Triennials.
Represented SA National Gallery, Cape Town.

KUMALO Sydney Alex

Born 1935 Johannesburg.
A sculptor and a painter of figures, heads, animals and mythological beasts. Works in bronze, terracotta, pencil, charcoal, watercolour, gouache and conté.
Studies 1952–57 Polly Street Art Centre, Johannesburg, under Cecil Skotnes (qv). Studied sculpture under Edoardo Villa (qv).
Profile 1957–65 a founder member of the Amadlozi Group. 1960 taught art and, on Cecil Skotnes' (qv) resignation in 1961, took over as official Art Organiser and Director of the Jubilee Social Centre Art School for four years (this had previously been called the Polly Street Art Centre).
Exhibitions He has participated in group exhibitions from 1957 in SA, Europe, South America and Australia; 1962 Egon Guenther Gallery, Johannesburg, first solo exhibition; 1965 Piccadilly Gallery, London, African Painters and Sculptors from Johannesburg; 1966 Grosvenor Gallery, London, joint exhibition with Cecil Skotnes (qv); 1979 Contemporary African Art in SA, touring exhibition; 1981 Republic Festival Exhibition; 1981 Standard Bank, Soweto, Black Art Today Exhibition; 1982 National Gallery, Gaborone, Botswana, Exhibition of SA Art; 1985 Goodman Gallery, Johannesburg, joint exhibition with Ezrom Legae (qv), Cecil Skotnes (qv) and Edoardo Villa (qv); 1985 Cape Town Triennial; 1986 Alliance Française, Pretoria, Historical Perspective of Black Art in SA Exhibition; 1988 Johannesburg Art Gallery, Vita Art Now.

Awards 1963 Phillip Frame Award, Art SA Today, NSA Gallery; 1967 Bronze Medal, Transvaal Academy, and a travel bursary for three months in the USA and Europe, as a guest of USSALEP.

Represented Durban Art Gallery; Johannesburg Art Gallery; Pretoria Art Museum; SA National Gallery, Cape Town; University of Fort Hare; University of South Africa; University of the Witwatersrand; William Humphreys Art Gallery, Kimberley.

Public Commissions 1960 Praying Woman, State Pavilion, Milner Park, Johannesburg; 1960 Eagle, Kitwe Hotel, Northern Rhodesia (Zambia); 1987 Natal Performing Arts Council.

References Art SA; SAA; 20C SA Art; SESA; SSAP; BSAK 1 & 2; Our Art 3; SA Art; Oxford Companion to 20C Art (under SA); 3Cs; AASA; LSAA; Echoes of African Art; *SA Panorama* January 1961, August 1967, July 1982 & June 1983; *Artlook* November 1966, February 1967 & December 1973.

KUMALO Temba Cyril Mokhethi see MOKHETHI KUMALO Temba Cyril

KUNENE Zenzele Selby I

Born 1952 Cato Manor, Natal.

Mainly a graphic artist of landscapes, figures and abstracts; also works in watercolour, ink, pencil and charcoal.

Studies c.1977 Rorke's Drift Art Centre, Natal, under Ada van de Vijver (qv) and Jules van de Vijver (qv); 1982–83 inservice training at the Natal Technikon, under Clive Truter (qv). 1978 granted a bursary from the SA Institute of Race Relations.

Profile A member of the SAAA. From 1983 a printing production clerk at Consol Plastics, Natal.

Exhibitions He has participated in group exhibitions at the University of Zululand.

KUPFERNAGEL Johanna Eleonore (Hanneli) (née Smuts)

Born 1931 Potchefstroom, Transvaal.

A painter of landscapes, harbour scenes, portraits and still life. Works in oil, watercolour, pastel, pencil and charcoal. 1984–85 a series of Cape and SWA/Namibia landscapes.

Studies 1948–50 Orange Free State Technical College, under Anna Hugo; 1967 a three-month course at the American Art School, Paris, France.

Profile A member of the SAAA. 1967 visited England, France, West Germany, The Netherlands, Belgium, Greece and Italy.

Exhibitions She has participated in several group exhibitions from 1975 in SA and one in London; 1968 Pretoria, first of five solo exhibitions held in Pretoria.

KUPHE Percy Ndithembile see KONQOBE Percy Ndithembile

L

LABUSCHAGNE Eugene
Born 1921 Volksrust, Transvaal.
A painter of landscapes, still life, figures and African tribal themes and scenes.
Works in oil.
Studies Briefly at the Michaelis School of Fine Art, under Lippy Lipshitz (qv);
1947–51 studied at a number of studios in Paris.
Exhibitions He has participated in group exhibitions from 1947 in Paris, Italy,
São Paulo, Zimbabwe and SA; 1951 Pretoria, first of several solo exhibitions.
Represented Hester Rupert Art Museum, Graaff-Reinet; Pretoria Art Museum;
William Humphreys Art Gallery, Kimberley.
References Art SA; SAA; 20C SA Art; SSAP; BSAK 1; AASA; *Fontein* vol 1
no 2, 1960.

LADAN Eduard Louis
Born 1918 Kalk Bay, Cape Province.
A painter, sculptor and graphic artist of still life, figures and abstract pieces.
Works in oil, watercolour, bronze, ciment fondu, wood and mixed media,
including nail and plastic constructions, as well as in various graphic media.
Studies 1937–39 Royal Academy of Fine Art, The Hague, The Netherlands.
Profile A member of the SAAA. 1969–77 contributing art writer and critic for
The Cape Times and *The Argus*. 1983 Art Advisor on the Advisory Board for SABC
TV1. He has travelled extensively in Europe and the Middle East.
Exhibitions He has participated in numerous group exhibitions from 1950 in SA
and once in Italy; 1964 Gallery 101, Johannesburg, first of 11 solo exhibitions
held in SA; 1981 Republic Festival Exhibition.
Represented Pietersburg Collection; SA National Gallery, Cape Town; Willem
Annandale Art Gallery, Lichtenburg.
References BSAK 1; AASA; *Artlook* July 1969 & October/November 1975;
Lantern March 1971.

LA GRANGE Marthinus
Born 1920 Aberdeen, Scotland.
An artist working in ink and wash depicting figures and animals.
Studies 1940–41 and 1954–55 Michaelis School of Fine Art, attaining a Diploma
in Fine Art; also studied in France and The Netherlands.
Profile 1965 a founder member of the Artists Guild, Cape Town.
Exhibitions He has participated in group exhibitions in SA; 1966 Cape Town,
solo exhibition.
Represented SA National Gallery, Cape Town; University of Cape Town;
University of South Africa.
References Register SA & SWA; SAP&D; BSAK 2; AASA.

LAIDLER Elise Lilian

Born 1915 Philipstown, Karoo, Cape Province.

A painter of landscapes, seascapes and abstract pictures. Works in oil, watercolour, ink and wash. A sculptor in clay.

Studies 1935 Natal Technical College, under Professor O J P Oxley (qv); 1942 clay modelling, Witwatersrand Technical College, under Elizabeth Macadam (qv).

Profile 1976 a member of the Somerset Society of Artists, England; 1984 a member of the Highway Art Group. Has lived in Cape Town, Johannesburg, Durban, Somerset in England and in Bulawayo in Zimbabwe. She has travelled throughout Europe. During the 1940s she was married to Johannes Oldert (qv), and is the mother of L Anton Benzon (qv).

Exhibitions She has participated in numerous group exhibitions in SA, Zimbabwe and England; *c.*1973, Neakes Gallery, Bulawayo, Rhodesia (Zimbabwe), first of five solo exhibitions.

LALITZKY Wladyslaw

Born 1935 Yugoslavia.

A painter of figures and landscapes. Works in oil and acrylic.

Studies 1960 Academy of Arts, Belgrade, Yugoslavia.

Profile Drew many illustrations for books and periodicals in Yugoslavia. For over 25 years designed stage sets and costumes for theatre and film. Lives in Johannesburg.

Exhibitions He has participated in numerous group exhibitions in Yugoslavia and from 1985 in SA.

Represented Museum of Art, Belgrade, Yugoslavia.

LAMB Elizabeth Dorothea (Elsa)

Born 1944 Willowmore, Cape Province.

A painter of a combination of creative landscapes, genre and figures with a socio-political content. Works in oil, acrylic, gouache, pencil, charcoal and in wax crayons. An etcher. In 1966 she carved wooden sculptures.

Studies 1963–66 Pretoria Technical College (Technikon), under Gunther van der Reis (qv), gaining National Fine Arts and Teachers Diplomas; 1966–67 Akademie der Bildenden Kunste, Munich, under Franz Xaver Fuhr (*b.*1898); 1975 l'Atelier 17, Paris, etching under Stanley William Hayter (*b.*1901); 1975–78 University of South Africa, where attained a BA in History of Art.

Profile A member of the SAAA and the SAAAH. 1967–68 a lecturer at the Pretoria Technical College (Technikon); 1969–73 taught at Pretoria School of Art, Ballet and Music; in 1976 she established, and presently continues to teach at, the Elsa Lamb Etching Studio, Pretoria; 1980–82 a part-time lecturer at the Pretoria Technikon and the University of Pretoria. 1967–69 a film set designer and craftsman for Emil Nofal and Jans Rautenbach Productions. Has written a number of newspaper reviews and essays for academic and professional purposes. 1970 visited Europe; 1974 travelled to Paris and Malaga, Spain; 1975 Paris; 1979 Paris and Amsterdam.

Exhibitions She has participated in several group exhibitions in SA from 1966 and in touring exhibitions in Europe and the USA.
Award 1968 First Prize Painting, New Signatures, SAAA, shared with Malcolm Payne (qv) and Alice Elahi (qv).
Represented Pretoria Technikon.
References BSAK 1; AASA; LSAA; *Artlook* September 1968.

LAMB Peter Percival William

Born 1905 Boksburg, Transvaal.
Died 1963 Johannesburg.
A painter of portraits and figures. Worked in oil and watercolour.
Studies c.1928 Witwatersrand Technical College, under Professor Austin Winter Moore (qv) and privately under Alfred Palmer (qv).
Profile During the late 1940s lived in Durban, where he painted the activities of the Indian community. 1957 visited the USA; 1958–62 lived in England, thereafter in Johannesburg. Married Doreen Lamb, the writer and broadcaster.
Exhibitions Participated in group exhibitions in SA, New York and London; 1944 Johannesburg, first of several solo exhibitions; 1963 Johannesburg, Memorial Exhibition; 1964 Adler Fielding Gallery, Johannesburg, Retrospective Exhibition; 1976 Galerie Bijou, Johannesburg, Retrospective Exhibition.
Represented Africana Museum, Johannesburg; Durban Art Gallery; Pretoria Art Museum; SA National Gallery, Cape Town; Victoria and Albert Museum, London, UK; William Humphreys Art Gallery, Kimberley.
Public Commissions Numerous portraits including those of Lord Nuffield, Sir Yehudi Menuhin, Anna Russell, General Sir Alan Cunningham and Archbishop Denis Hurley, who in 1957 commissioned him to paint a Zulu Madonna to promote interest in Roman Catholic missionary work. Painted murals in Piccadilly Cinemas in Johannesburg and Durban.
References SAA; AMC7; AASA; *SA Panorama* August 1958.

LAMPRECHT Gertruida Elizabeth (Elize)

Born 1943 Transvaal.
A painter and graphic artist of abstract pictures. Works in oil, gouache, ink, pencil, charcoal, mixed media and in various graphic media.
Studies 1980–86 The Art Studio, Pretoria, under Deline de Klerk (qv) and Willie Lottering (qv); also under Mimi van der Merwe (qv).
Profile From 1975 a member of the SAAA.
Exhibitions She has participated in many group exhibitions from 1980 in SA; 1985 SAAA, Pretoria, first of three solo exhibitions; 1987 SAAA, Pretoria, joint exhibition with the ceramic artist Neila Smit.

LANDSBERG (Ludwig Henrich) Otto (von)

Born 1803 Brunswick, Germany.
Died 1905 Rosebank, Cape Town.
Resided in SA from 1818.
A painter in oil, watercolour and tempera. Numerous pencil drawings. Painted landscapes, mainly of the Cape, and religious scenes after his visit to Europe in 1864, where he was strongly influenced by Rubens. These religious paintings are set in SA and peopled with South Africans. He made copies of the classic paintings of Rubens and Raphael as well as Ancient Greek and Roman statues.
Studies Thought to have been a student of Anton Anreith (qv).
Profile From 1831 a tobacconist who was well known for his snuff. 1847–51 taught music and drawing at the Tot Nut van't Algeneem School and also at the SA College, Cape Town. Co-founder of the Cape Musical Society. His picture of "Brandvlei Baths" was reproduced in Poortemans' series of lithographic drawings, 1835–57.
Exhibitions Participated in group exhibitions from 1851.
Represented Africana Museum, Johannesburg; Potchefstroom Museum; SA National Gallery, Cape Town; University of Stellenbosch.
Public Commission "Moses of the 10 Commandments", presented to the Cape Parliament, 1883.
References Simon A de Villiers, *Otto Landsberg 1803–1905*, 1974, C Struik, Cape Town; AMC3; DSAB; SESA; Pict Afr; BSAK 1; 3Cs.

LANG George Ernest

Born *c.*1907 London, England.
Arrived in SA in 1959.
A self-taught painter and graphic artist of landscapes, street scenes, portraits, genre, figures and wildlife. A miniaturist. Works in oil, watercolour, gouache and in various graphic media.
Profile A member of the Royal Miniature Society. 1959 visited Mozambique, thereafter based in Cape Town until his return to England. Married to Madge Lang.
Exhibitions 1959 Pieter Wenning Gallery, Johannesburg, first of several solo exhibitions held at this gallery.
Public Commission 1965 Prospector, Rand Mines, Commissioner Street, Johannesburg, jointly with his wife Madge Lang.

LANG Graham Charles

Born 1955 Bulawayo, Rhodesia (Zimbabwe)
Resided in SA from 1966.
A painter, graphic artist and sculptor of landscapes and figures. Works in oil, acrylic, watercolour, ink, wash, pencil, charcoal, various graphic media, ciment fondu and wood. 1984–86 a series entitled "Drought".

Studies 1976–79 Natal Technical College (Technikon), under Peter Schütz (qv), gaining a Higher Diploma in Education; 1985 Rhodes University, under Josua Nell (qv), where attained an MFA, majoring in sculpture.

Profile 1980–83 an art teacher at Amanzimtoti High School, Natal; 1984–86 a sculpture teacher at the Johan Carinus Art Centre, Grahamstown; 1987 a lecturer at the Orange Free State Technikon. A writer of poems and short stories. Has lived in Rhodesia (Zimbabwe), Pietermaritzburg, Durban and Grahamstown.

Exhibitions He has participated in many group exhibitions in SA from 1978; 1980 Hermit Gallery, Durban, first of nine solo exhibitions held in Durban, Cape Town, Johannesburg and Grahamstown.

Represented King George VI Art Gallery, Port Elizabeth; Natal Technikon.

Publication by Lang Wrote and illustrated *The Pilot Fish*, 1984, Vantage Press, New York, USA.

Reference *D'ARTS* March 1987.

LANGDOWN Amos

Born 1930 Plettenberg Bay, Cape Province.

A graphic artist and painter of landscapes, town scenes, genre and figures. Produces lithographs, woodcuts, etchings, drypoints, monotypes and copper engravings as well as paintings in oil.

Studies 1961 privately with Katrine Harries (qv); 1962–63 on a Government Scholarship at the Rijks Academy, Amsterdam, The Netherlands, under Professor Kuno Brinks, Jan Forrer and Ru van Rossem.

Profile 1953 an art master at the Athlone Training School, Paarl; 1972 Inspector of Arts for the Cape. Has illustrated several books and in 1970 made a three-month study tour of the USA.

Exhibitions He has participated in group exhibitions from the 1950s in West Germany, Italy, the USA and in SA; 1960 Cape Town, first of many solo exhibitions.

Represented William Humphreys Art Gallery, Kimberley.

References SAA; SESA; BSAK 1; 3Cs; AASA; LSAA.

LANGLEY Maureen

Born 1931 Bloemfontein.

A sculptor working in bronze, stone, wood, ivory and marble. 1973–76 a large series based on abstracted bird forms; 1977–80 a series of mythological subjects; 1981–84 a series based on fruit forms.

Studies 1958–60 part-time at the Michaelis School of Fine Art, under Lippy Lipshitz (qv); 1967–70 University of Natal, under Professor Jack Heath (qv) and Harry Atkins (qv), gaining a BA(Hons), majoring in English and Sculpture.

Profile From 1974 a member of the SAAA and from 1981 of the Artists Guild, Cape Town. 1972–74 an art teacher at Pietermaritzburg Girls High School; 1975–77 at St Anne's College, Hilton, Natal, and from 1981 a lecturer in life drawing and sculpture at the Ruth Prowse School of Art, Cape Town. 1979 spent four months at Pietrasanta, near Carrara, Italy, working with marble. She revisited Europe in 1984.

Exhibitions She has participated in several group exhibitions from 1961 in SA and once in Italy; 1973 Old Mill Gallery, Pietermaritzburg, first of nine solo exhibitions held in SA; 1977 University of Pretoria, solo exhibition; 1978 and 1980 University of Natal, solo exhibitions.
Represented Tatham Art Gallery, Pietermaritzburg.
Public Commissions 1970 plaster sculpture, University of Natal; 1983 Crucifixion and in 1986 a design for a stained glass window, St Alban's Anglican Church, Green Point, Cape Town.

LANGSCHMIDT Wilhelm Heinrich (Franz Ludwig)

Born 1805 Gustrow, Mecklenberg, Germany.
Died 1866.
Resided in SA from 1842.
A painter of portraits and scenes of Cape Town, a series of the Cape Malay Quarter. Worked in oil, pastel, watercolour and chalk.
Studies Under Professor Johann Kretschmar (1796–1847) in Berlin.
Profile A lithographer and drawing master in Long Street, Cape Town, retiring in 1851 to farm near Elgin in the Cape.
Exhibitions Participated in a group exhibition in 1851; 1948 Tate Gallery, London, SA Art Exhibition.
Represented Africana Museum, Johannesburg; SA Cultural History Museum, Cape Town; William Fehr Collection, Cape Town.
References Pict Art; BSAK 1 & 2; Art SA; 3Cs.

LANHAM Colin Temple

Born 1947 Johannesburg.
A painter of landscapes, birds and abstract pictures. Works in watercolour, egg tempera, acrylic, ink, pencil and charcoal. A graphic artist and a sculptor working in mixed media. 1967–70 produced abstract works; 1971–78 mountains isolated from their local context; 1979–85 conceptual landscapes and a symbolic, semi-surrealist bird series. From 1987 large-scale acrylic paintings and assemblages.
Studies 1966–67 and 1969–70 Natal Technical College, under Paul Stopforth (qv), gaining a National Art Teachers Diploma.
Profile 1966–70 a committee member of the NSA. From 1985 a member of the Swaziland Art Society. From 1973 Head of the Art Department, Waterford-Kamhlaba School, Swaziland. 1974 designed the set for "A Man for All Seasons", a play produced in Mbabane, Swaziland. 1970–71 visited Europe; 1978 visited France and Corsica.
Exhibitions He has participated in many group exhibitions from 1960 in SA; 1976 Walsh-Marais Gallery, Durban, first of two solo exhibitions.
Award 1967 P W Storey Award.
Public Commission 1986 five large watercolours for Protea Sun Hotel, Swaziland.

MAGGIE LAUBSER
Ducks and Arums 1936
Oil on Canvas 51 × 61 cm
Private

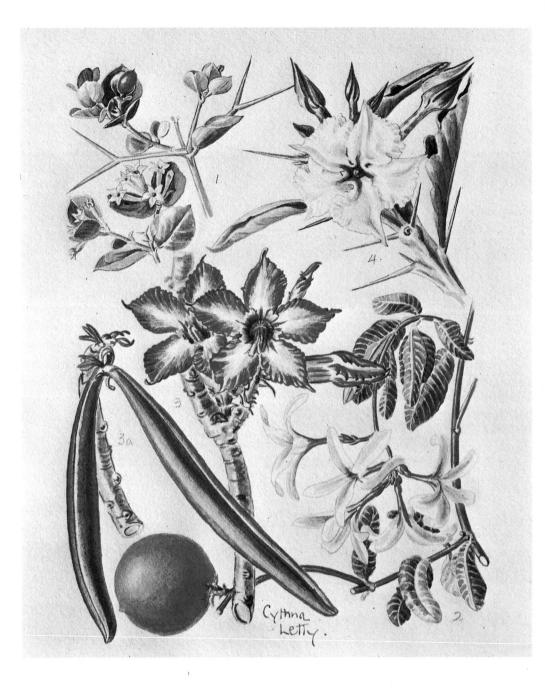

CYTHNA LETTY

(1) Carissa bispinosa
(2) Landolphia capensis
(3) Adenium obesum
(4) Pachypodium Saundersii
Watercolour 20 × 15 cm
The Botanical Research Institute

LANSDELL Annie Kathleen

Born 1888 Durban.
Died 1967 Pietermaritzburg.
A painter of botanical subjects. Worked in watercolour and ink.
Studies Three years at Natal Technical College, under W Tottendell Venner (qv); in London with W H Kenner.
Profile 1914 resident artist at the Natal Herbarium. 1917 the first artist on the staff of the Division of Botany, Pretoria (the Botanical Research Institute). Her illustrations include: 1914–20 plates for *Natal Plants*, by Medley Wood; 1921 all the plates for the first volume of *Flowering Plants of Africa*, her illustrations also being reproduced in subsequent issues; 1921–27 colour and ink illustrations for *Weeds of SA*; 1926 20 plates for the *Botanical Survey Memoir no 9*. Produced models of fruits and vegetables for scientific demonstrations. Lived in Durban and Pretoria.
Exhibitions Participated in group exhibitions from 1921 in SA; held a solo exhibition in the Natal Herbarium, Durban.
Represented The Imperial Institute, UK; Kew Gardens, Surrey, UK; Killie Campbell Africana Library, University of Natal, Durban; Mycological Institute, London, UK; Natal Herbarium, Durban.
References *SA Women's Who's Who*, 1914; SAA; AASA.

LATEUR Katrien Julienne Armande

Born 1952 Jadotville, Congo (Ukasi, Zaire).
Resided in SA from 1981.
A graphic artist of landscapes with figures and of abstract works. Creates etchings and collographs.
Studies 1967 Koninklijke Akademie, Ghent, Belgium; 1968–71 Koninklijke Kunstakademie, Brugge, Belgium.
Profile Employed as a graphic designer in an architectural firm. From 1982 a number of designs for murals in Pretoria, Johannesburg, Bethlehem, Uitenhage, Germiston and George. A trained jeweller.
Exhibitions She has participated in several group exhibitions in SA from 1982; 1983 Pretoria, first of four solo exhibitions.

LAUBSCHER Elizabeth Catharina (Elza)

Born 1920 Pretoria.
A painter and graphic artist of landscapes, seascapes, still life, wildlife and abstract pictures. Works in oil, watercolour, gouache, pencil, charcoal and in various graphic media, particularly monotypes. 1972–73 a series of Namaqualand flowers; 1977 experimented in abstract works; 1981 a series on the Greek islands.
Studies 1939–43 Witwatersrand Technical College, under Eric Byrd (qv) and Phyllis Gardner (qv), gaining a National Art Teachers Certificate; 1954 at the Central School of Art, London; 1963 Hendry Coets Studio, Paris; privately under Zakkie Eloff (qv), Robert Hodgins (qv) and Sidney Goldblatt (qv).

Profile From 1972 a council member of the SAAA; from 1982 a member of the WSSA. 1944 an art teacher at Klerksdorp High School; 1945–46 at Crosby Junior High School, Johannesburg; 1947 part-time at the Commercial High School, Pretoria; 1968 at Pretoria North High School. 1980 designed a tapestry for the Agricultural Union. A landscape gardener. 1954 and 1963 visited Europe; 1972 Rhodesia (Zimbabwe); 1977 the USA and in 1985 SWA/Namibia.

Exhibitions She has participated in numerous group exhibitions from 1947 in SA, West Germany, Italy and the USA; 1954 Cultura Gallery, Pretoria, first of 13 solo exhibitions; 1981 Republic Festival Exhibition.

Represented University of Amsterdam, The Netherlands; University of Bophuthatswana; University of Pretoria; Willem Annandale Art Gallery, Lichtenburg.

References SAA; BSAK 1; AASA; *Artlook* March 1972.

LAUBSCHER Frederik Bester Howard (Erik)

Born 1927 Tulbagh, Cape Province.

A painter of landscapes, seascapes, still life, figures, portraits and abstract pictures. Works in oil, acrylic, watercolour, ink, pencil and charcoal.

Studies 1946 Continental School of Art, Cape Town, under Maurice van Essche (qv); 1947–49 studied portrait drawing under Frank Slater RA in London, then attended the Anglo-French Art Centre, St Johns Wood, London, under C Venard (*b*.1913), A Clave (*b*.1913), J Aujame (1905–65), Jankel Adler (1895–1949), John Minton (1917–57), E Paolozzi (*b*.1924) and others; 1950–51 Académie Montmartre, Paris, under Fernand Léger (1881–1955).

Profile 1953 elected a member of the New Group. 1954 elected as a guest member of the International Arts Club. 1955 became a committee member of the SAAA, later a member of the National Fine Arts Committee. A member of the National Executive of SAAA and National Vice-President in 1965. 1952 began teaching with Alfred Krenz (qv) in Stellenbosch; 1953–55 ran the Continental School of Art, renamed the Contemporary School of Art, Cape Town. 1955 co-founded, with Marjorie Wallace (qv), the Cape Salon. During the 1950s and 1960s worked as a paint consultant to various firms. 1965 a founder member of the Artists Gallery. In 1966 he was the first South African to be awarded the Carnegie Scholarship, through which he spent three months on a study tour of the USA. 1969 Art Director of the Cape Town Art Centre. 1970 founded the Ruth Prowse Art Centre, Woodstock, Cape Town, which became the Ruth Prowse School of Art in 1975. 1970 a committee member of the National Art Teachers Association, Stellenbosch. 1973–74 art critic for *To the Point*. 1977 toured Europe. 1978 appointed Trustee to the Michaelis Collection, Old Town House, Cape Town. 1979 Founder Initiator of the Artists Guild and Chairman in 1980. 1980 a founder member of Cape Arts Forum. 1987 appointed a member of the SA National Gallery Council. Has also been a selector for a number of large national and international exhibitions. Married to Claude Bouscharain (qv).

Exhibitions He has participated in numerous group exhibitions from 1950 in France, SA, Italy, Brazil, Portugal, Belgium and the USA; solo exhibitions held in Cape Town, Johannesburg, Pretoria, Stellenbosch and in Geneva, Switzerland; 1960 and 1964 Quadrennial Exhibitions; 1970 University of Stellenbosch, Retrospective Exhibition; 1978 SAAA Gallery, Cape Town, joint exhibition with June te Water (qv); 1979 Cape Town Biennial, Invited Artist; 1981 Republic Festival Exhibition; 1981 University of Stellenbosch, solo exhibition; 1985 Drostdy Centre, Stellenbosch, joint exhibition with Claude Bouscharain (qv) and Stanley Pinker (qv).

Award 1972 Cape Arts Medal for Services to Art.

Represented Hester Rupert Art Museum, Graaff-Reinet; Pretoria Art Museum; SA National Gallery, Cape Town; University of Cape Town; University of the Orange Free State; University of Pretoria; University of Stellenbosch; University of the Witwatersrand; William Humphreys Art Gallery, Kimberley.

Public Commissions Numerous commissions including: 1970 a tapestry for the Nico Malan Theatre, Cape Town; 1971 acrylic mural, Jan Smuts Airport, Johannesburg; 1976 four mosaic panels, Tygerberg Hospital, Cape Town; 1977 mosaic panel, Melville Shopping Centre, Knysna; 1977–78 two mural panels, Medical Faculty, Tygerberg Hospital.

References Art SA; SAA; 20C SA Art; SAP&S; SSAP; Oxford Companion to Art (under SA); SSAP; BSAK 1 & 2; Our Art 3; SA Art; Oxford Companion to 20C Art (under SA); 3Cs; AASA; LSAA; *Artlook* September 1967.

LAUBSER Maria Magdalena (Maggie)

Born 1886 Malmesbury, Cape Province.
Died 1973 Strand, Cape Town.

A painter of landscapes, portraits, genre and still life. Her work is characterised by bold, bright colours and simplified subject matter. Worked in oil and occasionally in gouache. A large number of drawings and monotypes. Painted Cape farms and fishing villages; during the 1930s a series of birds and cats, while during the 1950s her work became more abstract.

Studies 1903 briefly under Professor Edward Roworth (qv); 1913–14 six months study in Laren, The Netherlands; 1914–19 Slade School of Art, London, under Henry Tonks (1862–1937), Ambrose McEvoy (1878–1927), Walter W Russell (1867–1949) and Philip Wilson Steer (1860–1942); 1922 occasional night classes in figure drawing under Professor Jachels in Berlin.

Profile Strongly influenced by the German Expressionists particularly Schmidt-Rotluff and Marc, with whom she was in contact. From 1922 a close friend of Irma Stern (qv). 1907 a member of the SA Society of Artists. 1938 a member of the New Group. 1912 worked as a teacher in the Transvaal; 1913 visited The Netherlands; 1914–19 lived in London, visiting Scotland, the English Midlands and SA; 1919–20 in Belgium and Germany; 1920–21 lived on Lake Garda and at San Vigilo, Italy; 1921–22 in SA; 1922–24 in Berlin, Germany, thereafter lived in the Transvaal and the Cape. A film on her life was made by the Union Department of Education and Rembrandt Ltd.

Exhibitions Participated in group exhibitions from 1909 in SA, Italy, Rhodesia (Zimbabwe), The Netherlands, Belgium, West Germany and the UK; 1925 Argus Gallery, Cape Town, first of many solo exhibitions held in SA; 1938 Stellenbosch, joint exhibition with Rene Graetz, Cecil Higgs (qv) and Lippy Lipshitz (qv); 1948 Tate Gallery, London, SA Art Exhibition; 1956, 1960 and 1964 Quadrennial Exhibitions; 1965 SAAA Gallery, Cape Town, Retrospective Exhibition; 1969 SA National Gallery, Cape Town, Pretoria Art Museum and Johannesburg Art Gallery, Retrospective Exhibition; 1975 University of Stellenbosch, Prestige Exhibition; 1975 Rand Afrikaans University, Prestige Exhibition; 1980 University of Stellenbosch, Prestige Exhibition; 1986 SAAA Gallery, Pretoria, Commemorative Exhibition; 1986 Silberberg Gallery, Tulbagh, Cape Province, Centenary Exhibition.

Awards 1946 Medal of Honour for Painting, SA Akademie vir Wetenskap en Kuns: 1947 Oscar Award, *Die Vaderland* newspaper; 1959 elected an Honorary Member of SA Akademie vir Wetenskap en Kuns; 1968 Medal of Honour, SAAA (Cape Region).

Represented Durban Art Gallery; Hester Rupert Art Museum, Graaff-Reinet; Johannesburg Art Gallery; Julius Gordon Africana Centre, Riversdale; King George VI Art Gallery, Port Eliabeth; National Museum, Bloemfontein; Potchefstroom Museum; Pretoria Art Museum; Rand Afrikaans University; Sandton Municipal Collection; SA Akademie vir Wetenskap en Kuns; SA National Gallery, Cape Town; University of the Orange Free State; University of Pretoria; University of South Africa; University of Stellenbosch; University of the Witwatersrand; William Humphreys Art Gallery, Kimberley.

References J Meintjes, *Maggie Laubser*, 1944, HAUM, Cape Town; J van Rooyen, *Maggie Laubser*, 1974, C Struik, Cape Town; *The Arts in SA*, edited by WHK, 1933–34, The Knox Printing & Publishing Company, Durban; KK; PSA; Collectors' Guide; Our Art 1, Art SA; SAA; 20C SA Art; SAP&S; Oxford Companion to Art (under SA); SAP&D; SESA; SSAP; BSAK 1 & 2; SA Art; Oxford Companion to 20C Art (under SA); 3Cs; AASA; LSAA; *SA Panorama* February 1969 & September 1973; *Artlook* December 1968, November 1969, June 1973, October 1973 & August/September 1975; *De Arte* April 1976; *SA Arts Calendar* March 1984 & Winter 1986.

LAVENDER Paul Guy

Born 1937 Port Elizabeth.

A painter of landscapes, still life and genre. Works in oil, acrylic, watercolour, gouache, wash, pencil and charcoal.

Studies Under John Muff-Ford (qv); 1957–60 at Port Elizabeth Technical College, gaining a National Diploma in Art and Design.

Profile A member of the WSSA and the Orange Free State Art Society. 1961–62 Head of the Art Department, Lawson Brown High School, Port Elizabeth; from 1963 Head of the Art Department at Michaelhouse, Balgowan, Natal. A number of his illustrations have appeared in newspapers. Has visited the UK.

Exhibitions He has participated in group exhibitions from 1953 in SA and London.

Represented University of Natal.

LAWRENCE Nina Dawn

Born 1947 Durban.

A creator of fabric sculptures using cotton, silk, wool, yarns, beads and bells. A painter in watercolour, gouache and wash; draws in pencil and charcoal.

Studies 1966–70 Natal Technical College, under Paul Stopforth (qv), gaining a National Teachers Diploma in Fine Art.

Profile 1971–72 taught at Durban Commercial High School; 1976 at Pinetown Junior Primary School. 1962–82 illustrated educational books for Juta & Co, Cape Town. 1982–85 produced jackets, belts and bags.

Exhibitions She has participated in several group exhibitions from 1978 in Natal.

Reference *Fair Lady* 16 October 1985.

LAWRENCE Robert Thomas Fredrick

Born 1933 White River, Eastern Transvaal.

A self-taught sculptor of wildlife and figures. Works in bronze.

Exhibitions He has participated in numerous wildlife group exhibitions in SA and in Texas, USA; 1973 Triad Gallery, Johannesburg, first of five solo exhibitions, two of which have been in Dallas, Texas, USA.

Represented Nelspruit Art Gallery; Pietersburg Collection.

Public Commission 1985 "Last Hunt", Jock of the Bushveld Camp, Kruger National Park.

LAWSON Cora Adeline

Born 1919 Pretoria.

A painter, of flowers, especially roses, and of landscapes, still life and portraits. Works in watercolour and oil.

Studies Mainly self-taught with some tuition from Barbara Sinclair, Marjorie Bowen (qv), Professor Alfred Ewan (qv), Margaret Burnard (qv) and George Boys (qv).

Profile An Associate of the WSSA and Chairman of the Natal Watercolour Society in 1982. Teaches art privately. Illustrated *Umkomaas Annals*, issued by the Womens Institute. A church organist. 1983 visited Italy with Marjorie Bowen (qv).

Exhibitions She has participated in many group exhibitions from 1973 in SA and in one in London; 1985 Studio 5, Rustenburg, Transvaal, solo exhibition.

Public Commission A watercolour painting for Scottburgh Library, Natal.

LAWSON Mari Meatha

Born 1929 Lindley, Orange Free State.

A painter and sculptor of portraits and figures. Works in oil, watercolour, ink, wash, pencil, ciment fondu and wood. From 1975 an ongoing series entitled "The Pickers".

Studies 1947–49 Witwatersrand Technical College, under James Gardner (qv), Phyllis Gardner (qv) and Elizabeth Macadam (qv), gaining a Diploma; during the 1960s and 1970s studied ceramics under John Edwards.
Profile 1950–52 worked in advertising and as a senior display artist for Stuttafords; 1952–57 worked as a Visualiser for Color Graphics; 1975–81 an Art Director for Doug Lawson and Associates. She has designed houses in Hermanus, Upington, and in Melville, Westdene, Sandhurst, Emmarentia and Rivonia, Johannesburg. 1940–50 studied music under Vincent Price and Professor Danza; 1938–50 studied drama and worked in radio. Has travelled throughout SA and lives in Johannesburg.
Awards 1947–49 several awards from the Witwatersrand Technical College, including the Most Outstanding Student Award of 1949.

LEA Philippa Ruth Delisle (Pippa)

Born 1963 Johannesburg.
A sculptor and painter working in wood and oil. Draws in pencil and pencil crayon. Symbolic imagery incorporating landscapes, figures and animals. From 1985 a series of painted wood sculptures and three-dimensional paintings.
Studies 1980–83 Natal Technikon, under Penny Siopis (qv), gaining a Higher Diploma in Fine Art and being awarded the Emma Smith Scholarship in 1982.
Exhibitions She has participated in several group exhibitions from 1985 in Durban, Pietermaritzburg and Cape Town; 1985 Cape Town Triennial; 1985 Karen McKerron Gallery, Johannesburg, solo exhibition; 1987 Karen McKerron Gallery, Johannesburg, joint exhibition with Beezy Bailey (qv) and Lulu Baily (qv).
Represented Natal Technikon; University of the Witwatersrand.

LECANIDES Maria Constantine

Born 1959 Salisbury, Rhodesia (Harare, Zimbabwe).
Resided in SA from 1963.
A painter of portraits, still life and genre. Works in oil and draws in pencil, pencil crayon, chalk and oil pastel.
Studies 1977–80 Michaelis School of Fine Art, painting under Stanley Pinker (qv), drawing under Marthinus la Grange (qv) and sculpture under Bruce Arnott (qv). Awarded the MacIver Scholarship for Women of Merit in 1978 and 1980.
Profile From 1983 a member of the Artists Guild. 1982–84 a lecturer and from 1984 a senior lecturer in the School of Art and Design, Cape Technikon.
Exhibitions She has participated in several group exhibitions in Cape Town.

LECLÉZIO Isabelle Marie Anne

Born 1964 Mauritius.
Resided in SA from 1982.
A painter and graphic artist of landscapes. Works in oil, watercolour, charcoal, pastel and in various graphic media.

Studies 1983–87 Natal Technikon, under Jeff Chandler (qv), gaining a National Diploma in Fine Art in 1985 and a Higher Diploma in Fine Art in 1987.
Profile From 1987 a member of the NSA.
Exhibitions She has participated in many group exhibitions from 1985 throughout SA.

LEE Catharine Agnes Rosalys (née Rivers)

Born Somerset, England.
Resided in SA from 1923.
A painter of still life, particularly flowers. Worked in oil.
Studies 1928–33 at the Michaelis School of Fine Art.
Profile Lived in Cape Town.
Exhibitions Participated in group exhibitions during the 1930s in SA.
Represented SA National Gallery, Cape Town.
Reference SAP&S.

LEE Frederick Richard RA

Born 1798 Barnstaple, Devon, England.
Died 1879 Harmon, Cape Province.
Resided in SA from 1876.
A painter of landscapes and seascapes.
Studies 1818 Royal Academy Schools, London.
Profile 1834 became an Associate of the Royal Academy and in 1838 a full Academician. Lived in London, Penshurst, Kent, and in 1858 in Pilton, near Barnstaple. Visited, by yacht, Gibraltar, Spain, France and the Italian islands; in 1870 the West Indies; in 1871 St Helena, Cape Town and Rio de Janeiro. 1872–76 lived part of each year in Devon, part on his yacht and part on various Cape farms. 1876 settled on the farm "Vleisbank", near Wellington, Cape Province. A friend of Abraham de Smidt (qv).
Exhibitions Participated in group exhibitions 1822–70 in the UK and in SA in 1871; 1871 Cape Town, joint exhibition with H W Hermann (qv).
Represented Galleries in Glasgow, Liverpool, Nottingham and Sheffield, UK; SA National Gallery, Cape Town; Tate Gallery, London, UK; Victoria and Albert Museum, London, UK.
References Pict Art; Bénézit; DBA; Pict Afr.

LEFTWICH Peter

Born 1913 London, England.
Resided in SA from 1924.
A painter of landscapes, portraits, still life and figures. Works in oil, egg tempera, pencil and charcoal.

Studies 1932–36 Michaelis School of Art, under Professor John Wheatley (qv).
Profile From 1942 a member of the NSA and in 1947 of the New Group. Since 1950 he has travelled extensively in Europe and to Egypt, the USA and Kenya.
Exhibitions He has participated in numerous group exhibitions from 1930 in SA, throughout the UK and in Paris; 1944 NSA Gallery, Durban, first of several solo exhibitions.
Award 1963 a prizewinner on Art SA Today.
Represented Durban Art Gallery.
Public Commissions Several portrait commissions for universities, portraits of other SA notabilities, and a number of murals, including one for the Edward Hotel, Durban.
References SAA; BSAK 1; AASA; *SA Panorama* March 1983.

LEGAE Ezrom Kgobokanyo Sebata

Born 1938 Johannesburg.
A painter and sculptor of figures, heads and animals. Works in oil, conté, bronze, clay and mixed media. 1977–78 "Chicken" series; 1979 "Freedom is Dead" series.
Studies 1959–60 Polly Street Art Centre, 1960–64 Jubilee Centre, Johannesburg, under Cecil Skotnes (qv) and Sydney Kumalo (qv); 1970 gained a travel scholarship from the US Exchange Programme; 1972 awarded a bursary from the Merit Grant Fund, USA.
Profile 1969 a member of the Amadlozi 69 Group. 1964–69 an instructor at the Jubilee Art Centre; a part-time teacher at FUBA. 1972–74 Director of the African Music and Drama Association Art Project. 1964 visited Central Africa.
Exhibitions 1965 Egon Guenther Gallery, Johannesburg, first of several solo exhibitions in SA; he has participated in many group exhibitions in SA from 1966 and in Belgium, The Netherlands, West Germany and South America; 1966 Republic Festival Exhibition; 1972 Republic Festival Exhibition; 1979 Contemporary African Art in SA; 1981 Standard Bank, Soweto, Black Art Today Exhibition; 1982 National Gallery, Gaborone, Botswana, Exhibition of SA Art; 1985 Tributaries, touring SA and West Germany; 1985 Goodman Gallery, Johannesburg, joint exhibition with Sydney Kumalo (qv), Cecil Skotnes (qv) and Edoardo Villa (qv).
Awards 1967 Oppenheimer Sculpture Prize, Art SA Today; 1979 Honorable Mention for Drawing, Valparaiso Bienale, Chile.
Represented Durban Art Gallery; Johannesburg Art Gallery; Pretoria Art Museum; SA National Gallery, Cape Town; University of Fort Hare; University of South Africa; University of the Witwatersrand; William Humphreys Art Gallery, Kimberley.
References SA Art; SESA; 3Cs; AASA; Echoes of African Art; *SA Panorama* July 1982.

LEGG Gordon Harold

Born 1932 East London.
A painter of landscapes and seascapes. Works in watercolour.
Studies 1950–53 Witwatersrand Technical College, under James Gardner (qv), gaining a Diploma.

Profile From 1975 a member of the WSSA. 1978 visited SWA/Namibia and in 1979 the Kalahari.
Exhibitions He has participated in numerous group exhibitions from 1973 in SA and twice in London; 1973 SAAA Gallery, Cape Town, first of 27 solo exhibitions.
Reference BSAK 2.

LEIBBRANDT Eben

Born 1915 Graaff-Reinet, Cape Province.
A painter, sculptor and graphic artist of figures, interiors, religious themes and abstract pictures. Works in gouache, stone, metal and in various graphic media, particularly etchings. 1962 a series of black and white paintings, using a roller and palette knife.
Studies 1937–40 Witwatersrand Technical College, under Eric Byrd (qv), gaining a National Art Teachers Certificate; 1953–55 sculpture at the Central School of Art, London; 1963–65 graphics at the Chelsea School of Art, London.
Profile During the early 1960s a senior Art Master at Forest High School, Johannesburg; 1968 Head of the Sculpture Department, Witwatersrand Technical College; 1970–74 a lecturer at the Witwatersrand Technical College. Early in his artistic career he illustrated the children's section of *Die Brandwag* for two years; he returned to this in 1948. 1975–77 lived in Spain; 1977–82 lived in SA, but did not exhibit; 1982 returned to Spain.
Exhibitions He has participated in group exhibitions in SA and in São Paulo, Venice, London, Canada, The Netherlands, West Germany and Spain; 1958 Lidchi Gallery, Johannesburg, first solo exhibition of paintings; 1965 first solo exhibition of etchings; 1968 Pretoria, first solo exhibition of sculpture.
Represented Ann Bryant Gallery, East London; Hester Rupert Art Museum, Graaff-Reinet; Johannesburg Art Gallery; King George VI Art Gallery, Port Elizabeth; Memorial University, Newfoundland, Canada; Pietersburg Collection; Pretoria Art Museum; Sandton Municipal Collection; SA National Gallery, Cape Town; University of South Africa.
Public Commissions Several mural, sculpture and mosaic commissions including: 1971 "The Family", sculpture, Jan Smuts Airport, Johannesburg; "The Family", Klerksdorp Municipality; three life-size Impala Antelope, White River.
References SAA; 20C SA Art; SAP&D; AASA; SASSK; *Artlook* September 1968 & September 1972.

LEIGH Derek Milton (Dick)

Born 1940 Pietermaritzburg.
A painter and graphic artist of landscapes, portraits, still life, seascapes, genre, figures, animals and abstract pictures. Works in oil, acrylic, watercolour, ink, wash, pencil, charcoal, conté and in various graphic media.
Studies 1959–61 University of Natal, under Professor Jack Heath (qv) and Jane Heath (qv), gaining a BA(FA); 1960–61 spent three weeks at l'Atelier André Lhote in Paris; 1962 gained a Higher Diploma in Education; 1987 gained an MA in the History of Art.

Profile 1968 a lecturer at the Natal Technical College; from 1969 a lecturer, subsequently a senior lecturer in the Department of Fine Art at the University of Natal.

Exhibitions He has participated in numerous group exhibitions in SA and West Germany; 1976 Durban Art Gallery, exhibition; 1985 Tributaries, touring SA and West Germany; 1985 Cape Town Triennial.

Represented Durban Art Gallery; Natal Technikon; Tatham Art Gallery, Pietermaritzburg; University of Natal.

LEONARD Joyce ARCA

Born 1909 Johannesburg.

A painter of portraits and still life. Works in oil.

Studies 1931–33 Royal College of Art, London, becoming an Associate in 1932.

Profile Ceased painting during the 1950s, since when she has dedicated her life to teaching art. She has taught at the following places: 1934–39 Johannesburg Teachers Training College; 1940–56 and 1970–77 the Fine Art and Architecture Departments of the University of the Witwatersrand; 1956–68 Witwatersrand Technical College; 1968–70 The Visual Arts Research Centre, Johannesburg; from 1978 through the Art Discussion Group. From 1974 she has been on the Selection Committee of the Johannesburg Art Gallery.

Exhibitions Exhibited in Johannesburg and London; 1948 Tate Gallery, London, SA Art Exhibition; 1952 Van Riebeeck Tercentenary Exhibition, Cape Town; 1956 Quadrennial Exhibition.

Represented Durban Art Gallery; Johannesburg Art Gallery; SA National Gallery, Cape Town.

References Collectors' Guide; AASA; SAA; SAP&S.

LE ROUX Le Roux Smith

Born 1914 Cape Town.

Died 1963 London.

Resided in SA until 1950.

A painter of landscapes. Worked in tempera, oil and watercolour. A large number of murals. Painted in a decorative, rhythmic style using African motifs.

Studies 1931 Michaelis School of Fine Art, under Professor John Wheatley (qv); Royal College of Art, London, under Professor Ernest W Tristram (1882–1952); Slade School of Art, London; British School of Art, Rome, under Colin Hardie and also at the British School of Art in Athens. Awarded a travel grant to Europe by the SA Government for special training in murals.

Profile 1938 a member of the New Group; 1948 a member of the International Art Club, SA; 1942 on the War Art Advisory Committee. Illustrated *Land van ons Vaderer* in 1943 and *Die Vlammende Fez* in 1945, both by I du Plessis. 1938 assisted with the British Pavilion at the Paris World Fair, gaining a Special Diploma from the French Government. 1943–49 Director of the Pretoria Art Centre and Curator of the Pretoria Art Collection; 1950–52 Deputy Keeper of the Tate Gallery, London; 1953 Assistant Director of the National Gallery, London, under Sir John Rothenstein (1872–1945); 1955 Art Advisor to Lord Beaverbrook; 1960 a buyer for various London galleries and leading collectors. During the 1950s an actor, critic and broadcaster with the BBC, also broadcast "London Letter" on the SABC. Son of the artist and writer J A Smith (qv).

Exhibitions Participated in group exhibitions from 1938 in the UK, SA and Rhodesia (Zimbabwe); 1941 Argus Gallery, Cape Town, a one-day solo exhibition; 1948 Tate Gallery, London, SA Art Exhibition.

Represented Durban Art Gallery; Pretoria Art Museum; SA National Gallery, Cape Town; SA National Museum of Military History, Johannesburg; William Humphreys Art Gallery, Kimberley.

Public Commissions Murals: with Eleanor Esmonde-White (qv), 1935–37 SA House, London and 1938 *SS Queen Elizabeth*; 1939 SA Mutual Building, Cape Town; 1948 *SS Pretoria Castle*; 1949 in The Netherlands, *SS Jagersfontein*; New Law Courts, Johannesburg; Dutch Reformed Church, Ladismith, Cape Province.

References Collectors' Guide; Art SA; SAA; 20C SA Art; AMC3; DSAB; SAP&S; BSAK 1 & 2; Enc S'n A; SA Art; 3Cs; AASA; *Die Huisgenoot* 14 November 1941; *Forum* 20 December 1941; *Standpunte* vol 9 no 3, 1954; *SA Panorama* September 1983.

LE ROUX Renée de Wet

Born 1927 Beaufort West, Cape Province.

A painter of abstract pictures. Works in acrylic, mixed media and occasionally in oil. Constructs collages. 1978 a series entitled "Graffiti" inspired by New York and District Six, Cape Town.

Studies 1944–47 Michaelis School of Fine Art, under Professor Edward Roworth (qv), gaining a Diploma in Commercial Art.

Profile A member of the SAAA; 1958 a founder member of the Bloemfontein Group; 1980 a founder and committee member of the Artists Guild, Cape Town. 1975–80 principal of a private art school for children in Llandudno, Cape Province; 1979–80 a lecturer at the Ruth Prowse School of Art, Cape Town. 1981–83 artist in residence to a firm of architects in Cape Town; 1983 and 1984 a number of large paintings commissioned for company headquarters in Cape Town and Stellenbosch. 1948–69 married to the SA writer Etienne Le Roux and lived in Koffiefontein, Orange Free State. 1954 travelled extensively in Europe; 1979 and 1980 travelled extensively in the USA.

Exhibitions She has participated in numerous group exhibitions from 1956 throughout SA and at the São Paulo Bienale; 1962 Roderick's Gallery, Bloemfontein, first of 12 solo exhibitions held in SA; 1964 Quadrennial Exhibition.

Represented Hester Rupert Art Museum, Graaff-Reinet; National Museum, Bloemfontein; Pietersburg Collection; Potchefstroom University for CHE; Pretoria Art Museum; SA National Gallery, Cape Town; University of the Orange Free State; University of Stellenbosch; William Humphreys Art Gallery, Kimberley.

References SAA; SAP&S; SAP&D; BSAK 1 & 2; 3Cs; AASA; LSAA; *Artlook* September 1971.

LESLIE Harry Charles

Active 1871–1903.

Resided in SA from 1881.

A painter of landscapes. Worked in oil and watercolour. Drew portraits in pencil.

Studies 1871–72 Slade School of Art, London, under Sir Edward Poynter (1836–1919); 1874–75 under Alphonse Legros (1837–1911).
Profile 1883–1903 first Art Master at the Port Elizabeth School of Art, also taught painting and drawing at Miss Brown's Riebeeck College, Uitenhage. Son of Charles Robert Leslie RA (1794–1859), a watercolourist.
Exhibitions Exhibited in London 1880–81.
Represented King George VI Art Gallery, Port Elizabeth.
Reference Port Elizabeth School of Art.

LE SUEUR Louis

Born 1942 Pretoria.
A sculptor, painter and graphic artist of landscapes, portraits, figures, still life, wildlife and abstracts. Works predominantly in wood, bronze, polyester resin, acrylic and mixed media, but also employs many other media. A number of collages during the 1970s.
Studies 1961 Dulcey Wisik Art School, Salisbury, Rhodesia (Harare, Zimbabwe); 1963 Witwatersrand Technical College, under George Boys (qv), Phil Kolbe (qv) and Attie Tromp; 1964 woodcarving privately under Peter Davis (qv); 1966 The Visual Arts Research Centre, Johannesburg, under George Boys (qv); 1971 bronze casting at Joubert's Foundry, Hartebeespoort, Transvaal and in 1982 at an art foundry in Sante Fe, New Mexico, USA.
Profile A former member of the Santa Fe Society of Art, USA and of Artists Equity, USA. Has taught art privately. A designer of tapestries, jewellery, posters, magazine covers, record sleeves and landscapes. A dancer and poet. Travelled extensively throughout the world during the 1960s, and during the late 1970s and early 1980s visited the USA. Has lived in New Mexico, USA, from 1983. Brother of the graphic designer Michel le Sueur. Briefly worked under the name Lewis Raseur.
Exhibitions He has participated in many group exhibitions from 1966 in SA and eight in the USA; 1966 Lidchi Gallery, Johannesburg, first of five solo exhibitions held in SA.
Award 1969 Bronze Medal for Sculpture, Transvaal Academy.
Represented Pretoria Art Museum.
References *Artlook* October 1967, May 1968 & November 1971; *Habitat* no 27, 1977.

LETTY Cythna (Mrs Forssman)

Born 1895 Standerton, Transvaal.
Died 1985 Pretoria.
A painter of South African flowers and plants, also a number of figure and landscape pictures. Worked in watercolour and pencil.
Studies A mainly self-taught artist who probably received art tuition from her mother Josina Letty (qv), Grace Battiss (qv) in Pretoria and George Crosland Robinson (qv) in Cape Town.

Profile 1925–27 joined the staff of the Onderstepoort Veterinary Research Institute; 1927–38 worked in the Botanical Division of the Department of Agriculture; 1945–50 worked full-time at the National Herbarium and part-time there between 1950–67; reappointed in 1968 to survey Arum Lilies for *Bothalia*, the Department's official journal. These departments are now named the Botanical Research Institute. During these 40 years, she completed over 750 plates for their publication *Flowering Plants of South Africa*. She was best known as an illustrator, with her work appearing in *Trees and Shrubs of the Kruger National Park*, *Grasses of the World* and *Medicinal and Poisonous Plants of Southern and Eastern Africa*. A number of her poems were published in *The Outspan*. Designed the Rhodesian silver sixpence, minted 1964 and the floral reverses of the SA half cent, ten cent, twenty cent and fifty cent decimal coins, minted in 1965. A botanist, with "Aloe Lettyae Reynolds" and "Crassula Lettyae Phillips" named after her, as well as the "Cythna Letty Nature Reserve" in the Barberton Mountains, Eastern Transvaal. 1920–25 lived in Cape Town, thereafter in Pretoria. Made several trips to the USA, Europe and the UK. Daughter of Josina Letty (qv), sister of Francis Freemantle (qv).
Exhibitions From 1937 participated in group exhibitions in the USA, the UK and SA; 1962 McFadyen Hall, Pretoria, first solo exhibition; 1974 SAAA Gallery, Pretoria, solo exhibition of 120 drawings from *Wild Flowers of the Transvaal*; 1974 "Green Greetings", SAAA Gallery, Pretoria, a group exhibition arranged as an 80th birthday tribute to her.
Awards 1970 Grenfell Medal of the Royal Horticultural Society of Great Britain for her paintings; in 1975 the University of the Witwatersrand conferred an Honorary Doctorate of Law upon her.
Represented Africana Museum, Johannesburg; Hunt Botanical Library, Pittsburgh, Pennsylvania, USA.
Publications by C Letty Author and illustrator of *Wild Flowers of the Transvaal*, 1962; *Trees of South Africa*, 1975, Tafelberg, Cape Town; *More Trees of South Africa*, 1980, Tafelberg, Cape Town; *Children of the Hours*, a book containing her poems and paintings, 1981, Ad Donker, Johannesburg.
References SAA; AMC; SESA; BSAK 1 & 2; AASA; *SA Panorama* April 1969, June 1980 & November 1984; *Suid Afrikaanse Oorsig* 28 Mei 1971.

LETTY Josina Christina (née Lindenberg)
Born 1861 Worcester, Cape Province.
Died 1938.
A painter of flowers. Worked in watercolour.
Profile 1892 lived on the Witwatersrand; 1899 moved to Natal; 1904–24 lived in the Transvaal; thereafter in the Western Cape. Mother of Cythna Letty (qv) and Francis Freemantle (qv).
Represented Botanical Research Institute, Pretoria.
Publications by J Letty Wrote and illustrated *Field Findings*, published in two volumes, 1908 and 1911, dealing with Transvaal veld flowers.
References SAA; AASA; *Bothalia* May 1966.

LE VAILLANT François

Born 1753 Paramaribo, Surinam, South America.
Died 1824 La Noue, Esternay, France.
Resided in SA 1781–84.
A painter of birds, other natural history subjects, landscapes, camp life and tribal peoples. Worked in watercolour.
Profile A French ornithologist, hunter and explorer who travelled in 1781–83 to the Eastern Cape, returning to Cape Town through the Karoo and the Outeniqua Mountains and in 1783–84 through the Northern Cape to the Orange River and SWA/Namibia. 1753–63 lived in Surinam; 1763–81 in Europe; 1785 returned to Europe, settling in France.
Represented Library of Parliament, Cape Town.
Publications by Le Vaillant Illustrated accounts of his trek, translated into English: *Travels into the Interior Parts of Africa*, 2 volumes, 12 copper-plates, 1790, London; *New Travels into the Interior Parts of Africa*, 3 volumes, 22 copper-plates, 1796, London; also wrote *Histoire naturelle des oiseaux d'Afrique*, 6 volumes, 300 copper engravings, 1796–1812, Paris. Several books on the birds of America and Asia.
References François Le Vaillant, edited by J C Quinton and A M Lewin Robinson, 2 volumes, 1973, Library of Parliament, Cape Town; Pict Art; Afr Repos; AMC3 & 7; DSAB; SESA; BSAK 1 & 2; Pict Afr; SA Art; 3Cs.

LEVSON Leon

Born 1881.
Died 1968.
A painter of landscapes, still life and flowers.
Profile Associated with the Transvaal Art Society. Better known for his photographs. 1926 in partnership with Ernest Lezard opened the Levson Gallery, Johannesburg. Father of Rhona Stern (qv).
Exhibition 1943 Gainsborough Gallery, Johannesburg, solo exhibition of photographs and paintings.
Reference AASA.

LEVY Ruth

Born Johannesburg.
A painter working in oil on paper until 1982 when she changed to acrylic. Up to the 1960s her work was figurative but she then turned to abstract, continuing this until 1975 when she returned once more to figurative works. An etcher. 1983 a series of portraits of friends; 1984–85 a series entitled "Environmental Abstracts"; 1985 a small satirical series entitled "Endangered Species".
Studies Witwatersrand Technical College, under James Gardner (qv), where gained a National Art Teachers Diploma.

Profile A former member of the SAAA; 1985 a member of the French Association of Women Painters. 1964 a lecturer at the Johannesburg Art School; 1965 a lecturer at the University of the Witwatersrand, also taught at the Braamfontein Study Centre, Johannesburg, the University of the Witwatersrand Centre for Continuing Education and privately. Designed a tapestry woven by Margaret Weavind. Visited London, Paris, Florence, West Africa and Zimbabwe.

Exhibitions She has participated in numerous group exhibitions in SA, London, Israel and Paris; Lidchi Art Gallery, Johannesburg, first of five solo exhibitions; 1981 Republic Festival Exhibition.

Represented Johannesburg Art Gallery; SA National Gallery, Cape Town.

References SAA; *Dictionary of Women Artists*, 1981, edited by Professor Lama Doumata of Colorado University, published in New York; AASA; *Artlook* May 1970; *Habitat* no 55, 1983.

LEWIS (Allan) Neville

Born 1895 Cape Town.
Died 1972 Stellenbosch.
A painter of portraits and figure compositions. Worked in oil. In later years produced a number of still life paintings.

Studies 1912 in Newlyn, Cornwall, UK, under Stanhope Forbes (1857–1948); 1914–16 Slade School of Art, London, under Henry Tonks (1862–1937), Philip Wilson Steer (1860–1942), Ambrose McEvoy (1878–1927) and Derwent Lees (1885–1931).

Profile 1920 a member of the New English Art Club; 1930 a member of the National Society; 1936 a member of the Royal Society of Portrait Painters; 1938 a member of the New Group. 1917–19 in the British Army in Flanders and Italy; 1919–38 lived in London; 1940–43 appointed an Official War Artist and designed the SA war postage stamps. His portrait of General George Brink was used on the cover of *Uncle George* by Carel Birkby, 1987, Jonathan Ball, Johannesburg. Made many visits to Spain and North America. Travelled extensively in SA, Botswana, Kenya and North Africa.

Exhibitions Participated in group exhibitions from 1923 in England, SA and Rhodesia (Zimbabwe); 1920 Carfax Gallery, London, first of several solo exhibitions held in Europe, SA and the USA; 1948 Tate Gallery, London, SA Art Exhibition; 1972–73 University of Stellenbosch, Memorial Exhibition.

Represented Africana Museum, Johannesburg; Arts Association SWA/Namibia Collection; Durban Art Gallery; Gallery of Modern Art, Madrid, Spain; Hester Rupert Art Museum, Graaff-Reinet; Imperial War Museum, London, UK; Johannesburg Art Gallery; Julius Gordon Africana Centre, Riversdale; Manchester Art Gallery, UK; National Gallery, London, UK; Pretoria Art Museum; SA National Gallery, Cape Town; SA National Museum of Military History, Johannesburg; Tate Gallery, London, UK; University of Cape Town; University of Stellenbosch; William Humphreys Art Gallery, Kimberley.

Public Commissions Numerous portrait commissions including those of King Alfonso XIII of Spain, King George II of Greece, Field-Marshals Lord Alexander, Lord Montgomery and J C Smuts, Sir Winston Churchill, Chief Tshekedi Khama, ex-Chief Albert Luthuli, State President C R Swart and various other SA notabilities.

Publication by Lewis Wrote and illustrated *Studio Encounters*, 1963, Tafelberg, Cape Town.

References Collectors' Guide; Our Art 2; Art SA; SAA; *Tate Gallery Catalogue—The Modern British Paintings, Drawings and Sculpture*, volume 1, 1964, Oldbourne Press, London; 20C SA Art; SAP&S; SSAP; Bénézit; SESA; DBA; BSAK 1 & 2; Enc S'n A; SA Art; 3Cs; AASA; N P C Huntingford, *The World War II Works of Neville Lewis*, July 1984, SA National Museum of Military History, Johannesburg; *Artlook* February 1967.

LEWIS Hester-Marié

Born 1957 Chingola, Northern Rhodesia (Zambia).

Resided in SA from 1958.

A sculptor of portraits, figures and abstract pieces. Works in bronze, ciment fondu, wood and ceramics. A stained glass artist and a graphic artist producing linocuts and silkscreens. 1982 a series entitled "The Mind of Man".

Studies 1979–81 Pretoria Technikon, under Koos den Houting (qv), Ian Redelinghuys (qv), Richard Adams (qv) and Gunther van der Reis (qv), gaining a National Diploma in Art and Design. 1986 studied part-time at the Witwatersrand Technikon.

Profile A member of the SAAA and the Heidelberg Culture Society. 1984 a part-time teacher at Brakpan Technical College; from 1985 taught sculpture, pottery and drawing privately in Heidelberg, Transvaal. 1975 visited Europe.

Exhibitions She has participated in several group exhibitions in the Transvaal from 1981.

Public Commission 1983–84 a portrait of Dr A G Visser for the hospital in Heidelberg, Transvaal.

LEWIS Rhoda Kathleen

Born 1908 England.

Resided in SA from 1909.

A painter of Cape houses and cottages, landscapes, seascapes, portraits and still life. Works in oil, watercolour, ink, wash and pencil.

Studies 1962–63 part-time courses in life drawing and portraiture at the Michaelis School of Fine Art, under Maurice van Essche (qv); 1965 at the Hayward Veal Art School, Reigate, Surrey, England.

Profile From 1960 a member of the SA Society of Artists and in 1968–72 a council member; from 1976 a member of the WSSA; 1985 a member of D'ARTS. 1958–72 lived in Cape Town, thereafter in Durban.

Exhibitions She has participated in numerous group exhibitions from 1960 in SA; 1968 Edrich Gallery, Stellenbosch, solo exhibition.

LEWIS Robin Kenneth
Born 1942 Johannesburg.
Died 1988 Muizenberg, Cape Province.
A self-taught sculptor of birds, fish and wildlife. Worked in various metals, particularly copper and brass. His early work is in wood, clay, plastic and stone.
Profile Spent twenty years working in advertising agencies as an art director through to a creative director. A life-long interest in birds led to him writing and illustrating a series of educational programmes on birds for Caltex Oil entitled "Know Your Birds"; these took the form of books, posters and audio-visuals. An ornithologist who also wrote and illustrated a book on the history, ecology and development of the now-proclaimed nature reserve of Saldanha Bay, Langebaan Lagoon. Became a full-time sculptor in 1979.
Exhibitions Participated in many group exhibitions in SA from 1970 and in the USA in 1986; 1984 Everard Read Gallery, Johannesburg, solo exhibition.

LIEBENBERG Dean
Born 1956 Cape Town.
A painter of landscapes, portraits, figures and still life. Works in oil, acrylic, ink, wash and pencil.
Studies 1977–80 Michaelis School of Fine Art, under Stanley Pinker (qv), gaining a BA(FA).
Profile From 1985 a member of the SAAA. 1981–84 taught at Vlaeberg Art School, Cape Town; from 1984 a lecturer at the School of Art and Design, Cape Technikon.
Exhibitions 1985 participated in a group exhibition in Cape Town; 1985 SAAA Gallery, Cape Town, solo exhibition.
Represented Willem Annandale Art Gallery, Lichtenburg.

LIEBENBERG Estelle Juliana
Born 1954 Bloemfontein.
A painter of landscapes and abstract pictures. Works in oil, acrylic, gouache, pastel, conté, pencil and charcoal.
Studies University of the Witwatersrand, under Cecily Sash (qv), Erica Berry (qv), Neels Coetzee (qv) and Joyce Leonard (qv), gaining a BA(FA) cum laude in 1975; 1976 University of the Witwatersrand, gaining a Higher Diploma in Education, and an Anya Millman Scholarship for Overseas Travel; 1980 gained an MA(FA) from the University of the Witwatersrand, having studied under Robert Hodgins (qv).
Profile 1978–79 Senior Bursar at the University of the Witwatersrand; 1980 a junior lecturer at the Rand Afrikaans University; from 1981 a lecturer in Painting and Art History at the University of Natal.
Exhibitions She has participated in several group exhibitions from 1981 in SA; 1981 Jack Heath Gallery, University of Natal, Pietermaritzburg, solo exhibition.
Award 1974 Henri Lidchi Prize for Drawing.
Represented Tatham Art Gallery, Pietermaritzburg.

LIGHTON Norman Charles Kingsley

Born 1904 Wonderboom, Pretoria.
Died 1981 Sea Point, Cape Town.
A self-taught bird artist.
Profile Illustrated *The Birds of South Africa* by Dr Austin Roberts, 1940—these plates were also used in the second edition in 1957, which appeared under the new title of *Roberts Birds of South Africa*, the third edition in 1970 and the fourth edition in 1978; *Birds of South Rhodesia* by Captain C D Priest; *Birds of East Africa and Somaliland* by Mackworth-Praed and Grant; *Some Protected Birds* by the Cape Province Conservation Department; *Blood Parasites and their Hosts* by the SA Institute of Medical Research, as well as an Afrikaans Children's Encyclopaedia for Nasionale Pers. A qualified architect with the Public Works Department, Pretoria. 1935 joined the Transvaal Museum, in order to work on illustrating *The Birds of South Africa*; during WWII worked as a physical training instructor in the SA Medical Corps; later an Assistant Provincial Architect in Cape Town, retiring in 1969.
References *The Paintings of Norman Lighton for Roberts Birds of South Africa*, edited by A V Bird, 1977, South African Natural History Publication Company, Cape Town; SAA; AMC7; SESA; BSAK 1; SA Art; AASA.

LINCOLN Thalia Nina

Born 1924 Cape Town.
A painter of botanical subjects and cosmic images. Works in coloured pencils.
Studies 1943–44 Michaelis School of Fine Art, under Professor Edward Roworth (qv).
Profile Portfolio of four flower prints, published in 1972 by Howard Swan, Johannesburg. Illustrated *Mimetes*, with text by Dr J P Rourke, 1982, Tiyan Publishers, Cape Town. A member of the Cape Town Symphony Choir. Has lived in Johannesburg and Durban, and Central and East Africa. Presently lives in Cape Town.
Exhibitions She has participated in several group exhibitions from 1972 in SA and once in London; 1974 Triad Gallery, Johannesburg, first of four solo exhibitions.
References AASA; *Artlook* May 1974.

LINDEQUE Leonard Nico (Len)

Born 1936 Brakpan, Transvaal.
Died 1980 Johannesburg.
A painter of portraits. Among the many well-known personalities he painted were J B Vorster, Ben Schoeman and many other Cabinet Ministers. Worked in mixed media.
Studies Witwatersrand Technical College, gaining a National Art Teachers Certificate and a Diploma in Fine Art.

Profile A cartoonist for SA newspapers including *Dagbreek*, *Die Vaderland* and *Rapport*. 1960 the Art Editor of the Afrikaanse Pers Publishing Company. 1977 an Official War Artist for the SA Navy. 1963, 1966 and 1967 visited the UK and the USA.
Exhibitions Participated in group exhibitions in 1973 and 1978.
Represented Pretoria Art Museum; SA National Museum of Military History, Johannesburg.
References BSAK 1 & 2; AASA; SASSK; *SA Panorama* November 1978 & June 1983.

LINDER Louise

Born 1960 Beira, Mozambique.
A sculptor of abstract pieces. Works in various metals and enamel paint.
Studies Michaelis School of Fine Art, gaining a BA(FA) in 1982, an Advanced Diploma in Fine Arts in 1983 and an MA(FA) in 1986.
Exhibitions 1987 exhibited at the University of the Witwatersrand; 1988 Johannesburg Art Gallery, Vita Art Now.
Represented University of Cape Town; University of the Witwatersrand.

LINDSAY Andrew John

Born 1956 Johannesburg.
A painter and graphic artist of figures. Works in oil, acrylic, watercolour, ink, wash, pencil, charcoal and in various graphic media.
Studies 1979–82 Witwatersrand Technical College (Technikon), under Jo Smail (qv), Robert Reedy (qv), Willem Boshoff (qv) and Marialda Marais, gaining a National Diploma in Art and Design.
Profile 1982–83 a member of the Possession Art Group; 1983 a founder member of the Skuzo Group and a co-ordinator of the Botswana Festival. 1983–84 a photography and drawing tutor at The Open School, Community Arts Programme, Johannesburg. A freelance photographer. 1984 set designs for a play by Don Mattera. 1985 a number of illustrations for periodicals. Nephew of David Lindsay (qv).
Exhibitions He has participated in group exhibitions from 1980 in Johannesburg.

LINDSAY David Norman

Born 1930 Johannesburg.
A painter of landscapes, wildlife and still life. Works in oil, acrylic and watercolour.
Studies Johannesburg Art School; Broken Hill Art School, Northern Rhodesia (Zambia).

Profile A member of the Courtyard Group and the WSSA. Illustrations for books, posters and calendars. A commercial and silkscreen artist. Uncle of Andrew Lindsay (qv).
Exhibitions He has participated in numerous group exhibitions in SA and Zambia; 1980 Sandown Gallery, Johannesburg, first of three solo exhibitions.

LINDSAY Thomas Mitchener

Resided in SA 1864–67.
A painter of landscapes. Worked in watercolour.
Studies South Kensington Art School, London, and Liverpool School of Art, UK.
Profile Taught art as a pupil-teacher at Liverpool School of Art; 1864–67 Principal of the Roeland Street School of Art, Cape Town and later Principal of the Belfast School of Art, Northern Ireland. During the 1880s he was the Curator of the Rugby Art Museum, England.
Exhibitions 1880–1910 participated in many group exhibitions in the UK.
References Pict Art; Pict Afr; DBA; AASA.

LINDSELL-STEWART Hilare Antoinette (Ann)

Born 1923 London, England.
Resided in SA from 1983.
A self-taught painter of semi-abstract landscapes and still life and of figurative portraits. Works in oil, pastel, wax crayon, ink and charcoal. 1965–75 depicted isolated figures in landscapes; 1970–80 a series entitled "Augustine"; 1978–84 a series of crowds; 1981 a series of people asleep and wrapped; 1980–85 a series of space, as seen in open, treeless landscapes.
Profile 1959–74 a member of the Pastel Society, London; from 1974 of "Circle" in Rhodesia (Zimbabwe). 1972–83 taught oil painting privately in Harare and from 1984 in Johannesburg. Lived in Zimbabwe 1950–83; frequent visits to Kent, England. In 1983 visited the USA and in 1984 Switzerland.
Exhibitions She has participated in numerous group exhibitions from 1954 in Wales, England, Scotland, France, Zimbabwe and SA; 1954 Rhodesia (Zimbabwe), first of 27 solo exhibitions held in Zimbabwe, Mozambique, Zambia, the UK, the USA, Switzerland and from 1964 in SA.
Represented Legislative Assembly, Harare, Zimbabwe; Municipal Gallery, Maputo, Mozambique; National Gallery, Harare, Zimbabwe; National Museum, Bulawayo, Zimbabwe; University of Zimbabwe.
Portrait Commissions 1956 Lord Llewellin, Governor-General of the Federation of Rhodesia and Nyasaland; 1956 Sir Peveril William-Powlett, Governor of Southern Rhodesia; 1960 Air Vice-Marshal Jacklin, Chief of Staff, Royal Rhodesian Air Force; 1965 Sir Winston Field, Prime Minister of Rhodesia; 1969 Air Vice-Marshal Harold Hawkins, Chief of Staff, Royal Rhodesian Air Force; 1977–81 several educationalists from the University of Rhodesia/Zimbabwe.
References BSAK; AASA; *Artlook* October 1969; *Habitat* no 8, 1974; *Arts Zimbabwe* 1981/82; *SA Arts Calendar* Spring 1985.

LIPKIN Aileen

Born 1933 Johannesburg.
Both a painter and sculptor of landscapes, portraits, still life, genre, figures and abstracts. Works in oil, acrylic, gouache, watercolour, ink, wash, pencil, charcoal, stainless steel, brass, perspex, fibreglass, polyester, polyurethane and glass. 1973 "Echo", a series of stained paper collages.
Studies 1949–50 Witwatersrand Technical College, under James Gardner (qv); 1959 six months at Arthur Goldreich Art School, Johannesburg, under Arthur Goldreich; 1960–62 Central School of Art, London, under Alan Davies (*b*.1920), Hans Hanstisdal, Alan Watson, Alan Reynolds and William Turnbull (*b*.1922).
Profile 1952–59 ran her own commerical art studio. 1963–66 taught art privately. From 1972 numerous illustrations for books published in Switzerland and SA, as well as for periodicals and brochures. In 1963 her painting "Woman on a Donkey" was reproduced. In 1976 a portfolio of sketches "From Bamako to the Dogon Country" was published by the Totem-Meneghelli Gallery, Johannesburg. 1984 tapestry design. 1960–64 lived in London, visiting many European countries. 1973–75 spent one month of each year in West Africa; 1979–80 spent four months in Egypt, visiting the Sinai Desert. 1984 and 1986 visited India. Lives in Johannesburg.
Exhibitions She has participated in numerous group exhibitions from 1960 in the UK, Portugal, Greece and SA; 1960 Lidchi Gallery, Johannesburg, first of 14 solo exhibitions, four of which have been held in London; 1970 Durban Art Gallery, Prestige Exhibition; 1978 National Museum, Bloemfontein, joint exhibition with Cecil Skotnes (qv) and Wendy Vincent (qv).
Represented Ann Bryant Gallery, East London; Johannesburg Art Gallery; King George VI Art Gallery, Port Elizabeth; Rand Afrikaans University; Sandton Municipal Collection; SA National Gallery, Cape Town; University of the Witwatersrand.
Public Commissions 1967 polyptych in oil, President Hotel, Johannesburg; 1972 steel mural, Provincial Administration Building, Pietermaritzburg; 1973 steel mural, Sable Building, Braamfontein, Johannesburg; 1976 stainless steel sculpture, "Growth", Exchange Square, President Street, Johannesburg.
References AASA; SSAP; *Artlook* February 1969 & June 1969; *Lantern* September 1972; *Habitat* no 5, 1973 & no 11, 1974.

LIPKIN Melissa

Born 1950 Johannesburg.
A painter of interiors, gardens, landscapes, still life, figures and portraits. Works in oil and acrylic.
Studies 1968–69 Camberwell School of Art, London; 1969–72 University of Sussex, under Quentin Bell and Hans Hess, gaining a BA with Honours in History and Theory of Art.

Profile Has lived in SA, Spain, England, France and the USA.
Exhibitions She has participated in several group exhibitions from 1985 in London, SA and the USA; 1974 Julian Simon Gallery, Johannesburg, solo exhibition; 1985 Everard Read Gallery, Johannesburg, joint exhibition with Sheila Jarzin-Levinson (qv); 1987 Read Stremmel Gallery, USA, solo exhibition.
Reference *Gallery* Spring 1985.

LIPSHITZ Israel-Isaac (Lippy) FRSA
Born 1903 Plungian, Lithuania (Lithuanian SSR).
Died 1980 Kiryat Tivon, Israel.
Resided in SA 1908–78.
A sculptor in bronze, clay, stone and from 1925 wood; also worked in ivory, marble, onyx, bone, horn, precious metals and semi-precious stones. A highly versatile artist producing high relief panels, free-standing sculpture, portraits, genre subjects, universal themes and abstract pieces. *c.*1932 made several drawings and produced works in various graphic media.
Studies 1922–25 Cape Town Art School, under Percy Thatcher and Charles S Groves (qv); 1925–26 Michaelis School of Fine Art, under Herbert V Meyerowitz (qv); 1928–29 Académie de la Grande Chaumière, Paris, under Antoine Bourdelle (1861–1929).
Profile 1938 a founder member of the New Group; 1949 a founder member of the Art Club of SA; 1961 an executive member of the SA Council of Artists. 1931 illustrated *Les Chansons du Vagabond* by Nesto Jacometti. 1933–37 shared Palm Studio with Wolf Kibel (qv), where they both taught art. 1949 published a monograph on Pieter Wenning (qv) with Gregoire Boonzaier (qv). 1952 Chief Advisor to the SA National Gallery, Cape Town. 1950–60 a visiting lecturer in sculpture, 1960–63 a senior lecturer and 1964–68 Associate Professor of Fine Art at the Michaelis School of Fine Art. 1928–32 lived in Paris; 1947–48 in the UK; 1949–78 in Cape Town, with visits to Israel in 1957 and Europe in 1961. In 1966 he spent six months travelling in Israel and throughout Europe. 1978–80 lived in Israel. Brother of Ada Lipshitz-Wolpe (qv) and father of Toni Lipshitz-Caspi (qv).
Exhibitions Participated in group exhibitions from 1929 in France, Italy, England, Greece, Yugoslavia, Zimbabwe, Brazil and throughout SA; 1932 Martin Melck House, Cape Town, first of many solo exhibitions held throughout SA and in London; joint exhibitions with Wolf Kibel (qv) from 1934 and from 1940 with Cecil Higgs (qv) and John Dronsfield (qv); 1938 Cape Town, joint exhibition with Russell Harvey (qv); 1938 Stellenbosch, joint exhibition with Rene Graetz, Cecil Higgs (qv), Maggie Laubser (qv) and John Dronsfield (qv); 1944 Durban Art Gallery, Retrospective Exhibition; 1948 Tate Gallery, London, SA Art Exhibition; 1956 and 1960 Quadrennial Exhibitions; 1968 Tatham Art Gallery, Pietermaritzburg, Durban Art Gallery and SA National Gallery, Cape Town, exhibition with John Dronsfield (qv) and Cecil Higgs (qv); 1968 SA National Gallery, Cape Town, Retrospective Exhibition; 1976 SA National Gallery, Cape Town, Retrospective Exhibition.

Awards 1953 Cape Tercentenary Foundation Certificate of Merit; 1959 First Prize, German Settlers Memorial Competition in East London; 1964 Medal of Honour for Sculpture, SA Akademie vir Wetenskap en Kuns; 1978 SA Association of Arts Medallion.

Represented Durban Art Gallery; Hester Rupert Art Museum, Graaff-Reinet; Johannesburg Art Gallery; King George VI Art Gallery, Port Elizabeth; National Gallery, Harare, Zimbabwe; Pretoria Art Museum; Rand Afrikaans University; SA Akademie vir Wetenskap en Kuns; SA National Gallery, Cape Town; Tatham Art Gallery, Pietermaritzburg; University of Cape Town; University of Stellenbosch; University of the Witwatersrand; William Humphreys Art Gallery, Kimberley.

Public Commissions 1960 German Settlers Monument, East London; 1962 six relief panels, Cape Provincial Library; bronze relief for Robertson Cape Memorial Gardens.

References Bruce Arnott, *Lippy Lipshitz*, 1969, A A Balkema, Cape Town; KK; Collectors' Guide; Our Art 2; Art SA; SAA; 20C SA Art; SAP&S; Oxford Companion to Art (under SA); SAP&D; IWAA; SESA; SSAP; BSAK 1 & 2; SA Art; Oxford Companion to 20C Art (under SA); 3Cs; AASA; LSAA; *Die Huisgenoot* 3 January 1941; *Lantern* May 1956; *Artlook* April 1967, February 1969 & June/July 1976; *SA Panorama* April 1978; Retrospective Exhibition Catalogue, 1968, SA National Gallery, Cape Town.

LIPSHITZ-CASPI Toni

Born 1930 Cape Town.

A lithographer.

Studies Under Lippy Lipshitz (qv); Continental School of Art, Cape Town, under Maurice van Essche (qv); 1953 Bezalel School of Art, Jerusalem.

Profile Settled in Israel in 1952. The daughter of Lippy Lipshitz (qv).

Exhibitions From 1952 she has exhibited in Israel; 1973 Cape Town, solo exhibition.

References SAA; AASA.

LIPSHITZ-WOLPE Ada

Born 1921 Cape Town.

A painter.

Studies University College, London, gaining a Teachers Certificate in Arts and Crafts; Michaelis School of Fine Art; Regent Street Polytechnic, London; Central School of Art, London; Trent Park School of Art and Isleworth Polytechnic, England.

Profile 1962 taught art to children at the Inter-Community School, Zurich. Sister of Lippy Lipshitz (qv).

Exhibitions During the 1940s exhibited in SA.

Reference SAA.

LITABE Makhoro Joseph
Born 1953 Bultfontein, Orange Free State.
A sculptor of figures, still life and abstract pieces. Works in wood.

LITTLEJOHNS John RBA RI
Born 1874 Orchard Hill, Bideford, Devon, England.
Known to have resided in SA during the 1940s and 1950s.
A painter of landscapes, trees, flowers, still life and portraits. Worked in oil, watercolour and pastel. Produced some clay model portraits.
Studies 1890 a pupil teacher at the School of Art, Bideford.
Profile 1919 a member of the Royal Society of British Artists and in 1939 of the Royal Institute of Painters in Water Colours. *c.*1906 lectured for 10 years for the London County Council. His paintings were reproduced by the Medici Society and John Bell & Company, Bond Street, London. 1896 lived in Swansea, 1906 in London, where he shared a studio with H E Compton ARBA; also lived in France. Travelled throughout SA.
Exhibitions Held a joint exhibition with Aubrey Fielding (qv) at the Durban Art Gallery; 1952 solo exhibition in Pretoria and in 1953 in Johannesburg.
Publications by Littlejohns Wrote and illustrated, among other books, the *Art for All* series, *The Technique of Watercolour Painting* and *The Technique of Pastels*.
References DBA; *The Studio*, 1922, London.

LIZAMORE John
Born 1950 Vereeniging, Transvaal.
A painter of landscapes, wildlife, portraits, figures and still life. Works in watercolour, gouache, ink, wash, pencil, charcoal, pastel and conté.
Profile A qualified teacher, attending Indiana University, USA, 1975–76. Numerous book illustrations and a tapestry design. 1970–73 involved in pottery. Since 1970 has lived in SWA/Namibia; visited Europe in 1976, 1978 and 1981–82.
Exhibitions He has participated in several group exhibitions from 1970; 1970 Little Theatre, Pretoria, first of five solo exhibitions held in SA, the USA and in SWA/Namibia.

LLOYD James
Died 1913.
Resided in SA from 1851.
A painter of landscapes and figures. Worked in watercolour and pencil.
Profile In 1853 advertised himself as a drawing and painting master. 1855 made sketches of events of interest in Natal for *The Illustrated London News*.
Represented Killie Campbell Africana Library, University of Natal, Durban.
Reference Pict Art.

LOCK Freida

Born 1902 Cheadle Hume, Cheshire, England.
Died 1962 London, England.
Resided in SA 1920–47.
A painter of still life and interiors, also a number of landscapes and figure studies. Worked in oil.
Studies 1932–34 Heatherley School of Art and Central School of Art, London.
Profile 1938 a founder member of the New Group. 1935–37 lived in Cape Town; 1947–49 lived in Zanzibar, Tanganyika (Tanzania) and in Lamu, Kenya; during the 1950s lived in Portugal.
Exhibitions Participated in group exhibitions from 1938; 1943 Argus Gallery, Cape Town, first solo exhibition; 1948 Tate Gallery, London, SA Art Exhibition.
Represented Durban Art Gallery; Johannesburg Art Gallery; King George VI Art Gallery, Port Elizabeth; SA National Gallery, Cape Town; University of South Africa; University of the Witwatersrand; William Humphreys Art Gallery, Kimberley.
References Collectors' Guide; Art SA; SAA; SAP&S; SSAP; BSAK 1 & 2; 3Cs; AASA; *Artlook* February 1972.

LOCKWOOD Geoffrey Michael

Born 1953 Johannesburg.
A painter of birds. Works in gouache.
Studies 1971–73 privately under Simon Calburn (qv).
Profile Illustrated his own book (see below) and in 1985 co-illustrated, with Kenneth Newman (qv), the fifth edition of *Roberts' Birds of Southern Africa*, John Voelcker Bird Book Fund, Cape Town. 1986 wrote and illustrated an article for *Fauna & Flora* periodical. Lectures on birds.
Exhibitions He has participated in many group exhibitions from 1976 in SA, Zimbabwe and the Seychelles; 1976 Look Out Gallery, Johannesburg, first of three solo exhibitions.
Publication by Lockwood *Garden Birds of Southern Africa*, 1981, Winchester Press, Johannesburg.

LONG Geoffrey Kellet

Born 1916 Durban.
Died 1961 London, England.
Resided in SA until 1954.
An artist producing drawings and the occasional expressionistic landscape in oil.
Studies 1932 Natal Technical College, then at the University of Natal, under Professor O J P Oxley (qv); 1934–36 Central School of Art, London, and at the Martin Bloch School of Contemporary Painting, London.

Profile A pictorial reporter. A theatre designer, working under Nugent Monk. 1938 a member of the New Group. A renowned WWII artist, being appointed an Official War Artist in 1941. Drew a series of drawings for *Life* magazine of the activities of the Italian Partisans. 1946–54 a lecturer at the University of Natal; 1954–61 a part-time lecturer in theatre design at the Central School of Art, London.

Exhibitions Participated in group exhibitions from 1941, and after 1954 in London; joint exhibitions with François Krige (qv); 1945 first of several solo exhibitions.

Represented Johannesburg Art Gallery; SA National Gallery, Cape Town; SA National Museum of Military History, Johannesburg.

Public Commissions 1935 assisted Eleanor Esmonde-White (qv) and Le Roux Smith Le Roux (qv) with murals at SA House, London; 1940 drawings of Iscor Steelworks, Pretoria.

References Collectors' Guide; SAA; SAP&S; BSAK 1 & 2; AASA.

LONG Marjorie

Born 1916 Durban.
Died 1979 Johannesburg.
A painter of portraits.

Studies University of Natal, under Professor O J P Oxley (qv); 1937 awarded the Emma Smith Scholarship and studied at the Westminster School of Art, London and at the Martin Bloch School of Contemporary Painting, London.

Profile A member of the SA Academy. 1942–45 taught at the Pretoria Art Centre; from 1946 lectured on art history at the University of the Witwatersrand. First married Christo Coetzee (qv) and then Professor I D MacCrone, Principal of the University of the Witwatersrand.

References SAA; BSAK; AASA.

LOSSGOTT Kurt

Born 1941 Nikolsburg, East Germany (now Czechoslovakia).
Resided in SA from 1964.
A sculptor of figures and animals. Works in all metals, particularly steel and bronze, as well as polyester, terracotta, bronze amalgam, wax and fabrics.

Studies 1956–71 worked in various metal-related industries in Switzerland, Germany and SA; 1971–72 Johannesburg College of Art.

Profile From 1968 a member of the Artists Market, Johannesburg. A jeweller. 1960–64 lived in Switzerland, visiting Algeria in 1963. Visited Cairo in 1970; Jerusalem, Istanbul and Athens in 1974; Finland, the USSR and Vienna in 1976 and London in 1980.

Exhibitions He has participated in several group exhibitions from 1968 in Johannesburg and Pretoria, and also exhibited in the USA and in Germany.

Awards 1973 Afrox Metalart (Amateur Category); 1981 Sculptor of the Year, West Rand Art Society.

Public Commissions 1972 Flying Owl, Zoo Entrance, Johannesburg; 1974 Peacock Fountain, Oriental Plaza, Johannesburg; 1976 Group of Sable Antelope, Ladysmith Provincial Hospital, Natal.
References BSAK 1; AASA; *Artlook* July 1970.

LOTTERING William (Willi)

Born 1956 Kimberley, Cape Province.
A painter of abstract works, figures and portraits, works in oil, ink, wash and mixed media such as leather, sand and steel.
Studies 1975–78 University of Pretoria, under Professor Nico Roos (qv), gaining a BA(FA); 1979 University of Pretoria, where attained a Higher Diploma in Education.
Profile From 1975 a member of the SAAA. 1980 co-founded The Art Studio, Pretoria, with Deline de Klerk (qv). 1980–81 a sculpture teacher at the Pretoria School of Art, Ballet and Music; 1981–83 a lecturer at the University of Pretoria. 1983–85 a lecturer at The Art Studio; 1986 a part-time lecturer at the Pretoria Technikon. 1987 a part-time lecturer at the University of Pretoria. From 1986 has written documentaries and dramas for radio, and also directed and acted in radio dramas. He has lived in Pretoria from 1975. Visited Europe in 1978–79. Married to Deline de Klerk (qv).
Exhibitions He has participated in numerous group exhibitions from 1978 held in SA; 1979 Ernst de Jong Gallery, Pretoria, first of eight solo exhibitions; 1982 Cape Town Triennial; 1984 Gallery 21, Johannesburg, first of several joint exhibitions with Deline de Klerk (qv).
Represented Pretoria Art Museum; University of the Witwatersrand Theatre.
Public Commissions Eight large paintings for Germiston Municipality; bust of Siegfried Mynhardt for the University of the Witwatersrand.
Happenings staged by Willi Lottering and Deline de Klerk (qv) "Colour Fields", April 1982; "Archaeological Finds", July 1983; "Sound and Expression", February 1984; "Human Ecology", November 1985.
Reference AASA.

LOUBSER Annette

Born 1953 Stutterheim, Eastern Province.
A painter of landscapes, figures, portraits, still life, genre and abstract pictures. Works in oil, acrylic, watercolour, gouache, ink, wash, pencil and charcoal. 1978–81 a series of black and white paintings and drawings; 1982–84 expressionistic paintings and drawings, organic and abstract forms; 1984 hard edge paintings of historical pieces.
Studies 1971–76 Rhodes University, under Professor Brian Bradshaw (qv), gaining a BA(FA) in 1974, an MFA in 1975 and a Higher Diploma in Education in 1976; 1982–83 on a British Council Scholarship, gained a Post-Graduate Diploma in stained glass and mural techniques from the Glasgow School of Art, Scotland, having studied under Jack Knox Cooper and John Clarke.

Profile From 1971 a member of the SAAA; 1972–77 a member of the Grahamstown Group. 1977–79 a lecturer at the Natal Technical College; 1979–82 a senior lecturer at the University of Fort Hare; 1984–85 lectured at the Community Arts Project, Cape Town; from 1985 an art teacher at St Martin's School, Rosettenville, Johannesburg. 1984 opened a stained glass studio in Cape Town for three months; also a photographer. Travelled throughout SA and to Zimbabwe, Botswana, Europe and South America.

Exhibitions She has participated in many group exhibitions from 1972 in SA, Scotland and Ecuador; 1978 Durban, first of three solo exhibitions of which one was held in Glasgow in 1983.

Represented Photographs in the Glasgow School of Art Collection, Scotland.

Public Commissions 1981 mural, Alice Municipality, Ciskei; 1982 mural, Fine Arts Department, University of Fort Hare.

LOURENS Amelia

Born 1965 Odendaalsrus, Orange Free State.

A graphic artist. Her works depict people, self-portraits, portraits, war, politics and her family.

Studies 1984–87 University of the Orange Free State, under Ben Botma (qv), attaining a BA in Plastic Arts.

Profile A pianist and potter. 1965–83 lived in Kroonstad, thereafter in Bloemfontein.

Exhibitions She has participated in several group exhibitions from 1980 in Belgium and SA.

LOUTIT Blythe Dulcie (Mrs Pascoe)

Born 1940 Pietermaritzburg.

Resided in SWA/Namibia from 1974.

A painter and graphic artist of landscapes, seascapes and wildlife. Works in watercolour, oil, ink and in various graphic media.

Studies 1970–71 guidance in botanical illustration from Cythna Letty (qv) and Herrat March (qv). Guidance in oils from Christine Marais (qv) and etching from Sue Williamson (qv).

Profile A member of the WSSA. Mainly a botanical illustrator, illustrating *The Acacia Species of Natal*, by J H Ross, 1972; *Compositae in Natal*, by O M Hilliard, 1977; *Walk Through the Wilderness*, by D Richards and Clive Walker (qv); *Trees & Shrubs of the Etosha National Park*, by C Berry, 1982; *Grasses of Southern Africa*, by L Chippendall and A O Crock, and *Grasses of South West Africa*, by M Muller, 1983. She has also written and illustrated a number of articles for newspapers and periodicals in SWA/Namibia and SA. 1974 lived in Etosha; from 1976 has lived on the Skeleton Coast of SWA/Namibia.

Exhibitions 1976 Windhoek, first of nine solo exhibitions held in SWA/Namibia; she has participated in several group exhibitions from 1978 in SA and SWA/Namibia.

Represented Arts Association SWA/Namibia Collection.

References PS/N; AASA.

LOUW Ulrich

Born 1935 Bloemfontein.

Studies Gained a Higher Diploma from the Johannesburg College of Education and spent one year at Luton School of Technology, England, studying drawing.

Profile 1963–66 worked at Luton School of Technology, England; 1966 taught at the Witwatersrand Technical College; 1970 taught at King Edward VII School, Johannesburg; taught at the University of the Witwatersrand during the 1970s. 1970 visited Europe.

Exhibitions He has participated in group exhibitions from 1966 in SA; 1968 The Gallery, Johannesburg, first solo exhibition.

Awards 1969 Argus Company Travel/Study Grant Award, Art SA Today; 1973 Oppenheimer Memorial Trust Award, Art SA Today, joint winner with Claude van Lingen (qv).

Represented Durban Art Gallery.

References AASA; *Artlook* December 1969 & January 1970.

LOUW Zan

Born 1964 Cape Town.

A wood-block printer of the daily life of people. Works in wood and ink. In 1986 she concentrated on life in the streets of Langa, Cape Town, producing "The Business Centre, Washington Street, Langa", a seven-part series, and "The New Flats, Langa", a three-part series.

Studies 1983–86 Michaelis School of Fine Art, under Professor Neville Dubow, where in 1985 she won the Irma Stern Scholarship, 1986 gained a BA(FA) with distinctions.

Profile Has travelled throughout Southern Africa.

Exhibitions 1986 participated in a group exhibition held at the University of Zululand; 1987 group exhibition, SA National Gallery, Cape Town; 1987 Market Gallery, Johannesburg, joint exhibition with Pohl Huÿzers (qv).

LOUWRENS Martin Stephen (Mat)

Born 1936 Newcastle, Natal.

A self-taught painter of historical buildings, landscapes, seascapes, portraits, wildlife and still life. Works in acrylic, watercolour, pastel and oil.

Profile Until 1978 a commercial artist in Johannesburg. From 1981 a member of the Artists Market and from 1985 of the Brush and Chisel Club. 1983 taught art in Ixopo, Natal. 1984 illustrated *Victorian Pietermaritzburg*, Village Publishers, Springfield, Durban. Lived in Durban until 1955, in Johannesburg until 1980, thereafter in Ixopo. 1976, 1980 and 1982 travelled to the UK and Sweden, having been commissioned by a Johannesburg-based company to paint their SA and overseas establishments.

Exhibitions 1978 Vereeniging, Transvaal, first of eight solo exhibitions.

LOWNDS Gordon Stafford

Born 1896 London, England.

Resided in SA from 1903.

An artist working in oil, watercolour, pastel and charcoal. Depicted landscapes and seascapes.

Studies Mainly self-taught with some advice from W G Wiles (qv).

Profile From 1926 a member of the East London Fine Art Society, of which he was the first Honorary Secretary and Treasurer and subsequently Life Vice-President. Until 1937 lived in East London; 1937–42 and 1950–56 lived in Johannesburg; 1942–49 in Tzaneen, Transvaal; 1956–70 lived in Durban; 1971–74 travelled extensively in SA and Rhodesia (Zimbabwe), thereafter lived in the Eastern Province.

Exhibitions Participated in numerous group and solo exhibitions from 1926.

Represented Ann Bryant Gallery, East London.

LUBISI Eric Magamana

Born 1946 Highlands, Pretoria South.

An artist using African symbols and traditions in his depictions of urban life. Works in oil, charcoal, in various graphic media and on woodpanels. 1970–79 "Winterveld" series.

Studies 1966–69 worked with Andrew Motjuoadi (qv) and Enos Makhubedu; 1970–77 encouraged by Walter Battiss (qv), but mostly self-taught.

Profile 1977 co-founder and organiser of the Studio des Independants, Pretoria, with Roy Ndinisa (qv); 1983 a founder member and Director of the Independant Visual Arts Council, Doornfontein, Johannesburg. 1978–83 cartoon illustrations for *The Eye*, published by the SA Bishops Conference. 1977 designed the stage and backdrop for "Divorce", a play by Oswald Msimanga. 1958–77 lived in Mamelodi, thereafter in Soshanguve, Transvaal.

Exhibitions 1968 joint exhibition with Richard Mbuyomba; 1970 Plaza Centre, Pretoria, first of two solo exhibitions; he has participated in group exhibitions from 1977 in Spain, the UK, Botswana, Australia and SA; 1987 FUBA Gallery, Johannesburg, joint exhibition with Roy Ndinisa (qv).

References *Phafa-Nyika*, edited by Ute Scholz, 1980, University of Pretoria; *Bonanza* September 1979.

LUCAS Thomas John Captain

Resided in SA 1848–62.

A painter of landscapes, tribal people and their genre, military life on the Eastern Cape Frontier and animals. Worked in watercolour, pen and pencil.

Profile A soldier in the Cape Mounted Rifles.

Publications by Lucas Wrote and illustrated *Pen and Pencil Reminiscences of a Campaign in SA*, quarto, 21 colour-tinted lithographs, 1861, Day & Son, London; *Camp Life and Sport in SA*; *Experiences of Kaffir Warfare with the Cape Mounted Rifles*, 1878, Chapman & Hall, London.

References Pict Art; SESA; Pict Afr; BSAK 2; SA Art.

LÜCKHOFF Carl A

Born 1914 Cape Town.
Died 1960 Cape Town.
A self-taught botanical artist.
Profile A professional medical doctor holding posts in Bloemfontein Hospital, Groote Schuur Hospital, Cape Town and as Chief Medical Officer to the SA National Life Assurance Company. 1950–53 wrote several literary works concerned with preservation in Cape Town. Illustrated *The Stapelieae*, by A White and B L Sloane, 1937, Pasadena, California; contributed plates to *Flowering Plants of Africa*, a quarterly publication by the Botanical Research Institute. A Trustee and Chairman of the National Botanic Gardens and a council member of the Botanical Society of SA.
Exhibitions 1945 first of several solo exhibitions held at the Schweikerdt Gallery, Pretoria.
Publications by Lückhoff Wrote and illustrated *Table Mountain, our National Heritage after 300 years*, 1951; *The Stapelieae of Southern Africa*, 1952; *The Malay Quarter and its People*, 1953, with I D du Plessis.
References SAA; DSAB; AASA.

LUDIK Jan

Born 1937 Douglas, Cape Province.
A painter of abstract pictures. Works in oil, gouache and pencil, makes abstract collages with mixed media and found objects. 1966–77 paintings of South End, Port Elizabeth.
Studies 1966–68 University of South Africa, under Professor Walter Battiss (qv).
Profile From 1966 a member of the SAAA. 1966–77 lived in Port Elizabeth, thereafter in Cape Town. 1980 and 1983 visited Europe and the USA.
Exhibitions He has participated in numerous group exhibitions from 1957 in SA; 1968 Port Elizabeth, first of many solo exhibitions.

LUGG Jack

Born 1924 Pretoria.
A painter and graphic artist working in oil, acrylic, watercolour, ink, pencil, charcoal and in various graphic media. A sculptor working in bronze, stone, wood, brick and ceramics.
Studies 1946–48 Natal Technical College, under Cecil Todd (qv) and Mary Stainbank (qv); 1949 on an Emma Smith Scholarship to the Camberwell School of Art, London, under Martin Bloch (1883–1954); 1951 l'Ecole des Beaux Arts, Paris, under Henri Matisse (1869–1954).
Profile From 1953 Head of Department of Art and Design, East London Technical College. A member of the Advisory Board for the Ann Bryant Art Gallery, East London. 1956–76 an External Moderator for National Diploma Examinations; 1965–85 a judge of the International Photography Competition, East London Salons. An illustrator and art critic for *The Daily Dispatch*, East London. From 1953 lived in East London, where his work has been influenced by the Xhosa people.

Exhibitions 1941 Pretoria, joint exhibition with Gabor Tallo and Elza Dziomba (qv); he has participated in numerous group exhibitions from 1950 in SA, the UK, the USA, West Germany, Israel, South America and Canada; 1952 Durban, joint exhibition with Gordon Balfour-Cunningham (qv); 1956 East London, first of 20 solo exhibitions held in SA; 1960 and 1964 Quadrennial Exhibitions; 1978 East London Technical College, Retrospective Exhibition; 1981 Republic Festival Exhibition; 1987 Pretoria Art Museum, Retrospective Exhibition; 1988 SAAA Gallery, Pretoria, exhibition of paintings and sculpture.
Represented Ann Bryant Art Gallery, East London; galleries in Boston, USA and in Israel; Hester Rupert Art Museum, Graaff-Reinet; Pretoria Art Museum.
Public Commissions Brick sculptures, Joan Harrison Municipal Swimming Pool, East London; designed a stained glass window for a chapel in East London; murals for schools in East London and for various companies.
References Art SA; SAA; 20C SA Art; BSAK 1; AASA; *Artlook* June 1969; *Lantern* June 1969; *SA Panorama* March 1976.

LURIE Hannah

Born 1930 Johannesburg.
A sculptor of figures, portrait busts and abstract pieces. Works in bronze, ciment fondu, terracotta, wood and in polyester resins. 1973 a series on "The Tokolosche"; from 1975 a series of cloaked figures; 1984 a series of women in hats; 1982 a series on "Limbo"; from 1982 a series on "The Age of Anxiety".
Studies 1956–61 part-time at the Natal Technical College, under Mary Stainbank (qv); 1962–65 terracotta techniques under Karin Jonzen (*b*.1914) in her studio, London.
Profile A member of the SAAA; 1966 elected to the council of the NSA, 1973–78 President and in 1985 elected Honorary Vice-President. Teaches art privately. A number of architectural designs and decorative doors and panels.
Exhibitions 1969 NSA Gallery, Durban, first of seven solo exhibitions held in Durban, Cape Town, Johannesburg and Pretoria; she has participated in numerous group exhibitions in SA from 1973.
Represented Pietersburg Art Gallery.
Public Commissions 1978 panel and tiles for Holy Trinity Church, Durban; 1978 Madonna for Our Lady of Lourdes Church, Westville; 1980 portrait bust of John Medley-Wood for the National Historic Society, Durban; 1981 portrait bust of James Mark McKen for Durban Municipality; 1984 portrait bust of Professor Elizabeth Sneddon for the Elizabeth Sneddon Theatre, Durban.
References AASA; *Habitat* no 48, 1982.

LUYT Arie Marthinus

Born 1879 Sliedrecht, The Netherlands.
Died 1951 Wassenaar, The Netherlands.
Resided in SA 1921–25 in Stellenbosch.
A painter of landscapes, still life, figures and animals, particularly horses. Worked in oil using subdued colours.

LIPPY LIPSHITZ
Annunciation 1949
Marble 44 cm High
Die Kunskamer

JUDITH MASON ATTWOOD
The Tombs of the Pharaohs of Johannesburg 1986
Oil & Pencil on Objets Trouvés 64 cm High
Tatham Art Gallery, Pietermaritzburg

Studies Hague Akademie vir Beeldende Kunste; 1905–08 Académie Julian, Paris, under Jean-Paul Laurens (1838–1921).

Profile Achieved considerable fame in The Netherlands. A member of the Pulchri Studio, The Hague, an art society in whose exhibitions he participated. Illustrations for *Stories vir die Kinders*, by C L Leipoldt, *Jaarboek vir Afrikaanse Kinders*, by M S Smith and for *Die Huisgenoot* magazine.

Exhibitions Participated in group exhibitions in SA and in 1944 in "Netherlands Art Exhibition of Paintings, Drawings, Etchings and Engravings", SA National Gallery, Cape Town.

Represented Gemeente Museum, The Hague, The Netherlands; Teylers Feund, Haarlem, The Netherlands.

Public Commissions Murals for KLM buildings in London, Amsterdam and The Hague.

References PSA; SAA; DSAB; AMC7; Bénézit; BSAK 1 & 2; AASA.

M

MAARTENS Marjorie

Born 1930 Bedford, Cape Province.
A painter of landscapes, seascapes and still life. Works in oil.
Profile A member of the Artists Market and Art Alfresco. Visited Europe, South America, Mauritius, the Canary Islands and East Africa.
Exhibitions She has participated in group exhibitions in SA.

MABASA Noria

Born 1938 Xigalo, Ramukhumba District, Northern Transvaal.
A self-taught sculptor of figures and portraits. Initially she carved wood figurines which she painted, while her later figurines are made in clay.
Profile A potter. Lives in the Vuwani District of Venda.
Exhibitions 1985 Tributaries, touring SA and West Germany; she has participated in group exhibitions from 1986 in Johannesburg; 1986 Goodman Gallery, Johannesburg, solo exhibition; 1987 Johannesburg Art Gallery, Vita Art Now.
Represented Pretoria Art Museum; SA National Gallery, Cape Town; University of Fort Hare; University of the Western Cape; University of the Witwatersrand.
Reference Echoes of African Art.

MABASO Dumisane Abraham

Born 1955 Soweto, Johannesburg.
A graphic artist producing etchings of figures. Paints abstract pictures, using acrylic.
Studies 1975–78 Rorke's Drift Art Centre, Natal; 1981 Witwatersrand Technikon.
Profile 1978–79 lectured at the Mofolo Art Centre, Soweto. 1980 Head of FUBA, later a part-time teacher there.
Exhibitions He has participated in group exhibitions during the 1980s in Johannesburg and Pretoria and in the USA, France and Sweden; exhibits his work at the Johannesburg Art Foundation; 1982 National Gallery, Gaborone, Botswana, Exhibition of SA Art; 1985 Tributaries, touring SA and West Germany; 1987 Johannesburg Art Foundation, joint exhibition with Bill Ainslie (qv), David Koloane (qv), Tony Nkotsi (qv) and Anthusa Sotiriades (qv).
Award Won a USSALEP award to work in the 1986 New York Triangle Workshop.
Represented Johannesburg Art Gallery.
Reference Echoes of African Art.

MABASO Richard Mzamani

Born 1950 Alexandra, Johannesburg.
A sculptor, working in wood and stone, of abstract expressionistic pieces. A painter in watercolour, oil and acrylic, of landscapes, portraits, still life, figures and abstract paintings. Draws in pencil and charcoal and produces silkscreens.

Studies 1985–87 Funda Centre, Soweto, under Steven Sack (qv) and Michael McIlrath (qv).
Profile The Resident Artist at the Funda Centre.
Exhibitions He has participated in group exhibitions from 1981 in SA; 1985 Tributaries, touring SA and West Germany; 1987 Johannesburg Art Gallery, Vita Art Now; 1987 Market Gallery, Johannesburg, solo exhibition.
Represented SA National Gallery, Cape Town.

MABERLY Charles Thomas Astley
Born 1905 Clifton, Bristol, England.
Died 1972 Duiwelskloof, Northern Transvaal.
Resided in SA from 1924.
A painter of wildlife and figures. Worked in watercolour, ink and pastel.
Profile Illustrated *Memories of a Game Ranger* by Harry Wolhuter, 1950; *The Call of the Bushveld* by A C White, 1954; *Snakes & Snake Catching in Southern Africa* by R Isemonger, as well as books by T V Bulpin, Anna Rothman, Bruce Kinloch and E Cronje Wilmot. He illustrated many wildlife brochures and periodicals and occasionally contributed articles. Colour and sepia birds and animals engraved on Commemoration Ware by Wedgwood & Company, England. 1925–36 annually spent 4–5 months in the Kruger National Park, Eastern Transvaal. Travelled extensively in Southern, Central and Eastern Africa.
Exhibitions Participated in several group exhibitions; 1953 Pieter Wenning Gallery, Johannesburg, first of four solo exhibitions; 1973 Johannesburg Public Library, Commemorative Exhibitions.
Publications by Maberly Wrote and illustrated *Nature Studies of a Boy Naturalist*, 1925, T Fisher Unwin, London; *What Buck is That?*, 1951, White, Bloemfontein; *Animals of Rhodesia*, 1959, Howard Timmins, Cape Town; *Animals of Southern Africa*, 1959, Howard Timmins, Cape Town; *Animals of East Africa*, 1960, Howard Timmins, Cape Town; *The Game Animals of Southern Africa*, 1963, Nelson, Johannesburg; *The World of Big Game*, with Penny Miller, 1969, Books of Africa, Cape Town.
References SAA; SESA; BSAK 1; AASA.

MACADAM Elizabeth Jane (Mrs Benson)
Born 1888 Kimberley, Cape Province.
Died 1976 Johannesburg.
A sculptor of portrait busts and figures. Worked in bronze, wood, brass and plaster. In addition she painted in watercolour and made a number of sepia and pencil drawings.
Studies 1910 Port Elizabeth Art School; 1911–14 Regent Street Polytechnic, London, where she was awarded many medals and a scholarship to the Royal Academy Schools.
Profile A member of the Johannesburg Sketch Club, the Transvaal Art Society and from 1949 of the Brush and Chisel Club. 1922–57 taught modelling at the Witwatersrand Technical College.

Exhibitions Participated in group exhibitions in England and SA; 1920 exhibited at the Royal Academy, London, and from 1921 annually at the SA Academy; 1943 Gainsborough Gallery, Johannesburg, first of over nine solo exhibitions.

Public Commissions Reverse side of the Coronation Medal for the Pretoria Mint; 1924 Air Force Eagle for the memorial to Captain Beauchamp-Proctor VC in Mafeking (Mafikeng, Bophuthatswana)—a replica of this stands on the Thames Embankment, London.

References SAA; AMC7; DBA (under Benson); BSAK 1 & 2; AASA; *SA Art News* 18 May 1961.

MACALA Benjamin Mzimkulu (Ben)

Born 1938 Bloemfontein.

Both a painter and sculptor of figures, urban life and abstract pieces. Works in oil, pencil, pastel, conté, charcoal, bronze, stone and ciment fondu.

Studies Under Ephraim Ngatane (qv); one year at the Jubilee Art Centre, Johannesburg, under Sydney Kumalo (qv) and Cecil Skotnes (qv).

Profile Taught art at the YWCA. 1980 went to Greece to represent South African artists.

Exhibitions He has exhibited throughout SA and in West Germany, Greece, the USA, Switzerland, Italy and the UK; 1965 Piccadilly Gallery, London, African Painters and Sculptors from Johannesburg; 1979 Contemporary African Art in SA, touring; 1981 Standard Bank, Soweto, Black Art Today Exhibition.

Represented King George VI Art Gallery, Port Elizabeth; SA National Gallery, Cape Town; University of Bophuthatswana; University of Fort Hare.

References SAP&S; SAP&D; SESA; BSAK 1 & 2; SA Art; 3Cs; AASA; Echoes of African Art; *Artlook* November 1967; *SA Panorama* July 1982.

MACDONALD Longford FIAL

Born 1905 County Durham, England.

Died 1957.

Resided in SA from *c.*1922.

A painter, etcher and graphic artist, working in oil, watercolour and in various graphic media. His subjects included landscapes, marine studies, still life and figures.

Studies Apprenticed to a stained glass expert, but mainly self-taught.

Profile A Life Fellow of the International Institute of Arts and Letters. Lived in Newcastle in the UK and in Durban.

Exhibitions Participated in group exhibitions from 1933 in SA; 1942 Johannesburg, first of several solo exhibitions.

Represented Ann Bryant Gallery, East London; Durban Art Gallery.

Reference AASA.

MACE Edward Clark Churchill

Born 1863 Leicestershire, England.
Died 1928 Cape Town.
Resided in SA from 1901.
A painter of landscapes and seascapes. Worked in watercolour and thin oil.
Studies In Australia under Charles Rolando (qv).
Profile A founder member of the SA Society of Artists and its secretary 1907–15.
Travelled extensively.
Exhibitions Participated in group exhibitions held in SA.
References SAA; SADNB; SSAP; BSAK 1 & 2; AASA; *ANN* September 1963.

MACGREGOR David F

Born 1912 Scotland.
Died 1983 Port Elizabeth.
A painter and sculptor of landscapes, figures and wildlife.
Studies Pratt Institute, New York.
Profile A lecturer in art and a former Head of the Sculpture Department at the
Witwatersrand Technical College. An illustrator, political and sports cartoonist,
art director and writer of children's stories. Prior to SA lived in Canada; 1971–83
lived in Port Elizabeth.
Exhibitions Participated in group exhibitions during the 1930s in Johannesburg.
Public Commissions 1964 Miners Memorial, Civic Centre, Braamfontein,
Johannesburg; 1966 Captain Carl von Brandis, Jeppe Street, Johannesburg;
1973 Confucius, Chinese High School, Port Elizabeth; Prospector, Rosettenville,
Johannesburg.
References BSAK 2; SA Art; SASSK; *SA Arts Calendar* May 1983.

MACHANIK Gail

Born 1944 UK.
An artist working in oil, ink, pencil, etching and lithography. Depicts land-
scapes, still life, figures and domestic animals.
Studies In Johannesburg, at the Michaelis School of Fine Art and at the
Accademia di Belle Arti, Perugia, Italy.
Profile A lecturer at the Centre for Continuing Education, University of the
Witwatersrand and at the Technical College in Germiston. Lived in Johannes-
burg and is presently living in Connecticut, USA.
Exhibitions She has participated in group exhibitions and held solo exhibitions
in SA and overseas; 1981 Republic Festival Exhibition.

MACINTOSH Robert James Leonard (Rob)

Born 1949 Johannesburg.
A self-taught painter of wildlife, landscapes, seascapes, portraits and still life.
Works in pastel, oil and gouache.

Profile 1979–80 an art director for marketing companies in Johannesburg. From 1964 a guitarist and singer with various groups. 1981 visited Chobe, Botswana; 1982 Etosha, SWA/Namibia; 1983 the USA; 1983 Savuti, Botswana; 1984 revisited SWA/Namibia and travelled to many SA game reserves.

Exhibitions He has participated in several group exhibitions from 1983 in SA; 1982 Port Shepstone, first of 10 solo exhibitions held in SA, the USA and Swaziland.

MACIVOR Monica (Mrs Freyburg)

Born 1881 Bushire, Persia (Iran).
Died 1939 London, England.
Resided in SA 1931–37.

A painter of landscapes, seascapes, flowers, genre and figures. Worked in oil, watercolour and pastel. Made a number of miniatures and presentation portraits.

Studies Académie Julian, Paris.

Profile 1918 a member of the SA Society of Artists. During the 1930s taught at the Witwatersrand Technical College. Married to the British artist Frank Freyburg.

Exhibitions Participated in group exhibitions from 1903 in Paris, London and SA; 1945 Gainsborough Gallery, Johannesburg, Memorial Exhibition.

Represented Johannesburg Art Gallery; University of Natal.

References *Who's Who in Art*, 1934; AMC4; DBA; BSAK 1 (under McIver) & 2; AASA.

MACKENNY Virginia Siobhan

Born 1959 London, England.
Resided in SA from 1972.

A painter of abstracted landscapes. Works in oil, acrylic and charcoal.

Studies 1977–80 University of Natal, under Professor Murray Schoonraad, Dick Leigh (qv), Jinny Heath (qv), Malcolm Christian (qv) and Mike Taylor, gaining a BA(FA).

Profile From 1984 a council member of the NSA; from 1985 a member of the SAAAH. In 1987 joined D'ARTS. 1980 a tutor in the history of art at the University of Natal; from 1984 a lecturer in painting, drawing and the history of art at the Natal Technikon.

Exhibitions She has participated in many group exhibitions from 1979 in SA; 1984 Café Geneve Gallery, Durban, solo exhibition; 1986 NSA Gallery, Durban, joint exhibition with Bronwen Findlay (qv) and Jeremy Wafer.

Represented Natal Technikon; Tatham Art Gallery, Pietermaritzburg.

MACLAGAN Tina

Born 1928 London, England.
Resided in SA from 1950.

A painter of portraits, still life, genre, mythology and abstract pictures. Works in oil.

Studies 1980–84 Michael Pettit School of Art, Cape Town, under Michael Pettit (qv).
Profile From 1985 a member of the SAAA. 1948–78 a professional medical photographer.
Exhibitions She has participated in several group exhibitions from 1980 in Cape Town.

MADGE Donald James (Don)

Born 1920 Stutterheim, Cape Province.
A painter and graphic artist of landscapes, seascapes, portraits and still life. Works in pastel, oil, watercolour, ink, pencil, charcoal and in various graphic media, particularly monotypes.
Studies 1937–40 Witwatersrand Technical College, under James Gardner (qv).
Profile 1947–60 lived in Pretoria; from 1960 in Cape Town. Has travelled extensively throughout SA. Father of James Madge (qv).
Exhibitions He has participated in numerous group exhibitions in SA and one in Australia; 1947 Kimberley, first of 24 solo exhibitions held in SA and one touring England and Wales; 1959 Durban Art Gallery, joint exhibition with Errol Boyley (qv) and W H Coetzer (qv); 1968 Durban Art Gallery, solo exhibition.
Represented Durban Art Gallery; Pretoria Art Museum; Queenstown Art Gallery; William Humphreys Art Gallery, Kimberley.
References BSAK 1 & 2; AASA.

MADGE James

Born 1963 Cape Town.
A painter and graphic artist of landscapes, seascapes, still life, figures and abstract pictures. Works in oil, acrylic, watercolour, gouache, ink, wash, pencil, charcoal and in various graphic media.
Studies 1980–83 Ruth Prowse School of Art, Cape Town, under Erik Laubscher (qv); tuition from his father, Don Madge (qv).
Profile A trained musician. Has travelled extensively in SA.
Exhibitions He has participated in group exhibitions in SA from 1984.

MADIBA Ezekiel (Boycie)

Born 1948 Pretoria.
A self-taught graphic artist producing woodcuts and silkscreens. He depicts figures, township scenes and religious themes.
Profile Lives in Mabopane, near Pretoria.
Exhibitions He has participated in group exhibitions at various embassies.
Represented University of Fort Hare.
Reference *Phafa-Nyika*, edited by Ute Scholz, 1980, University of Pretoria.

MADISIA Joseph Frank Herman
Born 1954 Lüderitz, SWA/Namibia.
A painter and graphic artist of portraits, still life, abstracts and pictures of social comment. Works in oil, watercolour, pastel, various graphic media and oil monotypes.
Studies A self-taught artist until 1982 when he attended a two-week watercolour course under Professor Edda Mally from Vienna, Austria; 1983–85 Windhoek Academy, graphic techniques under Demetrios Spirou (qv) and drawing under Marina Aguiar (qv).
Profile From 1983 a member of the Arts Association SWA/Namibia. 1983–85 a photographer and commercial artist for Namib Advertising and Public Relations; 1985–86 a commercial artist for Pronam Advertising; from 1986 a media technologist at Windhoek Academy. 1986 pen and ink drawings for *Metje & Ziegler Chronik* by Klaus J Becker.
Exhibitions He has participated in several group exhibitions from 1983 in SWA/Namibia; 1982 AMA Gallery, Windhoek, first of two solo exhibitions.
Awards 1983 Merit Award, STANSWA Biennale; 1985 Best Graphic, STANSWA Biennale.
Represented Africana Museum, Johannesburg; Arts Association SWA/Namibia Collection.
Public Commission 1984 "Namib Flight", West Air, Windhoek.

MAFA Pieter
Born 1938 Pietersburg, Northern Transvaal.
A self-taught painter and sculptor of figures. Works in oil and wood.
Exhibitions He has participated in group exhibitions from 1986 in Pretoria, Paris and Johannesburg; 1986 FUBA Gallery, Johannesburg, first of two solo exhibitions.
Award 1987 a prize winner in a FUBA competition.

MAGADLEDLA Fikile
Born 1952 Newclare, Johannesburg.
A self-taught artist of landscapes, figures and flowers. Works in acrylic, pencil and mixed media. A sculptor, whose early works were in terracotta and gas concrete, and later works in metal.
Profile From 1973 a full-time artist.
Exhibitions From 1973 he has participated in many group exhibitions held in SA; 1979 Goodman Gallery, Johannesburg, solo exhibition; 1981 Standard Bank, Soweto, Black Art Today Exhibition.
Represented SA National Gallery, Cape Town; University of Fort Hare.
References AASA; Echoes of African Art; *SA Panorama* July 1982.

MAGID Annette

Born 1950.

A painter and graphic artist. Works in oil, watercolour, etching and drypoint. 1975 drawing and watercolour series entitled "Paradise Lost"; a series of 12 drawings entitled "Prometheus" and a series entitled "Rose to Paper Bag".

Studies 1974 etching at Salzburg Academy, Austria, under Professor Otto Eglau. 1974 gained the Freda Lawenski Scholarship to study for an MA(FA).

Exhibitions She has participated in group exhibitions in SA; 1975 Gallery 21, Johannesburg, solo exhibition.

Reference *Habitat* no 15, 1975.

MAGNES David

Born 1963 SA.

A self-taught painter of equestrian studies, wildlife, landscapes, seascapes and children's portraits. Works in pastel.

Profile Designed the logo for the Winner's Enclosure, Turffontein Race Course and several race cards.

Exhibitions 1983 Turffontein Race Course, Johannesburg, first of five solo exhibitions.

MAGNI CASTELLANETA Stella

Born Bari, Italy.

Resided in SA from 1953.

A sculptor of figures in bronze. Produces mixed media drawings, etchings, monotypes and silkscreens. A designer and maker of ethnic jewellery.

Studies 1933 Accademia di Belle Arti, Brera, Italy, under Aldo Carpi (1886–1973) and Marino Marini (*b*.1901), attaining a Diploma; 1935–40 architecture at the Politecnico di Milano, Italy; 1952 ceramics in Professor Gronchi's studio in Florence, Italy.

Profile Has travelled extensively throughout the world.

Exhibitions She has held many solo exhibitions in SA, Italy and France.

References *Artlook* July 1969, September 1970 & March 1971.

MAHLANGU Judas

Born 1951 Brakpan, Transvaal.

A graphic artist of coloured etchings. Depicts landscapes, urban scenes, figures and religious themes.

Studies 1973–75 Rorke's Drift Art Centre; also worked with Bill Ainslie (qv) in Johannesburg for several years.

Profile A member of the Soweto Art Society and of the SAAA. Teaches in his own studio in KwaThema, East Rand, also in Soweto.

Exhibitions He has participated in numerous group exhibitions from 1973 in SA, the USA, West Germany and the UK; 1979 Contemporary African Art in SA, touring; 1979 Lidchi Gallery, Johannesburg, solo exhibition; 1981 Standard Bank, Soweto, Black Art Today Exhibition; 1985 Tributaries, touring SA and West Germany.
Represented University of Fort Hare.
References *Phafa-Nyika*, edited by Ute Scholz, 1980, University of Pretoria; AASA.

MAHLANGU Speelman

Born 1958 Katlehong, Transvaal.
A sculptor of figures. Works in clay, bronze and wood. A painter of figures and genre, working in oil, acrylic, ink, pencil, charcoal and mixed media.
Studies 1977–80 Katlehong Art Centre, under Rose Shakanovsky and Stanley Nkosi (qv).
Profile A member of the Katlehong Art Centre. 1977–81 a part-time teacher, from 1986 a full-time teacher at the Katlehong Art Centre. 1987 a graphic and sculpture teacher at the Ezebeleni Cripple Care Centre, Tokoza, East Rand. A designer of tapestries woven at the Katlehong Art Centre, also creates pots and makes relief murals in clay.
Exhibitions He has participated in numerous group exhibitions from 1977 in SA, West Germany and Israel; 1985 Tributaries, touring SA and West Germany.
Award 1980 First Prize, New Signatures, SAAA, Pretoria.
Represented Frankfurt Ethnology Museum, West Germany; University of Zululand.
Reference *SA Panorama* June 1985.

MAIL Cally

Born 1948 Transvaal.
A painter of wildlife, particularly birds, botanical studies and still life. Works in watercolour, gouache, ink and pencil.
Studies 1966–67 Rhodes University; 1968–69 Natal Technical College, under Bailey-Searle, where gained a Commercial Art Diploma.
Profile Has lived in the Eastern Transvaal from 1974.
Exhibitions She has held several solo exhibitions in the Eastern Transvaal from 1974 and two in Swaziland; participated in group exhibitions from 1982.
References BSAK 2; *Garden & Home* August 1978; *Rooi Rose* 20 October 1982.

MAINGANYE Avishoni

Born 1950 Phiphidi, Venda.
A painter and graphic artist of figures and surreal landscapes, with social-realistic themes and religious symbols. Works in oil and linocut. Makes sculptures in wood, bone and wire.

Studies Two years at the Rorke's Drift Art Centre. Presently studying for a BA(FA) through the University of South Africa.

Profile Lives in Venda, and in Soweto during semester.

Exhibitions He has participated in group exhibitions from 1982; 1985 Tributaries, touring SA and West Germany; 1986 Alliance Française, Pretoria, Historical Perspective of Black Art in SA Exhibition; 1988 FUBA Gallery, Johannesburg, solo exhibition.

Reference Echoes of African Art.

MAKHANYA Romeo Zamani

Born 1959 Durban.

A painter of landscapes and figures. Works in oil.

Studies 1979–84 University of Fort Hare, under Professor Michael Hallier (qv), gaining a BA(FA) (Hons); 1985 University of Fort Hare, under R Hoskyn.

Profile From 1986 a lecturer at the Ntuzuma College of Education, KwaMashu, Natal. In 1985 he illustrated a poetry collection by Richard Sibaya Nzimande and painted a composite representation of Fort Hare for the University brochure.

Exhibitions He has participated in several group exhibitions from 1980 held in the Eastern Cape.

Awards 1983 and 1984 awarded First Prize, Festival of African Art, University of Zululand; 1985 Second Prize, Rolfes Impressions '85, Johannesburg Art Gallery.

Represented University of Fort Hare.

MAKHATHINI Derrick Vusimuzi

Born 1962 Durban.

A painter of portraits, genre and figures. Works in oil, acrylic, watercolour, ink, wash, pencil and charcoal. Numerous cartoons and illustrations.

Profile 1987 a member of the Community Arts Workshop, Durban.

MAKHUBELA Billy

Born 1947 Duiwelskloof, Northern Transvaal.

A self-taught wire sculptor of vehicles, animals and machines.

Profile Works as a restorer of antique furniture. Since 1969 he has lived in Johannesburg.

Exhibitions He has participated in group exhibitions in SA; 1985 Valparaiso Bienale, Chile.

Reference De Kat September 1985.

MAKOANYANE Samuel

Born 1905 Near Parys, Orange Free State.

Died 1944 Lesotho.

A self-taught sculptor of animals, especially frogs and crocodiles, his later works being mainly of figures. His figures include those of children and historical persons, particularly Moshesh and Makoanyane. Worked in clay and wood, frequently using feathers.

Profile He lived in Koalabata, near Maseru, Lesotho.
Exhibitions Participated in group exhibitions from 1935 in the USA, France and SA.
Represented University of Fort Hare; William Fehr Collection, Cape Town.
Reference C C Damant, *Samuel Makoanyane*, 1951, Morija Book Depot, Lesotho.

MAKWALA Mohale Samson

Born 1942 Ofcolaco District, Eastern Transvaal.
A self-taught sculptor of figures, portraits, still life, wildlife and abstract pieces. Works in wood and stone.
Exhibitions He has participated in several group exhibitions from 1978.

MALAN Solomon Caeser

Born 1812 Merindol, France.
Died 1894 (buried in Bournemouth, England).
Resided in SA May–September 1839.
A painter of landscapes and figures. Worked in watercolour, sepia, ink and pencil.
Studies A number of lessons from his father but mainly self-taught.
Profile Illustrator of Austen Henry Layard's work *Nineveh & Babylon*, 1853, John Murray, London. An ecclesiastic, who travelled and worked in many parts of the world. 1834–37 lived in Oxford, England; 1837 in India, 1839 travelled in the Cape, returning to England via Arabia and Malta; 1841–42 visited the Near East and the Holy Land; from 1842 lived in England, with tours of Europe. In 1971 reproductions of 31 of his watercolours were published by the University of Stellenbosch.
Exhibition 1979 University of Stellenbosch, solo exhibition of his work.
Represented British Museum, London, England; University of Stellenbosch.
Publications by Malan Published books of a theological, historical and scientific nature, and in 1856 *Aphorisms on Drawing*, dedicated to James Duffield Harding, in 10 volumes. In the first volume entitled *India*, 60 of the 175 illustrations are of the Cape.
References B Booyens & O Schröder, *Solomon Caeser Malan, Aquarelles*, 1970, University of Stellenbosch, Human & Rousseau, Cape Town; BSAK 1; 3Cs; *Personality* 17 February 1966; *The Connoisseur* October 1968.

MALAN Wendy

Born 1945 Benoni, Transvaal.
A painter and graphic artist of landscapes, portraits and still life. Works in acrylic and in various graphic media.
Studies In 1968 gained an MFA from Rhodes University, having studied under Professor Brian Bradshaw (qv).

Profile During the 1960s a member of the Grahamstown Group. A set designer for films by Jans Rautenbach and Ashley Lazarus.

Exhibitions She has participated in numerous group exhibitions from 1964 in SA, Monaco, Austria, Israel, Australia, the Republic of China and West Germany; 1981 Republic Festival Exhibition; 1983 SAAA Gallery, Pretoria, first of four solo exhibitions; 1984 SAAA Gallery, Pretoria, joint exhibition with Gordon Vorster (qv), Dale Elliot (qv) and Ulrich Schwanecke (qv); 1985 SAAA Gallery, Pretoria, joint exhibition with Deline de Klerk (qv) and Christa Botha (qv).

Award 1969 New Signatures Painting Award.

References BSAK 1; AASA; *Artlook* September 1973.

MALEMANE Sello Lucas

Born 1949 Nelspruit, Eastern Transvaal.

A self-taught painter and graphic artist of landscapes, genre, figures, domestic animals, scenes from tribal life and of urban scenes. Works in oil, acrylic, watercolour, pastel and coloured pencil, also produces woodcuts.

Profile From 1974 has worked as a messenger in the Fine Arts Department of the University of South Africa. Lives in Mabopane, near Pretoria.

Exhibitions He has participated in group exhibitions from 1974 in Pretoria; 1979 Hoffer Gallery, Pretoria, first of two solo exhibitions.

Represented University of Pretoria; University of South Africa; William Humphreys Art Gallery, Kimberley.

Reference *Phafa-Nyika*, edited by Ute Scholz, 1980, University of Pretoria.

MALES June Erica

Born 1926 Bloemfontein.

A sculptor of figures and abstract pieces. Works in bronze, stone and wood.

Studies 1950–52 Michaelis School of Fine Art, under Maurice van Essche (qv) and Lippy Lipshitz (qv).

Profile She has travelled extensively throughout Africa and in Europe. Lives in the Cape.

Exhibitions She has participated in several group exhibitions in Johannesburg; 1976 SAAA Gallery, Johannesburg, first of three solo exhibitions, one of which was held in London in 1980.

Reference *Gallery* Autumn 1987.

MALOPE Solomon Lefika (Solly)

Born 1953 Pretoria.

An artist working in pastel, coloured pencils and charcoal of figures, portraits and abstract works.

Studies 1974 Ndaleni Educational Training School, under Craig Lancaster and Lorna Pearson; 1982–83 Lorenzo de Medici School, Florence, Italy, under Marco Paoletti. Gained two diplomas in art.

Profile From 1978 a member of the SAAA. 1981 taught art, drama and poetry at Atteridgeville Welfare Centre, Pretoria.

Exhibitions He has participated in numerous group exhibitions from 1979 in SA, West Germany and Italy; 1979 SAAA Gallery, Pretoria, first of several solo exhibitions in SA, the USA, Italy and Botswana.

Reference *Phafa-Nyika*, edited by Ute Scholz, 1980, University of Pretoria.

MALUMISE Phillip Lempa

Born 1958 Alexandra, Johannesburg.

A painter, sculptor and graphic artist of landscapes, figures, portraits, genre and abstracts. Works in acrylic, watercolour, various graphic media, metal, wood and ciment fondu.

Studies 1979–81 Rorke's Drift Art Centre, under Carl Bethke, Keith van Winkel and Jay Johnson.

Profile 1977 a member of the Creative Youth Association, affiliated to the Funda Centre; 1979 a founder member of Artimo; 1982–84 an art tutor at FUBA; from 1985 an art tutor at The Open School, Johannesburg. 1983 visited Swaziland.

Exhibitions He has participated in many group exhibitions from 1979 in SA, West Germany, Sweden, Denmark and the UK.

Represented University of Fort Hare; University of Zululand.

Reference Echoes of African Art.

MAMABOLO Pulane Jeannette (née Motaung)

Born 1952 Witsieshoek, QwaQwa.

A painter, graphic artist and sculptor of landscapes, portraits, still life, genre, figures, wildlife and abstracts. Works in oil, acrylic, watercolour, gouache, ink, pencil, charcoal, stone, wood, papier mache and in various graphic media.

Studies 1977 Ndaleni Educational Training School, under Lorna Pearson and Craig Lancaster, gaining an Art Diploma; 1978–82 University of Fort Hare, under Professor Michael Hallier (qv), attaining a BA(FA).

Profile From 1969 she has taught at several schools and colleges of education in QwaQwa. 1984–85 visited London, Paris, Rome, Basle, Brussels, Amsterdam, Luxembourg, Rotterdam and Haarlem. Wife of Thato Mamabolo (qv).

Exhibitions She has participated in several group exhibitions from 1977 in SA and one in Rome.

Represented University of Fort Hare.

MAMABOLO Thato Johannes

Born 1951 Delmas, Transvaal.

A sculptor of wildlife and abstract pieces, works in ciment fondu, wood and terracotta. A graphic artist.

Studies 1974 Ndaleni College of Education, under Lorna Pearson, gaining a Special Art Teachers Diploma; 1978–80 University of Fort Hare, under Professor Michael Hallier (qv), attaining a BA(FA); 1983–87 Birmingham Polytechnic, England, under Mrs Lea Elliot, where gained a Postgraduate Degree in Art Education and an MA(Art Education).
Profile 1975 an Assistant Teacher at the Katlehong Art Centre, Transvaal; 1981 taught in Tembisa, Kempton Park, Transvaal; 1981–85 taught at colleges of education in QwaQwa. 1983 visited Paris; 1984–85 visited Paris, Rome, Florence, Basle, Brussels and Amsterdam. Husband of Pulane Mamabolo (qv).
Exhibitions He has participated in several group exhibitions from 1974.
Represented University of Fort Hare.

MANAKA Faith Makgomo

Born 1952 Springs, Transvaal.
Both a painter and sculptor of landscapes and abstract works.
Studies 1978 Rorke's Drift Art Centre.
Profile A weaver, silkscreen printer and fashion designer. 1980 taught weaving at The Open School, Johannesburg. Has visited Zimbabwe.
Exhibitions She has participated in group exhibitions from 1979.

MANAKA Matsemela

Born 1956 Alexandra, Johannesburg.
A self-taught painter and graphic artist of portraits and genre. Works in oil, acrylic, pencil, charcoal, conté and in various graphic media, particularly lino and woodcuts.
Profile From 1981 a member of Artimo. 1984–86 Arts Administration Co-ordinator at the Funda Centre, Soweto; 1977–78 a school teacher; 1987 a drama teacher at the Funda Centre; 1986–87 Project Director of the Soyikwa Theatre Group. From 1977 a playwright, theatre director, designer and painter of sets, in which sphere he has had much acclaim. 1979–82 Co-ordinating Editor of *Staffrider* periodical, in which he published poems and essays. A member of the Market Gallery Advisory Board. He has visited the USA, France, The Netherlands, the UK, West Germany, Denmark, Zimbabwe, Senegal, Botswana and Lesotho.
Exhibitions 1978 Donaldson Orlando Community Centre, Soweto, first of four solo exhibitions; he has participated in many group exhibitions from 1980 in SA, Swaziland, West Germany, Sweden, Denmark, Scotland and England.
Plays by Manaka 1977 "The Horn", 1978 "Egoli—City of Gold", 1979 "Imbumba", 1980 "Blues Africa", 1981 "Vuka", 1982 "Pula", 1984 "Children of Asazi", 1986 "Domba", 1987 "Toro—The African Dream".
Publication by Manaka *Echoes of African Art*, 1987, Skotaville Publishers, Johannesburg.

MANGANYI Chabani Cyril

Born 1959 Mofolo, Soweto.

A painter and graphic artist of landscapes, portraits, still life, figures and abstract pictures. Works in oil, acrylic, watercolour, gouache, ink, wash, pencil, charcoal, gel, silkscreen, woodblock and etching. A sculptor of portraits, figures and abstract pieces. Works in wood, clay and plaster.

Studies Mofolo Art School, under Dan Rakgoathe (qv) and Cyril Kumalo (qv); 1979–81 Rorke's Drift Art Centre, under Carl Bethke, Keith van Winkel and Jay Johnson, where gained a Fine Arts Diploma; 1987 attended the Thupelo Art Workshop, Johannesburg.

Profile From 1982 Head of Fine Art, Mofolo Art School. 1984 illustrated a brochure for Soweto Libraries. 1986 a founder of Art Appreciation, Soweto. 1986 a council member of the Johannesburg Art Foundation. From 1977 a member of the Medupi Writers Association and from 1978 of the Mihloti Black Theatre. 1977–79 part of the Varikweru music group. 1980 sub-editor of *Jabula Journal*, Soweto. 1977–79 travelled to Lesotho, Botswana and Swaziland. 1987 moved to Pimville, Soweto.

Exhibitions He has participated in several group exhibitions from 1978.

Represented University of Zululand.

MANYONI Bhekisani

Born 1945 Greytown, Natal.

A graphic artist producing linocuts and woodcuts depicting figures and animals in their natural setting. Sculpts fantastical animals in clay.

Studies Three years at the Rorke's Drift Art Centre.

Profile After graduating from the Rorke's Drift Art Centre he remained there to teach children. He then moved to Swaziland for five years, where he co-founded an art training school. From *c.*1976 he has been an art supervisor at the Katlehong Art Centre, Transvaal. 1978 taught at the Cripple Care Centre in Newcastle, Natal.

Exhibitions He has participated in group exhibitions throughout SA and in Kenya and Swaziland; 1985 Tributaries, touring SA and West Germany.

References Frankfurt Ethnology Museum, West Germany; SA National Gallery, Cape Town; University of Fort Hare; University of South Africa; University of the Witwatersrand.

MAPHIRI Solomon

Born 1942 Johannesburg.

A sculptor of figures. Works in clay, bronze, stone and wood. He has also produced a number of drawings. 1972–73 worked in enamel.

Exhibitions He has participated in several group exhibitions in SA and London; 1965 Piccadilly Gallery, London, African Painters and Sculptors from Johannesburg; 1969 Gallery 101, Johannesburg, first of two solo exhibitions; 1979 Contemporary African Art in SA, touring; 1981 Standard Bank, Soweto, Black Art Today Exhibition.

Represented Pretoria Art Museum; University of Fort Hare.

References BSAK 1; AASA; *Bantu* June 1975; *SA Panorama* July 1982.

LEONARD MATSOSO
The King and His Indunas 1981
Crayon & Pastel on Paper 169 × 81,5 cm
Pretoria Art Museum

AZARIA MBATHA
Reconciliation 1968
Linocut 27 × 31 cm

JOHN MEYER
The Road to Nieu Bethesda 1981
Acrylic on Canvas 57 × 87 cm
H Kollrepp

BILLY MOLOKENG
Beauty of Africa 1988
Mixed Media on Paper 135 × 98 cm
The Everard Read Gallery

MAQHUBELA Louis Khehla

Born 1939 Durban.

A painter of symbolic figures, religious works, animals, birds and urban scenes. Works in oil, watercolour, conté, wash and mixed media. Creates monotypes and collages.

Studies Part-time at the Polly Street Art Centre, Johannesburg, under Cecil Skotnes (qv).

Profile Inspired by the poetry of Donne, Keats and Pope. 1967 studied in the European galleries and museums. 1973 lived and worked in Spain. 1978 settled in London.

Exhibitions He has participated in group exhibitions from 1959 in SA and London; 1962 Adler Fielding Gallery, Johannesburg, joint exhibition with Gerard Sekoto (qv) and Lucas Sithole (qv); 1965 Piccadilly Gallery, London, African Painters and Sculptors from Johannesburg; 1967 Adler Fielding Gallery, Johannesburg, first of several solo exhibitions; 1971 Lidchi Gallery, Johannesburg, joint exhibition with Sydney Kumalo (qv) and Geoffrey Armstrong (qv); 1974 Goodman Gallery, Johannesburg, joint exhibition with Leonard Matsoso (qv) and Sydney Kumalo (qv); 1979 Contemporary African Art in SA, touring; 1981 Standard Bank, Soweto, Black Art Today Exhibition.

Awards 1966 First Prize, Artists of Fame and Promise; 1969 Cambridge Shirt Award, Art SA Today.

Represented Africana Museum, Johannesburg; Johannesburg Art Gallery; Sandton Municipal Collection; SA National Gallery, Cape Town; University of Fort Hare; University of the Witwatersrand.

References Art SA; SAA; SESA; BSAK 1 & 2 (under Maghubela and Maqhubela); SA Art; Oxford Companion to 20C Art (under SA); 3Cs; AASA; Echoes of African Art; *SA Art News* 6 July 1961; *Artlook* March 1967, November 1968 & January 1970; *SA Panorama* July 1982.

MARAIS Amanda

Born 1958 Johannesburg.

A painter and graphic artist of landscapes, wildlife and abstract pictures. Works in oil, pencil and in various graphic media. A creator of collages.

Studies 1977–80 University of Pretoria, under Professor Nico Roos (qv), gaining a BA(FA).

Exhibitions She has participated in several group exhibitions from 1980; 1983 University of Pretoria, solo exhibition; 1986 Gallery 21, Johannesburg, joint exhibition with Guy du Toit (qv) and Erna Bodenstein-Ferreira (qv).

MARAIS (Anna) Christine

Born 1935 Bloemfontein.

A painter of landscapes, seascapes, still life, figures and wildlife. Works in oil, watercolour, gouache, ink and wash. Paints her own personal interpretation of the Namib Desert. 1979–86 a series on German Colonial Architecture; from 1986 a series on Namib flora.

Studies 1954–57 University of the Witwatersrand, under Charles Argent (qv), Joyce Leonard (qv), Cecily Sash (qv), Professor Heather Martienssen (1915–79) and Erica Berry (qv), gaining a BA(FA).

Profile A member of the SAAA from 1960 and of the Arts Association SWA/Namibia from 1970; 1964 a co-founder of the Rustenburg Art Society; 1976 a member of the Swakopmund Arts Association. 1958 taught at Jeppe Girls High School, Johannesburg. From 1965 has taught both children and adults in her own studio. In 1973 she created a mosaic for the Centaurn High School, Windhoek. An enamellist and from 1976 a designer of tapestries. 1963–70 lived in Rustenburg, Transvaal; 1970–76 in Windhoek; from 1976 in Swakopmund, SWA/Namibia. 1981 visited the Greek islands; 1983 Italy and in 1985 Spain.

Exhibitions She has participated in numerous group exhibitions from *c.*1964 in SA and SWA/Namibia; 1968 SAAA Gallery, Pretoria, first of 22 solo exhibitions held in SA and SWA/Namibia.

Represented Arts Association SWA/Namibia Collection; Rand Afrikaans University.

Publications by Marais A trilogy on German colonial architecture: *Swakopmund Our Heritage* in 1979, *Lüderitz Our Heritage* in 1981 and *Windhoek Our Heritage* in 1986; co-author of *Namib Flora*, 1986; all books published by Gamsberg, Windhoek.

Reference SA *Garden & Home* December 1986.

MARAIS Diedie

Born 1939 Kokstad, Natal.

A painter of landscapes, seascapes and close-up studies of trees and rock pools. Works in watercolour.

Studies 1958–61 Rhodes University, under Walter Battiss (qv), Cecil Todd (qv) and Alfred Ewan (qv), where gained a Fine Arts Diploma and an Art Teachers Certificate.

Profile From 1973 a member of the WSSA, becoming an Associate in 1984 and subsequently a Fellow. Chairman of the Johannesburg Branch of the WSSA in 1985–86. An occasional member of the SAAA. 1978–81 Senior Art Mistress at King David School, Victory Park, Johannesburg; 1983 taught for six months at Athlone Girls High School, Johannesburg; from 1983 has taught at St John's College, Johannesburg and from 1982 has designed and made costumes for their theatrical productions. She has painted and travelled throughout SA and in SWA/Namibia. 1987 visited Scotland.

Exhibitions She has participated in numerous group exhibitions from 1971 held in SA, London and West Germany; 1971 first of *c.*13 solo exhibitions held throughout SA; 1979 Gallery 21, Johannesburg, joint exhibition with Cynthia Ball (qv), Ulrich Schwanecke (qv) and Nicholas Garwood (qv).

Award 1971 a prize winner, New Signatures, SAAA, Pretoria.

Reference Artlook February 1975.

MARAIS Estelle Professor

Born 1943 Cradock, Eastern Cape.

A painter and graphic artist of landscapes, seascapes, portraits, figures, still life, mythological themes and city scenes. Works in oil, acrylic, watercolour, gouache, pastel, ink, wash, pencil, charcoal and in various graphic media.

Studies 1962–66 Rhodes University, under Professor Brian Bradshaw (qv), gaining a BA(FA); 1972 Rhodes University, under Professor Brian Bradshaw (qv), where attained an MFA.
Profile 1962–72 a member of the Grahamstown Group, 1979–80 of the EPSFA, 1978 of the NSA and in 1984 of the Lichtenburg Fine Arts Society. 1967–68 taught at the Kaffrarian School for Girls, King William's Town; 1969–70 and 1980 at the Johan Carinus Art Centre, Grahamstown; 1971–77 a lecturer, senior lecturer, then Head of the Fine Art Department, University of Fort Hare; 1978 Head of the Fine Art Department, Natal Technical College; 1981–83 a lecturer at Rhodes University; from 1984 Professor of Fine Art at the University of Bophuthatswana. Has lived in the Eastern Cape, Durban and Bophuthatswana. 1973–74 visited Greece, Italy, the UK, Turkey, West Germany, Spain, The Netherlands, Belgium and France; 1987 spent eight months working at the Cité Internationale des Arts, Paris, and travelling throughout France.
Exhibitions She has participated in numerous group exhibitions from 1963 in SA and France; 1971 Bedford City Hall, Eastern Cape, first of 11 solo exhibitions held in SA; 1979 Uitenhage, Eastern Cape, joint exhibition with Josua Nell (qv); 1981 Republic Festival Exhibition; 1987 Cité Internationale des Arts, Paris, joint exhibition.
Public Commissions Mural, University of Fort Hare; portrait, University of Port Elizabeth; four portraits, Rhodes University; landscape, University of the Transkei; two landscapes, University of Bophuthatswana.
References AASA; *SA Panorama* January 1976.

MARAIS Peter

Born (between 1900 and 1910 in the Cape).
A painter of landscapes, seascapes, flowers, trees, the Cape area and its buildings, particularly Cape Malay houses.
Studies Gained a Degree in Architecture from the University of Cape Town, and subsequently studied at the Michaelis School of Fine Art.
Profile An interior decorator.
Exhibitions He has participated in several group exhibitions in SA; 1948 Ermelo Town Hall, Transvaal, first of several solo exhibitions.
References BSAK 1; *Artlook* May 1970.

MARCH Herrat Lydia Erika

Born Ganda, Angola.
Resided in SA from 1969.
A painter of botanical studies, microbiological shapes, landscapes, still life and abstract pictures. Works in watercolour, gouache, ink, charcoal, pencil and crayon.
Studies 1957–61 University for Art and Design, Cologne, West Germany, under Professors Wolff and Schaffmeister, gaining a Diploma in Fine Art.

Profile 1981 a member of the WSSA. 1970–74 Senior Botanical Artist at the Botanical Research Institute, Pretoria, where her work was published in the journals *Flowering Plants of Africa* and *Bothalia* as well as in *The Survival Book* and *The Ferns of Southern Africa*. 1979–83 designed the A B Eksteen Museum for the Department of Transport. A trained photographer and a graphic and interior designer. 1949–50 lived in Portugal; 1950–61 in West Germany; 1962–69 in Canada, where she worked in the National Museum of Canada in Ottawa. Has travelled throughout Europe, the USA and Israel.

Exhibitions She has participated in several group exhibitions in SA, Canada and London; 1974 University of Pretoria, solo exhibition.

Reference AASA.

MARGALIT Nathan

Born 1950 Ramat Gan, Israel.

A painter and a carver working in oil on wood reliefs and using metal rods.

Studies 1971 gained a Certificate in Graphic Design, 1974 gained a BA(FA) and a Higher Diploma in Education from the Michaelis School of Fine Art; 1977 gained an MA(FA) from the Maryland Institute College of Fine Art, Baltimore, USA.

Profile A founder member and Vice-Chairman of the Artists Guild, Cape Town. From 1983 a lecturer at the Michaelis School of Fine Art.

Exhibitions He has participated in group exhibitions from 1977 in SA, the USA and West Germany; 1982 Cape Town Triennial; 1984 Gallery 21, Johannesburg, solo exhibition; 1985 Cape Town Triennial; 1985 Tributaries, touring SA and West Germany.

Represented SA National Gallery, Cape Town.

Reference AASA.

MARGETTS Patricia

Born 1957 Johannesburg.

Works in ink, pencil, pastel and crayon. Depicts genre and figures. Aspects of the grotesque and of caricature regarding the figure.

Studies 1980–83 University of the Witwatersrand, under Professor Alan Crump, gaining a BA(FA); 1987 registered for an MA(FA) at the University of the Witwatersrand.

Profile 1987 a member of the Johannesburg Art Foundation. 1978–79 lived in London. 1979 travelled in Europe and the USA; 1980 visted Australia and New Zealand.

Exhibitions She has participated in group exhibitions from 1987.

Reference AASA.

MARITZ Barry

Born 1928 Pietermaritzburg.

Trained as a painter, but has worked in graphic media from 1969. Creates etchings and woodcuts of landscapes and buildings. A number of series: 1979–82 "My Home & Garden"; 1982 "Zulu War"; 1983–84 "Natal Landscapes"; 1985 "Aspects of Old Durban".

Studies 1950–53 Rhodes University, under Cecil Todd (qv), gaining a BA(FA); 1954 gained a Higher Diploma in Education from the University of Cape Town; 1958 Central School of Art, London, under Hans Tisdal (*b*.1910); 1979–81 University of Natal, under Professor Murray Schoonraad, where attained an MA(FA).

Profile 1955 taught art at Kimberley Boys High School, Cape Province; 1956–57 a lecturer at the Orange Free State Technical College; in 1963 joined the staff of the Natal Technical College (Technikon), from 1966 a senior lecturer in printmaking there and 1974–76 Head of the Fine Art Department.

Exhibitions He has participated in numerous group exhibitions from 1957 in SA and London; 1957 Bloemfontein and Johannesburg, joint exhibitions with Anna Vorster (qv); 1974 Walsh-Marais Gallery, Durban, first of nine solo exhibitions held in Natal; 1974 William Humphreys Art Gallery, Kimberley, solo exhibition; 1981 Republic Festival Exhibition.

Represented Durban Art Gallery; Natal Technikon.

Reference AASA.

MARITZ Nicolaas

Born 1959 Pretoria.

A painter, graphic artist and sculptor of Euro-Afro microcosms. Works in acrylic, various graphic media, commercial paints and in ceramics. 1984–85 "Cultural Still Life", a series of eight paintings.

Studies 1978–81 Michaelis School of Fine Art, gaining a BA(FA).

Profile 1987 a lecturer at the Michaelis School of Fine Art. 1983–84 lived in London, UK, and again in 1985–86.

Exhibitions He has participated in several group exhibitions from 1976 in SA; 1976 EPSFA Gallery, Port Elizabeth, first of five solo exhibitions, one of which was held in London in 1984; 1987 Michaelis School of Fine Art, Cape Town, solo exhibition.

Represented Pretoria Art Museum.

MARKS-PATON Beverley Anne

Born 1962 Johannesburg.

A graphic artist.

Studies University of the Witwatersrand, gaining a BA(FA) in 1984 and a MA(FA) in 1987.

Profile Curator of Prints at the Johannesburg Art Gallery.

Exhibitions Exhibited at the University of the Witwatersrand in 1987; 1988 Johannesburg Art Gallery, Vita Art Now.

Awards 1982 Merit Award, New Signatures, SAAA, Pretoria; 1983 Heather Martienssen Prize, University of the Witwatersrand; 1984 Merit Award, Rolfes Impressions '84, Johannesburg Art Gallery.
Represented University of the Witwatersrand.

MARRIOTT Francis Pickford ARCA

Born 1876 Shropshire, England.
Died 1935 Port Elizabeth.
Resided in SA from 1903.
A painter and sculptor in the Pre-Raphaelite manner using wood, gesso, ivory, mother-of-pearl, enamel and silver. A number of panels and designs for stained glass.
Studies 1900 Royal College of Art, London, to which he was elected an Associate.
Profile 1918 a founder member of the Eastern Province Society of Arts and Crafts; 1918 a member of the SA Society of Artists. 1903 Principal of the Port Elizabeth Art School, which in 1927 was incorporated into the Port Elizabeth Technical College of which he became Vice-Principal.
Represented Brisbane Art Gallery, Queensland, Australia; King George VI Art Gallery, Port Elizabeth.
Public Commissions Memorial, Grey High School, Port Elizabeth; 1820 Settlers Memorial, Port Elizabeth City Hall (destroyed by fire in 1977).
References DBA; Alan McCullach, *Encyclopedia of Australian Art*, 1968 Hutchinson of Australia, Victoria; Port Elizabeth School of Art; AASA.

MARRIOTT Rosemarie

Born 1943 Kuruman, Northern Cape.
A painter and graphic artist of landscapes, seascapes, portraits, figures, still life and abstract pictures. Works in acrylic, watercolour, gouache, ink, wash, pencil, charcoal and in various graphic media.
Studies 1978 Centre for Continuing Education, University of the Witwatersrand, under Gail Machanik (qv); 1979–80 under Bill Ainslie (qv); 1982–84 under Hermine Spies (qv); 1983 under Professor Edda Mally from Vienna, Austria; 1984 under Ines Aab-Tamsen (qv); 1985 under Elizabeth Harington (qv); 1986 under John Clarke (qv).
Exhibitions She has participated in several group exhibitions from 1982 in Johannesburg and Pretoria; 1986 Gallery 21, Johannesburg, solo exhibition.

MARSCHALL Elsa (née Van Niekerk)

Born 1915 Ermelo, Transvaal.
A painter of abstracted landscapes, still life and figures. Works in oil.
Studies 1945 Witwatersrand Technical College, under Maurice van Essche (qv).

Profile 1979 study tour of Europe.

Exhibitions She has participated in many group exhibitions from 1956 in SA, São Paulo and New Orleans; 1956 Quadrennial Exhibition; 1957 Whippman's Gallery, Johannesburg, first of many solo exhibitions held in SA; 1960 and 1964 Quadrennial Exhibitions.

Represented Pretoria Art Museum; SA National Gallery, Cape Town; University of Potchefstroom for CHE; William Humphreys Art Gallery, Kimberley.

References Art SA; SAA; SAP&S; AASA; *Artlook* September 1967 & November 1970.

MARTIN Alfred Richard

Born 1874 Liverpool, England.
Died 1939 Johannesburg.
Resided in SA from 1916.

A painter of portraits, landscapes and figures. Worked in oil. Created a number of sculptures.

Studies Liverpool Academy, under Augustus John (1878–1961) and Robert Anning Bell (1863–1933); also at Westminster School of Art, London.

Profile A founder member of the Guild of Decorators, London. A member of the NSA; the SA Society of Artists; the SA Institute; the Liverpool Academy of Fine Arts; the Durban Art Gallery Advisory Committee and of the Designers Society, London. Decorated a number of P & O liners and designed scenic pieces for the Drury Lane Theatre, London. 1898 Clerk of Works responsible for the decoration of Liverpool Town Hall; 1916 joined the African Theatres Trust; from 1919 a senior lecturer at the Natal Technical College. An Examiner in Fine Arts for the University of Natal and the University of South Africa. Lived in Natal and from *c.*1930 in Johannesburg.

Exhibitions Participated in group exhibitions from 1907 in SA, the USA and the UK; 1927 New York, solo exhibition.

Represented Durban Art Gallery.

References *The Arts in SA*, edited by WHK, 1933–34, The Knox Printing & Publishing Company, Durban; SSAP; DBA; BSAK 1 & 2; AASA.

MARTIN Anthea Ruth

Born Durban.

A painter of still life. Works in watercolour, wash, pencil and charcoal. A fabric artist creating abstract collages in fabric, fibre and found objects.

Studies 1970 six months at the Art Students League, New York; 1977 part-time under Andrew Verster (qv) in Durban; 1978 under Fiona Kirkwood (qv); 1983 six months under Robert Reed, Yale University, Connecticut, USA; 1984–86 under Joyce Leonard (qv) in Johannesburg.

Profile A member of the WSSA.

Exhibitions She has participated in several group exhibitions from 1968 in SA; 1985 Grassroots Gallery, Westville, Natal, joint exhibition with Lorraine Wilson (qv); 1985 Laura Collection, Johannesburg, solo exhibition.

MARTIN-POVAL Lois (née Martin)

Born 1905 Somerset, England.
Resided in SA from 1952.
A painter of indigenous flowers, butterflies and insects.
Studies Liverpool School of Art, under George Marples (1869–1939); textile design at the Regent Street Polytechnic, London, under Harry George Theaker (1873–1954); also studied in Florence, Italy.
Profile During WWII taught art in Torquay, Devon, England. Five coloured plates of flowers, trees, moths and butterflies for Eric Rosenthal's *Encyclopedia of Southern Africa*, 1961, F Warne & Co., London; drew illustrations for the Botanical Research Institute's quarterly publication *Flowering Plants of Africa* and for *Veld and Flora*. Drew orthopaedic and other medical illustrations. Travelled in Europe.
Exhibitions She has participated in group exhibitions in SA; 1962 Durban, first of several solo exhibitions.
References SAA; AASA.

MARTINS Helen Elizabeth

Born 1898 New Bethesda, Cape Province.
Died 1976 New Bethesda, Cape Province.
A self-taught sculptor working in cement over wire mesh, decorated with paint and coloured glass.
Profile As a young woman she travelled throughout Europe and worked as a teacher in Graaff-Reinet. Later she began sculpting life-size animals and people which were placed in her garden. The play "Road to Mecca" by Athol Fugard was based on her later life.
References AASA; *ADA* no 5, 1988.

MASEKO Joseph Ramapulane (Joe)

Born 1940 Johannesburg.
A self-taught painter of portraits, figures, urban scenes and abstract pictures. Works in watercolour, oil, acrylic, gouache, pencil, charcoal, airbrush and pastel.
Profile A full-time artist from 1959. A member of Artists under the Sun. Lives in Johannesburg, visiting the Cape in 1975.
Exhibitions He has participated in many group exhibitions; 1970 Gallery 101, Johannesburg, first of several solo exhibitions; 1973 Hilton Hotel, Denver, Colorado, USA, solo exhibition; 1974 Swazi Trade Fair, joint exhibition with Lucky Sibiya (qv); 1988 Karen McKerron Gallery, Johannesburg, joint exhibition with Leonard Matsoso (qv) and Sheila Nowers (qv).

MASISO Mandla

Born Dukatolo, Germiston, Transvaal.
A self-taught painter and sculptor of portraits, figures and abstract pieces. Works in mixed media, crushed bone and traditional colouring minerals.

Profile From 1973 a member of the National Art Society and from 1975 of the Katlehong Art Society. In 1974 taught sculpture at Tsirwandindi in the Malagasy Republic; in 1978 taught in Johannesburg and in Benoni. An Administration Manager at the Katlehong Art Centre. 1976–79 produced several church murals and painted glass.
Exhibitions He has participated in many group exhibitions from 1969 in SA, Paris, Tel Aviv, Rio de Janeiro and in Nigeria; 1972 Little Gallery, Sandown, Johannesburg, first of two solo exhibitions; 1973 Triad Gallery, Johannesburg, joint exhibition with Morningstar Motaung (qv).
Represented Katlehong Town Council Collection.
Public Commission KwaNdebele Development Corporation.
References The Black Who's Who of Southern Africa Today; 1979/82, African Business Publications, Johannesburg; *SA Panorama* April 1979.

MASON Albert Edward

Born 1895 London, England.
Died 1950 Johannesburg.
Resided in SA from 1917.
A painter of portraits, landscapes and still life; also produced a number of sculptures. Worked in oil.
Studies St Martin's Lane Academy, London, under John Holt, and privately in Europe.
Profile Designed the first poster for the Johannesburg Publicity Association. 1927 taught commercial art and poster design at the Witwatersrand Technical College. A large number of illustrations for periodicals and for W S Chadwick's *Op die Spoor van ons Grootwild* in 1930 and *Slagoffers van die Rowers* in 1931. A number of reproductions published by E Schweikerdt, Pretoria. Trained in architecture at the Birkbeck College, University of London. Decoration designer and artistic adviser to the architect of The Colosseum, Johannesburg (demolished); 1937 decorative work for the Delhi Durbar in India.
Exhibitions Participated in group exhibitions from 1925 in the UK and SA; 1921 Cape Town, first of several solo exhibitions.
Represented Africana Museum, Johannesburg; Durban Art Gallery; National Cultural History Museum, Pretoria; National Museum of Wales, UK; Pretoria Art Museum; SA National Gallery, Cape Town.
Public Commission Three wall panels, Capitol Theatre, Pretoria.
References SAA; AMC4 & 7; DSAB; SAP&S; DBA; BSAK 1 & 2; SA Art; AASA.

MASON Hilda M ARCA (Mrs E Axelson)

Born 1909 Chile.
Resided in SA from 1936.
A painter, working in watercolour, oil, tempera and crayon; modelled sculptures and engraved.

Studies 1934–36 Royal College of Art, London, gaining an Associateship in Design and Certificates in Copper and Wood Engraving.

Profile Produced industrial designs, illuminations, murals and posters. Painted 12 miniature watercolours, depicting events in the life of Field-Marshal J C Smuts. 1937–38 a lecturer in drawing and design at the Port Elizabeth Technical College; 1938–40 a full-time lecturer in drawing, design and crafts, 1940–42 a part-time lecturer at the Witwatersrand Technical College; 1947 lecturer in charge of the Adult Education Art Department, at the Pretoria Technical College. A designer of coins: in 1959 designed the five shilling piece and in 1960 the one cent piece, also a number of medals. Illustrated *Western Cape Sandveld Flowers*, African Book Collectors, Pretoria. Lived in England, Switzerland, the Eastern Cape, Transvaal and in 1962 Newlands in the Cape.

Exhibitions Participated in group exhibitions from 1939 in SA; 1949 first of six solo exhibitions held in SA.

Represented SA National Gallery, Cape Town.

References SAP&D; BSAK 1; AASA.

MASON ATTWOOD Judith Seelawder

Born 1938 Pretoria.

A painter and graphic artist of symbolic and mythological landscapes, figures and portraits. Works in oil, pencil, various graphic media and with objets trouvés.

Studies 1957–60 University of the Witwatersrand, under Cecily Sash (qv), Erica Berry (qv) and Professor Heather Martienssen (1915–79), gaining a BA(FA).

Profile 1984–85 a member of the Patrons Trust. 1962–73 a junior lecturer at the University of the Witwatersrand; 1977 a junior lecturer in History of Art, Drawing and Painting at the University of the Witwatersrand. Has designed a number of tapestries. 1987 wrote an article for the first issue of *Art* magazine. 1980 and 1983 visited India and Nepal. Married to Bruce Attwood, the printer and publisher of *Art*.

Exhibitions She has participated in numerous group exhibitions in SA and in Italy, Greece, The Netherlands, Belgium, West Germany, Chile, Brazil and the USA; 1964 Gallery 101, Johannesburg, first of over 20 solo exhibitions; 1971 Durban Art Gallery, Prestige Exhibition; 1975 Pretoria Art Museum, Prestige Exhibition; 1978 Johannesburg Art Gallery, Prestige Exhibition; 1983 Rand Afrikaans University, Prestige Exhibition.

Represented Ann Bryant Gallery, East London; Arts Association SWA/ Namibia Collection; Durban Art Gallery; Hester Rupert Art Museum, Graaff-Reinet; Johannesburg Art Gallery; King George VI Art Gallery, Port Elizabeth; Pretoria Art Museum; Rand Afrikaans University; Tatham Art Gallery, Pietermaritzburg; SA National Gallery, Cape Town; University of Natal; University of the Orange Free State; University of Pretoria; University of South Africa; William Humphreys Art Gallery, Kimberley.

Public Commissions Tapestries: 1978 Royal Hotel, Durban; 1980 the State Theatre, Pretoria; 1985 the Sand du Plessis Theatre, Bloemfontein; 1986 the Playhouse, Durban.

References SSAP; SAP&S; BSAK 1 & 2; Our Art 3; SA Art; Oxford Companion to 20C Art (under SA); 3Cs; AASA; LSAA; *Artlook* September 1968, July 1972, May 1974 & August/September 1975; *Lantern* March 1975; *De Arte* October 1972 & September 1975; *Habitat* no 20, 1976.

MASSEY-HICKS Margaret Jane (Willy)

Born 1915 Bradford, Yorkshire, England.

Resided in SA from 1946.

A painter of animals, figures, portraits and genre. Works in watercolour, ink and wash. Additionally produces architectural drawings in watercolour.

Studies 1933–36 Wimbledon School of Art, England, under Gerald Cooper (*fl.*1928–40), gaining a London Board of Education Certificate in Drawing in 1934 and in Painting in 1935; 1936 Central School of Art, London, under Bernard Meninsky (1891–1950), on a special award.

Profile 1983 a portfolio entitled "Four Grahamstown Buildings" published by Howard Swan, Johannesburg. Numerous illustrations for over 45 books and for magazines, newspapers, Christmas cards and calendars. A number of felt appliqué figures on loan to the 1820 Settlers Museum, Grahamstown. 1956–57 lived in Europe.

Exhibitions She has participated in several group exhibitions from 1938 in London and SA; 1966 Gallery 101, Johannesburg, first of four solo exhibitions held in SA and London.

References BSAK 1; *Artlook* March 1969, September 1971 & August 1973; *Personality* August 1968; *SA Panorama* July 1970, September 1971 & December 1972.

MASWANGANYI Johannes

Born 1949 Msengi Village, Giyani, Gazankulu.

A carver of figures in wood.

Studies A self-taught artist, who was taught the art of carving by his father.

Exhibitions Exhibited at the Market Gallery, Johannesburg, in 1987; 1988 Johannesburg Art Gallery, Vita Art Now.

Represented Durban Art Gallery; SA National Gallery, Cape Town; University of the Witwatersrand.

MATHESON Gwendoline Jeanette

Born 1925 Johannesburg.

A self-taught painter of landscapes, seascapes and still life. Works mainly in watercolour, occasionally in oil.

Profile *c.*1960 a member of the Brush and Chisel Club; 1979 a member of the WSSA, becoming an Associate in 1983. A potter and draughtswoman. Travelled in Europe.

Exhibitions She has participated in numerous group exhibitions held in SA and London; 1983 St Andrews School, Johannesburg, first of two solo exhibitions in SA.

MATJIE Fani

Born 1953 Eastern Transvaal.

A sculptor of figures, birds and animals. Works in stone, ciment fondu, wood and bone. A graphic artist producing woodcuts and linocuts.

Studies 1982–83 bone and stone carving in Harare, Zimbabwe; 1984–85 Ndaleni Educational Training School.

Profile A member of the Katlehong Art Centre, Transvaal; 1986 taught carving there. Makes clay pots.

Exhibitions He has participated in numerous group exhibitions from 1974 in SA and once in Los Angeles, USA, in 1986; 1974 Pietersburg, first of four solo exhibitions.

Public Commission 1981 Elephant, Sudwala Caves, Eastern Transvaal.

MATOUSEK Vaclav Vilem (Vasek)

Born 1943 Prague, Czechoslovakia.

Resided in SA from 1972.

A painter and graphic artist of landscapes, figures, portraits, and abstract pictures. Works in oil, watercolour, ink, wash, pencil, charcoal, airbrush and in various graphic media.

Studies 1981–85 Cape Technikon, under Ulrich Binedell and Richard Mitchell (qv), gaining a National Diploma in Fine Art in 1983 and a Higher Diploma in Printmaking in 1985.

Profile 1985–86 a series of mandala serigraphs. 1982–83 a number of illustrations for *Sarie* magazine, Cape Town. From 1981 a decorator of pottery and a designer of tapestries. Has lived in West Germany and Iran, with visits to Russia and the Far East.

Exhibitions He has participated in several group exhibitions from 1967 in Czechoslovakia, France, Taiwan, West Germany and SA; 1971 West Germany, first of four solo exhibitions; 1988 Johannesburg Art Gallery, Vita Art Now.

Award 1984 Prize Winner, International Art and Fashion Competition, Paris, France.

Public Commission 1984 portraits of seventeenth-century Cape personalities, VOC Room, Cape Sun Hotel, Cape Town.

MATSOSE Jacob

Born *c.*1961 Sharpeville, Transvaal.

A painter and graphic artist of figures and religious scenes. Works in watercolour and in various graphic media.

Studies Graduated from Rorke's Drift Art Centre in 1977.

Exhibitions He has participated in group exhibitions in SA, the USA and West Germany.

MATSOSO Leonard

Born *c.*1949 Soweto, Johannesburg.

An artist depicting mythological animals, tribal rituals, myths, African legends, abstracted figures and urban life. Has worked in ink, conté, mixed media and in oil pastel.

Studies 1962–69 part-time at the Jubilee Centre, Johannesburg, under Cecil Skotnes (qv), Sydney Kumalo (qv), Bill Hart (qv) and Ezrom Legae (qv); 1972 part-time at the Bill Ainslie (qv) Studio.

Profile Large-scale works from 1975. 1972 visited London, Paris and Rome, having won the UTA Pavement Art Competition Travel Prize.

Exhibitions He has participated in group exhibitions from 1970 in SA, the USA, West Germany, Australia and in São Paulo, Athens and London; 1971 Goodman Gallery, Johannesburg, solo exhibition; 1971 Building Design Centre, Preston, UK, joint exhibition with Winston Saoli (qv) and Cyprian Shilakoe (qv); 1974 Goodman Gallery, Johannesburg, joint exhibition with Louis Maqhubela (qv) and Sydney Kumalo (qv); 1979 Contemporary African Art in SA, touring; 1981 Standard Bank, Soweto, Black Art Today Exhibition; 1981 Republic Festival Exhibition; 1985 Tributaries, touring SA and West Germany; 1988 Karen McKerron Gallery, Johannesburg, joint exhibition with Joe Maseko (qv) and Sheila Nowers (qv).

Award 1973 Special Award for drawing, São Paulo Bienale.

Represented Johannesburg Art Gallery; Pretoria Art Museum; Sandton Municipal Collection; SA National Gallery, Cape Town; University of Fort Hare; University of South Africa; University of the Witwatersrand.

Public Commission The State Theatre, Pretoria, bought five oil pastel murals.

References 3Cs; AASA; LSAA; Echoes of African Art; *Artlook* August 1971; *SA Panorama* July 1982 & June 1983; *Habitat* no 2, 1983.

MATTHEWS Thomas Herbert Professor

Born 1936 Johannesburg.

A painter of landscapes, seascapes, figures and still life. Works in oil and acrylic. 1977–81 a series of transparent figures; from 1981 a series of large flower pieces.

Studies 1959–64 Rhodes University, under Cecil Todd (qv), Walter Battiss (qv) and Brian Bradshaw (qv), where gained an MFA; 1969–71 University of South Africa, under Walter Battiss (qv), where gained a D Litt et Phil.

Profile 1964–74 a founder member of the Grahamstown Group; from 1985 a member of the SAAA. 1965–81 a junior, then a senior lecturer at Rhodes University; from 1981 Professor in History of Art at the University of Durban-Westville. 1975–85 wrote a number of articles for journals and has given public lectures in Grahamstown, East London, Durban and Johannesburg. 1955–56 visited Canada; 1956–58 lived in Sydney, Australia; 1970 and 1975 visited Paris; 1975–76 Spain and in 1976 Italy.

Exhibitions He has participated in numerous group exhibitions from 1964 in SA, Zimbabwe and twice in the USA; 1965 Rhodes Library, Grahamstown, first of four solo exhibitions held in SA; 1976 Pretoria, joint exhibition with David Grant (qv).

Award 1963 Purvis Prize, Rhodes University.

Represented Pietersburg Collection.

Public Commission 1978 mural in African Music Institute, Grahamstown.

Reference AASA.

MAULE Pamela (née Halestrap)

Born 1930 Essex, UK.
Died 1975.
A painter and graphic artist.
Studies Chelmsford Technical College School of Art, Essex, UK; Bath Academy of Art, Avon, UK, where obtained a Certificate in Education.
Profile Taught at schools in England and Rhodesia (Zimbabwe); 1970–74 taught textile printing at Port Elizabeth Technical College.
Exhibitions Participated in group exhibitions with the EPSFA.
Reference Port Elizabeth School of Art.

MAURICE Louis

Born 1917 Cape Town.
A sculptor of figures and figure groupings. Works in bronze, wood and ivory.
Studies 1938 a one-year course in child art, Zonnebloem, Cape Town; 1952–53 Slade School of Art, London.
Profile From 1937 a qualified school teacher.
Exhibitions He has participated in group exhibitions from 1942 in SA and in London; 1942 Cape Town, first of several solo exhibitions; 1944, 1950, 1952 and 1954, Cape Town, joint exhibitions with Gerard Sekoto (qv); 1956 Quadrennial Exhibition.
Represented Battersea Gardens, London.
References Art SA; SAA; SESA; BSAK 1; *South Africana* no 10, April 1958; *Artlook* April 1968; *Historia* December 1968.

MAUTLOA Kagiso Patrick

A painter, sculptor and a graphic artist of historical and socio-political pieces. Works in acrylic, metal and in various graphic media, particularly linocuts. Lives in Soweto, Johannesburg.
Studies Jubilee Art Centre, Johannesburg; Mofolo Art Centre, Soweto; two years at Rorke's Drift Art Centre.
Profile c.1978 taught at the Mofolo Art Centre, Soweto. Married to Bongiwe Dhlomo (qv).
Exhibitions He has participated in several group exhibitions; 1985 Tributaries, touring SA and West Germany.
Award First Prize in an OK Bazaar's Commerical Art Competition.

MAY David

Born 1953 Durban.
A sculptor working in clay and a graphic artist.
Studies 1974–75 BA Foundation in Ceramics, South Devon School of Art, Torquay, UK; 1976–78 Ruth Prowse School of Art, Cape Town, gaining a First Class Diploma in Fine Art (Ceramics and Graphics).

Profile 1979 a lecturer in ceramics at the Ruth Prowse School of Art, Cape Town. 1980–81 a lecturer in advanced ceramics at Potters Place, Cape Town. 1982 studio courses in handbuilding and Raku, Muizenberg, Cape Province.
Exhibitions He has participated in group exhibitions in SA from 1977; 1980 Gallery International, Cape Town, first of three solo exhibitions.

MAYER (Ernst Karl) Erich
Born 1876 Karlsruhe, Germany.
Died 1960 Pretoria.
Resided in SA from 1898.
A painter of scenes from Afrikaner life and of landscapes. Worked in oil and in watercolour from 1905. Designed tapestries and rugs and worked in various graphic media.
Studies 1894–96 Architecture at the Charlottenburg Technische Hochschule, Berlin; 1907 drawing and painting in Karlsruhe; 1909–11 Stuttgart; 1935–36 in Florence, Italy, under Galileo Chini (1873–1945) and Pietro Annigoni (*b*.1900)
Profile A member of the NSA, the Eastern Province Society of Artists and the Transvaal Society of Artists. A number of illustrations for newspapers and books including: *23 Jahre Sturm und Sonnenschein in Südafrika*, A Schiel, 1903, Brockhaus, Leipzig and *Nuwejaarfees op Palmietfontein* by Leon Maré. 1898 an assistant land-surveyor at Vrede in the Orange Free State; 1900–02 a POW on St Helena Island, Atlantic Ocean; 1902 repatriated to Germany; 1903–06 lived in SWA/Namibia; 1907–11 in Germany; 1911–14 lived in Port Elizabeth, Potchefstroom, Johannesburg and Pretoria; 1914–16 interned at Pietermaritzburg; from 1916 based in the Transvaal; 1920–25 in Johannesburg; 1926–28 in the Magaliesburg; 1928–31 toured SWA/Namibia in a caravan; 1931–60 lived in Pretoria. A trained architect working in Pretoria. Travelled on painting excursions with Olchert Braak (qv), Bernhard Hesselbarth (qv) and J H J Rabe (qv). In 1976 a commemorative issue of postage stamps of his work was issued.
Exhibitions Participated in group exhibitions from 1920 in SA, Rhodesia (Zimbabwe) and the UK; 1914 Johannesburg, first of several solo exhibitions; 1972 Pretoria Art Museum, Retrospective Exhibition; 1976 National Cultural History Museum, Pretoria and Holthausen Gallery, Pretoria, Commemorative Exhibitions.
Award 1943 Medal of Honour, SA Akademie vir Wetenskap en Kuns.
Represented Africana Museum, Johannesburg; Ann Bryant Gallery, East London; Durban Art Gallery; Johannesburg Art Gallery; Julius Gordon Africana Centre, Riversdale; King George VI Art Gallery, Port Elizabeth; National Museum, Bloemfontein; Potchefstroom Museum; Pretoria Art Museum; SA Akademie vir Wetenskap en Kuns; SA Cultural History Museum, Cape Town; University of Cape Town; University of the Orange Free State; University of Pretoria; University of South Africa; University of Stellenbosch; War Museum of the Boer Republics, Bloemfontein; Willem Annandale Art Gallery, Lichtenburg; William Humphreys Art Gallery, Kimberley.

Public Commissions *c*.1904 mural, Museum, Windhoek; 1907 painting on the façade of the Deutsche Afrika Bank, Windhoek; 1931 mural, Women's Residence, Johannesburg College of Education; 1934 mural, Staff Restaurant, Johannesburg Post Office; monument, High School, Krugersdorp, Transvaal; 1932–33 designed a knotted carpet, made by his wife Marga Gutter, for SA House, London.

References *Erich Mayer Album*, introduction by Professor H M van der Westhuysen, 1953, HAUM, Cape Town; PSA; Collectors' Guide; Our Art 1; Art SA; SAA, SADNB; 20C SA Art; AMC4 & 7; DSAB; SESA; BSAK 1 & 2; SA Art; Art SWA; 3Cs; AASA; LSAA; *Die Huisgenoot* 28 July 1944; *Fontein* vol 1 no 2, 1960; *SA Digest* 14 May 1976; *SA Arts Calendar* May 1983; *Erich Mayer*, 1972, Exhibition Catalogue, Pretoria Art Museum.

MBAMBO Wiseman

Born 1944.

A sculptor of figures. Works in wood.

Studies Trained at the Ndaleni Educational Training School, Natal.

Profile A school principal.

Exhibitions He has participated in group exhibitions from 1965 in Natal and Zululand.

Award 1967 Study Award, Art SA Today.

Represented Durban Art Gallery; University of Fort Hare.

References BSAK 1; AASA; *SA Panorama* April 1979.

MBATHA Azaria

Born 1941 Mahlabatini, Zululand, Natal.

A graphic artist, creating linocuts, silkscreens, etchings and serigraphs. Depicts Biblical subjects and figures.

Studies 1961 Lutheran Art and Craft Centre at Umpumulo, Natal; 1962–64 Rorke's Drift Art Centre, under the Swedish artist Peter Gowenius; 1965 gained a two-year scholarship to the Konstfachskolan, Stockholm, Sweden, where he designed tapestries (which his wife wove) and studied mural painting and enamel painting; 1977–80 studied social sciences at the University of Lund, Sweden.

Profile Began painting while he was a patient at the Lutheran TB Hospital. 1967–68 a teacher at Rorke's Drift Art Centre. Has lived in Sweden from 1969.

Exhibitions He has participated in group exhibitions from 1965 in SA, the UK, Sweden, Belgium, The Netherlands and West Germany; 1966 Sweden, first of several solo exhibitions held in Sweden; 1968 Cape Town, first of several solo exhibitions held in SA; 1981 Standard Bank, Soweto, Black Art Today Exhibition.

Awards 1965 Art SA Today Prize Winner; 1982 Bradford Art Biennale, UK, Prize Winner.

JOHN MUAFANGEJO
Oniipa New Printing Press 1975
Linocut

HUGO NAUDÉ
The Hex River Valley
Oil on Canvas 70 × 35 cm
Max Levenberg

Represented Arts Association SWA/Namibia Collection; Bradford Art Gallery, UK; Durban Art Gallery; King George VI Art Gallery, Port Elizabeth; Johannesburg Art Gallery; Malmö Museum, Malmö, Sweden; Museum of Modern Art, New York, USA; National Museum, Stockholm, Sweden; Pietersburg Collection; Pretoria Art Museum; Sandton Municipal Collection; SA National Gallery, Cape Town; University of Cape Town; University of Fort Hare; University of South Africa; William Humphreys Art Gallery, Kimberley.

Public Commissions Murals: Lutheran Mission and Lutheran Church, Vryheid, Natal; Esiqhomaneni Church, near Eshowe, Natal; Lutheran Church, Vosloorus, Transvaal.

Publication by Mbatha In the Heart of the Tiger, with text by Werner Eichel, 1986, Hammer, Wuppertal, Verlag der Vereinigten Evangelischen Mission, Wuppertal, West Germany.

References Oxford Companion to 20C Art (under SA); AASA; Echoes of African Art; *Artlook* October 1969; *SA Panorama* July 1982.

MBATHA Eric

Born 1948.

A graphic artist producing etchings and linocuts. Depicts figures.

Profile Taught at Rorke's Drift Art Centre during the late 1970s.

Exhibitions He has participated in group exhibitions from 1967 in SA; 1979 Contemporary African Art in SA, touring; 1981 Standard Bank, Soweto, Black Art Today Exhibition; 1972 Goodman Gallery, Johannesburg, solo exhibition.

Represented SA National Gallery, Cape Town; University of Fort Hare.

References BSAK 1; 3Cs; AASA; Echoes of African Art.

MBELE David

Born 1940 Johannesburg.

An artist working in charcoal, pastel and in various graphic media; also carves in wood. He depicts township scenes and figures.

Studies 1958 Polly Street Art Centre, Johannesburg, under Cecil Skotnes (qv).

Profile His work was reproduced on the cover of *South African Contemporary Artists*, 1980, Cape Town and the cover of *Contrast 51*, 1982, Cape Town. 1985 a painting of his was acquired for the collection of King Zwelithini of the Zulus.

Exhibitions He has participated in several group exhibitions from 1960 in SA, West Germany, Italy, the USA, Spain and France; 1961 Adler Fielding Gallery, Johannesburg, first of four solo exhibitions in SA.

Represented University of Fort Hare.

References BSAK 1 & 2; AASA; Echoes of African Art.

MBONGWA Daniel Themba

Born 1954 Ladysmith, Natal.

A self-taught sculptor of figures and wildlife. Works in wood.

Profile Encouraged by Michael Zondi (qv). 1970–73 lived at Umkomaas, Natal; 1974–78 at Weenen, Natal and from 1978 at Umlazi, Natal.
Exhibitions He has participated in several group exhibitions from 1976 in Natal.
Award 1982 Third Prize, Festival of African Art, University of Zululand.

MBUYISA Bekuyise Joel

Born 1948 Nongoma, Natal.
Mainly a self-taught sculptor of portraits and still life. Works in bronze, stone and wood.
Studies 1965 some art training at Nkamane Mission.
Profile A Minister of the Ethiopian Church.
Exhibitions He has participated in group exhibitions in SA from 1964 and once in West Germany.
Award 1965 Art SA Today Prize Winner.
Represented University of Fort Hare.
Reference BSAK 1.

McALLISTER Patricia Margaret

Born 1932 Bulawayo, Rhodesia (Zimbabwe).
A sculptor of figures. Works in stone, wood, lead, plaster and glass.
Studies 1950–52 and 1954 Natal Technical College, under Mary Stainbank (qv); 1954–55 Goldsmith's College, University of London, under Harold Parker (*b.*1896); 1960–61 on a bursary from the Italian Government at the Accademia di Belle Arti, Rome, under Professor Fazzini (*b.*1913).
Profile Taught sculpture privately. On her return to Rhodesia (Zimbabwe) in 1957 she worked with Lazarus Khumalo. 1962 lived in London.
Exhibitions Exhibited in Johannesburg in 1960; she has participated in group exhibitions in Rhodesia (Zimbabwe).
Reference SAA.

McCALLUM Robert (Rob)

Born 1954 Cape Town.
A painter of figures, landscapes and universal themes. Works in oil.
Studies Michaelis School of Fine Art, gaining a BA(FA) in 1980. 1985 research into art education at the University of Bophuthatswana, gaining a BEd in 1986.
Profile 1981–86 an art teacher at a multi-cultural school in Mmabatho, Bophuthatswana. 1987 an art teacher at the Connie Minchin Primary School in Mmabatho. He has participated in and organised numerous art exhibitions, festivals and workshops in Bophuthatswana. Has written numerous articles and publications about Art Education in Black schools in South Africa.
Exhibitions He has participated in numerous group exhibitions in SA and Bophuthatswana; 1983 Market Gallery, Johannesburg, first of two solo exhibitions held in Johannesburg; 1988 Johannesburg Art Gallery, Vita Art Now.

McCAW Terence John

Born 1913 Pilgrim's Rest, Eastern Transvaal.
Died 1978 Hout Bay, Cape Province.
A painter of Cape and Lesotho landscapes. Worked in oil. A series of the Cape Malay Quarter, Cape Town.
Studies 1930–33 Witwatersrand Technical College, under Sydney Carter (qv) and Emily Fern (qv); 1934–36 Central School of Art, London and Heatherley School of Art, London, under James Fitton (b.1899).
Profile A member of the SA Society of Artists; 1938 a founder member of the New Group. 1943–46 an Official War Artist in Egypt, Italy and France. 1934–37 lived in London, visiting Spain, Greece and Morocco; from 1937 lived at the Cape and regularly visited the Middle East and Europe, especially Italy.
Exhibitions Participated in group exhibitions from 1925 in SA, the UK, France, Italy, Belgium, Rhodesia (Zimbabwe), East Africa, Denmark and South America; 1935 Cape Town, first of several solo exhibitions held in SA, Ireland and Kenya; 1948 Tate Gallery, London, SA Art Exhibition; 1960 Quadrennial Exhibition; 1975 William Humphreys Art Gallery, Kimberley, solo exhibition; 1980 Lister Galleries, Johannesburg, Commemorative Exhibition; 1982–83 SA National Museum of Military History, Johannesburg, Retrospective Exhibition, on loan to SA National Gallery, Cape Town, University of Pretoria and King George VI Art Gallery, Port Elizabeth; 1985 Durban Art Gallery, Retrospective Exhibition.
Award 1935 First Prize, SA Railways Poster Competition.
Represented Ann Bryant Gallery, East London; Durban Art Gallery; Johannesburg Art Gallery; Julius Gordon Africana Centre, Riversdale; King George VI Art Gallery, Port Elizabeth; National Museum, Bloemfontein; Queenstown Art Gallery; SA Cultural History Museum, Cape Town; SA National Gallery, Cape Town; SA National Museum of Military History, Johannesburg; University of Cape Town; University of the Orange Free State; William Humphreys Art Gallery, Kimberley.
References Collectors' Guide; Art SA; SAA; SAP&S; SSAP; DBA; BSAK 1 & 2; Enc S'n A; SA Art; 3Cs; AASA; LSAA; *The World War II Works of Terence McCaw*, N P C Huntingford and R E Hardy, 1982, SA National Museum of Military History, Johannesburg; *SA Art Collector* December 1946.

McCLUNAN Bruce Patrick

Born 1956 Johannesburg.
A self-taught sculptor of animals and figures. Works in bronze and stone.
Profile A sign-writer. From 1977 he has lived in Zululand, Natal. Visited the Okavango, Botswana. His wife Erica paints children's portraits in oil.
Exhibitions He has participated in several group exhibitions from 1985.

McCORKINDALE Sheila Ruth ARCA (Mrs Powrie)

Born 1929 Germiston, Transvaal.
A painter working in acrylic, coloured dyes, gouache, pencil and crayons. An etcher and lithographer.

Studies 1947–50 Port Elizabeth Technical College, under Professor Jack Heath (qv); 1950–51 Michaelis School of Fine Art, under Professor Rupert Shephard (qv); 1951–54 Royal College of Art, London, under Professor Robin Darwin, later awarded an Associateship.

Profile *c.*1968–71 a temporary lecturer at the Michaelis School of Fine Art. 1955–60 lived and taught art in Cape Town and Durban; 1961 moved to Rhodesia (Zimbabwe); from 1966 has lived in Cape Town. Married to John Powrie (qv).

Exhibitions She has participated in group exhibitions from 1955 in SA, Brazil and Yugoslavia; 1956, 1960 and 1964 Quadrennial Exhibitions; has held several solo exhibitions in Cape Town, Durban, Port Elizabeth and Stellenbosch.

Represented Ann Bryant Gallery, East London; Hester Rupert Art Museum, Graaff-Reinet; Johannesburg Art Gallery; King George VI Art Gallery, Port Elizabeth; Pretoria Art Museum; SA National Gallery, Cape Town.

References Art SA; SAA; 20C SA Art; SAP&D; BSAK 1; 3Cs; AASA.

McCORMICK Harry

Born 1874 Komga, Cape Province.
Died 1917 (of wounds in a German POW camp).
A painter of landscapes, figures and military scenes. Worked in watercolour and ink.

Studies Although mainly self-taught, late in life studied in Paris.

Profile A war artist, though not in an official capacity, who followed the troops in the Anglo-Boer War. 1899 two of his sketches of the war were included in *The Illustrated London News*. 1900 a number of Anglo-Boer War scenes appeared in *The Art Annual*. His sketches were also used by *The Graphic*, London, *The State* and other journals. He contributed cartoons to *The Rand Daily Mail*. In 1907 he co-sponsored *African Art Journal* (one edition only). At the outbreak of WWI he travelled to Europe and joined the Artists Rifles.

Represented Africana Museum, Johannesburg.

References ACR Carter, *War Artists in South Africa*, 1900, The Art Annual, London; SADNB; AMC4; Natal Art; BSAK 1 & 2; SASSK; AASA.

McCREA Evelyn Joyce

Born 1905 Altona, County Dublin, Republic of Ireland.
Resided in SA from 1925.
A painter of figures and portraits. Works in oil and watercolour.

Studies In Dublin under Clare Marsh (*fl.*1899–1922); Dublin Metropolitan School of Art, Republic of Ireland, under John Keating (*b.*1899).

Profile Her portraits include those of Sir John Adamson, Lady Oppenheimer and a number of judges and school principals. A member of the Eastern Province Society of Arts and Crafts. Sporadically taught art at Rhodes University and Port Elizabeth Technical College. 1932 travelled in Africa; 1934 in Europe; 1949 and 1957–58 lived in Rhodesia (Zimbabwe). Travelled widely in SA. Lives in Grahamstown.

Exhibitions She has participated in group exhibitions with the SA Academy, the NSA and the Eastern Province Society of Arts and Crafts; 1936 Empire Exhibition, Johannesburg; also exhibited in the UK from 1934.
Award 1928 Karl Gundelfinger Award from the NSA.
Represented Africana Museum, Johannesburg; Albany Museum, Grahamstown; Rhodes University; SA National Gallery, Cape Town.
References SAP&S; DBA; BSAK 1 & 2; AASA; Port Elizabeth School of Art.

McGILL William James

Born 1934 Greytown, Natal.
A painter of landscapes, seascapes and still life. Works in watercolour.
Studies 1975 under Peter Lely in Spain.
Profile From 1960 he has taught art privately in Rustenburg, Transvaal; 1979–81 taught at the Rustenburg Technical College. Illustrated *Rustenburg Romance*, by Eric Rosenthal and *Disappearing Landscapes*, by Bill Mehue in 1979. In 1986 a portfolio of his prints was produced entitled "Bosman's Marico".
Exhibitions He has participated in many group exhibitions in SA; *c.*1962 Rustenburg, first of 16 solo exhibitions held in the Transvaal and Natal.
Represented Willem Annandale Art Gallery, Lichtenburg.

McGILL William Murdoch

Resided in SA *c.*1868–74.
A painter of landscapes and scenes of the early diamond fields of Pniel, Cape Province in 1873 and of Kimberley in 1874. Worked in watercolour.
Studies South Kensington School of Art, London.
Profile An assistant master at the Government School of Design, Lambeth, London. 1868–73 Principal of the Roeland Street School of Art, Cape Town, he also taught at the Diocesan College, Rondebosch, Cape Town. Contributed cartoons to *The Zingari*, a journal in Cape Town. 1874 returned to England.
Exhibitions Participated in group exhibitions in SA in 1869 and 1871, and in the UK from 1882; included in the exhibition "Founders of Painting at the Cape", 1957, SA National Gallery, Cape Town.
Represented William Fehr Collection, Cape Town.
References Pict Art; AMC7; Pict Afr; DBA; SASSK.

McILRATH Michael John

Born 1944 Pretoria.
A painter and graphic artist of allegorical, metaphorical and narrative figuration. Works in oil, acrylic, ink, wash, pencil, charcoal and in various graphic media. 1984 a series entitled "Meetings and Relationships".

Studies 1963–67 University of the Witwatersrand, under Professor Heather Martienssen (1915–79), Cecily Sash (qv), Robert Hodgins (qv) and Giuseppe Cattaneo (qv), gaining a BA(FA); 1971 Johannesburg College of Education, where gained a Higher Diploma in Education; 1982–83 University of South Africa; from 1986 at the Rand Afrikaans University, under Dr L Schmidt, where he has registered for an MA in History of Art.

Profile 1967–76 taught at Orange Grove Primary School, Johannesburg; 1977 a lecturer, then a senior lecturer at Athlone Boys High School and at the Johannesburg College of Education; 1985 author of and lecturer for the Teachers Art Project, Funda Centre, Soweto; 1987 a lecturer in Art Education at the Johannesburg College of Education. 1969–71 involved in stage designs and from 1984 in pottery.

Exhibitions He has participated in several group exhibitions from 1964 in Johannesburg; 1984 Carriage House Gallery, Johannesburg, first major exhibition.

McKEAN Margaret Shona (Dr)

Born 1936 Johannesburg.

A painter of abstracted figures. Works in oil, acrylic, gouache, ink, pencil and charcoal. An etcher.

Studies 1952–55 and 1958 University of the Witwatersrand, on a Transvaal Chamber of Mines Bursary, under Professor Heather Martienssen (1915–79), gaining a BA(FA) and an MA(FA) in 1958; 1956 gained a Higher Diploma in Education from the Johannesburg College of Education; 1959–61 Central School of Art, London, under Merlyn Evans (qv) and the Académie Julian, Paris, on a University of the Witwatersrand Council Post-graduate Scholarship. 1977 awarded a PhD from the University of the Witwatersrand.

Profile Until 1968 taught at various institutions, including at the University of the Witwatersrand, the Frank Joubert Art Centre, Cape Town, Parkview Senior School, Johannesburg and Athlone Girls High School, Johannesburg. From 1968 she has been Head of the Art Department at the Johannesburg College of Education.

Exhibitions She has participated in several group exhibitions from 1963 in SA; *c.*1971 Lidchi Gallery, Johannesburg, first of five solo exhibitions in SA; 1982 Cape Town Triennial; 1985 Cape Town Triennial; 1988 Johannesburg Art Gallery, Vita Art Now.

Awards 1954 Henri Lidchi Prize for Drawing, University of the Witwatersrand; 1955 Herbert Evans Prize for Painting, University of the Witwatersrand; 1971 Hajee Suliman Ebrahim Memorial Trust Award, Art SA Today.

Represented Durban Art Gallery; Johannesburg College of Education; SA National Gallery, Cape Town; University of the Witwatersrand.

References BSAK 1; Oxford Companion to Art (under SA); AASA.

McNAIRN Elizabeth Wyndom (Beth)

Born 1931 Piketberg, Cape Province.

A painter of interiors, landscapes, figures, portraits and still life. Works in oil, ink, pencil and charcoal. A number of graphic works.

Studies 1945–48 part-time under Florence Zerffi (qv) and at the Frank Joubert Art Centre, Cape Town. 1969–72 part-time at Port Elizabeth Technical College, under Joan Wright (qv) and Alexander Podlaschuc (qv); 1975–78 part-time at the Ruth Prowse School of Art, Cape Town, under Erik Laubscher (qv).

Profile 1970–73 a member of the Port Elizabeth Art Club, the EPSFA and the Grahamstown Watercolour Group; from 1975 a member of the SAAA. 1965–71 copper repoussé work, 1969 a mural for the 33rd International Arts and Crafts Exhibition in Italy, in which SA won the Gold Medal. A pianist. 1970–73 lived in the Eastern Cape; 1975–78 in Cape Town; 1978–81 in Johannesburg and from 1983 in Stellenbosch. 1973 and 1979 visited France.

Exhibitions She has participated in many group exhibitions from 1970 in SA; 1978 Nedbank Gallery, Killarney, Johannesburg, first of five solo exhibitions held in Johannesburg, Stellenbosch and Banhoek, Cape Province.

McNAUGHT DAVIS Sheila Emily Hayton (née Maasdorp)

Born 1922 Stellenbosch, Cape Province.

An artist depicting landscapes and seascapes. Works mainly in pastel, but also in oil, gouache and charcoal.

Studies 1952–56 Krenz School of Art, Cape Town, under Professor Alfred Krenz (qv); 1970–75 Ruth Prowse Art Centre, Cape Town, under Erik Laubscher (qv).

Profile 1970 a founder member of the Somerset West Art Group; from *c.*1975 a member of the SAAA. From 1960 lived in Somerset West. 1975 visited SWA/Namibia; 1984–85 the Drakensberg Mountains, Natal and in 1986 Plettenberg Bay, Cape Province. Comes from a family of professional artists.

Exhibitions She has participated in many group exhibitions from 1956 in SA; 1968 Edrich Gallery, Stellenbosch, first of five solo exhibitions in the Cape.

Represented University of Stellenbosch.

McWILLIAMS Herbert Hastings

Born 1907 Port Elizabeth.

Produced pen and ink drawings. Depicted war scenes.

Studies 1926–29 architecture at the Architectural Association, London, where gained a Diploma.

Profile A keen archaeologist and a practising architect.

Exhibitions Participated in group exhibitions during the 1930s in SA; 1973 King George VI Art Gallery, Port Elizabeth, Retrospective Exhibition; 1975 Durban Art Gallery, solo exhibition of drawings and watercolours from WWII; 1978 Umhlanga Sands Hotel, Natal, solo exhibition.

Represented King George VI Art Gallery, Port Elizabeth; SA National Museum of Military History, Johannesburg.

Reference 3Cs.

MEACHAM C S

A painter of landscapes and seascapes. Worked in oil.

Studies Between the ages of 16 and 24 he studied under E Harper in Birmingham, England.

Profile c.1917 a member of the SA Society of Artists. Lived in Cape Town and Johannesburg, retired in 1920 to Scotland.
Exhibitions Participated in group exhibitions in SA from 1910; exhibited with the Grahamstown Fine Arts Association in 1910 and 1917; 1918 Johannesburg, first solo exhibition held in SA.
Represented Albany Museum, Grahamstown.
Reference AASA.

MEERKOTTER Dirk Adriaan

Born 1922 Pietersburg, Northern Transvaal.
A painter and graphic artist of semi-abstract and abstract pictures. Works in oil, acrylic, watercolour, ink and in various graphic media. A ceramicist.
Studies 1944 Witwatersrand Technical College, under Maurice van Essche (qv).
Profile c.1948–58 a committee member of the Transvaal Art Society; from 1958 a member of the SAAA. 1959–62 an art critic for *Die Vaderland*; 1963–66 an art critic for *Die Transvaler*. A number of designs for stained glass windows for churches. From 1962 he has run his own pottery studio in Johannesburg. From 1973 several of his works have been reproduced in calendars. An organist and pianist. Study visits in 1982 to the USA; 1958, 1968, 1972 and 1978 to Europe; 1984–85 worked at the Cité Internationale des Arts, Paris.
Exhibitions He has participated in numerous group exhibitions from 1949 in SA, Italy, Switzerland, Austria, Israel, Peru, Australia, the USA, West Germany and Zimbabwe; 1950 Constantia Art Gallery, Johannesburg, first of over 12 solo exhibitions; 1956 and 1960 Quadrennial Exhibitions; 1978 Rand Afrikaans University, solo exhibition; 1981 Republic Festival Exhibition.
Represented Ann Bryant Gallery, East London; Durban Art Gallery; Hester Rupert Art Museum, Graaff-Reinet; Johannesburg Art Gallery; Pietersburg Collection; Potchefstroom Museum; Potchefstroom University for CHE; Pretoria Art Museum; Rand Afrikaans University; SA National Gallery, Cape Town; University of Durban-Westville; University of Natal; University of the Orange Free State; University of Pretoria; University of the Witwatersrand; Willem Annandale Art Gallery, Lichtenburg; William Humphreys Art Gallery, Kimberley.
Public Commissions Large ceramic murals: 1969 Potchefstroom University for CHE; 1980 the State Theatre, Pretoria; 1981 Library, Goudstad College of Education, Johannesburg; 1982 Municipal Offices, Phalaborwa, Eastern Transvaal; 1985 the Sand du Plessis Theatre, Bloemfontein.
References Art SA; SAA; 20C SA Art; BSAK 1 & 2; Our Art 3; 3Cs; AASA; LSAA; *Artlook* February 1967, April 1967, August 1968 & October 1970; *SA Panorama* October 1968; *Lantern* December 1973.

MEIJER Hester Laurika

Born 1934 Potgietersrus, Northern Transvaal.
An artist producing etchings, clay pieces and sculptural tiles.
Studies 1953–55 and 1960 Pretoria Technical College, under Thelma van Schalkwyk (qv) and Robert Hodgins (qv).

Profile From 1976 a member of the APSA. 1956–58 drawings of butterflies and insects for scientific works at the Transvaal Museum. A potter, exhibiting in SA and France.
Represented Corobrik Collection, University of Natal.

MEIJER Marianne Ingrid

Born 1935 The Netherlands.
Resided in SA from 1958.
A painter working in oil and pencil and a sculptor working in ciment fondu. Depicts landscapes, seascapes, portraits and produces abstract works. 1982–83 "Apple" series; 1985–86 "Tides" series.
Studies Privately under Andrew Verster (qv); part-time at the Natal Technikon, under Diana Kenton (qv); under Meta Orton (qv); extra-murally at the University of Natal.
Profile A member of the NSA, a council member from 1975 and President 1982–85. From 1983 an art critic and art columnist for *The Natal Mercury*. Daughter of the Dutch poet and playwright, Ed Hoornik.
Exhibitions She has participated in several group exhibitions from 1982 in Durban; 1983 NSA Gallery, Durban, solo exhibition.
Represented Durban Art Gallery.

MEINTJES Johannes Petrus

Born 1923 Riversdale, Cape Province.
Died 1980 Molteno, Cape Province.
A painter of portraits, figures, landscapes, still life and street scenes. Worked in oil, charcoal, pastel and watercolour, with a strong use of colour, later more surreal with use of symbols.
Studies 1938–43 under Florence Zerffi (qv) in Cape Town; 1945–47 etching at the Central School of Art, London; 1946–47 in Amsterdam; 1958 in Paris.
Profile 1945 taught art part-time at the SA College and the Jan van Riebeeck High School, Cape Town. 1945–47 worked part-time as an announcer and translator on the African Service of the British Broadcasting Corporation. A poet and writer of both books and magazine articles, winning numerous literary awards. 1938–45 lived in Cape Town; 1945–47 in Europe; 1947–65 in the Cape and Johannesburg; 1965–80 lived in Molteno, Cape Province, where he was the Librarian and Museum Curator. 1949 joint winner of "Most Original SA Painting", *Die Vaderland* newspaper.
Exhibitions Participated in group exhibitions in SA and in Rhodesia (Zimbabwe); 1944 Gainsborough Gallery, Johannesburg, first of numerous solo exhibitions held throughout SA; 1963 SAAA Gallery, Pretoria and Cape Town, Retrospective Exhibition; 1980 Library, University of Port Elizabeth, Memorial Exhibition.

Represented Africana Museum, Johannesburg; Hester Rupert Art Museum, Graaff-Reinet; Pretoria Art Museum; SA National Gallery, Cape Town; University of the Witwatersrand; War Museum of the Boer Republics, Bloemfontein; Willem Annandale Art Gallery, Lichtenburg; William Humphreys Art Gallery, Kimberley.

Some of the publications by Meintjes *Maggie Laubser*, 1944, J H de Bussy, Cape Town; *Lyrical Works*, 1948, Anreith Press, Cape Town; *Anton Anreith Sculptor 1754–1822*, 1951, Juta, Cape Town; *Complex Canvas*, 1960, Afrikaanse Pers, Johannesburg; *Die Dagboek van Johannes Meintjes*, three volumes, 1975, Bamboesberg Uitgewers, Molteno, Cape Province. He wrote 35 fictional and historical books.

References Art SA; SAA; 20C SA Art; BSAK 1 & 2; 3Cs; AASA; *SA Art News* 6 July 1961 & 20 July 1961; *Artlook* March 1971; *SA Panorama* July 1974.

MEIRING Johannes Henricus

Born 1934 Potchefstroom, Transvaal.

A painter and graphic artist of landscapes, town scenes and architectural subjects. Works in watercolour, ink, wash, pencil, charcoal and in various graphic media.

Studies 1952–58 University of Cape Town, under Professor Thornton White, where gained a BA in Architecture; 1962–63 on a German Exchange Scholarship, at the Akademie der Bildenden Kunste, Munich, under Professor Franz Nagel.

Profile 1984–85 Chairman of the Northern Transvaal Branch of the Simon van der Stel Foundation. A member of the Institute of SA Architects and the SAAA. 1981–82 a part-time lecturer at the School of Architecture, University of Pretoria. A practising architect, who received a Gold Medal from the Simon van der Stel Foundation for his efforts towards the preservation of South Africa's architectural heritage. Illustrations for Vivian Allen's book, *Kruger's Pretoria*, 1970, A A Balkema, Cape Town and three books by Ters van Huyssteen: *Footloose in Stellenbosch*, 1979, *Hart van die Boland*, 1983 and *Hugenoteland*, 1985, all published by Tafelberg, Cape Town. 1950–60 lived in Stellenbosch; 1960–62 in Cape Town; 1964–70 in Pretoria; 1970–78 in Johannesburg; from 1978 in Pretoria. Has frequently visited Europe, in 1974 the USA and in 1976 the Far East, the USA, Brazil and the Caribbean. Nephew of the architect, Professor A L Meiring.

Exhibitions He has participated in several group exhibitions from 1960 in SA and West Germany; 1964 Quadrennial Exhibition; 1967 Pretoria, first of eight solo exhibitions; 1981 Republic Festival Exhibition.

Represented Potchefstroom University for CHE; Pretoria Art Museum; Rand Afrikaans University; University of Stellenbosch.

Publications by Meiring *Boukunsskatte van SA*, 1976, Human & Rousseau, Cape Town; *Pretoria 125*, 1980, Human & Rousseau, Cape Town; *Early Johannesburg*, 1986, Human & Rousseau, Cape Town.

References AASA; *Artlook* April 1972; *Habitat* no 21, 1976.

MELLOR Bronwen Joan

Born 1945 Johannesburg.

A self-taught painter of wildlife, particularly of birds. Works in watercolour and gouache. A calligrapher.

Exhibitions She has participated in many group exhibitions from 1978 in Johannesburg and Bloemfontein. 1988 Yvonne Baxter Gallery, Sandton, Johannesburg, solo exhibition.

MELMAN Rosalind

Born 1935.

Died 1986.

A painter of faces, figures and heads. Worked in oil.

Studies Etching at the Stanley William Hayter Studio in Paris.

Profile A large number of drawings and commissioned portraits. Designed the stained glass windows in St Anthony's Church, Mafeking (Mafikeng, Bophuthatswana). Lived in Johannesburg.

Exhibitions Participated in group exhibitions in SA; 1977 Trevor Coleman Gallery, Johannesburg, solo exhibition; 1981 Republic Festival Exhibition.

Reference AASA.

MENPES Mortimer FRGS RE RBA

Born 1859 Port Adelaide, Australia.

Died 1938 (thought to have died in England).

Resided in SA *c*.1900.

A painter of landscapes, city scenes, genre and portraits (including one of Cecil Rhodes). Worked in watercolour, crayon and various other media. A large series of Orange Free State scenes. A celebrated etcher.

Studies School of Design, Adelaide, Australia; South Kensington School of Art, London, under Sir Edward John Poynter (1836–1919); during the 1890s became a follower and admirer of James A Whistler (1834–1903).

Profile A member of the Royal Society of British Artists and of the Royal Society of Painters and Etchers. A Fellow of the Royal Geographical Society. 1900 a war artist for *Black and White in SA*. An essayist and administrator of the Menpes Press, London. A well-travelled artist working in France, North Africa and India; visited Japan in 1887. Most of his life, however, was lived in London.

Exhibitions Participated in group exhibitions 1880–1913 in England and regularly at the Royal Academy and the Royal Society of Painters and Etchers; held a large number of solo exhibitions in London.

Represented Africana Museum, Johannesburg; Commonwealth National Gallery, fifty of his copies of Old Masters; SA National Gallery, Cape Town; William Fehr Collection, Cape Town.

Publications by Menpes *War Impressions; being a record in Colour*, etchings of SA transcribed by D Menpes, 1901, A & C Black, London; *Whistler as I Knew Him*, 1904, A & C Black, London.

References ACR Carter, *War Artists in South Africa*, 1900, The Art Annual, London; AMC4; Alan McCulloch, *Encyclopedia of Australian Art*, 1968, Hutchinson of Australia, Victoria; DVP; Pict Afr; Bénézit; DBA; BSAK 1 (under Mempes); SA Art; AASA (under Mempes).

MERKELL Alfred Martin

Born *c*.1888 Vryburg, Northern Cape.
Died *c*.1950.
A painter of landscapes, mining scenes and still life. Worked in oil and pastel.
Profile A friend of Hugo Naudé (qv), with whom he painted in Worcester, Cape Province.
Exhibitions Participated in group exhibitions from 1925; 1946 first solo exhibition held in Johannesburg.
Reference BSAK 1.

METCALF Victor Grant

Born 1916 Middlesbrough, Yorkshire (Cleveland), England.
Resided in SA from 1947.
A painter of portraits, figures and abstract pictures. Works in oil, ink and pencil.
Studies 1936–38 Constantine School of Art, Middlesbrough; 1938–39 Chelsea School of Art, London.
Profile A founder member of the SA Society of Industrial Artists and its President in 1956–57. 1948–55 a part-time lecturer at the Witwatersrand Technical College. 1943–46 a British Official War Artist in India and Burma; 1976–83 an Official War Artist in SWA/Namibia and SA, painting official portraits and pictures of military activities. An executive of an advertising agency. A calligrapher. A number of his illustrations appeared in *The Illustrated London News*.
Exhibitions 1946 New Delhi, India, first of several solo exhibitions.
Award Chief of Defence Force Distinguished Service Medal.
Represented SA National Museum of Military History, Johannesburg.
Public Commissions Numerous portraits for the SA Defence Force and of State Presidents.
References AASA; *SA Panorama* November 1978.

METCALFE Roland William

Born 1953 Johannesburg.
A painter and graphic artist of landscapes and interiors with people. Works in oil, acrylic and in various graphic media.
Studies 1972–74 Witwatersrand Technical College, where gained a National Diploma in Graphic Design.
Profile 1981–82 a part-time lecturer in graphic design at the Witwatersrand Technikon. Visited the UK and Nepal.

Exhibitions He has participated in several group exhibitions in Johannesburg; 1976 Space and Design, Johannesburg, joint exhibition with Philippa Hobbs (qv); 1983 Market Gallery, Johannesburg, first of two solo exhibitions.
Reference Habitat no 26, 1977.

METHVEN Cathcart William FRIBA

Born 1849 Edinburgh, Scotland.
Died 1925 Pietermaritzburg.
Resided in SA from 1888.
A painter of Natal landscapes, Durban Bay and other harbour scenes. Worked in oil and watercolour.
Studies Under a Mr Fothergill.
Profile Used ink, pencil and various graphic media to depict Durban Harbour, and for the commissioned surveys of Cape ports and the coast of Zululand. Prior to 1888 was Assistant Harbour Engineer in Greenock, Scotland, for 18 years, 1888–95 Engineer in Chief for Natal Harbour Works. A trained architect and surveyor, setting himself up as an architect in Durban in 1895. A member of the Pen and Pencil Club, Glasgow, Scotland and a Fellow of the Royal Institute of British Architects. 1905 co-founded the Natal Institute of Architects and the NSA, of which he was President for the following 12 years. He was also President of the SA Association for the Advancement of Science. He was responsible for the initiation of the Durban Art Gallery. Interested in music, particularly organs. After 1924 lived in Pietermaritzburg.
Exhibitions Participated in group exhibitions in Scotland and England from 1886 and later in SA; 1921 Lezards, Johannesburg, first solo exhibition in SA.
Award 1892 First Prize in Landscape, SA Drawing Club Exhibition.
Represented Africana Museum, Johannesburg; Durban Art Gallery; Tatham Art Gallery, Pietermaritzburg; University of Natal.
Publications by Methven Greenock and its Harbour, 1886; *Sketches of Durban and its Harbour*, 1891, P Davis Publishers, Durban.
References SADNB; DSAB; AMC7; Pict Afr; 3Cs; AASA.

MEYER André

Born 1953 Cape Town.
A sculptor of figures and abstract pieces. Works in ceramics and metal.
Studies 1971 Ruth Prowse Art Centre, under Erik Laubscher (qv) and Anna Vorster (qv); 1977 Cape Technical College (Technikon), gaining a Certificate in Commercial Art; 1979–81 Cape Technikon, under Michael Mitford-Barberton, Jan Vermeiren (qv) and Ulrich Binedell, where attained a National Diploma in Fine Art (Sculpture); 1981–82 Cape Technikon, under Michael Mitford-Barberton, gaining a Higher Diploma in Fine Art (Ceramic Sculpture).
Profile A member of the SAAA and the APSA. From 1982 an art technician at the School of Art and Design, Cape Technikon. A potter.

Exhibitions He has participated in several group exhibitions from 1984 in SA.
Reference Maarten Zaalberg, *The 1985 Year Book of Ceramics*, 1985, Perskor in conjunction with Corobrik, Cape Town/Johannesburg.

MEYER Carl Walter

Born 1965 Aliwal North, Cape Province.
A painter and graphic artist of landscapes, portraits, still life, wildlife and abstract pictures. Works in oil, acrylic, watercolour, gouache, ink, wash, pencil, charcoal and in various graphic media. Sculpts in wood.
Studies 1983–84 University of Pretoria, under Professor Nico Roos (qv) and John Clarke (qv); 1985–86 Staatliche Kunstakademie, Düsseldorf, West Germany, under Professor Michael Buthe.
Exhibitions He has participated in several group exhibitions from 1983 in SA and West Germany; 1986 Pierneef Gallery, Pretoria, solo exhibition.
Award 1985 First Prize for Painting, SAAA, Pretoria.

MEYER Jenny Anne

Born 1947 Yorkshire, England.
Resided in SA from 1953.
A painter of figures. Works in oil and acrylic.
Studies 1982–83 University of South Africa, under Leon du Plessis (qv), Keith Dietrich (qv) and Wendy Ross (qv); 1985 University of Natal, under Professor Terence King (qv); 1986–87 University of South Africa, under Debbie Bell (qv) and Nina Romm (qv), studying for a BA(FA).
Profile A member of the NSA and from 1984 an Associate of the WSSA. 1983 on the Tatham Art Gallery Fund-Raising Committee. A trained maths teacher, who taught this subject 1967–71. *c.*1978 travelled in the USA; 1984 in Europe and in 1985 to Israel.
Exhibitions She has participated in many group exhibitions from 1982 in SA; 1982 Pietermaritzburg, solo exhibition.

MEYER Jill

Born 1926 Johannesburg.
A painter of flowers. Works in oil and watercolour.
Studies Witwatersrand Technical College, under James Gardner (qv) and Douglas Portway (qv); Regent Street Polytechnic, London; also under Erica Berry (qv).
Exhibitions She participated in group exhibitions during the 1960s; 1961 Gallery 101, Johannesburg, solo exhibition.
Reference SAA.

MEYER John

Born 1942 Bloemfontein.

A painter of landscapes, town scenes, portraits, still life, seascapes and figures, in a realistic manner. Works in acrylic, watercolour and oil. 1970–74 "Highveldt" series; 1974-84 "Karoo" series; 1977–81 "Doornfontein" series; from 1977 US landscapes; 1979–80 flat colour series. From 1970 he has been commissioned to paint numerous private portraits.

Studies 1961 six months at the Witwatersrand Technical College, under Phil Kolbe (qv).

Profile 1967–72 a full-time professional illustrator. In 1982 his portrait of Dr R Koch was reproduced on the SA twenty cent stamp. 1961–67 lived in Johannesburg; 1967–69 in London; 1969–84 in Johannesburg; 1984–86 in Nevada, USA; 1987 returned to Johannesburg. 1975 visited Rhodesia (Zimbabwe); 1976 Europe; 1977, 1979 and 1981 the USA and Europe; 1982 the USA, Europe, Israel and Portugal; 1983 Kenya and Egypt; 1984 South East Asia, Burma and Thailand; 1988 the USA.

Exhibitions 1972 Everard Read Gallery, Johannesburg, first of 11 solo exhibitions held in SA, London, New York, Nevada and Toronto; he has participated in many group exhibitions from 1973 in SA and in Nevada, New York, Tennessee, New Orleans, New Jersey and Texas in the USA; 1983 Everard Read Gallery, Johannesburg, Retrospective Exhibition; 1986 invited to participate in "Landscape, Seascape, Cityscape 1960–1985", Contemporary Arts Center, New Orleans and the New York Academy of Art, New York; "Ten Contemporary Realists", Alice Bingham Gallery, Memphis, Tennessee and "Hadassah Annual Exhibition", Woodcliff Lake, New Jersey.

Represented Pretoria Art Museum; Willem Annandale Art Gallery, Lichtenburg; William Humphreys Art Gallery, Kimberley.

Public Commissions Portraits: 1972 Dr W J Busschau, Rhodes University; 1973 Dr J M Hyslop, Rhodes University; 1974 Dr F R Bozzoli, University of the Witwatersrand; 1975 Dr F Hill, University of the Witwatersrand; 1976 Dr N Diederichs, Vanderbijlpark Town Council; 1976 Dean Yeats, St John's College, Johannesburg; 1979 Dr N Diederichs, Rand Afrikaans University; 1981 President K Matanzima, Wild Coast Holiday Inn, Transkei; 1982 Mr A Murray, St John's College, Johannesburg; 1983 Mr S Krige, Woodmead School, Johannesburg; 1984 Governor R List, State Capitol, Nevada, USA; 1985 Walter Travis, US Golf Hall of Fame, New Jersey, USA; 1986 Babe Didrickson Zaharias, US Golf Hall of Fame, New Jersey, USA; 1986 Mr P Nixon, Woodmead School, Johannesburg; 1987 Dr G de Koch, SA Reserve Bank, Johannesburg. In addition to this he has received many portrait commissions from large corporations and private collectors in the USA, Sweden, the UK and throughout SA.

References AASA; LSAA; *The Condenser* 1977; *John Meyer in Retrospect*, 1983, Everard Read Gallery, Johannesburg; *Gallery* Summer 1983; *Arts Magazine* February 1985, New York; *Christian Science Monitor* 11 February 1985; *Landscape, Seascape, Cityscape 1960–1985*, 1986, Contemporary Arts Center, New Orleans.

MEYEROWITZ Eva Leone (née Lewin-Richter)

Born 1899 Berlin.

Resided in SA 1925–36.

A sculptor in stone, wood and bronze.

Studies 1919–23 Städtische Kunstgewerbe und Handwerker Schule, Berlin; 1922–25 Vereinigte Staatsschule für freie und angewandte Kunst, Berlin, under Professor Fritz Klimsch (1870–1960).

Profile 1926–29 occasionally taught woodcarving at the Michaelis School of Fine Art; 1929–33 taught at the SA School of Applied Art, Cape Town. Modelled the interiors of numerous cinemas. Published several books on ancient African history and culture. 1934–36 lived in Lesotho, Bloemfontein and London; 1936–44 lived in Ghana, travelled in West Africa. 1940 taught at the School of Arts and Crafts, Achimota College, Accra, Ghana. Later settled in London. 1944, 1954–55 and 1958–60 revisited SA. Married to Herbert V Meyerowitz (qv).

Exhibitions Exhibited in London.

Represented SA National Gallery, Cape Town.

Public Commissions Figures over the vestibule and above the entrance, SA National Gallery, Cape Town; putti for fountain, Botanical Gardens, Cape Town; lions' heads, Delville Wood Memorial, France; woodcarving of Lady Anne Barnard, Claremont Civic Centre, Cape Town; figures, Biet Hall, Dombashava College, Cape Town; reliefs in foyer, Bloemfontein City Hall.

References *The Arts in SA*, edited by WHK, 1933–34, The Knox Printing & Publishing Company, Durban; SAA; SAP&S; SESA; BSAK 1 & 2; *Personality* 8 October 1970.

MEYEROWITZ Herbert Vladimir

Born 1900 St Petersburg (Leningrad), Russia.
Died 1945 London.
Resided in SA 1925–36.

A sculptor of portraits. A woodcarver and a stonecarver, producing architectural work.

Studies 1919–22 Städtische Kunstgewerbe und Handwerker Schule, Berlin, under Professor Otto Hitzberger (*b*.1878); 1923–25 Vereinigte Staatsschule für freie und angewandte Kunst, Berlin.

Profile 1925–29 a lecturer in woodcarving at the Michaelis School of Fine Art. 1930 founder and, until 1933, co-director of the SA School of Fine and Applied Art, Cape Town, with A Sandor Konya (qv). 1933–36 lived in Lesotho, Bloemfontein and London. 1936–43 Supervisor of the School of Arts and Crafts, Achimota College, Accra, Ghana. Travelled throughout West Africa. From 1943 Acting Director of the West African Institute for Crafts, Industries and Social Studies. 1944 revisited SA. Married to Eva L Meyerowitz (qv).

Represented Rand Afrikaans University; SA National Gallery, Cape Town; University of Stellenbosch.

Public Commissions 1929–34 Hyman Liberman Doors and "Adam and Eve", stone carvings at the entrance, SA National Gallery, Cape Town; fanlights, University of Cape Town; statuette of Poet C J Langenhoven, for the four Provincial Administration Headquarters and for Parliament.

References *The Arts in SA*, edited by WHK, 1933–34, The Knox Printing & Publishing Company, Durban; Art SA; SAA; SADNB; SAP&S; SESA; BSAK 1 & 2; SA Art; 3Cs; AASA; LSAA.

MGUDLANDLU Gladys

Born 1925 Peddie, Ciskei.
Died 1979 Guguletu, Cape Province.
A self-taught painter of landscapes, figures, flora and fauna. Worked in gouache and oil.
Profile Had some guidance from Katrine Harries (qv). Began painting in 1952, in a naive style. Wrote and illustrated original African folktales, gained a Teachers Diploma from Lovedale College, Alice, and during 1968–78 taught art at Athlone Community School, Cape Town.
Exhibitions Exhibited widely in SA and abroad; 1961 Port Elizabeth, first of several solo exhibitions; 1979 Contemporary African Art in SA, touring.
Award 1963 Prize Winner, Art SA Today.
Represented King George VI Art Gallery, Port Elizabeth; University of Fort Hare.
References Art SA; SESA; BSAK 1 & 2; AASA; *Artlook* November 1972.

MHLABA Zwelidumile Mxgazi (Dumile)

Born *c.*1942 Worcester, Cape Province.
Resided in SA until 1968.
A self-taught artist of genre, figures, domestic animals, urban scenes, religious and allegorical themes. Draws in crayon, ink and charcoal. Created the well-known 2,5 m × 3 m charcoal drawing entitled "African Guernica". A sculptor of figures and heads in bronze and terracotta.
Profile He began drawing in 1963. 1979 Visiting Artist in Residence at the African Humanities Institute, University of California, Los Angeles, USA. Grew up in Johannesburg, moved to the UK in 1968.
Exhibitions He has participated in group exhibitions from 1965 in SA, São Paulo, Brazil and in the UK; 1966 Gallery 101, Johannesburg, first of two solo exhibitions held in Johannesburg; 1966 Durban Art Gallery, Invited Artist; 1969 Grosvenor Gallery, London, solo exhibition; 1979 Contemporary African Art in SA, touring; 1981 Standard Bank, Soweto, Black Art Today Exhibition.
Awards 1966 Merit Award, Art Prize '66, SA Breweries, Cape Town; 1971 First Prize in a competition organised by the African Studies Center, Los Angeles, USA.
Represented Ann Bryant Gallery, East London; Durban Art Gallery; Johannesburg Art Gallery; Pretoria Art Museum; SA National Gallery, Cape Town; University of Fort Hare.
Public Commission Began, in 1979, a mural for the University of California, Los Angeles, USA.
References SAP&D; SA Art; Oxford Companion to 20C Art; 3Cs; SSAP; SESA; P Schirmer, *Concise Illustrated SA Encyclopaedia*, 1980, CNA, Johannesburg; AASA (all under Dumile); Echoes of African Art; *Artlook* November 1966, June 1967 & November 1972; *SA Panorama* July 1975.

MICHALETOS Aleta Cecilia (Mrs Botha)

Born 1952 Pretoria.

A painter of landscapes, portraits, still life, interiors, genre and abstract pictures. Works in oil, watercolour, pencil, pen and ink. 1979–84 pastel-coloured paintings of African masks and flowers; 1983–84 "Anger and Passion" series; 1986–87 "Alethea" series.

Studies 1970 Architecture at the University of Pretoria; 1971–74 University of Pretoria, under Justinus van der Merwe (qv), Jean Beeton (qv), Raymond Andrews (qv), Eben van der Merwe (qv) and Professor Nico Roos (qv), gaining a BA(FA); 1979–80 began an MA(FA) at the University of Pretoria, under Professor Nico Roos (qv).

Profile A member of the SAAA. 1987 a guest lecturer at the University of Pretoria. In 1983 she established and presently continues to run an art gallery in Pretoria. A collector of art nouveau and art deco.

Exhibitions She has participated in many group exhibitions from 1972 in SA; 1976 SAAA Gallery, Pretoria, first of four solo exhibitions.

Public Commissions 1973 portrait of Dr D J Opperman, University of Pretoria; 1986 portrait of Dr H J Aschenborn, the State Library, Pretoria.

MICHELL Charles Cornwallis

Born 1793 Exeter, Devon, England.
Died 1851 Eltham, London, England.
Resided in SA 1828–48.

A painter of landscapes. Worked in watercolour, ink and wash. Produced drawings, etchings and engravings of Cape scenes and of genre.

Profile 1824 a drawing master at Sandhurst, Kent, UK. Contributed some of the illustrations for the book by his son-in-law, James E Alexander (qv), *Narrative of a Voyage and of a Campaign in Kaffirland*, 2 volumes, 1837, Henry Colbourn, London. Reproductions of his work appeared in *South Africa's Heritage*, 1962, Caltex. Designed St Paul's Church, Rondebosch and St John's, Bathurst, Cape Province. His drawing of Cradock's Pass was used on the SA penny stamp of 1938. An ex-artillery officer, who was Surveyor-General and Superintendent of Works at the Cape, 1828–48.

Represented Africana Museum, Johannesburg; William Fehr Collection, Cape Town.

References Pict Art; AMC4; SESA; Pict Afr; DSAB; 3Cs.

MICHELOW Berenice

Born 1930 Johannesburg.

A painter and graphic artist, working in oil, gouache, pencil, charcoal and in various graphic media. 1964–68 "Paintings Relating to Music"—structuring musical rhythm into visual colour and form; 1969 "Reality of Form"—reinter-pretation of organic shapes which led to the interest in human form; 1971 "Nudescapes"; 1977 "Flight" series; 1978 "Reflection of our Times"; 1979 "Focus"; 1983–85 "Everyday Landscapes".

Studies 1948–50 Witwatersrand Technical College, gaining a Diploma in Fine Arts; 1951–53 Central School of Art, London, under Laurence Irving (*b*.1897), Reginald Robert Thomlinson (*b*.1885) and Cochrane, where attained a Higher Diploma.

Profile A member of the SAAA; from 1968 an art lecturer at the Centre for Continuing Education, University of the Witwatersrand. 1954–60 theatre costumes and stage sets for productions in London and Johannesburg. Illustration for *Izwi 14*, February 1974 and the cover design for *Contrast 35*, December 1974. Travelled extensively.

Exhibitions She has participated in numerous group exhibitions from 1964 in SA, The Netherlands, Belgium, West Germany, Israel, Australia, Zimbabwe, Monaco, France, Chile, Greece and the USA; 1965 Lidchi Art Gallery, Johannesburg, first of 18 solo exhibitions in SA; 1980 University of Stellenbosch, Guest Artist; 1981 Republic Festival Exhibition; 1983 Rand Afrikaans University, Guest Artist; 1987 Johannesburg Art Gallery, Vita Art Now.

Awards 1963 Joint Winner, First Prize, OK Bazaars Multiple Competition; 1973 Phillip Frame Award, Art SA Today Exhibition.

Represented Boksburg Municipal Collection; California College of Arts and Crafts, USA; Department of National Education, Permanent Collection, Bonn, West Germany; Durban Art Gallery; Johannesburg Art Gallery; Pietersburg Collection; Potchefstroom University for CHE; Pretoria Art Museum; SA National Gallery, Cape Town; Sandton Municipal Collection; University of South Africa; University of the Witwatersrand; Willem Annandale Art Gallery, Lichtenburg; William Humphreys Art Gallery, Kimberley.

Public Commission 1985 a panel in oil "Between Reality and Illusion", the Sand du Plessis Theatre, Bloemfontein.

References SAGAT; BSAK 1 & 2; 3Cs; AASA; *Artlook* February 1968, July 1969, May 1971, September 1973 & December 1975/January 1976; *Lantern* July 1978; *Habitat* no 33, 1979; *SA Arts Calendar* September 1983.

MICHIE Elsie Ekren

Born 1906 Middelburg, Transvaal.
Died 1964 Johannesburg.
A painter of views of Johannesburg and landscapes. Worked in watercolour and occasionally in oil.
Studies 1924 art classes at the Tin Temple, Johannesburg, under Austin Winter Moore (qv); also under William Cook and J W Bramham in Johannesburg.
Profile A part-time artist who worked as a stockbroker's secretary.
Exhibitions Participated in group exhibitions 1955 and 1958.
Represented Africana Museum, Johannesburg.
Reference AMC7.

MIEDZINSKI Daniel

Born 1930 Johannesburg.
A painter and sculptor of figures, African mysticism, religious subjects, natural forms and abstract pieces. Works in acrylic, ink, wood and plaster.

Studies Spent three years at the Witwatersrand Technical College, as well as a further 18 months studying woodcarving.

Profile 1964 made the semi-abstract space film "Orion's Eye" and in 1967 the abstract film "Escape". Lived in Johannesburg.

Exhibitions Participated in group exhibitions held throughout the 1960s and 1970s; 1967 Gallery 101, Johannesburg, first of several solo exhibitions held in Johannesburg.

References Art SA; SAA; BSAK 1; *Artlook* January 1968, January 1970 & April 1972.

MIKULA Maggie

Born 1941 Durban.

A ceramic artist working in clay, metal, fibre and with beads. Her work is ethnically inspired.

Studies 1960–62 Natal Technical College, gaining a Diploma in Commercial Art.

Profile From 1977 a member of the SAAA and the APSA. A number of ceramic tile commissions. 1984 created jewellery pieces and metal work and in 1985 weavings. Travelled in Europe.

Exhibitions She has participated in numerous group exhibitions from 1978 in SA; 1983 Grassroots Gallery, Westville, Natal, first of three solo exhibitions.

Award 1984 Corobrik National Award.

Represented Durban Art Gallery.

References *Sgraffiti* nos 32 & 39.

MILES Frank

Born 1946 Rhodesia (Zimbabwe).

Resided in SA from 1972.

A self-taught sculptor of wildlife, figures and abstract pieces. Works in bronze and wood.

Profile 1973 visited Europe; 1974 the USA, Canada and Mexico. Casts his own bronze sculptures.

Exhibitions He has participated in several group exhibitions in Zimbabwe and SA.

MILLAIS John Guille

Born 1865 London, England.

Died 1931.

Visited SA *c.*1894.

An animal sculptor and painter of wildlife. Worked in watercolour, ink, wash and Chinese white.

Profile Contributed illustrations to *The Graphic*, London. A traveller and hunter. Lived in England. Son of the painter, Sir John Everett Millais (1829–96).

Represented Africana Museum, Johannesburg.
Publications by Millais Many books on natural history and big game including: *A Breath from the Veldt*, 1895, Henry Sothern, London, reprinted by Galago Publishers; *Wanderings and Travel*, 1919, Longmans Green, London; *Wild Life in Africa*, 1928, published privately.
References SADNB, AMC4; SESA; Pict Afr; Bénézit; DBA; BSAK 1.

MILLAR Harold Martel

Born 1865 Durban.
Died 1961 Durban.
A painter of birds. Worked in watercolour.
Profile A member of the original committee which founded the Durban Museum. Practised as an Attorney and had a keen interest in ornithology, entomology and taxidermy. 1955 the Freedom of the City of Durban was conferred on him for his work on birds and insects.
Represented Africana Museum, Johannesburg; Bird & Butterfly Collection, Durban Museum.
References SAA; AMC7; SESA; SA Art; AASA; *De Arte* April 1978.

MILLER Ralph Rillman

Born 1915 Wayne, Pennsylvania, USA.
Resided in SA from 1974.
A painter of landscapes, portraits, figures and still life. Works in oil. He has received numerous private portrait commissions in Cape Town.
Studies 1935 University of Washington, USA, sculpture under Alexander Archipenko (1887–1964); 1964 part-time at the Art Students League, New York, under Robert Phillips; 1971–72 drawing under N Simi in Florence, Italy.
Profile He grinds his own paint, makes the medium and prepares the ground on raw linen. A member of the SA Society of Artists. 1960–70 Director of the Museum of the City of New York, USA. 1973–74 a part-time lecturer at the University of Cape Town. 1975 painted a portrait of David Bloomberg for the cover of Bloomberg's book *Meet the People*. 1947–70 lived in New York; 1970–73 in Florence, Italy. Has travelled throughout Europe and the USA.
Exhibitions He has participated in numerous group exhibitions in the USA, Italy and SA; 1964 Hudson Valley Museum, Yonkers, New York, first of 15 solo exhibitions.
Represented Pietersburg Collection; University of Cape Town.
Reference AASA.

MILNE Peter W S

Born 1923 Durban.
A painter of wildlife, landscapes, seascapes and still life. Works in oil, acrylic and pastel. An aviation artist.

Studies Natal Technical College, gaining a National Teachers Certificate III in 1946.
Profile Visited London in 1974 and 1983.
Exhibitions He has participated in several group exhibitions in SA, the USA and the UK; 1973 Durban, first of six solo exhibitions.

MITCHELL Richard Jeffery

Born 1944 Plymouth, Devon, England.
Resided in SA from 1969.
A painter of landscapes, seascapes and abstract pictures. Works in oil, acrylic, watercolour, gouache, ink, wash, pencil and charcoal.
Studies 1961–65 Plymouth College of Art, UK, under Alexander McKenzie, where gained a National Diploma in Art and Design, Painting and Lithography; 1965–66 Brighton College of Art, Sussex, UK, under Ron Horton, gaining an Art Teachers Certificate.
Profile 1972–73 a committee member of the East London Branch of the SAAA; 1977–83 a member of the Cape Town Branch of the SAAA; from 1985 a committee member of the Cape Friends of Calligraphy. 1966–68 an art teacher at Marlow, Buckinghamshire, UK; 1969–70 an art teacher at the Johan Carinus Art Centre, Grahamstown; 1971–76 a lecturer at the East London Technical College; from 1977 a lecturer, then a senior lecturer at the Cape Technikon. Involved in the restoration and conservation of fine art works.
Exhibitions He has participated in several group exhibitions.

MITFORD-BARBERTON Ivan Graham ARCA ARBS FRGS

Born 1896 Glen Avon, Somerset East, Cape Province.
Died 1976 Cape Town.
A sculptor of portrait busts, animals and figures. Worked in wood, stone, bronze and ivory.
Studies 1919 and 1922 Grahamstown School of Art, under Professor F W Armstrong (qv); 1923–25 Royal College of Art, London, under Derwent Wood (1871–1926) and Henry Moore (1898–1986), where he was awarded an Associateship; later studied in Italy and France.
Profile An heraldic artist. 1938–61 a lecturer in sculpture at the Michaelis School of Fine Art. 1912–22 lived in Kenya, but schooled in Grahamstown, Eastern Cape; 1923–27 lived in Europe; 1927–30 returned to Kenya, working as a coffee planter; from 1930 lived in Cape Town. 1935 revisited Kenya. Travelled extensively in Europe, India, Ceylon (Sri Lanka) and Egypt. Grandson of Mary Elizabeth Barber (qv).
Exhibitions Participated in group exhibitions from 1930 in SA and Rhodesia (Zimbabwe); 1930 Cape Town, first of several solo exhibitions in SA and Kenya; 1948 Tate Gallery, London, SA Art Exhibition.

Represented Albany Museum, Grahamstown; Ann Bryant Gallery, East London; Durban Art Gallery; Johannesburg Art Gallery; Nairobi Art Gallery, Kenya; Nottingham Art Gallery, UK; SA Akademie vir Wetenskap en Kuns; SA National Gallery, Cape Town; University of Cape Town; University of Stellenbosch; William Humphreys Art Gallery, Kimberley.

Public Commissions Monument to the 1820 Settlers, Grahamstown; 1935 frieze, SA Mutual Building, Darling Street, Cape Town, as well as works in the Provincial Administration Building, Wale Street, Cape Town and the African Homes Trust Building, Cape Town; 1968–73 Jan Smuts statue, Adderley Street, Cape Town; equestrian statue of Wolraad Woltemade, SA Mutual, Pinelands, Cape Town; 1960 four springbok, Springs, Transvaal.

Publications by Mitford-Barberton *The Barbers of The Peak*, 1934, Oxford; *The Bowkers of Tharfield*, with his brother Raymond; *Ivan Mitford-Barberton: Sculptor*, autobiography, 1962, HAUM, Cape Town.

References *The Arts in SA*, edited by WHK, 1933–34, The Knox Printing & Publishing Company, Durban; Collectors' Guide; Pict Art; Art SA; SAA; DSAB; SAP&S; IWAA; SESA; BSAK 1 & 2; SA Art; 3Cs; AASA; LSAA; Phyllis Scarnell Lean, "Clay in his Hands", manuscript; *SA Panorama* September 1959 & August 1966.

MKWANE Haugai Mninikhaya

Born 1958 Welkom, Orange Free State.

A painter, sculptor and graphic artist of landscapes, portraits, still life, seascapes and wildlife. Works in acrylic, watercolour, pencil, charcoal, stone, wood and in various graphic media.

Profile From 1986 a member of the QwaQwa Artists Association. From 1981 a teacher in QwaQwa. An actor.

Exhibitions He has participated in group exhibitions from 1987.

MLANGENI Wandile Ignatius

Born 1966 Johannesburg.

A painter, sculptor and graphic artist of portraits and figures. Works in oil, acrylic, watercolour, ink, pencil, charcoal, pastel, wood and in various graphic media.

Studies 1985–87 Funda Centre, Soweto, under Charles Sokhaya Nkosi (qv).

Profile 1987 a part-time tutor at the Funda Centre, Soweto, Johannesburg.

Exhibitions He has participated in several group exhibitions from 1985.

MOCKE Johannes Bernardus

Born 1932 Carnarvon, Cape Province.

A painter of figures, portraits and abstract pictures. Works in oil and acrylic. 1980 a series of six acrylic paintings entitled "The Gifted Child".

Studies 1950–52 Michaelis School of Fine Art, under W Twine and Russell Harvey (qv), gaining a Certificate in Commercial Art; 1979–80 Cape Technikon, under S Slack, gaining a Higher Diploma in Graphic Design.

Profile 1953–71 a studio artist in advertising agencies in Cape Town; 1972–74 an art teacher at Grey High School, Port Elizabeth; from 1975 a senior lecturer at the Cape Technikon. 1956 book covers for Gerrie Radloff's adventure series, published by Tafelberg, Cape Town. A playwright, winning a number of prizes in this field. A translator of plays into Afrikaans, a theatre director, and a set and costume designer.

Exhibitions He has participated in several group exhibitions from 1978 in Cape Town.

MOEMA Sydney Patrick

Born 1954 Pretoria.

A painter and graphic artist of still life, figures and abstract pictures. Works in watercolour, ink, wash, pencil, charcoal and in various graphic media particularly etching and silkscreening. Carves in wood and weaves.

Studies 1976–77 Rorke's Drift Art Centre, under Jules van de Vijver (qv) and Ada van de Vijver (qv), gaining a Diploma in Fine Arts; 1983–84 on an Italian Scholarship at the Accademia di Belle Arti, under Brüno Orfei.

Profile 1980–82 illustrations for books, booklets and posters. 1983 an art teacher on local television for a youth education programme on art.

Exhibitions He has participated in several group exhibitions from 1977 in SA, Sweden, The Netherlands, West Germany, the UK and Italy; 1982 London, first of two solo exhibitions, the second being held in Stockholm, Sweden.

Represented Caritas-Pierckheimer Haus, Katholische Akademie, Bamberg, West Germany; Wallberger Institut, West Germany.

MOERANE Molaoa Philemon

Born 1945 Johannesburg.

A painter of landscapes, seascapes and abstract pictures. Works in watercolour, soluble coloured pencil and pencil. Sculpts in wood.

Studies 1968 Ndaleni Educational Training School, Natal, under Lorna Pearson, attaining an Art and Craft Specialist Teachers Diploma; 1985 a six-week course at the Funda Centre, Soweto, under Steven Sack (qv).

Profile Secretary of the QwaQwa Art Group. 1969–70 an art teacher in Soweto; from 1971 an art teacher at the Tshiya College of Education, Witsieshoek, QwaQwa. From 1972 he has made copper and enamel jewellery.

Exhibitions He has participated in group exhibitions from 1974.

MOGALE Dikobe Benedict Martins

Born 1956 Coronationville, Johannesburg.

A painter and graphic artist of portraits, figures and cartoons.

Works in oil, watercolour, ink, pencil and in various graphic media.

Profile Has illustrated short stories and poems for Ravan Press, Johannesburg, and produced drawings for *The Natal Witness* supplement, *Echo.*
Exhibitions He has participated in group exhibitions during the 1970s and 1980s in Australia and SA.
Reference SASSK.

MOGANO Phoshoko David

Born 1932 Pietersburg, Northern Transvaal.
A painter of rural and urban life. Works in watercolour and since 1985 occasionally in acrylic.
Studies 1959 Polly Street Art Centre, Johannesburg, under Cecil Skotnes (qv) and Sydney Kumalo (qv).
Profile From 1964 a member of the Artists Market.
Exhibitions He has participated in many group exhibitions from 1970 in Johannesburg; 1972 Foundation of Creative Art, Johannesburg, first of two solo exhibitions.
Represented Africana Museum, Johannesburg; University of Fort Hare.
Reference Echoes of African Art.

MOHL John Koenakeefe

Born 1903 Dinokana, Zeerust, Western Transvaal.
Died 1985 Zeerust, Western Transvaal.
A painter of landscapes, figures and of rural and urban life. Worked in oil.
Studies Windhoek School of Art, SWA/Namibia; five years in Düsseldorf, West Germany.
Profile A member of Artists under the Sun. Gave art classes in Sophiatown, Johannesburg.
Exhibitions Participated in group exhibitions from 1943; 1943 Transvaal Art Society, first of several solo exhibitions; 1963 Apollo Gallery, Johannesburg, joint exhibition with Mizraim Maseko, who produced works in leather; 1965 Piccadilly Gallery, London, African Painters and Sculptors from Johannesburg.
Award 1943 SA Academy of Art Award.
Reference Echoes of African Art.

MOKGOSI Nathaniel

Born 1946 Johannesburg.
A graphic artist, producing linocuts of figures and animals, with a religious theme.
Studies 1966 began his studies at the Jubilee Art Centre, Johannesburg.
Profile Taught at The Open School, Johannesburg. From 1970 a full-time artist living in Soweto.
Exhibitions He has participated in group and solo exhibitions in SA, the USA, Canada, Australia and West Germany.

MOKHACHANE Gibson

Born 1941 Witsieshoek, QwaQwa.

A painter working in watercolour and charcoal and a sculptor working in clay, depicting rural and urban life.

Exhibitions He has participated in many group exhibitions from 1979 in SA; 1982 first of six solo exhibitions.

Represented University of the Orange Free State.

MOKHELE Tanki Masupha

Born 1961 Mofolo, Soweto.

A painter, working in oil, ink and pencil; a sculptor in scrap metal and a graphic artist producing linocuts. His works are of semi-abstract portraits, figures and genre.

Studies 1982 part-time at the Mofolo Art Centre, under Cyril Manganyi (qv); 1986–87 on a bursary from the Funda Centre, at the University of South Africa.

Profile From 1986 a teacher at The Open School, Johannesburg. 1985 designed a poster for Lesotho, where he grew up.

Exhibitions He has participated in several group exhibitions from 1984 in Johannesburg.

Awards 1983 First Prize, Regional Bata International Art Competition; 1984 awarded Diploma of Merit, Bata International Art Competition.

Public Commission 1986 mural, Alexandra Art Centre, Johannesburg.

Reference Echoes of African Art.

MOKHETHI Peter Mokete

Born 1933 Parys, Orange Free State.

A painter and sculptor of landscapes, still life and figures. Works in watercolour, gouache, ink, pencil, charcoal, stone and wood.

Studies Ndaleni Educational Training School, under Lorna Pearson and Craig Lancaster, gaining an Art Diploma.

Profile From 1983 a teacher at the Bonamelo College of Education, QwaQwa.

MOKHETHI KUMALO Temba Cyril

Born 1950 Johannesburg.

A sculptor of figures and abstract pieces. Works in bronze.

Studies 1966–69 Jubilee Art Centre, Johannesburg, under Bill Hart (qv) and Ezrom Legae (qv); 1974–75 awarded a scholarship to the Museum of Fine Arts, Boston, Massachusetts, USA.

Profile 1975 an art instructor at the Mofolo Art Centre, Soweto.

Exhibitions He has participated in many group exhibitions in SA; 1969 Goodman Gallery, Johannesburg, first of three solo exhibitions.

Represented University of Fort Hare.

Reference BSAK 1.

MOKOENA Motsamai Paul

Born 1966 Sophiasdeel, Villiers District, Orange Free State.
Draws in pencil and pastel. Depicts landscapes, portraits, still life and figures.
Paints in oil and watercolour.
Studies 1985–86 Katlehong Art Centre, under Sue Kaplan and Napo Mokoena
(qv); 1987 arts and crafts at the Tshiya College of Education, Witsieshoek,
QwaQwa.
Profile From 1986 a member of the QwaQwa Association of Artists.
Exhibition 1986 Katlehong, group exhibition.

MOKOENA Mpho Samuel

Born 1940 Johannesburg.
A painter of landscapes and figures. Works in oil, acrylic, watercolour and
charcoal.
Studies Several lessons from Cecil Skotnes (qv).
Exhibitions He has participated in several group exhibitions from 1972 in
Johannesburg.

MOKOENA Napo J

Born Katlehong, Transvaal.
A painter and graphic artist of genre, figures and abstract pictures. Works in
acrylic, charcoal and in various graphic media.
Studies 1976–77 Tshiya College of Education, Witsieshoek, QwaQwa, under
Molaoa Moerane (qv).
Profile From 1973 a member of the Katlehong Art Society and Centre. 1978–86
taught at the Katlehong Art Centre, from 1986 Manager of the Katlehong Art
Centre. From 1983 many contributions to *Staffrider* magazine. Since 1979 he has
worked in wheel pottery. 1976–77 lived in Witsieshoek, QwaQwa.
Exhibitions He has participated in many group exhibitions 1969–79 and from
1985.

MOKOENA Tello Joseph

Born 1957 Paul Roux, Orange Free State.
A painter and a sculptor of landscapes and abstract pictures. Works in acrylic,
watercolour, ink, pencil, charcoal and ciment fondu.
Exhibitions Exhibits in QwaQwa.

MOLETSANE Johannes

Born 1959 Bloemfontein.
A painter of township life, African art, landscapes, portraits and figures. Works
in oil, watercolour and pastel.
Studies 1980–82 under Mpho Sam Mokoena (qv).

Profile A member of the Bloemfontein Art Society. Visited London in 1979.

Exhibitions He has participated in group exhibitions from 1979 in SA, the USA, the UK and Japan; 1979 Public Library, Bloemfontein, first of two solo exhibitions.

MOLLOY Sylvia (Mrs)

Born 1914 Durham, England.

Resided in SA from 1948.

A painter of landscapes, city scenes, figures and portraits. Works in oil.

Studies University of Durham, UK.

Profile A founder member, and in 1962 President, of the Johannesburg Society of Arts; a member of the Transvaal Art Society. Taught art in England, and from 1956 privately in her studio in Johannesburg. Designed the stained glass windows for the MOTH (Military Order of Tin Hats) Chapel, Johannesburg and St Michael and All Angels' Church, Pretoria. Lived in Burma, India and SA.

Exhibitions She has participated in group exhibitions in the UK, France, Australia and SA; held four solo exhibitions in SA.

Represented Africana Museum, Johannesburg; Ann Bryant Gallery, East London.

References SAA; AMC4; AASA.

MOLOKENG (Joshua) Billy

Born 1949 Alexandra, Johannesburg.

A painter of figures, heads and abstract pictures. Works in oil, watercolour, gouache, conté, pencil and charcoal.

Studies In 1971 studied under Peter Eliastam (qv).

Profile Has also designed tapestries and made leather sandals and belts. A music composer and singer, under the name Billy Africa.

Exhibitions 1968 Dorkey House, Braamfontein, Johannesburg, first of seven solo exhibitions, one of which was held in Braunschweig, West Germany in 1980; he has participated in several group exhibitions from 1971 in SA, Israel, West Germany, The Netherlands, Greece and Italy.

Award 1981 Republic Festival Painting Award.

Represented University of Fort Hare.

References AASA; Echoes of African Art; SA *Panorama* April 1979.

MOMBERG Anton

Born 1951 Pietersburg, Northern Transvaal.

A sculptor of portraits and figures. Works in bronze, wood, ceramics and polyester resin.

Studies Port Elizabeth Technikon, under Hillary Graham (qv) and Neil Rodger (qv), gaining a Teachers Diploma in Fine Art.

Profile From 1976 a member of the EPSFA and 1986 of the GAP Group. From 1981 a lecturer in Fine Art at the Port Elizabeth Technikon. 1975 visited London and Paris.
Exhibitions He has participated in several group exhibitions from 1980 in SA.
Public Commissions Bronze portraits: 1984 Heinz Betze, Port Elizabeth Technikon; 1985 Dr Danie Craven, University of Stellenbosch; 1986 Dr Danie Craven, Western Province Rugby Union, Cape Town.

MONYOBO Sepiriti Jeremiah

Born 1959 Clocolan, Orange Free State.
A painter of portraits. Works in oil, watercolour, oil pastel, pencil and charcoal. Carves wooden figures.
Profile A court interpreter in QwaQwa.

MOOIJ Jessica (née Tiggelman)

Born 1948 Amsterdam, The Netherlands.
Resided in SA from 1956.
A painter of wildlife, particularly of fish and birds, and of figures. Works in oil, watercolour, gouache, ink and wash. 1984 a series of pictures entitled "The Life Cycle of the Fish"; 1985–86 a series of women portrayed as dolls.
Studies 1967–70 University of Pretoria, under Professor Nico Roos (qv), gaining a BA(FA) and at the Pretoria Technical College, under Gunther van der Reis (qv); 1974 gained a Secondary School Teaching Diploma.
Profile A member of the EPSFA. 1970–74 worked as a heraldic artist for the SA Bureau of Heraldry, designing coats of arms for schools, municipalities etc. 1978–81 taught at Gelvandale Senior Secondary School, 1982 at David Livingstone Senior Secondary School, Port Elizabeth. From 1985 has taught art privately. 1970–78 created a number of works using the batik method. Travelled extensively in Europe.
Exhibitions She has participated in several group exhibitions from 1970 in SA; 1983 EPSFA Gallery, Port Elizabeth, first of two solo exhibitions held in SA.
Represented Rhodes University.

MOOLENSCHOT Geneviève Shirley

Born 1935 Pretoria.
A painter and sculptor of landscapes, portraits and figures. Works in watercolour, conté, pastel, ink, wash, pencil, charcoal, stone, wood and wax relief.
Studies 1953–55 on an Arthur May Scholarship at the Natal Technical College, gaining a National Diploma in Art and Commercial Design.
Profile During the early 1970s acted in two Audrey Culverwell productions. 1975, 1984 and 1985 visited SWA/Namibia; 1982 the Karoo.
Exhibition 1985 participated in a group exhibition in Durban.
Public Commission 1979 Roll of Honour 1899–1902, Citizens' Memorial, Platrand, Ladysmith, Natal.

MOOLMAN Hermanus Johannes (Manus)

Born 1955 Standerton, Transvaal.

A painter of landscapes and abstract pictures. Works in oil, watercolour, ink and wash.

Studies 1974–77 Potchefstroom University for CHE, under Professor G M Ballot, where gained a BA(FA).

Profile A member of the SAAA and the SAAAH. From 1982 an artist in the service of the Transvaal Provincial Administration Museum Service, Pretoria. 1984 stained glass work for Lichtenburg and Rustenburg museums, Transvaal. 1983 visited Europe.

Exhibitions He has participated in several group exhibitions from 1976 in SA; 1981 Pretoria, first of three solo exhibitions held in SA.

Represented Potchefstroom Museum; Potchefstroom Teachers Training College.

MOOLMAN Johann

Born 1950 Johannesburg.

A sculptor of figures, often combined with wood and steel structures and paper relief collages. Works in bronze, steel, lead, wood, painted plaster of Paris and with mud, textiles, bitumen and paper. A continuing theme of man and his relationship to the environment.

Studies 1970–73 Witwatersrand Technical College, where gained a Diploma in Fine Art; 1975–76 took an advanced course in sculpture at St Martin's School of Art, London.

Profile From 1974 on the temporary staff and later on the permanent staff of the Witwatersrand Technical College, until 1979, when he took up lecturing at the University of South Africa in sculpture, graphic printmaking and drawing.

Exhibitions He has participated in numerous group exhibitions held in SA; 1980 Gertrude Posel Gallery, University of the Witwatersrand, first of several solo exhibitions; 1981 Johannesburg Art Gallery, Guest Artist; 1985 Tributaries, touring SA and West Germany; 1986 University of the Orange Free State, joint exhibition with Sybille Nagel (qv), Debbie Bell (qv) and Keith Dietrich (qv); 1987 Gallery 21, Johannesburg, joint exhibition with John Clarke (qv), Jacobus Kloppers (qv), Erna Bodenstein-Ferreira (qv) and William Steyn (qv).

Represented Pretoria Art Museum; Rand Afrikaans University; SA National Gallery, Cape Town; University of the Orange Free State; University of South Africa; University of the Witwatersrand.

References AASA; *De Arte* April 1983.

MOORE Daphne

Born 1894 Britstown, Cape Province.

Depicted still life, portraits and figures. Known to have worked in monotypes.

Studies Spent six years studying at the Slade School of Art, London, under Henry Tonks (1862–1937) and at the Royal Academy Schools, London, under Charles Sims (1873–1926).

Profile From 1950 lived in Cape Town.

Exhibitions Participated in numerous group exhibitions in SA and the UK; 1960 Quadrennial Exhibition; numerous solo exhibitions held through the SAAA.
References SAA; AASA.

MOORE Edward Charles

Born 1883 Grahamstown.
Died 1946.
A painter of landscapes. Worked in oil.
Profile Lived in the Transvaal and Natal, before settling in the Cape.
Exhibitions Participated in group exhibitions from 1923 in Johannesburg and throughout SA; 1934 Grahamstown, solo exhibition.
Represented Africana Museum, Johannesburg; Albany Museum, Grahamstown; Ann Bryant Gallery, East London; University of Stellenbosch.
References AMC4; BSAK 1; AASA.

MOORREES Victor

Born *c*.1886 Malmesbury, Cape Province.
Died 1945 Cape Town.
A painter of landscapes, seascapes, street scenes, especially those of Cape Town and its Malay Quarter, and of flowers. Worked in oil. Produced a number of coloured woodcuts and aquatints.
Studies Studied in Grahamstown.
Profile Lived in SA, in York, UK and in the USA, where he studied psychology.
Exhibition 1945 Langton Gallery, Johannesburg, solo exhibition.
Represented SA National Gallery, Cape Town.
References SAP&S; BSAK 1; AASA (under Moorees).

MORLAND James Smith

Born 1846 Liverpool, England.
Died 1921 Cape Town.
Resided in SA from 1888.
A painter of landscapes, genre and figures. Worked in watercolour, pastel and oil. Painted scenes of England from memory.
Studies 1863–73 part-time at Liverpool North District School of Art, where gained two bronze medals.
Profile 1880 accepted as a full member of the Liverpool Academy of Arts. A member of the Liverpool Watercolour Society, and first President of the Liverpool Sketch Club. 1873–76 an assistant teacher at the Liverpool North District School of Art. 1897 a member of the SA Society of Artists and its first President 1902–04. 1898 Vice-President of the Owl Club, Cape Town (a society for literary and artistic appreciation). 1888 taught at Vredenberg High School for Girls, Good Hope Seminary, Rondebosch High School and Sea Point Girls High School, Cape Town. 1889–1902 founder, tutor and adjudicator of the SA Drawing Club. 1862–76 worked at a Liverpool firm of general merchants; 1876–88 lived in North Wales; 1888–1902 in Cape Town; 1902–05 in England; from 1905 in SA. Included in Edward Roworth's (qv) essay "Landscape Art in SA", 1917, Studio Publication, *Art of the British Empire Overseas*. Came from a family of well-known English artists. Mentor of Gwelo Goodman (qv).

Exhibitions Participated in group exhibitions from 1877 in England and SA; 1899 Cape Town, joint exhibition with Borge Stuckenberg (qv), George Winkles (qv) and Hugo Naudé (qv); 1906 Darters Gallery, Cape Town, solo exhibition; 1931 SA National Gallery, Cape Town, Commemorative Exhibition; 1977 SA National Gallery, Cape Town, Retrospective Exhibition.

Represented Albany Museum, Grahamstown; Glasgow Art Gallery, UK; Imperial Institute, London, UK; Julius Gordon Africana Centre, Riversdale; Liverpool Art Gallery, UK; Norwich Art Gallery, UK; Pretoria Art Museum; SA Cultural History Museum, Cape Town; SA National Gallery, Cape Town; William Fehr Collection, Cape Town; William Humphreys Art Gallery, Kimberley.

References Collectors' Guide; SAA; SADNB; SAP&S; SAP&D; SSAP; Pict Afr; Bénézit; DBA; BSAK 1 & 2; 3Cs; AASA; *J S Morland 1846–1921*, SA National Gallery, Cape Town, Catalogue, 1977.

MOROSS BALLEN Lynda see BALLEN Lynda

MORRIS Arthur Greenwood

Born 1922 Keighley, Yorkshire, England.
Resided in SA from 1947.
A self-taught painter of landscapes and seascapes, aircraft, figures and wildlife. Works in oil, watercolour, ink and wash. Makes wire sculptures of aircraft, yachts, birds etc.

Profile From 1984 a member of D'ARTS. Designed and made the Africa Trophy for the Mirror Dinghy World Championship. An art restorer. Formerly a commercial pilot and flying instructor. Cartoon strips and illustrations for *World Air News*; has also had various articles and verse published in both SA and the UK.

Exhibitions He has participated in several group exhibitions from *c.*1954 in SA; 1974 Cafe Wien (Genevé), Durban, first of seven solo exhibitions held in Natal.

Reference SASSK.

MORRIS Timothy William

Born 1941 England.
Resided in SA from 1965.
A painter of landscapes. Works in watercolour, gouache, ink, wash, pencil and charcoal.

Studies 1958–65 at Brighton School of Art; St Martin's School of Art, London; the University of London; Central School of Art, London, and Accademia di Belle Arti, Perugia, Italy. Gained a National Diploma in Design and an Advanced Diploma in Painting and Ceramics.

Profile Primarily a potter producing clay domestic ware. Has taught at various schools in the UK and at the Johannesburg College of Art. Visited Italy, Jordan, the USA and the UK.
Exhibitions He has participated in several group exhibitions in the UK and SA; 1981 Republic Festival Exhibition; has held seven solo exhibitions of his paintings.
Represented William Humphreys Art Gallery, Kimberley.
References BSAK 1; SA Art; 3Cs; AASA; *Artlook* August 1972; *SA Arts Calendar* Spring 1985; *Sgraffiti* no 35.

MOTAU Julian

Born 1948 Tzaneen, Northern Transvaal.
Died 1968 Alexandra, Johannesburg.
A painter and graphic artist of scenes in townships and of figures. Worked in ink, chalk, charcoal, various graphic media and occasionally in watercolour. A sculptor.
Studies Mainly self-taught with some guidance from Judith Mason (qv).
Profile Came to Johannesburg in 1963.
Exhibitions Participated in group exhibitions from 1965 in SA; 1967 Goodman Gallery, Johannesburg, solo exhibition; 1968 Pretoria, Commemorative Exhibition; his works were included in graphic exhibitions in Europe from 1971; 1979 Contemporary African Art in SA, touring; 1981 Standard Bank, Soweto, Black Art Today Exhibition.
Awards 1965 Certificate of Merit, SAAA, Pretoria; 1967 First Prize, New Signatures, SAAA, Pretoria.
Represented Pretoria Art Museum; SA National Gallery, Cape Town; University of Fort Hare; University of South Africa.
References SAP&D; SESA; SSAP; BSAK 1; 3Cs; AASA; LSAA; Echoes of African Art; *Artlook* August 1967 & February 1969; *De Arte* May 1968; *SA Panorama* May 1975 & July 1982.

MOTAUNG Morningstar

Born 1938 Germiston, Transvaal.
A painter of township genre, figures and portraits. Works in watercolour and oil.
Studies Studied briefly under Cecil Skotnes (qv).
Profile A founder member and past Chairman of the Katlehong Art Society.
Exhibitions 1961 Lidchi Gallery, Johannesburg, joint exhibition with Solomon Kaphioa; 1973 Triad Gallery, Johannesburg, joint exhibition with Mandla Masiso (qv); participated in group exhibitions in SA, the UK and the USA, and in 1979 in West Germany.
Public Commission Portrait of Dr H F Verwoerd for the East Rand Bantu Administration Building, Germiston, Transvaal.
References AASA; *Informa* vol 26 no 5.

MOTEANE Tumbi David

Born 1951 Germiston, Transvaal.
A sculptor of figures. Works in wood and clay. A graphic artist.
Studies 1979 Katlehong Art Centre, under Rosemary Shakanovsky; 1986 Funda Centre, Soweto, under Steven Sack (qv).
Profile From 1983 a member of the Katlehong Art Society. 1986 taught children at the Katlehong Art Centre.
Exhibitions He has participated in several group exhibitions from 1982 in SA.

MOTHUDI Thabo Gregory

Born 1936 Sophiatown, Johannesburg.
A painter, sculptor and graphic artist of landscapes, figures and abstract pieces. Works in oil, acrylic, pencil, various graphic media, wood, bronze and other metals.
Studies 1960–62 studied art on a scholarship, at the Africa Writing Centre, Kitwe, Northern Rhodesia (Zambia), under Ms M Murray; 1968 under Bill Ainslie (qv).
Profile 1974 a founder member of the National Art Society; 1983 a member of Easelspeak. 1976 a teacher and club leader at the Margaret Ballinger Creche, Naledi Extension, KwaXuma, Transvaal; 1982 taught at The Open School, Johannesburg. From 1962 illustrated several books of Christian literature. 1968 a layout artist and cartoonist for *Elethu* newspaper, Johannesburg. 1984–85 wrote a religious column for *The Sowetan*. A potter. 1980 visited the USA and West Germany.
Exhibitions Many group exhibitions in SA, the USA, Israel, West Germany, The Netherlands, Austria and France; 1970 Gallery 101, Johannesburg, first of six solo exhibitions held in Johannesburg; 1981 Standard Bank, Soweto, Black Art Today Exhibition.
Public Commission 1984 large sculpture entitled "Peace" for SA Council of Churches, Johannesburg.
References AASA; Echoes of African Art; *SA Panorama* July 1982 & June 1983.

MOTJUOADI Tshidiso Andrew

Born 1935 Pietersburg, Northern Transvaal.
Died 1968 Mamelodi, Pretoria.
A self-taught artist of figures and of scenes in townships. Worked in pencil, coloured inks and in various graphic media.
Profile Designed the background to the credit titles of the film "The Naked Prey" by Cornel Wilde in 1964.
Exhibitions 1963 Johannesburg, solo exhibition; participated in group exhibitions from 1965; 1965 Piccadilly Gallery, London, African Painters and Sculptors from Johannesburg; 1977 Johannesburg, Retrospective Exhibition of works found in his house on his death.

Award 1966 Prize Winner, Artists of Fame and Promise.
Represented Biet Giorgis Trust, USA; Pretoria Art Museum; SA National Gallery, Cape Town; University of Fort Hare; University of Zululand.
References SAA; SESA; SSAP; BSAK 1; SA Art; Oxford Companion to C20 Art (under SA); 3Cs; AASA; Echoes of African Art; *Artlook* February 1972.

MOTSWAI Thomas Tommy Trevor
Born 1963 Johannesburg.
An artist of brightly coloured urban scenes of city people. Works in pastel and in various graphic media.
Studies 1980 irregularly at FUBA, Johannesburg, and at Bill Ainslie's (qv) studio; 1982–83 worked as an assistant to Kurt Lossgott (qv), but mainly self-taught.
Profile A member of the Artists Market. A deaf mute, who studied for eleven years (1968–79) at the Kutlwanong School for the Deaf, where he has also taught art. Worked at Wynberg Pottery, Johannesburg.
Exhibitions He has participated in several group exhibitions from 1979 in SA and in 1986 in Monte Carlo; 1988 Goodman Gallery, Johannesburg, solo exhibition.
Awards 1985 Santam Bursary; 1987 Volkskas Atelier Merit Prize; 1987 Sol Plaatjies Graphic Art Award; 1987 Excelsior Award.
Represented Johannesburg Art Gallery; SA National Gallery, Cape Town; University of South Africa.

MOYAGA Nkoane Harry
Born 1954 Pietersburg, Northern Transvaal.
A painter and a sculptor of abstracted figures and of religious and philosophical subjects. Works in mixed media.
Studies Five years at a private art school run by Brother Bral, a Roman Catholic missionary, in Pietersburg; Bill Ainslie's (qv) studio.
Profile Lives in Hammanskraal, Pretoria.
Exhibitions 1976 Nedbank Gallery, Killarney, Johannesburg, solo exhibition; 1977 Stuttgart, West Germany, solo exhibition; 1981 Standard Bank, Soweto, Black Art Today Exhibition.
Reference *Phafa-Nyika*, edited by Ute Scholz, 1980, University of Pretoria.

MSIMANG George
Born 1948 Durban.
A painter and graphic artist of figures, portraits and genre, especially of urban life. Works in oil, watercolour, gouache and in various graphic media, particularly monotypes. Draws in charcoal, pastel, pencil, ink and wash.

Studies At Rorke's Drift Art Centre; 1971–75 Accademia di Belle Arti, Rome, on a grant from the Italian Government; 1985–86 Accademia di Belle Arti, Perugia, Italy, under Professor Sante Monachesi (*b*.1910), Duiglio Rossoni, Franco Gentilini (*b*.1909) and Roberto di Jullo.

Profile A number of illustrations for a series of modern short stories compiled by Wanna Fourie. Designs for ceramics. Lives in Durban.

Exhibitions He has participated in many group exhibitions from 1969 in SA, Italy, West Germany and the USA; 1969 NSA Gallery, Durban, first of several solo exhibitions held in SA, the USA, West Germany and Switzerland; 1979 Contemporary African Art in SA, touring.

Award 1971 Prize Winner, African Studies Center, University of California, USA.

Represented Durban Art Gallery; University of Fort Hare.

Public Commission 1979 mural in Glebelands African Beerhall, by the Natal Bantu Administration Board.

References BSAK 1; Echoes of African Art.

MTHOMBENI Petrus (also known as Peter)

Born 1962 Benoni, Transvaal.

A painter, sculptor and graphic artist of landscapes, portraits and figures. Works in acrylic, watercolour, pencil, charcoal, wood, ceramics and in various graphic media.

Studies 1984–86 Witwatersrand Technikon, gaining a National Diploma in Fine Art; 1987 studied ceramics at the Witwatersrand Technikon.

Profile 1987 a member of the APSA. Works as a self-taught signwriter and handyman in order to finance his studies.

Exhibitions He has participated in several group exhibitions in Johannesburg from 1983.

Award 1983 New Signatures Award for Graphic Art, SAAA.

MUAFANGEJO John Ndevasia

Born 1943 Etunda lo Nghadi, Angola.

Died 1987 Katutura, Windhoek, SWA/Namibia.

An artist best known for his linocuts of genre, figures, religious and historical scenes, African traditions, domestic and wild animals. His works make a personal, social or political comment and many of them contain an explanatory script. An etcher, weaver and sculptor.

Studies 1967–69 Rorke's Drift Art Centre, Natal, under Otto Lundbohm.

Profile A member of Arts Association SWA/Namibia. 1970–74 taught art at Odibo, Owambo; 1974 Artist in Residence, Rorke's Drift Art Centre. From 1971 illustrated books and pamphlets. 1957 moved to Epinga, SWA/Namibia; 1964 lived at Odibo, Owambo; 1977 Windhoek; 1986 Katutura. Visited London and Finland.

Exhibitions Participated in several group exhibitions from 1968 in SA, SWA/ Namibia, West Germany, the UK, Canada, Brazil and in Scandinavia; 1971 Kunstkabinette, Windhoek, first of several solo exhibitions; 1979 Contemporary African Art in SA, touring; 1981 Republic Festival Exhibition; 1987 Johannesburg Art Gallery, Vita Art Now; 1988 Standard Bank National Arts Festival, Grahamstown, Second Guest Artist.

Awards 1981 Republic Festival Graphics Award; 1983 Medal Winner, Seventh International Graphic Exhibition, Frechen, West Germany; 1985 Most Outstanding Artists Award, STANSWA Biennial, Windhoek; 1987 Vita Art Now, Quarterly Award Winner, jointly with Edoardo Villa (qv); 1988 Second Guest Artist Award, Standard Bank National Arts Festival.

Represented Ann Bryant Gallery, East London; Arts Association SWA/ Namibia Collection; Durban Art Gallery; Johannesburg Art Gallery; King George VI Art Gallery, Port Elizabeth; Pretoria Art Museum; SA National Gallery, Cape Town; University of Bophuthatswana; University of Fort Hare; University of South Africa; University of the Witwatersrand; William Humphreys Art Gallery, Kimberley.

References Bruce Arnott, *John Muafangejo*, 1977, C Struik, Cape Town; BSAK 1; Art SWA; 3Cs; AASA; Echoes of African Art; Olga Levinson, *John N Muafangejo*, 1988, Standard Bank National Arts Festival Exhibition Catalogue.

MUBAYI Sylvester

A sculptor of figures and animals. Works in stone and ceramics.

Studies At a workshop school in Salisbury, Rhodesia (Harare, Zimbabwe).

Exhibitions He has participated in group exhibitions from 1969 in Zimbabwe, SA and in Paris, France.

Award 1969 Oppenheimer Trust Award, Art SA Today.

Represented National Gallery, Harare, Zimbabwe.

Reference AASA.

MUFF-FORD John Waldemere Daniel

Born 1884 New Ferry, Cheshire, England.
Died 1981 Port Elizabeth.
Resided in SA from 1898.

A painter of landscapes and flower pieces. Worked in watercolour and oil.

Studies 1912 Northampton School of Art, UK; 1912–14 Regent Street Polytechnic and Royal Academy Schools, London; 1938–39 stained glass at the Central School of Art, London.

Profile A member and President for several years of the Orange Free State Society of Arts and Crafts, a member of the Eastern Province Society of Arts and Crafts; both societies conferred Honorary Life Membership on him. 1902–12 worked in the Department of Customs and Excise, Bloemfontein. 1920 established the Bloemfontein School of Art (private). 1925 hosted the Inaugural Convention of the SA Institute of Art. 1934 taught at Port Elizabeth Technical College Art School, 1936–46 its Principal; 1937 also taught at Grey High School, Port Elizabeth. 1898 lived in Belfast, Transvaal; 1902 in Bloemfontein; 1910–19 in London and from 1933 in Port Elizabeth. Married to Lily Muff-Ford, a flower painter.

Exhibitions 1920 Bloemfontein, first solo exhibition; participated in group exhibitions from 1925; 1968 Eastern Province Society of Arts and Crafts, Retrospective Exhibition; 1979 Port Elizabeth, Retrospective Exhibition.
Represented Africana Museum, Johannesburg; King George VI Art Gallery, Port Elizabeth.
References AMC6 (under Ford); BSAK 1 & 2; AASA.

MUKHUBA Nelson

Born 1925 Tshakhuma, Venda.
Died 1987 Tshakhuma, Venda.
A self-taught sculptor of figures, heads, animals and abstracts. Worked in wood and paint. From 1956 ceramic figures and relief sculptures.
Profile A member of Bozz Art. 1980 three of his sculptures were reproduced on an issue of Venda stamps. 1986 one of six artists chosen for a documentary film made on Venda artists. 1947–58 involved in various marabi music bands, cutting records with "The Zoutpansberg Merry Makers", "Nelson and the Phiri Boys" and "The Music Men". From 1977 a member of the Venda Traditional Dance Group. During the 1980s initiated and trained dancers and singers for the "Maholombe a Mutanda Bin Yuka" Group. 1945–58 lived in Sophiatown, thereafter in Tshakhuma.
Exhibitions Participated in several group exhibitions from 1970 in Venda, five in Johannesburg, one in Durban, one in Cape Town and two in West Germany; 1985 Tributaries, touring SA and West Germany; 1986 Bozz Art Foundation Exhibition, touring Johannesburg, Cape Town and Durban, with Dr Phatuma Seoka (qv), Heindrick Nekhofhe (qv) and Jackson Hlungwani (qv); 1987 Johannesburg Art Gallery, Vita Art Now.
Represented Africana Museum, Johannesburg; Durban Art Gallery; SA National Gallery, Cape Town; University of South Africa; University of the Witwatersrand.
References Echoes of African Art; *SA Arts Calendar* Autumn 1987; *ADA* no 3, 1987.

MULDER Wynand

Born 1946 Krugersdorp, Transvaal.
A painter, sculptor and graphic artist of abstracted landscapes, portrait busts and birds. Works in oil, acrylic, ink, pencil, charcoal, bronze, stone, ciment fondu, wood, painted steel, mixed media, housepaint duco and in various graphic media.
Profile 1974, 1975 and 1976, three-month study tours in Europe and in 1978, 1979, 1980, 1981 and 1982 in the USA; 1981 in the UK and West Germany and in 1982 in The Netherlands.
Exhibitions 1976 SAAA Gallery, Pretoria, first of 21 solo exhibitions held in SA, the USA, the UK, West Germany and Canada; he has participated in many group exhibitions from 1977 in SA, West Germany and the USA; 1981 Republic Festival Exhibition.

Represented City Hall, Washington DC, USA; University of Pretoria.
Public Commissions From 1976 numerous portrait busts of SA and USA notability, including in 1977 Professor Ernst van Heerden of the University of the Witwatersrand for the University of the Orange Free State; 1978 Ms Wena Naudé, Civic Theatre, Johannesburg; 1981 Ms Mimi Coertse, SABC.
References AASA; *Exclusive* vol 1 no 5, 1981; *Steel Construction* August 1983.

MULLAN Marie-Louise

Born 1944 Vereeniging, Transvaal.
A painter of still life and abstract pictures. Works in oil, acrylic, watercolour, gouache and ink.
Studies Pretoria Technical College, under Leo Theron (qv), Gunther van der Reis (qv), Tertia Knaap (qv) and Minette van Rooyen (qv), gaining a National Diploma in Graphic Art in 1965.
Profile An illustrator of children's books and a ceramicist. A founder member and Chairman for the first few years of the APSA. 1966–69 State Heraldic Artist for the State Archives, Pretoria. From 1970 an art editor and illustrator to various publishing companies in SA. Writes and illustrates her own books and has received numerous ceramic mural commissions.
Exhibitions She has participated in numerous group exhibitions from 1965 in SA; has held *c.*20 solo exhibitions in Pretoria and Johannesburg.
Public Commissions During the late 1970s 14 murals for St John Fisher Catholic Parish Church, Pretoria, and a large mural for the ZA Hospital in Pretoria.

MULLANY Margaret Mary St John (Peggy)

Born 1916 Pietermaritzburg.
A painter of landscapes, seascapes, animal portraits and still life. Works in watercolour, gouache and acrylic.
Studies 1964–68 watercolour under Craig White-Smith; 1967–70 watercolour under Alfred Ewan (qv).
Profile A member of the WSSA and the Midlands Arts and Crafts Society. A writer of short stories and poems. A trained singer, who sang in the Pietermaritzburg Philharmonic Choir. 1982 visited England.
Exhibitions She has participated in numerous group exhibitions in SA from 1963; 1970 Pietermaritzburg, first of four solo exhibitions.

MULLER Nola Louise

Born 1949 Cape Town.
A painter of landscapes, seascapes and nature. Works in watercolour and acrylic.
Studies 1976 studied the art of watercolour privately under Viola M Fitzroy (qv); studied jewellery at the Medici School of Art, Florence, Italy, under Tamio Fujimaro.

Profile A member of the WSSA. 1981 visited SWA/Namibia, 1984 the Eastern Transvaal and Tuscany, Italy. Annual visits to Savoie, France.

Exhibitions She has participated in several group exhibitions; 1978 Cape Gallery, Cape Town, first of nine solo exhibitions, one of which was held in SWA/Namibia and one in France.

MULLINS Lucy see WILES Lucy

MUNNIK (John) Andrew

Born 1943 Cape Town.

A painter working in oil, acrylic, ink, pencil and charcoal. Makes sculptures in paper and plaster of Paris for three-dimensional elements of his pictures. Depicts figures and figures interacting with architectural elements. 1986 a series of self-portraits with the emphasis on psychological confrontation.

Studies 1978 began a BA(FA) at the University of South Africa, under Nina Romm (qv), and J P van der Watt (qv), course still to be completed; 1981–82 Witwatersrand Technikon, under Willem Boshoff (qv) and M Marais, where attained a Diploma in Fine Art.

Profile 1960–66 a guitarist in a rock and roll band. 1967–81 a graphic designer and illustrator for various advertising agencies. From 1984 a lecturer in Fine Art at the Witwatersrand Technikon. 1977 travelled in Europe and the USA.

Exhibitions He has participated in several group exhibitions from 1984; 1986 Market Gallery, Johannesburg, first of two solo exhibitions.

Award 1983 Merit Award for Painting, New Signatures, SAAA.

Represented Potchefstroom Museum; University of the Witwatersrand.

MURCOTT Lionel Emmanuel

Born 1947 Northern Transvaal.

A painter and graphic artist of figures, portraits and abstract pictures. Works in oil, acrylic, watercolour, ink, wash, pencil, charcoal, conté crayon and in various graphic media. A maker of collages.

Studies 1968–70 University of Natal, under Jane Heath (qv), Dick Leigh (qv) and Aidron Duckworth, gaining a BA in English and Fine Art; 1980–83 Johannesburg Art Foundation, under Bill Ainslie (qv), Ricky Burnett (qv) and William Kentridge (qv).

Profile 1975–76 a member of the North Coast Art Group, Durban, and of the NSA. 1972–73 an art teacher at Eshowe Junior High School, Natal; 1975–76 at the George Campbell Technical High School, Durban; 1978–79 at Northcliff High School, Johannesburg; 1983–85 a part-time teacher at the Johannesburg Art Foundation; from 1986 an art teacher, specialising in craft, at the Johannesburg Art, Ballet and Music School. 1979 illustrations in *Reality*. 1984 cover for *Journal of a New Man*, by Lionel Abrahams, Ad Donker, Johannesburg. 1980–85 a member of the Writer's Workshop, from 1981 his poems have been published in *Sesame*, and in *Columbia Review* in Canada. Since 1986 he has had an interest in pottery.

Exhibitions 1972 Royal Hotel, Eshowe, Natal, joint exhibition with Wally Walters; he has participated in many group exhibitions from 1976 in SA; 1982 National Gallery, Gaborone, Botswana, Exhibition of SA Art; 1987 Johannesburg Art Foundation, joint exhibition with Gail Behrmann (qv), Dee Jacobs (qv), Charles Levin and Russel Scott.
Award 1984 Award for conté portrait, Festival of African Art, University of Zululand.

MURPHY Michael Vincent

Born 1943 England.
Resided in SA from 1952.
A painter and graphic artist of landscapes, still life and figures, with the occasional venture into the surreal. Series of railway trucks and steam engines. Works in oil, acrylic and the various graphic media.
Profile From 1980 a member of the EPSFA, its Vice-Chairman in 1986 and Chairman 1987–88.
Exhibitions He has participated in several group exhibitions from 1979 in SA; 1983 EPSFA Gallery, Port Elizabeth, first of two solo exhibitions held in Port Elizabeth; 1987 Karen McKerron Gallery, Johannesburg, joint exhibition with Simon Stone (qv).
Represented King George VI Art Gallery, Port Elizabeth.

MURRAY Andrew James Jowett

Born 1917 Tientsin, North China.
Resided in SA 1946–69.
A self-taught painter of landscapes, genre, figures, animals, flowers, buildings and Biblical subjects in the naive tradition. Worked in tempera.
Profile 1940–45 in the Royal Navy. 1946–50 worked in advertising in Durban. He began painting in 1956 whilst working as a religious journalist in Cape Town; in 1969 he became a full-time artist. In 1966 opened the Dorp Street Gallery in Cape Town. He later settled in London where many of his paintings were reproduced as postcards and greetings cards. Several visits to SA since 1970.
Exhibitions Participated in group exhibitions from 1960 in SA, the UK and Europe; 1963 Cape Town, first of several solo exhibitions held in SA and the UK.
Represented Hester Rupert Art Museum, Graaff-Reinet; Musée d'Art Naif de l'Ile de France, Paris, France; William Humphreys Art Gallery, Kimberley.
Public Commission 1973 UNICEF Christmas Card.
References AASA; Oto Bihalji-Merin & Nebojša-Bato Tomašević, *World Encyclopedia of Naive Art*, 1984, Frederick Muller, London.

MURRAY Angela Winsome

Born 1939 Durban.
A painter of figures and abstract pictures. Works in oil, acrylic, watercolour, gouache, ink, pencil and charcoal.

Studies University of the Witwatersrand, under Professor Heather Martienssen (1915–79), Charles Argent (qv), Joyce Leonard (qv), Erica Berry (qv), Cecily Sash (qv) and Marjorie Long (qv), gaining a BA(FA).
Profile An occasional member of the SAAA. Tapestry designs. A choral singer, opera singer, poet and journalist. Has travelled extensively throughout the world.
Exhibitions She has participated in several group exhibitions from 1962 in SA, Greece and Italy; 1964 SAAA Gallery, Pretoria, first of two solo exhibitions.
Represented Potchefstroom University for CHE.
Public Commission Tapestry design for Waterkloof Catholic Church, Pretoria.
References BSAK 1; *Artlook* May 1970.

MURRAY Margaret (Nina)

Born 1861 Scotland.
Died 1952 Pretoria.
Resided in SA from *c.*1905.
A painter of landscapes. Worked in watercolour.
Profile From *c.*1906 taught at the Diocesan School for Girls in Pretoria.
Exhibitions 1910–12 exhibited with the Individualists in Pretoria.
References BSAK 1 & 2; AASA.

MUSKAT Victoria

Born 1949 Johannesburg.
A painter of the rites and traditions of tribal Africa. Works in oil, ink, wax and airbrush.
Studies 1968–69 Johannesburg School of Art; 1970 l'Ecole des Beaux Arts, Paris; 1975–80 University of South Africa, gaining a BA(FA).
Profile 1982 visited New York; 1985 San Francisco, USA.
Exhibitions 1982 New York, solo exhibition; 1985 participated in a group exhibition in Johannesburg.

MVEMVE Lindiwe

Born 1958 Benoni, Transvaal.
A graphic artist producing linocuts of figures.
Studies 1977–78 Rorke's Drift Art Centre.
Profile In 1979 began studying to be a medical technician in Pietermaritzburg.
Exhibitions Has participated in group exhibitions in SA and West Germany.

MVUSI Selby

Born 1929 Pietermaritzburg.
Died 1967.
Carved in wood, drew in pencil and chalk. Depicted township and religious scenes.
Studies Ndaleni Educational Training School, under Alfred Ewan (qv) and Alan Atkins. An Arts graduate from Boston University, USA.

Profile A member of the NSA. Taught at Loram School, Durban, and in West and East Africa.
Exhibitions Participated in group exhibitions in SA; 1956 Quadrennial Exhibition.
References SAA; SESA; BSAK 1; AASA; *South Africana* September 1957.

MYBURGH Davydd

Born 1953 Pietersburg, Northern Transvaal.
A sculptor working in wood and mixed media.
Studies Gained a BA(FA) from the University of Natal in 1974.
Profile Has lectured at the University of the Witwatersrand and at the Witwatersrand Technikon, also taught at the Katlehong Art Centre. Wrote articles for *Sgraffiti*.
Exhibitions 1982 Cape Town Triennial; 1983 Gallery DC, Johannesburg, solo exhibition.
Award 1982 Merit Award, Cape Town Triennial.
Represented Touch Gallery, SA National Gallery, Cape Town.

MYCHREEST Ronald

Born 1920 Johannesburg.
A painter and a sculptor of landscapes, portraits, still life, seascapes, figures, wildlife and abstracts. Works in oil, acrylic, watercolour, gouache, ink, wash, pencil, charcoal, bronze, stone and wood.
Studies Continental School of Art, Cape Town, under Arthur Podolini (qv).
Profile A former Vice-President of the Transvaal Art Society; Chairman of the Transvaal Academy and a former Vice-President of the Southern Transvaal Branch of the SAAA. 1976–77 lectured in painting at the University of Pretoria. Has acted as a judge on national exhibitions.
Exhibitions He has participated in numerous group exhibitions from 1950 in SA, Zimbabwe, Italy, Switzerland, Belgium and Brazil; 1951 Herbert Evans Gallery, Johannesburg, first of eight solo exhibitions; 1956 and 1960 Quadrennial Exhibitions.
Represented Ann Bryant Gallery, East London; Hester Rupert Art Museum, Graaff-Reinet; Pretoria Art Museum; SA National Gallery, Cape Town; Willem Annandale Art Gallery, Lichtenburg; William Humphreys Art Gallery, Kimberley.
Public Commissions Three concrete panels, Goudstad College of Education, Johannesburg; three wood panels, Jan Smuts Airport, Johannesburg; two glass mosaics, Johannesburg General Hospital; stone mosaic, Badplaas recreational spa, Transvaal; wood and bronze sculpture, Venda Parliament Assembly Hall; wood and bronze panel, Gazankulu Parliament Assembly Hall; wood and copper panel, the State Theatre, Pretoria; panel and wood sculpture, the Sand du Plessis Theatre, Bloemfontein; two panels, Legislative Assembly Building, Lebowa.
References Art SA; SAA; 20C SA Art; SAP&S; BSAK 1 & 2; SA Art; 3Cs; AASA; LSAA.

MYENI Bekhi

A self-taught sculptor of insects and animals, particularly cattle, and of figures, trees and abstract pieces. Works in white or burnt wood.

Exhibitions He has participated in several group exhibitions in SA from 1982; 1985 Valparaiso Bienale, Chile.

Reference De Kat September 1985.

MZIMBA George Velaphi

Born 1959 Dube, Soweto.

A painter of portraits, genre, figures, abstracts, street scenes and township life. Works in oil, watercolour, ink and pastel. A series of paintings and sketches of underground scenes in gold mines. Sculpts in bronze.

Studies 1975–76 Mofolo Art Centre, Soweto, under Dan Rakgoathe (qv); 1978–80 under Bill Ainslie (qv).

Profile 1985 taught at the Thusong Youth Centre, Alexandra, Johannesburg; from 1986 has taught at The Open School, Johannesburg.

Exhibitions He has participated in group exhibitions from 1975 in SA and West Germany; 1981 SAAA Gallery, Carlton Centre, Johannesburg, first of several solo exhibitions held in SA, Swaziland, Northern Ireland, West Germany, SWA/Namibia and the USA.

Represented National Art Museum, Frankfurt, West Germany.

N

NAGEL Sybille Beatrix
Born 1955 Johannesburg.
Drawing and mixed media compositions, eclectic collages, photo romances.
Studies 1973 architecture at the University of Cape Town; 1974–77 Michaelis
School of Fine Art, under Kevin Atkinson (qv), gaining a BA(FA) and the
Michaelis Prize; 1979–80 awarded the Harry Crossley Bursary and the Jules
Kramer Music and Fine Art Grant for overseas study, travelling in Europe and
the USA; 1983 on a Human Sciences Research Council Bursary and a
University Senior Bursary at Freie Kunstschule, Hamburg, West Germany
under Günter Lierschoff; 1982–86 Fine Art at the University of the Witwa-
tersrand in order to complete her MA(FA).
Profile 1983–84 a founder member of the Possessions Arts Group. 1980–81 and
1984–85 a lecturer in the Department of Architecture, University of the
Witwatersrand; 1984 taught at The Open School, Johannesburg; 1985–86 a
lecturer at the University of South Africa.
Exhibitions She has participated in several group exhibitions in SA and West
Germany; 1981 Republic Festival Exhibition; 1985 Cape Town Triennial; 1985
Tributaries, touring SA and West Germany; 1986 University of the Orange Free
State, joint exhibition with Debbie Bell (qv), Johann Moolman (qv) and Keith
Dietrich (qv); 1986 Market Gallery, Johannesburg, first of two solo exhibitions;
1987 Johannesburg Art Gallery, Vita Art Now.
Award 1987 Merit Award, Delfin/FUBA Creative Quest.
Represented Durban Art Gallery; SA National Gallery, Cape Town.
Reference AASA.

NANACKCHAND Vedant
Born 1955 Durban.
A graphic artist producing coloured etchings.
Studies 1977 graduated in Fine Art from the University of Durban-Westville;
1978 gained an Honours Degree in Fine Art, specialising in TV Graphics. In
1979 he was awarded a British Council Scholarship.
Exhibitions He has participated in group exhibitions from 1977 in SA, Australia,
West Germany and the USA.
Reference AASA.

NAPIER Ruth
Born 1928 Stellenbosch, Cape Province.
A painter of portraits, still life, genre and figures. Works in oil and pencil.
Sculpts in cold bronze, ciment fondu and fibreglass.

Studies 1953–54 London College of Art, under Percy Bradshaw; 1968–71 ceramics at the Cape Technical College, under Peggy Clay; 1972–73 sculpture at the Cape Technical College, under M Mitford-Barberton; 1974–79 University of South Africa, under Alan Crump and Professor Rayda Becker, where gained a BA(FA).

Profile A member of the SAAA and the Artists Guild, Cape Town. 1968–74 a potter making utility ware and stoneware.

Exhibitions She has participated in many group exhibitions from 1979 in SA and once in 1986 in Canada; 1984 Atlantic Gallery, Cape Town, first of two solo exhibitions.

Public Commissions 1979 statue of St Michael, St Michael and All Angels Church, Elgin, Cape Province; 1984 statue of St Barnabas, Villiersdorp Roman Catholic Church, Cape Province.

NAUDÉ André

Born 1950 Johannesburg.

A painter of landscapes, still life, portraits and figures. Works in acrylic, watercolour, gouache, ink, wash, pastel, pencil and charcoal. 1987 series of paintings of various types of luggage and of his garden.

Studies 1969–72 University of Pretoria, under Professor Nico Roos (qv) and Professor Murray Schoonraad, where gained a BA(FA); 1973 Johannesburg College of Education, under Larry Scully (qv), attaining a Higher Diploma in Education.

Profile From 1984 a member of the SAAA. 1974–80 Art Master and Head of the Art Department, Northcliff High School, Johannesburg, 1981 taught at Damelin College and 1983–88 at Roedean School, Johannesburg. 1988 a part-time assistant at the Karen McKerron Gallery, Johannesburg. From 1985 began working in pottery and painted ceramics. 1980 and 1983 visited the USA; 1980 and 1984 Europe. In 1986 he spent four months in Paris at the Cité Internationale des Arts.

Exhibitions He has participated in many group exhibitions in SA; 1974 Municipal Library, Springs, first of 25 solo exhibitions; 1982 Cape Town Triennial; 1987 Johannesburg Art Gallery, Vita Art Now.

Represented SA National Gallery, Cape Town.

Reference AASA.

NAUDÉ Anna Catharina (Mrs De Wit)

Born 1922 Lichtenburg, Western Transvaal.

A painter of landscapes, seascapes, still life, figures, wildlife and abstract pictures. Works in oil, acrylic, watercolour, gouache, ink, wash, pencil, charcoal and pastel. Numerous portraits in pencil, charcoal, pastel, watercolour and oil, as well as small gouaches of indigenous plants.

Studies 1957–60 Pretoria Technical College, under Robert Hodgins (qv) and Zakkie Eloff (qv); 1958 modelling and sculpture privately under Leo Theron (qv).

Profile From 1955 a member of the SAAA and in 1976–78 a council member of the Northern Transvaal Branch. A singer and a translator of books into Afrikaans, some of which she has illustrated in ink and watercolour. 1922–33 lived in Lichtenburg; 1933–40 in Ventersdorp, Transvaal; 1940–78 in Pretoria; from 1978 in Hermanus, Cape Province.

Exhibitions She has participated in several group exhibitions in Pretoria from 1960; 1963 first of several solo exhibitions.

Represented National Museum for Afrikaans Literature, Bloemfontein; Prince Albert Museum, Cape Province.

NAUDÉ Burgert

Born 1928 Klerksdorp, Transvaal.

A painter working in oil, watercolour, ink, pencil and charcoal.

Profile A member of the SAAA. A trained architect practising in Bellville, Cape Province.

Exhibition 1959 Salisbury, Rhodesia (Harare, Zimbabwe), solo exhibition.

NAUDÉ (Pieter) Hugo

Born 1868 Worcester, Cape Province.

Died 1941 Worcester, Cape Province.

A painter of the flowering fields of Namaqualand, landscapes, seascapes, portraits, genre and figures. Painted in the Cape, Namaqualand, Drakensberg, Boland, Karoo and at Victoria Falls, Rhodesia (Zimbabwe). Worked in oil and very occasionally in watercolour. A series of the Cape Malay Quarter, Cape Town. 1897–1900 a number of silverpoint drawings. Numerous etchings.

Studies 1889–90 Slade School of Art, London, UK, under Alphonse Legros (1837–1911); 1890–94 and 1913 Art Academy, Munich, Germany, under Adolf Hölzel (1853–1934) and Franz von Lenbach (1836–1904); 1895 with the Barbizon Group at Fontainebleau, France; 1913 etching at the King's Road School, London.

Profile 1902 a founder member of the SA Society of Artists; 1932 a founder member of the National Academy of Fine Arts; 1938 a member of the New Group. Illustrated *In Die Kerkhof, A Story of Old Worcester*, 1906, Cape Town Times and *Stories of Jesus, The Friend of Little Children* written by his wife, Julie Naudé, 1923, Maskew Miller, Cape Town. 1936 designed a rock-garden for the Empire Exhibition in Johannesburg; designed the Garden of Remembrance in Worcester, Cape Province. 1889 travelled with the writer, Olive Schreiner, to Europe, initially living in England; 1890–94 in Germany; 1895 in Italy; 1896–1912 travelled extensively in SA, particularly to Namaqualand, Damaraland and to the Victoria Falls in Rhodesia (Zimbabwe); 1913 visited London, Germany and Israel; 1914 returned to Worcester. A friend of Alfred Merkell (qv), with whom he painted in Worcester. A well-known figure in the Scout Movement. Included in Edward Roworth's (qv) essay "Landscape Art in SA", 1917, Studio Publication, *Art of the British Empire Overseas*.

Exhibitions Participated in group exhibitions from 1890 in Europe and SA; 1899 Cape Town, joint exhibition with Borge Stuckenberg (qv), George Winkles (qv) and James Morland (qv); 1917 Cape Town, joint exhibition with Pieter Wenning (qv), Edward Roworth (qv) and Nita Spilhaus (qv); 1945 SA National Gallery, Cape Town, Memorial Exhibition; 1948 Tate Gallery, London, SA Art Exhibition; 1969 Retrospective Exhibition, which travelled throughout SA.

Award 1938 Medal of Honour, SA Akademie vir Wetenskap en Kuns.

Represented Africana Museum, Johannesburg; Albany Museum, Grahamstown; Ann Bryant Gallery, East London; Durban Art Gallery; Hugo Naudé House, Worcester; Johannesburg Art Gallery; King George VI Art Gallery, Port Elizabeth; Pretoria Art Museum; Queenstown Art Gallery; SA Akademie vir Wetenskap en Kuns; SA Cultural History Museum, Cape Town; SA National Gallery, Cape Town; Tatham Art Gallery, Pietermaritzburg; University of the Orange Free State; University of South Africa; University of Stellenbosch; University of the Witwatersrand; War Museum of the Boer Republics, Bloemfontein; William Humphreys Art Gallery, Kimberley; 1820 Settlers Memorial Museum, Grahamstown.

Public Commissions Numerous portrait commissions including those of President Steyn, General Louis Botha, Reverend William Murray and Reverend Andrew Murray. A landscape by Naudé was given by the Worcester Chamber of Commerce to SA House, London.

References Adèle Naudé, *Hugo Naudé*, 1974, C Struik, Cape Town; Collectors' Guide; K&K; PSA; Skone Kunste; Our Art 1; Art SA; SAA; SADNB; 20C SA Art; SAP&S; Oxford Companion to Art (under SA); SAP&D; SESA; SSAP; Bénézit; BSAK 1 & 2; SA Art; Oxford Companion to 20C Art (under SA); 3Cs; AASA; LSAA; *Tydskrif vir Wetenskap en Kuns* December 1940; *SA Art Collector* December 1946; *SA Panorama* November 1969.

NDABA Godfrey

Born 1947.

An artist producing charcoal and pastel drawings. Depicts figures, animals and urban life.

Studies Jubilee Centre, Johannesburg; 1969 Ndaleni Educational Training School, Natal, under Lorna Pearson.

Exhibitions He has participated in several group exhibitions in SA, Botswana, Israel, the UK, West Germany and the USA; 1972 New Hyde Park Gallery, Johannesburg, first solo exhibition; 1981 Standard Bank, Soweto, Black Art Today Exhibition.

Award 1969 First Prize on a University of Fort Hare Exhibition.

Represented University of Fort Hare.

References Echoes of African Art; *Artlook* September 1972; *SA Panorama* April 1979 & July 1982.

NDINISA Roy Solomon

Born 1954 Swaziland.

A graphic artist. Produces linocuts depicting figures.

KAREL NEL
Transmuter 1986
Drawing on Bonded Fibre Fabric 220 × 193 cm
Y Tessler

KENNETH NEWMAN
Bald Ibis at a Roost 1972
Gouache 50 × 36 cm
M P S Irwin

ANTHONY NKOTSI
No Solution 1987
Oil & Acrylic on Canvas 150 × 180 cm
Dr J P Nel

FRANS OERDER
Pretoria 1885
Oil on Canvas 114 × 165 cm
Pretoria Art Museum

Studies Guided by Eric Lubisi (qv) but otherwise self-taught.
Profile Co-founder and organiser of the Studio Des Independants, Pretoria, with Eric Lubisi (qv).
Exhibitions He has participated in several group exhibitions from 1972 in SA and West Germany; 1985 Tributaries, touring SA and West Germany; 1987 FUBA Gallery, Johannesburg, joint exhibition with Eric Lubisi (qv).
Reference Echoes of African Art.

NEETHLING Johannes Henoch (Jan)

Born 1938 London, England.
Resided in SA from 1940.
A painter and graphic artist of figures. Works in acrylic and in various graphic media. A number of sculptures in plaster of Paris.
Studies Pretoria Art School, gaining a Diploma in 1960.
Exhibitions He has participated in several group exhibitions in Johannesburg and one at the Pretoria Art Museum which travelled to the USA and West Germany; from 1970 several joint exhibitions with Robert Hodgins (qv).
Represented University of South Africa; University of the Witwatersrand.
References BSAK; AASA; *Artlook* January 1973.

NEKE Gael

Born 1946 Johannesburg.
A sculptor working in ceramics. 1981–84 a series entitled "Expressions of Being African"; 1985 "Veld and City" series; 1985–86 "Intransigence and Change" series.
Studies 1964–65 and 1968–69 University of the Witwatersrand, under Cecily Sash (qv), Judith Mason (qv), Giuseppe Cattaneo (qv), Robert Hodgins (qv) and Erica Berry (qv), gaining a BA(FA).
Profile From 1975 a member of the APSA and from 1978 a committee member. Since 1977 she has run a teaching studio in Northcliff, Johannesburg. 1984–85 a part-time lecturer in ceramics at the Witwatersrand Technikon. 1984 a regional ceramics judge in Transvaal; 1985 a national ceramics judge in Natal and in 1986 in the Transvaal. Writes articles for *Sgraffiti*. In addition to her sculptural work she used to produce domestic ware. 1983 visited India and Nepal; 1984–85 the USA; 1985 Peru and Brazil; 1985–86 Botswana and SWA/Namibia.
Exhibitions She has participated in numerous group exhibitions from 1977 in SA and West Germany; 1980 Potters Gallery, Hyde Park, Johannesburg, first of two solo exhibitions; 1985 Cape Town Triennial.
Awards From 1982 several ceramic awards, including the Corobrik Award in 1982 and many APSA regional and national awards.
Represented Durban Art Gallery; King George VI Art Gallery, Port Elizabeth; Pretoria Art Museum; University of Natal; Willem Annandale Art Gallery, Lichtenburg; William Humphreys Art Gallery, Kimberley.
References *Sgraffiti* November 1982 & March 1985.

NEKHOFHE Tshivhangwaho Hendrick

Born 1956 Tshisahulu, Venda.
A sculptor of figures and abstract pieces. Works in wood.
Profile From 1983 a member of the Venda Group and from 1984 of FUBA. A potter.
Exhibitions Began participating in group exhibitions in Venda and SA whilst still at school; 1986 Bozz Art Foundation Exhibition, touring Johannesburg, Cape Town and Durban, with Dr Phatuma Seoka (qv), Nelson Mukhuba (qv) and Jackson Hlungwani (qv).
Reference Echoes of African Art.

NEL (Humboldt) Hylton

Born 1941 N'kana, Northern Rhodesia (Zambia).
A ceramic artist, making primitive figures and moulded vases. Works in kaolin.
Studies Rhodes University, where in 1963·he gained a BA(FA); 1965–67 Koninklijke Academie voor Schone Kunsten en de Hogere Instituten, Antwerp, Belgium, on a two-year scholarship, obtaining a Diploma in Ceramics.
Profile A member of the East Cape Potters Association, of which he is also a judge. 1974 a part-time pottery lecturer and 1975–87 a full-time pottery lecturer at the Port Elizabeth Technikon; 1988 lecturing at the Michaelis School of Fine Art, Cape Town. 1977 a selector for the National Exhibition of Ceramics. 1969–73 lived and worked in England and Belgium.
Exhibitions Has participated in several group exhibitions from the 1960s; 1968 Dorp Street Gallery, Cape Town, joint exhibition with John Nowers (qv); 1982 held a solo exhibition at his home in Port Elizabeth; 1987 SAAA Gallery, Cape Town, joint exhibition with John Nowers (qv) and Sheila Nowers (qv).
Represented Durban Art Gallery; SA National Gallery, Cape Town; University of Natal.
References Port Elizabeth School of Art; *Sgraffiti* no 27; *De Arte* May 1970; *De Kat* September 1985.

NEL Karel Anthony

Born 1955 Pietermaritzburg.
Draws in graphite, conté crayon, Caran d'Ache, charcoal, pastel and sprayed pigment on bonded fibre fabric. Series of large drawings of still life, interiors and abstract works. A graphic artist. A sculptor of abstract pieces. Works in steel, bronze, wood and felt.
Studies 1974–77 University of the Witwatersrand, under Giuseppe Cattaneo (qv), Cecily Sash (qv), Neels Coetzee (qv), Judith Mason (qv), Erica Berry (qv), Nils Burwitz (qv), Michael Pettit (qv) and Joyce Leonard (qv), gaining a BA(FA); 1977–78, on a Montague White Bursary, at St Martin's School of Art, London, under Anthony Caro (*b*.1924), Phillip King (*b*.1934), Michel Bolus, Tim Scott (*b*.1937), Tony Smart, David Everson and Alan Gaulk.

Profile From 1980 has lectured in drawing, sculpture and papermaking at the University of the Witwatersrand. 1979 visited museums, private collections and educational institutions in America and Europe on a Montague White Travel Grant; 1982 travelled extensively in Europe for three months on an Olivetti Travel Grant; 1983 travelled to Greece and Turkey; 1986 drew in the Comoro Islands; 1988 in the USA.

Exhibitions He has participated in several group exhibitions from 1977 in SA and West Germany; 1980 Olivetti Gallery, Johannesburg, first of three solo exhibitions; 1982 Cape Town Triennial; 1983 Johannesburg Art Gallery, Guest Artist; 1985 Cape Town Triennial; 1985 Tributaries, touring SA and West Germany; 1987 Johannesburg Art Gallery, Vita Art Now.

Awards 1977 joint winner, Metalart Student Award; 1978 Prize for Sculpture, Metalart, open category; 1981 First Prize, Almaks Prize Stainless Steel Sculpture Competition; 1982 Rembrandt Gold Medal, Cape Town Triennial; 1986 Vita Annual Award Winner; 1987–88 awarded a Fulbright Placement and a University Council Fellowship for study and research in the USA.

Represented Durban Art Gallery; Johannesburg Art Gallery; Pretoria Art Museum; SA National Gallery, Cape Town; University of the Orange Free State; University of South Africa; University of the Witwatersrand.

Public Commissions 1985 mural/pastel drawing, the Sand du Plessis Theatre, Bloemfontein; 1985 a graphic work commissioned by the Johannesburg Art Gallery for the Centenary Portfolio.

References AASA; *Habitat* no 27, 1977; *Gallery* Summer 1981; *Style* December/January 1984.

NEL Peter (Zirk)

Born 1935 Pietersburg, Northern Transvaal.
Died 1985 London, England.
A painter of landscapes and abstracted pictures. Worked in oil. An etcher.

Studies 1956–57 Witwatersrand Technical College, under T O D Davies; 1958–60 Central School of Art, London, where obtained a Diploma in Etching.

Profile A member of the British Printmakers Council. Taught at the Central School of Art, London and in 1966 became Head of the Etching Department there. Lived in London but frequently visited and exhibited in SA.

Exhibitions Participated in group exhibitions from 1960 in the UK, the USA, Canada, West Germany and SA; 1960 Johannesburg, first solo exhibition held in SA; 1981 Republic Festival Exhibition.

Award 1967 Transvaal Academy Award for Etching.

Represented Ann Bryant Gallery, East London; Bolton Museum and Art Gallery, England; Bradford University, England; Bristol Museum, England; British Arts Council, London; Fitzwilliam Collection, Cambridge, England; Greenwich Gallery, England; Johannesburg Art Gallery; Manchester Education Committee, England; Pietersburg Collection; Pretoria Art Museum; SA National Gallery, Cape Town; Sunderland Museum and Art Gallery, England; University of South Africa; Walker Gallery, Liverpool, England; William Humphreys Art Gallery, Kimberley.

References SAA; BSAK 1; 3Cs; AASA; *Artlook* April 1968; *Gallery* Summer 1981.

NEL Mathijs Isak (Thijs)

Born 1943 Ellisras, Transvaal.

A painter and graphic artist of landscapes, interiors and still life. Works in oil, acrylic, watercolour, gouache, ink, wash, pencil, charcoal, wood and in various graphic media. A ceramicist.

Studies 1962–65 University of the Witwatersrand, under Giuseppe Cattaneo (qv), Professor Heather Martienssen (1915–79), Cecily Sash (qv), Erica Berry (qv) and Judith Mason (qv).

Profile A member of the SAAA. 1965 lectured in the history of art at the Witwatersrand Technical College. 1966–70 Art Editor of *Die Vaderland* newspaper. 1977–79 ran Ateljee Thijs Nel, Johannesburg. Has written plays and short stories, sung in an opera and designed stage sets for opera. 1970–73 lived at the Cité Internationale des Arts, Paris; 1973–75 in Meudon, France. 1978 visited Europe and India; 1980 spent three months in Paris working in the studio of Henri Deprest; has also travelled in the USA.

Exhibitions He has participated in numerous group exhibitions in SA, France, Zimbabwe and Botswana; 1967 Serendipity, Johannesburg, first of *c.*40 solo exhibitions, two of which were held in Paris; 1981 Johannesburg Art Gallery, Guest Artist; 1982 Rand Afrikaans University, Retrospective Exhibition.

Represented Johannesburg Art Gallery; Pietersburg Collection; Potchefstroom Museum; Rand Afrikaans University; Roodepoort Municipal Museum; Willem Annandale Art Gallery, Lichtenburg.

Public Commissions 1973 and 1974 murals for Education Nationale, France, in schools in Bois d'Arcie, Versailles and in Neuilly-sur-Marne.

References BSAK 2; AASA; Retrospective Exhibition Catalogue, 1982, Rand Afrikaans University.

NELL Josua Andries

Born 1935 Keetmanshoop, SWA/Namibia.

An extremely versatile artist, painting and sculpting in many media, with a wide-ranging subject matter. A series of large topographical Namib landscapes in oil.

Studies 1955–58 Rhodes University, under Professor Cecil Todd (qv), where gained a Diploma in Fine Art with distinctions.

Profile From 1958 a member of the EPSFA; 1961–77 a founder member of the Grahamstown Group; a member of the SAAA. 1959–62 a junior lecturer, 1963–66 a lecturer, 1967–82 a senior lecturer, from 1983 Associate Professor and acting Department Head (1982–84) of the Fine Arts Department of Rhodes University. From 1970 an external examiner for the University of Fort Hare, from 1980 for the Port Elizabeth Technikon, from 1985 for the Orange Free State Technikon and 1986 for the East London Technical College. 1958 and 1962 made backdrops for the Rhodes Theatre. Travelled extensively in the desert regions of SWA/Namibia.

Exhibitions He has participated in numerous group exhibitions from 1958 in SA and in 1967 at the Royal Academy in London; 1960 Albany Museum, Grahamstown, first of four solo exhibitions; 1979 Uitenhage, joint exhibition with Estelle Marais (qv); 1981 Republic Festival Exhibition; 1982 Cape Town Triennial; 1985 Cape Town Triennial.

Award 1958 Purvis Prize, Rhodes University.
Represented Pietersburg Collection.
Public Commissions Academic portrait commissions for universities and schools.
References SAA; 3Cs; AASA.

NERO Daryl Christopher

Born 1946 Pietermaritzburg.
Resided in SA until 1981.
A painter of landscapes, figures and wildlife. Works in watercolour, oil, ink, wash, pencil and charcoal.
Studies 1965–69 University of Natal, under Professor Jack Heath (qv) and Jane Heath (qv), gaining a BA(FA) in 1968 and a BA (Hons) in 1969; 1970–71 Croydon College of Art, London, under Clifford Frith; 1978–79 University of Natal, under Mike Taylor.
Profile From 1969 a member of the NSA. 1974–75 a part-time lecturer in Fine Art, University of Natal; 1977–80 a lecturer at the University of Durban-Westville. 1977–79 illustrations and cover designs for *Reality*. From 1972 involved in stage design. Runs a pottery studio in Raffingora, Zimbabwe. 1976 spent six months in Botswana; from 1981 he has lived in Zimbabwe.
Exhibitions He has participated in numerous group exhibitions in SA; 1970 NSA Gallery, Durban, first of 12 solo exhibitions held in SA, Zimbabwe and West Germany; 1976 National Gallery, Gaborone, Botswana, solo exhibition; 1979 National Gallery, Gaborone, Botswana, joint exhibition with the potter David Walters; 1983 Tatham Art Gallery, Pietermaritzburg, solo exhibition.
Represented Durban Art Gallery; National Gallery, Gaborone, Botswana; National Gallery, Harare, Zimbabwe.
Reference AASA.

NESBIT (George) Hunter Hardy

Born 1933 Johannesburg.
A painter of landscapes, seascapes, figures, portraits and abstract pictures. Works in many media.
Studies 1952–56 Witwatersrand Technical College, under James Gardner (qv), J W Bramham and T O D Davies, gaining a National Art Teachers Certificate; 1960–63 University of South Africa, through which he gained a BA(FA); 1981–83 on a Human Sciences Research Council Ad Hoc Grant at Port Elizabeth Technikon, where attained a National Diploma in Fine Art; 1984 awarded an Ernest Oppenheimer Memorial Trust Award and a Human Sciences Research Council Grant for Overseas Study to study the current practice in the field of architectural and autonomous stained glass in Europe and the USA.

Profile A member of the EPSFA; a former President and Eastern Province Representative of the SAAA; a member of the Historical Society of Port Elizabeth; a member of the SA Museums Association; an active member of the International du Vitrail, Chartres et Paris, France and an Associate of the International Institute for Conservation and Artistic Works, London. Has served on numerous committees including the Design Education Committee of the Design Institute of the SA Bureau of Standards; the Arts Committee of the Association of SA Technikons; various committees of the Port Elizabeth Technikon; on the Board of Trustees of the King George VI Art Gallery, Port Elizabeth and the Port Elizabeth Athenaeum Council. 1957 and 1959–65 Art Master at Roosevelt High School, Johannesburg; 1957–58 a supply teacher for the London County Council, England. 1966–69 a lecturer in drawing and painting, 1969–80 Head of the School of Art and Design, 1981–84 Assistant Director, then Director, School of Art and Design and from 1985 Head of the Department of Stained Glass and of Post-Diploma Studies, School of Art and Design, Port Elizabeth Technikon. From 1976 a stained glass painter and designer. A restorer of artworks. 1971/72 and 1973/74 led art student study tours in Europe; 1984 a six-month study tour of Europe and the USA. Married to Ruth Nesbit (qv).

Exhibitions He has participated in numerous group exhibitions from 1958 in London and SA; 1968 Port Elizabeth, first of three solo exhibitions; 1981 Republic Festival Exhibition; 1986 Beuster-Skolimowski Gallery, Pretoria, joint exhibition with Ruth Nesbit (qv).

Represented King George VI Art Gallery, Port Elizabeth; National Museum, Bloemfontein; Port Elizabeth Technikon; University of Port Elizabeth.

Public Commissions Numerous commissions for stained glass windows in churches in Bathurst, Stanger, Margate, Kei Road, Port Elizabeth, Vanderbijlpark and in Umtata, Transkei.

Publications by Nesbit *Port Elizabeth School of Art—A History 1882–1982*, 1982, Port Elizabeth Technikon; *Roy Carruthers*, 1982, Retrospective Exhibition Catalogue.

References Register SA & SWA; BSAK 1; Port Elizabeth School of Art; AASA; *SA Digest* 17 December 1971; *Artlook* December/January 1976; *SA Arts Calendar* April/May 1982, February/March 1983 and April/May 1983; *SA Panorama* August 1982; *De Kat* March 1987.

NESBIT Ruth Alice Clare (née Carter)

Born 1948 London, England.
Resided in SA from 1968.
A painter and graphic artist of landscapes, figures and abstract pictures. Works in oil, acrylic and in various graphic media.

Studies 1971–73 Port Elizabeth Technical College, under Alexander Podlashuc (qv), specialising in graphics.

Profile A calligrapher and professional ceramicist from 1978. 1977, 1983, 1984 and 1986 taught drawing, fashion drawing and experimental graphics on a part-time basis at the Port Elizabeth Technical College (Technikon); 1983 set up a screen-printing department at the Port Elizabeth Cripple Care Society. 1984 a six-month study tour of Europe and the USA. Married to Hunter Nesbit (qv).

Exhibitions She has participated in many group exhibitions from 1976; 1976 EPSFA Gallery, Port Elizabeth, solo exhibition; 1985 Cape Town Triennial; 1986 Beuster-Skolimowski Gallery, Pretoria, joint exhibition with Hunter Nesbit (qv).
Represented Port Elizabeth Technikon.
References Port Elizabeth School of Art; *De Kat* March 1987.

NEWALL Albert

Born 1920 Manchester, England.
Resided in SA from 1946.
A self-taught painter and graphic artist of landscapes until 1953 and thereafter of abstract pictures. Works in oil, watercolour, gouache, ink and in various graphic media. A sculptor working in ciment fondu. 1957–62 geometric compositions, based on Golden Section and related mathematical sequences; also the analysis of surface colour harmonics, based on his own colour helix.
Profile Until 1960 a member of the SAAA. A photographer and from 1964 an antique dealer. 1938–42 in the Royal Air Force, stationed in India, Malaya and Arabia.
Exhibitions He has participated in many group exhibitions from 1944 in the UK, SA, Brazil, Italy, Belgium, France and West Germany; 1949 Johannesburg, first of *c.*20 solo exhibitions; 1956 Quadrennial Exhibition.
Represented SA National Gallery, Cape Town; Museum of Modern Art, New York, USA.
Public Commission Sculpture, African Life Building, Cape Town.
Publication by Newall *Images of the Cape*, a book of photographs, 1961, Tafelberg, Cape Town.
References Art SA; SAA; SAP&S; BSAK 1 & 2; AASA; LSAA.

NEWMAN Beryl

Born 1920 Durban.
A painter of landscapes, often incorporating animals, birds and figures, and of portraits and figures. Works in oil, watercolour, gouache, ink, wash, pencil and charcoal; also makes collages.
Studies 1938–42 on a Campbell Memorial Scholarship at the Natal Technical College, under Merlyn Evans (qv), gaining a National Art Teachers Diploma.
Profile From 1940 a member of the WSSA; 1948–85 a member of the SAAA. Prior to 1942 taught art privately; 1942–45 an art teacher at St Mary's Diocesan School for Girls, Kloof, Natal; 1947–48 at Redhill School, Johannesburg; 1968–81 taught art and music at Greytown High and Junior Schools, Natal. 1920–45 lived in Durban; 1945–49 in Johannesburg; from 1949 in Greytown, Natal. Married to Alex Wagner (qv).
Exhibitions She has participated in numerous group exhibitions from 1941; 1946 Christie's Gallery, Pretoria, first of 24 joint exhibitions held with Alex Wagner (qv) in SA and of two held in Scotland in 1959; 1948 Tate Gallery, London, SA Art Exhibition.
Represented Durban Art Gallery.

Public Commissions Mural, Natal Technical College, with Merlyn Evans (qv) and Alex Wagner (qv), now demolished; 1967 oil painting, Greytown Municipal Offices.
References BSAK 1 & 2; AASA; *Artlook* September 1969.

NEWMAN Kenneth

Born 1924 Basingstoke, Hampshire, England.
Resided in SA from 1948.
A painter in gouache of birds.
Studies 1944–45 Regent Street Polytechnic Art School, London; 1946 Brighton School of Art, England.
Profile Illustrated part of the fourth edition of *Roberts Birds of South Africa*, 1978, and in conjunction with Geoff Lockwood (qv) the fifth edition renamed *Roberts' Birds of Southern Africa*, 1985, John Voelcker Bird Book Fund, Cape Town. Chairman of the Southern African Ornithological Society. 1955 and 1958 two seven-month trans-African safaris.
Exhibitions 1967 Pieter Wenning Gallery, Johannesburg, solo exhibition; he has participated in many group exhibitions from 1972 in the UK and SA; 1985 Switzerland, solo exhibition.
Represented Dublin Museum, Republic of Ireland; Willem Annandale Art Gallery, Lichtenburg.
Publications by Newman Garden Birds of South Africa, 1967, Purnell & Sons, Johannesburg; *Roadside Birds of South Africa*, 1969, Purnell & Sons, Johannesburg; *Birdlife in Southern Africa*, 1971, Purnell & Sons, Johannesburg; *Birds of the Kruger National Park*, 1980, Macmillan (SA), Johannesburg; *Newman's Birds of Southern Africa*, 1984, Macmillan (SA), Johannesburg; *Newman's Birds of Botswana*, 1988, Southern Book Publishers, Johannesburg.
References SESA; BSAK 1; SA Art; AASA; *Artlook* January 1969; *SA Panorama* June 1969.

NGATANE Ephraim

Born 1938 Lesotho.
Died 1971 Johannesburg.
A painter of township scenes, genre and abstract pictures. Worked in water-colour, gouache, charcoal and later in oil.
Studies 1952–54 Polly Street Art Centre, Johannesburg, under Cecil Skotnes (qv); 1954–56 in Johannesburg under Hall Duncan, an American missionary.
Profile Came to Johannesburg in 1942. Taught at the Jubilee Centre and in the late 1950s started his own art school. An accomplished alto saxophonist.
Exhibitions Participated in group exhibitions from 1960 in SA and internationally; 1962 Johannesburg, first of several solo exhibitions; 1965 Piccadilly Gallery, London, African Painters and Sculptors from Johannesburg; 1979 Contemporary African Art in SA, touring; 1981 Standard Bank, Soweto, Black Art Today Exhibition.
Represented Johannesburg Art Gallery; Pretoria Art Museum; Sandton Municipal Collection; University of Fort Hare; University of the Witwatersrand; William Humphreys Art Gallery, Kimberley.

Public Commissions With other members of the Polly Street Art Centre, murals in St Mary's Church in Orlando, Transvaal, in 1958 and the Mooki Memorial School in Orlando, Transvaal, in 1969.
References SAA; SESA; SSAP; BSAK 1 & 2; SA Art; 3Cs; AASA; Echoes of African Art; *Artlook* August 1967; *SA Panorama* July 1982.

NGCOBO Welcome

Born 1952 Izingolweni, Natal.
A sculptor working in wood and stone.
Exhibitions Has participated in group exhibitions in Natal and Transvaal.

NHLENGETWA Jabulane Sam

Born 1955 Payneville, Springs, Transvaal.
A painter, graphic artist and sculptor of urban life, portraits, figures, still life and abstract pieces. Works in oil, acrylic, watercolour, pencil, charcoal, various graphic media and clay; also creates collages.
Studies 1976 under Bill Ainslie (qv); 1977–78 Rorke's Drift Art Centre, under Jules van de Vijver (qv) and Ada van de Vijver (qv), gaining an Art Diploma.
Profile A set designer and graphic artist for the SABC. Teaches art privately in KwaThema, Transvaal.
Exhibitions He has participated in many group exhibitions from 1975 in SA, the USA, France and West Germany; 1985 England, solo exhibition; 1987 FUBA Gallery, Johannesburg, exhibition; 1988 Johannesburg Art Gallery, Vita Art Now.
Represented National Gallery, Gaborone, Botswana.
Reference Echoes of African Art.

NIEHAUS Elna (Mrs Van der Walt)

Born 1949 Pretoria.
A painter of landscapes, seascapes, portraits, figures, flowers and abstract pictures. Works in oil, watercolour, gouache, ink, pencil and charcoal. Creates woodcuts and batiks.
Studies 1968–71 Pretoria Teachers Training College, where gained a Teachers Higher Diploma in Education, specialising in art; 1972 a six-month course in graphic design at the London Polytechnic, England.
Profile A member of the Pretoria Art Society, the Western Transvaal Art Society and Pretoria Art in the Park. 1972 an art teacher at Krugersdorp High School, Transvaal. 1974–75 a graphic artist with the SABC TV. 1975–78 lectured on audiovisual media at the University of the Witwatersrand and later became Head of its Central Graphic Services. 1979–81 Founder and Principal of the Klerksdorp Academy of Arts and Crafts. A media advisor to the Graphic Department of the Transvaal Education Department Media Services.
Exhibitions She has participated in numerous group exhibitions from 1968 in SA and Israel; 1971 SAAA Gallery, Pretoria, solo exhibition.

NIELSEN Christian

Born 1948 UK.
Resided in SA from 1968.
A painter of landscapes, portraits and seascapes. Works in oil, watercolour, wash, oil pastel and soft pastel. 1971–73 a series on Swaziland; 1986 a series on Cape Dutch architecture and wine farms.
Profile A part-time artist who works as a branch manager for an estate agency in the Cape. 1968–75 lived in Johannesburg, with many visits to Swaziland; 1976 moved to Cape Town.
Exhibition 1986 Cape Town, solo exhibition.

NIEMANN Hendrik Christiaan

Born 1941 Bloemfontein.
A self-taught painter of landscapes, seascapes, portraits, still life and figures. Works in oil, watercolour, ink, wash, charcoal, pastel and mixed media.
Profile A former member of the Orange Free State Art Society. Has acted in a number of plays with the Bloemfontein Theatre Group.
Exhibitions He has participated in several group exhibitions from 1956 in SA; 1971 Bloemfontein, first of six solo exhibitions.

NKOSI Charles Sokhaya

Born 1949 Durban.
A painter and graphic artist of landscapes, genre, figures and abstract pictures. Works in oil, acrylic, watercolour, gouache, ink, wash, pencil, charcoal, wood, mixed media and in various graphic media; also creates collages.
Studies 1974–76 on a three-year study grant from the South African Institute of Race Relations at Rorke's Drift Art Centre, under the Swedish artist Otto Lundbohm, the American artists Gabrielle and Carl Ellertson, and Jules van de Vijver (qv).
Profile For his graduation he produced a 13-page portfolio entitled "Crucifixion". A textile designer and printer. 1981 a member of the NSA. 1980–81 an art tutor at the Durban Open School at Abangami; 1982 a graphic artist for SABC TV; from 1986 an art tutor at the African Institute of Art, Funda Centre, Soweto. 1981–82 designed two record sleeves; 1986 set designs for "Domba", a play by Matsemela Manaka (qv) which was produced at the Funda Centre, Soweto.
Exhibitions He has participated in group exhibitions from 1974 held throughout SA and in Sweden, West Germany, the USA and Botswana; 1977 NSA Gallery, Durban, joint exhibition with Duke Ketye (qv) and Michael Ntuli; 1979 Mariannhill Art Gallery, Natal, joint exhibition with Bongani Shange (qv); 1988 Johannesburg Art Gallery, Vita Art Now.
Award 1984 Second Prize Painting, African Arts Festival, University of Zululand.

Represented Ethnology Museum, Frankfurt, West Germany; Munich Museum, West Germany; University of Fort Hare; University of Zululand.
Public Commission 1978 three life-size murals, Glebe Tavern, Durban.
Reference Echoes of African Art.

NKOSI Stanley

Born 1945 Newcastle, Natal.
A sculptor of figures and animals, works in bronze and terracotta. A graphic artist.
Studies 1967 privately under Peter Haden in Johannesburg.
Profile c.1980 taught at the Katlehong Art Centre, Transvaal.
Exhibitions He has participated in many group exhibitions held in SA, the UK and the USA; several solo exhibitions held in the Transvaal; 1978 Atlanta, Georgia, USA, solo exhibition; 1981 Standard Bank, Soweto, Black Art Today Exhibition.
Awards c.1978–79 First Prize, Wildlife of the World Competition, Oklahoma, USA.
Represented University of Fort Hare.
References Sheila Keeble, *The Black Who's Who of Southern Africa Today*, 1979/82, African Business Publications, Johannesburg; Echoes of African Art; *SA Panorama* April 1979.

NKOTSI Anthony Molebatsi

Born 1955 Western Township, Johannesburg.
A painter, sculptor and graphic artist of landscapes, portraits, genre and abstract pieces. Works in oil, acrylic, watercolour, gouache, ink, wash, pencil, charcoal, wood and in various graphic media.
Studies 1978–79 Mofolo Art centre, Soweto, under Dumisane Mabaso (qv), Pat Mautloa (qv) and Daniel Gabashane (qv); 1980–83 Rorke's Drift Art Centre, under Keith van Winkel and Jay Johnson.
Profile 1983–85 a founder member of Skuzo, a printmaking workshop; from 1986 on the management committee of the Thupelo Art Project. A committee member of the Hammanskraal Art Project; Vice-Chairman of the Mabaso/ Nkotsi Printmaking Workshop. 1984–85 a printmaking teacher at The Open School, Johannesburg and in 1985 at FUBA; from 1986 Head of the Printmaking Department of the Johannesburg Art Foundation. 1985 tapestry designs for Phumalanga Tapestries, Swaziland.
Exhibitions From 1976 many group exhibitions held throughout SA and in France, Botswana and Sweden; 1987 Johannesburg Art Foundation, joint exhibition with Bill Ainslie (qv), David Koloane (qv), Dumisane Mabaso (qv) and Anthusa Sotiriades (qv); 1988 Goodman Gallery, Johannesburg, solo exhibition.
Represented Johannesburg Art Gallery.
Public Commission 1986 wood panel, Piggs Peak Hotel, Swaziland.

NOLTE Zelda Maria

Born 1929 Cape Town.
A sculptor of figures, animals and birds. Works in wood, cement and stone. A graphic artist producing woodcuts.
Studies 1948–51 Kunstgewerbeschule, Zürich, Switzerland; 1951–53 Michaelis School of Fine Art, under Lippy Lipshitz (qv).
Profile Has taught at several art establishments. Lived in Cape Town, presently living abroad.
Exhibitions During the 1960s participated in several group exhibitions in SA; 1960 Quadrennial Exhibition; 1964 Wolpe Gallery, Cape Town, exhibition of drawings and sculpture.
Represented SA National Gallery, Cape Town.
Public Commissions Relief sculpture, Rondebosch Boys High School, Cape Town; decorated door for a bank in Paarl, Cape Province; sculpture, Albion Hall, Newlands, Cape Town.
References SA Art, SAA; SAP&S; SAP&D; SESA; BSAK 1; 3Cs; AASA.

NOMANDLA X

Born 1941 Transkei.
A self-taught painter of everyday scenes of the Transkei, particularly of the district around Qumbu where he lives. Works in acrylic on board.
Profile Began painting in 1972.
Exhibitions He has participated in numerous group exhibitions in the Eastern Cape and in Johannesburg.

NORTCLIFFE Frank

Born 1902 Ireland.
Died 1970 Johannesburg.
Resided in SA from 1939.
A painter of landscapes and seascapes. Worked in oil.
Profile Lived in London before settling in SA. Widely travelled both abroad and in SA.
Exhibitions Participated in group exhibitions from 1937 in the UK and SA; 1939 first of several solo exhibitions held in Johannesburg and Cape Town.
Represented Belfast Art Gallery, Republic of Ireland.
References DBA; BSAK 1; AASA; *SA Panorama* November 1963.

NOVIS Maisie

Born 1925 Johannesburg.
A painter and graphic artist of landscapes, still life, figures and abstract pictures. Works in oil pastel, pastel, watercolour, gouache, wash, pencil, charcoal and in various graphic media.

Studies Witwatersrand Technical College, under James Gardner (qv) and Phyllis Gardner (qv).

Profile From 1980 a member of the Brush and Chisel Club, a committee member and Secretary/Treasurer; from 1982 a member and from 1985 an Associate of the WSSA; from 1983 a member of the Rustenburg Art Society. Since 1946 she has worked as a graphic artist in the advertising industry. From 1965 costume designs for modern dance productions; 1972–80 set and costume designs for the Ballet Jeunesse Company. A calligrapher.

Exhibitions She has participated in over 30 group exhibitions from 1981 held throughout SA and in SWA/Namibia.

Awards 1984 First Prize, Amfest Art Festival, Roodepoort, Transvaal; 1986 First Prize, Annual W H Coetzer Award.

NOWERS John Leask

Born 1940 Klerksdorp, Transvaal.

A sculptor, working in ceramics.

Studies 1959–62 graphic design at the Michaelis School of Fine Art, under May Hillhouse (qv), Neville Dubow, Russell Harvey (qv) and Katrine Harries (qv), gaining a Certificate in Graphic Design.

Profile From 1978 a lecturer in ceramics at the Michaelis School of Fine Art. 1963–75 lived in England, during which time he made several trips to Greece. Brother of Sheila Nowers (qv).

Exhibitions 1968 Dorp Street Gallery, Cape Town, joint exhibition with Hylton Nel (qv); he has participated in several group exhibitions from 1970 in SA, the UK and the USA; 1977 Goodman-Wolman Gallery, Cape Town, solo exhibition; 1982 Cape Town Triennial; 1985 Cape Town Triennial; 1987 SAAA Gallery, Cape Town, joint exhibition with Hylton Nel (qv) and Sheila Nowers (qv).

Award 1982 Merit Award, Cape Town Triennial.

Represented Durban Art Gallery; Touch Gallery, SA National Gallery, Cape Town.

References 3Cs; AASA; *Sgraffiti* no 42.

NOWERS Sheila Marion

Born 1942 Klerksdorp, Transvaal.

A painter of landscapes, portraits, still life, genre, domestic animals, interiors, street and beach scenes. Works in gouache, watercolour and pencil. Specialises in miniatures.

Studies 1962–65 Michaelis School of Fine Art, under Melvin Simmers (qv), Neville Dubow, Peggy Delport (qv) and May Hillhouse (qv), gaining a Diploma in Graphic Design.

Profile From 1982 a member of the SAAA. From 1970 numerous illustrations for magazines in SA. From 1980 a stamp designer for the Philatelic Bureau, winning the Carpendale Trophy in 1982. After gaining her Diploma, lived in England until 1970. Sister of John Nowers (qv).

Exhibitions She has participated in many group exhibitions from 1982 in SA; 1983 SAAA Gallery, Cape Town, first of four solo exhibitions held in SA; 1985 Cape Town Triennial; 1986 at the Royal Academy in London and on a group exhibition in Canada; 1987 SAAA Gallery, Cape Town, joint exhibition with Hylton Nel (qv) and John Nowers (qv); 1988 Karen McKerron Gallery, Johannesburg, joint exhibition with Joe Maseko (qv) and Leonard Matsoso (qv).
Represented Johannesburg Art Gallery; University of the Orange Free State.

NTANZI Mbongeni Dingani

Born 1966 Katlehong, Transvaal.
A graphic artist and sculptor of portraits, figures, and semi-abstract as well as abstract pieces. Works in ink, various graphic media, wood and clay.
Studies 1977 Katlehong Art Centre, under Davydd Myburgh (qv), Rosemary Schakanovsky and Stephen Risi; 1986–87 Funda Centre, Soweto.
Profile A member of the Katlehong Art Centre. 1986 an instructor at the Katlehong Art Centre. A writer, poet, musician and actor.
Exhibitions He has participated in several group exhibitions from 1978 in SA.

NTSHALINSHALI Bonnie

Born 1965 Winterton, Natal.
A scuptor of figures and animals. Works in ceramics.
Profile Assisted in her artistic career by Fee Halstead (qv) from 1985.
Exhibitions She has participated in many group exhibitions from 1985 in SA.
Represented Durban Art Gallery; SA National Gallery, Cape Town; University of South Africa; University of the Witwatersrand.

NTUKWANA Hargreaves

Born 1938 Johannesburg.
A painter and sculptor of figures and township life. Works in oil, gouache, ink, wash, pencil, charcoal, wood, plaster of Paris, clay and terracotta. A Witch Doctor series, a rural life series and a factory series.
Studies Polly Street Art Centre, Johannesburg, under Cecil Skotnes (qv); 1955–56 African School of Art, Rhodesia (Zimbabwe); 1960–62 privately under Cordelidos, in Toledo, Spain; 1971–73 privately under Professor Mel Edwards, in New York.
Profile Has lectured on SA art in New York and in Switzerland. 1984 a workshop teacher at the University of the Witwatersrand. 1979 designed clothes for "Black and White is Beautiful", a modelling show in Germany. A photographer and jazz musician who participated in the musical "King Kong". Designed the record sleeves for "Underground in Africa" by Dollar Brand in 1980; "Did You Tell Your Mother" by the Cape Town Jazz Musicians in 1982 and "Plum & Cherry" by Basil Manenberg Coetzee in 1984. 1984 designed a wine bottle label for a Swiss company bottling SA wine. Designs for rugs made in Lesotho, and for Christmas cards. 1971–73, 1981–82 and 1985 lived in the USA; 1973–74 travelled in Europe; 1977 in Switzerland; 1979 visited West Germany.

Exhibitions He has participated in several group exhibitions in SA, Europe, the USA, Lesotho and Zimbabwe; 1967 Adler Fielding Gallery, Johannesburg, first of over 15 solo exhibitions held in SA, France, Switzerland, West Germany, The Netherlands and the USA.

Represented Rutgers State University, New Jersey, USA; University of California, USA; University of Fort Hare; University of the Witwatersrand.

Public Commission 1986 mural for the Italian School, Johannesburg.

References BSAK 1 & 2; AASA; *Hit* May 1983.

NTULI Pitika

A sculptor and a painter of figures, socio-political and universal themes. Works in metal, wood, stone, found objects and mixed media.

Profile A poet, who is presently living in New York.

Reference Echoes of African Art.

NXUMALO Caiphas

Comes from the Msinga District, KwaZulu.

A sculptor using indigenous woods. A graphic artist producing woodcuts.

Studies c.1970 at Rorke's Drift Art Centre, Natal.

Exhibitions He has participated in group exhibitions in SA and in West Germany.

O

O'CONNOR Patrick

Born 1940 Bloemfontein.

A painter of figures. Works in oil and sprayed-on liquid silver. Two series entitled "Prometheus" and "Doors."

Studies 1960–64 University of the Witwatersrand, where attained a BA(FA).

Profile 1964 a lecturer at the University of Durban-Westville; 1971 a senior lecturer in painting at the Natal Technikon. 1977 emigrated to the Republic of Ireland, where he has taught at the Dunleary Art School and lectured at the Dublin Art College.

Exhibitions He has participated in many group exhibitions in SA, South America and Europe; 1968 Lidchi Gallery, Johannesburg, first of several solo exhibitions held in SA; 1969 NSA Gallery, Durban, joint exhibition with Andrew Verster (qv); 1969 Durban Art Gallery, joint exhibition with Joan Templer (qv) and Andrew Verster (qv).

Award 1969 Cambridge Shirt Award, Art SA Today.

Represented Durban Art Gallery; Johannesburg Art Gallery; Pietersburg Collection; Sandton Municipal Collection; SA National Gallery, Cape Town; University of South Africa; University of the Witwatersrand.

Public Commission 1973 mural, Natal Provincial Administration Building, Pietermaritzburg.

References SSAP; Oxford Companion to 20C Art (under SA); 3Cs; AASA; *Artlook* July 1968; *SA Panorama* February 1976.

OERDER Frans David

Born 1867 Rotterdam, The Netherlands.

Died 1944 Pretoria.

Resided in SA 1890–1908 and 1938–44.

A painter of landscapes, still life, horses, genre and portraits. Worked mainly in oil, but also used pastel, watercolour and conté. Produced a number of etchings.

Studies 1880–85 Rotterdam Academy of Art, under J Striening (1827–1903) and A H R van Maadijk; 1886 under Ernest Blanc-Garin (1843–1916) in Brussels; also in Italy.

Profile 1899 a War Artist for the Kruger Government. 1905 a member of the SA Society of Artists. 1894 an art teacher at the Staatsmeisjesskool, Pretoria; 1902 taught at the Government School, Pretoria, and later at the Girls High School, Pretoria. Prior to 1908 shared a studio with Anton van Wouw (qv) in Pretoria. A number of prints of his work were published by E Schweikerdt in Pretoria and by the New York Graphic Society, USA, including "Magnolias" and "Blossom-time", which were immensely popular. 1910 designed the December cover of *Die Brandwag*. Drew cartoons for newspapers. 1885 visited Italy on a travel bursary; 1890–1908 lived in Pretoria, 1896 spent six months in Zululand; 1903–05 visited the East Coast of Africa, Ibo in Northern Mozambique, and Zanzibar; 1908–38 lived in The Netherlands, revisiting Zanzibar en route; 1909–10 spent 18 months in Italy; 1938–44 lived in Pretoria. Travelled throughout SA. Married to Gerda Oerder (qv).

Exhibitions Participated in group exhibitions in The Netherlands and in SA, as well as posthumously in Rhodesia (Zimbabwe); 1896 first solo exhibition in SA; *c.*1908 Rotterdam, The Netherlands, first solo exhibition in Europe; 1950 Old Pretoria Art Gallery, Memorial Exhibition; 1965 Pretoria Art Museum, Retrospective Exhibition; 1977 Van Wouw House, Pretoria, Exhibition of War Paintings.

Awards 1885 King William III Gold Medal and Bursary; 1909 Silver Medal, International Exhibition, Amsterdam; 1920 Silver Medal, International Exhibition, Brussels.

Represented Africana Museum, Johannesburg; Albany Museum, Grahamstown; Den Bosch, Northern Brabant, The Netherlands; Durban Art Gallery; Johannesburg Art Gallery; King George VI Art Gallery, Port Elizabeth; Potchefstroom Museum; Pretoria Art Museum; SA National Gallery, Cape Town; Tatham Art Gallery, Pietermaritzburg; University of Cape Town; University of Pretoria; University of South Africa; University of the Witwatersrand; War Museum of the Boer Republics, Bloemfontein; William Humphreys Art Gallery, Kimberley.

Public Commissions A large number of portraits of SA notability including General Louis Botha. In 1906 he was commissioned to paint "Pretoria 1906" by the Pretoria City Council.

References K&K; Collectors' Guide; Our Art 1; Art SA; SAA; SADNB; 20C SA Art; AMC4&7; DSAB; SAP&S; Oxford Companion to Art (under SA); SAP&D; SESA; SSAP; BSAK 1 & 2; Enc S'n A; SA Art; 3Cs; AASA; SASSK; LSAA; *SA Art Collector* April 1947; *South Africana* May 1956; *SA Panorama* December 1964; *Artlook* August 1970; *De Arte* April 1975; Retrospective Exhibition Catalogue, 1965, Pretoria Art Museum.

OERDER Gerda (née Pitlo)

Born 1887 The Netherlands.
Died 1961.
Resided in SA from 1938.
A painter of flowers and landscapes. Worked in oil.
*Profile c.*1953 Curator of the Pretoria Art Museum. Married to Frans Oerder (qv).
Exhibition Included in the "SA Flora in Art" group exhibition held at the SA National Gallery, Cape Town in 1963.
Represented Pretoria Art Museum.
References Collectors' Guide; SSAP; Enc S'n A; AASA.

OESTERLEIN Charlotte Irene

Born 1920 Chester, Cheshire, England.
Resided in SA and SWA/Namibia from 1961.
A painter of landscapes, still life, seascapes, figures and wildlife. Works in oil, watercolour, gouache and pencil; also creates collages.

Studies Royal Drawing Academy, England; 1947–49 studied textile design and drawing at the London Polytechnic; 1956–59 Nairobi Technical College, Kenya, under Professor Baines; 1966–68 under Professor Otto Klar (qv) in Pretoria; 1976 under Professor Fabio Barraclough.

Profile 1956–60 a member of the East African Society of Arts, Nairobi, Kenya; 1968–75 a member of the Brush and Chisel Club and from 1970 of the SAAA. 1975–78 taught drawing and painting in oil at her Johannesburg studio. 1941–46 lived in Egypt and Palestine; 1950–61 in Kenya and Tanganyika (Tanzania). 1976 visited Canada; 1978 went on a study tour of Spain with Professor Fabio Barraclough. Lives in Cape Town.

Exhibitions She has participated in over 60 group exhibitions from 1957 held in Kenya, throughout SA and in Canada, the USA and the UK; 1971 Carlton Centre Gallery, Johannesburg, first of 19 solo exhibitions held in SA and one held in Canada.

Represented Nelspruit Art Gallery; Pietersburg Collection; Tzaneen Collection.

References BSAK 1; *Artlook* August 1971.

OLDERT Johannes

Born 1912 Rotterdam, The Netherlands.
Died 1984 Johannesburg.
Resided in SA from 1935.

A painter of landscapes, seascapes, still life, figures and abstract pictures. Worked in oil. A number of portrait busts in bronze, including those of the late King George VI and Queen Elizabeth in 1947 and Dr H F Verwoerd in 1960.

Studies One year at the Royal Academy, Rotterdam, under Koos den Hartog; Natal Technical College, under Merlyn Evans (qv) and Nils Andersen (qv); briefly under Ernest Ullmann (qv) in Johannesburg and at the Witwatersrand Technical College, under Eric Byrd (qv); Regent Street Polytechnic, London, under Harold Brownsword (*b*.1885).

Profile A member of the NSA. 1935 lived in Durban, later in Johannesburg. In 1949 he was living in the Cape, then returned to Johannesburg. Travelled in England and The Netherlands; in 1954 he made an extensive tour of Europe. During the 1940s married to Elise Laidler (qv). Father of L Anton Benzon (qv).

Exhibitions Participated in group exhibitions in SA from 1938; held numerous solo exhibitions in SA and Rhodesia (Zimbabwe).

Represented Ann Bryant Gallery, East London.

References Collectors' Guide; SAA; BSAK 1; AASA.

OLIVIER Andrew Christian

Born 1960 Postmasburg, Northern Cape Province.

A painter and graphic artist of diverse subjects, including figures and abstract pictures. Works in oil, watercolour, ink, pencil, charcoal, mixed media, and in various graphic media, particularly screenprints.

Studies 1981–84 University of Stellenbosch, under Professor Larry Scully (qv), Paul Emsley (qv) and Timo Smuts (qv), where gained a BA(FA); 1985–86 Hochschule der Kunst, West Berlin, West Germany, under K H Hödicke, K Oppermann and J Zylla, on a Human Sciences Research Council Scholarship and a Maggie Laubser Overseas Bursary; 1987 studying for an MA(FA).
Profile A photographer. 1987 a temporary lecturer in the history of art at the University of Natal. 1985–86 visited Paris, Venice, Vienna and Portugal. Frequent visits to the Kalahari Desert.
Exhibitions He has participated in several group exhibitions from 1985 in SA, West Germany and France; 1983 Stellenbosch, solo exhibition.

OLIVIER Gerhardus Cornelius

Born 1914 Senekal, Orange Free State.
A painter of landscapes. Works mainly in watercolour and occasionally in pastel, oil, pencil and charcoal.
Studies 1945 privately under W H Coetzer (qv); 1946 privately under Erich Mayer (qv).
Profile From 1969 a member of the Orange Free State Art Society. 1937–72 a teacher and Principal of various Orange Free State schools; 1973–80 a lecturer at the Bloemfontein Teachers Training College. Involved in both music and acting, taking part in operas. 1972–74 lectured in music at the Bloemfontein Teachers Training College. He has also composed a number of school songs and folksongs. Signs his work "Gerhardo".
Exhibitions 1968 Bloemfontein, first of six solo exhibitions held in Bloemfontein and Pretoria; he has participated in several group exhibitions in Bloemfontein from 1969.
Awards Several awards for watercolour, oil and landscape paintings at the Orange Free State and Goldfields Art Festivals.
Reference SA Arts Calendar May 1979.

OLLEMANS Frieda

Born 1915 Bloemfontein.
A sculptor of figures. Works in wood.
Studies 1937–39 Slade School of Art, London.
Profile 1941–43 Head of the Children's Art Centre, Cape Town, where she introduced puppet theatre.
Exhibitions She has participated in group exhibitions from the 1940s in SA, Rhodesia (Zimbabwe) and the USA; 1948 Tate Gallery, London, SA Art Exhibition; she has held solo exhibitions in SA and the USA.
Represented SA National Gallery, Cape Town; University of the Orange Free State; University of Stellenbosch.
References Collectors' Guide; SAA; SESA; BSAK 1 & 2.

OLLS Sonnett

Born 1946 Johannesburg.

A painter of landscapes, seascapes, portraits, still life, figures and abstract pictures. Works in oil, watercolour, ink and wash.

Studies 1965–67 Witwatersrand Technical College, gaining a Diploma in Graphic Art; 1986 University of South Africa.

Profile 1976 a founder of the Newcastle Art Society, Natal; 1985 a founder of the Standerton Art Society, Transvaal. An Associate of the WSSA, a member of the SAAA, the Brush and the Chisel Club, the Orange Free State Art Society and the Benoni Art Society. 1981 taught art at Newcastle High School and from 1976 has taught art privately. 1968–70 lived in Kimberley, Cape Province; 1970–75 in Louis Trichardt, Transvaal; 1975–83 in Newcastle, Natal, and from 1983 in Standerton, Transvaal. Painting holidays in Spain and Greece.

Exhibitions She has participated in numerous group exhibitions from 1968 held throughout SA and in West Germany, Portugal and the UK; 1976 Newcastle, Natal, first of 20 solo exhibitions.

Represented Benoni Municipal Collection; Newcastle Municipal Collection.

Public Commissions 1979 design of Mayoral Chain for Madadeni Township, Newcastle; 1983 mural, Newcastle Junior Primary School.

OLTMANN Walter

Born 1960 Rustenburg, Transvaal.

A sculptor of abstract pieces. Works in bronze, steel and wire. Draws in pencil.

Studies 1978–81 University of Natal, under Henry Davies and Bronwen Heath (qv), gaining a BA(FA); 1982–84 University of the Witwatersrand, under Willem Strydom (qv), where gained an MA(FA).

Profile 1984 a part-time sculpture tutor at the University of Natal; 1985 a sculpture tutor at the University of the Witwatersrand.

Exhibitions He has participated in several group exhibitions from 1980 held throughout SA; 1984 Milner Park, Johannesburg, solo exhibition; 1985 Cape Town Triennial.

Represented University of the Witwatersrand.

OPPENHEIM Annemarie

Born 1904 Schöneberg, Berlin, Germany.

Resided in SA 1939–53.

An artist working in oil, watercolour, ink, pencil and charcoal.

Studies Kunstgewerbeschule, Charlottenburg, Berlin, under Schafer; Reimannschule, Berlin, under Hermann Sandkuhl (*b*.1872); privately under Arthur Segal (1875–1944) in Berlin. In 1938 gained a Teaching Certificate from Berlin-Zehlendorf.

Profile 1939–53 a member of the SAAA; from 1960 a member of the Art Association Ticinese, Lugano, Switzerland. 1939–53 taught art privately in Johannesburg. 1967 a portfolio entitled "Berlin, 10 Watercolours" published by Felgentreff & Goebel, Berlin, in an edition of 1 000; in 1985 a portfolio of 33 watercolours and charcoal drawings of Berlin scenes was published. 1956 spent six months in Cannes, France; from 1956 has lived in Lugano, Switzerland and in West Berlin, Germany.

Exhibitions She has participated in numerous group exhibitions from 1926 in West Germany, SA, the UK and Switzerland; 1939 Gainsborough Gallery, Johannesburg, first of over 26 solo exhibitions held throughout SA and in Germany, SWA/Namibia and the USA; 1975 Rand Afrikaans University, solo exhibition.

Public Commission 1947 two of her watercolours depicting the Orange Free State were presented to Queen Elizabeth II by the City of Bloemfontein.

Represented Berlinische Gallery, Germany; Jewish Museum, Berlin, Germany; Johannesburg Art Gallery; Johannesburg Town Hall; Niedersächsisches Landesmuseum, West Germany; Pretoria Art Museum; Rand Afrikaans University; SA National Gallery, Cape Town.

References BSAK 1; AASA.

ORD Jennifer Mary

Born 1948 Springs, Transvaal.

A sculptor of three-dimensional structures inspired by African landscapes. These are symbolic in content. Works in wax, resin, clay, wood, stone, gauze and found natural objects. A graphic artist, produces both textile and paper silkscreens.

Studies Port Elizabeth Technical College; University of South Africa, gaining a BA(FA).

Profile A member of the EPSFA and the GAP Group. An artist working at the Port Elizabeth Museum.

Exhibitions She has participated in several group exhibitions from 1984; 1985 Karen McKerron Gallery, Johannesburg, solo exhibition.

ORDBROWN Joyce

Born 1894 Port Shepstone, Natal.

Died 1974 East London.

A painter working in oil and watercolour. Additionally painted murals, produced silkscreens and designed tapestries.

Studies 1909–11 Westminster and Lambeth Art Schools, London, under Walter Sickert (1860–1942) (Lambeth); 1914 Johannesburg Art School; Michaelis School of Fine Art, under Charles S Groves (qv) and Percy Thatcher, gaining an Art Teachers Diploma.

Profile 1913 a founder member of the Johannesburg Art School Club; 1916 first Secretary of the Johannesburg Sketch Club; 1939 a member of the New Group. In 1929 published "Johannesburg Street Scenes". Illustrated Johannesburg newspapers, school textbooks, periodicals and the book *Tales from the Kraals,* by M Murgatroyd, 1968. Taught at the Witwatersrand Technical College, the Grahamstown Training College, the Stellenbosch Technical College and at the University of Stellenbosch. 1918–26 lived in Zululand; 1943–48 lived in Salisbury, Rhodesia (Harare, Zimbabwe); in 1948 moved to Stellenbosch. 1918–29 she was Mrs Rutherford, she then became Mrs Grellier on her marriage to Henry Harley Grellier (qv).
Exhibitions Participated in group exhibitions and held solo exhibitions in SA.
Represented Africana Museum, Johannesburg; Pretoria Art Museum; University of Stellenbosch.
References SAA; AMC4; BSAK 1 & 2; SA Art; AASA.

ORMEROD Cecile Lynette (née Chiappini)

Born 1915 Cape Town.
A painter formerly of abstract works and presently of figurative works of plants in relation to gardens, streams, pools and mountains. Works in acrylic and ink; also creates collages.
Studies *c.*1933 South African School of Fine and Applied Arts, Cape Town, under Herbert V Meyerowitz (qv) and A Sandor Konya (qv).
Exhibitions She has participated in numerous group exhibitions from 1966 in SA; 1971 SAAA Gallery, Cape Town, first of three solo exhibitions.
Award 1967 Painting Prize, Cape Art '67 Exhibition, SA National Gallery, Cape Town.
Represented SA National Gallery, Cape Town.
Reference SAP&S.

ORMISTON Georgina

Born 1903 Chelmsford, Essex, England.
Died 1967 Durban.
Resided in SA from 1929.
A painter of abstract and semi-abstract pictures, highly textured with subdued colours. Worked in oil on board. Painted *c.*100 paintings during her professional life. Did not paint between 1927 and 1953.
Studies Briefly at the London School of Art and the Glasgow School of Art in the early 1920s. Later received tutelage from Gordon Vorster (qv).
Exhibitions 1958 Johannesburg, first of four solo exhibitions; participated in group exhibitions from 1965 in London and SA; 1966 Republic Festival Exhibition.
Represented Durban Art Gallery; Pretoria Art Museum; SA National Gallery, Cape Town; University of the Witwatersrand; William Humphreys Art Gallery, Kimberley.
References Art SA; SAA; 20C SA Art; SSAP; BSAK 1 & 2; Our Art 3; SA Art; 3Cs; AASA; *Fontein* vol 1 no 3, 1960; *SA Art News* 18 May 1961; *Artlook* July 1967.

ORTON Meta

Born 1912 Pietermaritzburg.
A painter and sculptor of figures, portraits and landscapes. Works in oil, mixed media, pencil, charcoal and ciment fondu.
Studies 1946 Natal Technical College; 1947 Michaelis School of Fine Art, under Edward Roworth (qv); 1948–50 and 1957–59 Byam Shaw School of Art, London, under Patrick Phillips (*b*.1907) and Brian Thomas.
Profile From 1956 a member of the NSA and founder in 1976 of the North Coast Art Group, of which she was Chairman in 1984–85. 1967–75 taught art privately in Umhlanga Rocks, Natal, and from 1976 at the North Coast Artists Workshop. 1957–67 lived in London, thereafter at Umhlanga, Natal. Has travelled extensively throughout the world.
Exhibitions She has participated in numerous group exhibitions from 1956 in SA and the UK; 1972 NSA Gallery, Durban, first of three solo exhibitions.
Represented Pietersburg Collection.
Publication by Orton *The World and Umhlanga Rocks*, 1983, True Art Printing, Durban.
References BSAK 1; *Artlook* February 1972.

OSBORN Joan Marga

Born 1928 Johannesburg.
A painter of landscapes. Works in oil.
Studies Under Judith Gluckman (qv) and Sidney Goldblatt (qv).
Profile 1963 lived in Cornwall, England; 1964 in Dublin, Republic of Ireland; 1965–71 on the Isle of Man, UK; 1971 returned to Johannesburg. Has travelled throughout Europe and to Japan.
Exhibitions She has participated in several group exhibitions from 1960 in SA and on the Isle of Man, UK; 1961 Whippman's Gallery, Johannesburg, first of three solo exhibitions held in SA and one in the UK.
Reference SAA.

OSSER Josef (Joe)

Born 1908 Alpen, Niederrhein, Germany.
Resided in SA from 1936.
A painter and graphic artist of landscapes, seascapes, portraits, figures, still life and genre. Works in oil, acrylic, watercolour, gouache, wash, ink, pencil, charcoal and in various graphic media.
Studies 1930 Düsseldorf Academy, Germany.
Profile A member of the SAAA. Co-founder and Chairman of the Studio Club, which later formed the nucleus of the Cape Town Art Centre, Green Point, at which he lectured, 1963–83.
Exhibitions He has participated in numerous group exhibitions from 1952 in SA and held several solo exhibitions.
Represented SA Cultural History Museum, Cape Town.

OSSMAN Carl Adolf Erwin

Born 1883 Loswitz, Dresden, Germany.
Died 1935 Windhoek, SWA/Namibia.
Resided in SWA/Namibia from 1913.
A painter of SWA/Namibian landscapes. Worked in oil, with the occasional work in tempera or watercolour.
Studies Munich Art Academy; etching under Franz Skarbina (1849–1910) and oil painting under Walter Leistikow (1865–1908) in Berlin.
Profile Influenced by the Jugendstil Movement 1895–1905. 1911 an illustrator for Scherl Berlin Publishers and for *Die Woche*, a weekly magazine. Sent by the publishing firm to SWA/Namibia. 1921 an album of nine works of pen and ink sketches was published by John Meinert. During WWI served in the Military Camel Corps. 1921 settled in Okahandja, SWA/Namibia. Numerous study tours in Europe.
Exhibitions 1917 Swakopmund, first of several solo exhibitions held in SWA/Namibia; had previously held a solo exhibition in Berlin; group exhibitions from 1933 in SWA/Namibia; 1975 Arts Association SWA/Namibia Gallery, Windhoek, Commemorative Exhibition; 1979 Arts Association SWA/Namibia Gallery, Windhoek, Retrospective Exhibition; 1983 Arts Association SWA/Namibia Gallery, Windhoek, joint Commemorative Exhibition with Otto Schröder (qv).
Represented Arts Association SWA/Namibia Collection; Pretoria Art Museum; University of Pretoria; University of South Africa.
References SAA; DSAB; BSAK 1; Art SWA; 3Cs; AASA.

OWEN Andrew John

Born 1961 Salisbury, Rhodesia (Harare, Zimbabwe).
Resided in SA from 1974.
A painter and graphic artist, working in oil and in various graphic media.
Studies 1980–83 Michaelis School of Fine Art, under André van Zyl (qv), Stanley Pinker (qv) and Peggy Delport (qv), gaining a BA(FA) in 1985.
Profile From 1985 a member of the Artists Guild, Cape Town. 1985 a lecturer at the Ruth Prowse School of Art, Cape Town.
Exhibitions He has participated in group exhibitions in Cape Town from 1986.

OWEN Owen

Born 1926 Reading, Berkshire, England.
Resided in SA from 1949.
A painter of landscapes, seascapes and wildlife. Works in acrylic and pastel.
Studies 1937–39 on a scholarship at the Beckenham School of Art, England; 1972–75 under Walter Westbrook (qv) in Kimberley.
Profile Until 1983 worked for a building society, thereafter a full-time painter.
Exhibitions He has participated in many group exhibitions from 1975 in Johannesburg; 1979 Lister Gallery, Johannesburg, solo exhibition.

OXLEY Oswald John Philip ARCA

Born 1888 Helmsley, Yorkshire, England.
Died 1955.
Resided in SA from 1919.
A painter of still life and landscapes. Worked in oil.
Studies Leicester School of Art, England; on a scholarship to the Royal College
of Art, London, where awarded an Associateship; gained the Carnegie Grant to
the USA to study art education.
Profile 1926 Vice-President of the SA Institute of Art. A member of the NSA.
Primarily a teacher, 1919 Art Organiser of the Natal Department of Education;
1921 Principal of the Natal Technical College Art School; 1923–52 Professor of
Fine Arts, University of Natal.
Exhibitions Participated in group exhibitions in SA and abroad.
Represented Durban Art Gallery.
References Art SA; BSAK 1; AASA.

P

PACKER Mary Dorothea Gwinnett (née Bompas)

Born 1892 Johannesburg.
Died 1977 Johannesburg.
A painter of landscapes, figures and buildings. Worked in oil, watercolour, ink, charcoal, crayon and gouache.
Studies 1917–19 Cape Town School of Art, under Charles Groves (qv) and George C Robinson (qv); 1924 Heatherley School of Art, London, under Iain MacNab (1890–*c*.1970); also under J H Amshewitz (qv) in Johannesburg.
Profile A member of the Johannesburg Sketch Club; a member and in 1969 an Executive Committee member of the SAAA (Southern Transvaal); a member of the Friday Club. 1920 a commercial artist for the Thorold Advertising Company, Johannesburg. In 1921 she joined *The Star* newspaper as an illustrator and in 1932 became the art critic, remaining in this position until her retirement in 1952. She continued to write occasional articles for *The Star* until 1969. Married Edgar Arnold Packer (*d*.1932), the cartoonist "Quip" of *The Star*. In 1924 she visited Europe. Throughout her life she travelled extensively in SA on painting trips, frequently with Emily Fern (qv). In the early 1950s she visited Kenya, Dar es Salaam and Zanzibar.
Exhibitions Participated in many group exhibitions in SA; 1936 Empire Exhibition, Johannesburg; 1950 Johannesburg, first of several solo exhibitions held in SA; 1977 Rand Afrikaans University, Memorial Exhibition.
Represented Africana Museum, Johannesburg.
References Collectors' Guide; SAA; AMC7; BSAK 1 & 2; AASA; SASSK; *ANN* September 1963; Rand Afrikaans University Memorial Exhibition Catalogue 1977.

PAGDEN Dulce Maud

Born 1895 Port Elizabeth.
A painter of figures. Worked in oil.
Studies Port Elizabeth Technical College, under Francis P Marriott (qv); in Cape Town under Maurice van Essche (qv), John Farley and Alfred Krenz (qv).
Exhibitions Participated in group exhibitions in SA; 1956 Quadrennial Exhibition.
Represented William Humphreys Art Gallery, Kimberley.
References SAA; BSAK 1; AASA.

PAGE Frederick Hutchison (Fred)

Born 1908 Utrecht, Natal.
Died 1984 Port Elizabeth.
A painter of landscapes, cityscapes, architectural studies, interiors and still life. Used tempera and after 1967 polymer-acrylic and ink. Worked in a whimsical manner with the use of stark white on a dark background. His paintings are infused with a strange light that is neither night nor day. A series of District Six, Cape Town. A graphic artist.

Studies 1945 took an art course by correspondence; 1946–47 part-time at the Port Elizabeth Technical College, under John Muff-Ford (qv) and Jack Heath (qv), where awarded a bronze medal.

Profile c.1947 to the early 1960s worked as a display artist in Port Elizabeth.

Exhibitions Participated in group exhibitions from 1948 with the EPSFA and in West Germany, the UK and Greece; 1960 Port Elizabeth, first of numerous solo exhibitions held throughout SA; 1965 Grosvenor Gallery, London, exhibited with 10 other artists; 1968 Durban Art Gallery, solo exhibition entitled "Artist of the Eastern Province"; 1975 King George VI Art Gallery, Port Elizabeth, Retrospective Exhibition; 1979 SAAA Gallery, Cape Town, 70th Birthday Commemorative Exhibition; 1983 Carriage House Gallery, Johannesburg, Retrospective Exhibition.

Represented Hester Rupert Art Museum, Graaff-Reinet; King George VI Art Gallery, Port Elizabeth; Pretoria Art Museum; Sandton Municipal Collection; SA National Gallery, Cape Town; University of the Orange Free State; William Humphreys Art Gallery, Kimberley.

References Art SA; SAA; 20C SA Art; SSAP; BSAK 1 & 2; SA Art; Oxford Companion to 20C Art (under SA); 3Cs; AASA; LSAA; *Artlook* April 1968 & December 1975/January 1976; *Gallery* Summer 1983; Retrospective Exhibition Catalogue, 1975, King George VI Art Gallery, Port Elizabeth.

PAGE Mary Maud

Born 1867 London, England.
Died 1925 Cape Town.
Resided in SA from 1911.
From 1915 numerous botanical paintings; also carved in wood and worked in enamel.

Studies Caudron Art School; botanically correct studies learnt from F Bolus in Cape Town.

Profile Her illustrations have been used in the following publications: *Flora of South Africa,* by Rudolph Marloth, 1913–32; *The Journal of the Botanical Society,* 1915, Kirstenbosch, Cape Town; *South African Botany,* by F W Storey and K M Wright, 1916, London; *Elementary Lessons in Systematic Botany,* by F Bolus, 1919, Cape Town; *Flowering Plants of SA*, volumes 6, 7 and 8, 1926–28, Pretoria; *The Flowering Plants of Africa,* a quarterly publication by the Botanical Research Institute; *The Genera of the Mesembryanthemaceae,* by H Herre, 1971, Cape Town, in which the illustrations of Beatrice Carter (qv) were also used. 1915–25 botanical artist to The Bolus Herbarium, University of Cape Town.

Exhibition 1966 Kirstenbosch Gardens, Cape Town, Botanical Exhibition.

Represented University of Cape Town.

References SAA; DSAB; AASA.

PAKATI Dumezweni

Born 1957 Griqualand East, Transkei.
A painter of landscapes. Works in oil, acrylic, watercolour and pencil.

Studies 1981–82 Rorke's Drift Art Centre, under Keith van Winkel and Jay Johnson.

Profile 1983 taught art at the Mpumalanga College of Education, Hammarsdale, Natal; 1986 at Phezulu High School. From 1983 involved in the organisation of exhibitions in Mpumalanga Township and at the Hebron College of Education, Bophuthatswana. 1984 co-editor and illustrator of *The Jabula Journal*. A History and English teacher. A poet, actor and author. 1984–86 lived in Bophuthatswana.

Exhibitions He has participated in several group exhibitions from 1981 held throughout SA and in the UK, The Netherlands and West Germany; 1984 University of the Witwatersrand, first of five solo exhibitions held in educational establishments.

PALMER Alfred RBA ROI

Born 1877 London, England.
Died 1951 London, England.
Resided in SA 1925–50.

A painter of landscapes—particularly of Natal and Lesotho—and of figures, genre and religious studies. Worked in pastel, oil and watercolour, drew preliminary charcoal and red chalk sketches, painted frescos in tempera, etched and also sculpted in bronze and plaster. His sculptures were mostly of universal themes.

Studies Royal Academy Schools, London, under John Singer Sargent (1856–1925); 1899 Académie Julian, Paris, under Jean Paul Laurens (1838–1921) and also under Marcel Baschet (1862–1941).

Profile 1912 a member of the Royal Society of British Artists; 1922 a member of the Royal Institute of Oil Painters; a member of the NSA and the SA Institute of Art. Illustrated *Seven Lost Trails* by Hedley Chilvers. Travelled extensively throughout the world and had studios in Florence, Berlin, Brussels and Paris at various times. Prior to SA lived in Kent and in London; 1940–44 lived in England.

Exhibitions Participated in group exhibitions from 1902 in England, Paris and throughout SA; 1914 London, first of several solo exhibitions in England and SA; 1953 Royal Society of British Artists Galleries, London, Memorial Exhibition.

Award 1929 Gundlefinger Award, NSA.

Represented Africana Museum, Johannesburg; Durban Art Gallery; Johannesburg Art Gallery; Pretoria Art Museum; William Humphreys Art Gallery, Kimberley.

Public Commissions 1929 mural, Durban Children's Hospital (since removed); 1930 sculpture, Johannesburg Railway Station; 1936 mural, Manners Mansions, Johannesburg, among others.

References AMC4; DBA; BSAK 1 & 2; SA Art; AASA; LSAA.

PANTELIAS Chrysanthos (Chris)

Born 1943 Khartoum, Sudan.
Resided in SA from 1967.

A sculptor, painter and graphic artist of landscapes and figures. Works in wood, oil, acrylic and in various graphic media.

Studies 1964–67 School of Fine and Applied Art, Khartoum Technical Institute, under Ibrahim Salahi.

Profile 1973–76 a part-time lecturer at the Witwatersrand Technical College; from 1980 a full-time lecturer in graphic design at the Witwatersrand Technical College. Has visited Egypt, the Sudan and Ethiopia.

Exhibitions He has participated in several group exhibitions from 1983 in Johannesburg; 1967 Khartoum, Sudan, solo exhibition.

PAPAGEORGE Georgie

Born 1941 Simonstown, Cape Province.

An artist working in oil, acrylic, watercolour, pencil, charcoal and in 3D elements such as wood and stone. A number of photographic works. 1979–84 a series on the gold mining industry.

Studies 1974–79 University of South Africa, under Alan Crump and Leon du Plessis (qv), gaining a BA(FA); 1980–81 Pretoria Technikon, under Ian Redelinghuys (qv), where attained a Higher Diploma in Graphics; from 1985 University of the Witwatersrand, under Professor Alan Crump, studying for an MA(FA).

Profile 1986 an art teacher at St Alban's College, Pretoria. 1980–85 several visits to the Okavango Swamps in Botswana, and to London; 1982 visited West Germany; 1983–85 several visits to Italy.

Exhibitions She has participated in several group exhibitions from 1978 in the Transvaal; 1980 Olivetti Gallery, Johannesburg, first of three solo exhibitions held in Johannesburg and Pretoria.

Awards 1979 Graphic Award, Betty Pack Festival; 1980 Graphic Award, New Signatures, SAAA, Pretoria.

Represented Pietersburg Collection.

PAPAS William Elias (Bill)

Born 1927 Ermelo, Eastern Transvaal.

A painter and graphic artist of landscapes, street scenes, portraits, seascapes and figures. Works in acrylic, watercolour, wash, ink and in various graphic media.

Studies After 1945 studied at the Witwatersrand Technical College, under Walter Battiss (qv); 1947–50 St Michael's School of Art, London, the Beckenham School of Art, Kent, England, and on a study tour of Europe.

Profile A political cartoonist. 1950–56 lived in Cape Town, where he worked as a newspaper artist for *The Cape Times* and wrote a column called "Papas in the Peninsula". 1957–59 lived in Johannesburg, where he contributed to *The Star*, *Drum*, *Dagbreek* and *Sondagnuus*. 1959 went to England, 1959–66 made regular contributions to the London *Sunday Times* and daily to *The Guardian*; 1966–70 his work appeared in *Punch*; 1970 moved to Greece, from 1978 he has spent part of each year sailing in a yacht.

Exhibitions He has exhibited in SA, England, Northern Ireland, Canada, Israel, USA, Zimbabwe and Greece.

Represented Africana Museum, Johannesburg; SA National Gallery, Cape Town.

Publications by Papas An author and illustrator of children's books, including *Mr Nero* with his brother Theodore; Wm Papas and A Sussens, *Under the Tablecloth, Papas looks at the Peninsula,* 1952, Maskew Miller, Cape Town. His illustrations have also appeared in other authors' books.

References Art SA; Register SA & SWA; SESA; AMC4; BSAK 1 & 2; AASA; SASSK; *SA Panorama* November 1959; *SA Art News* 4 May 1961.

PARAMORE Dorothy O'Neil

Born 1937 Blantyre, Nyasaland (Malawi).
Resided in SA from 1948.
A painter in oil and acrylic and a sculptor in steel of landscapes, seascapes, still life and abstract works.

*Studies c.*1960 adult education classes, Wimbledon Polytechnic, London; 1971 privately under the sculptor Karl Duldig (*b.*1902) in Australia.

Profile A trained English teacher. 1959–61 lived in England; 1971 in Australia. Has travelled throughout Europe, the Far East and the USA.

Exhibitions She has participated in several group exhibitions from 1973 in Johannesburg; 1980 Carlton Hotel, Johannesburg (under the auspices of the SAAA), first solo exhibition, the second being held at Drian Galleries, London, in 1982.

Represented Gdansk National Gallery, Poland.

PARAVANO Dino

Born 1935 Italy.
Resided in SA from 1947.
A painter of wildlife, landscapes, seascapes, still life and figures. Works in oil, acrylic, watercolour, pastel and pencil.

Studies 1952–53 Johannesburg Art School.

Profile From 1979 a member of the Society of Animal Artists, New York; a member of the WSSA. From 1978 a number of limited edition lithographs of his works have been published in SA and the USA.

Exhibitions 1968 Durban, first of 14 solo exhibitions held in SA and the USA; he has participated in numerous group exhibitions from 1971 in SA, the USA, Italy, the UK and Austria.

Awards 1983 Second Prize, International Wildlife Exhibition, Cincinnati, Ohio, USA; 1984 Best of Show Award, Society of Animal Artists Exhibition, New York, USA.

References BSAK 1; AASA; *Artlook* August 1970; *Safari* November/December 1980 & October 1982 (USA); *In the Clouds* May 1981; *Custos* November 1982; *SA Panorama* September 1981, February 1983 & June 1987; *Flying Springbok* June 1983.

PARKER Barbara
Born Cape Town.
A painter and graphic artist of landscapes, seascapes, portraits and figures. Works in oil, watercolour, gouache, ink, wash, pencil, charcoal and in various graphic media.
Studies Michaelis School of Fine Art, under Edward Roworth (qv), where awarded the MacIver Scholarship, the MacIver Prize and the Michaelis Prize in 1945 and gained a BA(FA) and an MA(FA) with honours; *c.*1970 Académie Goetz, Paris, under Henri Goetz (*b.*1909) and at l'Académie de la Grande Chaumière, Paris.
Profile Worked with Katrine Harries (qv), producing etchings. 1949–52 a junior lecturer in Fine Art, Michaelis School of Fine Art; 1952 a lecturer in art at St Cyprian's School, Cape Town; 1954 at Kingsmead College, Johannesburg; 1960–69 Johannesburg College of Education. During the 1960s drew a large number of illustrations for schoolbooks and children's books, some of which she also wrote. During the 1970s illustrated several issues of the schools' series by Dr A Bleksley in *The Rand Daily Mail*. 1968–72 wrote articles on artists for *Artlook*, in 1972 for *Lantern*, in 1974 for *Our Art 3* and in 1982 for *Gallery*. Has travelled throughout SA, SWA/Namibia and Europe.
Exhibitions She has participated in numerous group exhibitions from the late 1940s in SA and West Germany; 1972 Lidchi Gallery, Johannesburg, first of six solo exhibitions in SA and SWA/Namibia.
Public Commission 1975 panoramic frieze for projection in the Johannesburg Planetarium.
References BSAK 1; AASA.

PATON David
Born 1960 Germiston, Transvaal.
A painter and a sculptor in mixed media.
Studies 1984 gained a BA(FA) from the University of the Witwatersrand.
Exhibition 1985 Cape Town Triennial.
Awards 1984 Winner of the Silver Award, Rolfes Impressions '84, Johannesburg Art Gallery; 1984 First Prize Sculpture, New Signatures, SAAA, Pretoria.

PATON Juliana
Born 1915 Zeerust, Western Transvaal.
A painter of flowers, still life and landscapes. Works in acrylic, mixed media, watercolour, gouache, ink, wash and pencil.
Studies 1941–43 in Vereeniging, Transvaal, under K M Knight; 1944–48 in Vereeniging, under Doris Prentice; 1945–46 in Vanderbijlpark, Transvaal, under John Littlejohns (qv); 1969, 1971, 1975 and 1979 in Natal, under Alfred Ewan (qv); 1973 under Marjorie Bowen (qv); 1976 in Johannesburg, under George Boys (qv).

Profile 1946 a member of the SAAA; 1970 a member of the Brush and Chisel Club; 1972 a founder member of the WSSA, of which she became an Associate in 1977; also founded the Vereeniging Art Society and the Vaal Triangle Society of Arts and Crafts. From 1979 has taught art privately. 1973 travelled to Italy.
Exhibitions She has participated in numerous group exhibitions from 1945 throughout SA; 1972 Carlton Centre Gallery, Johannesburg, first of 15 solo exhibitions held in SA.
Represented Willem Annandale Art Gallery, Lichtenburg.
References BSAK 1 & 2; *Garden & Home* July 1982.

PATON Wallace FRIBA

Born 1874 London, England.
Died 1948 Durban.
Resided in SA from 1885.
A painter of landscapes and seascapes. Worked in pastel, watercolour and oil.
Studies Qualified as an architect in Durban.
Profile 1905 a founder member of the NSA; 1917 a member of the SA Society of Artists; 1926 an Executive Member of the SA Institute of Art. A fully trained architect and senior partner in Paton, Taylor, Bennet & Willies of Durban. A Fellow of the Royal Institute of British Architects. 1943 the Consulting Architect on the new Durban Railway Station. Lived in Durban.
Exhibitions Participated in group exhibitions in SA and at the Royal Academy, London; 1948 Tate Gallery, London, SA Art Exhibition.
Represented Durban Art Gallery; SA National Gallery, Cape Town.
References Collectors' Guide; SAA; Pict Afr; BSAK 1 & 2; SA Art; 3Cs; AASA.

PAUL Robert Fowler

Born 1906 Sutton, Surrey, England.
Died 1980 Harare, Zimbabwe.
Resided in Rhodesia/Zimbabwe from 1927.
A self-taught artist of landscapes of the Eastern Highlands of Zimbabwe, particularly the area around Nyanga. Worked in ink & wash, watercolour, mixed media and in oil and tempera mixed.
Profile During the late 1960s and the early 1970s he painted a series of the old buildings of Rhodesia (Zimbabwe) using gum resist. Influenced by the work of Ivon Hitchens (1893–1979) and John Piper (*b*.1903), from whom he learnt the technique of gum resist. He met Piper in 1926 and retained a life-long connection with him. In 1950 retired from the Army, becoming a full-time artist. Painted in the Transkei and in England.
Exhibitions Participated in numerous group exhibitions in Rhodesia (Zimbabwe) and on the National Gallery Annual Exhibitions and the Salisbury District Art Shows; 1960 Salisbury, Rhodesia (Harare, Zimbabwe), joint exhibition with Peter Birch; 1976 National Gallery, Salisbury (Harare), Retrospective Exhibition; 1980 Pretoria Art Museum, Retrospective Exhibition.

FRED PAGE
The Last Lamington 1973
Polymer on Canvas on Panel 112 × 130 cm
Pretoria Art Museum

CATHERINE PAYNTER
The Moon and Sixpence with Open Pomegranate 1987
Mixed Media on Canvas 60 × 50 cm
Private

MICHAEL PETTIT
The Black Rose of Summer 1986
Oil on Canvas 43 × 36 cm Painted Frame
Private

J H PIERNEEF
Lowveld 1945
Oil on Canvas 100 × 74 cm
Max Levenberg

Represented National Gallery, Harare, Zimbabwe.
Reference Rhodesia National Gallery Catalogue, 1976 Salisbury, Rhodesia (Harare, Zimbabwe).

PAYNE Malcolm John

Born 1946 Pretoria.
Both a painter and sculptor of figures and abstract work. Uses acrylic, watercolour, gouache, ink, wash, pencil, mixed media. Polystyrene, felt, plywood and many other media. 1979–85 "Occular Surgery", a series of drawings on black casein using aquarelle crayons.
Studies 1967–70 Pretoria Technical College, under Gunther van der Reis (qv), where gained a National Teachers Diploma; 1972–73 on a Montague White Bursary at St Martin's School of Art, London, under Anthony Caro (*b*.1924) and Phillip King (*b*.1934).
Profile A member of the SAAA. 1971 worked as a scenic artist and designer for PACT. 1972–75 a lecturer in graphic art and sculpture at the Witwatersrand Technical College and in 1977–79 at the University of the Witwatersrand. 1975 appointed a Moderator for the National Diploma in Art and Design, for the Department of National Education. 1978 an external examiner in sculpture for the University of South Africa. Designed the sets for Athol Fugard's plays "Boesman and Lena" in 1971 and "A Lesson from Aloes" in 1979. 1985 commissioned by the Johannesburg Art Gallery to produce prints for the Centenary Print Portfolio, published by the Brenthurst Press, Johannesburg. 1976 made a study tour of the USA and Europe.
Exhibitions He has participated in many group exhibitions from 1968 in SA and the UK; 1974 SAAA Gallery, Johannesburg, first of 12 solo exhibitions in SA; 1983 solo exhibition, touring SA; 1985 Cape Town Triennial; 1985 Tributaries, touring SA and West Germany; 1987 Johannesburg Art Gallery, Vita Art Now.
Awards 1968 First Prize with Elizabeth Lamb (qv) and Alice Elahi (qv), New Signatures, SAAA, Pretoria; 1971 Ernest Oppenheimer Memorial Trust Award, Art SA Today; 1976 Metalart Prize, open category; 1983 Five Roses Young Artist Award for Art.
Represented Boksburg Town Council; Durban Art Gallery; Johannesburg Art Gallery; Pretoria Art Museum; SA National Gallery, Cape Town; University of South Africa; University of Stellenbosch; University of the Witwatersrand.
Public Commission 1985 mural for the New Zoology Building, University of Cape Town.
References BSAK 1 & 2; AASA; LSAA; *Artlook* September 1968; *Habitat* no 12, 1977; *Gallery* Spring 1983; *SA Art Calendar* September 1983.

PAYNTER Catherine

Born 1949 Johannesburg.
A painter of landscapes, village scenes, underwater scenes, vegetation, animals and still life. Works in acrylic, watercolour and gouache.

Profile 1981–85 lived in Port St Johns, Transkei, thereafter at Greyton, Cape Province. 1970–85 several visits to Mozambique; 1971 visited Australia; 1973 visited Rhodesia (Zimbabwe); 1974 Spain; 1975 Iran and Israel; 1983 SWA/ Namibia; 1985 London and Northern Italy.

Exhibitions She has participated in several group exhibitions in SA; 1975 SAAA Gallery, Johannesburg, first of 10 solo exhibitions including, from 1980, annually at the Everard Read Gallery, Johannesburg.

References *Artlook* January/February 1977; *Habitat* no 25, 1977 & no 64, 1984; *Gallery* Summer 1981 & Winter 1986; *Flying Springbok* May 1985.

PEARSON Susan Caroline (Sue)

Born 1932 Winnipeg, Canada.

Resided in SA from 1949.

A painter of seascapes, flower studies and "mood" paintings. Works in watercolour.

Studies 1946–48 part-time at Winnipeg School of Art, Canada; 1950 studied History of Art at Rhodes University; 1982–87 under Rosalind Chidell-Braby (qv).

Profile From 1982 a member of the Highway Art Group's Committee, and from 1984 a member of the NSA and the Midlands Arts and Crafts Association. From 1984 a member of the WSSA, becoming an Associate in 1986.

Exhibitions She has participated in many group exhibitions from 1982 in Natal.

Awards 1984 and 1987 Mary Clark Trophy, Highway Art Group.

PEDLEY Margaret Alice (Peggy)

Born 1918 Johannesburg.

A painter of landscapes, seascapes and abstract pictures. Works in watercolour, oil, ink and wash.

Studies 1973–81 regular painting courses under Professor Alfred Ewan (qv); from 1982 several short courses under Ulrich Schwanecke (qv), George Boys (qv) and Marjorie Bowen (qv).

Profile From 1974 a member of the WSSA and an Associate from 1984. Many visits to the Drakensberg Mountains and several painting holidays in SA and England.

Exhibitions She has participated in numerous group exhibitions from 1975 in SA and twice in London.

PEERS Charles Andrew

Born 1954 Port Elizabeth.

A painter of landscapes; also executes imaginative animal sculpture/furniture pieces. Works in oil, gouache, pencil, wood, cardboard and papier mâché.

Studies 1973–76 Rhodes University, under Professor Brian Bradshaw (qv) and Josua Nell (qv), gaining a BA(FA) in sculpture and being awarded the Purvis Art Prize.

Profile 1973–76 a member of the Grahamstown Group. A prop maker for the State Theatre, Pretoria, and from 1986 a designer of sets, props and costumes for other theatre groups. Grandson of Charles E Peers (qv).
Exhibitions He has participated in several group exhibitions from 1973 in Grahamstown and Pretoria.
Commission 1977 carved relief panels for the coffin of Steve Biko.

PEERS Charles Ernest

Born 1874 Castlereagh, County Down, Northern Ireland.
Died 1944 Higgovale, Cape Town.
Resided in SA from 1904.
A painter of landscapes, scenes of Cape Town, Cape homesteads and a number of flower pieces. During the 1890s painted mostly maritime pictures. Worked in watercolour and pastel. A number of oils after 1922. Additionally worked in pen, wash and pencil and produced linocuts, lithographs and etchings.
Studies Liverpool School of Art, England; Slade School of Art, London.
Profile 1905 a member of the SA Society of Artists; 1926 a member of the SA Institute of Art; 1934 President of the Owl Club; 1935 President of the K Club; 1938–44 first President of the New Group; Chairman of the SA Fine Arts Association. 1930 two folios of lithographic drawings published by Brown & Davies, Durban, entitled "The Cape—twelve familiar scenes" and "Natal—a series of sketches" with an introduction by S W Pope; other prints of his work have been published. Produced a series of 100 drawings for the United Tobacco Company publication "Our Land", 1939, Cape Town. Illustrated *The Seven Wonders of Southern Africa*, by Hedley Chilvers and *The Coast of Hermanus*, by Will Costello. 1931 employed as a chrome-lithographer for Galvin & Sales, Cape Town. 1924 won *The Cape Times* poster competition. Grandfather of Charles A Peers (qv).
Exhibitions 1923 Lezards Gallery, Johannesburg, first solo exhibition; 1924 Taylor Art Gallery, Durban, joint exhibition with Allerley Glossop (qv); participated in group exhibitions from 1926; 1939 Cape Town, joint exhibition with J Pope Ellis; 1945 Memorial Exhibition in conjunction with the New Group; 1948 Tate Gallery, London, SA Art Exhibition; 1975 SA National Gallery, Cape Town, Commemorative Exhibition.
Represented Africana Museum, Johannesburg; Albany Museum, Grahamstown; Durban Art Gallery; Pretoria Art Museum; SA National Gallery, Cape Town; Tatham Art Gallery, Pietermaritzburg; University of Cape Town; William Humphreys Art Gallery, Kimberley.
References Collectors' Guide; PSA; Pict Art; Art SA; SAA; SADNB; SAP&D; AMC7; BSAK 1 & 2; Enc S'n A; 3Cs; AASA; LSAA; Commemorative Exhibition Catalogue, 1975, SA National Gallery, Cape Town.

PELL Joan see WINDER Joan

PEMBA George Mnyalaza Milwa

Born 1912 Hill's Kraal, Korsten, Port Elizabeth.
A painter of figures, portraits and of rural and urban genre. Works in watercolour, chalk and oil.

Studies 1931 watercolour classes for two weeks at the University of Fort Hare; 1937 a short course at Rhodes University, under Professor Austin Winter Moore (qv). 1937 and 1947 gained a scholarship from the Fort Hare African Trust.
Profile Trades as a General Dealer.
Exhibitions He has participated in group exhibitions in Port Elizabeth; 1979 Contemporary African Art in SA, touring; 1986 Alliance Française, Pretoria, Historical Perspective of Black Art in SA Exhibition.
Award 1979 awarded an Honorary Master of Arts Degree from the University of Fort Hare.
Represented University of Fort Hare.
References BSAK 1 & 2; 3Cs; Sheila Keeble, *The Black Who's Who of Southern Africa Today*, 1979/82, African Business Publications, Johannesburg; Contemporary African Art; Echoes of African Art; *SA Panorama* March 1977.

PENFOLD Denise Marcelle

Born 1961 Kitwe, Zambia.
Resided in SA from 1967.
A painter and graphic artist of both abstract and figurative pictures. Works in oil, acrylic, watercolour, gouache, ink, wash, pencil, charcoal and in various graphic media.
Studies 1979–82 Michaelis School of Fine Art, under Bruce Arnott (qv), Gavin Younge (qv), Peggy Delport (qv), Marthinus la Grange (qv), Jules van de Vijver (qv) and Stanley Pinker (qv), gaining a BA(FA).
Profile 1984 an Associate member of the Artists Guild, Cape Town. 1983–86 a lecturer in the School of Art & Design, Cape Technikon. 1971 visited London; 1983 toured Europe.
Exhibitions She has participated in several group exhibitions from 1982 in Cape Town.

PENN Jack

Born 1909 Cape Town.
A self-taught sculptor of portrait busts. Works in bronze, resin and ciment fondu.
Profile A fully trained surgeon.
Public Commissions Numerous portrait busts of medical notability in SA and the UK; busts of Field-Marshal J C Smuts, the late J B Vorster, and other SA figures for various airports; 1970 statue of Sister Henrietta Stockdale in the gardens of St Cyprian's Cathedral, Kimberley; bust of General Ridgway, West Point, USA.
References SESA, BSAK 1; AASA; *SA Panorama* December 1978.

PENNINGTON Paule

Born 1944 Belgium.
A painter of abstract and cosmic works. Uses acrylic.
Studies 1961–64 under William E Gladstone Solomon (qv) in Cape Town, but mainly self-taught.

Exhibitions She has participated in group exhibitions in SA; 1981 Republic Festival Exhibition; 1984 Belgica (SA) Club, Johannesburg, solo exhibition.
Represented Willem Annandale Art Gallery, Lichtenburg.

PENNINGTON Reg

Born 1941 Horwich, Lancashire, England.
Resided in SA from 1966.
Both a sculptor and painter of abstract pieces. Works in bronze, stone, ciment fondu, wood, steel, fibreglass, polyester resin, perspex, oil, acrylic, watercolour, gouache, ink and wash.
Exhibitions 1969 Johannesburg, first of eight solo exhibitions one of which was held in Israel; he has participated in several group exhibitions from 1970 in SA and in one in Israel.
Represented National Gallery, Gaborone, Botswana.
References *Artlook* November 1969 & December 1972.

PENSTONE Constance

Born 1865 Chesterfield, Derbyshire, England.
Died 1928 Glencairn, Cape Province.
Resided in SA from 1896.
A painter of landscapes, seascapes, figures and Cape homesteads. Worked in watercolour and gesso.
Studies Derbyshire School of Art, UK.
Profile Initially a cartoonist for *The Owl* and *The Cape Times* under the pseudonym "Scalpel". In 1920 a founder member and for many years a Council member of the SA Society of Artists. Prior to 1896 lived in Australia where she taught and in America where she designed the stained glass windows for Tiffany & Company. First married to Charles Penstone (1852–96), the newspaper illustrator, cartoonist and founder of *The Owl* and secondly to George Crosland Robinson (qv). Included in Edward Roworth's (qv) essay "Landscape Art in SA", 1917, Studio Publication, *Art of the British Empire Overseas.*
Exhibitions Participated in group exhibitions from 1902; 1902 Cape Town, first of several solo exhibitions held in SA.
Represented Africana Museum, Johannesburg; Albany Museum, Grahamstown; Durban Art Gallery; Julius Gordon Africana Centre, Riversdale; SA Cultural History Museum, Cape Town; SA National Gallery, Cape Town; William Fehr Collection, Cape Town.
References SADNB; AMC4; SAP&D; SSAP; Pict Afr; Bénézit; BSAK 1 & 2; Enc S'n A; 3Cs; AASA; SASSK.

PERKES-FRANKS Arlette

Born 1957 Johannesburg.
A painter, graphic artist and sculptor of landscapes, portraits, still life, genre, figures, wildlife, cityscapes and abstracts. Works in oil, acrylic, watercolour, gouache, ink, wash, pencil, charcoal, pastels, various graphic media and wood; also creates collages. A number of large series: in 1978 portraits of friends; 1979 "Triangles"; 1980 Oedipus body puppets (for a stage production by Barney Simon); 1983 "Myself & Metaphysical Africa"; 1984–86 "People & City Life".

Studies 1976–79 University of the Witwatersrand, under Ulrich Louw (qv), Paul Stopforth (qv), Robert Hodgins (qv), Terence King (qv), Malcolm Payne (qv) and Neels Coetzee (qv), gaining a BA(FA) (Hons).

Profile 1980 a costume designer and maker for the Baxter Theatre, Cape Town. 1981–82 an art teacher at Woodmead School, Johannesburg; 1983 an art teacher at the Johannesburg Art Foundation. 1984 various designs for theatre programmes, letterheads, logos, brochures and cards. 1985–86 illustrations for *Apartheid for Beginners*, 1986, Readers & Writers, England.

Exhibitions She has participated in several group exhibitions from 1978 in Johannesburg; 1983 Karen McKerron Gallery, Johannesburg, solo exhibition.

PERREVOS Patricia Gudrun

Born 1946 SA.

A self-taught painter of landscapes, portraits, still life, figures and wildlife. Works in oil, acrylic, watercolour, pencil and charcoal. In 1982 a large series of African heads and in 1983 of women.

Profile 1984 a member of the Omni-Art Association; 1985 a member of the Artists Market. 1976–82 Director and owner of a commercial art company in Johannesburg.

Exhibitions She has participated in several group exhibitions in SA; 1982 Crake Gallery, Johannesburg, solo exhibition.

PETTIT Michael Francis

Born 1950 Durban.

A painter of still life, often with recurring images and from 1983 of portraits. Works mostly in oil and occasionally in watercolour, gouache and pencil. Uses a wide range of styles and techniques. 1973–74 a large series entitled "Spirals and Strips".

Studies 1968–71 University of the Witwatersrand, under Cecily Sash (qv) and Robert Hodgins (qv), gaining a BA(FA) in 1971 and an MA(FA) in 1982.

Profile A member of the SAAA. 1973–77 a lecturer at the University of Durban-Westville; 1974 a part-time temporary lecturer at the University of the Witwatersrand; from 1979 Director of the Michael Pettit School of Art, Cape Town. 1975 created the stage designs of "The Firebird", for NAPAC in Durban and Pietermaritzburg; also created the stage design and dance choreography of "Journey" for the Jazzart Company, Cape Town, in 1979. 1981 designed a tapestry, woven by E Holden, for the University of Zululand. Moved to Cape Town in 1979. Several study tours in Europe and the USA.

Exhibitions He has participated in numerous group exhibitions from 1971 in SA, West Germany, SWA/Namibia and the USA; 1973 Durban, first of six solo exhibitions held throughout SA; 1979 Cape Town Biennial, Invited Artist; 1982 Cape Town Triennial; 1987 Johannesburg Art Gallery, Vita Art Now.

Award 1973 Cambridge Shirt Award, Art SA Today.

Represented Durban Art Gallery; King George VI Art Gallery, Port Elizabeth; Mangosuthu Technikon; Pietersburg Collection; Pretoria Art Museum; SA embassies in Brussels, Belgium and Washington DC, USA; SA National Gallery, Cape Town; University of the Orange Free State; University of Stellenbosch; University of Witwatersrand; University of Zululand.

References BSAK 1 & 2; 3Cs; AASA; LSAA; *Artlook* April 1974 & November/December 1976; *Habitat* no 7, 1974; *Cape Style* November 1985; *Living* October 1986; *SA Arts Calendar* Summer 1987; *Gallery* Autumn 1987.

PFAFF Uwe

Born 1947 Rye, Denmark.

Resided in SA from 1970.

A sculptor of figures. Works in wood. Often surrealistic, with disparate parts of the body joined.

Studies 1974 part-time study of painting at the Ruth Prowse Art Centre and the Cape Town Art Centre; 1977–78 part-time study of graphics and sculpture.

Profile Until 1979 worked as a mechanical design draughtsman, from 1980 a sculptor and furniture restorer. Grew up in Ravensburg, West Germany.

Exhibitions 1975 first of three solo exhibition; 1981 Republic Festival Exhibition; 1982 Cape Town Triennial.

Represented Durban Art Gallery.

References AASA; *Gallery* Autumn 1983.

PHALA Madi

Born 1955 Payneville, Springs, Transvaal.

A painter of figures, portraits and abstract pictures. Works in acrylic, watercolour and pencil, also sculpts in wood.

Studies A brief training in arts and crafts at Mafikeng Teachers Training College; a two-week workshop in September 1985 in Rustenburg under the American artist Peter Bradley, through USSALEP.

Profile 1977 a founder member of Bayajula Art Group, KwaThema, East Rand. A scenic artist and maker of models, masks, puppets and their sets for the SABC. Involved in poetry, music and acting.

Exhibitions He has participated in many group exhibitions from 1976 in the Transvaal and in Zululand; 1985 Tributaries, touring SA and West Germany; 1987 Johannesburg Art Foundation, joint exhibition with Bongiwe Dhlomo (qv), Reggie Bardavid (qv), Sam Nhlengetwa (qv) and Pat Mautloa (qv).

Represented University of Fort Hare.

Reference Echoes of African Art.

PHETOANE Mokone Johannes

Born 1961 Bultfontein, Orange Free State.

A painter, working in watercolour, and a graphic artist of still life.

Profile From 1986 a member of the QwaQwa Association of Artists.

Exhibition He has participated in group exhibitions from 1979.

PHILIP (William) Ronald

Born 1922 Pretoria.

A painter of landscapes, seascapes, portraits and figures. Works in oil and acrylic.

Studies 1939–41 and 1946 Rhodes University, under Professor A Winter Moore (qv), gaining a BA(FA) and a National Art Teachers Diploma. June–December 1961 studied in Italy on an Italian Government Scholarship.

Profile A member of the SAAA. 1946–49 an art teacher at the Pretoria Art Centre; 1950–62 an art teacher at Parktown Boys High, Johannesburg; 1962–70 lecturer, then senior lecturer, 1970–82 Director of the School of Art and Design, Witwatersrand Technical College (Technikon). 1946–55 a stage designer in Johannesburg. 1950–70 a part-time display and industrial designer. From 1982 a full-time painter in the Cape.

Exhibitions 1949 Beaux Arts Gallery, Johannesburg, first of three solo exhibitions; he has participated in many group exhibitions from 1952 in SA.

Represented Africana Museum, Johannesburg.

PHOSHOKO David Mothabeng

Born 1945 Pretoria.

Mainly a graphic artist of figures in landscapes, tribal customs and traditions. Produces woodcuts, mostly in black and white but occasionally in colour.

Exhibitions He has participated in group exhibitions from 1972 in Pretoria and in West Germany; 1976 Nedbank Centre, Pretoria, first of several solo exhibitions.

Reference *Phafa-Nyika*, edited by Ute Scholz, 1980, University of Pretoria.

PICKFORD MARRIOTT Francis see MARRIOTT Francis Pickford

PICTON-SEYMOUR Désirée Monica (Mrs Duckham)

Born 1923 London, England.

Resided in SA from 1940.

A painter and graphic artist of buildings and the built environment both real and imaginary. Works in oil, acrylic, watercolour, gouache, ink, wash and in various graphic media.

Studies Sutton and Cheam School of Art, Surrey, England; 1941–44 Michaelis School of Fine Art, under Professor Edward Roworth (qv), awarded the MacIver Scholarship.

Profile From 1945 a member of the SAAA; 1978 a committee member of the Vernacular Architecture Society; from 1977 a member of the Heritage Committee of the Cape Provincial Institute of Architects. 1985–86 a member of the National Monuments Council for the Western Cape; 1978–86 a part-time lecturer at the School of Architecture, University of Cape Town. Illustrated *Western Provincial*, by R I B Webster, 1950, Maskew Miller, Cape Town; *Transvaal Republican*, by R I B Webster, 1951, Maskew Miller, Cape Town, as well as numerous periodicals from 1945. 1958 designs for the ballet "Coppelia", performed in Cape Town. Has acted as an architectural historian for the restoration of several buildings in the Cape. Has travelled throughout Europe and in East and North Africa.

Exhibitions She has participated in numerous group exhibitions from 1945 in SA, the UK, West Germany, Zimbabwe and Yugoslavia; 1947 Ashbey Galleries, Cape Town, first of many solo exhibitions; 1956 and 1960 Quadrennial Exhibitions; 1981 Republic Festival Exhibition.

Award 1983 Cape Times Centenary Medal for Conservation of the Built Environment.

Represented Africana Museum, Johannesburg; Ann Bryant Gallery, East London; Durban Art Gallery; King George VI Art Gallery, Port Elizabeth; SA Cultural History Museum, Cape Town; University of Cape Town.

Publication by Picton-Seymour Victorian Buildings in SA, 1976, A A Balkema, Cape Town.

References Art SA; SAA; AMC7; SESA; BSAK 1 & 2; AASA; *SA Panorama* August 1959.

PIERCE-ATKINSON Patricia Mary

Born 1942 Enfield, Middlesex, England.
A painter of abstract pictures. Works in acrylic and mixed media.

Studies 1959–63 Michaelis School of Fine Art, gaining a BA(FA); 1983 attained an MA(FA).

Profile 1963–67 Head of the Children's Teaching Section of the Cape Town Art Centre; from 1964 has taught art privately. From 1973 a lecturer and Head of the Art Teacher Training Section of the Michaelis School of Fine Art. Married to Kevin Atkinson (qv).

Exhibitions She has participated in group exhibitions in SA from *c.*1965; 1967 Cape Town Art Centre, first of several solo exhibitions held in Cape Town; 1979 Cape Town Biennial, Invited Artist; 1981 SAAA Gallery, Cape Town, joint exhibition with Nathan Margalit (qv); 1982 Cape Town Triennial; 1983 University of Stellenbosch, joint exhibition with Kevin Atkinson (qv).

Represented SA National Gallery, Cape Town; University of South Africa; University of Stellenbosch.

References AASA; *Artlook* September 1970.

PIERNEEF Jacob Hendrik

Born 1886 Pretoria.
Died 1957 Pretoria.

A painter of landscapes and the occasional still life or figure; also painted homesteads, city views and mines. Worked in oil, casein, tempera and water-colour. A number of drawings, etchings, woodcuts (seldom after 1933) and linocuts.

Studies 1900 night classes in drawing under an architect at Hilversum, The Netherlands; 1901 Rotterdam Academy; 1905–08 under Frans Oerder (qv) in Pretoria; 1908 etching and wood engraving under George S Smithard (qv); 1911 the art of woodcut under Erich Mayer (qv).

Profile Influenced by the writings of Willem van Konijnenburg, particularly "De Aesthetische Idee" written in 1926. His work became increasingly more geometric, and his landscapes became structural with a strong use of line and simplified flat planes of colour, each painting being carefully composed. 1910–12 a member of The Individualists; 1917 a member of the SA Society of Artists. 1932–33 a founder member of the National Academy of Fine Arts (SA). Illustrations for a number of periodicals and books including *Die Brandwag* in 1917 and *The Independent* in 1919. A designer of tapestries as well as book and magazine covers. A number of reproductions were published by E Schweikerdt, Pretoria. 1912–20 a librarian at the Pretoria State Library; 1920–23 a lecturer in art at the Pretoria and Heidelberg Normal Colleges; 1950 a lecturer at the University of Natal. 1886–1900 lived in Pretoria; in 1900 his family were deported to The Netherlands, via the East African coast; in 1901 he visited Rome; 1902 returned to SA; 1923–24 lived in SWA/Namibia; 1925–26 in Europe, returning via the East African coast; 1933–35 lived in London, thereafter in SA. In 1972 a film on Pierneef's linocuts was made by Gordon Vorster (qv).

Exhibitions Participated in group exhibitions from 1911 in SA, once in Italy and once in Rhodesia (Zimbabwe); 1913 Pretoria, first of numerous solo exhibitions held in SA and The Netherlands; 1929 Johannesburg, joint exhibition with Fanie Eloff (qv); 1948 Tate Gallery, London, SA Art Exhibition; 1950 Pieter Wenning Gallery, Johannesburg, Retrospective Exhibition; 1953 Potchefstroom University for CHE, Retrospective Exhibition; 1964 Adler Fielding Gallery, Johannesburg, Pierneef Festival; 1965 Pretoria Art Museum, exhibition of the Dirk Lion-Cachet Collection; 1965 Johannesburg Art Gallery, exhibition of watercolours and drawings; 1970 Durban Art Gallery, "The Complete Wood-cuts of Pierneef" exhibition; 1972 Johannesburg Art Gallery, exhibition of watercolours; 1973 Pretoria Art Museum, exhibition of the Johannesburg Station panels; 1974–75 University of Stellenbosch, Rand Afrikaans University and Potchefstroom University for CHE, exhibition of the Marita J Pierneef Collection; 1980/81 Pretoria Art Museum, Johannesburg Art Gallery, Durban Art Gallery, William Humphreys Art Gallery, Kimberley, King George VI Art Gallery, Port Elizabeth and SA National Gallery, Cape Town, Pierneef and Van Wouw (qv) Retrospective Exhibition; 1982 Pretoria Art Museum, "The Pierneef Collection" Exhibition; 1984 Pretoria Art Museum, Commemorative Exhibition; 1987 Johannesburg Art Gallery, exhibition of the Johannesburg Station panels.

Awards 1935 first Medal of Honour for Painting, SA Akademie vir Wetenskap en Kuns; 1951 Honorary Doctorate, University of Natal; 1957 Honorary Doctorate of Philosophy, University of Pretoria; 1957 Honorary Membership of the SA Akademie vir Wetenskap en Kuns.

Represented Africana Museum, Johannesburg; Ann Bryant Gallery, East London; Arts Association SWA/Namibia Collection; Durban Art Gallery; Engelenberg House Art Collection, Pretoria; Johannesburg Art Gallery; King George VI Art Gallery, Port Elizabeth; National Cultural History and Open-Air Museum, Pretoria; National Museum, Bloemfontein; Pierneef Museum, Pretoria; Pietersburg Collection; Potchefstroom Museum; Pretoria Art Museum; Rand Afrikaans University; Sandton Municipal Collection; SA National Gallery, Cape Town; SWA/Namibia Administration Collection, Windhoek; University of Cape Town; University of Natal; University of the Orange Free State; University of Pretoria; University of South Africa; University of Stellenbosch; University of the Witwatersrand; William Humphreys Art Gallery, Kimberley.

Public Commissions 1924 mural, Ficksburg High School, Orange Free State; 1929–32 Johannesburg Railway Station panels; 1933–35 murals, SA House, London; 1937 mural, *SS Pretoria Castle*; 1940 two large pictures, Johannesburg Magistrates Courts; 1955 painting, Broadcast House, Johannesburg.

References J F W Grosskopf, *Pierneef—The Man and His Work*, 1945, J L van Schaik, Pretoria; F E G Nilant, *Die Hout- en Linosneë van J H Pierneef*, 1974, A A Balkema, Cape Town; A Bibliography by Sonia Smit, 1957, School of Librarianship, Cape Town; Skone Kunste; Collectors' Guide; PSA; Our Art 1; Art SA; SAA; 20C Art; SADNB; AMC4; DSAB; SAP&S; Oxford Companion to Art (under SA); SAP&D; SESA; SSAP; BSAK 1 & 2; Enc S'n A; Art SWA; SA Art; 3Cs; AASA; LSAA; *SA Art Collector* October 1946; *South Africana* February & December 1957; *SA Panorama* April 1958, May 1961, August 1963, February 1964, June 1982, September 1983 & January 1987; *De Arte* October 1968, September 1973 & April 1974; *Artlook* June 1973; *De Kat* August 1986 & December/January 1987; Commemorative Exhibition Catalogues, 1980 and 1984, Pretoria Art Museum.

PIETERS Jacobus (Jack)

Born 1886 Amsterdam, The Netherlands.
Died 1977 Durban.
Resided in SA from 1904.
A painter of still life, landscapes, seascapes, portraits, figures and flowers. Worked in oil.

Studies Under his uncle Evert Pieters of Laren at the Quelinius School, Amsterdam, for two years.

Profile A member of the SA Society of Artists and from 1949 a member of the Brush and Chisel Club. A member of the SA Institute of Arts and on the Durban Art Gallery Advisory Committee; 1941 President of the NSA. An art critic for *The Natal Mercury* under the nom-de-plume "Cerulean Blue". Lived in Pretoria and Cape Town, before finally settling in Durban.

Exhibitions Participated in group exhibitions in SA and in Europe from 1924; held numerous solo exhibitions in SA.

Represented Ann Bryant Gallery, East London; Durban Art Gallery; King George VI Art Gallery, Port Elizabeth; Pretoria Art Museum; William Humphreys Art Gallery, Kimberley.

Public Commissions A number of paintings of cricket grounds for the SA Cricket Association, four of which hang in the Memorial Hall, Lords, London.

References Collectors' Guide; SAA; BSAK 1 & 2; AASA; *SA Art Collector* August 1947.

PIKE (Rosalie) Barbara

Born 1933 Johannesburg.

A self-taught painter of landscapes, still life, figures and abstract pictures. Works in watercolour, pastel, wash, pencil and in charcoal.

Profile A trained botanist and zoologist who has drawn numerous botanical and scientific illustrations for newspapers and books. A member of the WSSA. 1957–58 artist to the Botany Department, University of the Witwatersrand; 1985 artist to the Geological Survey Museum, Pretoria. Illustrated *Wildflowers of the Witwatersrand* by A Lucas, 1971, Purnell, Cape Town and *Ferns of the Witwatersrand*, by F D Hancock and A Lucas, 1973, University of the Witwatersrand, Johannesburg. 1976–80 lived in SWA/Namibia.

Exhibitions She has participated in many group exhibitions in SA.

PILKINGTON George William

Born 1879 Sea Point, Cape Town.

Died 1958 St James, Cape Province.

A painter of marine, sea and coastal scenes. Worked in oil and watercolour.

Studies Mainly self-taught but studied briefly during the late 1890s under James Ford (qv) in Cape Town; 1923 life drawing classes at the Cape Town School of Art, under William G Bevington (qv) and Percy Thatcher.

Profile 1898–1923 a civil servant working as a Private Secretary to, among others, J W Sauer and Henry Burton. In 1924 began cotton farming, then briefly entered politics before becoming a full-time painter in 1925. Executed two sculptures in bronze depicting fishermen. A member of the SA Society of Artists. Editor of *The Cape*. 1905 co-founder of the Royal Cape Yacht Club. Lived in St James, where he had a studio in the old aquarium. Brother of Gordon Pilkington (qv).

Exhibitions Participated in group exhibitions held throughout SA, between 1932 and 1937 in England and once in Rhodesia (Zimbabwe); 1946 Maskew Miller Gallery, Cape Town, solo exhibition; held annual solo exhibitions in the Cape; 1953 Pieter Wenning Gallery, Johannesburg, solo exhibition.

Represented Africana Museum, Johannesburg; Ann Bryant Gallery, East London; Durban Art Gallery; Pretoria Art Museum; SA House, London; SA National Gallery, Cape Town; SA National Museum of Military History, Johannesburg; Tatham Art Gallery, Pietermaritzburg; William Humphreys Art Gallery, Kimberley.

Public Commission 1941 two murals in Cape Town Post Office.

Publication by Pilkington *Tales from South Africa's History for Little Ones*, Maskew Miller, Cape Town.
References Collectors' Guide; Art SA; SAA; SAP&S; SAP&D; AMC 7; SESA; BSAK 1 & 2; DBA; SA Art; AASA; SASSK.

PILKINGTON (Henry L) Gordon
Born 1886 Sea Point, Cape Town.
Died 1968 London, England.
Resided in London from 1951.
A self-taught painter of landscapes, town scenes and interiors. Worked in watercolour.
Profile 1917 a member of the SA Society of Artists. Trained as an architect under Sir Herbert Baker and Sir William Lorimer of Edinburgh, practised in Pretoria. Brother of George Pilkington (qv). Included in Edward Rosworth's (qv) essay "Landscape Art in SA", 1917, Studio Publication, *Art of the British Empire Overseas*.
Exhibitions Participated in group exhibitions in SA and in Europe from 1924; 1925 first solo exhibition held in Johannesburg.
Represented Pretoria Art Museum; William Humphreys Art Gallery, Kimberley.
Public Commission Designed the Durban War Memorial.
References Collectors' Guide; SAA; BSAK 1; AASA.

PILKINGTON Marjorie Florence (Mrs McDulling)
Born 1924 Transvaal.
A painter of still life, figures and abstract pictures. Works in watercolour, oil, acrylic, gouache, ink and wash. Series of pods, seeds, shells and shellscapes.
Studies Privately under Eileen Smithers, George Boys (qv) and Giuseppe Cattaneo (qv), in Johannesburg.
Profile A member of the WSSA, and an Associate from 1981. A member of the SAAA and the Brush and Chisel Club.
Exhibitions She has participated in numerous group exhibitions from 1973 in SA and once in London and West Germany; 1976 SAAA Gallery, Pretoria, solo exhibition.

PILTAN Marcelle (Mrs W Morley)
Died 1938.
A painter of landscapes and portraits. Worked in watercolour and pastel.
Profile 1910–12 a member of The Individualists. From 1912 taught drawing, still life and portraiture at the Johannesburg School of Art.
Exhibitions Participated in group exhibitions in SA.
Represented Pretoria Art Museum.
References BSAK 1 & 2 (under Pilton M); AASA.

PINKER Stanley

Born 1924 Windhoek, SWA/Namibia.
Resided in SA from 1930.
A painter of landscapes, figures and abstracted pictures. Works in oil, water-colour, charcoal and mixed media.
Studies 1947–50 Continental School of Art, Cape Town, under Maurice van Essche (qv); 1954–56 lithography at the Hammersmith School of Art, London, under Alistair Grant (*b*.1925).
Profile 1965 a founder member and sometime Chairman of the Artists Gallery, Cape Town. 1964 taught at the Cape Town Art Centre; from 1970 a lecturer at the Michaelis School of Fine Art. 1953 lived at Castagniers, Alpes Maritimes, France. 1954–64 lived in London, England. Has lived in Cape Town from 1964, and in 1976 spent three months in Paris.
Exhibitions He has participated in numerous group exhibitions from 1952 in SA, the UK, Europe, Brazil and Australia; 1954 SAAA Gallery, Cape Town, first of many solo exhibitions; 1958 London, solo exhibition; 1965 SAAA Gallery, Cape Town, joint exhibition with Helmut Starcke (qv); 1979 Cape Town Biennial, Invited Artist; 1985 Cape Town Triennial; 1985 Drostdy Centre, Stellenbosch, joint exhibition with Claude Bouscharain (qv) and Erik Laubscher (qv).
Award 1985 Rembrandt Gold Medal, Cape Town Triennial.
Represented Ann Bryant Gallery, East London; Durban Art Gallery; Johannes-burg Art Gallery; King George VI Art Gallery, Port Elizabeth; Pretoria Art Museum; SA National Gallery, Cape Town; Tatham Art Gallery, Pieterma-ritzburg; University of the Orange Free State; University of Stellenbosch.
References SSAP; SAP&S; SAP&D; AASA.

PITCHFORTH Roland Vivian RA RWS

Born 1895 Wakefield, Yorkshire, UK.
Died 1982 UK.
Resided in SA 1945–48.
A painter of landscapes, seascapes and military subjects. Worked in oil, gouache, and after 1945 only in watercolour.
Studies 1912–13 Wakefield School of Art; 1913–15 and 1919–21 Leeds School of Art; 1921–25 Royal College of Art, London, under Sir William Rothenstein (1872–1945) and Leon Underwood (*b*.1890).
Profile 1920–35 a member of the 7 + 5 Group, London; 1928–32 a member of the London Artists Association; 1929 a member of the London Group; 1942 became an Associate of the Royal Academy, in 1952 a Royal Academician and in 1957 an Associate of the Royal Society of Painters in Watercolours. In 1926 taught at the Camberwell School of Art, London; 1926–39 at the Clapham College of Art, London; 1930 at St Martin's School of Art, London; 1937–39 at the Royal College of Art, London; 1940–45 an Official War Artist to the Ministry of Information and the Admiralty; 1945–48 taught at the Witwa-tersrand Technical College; 1948 at the Chelsea School of Art, London. After completing his studies he visited Paris and in 1945 Ceylon (Sri Lanka) and Burma. 1948 returned to London.

Exhibitions Participated in group exhibitions in London and SA; a frequent exhibitor at the Royal Academy; 1928 London Artists Association, first of several solo exhibitions held in the UK and in SA; 1942 Wakefield, Retrospective Exhibition; 1946 Maskew Miller Gallery, Cape Town, solo exhibition.

Represented Africana Museum, Johannesburg; Durban Art Gallery; Johannesburg Art Gallery; SA National Gallery, Cape Town; Tate Gallery, London, UK; Victoria and Albert Museum, London, UK.

Public Commission In 1947 commissioned by the Johannesburg City Council to depict the scene outside the City Hall during the Royal Visit.

References SAA; DBA; BSAK 2; AASA; *Contemporary British Artists with Photographs by Walia*, 1979, edited by Charlotte Parry-Cooke, Bergstrom & Boyle Books, London.

PLAUT Faith Loy

Born 1925 Cape Town.

An artist working in fibre, of large wall hangings. Depicts life, in a semi-abstract manner.

Studies Slade School of Art, London, under Professor Randolph Schwabe (1885–1948); Central School of Art, London; graphic techniques at the Michaelis School of Fine Art, under Katrine Harries (qv).

Profile A member of the SAAA. 1949–50 lectured in design at the Michaelis School of Fine Art, thereafter at various training colleges, primary and nursery schools. 1926–48 lived in England.

Exhibitions 1949 Cape Town, first of six solo exhibitions; she has participated in several group exhibitions from 1950 in SA; 1981 Republic Festival Exhibition.

Award 1981 First Prize, Republic Festival Exhibition.

Represented Durban Art Gallery; SA National Gallery, Cape Town; University of Stellenbosch.

References BSAK 2; AASA; *Fair Lady* February 1983; *Gallery* Spring 1983.

POCOCK Fania E

Born 1897 Rondebosch, Cape Town.

Died 1976 Fish Hoek, Cape Province.

A sculptor of heads. Worked in bronze.

Studies Central School of Art, London.

Profile Studied music at the SA and Royal Colleges of Music. During WWII served with the SA Defence Force entertainment unit. Lived and worked briefly in the Latin Quarter in Paris.

Exhibitions Participated in group exhibitions in the UK and SA.

Represented SA National Gallery, Cape Town.

References DBA; *Portraits from the Permanent Collection Catalogue*, 1977, SA National Gallery, Cape Town.

PODLASHUC Alexander Cecil

Born 1930 Pretoria.

A painter and graphic artist of landscapes, still life, figures and portraits. Works in oil, acrylic, watercolour, gouache, ink, wash, pencil and in various graphic media.

Studies 1946 Michaelis School of Fine Art, under Melvyn Simmers (qv) and Edward Roworth (qv); 1947 Continental School of Art, Cape Town, under Maurice van Essche (qv); 1948–52 Central School of Art, London, under Keith Vaughan (*b*.1912), Victor Pasmore (*b*.1908), Gertrude Hermes (*b*.1901), Mervyn Peake (1911–68), William Roberts (*b*.1895) and Paul Hogarth, gaining a Diploma in Graphic Art. In 1972 he was awarded a Higher Diploma in Art and in 1982 a Masters Diploma in Technology.

Profile 1958–64 a member of the Bloemfontein Group. 1953 a part-time lecturer at the Pretoria Technical College; 1955–63 a part-time lecturer at the Orange Free State Technical College; from 1964 a lecturer, senior lecturer and subsequently Head of the Fine Art Department at the Port Elizabeth Technikon. 1953–64 produced a wide range of newspaper and magazine illustrations in the UK, The Netherlands and SA. June 1953–December 1954 worked for a press syndicate in Amsterdam drawing comic strips; 1955–64 a staff artist for the Magazine Publishing Division of the Argus Company. Has produced innumerable cartoons, illustrations and designs, and in 1978 a series of poems and woodcuts entitled "The Passion of Judas Iscariot". An art critic for the Port Elizabeth newspaper *Die Oosterlig*. Has lived in London, Amsterdam, Vienna and Munich. In 1973 spent six months in the Greek islands. Married to Marianne Podlashuc (qv).

Exhibitions He has held *c*.20 solo exhibitions from 1952; has participated in numerous group exhibitions from 1957 in SA, once in the USA in 1978–79 and once in West Germany in 1980; since 1961 regular joint exhibitions with Marianne Podlashuc (qv); 1978 University of South Africa, solo exhibition of "The Passion of Judas Iscariot"; 1981 Republic Festival Exhibition; 1985 Cape Town Triennial.

Represented Hester Rupert Art Museum, Graaff-Reinet; King George VI Art Gallery, Port Elizabeth; National Museum, Bloemfontein; Pietersburg Collection; Pretoria Art Museum; SA National Gallery, Cape Town; University of the Orange Free State; University of South Africa; William Humphreys Art Gallery, Kimberley.

References Art SA; 20C SA Art; BSAK 1; 3Cs; AASA; SASSK; LSAA; *De Kat* May 1986.

PODLASHUC Marianne

Born 1932 Delft, The Netherlands.
Resided in SA from 1953.

A painter and graphic artist of landscapes, portraits, genre and figures. Works in acrylic, watercolour, ink, wash, pencil and in various graphic media.

Studies 1949–52 Academie voor Beeldende Kunsten, Rotterdam.

Profile 1958–63 a member of the Bloemfontein Group. Has occasionally held part-time teaching posts in Applied Design and Interior Decoration at the Port Elizabeth Technikon. 1955–64 numerous illustrations for magazines and newspapers for the Argus Company. A detail from her painting "Three Days" was used as the cover illustration for Alan Paton's *Cry The Beloved Country*, published in the Penguin Classics series. During 1986 numerous illustrations for *De Kat*. Has travelled throughout the USA and in The Netherlands. Married to Alexander Podlashuc (qv).

Exhibitions She has participated in numerous group exhibitions from 1958 throughout SA; since 1961 has held regular joint exhibitions with Alexander Podlashuc (qv); 1977 William Humphreys Art Gallery, Kimberley, solo exhibition; 1981 Republic Festival Exhibition.

Represented Hester Rupert Art Museum, Graaff-Reinet; King George VI Art Gallery, Port Elizabeth; National Museum, Bloemfontein; Pretoria Art Museum; Sandton Municipal Collection; SA National Gallery, Cape Town; University of the Orange Free State; William Humphreys Art Gallery, Kimberley.

References Art SA; SAA; 20C SA Art; SAP&S; BSAK 1; 3Cs; AASA; LSAA; *De Kat* May 1986.

PODOLINI Arthur Volkmann

Born 1891 Hungary.

A painter of figures, portraits, genre and landscapes.

Studies 1908 studied in Budapest.

Profile A member of the SA Society of Artists and of the European and American Societies of Art. 1920 founded a school of art in Budapest and in 1933 was Principal of the School of Commercial and Fine Art in Cape Town. After 1946 taught at the Continental School of Art, Cape Town. Prior to WWI travelled throughout Europe; 1929–30 travelled in the USA.

Exhibitions Participated in group exhibitions in Budapest, Vienna, Stockholm and in SA; held solo exhibitions in Cape Town, Durban, Port Elizabeth and East London.

Represented Hungarian Museum of Fine Art.

References *The Arts in SA*, edited by WHK, 1933–34, The Knox Printing & Publishing Company, Durban; Bénézit; BSAK 1; AASA.

POHL Jack W

Born *c.*1878 Eastern Cape Province.

Died 1944.

A painter of landscapes, especially the scenery around Grahamstown and Port Elizabeth. Worked in oil.

Profile Worked as a photographer. Father of Robert Pohl (qv).

Exhibitions Exhibited at Lezards, Johannesburg, during the 1920s and 1930s.

Represented Albany Museum, Grahamstown; Johannesburg Art Gallery; Pretoria Art Museum; University of Stellenbosch.
References BSAK 1; AASA.

POHL Robert

Born 1917.
Died 1981 Brits, Transvaal.
A painter of landscapes. Worked in oil.
Profile 1945–46 travelled throughout the Northern and Eastern Transvaal and in Mozambique. The son of Jack Pohl (qv).
Exhibitions Participated in group exhibitions in SA; 1943 first of several solo exhibitions held in SA.
Represented University of Pretoria; University of Stellenbosch.
References BSAK 2; AASA; Solo Exhibition Catalogue, 1947, Stellenbosch.

POLS Pearl

Born 1944 Grahamstown.
A self-taught painter of flower studies and still life. Works in oil and acrylic.
Exhibitions She has participated in several group exhibitions from 1985 in SA; has held several solo exhibitions.

POMBEIRO Rodrigo Antonio do Nascimento

Born 1938 Mozambique.
Resided in SA from 1981.
A painter and graphic artist of landscapes, seascapes, wildlife and abstracts. Works in oil, gouache, ink, pencil and in various graphic media. A sculptor working in ciment fondu.
Studies Nucceo D'Arte, Mozambique.
Profile A founder and co-ordinator of TAM. A freelance interior and graphic designer. Has painted murals in Mozambique and Portugal. Has lived in Mozambique, the UK, Portugal and Canada, travelling to Italy, France, Switzerland and Spain.
Exhibitions He has participated in group exhibitions in Mozambique, Portugal, Canada and SA; 1960 Lourenço Marques (Maputo), Mozambique, solo exhibition.
Represented Maputo Municipality, Mozambique.

PONTIN Sue

Born 1935 Pietermaritzburg.
A painter of classical composers' ideas of their music. Works in oil. A large series on Scottish folk music and traditional ballads.

Studies University of the Witwatersrand, gaining a BA(FA); Witwatersrand Technical College, gaining a National Art Teachers Diploma; American Society of Arts, Connecticut, USA, where gained AFA (USA).
Profile A member of the Royal Academy of Arts, London, the Royal Society of Women Artists and the Royal Society of Painters in Oil. 1951–52 taught at Wyksham School, Pietermaritzburg. Involved in music, ballet and opera.
Exhibitions She has participated in many group exhibitions from 1964 in SA; has held solo exhibitions in SA and abroad.

POOLEY Elsa Susanna

Born 1947 Johannesburg.
A self-taught painter of botanical studies of wild flowers. Works in watercolour.
Profile A member of the NSA. An indigenous landscape gardener. 1965–74 lived in the Ndumu Game Reserve, Natal, 1974–84 in the St Lucia Reserve, Natal, and from 1984 on the South Coast of Natal.
Exhibitions She has participated in several botanical group exhibitions in SA; 1985 Things Gallery, Durban, solo exhibition.
Represented Killie Campbell Africana Library, University of Natal, Durban.

POORTERMANS Johannes Cornelius

Born 1786 Amsterdam, The Netherlands.
Died 1870 Paarl, Cape Province.
Resided in SA from 1833.
A painter of landscapes, town scenes and genre paintings, mainly of the Western Cape and Natal. His paintings are of historical importance. Worked in watercolour. Numerous lithographs.
Profile An engraver of maps. Assisted by L H O Landsberg (qv) and W H Langschmidt (qv). 1844–45 published a series, in monthly parts, of his own and other Cape lithographs. Prior to living in SA he lived in British Guiana (Guyana), The Netherlands, France, England and North America. When in SA he lived in the Cape, where he practised as a tobacconist; 1846 lived at Fish River; 1847–48 in Saldanha; 1849 at Piketberg, Cape Province.
Exhibition 1948 Tate Gallery, London, SA Art Exhibition.
Represented Africana Museum, Johannesburg; University of Pretoria; SA Library, Cape Town; William Fehr Collection, Cape Town.
References Pict Art; A Gordon Brown, *Christopher Webb Smith*, 1965, Howard Timmins, Cape Town; AMC4; Pict Afr; BSAK 1 & 2; 3Cs; SASSK.

PORTALUPI Thalassa

Born 1928 Germiston, Transvaal.
A painter of landscapes, seascapes, still life and wildlife. Works in watercolour, gouache, ink and wash. From 1983 Golden Gate series, Cosmos fields, seascapes and seagulls; 1985–86 a series of the Drakensberg Mountains.

Studies 1967 drawing at the Centre for Continuing Education, University of the Witwatersrand, under Zoe Smith; 1978 Sumi-e painting at the Johannesburg Council for Adult Education, under Sonya Allais and David Momberg; 1979–84 watercolour and drawing techniques, under various artists.

Profile From 1977 a member of the Artists Market and the Pretoria Arts and Crafts Association; from 1979 of the WSSA; from 1984 of the Boksburg Art Association; 1985 a member of the Brush and Chisel Club and the Vereeniging Art Society; 1987 a founder member of the Sumi-e Art Society of SA. An enamellist from 1974. 1969 and 1972 visited Italy. Has travelled throughout SA.

Exhibitions She has participated in many group exhibitions from 1982 in SA; 1982 Third Avenue Gallery, The Hill, Johannesburg, first of two solo exhibitions.

Publication by Portalupi Wrote "Enamelwork", a chapter of *Creative Hands*, 1983, Daan Retief, Pretoria.

PORTWAY Douglas Owen
Born 1922 Johannesburg.
Resided in SA until 1956.
A painter and graphic artist of landscapes, still life, portraits, figures and abstract pictures. Works in oil, watercolour, pencil, charcoal and in various graphic media.

Studies 1940–41 Witwatersrand Technical College, under Eric Byrd (qv) and Mary Davies (qv).

Profile 1956 co-founder and Chairman of the Contemporary Arts Society. 1942–45 an art teacher at the Witwatersrand Technical College; 1945–47 an instructor at the University of the Witwatersrand. Has designed various tapestries and murals in Johannesburg. 1956–65 lived in Ibiza, Spain; 1966 in The Netherlands and West Germany; 1967–82 in St Ives, Cornwall, England; from 1983 has lived in Bristol, England. Since 1973 he has spent part of each year in the Dordogne, France. Prior to 1959 married to Rosalind Hertslet (qv).

Exhibitions He has participated in numerous group exhibitions from c.1941 in SA, the UK, France, Switzerland, West Germany, Belgium, Spain, Italy, Greece and the USA; 1945 Constantia Gallery, Johannesburg, first of c.48 solo exhibitions, held in SA, the UK, Spain, West Germany, France and Switzerland; 1967 Pretoria Art Museum, Retrospective Exhibition.

Awards 1969 Bronze Medal, European Painting Prize, Belgium; 1971 Gold Medal, European Painting Prize, Belgium.

Represented Durban Art Gallery; Johannesburg Art Gallery; King George VI Art Gallery, Port Elizabeth; Manchester City Art Gallery, UK; Musée des Beaux Arts, Ostend, Belgium; National Gallery of Modern Art, Edinburgh, Scotland; National Gallery of Poland, Gdansk; National Museum, Warsaw, Poland; Pretoria Art Museum; Sandton Municipal Collection; SA National Gallery, Cape Town; School Art Loans, Leeds, UK; Tate Gallery, London, UK; Tatham Art Gallery, Pietermaritzburg; University of the Witwatersrand; Victoria and Albert Museum, London, UK; William Humphreys Art Gallery, Kimberley.

References G M Butcher, *Douglas Portway*, 1963, XXth Century Masters, London; Joseph Paul Hodin, *Douglas Portway: A Painter's Life*, 1983, Springwood, London; Collectors' Guide; Art SA; SAA; 20C SA Art; SAP&S; SAP&D; IWAA; SSAP; BSAK 1 & 2; SA Art; Oxford Companion to 20C Art (under SA); 3Cs; AASA; LSAA; Herbert Read, *Contemporary British Art*, 1964, Penguin Books, London; *Who's Who in Art*, 1969, London; *Encyclopedia Universale 'Seda' de la Pittura Moderna*, 1969, Rome; *Contemporary Artists*, edited by Colin Naylor and Genesis P-Orridge, 1977, London and New York; *Contemporary British Artists with Photographs by Walia*, 1979, edited by Charlotte Parry-Cooke, Bergstrom & Boyle Books, London; *The Studio* September 1952, October 1962 & July 1963, London; *Art International* 1959, Zurich; *Art News and Review* 17 January 1959 & 9 April 1960; *Apollo* March 1959, May 1960 & July 1965, London; *The Arts Review* July 1961, 14 July 1962, 6 October 1962, June 1963, January 1964, November 1968, November 1973, July 1978 & November 1979; *Connoisseur* January 1963 & January 1964; *Artlook* June 1967 & May 1972; *La Revue Moderne* December 1969; *Studio International* March 1970, London; *Art and Artists* February 1970, London; Retrospective Exhibition Catalogue, April 1967, Pretoria Art Museum.

POSTMA Laurika

Born 1903 Bethulie, Orange Free State.
Died 1987 Pretoria.
A sculptor of portrait busts and figures. Worked in bronze, marble, plaster of Paris, wood and different types of stone. Paints still life and portraits.
Studies Private art studies under John Muff-Ford (qv); 1935 nine months under Milly Steger (*b.*1881) in Berlin; 1939 six months under Professor Bernhard Bleeker (*b.*1881) in Munich, West Germany; 1939 under Professor Ingen Horzt, in The Hague, The Netherlands; 1939 Institut Supérieur des Arts Décoratifs, Brussels, Belgium, under Professor Oscar Jespers (1887–1970); later studied in Italy.
Profile Spent her childhood in Bloemfontein, later living in Pretoria. 1935 lived in Berlin and Munich; 1936–38 in SA.
Represented Pretoria Art Museum; War Museum of the Boer Republics, Bloemfontein.
Public Commissions 1939 Voortrekker Girl, Oranje Girls High School, Bloemfontein; 1940 busts of Presidents Steyn and Reitz, Orange Free State Provincial Administration Building, Bloemfontein; bust of J G Strydom, Transvaal Provincial Administration Building, Pretoria; President Paul Kruger, Pretorius Park, Krugersdorp, Transvaal; relief panels, Children's Monument, Bloemfontein; frieze, Voortrekker Monument, Pretoria; nymph, Afrikaans Hoër Meisiesskool, Pretoria; bust of Dr H F Verwoerd, SABC, Meyerton, Transvaal.
References SK; Art SA; SAA; SESA; BSAK 1 & 2; SA Art; AASA; *SA Panorama* May 1970.

POTGIETER Hans

Born 1942 Vereeniging, Transvaal.
A sculptor working in many media including wood, metal, perspex, fibreglass, acrylic and polyurethane. A painter.
Studies 1966 Johannesburg School of Art; 1967–68 The Visual Arts Research Centre, Johannesburg, under George Boys (qv).
Profile 1970–72 worked in the film industry. A part-time lecturer in photography at the Witwatersrand Technikon.
Exhibitions He has participated in group exhibitions from 1967 in SA; 1968 The Gallery, Johannesburg, joint exhibition with Neels Coetzee (qv); 1969 Goodman Gallery, Johannesburg, first solo exhibition.
Award 1969 First Prize Painting, Transvaal Academy.
Represented Johannesburg Art Gallery; Pretoria Art Museum; Rand Afrikaans University; SA National Gallery, Cape Town; University of the Witwatersrand.

POTGIETER Hendrik Christoffel FIAL

Born 1916 Paul Roux, Orange Free State.
A sculptor of human figures, portrait busts, animals and landscapes. Works in bronze, stone, wood, ivory and rhino horn.
Studies 1936–41 Witwatersrand Technical College, under James Gardner (qv), Elizabeth Macadam (qv) and Eric Byrd (qv), granted a scholarship for the full five and a half years.
Profile 1945–48 a member of the SAAA. From 1956 a Fellow of the International Institute of Arts and Letters. Has lived in Johannesburg and Pretoria and spent one year in Florence, Italy. Has travelled in France, Italy and Spain.
Exhibitions He has participated in group exhibitions from 1936 in SA and Zimbabwe; 1945 Johannesburg, first of about eight solo exhibitions.
Represented Pietersburg Collection; Willem Annandale Art Gallery, Lichtenburg.
Public Commissions 1942–48 historic marble frieze, Voortrekker Monument, Pretoria; 1963 "Liberty Curbed", Transvaal Provincial Administration Building, Pretoria; General de la Rey Equestrian Statue, Lichtenburg, Western Transvaal; Kurt von François, Windhoek; "Wekroep", Primrose, Germiston, Transvaal; "Conquered Victor", Skukusa, Kruger National Park; "Wording", Vanderbijlpark, Transvaal.

POTTER Mary Archdale (née Ogilvy)

Born 1912 Kandy, Sri Lanka (Ceylon).
Resided in SA from 1948.
A naive painter of icons. Works in oil. A sculptor of figures. Works in bronze, glass, stone and cement.
Studies 1970 joined the studio of Tadeusz Jaroszynski (qv) and Karin Jaroszynska (qv) in Johannesburg.

Profile From 1978 a member of the SAAA. 1913–28 and 1940–45 lived in the UK; 1928–31 studied the pianoforte in Paris, France; 1930–31 studied at Oxford University, England; 1946 lived in Brussels, Belgium. Has travelled throughout Europe.
Exhibitions She has participated in several group exhibitions from 1975 in SA and one in Belgium in 1980.

POULTNEY Barbara Ann

Born 1932 Manchester, England.
Resided in SA from 1939.
A painter of three-quarter length figure portraits and portrait heads, also paints landscapes, seascapes and abstract pictures. Works in oil, watercolour, pastel and pencil.
Studies 1950–53 University of Natal, under Professor O J P Oxley (qv) and Professor Jack Heath (qv), gaining a BA(FA); 1953–54 Central School of Art, London.
Profile From 1971 has taught art privately; 1986 an art teacher at the Centre for Continuing Education, University of the Witwatersrand. 1950–53 and 1970–73 worked in pottery.
Exhibitions She has participated in several group exhibitions from 1975; 1982 Total House, Johannesburg, solo exhibition.
Public Commission 1983 Business Woman of the Year Portrait.

POWELL (Yvonne) Jean (Wynn)

Born 1927 Nakuru, Kenya.
Resided in SA from 1946.
An artist of abstract pieces. Works in glass and vitreous enamel. Creates assemblages.
Studies 1946–48 Natal Technical College, under George Howe; 1948–51 University College, London, under Professor Cortiatu, gaining a Diploma in Art and Design; 1952 studied textile design at the Central School of Art, London, under Eduardo Paolozzi (*b.*1924); 1984 accepted as a member of SDSA, which is affiliated to world design groups.
Profile From 1966 a member of the NSA, of which she has been a Council member from 1969 and Vice-President in 1976. From 1984 a Council member of the SA Society of Designers. 1969–71 Chairman of the Natal Art Teachers Association. 1982–85 Vice-President of the Durban Hand Weavers and Spinners Guild. 1962–70 a part-time art teacher at various high schools in Durban; 1969–74 taught textiles and applied art at the University of Durban-Westville; 1971 and 1974 taught part-time in the Architecture Department of the University of Natal, Durban; from 1977 a lecturer in fine art and design, Natal Technikon. A weaver, and a designer of stained glass. 1952–55 worked as a designer in London, UK; 1956–58 worked as a designer in Nairobi, Kenya. 1969 visited the USA; 1971 visited Finland.

Exhibitions She has participated in group exhibitions from 1969 in SA and West Germany.

Award 1971 Phillip Frame Prize, Art SA Today.

Represented Natal Technikon; Pietersburg Collection; University of Durban-Westville.

Public Commissions Many architectural commissions for both private and public buildings.

Reference AASA.

POWELL-JONES Charles Graeme

Born 1889 Kent, England.

Died 1966.

Resided in SA from 1928.

A painter of landscapes and seascapes. Worked in oil.

Studies Newlyn School, Cornwall, England, under Dod Procter RA (1892–1972), Ernest Procter RA (1886–1935) and Wilfred de Glehn RA (1870–1951).

Profile A judge on SA Academy Exhibitions during the 1930s. Lived in Hermanus, Cape Province.

Exhibitions Participated in group exhibitions throughout SA and in the UK, Europe, North Africa, Rhodesia (Zimbabwe), Burma, India, Australia and New Zealand.

Represented Bulawayo Art Gallery, Zimbabwe; King George VI Art Gallery, Port Elizabeth; William Humphreys Art Gallery, Kimberley.

Public Commission Crucifixion, Pretoria Cathedral.

References SAA; BSAK 1; AASA.

POWRIE John Anthony

Born 1928 Cape Town.

A painter of figures. Works in oil. A muralist and a potter.

Studies Michaelis School of Fine Art, where awarded the Michaelis Prize in 1951; Central School of Art, London, under John Keith Vaughan (*b*.1912) and Hans Tisdall (*b*.1910).

Profile *c*.1956 a lecturer in art at the Cape Town Training College; a former lecturer at the Bulawayo Teachers College, Rhodesia (Zimbabwe). Married to Sheila McCorkindale (qv).

Exhibitions He has participated in group exhibitions from 1954 in London and SA; 1956 and 1960 Quadrennial Exhibitions; has held solo exhibitions in Cape Town and Port Elizabeth.

References Art SA; SAA.

PRATT Steven Raymond

Born 1950 Salisbury, Rhodesia (Harare, Zimbabwe).

A painter and graphic artist of landscapes, still life and abstract pictures. Works in oil, mixed media, ink, wash, pencil, charcoal and in various graphic media, particularly monoprint.

Studies 1968–71 and 1976 Rhodes University, under Professor Brian Bradshaw (qv), gaining a BA(FA) in 1971 and an MFA in 1976.

Profile Influenced by Zimbabwean rock art. 1974–75 an art teacher at Nagle House; 1977 at The High School; 1977–79 at Peterhouse, all in Marondera, Rhodesia (Zimbabwe). 1977–79 a number of set designs for plays. Lives in Harare, Zimbabwe.

Exhibitions He has participated in several group exhibitions in SA and Zimbabwe from 1969; 1973 Salisbury (Harare), first of two solo exhibitions.

Represented National Gallery, Harare, Zimbabwe.

PRELLER Alexis

Born 1911 Pretoria.
Died 1975 Pretoria.
A painter of figures, heads, torsos, animals, still life and classical antiquity. Worked in oil. 1952 "Mapogga" series; 1955–58 Hieratic figure compositions; during the 1960s abstract and semi-abstract paintings; 1962 theme of outer space and celestial images; 1965 gold paintings, abstract and classical Greek themes; 1969 intaglio (three-dimensional fibreglass moulds). Created four carvings in wood and sandstone and one totem pole.

Studies 1934–35 Westminster School of Art, London, under Mark Gertler (1892–1939); 1937 Académie de la Grande Chaumière, Paris, under Emil Othon Friesz (1879–1949); 1937 two months' study in Monte Carlo; 1946–47 a study trip to the London and Paris museums (especially interested in the Greek statues in the Louvre); 1953 studied murals and painting in Italy and Egypt.

Profile 1938 a founder member of the New Group; 1948 a member of the International Art Club, SA; 1961 an executive committee member of the SA Council of Artists. 1911–34 lived in Pretoria; 1934 in London; 1935 in London, travelling to Berlin, Hamburg, Antwerp, Tetuan, Cairo, Mombasa, Zanzibar and Pretoria; 1936 in Pretoria; 1937 in Paris, Monte Carlo, Swaziland and Zululand; 1938 in Pretoria; 1939 in the Belgian Congo (Zaire); 1940–42 with the SA Medical Corps in East and North Africa; 1943 a Prisoner of War in Italy and North Africa; 1944–54 in Pretoria; 1946–47 visited Paris and London; 1948 Zanzibar and the Seychelles; 1953 Italy and Egypt; 1954–56 lived at Hartbeespoort Dam, Transvaal; 1956–75 lived in the Brits area, Transvaal; 1968 visited Greece, Turkey and Italy; 1971 visited Greece as well as Rome and Florence in Italy.

Exhibitions 1935 Pretoria, first of numerous solo exhibitions held in Pretoria, Johannesburg and Cape Town; participated in group exhibitions from 1938 in SA, Rhodesia (Zimbabwe), Italy, Greece and Brazil; 1948 Tate Gallery, London, SA Art Exhibition; 1972 Pretoria Art Museum, Retrospective Exhibition; 1975 Johannesburg, Retrospective Exhibition.

Awards 1953 Molteno Award with Jean Welz (qv); 1955 Medal of Honour, SA Akademie vir Wetenskap en Kuns.

Represented Africana Museum, Johannesburg; Ann Bryant Gallery, East London; Durban Art Gallery; Hester Rupert Art Museum, Graaff-Reinet; Johannesburg Art Gallery; King George VI Art Gallery, Port Elizabeth; Pretoria Art Museum; Rand Afrikaans University; Sandton Municipal Collection; SA National Gallery, Cape Town; SA National Museum of Military History, Johannesburg; Tatham Art Gallery, Pietermaritzburg; University of the Orange Free State; University of Pretoria; University of South Africa; University of Stellenbosch; University of the Witwatersrand; William Humphreys Art Gallery, Kimberley.

Public Commissions 1959–62 mural, Transvaal Provincial Administration Building, Pretoria; 1953–55 mural, Receiver of Revenue Building, Johannesburg.

References Christi Truter, *Alexis Preller*, 1947, The Maroola Press, Pretoria; Collectors' Guide; PSA; Our Art 2; Art SA; SAA; 20C SA Art; Oxford Companion to Art (under SA); SAP&S; SAP&D; SSAP; SESA; BSAK 1 & 2; SA Art; Oxford Companion to 20C Art; 3Cs; AASA; LSAA; *South Africana* July 1956; *SA Panorama* February 1961, February 1966 & November 1972; *Artlook* October 1969 & February/March 1976; *De Arte* April 1976 & April 1985; *Habitat* no 18, 1976; Exhibition Catalogue, 1972, Pretoria Art Museum.

PRENDINI Pamela Janet Geraldine

Born 1950 Johannesburg.

A painter and graphic artist of figures. Works in oil, ink, gold leaf, pencil and in various graphic media, including monotypes and aerographs. 1984 a large series of male/female figures, combined with birds of prey; 1985 mixed media female Odalisques.

Studies 1967–70 University of the Witwatersrand, under Professor Heather Martienssen (1915–79), Cecily Sash (qv), Robert Hodgins (qv), Giuseppe Cattaneo (qv) and Erica Berry (qv), gaining a BA(FA); 1970–71 on an Elizabeth Macadam Scholarship for Painting at Brera Academy, Milan, Italy, under Professor Pompeo Borra (1898–1973) and Professor Domenico Cantatore (*b*.1906), gaining a Diploma in Painting; 1971–72 University of the Witwatersrand, History of Art under Professor Heather Martienssen (1915–79), Professor Elizabeth Rankin and Dr Rory Doepel, where attained BA (Hons); 1985–86 University of the Witwatersrand, under Professor Elizabeth Rankin, studying for an MA.

Profile From 1984 a member of the SAAA. 1973–75 a design lecturer at the Johannesburg Training College for the Clothing Industry; 1976–77 a part-time design lecturer at the Fashion Design and Management College, and at The Clothing College, Johannesburg; 1984–85 a lecturer in art history, drawing and graphic design, Natal Technikon. 1970 travelled to Italy, 1974 Greece and in 1977 West Germany.

Exhibitions She has participated in several group exhibitions from 1980 throughout SA; 1975 SAAA Gallery, Johannesburg, first of three solo exhibitions held in SA.

Represented Pretoria Art Museum.

Reference *Gallery* Winter 1985.

PRESS Naomi
Born 1927 Poland.
Resided in SA from 1933.
A sculptor of initially realistic works, which have become increasingly abstract. A large series of abstracted torsos; 1986 abstract pieces in steel. Works in bronze, stone, wood and stainless steel.
Studies 1960–65 under Sidney Goldblatt (qv); 1965–67 under Peter Hayden; 1969–73 under George Boys (qv); 1974 under Bill Ainslie (qv).
Profile From 1977 she has spent roughly one quarter of each year in New York; 1980 lived in Pietrasanta, Italy.
Exhibitions 1981 Goodman Gallery, Johannesburg, first of three solo exhibitions; she has participated in several group exhibitions in SA and from 1985 in the USA; 1988 Armstrong Gallery, New York, first USA solo exhibition.
Represented Andre Emmerich Park, New York State, USA.

PRETORIUS Annette
Born 1957 Pretoria.
A painter and graphic artist of imaginary landscapes. Works in acrylic, pencil and in various graphic media.
Studies 1980 University of Pretoria, under Professor Nico Roos (qv), gaining a BA(FA).
Profile A member of the SAAA. 1983 and 1985 a part-time lecturer at the University of Pretoria. 1982 began designing puppets; in 1985 produced a slide show to support puppet shows for the Little Marionette Company.
Exhibitions She has participated in numerous group exhibitions from 1981 in SA; 1981 Republic Festival Exhibition; 1982 Cape Town Triennial; 1982 University of Pretoria, first of two solo exhibitions; 1983 Gowlett Gallery, Cape Town, joint exhibition with John Clarke (qv); 1985 Cape Town Triennial; 1987 SAAA Gallery, Pretoria, joint exhibition with Johann du Plessis (qv).
Awards 1980 Graphic Award, New Signatures, SAAA, Pretoria; 1981 Travelling Scholarship Award, Republic Festival Exhibition; 1982 Silver Medal, Cape Town Triennial.
Represented King George VI Art Gallery, Port Elizabeth; SA National Gallery, Cape Town.
Reference AASA.

PRETORIUS Elfriede
Born 1953 Pretoria.
A painter of abstract pictures. Works in oil, acrylic, pencil, charcoal and mixed media. 1985–86 a series on "Fear", in relation to war situations and decision-making; 1987 a series on "Feminine Consciousness", fear and boundary situations.

Studies 1982–87 University of South Africa, gaining a BA(FA).
Profile From 1971 involved in teaching music to children. An organist.
Exhibitions She has participated in several group exhibitions from 1983.

PRETORIUS Fransiolentru (née Erasmus)

Born 1940 Krugersdorp, Transvaal.
A painter of still life, portraits and figures. Works in oil, acrylic, pastel, watercolour, pencil and charcoal. From 1985 a series of large-scale charcoal and pastel drawings of plant forms and flowers.
Studies Witwatersrand Technical College; University of the Orange Free State, where attained a BA(FA) in 1975, a Higher Diploma in Education in 1978 and a BEd in 1980.
Profile A member of the NSA and the SAAAH. 1976–78 taught art at secondary school level; 1979–81 an art lecturer at the Orange Free State Technical College (Technikon); 1981–85 Head of the Art History and Drawing Department, Natal Technikon; from 1986 part-time Associate Director of the Fine Art Department, Natal Technikon.
Exhibitions She has participated in many group exhibitions from 1973 in SA; 1985 Cafe Genevé, Durban, first solo exhibition.
Represented Natal Technikon; University of the Orange Free State.

PRETORIUS Marena (Kaffie)

Born 1941 Lambert's Bay, Cape Province.
A painter of landscapes, seascapes, still life and figures. Works in oil. Uses the fish as a symbol of simplicity, the seabird as a symbol of space and freedom and the goat as a symbol of earthiness.
Studies 1976 Los Angeles Art School, USA; 1983 under Andre van Zyl (qv) in Cape Town.
Profile From 1985 a member of the SAAA. Teaches art privately in Stellenbosch. 1983 illustrated Rona Rupert's *Ambraal hoe gaan dit nog?*, Tafelberg, Cape Town. Has travelled in both Europe and America.
Exhibitions She has participated in several group exhibitions from 1982 in SA; 1985 Edrich Gallery, Stellenbosch, first of two solo exhibitions.

PRICE Grete Elisa

Born Denmark.
Resided in SA from 1949.
A painter and graphic artist of abstract pictures. Works in oil, acrylic, ink, pencil, charcoal, egg tempera and in various graphic media.
Studies 1960 Pretoria Technical College, under Peter Eliastam (qv), Robert Hodgins (qv) and Zakkie Eloff (qv).
Profile A member of the SAAA from 1957. A potter. Has made many study tours of Europe.

Exhibitions She has participated in numerous group exhibitions from 1964 in SA and in Europe; 1969 SAAA Gallery, Pretoria, first of five solo exhibitions held in Pretoria and Johannesburg; 1981 Republic Festival Exhibition.
Represented Willem Annandale Art Gallery, Lichtenburg.
References BSAK 1; AASA; *Artlook* February 1969.

PRICE Shelagh

Born 1944 Fort Victoria, Rhodesia (Masvingo, Zimbabwe).
Resided in SA from 1968.
A painter of landscapes, seascapes, portraits, figures and still life. Works in watercolour.
Studies 1961–64 Natal Technical College, gaining a Diploma in Dress Designing and Fashion Art.
Profile From 1986 a member of the Artists Market and from 1987 of the WSSA. 1968–79 a fashion designer for various Johannesburg firms. From 1984 a full-time artist. Her work has been reproduced on calendars and cards. 1986 a series of six watercolours of Pilgrim's Rest were reproduced for the Wildlife Society; 1986 "Dog Roses" printed by Howard Swan, Johannesburg. 1965–67 lived in London; 1967 spent two months in Paris. 1968–79 regular visits to Europe and the USA. 1985 visited Israel.
Exhibitions 1985 Eden Mall Gallery, Johannesburg, first of three solo exhibitions; she participated in several group exhibitions in 1987.

PRIEST Cecil Damer

Settled in Rhodesia (Zimbabwe) in 1924.
Died 1955.
A bird artist. Worked in pencil and ink.
Profile An army officer in WWI with the Royal Dublin Fusiliers and the Nigerian Regiment.
Represented Africana Museum, Johannesburg.
Publications by Priest *The Birds of Southern Rhodesia*, 4 volumes, 1933–36, William Clowes, London; many of the black and white illustrations for this book were drawn by Priest.
Reference AMC7.

PRINCE Hilary

Born 1945 Johannesburg.
Resided in SA until 1966.
A painter working in oil and watercolour.
Studies Johannesburg School of Art; St Martin's School of Art, London, England.

Profile 1966–78 lived in the UK; 1978 moved to Canada. Presently living in Edmonton, Alberta, Canada.
Represented Alberta Art Foundation, Canada; Edmonton Art Gallery, Canada; University of Alberta, Canada.

PRINS Nico Peter Jacobus

Born 1945 Calitzdorp, Cape Province.
A sculptor and a painter of figures, landscapes and still life. Works in wood, stone, ciment fondu and oil.
Studies 1975 Ruth Prowse School of Art, Cape Town, under Erik Laubscher (qv); 1981 privately under June te Water (qv); 1982–85 Ruth Prowse School of Art, under Maureen Langley (qv).
Profile Moved to Ravensmead in the Cape in 1963. Has travelled throughout SA, SWA/Namibia and Mozambique, and in 1988 made a study tour of the UK.
Exhibitions He has participated in many group exhibitions from 1982 in SA, SWA/Namibia and the USA; 1983 Atlantic Gallery, Cape Town, first of three solo exhibitions held in the Cape.
Represented Parow Municipality.
Reference *Prisma* February 1988.

PRINSLOO Therésa

Born 1965 Ladysmith, Natal.
A painter of illusionistic scenes and fantasies. Works in oil, acrylic, ink, pencil, gauze and other textured surfaces, including adhesives.
Studies 1984–86 Pretoria Technikon, gaining a Diploma in Fine Art, 1987–88 studying for a Higher Diploma in Fine Art.
Profile From 1985 a member of the SAAA. A weaver, designer and maker of clothing and wall hangings. Has visited Hong Kong.
Exhibitions She has participated in many group exhibitions from 1984; 1986 Ivan Solomon Gallery, Pretoria, joint exhibition.
Award 1986 Ingram Anderson Award for Painting.

PRIOR Melton

Born 1845 London, England.
Died 1910 Chelsea, London, England.
Resided in SA from the 1870s to the early 1900s.
An artist working in black and white.
Studies In London and Florence, Italy.
Profile From 1868 a war artist with the *The Illustrated London News,* in which 298 of his pencil and wash sketches of scenes from various SA wars were printed, including those of the 1877–78 Ninth Frontier War, the 1879–80 Zulu War, the 1880–81 First Anglo-Boer War; the Jameson Raid in 1895, the Matabele Rebellion in 1896 and the 1899–1902 Second Anglo-Boer War. His works also appeared in *The Graphic* and *The Sketch.* A journalist. Son of, pupil of and assistant to the artist William Henry Prior (1812–82).

Represented Africana Museum, Johannesburg; University of Natal.
Publication by Prior *Memoirs of a War Correspondent*, posthumously in 1912, Arnold, England.
References Jane Carruthers, *Melton Prior—War Artist in Southern Africa 1895–1900*, 1987, The Brenthurst Press, Johannesburg; A C R Carter, *The Work of War Artists in SA*, 1900, Art Journal, London; AMC4&7; DSAB; Natal Art; Pic Afr; Bénézit; BSAK 1; SA Art.

PRITCHARD Tienie

Born 1938 Zoekmekaar, Northern Transvaal.
A sculptor of figures, portraits and wildlife. Works in bronze and stone.
Studies 1966–68 under Eugene-Leon Bouffa (qv) in Pretoria.
Profile 1983 visited New York, Washington DC, London and Paris; 1984 visited Italy and Berlin in West Germany; 1985 Italy.
Exhibitions He has participated in many group exhibitions from 1969 in SA; 1974 Lister Art Gallery, Johannesburg, solo exhibition.
Represented Pietersburg Collection.
Public Commissions Bronze statues: Family Group, Civitas Building, Pretoria; Steenbok Group, SABC Building, Silverton, Pretoria; "Tranquillity", Benoni Plaza, Transvaal; Communications Development Panel, SA Post Office (on permanent exhibition in Toronto, Canada); "Discovery of Gold", Volkskas, Pietersburg, Northern Transvaal; Fountain, Water Nymphs, Overvaal, Warmbaths, Transvaal; panel depicting SA in WWII and Korea, Delville Wood, France; George Harrison, Johannesburg Centenary. Bronze busts of: Johannes Joubert, Civic Centre, Johannesburg; Johan Rissik; Edouard Bok, Civic Centre, Boksburg, Transvaal; General J B M Hertzog, Union Buildings, Pretoria and Piet Joubert, Civic Centre, Pietersburg, among others.

PROSSER Christian

Born 1937 Johannesburg.
A painter of flowers, cityscapes, portraits and figures. Works in oil on a turpentine wash on paper.
Studies 1954–56 Da Vinci Art School, Johannesburg, under Carlo Sdoya (qv); 1963 privately under P Martini.
Profile A trained singer. 1964 lived in Rome, Zurich and Venice; 1978 in England and Zurich, Switzerland.
Exhibitions He has participated in several group exhibitions in SA; 1965 Gallery Atelier, Johannesburg, first solo exhibition.

PROWSE (Ethel) Ruth FRSA

Born 1883 Queenstown, Cape Province.
Died 1967 Cape Town.

A painter of portraits, figures, landscapes, genre and still life. Worked in oil. 140 known paintings and numerous pencil and chalk drawings. A large series of street scenes in Cape Town, particularly those of the Malay Quarter and District Six; a series of Karoo landscapes.

Studies 1897 in Cape Town under Ethel Edwards (qv); 1900 Cape Town Art School, under G C Robinson (qv); 1902 Slade School of Art, London, under Cope and Nichols; 1902 a crammer course at the South Kensington School of Art, London; 1903–06 awarded a scholarship to the Royal Academy Schools, London, studied under John Singer Sargent (1856–1925) and George Clausen (1852–1944); 1907 Atelier La Palette, Paris, under Guerin, and Atelier Colarossi, Montparnasse, Paris; 1938 Courtauld Institute, London, conducting research into restoration.

Profile 1909 a member of the SA Society of Artists; 1938 a founder member of the New Group and Chairman in 1952; 1952 founded the Seven Arts Club, of which she was Chairman until 1963. A Fellow of the Royal Society of Arts. In 1885 her family moved to Roodebloem, Woodstock, Cape Town. 1908–12 taught art in Cape Town; 1912–15 lived at Paarl; 1915–18 served as a nurse in Durban and Cape Town; 1928–56 Keeper of The Michaelis Collection, Old Town House, Cape Town; 1939–45 commissioned by the SA Government to paint military scenes. 1948–60 a Trustee of the SA National Gallery, Cape Town. Involved in the preservation of historic areas and homes in Cape Town. Her home "The Retreat", Woodstock, was bequeathed as an art centre to Cape Town. Wrote numerous articles on art and preservation. Travelled throughout SA and lived in Europe in 1902–08, 1923–25, 1938, 1942, 1952 and 1963. 1954 visited SWA/Namibia. Included in Edward Roworth's (qv) essay "Landscape Art in SA", 1917, Studio Publication, *Art of The British Empire Overseas*. The Ruth Prowse Trust Fund was set up after her death to provide scholarships for art students.

Exhibitions Participated in group exhibitions held throughout SA from 1902 and once in Rhodesia (Zimbabwe); 1923 joint exhibition with Florence Zerffi (qv) and Nita Spilhaus (qv); exhibited at the Royal Academy, London in 1938; 1956 Quadrennial Exhibition; held numerous solo exhibitions in SA; 1956 Michaelis School of Art, Cape Town, Retrospective Exhibition; 1961 SAAA Gallery, Cape Town, Retrospective Exhibition; 1968 SA National Gallery, Cape Town, Johannesburg Art Gallery and Pretoria Art Museum, Memorial Exhibition.

Awards 1953 Queen's Coronation Medal for Services to Art in SA; 1959 Tercentenary Foundation Medal for work on the preservation of historic buildings; 1965 SAAA (Cape), Special Medal of Honour for Services to Art.

Represented Durban Art Gallery; Hester Rupert Art Museum, Graaff-Reinet; Johannesburg Art Gallery; King George VI Art Gallery, Port Elizabeth; Pretoria Art Museum; SA Embassy, London, UK; SA National Gallery, Cape Town; SA National Museum of Military History, Johannesburg; University of Cape Town; University of Pretoria; William Humphreys Art Gallery, Kimberley.

References *The Arts in SA*, edited by WHK, 1933–34, The Knox Printing & Publishing Company, Durban; Collectors' Guide; PSA; Our Art 2; Art SA; SAA; 20C SA Art; AMC4; SAP&S; SAP&D; SESA; SSAP; DBA; BSAK 1 & 2; SA Art; 3Cs; AASA; LSAA; *Artlook* June 1967; *Gallery* Winter 1983; Ruth Prowse Memorial Exhibition Catalogue, 1968, SA National Gallery, Cape Town.

STANLEY PINKER
Can The Leopard Change the Colour of his Spots? 1985
Oil on Canvas on Board 48 × 43 cm
Lieschen Heinz

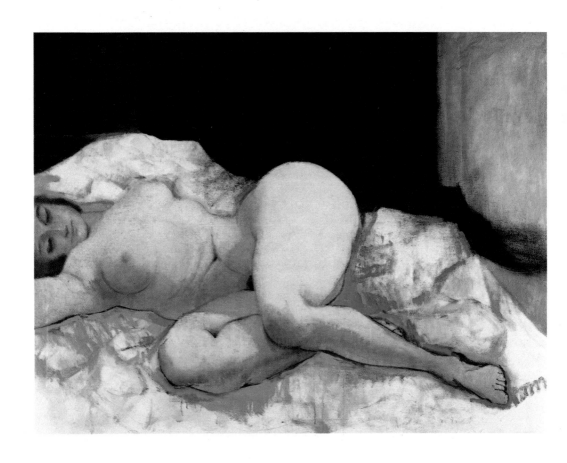

DOUGLAS PORTWAY
Reclining Nude 1988
Oil on Canvas 117 × 152 cm
The Everard Read Gallery

ALEXIS PRELLER
Hieratic Women 1955
Oil on Canvas 86,9 × 101,7 cm
Johannesburg Art Gallery

RUTH PROWSE
Buitengracht Street, Cape Town
Oil on Board 28,5 × 21,5 cm
Die Kunskamer

PRYOR Marjorie

Resided in SA from 1913.

A painter of landscapes, seascapes, flowers and city scenes. A series of the Malay Quarter in Cape Town. Worked in watercolour and oil.

Profile A member of the NSA and the Eastern Province Society of Arts and Crafts. Lived in Durban until 1920, when she moved to the Eastern Province.

Exhibitions Participated in group exhibitions throughout SA; 1925 Ashbey's Gallery, Cape Town, solo exhibition; 1945 Cape Town, joint exhibition with Mary E Best.

Reference AASA.

PUDI Ranko

Born 1950 Makapanstad, Transvaal (Makapaanstat, Botphuthatswana).

A self-taught painter and sculptor of figures in landscapes and of genre. Works in watercolour, ink, pencil, charcoal, crayon and wood.

Exhibitions He has participated in group exhibitions in SA from 1975; 1985 Tributaries, touring SA and West Germany.

Award 1979 Second Prize, New Signatures, SAAA.

References *Phafa-Nyika*, edited by Ute Scholz, 1980, University of Pretoria; Echoes of African Art.

PULÉ Calinka

Born 1941.

Died *c*.1984.

A painter of figures, still life, interiors and landscapes. Worked in oil and impasto; also produced pen and ink drawings.

Studies 1973 painting under Sidney Goldblatt (qv); 1974 the art of woodcut and silkscreen under Bill Ainslie (qv); 1975 Japanese brush technique under Yoko Dodd in the UK; 1977 studied under George Boys (qv).

Exhibitions Participated in group exhibitions in SA from 1978; 1979 Goodman Gallery, Johannesburg, first of several solo exhibitions.

PULON Heinz

Born 1930 Windhoek, SWA/Namibia.

A painter and graphic artist of the SWA/Namibian landscape and its wildlife, also depicts still life, figures and portraits. Works in watercolour, oil, pencil and in various graphic media. Particularly known for his etchings.

Studies 1951–54 Akademie der Bildenden Kunste, Munich, West Germany, under Professor H Kirchner, Professor Tiermann and Professor Lohwasser; 1958 studied in Munich.

Profile A designer of stained glass pieces.

Exhibitions 1948 Windhoek, first of 15 solo exhibitions held in SWA/Namibia; has participated in numerous group exhibitions from 1958 in West Germany, Italy, Brazil, Yugoslavia, the USA, Angola, SA and SWA/Namibia; 1958 SAAA Gallery, Pretoria, Johannesburg Art Gallery and SAAA Gallery, Cape Town, Exhibition of Gruppe Fùnf (Group Five) with Adolph Jentsch (qv), Fritz Krampe (qv), Otto Schròder (qv) and Joachim Voigts (qv); 1958 and 1985 held solo exhibitions in West Germany.

Awards 1963 Gold and Silver Medals, International Graphic Exhibition, Sa de Bandeira, Angola.

Represented Arts Association SWA/Namibia; SA National Gallery, Cape Town.

References Art SA; SAA; BSAK 1; Art SWA; AASA; PS/N.

PURCHASE Constance Elizabeth Margaret (Con) (Mrs Creel)

Born 1923 Kimberley.

A painter and graphic artist of landscapes, still life, genre, figures, allegorical and religious pieces. Works in oil, watercolour, ink, wash, pencil, oil pastel, and in various graphic media. Creates mosaics.

Studies 1943–46 Witwatersrand Technical College, under Maurice van Essche (qv), Ernest Renfield, James Gardner (qv) and Eric Byrd (qv), where gained a National Art Teachers Diploma.

Profile A founder and committee member of the Bellville Branch of the SAAA; a founder, Chairman in 1982 and Director 1984–85 of the Durbanville Cultural Society. 1947–48 an itinerant art teacher at various girls' high schools in the Cape. 1950–60 an art lecturer at the Barkly House Training Centre. Illustrated a series of English Readers for Xhosa scholars, published by the Oxford University Press, England. Designs stained glass windows, ceramic panels, wall hangings and tapestries. 1943–47 lived in Johannesburg; 1947–53 in Cape Town; from 1953 in Durbanville. 1962 visited Italy, Greece and Turkey; has also visited South America, Spain, the UK, Belgium and the Middle East.

Exhibitions She has participated in many group exhibitions from 1946; 1960–73 three exhibitions of mosaic work held in the Cape; 1980 SAAA Gallery, Bellville, first of three solo painting exhibitions; 1981 Republic Festival Exhibition; 1982 Durbanville, joint exhibition with Mimi van der Merwe (qv) and R Creel.

Public Commissions From 1960 numerous mosaic commissions for churches, educational establishments, hotels and clinics.

Reference AASA.

PURSER Lesley Helen

Born 1942 England.

Resided in SA from 1951.

A painter of landscapes, seascapes and still life. Works in oil, acrylic and watercolour.

Studies 1959–61 Natal Technical College, under George Howe, where gained a National Diploma in Commercial Art and Industrial Design; 1962 Canterbury College of Art, Kent, England, under A Martin, where attained a Diploma in Graphic Design.

Profile 1963 a lecturer in graphic design at the Natal Technical College. A professional graphic designer.

Exhibitions She has participated in several group exhibitions from 1975 in SA.

PURVIS Dennis Clifford

Born 1953 Pietermaritzburg.

A painter of landscapes, seascapes, city scenes, social comment and figures, extends his elemental images and symbols into three-dimensional paintings. Works in oil, oil pastel, tempera, crayon and paper, also a graphic artist. January–August 1985 a series entitled "Durban Healing"; August–December 1985 "Prediction Series"; from December 1985 "The Chosen Ones".

Studies 1972–75 Natal Technical College, under Barry Maritz (qv), Malcolm Christian (qv), Paul Stopforth (qv), Basil Friedlander (qv), Terry King (qv) and Dan Cook (qv), gaining a National Diploma in Fine Arts, majoring in graphic art; 1974 spent three months at the Witwatersrand Technical College, under Malcolm Payne (qv), before returning to Durban. 1987 began working towards a Higher Diploma in Fine Arts.

Profile 1985 a council member of the NSA; 1985 Director of the Cafe Genevê, Durban. 1985 began lecturing at the Community Arts Centre, Durban, appointed Head of Visual Arts in 1987. 1987 began lecturing in drawing and painting at the M L Sultan Technikon, Durban. 1975–85, with his wife Sue, ran a design and advertising agency in Durban. 1985 illustrated record sleeves for C & G Studios, Durban.

Exhibitions From 1984 he has participated in many group exhibitions in SA; 1985 Cafe Genevê, Durban, first of three solo exhibitions; 1985 NSA Gallery, Durban, Durban Daze Window Exhibition of hand-painted T-shirts, extending fine art into everyday objects; 1987 Potchefstroom Museum, solo exhibition.

Awards 1986 Merit Award, Volkskas Atelier Awards, Pretoria. His work was selected for the 1987 Volkskas national calendar.

Public Commission 1987 painting, E G Malherbe Library, University of Natal.

Represented Durban Art Gallery; Tatham Art Gallery, Pietermaritzburg.

References *Zig Zag* July 1985; *De Kat* May 1986; *Fair Lady* 17 September 1986.

PURVIS Patricia

A painter of landscapes, figures and flowers. Works in watercolour.

Profile A member of the SAAA and the Brush and Chisel Club. An Associate of the WSSA. Taught art privately. Lived in Johannesburg.

Exhibitions She has participated in group exhibitions in SA, SWA/Namibia and the UK; 1970 joint exhibition with Phyllis Luyt and Majorie Bowen (qv).

Represented Willem Annandale Art Gallery, Lichtenburg.

PUTTER Diedrik Johannes

Born 1938 Pretoria.

A self-taught sculptor of figures. Works in wood.

Profile A woodwork teacher at the W K du Plessis School for Epileptic Children, Springs, Transvaal. An authority on indigenous trees.

Exhibitions He has participated in group exhibitions and held solo exhibitions in Springs and Johannesburg.

Q

QUIN Maureen Vivian

Born 1934 Bloemfontein.

Primarily a sculptor of abstract pieces, portraits, figures and animals. Works in bronze and wood. Additionally paints landscapes and abstract pictures in oil and draws figures, portraits, landscapes and abstracts in pastel, pencil and charcoal. Prior to 1968 most of her work was in oil. 1982 a large series based on the Greek islands.

Studies 1952–55 Natal Technical College, under Mary Stainbank (qv), gaining a Diploma in Fine Art, with a distinction in sculpture; 1956–57 on an Emma Smith Bursary for overseas study, at Goldsmith's College, London, under Robert Jones.

Profile From 1970 a member of the SAAA. 1963–66 lived in Douglas, Cape Province; 1966–75 in Adelaide, Cape Province and from 1975 in Alexandria, Cape Province. 1981 visited the Greek islands.

Exhibitions 1961 Bloemfontein, first of over 20 solo exhibitions; she has participated in many group exhibitions from 1965 held throughout SA and in Zimbabwe, the UK and Monaco; 1981 Republic Festival Exhibition; 1987 University of the Orange Free State, solo exhibition.

Represented Ann Bryant Gallery, East London; Hester Rupert Art Museum, Graaff-Reinet; National Museum, Bloemfontein; University of the Orange Free State; Welkom Municipal Gallery.

Public Commissions 1965 panel depicting Unity, Douglas, Cape Province; 1968 Rescue Group, Red Cross Building, Port Elizabeth; 1972 panel, B & W Building, Vanderbijlpark, Transvaal; 1973 panel, Science Building, Potchefstroom University for CHE; 1976 carved door, Ichthyology Building, Rhodes University; 1980 Bronze of a Woman, Ermelo Civic Centre, Transvaal; 1980 portrait bust, Koot Kotze Building, Stutterheim, Cape Province.

References SAA; BSAK 1 & 2; AASA; *Artlook* February 1971, February 1973 & October/November 1974; *Garden & Home* September 1976; *Lantern* April 1980.

R

RABE Johannes Hendrik Jacobus (pseudonym Ebar)

Born 1907 Lindley, Orange Free State.

A painter and graphic artist of landscapes. Worked in oil, ink and the etching processes. A muralist.

Studies Witwatersrand Technical College, under Sydney Carter (qv).

Profile 1937–43 a freelance newspaper artist and cartoonist for *Die Vaderland, Die Brandwag, Die Transvaler, Die Huisgenoot* and later for *Jeugland*. Went on sketching trips with Erich Mayer (qv) and W H Coetzer (qv).

Exhibitions He has participated in many group exhibitions held in SA; has held several solo exhibitions since the 1940s.

Represented Pretoria Art Museum.

Public Commissions Paintings in the Transvaal Provincial Administration Building and the Reserve Bank in Pretoria.

References AASA; SASSK.

RABIE Anna Lilian Malherbe

Born 1925 Riversdale, Cape Province.

A painter of landscapes, seascapes, portraits, figures, still life and abstract pictures. Works in oil, acrylic and charcoal.

Studies Michaelis School of Fine Art, under Edward Roworth (qv), Ivan Mitford-Barberton (qv) and Melvin Simmers (qv), gaining a BA(FA) and being awarded the Michaelis Prize; also studied under Robert Hodgins (qv) in Pretoria.

Profile Has travelled extensively in Europe. Sister of the writer Etienne Le Roux.

Exhibitions She has participated in many group exhibitions from 1948 in SA; 1962 D S Vorster Art Gallery, Pretoria, first of two solo exhibitions held in SA; 1964 Quadrennial Exhibition.

References SAA; AASA.

RABIE William

Born 1963 Witbank, Transvaal.

A graphic artist producing serigraphs of figures.

Studies Gained a Diploma in Graphic Art in 1984 from the Vaal Triangle Technical College, Vanderbijlpark, Transvaal.

Profile A commercial silkscreen printer.

Exhibition 1985 Cape Town Triennial.

RAKGOATHE Daniel Sefudi

Born 1937 Randfontein, Transvaal.

An artist of metaphysical subjects. Works in oil, pencil and in various graphic media, particularly linocuts, etchings and aquatints. A number of series: "Moon-Bride and Sun-Bridegroom", "Unfolding Man", "Rain Queen", "Maternal Anxiety", "Cosmic Trinity", "Mystic Flute", "Mystical Awakening", "Mystery of Time", "Mystery of Space", "Horse People", "The Omen", "Ape Totem", "Symbol of Peace" and "Adoration".

Studies 1960 Ndaleni Educational Training School, Natal, under Peter Bell; 1967–69 Rorke's Drift Art Centre, under Olle Granath and Peter Gowenius; 1976–79 University of Fort Hare, under Professor Estelle Marais (qv), gaining a BA(FA); 1981–83 on a Fulbright Scholarship to the University of California, Los Angeles, USA, under Ray Brown, where attained an MA(FA).
Profile 1962–64 a teacher at the Botshabelo Teachers Training Centre, Middelburg; 1969–76 and 1980–81 a lecturer at the Mofolo Art Centre, Soweto; 1984 a lecturer at the Taung College of Education, Bophuthatswana.
Exhibitions He has participated in numerous group exhibitions from 1967 in SA, West Germany, Sweden, the UK, Australia, the USA and Japan; 1979 Contemporary African Art in SA, touring; 1981 Standard Bank, Soweto, Black Art Today Exhibition; has held several solo exhibitions in SA and in the USA.
Represented Durban Art Gallery; Museum of Modern Art, New York, USA; Pretoria Art Museum; University of Fort Hare.
References BSAK; E J de Jager, *Contemporary African Art*, 1973, Struik, Cape Town; AASA; Echoes of African Art; *SA Panorama* January 1977 & July 1982.

RAMPHOMANE Mpolokeng Raymond

Born 1955 Johannesburg.
A painter of landscapes, portraits, still life, figures and abstract pictures. Works in oil, acrylic, watercolour, ink, wash, pencil and charcoal.
Studies 1982 Rorke's Drift Art Centre, under Jay Johnson, gaining a Diploma in Fine Art.
Profile From 1986 a member of the Mofolo Art Centre, Soweto, presently its Chairman. 1983 taught at Zenzele (YWCA), Dube, Soweto. Involved in stained glass making and poetry writing.
Exhibitions He has participated in group exhibitions in Johannesburg from 1986.

RANCE Lucy Gertrude

Born 1872 King William's Town, Cape Province.
Died 1943 East London.
A painter of figures and genre. Worked in oil, watercolour and pastel.
Profile 1928–43 Chairman of the East London Society of Arts and Crafts. Lived and painted in the Ciskei until 1903 when she moved to East London.
Exhibitions Participated in a group exhibition in 1925 with the SA Academy; 1936 Johannesburg, Empire Exhibition.
Represented Ann Bryant Gallery, East London.
References SAA; AASA.

RANDELL Dorothy Mary

Born 1912 East London.
A sculptor of portrait busts and figures, working in bronze, wood and clay. A painter of urban landscapes, working in watercolour and pencil.

Studies 1929–32 Rhodes University, under Professor Austin Winter Moore (qv), gaining a BA(FA) and the Purvis Prize in 1932; 1936 Chelsea School of Art, London, under Henry Moore (1898–1986); 1961 sculpture at Kingston School of Art, London.

Profile 1938 a member of the East London Art Society, of which she was Secretary in 1940, Chairman in 1945 and is now an Honorary Life Member. 1982 illustrated *Gentlemen of the Law*, by George Randell, 1985 illustrated *Bench and Bar*, by George Randell, both published by the Randells. In addition she illustrated *History of the Methodist Church in Grahamstown*, by Leslie Hewson.

Exhibitions She has participated in numerous group exhibitions in SA and the UK; 1966 Grahamstown, solo exhibition.

Represented Ann Bryant Gallery, East London; Queenstown Library.

Public Commissions Ceramic rood screen, St Marks Anglican Church, East London; Figure of Christ the King, St Lawrence Church, East London; Madonna and Child, St Barnabas Church, Germiston, Transvaal; Madonna and Child, St Pauls Church, Port Alfred, Eastern Cape; several sculptural murals for public buildings in East London and King William's Town. A number of portrait heads for Rhodes University and other educational establishments.

Publications by Randell *We all Lived Here*, co-written with George Randell, 1977, published by the Randells; *Grahamstown Magic, exploring with a sketch book*, 1980, published by herself.

Reference AMC7.

RANKIN Joan

Born 1940 Johannesburg.

A painter and graphic artist of landscapes, still life, wildlife and abstract works. Works in oil, acrylic, watercolour, ink, airbrush, scraperboard, collage and in various graphic media. Creates fibre sculptures.

Studies 1957–58 Michaelis School of Fine Art, under Katrine Harries (qv) and Eleanor Esmonde-White (qv); 1959 Witwatersrand Technical College; 1968–78 privately under Sidney Goldblatt (qv).

Profile 1978–79 Chairman of the Johannesburg Spinners and Weavers Guild. 1981–86 privately published four books. 1986 illustrated M Thatcher's *Tselane*, Tafelberg, Cape Town, and in 1987 J Seed's *The Far Away Valley*, HAUM/Daan Retief, Cape Town, for which she won an award. Illustrated and printed two 1986 calendars, both limited to editions of 250. Involved in puppet theatre and the design of their programmes for the Civic Theatre, Johannesburg. A potter.

Exhibitions She has participated in several group exhibitions in SA; 1979 The Laura Collection, Johannesburg, first of six solo exhibitions held in Johannesburg and in 1986 in Cape Town.

Reference *Gallery* Spring 1983.

RAPHALALANI Meshack Matamela

Born 1950 Tshakhuma, Venda.

A sculptor of figures. Works in wood and occasionally in stone.

Studies Having completed a Primary Teaching Course, spent one year at the Ndaleni Educational Training School, Natal, studying art teaching methods.
Profile A teacher with the Department of Education. In 1986 his work was used on a set of Venda stamps.
Exhibition 1986 Helen de Leeuw, Johannesburg, solo exhibition.

RAPHOTLE Ramahlo Stanley

Born 1958 Orlando, Soweto.
A self-taught artist of landscapes, portraits, still life, genre, figures and abstract pictures. Works in watercolour, pencil and ballpoint.
Exhibition 1986 FUBA Gallery, Johannesburg, group exhibition.

RASEUR Lewis see LE SUEUR Louis

RAU Ronald Gilbert

Born 1948 Pretoria.
A painter of "landscape figures". Works in acrylic and watercolour. Large paintings derived from land or water plus figures and their shadows or reflections.
Studies 1966 Witwatersrand Technical College; 1967–69 Pretoria Technical College, under Gunther van der Reis (qv), gaining a National Art Teachers Diploma; 1981–82 Orange Free State Technikon, under Marita Swanepoel, where attained a Higher Diploma.
Profile Vice-President of the Orange Free State Branch of the SAAA. 1970–71 an art teacher at Eshowe High School, Natal; 1972–73 taught at Welkom High School, Orange Free State; 1974–80 a lecturer, then a senior lecturer at the Orange Free State Technikon; from 1981 Director of the School of Art and Design, Orange Free State Technikon. From 1984 he has served on the Committee for Cultural Affairs in Bloemfontein.
Exhibitions He has participated in numerous group exhibitions from 1969 in SA; 1970 Eshowe, Natal, first of three solo exhibitions.
Award 1969 First Prize for Painting, New Signatures, SAAA.
Represented Orange Free State Technikon.

RAUBENHEIMER Francis Alan

Born 1927 Heidelberg, Transvaal.
A painter of landscapes, seascapes, genre and still life. Works in watercolour and in ink and wash.
Studies Mainly self-taught but advised by Nerine Desmond (qv), Alfred Ewan (qv) and Anne Manduell.

Profile A member of the SAAA. Runs regular watercolour classes in Pieter-maritzburg. A Forest Conservation Officer. Has travelled throughout SA and lived in many different places in the Republic. Signs his paintings "Raub".
Exhibitions He has participated in numerous group exhibitions from 1967 in SA, West Germany and Portugal; 1970 Pietermaritzburg, first of 12 solo exhibitions.
Represented Killie Campbell Africana Library, University of Natal, Durban; Pietermaritzburg Public Library; Tatham Art Gallery, Pietermaritzburg.
References BSAK 1; AASA; *Artlook* December 1973; *SA Arts Calendar* July 1978 & August/September 1980.

RAUBENHEIMER Michele

Born 1957 Cape Town.
A sculptor of figures. Works in fibreglass resin and oil paint.
Studies 1978 gained a BA(FA) from the Michaelis School of Fine Art; 1983 gained an Advanced Diploma in Fine Art (Printmaking), Michaelis School of Fine Art; 1985 registered for an MA(FA) at the University of the Witwatersrand.
Exhibitions 1985 Cape Town Triennial.
Represented Touch Gallery, SA National Gallery, Cape Town.
Reference De Kat May 1986.

RAUTENBACH Laura

Born 1932 Bloemfontein.
A sculptor of portrait busts, full figures, religious works and animals, particu-larly horses and bulls. Works in wood, bronze, cold metal, stone, particularly marble and verdite, ciment fondu, plastic synthetics, fibreglass, plaster of Paris, welded steel and terrazzo. Occasionally paints portraits.
Studies 1950–53 Michaelis School of Fine Art, under Professor Rupert Shephard (qv), Maurice van Essche (qv), Katrine Harries (qv), Ivan Mitford-Barberton (qv) and Melvin Simmers (qv), gaining a Diploma.
Profile A member of the SAAA. A member and Secretary 1983–85 of the Orange Free State Art Society. Co-founder of the Bloemfontein Sketch Club. 1970–75 a lecturer in fine art, University of the Orange Free State. 1974–75 taught pottery and enamelling at the University of the Orange Free State. Thereafter taught art privately. A horse show-jumper, representing the Orange Free State for two years. Awarded Springbok Colours for hockey. She has travelled extensively in SA and to Zimbabwe; 1959 visited the UK, France and The Netherlands.
Exhibitions She has participated in many group exhibitions from 1952 in SA; has held solo exhibitions from 1970 in SA and SWA/Namibia; 1987 National Museum, Bloemfontein, Retrospective Exhibition.
Represented National Museum, Bloemfontein; University of Cape Town; University of the Orange Free State; Willem Annandale Art Gallery, Lichten-burg; William Humphreys Art Gallery, Kimberley.

Public Commissions 1953 portrait bust of Judge Toon van den Heever, Appeal Court, Bloemfontein; 1960 "Free State Farmer", Zastron Street, Bloemfontein; 1969 Merino Stud Breeders' Association Monument, Graaff-Reinet; 1969 Fifty Years' Commemoration Monument, Agricultural College, Glen, Orange Free State; 1970 bust of President Jim Fouché, Jan Smuts Airport, Johannesburg; 1971 President Jim Fouché, Raadsaal, Bloemfontein; 1973 Jim Fouché, as Minister, Verwoerd Building, Bloemfontein; 1973 Administrator Sampie Froneman, Verwoerd Building, Bloemfontein; 1976 "Bushbuck", Michaelhouse, Pietermaritzburg; 1979 President Nic Diederichs, Raadsaal, Bloemfontein; 1979 "Timeless Woman", Place for the Commemoration of the Day of the Covenant, Bloemfontein; 1979–80 "For Whom and What?", Military Museum, Bloemfontein; 1980 Centennial Monument, Dewetsdorp, Orange Free State; 1980 Dr Nak van der Merwe, Verwoerd Building, Bloemfontein; 1985 bust of Sand du Plessis, the Sand du Plessis Theatre, Bloemfontein; 1985 "Brahman Cow and Calf", Voortrekker Street, Bloemfontein; 1986 full figure of President F W Reitz, President Brand Street, Bloemfontein, among others.
References Kobus Smit, *Laura Rautenbach*, 1986, Laura Rautenbach, Bloemspruit; SAA; BSAK 1 & 2; AASA; *Sarie Marais* 26 June 1957; *SA Panorama* August 1969; *Farmer's Weekly* 22 October 1969; *Die Huisgenoot* 19 December 1969; *Fair Lady* 20 February 1974; *Die Landbouweekblad* 10 July 1981.

RAWBONE Kathleen May
Born 1910 Bareilly, India.
Resided in SA 1937–42 and from 1945.
A painter and graphic artist of landscapes, seascapes, portraits and still life. Works in oil, watercolour, pastel, wash, pencil, charcoal and in the etching process.
Studies 1942 Lucknow School of Art, India; 1943 Lahore School of Art, India; 1947 Continental School of Art, Cape Town, under Maurice van Essche (qv); 1965 Cape Town Art Centre, under Kevin Atkinson (qv); 1967 etching under Kevin Atkinson (qv); 1985 portraits under Francois Roux (qv).
Profile 1968–82 a member of the Cape Town Graphic Workshop. A member of the SAAA and the Somerset West Art Group. Visited Greece in 1966 and France in 1985 and 1986.
Exhibitions 1950 SAAA Gallery, Cape Town, first solo exhibition; she has also held a solo exhibition in England.
Award 1975 Phillip Frame Award for Graphics, Art SA Today.
Reference AASA (under Rawbone, Kay).

RAY Ute see GEVERS RAY Ute

READ Albert Everard
Born 1872 Nottingham, UK.
Died 1919 Johannesburg.
Resided in SA from *c*.1902.
A painter of landscapes, figures and animals. Worked in oil. Known for his English village scenes and views of South and East Africa.

Studies Four years under Sir W Q Orchardson RA (1835–1910), among other artists.

Profile A member of the London Arts and Crafts Society. A Director of Park Galleries, Nottingham. Opened the first antique and art business in Johannesburg. During WWI was wounded in East Africa.

Exhibitions Exhibited at the Royal Academy and in SA.

RECH-CASSARINO Severa

Born 1950 Italy.

Resided in SA from 1954.

A painter of mainly still life paintings, but also of portraits and allegorical plant and animal form compositions. Works in oil, watercolour and pencil.

Studies 1968–71 University of the Witwatersrand, under Cecily Sash (qv), Giuseppe Cattaneo (qv), Erica Berry (qv) and Robert Hodgins (qv), gaining a BA(FA); 1972 University of the Witwatersrand, where attained a Higher Diploma in Education.

Profile 1975–77 a lecturer at the Johannesburg College of Education; 1976 a part-time lecturer at the University of the Witwatersrand; 1979–82 a part-time lecturer at the Marist Brothers School, Linmeyer, Johannesburg, and at the Centre for Continuing Education, University of the Witwatersrand; 1986 taught art at St Barnabas College, Johannesburg, as well as privately. Frequent visits to Italy.

Exhibitions 1976 NSA Gallery, Durban, first of six solo exhibitions; she has participated in several group exhibitions from 1982 in SA.

Represented Johannesburg College of Education; University of Natal; University of the Witwatersrand.

REDDY Zainib

Born 1930 Poona, India.

Resided in SA 1955–67.

A painter of landscapes and figures. Works in oil and gouache.

Studies Sir Jamshedjee Jeejeebhoy School of Art, Bombay University, under A Bronsla and S B Palsikar.

Profile Lived in Durban until 1967 when she returned to Bombay; she subsequently moved to London.

Exhibitions She has participated in group exhibitions in SA from 1955; 1956 Durban, first of several solo exhibitions held in SA.

Award 1965 Cambridge Shirt Award, Art SA Today.

Represented Durban Art Gallery; Pretoria Art Museum; SA National Gallery, Cape Town.

References SAA; SAP&S; *South Africana* September 1958.

REDELINGHUYS Ian

Born 1949 Johannesburg.

A sculptor of abstract pieces. Works in bronze, steel, aluminium and brass. A graphic artist.

Studies Pretoria Technical College (Technikon), under Neels Coetzee (qv), Justinus van der Merwe (qv) and Alan Crump, gaining a National Diploma in 1971, a National Art Teachers Diploma in 1973 and a Higher Diploma in Sculpture in 1980. In 1987 he began studying for a Diploma in Technology.

Profile 1972–82 a lecturer and from 1982 a senior lecturer at the Pretoria Technikon. 1981, 1982 and 1983 visited the USA and Europe.

Exhibitions He has participated in several group exhibitions from 1970, exhibiting both his sculpture and graphic work; 1974 NSA Gallery, Durban, solo exhibition; 1980 Metalart Guest Artist Exhibition, with Neels Coetzee (qv), Johan van Heerden (qv), Gavin Younge (qv) and Edoardo Villa (qv); 1981 University of the Witwatersrand, joint exhibition with Johann Moolman (qv); 1983 Pretoria Art Museum, Johannesburg Art Gallery and the SA National Gallery, Cape Town, solo exhibitions; 1985 Cape Town Triennial; 1985 Tributaries, touring SA and West Germany.

Awards 1973 SA Institute of Architects Award; 1974 Metalart Prize, open category; 1977 Metalart Prize, open category, jointly with Willem Strydom (qv); 1979 Metalart Prize, closed category; 1975 Daily News Study Travel Award, Art SA Today.

Represented Durban Art Gallery; Pietersburg Collection; Potchefstroom University for CHE; Pretoria Art Museum; Rand Afrikaans University; SA National Gallery, Cape Town; University of Natal; University of the Witwatersrand.

Public Commissions 1984 bronze, "Telemechanique", Johannesburg; 1986 aluminium mobile, Mobil Oil SA, Cape Town.

References BSAK 1 & 2; 3Cs; AASA; LSAA.

REEDY Robert Eugene

Born 1941 Chico, California, USA.
Resided in SA from 1976.
A painter and sculptor of still life, figures and of geometric abstractions tending towards minimal art. Works in acrylic, watercolour, gouache, ink, wash, pencil, charcoal, mixed media and wood. Creates assemblages.

Studies 1962–71 Chico State College, USA, under Kenneth Morrow, John Ayres, Tom Griffith, Brian Paulson, Val Zarinus and Marion Epting, gaining a BA(FA) in 1967, a Californian Teaching Certificate in 1968 and an MA(FA) in 1971.

Profile 1968–70 Head of Department and a lecturer at Escalon High School, California; 1970–71 a teaching assistant at the Chico State College; 1978–81 a lecturer in art and design at the Witwatersrand Technical College (Technikon). A freelance design consultant. 1984–85 illustrated *All Flags Flying*, by William Sears, published by Baha'i Trust, Cape Town and Johannesburg.

Exhibitions He has participated in many group exhibitions from 1963 in California, Arizona and in Johannesburg; 1968 Chico, California, first of eight solo exhibitions, two of which have been held in Johannesburg.

REES Pippa Anne

Born 1954 Pretoria.
Draws Victorian and Edwardian buildings in ink and magic marker.

Studies Natal Technikon, under Barry Maritz (qv), Andrew Verster (qv) and Paul Stopforth (qv), gaining a National Diploma in Art and Design (graphic art).

Profile 1983 a lecturer in art and design at the M L Sultan Technikon, Durban.

Exhibitions 1982 Trevor Coleman Gallery, Johannesburg, first of two solo exhibitions.

REID Marie Lynn

Born 1945 Potchefstroom, Transvaal.

A painter of desert landscapes, seascapes, still life and figures. Works in watercolour, pastel, ink, wash and pencil.

Studies 1963–65 Rhodes University, under Professor Brian Bradshaw (qv) and Josua Nell (qv), gaining a BA(FA).

Profile A photographer. From *c.*1977 a member of the Swakopmund Art Association, also of the Arts Association SWA/Namibia and the WSSA. 1967 designed theatre décor in Klerksdorp, Transvaal. A layout artist for various SWA/Namibian publications. Has lived in SWA/Namibia from 1976.

Exhibitions She has participated in many group exhibitions from 1967 in SA and SWA/Namibia; 1979 Swakopmund Art Association Gallery, first of four solo exhibitions.

Represented Arts Association SWA/Namibia Collection.

REID Sarah M (Mrs)

A painter of landscapes and still life. Worked in oil.

Profile A teacher at the School of Art, Kimberley, in the early 1930s.

Exhibitions Participated in group exhibitions in Kimberley, with the Kimberley Athenaeum Club and in Johannesburg.

Reference AASA.

REINGOLD Estelle Ita

Born 1951 Cape Town.

A painter and graphic artist of landscapes, portraits, still life, figures and abstract pictures. Works in oil and acrylic and in pencil, charcoal, silkscreen and lithography.

Studies 1970–74 Michaelis School of Fine Art, under Neville Dubow, Stephen de Villiers (qv), Patricia Pierce-Atkinson (qv) and Peggy Delport (qv), attaining a BA(FA) and a Secondary School Teachers Diploma.

Profile From 1983 a member of the Artists Guild, Cape Town. 1975–78 an art teacher at the Cape Town Art Centre; 1975 Principal of a private art school in Cape Town. 1969, 1981 and 1985 visited North and South America; 1984 Israel; 1986 Europe.

Exhibitions She has participated in many group exhibitions in SA and one in Switzerland in 1985; 1978 Cape Town, first of five solo exhibitions, one of which was held in the USA in 1980.
Represented Pietersburg Collection.

REINHARDT Leslie Harold

Born 1933 Ventersdorp. Transvaal.
A painter of abstract pictures. Works in acrylic on hardboard, which is cut in relief.
Studies 1952–55 Witwatersrand Technical College, under Mary Davis (qv) and Phyllis Gardner (qv), gaining a National Art Teachers Certificate; 1961–64 University of South Africa, under Karin Skawran, where gained a BA(FA); 1984–85 Pretoria Technical College (Technikon), under Gunther van der Reis (qv), where attained a Diploma in Technology (FA).
Profile From 1967 a member of the Board of the SAAA. 1956–57 an art teacher at Athlone Boys High School, Johannesburg; 1958–65 an art teacher at Diamantveld High School, Kimberley; 1966-72 a lecturer, 1973–79 a senior lecturer and from 1980 Head of the Fine Art Department, Pretoria Technikon.
Exhibitions He has participated in numerous group exhibitions from 1958 in SA; 1972 Kimberley, first of four solo exhibitions; 1981 Republic Festival Exhibition.
Represented Potchefstroom University for CHE; Willem Annandale Art Gallery, Lichtenburg; William Humphreys Art Gallery, Kimberley.
Reference AASA.

RENECLE Bobbie (Mrs)

Born 1925 UK.
A painter of landscapes, seascapes, portraits, still life, wildlife and abstract pictures. Works in oil, watercolour, ink, wash, pastel and on scraperboard.
Studies 1942–45 Birmingham School of Arts and Crafts, England, under Bertram Francis, gaining Diplomas in Graphic Design and Fine Art; 1976–77 portraiture classes in Cape Town, under D Deacon-Moore.
Exhibitions She has participated in several group exhibitions from 1974 in the Cape Province; 1977 Hout Bay, Cape Province, first of nine solo exhibitions.

RENNIE Richard Alexander

Born 1932 Fort Victoria, Rhodesia (Masvingo, Zimbabwe).
Resided in SA from 1978.
A painter of landscapes. Works in watercolour. In addition to this he works in various graphic media.
Studies 1950–52 took a commercial art course at the Natal Technical College and gained a Diploma.

Profile From 1980 a member of the WSSA. A member of the Highway Art Group. An art gallery owner in Rhodesia (Zimbabwe) and later in Durban. A large number of reproductions of his work have been issued. 1984 visited the USA.
Exhibitions He has participated in numerous group exhibitions from 1974 in Rhodesia (Zimbabwe) and SA; 1979 Carlton Centre, Johannesburg, first of eight solo exhibitions in SA.

REPSOLD Louise

Born 1948 Zambia.
Resided in SA from 1962.
A self-taught painter of landscapes. Works in oil.
Profile From 1975 a member of the Artists Market. Lives in Brits, Transvaal.
Exhibitions She has participated in numerous group exhibitions from 1975.

REYNOLDS Patrick James

Born 1940 Pretoria.
A sculptor of figures, wildlife and religious pieces. Works in wood, bronze and ivory.
Exhibitions He has participated in several group exhibitions in SA.
Public Commissions A large figure of Jesus, Catholic Church, Overport, Durban; a large Nativity set, Lutheran Church, Greytown, Natal.

REYNOLDS Roy Peter

Born 1929 Eastleigh, Hampshire, UK.
Resided in SA from 1948.
A painter of portraits, still life, figures, wildlife and nudes, as well as historical and marine subjects. Works in oil, watercolour, ink, wash, pencil and conté. A sculptor, working in bronze, wood and silver.
Studies 1939–42 Moseley School of Art, Birmingham; 1943–44 Margaret Street College of Art, Birmingham; 1945–46 Royal College of Art, London.
Profile During the 1940s a member of the Royal Birmingham Society of Artists. From c.1981 an Official Artist to the SA Navy. 1952–54 taught at the Johannesburg Technical College, also at other art establishments in SA and England. Illustrations for *Sixty Miles of Pencil*, 1971, Gentry Books, London, and for various books published by the Hamlyn Publishing Group, Middlesex. Glass engraving of large windows for public buildings. 1948–63 lived in SA; 1963–80 in England; thereafter in SA. Has travelled extensively in Africa and Europe and to St Helena, the Arctic and Antarctic.
Exhibitions He has participated in many group exhibitions from 1940 in the UK, SA, Australia, the USA and Germany; 1952–53 John Orr's, Johannesburg, first of over 20 solo exhibitions held in England and SA; 1977 Brian Hatton Gallery, Hereford, England, Retrospective Exhibition; 1986 Admiralty House, Simonstown, Cape Province, Marine Exhibition.
Represented Buckingham Palace Royal Mews Collection, London.

NEIL RODGER
Infanta 1985
Oil on Canvas 122 × 90 cm
Noelle Bolton

NICO ROOS
Green Landscape 1983
Oil on Canvas 50 × 50 cm
Private

Public Commissions Numerous portrait commissions in both England and SA, including Dr D F Malan, for the University of Stellenbosch and in 1963 Prince Philip, Duke of Edinburgh, for the Affiliation of Youth Clubs. 1978 commissioned to paint a series of birds of prey for King Fahad of Saudi Arabia.
References BSAK 2; *De Kat* December/January 1987.

RICE Elsie (Mrs Garrett)

Born 1869 Elton, Derbyshire, UK.
Died 1959 Cape Town.
Resided in SA from 1933.
A painter of wild flowers, landscapes and seascapes of the Cape. Worked mainly in watercolour.
Studies Slade School of Art, London, and in Florence, Italy.
Profile Prior to 1933 taught art in England. Illustrated *Wild Flowers of The Cape of Good Hope*, with text by R H Compton, 1951, Cape Town and *Common SA Succulents*, with text by H Hall, 1955, Cape Town. A number of illustrations for the Botanical Society, SA. 1963 designed a series of postage stamps to commemorate the Golden Jubilee of Kirstenbosch Botanical Gardens, Cape Town.
Exhibitions 1920–29 exhibited in England.
References DSAB; DBA; SESA; AASA.

RIESER Dolf Eric

Born 1898 King William's Town, Cape Province.
A graphic artist of landscapes, figures, hunting scenes and flora. Produced lithographs, aquatints, etchings and engravings. 1961 African series.
Studies Began his art studies in 1923 in Germany; 1928–30 studied line and colour engraving in Paris.
Profile A member of the Royal Society of Painters, Etchers and Engravers. Taught printmaking privately in England. A visiting lecturer during the 1960s at the Michaelis School of Fine Art and at the University of the Witwatersrand. 1906 lived in Switzerland; 1923 Germany; 1928 France; in 1940 he went to England, where he settled in 1945.
Exhibitions He has participated in many group exhibitions in SA, Europe and the USA; 1956 Quadrennial Exhibition; 1960 SAAA Gallery, Cape Town, solo exhibition; has held solo exhibitions in SA, London, Paris and in Spain.
Represented Bibliothèque Nationale, Paris, France; SA National Gallery, Cape Town; Victoria and Albert Museum, London, UK.
References Art SA; SAA; SAP&D; BSAK 1; 3Cs; AASA.

RIPLEY Audrey Florence

Born 1930 Durban.
A painter of landscapes and still life. Works in acrylic, watercolour and pastel.
Profile From 1976 a member of the Highway Art Group, Natal, and from 1980 of the WSSA.
Exhibitions She has participated in numerous group exhibitions from 1976 in SA and London.

ROBERT Earl
Born England.
Died 1934 Johannesburg.
Resided in SA from 1892.
A painter of landscapes. Worked in watercolour and ink. A large series of paintings depicting the Premier Diamond Mines.
Profile A member of the Johannesburg Sketch Club. A large number of illustrations for newspapers including *The Cape Times*; drew cartoons for *The Star*, *The Rand Daily Mail* and *The Pretoria Press*. An Anglo-Boer War correspondent for *The Illustrated London News*. Edited and illustrated *The Ladysmith Bombshell*, and is thought to have been in Ladysmith during the siege. Illustrated *Die Afrikaner se Leesboek*, as well as other books. A poster maker for SA Railways and The Rand Show. Lived in Cape Town, moved to Johannesburg after the Boer War, where he gave art classes. Travelled throughout SA.
Exhibitions Participated in group exhibitions in Johannesburg; 1921 Johannesburg, third solo exhibition held in SA.
Represented Africana Museum, Johannesburg.
Public Commission Scenes of Lourenço Marques (Maputo), Mozambique, for the Portuguese Government.
References AMC4; SESA; BSAK 1 & 2; AASA; SASSK.

ROBERTS Carl Leopold
Born 1957 Bristol, UK.
Resided in SA from 1967.
A sculptor of figures and abstract pieces. Works in ceramics, bronze, stone and wood. 1984–85 a series of raku ceramic eggs.
Studies 1981–86 Rhodes University, under Josua Nell (qv), gaining a BA(FA) in 1984 and being awarded the Purvis Prize.
Profile Involved in pottery from 1981. Has lived in the UK, West Germany, Zambia, Zimbabwe, Tanzania and SA.
Exhibitions He has participated in many group exhibitions from 1981 in SA.
Represented Rhodes University.

ROBERTS Cecily
Born Pietersburg, Northern Transvaal.
A sculptor of wildlife and portraits. Works in bronze and ciment fondu.
Studies 1965–67 Witwatersrand Technical College, under David MacGregor (qv) and Eben Leibbrandt (qv).
Exhibitions She has participated in several group exhibitions in Johannesburg.

ROBERTSON Alexander
Born 1937 Wallsend, Northumberland, UK.
Resided in SA from 1968.
A painter of figures and landscapes. Works in acrylic.

Studies 1953–55 College of Art and Industrial Design, Newcastle, England.
Exhibitions From 1979 he has participated in two group exhibitions at the Crake Gallery, Johannesburg; 1980 Crake Gallery, Johannesburg, first of four solo exhibitions.

ROBERTSON James McCulloch RBC

Born 1869 Burnt Island, Fife, Scotland.
Died 1938 Newlands, Cape Province.
Resided in SA from 1912.
A painter of river scenes and landscapes. Worked in watercolour.
Profile 1917 a member of the SA Society of Artists. A member of the Royal British Colonial Society of Artists. Prior to 1901 worked in the family drapery business, on a sugar plantation in the West Indies and in a grocery store in Trinidad. 1901–12 a professional painter in Scotland. Included in Edward Roworth's (qv) essay "Landscape Art in SA", 1917, Studio Publication, *Art of the British Empire Overseas.*
Exhibitions Exhibited in SA and the UK.
Represented Durban Art Gallery; Julius Gordon Africana Centre, Riversdale; SA National Gallery, Cape Town.
References SAA; SAP&D; BSAK 1; AASA.

ROBERTSON Shirley Frances

Born 1920 East London.
A painter of landscapes, portraits, figures and still life. Works in watercolour.
Studies 1938–40 commercial art at the Witwatersrand Technical College, under James Gardner (qv), Phyllis Gardner (qv) and Eric Byrd (qv); August 1960, 1961 and 1962 life drawing and painting courses at the Witwatersrand Technical College, under Phil Botha (qv) and George Boys (qv).
Profile An Associate member of the WSSA. 1954–60 a member of the Vereeniging Art Society. Teaches art privately. 1982 a series of six watercolours of the University of the Witwatersrand, four of which were reproduced to mark its Diamond Jubilee.
Exhibitions She has participated in numerous group exhibitions from 1954 in SA and twice in London.
Represented Africana Museum, Johannesburg.

ROBINSON George Crosland

Born 1858 Huddersfield, Yorkshire, UK.
Died 1930 Cape Town.
Resided in SA 1885–90 and from 1895 until his death.
A painter of landscapes, seascapes, still life and portraits of SA notability, including those of Cecil Rhodes and President Paul Kruger. Worked in oil.
Studies Dresden Academy and in London, Paris, Berlin and in Italy.

Profile 1897 a founder member of the SA Society of Artists, and its President 1904–07, 1909–15 and 1924–25; 1901 a member of the SA Drawing Club. 1896 served in the Matabele War. From 1900 Principal of the Cape Town School of Art. 1882 lived in Paris; 1884 in London. Married to Constance Penstone (qv).
Exhibitions Participated in group exhibitions from 1879 in London, Paris, throughout SA and posthumously in Rhodesia (Zimbabwe).
Represented Africana Museum, Johannesburg; Albany Museum, Grahamstown; City Hall, Cape Town; House of Assembly, Cape Town; SA Cultural History Museum, Cape Town; SA National Gallery, Cape Town.
References SAA; SADNB; AMC4; DSAB; SAP&S; SSAP; Bénézit; DBA; BSAK 1 & 2; 3Cs; AASA; *Panorama* September 1983.

RODGER (John) Neil

Born 1941 Mowbray, Cape Province.
A painter of landscapes, portraits, figures, architecture and still life. Works in oil, watercolour and gouache. Draws in pencil and charcoal. A sculptor of figures and animals. Works in bronze, stone, ciment fondu, wood, polyester resin and ivory.
Studies 1961–63 and 1966 Michaelis School of Fine Art; 1963–66 on a study grant at the Rijks Academie voor Beeldende Kunsten, Amsterdam, under Sierk Schroeder; 1981–82 Rhodes University, under Thomas Matthews (qv), where gained an MFA cum laude.
Profile 1968–74 a member of the Grahamstown Group; from 1974 a member of the EPSFA. 1966–67 a part-time lecturer in drawing and painting at the Cape Technical College; 1967 Art Master at Wynberg Boys High School, Cape Town; 1968–74 a lecturer in fine art, Rhodes University; 1974–81 a lecturer, then a senior lecturer in fine art, Port Elizabeth Technical College; thereafter a full-time painter. 1980 a member of the selection board of the King George VI Art Gallery, Port Elizabeth. 1963–66 travelled throughout Europe; 1971 travelled to the UK, The Netherlands and Spain; 1986 visited the USA and England; 1987 spent five months painting portraits in Texas, USA; 1988 in the UK and Switzerland painting portraits.
Exhibitions He has participated in numerous group exhibitions from 1968 in SA, the USA and The Netherlands; 1968 Grahamstown, first of six solo exhibitions; 1981 Republic Festival Exhibition.
Award 1982 Five Roses Young Artist of the Year Award.
Represented George Municipal Collection; King George VI Art Gallery, Port Elizabeth; SA National Gallery, Cape Town; University of Pretoria; William Humphreys Art Gallery, Kimberley.
Public Commissions Mayoral portraits, Port Elizabeth; numerous portraits for educational institutions and large companies.
References 3Cs; AASA; LSAA.

ROESTORF Margaret

Born 1954 Port Elizabeth.
A painter of her own personal myth incorporating landscapes, portraits and animals. Works in acrylic, watercolour, pencil, charcoal and in mixed media on cloth.

Studies No formal training, but attended the Johannesburg Art Foundation and in 1985 the Joyce Leonard (qv) lecture groups.

Profile A writer of prose and poetry. Spent her childhood in Johannesburg; 1979–81 lived in Graz, Austria; 1984–87 in Maraisburg, Transvaal. 1988 living in Cape Town.

Exhibitions She has participated in many group exhibitions from 1981 in Austria, SA and Botswana; 1985 Carriagehouse Gallery, Johannesburg, first of two solo exhibitions; 1988 Johannesburg Art Gallery, Vita Art Now.

Represented Roodepoort Museum.

Publications by Roestorf *The Brown Book*, poetry, 1983, Kabelkarnimfe Press, Johannesburg; *On The Green*, poetry and drawing, 1985, The Hippogriff Press, Johannesburg; *The Dog of Air*, tales and paintings, 1987, The Hippogriff Press, Johannesburg.

ROETGER Liesa

Born 1957 Pretoria.

A painter working in oil, acrylic and egg tempera; draws in mixed media. A graphic artist working in various graphic media, particularly lithographs, etchings, woodcuts and silkscreens. Creates collages. An ongoing series on "Images from the Post Second War Years"; during late 1985 a series of cut-out paper dolls.

Studies 1975–78 University of Pretoria, under Professor Nico Roos (qv), Keith Dietrich (qv) and François de Nekker (qv), gaining a BA(FA); from 1983 at the Witwatersrand Technikon, under Philippa Hobbs (qv), Wendy Vincent (qv) and Sue Rosenberg (qv), in order to gain a Higher Diploma in Education, specialising in printmaking.

Profile From 1979 a member of the SAAA. 1978–80 taught both adult and children's classes privately, and was a guest lecturer at the Pretoria Technical College; 1981 a children's art teacher at Edenvale creche, Transvaal; 1982–83 a museum artist at the Africana Museum, Johannesburg; 1983–84 an art teacher at the Johannesburg Art Foundation; 1985 a part-time lecturer in printmaking at the Witwatersrand Technikon; 1987 a part-time lecturer at the University of Pretoria and at the Witwatersrand Technikon. A designer of posters for drama productions, she has also worked in the film industry since 1984.

Exhibitions She has participated in many group exhibitions from 1977 in SA and one in the UK; 1980 Gallery Y, Johannesburg, first of five solo exhibitions; 1985 Tributaries, touring SA and West Germany.

Represented Roodepoort City Council; University of Pretoria.

ROGIER Jean Marius

Born 1851 Grasse, France.
Died 1928 Wynberg, Cape Town.
Resided in SA from 1902.

A painter of landscapes and portraits.

Studies Ecole des Beaux Arts, Paris.

Profile Prior to 1902 lived in London. Taught at Rondebosch Girls High School, Cape Town.
Exhibitions Participated in group exhibitions from 1902 in the UK and SA.
Represented University of Cape Town.
References SAA; AASA.

ROGOFF Eileen

Born 1942 Vereeniging, Transvaal.
Best known for her paintings of old buildings, particularly those of Johannesburg and the Malay Quarter in Cape Town; she also depicts landscapes, portraits, still life and figures. Works in oil, watercolour, ink, pencil and charcoal.
Studies 1959–61 Johannesburg College of Education; 1962–63 Witwatersrand Technical College, gaining Primary and Junior School Teachers Certificates in 1962; studied for ten years under Cees Rietbroek and for three years under Sidney Goldblatt (qv).
Profile 1962–70 taught at King David Schools, Linksfield, Johannesburg. In 1980 she established her own art school in Johannesburg.
Exhibitions 1980 Nedbank Galleries, Johannesburg, first of three solo exhibitions, the third being held in Switzerland; she has participated in several group exhibitions from 1983 in SA and in New York, USA.
Represented Africana Museum, Johannesburg; Die Ou Kaaphuis Museum, Johannesburg.
Public Commissions 1984 Star Woman of the Year portrait, Johannesburg; 1985 commissioned by the Johannesburg Centenary Foundation to paint several paintings of the city.

ROLANDO Charles (Carlo)

Born 1844 Italy.
Died 1893 Melbourne, Australia.
Resided in SA 1881–85.
A painter of Cape landscapes; a large number of his paintings include ostriches. Worked in oil and watercolour.
Studies In Florence, Italy.
Profile Taught at the Cape Town School of Art. 1870–81 lived in England; 1881–85 in SA, thereafter in Australia.
Exhibitions Exhibited in SA 1881–85; 1886 participated in the Colonial and Indian Exhibition in London.
Awards 1881 Gold Medal for the best painting of Cape scenery; c.1884 received a Diploma from the President of the International Forestry Exhibition held in Edinburgh, Scotland.
Represented Africana Museum, Johannesburg; Johannesburg Art Gallery; Pretoria Art Museum; SA Cultural History Museum, Cape Town; SA National Gallery, Cape Town; William Fehr Collection, Cape Town.
References SADNB; AMC4; SAP&S; Bénézit; 3Cs; AASA; Alan McCulloch, *Encyclopedia of Australian Art*, reprinted 1977, Hutchinson, Victoria.

ROLFES Rita Louise 'T sas-

Born 1933 Albany, New York, USA.

Resided in SA from 1938.

A painter of landscapes and seascapes. Works in watercolour, ink and wash. 1969 a series on the Drakensberg Mountains; 1970 a series on the Okavango Swamps, Botswana; from 1977 paintings of private homes; 1985 a series on the Ben Lavin Nature Reserve, Northern Transvaal.

Studies 1951–54 Witwatersrand Technical College, gaining a Fine Arts Certificate; 1961–62 under Sidney Goldblatt (qv); 1962–63 under Karin Jaroszynska (qv); 1968–70 under George Boys (qv).

Profile From 1964 a member of the SAAA; from 1974 of the WSSA. From 1982 has taught art privately.

Exhibitions She has participated in several group exhibitions from 1963 with Artists under the Sun, Artists Market and the WSSA; 1971 Home and Art, Randburg, solo exhibition; since 1971 she has held several solo exhibitions in her own home.

Reference BSAK 1.

ROMAGNOLI (Henry Paul) Michael

Born 1933 Venice, Italy.

Resided in SA from 1938.

A painter of landscapes, seascapes, portraits and still life. Works in oil.

Studies 1951–52 and 1958–59 Accademia di Belle Arti, Florence, Italy, under Professor Conti; 1952 School of Architecture, University of Cape Town; 1953–56 Michaelis School of Fine Art, under Professor Rupert Shephard (qv), gaining a BA(FA).

Profile 1962–63 and 1965–66 a temporary junior lecturer in fine art at Rhodes University.

Exhibitions He has participated in several group exhibitions from 1958 in SA and one in Italy; 1964 Grahamstown Museum, solo exhibition.

Public Commission 1957 large mural on Barclays Bank (First National Bank) Stand at Goodwood Showgrounds, Cape Province.

Reference AASA.

ROMM Nina

Her creative work occurs on various levels: visual arts (painting, sculpture and multi-media), dance and performance. 1975 "The Pumpkin Cha-Cha" series.

Studies Gained a BA(FA) in 1972 from the Michaelis School of Fine Art and an MA(FA) in 1975; was awarded the MacIver Scholarship in 1973, the Jack Beattie Memorial Bursary and the Jules Kramer Fine Art Grant for Masters Study in 1974; also awarded the Sir Robert Kotzé Bursary for post-graduate study overseas, studying in 1978 at De Vrije Academie, Den Haag, The Netherlands; 1983 registered for a D Litt et Phil at the University of South Africa, on Performance Art–Rituals of Transformation; 1983 awarded a Human Sciences Research Council Grant for Post-Masters Research Overseas and a University of South Africa Doctoral Research Bursary for Overseas Study.

Profile 1977–80 a lecturer and 1980–87 a senior lecturer in the Department of History and Fine Art, University of South Africa. In May 1987 committed herself full-time to her own artistic work and to presenting creativity workshops: "the work might be termed an aerobics of the imagination, giving the individual a sense of renewed vitality which is not only physical but infiltrates the entire personality". 1984 spent six months in the USA, interviewing artists and scholars and attending performances and workshops in Los Angeles, New York and San Francisco.

Exhibitions She has participated in many group exhibitions in SA; 1975 SAAA Gallery, Cape Town, solo exhibition; 1985 Cape Town Triennial; 1985 Tributaries, touring SA and West Germany; 1986 Karen McKerron Gallery, Johannesburg, "Razzmatazz Mandala", joint exhibition with Valerie Bester (qv); 1988 Johannesburg Art Gallery, Vita Art Now.

Performances choreographed, directed and performed by Romm 1985 "Zen, Bananas and Rum", Market Theatre, Johannesburg; 1985 "With a Dab of Ylang-Ylang", Market Theatre, Johannesburg; 1987 "Posed Bods", Market Theatre, Johannesburg; 1987 "Strawberries and Cream on the Tail of the Hyena", Grahamstown Festival.

Represented King George VI Art Gallery, Port Elizabeth.

References *De Arte* April 1982 & September 1987; *De Kat* December/January 1987; *Ceramix* July 1987.

ROOD Linda Nancy

Born 1959 Eshowe, Zululand, Natal.

A printmaker of etchings and lithographs depicting figures and portraits. 1980–81 a series of masklike figures; 1982–85 a series entitled "An Analytical Exploration of the Human Form and its Relation to my Environment".

Studies 1979–80 Natal Technical College, under Barry Maritz (qv) and Stephen Inggs (qv), gaining a Diploma in Fine Art in 1979 and a National Diploma in Printmaking in 1980.

Profile 1981 a layout artist for the Republican Press, Durban. From 1983 a member of the Independent Visual Arts Council. 1984 an assistant at the Nicholas Treadwell Gallery, London; 1985 photographic assistant to Joe Alblas Photography, Durban. December 1982 illustrated the front cover of *Contrast*.

Exhibitions She has participated in several group exhibitions from 1981 in Durban; 1982 Elizabeth Gordon Gallery, Durban, first of two solo exhibitions, the second being held in Johannesburg.

ROODT Hilary Ann

Born 1944 Liverpool, UK.

Resided in SA in 1970–71 and 1978–82.

A painter of abstract pictures. Works in watercolour, sometimes combining watercolour with collage.

Studies 1975–78 under Jacqueline Bielmair and others in Brussels, Belgium; 1978–80 under Ines Aab-Tamsen (qv); 1980–81 evening classes at the Pretoria Technikon, under Willi Lottering (qv).

Profile From 1980 a member of the WSSA; from 1983 of the American Women's Club, Geneva, and of the United Nations Women's Guild, Geneva. 1971–78 lived in Belgium; from 1982 in Geneva, Switzerland. Married to a South African diplomat.

Exhibitions She has participated in many group exhibitions from 1980 held in SA, West Germany, the UK and Switzerland; 1981 Trevor Coleman Gallery, Johannesburg, first of four solo exhibitions, of which two have been held in Geneva.

ROOME John William

Born 1951 Pietersburg, Northern Transvaal.

A painter of landscapes, urban architecture and abstract pictures. Works in oil, acrylic, watercolour and gouache. Makes his own paper pulp. A maker of soft sculptures and an enamellist.

Studies 1971–75 Rhodes University, under Professor Brian Bradshaw (qv), gaining a BA(FA) in 1974 and an MFA in 1975.

Profile 1974–76 exhibited with the Grahamstown Group. 1978–79 co-established and ran the Stable Gallery in Durban with Jan Jordaan (qv). 1976 a lecturer in painting and history of art at Rhodes University; 1977 a lecturer in painting and history of art at the Natal Technical College (Technikon); from 1980 a senior lecturer in painting at the Natal Technikon. In 1983 began experimenting with papermaking and set up a papermaking unit at the Natal Technikon with Anthony Starkey (qv). 1980 visited the UK which stimulated interest in mural painting; 1983 visited the USA where he became interested in papermaking.

Exhibitions He has participated in numerous group exhibitions from 1974 held throughout SA; 1977 NSA Gallery, Durban, first of five solo exhibitions held in Durban; 1987 Strack van Schyndel Gallery, Johannesburg, joint exhibition with Peter Botha (qv).

Represented Durban Art Gallery.

ROOS Nicholas Oswald (Nico) Professor

Born 1940 Herbert District, Kimberley, Cape Province.

A painter of landscapes and abstract pictures. Works in oil, acrylic, watercolour, gouache and wash, draws in ink, pencil and charcoal.

Studies 1959 privately in Windhoek, SWA/Namibia, under Otto Schröder (qv); 1960–64 University of Pretoria, under Zakkie Eloff (qv), Anna Vorster (qv), Leo Theron (qv) and Gunther van der Reis (qv), gaining a BA(FA); 1964–69 informally under Adolph Jentsch (qv) in SWA/Namibia; gained an MA(FA) in 1970 and a D Phil in 1974 from the University of Pretoria.

Profile A member of the SAAA. 1964–66 an art teacher in Windhoek; 1967–68 a lecturer in art history, Potchefstroom University for CHE; from 1969 a lecturer in history of art at the University of Pretoria. 1972 established the Fine Arts Department at the University of Pretoria, of which he is the Professor. From 1972 a Council Member of the Pretoria Art Museum; from 1983 on the Arts Committee of the Department of Community Development; 1983 Commissioner to the Valparaiso Bienale held in Chile. Numerous visits to SWA/Namibia and the north-western Cape Province.

Exhibitions He has participated in numerous group exhibitions in SA and Zimbabwe; 1964 Windhoek, first of 14 solo exhibitions held in SWA/Namibia and SA; 1981 Republic Festival Exhibition.

Represented Arts Association SWA/Namibia Collection; Pretoria Art Museum; University of the Orange Free State; University of Pretoria; University of South Africa; William Humphreys Art Gallery, Kimberley.

Publication by Roos *Art in South-West Africa*, 1978, J P van der Walt, Pretoria.

References BSAK 1 & 2; AASA; LSAA; *Artlook* September 1968; *Insig* June 1988.

RORICH Jo

Born 1935 Viljoenskraal, Orange Free State.
Died 1985 Kommetjie, Cape Province.
A painter and graphic artist of landscapes and abstract pictures. Worked in oil, acrylic, ink, pencil, charcoal and in various graphic media. A sculptor working in bronze, stone and wood, who was well-known for her metal wall sculptures.

Studies 1960, 1962 and 1963, under Sidney Goldblatt (qv) in Johannesburg.

Profile A member of the SAAA and the Cape Artists Guild. 1961 and 1962 made study tours of Europe. Lived for many years on a farm in the northern Orange Free State, moving in 1981 to the Cape Peninsula.

Exhibitions Participated in numerous group exhibitions from *c.*1960 in SA; 1964 Adler Fielding Gallery, Johannesburg, first of *c.*eight solo exhibitions; 1980 University of the Orange Free State, Invited Artist; 1981 Republic Festival Exhibition.

Represented Potchefstroom University for CHE; University of the Orange Free State.

References BSAK 1 (under both Rorich and Roehrich) & 2; AASA; *Artlook* June 1968, March 1970 & December 1971.

ROSE-INNES Alexander

Born 1915 Beaufort West, Cape Province.
A painter of still life, portraits, figures and town scenes, particularly of the Cape Malay Quarter. Works in oil.

Studies During the 1930s and 1940s studied at the Port Elizabeth Technical College, under Francis Pickford Marriott (qv) and Professor Jack Heath (qv).

Profile Lives in Cape Town.

Exhibitions He has participated in many group exhibitions in SA and in Belgium; has held several solo exhibitions in the Cape from 1958; 1960 Quadrennial Exhibition.

Represented Hester Rupert Art Museum, Graaff-Reinet; SA National Gallery, Cape Town; Willem Annandale Art Gallery, Lichtenburg; William Humphreys Art Gallery, Kimberley.
References Art SA; SAA; AASA; *De Kat* February 1986; *SA Art Calendar* Autumn 1986.

ROSEN Frank

Born 1918 Bethal, Transvaal.
A painter and graphic artist of landscapes, fantasies and abstract pictures. Works in oil, watercolour, ink, wash, mixed media and produces aquatints and etchings.
Studies 1955 and 1957 Central School of Art, London.
Profile A Chartered Accountant and sportsman until 1955 when he became a professional painter. Wrote an article for the January 1972 issue of *Artlook*. 1960–66 lived alternately in London and SA; 1967 visited Europe; presently lives in London, annually visiting the USA.
Exhibitions He has participated in numerous group exhibitions from 1958 in SA, West Germany, Brazil, the UK, France, Monaco, Yugoslavia, Zimbabwe and The Netherlands; 1959 Lawrence Adler Gallery, Johannesburg, first of many solo exhibitions held in SA, Tel Aviv, Jerusalem, London and in Beverley Hills, California, USA; 1960 Quadrennial Exhibition; 1979 Californian Museum of Science and Industry, Los Angeles, USA, 35-year Retrospective Exhibition.
Represented SA National Gallery, Cape Town.
References Art SA; AASA; *Artlook* December 1967 & November 1968.

ROSENBERG Ronald Abraham

Born 1942 Johannesburg.
A sculptor of figures and abstract pieces. Works in metal.
Studies Witwatersrand Technical College, gaining a National Diploma in Industrial Design in 1965; 1979 gained a Higher Diploma in Art and Design with distinction.
Profile 1966–69 a product designer in the plastic industry; 1969–74 a freelance designer; 1974 appointed a lecturer at the Witwatersrand Technical College, in the Design Department; 1981 appointed a lecturer in the Fine Art and Sculpture Department. 1982 travelled throughout the USA and Europe; 1986 travelled extensively in the Far East.
Exhibitions He has participated in many group exhibitions from 1973 in SA; 1979 Market Gallery, Johannesburg, solo exhibition.
Award 1974 Metalart Prize, amateur category.
Represented Johannesburg Art Gallery; Rand Afrikaans University.
Reference AASA.

ROSENBERG Susan

Born 1954 Pietermaritzburg.
A painter and graphic artist. Works in mixed media on hand-made paper and produces etchings, drawings and collages.

Studies Gained a BA(FA) in 1976 from the University of Natal; 1978 attended workshops in Western and Japanese papermaking processes; 1979 gained an MA in Printmaking and Drawing from the University of Wisconsin, USA.

Profile Taught at the Witwatersrand Technikon; from 1985 she has lived in Oxford, UK, where she is a member of the Oxford Printmakers' Co-operative and the Oxford Artists Group.

Exhibitions 1982 Cape Town Triennial; 1983 Ernst de Jong Gallery, Pretoria, joint exhibition with Philippa Hobbs (qv); 1985 Cape Town Triennial; 1987 SA National Gallery, Cape Town and Goodman Gallery, Johannesburg, joint exhibition with Philippa Hobbs (qv), Lynda Moross-Ballen (qv) and Elizabeth Vels (qv).

Represented SA National Gallery, Cape Town; Wustum Museum of Art, Racine, Wisconsin, USA.

ROSS F B

An artist and etcher, whose ink drawings and coloured sketches depicted landscapes and city scenes of Cape Town and the UK.

Profile A member, and in 1902, Secretary of the SA Society of Artists. A cartoonist whose work appeared as early as 1896 in the *South African Review*, and 1908–10 in *The Cape*.

Exhibitions Participated in group exhibitions in Johannesburg from 1910.

Represented University of Cape Town.

References AASA; SASSK.

ROSS Wendy

Born 1944 Durban.

An artist creating land and sea art, as well as large sculptures made out of a variety of media including ceramics, paint, ciment fondu, wood, metal, canvas and horn.

Studies 1978 gained a BA(FA) and in 1986 an MA(FA) from the University of South Africa.

Profile Taught art privately. From 1980 has taught in the Department of History of Art and Fine Art, University of South Africa. A photographer and a potter who ran a pottery studio in Durban.

Exhibitions She has participated in group exhibitions from 1972 in SA and West Germany; 1981 SAAA Gallery, Pretoria, first of three joint exhibitions held with Marion Arnold (qv); 1982 Cape Town Triennial; 1985 Cape Town Triennial; 1985 Tributaries, touring SA and West Germany.

Represented University of South Africa; University of the Witwatersrand.

Reference De Arte September 1982.

ROSSOUW David Pierre

Born 1959 Johannesburg.

A painter, graphic artist and sculptor of portraits, figures, abstracts and mythological pieces. Works in oil, acrylic, watercolour, ink, wash, pencil, charcoal, various graphic media, bronze, stone, ciment fondu, wood, papier mâché, clay and steel.

Studies 1980 under Bill Ainslie (qv); 1981–84 University of the Witwatersrand, under Professor Alan Crump, gaining a BA(FA); 1983 awarded the Giovanna Milner Scholarship for overseas travel.

Exhibitions He has participated in several group exhibitions from 1982 in SA, the UK and the USA; 1981 Republic Festival Exhibition; 1985 Van Schalkwyk Gallery, Pretoria, first of two solo exhibitions; 1987 Johannesburg Art Gallery, Vita Art Now.

Awards 1981 Metalart Prize, student category; 1984 Second Drawing Prize, New Signatures, SAAA.

Reference AASA.

ROUPELL Arabella Elizabeth (née Piggott)

Born   1817 Newport, Shropshire, UK.
Died   1914 Swallowfield, Berkshire, UK.
Resided in SA 1843–45.

A painter of Cape landscapes and of portrait heads, as well as of botanical studies of flowers. Worked in watercolour, with some of her later works in oil.

Profile A member of the Regensburg Society of Arts and the Ratisbon Society of Arts, Germany. The plant *Protea Roupelliae* was named after her. Lived in England 1817–40, in India 1840–43 and 1845–53. Retired to England.

Exhibition 1951 Africana Museum, Johannesburg, exhibition of drawings.

Represented Africana Museum, Johannesburg; Bolus Herbarium Collection, University of Cape Town.

Publications by Roupell Two books of SA interest: *Specimens of the Flora of SA by a Lady*, an atlas folio of nine plates of the Cape and one of Sierra Leone, 1849, Shakespeare Press, London, with descriptions by Professor William Harvey, and *More Cape Flowers by a Lady*, a folio of 12 plates, 1964, SA Natural History Publications, Johannesburg, with text by Allan Bird.

References Pict Art; Afr Repos; SADNB; AMC4; DSAB; SESA; Pict Afr; BSAK 1 & 2; SA Art; *ANN* March 1951 & March 1952; *Quarterly Bulletin of the SA Library* September 1972.

ROUX (Jacobus) Francois

Born   1927 Fort Victoria, Rhodesia (Masvingo, Zimbabwe).
Resided in SA from 1967.

A painter of landscapes, seascapes, still life, genre, portraits and figures. Works in oil, Alkyd, watercolour, gouache and wash; draws in ink and pencil.

Studies 1943–45 Stellenbosch Technical College, under Siegfried Hahn (qv); 1946 Camberwell School of Art, London; 1947–51 Royal Academy Schools, London, under Philip Connard (*b.*1875), William Dring (*b.*1904), Bernard Fleetwood-Walker (*b.*1893) and Sir Henry Rushbury ·(1889–1968), gaining a Diploma in Painting.

Profile A member of the SAAA. 1970–78 a part-time lecturer in painting at the Cape Technikon, thereafter has taught art privately. 1946–51 lived in London and travelled extensively in Europe; 1951–67 lived in Rhodesia (Zimbabwe); from 1967 in Cape Town.

Exhibitions He has participated in group exhibitions from 1950 in the UK, Zimbabwe and SA; 1952 Fort Victoria, Rhodesia (Masvingo, Zimbabwe), first of several solo exhibitions held in Rhodesia (Zimbabwe); has held nine solo exhibitions in SA since 1973.

Represented Pietersburg Collection; SA National Gallery, Cape Town.

Public Commissions 1982 Portrait of the Mayor of Cape Town; 1982 Portrait of the Headmaster, Diocesan College, Cape Town; 1983 Portrait of Speaker J P du Toit, Houses of Parliament, Cape Town.

ROUX Janine

Born 1962 Port Elizabeth.

A painter of landscapes, portraits, genre and figures. Works in oil and watercolour, draws in pencil and charcoal.

Studies 1980–84 Port Elizabeth Technikon, under Neil Rodger (qv) and Hillary Graham (qv), gaining a Higher Diploma in Fine Art (painting); won a scholarship to study for a BA(FA) at The Cooper Union for the Advancement of Science and Art, Manhattan, New York, 1987–90.

Profile 1985–86 lived in Arizona, USA, Toronto, Canada and New York, USA. From 1987 living in New York.

Exhibitions She has participated in several group exhibitions from 1981 in SA.

Public Commissions 1984 large mural entitled "Broadcasting", foyer of the SABC, Port Elizabeth; 1985 large mural entitled "1930", Arthur's Steakghetti Restaurant, Port Elizabeth.

ROWETT Fiona Hilary Wilson

Born 1948 Pietermaritzburg.

A painter of landscapes, still life, seascapes and abstract pictures. Paints in watercolour and wash; draws in ink, pencil and charcoal.

Studies 1968–71 Michaelis School of Fine Art, under Maurice van Essche (qv), Stephen de Villiers (qv) and Neville Dubow, gaining a BA(FA).

Profile Influenced by Chinese and Japanese art. From 1979 a member of the WSSA and from 1983 of the Swaziland Art Society. 1972–73 an Art and English teacher, Plumstead High School, Cape Town; 1974 an Art and English teacher at Morgan High School, Rhodesia (Zimbabwe). 1976–77 lived in the Drakensberg Mountains; from 1983 has lived in Swaziland. Daughter of Alfred Ewan (qv).

Exhibitions She has participated in several group exhibitions from 1972 in SA and Swaziland; 1978 Blyvooruitsig, Transvaal, first of 13 solo exhibitions.

Represented Queenstown Municipal Collection.

Public Commission Three landscapes of Swaziland lowveld for the Commonwealth Development Corporation.

ROWORTH Edward

Born 1880 Heaton Moore, Lancashire, UK.
Died 1964 Somerset West, Cape Province.
Resided in SA from 1902.
A painter of Cape and Natal landscapes. His farm scenes often include an old homestead and oak trees. Additionally painted formal portraits. Worked in oil and pastel.

Studies During the mid 1890s studied under Tom Mostyn RBA (1864–1930) in Chorlton cum Hardy, near Manchester, and took a number of classes under Sir Hubert Herkomer (1849–1914) at Bushey, Hertfordshire, England; Slade School of Art, London, under Henry Tonks (1862–1937) and Frederick Brown (1851–1941); fresco painting in Florence, Italy.

Profile A member of the Mural Painters and Tempera Society, London; 1902 a founder member of the SA Society of Artists and its President 1908, 1918–20 and 1933–36; 1927 a council member of the SA Institute of Art; 1932 a member and later Chairman of the National Academy of Fine Arts (SA). 1902 ran a teaching studio in Berg Street, Cape Town. From 1935 Director and 1937–48 Professor of Fine Art at the Michaelis School of Fine Art; 1938–53 held the Chair of Fine Arts, University of Cape Town; 1930 a Trustee, 1939 Honorary Director, 1941–48 Director of the SA National Gallery, Cape Town. One of his paintings was reproduced by E Schweikerdt, Pretoria. Wrote an essay entitled "Landscape Art in SA" for the 1917 Studio Publication *Art of The British Empire Overseas*, incorporating his most favoured SA landscape artists. Father of Ivanonia Roworth (qv).

Exhibitions Participated in group exhibitions between 1902 and 1928 in the UK and from 1903 in SA; also exhibited in the USA and Rhodesia (Zimbabwe); 1903 Johannesburg, first of numerous solo exhibitions held throughout SA; 1917 Cape Town, joint exhibition with Pieter Wenning (qv), Hugo Naudé (qv) and Nita Spilhaus (qv).

Award 1935 King George V Silver Jubilee Medal for Services to Art in SA.

Represented Albany Museum, Grahamstown; Ann Bryant Gallery, East London; Durban Art Gallery; Johannesburg Art Gallery; Julius Gordon Africana Centre, Riversdale; King George VI Art Gallery, Port Elizabeth; National Museum, Bloemfontein; Pietersburg Collection; Queenstown Municipal Collection; SA Cultural History Museum, Cape Town; SA National Gallery, Cape Town; Tatham Art Gallery, Pietermaritzburg; University of Cape Town; University of the Orange Free State; University of Pretoria; University of Stellenbosch; War Museum of the Boer Republics, Bloemfontein; Willem Annandale Art Gallery, Lichtenburg; William Humphreys Art Gallery, Kimberley.

Public Commissions 1909 National Convention Group Portrait, House of Assembly, Cape Town; 1917 Fresco for St Philip's Church, Cape Town; 1934 six paintings for SA House, London; numerous portraits of SA notability, including Cecil Rhodes, Field-Marshal J C Smuts, Presidents Hofmeyr and Hertzog and in 1961 President C R Swart.

References Collectors' Guide; Our Art 1; Art SA; SAA; SADNB; 20C SA Art; AMC4; DSAB; SAP&S; SESA; SSAP; DBA; BSAK 1 & 2; Enc S'n A; SA Art; 3Cs; AASA; LSAA; *The Monitor* 8 November 1946.

ROWORTH Ivanonia (Mrs J Keet)

Born 1920 Richmond, Surrey, UK.
Resided in SA from 1920.
A painter of landscapes, portraits, figures and animals. Works in oil and watercolour. A muralist.
Studies 1934 Michaelis School of Fine Art, under Professor John Wheatley (qv) and Edward Roworth (qv), where awarded the Michaelis Prize; 1935 and 1950 fresco painting in Italy.
Profile 1942–44 taught drawing at the Michaelis School of Fine Art. Daughter of Edward Roworth (qv).
Exhibitions She has participated in group exhibitions and held several solo exhibitions in SA.
Represented SA National Gallery, Cape Town.
Public Commissions Several mural commissions, including six for the General Post Office in Cape Town.
References Collectors' Guide; SAP&D; BSAK 1; AASA.

RUBENS Leon

Born 1926 Potchefstroom, Transvaal.
A painter and graphic artist of landscapes, seascapes and still life. Works in oil, acrylic, watercolour, gouache, wash, ink, pencil, charcoal, wood and in various graphic media.
Studies 1946–47 commercial art at the Witwatersrand Technical College, under James Gardner (qv); 1948 commercial art at the Natal Technical College, under George Howe; 1956–59 Michaelis School of Fine Art, under Professor Rupert Shephard (qv), gaining a BA(FA).
Profile From 1970 a member of the SAAA. 1963–68 a lecturer at the East London Technical College; 1969–86 a senior lecturer at the Cape Technical College (Technikon). 1948–51 lived in London; has travelled throughout Europe and to the USA.
Exhibitions He has participated in many group exhibitions from 1976 in SA; 1985 SAAA Gallery, Cape Town, solo exhibition.

RUBIN Harold

Born 1932 Johannesburg.
An artist using chalk, ink and mixed media. Depicts figures. 1961 "Sharpeville" series; 1971 "The Beast and The Burden" series, which was published in *The American Review*, New York; 1976 "Crow" series, published by *Eked*, Tel Aviv.
Studies Studied drawing and painting under Rosa van Gelderen, Douglas Portway (qv) and in the studio of Herman Wald (qv).
Profile 1963 settled in Israel. 1979–82 a lecturer at the Bezalel School of Art, Jerusalem, Israel. A senior designer of architectural projects in Israel and at Ife, Nigeria.

Exhibitions He has participated in group exhibitions from 1956 held throughout SA and in Tel Aviv, London and New York; 1962 Gallery 101, Johannesburg, first of several solo exhibitions held in SA; 1986 Goodman Gallery, Johannesburg, exhibition of drawings and paintings.

Award 1969 Cambridge Shirt Award (Graphics), Art SA Today.

Represented Israel Museum; Johannesburg Art Gallery; SA National Gallery, Cape Town; University of the Witwatersrand; Utrecht Museum, The Netherlands.

Public Commissions 1971 executed a vitrage in Museum Yad—Mordechai, Israel; 1973 executed a vitrage in Rambam Hospital, Haifa, Israel.

References SAA; BSAK 1; *Artlook* February 1969 & September 1969.

RUNDLE Margaret Anne

Born 1932 Cape Town.

A painter of landscapes, portraits, still life and figures. Works in oil.

Studies 1947–49 Michaelis School of Fine Art, under Professor Edward Roworth (qv), Professor Rupert Shephard (qv) and W Twine, gaining a Certificate in Commercial Art.

Profile For many years a graphic artist and calligrapher. Lived in Cape Town until 1970 when she moved to Johannesburg. Ethel Dixie (qv) was her great-aunt and she is also related to Dorothy Barclay (qv).

Exhibitions She has participated in various group exhibitions in SA.

RUSKE Alicia Margaret (Peggy)

Born 1914 Bulawayo, Rhodesia (Zimbabwe).

Resided in SA from 1942.

A painter of floral paintings, landscapes, seascapes, figures and still life. Works in oil, acrylic, watercolour and wash, draws in ink, pencil and charcoal.

Profile From 1979 a member of the Fish Hoek Society of Artists and the SAAA. From 1980 has run a private watercolour painting group. Since 1950 has written short stories, many of which have been published and some broadcast. Chairman of the Fish Hoek Scribblers Club. 1948–68 involved in the Fish Hoek Dramatic Society. Visited the Transkei in 1980 and Natal in 1986.

Exhibitions She has participated in many group exhibitions from 1979 in the Cape Province.

S

SACHS Lily

Born 1914 Johannesburg.
A sculptor of figures and portraits. Works in bronze and ciment fondu.
Studies Witwatersrand Technical College, under Maurice van Essche (qv);
University of the Witwatersrand, under Willem de Sanderes Hendrikz (qv) and
Professor Heather Martienssen (1915–79); Académie Julian and Académie
Lhote, Paris; sculpture under Moses Kottler (qv).
Exhibitions 1966 Republic Festival Exhibition; 1966 Gallery 101, Johannesburg,
solo exhibition.
Public Commissions Designed a number of decorative features for Johannesburg
buildings, including the sculptural relief works on the Alexander Theatre,
Braamfontein; a piece of sculpture for a fountain in Commissioner Street,
Johannesburg; a column with relief figures in the Town Square, Lichtenburg,
Transvaal.
References SAA; SESA; AASA.

SACK Monty

Born 1924 Johannesburg.
A sculptor of abstract pieces and of constructions. Works in various metals and
creates torn paper and fabric collages. A series of Chinese and Hong Kong
scenes.
Profile 1954–57 a member of the Contemporary Art Society. A trained architect
who worked for the Schlesinger Organisation.
Exhibitions He has participated in several group exhibitions in Johannesburg;
1962 Whippman's Gallery, first of several solo exhibitions; 1981 Republic
Festival Exhibition.
Represented National Gallery, Harare, Zimbabwe.
References SAA; 3Cs; *Artlook* September 1967.

SACK Neil

Born 1929 Johannesburg.
A painter of semi-abstract and abstract pictures. Works in oil and watercolour.
Studies Natal Technical College; 1948–53 St Martin's School of Art, London.
Profile Prior to opening a gallery in Durban in 1955 he lectured at the University
of Natal. *c.*1953 illustrated *Mr Billing's World of Tropical Fish*, by Fay Alge. A
dancer in London and SA revues, a poet and writer. In 1955 he spent three
months in Corsica and Greece.
Exhibitions He has participated in group exhibitions from 1953 in Johannesburg
and Durban; 1953 Gallery Beaux-Arts, Johannesburg, first of several solo
exhibitions.
Reference SAA.

SACK Steven Joseph

Born 1951 Johannesburg.
A sculptor of landscapes, portraits and abstract pieces. Works in mixed media relief. 1977 a series of political portraits; 1979–80 "Cage" series; 1980–84 "House/Prison" series; 1985–86 a series of drawings of political landscapes and "The Daedallus" series.
Studies 1970–74 University of the Witwatersrand, under Neels Coetzee (qv), gaining a BA; 1979–82 University of South Africa, under Alan Crump, through which he attained a BA(FA).
Profile From 1985 a member of the SAAAH. 1978 an art tutor at Bill Ainslie's (qv) Studio; 1979–80 an art teacher at Hyde Park High School; from 1983 a lecturer at the University of South Africa; 1985–86 seconded from the University of South Africa to the Funda Centre, Soweto. 1986 a Trustee of the Patrons Trust; 1987 a Trustee of the African Institute of Art and the Katlehong Art Centre. Co-designed theatre sets, in 1976 for "Fantastical History of a Useless Man", in 1977 for "Woozebear" and in 1978 for "Randlord and Rotgut"; 1981 designed the set for "Marabi"; 1981–82 designed numerous sets for the University of the Witwatersrand Drama Department. From 1976 a member of the Junction Avenue Theatre Company, working as an actor, designer and administrator.
Exhibitions 1978 participated in several group exhibitions in SA and West Germany; 1982 National Gallery, Gaborone, Botswana, Exhibition of SA Art; 1985 Tributaries, touring SA and West Germany.
Represented University of the Orange Free State.

SACKS Lisa Jennifer

Born 1959 Johannesburg.
A sculptor of figures, portraits and genre. Works in clay, terracotta and bronze.
Studies 1973–76 Johannesburg Art, Ballet and Music School; 1980–81 Simi's School of Fine Art, Florence, under Signora Simi, and apprentice to Mario da Coreno in Varese, Italy.
Profile A trained doctor. Sister of Kim Sacks the ceramicist.
Exhibitions She has participated in several group exhibitions from 1979 in SA; 1979 The Firs, Rosebank, first of three solo exhibitions, the others being held in Rio de Janeiro, Brazil.

SALESSE André

Born 1910 Paris, France.
Died 1978 Ceres, Cape Province.
A painter of landscapes and street scenes. Worked in watercolour; also produced sepia drawings.
Studies Ecole des Beaux Arts, Paris; also studied printing and commercial art.
Profile 1977 President of the SAAA. In WWII served with the French Air Force, a POW escaping to SA in 1940 via Spain, Portugal and Mozambique. Lived in Cape Town.

Exhibitions Participated in group exhibitions in France and SA; 1977 Cottage Gallery, Cape Town, solo exhibition; 1978 Forum, Cape Town, joint exhibition with Aldo Gila.

Public Commissions Murals in the Reserve Bank, Bloemfontein; in 1933 commissioned by J W Schlesinger to decorate SA theatres, including The Alhambra in Cape Town, His Majesty's Theatre in Johannesburg and The Playhouse in Durban.

References BSAK 1 & 2.

SAMPSON Basil Fehrson Dr

Born In England.

A painter of landscapes. Worked in watercolour and oil.

Profile A member and in 1931 President of the NSA. 1931–32 on the Durban Art Gallery Advisory Committee. Lived in the UK and in Durban.

Exhibitions Participated in group exhibitions from 1923 in the UK and in SA.

References DBA; AASA.

SANDERSON John

Born 1820 Greenock, Scotland.

Died 1881 Durban.

Resided in SA from 1850.

A painter of scenes of Durban. Worked in watercolour, ink, wash and sepia.

Profile Drew political cartoons and pictures of historical events that took place in Durban and throughout Natal. Prior to 1850 a journalist in Glasgow; 1851 wrote for *The Weekly Times*, Durban; *c.*1853 worked for a general importer; 1871 editor, 1876–80 owner of *The Natal Colonist and Herald*. 1855–72 involved with Durban Town and Borough Councils, designing the Durban Borough Seal and the coats of arms for Durban and Pietermaritzburg. A littérateur, poet and politician. Former President of the Natal Agricultural Society and of the Public Library; a founder member of the Chamber of Commerce.

Exhibition 1858 exhibited at the Durban Fine Art Loan Exhibition.

Represented Local History Museum, Durban.

Publication by Sanderson *Polygamous Marriage among the Kaffirs of Natal and Countries Around*, 1878–79.

References Pict Art; DSAB; Natal Art; Pict Afr; BSAK 2; SASSK.

SANGWENI Phillmon Velangetshe

Born 1947 Vryheid, Natal.

A sculptor of figures, animals and still life pieces. Works in wood, as well as in stone, aluminium and copper.

Profile A jeweller.

Exhibitions He has participated in several group exhibitions from 1980 in SA.

Represented Durban Art Gallery.

SANTILHANO Sheila Gordon

Born 1936 Paisley, Renfrewshire, Scotland.

Resided in SA from 1967.

A painter of landscapes, seascapes, figures and animals. Works mainly in watercolour, but also in oil, pastel, pencil & wash, as well as in charcoal. 1974–75 yachting and seascape series; 1976–77 a series of small birds and animals; 1983–84 wildlife series.

Studies 1953–58 Glasgow School of Art, under Henry Hellier and Benno Schotz, gaining a BA(DA Scotland) in Art and Design.

Profile From 1985 a founder member and Chairman of the Vereeniging Art Society; a member of the WSSA, becoming an Associate in 1977; a member of the Brush and Chisel Club, the Artists Market, and formerly of the Vaal Triangle Art Society. 1976 Head of the Art Department, General Smuts High School, Vereeniging, Transvaal; from 1979 she has taught art privately. Designs and executes illuminated certificates. A potter.

Exhibitions She has participated in numerous group exhibitions from 1973 in SA, the UK, West Germany and Canada; 1973 Vereeniging, first of *c*.19 solo exhibitions.

Award 1952 silver medal for drawing and painting, Glasgow.

Represented Africana Museum, Johannesburg.

Public Commission 1985 a watercolour painting for the Oranje Vaal Administration Board.

Reference BSAK 2.

SANTRY Denis

Born 1879 Cork, Republic of Ireland.

Died 1960 Durban.

Came to SA in 1902 for health reasons.

A painter working in watercolour and gesso; also produced sketches, cartoons and metalwork.

Studies Cork School of Art, Republic of Ireland; awarded a bursary to attend the Royal College of Art, London.

Profile Elected a member of the SA Society of Artists. 1903–10 sketches and cartoons for *The Cape Press* under the pseudonym "Adam" and in 1904 for the *SA Review*; 1910–17 worked on the *Rand Daily Mail* and *The Sunday Times* in Johannesburg. Established the South African School of Art and Design in Cape Town. An architect and civil engineer. From 1917 lived briefly in the USA and the UK, then in Singapore. He returned to SA in 1945.

Exhibitions Participated in group exhibitions with the SAAA in 1903 and 1905.

Represented Africana Museum, Johannesburg; SA Cultural History Museum, Cape Town.

References SADNB; AMC4&7; BSAK 1 & 2; AASA; SASSK; *ANN* vol 15 no 7, September 1983.

SAOLI Winston

Born 1950 Acornhoek, Eastern Transvaal.

A painter, graphic artist and sculptor of figures and animals. Works in watercolour, ink, chalk, mixed media, various graphic media and in stone.

Studies Jubilee Centre, Johannesburg, under Bill Hart (qv) and Ezrom Legae (qv).

Exhibitions He has participated in group exhibitions from the late 1960s in SA, the UK and West Germany; 1969 Goodman Gallery, Johannesburg, first of several solo exhibitions; 1971 Building Design Centre, Preston, UK, joint exhibition with Leonard Matsoso (qv) and Cyprian Shilakoe (qv); 1979 Contemporary African Art in SA, touring; 1981 Standard Bank, Soweto, Black Art Today Exhibition.

Represented Johannesburg Art Gallery; University of Fort Hare; University of South Africa; William Humphreys Art Gallery, Kimberley.

References AASA; Echoes of African Art; *Artlook* May 1969, June 1970 & January 1971; *SA Panorama* July 1982.

SARGENT Bernard Maurice

Born 1921 Billericay, Essex, England.

Resided in SA from 1946.

A painter of landscapes, seascapes, portraits and wildlife. Works in oil, acrylic, watercolour, gouache and wash; draws in ink, pencil and charcoal.

Studies 1937 Worthing School of Art, Sussex, UK.

Profile 1927–32 a member of the Royal Drawing Society, Guildhall, London. A freelance commercial artist and illustrator.

Exhibitions He has participated in numerous group exhibitions from 1962 in SA and the USA; *c.*1962 Schweickerdt Gallery, Pretoria, solo exhibition.

References South Africa—a portrait in colour, *c.*1957, SA Tourism Board; SESA; BSAK 1; AASA.

SASH Cecily

Born 1924 Delmas, Transvaal.

Resided in SA until 1974, thereafter in Herefordshire, England.

A painter and graphic artist of still life and abstract pictures. Works in oil, watercolour, gouache, pencil, charcoal and in various graphic media, particularly etching. 1955–62 a series of birds (a recurring theme in her work); 1960 abstract works; 1965 interested in Op art; 1969 "Minoan" series and "Architectural Composition" series; 1970 "Metaphysical" series and "Medusa" series; 1972 "Phoenix" series; 1974 "Bird and Target" series; 1974–78 still life pieces; 1978–82 pencil drawings only.

Studies 1943–46 Witwatersrand Technical College, under Maurice van Essche (qv), gaining a National Art Teachers Certificate; 1948–49 Chelsea Polytechnic, London, under Henry Moore (1898–1986) and at the Camberwell School of Art, London, under Victor Pasmore (*b.*1908); 1952–54 part-time at the University of the Witwatersrand, attaining a BA(FA); 1953 mosaic and mural design in London; 1965 awarded an Oppenheimer Grant to research art education in Europe and the USA; 1972 University of the Witwatersrand, gaining an MA(FA).

Profile 1963 a founder member of the Amadlozi Group. 1952–58 an art teacher at Jeppe Girls High School, Johannesburg; 1955 a part-time lecturer, and from 1960–74 a full-time lecturer in design at the University of the Witwatersrand. 1979 opened the Granary Painting School, Leominster, Herefordshire, UK. A designer of tapestries woven at Aubusson, France and in SA.

Exhibitions She has participated in numerous group exhibitions from 1952 held throughout SA and in Italy, Brazil, the UK, Belgium, West Germany, The Netherlands and Greece; 1954 Whippman's Gallery, Johannesburg, first of numerous solo exhibitions held throughout SA; 1956, 1960 and 1964 Quadrennial Exhibitions; 1974 Pretoria Art Museum and Durban Art Gallery, Prestige Retrospective Exhibition; 1975 Rand Afrikaans University, Prestige Exhibition; 1978 London, first UK solo exhibition.

Awards 1966 Best Woman Artist, Artists of Fame and Promise; 1968 Bronze Medal, SA Breweries Art Prize; 1980 six tapestry designs for the SA Wool Board, Overall Winner and Silver Trophy, in their National Competition.

Represented Durban Art Gallery; Hester Rupert Art Museum, Graaff-Reinet; Johannesburg Art Gallery; King George VI Art Gallery, Port Elizabeth; Pietersburg Collection; Pretoria Art Museum; Sandton Municipal Collection; SA National Gallery, Cape Town; University of Natal, Durban; University of South Africa; University of the Witwatersrand; William Humphreys Art Gallery, Kimberley.

Public Commissions Numerous commissions, including: 1963 a large mosaic mural, Transvaal Provincial Administration Building, Pretoria; 1968 began mosaic mural, Jan Smuts Airport, Johannesburg. Mosaics commissioned for Cinerama, Johannesburg, Medical Arts Building, Johannesburg, a shopping centre in Germiston, Transvaal, a synagogue in Krugersdorp, Transvaal, the Transvaal Institute of Architects Building, Johannesburg and the Selwyn Segal Hostel, Johannesburg. A painted mural in the Sandton Civic Centre, Johannesburg. A tapestry in the Natal Provincial Administration Building, Pietermaritzburg.

References Our Art 2; Art SA; SAA; 20C SA Art; SAP&S; SAP&D; SSAP; BSAK 1 & 2; SA Art; Oxford Companion to 20C Art; 3Cs; AASA; *Insights— selected essays of Heather Martienssen*, introduction by Shirley Kossick, 1984, Ad. Donker, Johannesburg; LSAA; *SA Art News* 18 May 1961; *Artlook* November 1968, March 1971 & August/September 1974; *Habitat* no 2, 1973 & no 11, 1974; *SA Panorama* August 1974; *De Arte* 17 April 1975.

SASSOON Anne
Born 1943 Llandudno, Wales.
Resided in SA from 1949.
A painter and graphic artist of figures. Works in oil, watercolour, ink, pencil, charcoal and in various graphic media.
Studies 1963–64 Hornsey College of Art, London, under Michael Ayrton (1921–75).

Profile 1984–85 book covers for David Philip Publishers, Cape Town. Has written a number of articles for magazines. 1975–76 lived in America; 1986 in England. Visited New York in 1976; Botswana in 1983; the UK and Mozambique in 1984, and Israel in 1985.

Exhibitions She has participated in many group exhibitions from 1963 in SA and West Germany; 1968 Gallery 101, Johannesburg, first of three solo exhibitions held in Johannesburg; 1985 Cape Town Triennial; 1985 Tributaries, touring SA and West Germany.

Represented Johannesburg Art Gallery; University of the Witwatersrand.

References BSAK 1; *Artlook* February 1970.

SAUNDERS Katharine

Born 1824 England.
Died 1901 Tongaat, Natal.
Resided in SA from 1854.
A painter of Natal flora. Worked in watercolour.

Profile A botanist, with 16 species of plants named after her and her family. Married to James Saunders, founder of the Tongaat Sugar Estates.

Exhibitions 1854–1901 reguarly sent paintings for exhibition purposes to Kew Gardens, London.

References *Flower Paintings of Katharine Saunders*, 1979, Tongaat Group, Natal; AASA; *The Condenser 1979*, Tongaat Group, Maidstone, Natal.

SAVAGE Elaine

Born 1902 London, UK.
Resided in SA from 1936.
A painter of landscapes, tribal and traditional figures, and still life, particularly of flowers.

Studies Trained in England, France and Belgium.

Profile Taught at the Belgravia Art Centre, East London; 1937–44 taught at the East London Technical College. For many years on the Art Committee of the School of Arts and Crafts, Port Elizabeth Technical College. From 1944 a full-time painter.

Exhibitions Participated in group exhibitions held in SA; 1945 Lezards, Johannesburg, solo exhibition.

Represented Ann Bryant Gallery, East London; King George VI Art Gallery, Port Elizabeth.

References BSAK 1; Port Elizabeth School of Art; AASA.

SAWYER Ethel

Born Essex, UK.
Came to SA in 1902.
A portrait painter.

Studies South Kensington Art College, London, gaining an Art Teachers Certificate; Slade School of Art, London; Bushey School of Art, Hertfordshire, England, under Sir Hubert Herkomer (1849–1914), and in Paris.
Profile 1903 temporary head of the Port Elizabeth School of Art. Later lived at Wilderness, Cape Province.
Exhibitions 1898–1900 exhibited at the Royal Academy, London, and regularly with the NSA after 1902.
Represented Ann Bryant Gallery, East London; SA House, London, UK; SA National Gallery, Cape Town.
References *The Arts in SA*, edited by WHK, 1933–34, The Knox Printing & Publishing Company, Durban; SAP&S; DBA; AASA.

SCHADY Elsabé Karen

Born 1927 Cape Town.
A painter of landscapes, figures and abstract pictures. Works in oil. An etcher.
Studies 1945–48 University of Natal, under Professor O J P Oxley (qv) and Rosa Hope (qv), where gained a BA(FA); 1948–49 Central School of Art, London, under Bernard Meninsky (1891–1950).
Profile 1965–80 an art lecturer at the Pretoria Technical College (Technikon); 1980–82 Head of the Art Department, Pretoria Technikon.
Exhibitions She has participated in numerous group exhibitions from 1950 in SA, Spain, West Germany, Brazil and the USA; 1976 SAAA Gallery, Pretoria, joint exhibition with Jean Beeton (qv); 1976 SAAA Gallery, Pretoria, first of four solo exhibitions; 1981 Republic Festival Exhibition.
Represented Potchefstroom University for CHE; Pretoria Art Museum; University of the Orange Free State; Willem Annandale Art Gallery, Lichtenburg.
References AASA; LSAA.

SCHIMMEL Fred

Born 1928 Amsterdam, The Netherlands.
Resided in SA from 1948.
A painter working in oil, watercolour, gouache, ink, wash, pencil and charcoal. A graphic artist, making screenprints and woodcuts. 1977–81 a series of landscape-based screenprints. 1983 started experimenting in papermaking.
Studies 1946–47 Rietveld Akademie, Amsterdam.
Profile 1949–57 taught at the Polly Street Art Centre, Johannesburg. 1952 launched his own graphic studio and founded the Graphic Club of SA; 1956–57 lived in Melbourne, Australia, returning to SA via New Guinea, Manila, Hong Kong, Thailand, Pakistan, Kenya and Rhodesia (Zimbabwe); has also travelled extensively in Southern Africa and in Europe.
Exhibitions He has participated in numerous group exhibitions from 1960 in SA, Europe, the USA, Israel and Australia; 1964 Egon Guenther Gallery, Johannesburg, first of *c*.40 solo exhibitions held in SA, The Netherlands and West Germany; 1981 Republic Festival Exhibition; 1985 Potchefstroom University for CHE, solo exhibition.

Represented Durban Art Gallery; King George VI Art Gallery, Port Elizabeth; Potchefstroom Museum; Potchefstroom University for CHE; Pretoria Art Museum; Rand Afrikaans University; Sandton Municipal Collection; SA National Gallery, Cape Town; University of Cape Town; University of Durban-Westville; University of Natal; University of the Orange Free State; University of South Africa; University of the Witwatersrand; William Humphreys Art Gallery, Kimberley.

References SAGAT; BSAK 1 & 2; SA Art; 3Cs; AASA; LSAA; *Artlook* July 1967 & August 1969; *Lantern* November 1977; *In The Clouds* November 1979.

SCHIRMER Gustave E A

Born Rheydt, Rhineland, Germany.
A sculptor.

Studies Studied woodcarving in Landsberg and Flensburg, Schleswig-Holstein, Germany, under H Weddig; State School of Applied Art, Hamburg, studied sculpture under Professor Bossard and painting under Professor Adler; gained a Master Woodcarver's Diploma from Handwerkskammer, Frankfurt-on-Oder. An assistant sculptor to Professor George Wrba (1872–1939) at Dresden State Art Academy; then assistant to Professor Joseph Wackerle (*b*.1880) and Professor Karl Killer (*b*.1873) at Munich Art Academy, where he became a master student; also studied under Professor Moessel at Oviki Technical College.

Profile After his studies he taught at the Government School Workshops in Langsberg and made a study tour of Italy, Spain and France. Following this he came to SA. Until 1933 he worked as a sculptor, bronze caster, potter, mural decorator and goldsmith. In 1934 he taught wood and stone carving, and metalwork at the Michaelis School of Fine Art. A member of the South African School of Applied Art and an Associate of the Munich Academy, a member of the Master Woodcarvers Trade Guild and a Council Member of the SA Society of Artists and the Meldoic Society in Cape Town.

Represented University of the Orange Free State.

Public Commissions Stone carvings for the Delville Wood Memorial, Cape Town; wood carvings for the new Administration Building, University of Stellenbosch; sculptural works for the Colonial Orphan Chambers, Cape Town.

References The Arts in SA, edited by WHK, 1933–34, The Knox Printing & Publishing Company, Durban; SAA; BSAK 1 & 2.

SCHMULIAN Ruth Amy

Born 1944 Johannesburg.
A painter and graphic artist of portraits and figures. Works in oil, acrylic, watercolour and in various graphic media.

Studies 1962–66 Witwatersrand Technical College, under Joyce Leonard (qv), George Boys (qv), Claude van Lingen (qv) and Noel Bisseker (qv), gaining a National Art Teachers Diploma.

Profile 1967 taught at Potchefstroom Girls High School. 1979–85 Conservator of Paper at the Africana Museum, Johannesburg. 1967–69 lived in Europe.
Exhibitions She has participated in group exhibitions from 1966 in SA, Israel, Greece, Italy and the USA; 1979 Lidchi Gallery, Johannesburg, solo exhibition.
Represented Africana Museum, Johannesburg.

SCHOEMAN Erica Marie (Mrs Du Toit)

Born 1945 Pretoria.
A painter of landscapes, working in watercolour. A sculptor of figures carved in wood. A graphic artist.
Studies 1963–66 through the University of Pretoria, under Gunther van der Reis (qv), gaining a BA(FA) and an MA(FA).
Profile A member of the SAAA, the WSSA and the SAAAH. 1967 an art teacher at the Helpmekaar Hoër Meisieskool, Johannesburg; 1968 an art teacher at Menlo Park Hoërskool, Pretoria and in 1985 at Hoërskool Nelspruit. 1969–72 lived in Barberton, Transvaal; 1972–81 in Tzaneen, Transvaal; from 1981 in Nelspruit, Transvaal. 1983 visited SWA/Namibia.
Exhibitions 1972, 1976 and 1978 joint exhibitions in Pretoria and Cape Town with Marcella de Boom (qv); 1975 SAAA Gallery, Pretoria, first of three solo exhibitions; she has participated in numerous group exhibitions from 1976 in SA, West Germany, Spain and Portugal; 1979 NSA Gallery, Durban, exhibited with her sister, Carla Schoeman; 1981 Republic Festival Exhibition.
Represented Ermelo Municipal Collection; Pietersburg Collection.
Reference AASA.

SCHOLNICK Olivia

Born 1927 Williston, Cape Province.
A painter of landscapes, seascapes, their natural objects and textures. Works in acrylic, pastel, conté and pencil with wash. A graphic artist.
Studies 1965–68 Cape Town Art Centre, Green Point, under Kevin Atkinson (qv); graphic techniques with the Kevin Atkinson Graphic Group.
Profile A member of the Artists Guild, Cape Town. A trained musician.
Exhibitions She has participated in numerous group exhibitions from 1959 in SA, Zimbabwe, Belgium, The Netherlands, West Germany, Israel and Australia; 1966 Strand Street Gallery, Cape Town, first of 11 solo exhibitions; 1977 Gallery International, Cape Town, joint exhibition with Caroline van der Merwe (qv); 1979 National Museum, Bloemfontein, joint exhibition with Cecil Skotnes (qv), Thelma Chait (qv) and Lorraine Edelstein (qv); 1981 Republic Festival Exhibition; 1983 Gowlett Gallery, Cape Town, joint exhibition with June te Water (qv).
Represented Pretoria Art Museum; SA National Gallery, Cape Town; University of Stellenbosch.
References BSAK 1 & 2; Our Art 3; 3Cs; AASA.

SCHONEGEVEL Christiaan Carstens

Born 1808 Cape Town.
Died 1843 Cape Town.
A painter of miniatures. A lithographer.
Profile A compositor in the Government Printing Office. Produced a large, renowned hand-coloured aquatint of Table Bay, entitled "View of Cape Town and its Environs", which was engraved by N S Fielding, 1837. Brother of J M C Schonegevel (qv). A musician.
Represented William Fehr Collection, Cape Town.
References Pict Art; A Gordon Brown, *Christopher Webb Smith*, 1965, Howard Timmins, Cape Town; F R Bradlow, *Africana Books and Pictures*, 1975, A A Balkema, Cape Town; Pict Afr; 3Cs.

SCHONEGEVEL (Johan) Marthinus Carstens

Born 1819 Cape Town.
Died 1871 Cape Town.
Engraved on wood, copper and steel.
Profile A compositor for the Government until 1845 when he set up in the lithographic and printing trade; he made the famous lithograph of "The Anti-Convict Meeting of 1849". He lithographed the illustrations for and printed the first four issues of the Cape Town weekly *The Zingari*, which he founded. Gave lessons in art and music. Printed the earliest sheet music in Cape Town and the first book in Afrikaans. Brother of C C Schonegevel (qv).
Exhibition Participated in the 1851 First Annual Exhibition of Fine Arts in Cape Town.
Represented William Fehr Collection, Cape Town.
References Pict Art; DSAB; BSAK 2; F R Bradlow, *Africana Books and Pictures*, 1975, A A Balkema, Cape Town; Pict Afr; 3Cs; SASSK; *ANN* December 1962, June 1963 & December 1970.

SCHÖNFELDER Lorraine

Born 1952 Johannesburg.
A self-taught painter of still life and abstract pictures. Works in oil and ink.
Exhibitions She exhibited in Johannesburg in 1987.

SCHÖNFELDT Joachim Paulus

Born 1958 Pretoria.
A painter and sculptor of African art. Works in oil, acrylic, watercolour, ink, pencil, charcoal and wood.
Studies University of the Witwatersrand, gained a BA(FA) in 1980 and a Higher Diploma in Education in 1981.
Profile From 1977 has taken part in art performances. Since 1981 a member of Possession Art. From 1984 has worked for Meneghelli Galleries, Johannesburg.

Exhibitions He has participated in several group exhibitions from 1978; 1986 Gallant House, Johannesburg, solo exhibition; 1987 Johannesburg Art Gallery, Vita Art Now.

Award 1985 Haggie Prize, New Visions, Market Gallery, Johannesburg.

Represented University of South Africa; University of the Witwatersrand.

SCHRAUWEN Joan

Born 1940 Kimberley, Cape Province.

A painter and graphic artist of landscapes, still life, flora, fauna and abstract pictures. Works in oil, watercolour, ink, wash, pencil, charcoal and in various graphic media. Creates collages. 1983 "Veld" series i–xv, Frankfurt, West Germany; 1985 "Riverside" series i–ix, Houston, Texas, USA; "Wetlands" i–ix, Switzerland.

Studies 1959–61 University of the Orange Free State; 1984–85 graphics under Sue Williamson (qv).

Profile From 1982 a member of the SAAA. 1972–78 a potter in raku stoneware; 1985 papermaking and etching. 1966–68 lived in Jeffreys Bay, Cape Province; 1968–71 in Windhoek, SWA/Namibia, thereafter in Cape Town. Granddaughter of Tinus de Jongh (qv).

Exhibitions 1980 Grootmoddergat, Cape Town, first of *c*.10 solo exhibitions; has participated in several group exhibitions from 1982 in SA.

SCHRÖDER Otto Edward Henry FRSA

Born 1913 London, UK.

Died 1975 Stellenbosch, Cape Province.

Resided in SA from 1939.

A painter of landscapes, harbour and coastal scenes, figures and portraits. Worked in pastel and oil. Made metal and enamel wall decorations and designed stained glass windows.

Studies 1932–37 Landes Kunstschule, Hamburg, West Germany; 1934–38 privately under Oscar Boegel and portraiture under Hermann Junker (*b*.1867) in Hamburg; 1938 in Vienna, Austria.

Profile A Fellow of the Royal Society of Arts. 1947 co-founder, 1947–55 organising secretary and sometime Vice-President of the Arts Association SWA/Namibia, Windhoek. 1948 founded the Children's Art Centre, Windhoek, of which he was a Director until 1962; *c*.1965 co-founded the SWA Art Centre in Windhoek; a member of the South African Council of Artists and the International Society of Art Teachers, Paris. Wrote numerous articles on art which were published in periodicals. In 1958 he wrote, in conjunction with P A Hendriks (qv), a monograph on Adolph Jentsch (qv) which was published in Swakopmund, SWA/Namibia. 1962 Professor of Creative Art, 1963–75 First Dean of the Faculty of Fine Arts, lecturing in the History of Art, at the University of Stellenbosch. Four postage stamps depicting his paintings have been issued. 1919–38 lived in Germany; 1938 in Vienna, Austria; 1939–47 in the Cape, then in the Orange Free State and later interned at Baviaanspoort, Pretoria; 1947–62 in Windhoek, SWA/Namibia, and from 1963 in the Cape.

Exhibitions Participated in group exhibitions from 1940 in SWA/Namibia, SA, the UK, West Germany, Rhodesia (Zimbabwe), Brazil and Yugoslavia; 1948 Windhoek, first of numerous solo exhibitions held in SWA/Namibia, SA and in 1955 in Hanover, West Germany; 1956 & 1960 Quadrennial Exhibitions; 1958 SAAA Gallery, Pretoria, Johannesburg Art Gallery and SAAA Gallery, Cape Town, exhibition of Gruppe Fünf (Group Five), with Adolph Jentsch (qv), Fritz Krampe (qv), Joachim Voigts (qv) and Heinz Pulon (qv); 1976 Windhoek, Commemorative Exhibition; 1976 University of Stellenbosch, Commemorative Exhibition; 1983 Arts Association SWA/Namibia Gallery, Windhoek, joint Commemorative Exhibition with Carl Ossman (qv).

Represented Arts Association SWA/Namibia Collection; Johannesburg Art Gallery; Pretoria Art Museum; Sandton Municipal Collection; SA National Gallery, Cape Town; University of Cape Town; University of the Orange Free State; University of Stellenbosch.

Public Commissions Murals in Windhoek Airport and the Grand Hotel; mural, Tsumeb Town Offices.

References Art SA; SAA; SAP&D; BSAK 1 & 2; Art SWA; 3Cs; AASA; Commemorative Exhibition Catalogue, 1976, University of Stellenbosch.

SCHRÖDER William Howard

Born 1851 Cape Town.
Died 1892 Pretoria.
A painter of portraits and figures. Worked in watercolour and oil.

Studies Prior to 1865 while at Tot Nut van't Algemeen School, Cape Town, he was taught by the art master Charles Fanning (qv); 1866–72 part-time at the Roeland Street School of Art, Cape Town, under Thomas Mitchener Lindsay (qv) and W M McGill (qv); advised by Wilhelm Hermann (qv). Later studied under Donallier.

Profile A pencil and ink cartoonist and caricaturist in Cape Town, working part-time from 1870 and full-time from 1878 for such publications as *The Zingari*, *The Excalibur*, *Cape Punch*, *Het Volksblad*, *Cape Lantern*, *The Cape Argus* and his own publication *Knobkerrie*; 1889–90 in Johannesburg working for *Lantern*; from 1890 for *The Press* in Pretoria. A photographic colourist for S B Barnard in Cape Town. 1877–80 custodian of the SA Fine Arts Gallery, Cape Town.

Exhibitions Participated in group exhibitions from 1866 with the SA Fine Arts Society; 1886 Colonial and Indian Exhibition, London.

Awards 1872 First Prize for Best Amateur Watercolour, SA Fine Arts Society Exhibition; 1877 Gold Medal for Oil Painting, SA Fine Arts Society Exhibition.

Represented Africana Museum, Johannesburg; SA Cultural History Museum, Cape Town; SA National Gallery, Cape Town; William Fehr Collection, Cape Town.

Public Commissions Portraits of many well-known personalities including Cecil Rhodes, Jan Eloff, Saul Solomon, Carl von Brandis (1890) and President Paul Kruger (1890).

Publication by Schröder *The Schröder Art Memento*, edited by Leo Weinthal, 1894, published by Charles Cowan, The Press, Pretoria. This was the first review of SA Art.

References Pict Art; SADNB; 20C SA Art; AMC4&7; DSAB; Pict Afr; BSAK 1 & 2; 3Cs; AASA; SASSK.

SCHULER Hester

Born 1951 Salisbury, Rhodesia (Harare, Zimbabwe).
Resided in SA from 1975.
A painter of landscapes, seascapes and figures. Works in oil and acrylic. 1985 began sculpting figures, torsos and heads in ciment fondu and plaster of Paris – cast in fibreglass. 1984 a series of clowns.
Studies 1970–72 School of Art, Bulawayo Technical College, Rhodesia (Zimbabwe), where gained a Diploma in Applied and Commercial Design; 1979 sculpture privately under Ursula Fels.
Exhibitions 1979 Trevor Coleman Gallery, Johannesburg, first of five solo exhibitions held in Johannesburg and one in Port Elizabeth; she has participated in several group exhibitions from 1980 in Johannesburg.

SCHUMACHER Johannes

Born Rodenburg, Germany.
Resided in SA *c.*1770–89.
A painter of Cape scenes, extending to the Eastern and Northern Cape. Worked in watercolour.
Profile Listed as a soldier in the Cape Muster Rolls of 1770. 1776–77 as an artist, accompanied Hendrik Swellengrebel to the Eastern Cape. Assisted Colonel R J Gordon in his collection of drawings, now in the Rijksmuseum, Amsterdam, and accompanied him on his expeditions in 1777–78 to Bethulie, Northern Cape, and in 1779 up the Orange River past the Augrabies Falls. 56 Schumacher drawings from the Swellengrebel Collection, Breda, The Netherlands, were reproduced in *The Cape of Good Hope, 1776–1777, Schumacher's Water Colours,—a record of the journey of Hendrik Swellengrebel, 1777 explorer to the Eastern Cape*, 1951, introduction by A Hallema, published in The Hague, The Netherlands.
References Pict Art; Pict Afr; SESA; V S Forbes, *Pioneer Travellers of SA, a geographical commentary upon routes, records, observations and opinions of travellers at the Cape, 1750–1800*, 1965, edited by A Hallema.

SCHÜTTE Hermann

Born 1761 Bremen, Germany.
Died 1844 Cape Town.
Resided in SA from 1790.
A sculptor in the German Rococo style.
Studies Apprenticed to an architect in Hanover for seven years.

Profile A stonemason, architect and builder, who worked with Louis Michel Thibault and Anton Anrieth (qv). 1789 enlisted with the Dutch East India Company as a stonemason, 1791 left the company owing to an accident in the quarries on Robben Island in which he lost a hand and an eye. Thought to have designed, among many other public buildings: the Dutch Reformed Church and St Andrew's Church, Cape Town; 1811–14 the alterations to the Slave Lodge/Old Supreme Court, Cape Town; 1823 Green Point Lighthouse; 1836–41 Groote Kerk, Cape Town, designed and built with John Skirrow.
References Pict Art; Pict Afr; DSAB; *ANN* December 1958; *Historia* September 1964.

SCHUTTE Jan Harm Gysbert

Born 1949 Kroonstad, Orange Free State.
A painter and graphic artist who explores the relationship between surface and illusionistic depth/space. Works in oil, acrylic, watercolour, gouache, ink, wash, pencil, charcoal, wax crayons, spray paint, airbrush, collage and in various graphic media. Large series entitled "Aspects of the Anglo-Boer War" 1980–85 and "The Random Selection of Trash Found in Rubbish Bins".
Studies 1969–72 Witwatersrand Technical College, gaining a National Art Teachers Diploma; 1974–75 and 1978–84 through the University of South Africa, gaining a BA(FA).
Profile 1978–79 a founder member of the APSA in the Vaal Triangle; 1983 a founder member of the Vanderbijlpark Art Gallery Society; 1983–85 a member of the SAAA. From 1985 secretary of the fine arts section of the Kunswedstryd-vereniging van OVS (Art Competition Association of the Orange Free State). 1973–75 junior assistant at the Johan Carinus Art Centre, Grahamstown; 1973 a part-time lecturer at Rhodes University; 1975–76 a lecturer at the Natal Technical College; 1978–84 a lecturer, then Head of Department, School of Art and Design, Vaal Triangle Technikon; from 1984 a lecturer in the Department of Fine Arts, University of the Orange Free State. 1974–75 visited Europe; 1984 visited the UK. A cousin of Charles Gotthard (qv), and son of the author Jan H Schutte.
Exhibitions He has participated in several group exhibitions held in SA from 1972; 1972 Welkom, first of three solo exhibitions held in SA; 1985 Cape Town Triennial.
Represented Pretoria Art Museum; Vaal Triangle Technikon.
Public Commission 1984 a painting for the Bloemfontein City Council.

SCHÜTZ Peter

Born 1942 Glogau, Germany.
A sculptor of landscapes, city scenes, buildings, animals, trees, and of altered everyday objects. Works in wood and mixed media. A chair series with human elements.

HELEN SEBIDI
Mother Africa 1988
Pastel on Paper 160 × 130 cm
The Everard Read Gallery

CLÉMENT SERNEELS
Vernissage 1956
Oil on Canvas 70 × 90 cm
Denise Serneels

Studies 1965 Natal Technical College, gaining a National Diploma in Art and Design; 1971 gained a BA(FA) from the University of Natal, in 1973 a BA(FA)(Hons) and in 1982 an MA(FA). In 1962 he was awarded a Natal Technical College Bursary and in 1972 the Emma Smith Scholarship for Overseas Travel.

Profile 1975–82 a lecturer at the Natal Technical College (Technikon); from 1982 a lecturer at the University of the Witwatersrand.

Exhibitions He has participated in many group exhibitions from 1974 in SA; 1982 Cape Town Triennial; 1982 Market Gallery, Johannesburg, joint exhibition with Terence King (qv); 1983 University of the Witwatersrand, solo exhibition; 1984 Johannesburg Art Gallery, solo exhibition; 1985 Durban Art Gallery, Retrospective Exhibition; 1985 Cape Town Triennial; 1985 Tributaries, touring SA and West Germany; 1985 Valparaiso Bienale, Chile; 1986 Goodman Gallery, Johannesburg, joint exhibition with Penny Siopis (qv); 1987 Johannesburg Art Gallery, Vita Art Now.

Awards 1984 Standard Bank Young Artists Award; 1985 Merit Award, Cape Town Triennial; 1985 Best Foreign Entry, Valparaiso Bienale, Chile.

Represented Durban Art Gallery; Johannesburg Art Gallery; Mangosuthu Technikon; SA National Gallery, Cape Town; Tatham Art Gallery, Pietermaritzburg; University of Natal; University of South Africa; University of the Witwatersrand.

References AASA; *SA Arts Calendar* March 1984 & Spring 1985; *Gallery* Spring 1985; *De Kat* September 1985 & December/January 1986.

SCHWANECKE Ulrich Konrad Heinrich Valtin

Born 1932 Halberstadt, Germany.

Resided in SA from 1952.

A painter of landscapes, still life and occasionally of seascapes. Works in watercolour. 1971–73 painted semi-abstract paintings; from 1974 mainly deserts and semi-deserts. Numerous multi-panelled works.

Studies 1958 privately under Mrs Raath in Welkom, Orange Free State; 1960–62 Witwatersrand Technical College, under Jan Buys (qv), Cecil Skotnes (qv), George Boys (qv) and Bill Ainslie (qv); 1964–69 University of South Africa, under Professor Walter Battiss (qv), gaining a BA(FA).

Profile From 1975 a member of the WSSA, becoming a Fellow in 1979 and Chairman in 1977–79 and again in 1985. 1981 "The Edge of the Namib", a four-panelled print, reproduced by Howard Swan, Johannesburg. 1983 published *There are Places so Still . . .*, a limited edition book containing four graphics and two short stories. Many of his paintings have been reproduced. 1960 visited Central and West Africa; has made several visits to Lesotho, Greece, the USA and regular visits to SWA/Namibia.

Exhibitions He has participated in many group exhibitions in SA, the UK, the USA and West Germany; 1959 Welkom, Orange Free State, first of *c*.50 solo exhibitions held in SA and SWA/Namibia; he has also held two solo exhibitions in West Germany; 1965 Durban Art Gallery, solo exhibition; 1979 Gallery 21, Johannesburg, joint exhibition with Cynthia Ball (qv), Diedie Marais (qv) and Nicholas Garwood (qv); 1984 SAAA Gallery, Pretoria, joint exhibition with Dale Elliot (qv), Wendy Malan (qv) and Gordon Vorster (qv).

Represented Ann Bryant Gallery, East London; Arts Association SWA/ Namibia Collection; Pretoria Art Museum; Rand Afrikaans University; University of South Africa; Willem Annandale Art Gallery, Lichtenburg; William Humphreys Art Gallery, Kimberley.

References BSAK 1 & 2; AASA; *Artlook* February 1967, April 1970 & August 1971; *Lantern* September 1983; *Gallery* Summer 1983.

SCHWARZ Annette Louise

Born 1927 Orangeville, Orange Free State.

A painter of landscapes, figures and abstract works. Works in oil, acrylic, gouache and ink. 1983 painted "Rockey Street Poles"; 1982 series entitled "Documentation".

Studies 1960–63 Witwatersrand Technical College, gaining a Diploma in Commercial Art; 1966 The Visual Arts Research Centre, Johannesburg, under George Boys (qv); 1979–83 University of South Africa, gaining a BA(FA).

Profile A member of the Transvaal Art Society, of which she was a committee member 1968–70 and a lecture organiser and Public Relations Officer in 1969; a member of the SAAA. 1964–75 a part-time teacher at the Hope Convalescent Home, Johannesburg; from 1983 a part-time art therapy teacher at Glendale Training Centre, Cape Town. Her experience led her to write an article and give lectures on art for the retarded. Mother of the graphic artist and architect Allan David Schwarz.

Exhibitions She has participated in several group exhibitions from 1967 in SA; 1972 Foundation of Creative Art, Johannesburg, solo exhibition.

Public Commission 1985 mural for the Glendale Training Centre, Cape Town.

SCIALOM GREENBLATT Francine see GREENBLATT Francine Scialom

SCOTT Enid (Mrs Wollaston)

Born Kenilworth, Cape Town.

Both a sculptor and a painter, who lived in Bantry Bay, Cape Province.

Studies Michaelis School of Fine Art, under Professor John Wheatley (qv) and Herbert V Meyerowitz (qv); woodcarving and sculpture at Kunstgewerbeschule, Berlin; stonecarving at the Westminster School of Art, London.

References *The Arts in SA*, edited by WHK, 1933–34, The Knox Printing & Publishing Company, Durban; BSAK 1.

SCOTT Johan

Born 1960 Cape Town.

A painter and sculptor of genre. Works in enamel on canvas and ceramics.

Studies 1979 attended the Pretoria School of Art, Ballet and Music.

Profile 1982–84 taught ceramics at the Kraft Studio, Pretoria.

Exhibitions He has participated in several group exhibitions from 1979 held in Pretoria, Johannesburg, Durban and Cape Town; 1979 SAAA Gallery, Pretoria, first of 10 solo exhibitions held in Pretoria, Johannesburg and Cape Town.

SCOTT Louis

Born 1946 Edenville, Orange Free State.
A painter of landscapes, figures, wildlife and abstract pictures. Works in oil, acrylic, watercolour, ink and pencil.
Studies Informal art training in 1964 under Stefan Ampenberger (qv) and Iris Ampenberger (qv) in Thaba 'Nchu, Orange Free State; 1976 studied watercolour and oil painting under Hardy Botha (qv) in Melkbosstrand, Cape Province.
Profile A trained botanist, engaged in research at the Institute of Environmental Science at the University of the Orange Free State, where he is also a senior lecturer in the Botany Department. Has visited Marion Island (sub-antarctic), the Sonoran Desert in Arizona, USA, Spain and Greece. Son of the art critic and writer Dr F P Scott.
Exhibitions He has participated in several group exhibitions from 1976 throughout SA; 1982 Cape Town Triennial; 1985 Cape Town Triennial; 1986 Gallery 21, Johannesburg, solo exhibition; 1988 Johannesburg Art Gallery, Vita Art Now.
Represented National Museum, Bloemfontein; SA National Gallery, Cape Town; University of the Orange Free State; University of the Witwatersrand.
References AASA; *De Kat* December/January 1987.

SCULLY Laurence Vincent (Larry) Professor

Born 1922 Gibraltar.
Resided in SA from 1938.
A painter and graphic artist of abstract landscapes, cityscapes and seascapes. Numerous paintings derived from the desert. Works in oil, watercolour, ink, wash, pencil, charcoal and in various graphic media. Creates "photo-drawings", drawing in black pen on a photograph to outline, highlight or alter the image.
Studies 1944–45 part-time at the Pretoria Art Centre, under Le Roux Smith Le Roux (qv); 1947–50 University of the Witwatersrand, under Douglas Portway (qv), Charles Argent (qv), Joyce Leonard (qv) and Marjorie Long (qv), gaining a BA(FA); 1963 University of Pretoria, under Professor F G E Nilant, where attained an MA(FA) cum laude.
Profile An Honorary Life Member of the SAAA, 1969–74 Chairman of the Southern Transvaal Branch and in 1969–75 National Vice-President; 1954 a founder member of the Contemporary Art Society. 1967 and 1969 Chairman of the Transvaal Academy. 1970–75 a Johannesburg Aesthetics Committee member. 1951–65 Art Master at Pretoria Boys High School; 1964–65 an external

tutor for the University of South Africa; 1966–73 Head of the Art Department at the Johannesburg College of Education; 1976–84 Head and Professor of Fine Arts at the University of Stellenbosch and from 1984 Emeritus Professor of Fine Arts. 1961–75 chief examiner and later moderator of Matriculation Art Examinations for the Joint Matriculation Board of the Transvaal Education Department; 1971 an external examiner for the University of Natal, in 1981 for Rhodes University and in 1982 for Rhodes University and the Michaelis School of Art, Cape Town. 1951 designed costumes for the play "The Lady's Not for Burning", University of the Witwatersrand. Directed plays at Pretoria Boys High School. In 1957 created Multi-Image Performances, slide shows accompanied by classical music. 1973–75 a part-time art editor for *The Sunday Express,* Johannesburg. 1978–84 a Trustee of the SA National Gallery, Cape Town. 1957 and 1986 European study tours of art and architecture. Visits to Lesotho and SWA/Namibia.

Exhibitions He has participated in numerous group exhibitions from 1959 throughout SA, at the Venice and São Paulo Biennials and in the USA and West Germany; 1954 Whippman's Gallery, Johannesburg, joint exhibition with Cecil Skotnes (qv); 1962 SAAA Gallery, Pretoria, first of 33 solo exhibitions held in SA and SWA/Namibia; 1965 Pretoria Art Museum, Prestige Exhibition; 1973 William Humphreys Art Gallery, Kimberley, solo exhibition; 1974 National Gallery, Gaborone, Botswana, solo exhibition; 1975 National Museum, Bloemfontein, solo exhibition; 1981 Republic Festival Exhibition; 1982 New York, USA, solo exhibition.

Awards 1965 Oppenheimer Painting Award, Art SA Today; 1981 Photographic Prize, Republic Festival Exhibition.

Represented Ann Bryant Gallery, East London; Arts Association SWA/Namibia Collection; Contemporary Art Society, Tate Gallery, London; Durban Art Gallery; Hester Rupert Art Museum, Graaff-Reinet; Johannesburg Art Gallery; Johannesburg College of Education; National Gallery, Gaborone, Botswana; Pretoria Art Museum; Rand Afrikaans University; SA National Gallery, Cape Town; University of Cape Town; University of Durban-Westville; University of South Africa; University of Stellenbosch; University of the Witwatersrand; Willem Annandale Art Gallery, Lichtenburg; William Humphreys Art Gallery, Kimberley.

Public Commissions 1949 mural, N Knight Hospital, Transkei; 1971 Cityscape murals, Dudley Heights, Hospital Street, Johannesburg; 1972 Astral City, large canvases, Jan Smuts Airport, Johannesburg; 1978 Mandorla Murals, Konservatorium of Music, University of Stellenbosch; 1984 painting entitled "Flight" for SA Airway's 50th Anniversary; 1985 mural, Sun International, Aloe Ridge, Transvaal. Numerous portrait commissions for educational establishments and corporate headquarters.

References SAA; 20C SA Art; SAP&S; SSAP; BSAK 1 & 2; Our Art 3; SA Art; Oxford Companion to 20C Art (under SA); 3Cs; AASA; LSAA; *Artlook* August 1968, February 1970, June 1971, October 1971 & April 1974; *South African Garden & Home* February 1982; *SA Panorama* January 1984 & June 1985; *Flying Springbok* August 1984; *Gallery* Spring 1985; *SA Arts Calendar* Autumn 1987.

SDOYA Carlo

Born 1914 Rome, Italy.
Resided in SA from 1947.
A painter of landscapes, seascapes, still life, figures and portraits. Works in oil, watercolour, pencil and charcoal. Generally uses a palette knife.
Studies 1930–33 St Giacomo Art School, Rome; 1934–37 Fine Arts Academy, Rome, under Professors E Ballerini and R Bargellini.
Profile He has taught art privately in his own studio and from 1951 at his art school, the Da Vinci School of Fine Art, Johannesburg.
Exhibitions He has participated in numerous group exhibitions; 1953 Johannesburg, first of three solo exhibitions held in Johannesburg and SWA/Namibia.
References BSAK 1; AASA.

SEBIDI Mmakgabo Mapula Helen

Born 1943 Skilpadfontein, Hammanskraal, near Pretoria.
A painter of landscapes and figures. Works in oil and acrylic.
Studies 1969–70 privately under John Mohl (qv); 1985–86 Katlehong Art Centre, Transvaal; from 1986 at the Johannesburg Art Foundation, under Bill Ainslie (qv). 1988 awarded a scholarship for further study in the USA.
Profile A member of Artists under the Sun. From 1986 she has taught part-time at the Alexandra Art Centre. 1985 began creating large pots and sculpting in clay.
Exhibitions She has participated in numerous group exhibitions from 1977 in SA and the USA; 1986 FUBA Gallery, Johannesburg, solo exhibition; 1987 Johannesburg Art Gallery, Vita Art Now.
Represented Africana Museum, Johannesburg.
References Echoes of African Art; *Bona* September 1979; *Hit* August 1984.

SEBÖK Elizabeth (Mrs Borbereki-Kovacs)

Born 1908 Hajdudorog, Hungary.
Resided in SA 1950–70, thereafter in France.
A painter and graphic artist of landscapes, seascapes, still life, figures and abstract pictures. Works in oil and watercolour, also produces monotypes, mosaics and stained glass work.
Studies 1928–33 Academy of Fine Arts, Budapest, Hungary, where gained a Fine Arts Degree.
Profile 1966–69 director and owner of the Mona Lisa Gallery, Johannesburg. Has travelled in France, Italy, Spain and Hungary. Wife of Zoltan Borbereki (qv), mother of Daniel Kovacs (qv) and Barbara Borbereki (qv).
Exhibitions She has participated in numerous group exhibitions from 1948 in Italy, France and SA; 1973 Galerie Entremonde, Paris, first of several solo exhibitions.
Represented Durban Art Gallery; University of Pretoria.

Public Commissions Large mosaic panel, Addington Nurses' Home, Durban; stained glass window, Roman Catholic Cathedral, Kroonstad, Orange Free State; stained glass window, Roman Catholic Church, Parkview North, Johannesburg; stained glass window, Marist Brothers College, Inanda, Johannesburg; mosaic, Marist Brothers College, Observatory, Johannesburg.
References SAA; BSAK 1 & 2; AASA; LSAA; *SA Art News* 18 May 1961; *Artlook* September 1971.

SEGAL Arlene Florence

Born 1938 Johannesburg.
A sculptor of larger-than-life figures, portraits and abstract pieces. Works in fibreglass, reinforced concrete, bronze, stone and wood. A graphic artist.
Studies 1957–60 University of the Witwatersrand, under Professor Heather Martienssen (1915–79), Charles Argent (qv), Cecily Sash (qv) and Erica Berry (qv), gaining a BA(FA).
Profile Previously a member of the SAAA. 1961–62 an Itinerant Officer, teaching arts and crafts at recreation centres in Johannesburg. 1963–64 an art teacher at Parktown Boys High School, Johannesburg; 1964–69 a lecturer in history of art at the Greenoaks Finishing School. A Master of Environmental Planning, lecturing part-time in town planning and urban design at the University of the Witwatersrand from 1984. 1985 organising member of the Women's Art Festival, Market Theatre, Johannesburg. 1966 study tour of the Middle East, Greece, Turkey and Persia (Iran); 1970, 1972 and 1976 visited London; 1972 Israel; 1974 Europe; 1983 the USA; 1984 Portugal and Spain; 1985 Brazil and Paraguay.
Exhibitions She has participated in several group exhibitions in SA; 1965 Gallery 101, Johannesburg, first of six solo exhibitions held in SA.
Public Commission 1985 environmental sculpture fountain, Braamfontein Spruit Trust, Johannesburg.
References BSAK 1 & 2; *Artlook* June 1971.

SEGOGELA Mashego Johannes

Born 1936 Sekukuniland (Sekhukhuneland), Northern Transvaal.
A self-taught artist carving human figures and animals. Works in wood, sometimes finishing the piece with oil-stain varnish or paint. Several large group works, often depicting events from the Bible.
Profile Trained as a boiler-maker. Became a full-time artist in 1980.
Exhibitions He has participated in several group exhibitions from 1985; 1988 Goodman Gallery, Johannesburg, joint exhibition with Marion Arnold (qv), travelling to the Basle Art Fair, Switzerland.

SEKHWELA John Ngoako

Born 1955 Pietersburg, Northern Transvaal.
A painter and sculptor of figures and animals. Works in oil, acrylic, watercolour, ink, pencil and charcoal. 1987 began working in clay.

Studies 1983 FUBA, Johannesburg, under David Koloane (qv); 1983 Johannesburg Art Foundation, under Bill Ainslie (qv); 1987 Funda Centre, Soweto, under Lindi Solomons and at the Katlehong Art Centre, under Stephen Risi.

Profile A member of the Katlehong Art Society. 1987 taught children at the Katlehong Art Centre, Transvaal. In 1984 his poetry was published in books and periodicals.

Exhibitions He has participated in several group exhibitions from 1984 in Johannesburg; 1986 First Prize, Sol Plaatjie Exhibition, University of Bophuthatswana.

Represented University of South Africa.

Reference *Sesame* vol 5, 1985.

SEKOTO Gerard

Born 1913 Botshabelo Lutheran Mission Station, Middelburg, Transvaal. Resided in SA until 1947.

A painter of urban scenes, landscapes, genre and figures. Works in oil and gouache. 1924 a series on District Six, Cape Town; numerous paintings of Sophiatown, Johannesburg.

Studies *c.*1938 art part-time with Brother Roger Castle of St Peters School, Rosettenville, Johannesburg, but mainly self-taught. After 1947 studied at l'Académie de la Grande Chaumière and in other studios in Paris.

Profile A school teacher, trained at the Diocesan Teachers Training College, Pietersburg in 1930, who taught briefly at the Pietersburg Khaiso Secondary School. A pianist. Prior to 1947 he lived in Sophiatown outside Johannesburg and then in Cape Town. From 1947 he has lived in Paris. 1967–68 lived in Senegal. 1986, after a car accident, hospitalised in Hospital Dupuytren, Draveil. 1987 living at La Maison Nationale des Artistes, Nogent-sur-Siene, France.

Exhibitions He has participated in numerous group exhibitions from 1939 in SA, Zimbabwe and France, and continued to exhibit in SA after 1947; exhibited with the New Group; 1939 Marlborough Gallery, Johannesburg, first solo exhibition in SA, has also held solo exhibitions in Europe, Senegal and the USA; 1940, 1950, 1952 and 1954, Cape Town, joint exhibitions with Louis Maurice (qv); 1948 Tate Gallery, London, SA Art Exhibition; 1962 Adler Fielding Gallery, Johannesburg, joint exhibition with Louis Maqhubela (qv) and Lucas Sithole (qv); 1965 Piccadilly Gallery, London, African Painters and Sculptors from Johannesburg; 1986 Alliance Française, Pretoria, Historical Perspective of Black Art in SA Exhibition.

Award 1937 second prize in a national Bantu art competition.

Represented Johannesburg Art Gallery; Pretoria Art Museum; SA National Gallery, Cape Town; University of Fort Hare; University of South Africa; University of the Witwatersrand; William Humphreys Art Gallery, Kimberley.

Publication by Sekoto *Gerard Sekoto*, an autobiography, 1988, Dictum Publishing, Johannesburg.

References David Lewis, *The Naked Eye*, 1946, Paul Koston, Cape Town; Collectors' Guide; Our Art 2; Art SA; SAA; 20C SA Art; SAP&S; SESA; Contemporary African Art; SESA; BSAK 1 & 2; SA Art; Oxford Companion to 20C Art (under SA); 3Cs; AASA; Echoes of African Art; *SA Art News* 22 June 1961; *Art* March 1988.

SELEPE Daniel

Born 1946.

An artist depicting figures. Works in pencil, charcoal and wash.

Profile His work is reproduced on cards, published by Clifton Publications, Cape Town. Lives in Rondebosch, Cape Town.

Exhibitions He has exhibited in SA, Europe, Australia and SWA/Namibia.

SELHORST Josepha (Sister Mary Pientia)

Born 1914 Rietberg, Westphalia, Germany.

Resided in SA from 1938.

A painter of landscapes, portraits, still life, figures and abstract pictures. Works in oil, watercolour, gouache and wash, draws in ink, pencil and charcoal. A graphic artist, mosaicist and a designer of stained glass windows.

Studies 1941–47 University of Natal, under Rosa Hope (qv), Professor O J P Oxley (qv) and Geoffrey Long (qv), gaining a BA(FA); 1956–57 Düsseldorf State Academy, West Germany, under Professor Georg Meistermann (*b*.1911), attaining a testat.

Profile 1941–80 a lecturer and supervisor at Mariannhill Liturgical Art Centre; 1941–70 art lecturer at St Francis College, Mariannhill, Natal. 1951–52 made a study tour of European Romanesque churches and in 1956–57 of European Modern churches and museums. 1971–80 lived in Europe, studying mosaic work in Rome and Ravenna, Italy, and stained glass in Chartres, France. 1981–86 lived in The Netherlands, making African collages which are housed in a number of European museums; 1986 returned to SA. Sister of Professor Steve Selhorst of the Münster School of Art, West Germany.

Exhibitions She has participated in numerous group exhibitions from 1949 in SA and Italy; 1949 Durban, first of eight solo exhibitions of which five have been held in SA and three in West Germany; 1979 Jack Heath Gallery, Pietermaritzburg, Retrospective Exhibition.

Award 1973 Gold Medal, Cervo Riviera Exhibition, Institut Internationale pour l'Afrique, Milan and Rome, Italy.

Represented Durban Art Gallery; Killie Campbell Africana Library, University of Natal, Durban; Vatican Museum, Rome, Italy.

Public Commissions 1955 mural decoration, stained glass and mosaic, Hutchurch, Queenstown, Cape Province; 1958–59 stained glass for Queenstown Cathedral; 1960 stained glass for Church of the Assumption, Durban; 1967–68 stained glass for Bloemfontein Cathedral and 1950–70 for churches in Mariannhill, McKays Nek, Lady Frere and Bethlehem.

Publication by Selhorst UnKulunkulu Stories, 1975, Würzburg, West Germany.

References SAA; 3Cs; AASA; LSAA.

SELLERS Pauline Margaret

Born 1931 Johannesburg.

A painter and graphic artist of landscapes, figures, portraits and abstract pictures. Works in oil, mixed media, watercolour, gouache, ink, wash, pencil and in various graphic media.

Studies 1971–82 part-time, privately under Jane Heath (qv).

Profile From 1960 has had a keen interest in photography. From 1962 numerous anatomical illustrations. 1981 designs for stained glass windows. 1981–82 taught art privately. Has not painted since 1983. A full-time nurse and midwifery tutor. 1951 travelled throughout Europe.

Exhibitions She has participated in several group exhibitions in Natal; 1981 Republic Festival Exhibition.

Reference AASA.

SÉNÈQUE (Joseph Charles Louis) Clement

Born 1896 Phoenix, Mauritius.
Died 1930 Durban.
Settled in Durban in *c.*1908.

A painter of landscapes, harbour and city scenes, engineering and architectural subjects. Worked in oil and watercolour, drew in charcoal and pastel; also a graphic artist.

Studies Berea Academy, Durban; 1921–25 l'Ecole des Beaux Arts, Paris, under Professor Héraut and Alfred Agache, studying mainly architecture and town planning; 1923 Académie de la Grande Chaumière, Paris.

Profile A founder member of the NSA and a Council Member in 1925; 1925 founded the Durban Sketch Club; a Council Member of the SA Institute. 1915 an apprentice and 1918–21 articled to a firm of architects; 1924 an assistant to Alfred Agache, helping with the re-planning of Dunkirk, France. 1925–30 owned an architectural practice in Durban.

Exhibitions Participated in group exhibitions from 1918 in SA and from 1922 in Paris; 1925 Maison des Artistes, Paris, first solo exhibition; 1927 Lezard Gallery, Johannesburg, only solo exhibition held in SA; 1964 Pretoria Art Museum, Retrospective Exhibition; 1969 Tatham Art Gallery, Pietermaritzburg, Retrospective Exhibition; 1984 Johannesburg Art Gallery, SA National Gallery, Cape Town, Tatham Art Gallery, Pietermaritzburg, Durban Art Gallery and William Humphreys Art Gallery, Kimberley, Retrospective Exhibition.

Represented Durban Art Gallery; Johannesburg Art Gallery; National Museum, Bloemfontein; Pretoria Art Museum; SA National Gallery, Cape Town; Tatham Art Gallery, Pietermaritzburg; University of the Orange Free State; William Humphreys Art Gallery, Kimberley.

Publication by Sénèque Some Woodcuts by Clement Sénèque, 1926, Durban.

References Collectors' Guide; Our Art 2; Art SA; SAA; SADNB; SAP&S; BSAK 1 & 2; DSAB; BSAK; SA Art; 3Cs; AASA; Retrospective Exhibition Catalogue, 1964, Pretoria Art Museum.

SEOKA Phatuma Dr

Born 1922 Mojaji, Duiwelskloof, Lebowa.

A self-taught sculptor, who began working in horn and ceramics. In 1976 he started working in wood, particularly in corkwood and marula, retaining the shape of the piece of wood in his sculptures. He produced animal figures and later human figures and heads. His sculptures are often painted. He also works in stone, but less frequently.

Profile A member of Bozz Art. 1950–66 lived in Johannesburg, where he traded as a herbalist, from 1966 has lived in the Duiwelskloof area, where he has a barber-shop.

Exhibitions He has participated in several group exhibitions held in Lebowa and throughout SA; 1984 SA Contemporary Art, Johannesburg; 1985 Tributaries, touring SA and West Germany; 1986 Bozz Art Foundation Exhibition, touring Johannesburg, Cape Town and Durban, with Hendrik Nekhofhe (qv), Nelson Mukhuba (qv) and Jackson Hlungwani (qv); 1987 Goodman Gallery, Johannesburg, solo exhibition; 1987 Basle Art Fair, Switzerland; 1988 Johannesburg Art Gallery, Vita Art Now.

Represented Durban Art Gallery; Johannesburg Art Gallery; Pretoria Art Museum; Tatham Art Gallery, Pietermaritzburg.

SERNEELS Clément Edmond Théodore Marie

Born 1912 Brussels, Belgium.
Resided in SA 1961–80.
A painter of landscapes, seascapes, portraits, figures, nudes and still life, particularly flowers. Works in oil.

Studies 1926–28 l'Ecole Sain-Luc, Brussels; 1929–33 under Albert Philippot; 1934 Académie Royale de Belgique, under Alfred Bastien (1873–1955), where he gained a Diploma.

Profile 1936 received a travelling bursary to visit the Belgian Congo (Zaire), to which he returned in 1938 and where he lived until 1958. Visited SA for one year in 1945 and briefly on his way to the USA in 1948; 1951 revisited Europe; 1957 revisited Belgium. In 1980 he returned to Belgium.

Exhibitions He has participated in numerous group exhibitions from the early 1930s in Belgium, France, Belgian Congo (Zaire) and SA; 1937 Kinshasa, Belgian Congo (Zaire), first of numerous solo exhibitions held in Brussels, Paris, New York, Houston, Mexico and Lisbon; his frequent solo exhibitions in SA are held at the Everard Read Gallery, Johannesburg; 1964 Pretoria Art Museum, solo exhibition.

Represented Collection Etat Belge, Belgium; Pretoria Art Museum; Willem Annandale Art Gallery, Lichtenburg; William Humphreys Art Gallery, Kimberley.

References SAA; AMC4; SAP&D; BSAK 1 & 2; AASA; *Dictionaire Biographique des Artistes Belgiques*, 1987, Arto, Belgium; *Artlook* November 1966; Exhibition Catalogue, 1964, Pretoria Art Museum.

SETON-TAIT Adela (Ada)

A painter of portraits, flowers, landscapes, still life and miniatures. Worked in oil and watercolour.

Studies South Kensington Art School, London, under Sir Arthur S Cope RA (1857–1940); Slade School of Art, London.

Profile Until 1934 an art mistress at Jeppe High School, Johannesburg. Taught art at the Art Union, Johannesburg. In 1907 a portrait of a soldier painted by her was reproduced in the *African Art Journal.*

Exhibitions Participated in group exhibitions in London 1897–1901 and in SA from 1907; 1916 Levson's Studio, Johannesburg, solo exhibition.

Represented Africana Museum, Johannesburg.

References AMC7 (under Tait); DBA (under Tait); BSAK; AASA.

SEVERINO see BRACCIALARGHE Severino

SEYMOUR HADEN Francis (Toby)

Born 1891 Dundee, Angus, Scotland.
Died 1968 Pietermaritzburg.
Resided in SA from 1920.

A graphic artist who produced mezzotints, etchings and drypoints. His work depicts landscapes and buildings, mainly of the Natal area. Series of gold mines and Pietermaritzburg schools.

Profile Numerous commissions. A pianist and piano tuner. Lived in Pietermaritzburg and Johannesburg. Grandson of Sir Francis Seymour Haden (1818–1910) the surgeon, etcher, founder and first President of the Royal Society of Painter-Etchers.

Exhibitions Exhibited in SA and regularly with the SA Academy from 1932; also exhibited in the USA and the UK; 1970 Durban Art Gallery, joint exhibition of his and his grandfather's work.

Represented Africana Museum, Johannesburg; SA House, London, UK.

Reference Durban Art Gallery Brochure, 1970.

SHAKESPEARE Marjorie Kathleen

Born London.
Died *c.*1957.
Resided in SA from the early 1950s.

A painter of portraits, particularly children's, figures, landscapes, still life and interiors. Worked in oil.

Studies Birmingham School of Art, under B Fleetwood Walker RA (*b.*1893).

Profile An Associate of the Birmingham Society of Artists, and a member of the SAAA. Lived at Onrus River and Hermanus, Cape Province.

Exhibitions Exhibited at the Paris Salon in 1947, where she was awarded a commendation. Exhibited in London with the New English Art Club; participated in group exhibitions held throughout SA; 1953 and 1955 SAAA Gallery, Cape Town, solo exhibitions; 1954 held a solo exhibition in Durban and in 1955 in Bloemfontein; 1956 Quadrennial Exhibition.

Represented Johannesburg Art Gallery.

References SAA; BSAK 1; AASA.

SHANGE Bongani Peter

Born 1951 Pietermaritzburg.

A painter working in acrylic and watercolour and a sculptor in hardboard and aluminium of abstract works.

Studies 1976–77 Rorke's Drift Art Centre, under Jules van de Vijver (qv); 1981–82 Accademia di Belle Arti, Perugia, Italy, under Romeo Mancini and Gian Franco.

Profile From 1979 taught sculpture and graphics at the Community Arts Project, Cape Town. Has travelled in Italy, Austria, West Germany and Switzerland.

Exhibitions He has participated in group exhibitions throughout SA; held a solo exhibition in Cape Town.

Represented University of Fort Hare.

SHAWZIN Stella

Born Ogies, Transvaal.

A painter, graphic artist and sculptor, working in oil, acrylic, watercolour, gouache, ink, wash, pencil, charcoal, various graphic media, bronze, stone, wood, semi-precious stones and metals. Her pictures depict landscapes, sea-scapes, portraits, still life, figures, birds and insects. Her sculptures are of birds and insects. Series entitled "The Condition of Man".

Studies 57th Street Art Students League, New York, painting under Yasuo Kuniyoshi (1893–1953) and Du Mond, anatomy under George Bridgeman (1883–1954); painting under Martin Bloch in London; lithography at the Studio for Artists, Pratt Institute, New York, under Ponce de Leon and Sorrini; etching and engraving under Tony Harrison in London.

Profile A professional actress, singer and dancer appearing on the London stage and in films; has also worked in theatres in SA and Zimbabwe. Sister of the painter Alma Hayden and the writer Olga Levinson.

Exhibitions of Paintings She has participated in many group exhibitions from 1953 in London and Cape Town; 1953 Argus Gallery, Cape Town, first of four solo exhibitions held in London and Cape Town; 1964 Quadrennial Exhibition; 1981 Republic Festival Exhibition.

Exhibitions of Sculpture 1970 Lidchi Gallery, Johannesburg, first of six solo exhibitions held in Johannesburg, Cape Town and in London; she has partici-pated in many group exhibitions from 1973 in SA, the UK, the USA, Italy and Zimbabwe.

Represented Pietersburg Collection; Willem Annandale Art Gallery, Lichten-burg.

References Art SA; SAA; BSAK 1 & 2; AASA; *Artlook* February 1970.

SHEPHARD Rupert Norman

Born 1909 London, England.

Resided in SA 1948–63.

A painter of landscapes, portraits, still life, genre, figures and wildlife. Works in oil, watercolour, gouache, ink, wash, pencil and charcoal. A graphic artist creating coloured linocuts, lithographs and etchings.

Studies 1926–29 Slade School of Art, London, under Professor Henry Tonks (1862–1937), gaining a Slade Scholarship in 1928 and 1929 and a Slade Diploma in Fine Art in 1929. 1939 gained the Board of Education Art Teachers Diploma.
Profile From 1945 a member of the New English Art Club, London and from 1972 of the Royal Society of Portrait Painters. Elected an Honorary Academician, Accademia Fiorentina. 1945–48 a lecturer at St Martin's School of Art, London and at the Central School of Art, London; 1948–63 Professor of Fine Art and Director of the Michaelis School of Fine Art, Cape Town. 1945–46 an Official War Artist in England. 1956–63 Chairman of the Fine Arts Committee of the SAAA, Cape Town. A full-time painter from 1963 in England. 1986 illustrated *Pegeen Crybaby*, by Nicolette Devas, Grownow Press, London. Has written articles for *Leisure Painter* and *The Artist* in England. A writer, poet and potter. From 1963 regular visits to the South of France.
Exhibitions He has participated in numerous group exhibitions in the UK, SA, Italy, Brazil, Yugoslavia and the USA; 1939 Calmann Gallery, London, first solo exhibition; held seven solo exhibitions in Cape Town and three in Johannesburg; 1956 and 1960 Quadrennial Exhibitions; 1977 National Museum, Wales, solo exhibition.
Represented Ann Bryant Gallery, East London; Arts Council, London, UK; Print Room, British Museum, London, UK; Coventry Museum, UK; Imperial War Museum, London, UK; Johannesburg Art Gallery; King George VI Art Gallery, Port Elizabeth; National Museum, Wales; National Portrait Gallery, London, UK; Pretoria Art Museum; SA National Gallery, Cape Town.
Publications by Shephard *Capescapes*, 1954, F L Cannon, Cape Town; *Passing Scene*, colour linocuts, 1966, Stourton Press, London; *Cockcrow and other Verse*, 1977, Stourton Press, London.
References Collectors' Guide; SESA; *The Studio* July 1956.

SHER Jules

Born 1934 Johannesburg.
Resided in SA until 1964.
A painter of landscapes, waterscapes and still life. Works in oil, acrylic, ink, pencil and collage. 1959 painted in the abstract expressionist style; 1960–68 abstracted nude/landscape series; 1975–85 landscapes—horizon series; 1986–87 waterscapes—"Pittwater" series; 1988 waterscape—"Rottnest Island" series and landscape—"Bush Symbols" series.
Studies 1951–54 Witwatersrand Technical College, under Phyllis Gardner (qv) and T O D Davies; 1957–58 St Martin's School of Art, London, under Ted Gore and at the Central School of Art, London.
Profile 1956–59 studied in London, 1964–67 lived in London. Immigrated to Australia in 1967. Lived in Sydney until 1986, presently living in Perth, Western Australia.
Exhibitions He has participated in numerous group exhibitions from 1959 in SA, the UK, Australia and Korea; 1959 New Vision Gallery, London, first of six solo exhibitions held in the UK, SA and Australia.
References SAA; 20C SA Art; BSAK 1; AASA.

SHERMAN Louisa Elizabeth

Born 1955 Cape Town.

A painter of portraits and figures. Works in oil, watercolour and wash, draws in pastel and ink. A graphic artist. 1975 a series entitled "White Space" nos 1–4, a social comment on white suburbia.

Studies 1974–77 University of Stellenbosch, under Professor Larry Scully (qv), Paddy Bouma and Jochen Berger (qv), gaining a BA in Applied Art.

Profile From 1984 a member of the SAAA. 1980–81 a lecturer in the Department of Architecture, University of the Witwatersrand; 1983 Education Officer, SA National Gallery, Cape Town; from 1984 a lecturer at the Cape Technikon.

Exhibitions She has participated in several group exhibitions from 1985 in Johannesburg and Cape Town; 1985 Market Gallery, Johannesburg, joint exhibition with Gaby Cheminais (qv) and Angela Ferreira (qv).

SHEVEL Anne

Born Simonstown, Cape Province.

A painter of landscapes, figures and portraits. Worked in oil.

Studies Michaelis School of Fine Art, under Professor John Wheatley (qv) and Maurice van Essche (qv).

Profile A member of the Transvaal Art Society. Lived in Cape Town, in Europe and from 1936 in Johannesburg. 1958 visited Israel.

Exhibitions She has participated in group exhibitions from 1932.

Represented Africana Museum, Johannesburg.

References AMC4; BSAK 1; *SA Panorama* April 1958.

SHILAKOE Cyprian Mpho

Born 1946 Buchbeesreich, Eastern Transvaal.

Died 1972 Krugersdorp, Transvaal.

A sculptor of roughly carved wood figures. A graphic artist who produced etchings, linocuts, aquatints and worked in various other graphic media. Depicted township scenes and scenes of social realism. His themes are closely linked with African legends, death and reincarnation. His work is extremely symbolic. In 1972 began a series of totems.

Studies 1968–70 Rorke's Drift Art Centre, Natal.

Profile 1970–72 lived at the Lutheran Mission Station, Roodepoort, Transvaal.

Exhibitions Participated in group exhibitions in Sweden, West Germany, Denmark, Italy, the UK, the USA, Australia and SA; 1970 Goodman Gallery, Johannesburg, solo exhibition; 1971 Building Design Centre, Preston, UK, joint exhibition with Leonard Matsoso (qv) and Winston Saoli (qv); 1973 Goodman Gallery, Johannesburg, Memorial Exhibition; 1979 Contemporary African Art in SA, touring; 1981 Standard Bank, Soweto, Black Art Today Exhibition; 1982 National Gallery, Gaborone, Botswana, Exhibition of SA Art.

Award 1972 First Prize Graphics, African Art Exhibition, Los Angeles, USA.
Represented Durban Art Gallery; Johannesburg Art Gallery; King George VI Art Gallery, Port Elizabeth; Sandton Municipal Collection; SA National Gallery, Cape Town; University of Fort Hare.
References BSAK 1 & 2; 3Cs; AASA; Echoes of African Art; *Artlook* June 1971; *African Arts* vol VIII no 1, 1973; *SA Panorama* July 1975; *Bantu* December 1975.

SHILLER Joan

Born 1933 Pretoria.
A painter of landscapes, seascapes, wildlife and abstract pictures. Works in acrylic, watercolour, gouache, pencil and charcoal. 1982–83 sea-bed series; 1983–84 fabric-inspired series; 1986–87 life cycles.
Studies Witwatersrand Technical College, under James Gardner (qv); also under Andrew Verster (qv).
Profile An Associate member of the WSSA. 1985 and 1986 conducted two Design in Art workshops in Durban. Has travelled in the USA, Portugal, Spain, SWA/Namibia and Zaire.
Exhibitions She has participated in group exhibitions from 1965 held in SA and in London; 1983 Durban, first of three solo exhibitions.
Represented Durban Art Gallery; Margate Art Gallery.
Reference SA Arts Calendar August/September 1982.

SHLAMM Hans T

Born 1915 Breslau, Germany.
Resided in SA from 1936.
A painter of landscapes, city scenes and figures. Works in oil, watercolour, ink and wash.
Studies Reimann School, Berlin, and under Professor Brehaus.
Profile 1936 came to SA to work on the Empire Exhibition; also designed the interior of the Government Pavilion for the Pretoria Centenary Exhibition in 1955. An industrial and interior designer. Lived in Johannesburg, Tenerife, France, Mauritius and Lesotho.
Exhibitions Participated in group exhibitions in SA; 1953 Johannesburg, first of several solo exhibitions; 1956 and 1960 Quadrennial Exhibitions.
Reference SAA.

SHUTLER Shirley

Born 1929 Boksburg, Transvaal.
A painter of landscapes, seascapes, figures, portraits and still life. Works in oil, acrylic, watercolour, gouache, ink, pencil and charcoal. A collage maker and a sculptor of small figures. During the 1960s depicted dancing figures; the 1970s landscapes, flowers, nudes and portraits; the 1980s landscapes and fantasy figures.

Studies 1946–49, 1951 and 1954 Witwatersrand Technical College, under Phyllis Gardner (qv), Maurice van Essche (qv) and Joyce Leonard (qv), gaining a Diploma in Fine Art and a Teaching Diploma; 1964–65 under Sidney Goldblatt (qv); 1966 and 1968 under George Boys (qv).

Profile A founder member of the Benoni Art Society and Chairman in 1964. A life member of the Brush and Chisel Club. 1956–62 an art teacher at Boksburg Convent; 1965–72 at Christian Brothers College, Boksburg; 1957–80 Hillel High School, Benoni, and privately in her studio from 1963. 1968–72 a magazine illustrator for *Darling, The Sunday Express Woman's Magazine* and *Fair Lady*. During the 1950s and 1960s designed stage sets and costumes for East Rand theatres.

Exhibitions She has participated in numerous group exhibitions from 1950 in SA; 1962 Benoni, first of numerous solo exhibitions held in SA.

Reference BSAK 1 (under Shutley).

SIBISI Paul Michael

Born 1948 Umkhumbane, Durban.

A painter, graphic artist and sculptor of genre, figures and abstract pieces. Works in watercolour, gouache, ink, wash, pencil, charcoal, various graphic media and wood. From 1981 "Black Protest Art", a series of powerful urban images.

Studies 1968 on a Bantu Education Bursary at the Ndaleni Educational Training School, Natal, under Lorna Pearson; 1973–74 on an Institute of Race Relations Art Scholarship at Rorke's Drift Art Centre, Natal, under Otto Lundbohm, Malin Lundbohm, Carl Ellertson and Gabrielle Ellertson.

Profile 1980–84 a member of the SAAA. 1969–71 an art teacher at Appelsbosch Training College; 1975–77 at KwaThambo Combined School; 1977–85 at Mzuvele High School. A poet. 1984 visited the USA for one month on an Operation Crossroad Africa Grant; 1986–87 spent six months in the UK.

Exhibitions He has participated in numerous group exhibitions from 1968 throughout SA and in Botswana and the UK; 1973 Bojo Gallery, Durban, first of two solo exhibitions held in Durban; 1974 NSA Gallery, Durban, joint exhibition with Vuminkosi Zulu (qv); 1982 National Gallery, Gaborone, Botswana, Exhibition of SA Art; 1985 Tributaries, touring SA and West Germany; 1987 London, solo exhibition.

Award 1973 Graphic Art Award, Black Expo '73.

Represented Killie Campbell Africana Library, University of Natal, Durban; University of Fort Hare; University of Zululand.

SIBIYA Lucky Madlo

Born 1942 Vryheid, Natal.

A painter using themes from Zulu mythology, traditions and customs. Works in oil and powdered pigment on carved wood panels, paper or canvas. A sculptor creating free-standing sculptures in wood, bone and metal. A graphic artist, making serigraphs and woodcuts.

LUCKY SIBIYA
Flight 1987
Oil on Carved Wood Panel 90 × 70 cm
Private

ERIS SILKE
Malay Man
Acrylic on Board 64 × 53 cm
Die Kunskamer

PENNY SIOPIS
Aphrodite's Feast 1987
Oil on Canvas 159 × 128 cm
Private Collection, Stuttgart, West Germany

LUCAS SITHOLE
African Head
Carved Wood 71 cm High
The Everard Read Gallery

Wounded Buffalo
Resin 37 cm High × 78 cm
Private

Studies Some guidance from Cecil Skotnes (qv) and Bill Ainslie (qv), but mainly self-taught.

Profile 1975 produced 15 hand-printed woodcuts entitled "Umabatha", based on the play by Welcome Msomi, which were exhibited in London and Tel Aviv. From 1953 he has lived in the Transvaal, initially in Sophiatown, then in Soweto and presently in Hammanskraal. 1974 visited Europe and the USA.

Exhibitions He has participated in numerous group exhibitions held throughout SA and in Swaziland, the UK, Australia, Bostwana, France and the USA; 1971 Gallery 101, Johannesburg, first of many solo exhibitions; 1979 Contemporary African Art in SA, touring; 1981 Standard Bank, Soweto, Black Art Today Exhibition; 1985 Tributaries, touring SA and West Germany.

Represented Arts Association SWA/Namibia Collection; Durban Art Gallery; Sandton Municipal Collection; SA National Gallery, Cape Town; University of Fort Hare; University of the Witwatersrand; William Humphreys Art Gallery, Kimberley.

Public Commission Mural, Leratong Hospital, Krugersdorp, Transvaal.

References E J de Jager, *African Art*, 1979, Cape Town; SSAP; 3Cs; AASA; Echoes of African Art; *Artlook* June 1973; *Habitat* no 17, 1975; *SA Panorama* July 1982 & June 1983; *Southern Africa Today* May 1988.

SICKLE Mario Constant

Born 1952 Athlone, Cape Town.

A self-taught sculptor. Works in stone and wood. 1986 a series of eight large sculptures entitled "The Stone Throwers". A book illustrator, working in gouache, ink, wash, pencil and in various graphic media.

Studies 1982–85 The Foundation School of Art, Cape Town, under Barbara Pitt, gaining a Diploma in Graphic Design and Illustration.

Profile 1978 a founder member of the Bishop Lavis Art Centre, Cape Town; 1981 of the Vakaliza Art Association. 1986 founded The Art Gallery, Cape Town. Has designed 13 book covers for Maskew Miller Publishers, Cape Town, and illustrated *The New Fire*, by Jenny Seed, 1983, Human & Rousseau, Cape Town, *Sungura's Rope Trick*, 1986, Human & Rousseau, Cape Town and *Love David*, by Diane Case, Maskew Miller/Longman, Cape Town.

Exhibitions He has participated in numerous group exhibitions in Athlone, Cape Town.

SIEBERT Kim

Born 1958 Johannesburg.

An artist creating assemblages and collages of a wide variety of subjects. Works in oil, paper collage, found objects and oil pigments.

Studies 1977–80 Michaelis School of Fine Art, under Stanley Pinker (qv), where gained a BA(FA), was awarded a MacIver Scholarship for Post-Graduate Studies and gained a Higher Diploma in Education; 1982–84 Michaelis School of Fine Art, under Peggy Delport (qv), awarded the Harold Crossley Research Scholarship in 1983, the Jules Kramer Scholarship, the Irma Stern Scholarship and the MacIver Scholarship in 1984, gained an MA(FA).

Profile 1977–79 taught art to children at the Community Arts Project, Mowbray, Cape Town; 1986 a temporary lecturer at the University of Natal. 1987 Education Officer, Tatham Art Gallery, Pietermaritzburg. Has lived in Malawi, Zimbabwe, Durban, Cape Town and Pietermaritzburg. 1982 visited London and Paris.
Exhibitions She has participated in group exhibitions from 1984 in SA; 1985 Market Gallery, Johannesburg, solo exhibition; 1985 Cape Town Triennial.
Represented Durban Art Gallery.

SIEDLE Barbara Ann

Born 1946 Durban.
A painter of landscapes, animals and birds. Works in watercolour, ink, wash and pencil.
Studies 1964 Michaelis School of Fine Art; 1967–70 Akademie der Bildenden Kunste, Munich, West Germany, under Professor Kirchner.
Profile An Associate of the WSSA of which she was the Natal Chairman in 1982; a member of the NSA.
Exhibitions She has participated in numerous group exhibitions from 1982 in SA, West Germany, Italy, the UK and the USA; 1983 Sandown Gallery, Johannesburg, first of four solo exhibitions held in SA; 1985 Godalming Gallery, Surrey, UK, three-person exhibition.

SIHLALI Durant Basi

Born 1935 Germiston, Transvaal.
A painter, graphic artist and sculptor of figures, still life, genre, landscapes, seascapes and abstract works. Uses oil, acrylic, gouache, watercolour, wash, pencil, charcoal, various graphic media, wood and metal. 1975–85 gold and coal mining industry series of paintings, drawings and life-size sculptures.
Studies 1950–53 Chiawelo Art Centre, Moroka, Transvaal; 1953–58 Polly Street Art Centre, Johannesburg; 1955 Da Vinci School of Fine Art, Johannesburg, under Carlo Sdoya (qv); 1955–58 under Sidney Goldblatt (qv); 1965–66 under Ulrich Schwanecke (qv); 1985–86 Villa Arson Art School, Nice, France.
Profile From 1974 a member of the WSSA; 1980–85 a member of the Brush and Chisel Club. 1979–83 a part-time teacher at various Soweto art centres; from 1983 Head of the Fine Arts Department, FUBA. 1981 visited Athens, Greece and Palermo, Sicily. 1986 spent six months in Paris.
Exhibitions He has participated in numerous group exhibitions from 1952 throughout SA and in West Germany, Israel, Greece, the UK, the USA, France, Australia and Sicily; 1965 Piccadilly Gallery, London, African Painters and Sculptors from Johannesburg; 1966 Lidchi Gallery, Johannesburg, first of over 12 solo exhibitions held in Johannesburg; 1979 Contemporary African Art in SA, touring; 1981 Standard Bank, Soweto, Black Art Today Exhibition; 1982 National Gallery, Gaborone, Botswana, Exhibition of SA Art; 1988 Johannesburg Art Gallery, Vita Art Now.

Awards 1978 First Prize, Mariannhill Institute; 1982 Second Prize Sculpture, University of Zululand African Arts Festival; 1983 First Prize Graphics, University of Zululand African Arts Festival.

Public Commissions Works in the Tladi Anglican Church, Soweto in 1960 and in the Heidelberg Anglican Church in 1972.

Represented Africana Museum, Johannesburg; National Gallery, Gaborone, Botswana; Sandton Municipal Collection; University of Fort Hare; University of Zululand.

References BSAK 2; AASA; Echoes of African Art; *SA Panorama* July 1982 & June 1983.

SILKE Eris

Born 1947 Hungary.

Resided in SA from 1970.

A self-taught painter of fantasy people and stories set in a timeless world. Works in acrylic and pencil. 1982–85 a series of paintings inspired by the writing of Edgar Allan Poe.

Exhibitions She has participated in several group exhibitions from 1983 held in SA; 1977 SAAA Gallery, Cape Town, first of six solo exhibitions held in Cape Town and Johannesburg.

Represented SA National Gallery, Cape Town.

Reference *Gallery* Winter 1985.

SIMMERS (Robert) Melvin

Born 1907 Hampstead, London, England.

Resided in SA from 1924.

A painter of landscapes, seascapes, portraits, figures, genre, still life and wildlife. Works in oil, acrylic, watercolour, gouache, ink, wash, pencil and charcoal.

Studies 1925–31 Michaelis School of Fine Art, under Professor John Wheatley (qv) and Grace Wheatley (qv), awarded the Michaelis Prize in 1927; 1949–50 Slade School of Art, London, under William Coldstream (*b*.1908).

Profile 1933–47 a member of the SA Society of Artists, previously a member of the SAAA. 1933–36 secretary to Professor John Wheatley (qv), 1936–39 junior lecturer, 1940–72 lecturer in drawing and anatomy at the Michaelis School of Fine Art. 1933–39 art critic for *The Cape Times*. A number of illustrations for Longmans Green Publishers and numerous stage and costume designs for the theatre and ballet. A ballet dancer and actor. Numerous visits to London.

Exhibitions Participated in numerous group exhibitions from 1927 in SA and London; *c*.1931 Darters Gallery, Cape Town, first of several solo exhibitions held in SA and the UK.

Represented SA National Gallery, Cape Town.

References Art SA; SAP&S; SAP&D; BSAK 1 & 2; AASA.

SIMMONDS Victor F

Born 1909 Apsley, Hertfordshire, England.
Resided in SA from 1936.
A painter of landscapes, horses, seascapes, portraits and still life. Works in oil, watercolour, pencil and wash.

Studies 1925 privately under Philip Brandon Jones (1876–1944) in Berkhampsted, Hertfordshire.

Profile A member of the NSA during the 1950s and the Brush and Chisel Club *c.*1959. 1929–31 the vocalist in a dance band in England. 1945–51 lived in Durban; 1952–55 in the Orange Free State; 1955–58 in Durban; 1958–60 in the Orange Free State; 1961–62 in Pretoria; 1962–64 in Harrismith, Natal; from 1964 in the Royal Natal National Park. 1951 travelled extensively in Europe.

Exhibitions He has participated in several group exhibitions from 1949 to 1964 in SA and once in the UK in 1951; 1949 Tudor Galleries, Durban, first of 27 solo exhibitions held throughout SA and from 1964 exclusively at the Royal Natal National Park Hotel.

SIMON Edwine Simone

Born 1939 Luanshya, Northern Rhodesia (Zambia).
Resided in SA from 1942 and in the Cape from 1954.
Mainly a graphic artist producing etchings, silkscreens and woodcuts. Has also painted in oil, acrylic and mixed media.

Studies 1958–63 Michaelis School of Fine Art, under Katrine Harries (qv), May Hillhouse (qv), Lippy Lipshitz (qv) and Maurice van Essche (qv), gaining a BA(FA); 1964–65 on a MacIver Scholarship for Overseas Study at the Institute of Education, University of London, under Alfred Harris, gaining a Post-Graduate Certificate in Education, and part-time external study in the Etching Department of the Central School of Art, London.

Profile A founder member of the Artists Guild, Cape Town; a member of the SAAA and in 1978–80 a committee member for the Western Cape Branch. 1966–70 Assistant Art Director of the Cape Town Art Centre. From 1971 has taught at the Ruth Prowse Art Centre, Cape Town, becoming Vice-Principal in 1975 when it was renamed the Ruth Prowse School of Art; 1972–81 a part-time lecturer in design in the Occupational Therapy Department of the University of Cape Town; 1976 a part-time lecturer in graphics at the Mowbray Training College, Cape Town; 1982 a visiting lecturer in silkscreen techniques at the Cape Technikon. Has written articles and drawn illustrations for various periodicals and a number of book covers. Published two portfolios: 1976 photolithographs entitled "War & Terrorism" and in 1979 silkscreens entitled "Baxter". 1964 and 1968 visited Israel, the UK and parts of Europe.

Exhibitions She has participated in numerous group exhibitions from 1959 throughout SA and in Zimbabwe and Belgium; 1969 Cape Town Art Centre, first of six solo exhibitions held in Cape Town; 1981 Republic Festival Exhibition.

Represented National Museum, Bloemfontein.

References Register SA & SWA; BSAK 1 & 2; AASA; *Artlook* December 1971.

SIMONS Bridget Anne

Born 1953 Wynberg, Cape Town.

A painter of Cape Town buildings and harbour and of figures at/through real windows (assemblage). Works in oil, watercolour and mixed media.

Studies 1971–75 and 1979 Michaelis School of Fine Art, under Stanley Pinker (qv), Stephen de Villiers (qv) and Cecil Skotnes (qv), gaining a BA(FA) in 1975 and an Advanced Diploma in Fine Art in 1979.

Profile 1981–84 an associate member of the Artists Guild, Cape Town and from 1984 a full member. 1976–78 taught at the Frank Joubert Art Centre, Cape Town; 1980–83 a lecturer at the Ruth Prowse School of Art, Cape Town. 1971–72 visited the USA; 1974 and 1985 the UK and Europe; 1982 visited Australia.

Exhibitions She has participated in several group exhibitions from 1975 in Cape Town and in Windhoek, SWA/Namibia; 1976 SAAA Gallery, Cape Town, first of three solo exhibitions in the Cape.

Represented SA National Gallery, Cape Town.

SIMPSON John Churchill ARIBA MIA

Born 1911 Durban.

A painter of cityscapes, landscapes, seascapes, shipping, industrial developments and mining buildings, recording both past and current scenes. Works in watercolour, oil, acrylic, gouache, ink, wash, pencil and in charcoal.

Studies External studies at the Witwatersrand Architectural Association School of Architecture; Natal Technical College, gaining an Emma Smith Scholarship for Overseas Studies; further architectural studies in London.

Profile An Associate of the Royal Institute of British Architects. A Life Member of the Institute of SA Architects and President 1958–59. Book illustrations for *The Story of the Rand Club*, 1976, Johannesburg, and *Kalahari Wealth*, 1977, Purnell & Son, Cape Town.

Exhibitions He has participated in several group exhibitions in Durban and Johannesburg from 1938; 1973 Everard Read Gallery, Johannesburg, first of three solo exhibitions.

Represented Africana Museum, Johannesburg.

Public Commissions 1983, 1984 and 1985 several watercolours for the Natal Provincial Council; numerous corporate commissions.

References BSAK 2; AASA.

SIMPSON William Henry

Born 1843 UK.

Active until *c.*1914.

Resided in SA from 1881.

A painter of landscapes. Worked in oil and watercolour.

Studies South Kensington School of Art, London; Royal Academy Schools, London.

Profile A member of the SA Society of Artists. 1901–14 a member of the Grahamstown Fine Arts Association. 1881–1904 first Superintendent of the Grahamstown School of Art.

Exhibitions Until 1880 participated in group exhibitions in London; participated in group exhibitions in Grahamstown and Port Elizabeth from 1883.

Represented SA National Gallery, Cape Town.

References Pict Afr; DBA; SESA; AASA; *ANN* vol 13.

SINCLAIR Jan

Born 1935 London, England.

Resided in SA from 1981.

A self-taught painter of still life, particularly flowers. Works in oil.

Profile From 1982 a member of the SAAA. 1961–64 Head of the Young Artists Workshop, Salisbury, Rhodesia (Harare, Zimbabwe). 1946–81 lived in Rhodesia/Zimbabwe.

Exhibitions She has participated in several group exhibitions from 1967 in Mozambique, Zimbabwe, the UK and SA; 1971 Lidchi International Gallery, Salisbury, Rhodesia (Harare, Zimbabwe), first of seven solo exhibitions, two of which were held in Johannesburg.

Publication by Sinclair A *Rhodesian 12 months of Flowers*, 1978, Books of Rhodesia, Bulawayo.

References BSAK 2; *Garden & Home* July 1976 & November 1982.

SIOPIS Penelope

Born 1953 Vryburg, Northern Cape.

A painter of interiors and still life. Works in oil, pastel and mixed media. A series of tables laden with food and objects. 1986 "Act II" series, set in the Paris Opera.

Studies 1971–74 Rhodes University, gaining a BA(FA); 1975–76 Rhodes University, gaining an MFA with distinction; 1978–79 on a British Council Scholarship at Portsmouth Polytechnic, England, where attained a Post-Graduate Diploma.

Profile 1980–83 a lecturer at the Natal Technikon; from 1984 a lecturer in the Fine Arts Department of the University of the Witwatersrand. 1986 spent eight months at Cité Internationale des Arts, Paris.

Exhibitions She has participated in group exhibitions from 1975 throughout SA and in Switzerland, the USA and West Germany; 1978 Collectors Gallery, Johannesburg, first of seven solo exhibitions, of which two have been held in the UK; 1982 Cape Town Triennial; 1985 Cape Town Triennial; 1985 Tributaries, touring SA and West Germany; 1986 Goodman Gallery, Johannesburg, joint exhibition with Peter Schütz (qv); 1987 and 1988 Johannesburg Art Gallery, Vita Art Now.

Awards 1985 Merit Award, Cape Town Triennial; 1986 Volkskas Atelier Award; 1986 Anderson Capelli Research Award, University of the Witwatersrand; 1987 Vita Art Now Quarterly Award Winner and Merit Award Winner.

Represented Durban Art Gallery; Johannesburg Art Gallery; King George VI Art Gallery, Port Elizabeth; Natal Technikon; Pretoria Art Museum; Rhodes University; Roodepoort Museum; SA National Gallery, Cape Town; University of the Witwatersrand.
References AASA; *Gallery* Summer 1985; *SA Arts Calendar* Summer 1985–86 & Winter 1986; *De Kat* December/January 1986 & May 1986.

SITHOLE Lucas
Born 1931 KwaThema, Springs, Transvaal.
A sculptor of figures, heads, animals and mythological beasts and birds. Works in wood, bronze, stone and liquid steel.
Studies 1948 awarded a scholarship to Vlakfontein Technical College, Transvaal; 1959–60 Polly Street Art Centre, Johannesburg, under Cecil Skotnes (qv).
Profile Works as a full-time artist on the Swaziland/Zululand border.
Exhibitions He has participated in numerous group exhibitions from 1960 throughout SA and in London, Venice, Basle, Botswana and Zimbabwe; 1962 Adler Fielding Gallery, Johannesburg, joint exhibition with Louis Maqhubela (qv) and Gerard Sekoto (qv); 1965 Piccadilly Gallery, London, African Painters and Sculptors from Johannesburg; 1966 Adler Fielding Gallery, Johannesburg, first of many solo exhibitions; 1979 Rand Afrikaans University and Pretoria Art Museum, Retrospective Exhibition; 1979 Contemporary African Art in SA, touring; 1981 Standard Bank, Soweto, Black Art Today Exhibition; 1981 Republic Festival Exhibition; 1985 Tributaries, touring SA and West Germany; 1987 and 1988 Johannesburg Art Gallery, Vita Art Now.
Award 1968 Sculpture Prize, Venice Bienale.
Represented Durban Art Gallery; Museum für Volkerkunde, Frankfurt, West Germany; National Gallery, Gaborone, Botswana; Pretoria Art Museum; Rand Afrikaans University; SA National Gallery, Cape Town; University of Fort Hare; University of the Orange Free State; University of South Africa; University of the Witwatersrand.
Public Commissions Works for St Augustus Anglican Church, Thaba 'Nchu, Bophuthatswana; 1971 Wounded Buffalo, Bracken Mines, Evander, Transvaal.
References F F Haenggi, *Lucas Sithole 1958–79*, 1979, Gallery 21, Johannesburg; SESA; BSAK 1 & 2; *Who's Who in Southern Africa*, 1977–78 and 1978–79, Johannesburg; SA Art; Echoes of African Art; *Artlook* October 1970; *SA Panorama* August 1975; *African Art* August 1980, Los Angeles, California, USA; *Informa* December 1983.

SKEEN Julia Georgina St John (Mrs Marn)
Born 1956 Umtali, Rhodesia (Mutare, Zimbabwe).
Resided in SA from 1976.
A painter of figures and landscapes. Works in oil, watercolour, ink, wash and pencil.
Studies 1976–78 Rhodes University, under Professor Brian Bradshaw (qv).

Profile 1976–78 a member of the Grahamstown Group. 1983–84 taught privately through the Grassroots Gallery, Westville, Natal. From 1980 has lived in and painted the people and the scenery around Botha's Hill, Natal.
Exhibitions She has participated in several group exhibitions from 1979; 1984 Grassroots Gallery, Westville, solo exhibition.

SKILLETER Pat

Born 1922 Durban.
A painter of landscapes. Works in oil.
Studies Natal Technical College, under Eric Byrd (qv) and Merlyn Evans (qv).
Profile Travelled extensively in Europe and Africa. Wife of Philip Bawcombe (qv), with whom she has exhibited.
Exhibitions She has participated in group exhibitions from 1952 held throughout SA; 1957 and 1960 Greenwich Art Gallery, Johannesburg, solo exhibitions.
Represented Ann Bryant Gallery, East London.
Public Commissions Murals in Government buildings.
Reference Collectors' Guide.

SKOTNES Cecil Edwin Frans

Born 1926 East London.
An artist working in oil, acrylic, watercolour, gouache, stucco, ink, wash, pencil and charcoal. Engraved and incised painted-wood panels. A muralist and graphic artist. He depicts figures, still life, portraits and landscapes, and produces abstract works.
Studies 1946 under Henrich Steiner in Florence, Italy, as well as attending classes at the Witwatersrand Technical College; 1947–50 University of the Witwatersrand, under Professor Heather Martienssen (1915–79), Douglas Portway (qv) and Charles Argent (qv), gaining a BA(FA).
Profile 1953 appointed Secretary of the Johannesburg Local Committee for Non-European Adult Education and took control of the Polly Street Adult Centre, Johannesburg, establishing a black urban art school; 1963 appointed President of the SA Council of Artists; 1963 a founder member of the Amadlozi Group; 1966–68 Head of Damelin Art College; 1970 co-founder, with Walter Battiss (qv), of the African Council for Art; 1981 a part-time lecturer at the University of Stellenbosch; 1981 began art classes in Nyanga and District Six, Cape Town, for black artists; 1981 external examiner for the Michaelis School of Fine Art. In 1956 worked with Sydney Kumalo (qv) in the Kroonstad Roman Catholic Mission Church. Illustrated a book of poems entitled *Tales*, by Sinclair Beiles, 1972, Gryphon Poets, Johannesburg. 1973 produced a portfolio of 43 original three-colour woodcuts entitled "The Assassination of Shaka" with poems by Stephen Gray, published in 1974 by McGraw-Hill, Johannesburg;

1974 produced "The White Monday Disaster", a portfolio with Stephen Gray; 1975 "Baudelaire's Voyage to the Cape", a portfolio with Stephen Gray; 1975 memorial portfolio on the poet Charles Eglington. 1966 designed the Republic Festival commemorative series of stamps. Numerous illustrations for books and magazines. Has a great interest in music; appointed Chairman of the Johannesburg Bantu Music Festival in 1955 and has organised further festivals and created a music library. 1963 toured the USA; 1975 visited Belgium as a guest of the Belgian Government. Has lived in the Cape from 1978. 1982 visited Jerusalem as a guest of the Jerusalem Foundation. Father of John Skotnes (qv) and Pippa Skotnes (qv).

Exhibitions He has participated in numerous group exhibitions from 1948 in SA, Belgium, Italy, Austria, Zimbabwe, North and South America, Yugoslavia, the UK, Portugal, Spain, The Netherlands, West Germany, Greece and Israel; 1954 Whippman's Gallery, Johannesburg, joint exhibition with Larry Scully (qv); 1957 Pretoria Art Centre, first of 23 solo exhibitions held in SA; 1960 and 1964 Quadrennial Exhibitions; 1965 Grosvenor Gallery, London, first solo exhibition held in the UK; 1966 Grosvenor Gallery, London, joint exhibition with Sydney Kumalo (qv); 1972 Goodman Gallery, Johannesburg, joint exhibition of tapestries with Bettie Cilliers-Barnard (qv); 1972 Pretoria Art Museum, Retrospective Exhibition; 1974 Durban Art Gallery, exhibition of "The Assassination of Shaka"; 1978 National Museum, Bloemfontein, joint exhibition with Aileen Lipkin (qv) and Wendy Vincent (qv); 1979 National Museum, Bloemfontein, joint exhibition with Thelma Chait (qv), Olivia Scholnick (qv) and Lorraine Edelstein (qv); 1985 Goodman Gallery, Johannesburg, joint exhibition with Sydney Kumalo (qv), Ezrom Legae (qv) and Edoardo Villa (qv); 1985 Tributaries, touring SA and West Germany; 1987 Goodman Gallery, Johannesburg, joint exhibition with John Skotnes (qv); 1988 Johannesburg Art Gallery, Vita Art Now.

Awards 1965 Chamber of Mines Gold Medal, Transvaal Academy; 1968 Gold Medal, SA Breweries Biennial; 1972 Gold Medal, Third International Biennial of Graphic Art, Florence, Italy; 1976 Medal of Honour for Painting, SA Akademie vir Wetenskap en Kuns; 1976 set of commemorative medallions, 1820 Settlers National Monument Foundation for contribution to art in SA.

Represented Ann Bryant Gallery, East London; Durban Art Gallery; Hester Rupert Art Museum, Graaff-Reinet; Johannesburg Art Gallery; Johannesburg Central Library; Kettering Gallery, Northamptonshire, UK; King George VI Art Gallery, Port Elizabeth; National Museum, Bloemfontein; Pretoria Art Museum; Rand Afrikaans University; Royal Belgian Library Collection, Brussels, Belgium; Royal Danish Art Museum, Copenhagen, Denmark; Royal Museum of Fine Art, Denmark; SA National Gallery, Cape Town; Tatham Art Gallery, Pietermaritzburg; Uffizi Print Cabinet, Florence, Italy; University of Cape Town; University of the Orange Free State; University of South Africa; University of Stellenbosch; University of Uppsala, Sweden; University of the Witwatersrand; William Humphreys Art Gallery, Kimberley.

Public Commissions 1961 large mural, Thabong Catholic Mission Church, Orange Free State; 1965 large mural, Kroonstad Roman Catholic Cathedral, Orange Free State; 1966 large mural, Western Bank, African Life Centre, Johannesburg; 1984 SA Airways 50th Anniversary; 1985 carved panels, the Sand du Plessis Theatre, Bloemfontein; 1985 works in Kimberley Library; 1985–86 murals, 1820 Settlers Monument, Grahamstown.

References Art SA; SAA; 20C SA Art; SAP&S; SAP&D; AMC7; SSAP; BSAK 1 & 2; Our Art 3; SA Art; Oxford Companion to 20C Art; 3Cs; AASA; LSAA; *Artlook* February 1968, February 1969, January 1972, May 1972, April 1974, April 1975 & August/September 1975; *SA Panorama* July 1972, February 1974, June 1975 & January 1984; *Habitat* no 7, 1974 & no 56, 1983; *Gallery* Summer 1981 & Winter 1983.

SKOTNES John Anthony

Born 1952 Johannesburg.

A sculptor of figurative, mythological and anthropomorphical pieces. Works in bronze, copper, silver and brass.

Studies 1974–78 apprenticeship under Kurt Donau, qualifying as a goldsmith.

Profile 1975–83 a teacher at Yeoville recreation art classes, Johannesburg and 1978–79 part-time at a children's home. 1980 taught jewellery apprentices at the Germiston Technical College, Transvaal, and from 1983 at the Ruth Prowse School of Art, Cape Town. A goldsmith and silversmith. Has travelled in Europe and extensively in SA. Son of Cecil Skotnes (qv) and brother of Pippa Skotnes (qv).

Exhibitions He has participated in group exhibitions from 1986; 1986 Goodman Gallery, Johannesburg, solo exhibition; 1987 Johannesburg Art Gallery, Vita Art Now; 1987 Goodman Gallery, Johannesburg, joint exhibition with Cecil Skotnes (qv).

Public Commission 1986 Bronze Horse-Drawn Tram, Parade, Cape Town.

SKOTNES Pippa Ann

Born 1957 Johannesburg.

A printmaker depicting landscapes, interiors and objects revealing aspects of the South African way of life. 1983 a portfolio entitled "Imprints—Man's Impact on the SA Landscape", 1985 a portfolio entitled "Shelter".

Studies 1974–82 Michaelis School of Fine Art, gaining a BA(FA) in 1979, a Post-Graduate Diploma in Etching with distinction in 1980, and an MA(FA), with distinction, in 1983. For her studies she has been awarded the following scholarships: MacIver 1980, 1981 and 1982; Jules Kramer 1980 and 1982; Human Sciences Research Council Grant 1981; the Hugh and Win Walker Scholarship and the Harold Crossley Travel Grant, enabling her to go on a study tour of the USA and Europe 1981–82.

Profile From 1979 a member of the Artists Guild, Cape Town. From 1984 a part-time lecturer and MA(FA) Supervisor at the Michaelis School of Fine Art. From 1985 has held the John Platter wine label commission. Married to David Brown (qv); daughter of Cecil Skotnes (qv) and sister of John Skotnes (qv).

Exhibitions She has participated in many group exhibitions from 1980 in SA, the UK and the Republic of China; 1981 Goodman Gallery, Johannesburg, first of nine solo exhibitions; 1985 Tributaries, touring SA and West Germany; 1987 and 1988 Johannesburg Art Gallery, Vita Art Now.

Award 1987 H G Steyn Award for Excellence.

Represented Durban Art Gallery; Johannesburg Art Gallery; Pretoria Art Museum; Roodepoort Museum; SA National Gallery, Cape Town; University of Cape Town; University of South Africa; University of Stellenbosch; University of the Western Cape; University of the Witwatersrand.
References LSAA; *Fair Lady* September 1986; *Style* May 1988; *ADA* no 5, 1988.

SLINGSBY Robert Bevan

Born 1955 Cape Town.
A painter and a sculptor of landscapes, figures and abstract pieces. Works in oil, gouache, charcoal, stone, wood and synthetic resins. A graphic artist.
Studies 1976–81 Vrije Akademie, The Hague, The Netherlands, under George Lampe.
Profile A member of the SAAA. He is involved in the recording of the Rock Art of Southern Africa.
Exhibitions He has participated in numerous group exhibitions in SA, 14 in The Netherlands and two in West Germany; 1976 Gallery International, Cape Town, first of five solo exhibitions held in SA and six in The Netherlands; 1982 Cape Town Triennial; 1985 Cape Town Triennial; 1985 Tributaries, touring SA and West Germany.
Award 1975 New Signatures Award, SAAA.
Represented Artoteek, Dutch Municipal Collection, The Netherlands; Pietersburg Collection; Rand Afrikaans University; University of the Witwatersrand; William Humphreys Art Gallery, Kimberley.
References AASA; *De Kat* December/January 1986.

SLOMOWITZ Ilana

Born 1941 Johannesburg.
A ceramicist working in clay. Creates large murals.
Studies 1958–61 Witwatersrand Technical College, under George Boys (qv), Andrew Verster (qv), Joyce Leonard (qv) and John Edwards, gaining a Diploma in Commercial and Fine Arts.
Profile Has taught art privately. 1981 illustrations for Jill Johnson's book *South Africa Speaks*, Ad. Donker, Johannesburg.
Exhibitions She has participated in group exhibitions from 1961 in SA and Italy; 1962 Egon Guenther Gallery, Johannesburg, first solo exhibition.
Represented University of South Africa.
Public Commissions 1971 mural, City Centre, Johannesburg; 1975 mural, Cereal Centre, Johannesburg; 1982 mural, Jan Smuts Airport, Johannesburg and many commissions for corporate headquarters.
References AASA; *Artlook* February 1974; *Sgraffiti* Spring 1975.

SMAIL Johlyne (Jo)

Born 1943 Durban.
A painter of landscapes and abstract pictures. Works in acrylic, pencil, charcoal, chalk and oil sticks.

Studies 1975 gained a National Diploma in Art and Design and in 1978 a Higher Diploma in Art and Design from the Witwatersrand Technical College; 1982 studied at the Maryland Art Institute, Baltimore, USA.

Profile 1975 an art teacher at Pridwin School, Johannesburg; 1976 a part-time lecturer, 1977–81 a full-time lecturer at the Witwatersrand Technical College (Technikon); 1981–82 a lecturer at the University of the Witwatersrand. 1977 toured in Europe.

Exhibitions She has participated in group exhibitions from 1974 in SA and in 1978 in Israel and the USA; 1977 Fabian Fine Art, Cape Town, first of several solo exhibitions held in Cape Town and Johannesburg; 1978 University of the Witwatersrand, solo exhibition; 1981 Republic Festival Exhibition; 1984–85 Four Johannesburg Painters, a touring exhibition with Ilona Anderson (qv), Ricky Burnett (qv) and Robert Hodgins (qv); 1985 Cape Town Triennial; 1985 Tributaries, touring SA and West Germany.

Awards 1975 Eben Coetzee Award, Witwatersrand Technical College; 1975 Cambridge Shirt Award, Art SA Today.

Represented Durban Art Gallery; Johannesburg Art Gallery; Pretoria Art Museum; SA National Gallery, Cape Town; University of the Orange Free State; University of South Africa; University of Stellenbosch; University of the Western Cape; University of the Witwatersrand.

SMALLWOOD Heide-Marie

Born 1941 Kiel, Germany.
Resided in SA from 1965.
A sculptor of abstract pieces. Works in ceramics and vitreous enamels.

Studies 1962–65 Sir John Cass School of Art, London, under Carol Stewart; 1962–65 served an apprenticeship under Allan Wallwork, Greenwich, London.

Profile From 1972 a member of the NSA; from 1976 a member of the APSA. Since 1969 she has taught art privately. 1969–72 made vitreous enamel panels which were used on architectural façades and as interior furnishings. A potter. From 1980 a flautist in a Regimental Band and in the Durban City Orchestra. Has travelled in the UK, in Europe and throughout SA.

Exhibitions She has participated in numerous group exhibitions from 1972 in SA; 1981 Pretoria, first solo exhibition.

Represented Pots in Durban Art Gallery; Potchefstroom Museum.

Public Commission 1986 ceramic mural, Potchefstroom University for CHE.

SMART Desmond James

Born 1953 Pretoria.
A sculptor working in bronze, stone, ciment fondu and wood. Numerous pencil and ink drawings. Depicts landscapes and wildlife and sculpts abstract pieces.

Studies 1974–76 Natal Technical College (Technikon), under Gavin Younge (qv) and Peter Schütz (qv), gaining a National Diploma in Fine Art; 1977–78 Michaelis School of Fine Art, under Gavin Younge (qv) and Bruce Arnott (qv), where attained a Higher Diploma in Fine Art.

Profile A sculpture technician at the Natal Technikon.

Exhibitions He has participated in several group exhibitions from 1985.

SMIT Anton Sydney

Born 1954 Boksburg, Transvaal.

A self-taught sculptor of figures, heads, portraits and abstract pieces. Works in stone, ciment fondu, wood, bronze, ceramics, polymers and epoxy resins. A painter of aeroscapes, landscapes and abstract pictures. Works in oil, acrylic, ink, wash, pencil and charcoal. Combines the two in relief-painted ceramic murals and sculptures. 1981 a series of seven sculptures entitled "The Actor —Legends of the Mind".

Profile A member of the SAAA. A designer of pots for the Anorica Company, Pretoria.

Exhibitions He has participated in numerous group exhibitions from 1976 in SA; 1979 the Workshop Gallery, Pretoria, first of nine solo exhibitions held in SA.

Award 1979 First Prize, New Signatures Exhibition, SAAA, Pretoria.

Represented Pretoria Art Museum.

SMIT Peter

Born 1923 De Aar, Cape Province.

A photo-realist painter and graphic artist. Works in oil, acrylic, watercolour, gouache, ink, wash, pencil, charcoal and in various graphic media. Sculpts in wood.

Studies 1986 studying for a BA(FA) through the University of South Africa.

Profile From 1981 an Associate of the WSSA; from 1982 a member of the South Eastern and International Federation of Art Societies, England; also a member of the SAAA.

Exhibitions He has participated in several group exhibitions from 1980 throughout SA and twice in London.

SMIT Pierre Jacques Reverend

Born 1863 Leiderdorp, The Netherlands.

Died 1960 Pretoria.

Resided in SA from 1903.

A painter of birds, animals and reptiles.

Studies Taught by Joseph Smit (his father), a wildlife illustrator at the British Museum, London, and his colleague Joseph Wolf (1820–99).

Profile A member of the Eastern Province Society of Arts and Crafts. Numerous illustrations for books and catalogues in Europe, India and Egypt. Illustrations (from photographs) for *A Naturalist in the Transvaal*, by W L Distant, 1892, London; 1939–49, 105 colour plates of snakes for Dr Watt of the University of the Witwatersrand, used by Dr V Fitzsimons to aid his illustrations in *Snakes of SA*, 1962, Johannesburg; 24 colour plates for *Mammals of South Africa*, by Dr Austin Robert, 1951, published by the Trustees of "The Mammals of SA Book Fund", Cape Town, with a second edition in 1954. A Wesleyan Minister. 1865–1903 lived in the UK; 1906–32 in the Orange Free State and the Cape; 1932–53 in Port Elizabeth, where he retired from the Church.

Exhibitions Exhibited in the Eastern Province from *c.*1932; 1963 MacFadyen Hall, Pretoria, Centenary Exhibition.
Represented University of the Witwatersrand.
References SAA; DSAB; SESA; BSAK 1; AASA.

SMIT Wynand

Born 1922 Carolina District, Transvaal.
A painter and sculptor of landscapes, genre, figures and abstract pieces. Works in oil, acrylic, watercolour, pencil, bronze, stone and wood.
Studies 1940–46 University of Pretoria, under Professor A L Meiring; 1945 Witwatersrand Technical College, under James Gardner (qv) and Elizabeth Macadam (qv).
Profile 1957–63 a lecturer at the University of Pretoria. 1964 a committee member of the SA Art Academy; from 1968 a member of the SAAA, presently a Council Member of the Northern Transvaal Branch; from 1972 on the City of Pretoria Aesthetics Committee; 1973–86 a member of the State Art Advisory Committee (Johannesburg). A trained, practising architect and a member of the Institute of Architects and of the Council of Industrial Design from 1974. Involved in theatre designs as well as book and periodical illustrations. 1947–52 also involved in pottery. From 1954 has written articles on architecture. Has travelled extensively in North and South America, Canada, Europe and the Far East.
Exhibitions He has participated in numerous group exhibitions from 1964 in SA.
Public Commission 1983 mural, in collaboration with W Heimans, Jan Smuts Airport, Johannesburg.

SMITH Christopher Webb

Born 1793 Groomhill, Camberwell, England.
Died 1871 Florence, Italy.
Resided in SA 1837–39.
A painter of Cape scenes, figures and flowers. Worked in watercolour and pencil. Numerous sketches of the Cape.
Profile A civil servant in the Dutch East India Company. Based in India, but sent to SA on sick leave. 1811–42 lived in Bengal, India, where founded the Behar School of Athens with Charles D'Oyly (qv) in 1824 and practised lithography. 1843–45 in England; 1845–71 lived in Florence. Passed through Cape Town in 1842.
Exhibition 1964 Cambridge, England, Works of C W Smith Exhibition.
Represented House of Assembly, Cape Town; Library of Parliament, Cape Town; Three Albums in Newton Library, Cambridge, UK, consisting of "1815–31 Birds of India", 295 watercolours with descriptions; "1829–31 Indian Birds & Scenery", 191 watercolours with landscapes by C D'Oyly (qv); "1839–59 Birds, Flowers and Scenery of The Cape of Good Hope", 58 watercolours accompanied by notes.
Publications by Smith in collaboration with D'Oyly The Feathered Game of Hindostan, 1828 and Oriental Ornithology, 1829.

References A Gordon-Brown, *Christopher Webb Smith, An Artist at the Cape of Good Hope, 1837–39*, 1965, Howard Timmins, Cape Town; DSAB; Pict Afr; BSAK 1; SA Art; 3Cs; *ANN* December 1963; *Geographical Magazine* December 1963, London; *SA Panorama* July 1969; *Apollo* October 1975, London.

SMITH Johannes Anthoine

Born 1886 Aberdeen, Cape Province.
Died 1954 George, Cape Province.
A self-taught artist of seascapes and landscapes. Worked in oil. An etcher.
Profile A member of the Eastern Province Society of Arts; a Council Member of the SA Society of Artists. 1932 a founder member of the National Academy of Art (SA). 1933 a Government nominee for the Board of Trustees of the SA National Gallery, Cape Town. 1915 worked for a newspaper in Aberdeen, Cape Province; 1916–25 worked for Afrikaans periodicals and newspapers in Potchefstroom, Graaff-Reinet and Pietermaritzburg; 1925–40 worked for *Die Burger* newspaper, becoming the art critic. Father of Le Roux Smith Le Roux (qv).
Exhibitions Participated in group exhibitions in SA; 1929 Cape Town, first solo exhibition.
Represented Rand Afrikaans University; SA National Gallery, Cape Town; University of South Africa; University of Stellenbosch.
Publications by Smith Boer en Brit, 1917, *Van Bloedrivier na Paardekraal*, 1918 and *Ek Rebelleer*, 1939 (autobiographical).
References *The Arts in SA*, edited by WHK, 1933–34, The Knox Printing & Publishing Company, Durban; SAA; BSAK 1 & 2; AASA.

SMITH John

Born 1944 Worcester, Cape Province.
A painter of landscapes, seascapes, still life, genre and figures. Works in oil, watercolour, ink, wash, pencil, charcoal, airbrush and mixed media.
Studies 1972–73 privately under Johan Oldert (qv); 1973–74 a correspondence course in oil and watercolour; 1974 part-time at the Natal Technical College. He has also had assistance from Titta Fasciotti (qv).
Profile A member of the WSSA; of D'ARTS; and in 1974 Chairman of the Highway Art Group, Durban. Teaches art privately in Durban. A commercial artist and keen photographer. Two sets of prints of his work have been published by Howard Swan, Johannesburg.
Exhibitions He has participated in numerous group exhibitions in SA; 1976 Graham Gallery, Durban, first of six solo exhibitions held in SA.

SMITH Margaret Mary Professor

Born 1916 Indwe, Cape Province.
Died 1987 Grahamstown, Cape Province.
A self-taught painter of fish.

Profile Her paintings of fish have been included in *Die Afrikaanse Woordeboek*, the *Standard Encyclopedia of Southern Africa*, and *The Sea Fishes of Southern Africa*, by Professor J L B Smith (her husband) first published in 1949 and with subsequent editions, the latest of which she co-edited with P C Heemstra and which is published under the title *Smith's Sea Fishes*, 1986, Macmillan (SA), Johannesburg. She was the illustrator and co-author, with her husband, of *Old Fourlegs: the story of the Coelacanth*, 1956, and *The Fishes of the Seychelles*, 1963, and *Fishes of the Tsitsikama Coastal National Park*, 1967. Her illustrations also appeared in Rhodes University *Ichthyological Bulletins* Nos 1–26. She was the Director of the Institute of Ichthyology at Rhodes University until 1982, and thereafter Emeritus Professor. In 1987 she received the Order of Merit, Class I, Gold Medal awarded by the State President, for her services to science.
References SAA; *Who's Who of Southern Africa* 1987–88.

SMITH Richard John Templeton

Born 1947 Edinburgh, Scotland.
Resided in SA from 1958.
A painter of landscapes, seascapes, portraits, figures, still life and abstract pictures. Works in oil, acrylic, gouache, watercolour, ink, wash, pencil and charcoal. A graphic artist.
Studies 1966–68 Witwatersrand Technical College, gaining a National Diploma in Fine Art.
Profile 1968–70 a cartoonist for *The Sunday Times*; 1970–72 for *Punch* as well as animations for BBC Television; 1972–76 a cartoonist for the *Rand Daily Mail* and *The Sunday Tribune*; 1977–87 illustrations for *The Sunday Express, The Financial Mail, The Bloody Horse, Optima* and *Leadership SA*. Has designed book covers for Ravan Press, Bateleur Press and Macmillan (SA), Johannesburg. 1970–72 lived in England, 1976–77 visited Greece. 1987 visited the USA and the UK. Married to Liane Dutilleux (qv).
Exhibitions He has participated in several group exhibitions from 1970 in SA and the USA; 1972 Arts Theatre Club, London, first solo exhibition; has held two solo exhibitions in SA since his return; 1985 Cape Town Triennial; 1986 Everard Read Gallery, Johannesburg, joint exhibition with Paul Stopforth (qv) and Hillary Graham (qv).
Awards 1980 and 1983 Standard Bank Cartoonist of the Year Award.
Publication by Smith *Smith & Abbot's Greatest Hits*, a book of cartoons, 1974.
References SASSK; *Habitat* no 31, 1978.

SMITH Sylvia Rose

Born 1923 Sea Point, Cape Town.
A painter of landscapes, seascapes, still life, figures, birds and architectural subjects. Works in oil, acrylic, watercolour, ink, wash, pencil and in charcoal.
Studies 1939 art classes under Florence Zerffi (qv).

Profile From 1980 a member of the Hermanus Art Society, of which she was Chairman 1985–87. From 1982 a member of the WSSA and from 1985 of the SA Society of Artists. A trained architect who practised in the Cape until 1979. 1984 illustrated Maureen Cussins' poems in *Hermanus Sings*, Innerspace Publishers. 1949–59 lived in Worcester, thereafter at Hermanus, Cape Province.
Exhibitions She has participated in several group exhibitions in the Cape; 1981 Hermanus, first of six solo exhibitions held there.

SMITHARD George Salisbury

Born 1873 Litchurch, Derbyshire, England.
Died 1919 Johannesburg.
Resided in SA from 1901.
A painter of landscapes, figures and portraits. Worked in watercolour, pastel, oil and gouache, a number of pencil and charcoal drawings.
Studies On a bursary at the Slade School of Art, London; at the Académie Julian, Paris, under William A Bouguereau (1825–1905) and Gabriel Ferrier (1847–1914) and at the Koninklijke Academie voor Schone Kunsten en de Hogere Instituten, Antwerp, Belgium.
Profile Produced some of the earliest known etchings of the Cape. In 1905 published a folio of etchings entitled "A Folio of Cape Homesteads". 1907 a Council member of the SA Society of Artists; 1910 a founder member of the Johannesburg Art School; 1911 founded the SA Guild of Artists; 1910–12 a member of The Individualists; 1916 a member of the Johannesburg Sketch Club. Prior to 1901 taught at the Camberwell School of Art, the Central School of Art and at the Borough Polytechnic College, London; 1902 an illustrator for *The Cape Times*; 1908 a lecturer at the Normal College, Johannesburg and an inspector for the Normal Colleges in both Johannesburg and Heidelberg. He also taught art privately. 1908–17 an art teacher at the Teachers Training College, Johannesburg. Wrote a number of art reviews. 1873–1901 lived in Derby and in London, England; 1901–06 in Cape Town; 1906–08 in England; 1908–19 in Johannesburg. Included in Edward Roworth's (qv) essay "Landscape Art in SA", 1917, Studio Publication, *Art of The British Empire Overseas*.
Exhibitions Participated in group exhibitions in London and from 1902 in Cape Town and Johannesburg; 1908 Johannesburg, first of numerous solo exhibitions; 1964 SA National Gallery, Cape Town, exhibition.
Public Commission Four panels in tempera, Pretoria Railway Station.
Represented Johannesburg Art Gallery; Julius Gordon Africana Centre, Riversdale; Library of Parliament, Cape Town; Pretoria Art Museum; SA Cultural History Museum, Cape Town; SA National Gallery, Cape Town; William Humphreys Art Gallery, Kimberley.
References Collectors' Guide; SAA; SADNB; DSAB; SAP&S; SAP&D; DBA; BSAK 1 & 2; SA Art; 3Cs; AASA; *ANN* September 1963.

SMUTS Hanneli see KUPFERNAGEL Johanna Eleonore Smuts

SMUTS Lyn (Mrs Lubbe)

Born 1951 Bloemfontein.

A sculptor of pieces based on landscapes and the environment and of figures. Works in bronze, ceramics and ciment fondu. A graphic artist, producing etchings of SA iconography.

Studies 1969–72 Michaelis School of Fine Art, under Katrine Harries (qv) and Richard Wake (qv), gaining a BA(FA) and being awarded the MacIver Scholarship in 1972; 1973 University of Natal, where gained a BA(FA) with Honours in Sculpture; 1975–76 on a Belgian–SA Exchange Scholarship at the Koninklijke Academie voor Schone Kunsten, Ghent, Belgium, under Paul van Gijseghem (*b*.1935).

Profile From 1980 a member of the Artists Guild, Cape Town; from 1976 a member of the SAAA. 1973 an assistant lecturer in etching at the University of Natal; 1974–75 a lecturer in etching at the Cape Technikon; from 1980 a lecturer in etching and printmaking at the University of Stellenbosch. 1978–79 lived in New Haven, USA; 1986 visited London to study etchings.

Exhibitions She has participated in numerous group exhibitions throughout SA; 1976 SAAA Gallery, Cape Town, solo exhibition.

Award 1976 Tercentenary Award.

Represented University of Stellenbosch.

SMUTS Timotheus

Born 1944 Uniondale, Cape Province.

A painter and graphic artist of figures and mythological themes. Works in oil, watercolour, ink, wash and in various graphic media. Up to 1976 erotic/sexual themes; 1976–80 Bushman myth paintings; from 1980 Modern myth paintings.

Studies 1964–68 University of Stellenbosch, under Professor Otto Schröder (qv), gaining a BA(FA); 1971–72 Michaelis School of Fine Art, under Professor Neville Dubow, attaining an MA(FA) and in 1978 under Jules van de Vijver (qv), gaining an Advanced Diploma in Fine Arts.

Profile 1973–79 Principal of the Hugo Naudé Art Centre, Worcester, Cape Province; from 1982 a lecturer at the University of Stellenbosch.

Exhibitions 1970 William Humphreys Art Gallery, Kimberley, first of eight solo exhibitions held in SA; has participated in many group exhibitions from 1971 in SA.

Represented Durban Art Gallery; University of Stellenbosch.

Reference BSAK 1.

SNYCKERS Annette

Born 1945 Bloemfontein.

A painter and graphic artist of landscapes, figures and abstract pictures. Works in oil, acrylic, watercolour, gouache, ink, wash, pencil and in various graphic media. Theme of enlarged details of objects from nature. Works in clay, making pots and sculptural works.

Studies 1967 art classes at the University of Zürich, Switzerland.

Profile From 1976 a member of the APSA, Vice-Chairman and Public Relations Officer of the Northern Transvaal Branch; a member of the SAAA. Has written articles for *Sgraffiti*. 1967–70 lived in Switzerland. Numerous visits to Europe. 1984 visited SWA/Namibia; 1986 Botswana.

Exhibitions She has participated in numerous group exhibitions from 1977 in SA; 1978 SAAA Gallery, Pretoria, solo exhibition.

SOLBERG Nils Landmark FRSA

Born 1920 Melmoth, Zululand, Natal.

Died 1955 Durban.

A painter of still life and landscapes. Worked in watercolour, oil, pencil and pen. Produced a number of sculptures.

Studies 1936–42 part-time at the Natal Technical College, where in 1939 he won the Emma Smith Scholarship; 1946–48 on a Union Defence Force Grant at the Regent Street Polytechnic, London.

Profile 1954 a Fellow of the Royal Society of Arts and President of the NSA. A member of the Durban Sketch Club and Treasurer of the Natal Society of Industrial Artists of SA. A former Chairman of the Bantu, Indian and Coloured Arts, an art and music teaching group. A designer and commercial artist, whose work included posters for the Durban Publicity Association and SATOUR. Designed the Eshowe Coat of Arms. 1953 designed the plaques for the base, and produced the working drawings for the relief work of the Durban Field-Marshal J C Smuts Memorial. 1952 and 1955 designed Christmas stamps. A number of illustrations for periodicals. He was responsible for the cover design and layout of the book issued by the Durban Publicity Association to mark the centenary of the city. Whilst living in London he played the violin in the London Junior Orchestra. 1923–29 lived in Norway, thereafter in Durban. 1946–49 travelled in Europe.

Exhibitions Participated in group exhibitions from 1937 in SA and Europe; 1939 Durban, joint exhibition with Alex Wagner (qv); 1953 Van Riebeeck Gallery, Durban, first solo exhibition; 1955 Greenacres Exhibition Hall, Durban, Retrospective Exhibition entitled "The Nils Solberg Goodwill Exhibition"; 1967 Van Riebeeck Gallery, Durban, Retrospective Exhibition.

Represented Ann Bryant Gallery, East London; Durban Art Gallery; SA National Museum of Military History, Johannesburg.

References AASA; SASSK.

SOLKER Ismail

Born 1935 Cape Town.

Sculpts in pewter, plastic, steel and aluminium. Produces ink drawings of geometrical studies.

Studies 1955–56 School of Architecture, University of Cape Town.

Exhibitions He has participated in group exhibitions in SA; has held solo exhibitions in Cape Town and Johannesburg.

Represented SA National Gallery, Cape Town.

References Register SA/SWA; SAP&D.

SOLOMON J M

Born 1886 Paarl, Cape Province.

Died 1920 Cape Town.

A painter of portraits and a graphic artist.

Studies Diocesan College, Cape Town. Architecture through Sir Herbert Baker in Europe, particularly interested in Greek and Roman architecture; 1917 made a study tour of the USA, the UK, and France, looking at university architecture.

Profile Employed in the Cape Town office of the architect Sir Herbert Baker, working under F E Masey; after 1910 worked in the Johannesburg office; 1915–17 designed the new buildings of the University of Cape Town. 1913 served on the committee of the Johannesburg Art Gallery. He designed the cover for *The State* and drew many of the portraits published in this journal.

Represented Africana Museum, Johannesburg; SA National Gallery, Cape Town.

Publication by Solomon "Johannesburg—its Municipality, Art Endeavours, etc.", an article in *The Transvaal Leader*, 1910.

References SADNB; AMC4; DSAB; SAP&D; BSAK 1 & 2; 3Cs; AASA; SASSK; LSAA.

SOLOMON William Ewart Gladstone FRSA

Born 1880 Sea Point, Cape Town.

Died 1965 Johannesburg.

A painter of portraits, figures and nudes. Worked in oil and watercolour. A number of sepia drawings.

Studies Cope & Nicol's Art School, London and the Royal Academy Schools, London, where he won a Gold Medal in Painting and a travelling scholarship to study in France, Germany, Italy and The Netherlands.

Profile A Fellow of the Royal Society of Arts. A member of the SA Society of Artists. 1948 a founder member of the Brush and Chisel Club. Designed the décor for Pavlova's "Alenta Frescoes". During WWI he served with the Artists Rifles. 1936–41 lived in Bombay where he was the Principal of the Sir Jamshedjee Jeejeebhoy School of Art and curator of the Prince of Wales Museum, West India. Painted a portrait of Viceroy Lord Lloyd, wrote numerous articles on art and made numerous illustrations for books on India; 1941 returned to SA.

Exhibitions Participated in group exhibitions 1903–40 in the UK and in Paris and SA.

Represented Hull and Liverpool Art Galleries, England; SA National Gallery, Cape Town.

Publication by Solomon Wrote a biography on his father Saul Solomon, a printer, publisher and statesman in the Cape.

References SAA; SADNB; AMC4; DSAB; SAP&S; Bénézit; DBA; BSAK 1 & 2; AASA.

SOTIRIADES Anthusa

Born 1958 Cape Town.

Both a painter and sculptor of free-form abstract pieces. Works in acrylic, steel and sponge. From 1985 a series of wall sculptures in foam rubber and acrylic gel.

Studies 1982 Johannesburg Art Foundation, under Bill Ainslie (qv).
Profile From 1985 a committee member of the Thupelo Arts Project. From 1985 a secretary and co-ordinator of the USSALEP/Thupelo Black Artists' programme. 1984 taught art at the Johannesburg Art Foundation; 1986 at the Alexandra Art Centre and in 1987 at Sebokeng School.
Exhibitions She has participated in many group exhibitions in SA; 1987 Johannesburg Art Foundation, joint exhibition with Bill Ainslie (qv), David Koloane (qv), Dumisani Mabaso (qv) and Tony Nkotsi (qv).

SPANN Elizabeth Illingworth

Born 1949 Johannesburg.
A sculptor of figures, wildlife and abstract pieces. Works in bronze, clay and metal.
Studies 1972 the London School of Pottery, Johannesburg, under Gloria Holden, gaining a Diploma in Pottery.
Profile 1973–75 a teacher at the London School of Pottery, Johannesburg; from 1976 a teacher at, and owner of, the Magpie and Stump School of Pottery, Johannesburg.
Exhibitions She has participated in several group exhibitions from 1974 in SA; 1985 Beuster-Skolimowski Gallery, Pretoria, first of two solo exhibitions; 1987 Strack van Schyndel Gallery, Johannesburg, joint exhibition with Wendy Amm (qv) and Iris Vermont (qv).
Public Commissions 1978 ceramic wall plaques, Greenhills School, Johannesburg; 1979 ceramic wall plaques, Randpark Ridge School, Johannesburg.
Reference Habitat no 65, 1984.

SPEARS Frank Sydney

Born 1906 Walsall, Staffordshire, England.
Resided in SA 1928–*c*.1969.
A painter of landscapes, portraits, figures, genre, still life and religious pictures. Works in oil, watercolour, egg tempera, gouache, wash and in charcoal. Themes of "Immaculate Clowns", "Magicians", "Saints" and "Music".
Studies *c*.1915 Waverley Road School of Art, Birmingham, under Chaplin.
Profile 1945–47 President of the SA Society of Artists. Taught art privately. A specialist in architectural designs and a designer of stained glass. A number of illustrations for magazines and art publications. Involved in the dramatic arts. A broadcaster, opera singer, art critic and lecturer. Extensive travels in Europe. Visited the USA in 1949–50 and 1960–61. Lives in Hampshire, England.
Exhibitions He has participated in numerous group exhibitions from *c*.1932 in SA, the UK, Belgium, Zimbabwe, Italy and Brazil; 1935 Darter Gallery, Cape Town, first of 24 solo exhibitions held in SA; 1960 and 1964 Quadrennial Exhibitions; 1968 Stellenbosch, joint exhibition with Nell Kaye (qv); 1973 Drian Galleries, London, first of five solo exhibitions held in the UK; 1984 University of the Orange Free State, solo exhibition.

Represented Hester Rupert Art Museum, Graaff-Reinet; Johannesburg Art Gallery; National Gallery, Gdansk, Poland; Pretoria Art Museum; SA National Gallery, Cape Town; University of the Orange Free State; University of Stellenbosch; University of the Witwatersrand; William Humphreys Art Gallery, Kimberley.

Public Commissions *c.*1960 stained glass and bronze façade, Dutch Reformed Church Centre, Cape Town; stained glass and bronze façade, Thom Theatre, University of Stellenbosch; large Christ Altarpiece, Church of the Resurrection, Bonteheuwel, Cape Town.

References Art SA; SAA; 20C SA Art; SAP&S; SAP&D; BSAK 1 & 2; AASA; *Artlook* March 1968, October 1968 & August/September 1976.

SPIES Christiaan Coenraad (Chris)

Born 1951 Sabie, Eastern Transvaal.

A painter and graphic artist of landscapes, figures, abstract pictures and icons. Works in oil, acrylic, watercolour and in various graphic media. Occasionally sculpts. Several series including: "The History of the Bird", hand-printed wood engravings; "Fragments of Africa", "Erotica", "Beach Images", "Cape Images" and "Sea Images", all hand-printed silkscreens.

Studies 1972–75 University of Pretoria, under Ernst de Jong (qv), Raymond Andrews (qv), Eben van der Merwe (qv), Mike Edwards (qv) and Professor Nico Roos (qv), gaining a Diploma in Fine Arts.

Profile A member of the SAAA. Additionally works as a commercial artist.

Exhibitions He has participated in over 60 group exhibitions from 1976 throughout SA and in Australia; 1976 SAAA Gallery, Potchefstroom, first of 10 solo exhibitions held in SA; 1978 National Museum, Bloemfontein, solo exhibition; 1981 Republic Festival Exhibition.

Represented National Museum, Bloemfontein; Pietersburg Collection; Potchefstroom Museum; Potchefstroom University for CHE; Rand Afrikaans University; University of Durban-Westville; University of Natal; University of the Witwatersrand; Walter Battiss Art Gallery, Somerset East; Willem Annandale Art Gallery, Lichtenburg; William Humphreys Art Gallery, Kimberley.

SPIES Hermine Alida

Born 1950 Pretoria.

A painter and graphic artist of figures, landscapes and abstract pictures. Works in acrylic, watercolour, pastel, mixed media, crayon, pencil, charcoal and in various graphic media. 1983–84 "Jawbone" series.

Studies 1969–72 University of Pretoria, gaining a BA(FA); 1973–76 University of South Africa, under Frieda Harmsen, gaining a BA with Honours in Art History; 1974–76 on a Ministerial Exchange Bursary at the Koninklijke Academie voor Schone Kunsten, Ghent, Belgium.

Profile A member of the SAAA and the WSSA. Taught art in 1973 at the Transvalia High School, Vanderbijlpark; 1980 at the Johannesburg Council of Adult Education; 1979–85 privately in her own studio. 1978–79 an art critic for *Beeld*. 1950–74 lived in Pretoria; 1974–77 in Belgium and Paris, travelling throughout Europe; from 1977 in Johannesburg. 1982 on a UTA Artist Travel Bursary visited Venice, Kassel and Paris.

Exhibitions She has participated in numerous group exhibitions from 1976 in SA, SWA/Namibia, Belgium, the UK, West Germany, France and Japan; 1976 Egmont Gallery, Belgium, first of three solo exhibitions held in Belgium and 17 solo exhibitions held in SA and SWA/Namibia; 1981 Republic Festival Exhibition.

Represented Boksburg Municipality; Johannesburg Art Gallery; Pretoria Art Museum; SA Embassy, London, UK; William Humphreys Art Gallery, Kimberley.

SPILHAUS Arnold Wilhelm

Born 1845 Lübeck, Germany.
Died 1946 Cape Town.
Resided in SA from 1869.
A painter of landscapes. Worked in watercolour and oil.
Studies Self-taught, apart from three watercolour lessons from Constance Penstone (qv).
Profile Began painting in his 50s remaining, however, Chairman of and actively involved with the mercantile company he established in 1876. An uncle of Nita Spilhaus (qv).
Exhibitions Participated in exhibitions at the Cape Town Arts Association.
Represented SA National Gallery, Cape Town.
Reference SAP&S.

SPILHAUS Pauline Augusta Wilhelmina (Nita)

Born 1878 Lisbon, Portugal.
Died 1967 Cape Town.
Resided in SA from 1907.
A painter of landscapes, generally incorporating trees, scenes of Cape Town, portraits and of still life. Painted flowers during the war years when she was unable to leave her house. A series of the Cape Malay Quarter, Cape Town. Worked in oil and occasionally in watercolour. A number of drawings and etchings.
Studies 1896–1900 Lübeck School of Art and the Kunst Akademie, Munich, West Germany, under Friedrich Fehr (*b*.1862) and Adolf Holzel (1853–1934); Thanlow Swedish Painting School, Paris.
Profile 1907 a member of the SA Society of Artists. In 1900 a folio of her etchings of Lübeck was published. Two folios of her etchings entitled "Trees'" and "Cape Town" were published by *The Cape Times*. 1878–1907 lived in Lübeck, Germany; 1907 came to SA, returning to Germany during the mid 1920s. 1938–67 lived in SA. Included in Edward Roworth's (qv) essay "Landscape Art in SA", 1917, Studio Publication, *Art of The British Empire Overseas*. A distinctive signature of interlinking N and S. A niece of Arnold Spilhaus (qv).

Exhibitions Participated in group exhibitions from 1900 in France, Germany, SA, the UK and once in Rhodesia (Zimbabwe); 1917 Cape Town, joint exhibition with Pieter Wenning (qv), Edward Roworth (qv) and Hugo Naudé (qv); 1920 Johannesburg, first of several solo exhibitions; 1923 joint exhibition with Ruth Prowse (qv) and Florence Zerffi (qv).

Represented Albany Museum, Grahamstown; Durban Art Gallery; Johannesburg Art Gallery; King George VI Art Gallery, Port Elizabeth; Pretoria Art Museum; SA National Gallery, Cape Town; University of the Witwatersrand; William Humphreys Art Gallery, Kimberley.

References Collectors' Guide; Our Art 1; Art SA; SAA; 20C SA Art; SAP&S; SAP&D; SSAP; DBA; BSAK 1 & 2; SA Art; 3Cs; AASA; LSAA.

SPIROU Demetrios

Born 1949 Athens, Greece.
Died 1985 King Williamstown, Cape Province.
Resided in SA from 1971.
A painter working in mixed media. Mainly a graphic artist, depicting figures and landscapes.

Studies Worked in a pottery studio in Athens. 1974 gained a Diploma in Graphic Design from the East London Technical College, studying under Jack Lugg (qv); 1981 attained a Higher Diploma from the East London Technical College.

Profile From 1981 lectured at the East London Technical College.

Exhibitions Participated in group exhibitions in SA, the USA and in Europe; 1979 East London Society of Fine Arts Gallery, solo exhibition; 1981 Republic Festival Exhibition; 1982 Cape Town Triennial.

Represented Ann Bryant Gallery, East London; Arts Association SWA/Namibia Collection; Pretoria Art Museum; Queenstown and Border Museum; Tatham Art Gallery, Pietermaritzburg; University of the Orange Free State.

References AASA; *SA Arts Calendar* Summer 1985–86.

SQUIBB Ruth Audrey (Mrs Coles)

Born 1928 Portsmouth, England.
A painter of landscapes, still life, flowers and Cape houses. Works in oil.

Exhibitions She has participated in numerous group exhibitions in SA; 1981 Maud Street Gallery, Johannesburg, solo exhibition.

STADELMANN Ernest

Born Munich, Germany.
Resided in SA from 1951.
A painter of landscapes, still life and figures. Works in oil. A series on the Knysna Forest, Cape Province.

Studies Bayerische Akademie der Bildenden Künste, Munich, West Germany.
Exhibitions Prior to 1951 exhibited in the USA, the UK, France and Italy; from 1951 has exhibited mostly in Cape Town; 1956 and 1960 Quadrennial Exhibitions; has held solo exhibitions in Germany, the USA, the UK, France, Italy and SA.
References SAA; AASA.

STADLER Jennifer (Jenny)

Born 1938 Johannesburg.
A painter and graphic artist of abstract pictures, which often contain portrait, landscape and seascape elements. Works in oil, acrylic, watercolour, ink, wash, pencil, charcoal, koki pens, china markers, collage, sand, wood and in various graphic media.
Studies 1957–60 University of the Witwatersrand, under Cecily Sash (qv), gaining a BA(FA); 1969 life painting, for six months at the Brighton College of Art, Sussex, England; 1972 graphic art, on a part-time basis, at the Witwatersrand Technical College; 1974–75 studied graphic art at the Whitechapel Polytechnic College, London, and sculpture, drawing and painting at the Mary Ward Centre, London, under Rose Garrard and Kerry Trengrove.
Profile 1974 a member of the SAAA. 1983–84 a founder member of Possession Arts; 1985 on the Gallery Committee of the Johannesburg Art Foundation. 1963 an arts and crafts teacher at the Johannesburg Council for Adult Education; 1977–81 a teacher of painting, drawing and art history at the Johannesburg Art Foundation; from 1982 a lecturer in the Department of Architecture at the University of the Witwatersrand. 1949 visited France; 1948–49, 1968–69 and 1974–75 visited the UK.
Exhibitions She has participated in many group exhibitions from 1970 in SA; 1974 SAAA Gallery, Johannesburg, first of three solo exhibitions held in Johannesburg; 1985 Cape Town Triennial; 1985 Tributaries, touring SA and West Germany; 1987 University of the Witwatersrand, solo exhibition; 1988 Johannesburg Art Gallery, Vita Art Now.
Represented Durban Art Gallery; SA National Gallery, Cape Town; University of the Witwatersrand.

STAINBANK Mary Agnes ARCA

Born 1899 Bellair, Natal.
A sculptor of figures, heads, portraits, still life, scenes of African life, religious themes as well as semi-abstract and abstract pieces. Works in stone, marble, bronze, wood, cement and ceramics. A number of simplistic reliefs for buildings.
Studies 1918–22 Natal Technical College, under John Adams and Alfred Martin (qv); 1922–26 Royal College of Art, London, under Sir William Rothenstein (1872–1945), Frederick John Wilcoxson (*b*.1888), Leon Underwood (*b*.1890) and Ernest Cole, gaining an Associateship with distinction in 1925 and a Royal College of Art Scholarship 1925–26; studied bronze foundry work at a school of engineering in London.

Profile 1940–45 in charge of the Drawing Office of the SA Air Force, Pretoria, for which she received a special war service commendation. 1945–57 Head of the School of Sculpture at the Natal Technical College. 1958 travelled round the world visiting art galleries. Lives in Bellair, Natal, where she shared a studio with Wilgeforde Vann-Hall (qv).

Exhibitions She has participated in numerous group exhibitions in SA, Zimbabwe, the USA, Canada and Europe; 1948 Tate Gallery, London, SA Art Exhibition; 1960 and 1964 Quadrennial Exhibitions; has held solo exhibitions in London and throughout SA; 1988 Johannesburg Art Gallery, Retrospective Exhibition.

Represented Ann Bryant Gallery, East London; Durban Art Gallery.

Public Commissions Cement sculpture, Durban Defence Force Building; 1922 Bellair War Memorial; 1930 stone carving, Durban Government Offices; 1930 figures and faience panels, Children's Hospital, Durban; 1933 relief panels, Port Elizabeth Law Courts; cement frieze, Government Building, Port Elizabeth; 1938 plaques, Clubhouse, Natal Technical College; stone carving "Flower Sellers", Pine Street, Durban; 1970 cold bronze work, Marine Building, Durban; 1972 bronze figure of John Ross, John Ross Building, Durban and many other works for churches, schools and public offices throughout SA.

References Mary Webb, *Precious Stone*, 1985, Knox, Durban; *The SA Woman's Who's Who*, 1939, Biographies Ltd, Johannesburg; Collectors' Guide; Art SA; SAA; SESA; BSAK 1 & 2; AASA; *SA Panorama* April 1968.

STANDER Chrisman Joel Andries

Born 1943 Brits, Transvaal.

A painter and graphic artist of landscapes, still life and wildlife. Works in watercolour, ink, pencil and in various graphic media; also makes collages.

Studies 1962 Pretoria Technical College, under Peter Eliastam (qv), Zakkie Eloff (qv) and René Eloff (qv).

Profile 1973–81 a graphic illustrator for *Sarie* magazine. From 1981 an art director in the advertising industry. 1964–81 lived in Cape Town, thereafter in Johannesburg. 1984 visited Israel and Greece.

Exhibitions 1985 Carlton Centre, Johannesburg, first of three solo exhibitions.

STANDING Kathleen Joy

Born 1936 Ladysmith, Natal.

A self-taught sculptor of abstract pieces. Works in porcelain and raku.

Profile A member of the APSA. Teaches privately.

Exhibitions She has participated in several group exhibitions from 1972; 1979 first of three solo exhibitions held in her own studio.

STANFORD Cynthia

Born 1917 Cape Town.

A sculptor working in stone.

Studies 1936–39 University of Natal, under Professor O J P Oxley (qv), where attained a BA(FA); 1947 stone carving at the Witwatersrand Technical College, under James Gardner (qv).

Profile Taught at St Mary's Diocesan College, Natal. 1948 visited the UK, France and Italy. During the 1950s and 1960s lived in Cape Town.
Exhibitions Prior to 1952 exhibited with the NSA; 1956 Quadrennial Exhibition; 1964 Venice Biennale.
References SAA; AASA.

STANLEY Diana Heaton (Mrs Dominy)

Born Durban.
A painter of landscapes, portraits, still life, figures and abstract pictures. Works in oil, gouache, ink, wash, pencil, charcoal and in mixed media.
Studies 1959 University of Natal, under Professor Jack Heath (qv); 1960 Natal Technical College, under Bill Beekes, gaining a National Diploma in Fine Arts; 1961 Central School of Art, London; 1962 l'Académie de la Grande Chaumière, Paris.
Profile 1960 a member of the NSA. Teaches art privately. A weaver. Lives at and paints the people and scenery in the Valley of a Thousand Hills, Natal. 1982 visited SWA/Namibia.
Exhibitions She has participated in several group exhibitions from 1960 in Durban; Walsh-Marais Gallery, Durban, first of two solo exhibitions.
Award 1975 Cambridge Shirt Award, Art SA Today.
Reference AASA.

STARCKE Helmut

Born 1935 Offenbach on the Main, Germany.
Resided in SA from 1958.
A self-taught painter of landscapes, seascapes, plants and interiors. First worked in oil, then tempera and presently in acrylic on canvas. His works are generally on a large scale. A graphic artist creating serigraphs, he incorporates photographed material into his prints. 1968 "Karoo Travelogue" series; 1970 "Caprivi of My Mind" series.
Profile 1965 a founder member of the Artists Gallery, Cape Town and a founder member and Chairman in 1982 of the Artists Guild, Cape Town. Worked in advertising in West Germany and Cape Town. From 1975 a lecturer in graphic design at the Michaelis School of Fine Art. Numerous illustrations and designs of dust jackets for periodicals and books.
Exhibitions He has participated in numerous group exhibitions from 1961 in SA, West Germany, The Netherlands, Yugoslavia, Italy, Belgium, Brazil, Monaco, the UK and the USA; 1963 Cape Town, first of five solo exhibitions held in SA; 1979 Cape Town Biennial, Invited Artist; 1985 Cape Town Triennial; 1985 Tributaries, touring SA and West Germany.
Awards 1966 Bronze Medal, SA Breweries Exhibition; 1968 Silver Medal, SA Breweries Exhibition.

Represented Durban Art Gallery; Johannesburg Art Gallery; Pretoria Art Museum; Sandton Municipal Collection; SA National Gallery, Cape Town; University of Cape Town; University of the Orange Free State; University of South Africa.

References SAP&S; SESA; SSAP; BSAK 1 & 2; SA Art; Oxford Companion to 20C Art (under SA); 3Cs; AASA; LSAA; *Habitat* no 25, 1977.

STARKEY Anthony Roland

Born 1948 Durban.

A painter of realistic urban subject matter. Works in oil and mixed media.

Studies 1971 gained a BA(FA) from the University of the Witwatersrand; 1978 attained an MA(FA) from the University of the Witwatersrand.

Profile 1972–73 taught and painted in Durban; 1974–75 taught and painted in England. 1978 taught at Pretoria Boys High School; 1980 a senior lecturer on the Foundation Course of the Natal Technikon; from 1981 Head of the Painting Department, Natal Technikon. 1983 began experimenting with papermaking and set up the papermaking unit at the Natal Technikon with John Roome (qv).

Exhibitions He has participated in many group exhibitions in SA; 1973 NSA Gallery, Durban, first of several solo exhibitions held in SA; 1974 SAAA Gallery, Johannesburg, joint exhibition with Terence King (qv).

Represented Johannesburg Art Gallery; University of the Witwatersrand.

STASSEN Frans Johannes Nicolas

Born 1925 Kenhardt, Cape Province.

A self-taught painter of seascapes and landscapes, particularly of the Namib and Kalahari deserts. Works in oil and watercolour.

Profile A Minister in the Dutch Reformed Church. Has travelled throughout Southern Africa and in 1984 to the UK and Europe.

Exhibitions He has participated in several group exhibitions from 1971; 1972 first of two solo exhibitions.

STATHAM Caroline

Born 1947 Kempton Park, Transvaal.

A painter of satirical portraits. Works in oil, watercolour, gouache, ink, wash and pencil. Since 1980 a sculptor working in porcelain and mixed media.

Studies 1964 Commercial Art at the Pretoria Technical College; 1976–80 under George Boys (qv) in Johannesburg.

Profile From 1960 a member of the SAAA. Book illustrations for *Olifant en wys Muis* in 1974, *Krokodil se Tandpyn* in 1975, *Dom Tom die Plaaskneg* in 1976, *Sjimp en die Sjimpansee* in 1977 and *Die Twee Verwers* in 1978, all published by Daan Retief Publishers, Pretoria. 1955–64 lived in Rhodesia (Zimbabwe).

Exhibitions She has participated in several group exhibitions from 1984; 1986 SAAA Gallery, Pretoria, solo exhibition.

Public Commission 1984 two paintings, Christian Community Centre, Pretoria.

STAYT William John
Born 1903 Johannesburg.
A painter of landscapes and the fantastic. Worked in watercolour and oil.
Profile A founder member of the Friday Club, of which he was President in 1939.
1939 joined the SA Navy as a Physical Training Instructor. Worked for 20 years
in advertising with the Central News Agency and for 17 years as colour
consultant to a paint firm.
Exhibitions He has participated in group exhibitions with the SAAA from 1931;
1936 Empire Exhibition, Johannesburg.
References BSAK 1; AASA.

STEAD Jeanette
Born 1940 Johannesburg.
An artist depicting flowers. Works in pencil, ink and wash.
Studies 1955–56 commercial art, at the Natal Technical College.
Profile A member of the NSA. 1981 designed stamps for SA and Venda for the
International Orchid Conference.
Exhibitions She has participated in several group exhibitions in SA; 1967 T S
Taylor Gallery, Pietermaritzburg, first of c.10 solo exhibitions held in SA.

STEENBEEK Greta Jeannette Pierrette (Zenitha)
Born 1940 Leuven, Belgium.
A sculptor of abstract pieces. Works in bronze, ciment fondu, clay, ceramics and
glass. A painter of portraits. Works in acrylic, watercolour, gouache, ink, pencil
and charcoal.
Studies 1961–65 Academie voor Schone Kunsten, Leuven, Belgium, after which
she spent eight years in the studio of Willy Meysmans (b.1930).
Profile 1966–68 an Honorary member of Apollo in Belgium. 1973–77 a lecturer
in ceramics, University of Pretoria as well as teaching privately; 1976–77 taught
ceramic sculpture at the Kraft Studio, Pretoria. A designer for theatre, film and
television; she has also acted and sung in operettas. 1979 illustrations for the
periodical *Rachel*. A potter and enamellist. Study tours in The Netherlands,
France, Greece, the Greek islands and Italy.
Exhibitions She has participated in numerous group exhibitions from 1962 in
Belgium and SA; 1974 Arcadia Centre, Pretoria, first of two solo exhibitions;
1976 SAAA Gallery, Johannesburg, joint exhibition with Pieter Potgieter.
Represented Fort Klapperkop Museum, Pretoria.

STEER Ninetta (Nan)
Born 1935 London, England.
Resided in SA from 1936.
A painter, graphic artist and sculptor. Works in oil, acrylic, watercolour,
gouache, ink, wash, pencil, charcoal, various graphic media, wood and palm tree
seed pods.

Studies 1958–59 graphic art at the Witwatersrand Technical College, under Professor Robert Bain (qv); 1981–83 University of South Africa; also taught by Roy Reynolds (qv), Machiel Hopman, Marjorie Bowen (qv), Alfred Ewan (qv) and George Boys (qv).

Profile From 1973 a member of the WSSA, becoming an Associate and Chairman of the Eastern Transvaal Branch in 1987. From *c.*1974 a member of the SAAA. 1972–84 a member of the Artists Market Association. 1974 an art teacher at the Sandringham Primary School, Johannesburg; 1978–79 taught art privately in Johannesburg. Has travelled throughout SA and to Australia, New Zealand, the UK and the USA.

Exhibitions She has participated in many group exhibitions from 1971 in SA and once in London; 1976 P F C Gallery, Fairmount, Johannesburg, first of three solo exhibitions.

STERN Irma

Born 1894 Schweizer-Reneke, Transvaal.
Died 1966 Cape Town.

An artist depicting figures, portraits, heads, landscapes, flowers, still life, harbour views, scenes of the Cape Malay Quarter, cityscapes, genre and coastal subjects. Worked in many media including oil, tempera, watercolour, gouache, charcoal, ballpoint pen, conté, coloured inks and various graphic media. A number of sculptures of figures and heads, as well as ceramic pots and plates. Her most usual medium was oil which she used thickly with large brushstrokes; also known for the use of strong colours and dark outlines. She framed a number of her pictures in wood from Zanzibar door jambs.

Studies 1913 Weimar Academy, Germany, under Gari Melchers (1860–1932); 1914 Levin-Funcke Studio, Berlin, under Martin Brandenberg (*b.*1870); 1914 briefly at the Bauhaus, Weimar.

Profile 1916 a member of the November Group, Germany; 1918–19 a member of the Neue-Sezession, Germany, with whom she exhibited. From 1922 a close friend of Maggie Laubser (qv). 1931 a member of the SA Society of Artists; 1948 of the International Art Club SA. 1894–99 lived in SA; 1899–1903 in Germany; 1903–13 in SA, with visits to Europe; 1913–19 lived in Germany; 1919–22 in SA; 1922–26 in Germany and France, with visits to SA; 1926–66 in SA. Places visited: 1930 Madeira; 1937 Dakar, en route to Genoa; 1938 Dakar; 1939 Zanzibar; 1942 Belgian Congo (Zaire); 1945 Zanzibar; 1946 Central Africa; 1952 Madeira; 1955 Belgian Congo (Zaire); 1960 Spain; 1963 France; also travelled extensively throughout SA. Three films on her work have been made by the SA Department of Information. Prints of her work have been issued. In 1971 The Irma Stern Museum, situated in her house, was opened by the University of Cape Town.

Exhibitions Participated in group exhibitions from 1918 in Germany, SA, the UK, Switzerland, Italy, Rhodesia (Zimbabwe), Brazil, Yugoslavia and the USA; 1919 Galerie Gurlitt, Berlin, first of *c.*100 solo exhibitions held in Germany, Italy, France, Austria, Belgium, The Netherlands, the UK, Belgian Congo (Zaire) and SA; 1948 Tate Gallery, London, SA Art Exhibition; 1956 and

1960 Quadrennial Exhibitions; 1962 Grosvenor Gallery, London, Retrospective Exhibition; 1966 University of Stellenbosch, Memorial Tribute in the South African Art of the 20th Century Exhibition; 1967 Grosvenor Gallery, London, Memorial Exhibition; 1968 SA National Gallery, Cape Town, Pretoria Art Museum and Johannesburg Art Gallery, Memorial Exhibition entitled "Homage to Irma Stern".

Awards 1927 Prix d'Honneur at the International Exhibition, Bordeaux, France; 1952 Cape Tercentenary Molteno Grant; 1960 Guggenheim Foundation Regional Award for SA; 1963 Oppenheimer Award, Art SA Today; 1965 Medal of Honour, SA Akademie vir Wetenskap en Kuns.

Represented Africana Museum, Johannesburg; Ann Bryant Gallery, East London; Bielefeld Art Gallery, West Germany; Collection of Queen Elizabeth the Queen Mother, London, UK; Durban Art Gallery; Hester Rupert Art Museum, Graaff-Reinet; Irma Stern Museum, University of Cape Town; Johannesburg Art Gallery; Julius Gordon Africana Centre, Riversdale; King George VI Art Gallery, Port Elizabeth; Musée de l'Art Moderne, Paris, France; National Museum, Bloemfontein; Pretoria Art Museum; SA embassies in Geneva, The Hague, Madrid, Paris, London and Washington DC; SA National Gallery, Cape Town; Tatham Art Gallery, Pietermaritzburg; University of Cape Town; University of the Orange Free State; University of Pretoria; University of South Africa; University of Stellenbosch; University of the Witwatersrand; Willem Annandale Art Gallery, Lichtenburg; William Humphreys Art Gallery, Kimberley.

Publications by Stern Visionen: Zehn Steinzeichnungen, 1920, 10 lithographs, 40 copies, Hesperein Verlag, Berlin; *Congo*, 1943, Van Schaik, Pretoria; *Zanzibar*, 1948, Van Schaik, Pretoria; *Dhumella Morena*, lithographic works, Berlin, Fritz Gurlitt.

References Max Osborn, *Irma Stern*, Junge Kunst series of monographs, 1927, Verlag Klinkhardt und Biermann, Leipzig, Germany; Neville Dubow, *Irma Stern*, SA Library Series, 1974, C Struik, Cape Town; Joseph Sachs, *Irma Stern and the Spirit of Africa*, 1942, Van Schaik, Cape Town; L S Daneel, *A Guide to Sources on Irma Stern*, 1981, Human Sciences Research Council, Pretoria; Collectors' Guide; PSA; Our Art 1; Art SA; SAA; 20C SA Art; DSAB; SAP&S; Oxford Companion to Art (under SA Art); SAP&D; SESA; SSAP; Bénézit; DBA; BSAK 1 & 2; Enc S'n A; SA Art; Oxford Companion to 20C Art (under SA); 3Cs; AASA; LSAA; *South Africana* May 1957, June 1959 & December 1960; *SA Panorama* October 1965; *De Arte* May 1967; *Artlook* September 1967 & August 1968; *Gallery* Summer 1984; *Style* September 1984; *Homage to Irma Stern*, catalogue, 1968, Rembrandt van Rijn Art Foundation.

STERN Rhona

Born Johannesburg.

A self-taught sculptor of birds, torsos and portrait heads. Works in bronze.

Profile The author of *The Cactus Land* 1964, *The Bird Flies Blind* 1965, *Stop Half Way and Look at the View* 1969, all published by Michael Joseph Ltd, London; in the literature field she has won a number of prizes and has served on committees, panels, etc. A trained architect. Daughter of Leon Levson (qv).

Exhibitions She has participated in numerous group exhibitions in SA, the UK, Brazil, Zimbabwe and Monaco; has held numerous solo exhibitions in Johannesburg, Cape Town and London; 1960 and 1964 Quadrennial Exhibitions; 1981 Republic Festival Exhibition.

Represented Hester Rupert Art Museum, Graaff-Reinet; Pretoria Art Museum; Rand Afrikaans University; University of the Witwatersrand.

Public Commissions Field-Marshal J C Smuts, University of the Witwatersrand; bronze of Professor J C Middle-Shaw, Dental and Oral Hopsital, Johannesburg; "The Drum", African Theatres; Gates for Advisor House, Commissioner Street, Johannesburg; portrait busts of British Pioneers, University of the Witwatersrand; bronze of Sir Ernest Oppenheimer, Oppenheimer Memorial Park, Kimberley; fountain, Clarendon Park, Johannesburg; memorial bas-relief plaque of Mr R F Kennedy, Johannesburg Library; Eagle, Holiday Inn Airport Hotel, Jan Smuts, Johannesburg; portrait of Dr H F Verwoerd, Union Buildings, Pretoria; numerous portraits for corporations in SA.

References Art SA; SAA; 20C SA Art; Oxford Companion to Art (under SA); SESA; BSAK 1 & 2; SA Art; 3Cs; AASA; LSAA; *SA Art News* August 1961; *Artlook* November 1969; *SA Panorama* May 1974; *Habitat* no 18, 1976.

STEVENS Ingrid (Muffin)

Born 1952 Pretoria.

A painter of figures and still life. Her paintings are allegorical and symbolic. Works in oil and acrylic. A sculptor working in ceramics.

Studies 1971–73 Witwatersrand Technical College, under Spies Venter (qv), gaining a National Diploma in Ceramics; from 1981 studying for a BA(FA) on Merit Bursaries, through the University of South Africa, under Nina Romm (qv) and Keith Dietrich (qv).

Profile 1986 a committee member of the SAAA, Northern Transvaal Branch. 1974–76 a lecturer in ceramics at the Witwatersrand Technical College; from 1980 a lecturer in fine arts at Pretoria Technikon. A trained potter. 1976–77 lived in The Netherlands.

Exhibitions She has participated in several group exhibitions in SA; 1976 SAAA Galleries, Pretoria, first of three solo exhibitions, two of ceramics, and one of drawings held at Things Gallery, Johannesburg, in 1981.

Award 1976 Brickor Award for Ceramic Sculpture.

STEVENS Mark Gerald

Born 1956 Pretoria.

A painter, graphic artist and sculptor of landscapes, seascapes, portraits, figures, wildlife and abstract works. A recurring theme of social comment. Works in oil, acrylic, watercolour, gouache, ink, wash, pencil, charcoal, various graphic media, bronze, stone, ciment fondu, wood, clay, found objects and the encaustic processes; also uses photocopies and photographs.

Studies 1975–78 Pretoria Technical College (Technikon), under Ian Redelinghuys (qv), Koos den Houting (qv), Leslie Reinhardt (qv), Gunther van der Reis (qv) and Tertia Knapp (qv), gaining a National Diploma in Art and Design.

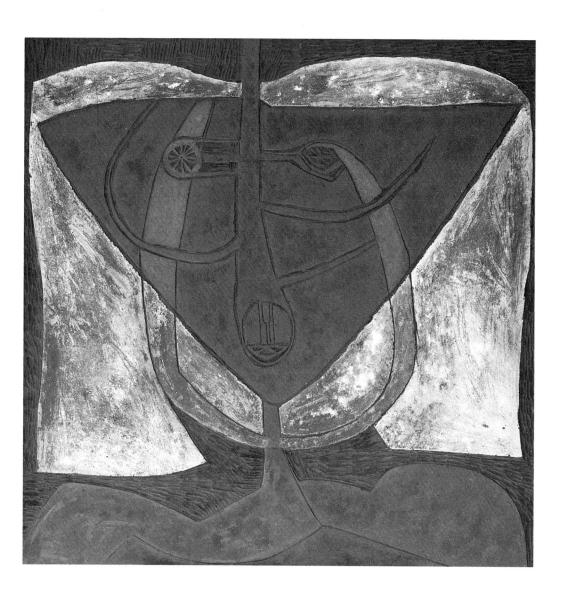

CECIL SKOTNES
The Bride 1968
Engraved & Carved Painted Wood Panel 91 × 91 cm
I J Kriel

RICHARD SMITH
Two Dancers 1988
Oil on Canvas 38 × 31 cm
Private

HELMUT STARKE
Welwitchia 1986
Oil on Canvas 124 × 174 cm
The Read Stremmel Gallery, Texas

IRMA STERN
Mangubetu Bride 1942
Oil on Canvas 141 × 86 cm
Die Kunskamer

Profile 1978 a member of the "Fook Island" group; from 1981 a founder member of "Seventy Miles per Hour and Standing Still"; 1985 founded TWAK (True White African Kaffir). 1981 taught sculpture and drawing part-time at the Pretoria Technikon; 1983 taught sculpture part-time at Pretoria Technikon. From 1984 involved in stage design, journal illustration and music. 1986 designs for jewellery with H Rautenbach. 1976 travelled in Europe.
Exhibitions He has participated in many group exhibitions from 1977 in SA and once in West Germany; 1977 private solo exhibition; 1982 Things Gallery, Johannesburg, first of two solo exhibitions.

STEVENSON Erica Crichton

Born 1926 Newcastle, Natal.
A painter and graphic artist of landscapes, seascapes, still life, figures and indigenous flora. Works in watercolour, ink, wash, pencil and in various graphic media.
Studies 1944–46 Witwatersrand Technical College, under James Gardner (qv) and Maurice van Essche (qv), gaining a Diploma in Art and Design.
Profile From 1979 a member of the WSSA, of which she was the Vice-President of the Natal Branch in 1986; from 1980 a member of the NSA; from 1983 a member of the Highway Group. 1971–83 Founder President of Ikebana Chapter 170, Ikebana International. A freelance commercial artist for over 30 years. 1967–73 and 1983–85 Editor and Co-Editor of the journal *Floral Notes*. 1970 travelled to Japan.
Exhibitions She has participated in many group exhibitions from 1980 in Natal and Cape Town.

STEWARD Elizabeth Ann (Lib)

Born 1935 Potchefstroom, Transvaal.
A painter working in oil, watercolour, pencil and fabric. 1981–82 "Flower" series; 1982–85 "African Shrine" series.
Studies 1978–79 under Jane Heath (qv) in Pietermaritzburg; 1980–83 extra-mural studies at the University of Natal, under Andrew Verster (qv) and Diana Kenton (qv).
Profile From 1977 a member of the NSA and from 1982 of the WSSA.
Exhibitions She has participated in several group exhibitions in Natal from 1977; 1982 Grassroots Gallery, Westville, solo exhibition.
Represented Durban Art Gallery.

STEWART Cecil Thornley FRSA

Born 1881 London, UK.
Died 1967 Port St Johns, Transkei.
Resided in SA from 1914.
A painter of landscapes, wildlife, portraits and seascapes. Worked in oil and watercolour.

Studies 1898–1904 Elmtree Road School of Art, St Johns Wood, London; also under Sir William Orchardson (1835–1910) and Albert Chevallier Tayler (1862–1925), in London.

Profile A Fellow of the Royal Society of Arts. An actor, newspaper reporter, cartoonist, stage manager, poet and lyric writer. 1905–13 taught art in India; 1914–24 farmed sugar in Zululand; 1924–32 worked as a miner; 1932–42 worked in advertising and copywriting; 1943 became a full-time artist, settling in Port St Johns. Travelled extensively in SA and Zimbabwe.

Exhibitions Participated in group exhibitions from 1928 in SA and Zimbabwe; 1943 Port St Johns, first of several solo exhibitions.

Represented Ann Bryant Gallery, East London.

References Collectors' Guide; SAA; BSAK 1 & 2 (also under Thornley); AASA.

STEWART James Struthers RSA

Born 1791 Edinburgh, Scotland.
Died 1863 Alice, Eastern Cape.
Resided in SA from 1833.

A painter of landscapes and portraits, particularly of 1820 Settler family members. Worked in oil and more rarely in watercolour.

Studies Drawing lessons at the Trustee's Academy, Edinburgh under John Graham (1754–1817); apprenticed to the engraver Robert Scott (1771–1841).

Profile 1830–58 a member of the Royal Scottish Academy, 1859 made an Honorary Member, shortly afterwards resigned. 1835 taught painting in Somerset East, Cape Province. Produced a large number of engravings, among which were "The Penny Wedding", original by Sir David Wilkie (1785–1841); 1820 "Circassian Captives" and 1824 "The Murder of Archbishop Sharpe", originals by Sir William Allan (1782–1850) and those in Thomas Pringle's books *African Sketches*, 1834 and *Poetical Works*, 1837. 1830–33 lived in London; 1834–54 farmed on the Eastern Frontier of the Cape Province and was the Justice of the Peace in Bedford in 1838 and later in Alice. In 1854 represented Queen Victoria in the first Cape Parliament. Great-grandfather of Molly Townsend (qv) and great-great-grandfather of Bill Ainslie (qv).

Exhibitions Participated in group exhibitions in London and Scotland.

Award 1830 Hope & Cockburn Award from the Royal Scottish Academy.

References Molly Townsend, *James Stewart, Royal Scottish Academician*, 1968, Government Printer, Botswana; Pict Art; DVP; Pict Afr; *ANN* vol 20 no 5, March 1973.

STEYN William James

Born 1957 Barberton, Eastern Transvaal.
A painter working in acrylic, ink and mixed media, also creates collages.

Studies 1977–81 University of Pretoria, under Professor Nico Roos (qv), John Clarke (qv) and Ernst de Jong (qv), gaining a BA(FA).

Profile From 1983 a member of the SAAA. A graphic designer. From 1985 his illustrations have been used on the covers of *Africa Insight*, the journal of the Africa Institute. 1986 editorial cartoons for *Die Vaderland* newspaper. 1987 illustrations for *Flying Springbok* and *De Kat*.

Exhibitions He has participated in several group exhibitions from 1983 in Pretoria and Johannesburg; 1983 SAAA Gallery, Pretoria, joint exhibition with Erna Bodenstein-Ferreira (qv); 1987 Gallery 21, Johannesburg, joint exhibition with John Clarke (qv), Johann Moolman (qv), Jacobus Kloppers (qv) and Erna Bodenstein-Ferreira (qv).

STEYNBERG Coert L ARCA FRSA FIAL

Born 1905 Hennops River, Transvaal.
Died 1982 Pretoria.
A sculptor of figures, portrait busts, masks, animals and metaphorical pieces. Worked in stone, marble, bronze, brass, copper, steel, ciment fondu and wood. Numerous large public sculptures and architectural relief work. In addition to this he created swirling metal abstract pieces and abstracted figures with the use of various materials including wire, sealing wax, coloured glass and ceramics.

Studies 1925–28 Rhodes University, under Professor Frederick Armstrong (qv), gaining an Art Teachers Diploma in 1927; 1928–30 Royal College of Art, London, under Professor Gilbert Ledward (1888–1960), Henry Moore (1898–1986) and Richard Garbe (1876–1957), becoming an Associate in 1929; 1930–34 studied art in Europe.

Profile A Fellow of the Royal Society of Arts. 1956 a Fellow of the International Institute for Arts and Literature; 1961 an Executive Committee Member of the SA Council of Arts; a member of the International Association of Plastic Arts and the SA Akademie vir Wetenskap en Kuns. 1942 designed the one franc and 50 centime coins for French Equatorial Africa. Designed the Springbok used on the SA 5 shilling coin of 1947 and subsequent years. 1930–34 lived in London, visiting Italy, France, The Netherlands, Germany and Austria; 1948 visited Central Africa. From 1952 made frequent visits to Europe. Lived in Pretoria. In 1988 The Steynberg Museum was opened in Pretoria.

Exhibitions Participated in group exhibitions from 1937 in SA, Belgium, The Netherlands, Zimbabwe and Italy; 1948 Tate Gallery, London, SA Art Exhibition; 1951 SA Akademie vir Wetenskap en Kuns, Pretoria, first of several solo exhibitions of his smaller works held throughout SA; 1956 Quadrennial Exhibition.

Awards Royal College of Art August Spencer Trophy for stone carving; 1939 Gold Medal for his design of a statue "The Role of Diamonds in SA"; 1953 Medal of Honour, SA Akademie vir Wetenskap en Kuns; 1953 "The Political Prisoner" prize, London; 1972 awarded an Honorary Doctorate from the University of Pretoria.

Represented Hester Rupert Art Museum, Graaff-Reinet; Potchefstroom Museum; Pretoria Art Museum; SA Akademie vir Wetenskap en Kuns; SA National Gallery, Cape Town; Steynberg Museum, Pretoria; University of the Orange Free State; University of Pretoria; University of Stellenbosch.

Public Commissions 1934 statue of Batholomew Dias, SA House, London; 1935–49 numerous memorials and statues of public figures in SA including in 1937 the Andries Pretorius Monument, Graaff-Reinet; 1939 Centenary Monument, Potchefstroom; 1942 Blood River Monument, Natal; 1942 Huguenot Monument, Franschhoek, Cape Province; 1946 General Louis Botha, Equestrian Statue, Union Buildings, Pretoria; 1949 Sarel Cilliers Statue, Kroonstad, Orange Free State; 1955 Andries Pretorius, Equestrian Statue, City Hall, Pretoria; 1960 Peace of Vereeniging Monument, Vereeniging, Transvaal; 1960 Piet Retief Statue, Pietermaritzburg; 1967 Pair of Lechwe, Lusaka Airport, Zambia; 1968 J G Strijdom Head, Strijdom Square, Pretoria.
Publication by Steynberg n' *Outobiografie*, 1982, Cum Books, Roodepoort.
References Edgar C L Bosman, *Coert Steynberg*, 1968, J L van Schaik, Pretoria; Collectors' Guide; KK; Our Art 1; Art SA; SAA; 20C SA Art; SAP&S; Oxford Companion to Art (under SA); SESA; BSAK 1 & 2; Enc S'n A; SA Art; 3Cs; AASA; *Lantern* May 1952; *SA Panorama* February 1957, November 1960, March 1963, February 1964, August 1972, June 1980 & September 1983; *Die Huisgenoot* 13 November 1959; *Fontein* vol 1 no 3, 1960; *SA Art News* 10 August 1961; *De Arte* 26 April 1982.

STEYNBERG Peter John

Born 1953 East London.
A painter of landscapes, portraits, still life, figures, wildlife and abstract pictures. Works in oil. 1985–87 a series on Rock Art.
Studies 1973–76 Rhodes University, under Professor Brian Bradshaw (qv); 1985–87 Rhodes University, under Professor Robert Brooks (qv), gaining an MFA.
Profile 1987 a member of the East London Fine Art Society. 1977–84 lived in Underberg, Natal; thereafter in Grahamstown.
Exhibitions He has participated in several group exhibitions from 1976 held throughout SA; 1987 1820 Settlers National Monument, Grahamstown, solo exhibition.

STEYNBERG Yvonne

Born 1928 Oudtshoorn, Cape Province.
A painter of landscapes and figures. Works in oil, gouache and wash.
Studies Port Elizabeth Technical College, under John Muff-Ford (qv), Walter Wiles (qv), Joan Wright (qv), Dorothy Kay (qv) and Professor Robert Bain (qv), gaining an Art Diploma; part-time at the Michaelis School of Fine Art.
Profile A journalist and interior designer. 1966 taught interior design classes at the Port Elizabeth Technical College. Has visited Europe, the USA and Argentina.
Exhibitions She has participated in several group exhibitions in SA and the USA; 1959 first of 52 solo exhibitions held in SA.
Represented C P Nel Museum, Oudtshoorn, Cape Province; Hester Rupert Art Museum, Graaff-Reinet; Molteno Museum, Cape Province; Port Elizabeth Technikon; Walter Battiss Museum, Somerset East; Welkom Technikon.
References BSAK 1; AASA; Port Elizabeth School of Art.

STIGLINGH Linda Alice

Born 1954 Transvaal.
A self-taught artist of representational and abstract works. Uses material dye, wax, bleach, wax crayons and watercolours.
Profile A member of the South African Arts Foundation.
Exhibitions 1983 Hermine Spies (qv) Studio Gallery, first of two solo exhibitions; she has participated in several group exhibitions in SA from 1984.

STOCK Francis

Born 1921 Edenburg, Orange Free State.
A painter of still life. Works in oil.
Studies University of Natal, where attained a BA(FA) in 1941.
Profile 1950–58 lived in Stockholm, Sweden and Paris, France.
Exhibitions He has participated in group exhibitions in SA; 1960 Quadrennial Exhibition.
Award 1959 Second Prize at the Pretoria Ideal Homes Exhibition.

STODEL Jennifer Ren

Born 1954 Cape Town.
A painter and graphic artist of landscapes, seascapes, portraits, figures, still life, genre and abstract pictures. Works in oil, watercolour, gouache, ink, pencil and in various graphic media. 1977–78 a series of "African Myth and Politics"; 1979–84 "Dynamics of Man and Woman"; 1985 Kalk Bay landscapes.
Studies 1973 under Pitika Ntuli (qv) in Swaziland; 1975–78 Ruth Prowse School of Art, Cape Town, under André van Zyl (qv) and Edwine Simon (qv); 1980 Michaelis School of Fine Art, under Kevin Atkinson (qv) and Nathan Margalit (qv).
Profile 1984 Founder and Director of the Creative Arts Studio. 1982–86 taught art privately. She has acted in and directed plays in SA. A designer of stage sets and of a record sleeve. During the 1970s her poems were published in *Contrast* magazine. 1974–76 lived in Namaqualand and SWA/Namibia; 1978 in Israel.
Exhibitions She has participated in several group exhibitions in SA from 1974; 1974 Royal Swazi Hotel, Swaziland, first of 10 solo exhibitions, of which one was held in London, four in SWA/Namibia, three in Cape Town and one in Johannesburg.
Represented Arts Association SWA/Namibia Collection.
Publication by Stodel Gemstones of South Africa.

STOKHUYZEN Frederike

Born 1938 Johannesburg.
A painter of landscapes and the South African flora and fauna. Works in oil, watercolour, pencil and wash. Uses a palette knife when working in oil.

Studies Rhodes University, under Cecil Todd (qv) and Walter Battiss (qv), gaining a BA(FA) in 1959.

Profile A member of the SAAA. 1961 an itinerant art teacher in the Cape Province; 1962 an art teacher at Herzlia, Cape Town. Has travelled extensively in SA and to SWA/Namibia, the UK, Canada and France.

Exhibitions 1960 Vanderbijlpark, Transvaal, first of 29 solo exhibitions held in SA and the UK; she has participated in numerous group exhibitions from 1964 in the UK, France, West Germany and SA; 1981 Republic Festival Exhibition.

References BSAK 1; AASA; *Artlook* April 1968 & January 1971.

STONE Simon Patrick

Born 1952 Lady Grey, Cape Province.

A painter of landscapes and figures. Works in oil, gouache, ink, charcoal, metal and the encaustic processes.

Studies 1973–78 Michaelis School of Fine Art, under Stanley Pinker (qv), gaining an Advanced Diploma in Fine Art in 1976 and awarded an Irma Stern Scholarship in 1976. 1979 made a study tour of Italian Renaissance Art in Italy.

Profile From 1985 a member of the Johannesburg Art Foundation. 1983 a part-time lecturer in lithography at the University of Witwatersrand; 1985 a part-time teacher at the Johannesburg Art Foundation. 1987 working on a series of paintings with Braam Kruger (qv).

Exhibitions 1978 Fabian Fine Art, Cape Town, first of four solo exhibitions held in SA; he has participated in several group exhibitions from 1980 in SA and Botswana; 1982 National Gallery, Gaborone, Botswana, Exhibition of SA Art; 1985 Cape Town Triennial; 1987 Karen McKerron Gallery, Johannesburg, joint exhibition with Michael Murphy (qv); 1988 Johannesburg Art Gallery, Vita Art Now; 1988 Gallery International, Cape Town, joint exhibition with William Kentridge (qv).

Award 1986 Merit Award, Volkskas Atelier Exhibition.

Represented SA National Gallery, Cape Town; University of South Africa.

References *De Kat* May 1986.

STOPFORTH Paul

Born 1945 Johannesburg.

A painter and a graphic artist of figures and portraits. Works in oil, charcoal, graphite, wax and the encaustic processes. 1980 a series of 20 drawings based on the death of Steve Biko.

Studies 1964–67 Witwatersrand Technical College, under Joyce Leonard (qv) and George Boys (qv), gaining a National Art Teachers Diploma; 1984–85 on a British Council Scholarship at the Royal College of Art, London, under Peter de Francia, John Golding and Michael Heindorff, gaining a Short Course Certificate.

Profile 1970 a member of the Theatre Council of Natal. 1976 a member of the Selection Committee of the NSA. 1977 a founder member and a Director of the Market Gallery, Johannesburg. 1968–71 a lecturer at the Natal Technical College; 1971–75 a part-time lecturer in fine arts at the University of Natal; 1976 a part-time lecturer in the Department of Architecture at the University of Natal, Durban; 1977 tutor, 1978 senior tutor, subsequently lecturer in painting and drawing at the University of the Witwatersrand until 1986. 1987 lived at Broederstroom, Transvaal. 1988 six months as Artist-in-Residence at Tufts University, Boston, USA, and six months in Paris.

Exhibitions He has participated in numerous group exhibitions from 1968 in SA and once in London; 1971 Walsh-Marais Gallery, Durban, first of seven solo exhibitions held in SA; 1981 Market Gallery, Johannesburg, joint exhibition with Michael Goldberg (qv); 1982 National Gallery, Gaborone, Botswana, Exhibition of SA Art; 1985 Tributaries, touring SA and West Germany; 1986 Everard Read Gallery, Johannesburg, joint exhibition with Hillary Graham (qv) and Richard Smith (qv); 1987 Johannesburg Art Gallery, Vita Art Now.

Awards 1971 Institute of Race Relations Award, Art SA Today; 1985 Rodney Burn Award for Figurative Drawing, Royal College of Art; 1986 Ian Haggie Award.

Represented Durban Art Gallery; Johannesburg Art Gallery; Pretoria Art Museum; SA National Gallery, Cape Town; University of the Witwatersrand.

References Avril Herber, *Conversations*, 1979, Bateleur Press; *The Council House*, edited by Lee Nordness, Perimeter Press Inc., Wisconsin, USA; BSAK 1; 3Cs; AASA; LSAA; photographic essay, *Art* December 1987.

STORK Annette Else

Born 1943 South Africa.

A painter, graphic artist and sculptor of portraits, figures, wildlife and abstract pieces. Works in oil, acrylic, gouache, ink, pencil, charcoal, various graphic media, wood and ceramics. 1980 a series on nature conservation; 1981 "Masks", a combination of ceramics and painting; 1984 a series on fertility.

Studies 1962–64 commercial art at the Witwatersrand Technical College, under Phil Botha (qv); 1966–67 an Advanced Course in Graphic Design, London College of Printing, UK.

Profile Numerous illustrations, book designs and dust jackets; 1965–66 and 1967–70 worked full-time in publishing.

Exhibitions 1980 Enthoven Gallery, Johannesburg, first of three solo exhibitions; 1981 Rand Afrikaans University, exhibition of "Masks".

Represented Rand Afrikaans University.

STRACK Peter-Burghard

Born 1940 Berlin/Lichterfelde, Germany.
Resided in SWA/Namibia from 1950.

A painter and graphic artist of religious and semi-religious dream-like subjects. Works in watercolour, coloured ink and in various graphic media.

Studies 1959–60 graphic art, Freie Kunstschule Stuttgart, West Germany, under Paul König; 1960–65 architecture and art at the Staatliche Akademie Baden-Württemberg, West Germany.
Profile 1974 a committee member, 1975–79 Vice-President, 1980 President, and from 1981 Honorary Life President of the Arts Association SWA/Namibia. Curator of the Permanent Collection of the Arts Association SWA/Namibia. A qualified, practising architect and an interior designer. A close friend of Adolf Jentsch (qv) for over twenty years. 1962 visited Rome; 1963 Turkey and Iran.
Exhibitions He has participated in many group exhibitions from 1967 in SWA/Namibia and once in Rhodesia (Zimbabwe); 1968 Windhoek, first of five solo exhibitions held in SWA/Namibia, one of which toured SA.
Represented Arts Association SWA/Namibia Collection.
Reference Art SWA.

STRAUSS Andre

Born 1937 Bloemfontein.
A painter of conceptual abstraction. Works in oil, acrylic, ink and pencil. A graphic artist.
Studies 1957–61 University of the Witwatersrand, under Charles Argent (qv) and Cecily Sash (qv), gaining a BA(FA)(Hons) in 1961 and a Higher Diploma in Education in 1962; 1986 registered for an MA(FA) at the University of the Witwatersrand.
Profile 1962 a lecturer at the Witwatersrand Technical College; 1964 head of the Art Department at Pretoria Boys High School. A photographer, designer and film maker. A writer of prose. 1986 made a three-month study tour of European galleries and collections.
Exhibitions He has participated in many group exhibitions from 1959 in SA; 1960 Quadrennial Exhibition; 1963 Lidchi Gallery, Johannesburg, first of five solo exhibitions held in Johannesburg.
Awards 1960 winner of both the painting and graphic sections of the Quadrennial Exhibition.
Represented University of South Africa.
References SAA; *Habitat* no 3, 1973.

STRAUSS Marié

Born 1955 Vereeniging, Transvaal.
A painter working in acrylic, ink, wash, pencil and charcoal.
Studies University of South Africa, under Nina Romm (qv) and Marion Arnold (qv).
Exhibitions She has participated in several group exhibitions from 1980 in SA; 1985 Karen McKerron Gallery, Johannesburg, first of three solo exhibitions.

STRAUSS Pamela

Born 1942 Pretoria.
A painter of still life. Works in oil and acrylic, draws in ink and pencil. 1973 a series of drawings based on nursery rhymes.

Studies Pretoria Technical College, under Robert Hodgins (qv), Zakkie Eloff (qv) and Peter Eliastam (qv).

Exhibitions She has participated in several group exhibitions from 1973 in Johannesburg, Pretoria and Cape Town.

Reference *Habitat* no 4, 1973.

STRICKLAND Anthony

Born 1920 Epsom, Surrey, England.

Resided in SA from 1959.

A painter of figures and landscapes. Works in oil, acrylic, ink, wash, pencil and charcoal. Sculpts in Cretan stone.

Studies 1935–38 Tonbridge Art School, Kent, UK.

Profile A member of the NSA and the Highway Art Group. Teaches art privately in Natal. 1942 lived in Ceylon (Sri Lanka); 1953–58 in Malaya (Malaysia).

Exhibitions He has participated in several group exhibitions from 1962 in SA; 1970 Lister Gallery, Johannesburg, first of 10 solo exhibitions held in SA.

Award 1963 Award, Art SA Today.

References BSAK 1; AASA; *Artlook* September 1970 & May 1974.

STROMSOE Frances Beryl

Born 1919 Johannesburg.

A painter of landscapes and seascapes. Works in oil and watercolour; also works with mosaic tiles and creates batiks.

Studies c.1937 Witwatersrand Technical College (Technikon); 1957–68 five courses on teaching child art; 1979–81 attended pottery classes at the Witwatersrand Technical College (Technikon); 1980–81 evening classes at the Witwatersrand Technikon.

Profile 1986–87 Chairman of the Art by the Sea Group, Margate. 1950–83 taught art at several schools. 1944 lived in Tanganyika (Tanzania). Has travelled throughout SA and extensively in Europe.

Exhibitions She has participated in several group exhibitions from 1934 in SA and in the UK.

STRUBEN Edith Frances Mary

Born c.1868 Pretoria.

Died 1936 Cape Town.

A painter of landscapes of the Transvaal and later of the Cape, who also painted flowers. Worked in watercolour.

Studies c.1901 Crystal Palace Art School, London; also in Paris and Rome and Cape Town.

Profile 1901 a committee member of the SA Drawing Club. A former Vice-President of the SA Society of Artists. Bequeathed the Edith Struben Scholarship to the University of Cape Town. Was actively involved in the preservation of old buildings in Cape Town, the Botanical Society of SA and in colour filming. Travelled in a caravan throughout SA. Revised and edited *Recollections of Adventures: pioneering and development in South Africa—1850-1911*, written by her father, Hendrik Wilhelm Struben, 1920.
Exhibitions Participated in group exhibitions from 1910 in SA and in the UK 1914–33.
Represented Africana Museum, Johannesburg; Pretoria Art Museum; SA National Gallery, Cape Town; University of Cape Town.
References SAA; SADNB; AMC4&7; DSAB; SAP&S; Pict Afr; DBA; BSAK 2; AASA.

STRYDOM Willem

Born 1945 Johannesburg.
A sculptor of abstract pieces. Works in wood, slate, bronze, steel and cast iron.
Studies 1972–75 Witwatersrand Technical College, gaining a Diploma in Fine Art and a Higher Diploma in Fine Art; 1977–78 St Martin's School of Art, London, under Phillip King (*b*.1934); University of Natal, where gained an MA(FA) in 1984.
Profile Worked as a photo-journalist with *The Star* newspaper for several years. 1979 taught sculpture and photography at the University of Natal. From 1980 a senior tutor in sculpture and photography at the University of the Witwatersrand.
Exhibitions He has participated in several group exhibitions held in SA; 1975 Thirteen Abel Road Gallery, Hillbrow, Johannesburg, solo exhibition; 1979 Hexagon Theatre Complex, University of Natal, Pietermaritzburg, solo exhibition; 1982 Johannesburg Art Gallery, Guest Artist; 1985 Cape Town Triennial; 1985 Tributaries, touring SA and West Germany.
Awards 1975 SAAA Award, Art SA Today; 1977 Metalart Award, open category, jointly with Ian Redelinghuys (qv).
Represented Durban Art Gallery; Johannesburg Art Gallery; Munich Gallery, West Germany; SA National Gallery, Cape Town; University of South Africa; University of the Witwatersrand.
Public Commission 1979 steel and brass sculpture, Standard Brass, Iron and Steel Corporation, Benoni, Transvaal.
References AASA; LSAA; *Habitat* no 27, 1977.

STUCKENBERG Borge

Born 1867 Denmark.
Died 1942.
Thought to have come to SA in 1896, although paintings of SA dated 1887 are known to exist.
A painter of landscapes. Worked in oil.
Studies 1883–89 Danish Academy.

Profile A member of the Society of Fine Arts.

Exhibitions Participated in the 1898 Second Exhibition of Fine Arts, Cape Town; 1899 Cape Town, joint exhibition with George M Winkles (qv), James S Morland (qv) and Hugo Naudé (qv); 1948 Copenhagen, Denmark, included in the Association of National Arts Exhibition.

Reference Register SA & SWA.

SUMNER Maud Eyston

Born 1902 Johannesburg.

Died 1985 Johannesburg.

A painter of landscapes, snowscapes, interiors, still life, city scenes, figures, portraits, religious scenes and semi-abstract paintings. Worked in oil and watercolour. Designs for stained glass windows and tapestries. A number of series of paintings including from 1953 flight series; 1954–57 desert series; 1965 SWA/Namibian series.

Studies Under Albert E Gyngell (qv), while at Roedean School for Girls, Johannesburg; 1925 briefly at Westminster School of Art, London, under Frank Dobson (*c*.1886–1963) and Bernard Meninsky (1891–1950); 1926 drawing lessons under the sculptor Naoum Aronson in Paris; 1926–29 Académie de la Grande Chaumière, Paris, under Georges Desvallières (1861–1950) and François Quelvée (1884–1967); 1929–32 Ateliers de l'Art Sacré, Paris, under Maurice Denis (1870–1943); 1932 briefly under André Lhote; *c*.1934 Académie de la Grande Chaumière, Paris, under Othon Friesz (1879–1949); 1938 Académie Ranson, Paris, under Roger Bissiere (1884–1964).

Profile 1926 shared a house with Maria Blanchard (1881–1932), influenced by the Intimists. A member of the Woman's International Art Club and from 1941 of the New Group. 1945 illustrated the Afrikaans translation of Shakespeare's *Hamlet*, Stewart, Cape Town. 1976 a print of her painting "Madonna & Child" was produced. 1902–22 lived in Johannesburg; 1922–25 at Oxford University, England (reading English Literature and Language, French, Greek and Latin); 1926–32 in Paris, with visits to SA and England; 1933–34 in SA; 1934–39 in Paris; 1939–41 in England, working as an ambulance driver; 1941–47 in Johannesburg; 1947–78 lived and worked mostly in Paris, but also in London and SA. In 1953 and 1954 visited Israel and in 1965 SWA/Namibia; from 1978 based in Johannesburg.

Exhibitions Participated in group exhibitions from 1932 in Italy, France, Belgium, the UK, the USA, Brazil, Greece, West Germany, SA and Rhodesia (Zimbabwe); 1932 Galerie Druet, Paris, first of over 70 solo exhibitions held in Paris, London, Oxford, Salisbury (Harare), Bulawayo and from 1942 throughout SA; 1948 Tate Gallery, London, SA Art Exhibition; 1964 Quadrennial Exhibition; 1964 the opening exhibition of the new Pretoria Art Museum, Prestige Exhibition; 1968 SAAA Gallery, Pretoria, Retrospective Exhibition; 1976 Pieter Wenning Gallery, Johannesburg, Fifty-Year Retrospective Exhibition; 1977 Pretoria Art Museum, Retrospective Exhibition; 1978 SA National Gallery, Cape Town, Retrospective Exhibition; 1980 Hoffer Gallery, Pretoria, Retrospective Exhibition; 1981 Republic Festival Exhibition; 1981 William Humphreys Art Gallery, Kimberley, exhibition.

Award 1971 Medal of Honour, SA Akademie vir Wetenskap en Kuns.

Represented Africana Museum, Johannesburg; Ann Bryant Gallery, East London; Arts Association SWA/Namibia Collection; Ashmolean Museum, Oxford, UK; Contemporary Art Society, London, UK; Durban Art Gallery; Hester Rupert Art Museum, Graaff-Reinet; Johannesburg Art Gallery; King George VI Art Gallery, Port Elizabeth; Municipal Museum of Modern Art, The Hague, The Netherlands; Musée de l'Art Moderne, Paris, France; National Museum, Bloemfontein; Pietersburg Collection; Potchefstroom Museum; Pretoria Art Museum; Rand Afrikaans University; Sandton Municipal Collection; SA Akademie vir Wetenskap en Kuns; SA National Gallery, Cape Town; Tatham Art Gallery, Pietermaritzburg; University of Cape Town; University of the Orange Free State; University of Pretoria; University of South Africa; University of Stellenbosch; University of the Witwatersrand; William Humphreys Art Gallery, Kimberley.

References Charles Eglington, *Maud Sumner*, 1967, Purnell & Sons SA, Cape Town; PSA; Collectors' Guide; Our Art 1; Art SA; SAA; 20C SA Art; AMC4&7; SAP&S; SAP&D; SSAP; Bénézit; BSAK 1 & 2; SA Art; Art SWA; Oxford Companion to 20C Art (under SA); 3Cs; AASA; *South Africana* May 1956, February 1957 & February 1959; *SA Panorama* May 1959; *Artlook* October 1967 & December 1969; *Habitat* no 9, 1974; *Gallery* Summer 1981; *SA Arts Calendar* March 1984; *De Arte* April 1985; *De Kat* August 1985.

SUZMAN Christine (née Egeland)

Born 1945 SA Embassy, Stockholm, Sweden.

A sculptor of animals, particularly of horses and birds. Works in bronze and ceramics. A series of ceramic horses in the tradition of the Chinese T'ang dynasty.

Studies *c.*1969–74 ceramic classes under Val and John Edwards.

Profile A number of illustrations for books and magazines.

Exhibitions 1971 Goodman Gallery, Johannesburg, first of three solo exhibitions.

References *Artlook* September 1971 & March 1973.

SWANEPOEL Nicolene Christine

Born 1962 Vanderbijlpark, Transvaal.

A painter and graphic artist of figures, animals, landscapes and mythological pictures. Works in oil, acrylic, pencil, mixed media on paper and in various graphic media.

Studies 1980–83 University of Pretoria, under Professor Nico Roos (qv), gaining a BA(FA).

Profile 1986 a member of the SAAA. 1984 illustrations for children's books for Daan Retief Publishers. 1985 worked as an arts journalist for *Die Transvaler*.

Exhibitions She has participated in several group exhibitions from 1984; 1986 SAAA Gallery, Pretoria, joint exhibition with her brother François Swanepoel, a photographer.

SWART Christopher Vernon

Born 1959 Stellenbosch, Cape Province.

A painter of portraits and figures. Works in oil, ink and pencil. From 1982 mainly working in airbrush. 1982 "Icon Analysis" series; 1983 "India Import" series.

Studies 1977–83 University of Stellenbosch, under Professor Larry Scully (qv) and Louis Jansen van Vuuren (qv), gaining a BA(FA) in 1981 and a BA(FA) (Hons) in 1982. Awarded the Maggie Laubser Bursary 1980–81 and the Ruth Prowse Bursary 1982–83.

Profile From 1986 has taught painting and art history at the Tygerberg Art Centre, Cape Province. 1982 stage designs for the H B Thom Theatre, Stellenbosch. 1984 travelled extensively in SWA/Namibia.

Exhibitions He has participated in several group exhibitions from 1980.

Award 1981 Cuesta Award, Stellenbosch.

Represented SA National Museum of Military History, Johannesburg.

SWART Gert Petrus

Born 1952 Durban.

A sculptor of animals, portrait heads, figures, anthropomorphic pieces, insectivorous pieces and objects with recurring tree, chair and bowl motifs. Works in wood, bronze, stone, ciment fondu and multi-media.

Studies 1982–83 Natal Technikon, under Andries Botha (qv) and Jeremy Wafer.

Profile From 1987 a member of the NSA. 1983–87 a co-founder of and teacher at the Community Arts Workshop, Durban.

Exhibitions He has participated in several group exhibitions from 1978 throughout SA; 1983 Gallery 567, Durban, first of two solo exhibitions.

Awards 1986 and 1987 the Hans Merensky Merit Awards for wood sculpture.

Represented Tatham Art Gallery, Pietermaritzburg.

SWART Ryno

Born 1945 Springbok, Namaqualand.

A painter of figures, landscapes and still life. Major themes of dancers, nudes, portraits, private mythology and the female observed. Works in oil, watercolour, pastel, pencil and charcoal.

Studies 1965–68 University of Stellenbosch, under Otto Schröder (qv), gaining a BA(FA); 1982 l'Ecole des Beaux Arts, Paris.

Profile 1969 a lecturer at the East London Technical College; 1970–79 a lecturer at the Witwatersrand Technical College; from 1984 a lecturer at the Ruth Prowse School of Art, Cape Town. 1971–76 worked in graphic design and produced a number of illustrations. 1972–73 worked in the film industry in Rhodesia (Zimbabwe), for which he won two awards. 1979 choreographed, by drawings, a ballet performed by PACT. 1977–78 spent a year in Paris; 1982 a seven-month trip to La Réunion, Mauritius, Greece, France and The Netherlands.

Exhibitions He has participated in several group exhibitions from 1979; 1979 Civic Theatre, Johannesburg, first of four solo exhibitions held in Johannesburg and Cape Town.

SWART Tjaart Johannes

Born 1933 SA.

A sculptor of portraits, figures and abstract pieces. Works in stone, ciment fondu, wood and ceramics.

Studies 1955–56 Cape Town Teachers Training College, gaining a Diploma in Art.

Profile 1957–65 an art teacher at the P J Olivier Art Centre, Stellenbosch; 1966 at Sarah Siddons School, Paddington, London; 1967 at the Ebury Bridge Boys High School, Victoria, London; 1968–69 at St Mary's, Kentish Town, London. 1970–82 a senior art lecturer at the Hewat Training College, Cape Town. 1970 opera costume designs for the Nico Malan Opera House, Cape Town.

Exhibitions 1967 Johannesburg, participated in a group exhibition; 1986 Grassroots Gallery, Westville, Natal, solo exhibition.

SWIFT Tony

Born 1951 Cape Town.

A painter and graphic artist of landscapes, portraits, still life, genre and abstract pictures. Works in oil, watercolour, gouache, ink, wash, pencil, charcoal and in various graphic media. Several series including: 1972 "Multiple Images"; 1978 "Piano"; 1980 "Papagalo"; 1984 "Settlement".

Studies 1969–75 Rhodes University, under Professor Brian Bradshaw (qv). Awarded the Rhodes University Art Scholarship 1969–72 and gained an MFA in 1975.

Profile 1969 a member of the Grahamstown Group; from 1974 a member and 1978–81 a committee member of the East London Fine Arts Society; a member of the SAAA. 1974–85 Head of the Art Department, Cambridge High School, East London; from 1986 Principal of the Johan Carinus Art Centre, Grahamstown. 1979–85 Chairman of the East London Schools Art Committee. 1983 stage designs for the Guild Theatre, East London. 1971, 1973 and 1975 visited SWA/Namibia.

Exhibitions He has participated in numerous group exhibitions from 1969 in SA; 1981 Republic Festival Exhibition; 1983 Port Elizabeth, joint exhibition with David Grant (qv); 1985 held a solo exhibition in a private house.

Represented Hood Point Collection of Eastern Cape Contemporary Art.

Reference AASA.

SYME William

Born 1820 Cape Town.

Died 1866.

A painter of landscapes. Worked in oil. Produced a number of etchings. His engravings on copper are of military activities of the Boer/Basuto war.

Studies 1853 photography in Edinburgh under Thompson and Ross.
Profile A coppersmith and collodion photographer, who owned his own photographic business in Cape Town 1854–57. Lived in Cape Town, travelled to Europe in 1853.
Exhibitions Participated in group exhibitions held in Cape Town from 1851.
References Pict Art; Pict Afr; BSAK 1.

SYMONDS Henry

Born 1949 Kimberley, Cape Province.
A landscape artist. Works in acrylic and enamel on canvas; also draws.
Studies 1970–73 Michaelis School of Fine Art, gaining a BA(FA); 1979 gained an MA (Art Education) from the Rhode Island School of Design, Providence, USA.
Profile Teaches art in Cape Town.
Exhibitions He has exhibited in the USA, The Netherlands, West Germany and SA; 1982 Cape Town Triennial; 1984 Gallery International, Cape Town, solo exhibition; 1985 Cape Town Triennial.
Represented SA National Gallery, Cape Town.
Reference AASA.

T

TAIT Adela Seton see SETON-TAIT Adela

TAIT Pauline Hannah
Born 1922 Detroit, Michigan, USA.
Resided in SA from 1949.
A painter of landscapes and space/atmosphere. Works in watercolour.
Studies Mainly self-taught, with a number of lessons from Marjorie Bowen (qv).
Profile From 1977 a member of the WSSA and from 1979 of the Artists Market, Johannesburg. 1973–77 lived in the Transkei.
Exhibitions She has participated in numerous group exhibitions from 1978 in SA and once in the USA; 1983 East London, solo exhibition.

TASKER (Audrey) Rita
Born 1945 Lancaster, Lancashire, England.
Resided in SA from 1950.
A sculptor working in ceramics. 1977–80 vessels, 1980–83 landscapes, from 1984 process art, 1985–86 funerary columns, 1987 figures.
Studies 1974–77 Witwatersrand Technical College (Technikon), under Spies Venter (qv) and Suzette Munnick, gaining a National Diploma in Art and Design; 1984–86 Witwatersrand Technikon, under Suzette Munnick, where attained a Higher Diploma in Ceramic Sculpture.
Profile From 1975 a member of the APSA, a committee member in 1980–81. 1978–79 and 1984–85 a ceramics lecturer at the Witwatersrand Technikon; from 1987 at the Vaal Triangle Technikon. Since 1976 she has also produced functional pottery. Has written numerous articles for *Sgraffiti*, an APSA publication.
Exhibitions She has participated in numerous group exhibitions from 1976 in SA; 1979 Helen de Leeuw, Johannesburg, first of four solo exhibitions held in Johannesburg and Pretoria.
Represented Corobrik Collection, University of Natal; Johannesburg Art Gallery; Linder Collection, Johannesburg College of Education; Touch Gallery, SA National Gallery, Cape Town.

TATHAM Susan Kathleen
Born 1956 Langebaanweg, Cape Province.
An artist depicting figures and abstract pictures. Works in mixed media and in various drawing and graphic media.

WILLEM STRYDOM
Otjittinduua II 1985–1987
Belfast Granite and Bronze 400 cm High
Johannesburg Art Gallery

MAUD SUMNER
Red Venice 1952
Oil on Canvas 89,2 × 105,2 cm
Johannesburg Art Gallery

Studies 1974–76 Pretoria Technical College, under Ian Redelinghuys (qv) and Gunther van der Reis (qv); 1977 Port Elizabeth Technical College, under Robert Brooks (qv); 1978–79 Michaelis School of Fine Art, under Jules van de Vijver (qv).
Profile From 1986 a member of the Society of Designers in SA. From 1980 a lecturer in clothing design at the Cape Technikon.
Exhibitions She has participated in many group exhibitions from 1982 in SA; 1982 Cape Town Triennial.
Award 1976 First Prize for Graphic Art, SAAA, Pretoria.
Reference AASA.

TAYLOR (Alfred) Gordon

Born 1891 Pretoria.
Died 1971.
A mainly self-taught painter of landscapes, marine scenes and later, of animals, particularly racehorses. Worked in oil and watercolour, drew in pastel, charcoal and pencil.
Studies 1930 under George W Pilkington (qv).
Profile Educated in England at Eton and at the Woolwich Military Academy, he served in WWI in France, was wounded and lost a leg. From 1919 to the early 1930s he farmed in the Ceres district. After 1930 he began painting professionally. From 1940 he served on the General Staff of the Union Defence Force. Throughout WWII the subject matter of his artistic work was military, his marine scenes being of particular significance. 1944 appointed Official War Artist to the SA Naval Forces. Saw service in the Middle East and North Africa, recording scenes of the desert war. A Steward of the SA Turf Club. Wrote a series of illustrated letters during 1914–16 signed "A Subaltern RFA" for *Country Life* magazine.
Exhibitions Participated in group exhibitions in the UK, Pretoria and Johannesburg; 1932–51 numerous solo exhibitions held in Cape Town, East London and Pretoria.
Award 1918 Chevalier Ordre de la Couronne, Belge.
Represented Ann Bryant Gallery, East London; SA National Gallery, Cape Town; SA National Museum of Military History, Johannesburg.
Public Commissions 1945 paintings for SA Railways; racing pictures for SA Turf Clubs.
References SAP&S; BSAK 1; SA Art; SAA; AASA.

TAYLOR Janet

Born 1928 Germiston, Transvaal.
A painter of landscapes, animals, birds and flowers. Works in watercolour.
Studies 1946–48 Witwatersrand Technical College, under James Gardner (qv), gaining a Diploma in Commercial Art.
Profile From 1979 a member of the WSSA. From *c.*1981 a member of the Brush and Chisel Club.
Exhibitions She has participated in several group exhibitions from 1979 in SA and London; 1979 held the first of three solo exhibitions.

TAYLOR Lorna

Born 1941 Johannesburg.
A graphic artist.
Studies 1959–62 University of the Witwatersrand, where gained a BA(FA); 1963–65 on a two-year post-graduate scholarship at Brera Academy and Grafica Workshop, Milan, Italy; 1965–67 Atelier 17, Paris.
Profile Experimented in Op art. In 1969 she settled in Europe.
Exhibitions She has participated in many group exhibitions in SA and Europe; 1968 Lidchi Gallery, Johannesburg, first solo exhibition.
Represented Johannesburg Art Gallery; National Library, Paris, France; SA National Gallery, Cape Town; University of the Witwatersrand; Victoria and Albert Museum, London, England.
References 3Cs; AASA.

TAYLOR Roy Cecil

Born 1919 Queenstown, Cape Province.
From 1952 a self-taught painter of landscapes and seascapes. Works in oil.
Profile 1940–65 a professional clarinettist and saxophonist of both jazz and classical music. 1940–45 a member of an Army band; 1959–64 of a Naval band in Simonstown, Cape Province. 1921–48 lived in East London, 1948–58 in Johannesburg, 1959–64 in Cape Town and from 1965 in Natal.
Exhibition 1957 Herbert Evans Gallery, Johannesburg, solo exhibition.

TAYLOR Sydney ARBC

Born 1870 London.
Died 1952 Cape Town.
A painter of landscapes. Worked in oil, watercolour and pastel. His paintings generally include Cape homesteads.
Studies Royal College of Art, London.
Profile Came to SA as an artist-correspondent. An Associate of the Royal British Colonial Society of Artists; 1930–32 and 1937–39 President of the SA Society of Artists; 1932 a founder member of the National Academy of Fine Arts (SA); a member of the NSA. Included in Edward Roworth's (qv) essay "Landscape Art in SA", 1917, Studio Publication, *Art of the British Empire Overseas*.
Exhibitions 1924 British Empire Exhibition, Wembley, England; 1936 Empire Exhibition, Johannesburg; participated in group exhibitions in London in 1938; 1946 Cotswold Gallery, Cape Town, solo exhibition.
Represented Ann Bryant Gallery, East London; Durban Art Gallery; SA Cultural History Museum, Cape Town; SA National Gallery, Cape Town; University of Cape Town; War Museum of the Boer Republics. Bloemfontein.
References *The Arts in SA*, edited by WHK, 1933–34, The Knox Printing & Publishing Company, Durban; DBA; SAP&D; BSAK 1 & 2; AASA.

TEALE Julia
Born 1960 Shipley, England.
A painter working in oil.
Studies Gained a National Diploma in Fine Art in 1982 and a Higher Diploma in Fine Art (cum laude) in 1983 from the Natal Technikon; 1985 registered at the University of the Witwatersrand.
Exhibitions 1985 Cape Town Triennial; 1985 NSA Gallery, Durban, solo exhibition.
Represented Natal Technikon.

TEFFO Madimetja Michael
Born 1957 Pretoria.
A self-taught sculptor of figures, portraits and abstract pieces. Works in wood. Paints in watercolour, draws in ink and pencil, and produces woodcuts.
Profile 1984 an art teacher at the Diocesan School for Girls, Pretoria.
Exhibitions He has participated in several group exhibitions in SA, Botswana, the USA and West Germany; 1978 SAAA Gallery, Pretoria, first of six solo exhibitions; 1982, National Gallery, Gaborone, Exhibition of SA Art; 1985 Tributaries, touring SA and West Germany.
Represented Durban Art Gallery; Medical University of SA; Potchefstroom University for CHE; University of Pretoria.
References *African Insight* vol 14 no 2, 1984; *Lantern* January 1985.

TEMPLER (Kathleen) Joan
Born 1929 Edenburg, Orange Free State.
Resided in SA until 1969.
A painter of abstract pictures. Works in mixed media.
Studies 1943–47 Pretoria Art Centre, under Le Roux Smith Le Roux (qv) and Marjorie Long (qv); 1948–51 on a scholarship at the University of Natal, gaining a BA(FA), studying under Geoffrey Long (qv); 1969 studied at Columbia University, New York, USA.
Profile 1943–47 a member of the Young Arts Group. A member of the NSA. 1953–54 and 1958–62 taught at Pretoria Girls High School, 1955 at Johannesburg Girls High School. 1965 a lecturer in visual communications at the School of Architecture, University of Natal, Durban. 1956–57 a scenic designer for the Marlowe Theatre, Canterbury, England, on her return designed sets for SA theatres. In 1968 began experimenting with vitreous enamels. 1956–57 lived in England; 1957–65 in Pretoria; 1965–69 in Durban; 1969–73 in New York, USA; 1973 in Atlanta, Georgia, USA; presently living in the UK. Married to the architect John Templer.
Exhibitions Participated in group exhibitions in SA; 1966 Pretoria, first of several solo exhibitions; 1969 Durban Art Gallery, joint exhibition with Patrick O'Connor (qv) and Andrew Verster (qv).

Award 1967 Oppenheimer Painting Prize, Art SA Today.
Represented Durban Art Gallery.
Public Commissions 1959 mural, Pretoria Showgrounds; murals for Volkskas in Humansdorp, Cape Province, and Roodepoort, Transvaal; several murals in private and commercial buildings in Pretoria and Durban; 1971 mural installed in Jan Smuts Airport, Johannesburg.
References SAA; AASA.

TEN KROODEN Lynette

Born 1955 Pretoria.
A painter and graphic artist of landscapes and abstract pictures. Works in oil, acrylic, watercolour, pencil, wash and in various graphic media.
Studies 1974–78 University of Pretoria, under Professor Nico Roos (qv), gaining a BA(FA); registered for an MA(FA) in 1979.
Profile From 1979 a member of the SAAA. A graphic artist for the Council of Psychiatric Research.
Exhibitions She has participated in several group exhibitions from 1979 in SA; *c.*1983 Pietersburg, first of four solo exhibitions.

TENNANT Alice (née Aubry)

Born 1890 Paris, France.
Died 1976 Cape Town.
Resided in SA from *c.*1922.
A painter of flowers, landscapes, animals and figures, particularly of children playing. Worked in oil, pastel, gouache, ink and watercolour. Numerous drawings.
Studies Académie de la Grande Chaumière, Paris.
Profile Illustrated a number of children's books, wrote and illustrated a children's section of *The Cape Argus*. An opera singer. 1922–43 lived in Stellenbosch and Jonkershoek, from 1943 in Newlands, Cape Town.
Exhibitions Participated in group exhibitions from 1905 in Paris, France, Rhodesia (Zimbabwe) and in SA; 1922 Cape Town, first of several solo exhibitions; 1956 and 1960 Quadrennial Exhibitions.
Represented Hester Rupert Art Museum, Graaff-Reinet; King George VI Art Gallery, Port Elizabeth; Pretoria Art Museum; SA National Gallery, Cape Town; University of Pretoria; University of Stellenbosch.
References Collectors' Guide; PSA; Art SA; SAA; 20C SA Art; SAP&S; SAP&D; BSAK 1 & 2; AASA.

TERBLANCHE Jacobus Filipus (Philip)

Born 1930 Tzaneen, Northern Transvaal.
Died 1985 The Cape.
A painter of landscapes, portraits, still life and historic buildings, especially in Cape Town. Worked in oil.

Studies 1955–59 at St Martin's School of Fine Art, London, under Sir Francis Rhodes and the Camberwell School of Art, London, under Richard Eurich (*b*.1903).

Profile c.1960–64 Art Director of the Rhodesian Television Service, prior to joining the SABC. 1966–75 a lecturer at the Cape Technical College; 1976 taught in Worcester, Cape Province. 1955 hitchhiked from SA to London.

Exhibitions Participated in group exhibitions in SA and in the UK; 1957 London, first of many solo exhibitions held in the UK and throughout SA; 1981 Republic Festival Exhibition.

Represented SA Cultural History Museum, Cape Town.

Public Commissions Many portrait commissions both public and private. 1969 portraits of 10 famous Boer War Generals for the SA Defence Force Danie Theron Combat School, Kimberley.

References BSAK 1; AASA.

TE WATER June

Born 1924 Pretoria.

A sculptor of abstract pieces. Works in bronze, stone, ciment fondu and wood.

Studies 1942–44 Michaelis School of Fine Art, under Ivan Mitford-Barberton (qv); 1945–47 under Florencio Cuairan (qv); 1956–58 Michaelis School of Fine Art, under Lippy Lipshitz (qv).

Profile A member of the SAAA and from 1980 a founder member of the Artists Guild. 1976–81 a lecturer at the Ruth Prowse School of Art, Cape Town; 1976 taught the blind at the Touch Gallery, SA National Gallery, Cape Town. Teaches art privately. 1929–39 lived in London. Daughter of C T te Water, Foundation President of the SAAA.

Exhibitions She has participated in numerous group exhibitions from 1958 in SA, Brazil, the USA and Italy; 1959 SAAA Gallery, Cape Town, first of six solo exhibitions held in SA; 1960 Quadrennial Exhibition; 1978 SAAA Gallery, Cape Town, joint exhibition with Erik Laubscher (qv); 1981 Republic Festival Exhibition; 1983 Gowlett Gallery, Cape Town, joint exhibition with Olivia Scholnick (qv).

Award 1981 Sculpture Prize, Republic Festival Exhibition, Durban.

Represented Pietersburg Collection; University of Pretoria; William Fehr Collection, Cape Town.

Public Commissions 1973 "Time", Langenhoven Memorial Library, Oudtshoorn, Cape Province; 1976 portrait of Dr C T te Water, University of Pretoria; 1976 portrait of Dr D F Malan, *Die Burger* newspaper.

References Art SA; SAA; Register SA & SWA; BSAK 1; AASA; 3Cs; *Gallery* Spring 1983.

THACKWRAY James Vicary

Born 1919 Dordrecht, Eastern Cape.

A painter of figures, landscapes, seascapes, portraits, still life, genre and abstract pictures. Works in oil, acrylic, watercolour and charcoal. A graphic artist producing monotypes. Known for his paintings of rural people of the Cape in their environment.

Studies 1937 extra-murally at the Michaelis School of Fine Art, under Professor Edward Roworth (qv) and Melvin Simmers (qv); studied life drawing under Maurice van Essche (qv) and Alfred Krenz (qv).
Profile A member of the SAAA. Works as an art director for a textile screenprinting company.
Exhibitions 1948 Ashbey Galleries, Cape Town, first of 10 solo exhibitions held in SA; he has participated in numerous group exhibitions from 1952 in SA.
Represented Willem Annandale Art Gallery, Lichtenburg.

THERON Guillaume

Born 1947 Pietersburg, Northern Transvaal.
A sculptor of figures and abstract pieces. Works in stone, ciment fondu, wood, concrete, stainless steel and chrome resin. A graphic artist. 1971–79 a series for the Industrial Sculpture Park, Pietersburg, these pieces being executed in industrial waste material.
Studies 1963–67 Pretoria Technical College, under Gunther van der Reis (qv), Eugene-Leon Bouffa (qv) and Koos den Houting (qv), gaining a National Diploma in Art and Design.
Profile A member of the SAAA. 1980–81 conducted an art school in Pietersburg. From 1985 has made handknotted, painted, fibre wall hangings. 1974 spent three months in Paris. 1974 toured Scandinavia, Europe, Turkey, Israel and the Middle East.
Exhibitions He has participated in many group exhibitions from 1967 in SA and in a graphic exhibition in the USA; 1973 SAAA Gallery, Pretoria, first of 14 solo exhibitions; 1981 Republic Festival Exhibition.
Public Commissions 1968 three wood relief panels, Jan Smuts Airport, Johannesburg; 1971 wood relief, Civitas Building, Pretoria; 1971 three wood panels, Information Bureau, Pietersburg.
Reference AASA.

THERON Leo

Born 1926 Pretoria.
An artist working with thick stained glass slabs in reinforced concrete. His works are both figurative and abstract. Paints in oil and watercolour, his paintings being strongly influenced by his stained glass work.
Studies 1945–50 Rhodes University, under Professor Austin Winter Moore (qv) and Jack Heath (qv), gaining a BA(FA) (Hons); 1950–53 l'Ecole des Beaux Arts, Paris, under De la Haille and at l'Académie Julian, under Emile Sabouraud (*b*.1900); 1952 mural painting in Italy on an Italian Travel Bursary.
Profile From 1979 an Honorary Member of the Jacob Burckhardt Academy, Rome. 1958–65 a lecturer at the Pretoria Technical College. 1964 awarded a study bursary from the French Government to visit stained glass studios in France. Study tours of Spain, West Germany, The Netherlands and Switzerland.
Exhibitions 1953 SAAA Gallery, Cape Town, first of several solo exhibitions of his paintings; he has exhibited a number of paintings on group shows in SA from 1956; 1956 and 1960 Quadrennial Exhibitions.

Award 1978 Medal of Honour for painting, SA Akademie vir Wetenskap en Kuns, jointly with Bettie Cilliers-Barnard (qv).

Represented Hester Rupert Art Museum, Graaff-Reinet; University of Stellenbosch.

Public Commissions Numerous public commissions including 1972–74, Tower Block, SABC Building, Johannesburg; over 112 churches in SA, SWA/Namibia and Zimbabwe contain windows designed and executed by Theron including: Christ the King Catholic Church, Queenswood, Pretoria and Burgerspark Dutch Reformed Church, City Centre, Pretoria; 1979 stained glass window, donated by SA ex-servicemen, Church of Santa Maria delle Grazie, Ponticelli, Italy; he has also executed commissions for the University of South Africa, the University of Pretoria, Jan Smuts Airport, Johannesburg, the Ermelo and Pietersburg Civic Centres as well as the Hillbrow Post Office, Johannesburg.

References Art SA; SAA; 20C SA Art; BSAK 1 & 2; SA Art; AASA; LSAA; *Lantern* September 1967; *Artlook* November 1969; *SA Panorama* December 1969, December 1975, August 1979 & December 1986.

THEYS Conrad Nagel Doman

Born 1940 Montague, Cape Province.

A painter and graphic artist of landscapes, portraits, still life and genre. Works in oil, watercolour, ink-wash, pencil, charcoal, pastel and in various graphic media. 1976 a series entitled "A Place I Know", scenes of Elsiesriver, Cape Province.

Studies 1969–70 privately under Gregoire Boonzaier (qv); 1981–82 Ruth Prowse School of Art, Cape Town, under Edwine Simon (qv).

Profile From 1981 a committee member of the SAAA (Bellville); from 1982 a member of the Artists Guild and a committee member 1985–86. 1961–74 an art teacher at Loeriesfontein, Elsiesriver and Bellville, Cape Province. 1940–44 lived in Montague; 1944–47 and 1954–59 in Paarl, Cape Province; 1947–54 and 1962–66 in Loeriesfontein; 1960–61 in Oudtshoorn, Cape Province, and from 1967 in Bellville. Visits to Namaqualand and SWA/Namibia.

Exhibitions He has participated in many group exhibitions from 1969 in SA; 1978 Edrich Gallery, Stellenbosch, first of 10 solo exhibitions held throughout SA.

Represented National Gallery, Gaborone, Botswana; Pietersburg Collection; Willem Annandale Art Gallery, Lichtenburg.

Public Commissions 1975 an oil painting, Cape Divisional Council; 1979 an oil painting, Department of Health, Cape Town.

References AASA; *SA Panorama* November 1974.

THOMSON Nichola Carol

Born Eastbourne, Sussex, England.

Resided in SA from 1983.

A self-taught painter of wildlife. Works in acrylic and ink. A series of prints entitled "Big Five Cats".

Profile 1960–83 lived in Zimbabwe. Presently lives in Natal. Has travelled to Kenya.

Exhibitions She has participated in numerous group exhibitions from 1979 in Zimbabwe and SA; 1987 NSA Gallery, Durban, joint exhibition with A Minnie Cook (qv) and Jan Zaal (qv).

THORNLEY STEWART Cecil see STEWART Cecil Thornley

THURLOW Eunice Dorothea

Born 1925 Durban.

A painter, graphic artist and sculptor of landscapes, seascapes, wildlife, still life, figures, portraits and genre. Works in oil, acrylic, watercolour, gouache, ink, wash, pencil, charcoal, various graphic media and ciment fondu.

Studies 1943–46 Natal Technical College.

Profile From 1975 a member of the SAAA; from 1976 of the North Coast Art Group; from 1978 of the WSSA, subsequently becoming an Associate. 1964–67 lived in Welkom, Orange Free State, thereafter in Natal. 1985 visited Spain.

Exhibitions She has participated in many group exhibitions from 1948 in SA and once in West Germany and the UK; 1958 in a private gallery, Durban, first of six solo exhibitions held in SA.

Represented Killie Campbell Africana Library, University of Natal, Durban; Willem Annandale Art Gallery, Lichtenburg.

TIMLIN William Mitcheson RIBA

Born 1893 Ashington, Northumberland, England.

Died 1943 Kimberley, Cape Province.

Resided in SA from 1912.

An artist who worked in oil, ink, wash, watercolour and pastel. An etcher. His best-known works are his watercolour fantasies filled with fairytale-like figures; also painted landscapes.

Studies Armstrong College of Art, Newcastle, England; architecture and art in Kimberley.

Profile 1914 founded the art section of the Athenaeum Club, Kimberley; 1932 a founder member of the National Academy of Fine Arts (SA); a member of the SA Society of Artists and the SA Institute of Artists. A licentiate of the Royal Institute of British Architects. Designed the first cover for *The Outspan* magazine and provided a number of its illustrations; also designed seals, theatre programmes and sets. Illustrated numerous books including *Out of the Crucible* by Hedley Chilvers as well as *Kees van Die Kalahari* and others by G C & S B Hobson. An architect in partnership with Greatbatch in Kimberley. 1936 and 1939 visited Java, via Zanzibar.

Exhibitions Participated in group exhibitions in SA and the USA; 1914 first of several solo exhibitions held in Cape Town, Johannesburg and Kimberley; 1964 William Humphreys Art Gallery, Kimberley, Memorial Exhibition; 1966 Pieter Wenning Gallery, Johannesburg, posthumous exhibition; 1977 William Humphreys Art Gallery, Kimberley, Memorial Exhibition.

Represented Albany Museum, Grahamstown; Durban Art Gallery; Johannesburg Art Gallery; King George VI Art Gallery, Port Elizabeth; National Museum, Bloemfontein; Pretoria Art Museum; William Humphreys Art Gallery, Kimberley.

Public Commission 1933 Auditorium of the Johannesburg Colosseum Theatre (demolished).

Publications by Timlin *The Ship that Sailed to Mars*, 1923, George G Harrap & Company, London (a film of this book was made in the USA); *South Africa, a series of pencil sketches by William Timlin*, introduction by G E Chittenden, 1927, A & C Black, London; *The Building of a Fairy City*, unfinished.

References Collectors' Guide; SAA; Afr Repos; SESA; BSAK 1 (under M Timlin) & 2; Enc S'n A; 3Cs; AASA.

TITCOMBE Stewart

Born 1898.
Died 1965 Port Elizabeth.
A painter of marine subjects, buildings and portraits. Worked in oil, watercolour and pastel.

Profile Served in the Navy for a number of years prior to WWI. Lived in Port Elizabeth.

Exhibitions 1958 Greenwich Gallery, Johannesburg, first of several solo exhibitions; participated in group exhibitions in SA from 1960.

References SA Art; AASA.

TITLEY Maria (née Braunstein)

Born 1959 Salisbury, Rhodesia (Harare, Zimbabwe).
Resided in SA from 1980.
A painter of figures, portraits and wildlife. Works in oil, watercolour, pencil, wash and charcoal.

Studies 1980–82 Port Elizabeth Technikon, under Leon de Bliquy (qv), Neil Rodger (qv) and Hillary Graham (qv), gaining a National Diploma in Painting; 1983 Cape Technikon, under Jan Vermeiren (qv), gaining a Higher Diploma in Painting.

Profile 1982 a member of the EPSFA. Yearly visits to Zimbabwe. 1978 spent four months in Austria where she became influenced by Germanic romanticism. Has lived in Johannesburg from 1984. Married to Roger Titley (qv).

Public Commission 1983 The Fourteen Stations of the Cross, Elsiesriver Catholic Church, Cape Province.

TITLEY Roger Humphrey

Born 1960 Johannesburg.

A sculptor of satirical figures. Works in stone, ciment fondu, wood and fibreglass. A graphic artist.

Studies 1981–82 Port Elizabeth Technikon, under Leon de Bliquy (qv) and Hillary Graham (qv); 1983 Cape Technikon, under Jan Vermeiren (qv). Attained a National Diploma in Fine Art, specialising in graphics.

Profile 1983 a member of the EPSFA. 1984 taught sculpture at the Johannesburg Art Foundation; from 1984 has taught sculpture and graphics at FUBA. A freelance cartoonist. A number of his cartoons and illustrations have appeared in books and journals including in 1985–86 in *The Financial Mail* and *Business Day*. 1971–81 lived near Knysna, Cape Province and from 1984 in Johannesburg, yearly visits to Zimbabwe. Married to Maria Titley (qv).

Public Commission Three body casts for the Africana Museum, Johannesburg.

TODD Andrew

Born 1947.

A sculptor and a graphic artist. Creates metal constructions and works in various graphic media.

Profile Taught at the Witwatersrand Technical College.

Exhibitions He has participated in group exhibitions from the 1960s in SA, The Netherlands, Belgium and West Germany; also held solo exhibitions in SA.

Awards 1967 Sculpture Prize, SAAA, Pretoria; 1968 Graphics Prize, SAAA, Pretoria; 1971 Cambridge Shirt Award, Art SA Today.

Public Commission c.1968 relief mural for the Administration Block, Pretoria Technikon.

References BSAK 1; AASA.

TODD Cecil ARCA FRSA

Born 1912 Leeds, Yorkshire, England.

Resided in SA 1946–59.

A painter of still life, figures and religious pictures. Works in oil. A muralist and mosaic artist.

Studies 1930–34 Hull School of Art and the Royal College of Art, London, under Sir William Rothenstein (1872–1945), Gilbert Spencer (*b*.1892) and Eric Ravilious (1908–42).

Profile An Associate of the Royal College of Art and a Fellow of the Royal Society of Arts. 1946–49 a senior lecturer at the Natal Technical College; 1950–59 Professor of Fine Art at Rhodes University; 1959 Professor of Fine Art at the University of Makerere, Kampala, Uganda.

Exhibitions Exhibited in London at the Royal Academy, the Tate Gallery and with the New English Art Club; participated in group exhibitions in SA and Rhodesia (Zimbabwe) from 1948; 1956 and 1960 Quadrennial Exhibitions.

Represented Pretoria Art Museum.
Public Commissions 1961 mosaic mural, National Theatre, Kampala, Uganda; 1962 mosaic mural, Bank of India, Uganda.
References Art SA; SAA; BSAK 1 & 2; AASA.

TODD Guy Maurice Charles FRGS

Born 1925 Tientsin, China.
Resided in SA from 1959.
A painter of landscapes and seascapes. Works in watercolour.
Profile A member of the British Watercolour Society and a Fellow of the Royal Geographical Society. Taught privately in Plettenberg Bay and with the Fish Hoek Art Society. Opened the Seascape Gallery in Fish Hoek. Lived in the UK; 1943–46 served in the Royal Naval Volunteer Reserves as a Sub-Lieutenant, Submarines. Settled in Rhodesia (Zimbabwe) in 1947, later moving to Plettenberg Bay and Fish Hoek.
Reference *Who's Who of Southern Africa*, 1987–88, Johannesburg.

TOLLAST Robert

Born 1915 London.
Resided in SA 1950–*c*.1960. Several visits thereafter.
A painter of portraits. Works in oil, watercolour and pastel.
Studies Westminster School of Art, under Mark Gertler (1892–1939) and privately under Henry Tonks (1862–1937).
Profile 1950 lectured at the University of the Witwatersrand. Acted with the Oxford Repertory Theatre, England and occasionally in Johannesburg. A broadcaster of radio plays for the SABC. During the early 1950s spent some time in Majorca. Lives in the UK.
Exhibitions He has participated in numerous group and solo exhibitions in the UK; 1953 Pieter Wenning Gallery, Johannesburg, first of several solo exhibitions held in Johannesburg.
References SAA; Collectors' Guide; AASA.

TOMLIN William A

A painter of landscapes and buildings, marine scenes and portraits. Worked in watercolour. Produced a number of black and white studies.
Profile A member, and in 1917 and 1919 secretary of the Johannesburg Sketch Club. Travelled in SA and visitied Madeira. Lived in Johannesburg.
Exhibitions Participated in group exhibitions in SA from 1916.
Represented Africana Museum, Johannesburg.
Reference AMC7.

TOMLINSON David Allen

Born 1941 Cape Town.
A sculptor of wildlife, particularly birds. Works in ceramics finished in acrylic, as well as in bronze.

Studies 1959 Cape Technical College.

Profile 1961–86 initially worked in the advertising industry, later owned and operated an advertising agency, winning awards for creativity in New York and SA. From 1986 a full-time sculptor. Has a passionate interest in wildlife, particularly ornithology. 1941–63 lived in Cape Town; 1963–86 in Johannesburg; thereafter near Balgowan, Natal.

Exhibitions He has participated in several group exhibitions from 1985; 1987 Everard Read Gallery, Johannesburg, solo exhibition.

TOSE Martin Qgibinsizi

Born 1958 Germiston, Transvaal.

A painter, graphic artist and a sculptor of figures, wildlife, genre, landscapes and abstract pieces. Works in mixed media, acrylic, wash, pencil, charcoal, various graphic media, wood and bronze. A series of paintings entitled "Bushmans Graffiti", 1983 a series of sculptures entitled "Conversation".

Studies 1975–77 The Open School, Johannesburg, under Nats Mokgosi (qv); 1977–80 Katlehong Art Centre, under Thato Mamabolo (qv).

Profile A member of the Katlehong Art Society. From 1984 has taught sculpture and painting at the Katlehong Art Centre, Transvaal.

Exhibitions He has participated in many group exhibitions from 1978 in SA.

Award 1978 Awarded the Most Promising Sculptor Award from the Ministry of Education, on a Katlehong Art Centre Exhibition.

References Echoes of African Art; *SA Panorama* April 1979.

TOTTENDELL VENNER W H see VENNER William H Tottendell

TOWNSEND Mary Edith (Mollie) (née Stewart)

Born 1921 Smithfield, Orange Free State.

A painter, sculptor and graphic artist of figures, landscapes and seascapes. Works in oil, acrylic, watercolour, crayon, ink, wash, bronze, plastics and in various graphic media. 1983 a series of horizontal seascapes; from 1986 a series of African/European symbolism.

Studies 1939 privately under Florence Zerffi (qv) in Cape Town; 1965–66 History of Art through the University of South Africa, under Frieda Harmsen and Karin Skawran; 1968 l'Académie de la Grande Chaumière, Paris; 1971–75 Michaelis School of Fine Art, under Richard Wake (qv), Bruce Arnott (qv), Katrine Harries (qv) and Jules van de Vijver (qv), gaining a BA(FA).

Profile From 1971 a member of the SAAA; 1984–86 a founder member of the Upington Art Society; 1955 taught art privately in Northern Rhodesia (Zambia); 1968–69 in Gaborone, Botswana; 1985 in Upington, Cape Province. 1965 and 1968 stamp designs for the Botswana Government. From 1955 she has been involved in stage design and production, and has acted with various amateur dramatic societies. 1948–53 lived in Port Elizabeth; 1954–57 in Ndola, Northern Rhodesia (Zambia); 1957–62 in Francistown, Botswana; 1962–65 in Mafeking, Cape Province (Mafikeng, Bophuthatswana); 1965–71 in Gaborone, Botswana; 1971–77 in Cape Town; 1977–83 in Hout Bay, Cape Province; from 1983 in Upington, Cape Province. 1968 toured Europe; 1984 spent four months in Paris at the Cité Internationale des Arts. Great-grand-daughter of James Stewart (qv).
Exhibitions 1949 Redhouse, Port Elizabeth, first of seven solo exhibitions held in SA and Zambia; she has participated in many group exhibitions from 1963 in SA, Italy, France and Norway; 1970 National Gallery, Gaborone, Botswana, solo exhibition.
Award 1980 medal awarded by Fédération Internationale Culturelle Feminine for an etching exhibited in Ancona, Italy.
Represented National Gallery, Gaborone, Botswana; University of Natal.
Publication by Townsend *James Stewart, Royal Scottish Academician*, 1968, Government Printer, Botswana.

TREASURE Douglas

Born 1917 Adelaide, Cape Province.
A painter of landscapes. Works in watercolour.
Studies 1935–38 Port Elizabeth Technical College, under John Muff-Ford (qv).
Profile 1935–38 lived in Port Elizabeth; 1938–52 in Johannesburg and from 1953 in Cape Town.
Exhibitions He has participated in numerous group exhibitions from 1939 throughout SA, in the UK in 1954 and in Australia in 1960; 1943 Johannesburg, first of 10 solo exhibitions held in Johannesburg, five in Cape Town and one in London.
Represented Ann Bryant Gallery, East London; Pietersburg Collection.
References BSAK 1; AASA.

TRETCHIKOFF Vladimir Griegorovich

Born 1913 Siberia, Russia.
Resided in SA from 1946.
A self-taught painter of figures, portraits, genre, still life and wildlife. Works in oil, watercolour, ink, pencil and charcoal.
Profile From 1946 a member of the SAAA. In 1942 a propaganda artist for the British Ministry of Information in Singapore. Reproductions of many of his paintings have been immensely popular. Has lived in Russia, Manchuria, China, Malaya, the UK, the USA and Canada. 1978–81 the subject of three documentary films made by the BBC, the SABC and Eurovision.
Exhibitions 1933 Shanghai, China, first of 52 solo exhibitions held in Asia, SA, the UK, the USA and Canada.

Award 1939 Medal, Gallery of Science and Art, New York.
Publication by Tretchikoff With A Hocking, *Pigeon's Luck*, 1973, Collins, London.
References Richard Buncher, *Tretchikoff*, 1950, Howard Timmins, Cape Town; George Harrap, *Art of Tretchikoff*, 1973, Howard Timmins, Cape Town; Collectors' Guide; SAA; IWAA; BSAK 1 & 2; AASA; *SA Panorama* November 1976.

TREVOR Harry

Born 1922 Johannesburg.
Died 1970 London, England.
Resided in England from 1947.
A painter of abstracted landscapes, city scenes, figures, nudes and still life. Worked in oil, pastel and watercolour. A series of the Malay Quarter, Cape Town. Prior to 1948 painted several murals.
Studies Briefly at the Michaelis School of Fine Art in 1939.
Profile c.1939–40 shared a studio in Cape Town with Willem Gravett (qv) and the painter and graphic artist, Israel Traub (*b*.1908). Lived in Cape Town and Johannesburg. Travelled extensively in the UK and Europe. Lived for some time in Cornwall and in the South of France.
Exhibitions 1940–47 participated in group exhibitions in SA; 1948 Tate Gallery, London, SA Art Exhibition; 1968 Silberberg Gallery, Cape Town, solo exhibition of his works from the Silberberg Collection.
References D Lewis, *The Naked Eye*, 1946, Paul Koston, Cape Town; BSAK 2; AASA; *Jewish Affairs* November 1972.

TROBEC Vittoria

Born 1922 Italy.
Resided in SA from 1957.
A painter of landscapes, fine-detailed plant and berry studies and more complex still life pictures. Works in watercolour, gouache, ink and wash.
Studies Privately under Severa Rech-Cassarino (qv), Ivy Botha and John Galloway.
Profile A potter. A writer of both poetry and prose in Italian. In 1979 her writings were published in the Italian newsaper *La Voce*. 1922–42 lived in Trieste, Northern Italy; 1942–57 in Florence, Italy, thereafter in Johannesburg.
Exhibitions She has participated in several group exhibitions in the Transvaal from 1983.

TROLLIP Henry William

Born 1858 Somerset East, Cape Province.
Died 1933.
A self-taught painter of landscapes of the Cape Province. Worked in watercolour and more rarely in oil.

Profile Served as a Lieutenant in Nesbitt's Horse in the Anglo-Boer War. An Attorney and a Justice of the Peace and, while living in Bedford, Cape Province, Secretary of the Bedford Divisional Council. 1881–1914 lived in Bedford, Cape Province, later in Cape Town.
Exhibitions Participated in group exhibitions in Port Elizabeth and Cape Town; 1924 British Empire Exhibition, Wembley, England.
Represented William Fehr Collection, Cape Town.
Reference AASA.

TROTTER Alys Fane (née Keatinge)

Born 1863 Teffont Ewyas, Salisbury, Wiltshire, England.
Died 1961 Teffont Ewyas, Salisbury, Wiltshire, England.
Resided in SA 1894–96.
Numerous pencil drawings of landscapes and the homesteads around Cape Town.
Studies Slade School of Art, London, under Professor Alphonse Legros (1837–1911) and in Rome.
Profile Her husband was the Electricity Advisor to the Cape Government. On her return to England she contributed to *Cornhill Magazine* and *Punch*. A writer of poetry. Travelled extensively in France and Italy.
Awards 1951 Gold Medal from the National Monuments Council for her work in the Cape; 1956 Silver Medal from the SA Historical Monuments Commission in London.
Represented Old Parsonage Museum, Paarl, Cape Province; SA Cultural History Museum, Cape Town; William Fehr Collection, Cape Town.
Publications by Trotter Wrote and illustrated the history of old Cape Dutch houses published in *The Cape Times*—Christmas Number, 1898; *Old Colonial Houses of the Cape of Good Hope*, illustrated and described by Alys Fane Trotter, with a chapter on the origins of old Cape architecture by Herbert Baker, 1900, Batsford, London; *Old Cape Colony, a chronicle of her men and houses from 1652 to 1806*, 1903, reprinted 1928, Maskew Miller, Cape Town; a number of volumes of poetry including *Nigel and Other Verse*, 1918, *Houses and Dreams*, 1924 and *The Old Village*, 1929.
References SADNB; BSAK 1; Enc S'n; AASA.

TRULL Thomas Rafael

Born 1904 Vigo, Spain.
Resided in SA from 1930.
A painter of landscapes and seascapes. Works in watercolour and oil.
Studies Michaelis School of Fine Art, under Professor John Wheatley (qv) and Grace Wheatley (qv).
Profile A member of the SA Society of Artists. Has lived in Spain, the UK, Portugal, the Azores Islands, Aden and Zanzibar.
Exhibitions From 1954 he has exhibited four times in Cape Town.
References SAA; AASA.

TRUTER Barry René

Born 1947 Ladysmith, Natal.

An artist creating lathe-turned and papier mâché sculptures, painted tins, stained glass pieces, silkscreens, woodcuts, etchings and drawings of erotica. His works are often abstract, surrealistic and humorous.

Studies 1968–70 Natal Technical College (Technikon), under Barry Maritz (qv), gaining a National Diploma in Art and Design; 1973–75 Natal Technical College (Technikon), under Cliff Bestall (qv), gaining a National Teachers Diploma in Art; 1980–83 Natal Technikon, where attained a Higher Diploma in Art and Design.

Profile A member of the NSA. 1971 a part-time lecturer in graphic design, 1973–76 a full-time lecturer in graphic design, 1977–84 taught the Fine Art Foundation Course and from 1984 a printmaking lecturer, at the Natal Technikon. 1947–65 lived in Ladysmith, 1966–67 in Bergville, Natal, thereafter in Durban. Has travelled extensively in Europe and Southern Africa, as well as to Mauritius.

Exhibitions He has participated in many group exhibitions from 1975 in SA; 1977 NSA Gallery, Durban, first of three solo exhibitions held in Natal; 1985 Tributaries, touring SA and West Germany.

Represented Natal Technikon.

TRUTER Clive Theodore

Born 1955 Pietermaritzburg, Natal.

Primarily a printmaker of silkscreens and lithographs; also paints figures and animals. Paints in oil and draws in crayon.

Studies 1974–78 University of Natal, under Professor Raymund van Niekerk, gaining a BA(FA) in 1977 and a Higher Diploma in Education in 1978.

Profile A member of the NSA. 1979 an art teacher at Richards Bay High School, Natal; from 1980 a lecturer in printmaking at the Natal Technikon.

Exhibitions He has participated in several group exhibitions from 1981 in Natal; 1983 Gallery 567, Durban, first of three solo exhibitions held in Durban.

'TSAS-ROLFES Rita see ROLFES Rita Louise 'Tsas-

TSHABALALA Mbekwa Paulos

Born 1954 Villiers, Orange Free State.

A painter and sculptor of landscapes, seascapes, still life and abstract pieces. Works in watercolour and wood.

Studies 1974–75 Tshiya College of Education, Witsieshoek, QwaQwa, under Philemon Moerane (qv); 1977 Ndaleni Educational Training School, Natal, under Lorna Pearson and Craig Lancaster.

Profile From 1986 a member of the QwaQwa Art Association. 1976–86 taught art in Witsieshoek. 1986 an art-inspector organising art guidance courses in Witsieshoek, QwaQwa.

TSOLO Gabriel

Born 1950 Sasolburg, Orange Free State.
A painter, graphic artist and sculptor of portraits, genre and abstract pieces. Works in oil, acrylic, watercolour, ink, pencil, charcoal, various graphic media, metal, wood, clay and found objects.
Studies 1960 privately under Ephraim Ngatane (qv); 1978 Johannesburg Art Foundation, under Bill Ainslie (qv).
Profile From 1973 a member of the Katlehong Art Society and Centre. 1980 Guest Artist, 1985 an art teacher and from 1986 the exhibition co-ordinator of the Katlehong Art Centre. From 1986 Manager of the Katlehong Art Gallery, Germiston. 1984 a potter, 1985 a designer of tapestries.
Exhibitions He has participated in many group exhibitions from 1969 held throughout SA and in Los Angeles, USA; 1985 FUBA Gallery, Johannesburg, solo exhibition.
Represented National Library, Mbabane, Swaziland.
Reference Echoes of African Art.

TSOTETSI Jacob Phumulo

Born 1959 Standerton, Transvaal.
A graphic artist of portraits and figures; also draws in pencil.
Profile From 1986 a member of the QwaQwa Art Association. Since 1980 he has taught art at Boitelo Senior Primary School, QwaQwa.

TURTON Allan Wilberforce FRSA

Born 1918 Dundee, Natal.
A painter of portraits and landscapes. Works in oil, acrylic and watercolour.
Studies 1940–44 University of Natal, under Professor O J P Oxley (qv) and Rosa Hope (qv); 1961 privately in the UK under Edward Halliday, a member of the Royal Society of Portrait Painters.
Profile 1970 elected a Fellow of the Royal Society of Arts. 1955–69 an art teacher at Durban High School; 1970–74 an art lecturer at Edgewood College of Education, Pinetown, Natal. A trained musician.
Exhibitions 1949 Pietermaritzburg, first of five solo exhibitions.
Public Commissions Numerous portrait commissions for the Church of England; Rhodes University; University of Bophuthatswana; University of Natal; as well as many corporations.

TURVEY Reginald Ernest George

Born 1882 Ladybrand, Orange Free State.
Died 1968 Durban.

A painter of landscapes in a traditional English manner, portraits, interiors and of animals derived from Bushmen drawings as well as of rhythmic semi-abstract pictures. Worked in oil, pastel and watercolour.

Studies 1902 painting lessons from Frans Oerder (qv) in Pretoria; 1903–06 Slade School of Art, London, under Henry Tonks (1862–1937), Philip Wilson Steer (1860–1942) and Frank Brangwyn (1867–1956), awarded the Wilson Steer prize for portrait painting in 1904; 1906–10 London School of Art, under John Macallan Swan (1847–1910) and George Washington Lambert (1873–1930)

Profile From 1935 a follower of the Baha'i religion, having been introduced to the teachings by the American painter Mark Tobey (1890–1976). 1911–12 taught at the Natal Technical College. January–May and August 1946 illustrated short stories by Herman Charles Bosman in *SA Opinion*. Owing to arthritis and failing eyesight he was forced to stop painting in 1965. 1903–10 lived in England, visiting Europe in 1906; 1910–11 lived in Japan with the artist, potter and writer Bernard Leach (*b.*1887); 1911–13 in Ladybrand and Durban; 1913–17 farmed with his family at Nakuru, Kenya; 1917–24 lived in Natal, revisiting Kenya in 1922; 1924–32 in St Ives, Cornwall, England, working at the Allison Studio, later moving to Carbis Bay, Cornwall, next door to Bernard Leach; visited SA in 1928 and Italy in 1931; 1933–40 lived in Totnes, Devon, England, 1937 visited SA; 1940–42 in Eerste Rivier, Cape Province, where he shared a studio with the artist Charles Wedgewood; 1942 settled in Johannesburg, moving to Honeydew in 1953. 1963 visited England. Grandson of the 1820 Settler artist, Edward Turvey.

Exhibitions Participated in group exhibitions from 1909 in the UK, France and SA; 1928 Durban Art Gallery, first of several solo exhibitions held in SA; 1937 Bloomsbury Gallery, London, solo exhibition; 1945 first of several joint exhibitions with Charles Wedgewood; 1968 Lidchi Gallery, Johannesburg, Retrospective Exhibition; 1975–76 Pretoria Art Museum and SA National Gallery, Cape Town, Memorial Exhibition, 50 works of which toured SA in 1976; 1986–87 Durban, Ladybrand, Bloemfontein, Kimberley, Grahamstown and Johannesburg, touring exhibition.

Represented Durban Art Gallery; Hester Rupert Art Museum, Graaff-Reinet; King George VI Art Gallery, Port Elizabeth; Pretoria Art Museum; SA National Gallery, Cape Town; Tatham Art Gallery, Pietermaritzburg; University of the Witwatersrand; William Humphreys Art Gallery, Kimberley.

References *Reginald Turvey/Life and Art*, edited by Lowell Johnson, 1986, George Ronald, Oxford, UK; SAA; DSAB; SAP&S; DBA; BSAK 1 & 2; AASA; *De Kat* August 1987; Memorial Exhibition Catalogue, 1975, Pretoria Art Museum.

TYRRELL Barbara Eleanor Harcourt (Dr Jurgens)

Born Durban.

A painter and graphic artist of landscapes, seascapes, figures, portraits, still life, genre, wildlife and abstract pictures. Works in oil, acrylic, watercolour, ink, wash, pencil and in various graphic media. A large series of African tribal dress.

Studies University of Natal, under Professor O J P Oxley (qv), gaining a BA(FA) and a PhD (honoris causa).

Profile Has taught art at the Natal and Port Elizabeth Technical Colleges (Technikons). Illustrated Peter Jurgens' *African Heritage*, 1985, Macmillan (SA), Johannesburg. She has travelled extensively throughout Southern Africa. Lives in Muizenberg, Cape Province.

Exhibitions She has participated in several group exhibitions; 1948 Tate Gallery, London, SA Art Exhibition; occasionally holds solo exhibitions in Pretoria.

Award CSIR Award for Tribal Dress Study.

Represented Africana Museum, Johannesburg; Bulawayo Museum, Zimbabwe; Duggin Cronin Museum, Kimberley; Killie Campbell Africana Library, University of Natal, Durban; Livingstone Museum, Zambia; Pretoria Cultural Museum; Royal Empire Society, London, England.

Publications by Tyrrell *Tribal Peoples of Southern Africa*, 1968, Books of Africa Ltd, Cape Town and *Suspicion is My Name*, 1971, T V Bulpin, Cape Town.

References Collectors' Guide; Art SA; SAA; AMC5; SESA; BSAK 1 & 2; SA Art; AASA; *SA Panorama* August 1965.

U

ULLMANN Ernest

Born 1900 Munich, Germany.
Died 1975 Sandton, Johannesburg.
Resided in SA from 1936.

A sculptor of figures and animals. Worked in wood, ciment fondu, hessian, wire, wax and bronze. Designed stained glass pieces and tapestries sewn by his wife Joyce Esson. A number of drawings, oil paintings, caricatures of political figures and works in various graphic media. His pictures are known for their simplified forms and strong, dark outline.

Studies *c.*1919 University of Munich, history of art under Professor Popp and Heinrich Wolffin and in Berlin under Stanislaus Stückgold (1868–1933); later at the Academy of Fine Arts, Munich, under Professor Bleecker.

Profile Art Editor and illustrator for *Auslandspost* 1919–20, *Mitropa Zeitung* 1933–35 and *The Forum* 1938–46. From 1939 wrote articles for *SA Architectural Record* and *Jewish Affairs*. From 1928 illustrated and designed books and dust jackets in Canada, Germany, South America, the UK and the USA. An interior designer in Munich 1920–27, in Berlin 1927–35 and from 1936 in Cape Town, Durban, Johannesburg, Port Elizabeth and Kitwe, Zambia, decorating offices, theatres, cinemas, hotels, hospitals and a synagogue. Designed exhibition pavilions in Germany 1922–34 and from 1936 for exhibitions in SA, Angola, SWA/Namibia, Rhodesia (Zimbabwe), Switzerland and the UK. Designed theatre sets, official guides, calendars and stamps, including a set of eight stamps, in 1937, depicting the Kruger Park. Designed posters, including the Johannesburg Golden Jubilee Celebration Poster in 1936, the winning entry in a competition. Made puppets for Simba Toys. An industrial designer. 1960 visited Israel. His property in Sandton, Johannesburg, has become a public park.

Exhibitions Participated in group exhibitions in the UK, Austria, Switzerland, Germany, Rhodesia (Zimbabwe), Israel and throughout SA; 1920 Wiesbaden, Germany, first of numerous solo exhibitions in Germany and from 1956 in SA; 1964 Quadrennial Exhibition.

Awards 1953 Queen's Coronation Medal; 1975 Citizen of the Year, Sandton, Johannesburg.

Represented Africana Museum, Johannesburg; Hester Rupert Art Museum, Graaff-Reinet; Imperial Institute, London, England; Johannesburg Art Gallery; National Museum, Bloemfontein; Pietersburg Collection; Pretoria City Hall; SA Embassy, Paris, France; Sandton Municipal Collection; SA Police Museum, Pretoria; University of Bologna Library, Italy; William Humphreys Art Gallery, Kimberley.

Public Commissions In Johannesburg: Young Buck, CNA Fountain, Jan Smuts Avenue; Sitting Girl, Mother and Daughter, and Young Love, Mutual Square, Rosebank; The Playmakers, Civic Theatre; Family Group, Star Fountain, Library Square; Mannequins, W & A Building, Siemert Road; Boy & Fishes, Merchandise Centre; Antelope, Johannesburg Botanical Gardens; Girl and Horse, SPCA Centre, Booysens. In Pretoria: Black Wildebeeste, Voortrekker

Monument. In Durban: Black Wildebeeste and Young, Lever Brothers Fountain; Listening, SABC Centre, Kingsmead. In Zambia: Impalas, Hotel Edinburgh Terrace, Kitwe; Dag Hammarskjöld Fountain, Ecumenical Centre, Kitwe. Murals in Bloemfontein, Cape Town, Johannesburg, Pretoria and Piet Retief. Tapestries, designed by him and made by his wife, in Amersfoort, Evander, Johannesburg, Potchefstroom, Pretoria and Stellenbosch in SA and in Bologna, Italy, Paris, France and Kitwe, Zambia.

Publications by Ullmann *Photographische Vergroesserung*, with R Mayrshoffer, 1914, Verlag Hachmeister & Thal, Leipzig, Germany; *Designs on Life*, autobiography, 1970, Howard Timmins, Cape Town.

References Art SA; SAA; 20C SA Art; AMC5&7; SESA; BSAK 1 & 2; SA Art; 3Cs; AASA; SASSK; LSAA; *SA Panorama* July 1964 & February 1971; *Artlook* December 1968, July 1971 & February 1973.

ULYATE Sheila

Born 1912 Cape Town.

A painter and a graphic artist of landscapes, portraits, figures, flowers and township scenes. Works in oil and various graphic media. A series on clowns.

Studies Witwatersrand Technical College, under W J Braham; studied in The Netherlands under A Kraan.

Profile A member of the Transvaal Art Society.

Exhibitions She has participated in group exhibitions in SA and in Zimbabwe; 1964 Quadrennial Exhibition.

Represented Africana Museum, Johannesburg; SA National Museum of Military History, Johannesburg.

References Register SA/SWA; AASA.

URANOVSKY Meyer

Born 1939 Cape Town.

A painter of figures, the human psyche and nature. Works in oil, acrylic, charcoal, shellac and pigment.

Studies 1958–60 Michaelis School of Fine Art, under Maurice van Essche (qv), Russell Harvey (qv) and Lippy Lipshitz (qv); 1968 on a Montague White Bursary at Atelier 17, Paris, under Stanley William Hayter (b.1901).

Profile A musician, 1957–76 played the bongos and mandolin for the Flamenco-Jazz group "Brazilia". 1960–65 worked as a graphic designer for various companies in Cape Town, Johannesburg and London, England. 1977–83 involved in the restoration and renovation of Victorian terrace houses in Gardens, Cape Town. From 1984 has made a number of veneered violin cases. 1960–61 visited London; 1967 Israel; 1985 and 1987 New York.

Exhibitions He has participated in several group exhibitions from 1965 in SA and one touring the USA and West Germany; 1966 Wolpe Gallery, Cape Town, first of four solo exhibitions, one of which was held in New York.

Award 1965 Cape Salon prize.
Represented University of Stellenbosch.
Reference *Sarie Marais* 3 October 1979.

UTTRIDGE Sandra Hillary

Born 1943 Cape Town.
A sculptor of large murals and smaller works depicting seascapes, landscapes and still life, as well as abstract pieces. Works in glazed ceramics. 1978 began sculpting in clay, and working in soapstone and wood.
Profile 1981 joined Nelius Britz (qv) in his studio.
Exhibitions She has participated in group exhibitions from 1979 held throughout SA; 1982–83 Shell Gallery, Cape Town, first of eight joint exhibitions with Nelius Brits (qv).
Public Commissions Several murals and fountains for corporate headquarters in Cape Town, Johannesburg and Paarl, Cape Province.
Reference *SA Panorama* March 1987.

V

VAN ALPHEN Willem Daniel de Vignon
Born 1815 Leyden, The Netherlands.
Died 1871 Willowmore, Cape Province.
Resided in SA from *c*.1854.
A painter of landscapes. Worked in bistre and watercolour.
Profile A former officer of the Dutch Military Engineers. Travelled and painted in the Cape and the Eastern Province during the 1860s. 1865 lived and painted in Knysna.
Represented Africana Museum, Johannesburg; Library of Parliament, Cape Town; William Fehr Collection, Cape Town.
Publications by Van Alphen *Twelve Views of The Knysna*, photographed by Lawrence and Selkirk, 1866, Juta, Cape Town; *Knysna Forest Scenery*, with sketches by Van Alphen, introduction by D Bax, 1957, A A Balkema, Cape Town.
References Pict Art; SADNB; AMC5; Pict Afr; BSAK 1; 3Cs.

VAN ASSELT Gerda
Born 1927 Latvia (Latvian SSR).
Resided in SA from 1936.
A painter of abstracts, still life, landscapes, seascapes and city scenes. Works in oil, acrylic and watercolour.
Studies Witwatersrand Technical College.
Profile 1968–75 a member of the Transvaal Art Society. 1968 and 1970 study tours in the USA; 1974 made a study tour to Europe. Has travelled to Mozambique, Malawi and the Seychelles.
Exhibitions 1967 Mona Lisa Gallery, Johannesburg, first of six solo exhibitions held in Johannesburg and Cape Town; she has participated in many group exhibitions from 1968 in SA.
References BSAK 1; *Artlook* July 1970.

VAN BLOMMESTEIN Peter Daniel
Born Pretoria.
A painter of landscapes, seascapes, still life and abstract pictures. Works in oil and watercolour.
Studies 1948–53 Continental School of Art, Cape Town, under Maurice van Essche (qv).
Profile Spent 12 years travelling in a caravan throughout SA, SWA/Namibia and Rhodesia (Zimbabwe). 1978–79 travelled in France and the UK.
Exhibitions He has participated in numerous group exhibitions from 1948 in SA, the USA and Australia; 1981 Republic Festival Exhibition.

Award President Award, Salmagundi Exhibition, New York, USA.
Represented Nylstroom Municipal Collection; Pietersburg Collection.
References BSAK 2; AASA.

VAN DEN BERG Clive

Born 1956 Zambia.
Resided in SA from 1966.
A painter of landscapes and portraits. Works in oil, acrylic, watercolour, pastel, pencil and charcoal. 1982–83 "Monument" series; 1983 "Cenotaph" series; 1983 "Oasis" series; 1984 "Sacred Site" series; 1985 "Oasis" series 2.
Studies 1975–79 University of Natal, under Andrew Verster (qv), Mike Taylor, Bronwen Heath (qv), Dick Leigh (qv) and Malcolm Christian (qv), gaining a BA(FA). 1979 awarded the Emma Smith Scholarship for Overseas Study.
Profile A member of the NSA, of which he was Vice-President 1984–85. 1982 lectured at the University of Natal; from 1983 a lecturer at the Natal Technikon. A number of architectural designs. Has written various articles and reviews for newspapers and journals. 1987 spent six months at Cité Internationale des Arts, Paris.
Exhibitions He has participated in numerous group exhibitions in SA; 1982 NSA Gallery, Durban, first of four solo exhibitions; 1985 Cape Town Triennial; 1985 Tributaries, touring SA and West Germany; 1985 SAAA Gallery, Pretoria, joint exhibition with Bronwen Findlay (qv) and Andrew Verster (qv); 1988 Johannesburg Art Gallery, Vita Art Now.
Awards 1979 New Signatures Award, SAAA; 1985 First Prize, Image of Natal Competition; 1985 First Prize, Paper Works, NSA; 1987 winner of the Volkskas Atelier Award.
Represented Durban Art Gallery; Johannesburg Art Gallery; Mangosuthu Technikon; Margate Municipal Collection; Natal Technikon; National Museum, Bloemfontein; Pretoria Art Museum; SA National Gallery, Cape Town; Tatham Art Gallery, Pietermaritzburg; University of Natal; University of South Africa; University of the Witwatersrand; William Humphreys Art Gallery, Kimberley.
Public Commissions 1986 fountain, Durban City Park; 1987 art work, Mangosuthu Technikon, Durban.
Reference BSAK 1.

VANDER HEUL-GRIFFITHS Yvonne Christine

Born 1939 Cape Town.
A painter and graphic artist of landscapes, seascapes, figures, portraits and still life. Works in oil, watercolour, ink, wash, pencil, charcoal and in various graphic media.
Studies 1958 commercial art at the Michaelis School of Fine Art; 1960–62 drawing and sculpture at the Regent Street Polytechnic Night School, London; 1965–66 part-time architecture and painting at the Hammersmith College of Art, London; 1969–70 obtained a Diploma from the London School of Fashion; 1976–80 at the Michaelis School of Fine Art, under Neville Dubow and Cecil Skotnes (qv), gaining a BA(FA) in 1976 and being awarded the MacIver Scholarship in 1977.

Profile From 1982 a member of the Artists Guild; from 1983 a member of the SAAA. 1982–83 taught art part-time at the Community Arts Project, Cape Town. Teaches art privately. From 1973 a designer of sets and costumes for plays and ballets. A shop window display designer, having won a number of awards in this field. 1960–72 lived in England; 1982 lived in Brazil; 1983–84 lived in West Germany. Has travelled throughout Europe and in the Americas.
Exhibitions She has participated in many group exhibitions from 1979 in SA and Germany; 1981 Watershed Gallery, Cape Town, first of three solo exhibitions held in Cape Town and Brazil.

VAN DER LINDE Martiens

Born 1924 Griquatown, Cape Province.
A self-taught painter of landscapes and seascapes in watercolour; fantastical works in acrylic; figures and abstract works in oil and charcoal.
Profile From 1979 a member of the SAAA. 1986 visited SWA/Namibia.
Exhibitions 1977 Municipal Hall, Citrusdal, Cape Province, first of 12 solo exhibitions held in SA; he has participated in several group exhibitions from 1978 in SA.

VAN DER MADE Bertha Sophia Henrietta (Mrs Lurie)

Born 1928 Grootfontein, SWA/Namibia.
A painter of landscapes, seascapes, figures, portraits and still life. Works in oil and watercolour. A graphic artist.
Studies 1948–52 Michaelis School of Fine Art, under Professor Edward Roworth (qv), Professor Rupert Shephard (qv), Maurice van Essche (qv), Katrine Harries (qv), Melvin Simmers (qv), Eleanor Esmonde-White (qv) and Ivan Mitford-Barberton (qv), gaining a BA(FA).
Profile A member of the WSSA and the SAAA, of which she was the Secretary in Pretoria 1965–66. 1954 an art teacher at Potchefstroom Girls High School; 1956 at Rondebosch Boys High and the Frank Joubert Art Centre, Cape Town; 1961–62 taught pottery at Ellis Robbins Boys School, Salisbury, Rhodesia (Harare, Zimbabwe); 1963–64 a crafts teacher at Pretoria Teachers Training College; 1970–80 founded and taught at the Arts & Crafts Centre, Swakopmund. 1965 drew plant illustrations for D K Shone & R B Drummond's *Poisonous Plants of Rhodesia* (under her married name). Has visited the Seychelles and Hong Kong.
Exhibitions She has participated in several group exhibitions in SWA/Namibia; 1970 Arts Association SWA/Namibia Gallery, Windhoek, first of five solo exhibitions held in SWA/Namibia.
Represented Arts Association SWA/Namibia Collection.

VAN DER MERWE Anita

Born 1958 Pretoria.
A painter of figures, wildlife and abstract pictures. Works in mixed media.

Studies 1978–79 Pretoria Technical College, gaining a Diploma in Graphic Design.
Profile A member of the SAAA. 1983 produced a ten-minute children's programme for Anglia Television, UK. 1985 illustrations for *Excellence* magazine. A trained actress and film director. 1982 lived with and studied the Bushmen in the Central Kalahari Desert.
Exhibitions She has participated in several group exhibitions in SA from 1980; 1983 Rembrandt Gallery, Johannesburg, first of two solo exhibitions; 1986 Everard Read Gallery, Johannesburg, joint exhibition with Arlene Amaler-Raviv (qv) and Karin Dando (qv).
Award 1980 First Prize for Drawing, New Signatures, SAAA.

VAN DER MERWE Banie

Born 1903 Grahamstown, Cape Province.
Died 1972 Windhoek, SWA/Namibia.
A painter of landscapes. Worked in oil and tempera.
Studies Part-time under Professor F W Armstrong (qv) of Rhodes University, but mainly self-taught.
Profile 1925 settled in SWA/Namibia. 1947–49 the first full-time art educationalist in Windhoek. 1949–52 taught at various SWA/Namibian schools; 1952–65 an art teacher at Windhoek High School.
Exhibitions Participated in group exhibitions from 1946 in SWA/Namibia, Cape Town and Pretoria; 1966 Arts Association SWA/Namibia Gallery, Windhoek, solo exhibition.
Represented SWA/Namibian Administration, Windhoek.
References BSAK 1 & 2; Art SWA.

VAN DER MERWE Caroline (née Overdyck)

Born 1932 Iringa, Tanganyika (Tanzania).
Resided in SA from 1952.
A sculptor of figures. Works in stone, bronze and ciment fondu. Paints in gouache and draws in ink with wash, pencil and charcoal; also an etcher. Began with bird forms, developing through abstracted female figures to the male torso.
Studies Natal Technical College, under George Howe; 1965–67 Michaelis School of Fine Art, under Lippy Lipshitz (qv), Bill Davis (qv) and Richard Wake (qv).
Profile From 1967 a member of the SAAA, from 1980 of the Artists Guild. 1972–77 taught art at the Cape Town Art Centre; 1972–76 at the Touch Gallery, SA National Gallery, Cape Town. 1976 first visit to Carrara, Italy, and an extensive tour of the USA; 1978 and 1980 travelled in Europe; 1983–85 lived in Pietrasanta, Italy; since 1985 she has spent six months of each year in Pietrasanta and six in Cape Town.

Exhibitions She has participated in numerous group exhibitions from 1969 in SA, the UK and Italy; 1973 SAAA Gallery, Cape Town, first of 14 solo exhibitions held in SA, West Germany and Italy; 1977 Gallery International, Cape Town, joint exhibition with Olivia Scholnick (qv); 1985 participated in the 7th Dante Biennale, Ravenna, Italy.

Represented Pietersburg Collection; Pietrasanta Permanent Collection, Italy; Pretoria Art Museum; SA National Gallery, Cape Town; University of the Western Cape.

Public Commissions Monument to the Fallen, Bellville, Cape Province; Crucifix for a Chapel, George, Cape Province.

References AASA; *Lantern* April 1978.

VAN DER MERWE Eben

Born 1932 Bloemfontein.

A self-taught painter of landscapes, portraits, figures, still life and abstract pictures. Works in oil, acrylic, pastel, Alkyd, gouache, pencil and Dalle-de-Verre.

Profile Trained as a commercial artist and as a typographer. 1958 a founder member of the Bloemfontein Group. A designer and maker of stained glass windows. Moved to Johannesburg in 1961, where he worked as a typographer, a visualiser and a designer in advertising agencies, and as an art director for the magazine section of the Argus Group until 1970. 1972–76 a lecturer in painting and applied design at the University of Pretoria. Since 1976 a full-time artist, concentrating on painting and the design and construction of Dalle-de-Verre windows. 1966 travelled to the UK and Europe to study the design and construction of slab-glass windows. 1976 made a study tour of the UK and Europe.

Exhibitions He has participated in numerous group exhibitions from *c.*1948 in SA, Venice and São Paulo; 1960 and 1964 Quadrennial Exhibitions; 1967 held his first solo exhibition at his home in Bloemfontein; 1973 Pretoria, joint exhibition with Mike Edwards (qv); 1974 SAAA, Pretoria, solo exhibition; 1980 National Museum, Bloemfontein, solo exhibition; 1981 Republic Festival Exhibition; 1986 University of the Orange Free State, exhibition.

Represented Hester Rupert Art Museum, Graaff-Reinet; National Museum, Bloemfontein; Pretoria Art Museum; SA National Gallery, Cape Town; University of the Orange Free State; University of Stellenbosch; War Museum of the Boer Republics, Bloemfontein; William Humphreys Art Gallery, Kimberley.

Public Commissions 1966–69 designed the stained glass which covers the 12-storey west façade of the Orange Free State Provincial Administration Building, Bloemfontein, constructed by Michael Edwards (qv); stained glass, Universitas Hospital Chapel, Bloemfontein; stained glass, Jan Smuts Airport, Johannesburg; stained glass, Post Office Tower, Hillbrow, Johannesburg; 1983 stained glass façade, New Library Building, University of the Orange Free State, Bloemfontein; also stained glass work for several Roman Catholic and Dutch Reformed churches in SA; four landscape paintings, Delville Wood Museum, France.

References SAA; *Artlook* November 1968.

VAN DER MERWE Justinus Benedictus

Born 1931 Marikana, Transvaal.

A sculptor. Works in bronze, stone, ciment fondu, wood, corten steel and stainless steel. 1967–69 a geometric series; from 1969 a series entitled "Towards Industrial Sections", the minimalising of engineering forms.

Studies 1952–56 Witwatersrand Technical College, under James Gardner (qv) and Professor Robert Bain (qv), gaining a National Art Teachers Diploma; 1958–61 University of South Africa, under Karin Skawran, gaining a BA(FA); 1978–84 University of Natal, under Professor Murray Schoonraad, where attained an MA(FA).

Profile 1956–57 taught art at the Michael Brink High School, Pretoria; 1958–61 a lecturer at the Orange Free State Technical College; 1961–63 a lecturer at the Natal Technical College; from 1963 Head of Department and Director of the School of Art, Pretoria Technical College (Technikon). 1964–65 travelled extensively in Europe; 1980 and 1982 visited the USA and Canada.

Exhibitions He has participated in numerous group exhibitions from 1959 throughout SA; 1959 Orange Free State Technical College, first of nine solo exhibitions; 1970 Herbert Evans Gallery, Johannesburg, joint exhibition with Hans Bilgeri (qv); 1981 Republic Festival Exhibition.

Represented Pietersburg Collection; Potchefstroom University for CHE.

Public Commissions 1963–64 busts of Dr D F Malan, Presidents Paul Kruger and M W Pretorius for the Transvaal Administration Building, Pretoria; 1968 bust of F H Odendaal, F H Odendaal High School, Pretoria; 1980 bust of J Ferreira, Department of Justice, Pretoria.

References BSAK 1; AASA.

VAN DER MERWE Mimi

Born 1934 Malmesbury, Cape Province.

An etcher of figures and portraits.

Studies 1955–57 Stellenbosch Technical College, under Edith ten Kate; 1959–60 l'Ecole des Beaux Arts, Brussels, Belgium, under Claude Lyr (b.1916); 1960–61 on a study bursary from the French Government at l'Ecole des Beaux Arts, Paris, under Jean E Bersier.

Profile 1968–79 a member of the Artists Guild, Cape Town. Taught art at several schools before becoming Head of the Art Department of the Zonnebloem Training College, Cape Town, in 1967. 1960–70 contributed illustrations to *Contrast* and in 1985 to *Die Suid-Afrikaan*. Since 1979 she has lived in Pretoria, where in 1984 she opened an etching studio at which she teaches.

Exhibitions She has participated in several group exhibitions from 1961 in SA and in Paris; 1963 SAAA Gallery, Cape Town, first of nine solo exhibitions; 1981 Republic Festival Exhibition; 1982 Durbanville, Cape Province, joint exhibition with Constance Purchase (qv) and R Creel.

Represented Ann Bryant Gallery, East London; Johannesburg Art Gallery; Pretoria Art Museum.

Reference AASA.

VANDERPLANK Helen Joyce

Born 1919 Cheltenham, Gloucestershire, England.
Resided in SA from 1963.
A self-taught painter of animals, invertebrates and flowers, particularly wild flowers. Works in oil, watercolour, pastel, pencil and ink.
Profile Illustrated six volumes of a natural history series by Dr F M Haworth, published by London University Press, UK. Simulates wild flowers in silk and wax. 1985 a set of six tree-flower paintings, printed and produced by the 1820 Settlers Memorial Foundation, Grahamstown.
Exhibitions She has participated in several group exhibitions in SA from 1978.
Represented University of Cape Town.

VAN DER REIS Gunther Friedrich Julius

Born 1927 Hamburg, Germany.
Resided in SA from 1937.
A painter, working in oil, acrylic and pencil. During the late 1950s and early 1960s his work related to landscapes; in the 1960s he used polyvinyl acetate to achieve reliefs; from the late 1960s and during the 1970s he developed a personalised African symbolism, using steel and later stainless steel. Since the late 1970s he has been working on a series of helmets, in paint, epoxy and bronze. An etcher.
Studies 1947–52 Michaelis School of Fine Art, under Professor Rupert Shephard (qv), Katrine Harries (qv), Lippy Lipshitz (qv) and Eleanor Esmonde-White (qv), gaining a BA(FA) in 1951 and a Secondary Teachers Certificate in 1952; received his MA(FA) in 1979 from the University of Pretoria.
Profile A committee member of the SAAA, from 1980 Vice-Chairman of Northern Transvaal Branch. 1953–54 an art teacher at SA College Schools Junior School, Cape Town; 1954–56 an art teacher at Maitland High School, Cape Town; 1956–61 an art lecturer at the Art Centre, Pretoria and at the Pretoria Normal College; 1962 art lecturer and from 1972 senior lecturer in fine art at the Pretoria Technical College (Technikon).
Exhibitions He has participated in numerous group exhibitions from 1954 in SA, Austria, Israel, Zimbabwe, Brazil, Italy, Portugal, the USA, West Germany, Spain, Yugoslavia and Australia; 1959 SAAA Gallery, Pretoria, first of 15 solo exhibitions held in SA; 1964 Quadrennial Exhibition; 1967 Pretoria Art Museum, joint exhibition with Armando Baldinelli (qv); 1967 William Humphreys Art Gallery, Kimberley, solo exhibition; 1977 Rand Afrikaans University, solo exhibition; 1981 Republic Festival Exhibition; 1985 Cape Town Triennial.
Awards 1966 Bronze Medal, First SA Breweries Biennale; 1968 Silver Medal, Second SA Breweries Biennale.
Represented Ann Bryant Gallery, East London; Durban Art Gallery; Göttingen University, West Germany; Hester Rupert Art Museum, Graaff-Reinet; King George VI Art Gallery, Port Elizabeth; Pietersburg Collection; Potchefstroom Museum; Potchefstroom University for CHE; Pretoria Art Museum; Rand Afrikaans University; Sandton Municipal Collection; SA National Gallery,

Cape Town; Tatham Art Gallery, Pietermaritzburg; University of Natal; University of the Orange Free State; University of South Africa; University of Stellenbosch; University of the Witwatersrand; Willem Annandale Art Gallery, Lichtenburg; William Humphreys Art Gallery, Kimberley.

Public Commissions 1972 corten steel mural, Kempton City; 1973 stainless steel mural, Jan Smuts Airport, Johannesburg; 1976 stainless steel mural, Abattoir Commission Building, Pretoria; 1977 steel mural, German School, Pretoria; 1985 two epoxy panels, the Sand du Plessis Theatre, Bloemfontein.

References SAA; 20C SA Art; Register SA & SWA; SAP&S; SAP&D; SSAP; SAGAT; BSAK 1 & 2; Our Art 3; SA Art; Oxford Companion to 20C Art (under SA); 3Cs; AASA; LSAA; *SA Panorama* January 1968; *Artlook* April 1968 & August 1969; *Lantern* December 1969; *Gallery* Winter 1984; *Garden & Home* January 1985; *Gunther van der Reis,* June 1967, Pretoria Art Museum; *Gunther van der Reis,* Exhibition Catalogue, September 1977, Rand Afrikaans University.

VAN DER RIET Helga

Born 1932 Estcourt, Natal.

A sculptor.

Studies Michaelis School of Fine Art, under Lippy Lipshitz (qv), gaining a BA(FA); welded sculpture and bronze casting under Leslie Thornton and at the Central School of Art, London.

Exhibitions Participated in group exhibitions in SA and in the UK during the 1950s and 1960s.

Public Commissions "Christ of the Sacred Heart" and "Madonna and Child", St Joseph's Catholic Church, De Doorns, Cape Province.

References SAA; SESA.

VAN DER WALT Clementina Unity Gough

Born 1952 Johannesburg.

A ceramic artist of abstract works, using the vessel format to express personal, social and political concepts.

Studies 1970–73 Hebrew University of Jerusalem, gaining a BA (History of Art); 1974–75 Bezalel Academy of Art & Design, Jerusalem, under Lydia Zavatsky and Pinchas Cohen Gan; 1976–77 Witwatersrand Technical College (Technikon), under Spies Venter (qv), gaining a National Diploma in Ceramics; 1983–84 Witwatersrand Technikon, under Suzette Munnick, where attained a Higher Diploma in Ceramics.

Profile From 1975 she has also made studio pottery. From 1983 a ceramics lecturer at the Witwatersrand Technikon. 1985–86 a member of the Advisory Board of the Market Gallery. 1970–75 lived in Israel. Visited Europe in 1972 and 1975, and both Europe and Israel in 1983.

Exhibitions She has participated in numerous group exhibitions from 1976 in SA; 1983 Things Gallery, Johannesburg, first of three solo exhibitions; 1985 Cape Town Triennial; 1985 Market Gallery, Johannesburg, joint exhibition.

Represented Johannesburg Art Gallery; Touch Gallery, SA National Gallery, Cape Town.
References De Kat December/January 1986; *Sgraffiti* no 42.

VAN DER WALT Ronnie

Born 1951 Cape Town.
A sculptor of fantasical birds and of gnomes. Works in clay.
Studies 1972–74 studied fine art at the Witwatersrand Technical College.
Profile 1979 established Things Gallery in Melville, Johannesburg, a ceramic studio and shop, which today has branches in both Johannesburg and Durban.
Exhibitions He has participated in group exhibitions and held solo exhibitions in SA; 1986 first of two solo exhibitions held at the Everard Read Gallery, Johannesburg.
Awards 1976 First Prize, Brickor National Ceramic Exhibition; 1977 First Prize, Oude Libertas National Ceramic Exhibition.

VAN DER WAT Hannatjie (née Schabort)

Born 1923 Frankfort, Orange Free State.
A painter, graphic artist and sculptor of abstract pieces. Works in oil, acrylic, various graphic media, stoneware and steel. 1977 "Homage to Rand Afrikaans University", a series of 16 oil paintings.
Studies 1941–44 Witwatersrand Technical College, under Maurice van Essche (qv), gaining a National Art Teachers Diploma; 1962–66 privately under Sidney Goldblatt (qv).
Profile 1945 an art teacher at Fakkel Hoërskool, Johannesburg; 1955 an art teacher at Hoër Volkskool, Heidelberg, Transvaal. 1974 designed a tapestry for Dorothy Neser. Lives in Johannesburg. From 1952 frequent tours overseas.
Exhibitions She has participated in numerous group exhibitions from 1963 in SA, the USA, Israel, West Germany, France, Greece and Italy; 1964 Quadrennial Exhibition; 1966 Adler Fielding Gallery, Johannesburg, first of seven solo exhibitions; 1977 Rand Afrikaans University, Prestigious Retrospective Exhibition; 1979 SAAA Gallery, Pretoria, Prestigious Retrospective Exhibition; 1981 Republic Festival Exhibition; 1984 Rand Afrikaans University, exhibition.
Award 1967 Cambridge Shirt Award, Art SA Today.
Represented Durban Art Gallery; Pietersburg Collection; Potchefstroom University for CHE; Pretoria Art Museum; Rand Afrikaans University; Touch Gallery, SA National Gallery, Cape Town; Willem Annandale Art Gallery, Lichtenburg; Witwatersrand Technikon.
Public Commissions 1965 mosaic mural, Helpmekaar Hoër Meisieskool, Johannesburg; 1978 abstract tubular steel sculpture, Pietersburg Municipal Sculpture Park.
References Register SA & SWA; SAP&S; G Clark & L Wagner, *Potters of Southern Africa*, 1974, C Struik, Cape Town; BSAK 1 & 2 (under Van der Watt); SA Art; AASA; *Lantern* December 1977–February 1978.

VAN DER WATT Jacobus Petrus

Born 1943 Pretoria.

A painter, sculptor and graphic artist of the SA landscape, people and animals. Works in oil, acrylic, charcoal, bronze, stone, wood, lead, fibreglass, natural fibres and in various graphic media.

Studies Pretoria Teachers Training College, gaining a National Art Teachers Diploma in 1964; University of South Africa, attaining a BA(FA) in 1976 and an MA(FA) in 1983.

Profile 1982 Founder and Chairman of Prisma Art Society, Alberton, Transvaal. 1965–77 taught art at Die Hoërskool, Alberton; from 1978 a lecturer in fine art at the University of South Africa. He has written a number of articles on artists and has worked in the film industry.

Exhibitions He has participated in several group exhibitions from 1978 in SA; 1980 SAAA Gallery, Pretoria, joint exhibition with Joey de Jager (qv); 1983 University of South Africa, solo exhibition.

Represented Pretoria Art Museum.

VAN DER WESTHUIZEN Pieter

Born 1931 Pretoria.

A painter and graphic artist of landscapes, portraits, still life, genre, figures and abstract pictures. Works in oil, watercolour, ink, pencil, charcoal and in various graphic media.

Studies 1959–62 University of South Africa, under Leo Theron (qv), Zakkie Eloff (qv) and Robert Hodgins (qv); 1969 under Alfred Krenz (qv); 1971 at the Ruth Prowse Art Centre, Cape Town, under Erik Laubscher (qv); 1979–80 Koninklijke Academie voor Schone Kunsten en de Hogere Instituten, Antwerp, Belgium; 1982 Stedelijke Academie, Ghent, Belgium.

Profile 1978–80 an art lecturer at Worcester Technical College, Cape Province. Visited Belgium in 1979–80, 1982, 1983 and 1985; visited Japan 1984 and 1985–86.

Exhibitions He has participated in numerous group exhibitions in SA, Belgium, the USA and the UK; 1970 Cape Town, first of several solo exhibitions held in SA, Belgium and Japan.

Represented Willem Annandale Art Gallery, Lichtenburg.

Reference *Gallery* Summer 1982.

VAN DER WESTHUIZEN Sonia

Born 1946 Cape Town.

A painter of landscapes, seascapes, portraits, still life and abstract pictures. Works in oil, acrylic, watercolour, gouache, ink, wash, pencil, pencil crayons, pastel, mixed media and clay.

Studies 1964–66 University of Stellenbosch; 1981–84 Cape Technikon, under Jan Vermeiren (qv), Stan Slack, Michael Mitford-Barberton and Leon Rubens (qv), gaining a National Diploma in Graphic Design in 1983 and a Higher Diploma in Graphic Design in 1984.

GUNTHER VAN DER REIS
Helmet for an African King
Epoxy, Acrylic & Oil 177 × 190 cm
Pretoria Art Museum

JOHAN VAN HEERDEN
Untitled 1987
Stainless Steel 5 × 7,5 × 3 meters
Reserve Bank, Pretoria

Profile From 1987 a member of the SAAA. From 1985 a lecturer at the East London Technical College. 1982 illustrated *History Makers* for Rössing Uranium, SWA/Namibia. Until 1985 lived in Stellenbosch, thereafter in East London. 1973–74 travelled in Europe.

Exhibitions 1987 Stellenbosch, first of two solo exhibitions.

VAN DE VIJVER Ada

Born 1947 Jakarta, Indonesia.

Resided in SA *c.*1975–84.

An artist producing etchings, aquatints, drawings and collages with a socio-political content. 1982 a portfolio of eight copper-plate aquatints entitled "Separate Freedoms"; 1983 a portfolio of black and white etchings entitled "Masque".

Studies 1965–69 Academie voor Kunst en Industrie, Enschede, The Netherlands; 1969–70 Akademia Sztuk Pieknych, Warsaw, Poland; 1972–74 Jan van Eyck Academie, Maastricht, The Netherlands.

Profile 1976–78 taught at Rorke's Drift Art Centre, Natal; 1983 a part-time lecturer at the Michaelis School of Fine Art. Married to Jules van de Vijver (qv).

Exhibitions She has participated in group exhibitions during the 1970s and 1980s in SA; 1982 Cape Town Triennial; 1982 Gowlett Gallery, Cape Town, solo exhibition; 1983 Cape Town, joint exhibition with Jules van de Vijver (qv); 1984 SAAA Gallery, Pretoria and Goodman Gallery, Johannesburg, joint exhibition with Jules van de Vijver (qv).

Award 1982 Merit Award, Cape Town Triennial.

Represented Durban Art Gallery; Pretoria Art Museum; SA National Gallery, Cape Town; University of the Orange Free State; University of South Africa.

References AASA; *SA Arts Calendar* November 1983.

VAN DE VIJVER Jules

Born 1951 De Bilt, The Netherlands.

Resided in SA 1967–84.

A graphic artist producing silkscreens of landscapes. Uses Zulu history as his source material. Several series including "Isandhlwana 1879–1979"; "Birds" 1983 and "Tracks" 1983.

Studies 1970 briefly at the Michaelis School of Fine Art; 1971–74 printmaking at the Jan van Eyck Academie, Maastricht, The Netherlands.

Profile 1975 a part-time lecturer at the Michaelis School of Fine Art; 1976–78 Principal of the Rorke's Drift Art Centre, Natal; 1978 took over the Printmaking Department at the Michaelis School of Fine Art on the death of Katrine Harries (qv), a permanent member of staff 1981–83. Married to Ada van de Vijver (qv).

Exhibitions He has participated in group exhibitions in SA during the 1970s and 1980s; 1980 University of Stellenbosch, solo exhibition; 1982 Cape Town Triennial; 1983 Cape Town, joint exhibition with Ada van de Vijver (qv); 1984 SAAA Gallery, Pretoria and Goodman Gallery, Johannesburg, joint exhibition with Ada van de Vijver (qv).

Award 1981 Five Roses Young Artist Award.
Represented Durban Art Gallery; National Museum, Bloemfontein; Pretoria
. Art Museum; SA National Gallery, Cape Town; University of the Orange Free
State; University of Stellenbosch; University of the Witwatersrand.
References AASA; *Gallery* Spring 1982; *SA Arts Calendar* November 1983.

VAN DUYN-MOL Linda

Born 1950 Johannesburg.
A self-taught painter of landscapes, seascapes, still life, portraits, figures, genre,
wildlife, abstract pictures and child art. Works in oil, watercolour, acrylic, ink,
wash, pencil and charcoal.
Profile A display artist, interior decorator and muralist. From 1985 a member of the
NSA. Numerous illustrations for books and periodicals. She has travelled extensively in Europe.

VANE Kathleen Airini The Honourable (née Mair)

Born 1891 New Zealand.
Died 1965 Auckland, New Zealand.
Visited SA 1935 and 1938.
A painter of landscapes. Worked in watercolour and tempera.
Studies Ecole des Beaux Arts, Paris, and under Samuel J Lamorna Birch
(1869–1955).
Profile Lived in the UK and New Zealand. Visited and painted in the UK,
Canada, Malta and Egypt. In 1935 painted Cape scenery and in 1938 mainly
Cape Dutch homesteads.
Exhibitions Participated in group exhibitions in the UK and in SA.
Represented Public galleries in Dunedin and Sargent in New Zealand; SA
National Gallery, Cape Town.
References SAP&D; Bénézit; DBA; *Who's Who in Art*, 1934.

VAN ELLINCKHUIJZEN Jacobus Johannes

Born 1942 Pretoria.
A self-taught painter and sculptor of landscapes, portraits, figures, still life,
seascapes, wildlife, metaphysical space art and three-dimensional stereoscopic
work. Uses oil, acrylic, watercolour, gouache, ink, wash, pencil, charcoal,
airbrush, polyester resin and dunesand casting. Works based on Einsteinian
relativity concepts, giving visual expression to space/time.
Profile A member of the SWA/Namibian Art Association and the Swakopmund Art
Association. 1971–80 artist to the Nature Conservation and Tourism Board,
SWA/Namibia, thereafter a full-time artist. 1983–86 produced 12 series of postage
stamp designs for the Philatelic Services of SA, Ciskei and SWA/Namibia.
Architectural designs for Hardap Dam Recreational Area and Gross Barmen Hot
Springs, SWA/Namibia. A concert guitarist and writer of private philosophies and
poetry.

Exhibitions He has participated in many group exhibitions from 1981 in SWA/Namibia; 1981 Swakopmund, solo exhibition.
Represented Pretoria Art Museum.

VAN ENTER Johannes Frederick

Born 1923 Vryburg, Cape Province.
A painter of landscapes, portraits, still life, figures, genre and wildlife. Works in oil, acrylic, gouache and pencil.
Studies 1945–46 privately under Professor Steiner in Italy; 1963–67 Old Mill Art School, Elizabethtown, USA, under E Stanley Turnbull, S Ohrvel Carlson, Jossey Bilan and S Ralph Maurello.
Profile From 1985 a member of the Verwoerdburg Art Society. 1947–81 worked in advertising. 1967–68 a guest teacher at the Old Mill Art School, USA. 1986 published a series of lectures entitled "Learning to Paint". Has lived in SA, Italy, the USA and Canada. Father of Mike van Enter (qv).
Exhibitions He has participated in several group exhibitions from 1967 in Canada and SA.
Public Commissions From 1967 several portrait commissions of business and social personalities in Canada and SA.

VAN ENTER Michael Juan (Mike)

Born 1958 Cape Town.
A sculptor of figures, portraits and human kinetic sculptures. Works in polychrome metal, stainless steel, bronze and wood. Paints his sculptures in oil.
Studies Polytechnic Laval, Canada; Johannesburg Art, Ballet and Music School.
Profile Practises as a commercial artist. 1986 a founder member of the Fusionist Society of Artists. During the 1960s and 1970s lived in Canada. Son of J F van Enter (qv).
Exhibitions He has participated in several group exhibitions in SA from 1985.

VAN ESSCHE Maurice Charles Louis

Born 1906 Antwerp, Belgium.
Died 1977 Thonon, Lake Geneva, France.
Resided in SA 1940–71.
A painter of portraits, figures, landscapes, still life and genre scenes. Worked in oil, gouache, watercolour and also drew. A lithographer. Painted numerous series including "Tribal Life", "The Karoo", "Cape Fishermen", "Clowns" and "Man in Africa".

Studies 1924 Brussels Academy of Fine Art, Belgium, under James Ensor (1860–1949); 1925 worked in a stained glass studio; 1926 in the studio of a wallpaper manufacturer; 1933 under Henri Matisse (1869–1954) at Cimiez in the South of France and in Paris.

Profile After 1926 worked as a freelance cartoonist. 1930 a member of La Jeune Peinture Belge Group; 1940 a member of the New Group; 1946 a committee member of the SAAA; 1948 a founder member of the International Art Club SA; 1958 appointed Commissioner for SA at the Venice Biennial; 1961 an executive committee member of the SA Council of Artists. 1964 appointed National Chairman of the Fine Arts Committee, SAAA. 1943–45 a lecturer at the Witwatersrand Technical College; 1946 Founder and first Principal of the Continental School of Art, Dean Street, Gardens, Cape Town; 1952–53 a temporary lecturer, 1954–58 a lecturer, 1958–63 a senior lecturer, 1964–70 Professor and Director of the Michaelis School of Fine Art, University of Cape Town and Dean of the Faculty of Arts. In 1967 his painting entitled "Congo" (Zaire) was reproduced by E Schweickerdt, Pretoria; "Coons Carnival", a set of 10 linocuts, was published by Koster, Cape Town. Designed wallpaper. 1906–11 lived in Antwerp, Belgium; 1911–39 in Brussels, with visits to Paris; 1939–40 in the Belgian Congo (Zaire), on a Government-sponsored painting expedition; 1940–71 lived in SA; 1971–77 in France, on the Swiss border.

Exhibitions 1927 Galerie la Cimaise, Brussels, first of numerous solo exhibitions held in Belgium and France; he continued to hold solo exhibitions in Belgium after moving to SA; participated in group exhibitions from 1930 in The Netherlands, Belgium, France, Belgian Congo (Zaire), the UK, Italy, Brazil, Yugoslavia, Rhodesia (Zimbabwe), Switzerland, the USA and from 1941 in SA; 1939 and 1955 Belgian Congo (Zaire), solo exhibitions; 1941 Argus Gallery, Cape Town, first of over 15 solo exhibitions held in SA; 1948 Tate Gallery, London, SA Art Exhibition; 1956 and 1960 Quadrennial Exhibitions; 1958 New York, USA, solo exhibition; 1968 Durban Art Gallery, exhibition of drawings; 1969 Petit Palais, Geneva, Switzerland, solo exhibition; 1974 SA National Gallery, Cape Town and Pretoria Art Museum, Retrospective Exhibition.

Awards 1930 Silver Medal, International Exhibition, Antwerp, Belgium; 1951 title of "Chevalier de Leopold II" awarded by King Baudouin of Belgium; 1966 Medal of Honour, SA Akademie vir Wetenskap en Kuns; 1972 Title of "Officer of the Order of Leopold II" awarded by King Baudouin of Belgium.

Represented Bezalel Gallery, Jerusalem, Israel; Durban Art Gallery; Hester Rupert Art Museum, Graaff-Reinet; Johannesburg Art Gallery; King George VI Art Gallery, Port Elizabeth; Museum of Graphic Art, Brussels, Belgium; Pretoria Art Museum; SA Akademie vir Wetenskap en Kuns; SA National Gallery, Cape Town; University of Natal; University of the Orange Free State; University of South Africa; University of the Witwatersrand; William Humphreys Art Gallery, Kimberley.

References Carl Buchner, *Van Essche*, 1967, Tafelberg, Cape Town; Collectors' Guide; Our Art 2; Art SA; SAA; 20C SA Art; SAP&S; SAP&D; SSAP; BSAK 1 & 2; Enc S'n A; Oxford Companion to 20C Art (under SA); 3Cs; AASA; LSAA; *Artlook* January 1969; *SA Panorama* September 1971; Retrospective Exhibition Catalogue, 1974, Pretoria Art Museum.

VAN GOGH Joan

Born 1939 Johannesburg.
A painter of landscapes, still life, figures and wildlife. Works in watercolour. In recent years she has painted mainly botanical studies.
Studies Privately under Erica Berry (qv).
Profile A member of the WSSA. 1977 an art teacher at Glenoaks Remedial School, Johannesburg. Illustrated Margaret Roberts' *Book of Herbs*, 1983, Jonathan Ball Publishers, Johannesburg and *Growing Herbs with Margaret Roberts*, 1985, Jonathan Ball Publishers, Johannesburg.
Exhibitions 1978 Nedbank Gallery, Killarney, Johannesburg, first of two solo exhibitions; 1987 participated in a group exhibition at the Sanderling Gallery, Johannesburg.

VAN GRAAN Riena

Born 1934 Cape Town.
A painter of landscapes, recently incorporating figures, and occasionally of still life pictures. Works in oil, acrylic, pastel, aquarelle, pencil, watercolour and charcoal.
Studies 1953–55 University of Pretoria, gaining a BA in History of Art; 1955 modelling, privately under Elly Holm (qv); 1960–61 and 1963 Pretoria Technical College, evening classes under Zakkie Eloff (qv), Johanna Wassenaar (qv) and Elza Botha (qv); 1964–67 on an Italian Government Scholarship at the Academy of Fine Arts, Florence, Italy, under Primo Conti (*b.*1900).
Profile A member of the SAAA and of the APSA. 1968–76 Gallery Director of the SAAA Gallery, Pretoria. 1977–78 a part-time lecturer at the University of Pretoria. 1969–72 an art critic for *Die Transvaler*, 1974–81 for *Beeld*; has also written articles for various publications and art catalogues. Editor of *Lantern*. 1958 visited Egypt and Europe, including the UK and Scandinavia; 1983 visited Greece.
Exhibitions She has participated in numerous group exhibitions from 1964 in SA, Italy and the UK; 1974 SAAA Gallery, Pretoria, first of seven solo exhibitions held in Pretoria, Durban and Potchefstroom; 1981 Republic Festival Exhibition.
Represented Pietersburg Collection; Willem Annandale Art Gallery, Lichtenburg.
References BSAK 2; AASA.

VAN HALTER François

Born 1923 Ghent, Belgium.
Resided in SA from 1952.
A painter of landscapes, portraits, figures, still life, genre and abstract pictures. Works in oil, watercolour, ink, pencil and charcoal.
Studies Comes from an artistic family, by whom he was given lessons in his childhood, otherwise self-taught.

Profile 1966 a member of the SAAA. 1970 opened the François van Halter School of Art, Johannesburg. During the 1930s and 1940s wrote both poetry and prose and acted with the Richard Stevens Group in Belgium. Nephew of the artist Joseph van Halter and cousin of Achilles Lammens (1888–1969).
Exhibitions He has participated in several group exhibitions from 1966 in SA and Belgium; from 1967 he has held nine solo exhibitions, often in private residences.
Represented Potchefstroom University for CHE.

VAN HEERDEN Johan

Born 1930 Bethal, Transvaal.
A sculptor of figures and abstract pieces. Works in bronze, stone, ciment fondu, wood, stainless steel and aluminium. A painter and graphic artist, working in oil, acrylic, ink, pencil, charcoal and in various graphic media.
Studies 1947–50 Orange Free State Technical College; 1952–55 sculpture at l'Académie de la Grande Chaumière, Paris, under Edouard Macavoy (*b*.1905) and Ossip Zadkine (1890–1967), and etching and life drawing at l'Ecole des Beaux Arts, under Edouard Goerg (1893–1969).
Profile From 1957 a member of the SAAA. 1958–64 a lecturer in sculpture at the Pretoria Technical College; 1969–79 a lecturer in sculpture, basic design and jewellery at the Witwatersrand Technical College. During the late 1950s and early 1960s acted in films.
Exhibitions He has participated in numerous group exhibitions from 1950 throughout SA and in France, West Germany, Brazil, Yugoslavia, Italy, the USA, Rhodesia (Zimbabwe) and Argentina; 1955 Lidchi Art Gallery, Johannesburg, first of 13 solo exhibitions held in SA; 1956 and 1960 Quadrennial Exhibitions; 1963 SAAA Gallery, Pretoria, 10 Years' Retrospective Exhibition; 1977 Metalart Guest Artist; 1980 Metalart Guest Artists Exhibition, with Edoardo Villa (qv), Neels Coetzee (qv), Ian Redelinghuys (qv) and Gavin Younge (qv); 1981 Republic Festival Exhibition.
Awards 1956 Guggenheim Award, Paris and New York; 1973 Metalart Prize, open category; 1976 Metalart Prize, closed category.
Represented Hester Rupert Art Museum, Graaff-Reinet; Johannesburg Art Gallery; Natal Technikon; Pretoria Art Museum; Rand Afrikaans University; SA National Gallery, Cape Town; University of Stellenbosch; Willem Annandale Art Gallery, Lichtenburg.
Public Commissions Numerous public commissions including: 1966 wooden sculpture, University of South Africa; 1966 sculpture and four panels, University of the Orange Free State; 1971 stainless steel cross, Kenridge Hospital, Parktown, Johannesburg; 1972–74 stainless steel sculpture, Department of the Interior (Home Affairs), Pretoria; 1974 stainless steel sculpture, Synagogue Remembrance Hall, Vereeniging, Transvaal; 1977 bronze trophy, Rand Afrikaans University; 1978 entrance portal, Hoër Tegniese Skool, Pretoria-Tuine; 1979 stainless steel sculpture, Volkskas Building, Pretoria; 1980 stainless steel sculpture, the State Theatre, Pretoria; 1981–82 stainless steel sculpture, Civic Centre, Cape Town; 1982 stainless steel sculpture, Pietersburg; 1984 bronze, SA Airways; 1987 stainless steel sculpture, Reserve Bank, Pretoria.

References Art SA; 20C SA Art; SAP&D; BSAK 1 & 2; SA Art; 3Cs; AASA; LSAA; *Artlook* September 1967, May 1969, December 1969 & September 1971; *Habitat* no 27, 1977; *Flying Springbok* October 1984; *Art* March 1988; *Johan van Heerden*, 1977, Afrox Metalart Guest Artist Catalogue.

VAN HEERDEN Johannes Lodewicus

Born 1945 Cradock, Eastern Province.

A painter of landscapes. Works in oil, watercolour, pencil and charcoal. A graphic artist and photographer. Series entitled "The Metaphysical Forces" in 1973 and "Karoo Images" in 1984.

Studies 1963–66 and 1973 Rhodes University, under Professor Brian Bradshaw (qv), gaining a BA(FA) in 1966 and an MFA in 1974; 1971 graphics part-time at Hull Regional College of Art, England, under Walter Chamberlain.

Profile 1963–66 and 1973 a member of the Grahamstown Group. 1973 a lecturer at the University of Fort Hare; 1974–77 a lecturer at Lovedale College, Ciskei; from 1978 a senior lecturer at the University of Durban-Westville. 1969 and 1982 visited Crete.

Exhibitions He has participated in many group exhibitions from 1960 in SA; 1972 SAAA Gallery, Cape Town, first of five solo exhibitions.

Represented Ann Bryant Gallery, East London; Natal Technikon.

VAN HEERDEN Louis

Born 1941 Pietersburg, Northern Transvaal.

A painter of landscapes, still life, portraits and abstract pictures. Works in oil, watercolour, charcoal and mixed media. A series of paintings inspired by Greek literature; 1988 series entitled "Passage through a French Garden".

Studies University of Pretoria, gaining a BA(FA); postgraduate studies at the Academie voor Beeldende Kunsten, Amsterdam.

Profile Taught for 12 years at Pretoria Boys High School. A former National President of the SAAA. He has lived in Johannesburg from 1979, visiting Switzerland *c.*1984. 1988 spent some months painting at Cité Internationale des Arts, Paris.

Exhibitions He has participated in group exhibitions from the 1970s in SA; 1974 Triad Gallery, Johannesburg, first of many solo exhibitions held in SA; 1981 Republic Festival Exhibition; 1981 NSA Gallery, Durban, joint exhibition with Titia Ballot (qv); 1982 University of Stellenbosch, Guest Artist; 1987 Johannesburg Art Gallery, Vita Art Now.

Represented Durban Art Gallery; Tatham Art Gallery, Pietermaritzburg; Willem Annandale Art Gallery, Lichtenburg.

Reference AASA.

VAN HEERDEN Pieter Gerhardus (Piet)

Born 1917 Malawi.

Resided in SA from 1927.

A painter of landscapes, figures and portraits. Works in oil, ink, wash, pencil and charcoal.

Studies Studied briefly under Hugo Naudé (qv), but mainly self-taught.

Profile 1952 gave part-time life classes at the Michaelis School of Fine Art. From 1965 has lived in Somerset West, Cape Province.

Exhibitions He has participated in numerous group exhibitions from 1945 in SA; 1944 Cape Town, first of 17 solo exhibitions held in SA; 1948 Tate Gallery, London, SA Art Exhibition; 1956 Quadrennial Exhibition.

Represented Ann Bryant Gallery, East London; Durban Art Gallery; Julius Gordon Africana Centre, Riversdale; University of Cape Town; University of Pretoria; University of Stellenbosch.

Public Commission 1952 portrait of the Speaker of the House of Assembly, Mr J H Conradie.

References Collectors' Guide; Art SA; BSAK 1; AASA.

VAN LINGEN Claude

Born 1931 Vereeniging, Transvaal.

An artist of abstract pieces. Works in oil, acrylic, gouache, pencil, various graphic media and from 1971 in polyurethane foam. Creates constructions of canvas, plastic and other media. Several series including in 1973 "Flexibles" using foam, and in 1974 "VV" consisting of 24 pencil drawings.

Studies 1949–52 Witwatersrand Technical College, under Phyllis Gardner (qv), T O D Davies and W J Bramham, gaining a National Art Teachers Diploma; 1961 Académie Notre Dame des Champs, Paris, under Henri Goetz (*b.*1909) and Selim Turan; 1980 Pratt Institute, New York, gaining an MA(FA).

Profile 1953–64 taught at Meyerton High School, near Johannesburg; 1965 a lecturer, 1970 a senior lecturer and subsequently Head of the Fine Art Department, Witwatersrand Technical College. An art critic. 1978 settled in New York, USA.

Exhibitions He has participated in group exhibitions from 1954 in SA, at São Paulo, Brazil and in the USA; 1962 Gallery 101, Johannesburg, first of several solo exhibitions held in SA; 1966 Republic Festival Exhibition; 1968 Durban Art Gallery, joint exhibition with Nico van Rensburg (qv); 1981 Republic Festival Exhibition.

Award 1973 joint winner of the Ernest Oppenheimer Memorial Trust Award, Art SA Today.

Represented Hester Rupert Art Museum, Graaff-Reinet; Johannesburg Art Gallery; University of the Witwatersrand; William Humphreys Art Gallery, Kimberley.

References SAA; BSAK 1; 3Cs; AASA; *Artlook* July 1970 & August/September 1974; *To the Point* 26 August 1972, 25 August 1973 & 18 June 1976; *Habitat* no 4, 1973; *SA Panorama* February 1976.

VAN LINGEN Gail Kathleen (Mrs Stubbs)

Born 1946 Johannesburg.

A painter of landscapes, seascapes, city scenes, still life and wildlife. Works in oil and watercolour.

Studies 1964–67 University of the Witwatersrand, under Giuseppe Cattaneo (qv), Cecily Sash (qv), Judith Mason (qv) and Erica Berry (qv), gaining a BA(FA).

Profile 1959–64 lived in Natal; 1968–70 in London; thereafter in Johannesburg. 1971–73 ran a children's art school called "The Young at Art" in Illovo, Johannesburg. Has visited France, Portugal, India, the Seychelles, Hong Kong, Kenya, Botswana, Israel and Singapore.

Exhibitions 1974 Balalaika Hotel, Johannesburg, first of nine solo exhibitions held in SA and in London; she has participated in numerous group exhibitions from 1975 in SA, the UK and once in Dubai in 1985.

Reference *Habitat* no 66, 1985.

VAN NAZARETH Herman Antoine Julien Henri

Born 1936 Evergem, East Flanders, Belgium.
Resided in SA 1965–74.

A painter, graphic artist and sculptor. Depicts landscapes, portraits, still life, seascapes, genre and figures, also creates abstract pieces. Works in oil, acrylic, watercolour, gouache, ink, wash, pencil, charcoal, various graphic media, bronze, stone, ciment fondu and wood. Began sculpting in 1965. 1967–71 a series of heads and nude torsos.

Studies 1961–62 still life painting, Koninklijke Academie, Ghent, Belgium; 1963–64 figure painting, Koninklijke Academie voor Schone Kunsten en die Hogere Instituten, Antwerp, Belgium; 1965–67 sculpture, Michaelis School of Fine Art, under Professor Lippy Lipshitz (qv), on a bursary from the Belgian/SA Cultural Accord.

Profile 1965 a founder member of the Artists Gallery. Several tapestry designs from 1970. 1965–74 lived in SA, thereafter in Italy and Belgium, visiting SA for several months each year.

Exhibitions He has participated in numerous group exhibitions from 1961 in Belgium, Denmark, West Germany, SA, Brazil, Argentina, France, Italy and the UK; 1963 Deurne, Belgium, first of over 20 solo exhibitions held in Belgium and SA; 1964 Deinze Museum, Antwerp, solo exhibition; 1972 William Humphreys Art Gallery, Kimberley, solo exhibition; 1976 Pretoria Art Museum and Durban Art Gallery, Retrospective Exhibition; 1977 Durban Art Gallery, solo exhibition; 1982 Cape Town Triennial; 1985 Cape Town Triennial.

Awards 1972 Special Prize from the Koninklijke Academie voor Schone Kunsten en die Hogere Instituten, Antwerp, Belgium; 1973 Bronze Medal for Painting, Ostend, Belgium; 1974 Anto Carte Prize, Palace of Fine Art, Brussels, Belgium.

Represented Belgian Government, Belgium; King George VI Gallery, Port Elizabeth; Museum van Deinze en de Leiestreek, Antwerp, Belgium; Pretoria Art Museum; Sandton Municipal Collection; SA National Gallery, Cape Town; University of Leuven, Belgium; University of the Witwatersrand; William Humphreys Art Gallery, Kimberley.

References SAP&D; SSAP; BSAK 1 & 2; AASA; LSAA; *Artlook* November 1967 & May 1969; Retrospective Exhibition Catalogue, 1976, Pretoria Art Museum.

VANN-HALL (Florence) Wilgeforde (Agnes) ARCA

Born 1894 Leicester, England.
Died 1981 Bellair, Natal.
Resided in SA from 1926.
A painter of landscapes, portraits, seascapes, figures and abstract pictures. Worked in oil, watercolour, pencil and charcoal; particularly well-known for her work in stained glass in both London and SA.
Studies 1918–21 Liverpool School of Art, gaining a scholarship; 1921–24 Royal College of Art, London, under Sir William Rothenstein (1872–1945) and Professor E W Tristram (1882–1952), becoming an Associate and gaining a scholarship for a further year's study in teacher training and stained glass.
Profile 1925 designed costumes for the Empire Exhibition, London. 1940–45 served in the Drawing Office of the SA Air Force, Pretoria. 1945–70 lectured in drawing and painting at the Natal Technical College. A trained pianist. 1958 travelled around the world. Lived in Bellair and shared a studio with Mary Stainbank (qv).
Exhibitions Participated in group exhibitions with the NSA and throughout SA.
Public Commissions Portrait, Natal Provincial Administration Building, Pietermaritzburg; mural of the family history, Coedmore, Bellair, Natal; painted tiles in Port Elizabeth Law Courts and in the Estcourt Post Office, Natal. Stained glass windows at Addington Children's Hospital, Durban; The Children's Hospital, East London; St James's Church, Durban; St Anne's College, Hilton, Natal; All Saints' Church, Bellair, Natal; St Paul's Church, Scottburgh, Natal; Christ Church, Umkomaas, Natal; among many others.
References BSAK 1 (under Hall Vane); AASA; *SA Panorama* December 1969.

VAN NIEUWENHUIZEN Olga Joyce

Born 1940 Kitale, Kenya.
Resided in SA from 1959.
A painter of landscapes, still life and genre. Works in acrylic, watercolour, ink and wash.
Studies 1959–61 Pretoria Technical College, under Albert Werth (qv), Peter Eliastam (qv), Ernst de Jong (qv), Leo Theron (qv) and Zakkie Eloff (qv), gaining a Commercial Art Diploma.
Profile From 1975 a member of the SAAA. From 1985 a member of the EPSFA.
Exhibitions She has participated in many group exhibitions from 1975 in SA; 1975 SAAA Gallery, Pretoria, first of eight solo exhibitions held in SA.

VAN NOUHUYS Jan Jozua

Born 1903 Ternate, the Moluccas.
Died 1940.
Resided in SA from 1921.
A painter and graphic artist depicting landscapes, still life, portraits, figures and genre. Worked in watercolour, oil, crayon and in various graphic media.

Studies Trained as a botanist. Private art lessons with M Winkel in Rotterdam.
Profile A large number of etchings—greatly influenced by Pieter Wenning (qv), whose etching press he obtained in 1931. Worked for the Pretoria Parks Department, the National Botanical Gardens, Pretoria, and for an aircraft corporation. Lived in The Netherlands and SA, 1935–36 visited France, where he studied in a Paris studio, sketching models. Joined the Union Defence Force in 1938.
Exhibitions 1936 participated in the Empire Exhibition, Wembley, UK; 1944 MacFadyen Hall, Pretoria, Memorial Exhibition; 1973 Pretoria Art Museum, Memorial Exhibition.
Represented Pretoria Art Museum.
References BSAK 1; AASA; *Jan van Nouhuys 1903–1940*, 1973, Pretoria Art Museum.

VAN RENSBURG Nico J J

Born 1935 Ladybrand, Orange Free State.
A painter and graphic artist of landscapes, portraits, seascapes, still life, genre, figures, wildlife, abstract pictures and personal experiences. Works in oil, acrylic, watercolour, gouache, ink, wash, pencil, charcoal and in various graphic media. Uses the child art symbol extensively. A sculptor of mixed media soft sculptures. 1974 a series entitled "Raka".
Studies 1956–59 Witwatersrand Technical College (Technikon), under Professor Robert Bain (qv), Joyce Leonard (qv), Phil Kolbe (qv) and Phil Botha (qv), gaining a National Art Teachers Diploma; 1978–79 Witwatersrand Technical College (Technikon), gaining a Higher Diploma in Fine Art.
Profile 1966–67 a member of the Sestigers Group. 1960–64 an art teacher at Hoër Volkskool, Potchefstroom; 1965–70 a lecturer in painting and drawing, 1970–76 a senior lecturer, 1978–82 Head of the Fine Art Department and from 1983 Director of the School of Art and Design, Witwatersrand Technikon. An art advisor to companies and an art critic for *Die Vaderland, Die Transvaler, Beeld* and the SABC. He has also written articles for *Lantern, Flying Springbok* and *Artlook*. A singer. Has travelled to the major art centres in the world.
Exhibitions He has participated in numerous group exhibitions from 1959, in SA and in West Germany, Italy and the UK; 1968 Durban Art Gallery, joint exhibition with Claude van Lingen (qv); 1968 The Gallery, Johannesburg, first of 10 solo exhibitions; 1981 Republic Festival Exhibition.
Represented Johannesburg Art Gallery; Johannesburg College of Education; Pietersburg Collection; Rand Afrikaans University; Sandton Municipal Collection; University of the Witwatersrand; Witwatersrand Technikon.
References BSAK 1 & 2; AASA.

VAN RENSBURG Susan

Born 1957 Pretoria.
A painter of landscapes, portraits, still life and figures. Works in oil, acrylic, watercolour, gouache, ink, charcoal and pencil.

Studies 1975–79 University of Pretoria, under Professor Nico Roos (qv), gaining a BA(FA); 1987 attained an MA(FA) from the University of Pretoria, studying under Professor Nico Roos (qv).
Profile 1979–82 lived in Brussels, Belgium; 1983–86 in The Hague, The Netherlands, where she became a member of The Hague Art Society. Currently living in Johannesburg. 1985 visited Spain, and Israel; 1986 Sardinia and Corsica.
Exhibitions She has participated in several group exhibitions from 1979 in SA and The Netherlands; 1983 University of Pretoria, first solo exhibition; she has also held a solo exhibition in The Hague.
Reference AASA.

VAN ROOYEN Minette (Mrs Schuiling)

Born 1934 Rustenburg, Transvaal.
A painter of landscapes, seascapes, still life, portraits and genre. Works in watercolour, ink and wash. Sculpts in clay and is a well-known potter working under her married name, Schuiling.
Studies 1952–55 Pretoria Technical College, under Thelma van Schalkwyk, Robert Hodgins (qv) and Dulcie Campbell; 1956–57 St Martin's School of Art, London; 1957–58 Munich Academy, West Germany, under Professor Erich Glette (*b*.1896).
Profile 1982–85 Northern Transvaal and National Chairman of the APSA. 1960–62 a lecturer at the Pretoria Technical College. From 1972 has taught pottery privately. 1978 a part-time lecturer at the University of Pretoria. 1981 visited Japan, 1983 Greece and SWA/Namibia, 1985 Botswana. A cousin of Dick Findlay (qv).
Exhibitions She has participated in numerous group exhibitions in Johannesburg and in West Germany; 1951 University of Pretoria, first of *c*.18 solo exhibitions held in SA; 1981 Republic Festival Exhibition.
Represented Pietersburg Collection; Pretoria Art Museum; University of Pretoria; Willem Annandale Art Gallery, Lichtenburg.
References BSAK 1; AASA; *Artlook* May 1969; *SA Arts Calendar* Spring 1986.

VAN SCHALKWYK Frieda Thea

Born 1935 Pretoria.
A painter and graphic artist of abstract pictures. Works in oil on paper and produces monotypes.
Studies 1953–57 University of Pretoria, under Professor F G E Nilant, Walter Battiss (qv) and George Boys (qv), gaining a BA(FA) cum laude in 1956 and a Higher Teachers Diploma in 1957.
Profile A member of the SAAA. 1959 an itinerant art teacher at the Frank Joubert Art School, Cape Town. From 1984 a lecturer in art appreciation at St Alban's College, Pretoria. Since 1980 she has written several articles for *Lantern*.
Exhibitions She has participated in several group exhibitions from 1980; 1984 Evita Gallery, Pretoria, solo exhibition.

VAN SCHOUWENBURG Gerrit Coenraad

Born 1956 Bloemfontein.

A painter, graphic artist and sculptor of landscapes, seascapes, portraits, still life, figures, wildlife and abstract pieces. Works in oil, acrylic, watercolour, gouache, tempera, ink, wash, pencil, charcoal, various graphic media, bronze, stone, ciment fondu and wood.

Studies 1975–79 University of the Orange Free State, under Professor Teurlinckx, Laura Rautenbach (qv) and Leon de Bliquy (qv), gaining a BA(FA) in 1978 and a Diploma in Higher Education in 1979.

Profile From 1975 a member of the Orange Free State Art Society; from 1978 of the SAAA. 1982–83 an art teacher at the Oranje Meisieskool, Bloemfontein; 1984–85 a lecturer at the Orange Free State Technikon.

Exhibitions He has participated in many group exhibitions from 1977 in SA and Australia; 1978 University of the Orange Free State, first of two solo exhibitions held in Bloemfontein.

Represented University of the Orange Free State.

Public Commission 1981–82 murals, Military Museum, Bloemfontein.

VAN SOMEREN Edmund Lawrence Major ROI

Born 1875 Bangalore, India.

A painter of landscapes, figures and portraits. Worked in oil.

Studies Royal Academy Schools, London, where he obtained two Silver Medals and won the Landseer Scholarship.

Profile 1909 a member of the Royal Institute of Oil Painters and in 1929 an Honorary Retired Member. Lived in London and the home counties and, while in SA, in Grahamstown.

Exhibitions 1903 participated in the SA Society of Artists' exhibition in Cape Town and in 1905 in the Grahamstown Fine Art Association annual exhibition; 1903 Grahamstown, joint exhibition with F W Meason.

Represented Albany Museum, Grahamstown.

References DBA; AASA (under Vornsomeren).

VAN VELDEN (Willem) Louvain

Born 1950 Rustenburg, Transvaal.

A self-taught sculptor of animals. Works in bronze and wood. A potter and occasionally a painter in watercolour and oil.

Profile A trained nature conservationist, initially working for the National Parks Board and from 1981 for the Bophuthatswana Parks Board.

Exhibitions He has participated in several group exhibitions in Natal and Johannesburg from 1977; 1977 Durban, first of four solo exhibitions of his paintings; began exhibiting sculpture in 1979.

VAN VUUREN André François

Born 1945 Benoni, Transvaal.
A painter of abstracted figures, landscapes and abstract pictures. Works in oil and watercolour. 1970–79 abstract expressionistic paintings using muted tones; 1974–80 simplified, isolated objects in deserted, idealised environments; 1978 a series entitled "Past and Silence", based on a visit to the Transkei. In 1981 he began using brighter colours in his depiction of the debilitating problems of our times.
Studies 1965–68 Johannesburg School of Art, under George Boys (qv); 1969–71 The Visual Arts Research Centre, Johannesburg, under George Boys (qv).
Profile 1985 made a study tour of West Germany.
Exhibitions He has participated in numerous group exhibitions from 1969 in SA, the UK and West Germany; 1970 Little Gallery, Johannesburg, first of 13 solo exhibitions held in SA.
References BSAK 1; *Artlook* August 1971; *Van Vuuren*, 1987, catalogue, Johannesburg.

VAN VUUREN Lukas ARCA

Born 1939 Bethlehem, Orange Free State.
An artist producing two- and three-dimensional pieces, silkscreens on polystyrene and holograms. Minimalistic. Works in mixed media, including wax, pencil, airbrush, light, perspex, acrylic, polystyrene, ink, pastel, plastic and Kodalith.
Studies 1958–61 Pretoria Technical College, gaining a Diploma in Fine Art, majoring in painting and graphics in 1961, and a National Art Teachers Diploma in 1962; 1962–65 on a scholarship at the Royal College of Art, London, becoming an Associate in 1965.
Profile 1965–66 Director of Fine Arts at the American College in Leysin, Switzerland; 1967 Director of the Fine Arts Department at the Desert Sun School, California; 1968–69 Assistant Professor of Fine Arts at Scripps College, Claremont, California; 1970–73 Artist-in-Residence at the California Institute of Technology, Pasadena, California; 1975–77 a senior lecturer at the University of Natal; 1977–82 founded and taught at the Cape Town Institute of Art.
Exhibitions He has participated in group exhibitions from 1959 in SA, the UK and the USA; 1960 Vorster Gallery, Pretoria, first of over 15 solo exhibitions held in SA, Switzerland and the USA; 1981 Republic Festival Exhibition; 1982 Cape Town Triennial; 1984 University of the Orange Free State, solo exhibition.
Represented Durban Art Gallery; Long Beach Museum of Modern Art, California, USA; National Museum, Bloemfontein; Pretoria Art Museum; SA National Gallery, Cape Town; Tatham Art Gallery, Pietermaritzburg; University of the Orange Free State.
Reference *Gallery* Winter 1982; *Lukas van Vuuren*, Vega Art Enterprises, Cape Town; *Lukas van Vuuren*, 1984, Gallery International, Cape Town.

VAN WOUW Anton

Born 1862 Driebergen, near Utrecht, The Netherlands.
Died 1945 Pretoria.
Resided in SA from 1890.

A sculptor of the human figure (shoulder, half and full length), portraits, small sculptures depicting life in SA during his period and of large public monuments. Worked in bronze. His bronzes were cast in Italy by Nisini and Massa of Rome and Marinelli of Florence, occasionally by A Prowaseck in The Netherlands and later by Vignali in Pretoria. A large number of inferior, posthumous casts and surmoulages do exist. A painter in oil of landscapes, portraits and still life. Numerous drawings and murals.

Studies *c.*1874–89 night classes at Acadamie van Beeldende Kunsten, Rotterdam, The Netherlands; 1874–75 under Joseph Grave in his studio.

Profile During his life worked as a gunsmith and house-decorator and taught art both privately and in schools. Prior to 1908 shared a studio with Frans Oerder (qv). In 1917 became a member of the SA Society of Artists. 1932 a founder member of the National Academy of Art (SA). A member of the SA Akademie vir Wetenskap en Kuns. Designed the Zuid-Afrikaansche Republiek Coat of Arms for the Volksraad, Pretoria, as well as other ornamental work for buildings. From 1892 drew cartoons for *The Pretoria Press*. 1910 designed the first cover of *Die Brandwag* periodical and thereafter drew numerous illustrations for this publication. 1862–64 lived in Driebergen; 1864–89 in Rotterdam; 1889 arrived in Mozambique; 1890–1908 lived in Pretoria; 1908–38 in Johannesburg; 1938–45 in Pretoria. 1895 visited Mozambique; 1896–99 visited Italy and The Netherlands in order to supervise the casting of the Paul Kruger Monument.

Exhibitions 1908 Fine Art Society, Pretoria, solo exhibition; 1909 participated in a group exhibition with the Fine Art Society, London; 1948 Tate Gallery, London, SA Art Exhibition; 1953 Rhodes Centenary Exhibition, Salisbury, Rhodesia (Harare, Zimbabwe); 1976 University of Pretoria, Retrospective Exhibition; 1980–81 Pretoria Art Museum, Johannesburg Art Gallery, Durban Art Gallery, William Humphreys Art Gallery, Kimberley, King George VI Art Gallery, Port Elizabeth and SA National Gallery, Cape Town, Pierneef (qv) and Van Wouw Retrospective Exhibition.

Awards 1913 received the Medal of Order of Orange-Nassau from the Government of The Netherlands; 1936 awarded an Honorary Doctorate from the University of Pretoria; 1937 awarded the Medal of Honour for Sculpture, SA Akademie vir Wetenskap en Kuns.

Represented Africana Museum, Johannesburg; Durban Art Gallery; Engelenberg House Art Collection, Pretoria; Johannesburg Art Gallery; King George VI Art Gallery, Port Elizabeth; Potchefstroom Museum; Pretoria Art Museum; Rand Afrikaans University; SA National Gallery, Cape Town; Tatham Art Gallery, Pietermaritzburg; University of the Orange Free State; University of Pretoria; University of Stellenbosch; Van Wouw House, Pretoria; War Museum of the Boer Republics, Bloemfontein; William Humphreys Art Gallery, Kimberley.

Public Commissions Numerous public monuments including: 1896–99 Paul Kruger Monument, Church Square, Pretoria; 1912 Woman's Monument, Bloemfontein; 1915 Jan Hofmeyr statue, Cape Town; 1923 General Louis Botha statue, Durban; 1925 History of Transport frieze, Johannesburg Railway Station; 1929 Reverend Andrew Murray, Cape Town; 1929 President M T Steyn, University of the Orange Free State; 1938 Mother and Children, Voortrekker Monument, Pretoria. Numerous portrait busts including those of President M W Pretorius and Cornelis Delfos, Transvaal Administration Building, Pretoria.

References Morris J Cohen, *Anton van Wouw, Sculptor of South African Life*, 1938, Radford Adlington, Johannesburg; *Anton van Wouw en die Van Wouwhuis*, 1981, Butterworth, Durban; K & K; Skone Kunste; Collectors' Guide; Our Art 1; Art SA; SAA; Fay Jaffe, *They Came to South Africa*, 1963, Howard Timmins, Cape Town; SADNB; AMC5&7; DSAB; Oxford Companion to Art (under SA); SAP&S; SESA; SSAP; Pict Afr; Bénézit; BSAK 1 & 2; Enc S'n A; SA Art; 3Cs; AASA; SASSK; LSAA; *Die Huisgenoot* 24 December 1943; *De Arte* October 1968; *Antiques in South Africa* no 5, Summer 1979; *SA Panorama* July 1982.

VAN WYK Dirk Andries

Born 1953 Northern Rhodesia (Zambia).
Resided in SA from 1963.
A self-taught painter of landscapes, seascapes, buildings, still life, figures, wildlife and abstract pictures. Works in oil, acrylic, watercolour, ink, wash, pencil, charcoal and airbrush. Carves and paints ostrich egg shells.
Profile 1984 a member of the Brush and Chisel Club, Johannesburg. 1985 taught sketching and the art of watercolour at evening classes, George College, Cape Province. His paintings have been reproduced on calendars printed by Swan Publications, Durban. 1978 lived in SWA/Namibia; 1979 in Rhodesia (Zimbabwe); 1979 in the Eastern Transvaal; from 1981 in Cape Province. In 1982 visited the Transkei; 1983 visited Stellenbosch, painting Cape homesteads.
Exhibitions He has participated in several group exhibitions from 1983; 1983 Montfleur Gallery, George, first of three solo exhibitions.
Public Commission 1980–81 three paintings for The 44 Parachute Brigade, Pretoria.

VAN WYK Hendrik Johannes

Born 1923 Benoni, Transvaal.
A painter and sculptor of landscapes, seascapes, still life, figures and abstract pieces. Works in acrylic and bronze.
Studies 1955–59 East London Technical College, under Jack Lugg (qv).
Profile 1959–76 a practising electrical engineer, thereafter a full-time artist. 1940–46 lived in Cape Town; 1946–59 in East London, 1960–65 in Port Elizabeth, presently resident in Reitz, Orange Free State. Has travelled in Europe.
Exhibitions He has participated in several group exhibitions from 1959 in SA; 1980 Gallery 21, Johannesburg, first of five solo exhibitions held in SA.

VAN ZIJL André

Born 1951 Salisbury, Rhodesia (Harare, Zimbabwe).
A painter of figures, landscapes and animals. Works in oil, mixed media, ink and wash. A sculptor.

ANTON VAN WOUW
The Skapu Player
Bronze, Nisini Foundry, Roma, 30 cm High
The Everard Read Gallery

JAN VERMEIREN
African Bull
Oil on Canvas 150 × 120 cm
Private

ANDREW VERSTER
Kevin–Orange 1986
Oil on Canvas 152 × 91 cm
Durban Art Gallery

EDOARDO VILLA
Encounter with Colour 1987
Steel Colour Patina 97 × 50 cm
Artist

Studies 1968–71 and 1975 Michaelis School of Fine Art, gaining a Certificate in Fine Art in 1971 and an Advanced Diploma in Design in 1975.

Profile Has taught at the Ruth Prowse School of Art and at the Michaelis School of Fine Art, Cape Town. From 1979 a teacher and presently Director of the Art & Design Studio, Cape Town. Since 1981 he has taught art privately. 1984 travelled to Europe and the USA.

Exhibitions He has participated in several group exhibitions from 1978 in SA; 1972 SAAA Gallery, Cape Town, first of 16 solo exhibitions; 1985 Tributaries, touring SA and West Germany; 1988 Johannesburg Art Gallery, Vita Art Now.

Represented Durban Art Gallery; Johannesburg Art Gallery; Natal Technikon; National Museum, Bloemfontein; Pretoria Art Museum; SA National Gallery, Cape Town; University of Cape Town; University of South Africa; University of the Witwatersrand.

References *Gallery* Spring 1982; *De Kat* December/January 1987.

VAN ZYL Adriaan

Born 1957 Vredenburg, Cape Province.

A painter of landscapes, portraits and figures. Works in oil. Creates assemblages.

Studies 1976–80 University of Stellenbosch, gaining a BA(FA) (Hons).

Profile 1981 illustrated a children's book by Hester Heese called *Kobus het 'n Blom*, Qualitas, Cape Town. 1987 travelled to the USA and France.

Exhibitions He has participated in many group exhibitions from 1977 in SA; 1981 Republic Festival Exhibition.

Award 1983 Katrine Harries Gold Medal for Illustration.

VAN ZYL Lynne Rae (née Marshall)

Born 1956 East London.

Draws portraits and figures in charcoal, pencil and conté. Has also worked in oil, watercolour, ink, wash and pencil crayon. Depicts still life and produces abstract pictures. 1987 "PACT Ballet", a series of drawings exhibited in Pretoria and Johannesburg.

Studies 1974–78 University of the Witwatersrand, under Robert Hodgins (qv), Neels Coetzee (qv) and Giuseppe Cattaneo (qv), gaining a BA(FA)(Hons).

Profile Established her own art studio in Johannesburg in 1980. 1978 spent nine months in Italy and travelling throughout Europe; 1984 visited London.

Exhibitions She has participated in several group exhibitions from 1985 in SA; 1985 Spring Street Gallery, Knysna, Cape Province, solo exhibition; 1987 Shell Gallery, Johannesburg, joint exhibition.

VARNEY Anna Madeleine

Born 1959 Johannesburg.

A painter of abstract pictures. Works in acrylic and in mixed media, including such materials as gel and sand.

Studies 1983 Johannesburg Art Foundation, under Bill Ainslie (qv).
Profile 1985 taught at the Johannesburg Art Foundation and in 1986 at the Alexandra Art Centre; also teaches art privately. In 1985 her prose poetry was published in *Sesame* magazine (no 6). Daughter of Neville Varney (qv) and niece of Fayetta Varney (qv) and Arthur Cantrell (qv).
Exhibitions She has participated in several group exhibitions from 1984 in SA.

VARNEY Fayetta (Mrs Cantrell)

Born 1922 Pretoria.
Died 1974 East London.
A painter of portraits and abstract pictures. Worked in oil and acrylic, also created collages.
Studies 1947–50 under Arthur Podolini (qv) in Cape Town.
Profile 1964–71 a member of the Bloemfontein Group. A member of the SAAA. *c.*1964 opened Gallery One in Bloemfontein. *c.*1965 opened the Varney–Cantrell School of Free Expression in Bloemfontein. 1968–72 taught at the Orange Free State Technical College. 1956–58 designed several tapestries and appliqué hangings for both public and private commissions in London. 1955 lived in London and Paris; 1956 in Madrid and Lisbon; 1957 in Jamaica; 1961 French Congo (Republic of Congo). Sister of Neville Varney (qv), aunt of Anna Varney (qv) and wife of Arthur Cantrell (qv).
Exhibitions 1952 Durban, first of over 12 solo exhibitions held in SA, Madeira, the UK, Portugal and SWA/Namibia; participated in numerous group exhibitions from 1953 in SA, the UK, France, Spain, Jamaica and the French Congo (Republic of Congo); 1964 Quadrennial Exhibition.
Represented National Museum, Bloemfontein; SA National Gallery, Cape Town; William Humphreys Art Gallery, Kimberley.
Public Commission 1957 jointly with Arthur Cantrell (qv), a mural in the Yacht Club, Montego Bay, Jamaica.
References SAA; SAP&S; BSAK 1; AASA; *Artlook* May 1971.

VARNEY Neville

Born 1926 Eshowe, Zululand.
Died 1966 Bloemfontein.
A painter of landscapes, figures and religious themes. Worked in oil.
Studies Although he had some private art training under Gert Brusseau (qv) in Johannesburg, he was mainly self-taught.
Profile An Associate of the Bloemfontein Group. Lived for varying periods in London, Paris (*c.*1950), St Ives, Cornwall (*c.*1953) and in Minorca, Spain (*c.*1961–63). Brother of Fayetta Varney (qv) and father of Anna Varney (qv).
Exhibitions 1953–65 participated in group exhibitions in SA and the UK; 1960 Quadrennial Exhibition; 1963 Chiltern Gallery, London, solo exhibition.
Represented National Museum, Bloemfontein; Pentwith Gallery, St Ives, Cornwall, England; SA National Gallery, Cape Town; William Humphreys Art Gallery, Kimberley.

Public Commissions Murals for the Copper Commission, London; with Arthur Cantrell (qv), a Crucifixion Triptych in wood and metal for the Chapel D'Amador, Funchal, Madeira.
References SAA; SAP&S; BSAK 1; AASA.

VAUGHAN Patricia Mary (Mrs Wiles) (née Wagstaffe)
Born 1922 London, England.
Resided in SA from 1923.
A painter of wildlife, landscapes and seascapes. Works in watercolour. From 1979 a number of triptychs, often on a large scale.
Studies 1941 and 1945–46 Rhodes University, under Professor Austin Winter Moore (qv), gaining a BA(FA); 1948–49 Slade School of Art, London.
Profile 1950–55 a member of the SAAA; 1962–68 a member of the NSA. From 1980 a member of the Society of Animal Artists, USA. 1947 an art teacher for the Rhodesian Education Department (Zimbabwe). Has travelled throughout Southern Africa and to Kenya in c.1960. Wife of Paul Wiles (qv) and mother of Shayne Haysom (qv).
Exhibitions She has participated in numerous group exhibitions from 1950 in SA and the USA; 1977 Everard Read Gallery, Johannesburg, solo exhibition.
References SAA (under Wiles); AASA (under Wiles); LSAA.

VAUGHAN-WILLIAMS Mary ARCA (Mrs Albino)
Born 1913 Clocolan, Orange Free State.
A painter and graphic artist of landscapes, figures, portraits, still life and semi-abstract pictures. Works in oil, watercolour, gouache, pencil and in various graphic media, particularly linocuts.
Studies Witwatersrand Technical College; 1936–39 Royal College of Art, London, under Gilbert Spencer (b.1892) and Sir William Rothenstein (1872–1945), becoming an Associate; 1953 spent six months at the Slade School of Art, London, studying under Sir William Coldstream (b.1908).
Profile A guest member of the New Group. 1943 settled in Natal, moving to the Cape in 1965.
Exhibitions She has participated in group exhibitions in SA, Rhodesia (Zimbabwe) and the UK; 1943 Gainsborough Gallery, Johannesburg, first of many solo exhibitions held throughout SA; 1948 Tate Gallery, London, Exhibition of SA Art; 1960 Quadrennial Exhibition.
References Collectors' Guide; SA Art; SAA; BSAK 1 & 2; AASA.

VELS Elizabeth Margaret
Born 1937 Pietermaritzburg.
A painter of abstract and Biblical pictures. Works in oil, acrylic, watercolour, gouache, ink and wash. c.1972 "Tutankhamen" series; 1973–74 "Umnagazi" series; 1976–77 "Garment of Praise" series; 1979–80 "Nkosi Sikelel' iAfrika" series; 1982–83 "Exodus" series; 1984–85 "The Passover Project".

Studies 1968–71 Witwatersrand Technical College (Technikon), under Phil Botha (qv), gaining a National Art Teachers Diploma; 1982–83 Witwatersrand Technikon, under Willem Boshoff (qv), attaining a Higher Diploma (paper-making).

Profile 1972 taught art history at the Witwatersrand Technical College (Technikon); 1972–84 a part-time lecturer in painting, Witwatersrand Technikon. Teaches art privately. A potter. 1978 visited Kassel, West Germany; 1980 Italy; 1982 Ireland.

Exhibitions She has participated in numerous group exhibitions from 1971 in SA and in West Germany, Israel, the USA, Italy and Greece; 1977 SAAA Gallery, Johannesburg, first of six solo exhibitions held in Johannesburg and Pretoria; 1981 Republic Festival Exhibition; 1985 Johannesburg Art Gallery, Guest Artist; 1985 Cape Town Triennial; 1987 and 1988 Johannesburg Art Gallery, Vita Art Now; 1987 SA National Gallery, Cape Town and Goodman Gallery, Johannesburg, joint exhibition with Linda Moross Ballen (qv), Philippa Hobbs (qv) and Susan Rosenberg (qv).

Represented Durban Art Gallery; Johannesburg Art Gallery; Pretoria Art Museum; SA National Gallery, Cape Town; University of the Witwatersrand; Witwatersrand Technikon.

References BSAK 2; AASA.

VENNER William H Tottendell

Born England.

A painter of landscapes. Worked in oil and pastel.

Studies Royal Academy Schools, London, and in Paris.

Profile During the 1890s an art master at the Durban Art School. Retired to the Northern Transvaal.

Exhibitions Participated in group exhibitions at the Royal Academy and in 1926 in Johannesburg.

References DBA; AASA.

VENTER Deon

Born 1953 Despatch, Port Elizabeth.

A sculptor of large clay and wood sculptures. A painter working in oil, acrylic and charcoal. 1983–85 life-size hollow-built clay pieces, 1985–87 larger-than-life-size wood carvings and door panel paintings.

Studies 1974–76 Port Elizabeth Technical College (Technikon), under Hillary Graham (qv) and Hylton Nel (qv), gaining a Diploma in Fine Art (Sculpture).

Profile From 1976 a member of the APSA and from 1977 of the EPSFA; 1977–78 a founder member of Y-U-VOOZ Group, Port Elizabeth; 1984–86 a member of the GAP Group; 1986 a founder member of Ecca One. 1976–83 a studio ceramicist producing utilitarian stoneware and ceramic sculpture. 1983–86 a lecturer in ceramics and sculpture at the Port Elizabeth Technikon and from 1987 at the University of Fort Hare. Married to Kathy Venter (qv).

Exhibitions He has participated in numerous group exhibitions from 1977 in SA and in 1986 in Vancouver, Canada; 1984 Beuster-Skolimowski Gallery, Pretoria, first of three joint exhibitions with Kathy Venter (qv).
Award 1986 First Prize, Hans Merensky Sculpture Award.
Represented King George VI Art Gallery, Port Elizabeth; Pretoria Art Museum; University of Natal.
Reference *Sgraffiti* no 35.

VENTER Julian

Born 1958 Pretoria.
A sculptor and painter of landscapes, portraits and animals. Works in wood, metal, plastic, oil, acrylic, watercolour, ink, pencil and charcoal.
Studies 1982–84 Pretoria Technikon, under Gunther van der Reis (qv), Leslie Reinhardt (qv) and Justinus van der Merwe (qv), gaining a Diploma in Fine Art.
Profile 1985 a drawing teacher at Leggats Design Academy, Johannesburg. 1985 illustrated Farnsi Phillips' *77 Stories van 'n Clown*, HAUM, Cape Town.
Exhibitions He has participated in several group exhibitions from 1979 in SA; 1985 Gallery 21, Johannesburg, joint exhibition with Izak de Villiers (qv).

VENTER Kathleen Mary (Kathy)

Born 1951 White River, Eastern Transvaal.
A sculptor in clay of Biblical themes, spiritual experiences and from 1982 of life-size hollow-built figures.
Studies 1974–76, 1978 and 1984 Port Elizabeth Technikon, under Hylton Nel (qv) and Phil Kolbe (qv), attaining a National Diploma in Fine Art (sculpture) in 1976, a Higher Diploma (ceramic sculpture) in 1978 and a Diploma in Technology (ceramic sculpture) in 1984.
Profile From 1977 a member of the APSA and the EPSFA; from 1984 of the GAP Group and from 1986 of Ecca One. From 1976 a studio ceramicist producing utilitarian ware and ceramic sculpture. Married to Deon Venter (qv).
Exhibitions She has participated in several group exhibitions from 1977 in SA; 1984 Beuster-Skolimowski Gallery, Pretoria, first of three joint exhibitions with Deon Venter (qv).
Represented Port Elizabeth Technikon; Pretoria Art Museum.
Reference *Sgraffiti* no 35.

VENTER (Philip) Spies

Born 1935 Port Elizabeth.
A sculptor in bronze, mixed media and porcelain of abstract works.
Studies 1954–57 Port Elizabeth Technical College (Technikon), under John Hooper (qv), Professor Robert Bain (qv) and Joan Wright (qv); 1963–64 on a British Council Scholarship at St Martin's School of Art, London, under Phillip King (*b.*1934) and Anthony Caro (*b.*1924).

Profile 1958 an art teacher at Eunice Girls High School, Bloemfontein; 1960 a lecturer in ceramics and sculpture at the Port Elizabeth Technical College (Technikon) and 1961–62 at the University of Stellenbosch; 1965–81 a senior lecturer and Head of the Ceramics Department, Witwatersrand Technical College (Technikon). A potter and co-partner of The Wayside Inn, Waterval Onder, Eastern Transvaal. 1959 a study tour in England, Italy and The Netherlands on an E R Searle Study Bursary.
Exhibitions He has participated in many group exhibitions from 1958 in SA.
Award 1975 Best Sculpture, Brickor Prize.
Represented Johannesburg Art Gallery; Touch Gallery, SA National Gallery, Cape Town.
Public Commissions Many public commissions including a bust of Professor Cillie, Cillie High School, Port Elizabeth; bas-relief mural for a church in Vereeniging, Transvaal; Pierce Nicholson Award sculpture, PACOFS, Bloemfontein; Stanley R Jones plaque, Alexander Theatre, Johannesburg.
Reference BSAK 1.

VERBOOM Nico

Born 1927 The Netherlands.
A painter, sculptor and graphic artist of portraits and portrait busts, figures and landscapes.
Studies 1946–50 Academy of Arts, The Hague, The Netherlands.
Profile 1965 a founder member of the Artists Gallery, Cape Town; 1986 Director of the Verboom Studio, Cape Town.
Exhibitions He has participated in group exhibitions in SA; 1965 SAAA Gallery, Cape Town, solo exhibition.
Awards 1965 First Prize, Escom Emblem Competition; 1967 Third Prize Graphic Art, Cape Salon.
Represented SA National Gallery, Cape Town; University of Stellenbosch.
Public Commissions Mural, National Bank, New York, USA; numerous portraits in SA.
References Register SA/SWA; BSAK 1 & 2; AASA; *Fontein* Summer 1960; *Artlook* July 1970.

VERGUNST Nicolaas Maarten

Born 1958 Cape Town.
A painter and graphic artist of figurative, mythological and historical themes. Works in oil, pastel, ink, crayon, water-soluble pencil, mixed media and in various graphic media; also sculpts. A series entitled "Europeans in Africa—Images of Colonialism and Class Conflict", and a second series entitled "The Dragonslayers—Images of Political Praxis and Revolutionary Struggle".
Studies 1977–80 University of Stellenbosch, under Professor Larry Scully (qv), Louis Jansen van Vuuren (qv) and Jan Vermeiren (qv), gaining the 1977 Henri Lidchi Award, the 1978–79 Maggie Laubser Scholarship and, in 1980, a BA(FA) and a Higher Diploma in Education; 1986 began his postgraduate studies for a Masters Degree at the University of Natal.

Profile From 1980 a member of the SAAA. 1983 co-ordinator of the Art and Ideology Discussion Forum. 1986 a founder of the Adult Art Association, Grahamstown. 1981 taught at Camphill School and Farm Community, Hermanus, Cape Province; 1983 at the Johan Carinus Art Centre, Grahamstown and lectured in the Departments of Journalism and Media Studies, Rhodes University. Several illustrations and reviews for journals and magazines from 1985.

Exhibitions He has participated in many group exhibitions from 1978; 1981 Republic Festival Exhibition; 1984 Grahamstown, first of two solo exhibitions.

Reference AASA.

VERMEIREN Jan

Born 1949 Bornem, Belgium.

Resided in SA from 1975.

An artist working in oil, lithography, etching and mural painting.

Studies 1968–71 Koninklijke Academie voor Schone Kunsten en de Hogere Instituten, Antwerp, Belgium; 1971 engraving, on a study bursary, in Belgrade, Yugoslavia; 1971–74 Koninklijke Academie voor Schone Kunsten en de Hogere Instituten, Antwerp, Belgium, where attained a Degree in Graphic Art.

Profile 1976–81 a committee member of the SAAA, Cape Town Branch; 1982–85 a committee member of the Artists Guild. Numerous illustrations for books, children's books and periodicals. 1973–74 a guest lecturer in lithography in the Cape. 1979–81 a part-time lecturer at the University of Stellenbosch; 1981–87 a lecturer at the Cape Technikon. 1968–75 lived in Antwerp. 1987 visited Belgium.

Exhibitions He has participated in numerous group exhibitions from 1969 held in Belgium, Yugoslavia, SA, the USA, West Germany and SWA/Namibia; 1969 Dendermonde, Belgium, first of three solo exhibitions held in Belgium and 11 in SA; 1981 Republic Festival Exhibition; 1985 Tributaries, touring SA and West Germany.

Represented Durban Art Gallery; National Museum, Bloemfontein; Pretoria Art Museum; Sterckshof Museum, Antwerp, Belgium; University of the Orange Free State.

Public Commissions 1979 Bacchus mural, De Waal Hotel, Cape Town; 1983 Fantasia mural, Drama Theatre, University of the Orange Free State.

Reference AASA.

VERMEULEN Leon

Born 1956 Knysna, Cape Province.

A painter working in mixed media.

Studies 1974–77 University of Stellenbosch; 1978–79 in Haarlem, The Netherlands.

Profile A member of the Artists Guild. 1983–84 a lecturer at the Ruth Prowse School of Art, Cape Town; from 1985 a drawing teacher at the Cape Technikon. Lives in the Cape.

Exhibitions He has participated in group exhibitions in SA from the late 1970s; he has held numerous solo exhibitions from 1980; 1981 Republic Festival Exhibition.
Represented University of Stellenbosch.

VERMEULEN-BREEDT Marié

Born 1954 Pretoria.
A painter of portraits, figures and still life. Works in oil, watercolour, ink, wash and pencil.
Studies 1972–76 University of South Africa, under Karin Skawran, gaining a BA(FA); 1976 Hammersmith Art School, London, under George Israels and Kingsley Sutton.
Profile From 1978 a member of the SAAA; 1981 of the WSSA and the National Portrait Society, London, and from 1985 of the SAAAH. A book illustrator, who in 1982 designed a tapestry. 1971, 1976 and 1981 visited Europe.
Exhibitions She has participated in several group exhibitions from 1967 in SA and in one in Paris; 1974 Pretoria, solo exhibition.
Represented Municipalities of Bethal, Bloemfontein, Ermelo and Middelburg.
Public Commissions 1982 portrait of President P W Botha, Middelburg Municipality; 1985 portraits of Professor Hoek and Dr J Howell, University of Pretoria.

VERMONT Iris

Born Johannesburg.
A painter of landscapes and seascapes. Works in oil. 1983–84 skyscape series; 1985 SWA/Namibia landscapes; Highveld landscapes.
Studies 1975 Centre for Continuing Education, University of the Witwatersrand, under Gail Machanik (qv); 1976–77 privately under Gail Machanik (qv).
Profile From 1975 a member of the SAAA. Married to Laurie Vermont, former Chairman of the WSSA and an Executive member of the SAAA. 1984 visited SWA/Namibia.
Exhibitions 1979 Garlicks, Rosebank, Johannesburg, first of 10 solo exhibitions held in SA; she has participated in group exhibitions from 1985; 1987 Strack van Schyndel Gallery, Johannesburg, joint exhibition with Wendy Amm (qv) and Elizabeth Illingworth Spann (qv).
Represented Pietersburg Collection; Pretoria Art Museum.
References *Gallery* Autumn 1983 & Spring 1985.

VERSCHOYLE Anna

Born 1920 Cheshire, England.
Died 1972 Cape Town.
Resided in SA from 1944.
A painter of semi-abstract landscapes and pure abstract pictures. Initially worked in oil and from 1971 in acrylic. A graphic artist who also designed a number of mosaics, having studied this art in Italy.

Studies 1953–58 under Alfred Krenz (qv) in Cape Town.

Profile A fully-trained town planner, who worked in Cape Town and lectured at the University of Cape Town during the 1960s. 1965 a founder member of the Artists Gallery, Cape Town. 1966–72 a member of the SA Institute of Town Planners and an Associate of the Town Planning Institute of Great Britain. Travelled in France, Italy, Greece, Turkey and the Scandinavian countries.

Exhibitions Participated in group exhibitions from 1956 in SA; 1956, 1960 and 1964 Quadrennial Exhibitions; 1958 SAAA Gallery, Cape Town, first of three solo exhibitions.

Represented Hester Rupert Art Museum, Graaff-Reinet; SA National Gallery, Cape Town.

References Art SA; SAA; 20C SA Art; SAP&S; BSAK 1; AASA.

VERSTER Andrew Clement

Born 1937 Johannesburg.

A painter of figures, landscapes, portraits, still life, beach scenes and views through windows. Works in oil, pencil and watercolour. A graphic artist, producing etchings and combining photography and serigraphs.

Studies 1955–59 Camberwell School of Art, London, gaining a National Diploma in Design; 1959–60 Reading University, UK, gaining an Art Teachers Diploma.

Profile 1961 taught at the Witwatersrand Technical College; 1962 taught for six months at the Michaelis School of Fine Art; 1962–71 a lecturer at the University of Durban-Westville; 1971–76 lectured at the Natal Technical College, becoming Head of the Division of Art. From 1976 an art critic for *The Daily News*, Durban, with a regular column in *The Argus*, Cape Town. A writer and art critic for various other publications. From 1978 an art advisor and designer for the architects Hallen, Theron and Partners, Durban. Since 1979 he has designed several tapestries. 1980–81 stage décor for ballet and theatre in Durban. 1970 spent seven months in London; 1985 and 1987 lived at Cité International des Arts, Paris.

Exhibitions He has participated in numerous group exhibitions throughout SA and in Austria, Israel, Greece, Italy, the UK, West Germany, South Korea, Australia, Belgium, The Netherlands, Switzerland and the USA; 1967 Johannesburg, first of over 30 solo exhibitions; 1969 Durban Art Gallery, joint exhibition with Patrick O'Connor and Joan Templer (qv); 1969 NSA Gallery, Durban, joint exhibition with Patrick O'Connor (qv); 1975 University of Natal, Retrospective Exhibition; 1985 Tributaries, touring SA and West Germany; 1985 SAAA Gallery, Pretoria, joint exhibition with Bronwen Findlay (qv) and Clive van den Berg (qv); 1987 Johannesburg Art Gallery, Vita Art Now; 1987 Durban Art Gallery and touring, Retrospective Exhibition.

Awards 1963 Special Award, Art SA Today; 1967 Cambridge Shirt Award, Art SA Today.

Represented Durban Art Gallery; Johannesburg Art Gallery; King George VI Art Gallery, Port Elizabeth; Mangosuthu Technikon; Natal Technikon; Pietersburg Collection; Pretoria Art Museum; Sandton Municipal Collection; SA National Gallery, Cape Town; Tatham Art Gallery, Pietermaritzburg; University of Natal; University of the Orange Free State; University of South Africa; University of Stellenbosch; University of the Witwatersrand; William Humphreys Art Gallery, Kimberley.

Public Commissions Numerous public commissions, including the 1974 etched stainless steel panel, Natal Provincial Administration Building, Pietermaritzburg; 1977–78 etched aluminum mural, Tongaat-Huletts Sugar, La Lucia, Natal; 1978 baked enamel doors, St John the Divine, Umbogintwini, Natal; 1980–81 concrete relief murals and etched glass screen-wall, Mangosuthu Technikon, Umlazi, Natal; 1981 sgraffito mural, Hotel Cecil, Bloemfontein.

References SSAP; 3Cs; AASA; LSAA; *Artlook* August 1967 & February/March 1976; *De Kat* May 1986; *SA Arts Calendar* Autumn 1987; *Art* March 1988.

VERWEY Daan

Born 1955 Beaufort West, Cape Province.

A self-taught sculptor of torsos. Works in ceramics.

Profile A potter, making vessels.

Exhibitions He has participated in group exhibitions from 1984 in the Cape; 1986 Gallery International, Cape Town, joint exhibition with Rochelle Beresford (qv).

VICTOR Diane Veronicique

Born 1964 Witbank, Transvaal.

A graphic artist producing etchings (mezzotints and aquatints). Draws in pencil and charcoal, and paints murals.

Studies 1983–86 University of the Witwatersrand, under Professor Alan Crump, awarded the Anya Millman Travel Scholarship in 1985 and attained a BA(FA) in 1986.

Profile Illustrations for *Frontline* March 1987.

Exhibitions She has participated in several group exhibitions from 1985 in SA; 1987 Melville Place Gallery, Johannesburg, four-person graphics exhibition.

Awards 1986 Overall Winner and Graphics Prize, New Signatures, SAAA; 1987 Graphics Prize, Rolfes Impressions '87, Johannesburg Art Gallery; 1988 Volkskas Atelier Award, SAAA.

Represented University of the Witwatersrand.

Reference *SA Arts Calendar* June 1988.

VILJOEN Hercules David

Born 1957 Stampriet, SWA/Namibia.

A painter working in oil and acrylic and a sculptor working in wood and polyester resin. His work is conceptual, metaphorical and concerns intercultural relationships and social comment.

Studies 1977–81 University of Stellenbosch, under Professor Larry Scully (qv), where he was awarded the Maggie Laubser Bursary in 1981 and gained a BA(FA) (Hons) cum laude; 1984–86 University of South Africa, under Professor Leon du Plessis (qv).

Profile From 1984 a member of the Arts Association SWA/Namibia and in 1986 a committee member. 1986 on the art committee of the Department of Civic Affairs, SWA/Namibia; 1987 a founder member of the Art Promotion Body, SWA/Namibia. From 1984 a lecturer and in 1987 acting Chairman, Department of Fine Arts, Academy, Windhoek. 1985 visited the Okavango Swamps, Botswana.

Exhibitions He has participated in many group exhibitions from 1980 in Cape Town, SWA/Namibia and in 1982 in West Germany; 1982 SAAA Gallery, Cape Town, solo exhibition.

Represented University of Stellenbosch.

VILLA Edoardo

Born 1920 Bergamo, Italy.

Resided in SA from 1942.

A sculptor of anthropomorphic images with an African theme. Works in steel, brass, copper and bronze. His sculptures are sometimes painted.

Studies Andrea Fantoni Art School, Bergamo, under Minotti, Barbieri and Lodi; also in Milan and Rome.

Profile A member of the SAAA. 1961 a committee member of the SA Council of Artists. A member of the Contemporary Art Society. 1963 a founder member of the Amadlozi Group.

Exhibitions He has participated in numerous group exhibitions from 1947 in SA and in Italy, Brazil, the USA, the UK, Greece, Zimbabwe and Chile; 1947 Johannesburg Public Library, first of 22 solo exhibitions held in SA, Zambia and Zimbabwe; 1953 Vanguard Booksellers, Johannesburg, joint exhibition with Douglas Portway (qv); 1953, 1960 and 1964 Quadrennial Exhibitions; 1964 Pretoria Art Museum, open-air exhibition; 1965 Durban Art Gallery and Pretoria Art Museum, solo exhibition; 1970 Pretoria Art Museum and Johannesburg Art Gallery, solo exhibition of works created 1960–70; 1976 Rand Afrikaans University, solo exhibition; 1977 Guest Artist, Metalart Competition; 1980 Metalart Guest Artists Exhibition, with Neels Coetzee (qv), Ian Redelinghuys (qv), Johan van Heerden (qv) and Gavin Younge (qv); 1980 Rand Afrikaans University, Retrospective Exhibition; 1981 Republic Festival Exhibition; 1982 Cape Town Triennial; 1984 University of the Witwatersrand, solo exhibition; 1985 Tributaries, touring SA and West Germany; 1985 Goodman Gallery, Johannesburg, joint exhibition with Sydney Kumalo (qv), Ezrom Legae (qv) and Cecil Skotnes (qv); 1986 Amadlozi Art Centre, Johannesburg, joint exhibition with Giuseppe Cattaneo (qv); 1988 Johannesburg Art Gallery, Vita Art Now; 1988 Standard Bank Festival of the Arts, 1820 Settlers National Monument, Grahamstown, Guest Artist.

Awards 1959 First Prize, Artists of Fame and Promise, Lawrence Adler Gallery, Johannesburg; 1965 Silver Medal, Transvaal Academy, Johannesburg; 1966 Silver Medal, SA Breweries Exhibition, Cape Town; 1969 Gold Medal, Chamber of Mines Award and Olivetti First Prize, Transvaal Academy, Johannesburg; 1979 Gold Medal, SA Akademie vir Wetenskap en Kuns; 1987 Vita Quarterly Award Winner with John Muafangejo (qv).

Represented Durban Art Gallery; Hester Rupert Art Museum, Graaff-Reinet; Johannesburg Art Gallery; King George VI Art Gallery, Port Elizabeth; National Gallery, Harare, Zimbabwe; Pietersburg Collection; Pretoria Art Museum; Rand Afrikaans University; Sandton Municipal Collection; SA Akademie vir Wetenskap en Kuns; SA National Gallery, Cape Town; University of Natal; University of South Africa; University of the Witwatersrand.

Public Commissions 1979 "Suspended Sculpture", painted steel, Warmbaths Recreation Centre; 1981 "The Knot", painted steel, Civic Centre, Cape Town; 1981 "Suspended Sculpture", brass, copper and steel, City Hall, Port Elizabeth; 1983 "Standing Form", bronze, Town Gardens, City Hall, Durban. Numerous corporate commissions throughout SA.

References L Watter, *Villa*, 1967, Phillip Steyn, Johannesburg; K Skawran, *Edoardo Villa*, 1976, Afrox, Johannesburg; *Edoardo Villa, Sculpture*, edited by E P Engel, 1980, United Book Distributors, Johannesburg; Art SA; SAA; 20C SA Art; SAP&S; Oxford Companion to Art (under SA); SESA; SSAP; BSAK 1 & 2; Our Art 3; SA Art; Oxford Companion to 20C Art; 3Cs; AASA; LSAA; *Fontein* vol 1 no 1, 1960 & vol 1 no 3, 1960; *SA Art News* 18 May 1961 & 22 June 1961; *Artlook* January 1967, July 1967, September 1967, October 1968, June 1970, December 1970, September 1972 & June/July 1976; *SA Panorama* September 1970, December 1976, November 1980 & January 1984; *De Arte* May 1971; *Habitat* nos 8, 9 & 19, 1974; *De Kat* February 1987; *Villa 88*, 1988, 1820 Settlers National Monument, Grahamstown.

VILLET (Jean) Carolus Johannes

Born 1817 Cape Town.
Died After 1870 Cape Town.
A painter of flowers. Worked in gouache.

Studies Thought to have studied under P J Verreaux, a Cape Town naturalist, taxidermist and artist.

Profile 1848 offered painting and drawing lessons in Cape Town. He was in partnership with his father, who had a seed business, a botanical garden and a menagerie. Lived in Cape Town.

Exhibitions 1858 participated in Third Exhibition of Fine Arts, Cape Town.

References Pict Art; Pict Afr.

VINCENT Nancy

Born 1895 Cape Town.
A sculptor of figures. Worked in bronze.

Studies Cape Town School of Art, under Charles S Groves (qv) and Percy Thatcher; Cape Technical College, winning a Giovanna Milner Scholarship for Overseas Study; Slade School of Art, London, under Henry Tonks (1862–1937); sculpture under James Harvard Thomas (1854–1921) in London; Chelsea Polytechnic, London; Westminster School of Art, London, under Frank Dobson (1888–1963); later studied in Paris and in Rome.

Profile The first woman to open a sculpture studio in Cape Town.

Exhibitions Participated in group exhibitions in SA and in England 1927–36.
Represented SA National Gallery, Cape Town.
Public Commission Two figures for the Voortrekker Memorial Hall, Pretoria.
References Art SA; SAA; SAP&S; SESA; DBA; BSAK 1; AASA.

VINCENT Wendy Joan
Born 1941 Pretoria.
A painter and graphic artist of landscapes and abstract landscapes. Works in oil, acrylic and lithography.
Studies 1958–59 Natal Technical College, under Harold Strachan and Hugh Dent (qv); 1960–61 Witwatersrand Technical College (Technikon), under Joyce Leonard (qv) and George Boys (qv), gaining a National Art Teachers Certificate; 1965 Art Students League, New York, under Harry Sternberg (*b.*1904); 1969–71 lithographic workshops, Paris, under Desjobert and Detruit.
Profile 1983–85 a part-time lecturer in graphic printmaking at the Witwatersrand Technikon. 1981 commissioned to engrave 12 engravings for the de-luxe limited edition of Olive Schreiner's "The Hunter", published by Egon Guenther, Johannesburg. 1946–58 lived in Rhodesia (Zimbabwe); has travelled throughout Southern Africa. She has lived in England since 1986, but continues to visit SA.
Exhibitions She has participated in numerous group exhibitions from 1962 in SA, Austria, Israel, Australia, West Germany, the USA, Switzerland and Spain; 1974 NSA Gallery, Durban, first of six solo exhibitions; 1976 Rand Afrikaans University, solo exhibition; 1978 Bloemfontein Art Museum; joint exhibition with Cecil Skotnes (qv) and Aileen Lipkin (qv); 1981 Republic Festival Exhibition.
Represented New York Library, New York, USA; Philadelphia Art Museum, USA; Pretoria Art Museum; Rand Afrikaans University.
References BSAK 2; AASA; LSAA; Lamia Doumato, *Dictionary of Women Artists*, New York; *Artlook* February 1975; *Living* June 1985.

VISAGIE Johannes Jacobus Frederick (Hansie)
Born 1958 Lusaka, Northern Rhodesia (Zambia).
Resided in SA from 1964.
A painter, graphic artist and sculptor of abstract works and abstracted figures and landscapes. Works in oil, acrylic, mixed media, gouache, ink, pencil, various graphic media, wood, papier mâché and found objects.
Studies 1975 Pretoria School of Art, Ballet and Music; 1981 University of Pretoria, gaining a BA(FA).
Profile From 1985 a part-time lecturer at the University of Pretoria. Has designed various marionettes and puppets for the SABC, and has been involved in the design of scenery and costume for both the SABC and for theatres. Established The Little Marionette Company in 1975, from 1976 has been a member of the Union Internationale de la Marionette. 1980–81, 1983 and 1985 visited the USA, Europe and the UK.
Exhibitions He has exhibited his marionettes and paintings from 1980 in SA.

VISSER Joey

Born 1930 Mount Frere, Transkei.
A painter of indigenous flora. Works in watercolour, ink and charcoal.
Studies 1948 Witwatersrand Technical College, under James Gardner (qv).
Profile 1958–59 secretary of the East London Fine Arts Society; from 1961 a member of the SAAA and the EPSFA. 1952–58 lived in Durban; 1958–59 in East London; 1960 in Johannesburg; 1961–82 in Pretoria; from 1982 in the Karoo. 1962 visited Europe; 1969 the USA; 1985 the Greek islands.
Exhibitions She has participated in several group exhibitions from 1955 in SA and twice in London; 1977 Hoffer Gallery, Pretoria, first of seven solo exhibitions.
Reference BSAK 2.

VISSER Johannes Petrus (Jan)

Born 1933 Windhoek, SWA/Namibia.
A painter and graphic artist of landscapes, seascapes, still life, architectural themes, animals, symbolic landscapes, figures and portraits. Works in oil, gouache, pencil, charcoal, pastel and in various graphic media. Uses the Pointillist technique.
Studies At the Hugo Naudé Art Centre, Worcester, under Jean Welz (qv); 1964–70 privately under Alfred Krenz (qv) and through the University of South Africa, for three years; 1971–73 graphic art under Anna Vorster (qv).
Profile From 1979 a member of the SAAA. 1980 a founder member of the Artists Guild in Cape Town. 1981–82 and from 1986 a lecturer at the Ruth Prowse School of Art, Cape Town. A qualified lawyer, practising as such 1958–68. 1974 visited Europe, working in the graphic studio of Stanley William Hayter (b.1901) in Paris and at the Van Gogh Museum in Amsterdam. 1977–78 made a study tour in Europe.
Exhibitions 1970 Artists Gallery, Cape Town, first of 11 solo exhibitions; he has participated in numerous group exhibitions from 1971 in SA, the USA and Europe; 1981 Republic Festival Exhibition.
Represented Pretoria Art Museum; University of the Orange Free State; University of Stellenbosch; Willem Annandale Art Gallery, Lichtenburg; William Humphreys Art Gallery, Kimberley.
Reference *Artlook* September 1972.

VOIGT Harold Frederick

Born 1939 Johannesburg.
A painter of landscapes, abstract works and the human figure. Concentrates on textural qualities, light and colour, derived from the African landscape. Often uses primitive African motifs. Works in a wide range of mixed-media techniques incorporating sand, marble dust, wax and oil. 1974 a series entitled "The Animal in Africa"; 1975–79 "The African Landscape"; 1981 "The Landscape and Impressions of Greece"; 1982–85 "The African Landscape"; 1986 "The Female Figure"; from 1986 abstract work derived from the colours and textures of Africa.

Studies 1957 briefly studied architecture at the University of the Witwatersrand; 1965 and 1972 studied painting under Bill Ainslie (qv).
Profile Worked as Creative Director of a Johannesburg advertising agency, and wrote and produced documentary and feature films before turning to full-time painting in 1973. From 1974 he has been based in the Eastern Transvaal Lowveld. 1966 travelled to New York, Paris, Rome and London; 1975 New York and London; 1978 London and West Germany; 1981 London, Paris, Rome, Florence and Greece; 1984 New York and Spain; 1986 London, Paris, West Germany, Austria and Italy; 1986 New York, Texas and Louisiana, USA. Married to Leigh Voigt (qv).
Exhibitions He has participated in several group exhibitions from 1971 in Johannesburg; 1973 Gallery 21, Johannesburg, first of six solo exhibitions held in SA; 1986 Everard Read Gallery, solo exhibition; 1987 Johannesburg Art Gallery, Vita Art Now.
Represented Nelspruit Art Gallery; William Humphreys Art Gallery, Kimberley.
References AASA; *Artlook* July 1973; *Habitat* no 4, 1973; *To the Point* 8 February 1974.

VOIGT Leigh

Born 1943 Johannesburg.
A painter of wildlife, landscapes, still life and portraits. Works in watercolour, ink and pencil.
Studies 1961–62 Witwatersrand Technical College, under Joyce Leonard (qv), Andrew Verster (qv) and George Boys (qv).
Profile 1981–84 Curator of the Nelspruit Art Gallery. An illustrator, whose work has been reproduced in periodicals, newspapers and the following books: Marguerite Poland, *Mantis and The Moon*, 1979 and *Once at KwaFubesi*, 1981, both published by Ravan Press, Johannesburg; Sue Hart, *In the Wild*, 1974, *Back in the Wild*, 1977, both published by Collins, Johannesburg and *Nature's ABC*, 1979, Via Afrika, Parow, Cape Province; Nan Wrogeman, *Cheetah Under The Sun*, 1975, and Ted Townsend, *Foxtails*, 1988, HAUM/Daan Retief, Cape Town. 1983 designed a tapestry for Marguerite Weavind. 1981 visited Greece. Wife of Harold Voigt (qv); daughter of Barbara Jeppe (qv) and sister of Carl Jeppe (qv).
Exhibitions 1967 Lloys-Ellis Gallery, Johannesburg, first of nine solo exhibitions held in SA and one in Canada in 1981; she has participated in numerous group exhibitions from 1970 in SA, once in Canada in 1974 and in the USA and West Germany in 1978–79.
Represented Nelspruit Art Gallery.
References *Artlook* December 1971; *SA Panorama* April 1976.

VOIGTS (Gustav Adolf) Joachim

Born 1907 Windhoek, SWA/Namibia.
A painter and graphic artist of dunes and desert landscapes, seascapes, figures and wildlife. Works in oil, watercolour, ink, charcoal, woodcuts and linocuts.

Studies 1926–28 Kunstgewerbeschule, Braunschweig, Germany, under Professor H Ernst and G Clausen; 1929–31 Landeskunstschule, Hamburg, Germany, under Professor C O Czeschka; 1936–37 Akademie München, Munich, Germany, under Professor Ehmicke.

Profile 1950 a co-founder of the Arts Association SWA/Namibia, of which he is a committee member. 1947–77 a farmer in SWA/Namibia. Since 1948 he has produced a yearly calendar of wildlife woodcuts. 1907–14 lived in Windhoek; 1914–28 in Braunschweig, Germany; 1928–31 in Hamburg, Germany; 1931–40 in Windhoek; 1940–46 in an internment camp in Andalusia, Spain; 1946–85 lived on a farm 70km northeast of Windhoek; thereafter in Windhoek. 1952 visited Paris, London, Rome and Florence; 1960 visited Paris, Madrid, Rome and Amsterdam; 1980 visited Athens.

Exhibitions He has participated in numerous group exhibitions from 1931 in Germany, Brazil and SWA/Namibia; 1956 Quadrennial Exhibition; 1958 SAAA Gallery, Pretoria, Johannesburg Art Gallery and SAAA Gallery, Cape Town, exhibition of Gruppe Fünf (Group 5), with Adolph Jentsch (qv), Otto Schröder (qv), Fritz Krampe (qv) and Heinz Pulon (qv).

Awards 1981 Second Prize, 1983 First Prize, 1985 First Prize for Watercolour, STANSWA Competition.

Represented SA National Gallery, Cape Town.

Publications by Voigts SWA *Fables*, 1978, Gamsberg Publishers, Windhoek, SWA/Namibia; *Animal Rhymes*, 1987, Gamsberg Publishers, Windhoek, SWA/Namibia.

References SAA; SAP&D; BSAK 1 & 2; Art SWA; 3Cs; AASA.

VOLBEHR Ernst

Born in Germany.

Resided in SWA/Namibia 1908–12.

A painter of landscapes, particularly of the diamond rush and of tribal figures. Worked in oil.

Profile Most of his work returned with him to Germany.

Exhibitions He was the first artist to hold an exhibition in SWA/Namibia, a one-day event in Swakopmund.

Represented Arts Association SWA/Namibia Collection.

References BSAK 1; Art SWA; *Garden & Home* October 1984.

VOLSCHENK Jan Ernst Abraham

Born 1853 Riversdale, Cape Province.

Died 1936 Riversdale, Cape Province.

A self-taught painter of landscapes in a detailed and realistic manner. Scenes of veld and mountain, particularly of the Langeberg Range. Worked in oil and very occasionally in watercolour. A number of wood-engravings.

HAROLD VOIGT
Untitled 1986
Mixed Media on Canvas 190 × 140 cm
Dr & Mrs G Schlosser

GORDON VORSTER
The Nossob River 1988
Watercolour 65,5 × 95,5 cm
The Everard Read Gallery

Profile 1894–1902 a member of the SA Drawing Club; 1906 a member of the SA Society of Artists. 1931 an Honorary Member of the SA Akademie vir Wetenskap en Kuns. 1932 a founder member of the National Academy of Arts (SA). 1893 a study trip to the UK, France, The Netherlands, Germany, Italy and Switzerland with the Reitz family. Until 1904 worked as a book-keeper for Reitz & Versveld, Attorneys in Riversdale, thereafter painted full-time. In 1924 the first of several of his landscapes was reproduced by E Schweickerdt, Pretoria. In 1940 Riversdale Primary School was named after him. A coleopterist. Father of Vera Volschenk (qv).
Exhibitions Participated in group exhibitions from 1879 in SA, the UK and posthumously in Rhodesia (Zimbabwe); *c.*1925 Lezards Gallery, Johannesburg, solo exhibition; 1945 SA National Gallery, Cape Town, Memorial Exhibition; 1953 Pieter Wenning Gallery, Johannesburg, Retrospective Exhibition.
Represented Africana Museum, Johannesburg; Albany Museum, Grahamstown; Durban Art Gallery; Johannesburg Art Gallery; Julius Gordon Africana Centre, Riversdale; King George VI Art Gallery, Port Elizabeth; National Museum, Bloemfontein; Pretoria Art Museum; SA National Gallery, Cape Town; University of the Orange Free State; University of Stellenbosch; Willem Annandale Art Gallery, Lichtenburg; William Humphreys Art Gallery, Kimberley.
References Collectors' Guide; Our Art 1; Art SA; SAA; SADNB; 20C SA Art; AMC5; DSAB; SAP&S; Oxford Companion to Art (under SA); SSAP; Pict Afr; DBA; BSAK 1 & 2; Enc S'n A; SA Art; 3Cs; AASA; LSAA; *Die Huisgenoot* 21 February 1936 & 25 June 1954; Memorial Exhibition catalogue, 1945, SA National Gallery Cape Town.

VOLSCHENK Pierre Dr
Born 1926 Paardekop (Perdekop), Transvaal.
Both a painter and sculptor of landscapes, portraits, still life, seascapes, genre, figures and wildlife. Works in oil, watercolour, wash, bronze and ceramics.
Studies 1949–54 University of South Africa, where gained a BA(FA); 1961 University of South Africa, where gained BA(FA) (Hons); 1964 University of South Africa, gaining an MA(FA); 1971 University of Pretoria, attaining a PhD.
Profile 1949–52 an art lecturer for the Institute for Black Education, Middelburg, Transvaal; 1953–56 a ceramics lecturer at the Witwatersrand Technical College; 1957–63 a lecturer/teacher for the Transvaal Education Department; 1964–74 Senior Inspector for Art Education with the Department of Coloured Affairs, Cape Town; 1975–86 Professor and Head of Department of Fine Arts at the University of Durban-Westville. A designer and maker of National Sporting trophies. Creates functional and non-functional ceramic objects. 1962 wrote the script and monitored a film on Coloured people's art entitled "Art in Life and Life in Art". 1975 an art critic for *Die Burger*, from 1975 contributed to talks on art broadcast by the SABC. 1974 visited the UK; 1975 Belgium, West Germany and France; 1980 and 1981 the USA. 1987 retired to Gordon's Bay, Cape Province.
Exhibitions He has participated in numerous group exhibitions throughout SA; 1958 Tshipise, Northern Transvaal, first of 30 solo exhibitions held throughout SA and in West Germany, Spain and Portugal.

Represented Pietersburg Collection.
Public Commissions Numerous commissioned portraits in oil or bronze. 1968 ceramic panels for Tshipise Mineral Baths, Northern Transvaal; 1970 oil portrait of Dr Danie Craven, SA Rugby Board; 1979 three bronze portraits for the National Museum for Afrikaans Literature, Bloemfontein; 1987 bronze portrait of Professor D Swiegers, University of Pretoria.
References BSAK 1; AASA.

VOLSCHENK Vera (Mrs Hayward)

Born 1899 Riversdale, Cape Province.
A self-taught painter of landscapes, seascapes and still life. Works in oil.
Profile Trained as a school teacher, she taught art at Oudtshoorn Training College, Cape Province. She began painting seriously in 1936, after the death of her father, J E A Volschenk (qv). Travelled and painted extensively throughout SA. Lived from 1923 in the Aberdeen district and from 1948 in Stilbaai, Cape Province.
Exhibitions She has participated in group exhibitions in Cape Town, Johannesburg and Pretoria; 1939 Johannesburg, first of many solo exhibitions held throughout SA; 1947 and 1953 joint exhibitions with her daughter, Helene Volschenk Hayward, a trained but non-professional artist; 1974 Stilbaai City Council mounted a Retrospective Exhibition to mark her 75th birthday.
Represented Julius Gordon Africana Centre, Riversdale.
References Collectors' Guide; Art SA; BSAK 1 & 2; AASA; *Lantern* July 1982.

VON GLEHN Roswitha Valeska

Born 1928 Riga, Latvia (Latvian SSR).
Resided in SA from 1952.
A painter and graphic artist of wildlife, landscapes, figures and abstract pictures. Works in oil, ink and in various graphic media, particularly woodcuts. 1976 a series of six etchings entitled "Remembering Minos". Until 1979 produced mainly graphic work.
Studies 1960–62 part-time at the Witwatersrand Technical College; 1966 The Visual Arts Research Centre, Johannesburg, under George Boys (qv); also studied under Karin Jaroszynska (qv) and Albert Christoph Reck.
Profile From 1969 a member of the SAAA. Since 1976 she has produced a calendar annually. 1973 conducted an art tour of Moscow and Leningrad; 1974 visited New York and Washington DC; 1976 conducted an art tour of Crete; 1983 visited Japan and Taiwan.
Exhibitions 1971 SAAA Gallery, Durban, first of 11 solo exhibitions three of which were held in West Germany; she has participated in many group exhibitions from 1976 in SA and in West Germany, Italy, Brazil, France and Spain; 1981 Republic Festival Exhibition.
Represented Willem Annandale Art Gallery, Lichtenburg.
References BSAK 1 & 2; AASA; *Artlook* March 1973 & October/November 1974.

VON HOENSBROECH Irmgard Graefin (Countess)

Born 1899 Cologne, Germany.
Resided in SWA/Namibia from 1930 and in SA from 1953.
Draws portraits in charcoal.
Studies 1918–19 Kunstgewerbeschule, Cologne; 1926 under Professor Seewald in Cologne and Munich; 1956 sgraffito under Otto Gerster in Cologne; 1958 under André Lhote (1885–1962), in Paris.
Profile Introduced sgraffito to SA.
Exhibitions 1926 Galerie Casparie, Munich, Germany, first solo exhibition; she has exhibited in Europe from 1926 and in SA from 1946; 1956 and 1960 Quadrennial Exhibitions.
References SAA; AASA.

VON MALTITZ (Elizabeth) Amalie

Born 1940 Springs, Transvaal.
A sculptor of figures, portraits and abstract pieces. Works in bronze, stone, wood and clay. 1973–74 "Flight" theme; 1980–84 "Dancers"; from 1985 "Group, Situations" theme.
Studies 1959–62 Michaelis School of Fine Art, under Lippy Lipshitz (qv) and Katrine Harries (qv), gaining a BA(FA); 1963–65 Fine Art Academy, Stuttgart, West Germany, under Professor Daudert and Schellenberger; 1976–82 Rand Afrikaans University, under Professor E P Engel, attaining a BA (Hons) in 1977 and an MA (History of Art) in 1982.
Profile From *c.*1966 a member of the SAAA. 1966 Recreation Officer, Yeoville Recreation Centre; 1967–72 taught sculpture at the Johannesburg Council for Adult Education. 1974–83 an exhibition organiser and from 1983 senior exhibition organiser at the Rand Afrikaans University. 1959–62 lived in Cape Town; 1963–65 in Stuttgart, West Germany; thereafter in Johannesburg, with numerous visits to the Transkei. 1965 visited Italy; 1983 New York; 1985 Greece. Daughter of Gerda von Maltitz (qv).
Exhibitions She has participated in several group exhibitions from 1968; 1970 El Greco Gallery, Johannesburg, solo exhibition.
Public Commission 1961–62 designed the colour-film windows for Aasvoëlkop Dutch Reformed Church, Northcliff, Johannesburg.
Reference *Artlook* June 1970.

VON MALTITZ Gerda de Waal (née De Kock)

Born 1911 Heilbron, Orange Free State.
A mainly self-taught painter who attended life-drawing classes in Johannesburg. Works in oil and watercolour, painting landscapes, still life, seascapes and portraits.
Profile From 1948 a member of the SAAA; a member of the WSSA. 1935–37 an art teacher at Harrismith High School, Orange Free State; 1937–39 at Voortrekker High School, Boksburg, Transvaal. 1963 and 1984 travelled round the world; has also made frequent visits to Europe, the Americas, Australia and New Zealand. Mother of E Amalie von Maltitz (qv).

Exhibitions c.1950 Heidelburg, first of 24 solo exhibitions held in SA and in France, the UK, the USA, West Germany and Sweden; c.1950 Springs, Transvaal, joint exhibition with Mascha Braunger (qv); she has participated in many group exhibitions from 1964 in SA and in West Germany and the UK; 1981 Republic Festival Exhibition.

Represented Rand Afrikaans University; University of Pretoria; Willem Annandale Art Gallery, Lichtenburg.

References SA Panorama February 1959; *Artlook* March 1971.

VON MICHAELIS Heinrich H J (Heinie)

Born 1912 Berlin, Germany.
Resided in SA from 1927.
A painter of birds, particularly birds of prey, and of animals, especially horses, also paints figures, portraits, flowers, landscapes and seascapes. Works in oil, acrylic, watercolour, gouache, ink, wash and pencil. A sculptor in bronze and stone.

Studies Painting at the Academy of Art, Munich, Germany; 1934–36 sculpture at the Accademia di Belle Arti, Rome, Italy.

Profile A well-known glider pilot and naturalist, living in Somerset West, Cape Province.

Exhibitions He has participated in group exhibitions from 1937 in SA, once in Rhodesia (Zimbabwe) and in the USA; 1943 first of several solo exhibitions held in SA and London.

Award 1962 a Merit Award for his contribution to the study of bird life in SA, Cape Tercentenary Foundation.

Represented Ann Bryant Gallery, East London; SA National Gallery, Cape Town; William Humphreys Art Gallery, Kimberley.

Publications by Von Michaelis Birds of the Gauntlet, Hutchinson, London; *Wings of the Wild*, 1953, Central News Agency, Cape Town; *Our Birds*, second series, with Allan Bird.

References Collectors' Guide; Art SA; SESA; BSAK 1; SA Art; AASA; *SA Panorama* May 1965.

VON MOLTKE Monika Nona Paula

Born 1934 Breslau, Germany.
Resided in SA from 1950.
A painter and graphic artist of figures, portraits and animals; concepts that describe the transpersonal, holistic, archetypal and psychological aspects in art. Works in oil, watercolour, gouache, ink, wash, pencil, charcoal and in various graphic media, particularly monotypes.

Studies 1951–53 Witwatersrand Technical College; 1961 privately under Karin Jaroszynska (qv); 1962 privately under Albert Christoph Reck; 1963 Sommer Academy, under Oskar Kokoschka (1886–1980) in Salzburg, Austria; 1966 The Visual Arts Research Centre, Johannesburg, under George Boys (qv).

Profile From 1980 a member of the SAAA. 1975–78 an art teacher at a high school in Hamburg, West Germany; 1982 an art teacher at FUBA, Johannesburg. 1987 "Three Moons", 100 signed prints. 1973–78 lived in Hamburg, West Germany. Has visited East and West Africa and SWA/Namibia.
Exhibitions 1969 Lidchi Gallery, Johannesburg, first of 11 solo exhibitions one of which was held in SWA/Namibia and three in West Germany.
Public Commission 1982 painted the portrait of The Star Woman of the Year.
References T L Holdstock, *Transpersonal Art. The Paintings of Monika von Moltke*, 1986, Africa Transpersonal Association, Johannesburg; BSAK 1; *Artlook* August 1969 & August 1971; *Gallery* Winter 1986 & Autumn 1987; *SA Arts Calendar* Summer 1987.

VOORVELT David Paul

Born 1947 Kitale, Kenya.
Resided in SA from 1963.
A self-taught painter of landscapes, portraits, still life, animals and abstract pictures. Works in acrylic, ink, wash, crayon and pencil. A poem accompanies each painting exhibited.
Profile An ichthyological illustrator, co-illustrating *Smith's Sea Fishes of Southern Africa*, 1986, Macmillan (SA), Johannesburg; also illustrated several scientific papers.
Exhibitions He has participated in several group exhibitions from 1984 in the Eastern Cape; 1985 Grahamstown, solo exhibition.

VORSTER Anna

Born 1928 Hartbeesfontein, Transvaal.
A painter and graphic artist of landscapes, seascapes, portraits, still life, genre and figures. Works in oil, watercolour, gouache, ink, pencil, charcoal and in various graphic media. Abstracted compositions based on realistic drawings and watercolours. A number of series: 1956–60 industrial and town scenes of Johannesburg; 1961–62 rock formations of the Transvaal; 1963–65 paintings and drawings of classical Greece and Greek dramatic characters; 1965–69 a series on the Namib Desert; 1971–73 figure paintings set in Cape Town; 1974–75 yacht paintings set in Cape Town; 1978–88 extended series of drawings, watercolours and oil paintings of the Drakensberg mountains.
Studies 1948–51 University of the Witwatersrand, under Professor Heather Martienssen (1915–79), Charles Argent (qv), Dr Maria Stein-Lessing (1905–61) and Joyce Leonard (qv), gaining a BA(FA); 1952–54 on a Union Post-Graduate Scholarship at the Slade School of Fine Art, London; Académie Lhote, Paris; 1964 under Stanley William Hayter (*b*.1901) at Atelier 17, Paris.

Profile From 1983 an Executive member of the SAAA and a founder member of the Bellville Branch; 1985 editor of the *SA Arts Calendar*, SAAA, Pretoria. 1957–62 a lecturer in drawing and painting at the Technical Colleges in Bloemfontein, Johannesburg and Pretoria; 1967–69 a lecturer in fine art and the history of art at the University of South Africa; 1971 taught at the Ruth Prowse Art Centre, Cape Town; in addition to this she taught art privately. 1965 designed the programme for the PACT production of "Electra" and in 1972 of "Uncle Wanja". Designed stained glass window for The Assembly of God Church, Park Street, Pretoria. Wrote art criticism and articles for the following daily newspapers: 1957–62, 1965 and 1970 *Die Transvaler*; 1974–75 *The Cape Argus* and 1977–78 *Beeld*. 1956–60 lived in Johannesburg; 1960–61 in Pretoria; 1961–63 in Johannesburg; 1963–64 in Greece and Crete; 1965–66 in SWA/Namibia; 1967–70 in Pretoria; 1971–75 in Cape Town; thereafter in Pretoria. 1960 visited the Greek islands, Turkey and Israel.

Exhibitions She has participated in many group exhibitions from 1950 in SA, Brazil, the UK, Italy, West Germany, Greece and the USA; 1953 Association of International Artists Gallery, London, first of 31 solo exhibitions, the remaining 30 having been held in SA; 1956, 1960 and 1964 Quadrennial Exhibitions; 1965 Pretoria Art Museum, Retrospective Exhibition; 1970 Rand Afrikaans University, solo exhibition; 1981 Republic Festival Exhibition; 1983 Rand Afrikaans University, Retrospective Exhibition; 1985 University of the Orange Free State, solo exhibition.

Represented Africana Museum, Johannesburg; Durban Art Gallery; Hester Rupert Art Museum, Graaff-Reinet; Johannesburg Art Gallery; National Museum, Bloemfontein; Pretoria Art Museum; Rand Afrikaans University; SA embassies in São Paulo, Washington DC and Bonn; SA National Gallery, Cape Town; University of Durban-Westville; University of the Orange Free State; University of Pretoria; University of South Africa; Willem Annandale Art Gallery, Lichtenburg; William Humphreys Art Gallery, Kimberley.

References Le Riche Kruger, *Anna Vorster, A Biography*, 1983, Cum Books, Roodepoort; Art SA; SAA; 20C SA Art; Oxford Companion to Art (under SA); SAP&D; BSAK 1 & 2; Our Art 3; Art SWA; SA Art; 3Cs; AASA; LSAA; *The Studio* November 1953; *SA Art News* 4 May 1961; *Lantern* September 1962; *Artlook* May 1968, April 1969 & August 1973; *SA Arts Calendar* March 1983 & Autumn 1986.

VORSTER Enslin

Born 1934 Boksburg, Transvaal.
A painter of landscapes, portraits, still life, seascapes, genre, figures and wildlife. Works in oil, watercolour, gouache, ink, wash, pencil and charcoal.

Studies 1951 Witwatersrand Technical College, under James Gardner (qv).

Profile 1980 designed a tapestry depicting the history of Benoni for Benoni Town Council. 1974–76 lived in the Eastern Transvaal; 1976–77 in George, Cape Province; thereafter in the Transvaal. 1984 made a study tour of the USA.

Exhibitions He has participated in numerous group exhibitions from 1970 in SA and once in 1977 in Australia and in 1985 in the USA; 1972 Pietersburg, first of *c*.11 solo exhibitions held in SA.

Represented Boksburg Municipality.

VORSTER Gordon Frank

Born 1924 Warrenton, Northern Cape.

Died 1988 Broederstroom, Transvaal.

A painter of landscapes, wildlife, portraits, figures and abstract pictures. Worked in oil on masonite or canvas and in watercolour, acrylic, gouache, ink and wash. A graphic artist. 1976–87 a series of 30 paintings entitled "Genesis".

Studies 1944–45 private study in Florence and Rome, Italy; 1947–49 University of the Witwatersrand, under Joyce Leonard (qv), Professor Heather Martienssen (1915–79), Douglas Portway (qv) and Dr Maria Stein-Lessing (1905–61).

Profile 1976–78 a lecturer in portraiture at the Witwatersrand Technical College. A writer of both poetry and prose. 1950–63 Art Director of Killarney Film Studios. A professional scriptwriter and a producer and director of films. An actor who was awarded the 'Oscar' of the Motion Picture Producer's Association, SA, for his performance in "Pappa Lap"; also acted in "The Guest", which was honoured at the Locarno Film Festival, Switzerland. He won two *Star Tonight!* awards for "The Story of an African Farm" and "The Pain"; his film "Sarah" was featured in the International Film Critics' Recall Season. He travelled extensively in sub-equatorial Africa as a film producer. Frequently visited the Kalahari and the Kruger National Park. Was married to Gina Hall (qv).

Exhibitions Participated in numerous group exhibitions from 1953 in SA, Zimbabwe, France, The Netherlands, Belgium, West Germany, Italy, the USA and the UK; 1954 Johannesburg, first of over 100 solo exhibitions held in SA; 1960 Quadrennial Exhibition; 1966 Lexington Gallery, New York, solo exhibition; 1984 SAAA Gallery, Pretoria, joint exhibition with Dale Elliot (qv), Wendy Malan (qv) and Ulrich Schwanecke (qv); 1987 Rand Afrikaans University, Prestige Exhibition.

Represented Ann Bryant Gallery, East London; Hester Rupert Art Museum, Graaff-Reinet; King George VI Art Gallery, Port Elizabeth; Potchefstroom Museum; Pretoria Art Museum; Rand Afrikaans University; SA National Gallery, Cape Town; University of the Orange Free State; University of South Africa; Willem Annandale Art Gallery, Lichtenburg; William Humphreys Art Gallery, Kimberley.

Publications by Vorster *The Textures of Silence*, 1983, Howard Timmins, Cape Town—a novel which won the Golden Cape Prize; *The Blood River Bible*, to be published in 1989.

References SAA; Our Art 2; AASA; *Fontein* vol 1 no 1, 1960; *SA Panorama* May 1966 & June 1983; *Artlook* November 1966, February 1967, August 1969 & May 1970; *De Kat* June 1987.

VORSTER Johanna (Joe)

Born 1887 Philipstown, Cape Province.

Died 1945 Cape Town.

Mainly a self-taught sculptor of portraits and figures of the various tribal peoples of SA, SWA/Namibia, Mozambique and the Belgian Congo (Zaire). Worked in clay and plaster of Paris.

Studies Studied very briefly under Ivan Mitford-Barberton (qv) in 1934.

Profile A qualified nursing sister, working in District Six, Cape Town, who began sculpting in 1930. In 1934 African Mirror made a short film about her, which was shown in cinemas throughout the country. 1908–34 lived in Cape Town and from 1934 alternately in the Transvaal and Cape Town. 1934 visited Mozambique.

Exhibitions Participated in group exhibitions in SA from 1930.

Represented Cultural History Museum, Pretoria; SA House, London, England; William Fehr Collection, Cape Town.

Public Commission 1934 portrait busts for the Portuguese Government in Mozambique.

References Naxa Pillman, *African Portrait*, 1976, Keartland, Johannesburg; BSAK 1; *Lantern* September 1969.

VORSTER Margaret

Born 1953 Durban.

A painter and graphic artist of landscapes, portraits and abstract pictures. Works mostly in oil, but also in watercolour, gouache, ink, wash, pencil, charcoal, pastel and in various graphic media.

Studies 1975–79 University of South Africa, under Karin Skawran, Rayda Becker and Leon du Plessis (qv) gaining a BA(FA); 1980–84 University of the Witwatersrand, under Robert Hodgins (qv), gaining an MA(FA) cum laude.

Profile A member of the Southern African Museums Association and the SAAAH. In 1982 she became a professional officer at the Johannesburg Art Gallery. 1988 teaching at the University of the Witwatersrand. 1975 visited Los Angeles; 1979 London; 1985 travelled throughout Europe.

Exhibitions She has participated in many group exhibitions from 1978 in SA and once in West Germany; 1980 Market Gallery, Johannesburg, first of several solo exhibitions; 1985 Cape Town Triennial; 1985 Tributaries, touring SA and West Germany; 1988 Standard Bank Festival of the Arts, 1820 Settlers National Monument, Grahamstown, and touring SA, solo exhibition.

Awards 1987 Merit Award, Standard Bank National Drawing Competition; 1988 Standard Bank Young Artist Award.

Represented Johannesburg Art Gallery; Pretoria Art Museum; SA National Gallery, Cape Town; University of South Africa; University of the Witwatersrand.

Reference *Femina* July 1988.

VOS Hendrik Egbert (Henk)

Born 1946 Amsterdam, The Netherlands.

A painter of equestrian subjects and wildlife. Works in oil, ink and pastel.

Studies 1965–66 studied commercial art at the Witwatersrand Technical College.

Profile From 1969 numerous calendars of his work have been published, as well as a number of limited edition prints. Lives in Natal.

Exhibitions 1975 Collectors Gallery, Johannesburg, first of three solo exhibitions held in Johannesburg; he has participated in several group exhibitions from 1977 in SA, Zimbabwe, London and New York.

VOSLOO Nicolaas Phillipus Lourens

Born 1942 East London.

A painter, graphic artist and sculptor of landscapes, seascapes, figures, portraits, wildlife and abstract pieces. Works in oil, acrylic, watercolour, gouache, wash, pencil, various graphic media, mixed media (skin, bone, beads etc.), ceramics and bronze.

Studies 1960–63 Witwatersrand Technical College, under Phil Botha (qv) and Anna Vorster (qv).

Profile From 1982 a member of the Society of Animal Artists, New York. 1968–75 a lecturer at the Witwatersrand Technical College. He has illustrated a number of magazines and pamphlets. Has travelled extensively in Southern Africa and to the USA.

Exhibitions He has participated in several group exhibitions in SA from 1978 and three in the USA; 1979 Studio 5 Gallery, Rustenburg, Transvaal, first of four solo exhibitions held in SA and two held in the USA.

Award 1986 New York Animal Art Association Medal.

Represented Roodepoort Municipal Collection.

Reference *Habitat* no 56, 1983.

VYVYAN Dorothea M (Mrs Percival)

Born 1875 Charterhouse, England.

A painter of landscapes, particularly of Natal and Zululand. Worked in watercolour and pastel.

Studies Slade School of Art, London; Westminster School of Art, London; Sir Frank Brangwyn's School of Art, London, and in Italy.

Profile A Council member of the NSA. Lived in Richmond, Natal. Her unpublished diaries are kept at the Killie Campbell Africana Library, University of Natal, Durban.

Exhibitions Participated in group exhibitions at the Royal Academy three times 1921–32 and in provincial galleries in England; participated in the 1924 British Empire Exhibition, Wembley, London, and in group exhibitions in 1925 with the SA Academy and in 1928 at Lezards Gallery, Johannesburg; 1928 Lezards Gallery, Johannesburg, solo exhibition.

Represented Ann Bryant Gallery, East London; Johannesburg Art Gallery; National Museum, Bloemfontein; SA National Gallery, Cape Town.

References DBA; BSAK 1 & 2; AASA.

W

WAGENAAR Anne Locke (née Chowles)

Born 1919 Alexandria, Cape Province.

A painter of landscapes, seascapes, still life and portraits. Works in oil, watercolour and pencil. Several series, including "Spruite", "Farm Roads", "Farm Dams", "Old Boats" and "Bushman Ruins and Caves".

Studies 1936–39 Grahamstown Training College, under Professor Austin Winter Moore (qv); 1941–42 Port Elizabeth Technical College, under Joan Wright (qv).

Profile From 1953 a member of the Aliwal North Art Club; from 1954 of the Queenstown and Orange Free State Art Societies and Bushmans Art Club; from 1958 of the East London Art Society. 1981 became an Associate of the WSSA. Has written a number of articles for art publications. Plays the organ. Lives in Jamestown, Cape Province. 1956 visited the UK.

Exhibitions She has participated in numerous group exhibitions from 1953 in SA, twice in London and once in West Germany; 1970 SAAA Gallery, Pretoria, first of four solo exhibitions.

Represented University of Pretoria; Willem Annandale Art Gallery, Lichtenburg.

Reference BSAK 2.

WAGNER Alexander Quinn

Born 1920 Johannesburg.

A painter of portraits, figures and abstract pictures. Works in oil, watercolour, gouache, ink, pencil and charcoal. Makes constructions in wood, ivory and precious metals and stones.

Studies 1937–40 Natal Technical College, under Professor O J P Oxley (qv), George Howe and Merlyn Evans (qv).

Profile From 1937 a member of the NSA. 1942 designed a series of SA war stamps. 1946–49 taught at the Ray Art School for Adults, Johannesburg. 1920–40 lived in Durban; served in Italy, Palestine, Algeria and Egypt during WWII, later visited Lebanon and Syria. 1945–49 lived in Johannesburg; thereafter in Greytown, Natal. Married to Beryl Newman (qv).

Exhibitions He has participated in several group exhibitions from 1938 in SA, the UK, The Netherlands and Belgium; 1939 Durban Art Gallery, joint exhibition with Nils Solberg; has held 24 joint exhibitions with Beryl Newman (qv) in SA and two in Scotland in 1959; 1948 Tate Gallery, London, SA Art Exhibition; 1960 Johannesburg, first solo exhibition.

Represented Durban Art Gallery; Killie Campbell Africana Library, University of Natal, Durban; University of Natal, Pietermaritzburg.

Public Commission Mural, Natal Technical College, with his teacher Merlyn Evans (qv) and Beryl Newman (qv) (demolished).

References Art SA; SAA; BSAK 1 & 2; AASA; *SA Architectural Record* July 1949; *Artlook* September 1969; *Lantern* December 1979.

WAHER Roman

Born 1909 Tartu, Estonia (Estonian SSR).
Died 1975 Cape Town.
Resided in SA from 1964.
A graphic artist, creating lithographs, woodcuts and etchings.
Studies 1930–35 Higher Art School, Pallas, Tartu, Estonia; 1936–37 Academy for Graphic Arts, Leipzig, Germany.
Profile 1937–39 a lecturer at the Pallas Art School, Tartu. 1945–63 worked as a graphic designer. 1964–74 taught in the graphic design department of the Michaelis School of Fine Art, becoming a senior lecturer in 1970. Illustrated *Wines of SA*, by A G Bagnold, 1961, KWV, Paarl.
Exhibitions Participated in several group exhibitions in SA.
Publication by Waher Edited and completed F L Alexander's (qv) book *South African Graphic Art and its Techniques*, 1974, Human & Rousseau, Cape Town.
References 3Cs; AASA.

WAITE Maisie

Born 1906 Kent, England.
Died 1986 Johannesburg.
Resided in SA from 1946.
A painter of landscapes and seascapes. Worked in watercolour.
Studies Under her father Harold Waite, who was Head of the Canterbury School of Art, Kent, England and at l'Académie de la Grande Chaumière, Paris.
Profile A Fellow of the WSSA. Prior to 1946 taught in England for 10 years. 1946–70 Art Mistress at Kingsmead Girls School, Johannesburg, 1953–56 and 1961–67 Vice-Headmistress. Designed and made costumes for Kingsmead theatre productions.
Exhibitions Participated in numerous group exhibitions held in SA and the UK; held a number of solo exhibitions in Johannesburg.
References BSAK 1; AASA; Margot Bryant, *The Kingsmead Heritage*, The Kingsmead Foundation, Johannesburg; *Artlook* August 1971.

WAKE Richard Henry

Born 1935 Cape Town.
Resided in SA until 1973.
A sculptor of figures, portraits and abstract pieces. Works in bronze, aluminium and other metals.
Studies Studied under Florence Zerffi (qv); 1954–57 Michaelis School of Fine Art, under Lippy Lipshitz (qv), where attained a BA(FA); 1958–59 Staatliche Akademie der Bildenden Kunste, Stuttgart, West Germany, under Professor Otto Heim; 1960–61 l'Ecole Supérieure des Beaux Arts, Paris, under Professor Louis Leygue (*b*.1905).
Profile 1965 a founder member of the Artists Gallery, Cape Town. 1963–73 a lecturer at the Michaelis School of Fine Art. An art consultant, with Neville Dubow and Kevin Atkinson (qv), for the Beachfront Redevelopment Scheme, Muizenberg, Cape Province. 1971 produced an art happening of a set of six plaster-cast figures which were placed on a beach and subsequently washed away. 1973 emigrated to West Germany, where he has continued to teach.

Exhibitions He has participated in group exhibitions during the 1960s and early 1970s in SA and at the Venice and São Paulo Biennials; 1965 Worcester, Cape Province, first solo exhibition; 1966 Republic Festival Exhibition; 1970 Goodman Gallery, Johannesburg, joint exhibition with Kevin Atkinson (qv).

Awards 1957 Michaelis Prize; 1963 Oppenheimer Sculpture Prize, Art SA Today; 1966 Bronze Medal, SA Breweries Art Prize; 1971 Natal Provincial Institute of Architects Award, Art SA Today. During the late 1960s awarded the Deutscher Akademischer Austauschdienst Bursary, the Montague White Bursary and the Cape Tercentenary Grant for Travel in the USA.

Represented Hester Rupert Art Museum, Graaff-Reinet; King George VI Art Gallery, Port Elizabeth; SA National Gallery, Cape Town; University of Cape Town; University of the Witwatersrand.

Public Commissions Several architectural and sculptural commissions. 1970 a relief mural, joint winner with Kevin Atkinson (qv) of the 1820 Settlers Memorial Monument Competition.

References Art SA; SAA; 3Cs; AASA; *Artlook* February 1971.

WALCOTT Colleen Bridget

Born 1959 Cholo, Nyasaland (Malawi).
Resided in SA from 1980.

A painter and graphic artist of landscapes, wildlife and the domestic dog in the wilderness and in its domestic environment. Works in oil, watercolour, ink, pencil, crayon and in various graphic media.

Studies 1980–83 Natal Technikon, under Penny Siopis (qv), gaining a National Diploma in Fine Art in 1982 and a Higher Diploma in Fine Art in 1983.

Profile A member of the NSA. 1964–80 lived on a farm in north-eastern Rhodesia (Zimbabwe).

Exhibitions She has participated in many group exhibitions from 1979 in Rhodesia (Zimbabwe) and SA; 1985 Cafe Genevé Gallery, Durban, solo exhibition.

Represented Natal Technikon.

WALD Herman

Born 1906 Cluj Kolozsvar, Hungary.
Died 1970 Rhodesia (Zimbabwe).
Resided in SA from 1937.

A sculptor of portrait busts, animals and figures. A number of Biblical scenes. Worked in bronze, wood, marble, terracotta and fibreglass. Produced large, simplified, monumental works as well as smaller, more detailed pieces.

Studies 1924–28 Budapest Academy, Hungary, under Strobl; 1928–31 School of Arts and Crafts, Vienna, under Anton Hanak (1873–1934); 1931 in Berlin; 1932–33 in Paris and London.

Profile A founder member of the Brush and Chisel Club. 1933 taught sculpture at the Men's Working College, London, later taught in Johannesburg. Died in Salisbury (Harare), while working on a commission.

Exhibitions Participated in group exhibitions from 1930 in Vienna, London, Paris, New York and SA; 1938 Johannesburg, first of numerous solo exhibitions; 1952 New York, solo exhibition; 1971 Johannesburg, Memorial Exhibition.

Represented Cultural Congress Art Gallery, New York, USA; SA National Museum of Military History, Johannesburg.

Public Commissions Portrait busts of Albert Schweitzer, Albert Einstein, Sir Ernest Oppenheimer and Dr Chaim Weitzman among others. Numerous memorials and statues such as the following works in Johannesburg: Memorial to the Jewish Dead of World War II; 1956 Memorial to the Heroes of Warsaw, Westpark Cemetery; 1957 Kria, Witwatersrand Jewish Aged Home; Wings of the Shechinah, Berea Jewish Synagogue; 1960 Oppenheimer Fountain of Impala; sculptural decorations for five cinemas. Other commissions include in 1960 the Diamond Pioneers Fountain, Kimberley; 1951 the Kiaat panel, Jewish Community, Springs and 1971 Lumberjack, Ellerine Centre, Germiston.

References SAA; SESA; BSAK 1 & 2; SA Art; AASA; *SA Panorama* November 1968; *Artlook* March 1969 & August 1970; Catalogue of Memorial Exhibition, 1971, Johannesburg.

WALDECK Christiaan

Born 1960 Pretoria.

A painter, sculptor and graphic artist, working in oil, watercolour, ink, wash, pencil, charcoal, bronze, steel, stone, ceramics and in various graphic media. 1982 a series of portraits in oil; 1983 a series of horses in bronze and ceramics; 1983 "Apocalypse" series in oil; 1984 "Word Image" series of drawings and poetry; 1986 a series of miniatures in oil.

Studies 1978 Pretoria School of Art, Ballet and Music; 1985 Pretoria Technikon, under Ian Redelinghuys (qv).

Profile 1978–80 Artistic Chairman of the Kwanza Poetry and Art Society. 1981 and 1983–85 a lecturer at, and manager of, the Kraft Ceramic Studio, Pretoria. A potter. 1980 spent four months in Swaziland; 1982 in Cape Town; 1985 spent three months at Pietrasanta, Carrara, Italy, working as an assistant to David Middlebrook, and learning marble techniques; 1986 spent three months in London.

Exhibitions Has participated in many group exhibitions from 1976 in SA and one in Italy; 1985 Ivan Solomon Gallery, Pretoria, first of two solo exhibitions.

Represented Pretoria Art Museum.

WALES-SMITH (Arthur) Douglas

Born 1888 Bengal, India.

Died 1966 SA.

Resided in SA from 1948.

A self-taught painter of naval scenes of WWI & II, and of portraits (generally from photographs), also painted flowers and landscapes. Worked in oil, watercolour and pastel.

Profile Retired as a Captain in the Royal Navy prior to WWII, but returned as a Commander in the Naval Ordnance Department, being appointed a Royal Naval War Artist 1939–45. A member of the Society of Marine Artists and the Royal Pastel Society. An illustrator working for English magazines. Initially signed his work D W Smith, later Douglas Wales and after 1948 Douglas Wales-Smith.

Exhibitions Participated in group exhibitions in London 1929–40 and in Paris and SA; 1952 Van Riebeeck Festival Exhibition; 1953 Maskew Miller Art Gallery, Cape Town, solo exhibition.

Represented National Maritime Museum, Greenwich, England; University of Cape Town.

References Art SA; Register SA & SWA; E H H Archibald, *Dictionary of Sea Painters*, 1980, Antique Collector's Club, Woodbridge, Suffolk, England; Bénézit; DBA; AASA.

WALFORD Margaret Frances

Born 1913 Aligarh, Uttar Pradesh, India.
Resided in SA from 1947.
A painter and graphic artist, working in oil, acrylic, gouache, charcoal and in various graphic media.

Studies Académie de la Grande Chaumière, Académie Julian and the New York School of Art, Paris; the Bournemouth College of Art, UK.

Profile Prior to 1940 involved in costume design. 1927–32 lived in France; 1965–80 in Italy; presently living in Natal. In 1965, 1967 and 1972 visited Greece.

Exhibitions She has participated in group exhibitions in SA and Italy.

WALGATE Marion Blaire ARCA

Born 1886 Arbuthnot, Kincardineshire, Scotland.
Died 1975 Fish Hoek, Cape Province.
Resided in SA from 1920.
A sculptor of busts, figures, statuettes and bas-reliefs. Worked in bronze. Painted and drew landscapes and seascapes in watercolour and pastel. Sewed a number of embroideries.

Studies 1902–06 Gray's School of Art, Aberdeen, Scotland; 1907–10 Royal College of Art, London, under W R Lethaby (1857–1931), becoming an Associate.

Profile 1932 a founder member of the National Academy of Art (SA). A designer of coins. Prior to 1920 lived in London.

Exhibitions Between 1913 and 1932 she exhibited at the Royal Academy four times; 1933 Martin Melck House, Cape Town, solo exhibition.

Represented SA National Gallery, Cape Town; University of Cape Town.

Public Commissions Numerous commissions, including: 1932 statue of Cecil Rhodes, University of Cape Town (replica in Harare)—this was sculpted in the studio of John Tweed in London; Proctor Memorial, Hiddingh Hall, Cape Town; Peringuet Memorial, SA Museum, Cape Town; bust of Dr W J Viljoen, Cape Provincial Administration Building, Cape Town; bust of Field-Marshal J C Smuts donated by the University of Cape Town to the Smuts Family; Jagger Memorials, City Hall, Cape Town and the University of Cape Town.

References *The Arts in SA*, edited by WHK, 1933–34, The Knox Printing & Publishing Company, Durban; SAA; SAP&S; SESA; BSAK 1 & 2; DBA.

WALKER Clive

Born 1936 Johannesburg.

A painter of wildlife. Works in watercolour.

Studies During the 1950s attended evening classes at the Witwatersrand Technical College; 1959–60 briefly at St Martin's School of Art, London, England. Mainly self-taught.

Profile 1969 Vice-Chairman of the SAAA, Southern Transvaal Branch. A conservationist and educationist who has written numerous articles and three books on wildlife (see below). Founder, Trustee & Honorary Life Member of the Endangered Wildlife Trust. Has travelled to Kenya, SWA/Namibia, Botswana, Zimbabwe and Mozambique.

Exhibitions 1970 Pretoria, first solo exhibition in SA, has also held solo exhibitions in London in 1974 and in the USA in 1982; he has participated in several group exhibitions from 1971 in SA, one in the USA in 1973 and one in Australia in 1976.

Publications by Walker *Walk Through the Wilderness*, 1974 and *Signs of The Wild*, 1981, C Struik, Cape Town; *Twilight of the Giants*, 1984, Sable, Johannesburg.

References BSAK 1 & 2; AASA; *Artlook* December 1969 & February 1972; *SA Panorama* February 1971 & April 1976.

WALLACE Helen

Born England.

Died 1933 England.

A painter of landscapes. Worked in watercolour and oil.

Profile An art teacher at King William's Town Collegiate School for Girls during the 1890s, taught at East London Girls High School until 1920, thereafter ran her own teaching establishments in East London and Durban. A founder member of the East London Society of Arts and Crafts and Chairman 1926–28.

Exhibitions Participated in group exhibitions in SA and in the UK. 1927 Inaugural Exhibition of the SA Institute, Durban.

Represented Ann Bryant Gallery, East London; Durban Art Gallery.

Reference AASA.

WALLACE Marjorie

Born 1925 Edinburgh, Scotland.

Resided in SA from 1955.

A painter of genre, figures, portraits and still life. Works in oil and gouache.

Studies 1942–47 Edinburgh College of Art, under Sir William George Gillies (1898–1973) and John Maxwell, gaining a Diploma in Drawing and Painting in 1946, Postgraduate Honours in 1947 and awarded the 1947 Andrew Grant Travelling Scholarship.

Profile 1955 co-founder of the Cape Salon, with Erik Laubscher (qv). 1956–66 a committee member of the SAAA, Cape Town; 1962–66 a central committee member of the SAAA; 1965 a founder member of the Artists Gallery, Cape Town; 1979 a founder member of the Artists Guild, Cape Town. Numerous illustrations for books by Jan Rabie, Freda Linde and Paul Berne. 1947–55 lived in Paris and 1958–59 spent several months there; 1966–67 spent five months in the USA; 1967–70 lived in Crete; 1985 spent nine months in Greece. Visited Israel in 1967 and 1974. In 1955 married the writer Jan Rabie.

Exhibitions She has participated in numerous group exhibitions from 1947 in Edinburgh, London, Paris, Ghent and throughout SA; 1952 Galerie Olga Bogroff, Paris, first of two solo exhibitions held in Paris, two in Scotland, one in London and 19 in SA; 1960 and 1964 Quadrennial Exhibitions; 1981 Republic Festival Exhibition.

Award 1981 awarded one of the three painting prizes on the Republic Festival Exhibition.

Represented Hester Rupert Art Museum, Graaff-Reinet; Julius Gordon Africana Centre, Riversdale; Pretoria Art Museum; SA National Gallery, Cape Town; University of the Orange Free State; University of Stellenbosch; Willem Annandale Art Gallery, Lichtenburg; William Humphreys Art Gallery, Kimberley.

References Art SA; SAA; SAP&S; SESA; BSAK 1 & 2; *Sarie Marias* 20 May 1970; *Artlook* June 1971.

WALLER Agnes Helen (née Thorne)

Born 1883 Greenwood Park, Durban.

Died 1974 Greenwood Park, Durban.

A painter of flowers and landscapes. Worked in oil and watercolour. In the latter part of her life she made a number of mosaics using broken china.

Studies 1904–05 under W H Tottendell Venner (qv).

Profile 1905 a founder member of the NSA. *c.*1925 painted a collection of Natal wild flowers for the Natal Technical College.

Exhibitions Participated in several group exhibitions from 1905.

Represented Local History Museum, Durban.

WALLER Penelope Mary (Penny)

Born 1940 Stirling, Scotland.

Resided in SA from 1961.

A painter of landscapes, seascapes, still life, figures, portraits and abstract pictures. Works in oil, watercolour, gouache, ink, wash, pencil and charcoal.

Studies From 1971 took various courses under Jane Heath (qv).
Profile From 1980 a member of the NSA; from 1983 a committee member of the Midlands Arts and Crafts Society. Has visited Brazil, Italy and France.
Exhibitions She has participated in many group exhibitions from 1972 in Natal.

WALSH Aidan Victor

Born 1932 Durban.
A painter of landscapes, portraits and figures. Works in oil. A ceramicist and batik artist.
Studies 1948–50 Natal Technical College, under Julia Shum and Cecil Todd (qv); 1956–57 Hammersmith School of Art, London, under Carel Weight (*b*.1908).
Profile From 1967 a member of the NSA. 1959–60 an art teacher at the Natal Technical College; 1959–66 an art teacher at Kearsney College, Botha's Hill, Natal. 1961–79 Director of the Walsh-Marais Gallery, Durban; 1979–87 Curator of the NSA Gallery, Durban; thereafter a full-time painter. 1976 and 1981 designed and executed the batik costumes for productions of "A Midsummer Night's Dream" in Grahamstown and Pretoria. 1986 spent three months at Cité Internationale des Arts, Paris.
Exhibitions He has participated in several group exhibitions from 1954 in SA; 1987 Gallery International, Cape Town, solo exhibition.
Represented Durban Art Gallery (batik).
Public Commissions 1972–73 portraits of the Natal Administrators, Natalia, Pietermaritzburg; 1983 batik mural for Mangosuthu Technikon, Umlazi, Natal.

WALSH Shirley Margaret

Born 1959 Salisbury, Rhodesia (Harare, Zimbabwe).
Resided in SA from 1983.
A self-taught painter of birds, specialising in the raptors. Works in watercolour, gouache and pencil.
Profile 1982 illustrated a calendar in Zimbabwe.
Exhibitions She has participated in several group exhibitions from 1983 in SA and in the USA.

WARD Edith

A painter of landscapes. Worked in watercolour and oil.
Profile President of the NSA in 1935.
Exhibitions Participated in group exhibitions with the NSA; 1936 Empire Exhibition, Johannesburg; 1937 participated in a group exhibition at the Gainsborough Gallery, Johannesburg.
References BSAK 1 & 2; AASA.

WARD Richard
Born 1934 Jhansi, Uttar Pradesh, India.
Resided in SA from 1969.
A painter of landscapes, seascapes, still life and figures. Works in watercolour, gouache, ink, wash, pencil and charcoal.
Studies 1950–52 Bournemouth College of Art, England, gaining an Intermediate Certificate in Art; 1954–56 Winchester Art School, England, under D Pare, attaining a National Diploma in Design (Illustration); 1984–85 Peninsula Technikon, under P Fourie, attaining a Higher Diploma in Design (Illustration).
Profile From 1980 a member of the Society of Designers in SA and from 1986 of the SAAA. 1982 lectured at the Cape Technikon; from 1983 a lecturer in graphic design at the Peninsula Technikon. 1986 a member of the Design Council's joint standing committee on Design Education, SA Bureau of Standards, Pretoria. From 1969 designs and illustrations for advertising and publishing companies, greeting cards and books. Several series of prints. 1964–68 lived in Kenya.
Publication by Ward Wrote and illustrated *Willie and the Game Warden*, 1968, East African Wildlife Society, Kenya.

WASSENAAR Johanna (Mrs Du Toit)
Born 1896 Middelburg, Transvaal.
Died 1971 Pretoria.
A sculptor of portrait busts. Worked in bronze. A painter of portraits, particularly children's, and of still life, figures and occasionally landscapes. Worked in oil, watercolour and pastel.
Studies In Munich, Germany and Vienna, Austria; 1921–24 and 1957–58 in Amsterdam, The Netherlands.
Profile In 1949 a member of the Brush and Chisel Club. A number of lithographs. 1956–58 lived in Europe. During the 1960s taught art in Pretoria.
Exhibitions Participated in group exhibitions in the UK and SA; 1966 Republic Festival Exhibition.
Represented Pretoria Art Museum; University of the Orange Free State; University of Pretoria; University of Stellenbosch.
Public Commissions Portrait busts of Dr H F Verwoerd and President C R Swart, Transvaal Provincial Administration Building, Pretoria; General J B M Hertzog, University of the Orange Free State, Bloemfontein; Mr Bischoff, Rondalia Holiday Resort, Hibberdene, Natal; Dr P J du Toit (her husband), Director of the Veterinary Research Institute, Onderstepoort, Transvaal; numerous portrait commissions including those of B J Vorster and Dr Willie Hofmeyr. Oil portraits of Mr Bosman, Manager, Volkskas Headquarters, Pretoria; Dr Van Wyk, Director, Pretoria Teachers Training College.
References BSAK 1 & 2; AASA; *SA Panorama* February 1964.

WASSERFALL Hilda Edith
Born 1933 Piet Retief, Transvaal.
A painter and sculptor of landscapes, still life, figures and near-focus outdoor studies. Works in oil, acrylic, watercolour, stone and wood.

Studies 1951–54 Michaelis School of Fine Art, under Professor Rupert Shephard (qv), Lippy Lipshitz (qv), Maurice van Essche (qv), Eleanor Esmonde-White (qv) and Katrine Harries (qv), gaining a BA(FA).
Profile A member of the Arts Association SWA/Namibia and the WSSA. In 1976 designed a number of abstract and animal tapestries. Has lived in Windhoek from 1955. 1977 visited Paris.
Exhibitions She has participated in many group exhibitions from 1966 in SA and SWA/Namibia; 1970 Windhoek, first of four solo exhibitions held in Windhoek.
Award 1985 Prize for Best Acrylic Work, STANSWA.
Represented Arts Association SWA/Namibia Collection; Pretoria Art Museum; SWA Administration Collection; Willem Annandale Art Gallery, Lichtenburg; Windhoek Municipal Collection.
References Art SWA; PS/N.

WATERS Athelene Jeanette

Born 1936 Johannesburg.
A painter of landscapes, still life, genre and abstract pictures. Works in oil, acrylic, watercolour, gouache, ink, wash, pencil and charcoal.
Studies 1970–73 under Meta Orton (qv); 1974–81 University of South Africa, under Nina Romm (qv), Alan Crump and Marion Arnold (qv), gaining a BA(FA) with Honours in History of Art; 1978 privately under Basil Friedlander (qv) and also under him at the Natal Technikon in 1980.
Profile A member of the NSA and the North Coast Art Group. 1982 and 1984 a part-time lecturer in drawing and history of art at the Natal Technikon. Teaches art privately. Has lived in Durban from 1967.
Exhibitions She has participated in several group exhibitions from 1981 in SA.

WATSON Beatrice

Born 1952 Santiago, Chile.
Resided in SA from 1981.
A painter of landscapes, seascapes, portraits, still life, figures and abstract pictures. Works in watercolour, ink, pencil and charcoal.
Profile A member of the WSSA. 1952–79 lived in Chile. 1975 visited Europe; 1983 Botswana and SWA/Namibia; 1985 Canada; 1986 SWA/Namibia. Sister of the Canadian artist Monica Shelton.
Exhibitions 1985 Nedbank, Randburg, first of two solo exhibitions; she has participated in group exhibitions from 1987 in Johannesburg.

WATSON Gordon David

Born 1951 Durban.
A sculptor of figures, animals and abstract pieces. Works in wood and stone.
Profile A silversmith. From 1975 has lived at Knysna, Cape Province.
Exhibitions He has participated in several group exhibitions from 1974 in SA and Italy.

WATSON Olivia (Mrs Burdett Coutts)

Born 1944 Pietersburg, Northern Transvaal.

A painter and graphic artist of landscapes, figures, nudes and abstract pictures.

Studies 1962–66 University of the Witwatersrand, under Professor Heather Martienssen (1915–79), Cecily Sash (qv), Giuseppe Cattaneo (qv) and Judith Mason (qv), gaining a BA(FA); 1967 on a Giovanna Milner Bursary, three months at the School of Painting of Maestro Reggiani at the Brera Academy, Milan, Italy, and on an Olivetti Bursary at the School of Fresco Painting at the Castle of Sforzesco in Milan and under Maestro Saetti at the School of Painting of the Venetian Academy of Fine Art, Venice, Italy.

Profile Lives alternately in Johannesburg, Harare, Zimbabwe and in New York, USA. 1965 visited Italy, 1966 the Middle East.

Exhibitions She has participated in group exhibitions in SA, Italy, Switzerland, the UK, Austria, Israel, Zimbabwe, the USA and Australia; 1965 Olivetti Gallery, Johannesburg, first of many solo exhibitions held in SA and in Italy.

Awards 1968 Merit Award, SA Breweries; 1969 Gold Medal at the First International Biennale of Contemporary Art, Italy.

Represented Burdeke, Zurich, Switzerland; Il Traghetto, Venice, Italy; SATOUR, Rome, Italy.

References *Artlook* February 1968 & March 1970.

WATSON Stephanie

Born 1927 Livingstone, Northern Rhodesia (Maramba, Zambia).

Resided in SA from *c*.1934.

A painter and graphic artist of seascapes and abstract pictures. Works in oil, acrylic, pastel, ink and in various graphic media.

Studies Witwatersrand Technical College, under Joyce Leonard (qv) and George Boys (qv) and at The Visual Arts Research Centre, Johannesburg.

Profile A member of the Artists Guild, Cape Town. From 1978 a lecturer at the Ruth Prowse School of Art, Cape Town; 1981–83 a lecturer at the Strand Technical College; she has also taught at studios in Gordons Bay and Grabouw, Cape Province. Designed sets for Springs Theatre, Transvaal. Has travelled to Mauritius, Egypt and India.

Exhibitions She has participated in numerous group exhibitions from 1966 in SA, Switzerland, Peru, Australia, the USA, Germany, Austria, the UK, Belgium, Spain and Monaco; 1967 Stuttafords, Johannesburg, first of 19 solo exhibitions held throughout SA; 1968 Mona Lisa Gallery, Johannesburg, joint exhibition with Naomi Kark (qv); 1981 Republic Festival Exhibition.

Represented Pietersburg Collection; Pittsburgh and Philadelphia Museum, Pennsylvania, USA; SA National Gallery, Cape Town.

References *Artlook* June 1969 & October 1970.

WEBB Pamela Constance

Born 1931 Johannesburg.

A painter of landscapes, seascapes, still life, figures, wildlife and abstract pictures. Works in oil, acrylic, watercolour, gouache, ink, wash, pencil and charcoal.

Studies 1970–74 Witwatersrand Technical College, under Nico van Rensburg (qv) and Noel Bisseker (qv); privately under Sidney Goldblatt (qv); 1974 and 1976 under Dino Paravano (qv); 1980 under Cynthia Ball (qv).

Profile From *c.*1975 a member of the WSSA. From 1984 Curator of the Sandton Municipal Art Collection. Has travelled extensively.

Exhibitions She has participated in numerous group exhibitions from 1979 in SA.

WEBBER Peter Graham

Born 1931 Johannesburg.

A painter and graphic artist of space and of man and vehicle in space. Works in oil, acrylic, watercolour, gouache, sand, steel and in various graphic media. Additionally a sculptor. 1967 a series on space travel; 1976 "Summer of '76", scenes of Majorca; 1978–79 "African Evolution", scenes of desert and space.

Studies 1954–56 St Martin's School of Art, London, England; *c.*1956–60 Toronto Art School, Canada.

Profile From 1984 a member of the Artists Guild, Cape Town. A well-known photographer. 1960–65 lived in Ibiza and Spain. 1976 spent six months on the island of Majorca, Spain.

Exhibitions He has participated in numerous group exhibitions in Spain, the UK, Australia, Zimbabwe, France, Brazil, West Germany and throughout SA; 1962 Ibiza, Spain, first solo exhibition; 1965 Lidchi Gallery, Johannesburg, first of several solo exhibitions held in SA; 1981 Republic Festival Exhibition.

Represented Johannesburg Art Gallery; Pretoria Art Museum; SA National Gallery, Cape Town; University of South Africa.

References SAP&S; BSAK 1 & 2; 3Cs; AASA; *Habitat* no 14, 1975 & no 25, 1977.

WEBB SMITH Christopher see SMITH Christopher Webb

WEHDEMANN Clemenz Heinrich

Born 1762 Breda-Resa, Hanover, Germany.

Died 1835 Baviaans River, Cape Province.

Resided in SA from 1784.

A self-taught painter of trees, plants and animals. Worked in watercolour, black ink and pencil. He also carved sets of "Tree Books", the volumes being made from the wood of a particular tree and containing a description, the seed and a painting of the tree.

Profile From 1795 gave drawing lessons in Cape Town and, after moving to Sundays River, taught in Grahamstown. Established a circulating library in Cape Town, and from *c.*1810 was a forest botanist at Plettenberg Bay and later at Sundays River.

Represented Botanical Research Institute, Pretoria; British Museum, London, England; Kew Gardens, Surrey, England.
References DSAB; Pict Afr.

WEIERSBYE Ingrid Birgitte

Born 1954 London, England.
Resided in SA from 1979.
A self-taught painter of environmental subjects and wildlife. Works in oil, acrylic and gouache.
Profile In 1977 a series of bird prints published in Rhodesia (Zimbabwe); 1981 a limited edition of bird prints published for the Endangered Wildlife Trust, Johannesburg; 1982 a set of four large mammal prints published by Harold Swan, Johannesburg. Prior to 1979 lived in Rhodesia (Zimbabwe). Has travelled throughout Southern Africa and is married to a Natal Parks Board ecologist.
Exhibitions She has participated in numerous group exhibitions from 1975 in Zimbabwe and SA; 1978 Salisbury, Rhodesia (Harare, Zimbabwe), solo exhibition.
Reference "Women in the Bush", *Darling*, 1983.

WEIGHTMAN Maurice (Nick)

Born 1907 Hounslow, Middlesex, England.
Died 1969 Port Elizabeth.
Resided in SA from 1947.
A painter and graphic artist who worked in watercolour, gouache and in various graphic media. 1931 series on Mary Shelley's *Frankenstein* and Edgar Allan Poe's *William Wilson*.
Studies Slade School of Art, London.
Profile After 1933 worked exclusively on theatre and costume design. Worked in an advertising agency as a studio manager, and from 1957 as an art critic, book and cinema reviewer for *The Evening Post*, Port Elizabeth.
Exhibition 1977 King George VI Art Gallery, Port Elizabeth, Memorial Exhibition.
Represented King George VI Art Gallery, Port Elizabeth.
Reference Lantern December 1976–February 1977.

WEISS Hans

Born 1912.
Died 1971.
A painter of landscapes.
Profile 1954 a member of the Contemporary Art Society. Lived in Pretoria and at Welkom in the Orange Free State.
Exhibitions Participated in group exhibitions from 1935.
Reference AASA.

WEITZ Anthony William
Born 1953 Cape Town.
A painter of landscapes, still life, portraits and figures. Works in oil, acrylic, gouache, charcoal and pastel.
Studies 1972–74 Witwatersrand Technical College, gaining a Diploma in Graphic Design; 1977–78 Pennsylvania Academy of Fine Arts, USA, gaining a Certificate in Fine Art; 1967 and 1977 extra-curricular courses in philosophy and fine art, through the University of South Africa and the Pennsylvania State University, USA.
Profile 1986 Chairman of the Illustrators Association of SA. 1975 a lecturer in presentation drawing, Witwatersrand Technical College; 1976 a lecturer in graphic design at the Ruth Prowse School of Art, Cape Town. An illustrator working in the advertising industry. Editorial and advertising work published regularly from 1976.
Exhibitions He has participated in several group exhibitions from 1975 in SA and once in the USA; 1986 Shell Gallery, Johannesburg, solo exhibition.
Reference Art Director no 1.

WELZ Jean Max Friedrich
Born 1900 Salzburg, Austria.
Died 1975 Cape Town.
Resided in SA from 1937.
A painter of still life, flowers, portraits, nudes and landscapes. Worked in oil, pastel, watercolour, charcoal, pencil and Indian ink. Two portrait busts in ciment fondu. A graphic artist. Began painting in 1940, becoming more abstracted during the 1950s and 1960s.
Studies 1915 Realschule, Salzburg, Austria; 1918 architecture at the Academy of Associated Arts, Vienna, under Oskar Strnad and Josef Hoffmann. As a painter, however, he was mainly self-taught.
Profile 1942 a member of the New Group; 1943–48 Principal of the Hugo Naudé Art Centre, Worcester, where he gave lectures on art and held art classes for children. 1948 the Worcester organiser of the SAAA. Wrote a number of articles on Art. 1975 a portfolio of 10 colour prints and one black and white print was published in an edition of 300. 1900–18 lived in Salzburg, Austria; 1918–25 in Vienna, Austria, where he qualified as an architect; 1925–36 in Paris where he worked as an architect for Robert Mallet-Stevens and Raymond Fischer, in L'Esprit Nouveau style with Adolf Loos, and with Le Corbusier and Amédée Ozenfant. 1937–39 in Johannesburg, working under Professor Pearse in the Department of Architecture at the University of the Witwatersrand, he was involved in the designing of the Bernard Price Institute of Geophysical Research and the entrance foyer and door of the Great Hall; 1939–41 lived near Barrydale, Cape Province; 1941 De Wet, Cape Province; 1942–69 in Worcester, Cape Province; 1969–75 in Rondebosch, Cape Town.

Exhibitions Participated in group exhibitions from 1942 throughout SA and in Brazil, Italy, Rhodesia (Zimbabwe), The Netherlands and the USA; 1942 Cape Town, first of numerous solo exhibitions held throughout SA; 1945 Constantia Gallery, Johannesburg, joint exhibition with Elsa Dziomba (qv); 1945 Argus Gallery, Cape Town, joint exhibition with Paul du Toit (qv); 1948 Tate Gallery, London, SA Art Exhibition; 1965 Galerie Welz, Salzburg, Austria, Retrospective Exhibition; 1969 SAAA Gallery, Worcester, Cape Province, Retrospective Exhibition; 1970 SA National Gallery, Cape Town, and Johannesburg Art Gallery, Retrospective Exhibition; 1976 SA National Gallery, Cape Town, Commemorative Exhibition; 1977 Pieter Wenning Gallery, Johannesburg, Memorial Exhibition; 1983 Hugo Naudé Centre, Worcester, Retrospective Exhibition.

Awards 1947 Silver Medal, SA Academy; 1953 Molteno Award with Alexis Preller (qv); 1969 Medal of Honour for Painting, SA Akademie vir Wetenskap en Kuns.

Represented Albertina Museum, Vienna, Austria; Ann Bryant Gallery, East London; Hester Rupert Art Museum, Graaff-Reinet; Hugo Naudé House, Worcester; Johannesburg Art Gallery; King George VI Art Gallery, Port Elizabeth; National Museum, Bloemfontein; Pietersburg Collection; Pretoria Art Museum; Rand Afrikaans University; Sandton Municipal Collection; SA Akademie vir Wetenskap en Kuns; SA National Gallery, Cape Town; Tatham Art Gallery, Pietermaritzburg; University of Cape Town; University of the Orange Free State; University of South Africa; University of Stellenbosch; University of the Witwatersrand; William Humphreys Art Gallery, Kimberley.

Public Commissions A number of architectural commissions in Worcester during the 1950s and 1960s, including the entrance to the sports field, the Union Festival Monument in Church Square and The Little Theatre.

References PSA; Collectors' Guide; Our Art 1; Art SA; SAA; 20C SA Art; SAP&S; SAP&D; SSAP; SESA; BSAK 1 & 2; SA Art; Oxford Companion to 20C Art (under SA); 3Cs; AASA; LSAA; *Artlook* December 1966 & November 1970; *SA Panorama* October 1970; *De Arte* April 1976; Retrospective Exhibition Catalogue, 1970, Johannesburg; Johanna de Villiers, *Jean Welz*, catalogue, 1977, Cape Town.

WENNING Pieter Willem Frederik

Born 1873 The Hague, The Netherlands.
Died 1921 Pretoria.
Resided in SA from 1905.

1905–09 painted and drew scenes around Pretoria in watercolour and crayon; 1909 began working in oil, painted 300–400 oil paintings mainly between 1916–21. Well-known for his landscapes, which frequently incorporated homesteads, Wenning also painted street scenes, especially of the Malay Quarter, Cape Town, still life, portraits, figures and genre paintings. His work is characterised by a heavy, dark outline and impasto paint. Numerous pencil, charcoal and ink drawings. From 1913 produced a large number of etchings on his own press, including a series entitled "Johannesburg Impressions" in 1913 and a number of etchings on cards and headed paper in 1915.

Studies The son of an art master living in Leeuwarden, The Netherlands. A pupil at Rijks Hoogere Burgerschool, Leeuwarden, where he was taught and encouraged by the Art Master, Bubberman. Learnt the art of woodcuts from Erich Mayer (qv).

Profile A friend of D C Boonzaier (qv), whose collection of oriental objets d'art influenced Wenning and appeared in his paintings. 1911 a member of The Individualists; 1917 a member of the SA Society of Artists. 1931 a print entitled "Malta Farm" was published by E Schweickerdt, Pretoria. 1873–1905 lived in The Netherlands, where he worked as a foreign correspondent for Hollandsch Ijzeren Spoorweg Maatschappij, and visited England, Scotland, France, Switzerland and Germany; 1905 visited Tenerife on his way to SA; 1905–15 worked at J H de Bussy & Co, booksellers, publishers and from 1911 sellers of artists' materials and prints in Pretoria and Johannesburg. 1905–13 lived in Pretoria; 1913–15 in Johannesburg, after leaving the employment of De Bussy & Co, he worked briefly at A B Pringle Fine Art Gallery in Eloff Street; 1915–17 lived in Pretoria, employed by Van Schaik's Bookshop. Visited Cape Town in 1913, in 1915 and for three months in 1916; from 1917 based in Cape Town, with several visits to Pretoria and in 1917 to Mozambique and Zanzibar; 1918 visited Durban and in 1919 Nelspruit, Potgietersrus, Nylstroom and Pietersburg. Included in Edward Roworth's (qv) essay "Landscape Art in SA", 1917, Studio Publication, *Art of The British Empire Overseas*.

Exhibitions Participated in group exhibitions from 1880 in The Netherlands and from 1910 in SA; 1916 Cape Town, first of several solo exhibitions held in Cape Town and Johannesburg; 1917 Cape Town, joint exhibition with Edward Roworth (qv), Hugo Naudé (qv) and Nita Spilhaus (qv); 1925 Cape Town, Memorial Exhibition; 1931 SA National Gallery, Cape Town, Memorial Exhibition; 1946 Pieter Wenning Gallery, Johannesburg, Memorial Exhibition; 1948 Tate Gallery, London, SA Art Exhibition; 1967 Pretoria Art Museum and SA National Gallery, Cape Town, Commemorative Exhibition; 1968 Retrospective Exhibition, Cape Town; 1973 Johannesburg Art Gallery, "Homage to Pieter Wenning" Exhibition; 1973 SA National Gallery, Cape Town, Centenary Exhibition.

Represented Durban Art Gallery; Johannesburg Art Gallery; Julius Gordon Africana Centre, Riversdale; King George VI Art Gallery, Port Elizabeth; Pretoria Art Museum; Pretoria City Hall; Rand Afrikaans University; SA National Gallery, Cape Town; The Hague Museum, The Netherlands; University of Pretoria; University of South Africa; University of the Witwatersrand; William Humphreys Art Gallery, Kimberley.

Public Commissions 1902 bust of President Paul Kruger for Transvaalsche Vereeniging, Amsterdam, The Netherlands; 1917 painting of the Women's Memorial, Bloemfontein, presented to the wife of President M T Steyn; 1918 "Stations of the Cross", Roman Catholic Church, Durban.

Publication by Wenning Article entitled "Kunst in Zuid-Afrika" for *Neerlandia*, September 1913.

References Gregoire Boonzaier and Lippy Lipshitz, *Wenning*, 1949, Unie-Volks Pers, Cape Town; J du P Scholtz, *D C Boonzaier en Pieter Wenning*, 1973, Tafelberg, Cape Town; Harco Wenning, *My Father*, 1976, Howard Timmins, Cape Town; KK; Collectors' Guide; Our Art 1; Art SA; SAA; SADNB; 20C SA

Art; DSAB; SAP&S; Oxford Companion to Art (under SA); SAP&D; SESA; SSAP; BSAK 1 & 2; Enc S'n A; SA Art; 3Cs; AASA; LSAA; *Die Huisgenoot* April 1921, November 1944, January 1945 & May 1961; *Aurora* September 1949; *Lantern* June 1961; *SA Panorama* May 1963; *Artlook* March 1967; A J Werth (qv), Commemorative Exhibition Catalogue, 1967, Pretoria Art Museum.

WENTZEL Roland Theodore

Born 1907 Germany.

Resided in SA from 1937.

A self-taught painter of landscapes and seascapes. Works in watercolour. Additionally makes copper engravings.

Profile 1952–64 a member of the SAAA. Has written a number of short stories and articles. 1937–72 worked for an advertising agency.

Exhibitions 1952 Cape Town, first of four solo exhibitions.

Publication by Wentzel There Are More Things, 1951, Nasionale Pers, Cape Town.

Reference BSAK 1.

WERBELOFF Marjory Jess (née Kussel)

Born 1921 Port Elizabeth.

A painter depicting old buildings. Works in watercolour, ink and wash. A graphic artist, making linocuts and etchings. A creator of mosaics, pottery and jewellery. 1956–80 a large series of Cape Town buildings; 1970–75 of Grahamstown buildings; 1970–80 a series of linocuts of birds.

Studies 1938 six months at the University of the Witwatersrand, under Willem de Sanderes Hendrikz (qv); 1938 six months at Rhodes University, under Professor Austin Winter Moore (qv); 1939–41 Port Elizabeth Technical College, under John Muff-Ford (qv) and Barbara Tyrrell (qv). In 1941 gained a BA(FA) from Rhodes University.

Profile From 1947 a member of the SAAA. A founder member of the Vernacular Architecture Society of SA. 1942–46 taught part-time at the Port Elizabeth Technical College; 1943 taught at the Holy Rosary Convent, Port Elizabeth; c.1968–70 taught at the Union of Jewish Women, Cape Town; teaches both children and adults privately. 1985 published a series of greeting cards of 10 Cape Town buildings. 1921–47 lived in Port Elizabeth, thereafter in Cape Town.

Exhibitions c.1945 Port Elizabeth, joint exhibition with her sister Rhoda Pepys; she has participated in several group exhibitions from 1986 in Cape Town.

WERTH Albert Johannes Dr

Born 1927 Bethlehem District, Orange Free State.

A painter and graphic artist of landscapes, seascapes, portraits, still life, genre and abstract pictures. Works in watercolour, oil, ink, wash, pencil, charcoal and in various graphic media.

Studies 1952 gained an MA in the History of Art from the University of Pretoria, having studied under Professor M Bokhorst; 1973 gained a DPhil in the History of Art from the University of Pretoria, having studied under Professor F G E Nilant.

Profile From 1963 a member of the SAAA and from 1984 of the SAAAH. 1951 a part-time lecturer in the History of Art at the University of Pretoria; 1953–58 a graphic designer for SA Airways; 1959–60 a lecturer, 1960–63 Head of the Art Department, Pretoria Technical College. From 1963 Director of the Pretoria Art Museum and Melrose House and from 1981 a part-time lecturer in Museum Studies at the University of Pretoria. Chairman of the Arts Committee of the SA Akademie vir Wetenskap en Kuns. Has travelled throughout Europe and the USA.

Exhibitions He has participated in group exhibitions in SA; 1946 University of Pretoria, first of *c*.12 solo exhibitions held in SA.

Award Promotion of SA Art Medal from the SA Akademie vir Wetenskap en Kuns.

Represented Pretoria Art Museum; Willem Annandale Art Gallery, Lichtenburg.

References IWAA; BSAK 1 & 2; AASA; LSAA; *Habitat* no 19, 1976.

WESSELS Annemarie

Born 1950 Heilbron, Orange Free State.

A painter of figures and portraits. Works in oil, acrylic, ink and pencil.

Studies 1969–72 through the University of Pretoria, under Gunther van der Reis (qv) and Leslie Reinhardt (qv), gaining a BA(FA).

Profile 1973 a temporary lecturer at the University of Pretoria. In 1980 illustrated a number of children's books for Daan Retief Publishers, Pretoria. Visited Germany in 1970, 1975, 1979 and 1986; and Paris in 1986.

Exhibitions 1975 at a private venue in Pretoria, first of four solo exhibitions held in SA; she has participated in several group exhibitions from 1982 in SA and France; 1983 University of Natal, Pietermaritzburg, first of two joint exhibitions with Piet Brink (qv).

WESSELS Margaretha S (Rhé)

Born 1950 Pretoria.

A sculptor of a combination of figures, man-made elements and abstract elements. Works in ceramics and mixed media. 1987–88 a series of decorative sculptures based on vessel shapes.

Studies 1968–70 Michaelis School of Fine Art, under Neville Dubow, gaining a Diploma in Graphic Design; 1975 Port Elizabeth Technical College, under Alexander Podlashuc (qv), gaining a Higher Diploma in Graphic Design; 1981–83 studied fine art at the Witwatersrand Technikon, under Suzette Munnick, gaining a Diploma in Fine Art (ceramics); 1987 completing a Higher Diploma in Fine Art (ceramics) at the Witwatersrand Technikon.

Profile 1973–76 a lecturer at the Port Elizabeth Technical College; 1977–87 a senior lecturer and in 1988 a part-time lecturer in graphic design at the Witwatersrand Technikon.

Exhibitions She has participated in several group exhibitions from 1981 in SA; 1975 Port Elizabeth, solo exhibition.

Represented SA National Gallery, Cape Town.

WEST Marjorie

Born 1945 Thabazimbi, Transvaal.

A self-taught painter of landscapes, seascapes and portraits. Works in oil, watercolour and pencil.

Profile Has taught art privately from 1980. Lives in Cape Town.

Exhibitions 1979 Market Gallery, Johannesburg, first of two solo exhibitions held in Johannesburg; she has participated in several group exhibitions from 1982 in Cape Town.

WESTBROOK Walter Edward

Born 1921 Pretoria.

A painter and graphic artist of landscapes, portraits, still life and figures. Works in oil, acrylic, watercolour, wash, pencil, charcoal, linocuts and silkscreens. Series of religious works, and landscapes of arid regions. He also works in clay, wood and fibreglass.

Studies 1937–38 in Pretoria under Walter Battiss (qv); 1943–44 under Francisco Caprioli in Rome, Italy; 1946 at various schools in London; 1947–49 part-time at Pretoria Technical College.

Profile A member of the SAAA and the Bloemfontein Group. 1968–76 taught adult art classes at the Northern Cape Technical College, Kimberley; 1970–74 an art master in Kimberley. 1971–76 set designs for Gilbert & Sullivan operas. Has travelled in Europe and to Egypt.

Exhibitions He has participated in numerous group exhibitions from 1947 throughout SA and in West Germany, Spain, Portugal, the UK and Zimbabwe; 1947 Pretoria, first of numerous solo exhibitions held in SA; 1964 Quadrennial Exhibition; 1981 Republic Festival Exhibition; 1981 Kimberley and Bloemfontein, Retrospective Exhibition; 1986 Pretoria, Retrospective Exhibition.

Represented National Museum, Bloemfontein; Pietersburg Collection; Potchefstroom Museum; Pretoria Art Museum; Rand Afrikaans University; SA National Gallery, Cape Town; SA National Museum of Military History, Johannesburg; University of the Orange Free State; University of Pretoria; University of South Africa; Willem Annandale Art Gallery, Lichtenburg; William Humphreys Art Gallery, Kimberley. Various SA embassies in Europe and South America.

Public Commissions A number of commissions including: 1966 mural, Orange Free State Provincial Administration Building, Bloemfontein; mural, St James's Church, Kimberley; 1971 a painting commissioned by Southern Life and presented to Kimberley on the city's centenary.

References SAA; SAP&S; BSAK 1 & 2; 3Cs; AASA; SASSK; *SA Panorama* November 1977.

WESTHOVEN William

Born 1842 Cape Town.
Died 1925.
A painter of landscapes. Worked in oil and watercolour.
Profile Illustrated *The Cape Peninsula, pen and colour sketches, described by Rene Juta, painted by W Westhoven*, published by Black, London, and in 1910 by J C Juta, Cape Town. A qualified engineer, who worked for the Public Works Department of the Cape Government from 1882.
Exhibitions Participated in group exhibitions from 1903 in Cape Town and Pretoria.
References SADNB; AASA.

WEYERS Evette

Born 1946 Durban.
A sculptor of personalised, figurative mythologies. Works in clay, found objects, steel, wood, acrylic, ink, pencil and charcoal.
Studies Pretoria Technical College, gaining an Art Diploma, majoring in Ceramics.
Profile A member of D'ARTS and the APSA. A lecturer in ceramic sculpture, in 1977 at the Witwatersrand Technical College and in 1986 at the Pretoria Technikon. Produces the occasional documentary film for the SABC TV. Presently living alternately in the USA and SA. Has visited Mozambique and the Red Sea. Married to the actor Marius Weyers.
Exhibitions She has participated in group exhibitions from 1977; 1979 first of six solo exhibitions; 1987 Verwoerdburg Association of Arts Gallery, joint exhibition with Johann du Plessis (qv), Guy du Toit (qv) and Maryna Huyser (qv); 1987 Strack van Schyndel Gallery, Johannesburg, joint exhibition with Michelle Davies and Sylvia Kaplan (qv).
Award 1986 First Prize, sculpture category, Corobrik National Competition.

WHALE R H

Born Birmingham, England.
Died 1909.
A painter of landscapes. Worked in oil.
Profile A founder member of the SA Society of Artists. Lived in Cape Town.
Exhibitions Participated in group exhibitions in Cape Town.
Represented Albany Museum, Grahamstown; SA National Gallery, Cape Town; University of Cape Town.
References AASA; 80th Anniversary Exhibition of the SA Society of Artists Catalogue, November 1982, SA National Gallery.

WHEATLEY (Edith) Grace RMS RWS RSPP (née Wolfe)

Born 1888 London, England.
Died 1970 London, England.
Resided in SA 1925–38.
A painter of portraits and fauna. Worked in watercolour. She also sculpted.

Studies 1906–08 Slade School of Art, London; the School of Animal and Landscape Painting, London; later also studied at Atelier Colarossi in Paris.

Profile 1910 an Associate and in 1913 a full member of the Royal Society of Miniature Painters; 1921 a member of the New English Art Club; 1945 an Associate and in 1952 a full member of the Royal Society of Painters in Watercolour; 1955 a member of the Royal Society of Portrait Painters. 1925–37 an assistant lecturer in painting, drawing and pottery at the Michaelis School of Fine Art. Prior to 1925 she lived in London and Penzance, Cornwall. Returned to the UK in 1938. Married to Professor John L Wheatley (qv).

Exhibitions Participated in group exhibitions in the UK; 1933 Greatorex Gallery, London, first solo exhibition.

Represented British Museum, London, England; SA National Gallery, Cape Town; Tate Gallery, London, England; University of Cape Town; Walker Gallery, Liverpool, England.

Public Commissions 1929–30, with her husband, responsible for the decorating of the ceiling and walls of the Entrance Gallery to the SA National Gallery, Cape Town; a sculpture for the New Law Courts, Cape Town.

References SAA; *Tate Gallery Catalogue—The Modern British Paintings, Drawings and Sculpture*, volume 2, 1964, Oldbourne Press, London; DSAB (under J L Wheatley); SAP&S; SAP&D; Bénézit (under Wheatly); DBA; AASA.

WHEATLEY John Laviers RE ARA RWS

Born 1892 Abergavenny, Wales.
Died 1955 Wimbledon, London, England.
Resided in SA 1925–38.
A painter of portraits, figures and genre. Worked in oil, watercolour, pencil and ink. An etcher.

Studies 1912–13 Slade School of Art, London, under Walter Sickert (1860–1942) and Stanhope Forbes (1857–1948).

Profile 1917 a member of the New English Art Club; 1921 an Associate of the Royal Society of Painter-Etchers and Engravers; 1932 a founder member of the National Academy of Arts (SA). 1945 an Associate of the Royal Academy; 1946 a member of the Royal Fine Art Commission; 1947 a member of the Royal Society of Painters in Watercolour. 1918–20 served in the Artists' Rifles as an Official War Artist; 1920–25 lectured at the Slade School of Art, London; 1925–37 Principal and Professor of the Michaelis School of Fine Art; 1935–36 First Honorary Director and Chairman of the Board of Trustees, SA National Gallery, Cape Town; 1938–48 Director of the Sheffield Art Gallery, UK; 1941–42 commissioned to paint war portraits; 1948–50 Director of the National Gallery of British Sports and Pastimes, UK. Prior to 1925 lived in London and Penzance, Cornwall. Married to Grace Wheatley (qv).

Exhibitions Participated in group exhibitions from 1917 in England and later in SA. 1922 Grosvenor Gallery, London, joint exhibition with Muirhead Bone (1876–1953).

Represented Manchester Art Gallery, England; SA National Gallery, Cape Town; Tate Gallery, London, England; University of Cape Town.

Public Commission 1929–30, with his wife, responsible for the decorating of the ceiling and walls of the Entrance Gallery of the SA National Gallery, Cape Town.

References SAA; *Tate Gallery Catalogue—The Modern British Paintings, Drawings and Sculpture*, volume 2, 1964, Oldbourne Press, London; SADNB; DSAB; SAP&S; SAP&D; Bénézit (under Wheatly); DBA; BSAK 1 & 2; SA Art; AASA.

WHIPPMAN Matthew (Taffy)

Born 1901 Pontypridd, Wales.
Died 1973 Johannesburg.
Resided in SA from 1920.

A painter of semi-abstract paintings of flowers, landscapes and seascapes; a number of figure studies and portraits. Worked in oil, pastel and watercolour. An etcher.

Studies Mainly a self-taught artist but had lessons in etching 1930–31 at the Witwatersrand Technical College, under Professor F W Armstrong (qv).

Profile After an initial stay in the Eastern Province, lived in Johannesburg where he encouraged young artists. In 1945 he acquired Rand Picture Framers and in 1950 opened Whippman's Gallery in Johannesburg.

Exhibitions Participated in group exhibitions from 1946; 1953 Johannesburg, first of several solo exhibitions held in Johannesburg and Bloemfontein; 1965 Grosvenor Gallery, London, group exhibition; 1971 William Humphreys Art Gallery, Kimberley, Prestige Exhibition; 1971 Johannesburg Art Gallery, exhibition of selected works; 1974 Johannesburg Art Gallery, Memorial Exhibition; 1977 Pretoria Art Museum, exhibition of selected works.

Represented Hester Rupert Art Museum, Graaff-Reinet; Johannesburg Art Gallery; Pretoria Art Museum; Rand Afrikaans University; Sandton Municipal Collection; SA National Gallery, Cape Town; University of the Witwatersrand; William Humphreys Art Gallery, Kimberley.

References Collectors' Guide; Art SA; SAA; 20C SA Art; SSAP; BSAK 1 & 2; SA Art; AASA; *SA Art News* 4 May 1961; *Artlook* November 1967 & June 1972; *Lantern* August 1977.

WHITE Adèle

Born 1931 Cape Town.
Died 1987 Johannesburg.
A painter of landscapes.

Studies 1948–53 at the Michaelis School of Fine Art, under Maurice van Essche (qv), where awarded the MacIver Scholarship for painting; 1953–55 at the Koninklijke Academie voor Schone Kunsten en de Hogere Instituten, Antwerp, Belgium, where won the Philip Opperman prize in 1955. 1959 gained an National Art Teachers Certificate.

Profile Taught at Jeppe High School for Girls, Johannesburg, Redhill School, Johannesburg, and in Hackney in the East End of London. 1955 made a study tour of North Italy. 1956 returned to Cape Town, moving to Johannesburg in 1957 for five years. 1961–63 lived in Europe. In 1964 worked as a social group worker at various children's centres.

Exhibitions Participated in group exhibitions from the 1950s in SA and Belgium, and from 1964 in London; 1956 SAAA Gallery, Cape Town, first of many solo exhibitions; 1960 Quadrennial Exhibition.
Represented Pretoria Art Museum.
References Art SA; SAA; BSAK 1; AASA; *SA Art News* 6 April 1961.

WHITE Donna Marita

Born 1953 Pietermaritzburg.
A painter of figures. Works in oil.
Studies 1970–75 University of Natal, under Raymund van Niekerk, gaining a BA(FA) in 1975 and a Higher Diploma in Education in 1976; 1982 Johannesburg Art Foundation.
Profile 1977–79 an art teacher at the Grosvenor Girls High School, Bluff, Durban.
Exhibitions She has participated in many group exhibitions from 1971 in SA; 1978 NSA Gallery, Durban, first of two solo exhibitions held in SA; 1983 Crake Gallery, Johannesburg, joint exhibition with Laraine Campbell (qv) and Cecily Grant (qv).
Reference LSAA.

WHITTALL John St Clair

Born 1937 Nakuru, Kenya.
Resided in SA from 1969.
A sculptor of figures, wildlife and abstract pieces. Works in wood.
Studies Informal art studies under George Gabb in Belize, Central America.
Profile 1961–69 lived in Belize working in the hardwood industry. From 1969 he has worked in publishing.
Exhibitions Participated in several group exhibitions from 1971 in SA; 1977 Ann Zinn Gallery, Cape Town, solo exhibition.

WICHGRAF Fritz

Born 1853 Potsdam, Germany.
Died *c.*1920 Germany.
Resided in the Transvaal 1896–1900.
A painter of portraits of SA notability; numerous landscapes, paintings depicting early Boer life, genre and historical scenes. Worked in oil and watercolour.
Studies In Weimar, Germany, under Professor Albert Baur (1835–1906), in Vienna, Austria, under Heinrich von Angeli (1840–1924) and in Munich, Germany, under Professor Wilhelm von Diez (1839–1907) and Professor Ludwig von Lofftz (1845–1910).
Exhibitions Exhibited in Vienna in 1887; 1898 Johannesburg, solo exhibition; participated in group exhibitions in Berlin 1904–07.

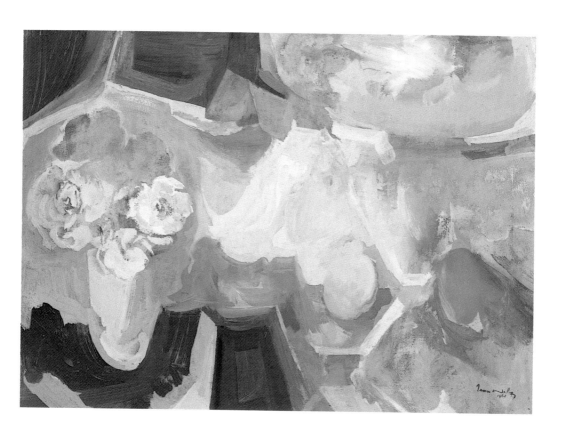

JEAN WELZ
Rococo 1964
Oil on Canvas 65 × 90,5 cm
Johannesburg Art Gallery

PIETER WENNING
Jour d'Hiver 1915
Oil on Plywood Panel 55 × 72 cm
Johannesburg Art Gallery

Represented Africana Museum, Johannesburg; Johannesburg Art Gallery; University of Pretoria.

Public Commission 1900 "Boer Deputation", by the Zuid-Afrikaansche Republiek Government, for display at the Paris Exhibition in 1900, now in the Transvaal Provincial Administration Building, Pretoria (several prints have been made of this work).

References SADNB; AMC5; DSAB; Pict Afr; Bénézit; BSAK 1 & 2; Enc S'n A; SA Art; 3Cs; AASA; *Historia* June & September 1961; *ANN* September 1963; *SA Panorama* February 1964.

WIID Siebert Christiaan

Born 1927 Wellington, Cape Province.

A painter of landscapes and abstract pictures. Works in oil, watercolour and gouache.

Studies 1955 one month at the Art Academy, Vienna, under Professor Matejkafelden and six months at l'Académie de la Grande Chaumière, Paris, under Yves Brayer (*b*.1907); 1973 five months at l'Académie de la Grande Chaumière, Paris.

Profile A member of the SAAA. A qualified, practising architect.

Exhibitions He has participated in several group exhibitions from 1956 in SA; 1956 Quadrennial Exhibition; 1956 held a solo exhibition.

References BSAK 1; AASA.

WILES Brian Hugh

Born 1923 Alexandria, Cape Province.

A painter of landscapes and seascapes. Works in oil. 1977–80 a series entitled "Cycle of 10".

Profile Owns and runs The Gallery, Leisure Isle, Knysna, Cape Province. Since 1972 he has travelled to Madagascar, Mauritius, Thailand, Hong Kong, Italy, Israel, the UK, Austria and India. Son of W G Wiles (qv), nephew of Frank Wiles (qv), brother of Paul Wiles (qv). Married to Lucy Wiles (qv).

Exhibitions He has participated in several group exhibitions from 1959 in SA; he has held numerous solo exhibitions at his gallery in Knysna; 1959 Pieter Wenning Gallery, Johannesburg, Wiles Group Exhibition.

Reference *SA Panorama* October 1959.

WILES (Francis Edmund) Frank

Born 1881 Cambridge, England.

Died 1963 Grahamstown, Cape Province.

While in SA resided in Cape Town.

A painter of portraits and landscapes. Worked in oil.

Studies 1901 Cambridge School of Art; also in London under Walter Sickert (1860–1942).

Profile Known to have illustrated books and magazines while in England. Brother of W G Wiles (qv) and son of the sculptor Henry Wiles, uncle of Brian Wiles (qv) and Paul Wiles (qv).
Exhibitions Exhibited at the Royal Academy, London, five times between 1912 and 1930; 1959 Pieter Wenning Gallery, Johannesburg, Wiles Group Exhibition.
Represented House of Assembly, Cape Town; Houses of Parliament, Harare, Zimbabwe.
Public Commissions Portraits of Governors and Prime Ministers of SA and Rhodesia (Zimbabwe).
References SAA; DBA; BSAK 1; AASA; LSAA; *SA Panorama* October 1959.

WILES Lucy Mary (née Townsend)
Born 1920 Johannesburg.
A painter and a graphic artist of landscapes, figures, portraits and still life. Works in oil, watercolour and in various graphic media.
Studies Briefly at the Natal Technical College, under Professor Cecil Todd (qv).
Profile A founder member of the Queenstown Art Society. Illustrated Winifred Tapson's book *Old Timer* and Brigadier Day's *Brigadier to Barman*. Paints and glazes tiles, and makes Xhosa figure friezes, prints and Christmas cards. 1946–54 lived in the Transkei, thereafter in Knysna, Cape Province. Since 1972 she has travelled to Madagascar, Mauritius, Thailand, Hong Kong, Italy, Greece, Israel, the UK, Germany and India. Married to Brian Wiles (qv). Her earlier works are signed Lucy Mullins.
Exhibitions She has participated in numerous group exhibitions from 1959 in SA and once in London; 1959 Pieter Wenning Gallery, Johannesburg, Wiles Group Exhibition; 1961 Pieter Wenning Gallery, Johannesburg, first of two solo exhibitions held there; she has also held numerous solo exhibitions at The Gallery, Leisure Isle, Knysna.
Represented Queenstown Municipal Collection; William Humprheys Art Gallery, Kimberley.
Reference *SA Panorama* October 1959.

WILES Patricia see VAUGHAN Patricia

WILES Paul
Born 1919 Uitenhage, Cape Province.
A painter of landscapes and wildlife. Works in oil and acrylic.
Studies 1937–39 and 1946 Rhodes University, under Professor Austin Winter Moore (qv), gaining a BA(FA); 1948–49 Slade School of Art, London, under Professor Charlstone.

Profile 1950–55 a member of the SA Society of Artists; 1962–68 of the NSA, serving one year as Chairman. 1947–48 an art teacher for the Rhodesian (Zimbabwe) Education Department. 1950–70 worked in advertising, establishing the agency Kenyon Wiles (Pty) Ltd. Husband of Patricia Vaughan (qv); father of Shayne Haysom (qv), brother of Brian Wiles (qv), son of W G Wiles (qv) and nephew of Frank Wiles (qv).
Exhibitions He has participated in several group exhibitions from 1950 in SA and twice in the USA; 1959 Pieter Wenning Gallery, Johannesburg, Wiles Group Exhibition; 1975 Everard Read Gallery, Johannesburg, solo exhibition.
Represented University of Cape Town.
References SAA; AASA; LSAA; *SA Panorama* October 1959.

WILES Walter Gilbert

Born 1875 Cambridge, England.
Died 1966 Knysna, Cape Province.
Resided in SA from 1902.
A painter of seascapes, landscapes and occasionally portraits. Worked in oil, watercolour and pastel.
Studies 1890 in France; 1911 in London.
Profile 1918 an original committee member of the EPSFA. A member of the SA Society of Artists. An ostrich farmer near Uitenhage, who began painting in watercolour in his spare time, later lived on Leisure Isle, Knysna. 1939 published a pamphlet entitled "Art—Its Spiritual Meaning—an antidote to Modernism". Son of the sculptor Henry Wiles. Brother of Frank Wiles (qv), father of Brian Wiles (qv) and Paul Wiles (qv), and grandfather of Shayne Haysom (qv).
Exhibitions Participated in group exhibitions in SA; 1920 first of several solo exhibitions held in SA; 1924 British Empire Exhibition, Wembley, London; 1959 Pieter Wenning Gallery, Johannesburg, Wiles Group Exhibition.
Represented Albany Museum, Grahamstown; Ann Bryant Gallery, East London; Durban Art Gallery; Julius Gordon Africana Centre, Riversdale; Pretoria Art Museum; Queenstown Municipal Collection; SA National Gallery, Cape Town; William Humphreys Art Gallery, Kimberley.
Public Commissions 1930 Portrait of F P Marriott (qv) for the Port Elizabeth Technical College; 1947 several paintings of the Royal Tour to South Africa.
References Collectors' Guide; SAA; SAP&D; BSAK 1 & 2; SA Art; AASA; LSAA; *SA Panorama* October 1959.

WILLE Marjorie

Born 1899 Bloemfontein.
Died 1981 Cape Town.
A painter of flowers and botanical illustrations.
Studies Cape Town Technical College; Regent Street Polytechnic, London, England.

Profile Her interest in flora extended to garden design and exhibiting in and judging flower shows. Her work was reproduced by Howard Swan, Johannesburg.

Exhibitions Participated in group exhibitions at Kirstenbosch, Cape Town.

Publication by Wille *Patterns in the Garden.*

Reference AASA.

WILLIAMSON Susan Mary (Sue)

Born 1941 Lichfield, Staffordshire, England.

Resided in SA from 1948.

A printmaker of socio-political works. 1978 a series of the Modderdam postcards (banned); 1981 "The Last Supper", a mixed-media installation comprised of fragments of demolished buildings and abandoned possessions from District Six, Cape Town, exhibited at the Gowlett Gallery, Cape Town; from 1982 "A Few South Africans", a portfolio of 17 (to 1988) photo-silkscreens depicting SA women involved in the struggle for liberation.

Studies 1966–69 Art Students League, New York, under Thomas Fogarty, Seong Moy (*b.*1921) and John Groth; 1971–73 Ruth Prowse Art Centre, under Erik Laubscher (qv); 1982–83 Michaelis School of Fine Art, under Jules van de Vijver (qv), gaining an Advanced Diploma in Fine Art with distinction.

Profile From 1981 a member of the Artists Guild, Cape Town, 1982–83 a committee member. From 1984 has taught etching and screenprinting at the Graphic Workshop, Cape Town. Has designed record covers and posters for music groups. 1970–72 wrote a weekly column in *The Sunday Tribune*, Durban; since 1972 she has written several articles for periodicals. 1964–69 lived in New York. Presently lives in Cape Town.

Exhibitions She has participated in numerous group exhibitions from 1968 in the USA, SA, Italy, the UK and West Germany; 1975 Nedart, Sea Point, Cape Town, first of six solo exhibitions, two of which were held in the USA; 1982 National Gallery, Gaborone, Botswana, Exhibition of SA Art; 1985 Tributaries, touring SA and West Germany.

Represented Durban Art Gallery; Pietersburg Collection; University of Cape Town.

Reference *Vulva* February 1985.

WILLY see MASSEY HICKS Margaret

WILSON Clarence

Born 1931 Toronto, Canada.

Died 1985 New York, USA.

Resided in SA from 1964.

A painter of portraits, still life, decorative panels and large murals. Worked in egg tempera.

Studies Ontario Art School, Canada, and Chicago Institute of Art, Illinois, USA.

Profile Designed film sets, including those for "Majuba" and "The Professor and the Beauty Queen" by Jamie Uys, also designed stage costumes. An interior decorator and an actor. Prior to 1964 visited Japan and travelled extensively in the Far East and Europe. *c.*1971 spent eight months in the Philippines, where he painted portraits of the Marcos family. Lived in Johannesburg, London and New York.

Exhibitions Participated in group exhibitions in SA; 1966 first of several solo exhibitions held in SA.

References BSAK 1 & 2; AASA; *Artlook* February 1969; *Habitat* no 26, 1977; *Interior Design* September 1983.

WILSON Lorraine Frances

Born 1944 Durban.

A painter of landscapes and abstract pictures. Works in watercolour.

Studies 1963–64 Natal Technical College, ceramics under James Hall; 1965 ceramics at the University of London.

Profile From 1970 a member of the NSA; from 1975 of the APSA and from 1978 of the WSSA of which she is presently an Associate. Has taught pottery from 1970.

Exhibitions She has participated in numerous group exhibitions from 1975 in Southern Africa and once in London; 1982 Grassroots Gallery, Westville, Natal, first of three solo exhibitions; 1985 Grassroots Gallery, Westville, Natal, joint exhibitions with Anthea Martin (qv).

Award 1977 P W Storey Trophy.

WILSON Norman Octavius Dr

Born 1871 Wandsworth, London, England.

Died 1940 Rondebosch, Cape Town.

Resided in SA from 1899.

A painter of landscapes. Worked in watercolour.

Profile A member of the SA Society of Artists. A practising doctor who lived in Cape Town.

Exhibitions Participated in group exhibitions with the SA Society of Artists; 1924 British Empire Exhibition, Wembley, London.

Represented SA National Gallery, Cape Town.

References SAP&D; AASA.

WILSON Ronald John Beverly

Born 1939 Dunnottar, Transvaal.

A painter of portraits, landscapes, seascapes, still life and wildlife. Works in oil, watercolour, pencil and charcoal. 1985 a series entitled "Jenny at Emmarentia Dam".

Studies Privately under Paul Bosman (qv), Giuseppe Cattaneo (qv) and Dino Paravano (qv).
Profile From 1979 a member of the Artists Market. 1980 a member of the Selection and Purchasing Committee of the SABC Art Collection. From 1965 numerous records of his folk music and children's songs have been cut. Many visits to SWA/Namibia. Nephew of Rhoda Lewis (qv).
Exhibitions He has participated in several group exhibitions from 1969 in SA.

WINDER Elsie Joan (née Pell)

Born 1915 Pretoria.
Died 1988 Johannesburg.
A painter and a sculptor who worked in oil, watercolour, pencil, bronze, wood and plaster of Paris. Depicted landscapes, portraits, still life, seascapes, figures, city scenes, particularly of Johannesburg, and flowers in a semi-botanical manner.
Studies 1932–34 awarded a three-year bursary to the Witwatersrand Technical College, studying under Professor F W Armstrong (qv), Sydney Carter (qv), Elizabeth Macadam (qv), James Gardner (qv) and Phyllis Gardner (qv); later took evening classes under Eric Byrd (qv) and Emily Fern (qv).
Profile c.1939 a member of the Friday Club; c.1942–60 a member of the Transvaal Academy; 1986 a member of the WSSA. c.1947 taught at the Witwatersrand Technical College. A calligrapher and commercial artist. 1951 married Henry E Winder (qv).
Exhibitions Participated in numerous group exhibitions from the 1940s.
References AMC4; BSAK 1; *SA Architectural Record* 3 January 1950.

WINDER Henry Edward FRSA (Teddy)

Born 1897 London, England.
Died 1982 Johannesburg.
Resided in SA from 1902.
A cartoonist working in pencil, ink and in various graphic media.
Studies Slade School of Art, London, under Professor Henry Tonks (1862–1937).
Profile He was instrumental in the foundation of the SAAA. 1937 a committee member and 1940–47 President of the Transvaal Art Society; on its affiliation to the SAAA remained President of the Southern Transvaal Branch until 1960. 1954 elected a Fellow of the Royal Society of Arts. From 1920 worked for the *Rand Daily Mail*, the *Sunday Times*, the *Sunday Express*, the *Financial Mail*, *The Outspan*, *The Nongqai* and the English publications the *London News Chronicle*, *Motor* and *Sketch*. 1925 began the first children's comic strip in SA entitled "Duggie, Lammie and Hi Ti", which was published in the *Rand Daily Mail*; he was also the art critic H E W for the same newspaper. Illustrated *No Ordinary Woman*, Thelma Gutsche, 1966, Howard Timmins, Cape Town. Married to Joan Winder (qv).
Represented Africana Museum, Johannesburg.
References AMC5&7; BSAK 1 & 2; AASA; SASSK.

WINK Peter William

Born 1949 Pretoria.

A sculptor of figures. Works in wood, stone and bronze. A painter of landscapes, seascapes, still life, wildlife and abstract pictures. Works in oil, acrylic, watercolour, ink, wash, pencil and charcoal.

Studies Evening classes at the Natal Technical College, under Gillian Chase (qv).

Profile A member of the NSA and D'ARTS. Has travelled throughout SA and to SWA/Namibia.

Exhibitions He has participated in many group exhibitions from 1973 in SA; 1981 Republic Festival Exhibition.

Award 1984 Gold Medal for Sculpture, Queensburgh Festival of Arts.

Reference AASA.

WINKLES George Matthias

Born 1859 Birmingham, England.

Died 1928.

Resided in SA from 1889.

A painter of portraits, landscapes and still life. Worked in oil and pastel.

Studies In England, Antwerp and Paris.

Profile 1902 a co-founder of the SA Society of Artists.

Exhibitions Participated in group exhibitions from 1877 in the UK and SA; 1899 Cape Town, joint exhibition with Borge Stuckenberg (qv), James S Morland (qv) and Hugo Naudé (qv).

Represented SA National Gallery, Cape Town; William Humphreys Art Gallery, Kimberley.

Public Commissions Numerous portrait commissions of SA notability, including Ada Morris and in 1920 W J Thorn, the Mayor of Cape Town.

References SAP&S; SSAP; Pict Afr; DBA; AASA; *De Arte* April 1978.

WINTER MOORE Austin

Born 1889 Sheffield, Yorkshire, England.

Resided in SA *c*.1926–50.

A painter of landscapes. Worked in watercolour. A number of ink drawings.

Studies Nottingham School of Art and the Royal Academy Schools, London.

Profile 1927–29 Principal of the Witwatersrand Technical College Art School; 1928–29 Curator of the Johannesburg Art Gallery; 1929–50 Professor of Fine Arts, Rhodes University. Returned to England in 1950, but continued to visit SA regularly.

Exhibitions Participated in group exhibitions at the Royal Academy and in SA; 1936 Empire Exhibition, Johannesburg.

Represented Albany Museum, Grahamstown; Johannesburg Art Gallery; 1820 Settlers Memorial Museum, Grahamstown.

References AMC4; BSAK 1; AASA.

WISE Thelma Juliana

Born 1921 Pretoria.

A painter and graphic artist of still life and abstract pictures. Works in oil and in coloured etching.

Studies 1938–41 Witwatersrand Technical College, under Eric Byrd (qv) and Mary Davies (qv), gaining a National Art Teachers Certificate; 1958–59 under Sidney Goldblatt (qv); graphics at l'Atelier 17, Paris, under William Stanley Hayter (*b*.1901).

Exhibitions She has participated in group exhibitions from the 1950s in SA; 1960 Quadrennial Exhibition; 1966 Republic Festival Exhibition.

References SAA; *Artlook* February 1971.

WITHERS Honorine Margaret FRGS (Mabel)

Born 1870 London, England.

Died 1956.

Resided in SA from 1910 at Wilderness, Cape Province.

A painter of landscapes and figures set in the Transkei. Worked in watercolour.

Studies Royal College of Art, London.

Profile A member of the SA Society of Artists. *c*.1945 gave art lessons in her Johannesburg studio. 1915–20 lived in Australia. Travelled to Kenya, Zimbabwe, Uganda, Cyprus, Mauritius, New Zealand, Australia and extensively throughout SA.

Exhibitions 1904–10 exhibited in London; 1920 Johannesburg, exhibition of Australian landscapes, the first of several solo exhibitions held in SA; 1924 British Empire Exhibition, Wembley, London; participated in group exhibitions 1925–39 with the SA Academy, and during the 1940s and 1950s with the Brush and Chisel Club.

Represented National Museum, Bloemfontein.

References SADNB; DBA; BSAK 1; AASA; Allister Macmillan, ed., *The Golden City, Johannesburg* (undated), Collingridge, London.

WITKIN Aaron

Born 1934 Johannesburg.

A painter of abstract paintings. Works in oil.

Studies Several lessons under G J Brusseau (qv) in Johannesburg; Central School of Art and the Chelsea School of Art, London.

Profile 1955–58 lived in London; 1958–59 in Johannesburg; 1959–62 in London; 1962–67 in Israel, where worked as an assistant to Dr Sandberg at the Israel Museum, Jerusalem and taught at an art school in Tel Aviv; in 1967 returned to London. Brother of Isaac Witkin (qv).

Exhibitions He has participated in group exhibitions from *c*.1955 in SA, the UK, Israel and France; 1967 Lidchi Gallery, Johannesburg, solo exhibition.

Award 1967 Aika Memorial Prize, Israel Museum, Jerusalem.

References SAA; BSAK 1; AASA; *Artlook* April 1967, June 1967, November 1967 & December 1967.

WITKIN Isaac

Born 1936 Johannesburg.

A sculptor.

Studies St Martin's School of Art, London, under Anthony Caro (*b*.1924).

Profile An assistant to Herman Wald (qv) in Johannesburg and a ceramics designer prior to emigrating to London *c*.1962. In London he worked as an assistant to Henry Moore (1898–1986) and taught at Maidstone and St Martin's Schools of Art. On moving to the USA he became Artist-in-Residence at Bennington College, Vermont. Revisited SA in 1981. Brother of Aaron Witkin (qv).

Exhibitions Has exhibited in London but not in SA.

Represented Tate Gallery, London.

References SAA; AASA.

WOLFE Edward RA

Born 1897 Johannesburg.

Died 1982 London, England.

A painter of landscapes, still life, figures and flowers, also a painter of portraits, particularly children's, and the occasional abstract picture. Worked in oil, using strong colours.

Studies 1914–16 in Johannesburg, under George S Smithard (qv); 1916 Regent Street Polytechnic, London, on a scholarship; 1917–19 Slade School of Art, London, under Henry Tonks (1862–1937) and Philip Wilson Steer (1860–1942).

Profile 1917 met Roger Fry (1886–1934) and joined the Omega Workshops; 1923 a member of the London Group; a member of the National Society; 1926–31 a member of the 7 & 5 Society; a member of the London Artists Association; a member of the Johannesburg Sketch Club; 1938 a member of New Group. 1971 became a Royal Academician. 1980 12 illustrations for Solomon's "Song of Songs", printed by Whittington Press, Andoversford, UK, in a limited edition of 250. 1931 and 1933 stage designs for G B Cochran Productions and in 1938 for James Laver. 1907–09 lived in England; 1910–13 toured SA as a child actor; 1914–16 lived in Johannesburg; 1917–19 in London; 1919–21 in SA; 1921 in London; 1922 in Paris and Spain; 1923–25 in Italy; 1925–34 in London; 1928 in Spain and Morocco; 1934 spent six months in New York; 1934–36 lived in Mexico; 1936–40 in London; 1940 in Dorset, where he joined the BBC; 1941–45 in Bristol, working as a censor for the BBC; 1944–46 in Portmeirion, Wales; 1946 visited Ischia, Italy; 1946–56 in London; 1956–58 in SA; 1958–64 in Rotherhithe, England and in Wales; 1964–67 based in London with visits to Spain, France, Italy, Tunisia, Gozo Island and Greece; 1967–82 in London.

Exhibitions Participated in group exhibitions from 1918 with the London Group in England, and in Europe, the USA and SA; 1918 Omega Workshops, London, first of numerous solo exhibitions held in the UK, the USA and Europe; 1920 Leon Levson Gallery, Johannesburg, first of numerous solo exhibitions held in SA; 1925 first of several exhibitions held at the Mayor Gallery, London; 1936 Empire Exhibition, Johannesburg; 1948 joint exhibition with Enslin du Plessis (qv); 1967 British Arts Council, London, and in Norwich, Wolverhampton and Derby, touring Retrospective Exhibition; 1986 Odette Gilbert Gallery, London, Retrospective Exhibition.

Represented Abbot Hall Art Gallery, Kendal, England; Belfast Museum and Art Gallery, Northern Ireland; Bootle Museum and Art Gallery, England; Clifton College, Bristol, England; civic halls of Bradford, Dublin and Hull, Great Britain; Geffrye Museum, London; Johannesburg Art Gallery; King George VI Art Gallery, Port Elizabeth; Manchester Art Gallery, England; National Museum of Wales, Cardiff; National Portrait Gallery, London, England; SA National Gallery, Cape Town; Tate Gallery, London, England; Whitworth Art Gallery, University of Manchester, England; William Humphreys Art Gallery, Kimberley; York Art Gallery, England.

Public Commissions A large number of portrait commissions.

References John Russell Taylor, *Edward Wolfe*, 1986, Trefoil Books for Odette Gilbert Gallery, London; Art SA; SAA; *Tate Gallery Catalogue—The Modern British Paintings, Drawings and Sculpture*, volume 2, 1964, Oldbourne Press, London; SAP&S; Oxford Companion to Art; Bénézit; DBA; SAP&S; BSAK 1 & 2; AASA; *South Africana* January 1956; *The Connoisseur* December 1981; *Retrospective Exhibition of Paintings and Drawings,* 1967, British Arts Council Catalogue.

WOLTER Ruth

Born 1928 Döbeln, Saxony, Germany.
Resided in SWA/Namibia and SA from 1950.
A sculptor of figures, wildlife and abstract pieces. Works in wood, bronze, ciment fondu and sgraffito.

Studies 1946–48 Dresden Art Academy, under Professor Braun; 1948–50 privately in Dresden, under Professor Melzer and in Döbeln, under Alex Pitschman and Theo Thomas.

Profile A member of the SAAA. Presently living in Pretoria.

Exhibitions 1952 Gobabis High School, SWA/Namibia, first of 10 solo exhibitions held in SWA/Namibia and SA; she has participated in several group exhibitions from 1964 in SWA/Namibia, SA and once in Austria.

Public Commissions Numerous public commissions, including: 1964 64 panels, New Legislative Buildings, Windhoek; 1965 large panel, Okaukuejo, Etosha; 1966 five large panels for the Municipality, Windhoek; 1966 Baptismal Font, Dutch Reformed Church, Windhoek; 1967 panel, Library, Walvis Bay; 1967 panel, Potchefstroom University for CHE; 1972 large panel, VIP Lounge, Jan Smuts Airport, Johannesburg; 1975 Sarcophagus and Pulpit, Windhoek Crematorium; 1979 sculpture, Postal Headquarters, Pretoria; 1986 sgraffito, Technical School, Sasolburg, Orange Free State.

Publication by Wolter *Houtsnywerk*, 1985, Tafelberg, Cape Town.

References Art SWA; AASA.

WOODROW Mervyn

Born 1932 Boksburg, Transvaal.
A painter of landscapes and figures. Works in oil.

Studies University of the Witwatersrand, under Professor Heather Martienssen (1915–79), Charles Argent (qv) and Dr Maria Stein-Lessing (1905–61).

Profile Taught at King Edward VII School, Johannesburg; the Louis Trichardt High School, Transvaal, and in 1961–62 lectured in English Literature at the Pretoria College of Education.

Exhibitions He has participated in group exhibitions from the 1950s in SA; 1969 SAAA, Pretoria, first of several solo exhibitions held throughout SA.

Represented Willem Annandale Art Gallery, Lichtenburg.

Reference SAA.

WREN-SARGENT Walter George

Born 1908 Port Elizabeth.

Died 1962 Port Elizabeth.

A painter who worked in oil and watercolour. His style ranged from realism to semi-abstract.

Studies Educated in England, studied engineering prior to art at the Regent Street Polytechnic and art at the Slade School of Art, London.

Profile 1938 a member of the New Group. Worked on Spitfire planes at Vickers, UK, and later as an illustrator in advertising. During WWII joined the SA Air Force. During the 1950s lived mainly in Zanzibar and in the Seychelles. Lived at Plettenberg Bay, Cape Province.

Exhibitions Participated in group exhibitions in SA, Norway, Sweden, Denmark (where he won a gold medal), and in London and New York; 1962 Port Elizabeth, solo exhibition; 1963 Cape Town, Memorial Exhibition; 1966 Republic Festival Exhibition.

Represented SA National Gallery, Cape Town.

Public Commissions Murals for the Franciscan Convent, Swellendam and churches in Steenberg and Grassy Park, Cape Town.

References SADNB; SAP&S; SAP&D; BSAK 1 (under Sargent Wren); SA Art; AASA; *SA Art News* 4 May 1961.

WRIGHT Henry Charles Seppings

Born 1849 Stithians, Cornwall, England.

Died 1937 England.

Thought to have resided in SA 1871–77.

A painter of portraits and landscapes, in particular scenes of the diamond fields at Kimberley in 1876 and Bloemfontein in 1876–77, and the gold mines at Pilgrim's Rest, Kuruman and Lesotho. Worked in watercolour and oil.

Profile A lithograph by him of Bloemfontein in *c*.1876 has been reproduced. Illustrated Klipdrift (now Barkly West), Cape Province, for *Some Dreams Come True* by A F Williams. From 1895 a war correspondent and artist for *The Illustrated London News*, covering campaigns in Sudan, South America, West Africa, Japan and SA, also covered WWI. He wrote a number of books on his experiences.

Exhibitions Participated in group exhibitions in London 1883–88. In 1907 a number of his SA pictures were placed on exhibition to inaugurate the Alexander McGregor Memorial Museum in Kimberley.

Represented Albany Museum, Grahamstown; McGregor Memorial Museum, Kimberley; William Fehr Collection, Cape Town.
References Pict Afr; SADNB; DSAB; DBA; AASA.

WRIGHT (Dorothy) Joan

Born 1911 Pretoria.

A painter and graphic artist of landscapes, figures, city scenes and geometric compositions. Works in oil and in various graphic media including monotype.

Studies 1929–32 Port Elizabeth Technical College, under Francis Pickford Marriott (qv) and Phyllis Gardner (qv), gaining a National Art Teachers Certificate; also studied at the Regent Street Polytechnic, London, under Norman Blamey (*fl.*1938–40) and Heatherley School of Art, under Ian Macnab (1890–1967) in England; received a BA(FA) from the University of South Africa in 1955; 1963 studied picture restoration in The Netherlands.

Profile A member of the EPSFA. From 1941 taught at the Port Elizabeth Technical College; 1961–67 an External Examiner in Fine Art for the University of Natal; 1963–72 Vice-Principal of the Port Elizabeth Technical College Art School. During the 1930s lived in Nyasaland (Malawi). Has travelled throughout Europe. The daughter of Dorothy Kay (qv).

Exhibitions She has participated in group exhibitions in SA, West Germany, Yugoslavia and Italy; 1960 and 1964 Quadrennial Exhibition.

Represented Ann Bryant Gallery, East London; King George VI Art Gallery, Port Elizabeth; SA National Gallery, Cape Town.

References Art SA; SAA (under Dorothy Wright); SAP&S; BSAK 1 & 2; Port Elizabeth School of Art; AASA.

WYLDE Geoffrey Spenser

Born 1903 Port Elizabeth.

A painter of portraits and figures. Works in oil, watercolour and pastel. An etcher.

Studies 1925–26 Michaelis School of Fine Art, under Professor John Wheatley (qv).

Profile A member of the Pastel Society, the United Society of Artists, the Chelsea Arts Club and the London Sketch Club. 1927–31 held a temporary post in the Department of Architecture at the University of Cape Town, 1931–35 a junior lecturer at the Michaelis School of Fine Art, where he taught drawing and painting from life. Taught art in London and in 1950–53 at the Sir John Cass School of Art. Lived in Cape Town and visited London in 1932 where he joined "The Twenties Group"; he then emigrated to London in the latter half of the 1930s, but continued to paint in SA on his frequent visits.

Exhibitions He has participated in many group exhibitions in SA and the UK; held solo exhibitions in SA during the 1950s.

Represented Kings College, Cambridge, England; SA National Gallery, Cape Town.

Public Commissions Numerous portrait commissions including the Mayor of Cape Town in 1970.

References *The Arts in SA*, edited by WHK, 1933–34, The Knox Printing & Publishing Company, Durban; SAA (under Wilde); SAP&D; IWAA; DBA; BSAK 1; SA Art (under Wilde); AASA.

X

XABA Gladys

Born 1943 Dundee, Natal.
A sculptor of mythical animals. Works in clay.
Profile 1973 joined the Katlehong Art Centre, Transvaal. Designs and weaves tapestries.
Exhibitions She has participated in several group exhibitions in SA.

XABA Leonard

Born 1964 Wasbank, Natal.
A sculptor of animals and figures. Works in clay.
Studies Studied at the Katlehong Art Centre, Transvaal.
Exhibitions He has participated in group exhibitions in SA.

XABA Nhlanhla Arthur

Born 1960 Payneville, Springs, Transvaal.
A painter of figures and abstract pieces. Works in oil, acrylic, wash, pencil and charcoal.
Studies 1975–79 studied under Madi Phala (qv); 1984 began studying for a BA(FA) at the University of South Africa, through Funda in Soweto.
Profile 1987 member of Artimo. 1987 teaches art at The Open School, Johannesburg. 1979–82 involved in acting and poetry reading.
Exhibitions He has participated in several group exhibitions from 1979 in SA.
Reference Echoes of African Art.

XENIDES Valentinos

Born 1928 Athens, Greece.
Resided in SA from 1960.
A painter and a sculptor.
Studies Studied painting privately; as a sculptor he is self-taught.
Exhibitions He has participated in group exhibitions in SA and Greece; 1954 Athens, solo exhibition; 1963 Cape Town, solo exhibition.
Public Commissions Statues and portrait busts for buildings in Johannesburg.
References Register SA/SWA; BSAK 1; *Fontein* Summer 1960.

Y

YATES James Charles

Born 1944 Johannesburg.

A painter of landscapes, seascapes, still life and abstract pictures. Works in oil.

Studies 1960 briefly under Machiel Brandenberg (qv).

Profile Has travelled throughout Southern Africa.

Exhibitions 1967 Muizenberg, Cape Province, first of *c.*18 solo exhibitions held in SA; he has participated in several group exhibitions from 1975 in the Cape.

Represented University of Stellenbosch.

YOUNG Kathleen Edith May

Born 1905 Queenstown, Cape Province.

A self-taught painter of landscapes, seascapes, portraits and still life. Works in oil and watercolour.

Exhibitions She has participated in several group exhibitions from 1971.

YOUNGE (James) Gavin (Forrest)

Born 1947 Bulawayo, Rhodesia (Zimbabwe).

Resided in SA from 1955.

A sculptor working in bronze, stone, ciment fondu and wood. A painter and graphic artist working in oil, pencil, charcoal and in various graphic media.

Studies 1965–68 Witwatersrand Technical College, under Joyce Leonard (qv), gaining a National Art Teachers Diploma; 1972–76 University of South Africa, under Karin Skawran, attaining a BA in Philosophy and Art History.

Profile 1976–78 co-founder of the Community Arts Project, Cape Town, presently a trustee; currently a member of the SAAA. 1972–73 a part-time lecturer in graphics at the University of Natal; 1973–75 a lecturer, then a senior lecturer in sculpture at the Natal Technical College; from 1975 a senior lecturer in sculpture at the Michaelis School of Fine Art. 1980–84 produced three television documentaries.

Exhibitions He has participated in numerous group exhibitions from 1971 throughout SA and in Australia, Botswana, West Germany and the USA; 1971 Lidchi Gallery, Johannesburg, first of eight solo exhibitions held in SA; 1977 San Francisco, California, USA, solo exhibition; 1979 Metalart Competition, Guest Artist; 1980 Metalart Guest Artists Exhibition, with Neels Coetzee (qv), Ian Redelinghuys (qv), Edoardo Villa (qv) and Johan van Heerden (qv); 1982 Cape Town Triennial; 1982 National Gallery, Gaborone, Botswana, Exhibition of SA Art; 1985 Cape Town Triennial; 1985 Tributaries, touring SA and West Germany; 1986 1820 Settlers National Monument, Grahamstown, University of the Witwatersrand, University of South Africa, Tatham Art Gallery, Pietermaritzburg and University of Cape Town, solo exhibition; 1987 Johannesburg Art Gallery, Vita Art Now.

Awards 1971 Institute of Race Relations Award, Art SA Today; 1973 Cambridge Shirt Award, Art SA Today; 1978 Metalart Prize, closed category; 1983 University of Cape Town Merit Award; 1986 Standard Bank Young Artist of the Year Award.

Represented Durban Art Gallery; Johannesburg Art Gallery; National Gallery, Gaborone, Botswana; SA National Gallery, Cape Town; University of Cape Town; University of South Africa; University of the Witwatersrand.

Public Commissions 1983 "Deep Continent", Standard Bank, Johannesburg; 1984 "From Hoerikwagga", University of Cape Town; 1985 "Talion", Johannesburg Art Gallery.

References BSAK 1 & 2; 3Cs; AASA; LSAA; *Habitat* no 32, 1978; *De Kat* December/January 1986; 1986 Standard Bank Young Artist of the Year Catalogue.

YSSEL Frederik Johannes (Basie)

Born 1956 Pretoria.

A painter, graphic artist and sculptor of abstract pieces. Works in watercolour, gouache, ink, wash, pencil, charcoal, various graphic media, bronze, ciment fondu, wood and steel.

Studies 1976–79 Pretoria Technical College (Technikon), under Koos den Houting (qv), Ian Redelinghuys (qv) and Richard Adams (qv), gaining a National Diploma in Art and Design (sculpture) in 1978 and a Higher Diploma in Art (sculpture) in 1979.

Profile 1981–83 a temporary lecturer and from 1984 a lecturer at the Pretoria Technikon. From 1977 has made several visits to SWA/Namibia, Namaqualand and the Richtersveld in the Northern Cape.

Exhibitions He has participated in several group exhibitions from 1981 in SA; 1981 SAAA Gallery, Pretoria, solo exhibition; 1981 Republic Festival Exhibition; 1982 Gallery 21, Johannesburg, joint exhibition with Koos den Houting (qv); 1985 Ivan Solomon Gallery, Pretoria, joint exhibition with A Schönfeldt.

Awards 1979 First Prize Sculpture, New Signatures, SAAA, Pretoria.

Reference AASA.

YUDELOWITZ Ruth MBE

Born 1914 Johannesburg.

A painter of landscapes, portraits, figures and wildlife. Works in oil, watercolour, ink, wash, pencil and charcoal.

Studies 1932–38 Witwatersrand Technical College, under James Gardner (qv); 1943–44 studied architecture at the University of Cape Town; 1946–49 at the Central School of Art, London, UK, and the Royal Academy of Art, Stockholm, Sweden.

Profile From 1934 illustrated numerous books for Government offices, in SA, Kenya and the UK. During WWII joined the SA Womens Auxiliary Service and the SA Coastal Artillery Command. Has painted many murals and designed textiles. In 1963 appointed a Member of the Order of the British Empire for services to Her Majesty's Overseas Civil Service, from which she retired in 1964. She has not painted since the late 1970s.
Exhibitions She has participated in several exhibitions from 1940.
Reference BSAK 1.

Z

ZAAL Jan Professor

Born 1925 Utrecht, The Netherlands.

Resided in SA from 1936.

A painter of landscapes and cityscapes. Works in oil and acrylic.

Studies 1966–69 Sacramento City College, California, USA, under Wayne Thiebaud (*b.*1920); 1973–74 University of South Africa.

Profile From 1980 a member of the SAAA. A Professor of English at the University of Zululand, Umlazi, Natal. 1965 visited Chicago; 1965–69 lived in San Francisco; 1973 made an art tour of European cities; 1976 visited New York and Washington DC, USA.

Exhibitions He has participated in group exhibitions from 1968 in the USA and in Durban; 1987 NSA Gallery, Durban, joint exhibition with A Minnie Cook (qv) and N Carol Thomson (qv).

ZANDER Konrad Erhard

Born 1920 Windhoek.

A painter of wildlife. Works in acrylic, watercolour and ink.

Studies Prior to WWII studied under Johannes Blatt (qv) in Swakopmund, SWA/Namibia; 1965 a number of art lessons in West Germany.

Profile A member of the Arts Association SWA/Namibia. A number of his works have been used in calendars and on cards. A designer of wool carpets. 1947–84 a farmer in north-west SWA/Namibia.

Exhibitions 1959 Grootfontein, SWA/Namibia, first of 20 solo exhibitions held in SWA/Namibia, SA and West Germany; he has participated in many group exhibitions from 1960 in SWA/Namibia, SA and West Germany.

Award 1968 Prince Bernhard Medal in Bronze, Interfanne Exhibition, West Germany.

Represented Arts Association SWA/Namibia Collection; Willem Annandale Art Gallery, Lichtenburg.

References Art SWA; AASA.

ZENITHA see STEENBEEK Greta

ZERFFI Florence Louise Josephine

Born 1882 London, England.

Died 1962 London, England.

Resided in SA 1916–56.

A painter of still life, interiors, landscapes, portraits, street scenes of Cape Town and a number of night scenes. Worked in oil, watercolour, gouache, ink, charcoal and pastel. A series of the Cape Malay Quarter. Painted mostly indoors owing to her dislike of the harsh SA light. Numerous linocuts.

Studies Technical School, Stockport, England; 1906–16 in Berlin, at the Königliche Kunstgewerbeschule, under Professor Emil Orlik (1870–1932), Professor Otto Marcus (*b*.1863), Leo von Konig (1871–1944) and Professor Georg Tippel, awarded a Silver Medal; also privately under Professor Emil Doepler.

Profile 1916 a member of the SA Society of Artists; 1922 a founder member of the K Group; 1938 a founder member of the New Group; a member of the Eastern Province Society of Artists. Illustrations for *Die Burger, Die Huisgenoot* and the book *Die Eensame Hoop*, by C J Langenhoven, 1922. Was involved in the preservation of buildings in Cape Town. 1921–24 Curator of The Michaelis Collection, Cape Town; 1929–56 taught painting privately and at the Wynberg Girls and Boys High Schools and the South African College Schools in Cape Town. 1956 moved to London. 1924 married Harry Stratford Caldecott (qv).

Exhibitions Participated in group exhibitions from 1916; held numerous solo exhibitions; 1923 joint exhibition with Ruth Prowse (qv) and Nita Spilhaus (qv); 1925 Ashbey's Gallery, Cape Town, joint exhibition with Harry Stratford Caldecott (qv); 1953 Rhodes Centenary Exhibition, Bulawayo, Rhodesia (Zimbabwe); 1957 SAAA Gallery, Cape Town, Retrospective Exhibition; from 1959 exhibited in London; 1982 SA National Gallery, Cape Town, Commemorative Exhibition.

Represented Durban Art Gallery; Johannesburg Art Gallery; Pretoria Art Museum; SA National Gallery, Cape Town; University of the Orange Free State; University of Pretoria; University of Stellenbosch; William Humphreys Art Gallery, Kimberley.

References J du P Scholtz, *Strat Caldecott*, 1970, A A Balkema, Cape Town; PSA; Collectors' Guide; Art SA; SAA; SADNB; 20C SA Art; DSAB; SAP&S; SAP&D; SESA; SSAP; BSAK 1 & 2; 3Cs; AASA; LSAA.

ZIQUBU Ephraim

Born 1948 Rorke's Drift, Natal.
A sculptor of mythical animals. Works in clay.
Studies Rorke's Drift Art Centre, Natal.
Profile A member of the Katlehong Art Centre, Transvaal.
Exhibitions He has partcipated in group exhibitions in SA; 1985 Tributaries, touring SA and West Germany.

ZONDI Michael

Born 1926 Msinga, Natal.
A sculptor of figures. Works in wood.
Studies Trained as a cabinet maker at a mission school in Dundee, Natal. Gained a Teachers Diploma in Woodwork.
Profile 1952–56 a teacher at the Dundee Trade School; 1956–63 at Edenvale Vocational School, Transvaal. 1967–72 a programme promoter for African arts and crafts, Department of Information, Durban.

Exhibitions He has participated in group exhibitions from 1961 in SA, Italy and Austria; 1979 Contemporary African Art in SA, touring; 1981 Standard Bank, Soweto, Black Art Today Exhibition.

Awards 1965 Phillip Frame Award, Art SA Today; 1966 Bronze Medal, Sculpture, Republic Festival Exhibition.

Represented Durban Art Gallery; SA National Gallery, Cape Town; University of Fort Hare; University of Stellenbosch.

References BSAK 1; 3Cs; AASA; Echoes of African Art; *The Condenser* December 1966; *SA Panorama* February 1975 & July 1982.

ZULU Ndabenhle William

Born 1958 Mondlo, Natal.

An artist depicting figures and portraits. Works in watercolour, ink, pencil and in various graphic media.

Studies 1977–78 Rorke's Drift Art Centre, Natal, under Jules van de Vijver (qv), Ada van de Vijver (qv) and Eric Mbatha (qv), where he obtained an Art Certificate.

Profile A weaver and a photographer.

Exhibitions He has participated in several group exhibitions from 1982.

ZULU Sandile Conrad

Born 1961 Ixopo, Natal.

A painter and graphic artist of landscapes, figures, portraits and abstract pictures. Works in oil, acrylic, watercolour, gouache, ink, wash, pencil, charcoal and in various graphic media. Makes collages and works in pottery.

Studies 1982 Rorke's Drift Art Centre, Natal, gaining a Diploma; 1983 on a bursary from the African Bursary Fund at the Natal Technikon.

Profile 1984 taught at St Joseph's Art Workshop and the Community Art Workshop, Durban. A poet.

Exhibitions He has participated in several group exhibitions in Natal and once in Swaziland in 1983.

ZULU Thabani Derrick

Born 1950 Eshowe, Natal.

A painter and graphic artist of landscapes, portraits, still life, figures, abstract works and genre, particularly of urban life. Works in oil, ink, pencil, charcoal and in various graphic media.

Studies 1972 Ndaleni Educational Training School, Natal; presently studying for a BA(FA) through the University of South Africa.

Profile 1977–80 taught at Ohlange High School; 1980–82 an art teacher at Umzuvele High School; from 1983 an art teacher at Esikhawini College of Education, Natal. 1986 on the subject committee for Art, Department of Education, Transvaal. 1981 designed a record cover for Sipho Gumede.

Exhibitions He has participated in several group exhibitions from 1980.
Award 1981 First Prize in Drawing and Painting, University of Zululand Festival of African Art.
Public Commissions 1979 mural and portrait of the Founder of the Ohlange High School; 1981 Founder's portrait, Dr Dube High School.

ZULU Vuminkosi

Born 1948 KwaZulu, Natal.
A graphic artist.
Studies 1970–72 Rorke's Drift Art Centre, Natal.
Exhibitions He has participated in numerous group exhibitions in SA and overseas; 1979 Contemporary African Art in SA, touring; 1985 Tributaries, touring SA and West Germany.
Award 1973 Hajee Suliman Ebrahim Memorial Trust Award, Art SA Today.
Represented Ann Bryant Gallery, East London; SA National Gallery, Cape Town; University of Fort Hare; University of South Africa.
Reference AASA.

ZUNGU Tito

Born *c.*1946 Mapumulo District, KwaZulu, Natal.
An artist of cityscapes, aeroplanes and ships. Works in ballpoint pen and koki pen.
Profile Began drawing on the backs of envelopes, later producing larger drawings with the frame and mount becoming part of the whole picture. 1976 invited by *African Arts Magazine*, University of California, Los Angeles, to design the cover for its US Bicentennial issue.
Exhibitions He has participated in several group exhibitions from 1965 in Durban and Johannesburg; 1982 University of the Witwatersrand, solo exhibition; 1985 Tributaries, touring SA and West Germany; 1987 Primitive Arts and Antiques, Rosebank, Johannesburg, solo exhibition; 1988 Johannesburg Art Gallery, Vita Art Now.
Award 1971 prizewinner, Art SA Today.
Represented Durban Art Gallery; Johannesburg Art Gallery; SA National Gallery, Cape Town; Tatham Art Gallery, Pietermaritzburg; University of Fort Hare; University of South Africa; University of the Witwatersrand.
References BSAK; AASA; *SA Arts Calendar* March 1983.

ZWAAF George

Born 1909 Scheveningen, The Netherlands.
Resided in SA from 1948.
Depicts portraits and flowers.
Profile A founder member of the Natal Group.
Exhibitions Has exhibited his work in Durban.
References SAA; AASA.

ZYLLA Manfred

Born 1939 Augsburg, Germany.

Resided in SA from 1970.

A painter and a graphic artist of landscapes, portraits, still life, figures, genre and of pictures containing socio-political comment. Works in oil, acrylic, watercolour, ink, pencil, wood and in various graphic media. Creates mosaics.

Studies 1959–60 life drawing at a night school in Augsburg, West Germany, under Butz, however, he is mainly self-taught.

Profile From 1980 a member of the SAAA. 1981–84 taught printmaking at the Michaelis School of Fine Art; from 1985 a part-time teacher in etching at the Community Arts Project, Cape Town. A number of illustrations for books and periodicals. Has travelled throughout Europe and in 1972 to India, Nepal, Pakistan, Afghanistan, Turkey, Iran and Egypt.

Exhibitions He has participated in numerous group exhibitions from 1950 in West Germany, SA and Botswana; 1965 Ulm, West Germany, first of seven solo exhibitions held in West Germany and SA; 1982 National Gallery, Gaborone, Botswana, Exhibition of SA Art; 1985 Tributaries, touring SA and West Germany.

Represented Augsburg Archives, West Germany; Durban Art Gallery; National Gallery, Gaborone, Botswana; New Hospital, Munich, West Germany; SA National Gallery, Cape Town.

Publication by Zylla "Inter-Action", 1982, a report of a "happening" at the Community Arts Project, Cape Town.

ZYTKOW Sonja Janina

Born 1952 Johannesburg.

A sculptor and painter of humorous animals. Works in ceramics, clay, acrylic, watercolour and gouache. 1975–78 a series entitled "The Travels of Huberta the Hippo"; 1980–85 a series of birds; from 1985 a series of crocodiles.

Studies 1971–72 Cardiff College of Art, Wales; 1972–75 Sheffield College of Art, UK, gaining a BA(FA) (Hons); 1976–78 California College of Art, USA, under Viola Frey and David Middlebrook, attaining an MFA in ceramic sculpture.

Profile 1978 an assistant lecturer at the California College of Art, USA; 1978 visiting lecturer at Cardiff, Sheffield and North London Colleges of Art, UK; 1979 visiting lecturer, Exeter College of Art, UK; 1981–84 a part-time lecturer in the Ceramics Department of the Witwatersrand Technikon; 1986 visiting lecturer, Sheffield College of Art, UK. 1983, with Ros O'Connor, established "Ceramic Designs", a commercial ceramic factory; 1985–86 produced and directed a documentary film on transitional art in Venda. 1955–69 lived in Zambia; 1969–75 in the UK; 1976–79 in the USA; thereafter in SA.

Exhibitions 1971 Kitwe, Zambia, first of seven solo exhibitions held in Zambia and SA; she has participated in numerous group exhibitions from 1972 in Zambia, the UK, the USA and SA; 1985 Cape Town Triennial; 1987 Johannesburg Art Gallery, Vita Art Now.

Represented William Humphreys Art Gallery, Kimberley.

References *Style* September 1986; *Sgraffiti* no 42.

FAMILY TREES

King/Everard family tree

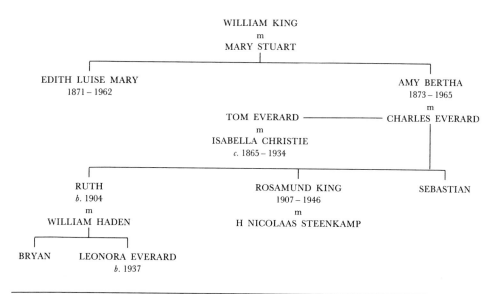

WILLIAM KING
m
MARY STUART

EDITH LUISE MARY
1871 – 1962

AMY BERTHA
1873 – 1965
m

TOM EVERARD ———————— CHARLES EVERARD
m
ISABELLA CHRISTIE
c. 1865 – 1934

RUTH
b. 1904
m
WILLIAM HADEN

ROSAMUND KING
1907 – 1946
m
H NICOLAAS STEENKAMP

SEBASTIAN

BRYAN   LEONORA EVERARD
b. 1937

Wiles family tree

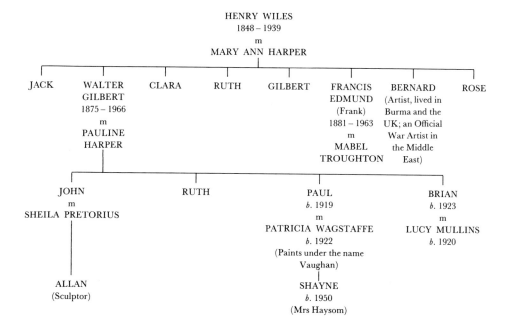

HENRY WILES
1848 – 1939
m
MARY ANN HARPER

JACK   WALTER
         GILBERT
         1875 – 1966
         m
         PAULINE
         HARPER

CLARA   RUTH   GILBERT   FRANCIS
                                EDMUND
                                (Frank)
                                1881 – 1963
                                m
                                MABEL
                                TROUGHTON

BERNARD
(Artist, lived in
Burma and the
UK; an Official
War Artist in
the Middle
East)

ROSE

JOHN
m
SHEILA PRETORIUS

RUTH

PAUL
b. 1919
m
PATRICIA WAGSTAFFE
b. 1922
(Paints under the name
Vaughan)

BRIAN
b. 1923
m
LUCY MULLINS
b. 1920

ALLAN
(Sculptor)

SHAYNE
b. 1950
(Mrs Haysom)

Dates denote an artist.

SELECT BIBLIOGRAPHY

Published Works

A Dictionary of Art and Artists, Peter and Linda Murray, 4th edition 1976, Penguin Books, Middlesex, England.

A Dictionary of British Animal Painters, J C Wood, 1973, F Lewis, Leigh-on-Sea, UK.

A Dictionary of Victorian Painters, Christopher Wood, 1971, The Antique Collectors' Club, Woodbridge, Suffolk, UK.

A Guide to Sources on Irma Stern, L S Daneel, 1981, Human Sciences Research Council, Pretoria.

Abraham de Smidt 1829–1908, Marjorie Bull, 1981, Printpak, Cape Town.

Adolph Jentsch, Olga Levinson, 1973 and 1974, Human & Rousseau, Cape Town.

African Portrait. The Life and Sculpture of Sister Joe Vorster, Naxa Pillman, 1976, Keartland, Johannesburg.

Africana Books and Pictures, Frank R Bradlow, 1975, A A Balkema, Cape Town.

Africana Repository, R F Kennedy, 1965, Juta & Co., Johannesburg.

Akademie 75, Akademie vir Wetenskap en Kuns, 1975, Pretoria.

Alexis Preller, Christi Truter, 1947, The Maroola Press, Pretoria.

Animal Art of Etosha, Department of Agriculture and Nature Conservation, SWA/Namibia, in collaboration with the Southern African Nature Foundation, 1986, Windhoek/Stellenbosch.

Anna Vorster A Biography, Le Riche Kruger, 1983, CUM Books, Roodepoort.

Anton Anreith, Africa's First Sculptor, C de Bosdari, 1954, A A Balkema, Cape Town.

Anton Anreith. Sculptor 1754–1822, J P Meintjes, 1951, Juta, Cape Town.

Anton van Wouw 1862–1945 en die Van Wouwhuis, Universiteit van Pretoria, 1981, Butterworth, Durban/Pretoria.

Anton van Wouw, Sculptor of South African Life, Morris J Cohen, 1938, Radford Adlington, Johannesburg.

Armando Baldinelli, Albert Werth, 1974, Gallery 21, Johannesburg.

Art and Articles in honour of Heather Martienssen, edited by F Harmsen, 1973, A A Balkema, Cape Town.

Art and Artists of South Africa, Esmé Berman, 1983, A A Balkema, Cape Town.

Art in South Africa, Painting, Sculpture and Graphic Work since 1900, F L Alexander, 1962, A A Balkema, Cape Town.

Art in South West Africa, Nico Roos, 1978, J P van der Walt, Pretoria.

Baines on the Zambesi, Edward C Tabler, 1982, Brenthurst Press, Johannesburg.

Baldinelli, Umbro Apollonio, 1964, Edizione d'Arte Moderna, Rome, Italy.

Barbers of the Peak, I Mitford-Barberton, 1934, Oxford University Press, Oxford, UK.

Battiss in the Hadhramaut – Sketches of Southern Arabia, Murray and Elzabé Schoonraad, 1985, Elmur Publications, Pretoria.

Battiss 75, Murray Schoonraad and Peter Duminy, 1981, D & S Publishers, Pietermaritzburg.

Bibliografie: Suid-Afrikaanse Kunstenaars, F G E Nilant & M Schoonraad, 2 vols, 1976 & 1986, Kunsargief, Universiteit van Pretoria, Pretoria.

British Settlers in Natal 1824–1857, a biographical register, Shelagh O'Byrne Spencer, 2 vols, 1981 & 1983, University of Natal Press, Pietermaritzburg.

Catalogue of Pictures in the Africana Museum, R F Kennedy, 7 vols, 1966–1972, Africana Museum, Johannesburg.

Cecil Higgs, Victor Holloway, 1974, South African Art Library, C Struik, Cape Town.

Christopher Webb Smith. An Artist at the Cape of Good Hope 1837–1839, A Gordon-Brown, 1965, Howard Timmins, Cape Town.

Claude Bouscharain, Bruce Arnott, 1977, South African Art Library, C Struik, Cape Town.

Coert Steynberg, Edgar C L Bosman, 1968, Suid-Afrikaanse Kunsmonografie, J L van Schaik, Pretoria.

Coert Steynberg 'n Outobiografie, Coert Steynberg, 1982, CUM Books, Roodepoort.

Complex Canvas, J P Meintjes, 1960, Afrikaner Pers, Johannesburg.

Contemporary African Art, E J de Jager, 1973, C Struik, Cape Town.

Contemporary Artists, edited by C Naylor and G P-Orridge, 1977, St James Press, London, UK.

Contemporary British Artists, edited by C Parry-Crooke, 1979, Bergstrom & Boyle Books, London, UK.

D C Boonzaier en Pieter Wenning Verslag van 'n Vriendskap, J du P Scholtz, 1973, Tafelberg, Cape Town.

Designs on Life, E Ullman, 1970, Howard Timmins, Cape Town.

Dictionary of Military Abbreviations, British Empire and Commonwealth, P K B Scott, 1982, Tamarisk Books, Hastings, UK.

Dictionary of Sea Painters, E H Archibald, 1980, The Antique Collectors' Club, Woodbridge, Suffolk, UK.

Dictionary of South African Biographies, edited by C Beyers, 5 vols, 1968–1987, Human Sciences Research Council, Pretoria.

Dictionnaire Critique et Documentaire des Peintres, Sculpteurs, Dessinateurs et Graveurs, E Bénézit, vols 1–10, nouvelle edition 1976, Librairie Gründ, Paris, France.

Die Dagboek van Johannes Meintjes, Johannes Meintjes, 3 vols, 1975, Bamboesberg Uitgewers, Molteno, Cape Province.

Die Hout- en Linoseë van J H Pierneef, F G E Nilant, 1974, A A Balkema, Cape Town.

Directory of Publishing in Great Britain, the Commonwealth, Ireland, Pakistan and South Africa, Cassell and the Publishers Association, 1983, Cassell, London.

Echoes of African Art, A Century of Art in South Africa, Matsemela Manaka, 1987, Skotaville Publishers, Johannesburg.

Edoardo Villa Sculpture, edited by E P Engel, 1980, United Book Distributors, Johannesburg.

Edward Wolfe, J Russell-Taylor, 1986, Trefoil Books, London.

Encyclopedia of Southern Africa, E Rosenthal, 7th edition 1978, Juta & Co., Cape Town.

Encyclopedia of Australian Art, Alan McCulloch, reprint with corrections 1977, Hutchinson Group (Australia), Richmond, Victoria, Australia.

English Art and Modernism 1900–1939, Charles Harrison, 1981, Allen Lane, London.

Esias Bosch, Andree Bosch and Johann de Waal, 1988, C Struik–Winchester, Cape Town.

François Krige Drawings Tekeninge, François Krige, introduction by Willem Gravett, 1971, Tafelberg, Cape Town.

François Le Vaillant, edited by J C Quinton and A M Lewin Robinson, 2 vols, 1973, Library of Parliament, Cape Town.

Frans Claerhout, F P Scott, L Roppe, P Rock and F Jonckheere, 1975, Vriende Frans Claerhout Hasselt Belgie, Drukkerij-Uitgeverij Lannoo, Belgium.

Frans Claerhout – Catcher of the Sun, Leon Strydom, 1983, Tafelberg, Cape Town.

Frederick I'Ons – Artist, J Redgrave and E Bradlow, 1958, Maskew Miller, Cape Town.

Gerard de Leeuw, Matthys J Strydom, 1979, Suidkaap-Uitgewery, George.

Gregoire Boonzaier, F P Scott, 1964, Tafelberg, Cape Town.

Guide to the Museums of Southern Africa, Hans Fransen, 1978, Galvin & Sales (Pty) Ltd (for the Southern African Museums Association), Cape Town.

Gwelo Goodman – South African Artist, Joyce Newton-Thompson, 1951, Howard Timmins, Cape Town.

Heinrich Egersdorfer, Eric Rosenthal, 1960, Nasionale Boekhandel, Cape Town.

Hendrik Pierneef The Man and his Work, J F W Grosskopf, 1947, J L van Schaik, Pretoria.

Hugo Naudé, Adèle Naudé, 1974, South African Art Library, C Struik, Cape Town.

In the Heart of the Tiger, Azaria Mbatha, with text by Werner Eichel, 1986, Verlag der Vereinigten Evangelischen Mission, Wuppertal, Hammer, Wuppertal, West Germany.

Insights, selected essays by Heather Martienssen, edited by S G Kossick, 1984, Ad Donker, Johannesburg.

International Who's Who in Art and Antiques, Ernest Kay, 1972, Melrose Press, Cambridge, UK.

Irma Stern, Max Osborn, 1927, Klinkhardt und Bierman, Leipzig, Germany.

Irma Stern, Neville Dubow, 1974, South African Art Library, C Struik, Cape Town.

Irma Stern and the Spirit of Africa, Joseph Sachs, 1942, J L van Schaik, Pretoria.

Irmin Henkel, M Henkel and K Skawran, 1983, Butterworth, Durban/Pretoria.

Ivan Mitford-Barberton – Sculptor, Ivan Mitford-Barberton, 1962, HAUM, Pretoria.

Jock – The Art of Edmund Caldwell, 1978, text by Jan Meiring, and *The Art of Edmund Caldwell*, volume 2, 1982, text by F R Bradlow, Frank Read Press, Mazoe, Zimbabwe.

John Muafangejo, Bruce Arnott, 1977, South African Art Library, C Struik, Cape Town.

Katrine Harries, Life and Work, J du P Scholtz, 1978, Tafelberg, Cape Town.

Kromdraai, F M Claerhout, 1972, Errol Marks Uitgewers, Pretoria.

Kuns en Kunswaardering, A C Bouman, 1942, J L van Schaik, Pretoria.

Kuns in Suid-Afrika, A C Bouman, 1938, HAUM, Cape Town.

Kunsgeskiedenis – Skilderkuns, B van Niekerk, 1942, Nasionale Pers, Bloemfontein.

Laura Rautenbach, Kobus Smit, 1986, Laura Rautenbach, Kerelaw.

Lippy Lipshitz, a biographical commentary and documentation of the years 1903–1968 with catalogue raisonné of sculptures, Bruce Arnott, 1969, A A Balkema, Cape Town.

Looking at South African Art, A guide to the study and appreciation of art, Frieda Harmsen, 1985, J L van Schaik, Pretoria.

Lucas Sithole 1958–1979, F F Haenggi, 1979, Gallery 21, Johannesburg.

Lyrical Works, J P Meintjes, 1948, Anreith Press, Cape Town.

Maggie Laubser, J P Meintjes, 1944, J H du Bussy/HAUM, Cape Town.

Maggie Laubser, Johan van Rooyen, 1974, South African Art Library, C Struik, Cape Town.

Malay & Cape Sketches, Leng Dixon, with introduction by Ruth Prowse, 1952, Maskew Miller, Cape Town.

Maud Summer, Charles Eglington, undated, Purnell & Sons, Cape Town.

Maurice van Essche, Carl Buchner, 1967, Tafelberg, Cape Town.

Moses Kottler, His Cape Years, J du P Scholtz, 1976, Tafelberg, Cape Town.

My Father, Harco Wenning, 1976, Howard Timmins, Cape Town.

My Kwas Vertel, W H Coetzer, 1947, Boek-en-Kunssentrum, Johannesburg.

Natal Art before Union, J A Verbeek, 1974, University of Natal Library, Pietermaritzburg.

Ons Erfenis, V de Kock, 1960, Nasionale Boekhandel, Cape Town.

Oor Skilders en Skrywers, J du P Scholtz, 1979, Tafelberg, Cape Town.

Otto Landsberg 1803–1905, 19th Century South African Artist, Simon A de Villiers, 1974, C Struik, Cape Town.

Our Art 1, undated *c.*1960; *Our Art 2*, 1961; *Our Art 3*, undated *c.*1978, Foundation for Education, Science and Technology, Pretoria.

Painters of South Africa, A C Bouman, 1948, HAUM & J H de Bussy, Cape Town, Amsterdam and Pretoria.

Painters SWA/Namibia, L Heinze and U Oldorf, 1983, CUM Books, Roodepoort.

Pen sketse/Sketches, W H Coetzer, 1982, CUM Books, Roodepoort.

Phafa-Nyika, Contemporary Black Art in South Africa with special reference to the Transvaal, edited by Ute Scholz, 1980, Archives, Department of History of Art, University of Pretoria, Pretoria.

Pictorial Africana A survey of old South African paintings, drawings and prints to the end of the nineteenth century with a biographical dictionary of one thousand artists, A Gordon-Brown, 1975, A A Balkema, Cape Town.

Pictorial Art in Southern Africa during Three Centuries to 1875, with notes on over four hundred artists, A Gordon-Brown, 1952, Charles J Sawyer, London.

Pioneers of Rhodesia, Edward C Tabler, 1966, C Struik, Cape Town.

Port Elizabeth School of Art, A History 1882–1982, Hunter Nesbit, 1982, Port Elizabeth Technikon, Port Elizabeth.

Portraits of Game and Wild Animals of Southern Africa, W Cornwallis Harris, with introduction by Edmund C Tabler, 1969, A A Balkema, Cape Town.

Potters of Southern Africa, C Clark and L Wagner, 1974, C Struik, Cape Town.

Pranas Domsaitis, Elsa Verloren van Themaat, 1976, South African Art Library, C Struik, Cape Town.

Reginald Turvey/Life and Art, edited by Lowell Johnson, 1986, George Ronald, Oxford, UK.

Register of South African and South-West African Artists 1900–1969, South African Association of Arts, 1969, Cape Town.

Rust en Vreugd, A Pictorial Narrative, Guide to the Collection, W Fehr, 1965 William Fehr Collection, Cape Town.

Sketches by Ida Mae Stone and Harry Clayton, Anna H Smith, 1976, Ad Donker, Johannesburg.

Sketse en Gedagtes vir die Simfonie van die Sonnevanger, F M Claerhout, undated *c.*1982–83, Roman Catholic Mission, Tweespruit.

Skone Kunste in Suid-Afrika, P J Nienaber, 1951, Afrikaanse Pers-Boekhandel, Johannesburg.

Solomon Caesar Malan Akwarelle, B Booysens and O Schröder, 1970, Human & Rousseau, Cape Town.

South African Art, James Ambrose Brown, 1978, Macdonald Heritage Library Series, Macdonald, South Africa.

South African Artists 1900–1962, Harold Jeppe, 1963, Afrikaanse Pers-Boekhandel, Johannesburg.

South African Dictionary of National Biography, Eric Rosenthal, 1966, Frederick Warne, London.

South African Graphic Art and its Techniques, F L Alexander, completed and edited by Roman Waher, 1974, Human & Rousseau, Cape Town.

South African Painting and Sculpture Catalogue, compiled by M Bull, 1970, South African National Gallery, Cape Town.

South African Prints and Drawings Catalogue, compiled by M Bull, 1971, South African National Gallery, Cape Town.

Standard Encyclopaedia of Southern Africa, edited by D J Potgieter, 12 vols from 1970, Nasionale Boekhandel, London.

Stillewes/Still Lifes, W H Coetzer, 1982, CUM Books, Roodepoort.

Strat Caldecott, J du P Scholtz, 1970, A A Balkema, Cape Town.

Suid-Afrikaanse Spot- en Strookprent- kunstenaars, M Schoonraad en E Schoonraad, 1983, CUM Books, Roodepoort.

Sydney Carter, Elizabeth Carter, 1948, The Swan Press, Johannesburg.

Tate Gallery Catalogue – The Modern British Paintings, Drawings and Sculpture, vols 1 & 2, 1964, Oldbourne Press, London.

The Arts in South Africa, edited by WHK, 1933–34, The Knox Printing & Publishing Co., Durban.

The Birds of South Africa painted by Thomas Baines, R F Kennedy, 1975, Winchester Press, Johannesburg.

The Black Who's Who of Southern Africa Today, Sheila Keeble, 1979–82, African Business Publications, Johannesburg.

The Brenthurst Baines, Marius and Joy Diemont, 1975, Brenthurst Press, Johannesburg.

The Cape Sketchbooks of Sir Charles D'Oyly, introduction by A Gordon-Brown, 1968, A A Balkema, Cape Town.

The Collectors' Guide to South African Artists, E W Read, 1953, Pieter Wenning Gallery/ Everard Read Gallery, Johannesburg.

The Concise Illustrated South African Encyclopaedia, Peter Schrimer, 1980, Central News Agency, Johannesburg.

The Dictionary of British Artists 1880–1940, J Johnson and A Greutzner, 1976, The Antique Collector's Club, Woodbridge, Suffolk, UK.

The Kingsmead Heritage, Margot Bryant, undated, The Kingsmead Foundation, Johannesburg.

The Naked Eye, D Lewis, 1946, Paul Koston, Cape Town.

The Oxford Companion to Art, edited by Harold Osborne, 1970, Oxford University Press, Oxford, UK.

The Oxford Companion to Twentieth Century Art, edited by Harold Osborne, 1981, Oxford University Press, Oxford, UK.

The Paintings of J H Amshewitz RBA, Sarah Briana Amshewitz, 1951, B T Batsford Ltd, London.

The Pocket Dictionary of Art Terms, Julia Ehresmann (revised and enlarged by James Hall), 1980, John Murray (Publishers) Ltd, London.

The Story of South Africa House, R Macnab, 1983, Jonathan Ball, Johannesburg.

The Story of South African Painting, Esmé Berman, 1974, A A Balkema, Cape Town.

The Story of the British Settlers of 1820 in South Africa, H E Hockley, 2nd edition 1957, Juta & Co., Cape Town.

The Women of Bonnefoi, Frieda Harmsen, 1980, J L van Schaik, Pretoria.

They Came to South Africa, Fay Jaffe, 1963, Howard Timmins, Cape Town.

Thomas Baines, his art in Rhodesia, J P R Wallis, 1956, Central African Archives, Salisbury, Rhodesia (Harare, Zimbabwe).

Thomas Baines, his life and explorations in South Africa, Rhodesia and Australia 1820–1875, J P R Wallis, with captions and a new introduction by F R Bradlow, 1976, A A Balkema, Cape Town.

Thomas Bowler, His Life and Work, Frank R Bradlow, 1967, A A Balkema, Cape Town.

Thomas Bowler in Mauritius, a detail in the history of contacts between The Cape of Good Hope and Mauritius, 1866–68, Frank R Bradlow, 1970, A A Balkema, Cape Town.

Thomas Bowler of The Cape of Good Hope, his life and works with a catalogue of extant paintings, Frank and Edna Bradlow, 1955, A A Balkema, Cape Town.

Three Centuries of South African Art, Hans Fransen, 1982, Ad Donker, Johannesburg.

Tretchikoff, Richard Buncher, 1950, Howard Timmins, Cape Town.

Twentieth Century South African Art, introductions by M Bokhorst and H Martienssen, 1966, Human & Rousseau, Pretoria.

W H Coetzer 80, W H Coetzer, 1980, CUM Books, Roodepoort.

Walter Battiss, M Schoonraad, 1976, South African Art Library, C Struik, Cape Town.

War Artists in South Africa, A C R Carter, 1900, The Art Annual, London.

Wenning, G Boonzaier and L Lipshitz, 1949, Unie-Volkspers Beperk, Cape Town.

Who's Who in Art, numerous editions, The Art Trade Press Ltd, Havant, Hants, UK.

Wolf Kibel – A brief sketch of his life and a critical assessment of his work, Neville Dubow and Frieda Kibel, 1968, Human & Rousseau, Pretoria.

World Encyclopaedia of Naive Art, edited by O Bihalji-Merin and N B Tomašević, 1984, Frederick Muller, London.

Zakkie Eloff, Drawn From Life, Sue Hart, 1982, Chris van Rensburg Publications, Johannesburg.

Zoltan Borbereki – Sculptures in Semi-Precious Stones, F Haenggi, 1981, Gallery 21, Johannesburg.

Individual Catalogues

These are listed under the name of the artist rather than by title.

Keith Alexander: *Keith Alexander: The artist & his work*, undated, Elizabeth White & Associates, Johannesburg.

Marion Arnold: *Marion Arnold – Encounters*, 1985, The Standard Bank Young Artists Award, 1820 Settlers National Monument, Grahamstown, text by Karin M Skawran.

Armando Baldinelli: *Armando Baldinelli Yesterday and Today*, 1984, University of the Witwatersrand, Johannesburg, article by Professor Reingard Nethersole.

Armando Baldinelli: *Armando Baldinelli, Part of South Africa's heritage*, 1987, Matignon Fine Art, Johannesburg.

Philip Bawcombe: *The World War II works of Philip Bawcombe*, 1981, SA National Museum of Military History, Johannesburg, foreword by G B Duxbury.

Gregoire Boonzaier: *Gregoire Boonzaier*, 1985, University of Pretoria, foreword by Professor D M Joubert.

Ben Burrage: *The World War II works of Burrage*, 1981, SA National Museum of Military History, Johannesburg, foreword by G B Duxbury.

Nils Burwitz: *Nils Burwitz 1960–1985*, 1985, Palau Solleric, Palma, Spain, text in Spanish by José Corredor-Matheos and Zoran Krzisnik.

Norman Catherine: *Norman Catherine 1986/87 Recent paintings, sculpture and assemblages*, 1987, Goodman Gallery, Johannesburg, foreword by Raymund van Niekerk, review by John Howell.

Giuseppe Cattaneo: *Retrospective Exhibition Catalogue*, 1977, University of the Witwatersrand, Johannesburg.

Bettie Cilliers-Barnard: *Bettie Cilliers-Barnard*, 1974, SAAA, Pretoria, text by A J Werth.

Christo Coetzee: *Christo Coetzee*, 1983, Pretoria Art Museum, foreword by A J Werth.

Tinus de Jongh: *Tinus de Jongh Memorial Gallery*, undated, Lanzerac, Stellenbosch.

Nel Erasmus: *Nel Erasmus, Retrospective Exhibition Catalogue*, 1985, The University of the Orange Free State, Bloemfontein, foreword by Albert Werth, introduction by Marina Hough, text by Elza Miles, Raymund van Niekerk, Esmé Berman and Nel Erasmus.

Francine Scialom Greenblatt: *Francine Scialom Greenblatt*, 1985, Gabrielle Bryers Gallery, New York, text by John Gruen.

August Hammar: *August Hammar*, 1985, Natal Arts Trust, Natal.

Irmin Henkel: *Irmin Henkel*, 1971, Pieter Wenning Gallery, Johannesburg.

Robert Hodgins: *Images 1953–1986*, 1986, The Standard Bank Guest Artist, 1820 Settlers National Monument, Grahamstown, articles by Alan Crump, Elizabeth Rankin and Marion Arnold.

Tadeusz Jaroszynski: *Jaroszynski*, 1979, Galerie Romaner, Paris, text in French by Pierre Mazars.

Fritz Krampe: *Fritz Krampe 1913–1966*, 1967, SA National Gallery, Cape Town.

William Kentridge: *William Kentridge 1987*, The Standard Bank Young Artist Award, 1820 Settlers National Monument, Grahamstown, text by Elza Miles and Alan Crump.

François Krige: *The Official World War II works of François Krige*, 1980, SA National Museum of Military History, Johannesburg, foreword by G B Duxbury.

Neville Lewis: *The Official World War II works of Neville Lewis*, 1984, SA National Museum of Military History, Johannesburg, foreword by N P C Huntingford and R E Hardy.

Terence McCaw: *Terence McCaw '71*, 1971, Pieter Wenning Gallery, Johannesburg.

John Meyer: *John Meyer in retrospect*, 1983, The Everard Read Gallery, Johannesburg, introduction by Everard Read, interview by Jennifer Hobbs.

John Muafangejo: *John Ndevasia Muafangejo*, 1988, The Standard Bank Second Guest Artist Award, 1820 Settlers National Monument, Grahamstown, introduction by Alan Crump, text by Olga Levinson.

Hugo Naudé: *Catalogue of Works in The Hugo Naudé Art Centre*, The Hugo Naudé Art Centre, Worcester, introduction by Gerda Engelbrecht.

Thijs Nel: *Thijs Nel*, 1982, Rand Afrikaans University, Johannesburg.

Annemarie Oppenheim: *Annemarie Oppenheim Berlin Vedutas*, 1984, Press and Information Office of Land Berlin, foreword by Eberhard Diepgen, text by Walter Heuder.

J H Pierneef: *J H Pierneef – Pretorian, Transvaler, South African*, 1986, Pretoria Art Museum, foreword by A J Werth, text by Rina de Villiers.

J H Pierneef: *Pierneef – Van Vouw*, 1980, The Rembrandt van Rijn Art Foundation, Stellenbosch, text by A J Werth and Murray Schoonraad.

Clement Sénèque: *Retrospective Exhibition Catalogue*, 1984, Johannesburg.

Irma Stern: *Irma Stern 1894–1966, Memorial Exhibition*, 1967, Grosvenor Gallery, London, UK.

Cecil Thornley Stewart: *C Thornley Stewart*, 1960, Pieter Wenning Gallery, Johannesburg, text by Everard Read, Cecil Thornley Stewart and Pat Stewart.

Johan van Heerden: *Afrox Metalart*, 1977, introduction by A J Werth, article by Edward Russell-Walling.

Herman van Nazareth: *Herman van Nazareth*, 1976, Pretoria Art Museum, foreword by A J Werth, text by J du P Scholtz.

Jan van Nouhuys: *Jan van Nouhuys 1903–1940*, 1973, Pretoria Art Museum.

André van Vuuren: *Van Vuuren*, 1987, André van Vuuren, Johannesburg, foreword by George Boys.

Lukas van Vuuren: *Lukas van Vuuren*, 1984, Gallery International, Cape Town, introduction by Esther Rousso.

Lukas van Vuuren: *Lukas van Vuuren*, Vega Art Enterprises, Cape Town.

Anton van Wouw: *Pierneef – Van Wouw*, 1980, The Rembrandt van Rijn Art Foundation, Stellenbosch, text by A J Werth and Murray Schoonraad.

Edoardo Villa: *Villa 88*, The Standard Bank Guest Artist, 1820 Settlers National Monument, Grahamstown, text by Alan Crump and Raymund van Niekerk.

J E A Volschenk: *Jan Ernest Abraham Volschenk 1853–1936*, 1945, SA National Gallery, Cape Town, foreword by Ernest Lezard, text by L Gordon.

Anna Vorster: *Anna Vorster*, 1985, University of the Orange Free State, Bloemfontein, text by Anna Vorster, Elza Miles and Lydia M de Waal.

Jean Welz: *Jean Welz*, 1977, introduction by Johanna de Villiers, Cape Town.

Pieter Wenning: *Pieter Wenning Memorial Exhibition*, 1946, Pieter Wenning Gallery, Johannesburg, text by P Anton Hendriks, *The Cape* and Bernard Lewis.

Pieter Wenning: *Pieter Wenning 1873–1921*, 1967, Pretoria Art Museum, text by A J Werth.

Matthew Whippman: *Matthew Whippman*, 1967, Pieter Wenning Gallery, Johannesburg, text by Charles Eglington.

Edward Wolfe: *Retrospective Exhibition of Paintings and Drawings Catalogue*, 1967, Art Council (UK), foreword by Gabriel White, articles by Bryan Robertson and Richard Hughes.

Gavin Younge: *Gavin Younge – Koperberg*, 1986, The Standard Bank Young Artists Award, 1820 Settlers National Monument, Grahamstown, introduction by Alan Crump.

Group Catalogues

Africana Pictures from the Permanent Collection of the King George VI Art Gallery, 1987, King George VI Art Gallery, Port Elizabeth, introduction by Melanie Hillebrand.

Art Collection of the University of South Africa, Catalogue no. 1, 1961–79, University of South Africa, Pretoria, introduction by Karin M Skawran.

Art from the Cape, undated, Rand Afrikaans University, Johannesburg, introduction by Amalie von Maltitz.

Art in South Africa, A Short Survey, a special issue of *Report from South Africa*, July/August 1972, Director of Information, SA Embassy, London, UK.

Art of Portrait, undated, Pretoria Art Museum.

Aviation Art '87, 1987, Total Gallery, Johannesburg, foreword by Cmdt A E Smit.

Cape Town Biennial, 1979, SAAA, SA National Gallery, Cape Town, preface by Simon Rappaport and Raymund van Niekerk.

Cape Town Triennial, 1982, Rembrandt van Rijn Art Foundation, SA National Gallery, Cape Town, preface by Raymund van Niekerk.

Cape Town Triennial, 1985, Rembrandt van Rijn Art Foundation, SA National Gallery, Cape Town, preface by Raymund van Niekerk, article by Alan Crump.

Irma Stern Museum, Catalogue of the Collections, undated, University of Cape Town, foreword by D P Inskip, introduction by J du P Scholtz, evaluation by N E Dubow.

Johannesburg Art and Artists: Selections from a Century, 1986, Johannesburg Art Gallery, foreword by Christopher Till, compiled by Sheree Lissoos.

Lecturers, School of Art & Design, Port Elizabeth Technikon, 1986, University of the Orange Free State Art Gallery, Bloemfontein.

Lecturers, School of Art & Design, Technikon Orange Free State, 1986, University of the Orange Free State Art Gallery, Bloemfontein.

Paris and South African Artists 1850–1965, 1988, SA National Gallery, Cape Town, preface by Raymund van Niekerk, introduction by Lucy Alexander, text by Lucy Alexander, Emma Bedford and Evelyn Cohen.

Quadrennial Exhibition of SA Art Catalogues, 1956, 1960 & 1964, organised by the SAAA.

Republic Festival Arts Exhibition, 1981, Durban.

Sanlam Art Collection, Catalogue of Paintings and Sculpture, 1986, Sanlam, Cape Town.

South African Art, 1948–49, SAAA, Cape Town, foreword by C T te Water.

South African Contemporary Realism, 1983, Pretoria Art Museum, introduction by Gerda Engelbrecht.

South African Paintings 1898–1941 from the Grahamstown Fine Art Association Collection, 1985, 1820 Settlers Memorial Museum, Grahamstown, introduction by Robert Brooks.

South African paintings and drawings from the collections of The Friends of the Johannesburg Art Gallery, 1981, Johannesburg Art Gallery, foreword by Pat Senior.

Technikon Pretoria Art Lecturers/Kunsdosente, 1987, Pretoria Art Museum.

Tributaries, A view of contemporary South African art, 1985, BMW (South Africa), Johannesburg, introduction by Ricky Burnett.

University of South Africa Art Lecturers, 1986, University of South Africa, Pretoria, introduction by L du Plessis.

Vita Art Now, 1987, AA Mutual, Johannesburg Art Gallery, introduction by Marilyn Martin.

Vita Art Now, 1988, AA Mutual, Johannesburg Art Gallery, introduction by Rayda Becker.

William Fehr Collection, revised inventory for The Castle, 1977, The Castle of Good Hope, Cape Town.

William Humphreys Art Gallery Check List of the Permanent Collection, 1987, Kimberley.

9 Art Lecturers, 1986, Pretoria Art Museum, introduction by Nico Roos.

100 years of Natal Art, undated, Technikon Natal, Durban, foreword by Herman du Toit.

Selected Periodicals

Africana Notes and News, Africana Museum, Johannesburg

Apollo, London

Aquarelle, WSSA, Johannesburg

Art, Bruce Attwood, Broederstroom

Art Design Architecture, Jennifer Sorrell, Vlaeberg

Art Director, DADA Publishing, Johannesburg

Artlook, (defunct)

Cosmopolitan, Jane Raphaely, Cape Town

De Arte, Department of Art History and Fine Art, University of South Africa, Pretoria

De Kat, Living in SA (Pty) Ltd, Sandton, Johannesburg

Fair Lady, National Media, Cape Town

Flying Springbok, South African Airways, Johannesburg

Fontein, (defunct)

Gallery, Seven Arts Publishers (Pty) Ltd, Johannesburg

Habitat, Index Publishers, Johannesburg

Historia, The Historical Society of South Africa, Department of History, University of Pretoria

Lantern, Foundation for Education, Science and Technology, Pretoria

Living, Living in SA (Pty) Ltd, Sandton, Johannesburg

Sgraffito, APSA, Craighall, Johannesburg, (defunct, now replaced by *Ceramix*)

South Africana, (defunct)

South African Art Collector, (defunct)

South African Arts Calendar, SAAA, Pretoria

South African Panorama, Department of Information, Pretoria

Style, CTP, Johannesburg

USEFUL ADDRESSES

African Art Centre
8 Guildhall Arcade
35 Gardiner Street
Durban
4001

Africana Museum
Market Square
Johannesburg
2001

Albany Museum
Somerset Street
Grahamstown
6140

Aleta Michaletos Gallery
20a The Loop
Lynnwood
Pretoria
0081

Alexandra Art Centre
P O Box 357
Marlboro
2063

Ann Bryant Gallery
9 St Marks Road
corner Oxford Street
P O Box 11008
Southernwood
East London
5213

Anthony Adler Gallery
164b Russell Road
Port Elizabeth
6001

Anton van Wouw House
c/o Department of History of Art
University of Pretoria
corner Clark and Rupert Streets
Brooklyn
Pretoria
0181

The Art Foundation
see Johannesburg Art Foundation

The Art Gallery Association of the Vaal Triangle
Andries Potgieter Boulevard
P O Box 2662
Vanderbijlpark
1900

Art in the Parks Association
a member of the Afrikaanse Kunsvereniging
Pretoria

Artists Market Association
P O Box 93024
Yeoville
Johannesburg
2143

Arts Association SWA/Namibia
109 Leutwein Street
P O Box 994
Windhoek
Namibia

Associated Potters of Southern Africa
P O Box 41535
Craighall
Johannesburg
2024

Atlantic Art Gallery
71 Burg Street
corner Church Street
Cape Town 8001

Belgravia Art High School
56 Belgravia Crescent
East London
5213

Benoni Art Society
P O Box 12336
Benoryn
1504

Beuster-Skolimowski Gallery
106 Arcadia Centre
Beatrix Street
Arcadia
Pretoria
0083

Boksburg Art Association
P O Box 9354
Cinda Park
1463

Botanical Research Institute
2 Cussonia Road
P O Box X101
Pretoria
0001

The Brush and Chisel Club
P O Box 68309
Bryanston
Johannesburg
2021

The Cafe Genevé Gallery of Artists
First Floor
Old Well Arcade
384 Smith Street
Durban
4001

Cannon and Findlay
110 Commercial Road
P O Box 333
Pietermaritzburg
3200

The Cape Gallery
60 Church Street
Cape Town
8001

Cape Technikon
P O Box 652
Cape Town
8000

Cassirer Fine Art
13 Mutual Square
169 Oxford Road
Rosebank
Johannesburg
2196

Centre for Continuing Education
University of the Witwatersrand
1 Jan Smuts Avenue
Johannesburg
P O Wits
2050

The Chelsea Gallery
The Old Town House
Durban Road
Wynberg
Cape Town
7800

Claerhout-Ampenberger House
Tweespruit
9770

Coert Steynberg Museum
465 Berg Avenue
Pretoria North
0182

Community Arts Project
Arts Resource Centre
Chapel Street
District Six
P O Box 168
Rondebosch
Cape Town
7700

Community Arts Project
B210 Walnut Road
Durban
4001

Coppin Johnson Gallery
150 West Street
Durban
4001

C P Nel Museum
Voortrekker Road
P O Box 453
Oudtshoorn
6620

Crake Gallery
35a Grant Avenue
Norwood
P O Box 95009
Grant Park
Johannesburg
2051

Ditike Craft Centre
P O Box 9
Sibasa
Republic of Venda

Dorp Street Gallery
Dorp Street
Stellenbosch
7600

Drostdy Museum
18 Swellengrebel Street
Swellendam
6740

Durban Art Gallery and Museum
City Hall
Smith Street
P O Box 4085
Durban
4000

Durban Arts Association
6 Silverton Road
Durban
4001

Eastern Province Society of Fine Arts
Arts Hall
Park Drive
Port Elizabeth
6001

The East London Fine Arts Society
Ann Bryant Gallery
Oxford Road
P O Box 11008
Southernwood
East London
5213

East London Museum
319 Oxford Street
East London
5201

East London Technical College
Lukin Road
East London
5201

Elizabeth Gordon Gallery
18 Windermere Road
Durban
4001

Engelenburg House Art Collection
corner Hamilton and Edmunds Streets
P O Box 538
Pretoria
0001

Ernst de Jong Studio Gallery
366 Hill Street
Hatfield
Pretoria
0083

The Everard Read Gallery
(formerly The Pieter Wenning Gallery)
6 Jellicoe Avenue
Rosebank
Johannesburg
Private Bag 5
Parklands
2121

Fish Hoek Art Society
c/o 28a Teubes Road
Kommetjie
7975

Fort Beaufort Museum
Durban Street
P O Box 94
Fort Beaufort
5720

Frank Joubert Art Centre
Vredenhof
Keurboom Road
Newlands
7700

Fransie Pienaar Museum
16 Church Street
Prince Albert
6930

FUBA Gallery
66 Wolhuter Street
Newtown
Johannesburg
2001

Funda Centre
Zone 6
Diepkloof
P O Box 359
Orlando
1804

Gallery International
13 Hout Street
Cape Town
8001

Gallery 21
Third Floor
Victory House
34 Harrison Street
corner Fox Street
Johannesburg
P O Box 41037
Craighall
2024

Gallery 709
25 Adderley Street
Cape Town
8001

Gencor Gallery
c/o Rand Afrikaans University
Auckland Park
P O Box 524
Johannesburg
2000

Gertrude Posel Gallery
Senate House
University of the Witwatersrand
1 Jan Smuts Avenue
Johannesburg
P O Wits
2050

Goodman Gallery
3b Hyde Square
North Road
Hyde Park
2196

Grassroots Gallery
119a Jan Hofmeyr Road
P O Box 570
Westville
3630

Helen de Leeuw
16 Hyde Park Corner
Jan Smuts Avenue
Hyde Park
P O Box 41461
Craighall
2024

Hester Rupert Art Museum
Church Street
Graaff-Reinet
6280

Highway Art Group
5 Braby Place
Cowies Hill
3610

Hoffer Gallery
8b SAAV Building
corner Andries and Schoeman Streets
Pretoria
0002

Hugo Naudé Art Centre
86 Tulbagh Street
Worcester
6850

Human Sciences Research Council
134 Pretorius Street
Private Bag X41
Pretoria
0001

Inscape Study Centre
261 Oxford Road
Illovo
P O Box 785148
Sandton
Johannesburg
2146

Irma Stern Museum
c/o The University of Cape Town
The Firs
Cecil Road
Rosebank
7700

Ivan Solomon Gallery
c/o Pretoria Technikon
420 Church Street
Pretoria
0002

Jack Heath Gallery
c/o The Fine Arts Department
The University of Natal
P O Box 375
Pietermaritzburg
3200

Johan Carinus Art Centre
Grant House
Beaufort Street
Grahamstown
6140

Johannesburg Art, Ballet and Music School
17 Hoofd Street
Braamfontein
2001

Johannesburg Art Foundation
(The Art Foundation)
6 Eastwold Way
Saxonwold
Johannesburg
2196

Johannesburg Art Gallery
Joubert Park
P O Box 23561
Johannesburg
2000

Johannesburg College of Education
27 St Andrews Road
Parktown
2193

Johannesburg Council for Adult Education
P O Box 87334
Houghton
2041

**Johannesburg Spinners and Weavers
Guild**
P O Box 52570
Saxonwold
2132

Johannesburg Teachers Training College
Bunting Road
Private Bag X27
Auckland Park
2006

Julius Gordon Africana Centre
Versveld House
Long Street
P O Box 29
Riversdale
6770

Karen McKerron Gallery
42 Mandeville Road
P O Box 6948
Bryanston
Johannesburg
2021

Katlehong Art Centre
Maphiki Street
Katlehong
P O Box 57
Germiston
1400

Killie Campbell Africana Library
University of Natal
220 Marriott Road
Berea
Durban North
4051

King George VI Art Gallery
1 Park Drive
Port Elizabeth
6001

King Williams Town Art Society
contactable through the King Williams Town
Round Table

Knysna Arts and Crafts Society
7 Green Street
Knysna
6570

Die Kunskamer
14 Burg Street
Cape Town
8001

Lichtenburg Art Society
P O Box 1794
Lichtenburg
2740

Local History Museum
Old Court House
Aliwal Street
Durban
4001

Mangosuthu Technikon
P O Box 12353
Jacobs
4026

Margate Art Centre and Gallery
5 United Building
Margate
4275

Market Gallery
corner Bree and Wolhuter Streets
Newtown
Johannesburg
2001

McGregor Museum
Egerton Road
Kimberley
8301

Michaelis Art Library
Elizabeth House
Pritchard Street
Johannesburg
2001

Midlands Arts and Crafts Centre
28 Prince Albert Street
Pietermaritzburg
3201

M L Sultan Technikon
P O Box 1334
Durban
4000

Mofolo Art Centre
Soweto City Council
Private Bag X10
KwaXuma
1868

Natalie Knight Gallery
8 Hyde Park Centre
Jan Smuts Avenue
Hyde Park
P O Box 1793
Johannesburg
2000

National Art Society
P O Box 41221
Craighall
2024

National Botanic Gardens
Kirstenbosch
Claremont
Cape Town
7700

National Cultural History and Open-Air Museum
Boom Street
Pretoria
0002

National Museum
36 Aliwal Street
P O Box 266
Bloemfontein
9300

National Museum for Afrikaans Literature
Old Government Building
President Brand Street
Bloemfontein
9301

Ndaleni Educational Training School
Art Department
Ndaleni
Richmond
3780

Nelspruit Art Gallery
Louis Trichardt Street
P O Box 45
Nelspruit
1200

North Coast Art Group
106 Costa do Sol
Park Drive
Umhlanga Rocks
4320

NSA Gallery
Boulevard Level
Overport City
Ridge Road
P O Box 37408
Durban
4067

Nyanga Art Centre
corner Qumbu and Sibini Avenue
Nyanga
c/o P O Box 73
Claremont
7735

The Old House Museum
31 St Andrew's Street
Durban
4001

The Open School
Cambridge Mansions
Sauer Street
Johannesburg
2001

Orange Free State Technikon
Private Bag X20539
Bloemfontein
9300

Peninsula Technikon
P O Box 1906
Bellville
7535

Pierneef Museum
Vermeulen Street
Pretoria
0002

Pietersburg Collection
c/o Pietersburg Town Council
Civic Centre
Mare Street
P O Box 111
Pietersburg
0700

The Plettenberg Bay Arts Association
P O Box 1118
Plettenberg Bay
6600

Port Elizabeth Technikon
Private Bag X6011
Port Elizabeth
6000

Possession Arts Group
P O Box 15905
Doornfontein
Johannesburg
2028

Potchefstroom Museum
c/o Potchefstroom Municipality
Gouws Street
P O Box 113
Potchefstroom
2520

Potchefstroom University for Christian Higher Education
corner Jooste and Hoffman Streets
The Bult
P O Box X6001
Potchefstroom
2520

Potchefstroom University for CHE Art Gallery
Department of History of Art
Third Floor
Ferdinand Postma Library Building
Potchefstroom
2520

Pretoria Art Museum
Arcadia Park
Arcadia
Pretoria
0083

Pretoria School of Art, Ballet and Music
36 University Road
Brooklyn
0181

Pretoria Technikon
420 Church Street
Pretoria
0002

Prisma Art Society of Alberton
P O Box 1543
Alberton
1450

Queenstown Art Gallery
(J C Marshall Art Gallery)
Ebden Street
Queenstown
5320

Queenstown Art Society
c/o 116 Berry Street
Queenstown
5320

Queenstown and Frontier Museum
13 Shepstone Street
P O Box 296
Queenstown
5320

Rand Afrikaans University
Auckland Park
P O Box 524
Johannesburg
2000

Rembrandt van Rijn Gallery
31 Dorp Street
Stellenbosch
7600

Rhodes University
P O Box 94
Grahamstown
6140

Roodepoort Municipal Museum
18 Dieperink Street
P O Box 217
Roodepoort
1725

Rorke's Drift Art Centre
Private Bag 2610
Dundee
Natal
3000

The Rustenburg Art Society
P O Box 52
Rustenburg
0300

The Ruth Prowse School of Art
(1970–75 called the Ruth Prowse Art Centre)
The Retreat
5 Elson Road
Rondebloom
P O Box 89
Woodstock
Cape Town
7925

SABC Art Collection
c/o SABC
Henley Road
Auckland Park
Johannesburg
2092

The Sanderling Gallery
7 Smal Street
Johannesburg
Private Bag 5
Parklands
2121

Sandton Municipal Collection
Norscot Manor House
Penguin Drive
Norscot Manor
P O Box 78001
Sandton
2146

Schweickerdt Art Gallery
89 Queen Street
P O Box 697
Pretoria
0001

Shell Art Gallery
51 Plein Street
Johannesburg
2001

Somerset West Art Group
17 Pinewoods Street
Somerset West
7130

The South African Arts Calendar
P O Box 6188
Pretoria
0001

The South African Association of Arts
a. c/o Public Library
   Kruskal Avenue
   Bellville
   7530
b. P O Box 2198
   Bloemfontein
   9300
c. 35 Church Street
   Cape Town
   P O Box 15218
   Vlaeberg
   8018
d. P O Box 2536
   Klerksdorp
   2570
e. P O Box 20147
   Noordbrug
   Potchefstroom
   2522

f. Momentum Centre
   343 Pretoria Street
   P O Box 1024
   Pretoria
   0001
g. P O Box 422
   Worcester
   6850

for Durban *see* NSA Gallery
for Lichtenburg *see* Lichtenburg Art Society
for Windhoek *see* Arts Association
   SWA/Namibia

South African Cultural History Museum
Old Supreme Court Building
49 Adderley Street
Cape Town
8001

South African National Gallery
The Gardens
Government Avenue
P O Box 2420
Cape Town
8000

**South African National Museum of
Military History**
Erlswold Way
P O Box 52090
Saxonwold
Johannesburg
2132

South African Society of Artists
Athenaeum
Camp Ground Road
Newlands
7700

Standard Bank SWA Limited
P O Box 3327
Windhoek
Namibia

Standerton Art Society
P O Box 1371
Standerton
2430

Strack van Schyndel Gallery
30 Mutual Square
Oxford Road
Rosebank
Johannesburg
2196

Strydom and Jordaan Gallery
79 Mark Street
P O Box 144
George
6530

Suid-Afrikaanse Akademie vir Wetenskap en Kuns
P O Box 538
Pretoria
0001

Sumi-e Art Society of South Africa
16 Pamplona
15 Main Street
Townsview
Johannesburg
2197

SWA/Namibia Administration
P O Box 13186
Windhoek
Namibia

SWA/Namibia Museums and Monuments
P O Box 1203
Windhoek
Namibia

Tatham Art Gallery
Pietermaritzburg City Hall
333 Church Street
P O Box 321
Pietermaritzburg
3200

Things Gallery
9c 7th Street
Melville
Johannesburg
2092

Tinus de Jong Memorial Gallery
Lanzerac Rawdon's Hotel
Jonkershoek Road
Stellenbosch
7600

Total Gallery
Total House
corner Smit and Rissik Streets
Braamfontein
2001

Transvaal Education Museum
185 Gerhard Moerdyk Street
Sunnyside
Private Bag X434
Pretoria
0001

Transvaal Museum
Paul Kruger Street
P O Box 413
Pretoria
0001

Transvaal Provincial Administration
Library and Museum Service
Private Bag X288
Pretoria
0001

University of Bophuthatswana
Private Bag X2046
Mafikeng
8670

University of Cape Town
Michaelis School of Fine Art
Private Bag
Rondebosch
7700

University of Durban-Westville
Private Bag X54001
Durban
4000

University of Fort Hare
Private Bag X1314
Alice
Republic of Ciskei

University of Natal
Department of Fine Arts
P O Box 375
Pietermaritzburg
3200

University of the North
Private Bag X5090
Pietersburg
0700

University of the Orange Free State
Stegmann Gallery
P O Box 339
Bloemfontein 9000

University of Pretoria
Corner Lynnwood and University Roads
Brooklyn
Pretoria
0002

University of South Africa
Muckleneuk Ridge
P O Box 392
Pretoria
0001

University of Stellenbosch
Stellenbosch
7600

University of Stellenbosch Gallery
corner Bird and Dorp Streets
Stellenbosch
7600

University Vista Soweto
Koma Street
Dhlmini
P O Box X03
Tshiawelo
1818

University of the Western Cape
Private Bag X17
Bellville
7530

University of the Witwatersrand
1 Jan Smuts Avenue
Johannesburg
P O Wits
2050

University of Zululand
Umlazi Campus
Private Bag 10
Isipingo
4110

Upper South Coast Art Association
P O Box 104
Winklespruit
4145

Vaal Triangle Technikon
Private Bag X021
Vanderbijlpark
1900

Verboom Studio
5 Highfield Street
Green Point
Cape Town
8001

Vereeniging Art Society
P O Box 2313
Vereeniging
1930

Voortrekker Monument Museum
Voortrekker Monument
Monument Koppie
Pretoria
0002

Walter Battiss Art Gallery
Paulet Street
Somerset East
5850

War Museum of the Boer Republics
National Women's Monument Grounds
P O Box 704
Bloemfontein
9300

The Watercolour Society of South Africa
14 West Street
East Town
Johannesburg
2195

Willem Annandale Art Gallery
c/o Lichtenburg Art Society
P O Box 1794
Lichtenburg
2740

William Fehr Collection
c/o Rust en Vreugd
78 Buitenkant Street
Cape Town
8001
and
The Castle of Good Hope
Grand Parade
Cape Town
8001

William Humphreys Art Gallery
Civic Centre
P O Box 885
Kimberley
8300

Witwatersrand Technikon
P O Box 3293
Johannesburg
2000

Wolpe Gallery
501 Impala House
27 Castle Street
Cape Town
8001

Worcester Museum
21 Baring Street
P O Box 557
Worcester
6850

The Zululand Society of Arts
P O Box 117
Eshowe
3815

The 1820 Settlers Memorial Museum
c/o The Albany Museum
Somerset Street
Grahamstown
6140

ABBREVIATIONS

Italics denotes the title of a book or periodical. Full details of publication can be found in the Select Bibliography.

A

AASA	*Art and Artists of South Africa*, 1983
ADA	*Art Design Architecture*
AFA	Associate of Fine Art
Afr Repos	*Africana Repository*, 1965
AMC1	*Catalogue of Pictures in the Africana Museum A–B*, 1966
AMC2	*Catalogue of Pictures in the Africana Museum C–D*, 1967
AMC3	*Catalogue of Pictures in the Africana Museum E–L*, 1967
AMC4	*Catalogue of Pictures in the Africana Museum M–S*, 1968
AMC5	*Catalogue of Pictures in the Africana Museum T–Z*, 1968
AMC6	*Catalogue of Pictures in the Africana Museum A–G*, 1971
AMC7	*Catalogue of Pictures in the Africana Museum H–Z*, 1972
ANN	*Africana Notes and News*
APSA	Associated Potters of Southern Africa
ARCA	Associate of the Royal College of Art
ARIBA	Associate of the Royal Institute of British Architects
Artimo	Art in Motion
Art SA	*Art in South Africa since 1900*, 1962
Art SWA	*Art in South West Africa*, 1978

B

b.	born
BA(FA)	Bachelor of Art (Fine Art)
BA(FA) (Hons)	Bachelor of Art (Fine Art) (Honours)
BANKOVS	Bank van die Oranje Vry Staat
BBC	British Broadcasting Corporation
BEd	Bachelor of Education
Bénézit	*Dictionnaire des Peintres, Sculpteurs, Dessinateurs et Graveurs*, 1976
BSAK	*Bibliografie Suid-Afrikaanse Kunstenaars*, volumes 1 & 2, 1976, 1986
BSc	Bachelor of Science

C

c.	circa
C	century
CAPAB	Cape Performing Arts Board
CHE	Christian Higher Education
Co	Company
Collectors' Guide	*The Collectors' Guide to SA Artists*, 1953
CSIR	Council for Scientific and Industrial Research

D

DA	Doctor of Art
D'ARTS	Durban Arts
DBA	*The Dictionary of British Artists*, 1976

DLitt	Doctor of Literature
DPhil	Doctor of Philosophy
Dr	Doctor
DSAB	*Dictionary of South African Biographies*, 1968–87
DVP	*A Dictionary of Victorian Painters*, 1971

E

Echoes of African Art	*Echoes of African Art*, 1987
Enc S'n A	*Encyclopedia of Southern Africa*, 1978
EPSFA	Eastern Province Society of Fine Art

F

FIAL	Fellow of the International Institute of Arts and Letters
fl.	flourished
FLS	Fellow of the Linnaean Society
FRCS	Fellow of the Royal College of Surgeons
FRGS	Fellow of the Royal Geographical Society
FRIBA	Fellow of the Royal Institute of British Architects
FRSA	Fellow of the Royal Society of Arts
FUBA	Federated Union of Black Artists

G

GAP	Grahamstown, Alice and Port Elizabeth (a combining of the students and staff of their Universities and Technikon)

I

IWAA	*International Who's Who in Art and Antiques*, 1972

K

KK	*Kuns en Kunswaardering*, 1942
KWV	Ko-operatiewe Wijnbouwers Vereniging van Suid-Afrika

L

Ltd	Limited
LSAA	*Looking at South African Art*, 1985

M

MA(FA)	Master of Art (Fine Art)
MBE	Member (of the Order) of the British Empire
MFA	Master of Fine Art – from Rhodes University
MIA	Member of the South African Institute of Architects

N

NAPAC	Natal Performing Arts Council
Natal Art	*Natal Art before Union*, 1974
no	number
NSA	Natal Society of Arts

O

OBE	Officer (Order) of the British Empire
Our Art 1	*Our Art 1, c.*1960
Our Art 2	*Our Art 2,* 1961
Our Art 3	*Our Art 3, c.*1978
Oxford Companion to Art	*The Oxford Companion to Art,* 1970
Oxford Companion to 20C Art	*The Oxford Companion to Twentieth Century Art,* 1981

P

PACOFS	Performing Arts Council of the Orange Free State
PACT	Performing Arts Council of the Transvaal
PhD	Doctor of Philosophy
Pict Afr	*Pictorial Africana,* 1975
Pict Art	*Pictorial Art,* 1952
Port Elizabeth School of Art	*Port Elizabeth School of Art, A History 1882–1982,* 1982
POW	Prisoner of War
PSA	*Painters of South Africa,* 1948
PSN	*Painters SWA/Namibia,* 1983
Pty	Proprietary

Q

qv	quod vide (which see, used for cross references)

R

RA	Royal Academician
RBA	Royal Society of British Artists
RBC	Royal British Colonial Society of Artists
RE	Royal Society of Painters and Etchers
Register SA & SWA	*Register of South African and South-West African Artists,* 1969
RIBA	Royal Institute of British Architects
RMS	Royal Society of Miniature Painters
ROI	Royal Institute of Oil Painters

S

SA	South/Southern Africa
SAA	*South African Artists 1900–1962,* 1963
SAAA	South African Association of Arts
SAAAH	South African Association of Art Historians
SA Art	*South African Art,* 1978
SABC	South African Broadcasting Corporation
SADNB	*South African Dictionary of National Biography,* 1966
SAGAT	*South African Graphic Art and its Techniques,* 1974
SANCA	South African National Council for Alcoholism and Drug Abuse
SAP&D	*South African Prints and Drawings,* 1971
SAP&S	*South African Painting and Sculpture,* 1970

SASSK	*Suid-Afrikaanse Spot- en Strookprent- kunstenaars*, 1983
SATOUR	South African Tourist Corporation
Sc Nat	Bachelor of Natural Sciences
SDSA	Society of Designers, South Africa
SEIFSA	Steel and Engineering Industries Federation of South Africa
SESA	*Standard Encyclopaedia of Southern Africa*, volumes 1–12, from 1970
SK	*Skone Kunste*, 1951
SSAP	*The Story of South African Painting*, 1974
SSR	Soviet Socialist Republic
St	Saint
STANSWA	Standard Bank SWA Ltd
SUKOVS	Streekraad vir Uitvoerende Kunste, Oranje-Vrystaat
SWA	South West Africa
SWALU	South West Africa Labour Union
SWAWEK	SWA Akademie vir Wetenskap en Kuns

T

TAM	Tertulia de Artistas Moçambicanos
TB	Tuberculosis

U

UK	United Kingdom
UNESCO	United Nations Educational, Scientific and Cultural Organisation
UNICEF	United Nations Children's Fund – formerly United Nations International Children's Emergency Fund
USA	United States of America
USSALEP	United States–South African Leader Exchange Programme
UTA	Union de Transport Aeriens

V

VC	Victoria Cross
VOC	Vereenigde Oost-Indiese Compagnie
vol	volume

W

WSSA	Watercolour Society of South Africa
WWI	First World War
WWII	Second World War

Y

YMCA	Young Men's Christian Association
YWCA	Young Women's Christian Association

Z

ZA	Zuid Afrikaansche

FIGURES

3Cs   *Three Centuries of South African Art,* 1982
20C SA Art   *Twentieth Century South African Art,* 1966